MOON HANDBOOKS

SOUTHERN CALIFORNIA

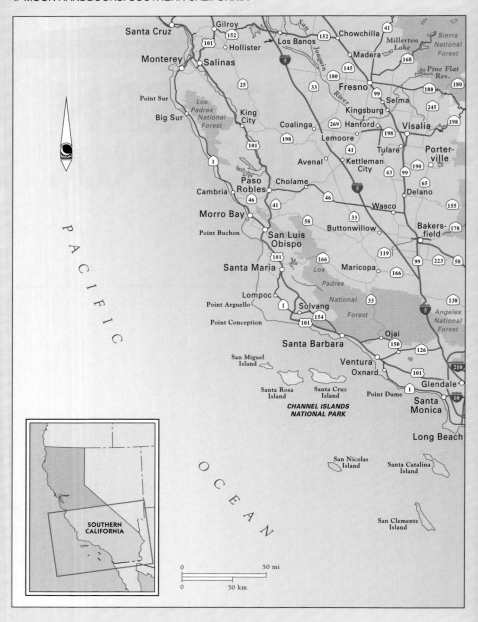

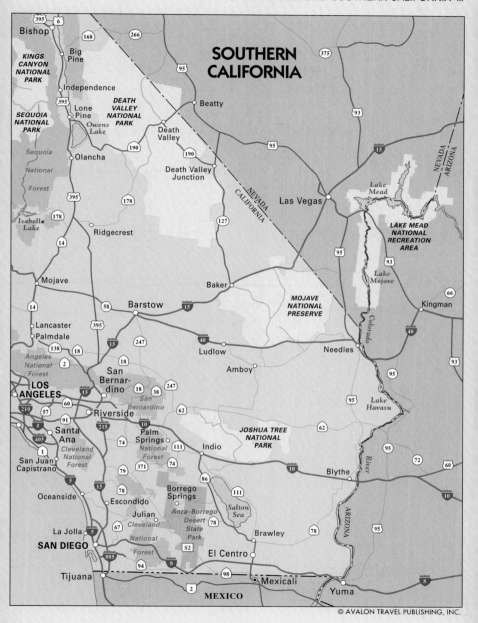

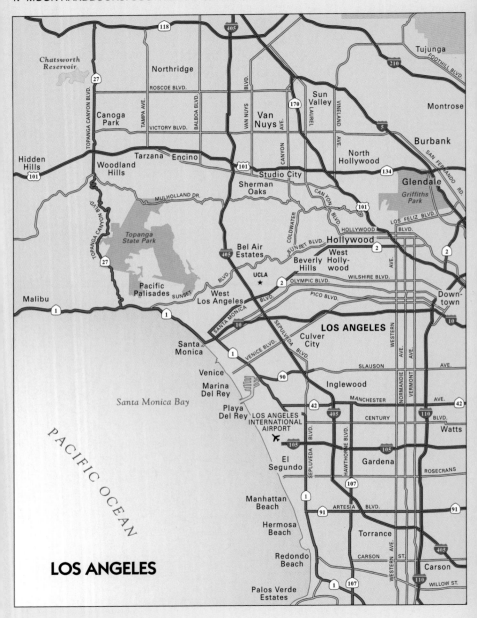

LOS ANGELES

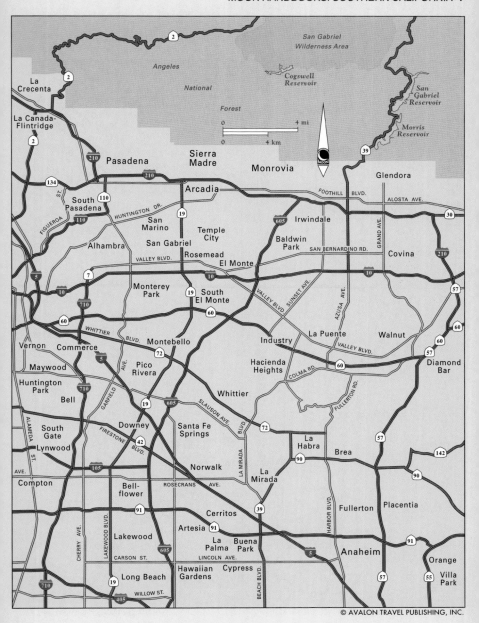

San Gabriel
Wilderness Area

Angeles

Cogswell
Reservoir

National

San Gabriel
Reservoir

Forest

Morris
Reservoir

0   4 mi

0   4 km

La
Crecenta

La Canada-
Flintridge

Pasadena

Sierra
Madre

Monrovia

Glendora

South
Pasadena

Arcadia

FOOTHILL   BLVD.

ALOSTA AVE.

HUNTINGTON DR.

San
Marino

Temple
City

Irwindale

Covina

Alhambra

San Gabriel

Baldwin
Park

SAN BERNARDINO RD.

VALLEY BLVD.

Rosemead

El Monte

Monterey
Park

South
El Monte

Industry

La Puente

Walnut

Vernon

Commerce

WHITTIER   BLVD.

Montebello

Hacienda
Heights

COLMA RD.

Diamond
Bar

Maywood

Pico
Rivera

Huntington
Park

Bell

Whittier

SLAUSON   AVE.

South
Gate

Downey

Santa Fe
Springs

La Habra

Brea

Lynwood

Norwalk

La
Mirada

Compton

Bell-
flower

ROSECRANS   AVE.

Fullerton

Placentia

Cerritos

Artesia

Lakewood

CARSON ST.

La
Palma

Buena
Park

Anaheim

Orange

Long Beach

Hawaiian
Gardens

Cypress

Villa
Park

WILLOW ST.

LINCOLN AVE.

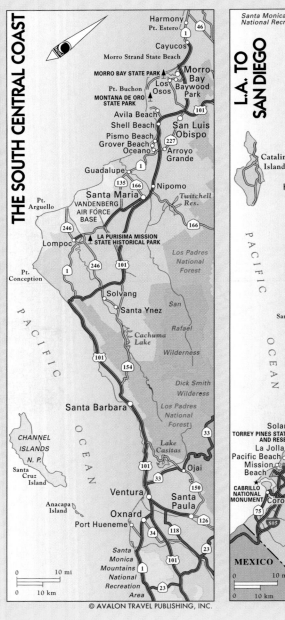

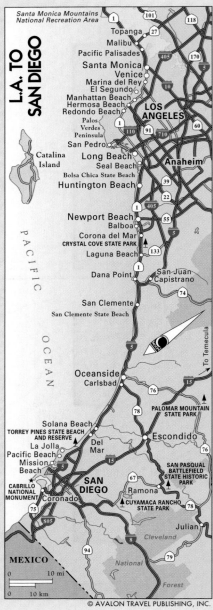

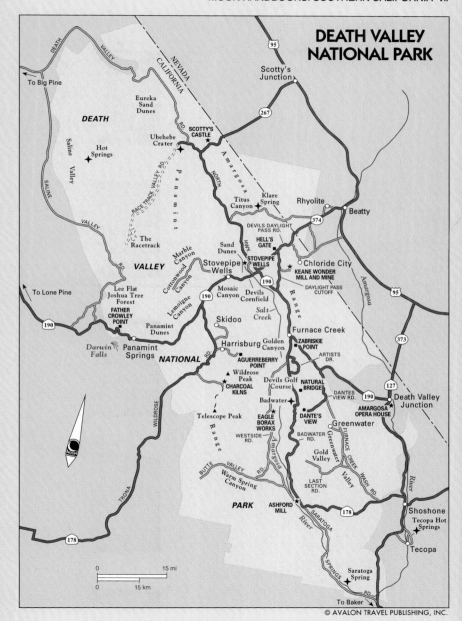

DEATH VALLEY NATIONAL PARK

To Big Pine

DEATH

Eureka Sand Dunes

Saline Valley

Hot Springs

Ubehebe Crater

SCOTTY'S CASTLE

Scotty's Junction

95

267

RACE TRACK VALLEY RD.

The Racetrack

Titus Canyon

Klare Spring

Rhyolite

Beatty

374

DEVILS DAYLIGHT PASS RD.

HELL'S GATE

Marble Canyon

Sand Dunes

VALLEY

Cottonwood Canyon

Stovepipe Wells

STOVEPIPE WELLS

Chloride City

KEANE WONDER MILL AND MINE

DAYLIGHT PASS CUTOFF

95

To Lone Pine

Lee Flat Joshua Tree Forest

FATHER CROWLEY POINT

Lemoigne Canyon

190

190

Mosaic Canyon

Devils Cornfield

Salt Creek

Skidoo

Amargosa Range

Furnace Creek

373

Darwin Falls

Panamint Springs

Panamint Dunes

NATIONAL

Harrisburg

AGUERREBERRY POINT

Wildrose Peak

CHARCOAL KILNS

Golden Canyon

ZABRISKIE POINT

ARTISTS DR.

Devils Golf Course

NATURAL BRIDGE

DANTES VIEW RD.

127

190

Death Valley Junction

AMARGOSA OPERA HOUSE

WILDROSE RD.

Telescope Peak

Panamint Range

EAGLE BORAX WORKS

Badwater

DANTE'S VIEW

WESTSIDE RD.

BADWATER RD.

Greenwater

Greenwater Valley

Gold Valley

FURNACE CREEK WASH RD.

TRONA

BUTTE VALLEY RD.

Warm Spring Canyon

Amargosa River

LAST SECTION RD.

178

PARK

ASHFORD MILL

SARATOGA SPRINGS RD.

River

Shoshone

Tecopa Hot Springs

Tecopa

178

Saratoga Spring

River

To Baker

MOON

| 0 | 15 mi |
| 0 | 15 km |

© AVALON TRAVEL PUBLISHING, INC.

DEATH VALLEY

CALIFORNIA

NEVADA

NORTH HWY.

Amargosa

PANAMINT

SALINE VALLEY

Devils Canyon

MOON HANDBOOKS

SOUTHERN CALIFORNIA

INCLUDING GREATER LOS ANGELES, DISNEYLAND, SAN DIEGO, DEATH VALLEY, AND OTHER DESERT PARKS

SECOND EDITION

KIM WEIR

AVALON
TRAVEL

MOON HANDBOOKS: SOUTHERN CALIFORNIA
SECOND EDITION

Kim Weir

Published by
Avalon Travel Publishing
5855 Beaudry St.
Emeryville, CA 94608, USA

ISBN: 1-56691-333-0
ISSN: 1535-7430

Please send all comments,
corrections, additions,
amendments, and critiques to:

**MOON HANDBOOKS:
SOUTHERN CALIFORNIA
AVALON TRAVEL PUBLISHING
5855 BEAUDRY ST.
EMERYVILLE, CA, USA**
email: atpfeedback@avalonpub.com
website: www.travelmatters.com

Printing History
1st edition—1999
2nd edition—November 2001
5 4 3 2 1

Editor: Rebecca K. Browning
Series Manager: Erin Van Rheenen
Copy Editor: Jean Blomquist
Proofreader: Julie Leigh
Graphics: Melissa Sherowski
Production: Alvaro Villanueva, David Hurst
Map Editor: Naomi Dancis
Cartography: Chris Folks, Ben Pease, Mike Morgenfeld, Kat Kalamaras
Indexer: Emily Lunceford

Front cover photo: Mission San Diego de Alcala © 1992 Michele Burgess

Distributed by Publishers Group West

Printed in USA by R.R. Donnelley

The real voyage of discovery
consists not in seeking new landscapes
but in having new eyes.
—Marcel Proust

CONTENTS

GREATER SOUTHERN CALIFORNIA

UP THE COAST FROM L.A. ....589~649

MAPS

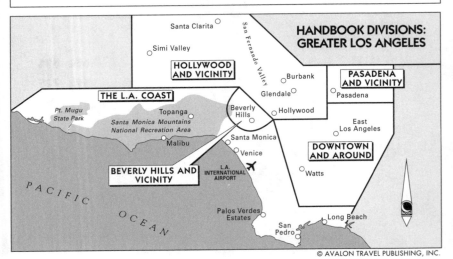

HANDBOOK DIVISIONS: GREATER LOS ANGELES

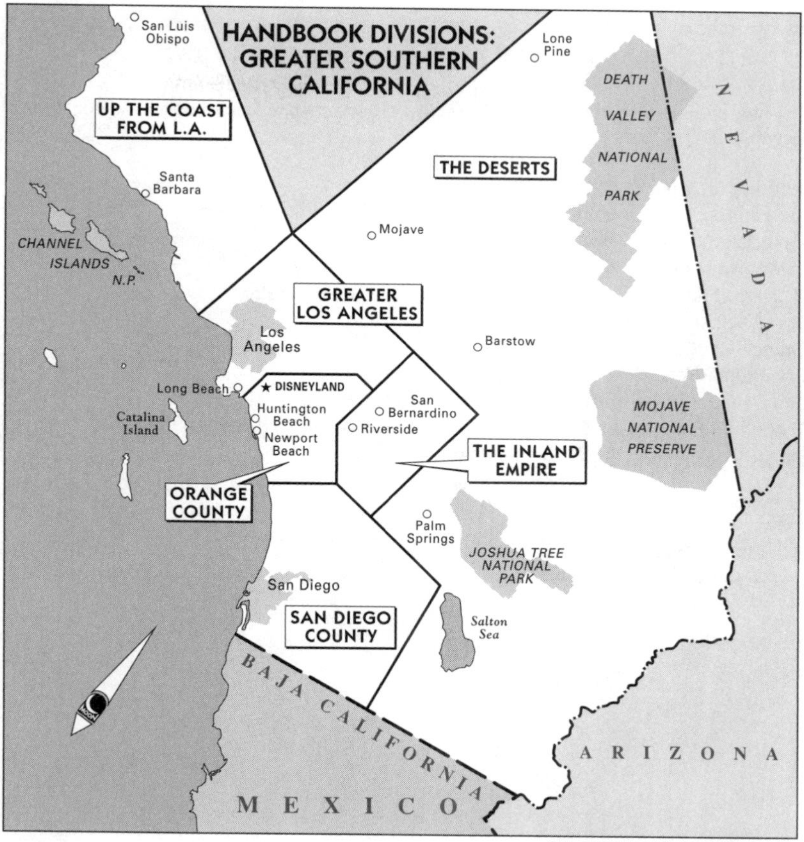
HANDBOOK DIVISIONS: GREATER SOUTHERN CALIFORNIA
San Luis Obispo
UP THE COAST FROM L.A.
Santa Barbara
CHANNEL ISLANDS N.P.
Lone Pine
DEATH VALLEY NATIONAL PARK
NEVADA
THE DESERTS
Mojave
GREATER LOS ANGELES
Los Angeles
Barstow
Long Beach
★ DISNEYLAND
Huntington Beach
Newport Beach
Catalina Island
San Bernardino
Riverside
THE INLAND EMPIRE
MOJAVE NATIONAL PRESERVE
ORANGE COUNTY
Palm Springs
JOSHUA TREE NATIONAL PARK
San Diego
SAN DIEGO COUNTY
Salton Sea
BAJA CALIFORNIA
ARIZONA
MEXICO

© AVALON TRAVEL PUBLISHING, INC.

MAP SYMBOLS

═	Divided Highway	○	City/Town	✈	Airport
═	Primary Road	●	Accommodation	↟	State Park
═	Secondary Road	▼	Restaurant/Bar	▲	Mountain
┄	Dirt Road	★	Point of Interest	✦	Unique Natural Feature
– – –	Trail	■	Other Location	≋	Waterfall
⛊	Interstate	⛳	Golf Course	▨	Volcanic Landform
⛉	U.S. Highway			⬚	Dry Lake

ABOUT THE BANNERS

The historic images that illustrate the beginning of each chapter in this book come from the collection of Aislinn Race.

Introduction: *Irrigation ditches*
Introduction: Greater Los Angeles: *A Palm-Girt Avenue, Los Angeles*
Pasadena: *Orange Grove Avenue, Pasadena*
Downtown and Around: *Broadway, downtown Los Angeles*
Hollywood and Vicinity: *Midwinter in Southern California*
The Westside: *Pier at Santa Monica*
Orange County: *Surf with ship*
San Diego: *Hotel Coronado*
The Deserts: *Horse and buggy among Joshua trees*
The Inland Empire: San Bernardino and Riverside: *Magnolia Avenue, Riverside*
Up the Coast from L.A.: *Santa Barbara Mission*

All banners courtesy of Aislinn Race.

EXPRESS YOURSELF

Not on just any topic, though. This being California, most things change faster than traffic lights. Because of this unfortunate fact of life in the fast lane of travel writing, comments, corrections, inadvertent omissions, and update information are always greatly appreciated. Though every effort was made to keep all current facts corralled and accounted for, it's no doubt true that *something* (most likely, a variety of things) will already be inaccurate by the time the printer's ink squirts onto the paper at press time.

Just remember this: whatever you divulge may indeed end up in print—so think twice before sending too much information about your favorite hole-in-the-wall restaurant, cheap hotel, or "secret" world's-best swimming hole or hot springs. Once such information falls into the hands of a travel writer, it probably won't be a secret for long. Address all correspondence to:

Moon Handbooks: Southern California
c/o Avalon Travel Publishing
5855 Beaudry St.
Emeryville, CA 94608, USA
email: atpfeedback@avalonpub.com
(please put book title in subject line)
http://www.travelmatters.com

ABBREVIATIONS

BLM—Bureau of Land Management
PCH—Pacific Coast Highway
L.A.—Los Angeles
LAPD—Los Angeles Police Department
BH—Beverly Hills

SOUTHERN CALIFORNIA DREAMING: REVISITING THE HUMBLE ORANGE

My grandfather was a citrus grower. A Kansas farm boy with an eighth-grade education and much grander dreams, he came to Southern California to achieve them after doing time in the trenches during World War I. He worked hard at it, too, first opening an Indian motorcycle dealership in Lordsburg (present-day La Verne) and then, through another partnership, a tractor business in Pomona. Eventually he bought a small orange grove in Pomona, and later another, with its own farmhouse, in Upland.

My mother's childhood was scented with citrus blossoms. It was an idyll that included occasional cuts and scratches and a workingman's tan. By age 10 she'd learned to drive both truck and tractor. Along with her brother and sister she worked in the orchards and the packing shed after school and on weekends. In those days, my mother told me, properly packing fruit meant that she and her siblings carefully wrapped each orange in tissue paper.

Thanks to oranges, there was money for college. So sometime in the middle of World War II my mother drove off the ranch and on to UCLA in a battered old pickup truck her father had spruced up with leftover bathroom paint.

Magnify my family's simple story by the multitude of others who tell a similar tale and an entire chapter of Southern California history is written.

The humble orange has long been a symbol of the Southern California dream. The image itself was hardly homegrown, however. It was crated up for wholesale consumption throughout the United States by advertising executives employed by the California Fruit Growers Exchange, known for its trademark "Sunkist" brand. High drama was part of the hard sell. In 1907, for example, the Southern Pacific Railroad and the Lord and Thomas agency of Chicago jointly sponsored the Orange Train to Iowa to promote "Oranges for Health—California for Wealth." Next came direct mail—a sales technique pioneered by Lord and Thomas, incidentally—along with ever more sophisticated campaigns aimed at selling both California and its oranges by promoting the middle-class mores of respectability, prosperity, domestic bliss, and glowing good health. An imaginative new genre of de facto folk art, those colorful, stylized art-deco orange crate labels, delivered the myth directly into subterranean layers of the American psyche.

This particular California sales job was spectacularly successful. By 1914 national per capita consumption of oranges reached an annual average of 40, an astounding increase from the near-zip totals of 30 years earlier.

Oranges—the idea of oranges—brought my grandfather to California. The physical fact of oranges, the modest prosperity the annual orange harvest promised, paid my mother's way through UCLA. And my mother was the first in the immediate family, though far from the last, to go to college. That is the lasting legacy of my family's life in the orange groves, because by the 1960s and 1970s only remnants of that idyllic life remained in Southern California. That dream had largely been paved over, though here and there orange and lemon groves still survive, leafy oases in an asphalt desert. So long as a single citrus tree still stands somewhere in Southern California, my grandfather's dream continues.

The symbols of the dream—the Southern California dream, the California dream, the American dream of unlimited future possibilities—constantly change. In early settlement days, adobe ranchos and herds of free-ranging longhorns painted the prettiest imaginable picture of the good life. During California's era of yeoman agriculture, it was orange groves, avocados, and lima beans. Then fields of oil derricks. Then the fantasy of overnight fame and fortune as a movie star. After World War II the dream was subdivided single-family residential and generously subsidized by the U.S. defense and aerospace industries.

In an age that measures value in dollars and the Western frontier more accurately in cyberspace than space, the dream now seems to require every conceivable consumer comfort and online computers, cellular phones, faxes, pagers, and other accessories for faster and more, if not better, communication.

So goes the dream.

INTRODUCTION

COURTESY AISLINN RACE

INTRODUCTION
CALIFORNIA AS MYTH

California is a myth—a myth in the sense of a traditional tale told to impart truth and wisdom, and in the fanciful sense of some extravagant storybook fiction. Californians happen to like the quirky character of the state they've chosen to live in. Whether or not they realize it, California as myth is exactly why they're here—because in California, even contradictions mean nothing. In California, almost everything is true and untrue at the same time. In California, people can pick and choose from among the choices offered, as if in a supermarket, or create their own truth. Attracted to this endless sense of creative possibilities—California's most universal creed, the source of the ingenuity and inventiveness the state is so famous for—people here are only too happy to shed the yoke of tradition, and traditional expectations, that kept them in harness elsewhere.

Californians tend to think life itself is a California invention, but "lifestyle" definitely is: people come to California to have one. Coming to California, novelist Stanley Elkin observes, "is a choice one makes, a blow one strikes for hope.

No one ever wakes up one day and says, 'I must move to Missouri.' No one chooses to find happiness in Oklahoma or Connecticut." And according to historian Kevin Starr, "California isn't a place—it's a need." Once arrived in California, according to the myth, the only reason to carry around the baggage of one's previous life is because one chooses to.

But it would be naive to assume that this natural expansiveness, this permission to be here now, is somehow new in California. It may be literally as old as the hills, oozing up through the rocks and soil like psychic black gold. Native peoples, the first and original laid-back Californians, knew this. Busy with the day-to-day necessities of survival, they nonetheless held the place in awe and managed to honor the untouchable earth spirits responsible for creation. The last remembered line of an ancient Ohlone dancing song—"dancing on the brink of the world"—somehow says it all about California.

As a place, California is still a metaphor, for Shakespeare's "thick-coming fancies" as well as for those awesome mysteries that can't be taken in by the five senses. People come here to sort it all out, to somehow grasp it, to transform themselves and the facts of their lives—by joining in the dance.

CALIFORNIA AS EUROPEAN MYTH

Native peoples had many explanations for how the land and life in California came to be, almost as many stories as there were villages. But it's a stranger-than-fiction fact that California as a concept was concocted in Europe, by a Spanish soldier turned romance writer.

The rocky-shored island paradise of California, according to the 1510 fictional *Las Sergas de Esplandían* by Garcí Ordóñez de Montalvo, overflowed with gold, gems, and pearls, was inhabited by griffins and other wild beasts, and "peopled by black women, with no men among them, for they lived in the fashion of Amazons" under the great Queen Calafia's rule. With such fantastic images seared into the European imagination, it's no wonder that Cortés and his crew attached the name California to their later territorial claims from Baja California north to Alaska.

THE MYTH OF NORTHERN AND SOUTHERN CALIFORNIA

While California is still a destination of the imagination and a rich land indeed, its true wealth is (and always was) its breathtaking beauty, its cultural creativity, and its democratic dreams.

The primary political fact of life here is that California is one state. Technically indisputable, this fact is nonetheless widely disputed. Californians themselves generally view the state as two distinct entities: Northern California, centered in sophisticated San Francisco, and the continuous sprawl of Southern California south of the Tehachapi Mountains, its freeways spreading out from its Los Angeles heart like the spokes of a bent and broken wheel.

According to the myth that successfully populated Southern California, simple, neighborly, nature-oriented living amid sunny gardens and citrus groves would save civilization from the mass-production mindset of industrialism— almost shocking to contemplate now, when one sees what's become of that idea. Yet this is also the land of the American dream made manifest, where the sun always shines—on the degenerate and deserving alike, the ultimate in California-style social democracy—and where even the desert itself is no limitation since, thanks to the wonders of modern engineering, water can be imported from elsewhere. In the newer Southern California myth, style is more important than substance and image is everything, cultural truths shaped in large part by Hollywood and the movies. Life itself is defined by humanity—by an artificial environment of pavement and plastic technologies manufactured by human need and vanity, by the worship of physical beauty in human form, and by the relentless search for the ultimate in hedonistic diversion and novelty. An engineered Eden ruled by Midwestern social and political mores, Southern California worships everything new—from new beliefs and ideas and commercially viable images transmitted via its own film and media industries to art and innovation for their own sakes—and rarely questions the intrinsic value of cosmetic change. The main moral question in the southstate is not "Is it important?" or "Is it right?" but: "Is it new?"

Northern California's mythic soul is represented by nature in all its contradictions—the rugged outdoors and the rugged individualist struggling for survival, the simple beauty of humanity in nature as well as more complicated relationships that result from humanity's attempts to change and control nature's inherent wildness. The collective and personal histories of Northern California suggest secessionism, rebellion, and the high-technology innovations largely responsible for today's global culture. Northern California is also about human awareness in nature, and a modern consciousness seemingly sprung fully formed from nature worship: holistic health and get-in-touch-with-yourself psychological trends; mandatory physical fitness, as if to be ready at a moment's notice to embark upon ever more challenging outdoor adventures; natural foods and a regionally focused appreciation of fresh produce and fine wines. Life in Northern California is defined by outdoor-oriented, socially responsible narcissism—and symbolized by an upwardly mobile young professional couple nudging their new, gas-guzzling four-wheel drive onto well-engineered highways leading out of the city and into the wilderness.

Yet in many ways the two ends of the state are becoming one. Despite regional chauvinism, southstate-style growth, with all its attendant problems, is fast becoming a fact of life in the north; within several decades, almost as many people will live in Northern California as in the south. In all parts of the state, growth is away from major cities and into the suburbs—a fact that is influencing political trends as well. Northern California, traditionally more liberal than Southern California, is becoming more Republican, while the southstate's increasing concerns over health and environmental issues are liberalizing urban political trends. And though Northern California politicians tend to openly oppose any increased water shipments to Southern California, most are much quieter about supporting water engineering feats designed to meet the needs of the northstate's own suburban growth.

Californians themselves still see most statewide social, political, and "style" differences in terms of north versus south regionalism. The time-honored historical issue of politically splitting California into two separate states—an idea now at least rhetorically quite popular in the rural north, though the state's first secessionism arose in the south—still comes up regularly. But the actual facts about modern-day California suggest a different reality. Life here is, and will be continue to be, defined by the conflicting cultures of minority-dominated urban areas, more conservative Sun Belt suburbs created by "white flight," and declining, truly rural resource-based communities.

CALIFORNIA AS "FIRST IN THE NATION"

California's most obvious "first" is its population. Half of the people living in the West, the fastest-growing region of the nation, live in California. Number one in the nation now—with more than 34 million people—California's population at current growth rates will be nearly 40 million by the year 2005, nearly 50 million by 2030 (some say 2020 or 2025), and 60 million by 2040. Or more. The state has been growing so rapidly during the past decade, largely because of legal and ille-

gal immigration, that demographers can't keep up. Keeping tabs on Californians has been complicated further by their increasing migration, in recent years, to other states; more than 1.1 million left in the early 1990s, though that trend has slowed.

The sheer heft of California humanity makes it first in the nation in immigration (both legal and illegal), first in bomb threats and investigations, first in firearm-related violent crime, and first in prison budgets. Largely because of Southern California population pressures, California also ranks shockingly high for endangered and threatened species. Yet California boasts more Nobel Prize laureates than any other state, more engineers and scientists, and more research labs, colleges, and universities.

California is also number one in construction-related business contracts and leads the nation in number of millionaires, though it no longer tops the nation's lists for livable cities or average personal incomes. Despite the crush of its urban population, California usually makes more money in agriculture than any other state, and produces —and consumes—most of the country's wine.

The land has its own firsts-and-bests, since California boasts the highest point in the contiguous United States (Mt. Whitney) and the lowest (Death Valley). California is also home to the world's largest living thing, the Sequoia big tree; the world's tallest, the coast redwood; and the world's oldest, the bristlecone pine. Depending upon how one defines individuality, however, two of the latter records may fall. One particular subterranean fungus in Michigan, sprouting multiple mushrooms, spans at least 37 acres, is estimated to weigh 220,000 pounds, and may have been alive since the end of the last Ice Age.

Common wisdom in the United States holds that "as California goes, so goes the nation." As with most California legends, there is at least some truth to this. California is quite often the national trendsetter, from fads and fashions in political or social beliefs to styles in cars and clothes. In its endless pursuit of style, California searches for its identity, for some explanation of itself. California is constantly inventing and reinventing its own mythology. Yet few states so far are following California's lead in eliminating affirmative action programs and attempting to withhold public services from immigrants.

The Free Speech Movement, the philosophical foundation supporting both civil rights and anti-Vietnam War activism, took root in California. But so did the New Republicanism (best represented by Richard Nixon and Ronald Reagan), a reactionary trend toward social control that arose at least as an indirect result. California is usually first in the nation for new religious and spiritual trends, too, from New Age consciousness to televangelism.

California is the birthplace of the motel, the climate-controlled shopping mall, suburban sprawl, and a lifestyle almost entirely dependent upon cars and elaborately engineered highway and freeway systems. But California is also first in the nation in car thefts and in marijuana cultivation. It's home to the back-to-the-land culture and spawning ground for the philosophy of bioregionalism, too, decrying all things homogenized, unnatural, unnecessarily imported, and plastic. For every action in California, there is also a reaction.

CONTEMPORARY CALIFORNIA FACTS AND FANCY

Among common misconceptions about the state is the one the rest of the world tenaciously clings to—that everyone in California is laid-back, liberal, blond, rich, and well educated.

California as Laid-Back

California may be casual, but it's not exactly relaxed. Despite the precedents set by native peoples and early Californios (those of Spanish descent born in the pre-United States period), most of the state's modern residents are hardly content to live in leisure. In their frantic rush to accumulate, to stay in style, to just keep up with the state's sophisticated survival code and incredible rate of change, Californians tend to be tense and harried. And now that Californians have remembered—and reminded the rest of the world—that rest and relaxation are necessary for a well-rounded life, people here pursue recreation with as much vengeance as any other goal. Just sitting around doing nothing isn't against the law in California, but it's definitely déclassé.

California as Liberal

If people in California aren't particularly laid-back, they aren't particularly liberal either. After all, California created both Richard Nixon and Ronald Reagan. The truth is, California has never committed itself to any particular political party. Democratic legislators still predominate in California's Senate and Assembly—a surprise in 1996, considering the general Republican drift elsewhere—and Democrats, after losing ground in 1994, regained strength in the U.S. House of Representatives in 1996 and, in 2000, both houses of the state legislature as well. California also strongly supported Vice President Al Gore in the 2000 presidential race. Some blame Republican Governor Pete Wilson, described by national columnist Anthony Lewis as "the premier gutter politician of our day," since Wilson's reactionary anti-immigrant reelection campaign of 1994 and his activist anti-affirmative action stance in 1996 made Latino citizens—and other voters—angry enough to vote Democratic in a big way. Perhaps it was only fitting that Fresno's Cruz Bustamante, the first Latino speaker of the state Assembly, took office in 1996. Subsequently there was a rapid decline in the Republicans' recent race-baiting politicking —but not enough to slow the statewide decline in Republican influence.

In November 1998, California elected a Democratic governor, Gray Davis, by a whopping 20-percentage point margin, though the state has supported only Republicans in that office since the departure of "Governor Moonbeam," Jerry Brown, in the late 1970s. And Cruz Bustamante was elected lieutenant governor, the first Latino in the 20th century elected to statewide office. In the same election, the previously ascendant Christian conservatives in the Republican Party lost big. In 1998 California also elected its first Green Party candidate, Audie Bock, to the state Assembly. Bock subsequently lost that seat to a Democratic challenger.

Even in 1992, when Republicans otherwise dominated state politics, California was first in the nation to elect women—both Democrats, Barbara Boxer and Dianne Feinstein—to fill its two U.S. Senate seats, outdoing all other states, cities, and municipalities in paying homage to "the year of the woman." And California overwhelmingly supported Governor Bill Clinton, a Democrat, in the 1992 presidential election. President Clinton's support, though still a majority, was substantially less in the 1996 election. Yet the Democrats' previous declines and Republican dominance on the national level have diminished the state's traditional political clout in the United States, at least in the short term, because of the loss of key committee chairs and committee rankings once held by California Democrats.

Occasional flamboyant public figures and longstanding double-edged jokes about the land of "fruits and nuts" aside, predicting the direction in which political winds will blow here is difficult. Until recently, pollsters detected a steady trend toward increasing identification with the Republican Party among the state's voting-age population. Generally speaking, the political labels of Democrat and Republican mean little in California. People here tend to vote on the basis of enlightened economic interest, personal values, and "political personality."

But if the New Republicanism has been quite comfortable in California, so is the orthodoxy of no orthodoxy. Values, political and social, are discarded as easily as last year's fashions. (Californians don't oppose tradition so much as they can't find the time for it.) The state's legendary liberalness is based on the fact that, like social voyeurs, Californians tolerate—some would say encourage—strangeness in others. Rooted in the state's rough-and-tumble gold rush history, this attitude is almost mandatory today, considering California's phenomenal cultural and ethnic diversity.

California as Blond

Despite the barrage of media and movie images suggesting that most Californians are blond and tan and live at the beach, not much could be further from the truth. Caucasians or "Anglos" predominate, ethnically, yet California's population has represented almost every spot on the globe since the days of the gold rush. More than 240 identified cultures or ethnicities have been identified in California. Blacks, Asians, and those of Hispanic descent predominate among the state's diverse minority populations—and by the turn of the 21st century, according to demographic projections, California's collective "minority" populations had become the majority. This occurred earlier in major cities, including Los Angeles, East Los Angeles, Fresno, Oakland, and San Francisco, and in many public school classrooms.

California's Asian population, now representing almost 10 percent of the total, will grow slightly. Its Latino population, now approximately 28 percent, will increase to 50 percent by the year 2040 (some say this demographic event will occur much sooner). Blacks in California will remain at a fairly stable population level, demographers project, about 7 percent of the population, as will Native Americans at around 1 percent.

No matter what color they started out, people in Paradise have been getting a bit gray; throughout the 1980s, retirees were California's fastest-growing age group. But just as it seemed the Golden State's stereotypical golden glow of youth was on the wane came the news that the population is actually getting younger, helped along by the arrival of five million preschoolers since 1990. And that trend underscores the others. According to the most recent U.S. census—already inadequate for keeping pace with the state's fast-changing face—in 1990 70 percent of the state's 60-year-olds were white and 55 percent of the 10-year-olds were ethnic minorities.

California as Rich

Though California is the richest state in the union, with a bustling economy of nation-state status and an average per-capita personal income of $22,000, the gap between the very rich and the very poor is staggering—and shocking to first-time visitors in major urban areas, since the despair of homelessness and poverty is very visible on city streets.

The news in 1995 that the United States is now the most economically stratified of all industrialized nations—with the top 20 percent of the population controlling 80 percent of the nation's wealth—barely raised an eyebrow in California. Neither did the word in 1996, with the state's economy once again booming, that California has the largest gap between rich and poor in the world because of precipitous declines in wages and income among the working poor. The widest income disparities are in Los Angeles.

Interpretations of U.S. census data suggest that California is becoming two states—or at least two states of mind. One California is educated, satisfied, and safe. The other is young, uneducated, immigrant (many do not speak English), restless, and impoverished. The ranks of the upper-income professional class (household income $50,000 or above) increased almost 10 percent between 1980 and 1990, to 33 percent—a phenomenon partly attributed to greater numbers of working women. (It's also striking to note that 18 percent of all U.S. households with an annual income of $150,000 or more are in California.) During that same decade, the state's middle-income households shrank from 35 percent to 33 percent, and the number of low-income households also declined, from 41 percent to 34 percent. But the numbers of the actual poor increased, from 11.4 percent to 12.5 percent.

Contradicting the skid row–alcoholic image of street life, almost one-third of the homeless in California are under age 18. But almost more disturbing is California's unseen poverty. Not counting those who are turned away because there isn't enough to go around, more than two million people—almost one in every 10 Californians—regularly require food from public and private charitable organizations just to survive; on any given day in the Golden State, a half-million people stand in line to get a free meal at a soup kitchen or commodity pantry. Minors, again, are California's largest class of hungry people. More than one in every four children in the Golden State live in poverty.

California as Well Educated

California has long been committed to providing educational opportunity to all citizens—a commitment expressed in once-generous public school funding as well as public financing for the nine (soon 10) campuses of the prestigious University of California, 23 California State University (CSU) campuses (CSU recently acquired the Maritime Academy), and the 106 independent California Community College (CCC) campuses. But because of the obvious educational impacts of increased immigration—80 separate languages are spoken at Los Angeles schools, at least 40 at Hollywood High alone—and the unofficial reality of socially segregated schools,

uneven early educational opportunities are a fact of life even in well-intentioned California. Until recently the situation has been steadily worsening, with California spending $900 less per public school student than the national average; ranked 40th in per-pupil spending; and burdened with the nation's highest student-teacher ratios. Faced with a projected 18 percent enrollment increase in elementary and high schools by 2006, California has lately turned its attention to improving public schools—both with increased levels of funding and increased performance testing.

Previous declines in public school performance, coupled with increasingly stringent entrance requirements at both University of California and California State University campuses, have led critics such as former state Assemblymember and Senator Tom Hayden of Santa Monica to suggest that California's current public education policies are creating a "de facto educational apartheid." Though California's two-year community colleges are providing more four-year college preparation courses and are increasingly encouraging students to transfer to state universities, most minority groups in California are vastly underrepresented even in public universities.

The state's recent budget crisis meant significant cuts in public financial support for education; fees at public universities (California educators and legislators never say "tuition") have increased rapidly. With the general public financing a diminishing share of the cost of each student's college education, there isn't enough opportunity to go around. Just to keep pace with current and anticipated demand early in the new century, the University of California needs three new campuses, the California State University system needs five, and the California Community Colleges need 28. According to a gloomy 1996 report by the nonprofit RAND think tank in Santa Monica, all three levels of California public higher education will be in deep financial crisis yet challenged to absorb a record 2.3 million potential students by 2010.

Overall trends in education, economics, and employment patterns suggest that California is evolving into a two-tiered society dominated by an affluent and well-educated Anglo-Asian "overclass." Those who make up the underclass and who compete for relatively low-paying service jobs will increasingly be immigrants or the functionally illiterate. According to Bill Honig, former state superintendent of public instruction, about 60 percent of California's public school students leave school without being able to read well enough to compete in California's increasingly complex, technology-oriented job market.

THE LAND: AN ISLAND IN SPACE AND TIME

California's isolated, sometimes isolationist human history has been shaped more by the land itself than by any other fact. That even early European explorers conceived of the territory as an island is a fitting irony, since in many ways —particularly geographically, but also in the evolutionary development of plant and animal life— California was, and still is, an island in both space and time.

The third-largest state in the nation, California spans 10 degrees of latitude. With a meandering 1,264-mile-long coastline, the state's western boundary is formed by the Pacific Ocean. Along most of California's great length, just landward from the sea, are the rumpled and eroded mountains known collectively as the Coast Ranges.

But even more impressive in California's 158,693-square-mile territory is the Sierra Nevada range, which curves like a 500-mile-long spine along the state's central-eastern edge. Inland from the Coast Ranges and to the north of California's great Central Valley are the state's northernmost mountains, including the many distinct, wayward ranges of the Klamaths— mountains many geologists believe were originally a northwesterly extension of the Sierra Nevada. Just east of the Klamath Mountains is the southern extension of the volcanic Cascade Range, which includes Mount Shasta and Lassen Peak.

This great partial ring of mountains around California's heartland (with ragged eastern peaks reaching elevations of 14,000 feet and higher) as well as the vast primeval forests that once almost suffocated lower slopes, have always influenced the state's major weather patterns—and have also created a nearly impenetrable natural barrier for otherwise freely migrating plant and animal species, including human beings.

But if sky-high rugged rocks, thickets of forest, and rain-swollen rushing rivers blocked migration to the north and east, physical barriers of a more barren nature have also slowed movement into California. To the south, the dry chaparral of the east-west Transverse Ranges and the northwest/southeast-trending Peninsular Ranges impeded northern and inland movement for most life forms. The most enduring impediment, however, is California's great southeastern expanse of desert—including both the Mojave and Colorado Deserts—and the associated desert mountains and high-desert plateaus. Here only the strong and well adapted survive.

EARTHQUAKES, VOLCANOES, AND CRUSTY PLATES

Perched along the Pacific Ring of Fire, California is known for its violent volcanic nature and for its earthquakes. Native peoples have always explained the fiery, earth-shaking temperament of the land quite clearly, in a variety of myths and legends, but the theory of plate tectonics is now the most widely accepted scientific creation story. According to this theory, the earth's crust is divided into 20 or so major solid rock (or lithospheric) "plates" upon which both land and sea ride. The interactions of these plates are ultimately responsible for all earth movement, from continental drift and landform creation to volcanic explosions and earthquakes.

Most of California teeters on the western edge of the vast North American Plate. The adjacent Pacific Plate, which first collided with what is now California about 250 million years ago, grinds slowly but steadily northward along a line more or less defined by the famous San Andreas Fault (responsible for the massive 1906 San Francisco earthquake and fire as well as the more recent shake-up in 1989). Plate movement itself is usually imperceptible: at the rate things are going, within 10 million years Los Angeles will slide north to become San Francisco's next-door neighbor. But the steady friction and tension generated between the two plates sometimes creates special events. Every so often sudden, jolting slippage occurs between the North American and Pacific Plates in California—either along the San Andreas or some other fault line near the plate border—and one of the state's famous earthquakes occurs. Though most don't amount to much, an average of 15,000 earthquakes occur in California every year.

A still newer theory augments the plate tectonics creation story, suggesting a much more fluid local landscape—that California and the rest of the West literally "go with the flow," in particular the movement of hot, molten rock beneath the earth's crust. "Flow" theory explains the appearance of earthquake faults where they shouldn't be, scientists say, and also explains certain deformations in the continental crust. According to calculations published in the May 1996 edition of the journal *Nature,* the Sierra Nevada currently flows at the rate of one inch every three years.

CALIFORNIA CREATION: WHEN WORLDS COLLIDE

In ancient times, some geologists say, the American Southwest was connected to Antarctica. This new theory, presented in 1991 by researchers at the University of California at Davis and the University of Texas, suggests that 500–700 million years ago a "seam" connected the two continents; Antarctica's Transatlantic Mountains were contiguous with the western edge of the Sierra Nevada, parts of Idaho, and the Canadian Rockies. The geological similarities between the now far-flung rock formations are unmistakable. Yet at that time the North American continent was missing California. Some geologists theorize that California came along later; certain rock formations now found south of the equator match those of California's Coast Range.

Wherever its raw materials originally came from, California as land was created by the direct collision, starting about 250 million years ago, of the eastward-moving Pacific Plate and the underwater western edge of the North American Plate—like all continents, something like a floating raft of lighter rocks (primarily granite) attached to the heavier, black basalt of the earth's mantle. At first impact, pressure between the two plates scraped up and then buckled offshore oceanic sediments into undulating ridges of rock, and an eventual California shoreline began to build.

But the Pacific Plate, unable to follow its previous forward path against such North American resistance, continued on its way by first plunging downward, creating a trough that soon began filling with oceanic basalts, mud, and eroded sediments from what is now Nevada. Sinking (or subducting) still farther beneath the North American Plate, some of these trench sediments slipped into the hot core (or athenosphere) beneath the earth's lithosphere and melted—transformed by heat into the embryonic granitic backbone of the Sierra Nevada and other metamorphic mountains that slowly intruded upward from the inner earth.

Approximately 140 million years ago, the northern section of what would later be the Sierra Nevada started to shift westward along the east-west tectonic fault line known as the Mendocino Fracture—the genesis of the Klamath Mountains. The Pacific Ocean, sloshing into the area just north of the infantile Sierra Nevada, brought with it the sediments that would create California's northeastern Modoc Plateau—a high-plains landscape later transformed by volcanic basalt flows and "floods."

About 60 million years ago, California's modern-day Sierra Nevada was a misshapen series of eroded ridges and troughs sitting on the newly risen edge of the continent. The violent forces generated by continuing plate confrontation, including sporadic volcanism and large-scale faulting, pushed the state's mountains slowly higher. Remaining ocean sediments later rose to create first the Coast Ranges, as offshore islands about 25 to 30 million years ago, and eventually an impressive, 450-mile-long inland sea, which, once filled with sediment, gradually evolved into the marshy tule wetlands recognizable today as California's fertile Central Valley.

Though California's creation has never ceased —with the land transformed even today by volcanic activity, earthquake shifts, and erosion—the landscape as we know it came fairly recently. According to the widely accepted view, about 10–16 million years ago the Sierra Nevada stood tall enough (approximately 2,000 feet above sea level) to start changing the continent's weather patterns: blocking the moisture-laden winds that had previously swept inland and desiccating the once-lush Great Basin. Then, one million years ago, the Sierra Nevada and other fault-block ranges "suddenly" rose to near their current height. By 800,000 years ago, the mountains had taken on their general modern shape—but fire was giving way to ice. During the million-year glaciation period, particularly the last stage from 100,000 to 30,000 years ago, these and other California landforms were subsequently carved and polished smooth by slow-moving sheets of ice. Vestigial glaciers remain in some areas of the Sierra Nevada and elsewhere.

A "countercultural" view of Sierra Nevada creation is emerging, however. According to this theory, based on research done in the southern Sierra Nevada, the range reached its zenith about 70 million years ago—massive mountains, as tall as the Andes, looming large during the last days of the dinosaurs. The height of the Sierra Nevada, once reaching 13,000 feet, has been declining ever since—a loss of about a quarter-inch in the course of a single person's lifetime—because erosion has proceeded faster than the forces of ongoing creation.

Though vegetation typical of the late Ice Age has largely vanished and mastodons, saber-toothed cats, and other exotic animals no longer stalk the land, the face of the California landscape since those bygone days has been transformed most radically by the impact of humanity—primarily in the past century and a half. Building dams and "channeling" wild rivers to exploit water, the state's most essential natural resource; harvesting state-sized forests of old-growth trees; hunting animals, to the edge of extinction and beyond, for fur and pelts; digging for, and stripping the land of, gold and other mineral wealth; clearing the land for crops and houses and industrial parks: all this has changed California forever.

FROM FIRE TO ICE: THE CALIFORNIA CLIMATE

California's much-ballyhooed "Mediterranean" climate is at least partially a myth. Because of extremes in landforms, in addition to various microclimatic effects, there are radical climatic differences within the state—sometimes even within a limited geographic area. But California as a whole does share most of the classic characteristics of Mediterranean climates: abundant sunny days year-round, a cool-weather coast, dry summers, and rainy winters. California, in fact, is the only region in North America where summer drought and rainy winters are typical.

Between the coast and the mountains immediately inland, where most of the state's people live, temperatures—though cooler in the north and warmer to the south—are fairly mild and uniform year-round. Because of the state's latitudinal gradation, rain also falls in accordance with this north-south shift: an average of 74 inches falls annually in Crescent City, 19–22 inches in San Francisco, and less than 10 inches in San Diego. When warm, moist ocean air blows inland over the cool California Current circulating clockwise above the equator, seasonal fog is typical along the California coast. Summer, in other words, is often cooler along the coast than autumn. (Just ask those shivering tourists who arrive in San Francisco every June wearing Bermuda shorts and sandals.)

Inland, where the marine-air influence often literally evaporates, temperature extremes are typical. The clear, dry days of summer are often hot, particularly in the Central Valley and the deserts. (With occasional freak temperatures above 130°F, Death Valley is aptly named.) In winter, substantial precipitation arrives in Northern California—especially in the northwest "rain belt" and in the northern Sierra Nevada—with major storms expected from October to May. In the High Sierra, the average winter snowpack is between 300 and 400 inches; California's northern mountains "collect" most Pacific Ocean moisture as rain. Wrung out like sponges by the time they pass over the Sierra Nevada and other inland mountains, clouds have little rain or snow for the eastern-slope rainshadow.

Since the 1970s California's climate patterns have been increasingly atypical—which may be normal, or may be early local indications of global warming. The reason no one knows for sure is because the state's "average" weather patterns were largely defined between the 1930s and the 1970s, a period of unusually stable weather conditions, it now appears. Complicating the question further is new scientific research suggesting that California climate has been characterized, since ancient times, by alternating cycles of very wet and very dry weather—200- to 500-year cycles. Epic droughts have been traced to the Middle Ages, and just 300 years ago California experienced a drought lasting 80–100 years. California's last century and a half, it turns out, represents one of the wettest periods in the past 2,500 years.

The increasing scientific consensus is that global warming is indeed having a major impact on California weather. Since the late 1970s El Niño "events" have increased noticeably, bringing warmer offshore waters and heavy storms in California and the Southwest. But in other years —drought times for California—"La Niña" occurs, with colder offshore waters and storms tracking into the Pacific Northwest. Being whipsawed between periods of torrential rains and flooding (yet subnormal snowpack) and devastating drought seems to be California's future—a future almost certain to feature disrupted water supplies, even without a 100-year drought.

CALIFORNIA FLORA: BLOOMING AT THE BRINK

"In California," observed writer Joaquin Miller, "things name themselves, or rather Nature names them, and that name is visibly written on the face of things and every man may understand who can read." When explorers and settlers first stumbled upon California's living natural wonders, they didn't "read" landforms or indigenous plants and animals in the same way native peoples did, but they were quite busy nonetheless attaching new names (and eventually Latin terminology) to everything in sight. From the most delicate ephemeral wildflowers to California's two types of towering redwoods, from butterflies and birds to pronghorn, bighorn sheep, and the various sub-

species of grizzly bear, the unusual and unique nature of most of the territory's life forms was astonishing. California's geographical isolation— as well as its dramatic extremes in landforms and localized climates—was (and still is) largely responsible for the phenomenal natural divergence and diversity originally found here.

Former President Ronald Reagan, while still governor of California and embroiled in a battle over expanding redwood parks, unwittingly expressed the old-and-in-the-way attitude about the state's resources with his now-famous gaffe, widely quoted as: "If you've seen one redwood, you've seen 'em all." (What Reagan actually said was: "A tree is a tree—how many more do you need to look at?") But his philosophy, however expressed, is the key to understanding what has happened to California's trees, other native flora, and animal species.

Even today, the variation in California's native plant life is amazing. Nearly 5,200 species of plants are at home in the Golden State—symbolized by the orange glow of the California poppy—and over 30 percent of these trees, shrubs, wildflowers, and grasses are endemic. (By comparison, only 13 percent of plant life in the northeastern United States, and 1 percent of flora in the British Isles, are endemic species.) In fact, California has greater species diversity than the combined totals of the central and northeastern United States and adjacent Canada—an area almost 10 times greater in size.

But to state that so many plant species survive in California is not to say they thrive. The economic and physical impact of settlement have greatly stressed the state's vegetative wealth since the days of the gold rush, when the first full-scale assaults on California forests, wetlands, grasslands, and riparian and oak woodlands were launched. The rate of exploitation of the state's 380 distinct natural communities has been relentless ever since. Half of the state's natural terrestrial environments and 40 percent of its aquatic communities are endangered, rare, or threatened.

Some of the state's most notable natural attractions are its unique trees—entire forests nearly toppled at the edge of extinction. California's *Sequoiadendron giganteum*, or giant sequoia, grows only in limited surviving stands in the Sierra Nevada—saved as much by the brittleness of its wood as by the public outcry of John Muir and other enlightened 19th-century voices. But the state's remaining virgin forests of *Sequoia sempervirens,* the "ever-living" coast redwoods, are still threatened by clearcutting, a practice that also eliminates the habitat of other species. The same conservation-versus-economic expediency argument also rages over the fate of the few remaining old-growth outposts of other popular timber trees. And decades of fire suppression, logging, grazing, and recreational development in California's vast forests of ponderosa pines, combined with the state's recent drought, have led to insect infestations, tree disease, and death—and a tinder-dry, fuel-rich landscape more vulnerable than ever to uncontrollable fires. Even trees without notable economic value are threatened by compromises imposed by civilization. Among these are the ancient bristlecone pines near the California-Nevada border—the oldest living things on earth, some individuals more than 4,000 years old—now threatened by Los Angeles smog, and the gnarled yet graceful valley oak. An "indicator plant" for the state's most fertile loamy soils, even the grizzled veteran oaks not plowed under by agriculture or subdivision development are now failing to reproduce successfully.

And while the disappearance of trees is easily observed even by human eyes, other rare and unusual plants found only in California disappear, or bloom at the brink of eternity, with little apparent public concern. A subtle but perfectly adapted native perennial grass, for example, or an ephemeral herb with a spring blossom so tiny most people don't even notice it, are equally endangered by humankind's long-standing laissez-faire attitude toward the world we share with all life.

Only fairly recently, with so much of natural California already gone for good, have public attitudes begun to change. No matter what Ronald Reagan says, and despite the very real economic tradeoffs sometimes involved, most Californians—and usually the state's voters—strongly support conservation, preservation, and park expansion proposals whenever these issues arise. Yet urban and suburban sprawl and commercial development continue unabated throughout California, with little evidence that the general public connects its personal and political choices with a sense of shared responsibility for the state's continued environmental decline.

CALIFORNIA FAUNA: A LONELY HOWL IN THE WILDERNESS

The Golden State's native wildlife is also quite diverse and unique. Of the 748 known species of vertebrate animals in California, 38 percent of freshwater fish, 29 percent of amphibians, and 9 percent of mammals are endemic species; invertebrate variation is equally impressive. But with the disappearance of quite specific natural habitats, many of these animals are also endangered or threatened.

One notable exception is the intelligent and endlessly adaptable coyote, which—rather than be shoved out of its traditional territory even by suburban housing subdivisions—seems quite willing to put up with human incursions, so long as there are garbage cans to forage in, swimming pools to drink from, and adequate alleys of escape. Yet even the coyote's lonely late-night howl is like a cry for help in an unfriendly wilderness.

The rapid slide toward extinction among California's wild things is perhaps best symbolized by the grizzly bear, which once roamed from the mountains to the sea, though the wolf, too, has long since vanished from the landscape. The Sierra Nevada bighorn sheep, the San Joaquin kit fox, the desert tortoise, and the California condor—most surviving birds are maintained now as part of a zoo-based captive breeding program—are among many species now endangered. Upward of 550 bird species have been recorded in California, and over half of these breed here. But the vast flocks of migratory birds (so abundant they once darkened the midday sky) have been thinned out considerably, here and elsewhere, by the demise of native wetlands and by toxins.

The fate of the state's once-fabled fisheries is equally instructive. With 90 percent of salmon spawning grounds now gone because of the damming of rivers and streams, California's commitment to compensatory measures—fish hatcheries and ladders, for example—somehow misses the point. Now that humans are in charge of natural selection, the fish themselves are no longer wild, no longer stream-smart; many can't even find their way back to the fisheries where they hatched out (in sterile stainless steel trays). California's once-fabled marine fisheries are also in dire straits because of the combined effects of overfishing, pollution, and habitat degradation, a subject of only very recent political concern.

However, some California animals almost wiped out by hunters, habitat elimination, and contamination are starting out on the comeback trail. Included among these are native elk and the antelope-like pronghorn populations, each numbering near 500,000 before European and American settlement. Also recovering in California is the native population of bighorn sheep—probably never numbering more than 10,000—that now clambers over craggy high peaks in small groups collectively totaling about 5,000 in recent years (numbers have since declined because of disease). Among marine mammals almost hunted into oblivion but now thriving in Califor-

nia's offshore ocean environments are the northern elephant seal and the sea otter. And in 1994 the California gray whale was removed from the federal endangered species list—the first marine creature ever "delisted"—because its current population of 21,000 or so is as high, historically speaking, as it ever was.

Until recently, California's predators—always relatively fewer in number, pouncing from the top of the food chain—fared almost as poorly as their prey, preyed upon themselves by farmers, ranchers, loggers, and hunters. Though the grand grizzly hasn't been seen in California for more than a century, California's black bear is still around—though increasingly tracked and hunted by timber interests (for the damage the bears inflict on seedling trees) and poachers out to make a fast buck on gall bladders popular in Asian pharmacology. Of California's native wildcats, only the mountain lion and the spotted, smaller bobcat survive. The last of the state's jaguars was hunted down near Palm Springs in 1860.

THE HISTORY OF THE GOLDEN DREAM

Europeans generally get credit for having "discovered" America, including the mythic land of California. But a dusty travel log tucked away in Chinese archives in Shenshi Province, discovered in the 19th century by an American missionary, suggests that the Chinese discovered California—in about 217 B.C. According to this saga, a storm-tossed Chinese ship—misdirected by its own compass, apparently rendered nonfunctional after a cockroach got wedged under the needle—sailed stubbornly for 100 days in the direction of what was supposed to be mainland China. (The navigator, Hee-li, reportedly ignored the protests of his crew, who pointed out that the sun was setting on the wrong horizon.) Stepping out into towering forests surrounding an almost endless inlet at the edge of the endless ocean, these unwitting adventurers reported meetings with red-skinned peoples—and giant red-barked trees.

Conventional continental settlement theory holds that the first true immigrants to the North

American continent also came from Asia—crossing a broad plain across the Bering Strait, a "bridge" that existed until the end of the Ice Age. Archaeologists agree that the earliest Americans arrived more than 11,500 years ago, more or less in sync with geologists' belief that the Bering bridge disappeared about 14,000 years ago. Circumstantial support for this conclusion has also come from striking similarities—in blood type, teeth, and language—existing between early Americans and Asians, particularly the northern Chinese. But recent discoveries have thrown all previous American migration theories into doubt.

In 1986, French scientists working in Brazil discovered an ancient rock shelter containing stone tools, other artifacts, and charcoal that was at first carbon-dated at approximately 32,000 years old. (A subsequent announcement, that the discovery was actually more than 45,000 years old, shocked archaeologists and was widely discredited.) Wall paintings suggest that cave art developed in the Americas at about the same time it did in Europe, Asia, and Africa. Preliminary evidence of very early human habitation (possibly as long ago as 33,000 years) has also been found in Chile. Subsequent Chilean finds at Monte Verde, dated authoritatively to 10,900 to 11,200 years ago, were announced in 1997—setting off a flurry of searches for still earlier sites of human habitation.

So the question is: if migration to the Americas was via the Bering Strait, and so long ago, why hasn't any similar evidence been discovered in North America? The mummified, mat-wrapped body of an elderly man discovered in 1940 in Spirit Cave near Fallon, Nevada, has subsequently been dated as 9,415 years old—making this the only Paleonoid (more than 8,500 years old) ever found in North America; the body was particularly well preserved by the desert climate. And a human skull dated as 9,800 years old has been discovered on Canada's Prince of Wales Island. Both of these finds are thought to bolster the Bering Straits land bridge theory—as does the Monte Verde discovery in Chile, if the first American arrivals were fishing people who worked their way down the continental coastline to settle, first, in South America. Some suggest that signs of earlier human habitation in North America have been erased by climatic factors, or by glaciation. But no one really knows. One thing is certain: most archaeologists would rather be buried alive in a dig than be forced to dust off and reexamine the previously discredited "Thor Heyerdahl theory" of American settlement: that the first immigrants sailed across the Pacific, landed in South America, and then migrated northward.

CALIFORNIA'S FIRST PEOPLE

However and whenever they first arrived in California, the territory's first immigrants gradually created civilizations quite appropriate to the land they had landed in. "Tribes" like those typical elsewhere in North America did not exist in California, primarily because the political unity necessary for survival elsewhere was largely irrelevant here. Populations of California native peoples are better understood as ethnic or kinship or community groups united by common experience and shared territory.

Though no census takers were abroad in the land at the time, the presettlement population (about 500 groups speaking 130 dialects) of what is now California is estimated at about 250,000—a density four to eight times greater than early people living anywhere else in the United States. Before their almost overnight decimation—from settlement, and attendant disease, cultural disintegration, and violence—California's native peoples found the living fairly easy. The cornucopia of fish, birds, and game, in addition to almost endlessly edible plant life, meant that hunting and gathering was not the strict struggle for survival it was elsewhere on the continent. Since abundance in all things was the rule, at least in nondesert areas, trade between tribal groups (for nonlocal favorite foods such as acorns, pine nuts, or seafood and for nonlocal woods or other prized items) was not uncommon. Plants and animals of the natural world were respected by native peoples as kindred spirits, and a deep nature mysticism was the underlying philosophy of most religious traditions and associated myths and legends.

Most California peoples were essentially nonviolent, engaging in war or armed conflict only for revenge; bows and arrows, spears, and harpoons were used in hunting. The development of basketry, in general the highest art of native populations, was also quite pragmatic; baskets of specific shapes and sizes were used to gather and to store foods and for cooking in. Homes, boats, and clothing were made of the most appropriate local materials, from slabs of redwood bark and animal hides to tule reeds.

Time was not particularly important to California's first immigrants. No one kept track of passing years, and most groups didn't even have a word for "year." They paid attention, however, to the passage of the moons and seasons—the natural rhythm of life. Many native peoples were seminomadic, moving in summer into cooler mountain regions where game, roots, and berries were most abundant, and then meandering down into the foothills and valleys in autumn to collect acorns, the staff of life for most tribes, and to take shelter from winter storms.

But there was nowhere to hide from the whirling clouds of change that started sweeping into California with the arrival of early explorers and missionaries, or from the foreign flood that came when the myth of California gold became a reality. Some native peoples went out fighting: the 19th-century Modoc War was one of the last major Indian wars in the United States. And others just waited until the end of their world arrived. Most famous in this category was Ishi, the "last wild man in America" and the last of his Yahi people, captured in an Oroville slaughterhouse corral in 1911. Working as a janitor as a ward of the University of California until his death five years later from tuberculosis, Ishi walked from the Stone Age into the industrial age with dignity and without fear.

FOREIGNERS PLANT THEIR FLAGS

The first of California's official explorers were the Spanish. Though Hernán Cortés discovered a land he called California in 1535, Juan Rodríguez Cabrillo—actually a Portuguese, João Rodrigues Cabrilho—first sailed the coast of Alta California ("upper," as opposed to "lower" or Baja California, which then included all of Mexico) and rode at anchor off its shores.

But the first European to actually set foot on California soil was the English pirate Sir Francis Drake, who in 1579 came ashore somewhere along the coast (exactly where is still disputed, though popular opinion suggests Point Reyes) and whose maps—like others of the day—reflected his belief that the territory was indeed an island. Upon his return to England, Drake's story of discovery served primarily to stimulate Spain's territorial appetites. Though Sebastián Vizcaíno entered Monterey Bay in 1602 (18 years before the Pilgrims arrived at Plymouth), it wasn't until 1746 that even the Spanish realized California wasn't an island. It wasn't until 1769 and 1770 that San Francisco Bay was discovered by Gaspar de Portolá and the settlements of San Diego and Monterey were founded.

Though the Spanish failed to find California's mythical gold, between 1769 and 1823 they did manage to establish 21 missions (sometimes with associated presidios) along the Camino Real or "Royal Road" from San Diego to Sonoma. And from these busy mission ranch outposts, maintained by the free labor of "hea-

then" natives, Spain grew and manufactured great wealth.

But even at its zenith, Spain's supremacy in California was tenuous. The territory was vast and relatively unpopulated. Even massive land grants—a practice continued under later Mexican rule—did little to allay colonial fears of successful outside incursions. Russian imperialism, spreading east into Siberia and Central Asia, and then to Alaska and an 1812 outpost at Fort Ross on the north coast, seemed a clear and present danger—and perhaps actually would have been, if the Russians' agricultural and other enterprises hadn't ultimately failed. And enterprising Americans, at first just a few fur trappers and traders, were soon in the neighborhood.

As things happened, the challenge to Spain's authority came from its own transplanted population. Inspired by the news in 1822 that an independent government had been formed in Baja California's Mexico City, young California-born Spanish ("Californios") and independence-seeking resident Spaniards declared Alta California part of the new Mexican empire. By March of 1825, when California proper officially became a territory of the Republic of Mexico, the new leadership had already achieved several goals, including secularizing the missions and "freeing" the associated native neophytes (not officially achieved until 1833), which in practice meant that most became servants elsewhere. The Californios also established an independent military and judiciary, opened the territory's ports to trade, and levied taxes.

During the short period of Mexican rule, the American presence was already prominent. Since even Spain regularly failed to send supply ships, Yankee traders were always welcome in California. In no time at all, Americans had organized and dominated the territory's business sector, established successful ranches and farms, married into local families, and become prominent citizens. California, as a possible political conquest, was becoming increasingly attractive to the United States.

Gen. John C. Frémont, officially on a scientific expedition but perhaps acting under secret orders from Washington (Frémont would never say), had been stirring things up in California since 1844—engaging in a few skirmishes with the locals or provoking conflicts between Californios and American citizens in California. Though the United States declared war on Mexico on May 13, 1846, Frémont and his men apparently were unaware of that turn of events and took over the town of Sonoma for a short time in mid-June, raising the secessionist flag of the independent—but very short-lived—Bear Flag Republic.

With Californios never mustering much resistance to the American warriors, Commodore John C. Sloat sailed unchallenged into Monterey Bay on July 7, 1848, raised the Stars and Stripes above the Custom House in town, and claimed California for the United States. Within two days, the flag flew in both San Francisco and Sonoma, but it took some time to end the statewide skirmishes. It took even longer for official Americanization—and statehood—to proceed. The state constitution established, among other things, California as a "free" state (but only to prevent the unfair use of slave labor in the mines). This upset the balance of congressional power in the nation's anti-slavery conflict and indirectly precipitated the Civil War. Written in Monterey, the new state's constitution was adopted in October of 1849 and ratified by voters in November.

General John C. Frémont declared California independent of Mexico and raised the flag of the shortlived Bear Flag Republic.

GOLD IN THEM THAR HILLS

California's legendary gold was real, as it turned out. And the Americans found it—but quite by accident. The day James Marshall, who was building a lumber mill on the American River for John Sutter, discovered flecks of shiny yellow metal in the mill's tailrace seemed otherwise quite ordinary. But that day, January 24, 1848, changed everything—in California and in the world.

As fortune seekers worldwide succumbed to gold fever and swarmed into the Sierra Nevada foothills in 1849, modern-day California began creating itself. In the no-holds-barred search for personal freedom and material satisfaction (better yet, unlimited wealth), something even then recognizable as California's human character was also taking shape: the belief that anything is possible, for anyone, no matter what one's previous circumstances would suggest. Almost everyone wanted to entertain that belief. (Karl Marx was of the opinion that the California gold rush was directly responsible for delaying the Russian revolution.) New gold dreamers—all colors and creeds—came to California, by land and by sea, to take a chance on themselves and their luck. The luckiest ones, though, were the merchants and businesspeople who cashed in on California's dream by mining the miners.

Because of the discovery of gold, California skipped the economically exploitive U.S. territorial phase typical of other Western states. With almost endless, indisputable capital at hand, Californians thumbed their noses at the Eastern financial establishment almost from the start: they could exploit the wealth of the far West themselves. And exploit it they did—mining not only the earth, but also the state's forests, fields, and water wealth. Wild California would never again be the same.

Almost overnight, "civilized" California became an economic sensation. The state was essentially admitted to the union on its own terms—because California was quite willing to go its own way and remain an independent entity otherwise. The city of San Francisco grew from a sleepy enclave of 500 souls to a hectic, hellbent business and financial center of more than 25,000 within two years. Other cities built on a foundation of prosperous trade included the inland supply port of Sacramento. Agriculture, at first important for feeding the state's mushrooming population of fortune hunters, soon became a de facto gold mine in its own right. Commerce expanded even more rapidly with the completion of the California-initiated transcontinental railroad and with the advent of other early communications breakthroughs such as the telegraph. California's dreams of prosperity became self-fulfilling prophecies. And as California went, so went the nation.

SOUTHERN CALIFORNIA'S GOLDEN AGE

There was gold in Southern California, too—and it was actually discovered first, at Placerita Canyon not far north of Mission San Fernando. But the subsequent discovery at Sutter's Mill soon dwarfed Southern California's gold rush–era mining finds. The bonanza here came from inflated beef prices and otherwise supplying the booming northstate goldfields. The boom went bust in the mid-1850s, and depression came to California. Only the arrival of the railroads awakened Southern California from its social and economic slumber. Lured by well-promoted tales and photographs of the salubrious sunny climate—a place where oranges grew in people's backyards, where even roses bloomed in winter—migrants arrived by the trainloads, particularly from the Midwest, throughout the 1880s. Soon agriculture, with orchards and fields of crops stretching to every horizon, became Southern California's economic strength. Real estate developments and grand hotels, often built on land owned by the railroad barons, soon boomed as well. In the late 1800s, oil was discovered throughout the greater Los Angeles basin, creating still more regional wealth.

As a land with little annual rainfall, its vast underground aquifers already well on the way to depletion because of agricultural irrigation and urban use, by the early 1900s Los Angeles was quickly running out of water. Yet the inventiveness of self-taught water engineer William Mulholland, soon an international celebrity, eliminated any prospect of enforced limits on growth. When the floodgates of the famed Los Angeles Aqueduct first opened, to great public acclaim, in 1913, Southern California had made its first monumental step toward eliminating the very idea of limits. Mulholland's engineering miracle, which

successfully tapped into Owens Valley water supplies that originated 250 miles to the north, also tapped into the southstate's social imagination. In no time at all the "desert" was in full bloom, landscaped with lush lawns, ferns, roses, and palm trees and populated by happy, healthy families frolicking in the sunshine.

That image, translated to the world's imagination via Hollywood's movie industry in the 1920s and subsequent years, essentially created the Southern California of today. Massive growth followed World War II, when Los Angeles began to create itself as an industrial and technological superpower—one soon beset by traffic, pollution, and social problems befitting its size.

Yet for all its current challenges Southern California is still a surprisingly optimistic place. For every problem there is a solution, according to traditional southstate thinking.

DREAMING THE NEW GOLD DREAM

California as the land of opportunity—always a magnet for innovation, never particularly respectful of stifling and stodgy tradition—has dictated terms to the rest of the country throughout its modern history. Even with the gradual arrival of what the rest of the world could finally recognize as civilization, which included the predictable phenomenon of personal wealth translated into political power, California's commitment to prosperity and change—sometimes for its own sake—has never waned.

From the founding of the Automobile Club of Southern California in 1900 to the construction of Yosemite's Hetch Hetchy Dam (to slake San Francisco thirst) in 1923; from the establishment of the first Hollywood movie studio in 1911 to the 1927 transmission, from San Francisco, of the first television picture; from the completion in 1940 of the world's first freeway to the opening of Disneyland in 1955; from the 1960s' Free Speech Movement, the rise of Black Power in the wake of the Watts riots in 1965, and the successes of César Chávez's United Farm Workers Union to the Beat poets, San Francisco's Summer of Love and the oozing up of New Age consciousness; from California's rise as leader in the development of nuclear weapons and defense technology to the creation of the microchip and personal computer: California history is a chronicle of incredible change, a relentless double-time march into the new.

"All that is constant about the California of my childhood," writes Sacramento native Joan Didion in an essay from *Slouching Towards Bethlehem,* "is the rate at which it disappears."

CALIFORNIA GOVERNMENT: THE BEST THAT MONEY CAN BUY

California's political structure is quite confusing, with thousands of tax-levying governmental units—including special districts, 58 county governments, and hundreds of cities both large and small—and a variety of overlapping jurisdictions. Based on the federal principle of one-person, one-vote and designed with separate executive, judicial, and legislative (Assembly and Senate) branches, the game of state-level California government is often quite lively, almost a high form of entertainment for those who understand the rules. The use and abuse of public resources is the ultimate goal of power-brokering in the Golden State, affecting statewide and local economies as well as the private sector and creating (or abandoning) commitments to social justice and various human rights issues many Californians still hold dear.

The popularity of unusually affable, charismatic, and highly visible California politicians, from Ronald Reagan to Jerry Brown, would suggest that Golden State politics generally takes place in the entertainment arena. Nothing could be further from the truth. Though Californians are committed to the concept of public initiatives and referenda on major issues—politicians be damned, basically—most decisions affecting life in California are still made in the time-honored behind-the-scenes tradition of U.S. politics, with backroom deal-making conducted something like a poker game. In order to know the score, you have to know the players and what cards they hold.

Those in the know contend that the California Legislature, considered the best state-level legislative body in the nation as recently as 1971, has steadily been careening downhill, in terms of effectiveness and ethics, ever since—largely because of "juice," or the influence of lobbyists and special interest money. According to veteran *Sacramento Bee* political reporter and columnist Dan Walters: "Votes are bought, sold, and rented by the hour with an arrogant casualness. There are one-man, one-vote retail sales as well as wholesale transactions that party leaders negotiate for blocs of votes."

Though from some perspectives California voters—and nonvoters—are largely responsible for the seemingly insoluble problems the state now faces, polls indicate that Californians increasingly distrust their politicians. From his years observing the species from the 19th-century Washington, D.C., press gallery, Mark Twain offered this fitting summary, a quote from a fictitious newspaper account in his novel, *The Gilded Age:* "We are now reminded of a note we received from the notorious burglar Murphy, in which he finds fault with a statement of ours that he had served one term in the penitentiary and one in the U.S. Senate. He says, 'The latter statement is untrue and does me great injustice.'"

Given California voters' current penchant for taking matters into their own hands, no matter how disastrously, it came as no surprise in 1992 when California became one of the first states in the nation to pass a "term limitations" law, restricting its Assembly members to maximum six-year terms in office and limiting the terms of governor, state senators, and other constitutional officers to eight years. Another initiative, put before the voters in 1990 as Proposition 140, cut the Legislature's operating budget by $70 million, about 38 percent. It has been upheld as constitutional by the State Supreme Court.

THE GLITTER OF THE GOLDEN STATE ECONOMY

If the lure of gold brought pioneers to California, the rich land, its seemingly endless resources, and the state's almost anarchistic "anything goes" philosophy kept them here. The Golden State has essentially become a nation-state—an economic superpower, the fifth-largest (or sixth or seventh, depending on the comparison data) economy in the world. A major international player in the game of Pacific Rim commerce, California's cry is usually "free trade," in contrast to the philosophy of high-tariff trade protectionism typically so strong elsewhere in the United States. And with so much financial clout, California is often the tail that wags the dog of U.S. domestic and foreign economic and political policy. No one ever says it out loud, but California could easily secede from the union, only too happy to compete as an independent entity in the world market. This seemed especially true in the late 1990s, as California emerged stronger than ever after an economic slump, buoyed by booming exports to both Japan and Mexico.

Though industry of every sort thrives in California, agriculture has long been the state's economic mainstay. ("The whole place stank of orange blossoms," observed H. L. Mencken on a Golden State visit.) Though most Southern California citrus groves have long since been paved over for parking lots and shopping malls—those disturbed by California's proclivity for bulldozing the past in the name of progress have coined a verb for it: "to californicate"—agriculture in pockets of Southern California and in Northern California is still going strong. Because of the large size and concentrated ownership of farm and ranch lands, helped along by public subsidies of irrigation engineering projects, agriculture in California has always been agribusiness. In its role as agricultural nation-state, California produces more food than 90 percent of the world's nations, a $25 billion annual business.

The economic spirit of the northstate, suggested philosopher George Santayana in a 1910 Berkeley speech, is best summed up by the immense presence of nature in Northern California—nature in tandem with engineering and technology. Now that the roughshod, rough-and-tumble days of man against nature are no longer widely condoned, Californians increasingly expect technology to respect nature's standards. In Northern California particularly, but increasingly in Southern California, information is the cleanest industry of all. It seems no coincidence that both the microchip and the personal computer were born here.

Yet California, northern and southern, is industrious in all ways. Travel and tourism is a major industry—now promoted, since California has started to lose ground in the tourist sweeps to other Western states—with annual revenues in the $52 billion range. Growth itself is a growth industry in California, with all aspects of the construction trade generating an average $30 billion in business annually. Revenues generated by California's top 100 privately held companies—including Bechtel Group, Hughes Aircraft, USA Petroleum (and other oil companies), Twentieth-Century Fox Films (and other media giants), Purex Industries, Denny's Inc., Raley's, both the AAA-affiliated Automobile Club of Southern California and the California State Automobile Association, and a long string of agricultural cooperatives as well as health- and life-insurance companies—approach $100 billion annually.

A U.S. capital of finance and commerce, the state is also the world's high-technology headquarters. Helped along by state-supported University of California labs and research facilities, California has long been a leader in the aerospace and weapons development industries. Including military bases and research, testing, and surveillance sites, about 80 outposts of nuclear weaponry are—or were—based in California; recent federal cuts in defense spending have slowed business considerably.

THE PEOPLE— ALWAYS ON THE MOVE

Everyone is moving to California and vicinity, it seems. According to American Demographics, the geographic center of the U.S. population moves 58 feet farther west and 29 feet to the south every year. (Recent bad times in California slowed that trend temporarily, as Californians left to find jobs elsewhere, but that loss has been overshadowed by increased immigration.) Be that as it may, some people consider Californians among the most obnoxious people on earth, and this is not necessarily a new phenomenon.

To some, the state is a kind of cultural purgatory, settled (in the words of Willard Huntington Wright) by "yokels from the Middle West who were nourished by rural pieties and superstitions." Others consider, and have always considered, Californians as somehow inherently unstable. "Insanity, as might be expected, is fearfully prevalent in California," Dr. Henry Gibbons stated before San Francisco's local medical society in 1857. "It grows directly out of the excited mental condition of our population, to which the common use of alcoholic drink is a powerful adjunct." The general outside observation today is that if Californians aren't talking about themselves—and about accomplishing their latest career, financial, fitness, or psychospiritual goals—they talk about California. New Englander Inez Hayes Irwin defined those afflicted with Californoia in her 1921 book *Californiacs:*

> *The Californiac is unable to talk about anything but California, except when he interrupts himself to knock every other place on the face of the earth. He looks with pity on anybody born outside of California, and he believes that no one who has ever seen California willingly lives elsewhere. He himself often lives elsewhere, but he never admits that it is from choice.*

There may be more than a shred of truth in this, even today; pollsters say one out of every four Californians would rather live elsewhere—for the most part, either in Hawaii or Oregon. But many who live and work in California are not native Californians. This is almost as true today as it ever was; at least one-third of contemporary Californians were born somewhere else. Somehow, California's amazing cultural and ethnic diversity is the source of both its social stability and its self-renewal.

Perhaps because of misleading portrayals of California's past, in the media and the movies as well as the history books, a common misconception is that the impact and importance of California's ethnic populations is relatively recent, a post–World War II phenomenon. But many peoples and many races have made significant contributions to California culture and economic development since the days of the gold rush—and since the decimation of native populations.

Blacks and Hispanics, despite attempts (official and otherwise) to prevent them from dreaming the California dream, were among the first to arrive in the goldfields. The Chinese, who also arrived early to join the ranks of the state's most industrious citizens, were relentlessly persecuted despite their willingness to do work others considered impossible—including the unimaginable engineering feat of chiseling a route over the forbidding Sierra Nevada for the nation's first transcontinental railroad. And when the state's boom-bust beginnings gave way to other possibilities, including farming, ranching, and small business enterprises, California's minorities stayed—helping, despite the realities of subtle discrimination and sometimes overt racism, to create the psychological pluralism characteristic of California society today.

DOING THE DREAM: PRACTICALITIES

California is crowded—both with people trying to live the dream on a permanent basis and with those who come to visit, to re-create themselves on the standard two-week vacation plan. Summer, when school's out, is generally when the Golden State is most crowded, though this pattern is changing rapidly now that year-round schools and off-season travel are becoming common. Another trend: "mini-vacations," with workaholic Californians and other Westerners opting for one- to several-day respites spread throughout the year rather than traditional once-a-year holidays. It was once a truism that great bargains, in accommodations and transport particularly, were widely available during California's nonsummer travel season. Because of Southern California's mild coastal temperatures and popular wintertime sports and desert recreational possibilities, this is not necessarily true. Early spring and autumn can be the best times to travel.

Spontaneous travel, or following one's whims wherever they may lead, was once feasible in Southern California. Unfortunately, given the immense popularity of many southstate attractions and destinations, those days are long gone. Particularly for those traveling on the cheap and for travelers with special needs or specific desires, some of the surprises encountered during impulsive adventuring may be unpleasant. If the availability of specific types of lodgings (including campgrounds) or eateries, or if transport details, prices, hours, and other factors are important for a pleasant trip, the best bet is calling ahead to check details and/or to make reservations. (Everything changes rapidly in California.) For a good overview of what to see and do in advance of a planned trip, including practical suggestions beyond those in this guide, also contact the chambers of commerce and/or visitor centers listed. Other good sources for local and regional information are bookstores, libraries, sporting goods and outdoor supply stores, and local, state, and federal government offices.

BEING HERE: BASIC TRUTHS

Conduct and Custom: Smoking, Drinking, and General Truths

Smoking is a major social sin in California, often against the law in public buildings and on public transport, with regulations particularly stringent in urban areas. People sometimes get violent over other people's smoking, so smokers need to be respectful of others' "space" and smoke outdoors when possible. Smoking has been banned outright in California restaurants and bars, and smoking is not allowed on public airplane flights, though nervous fliers can usually smoke somewhere inside—or outside—airline terminals. Many bed-and-breakfasts in California are either entirely nonsmoking or restrict smoking to decks, porches, or dens; if this is an issue, inquire by calling ahead. Hotels and motels, most commonly in major urban areas or popular tourist destinations, increasingly offer nonsmoking rooms (or entire floors). Ask in advance.

The legal age for buying and drinking alcohol in California is 21. Though Californians tend to (as they say) "party hearty," public drunkenness is not well tolerated. Drunken driving—which means operating an automobile (even a bicycle, technically) while under the influence—is definitely against the law. California is increasingly no-nonsense about the use of illegal drugs, too, from marijuana to cocaine, crack, and heroin. Doing time in local jails or state prisons is not the best way to do California.

English is the official language in California, and even English-speaking visitors from other countries have little trouble understanding California's "dialect" once they acclimate to the accents and slang expressions. (Californians tend to be very creative in their language.) When unsure what someone means by some peculiar phrase, ask for a translation into standard English. Particularly in urban areas, many languages are commonly spoken, and—even in English—the accents are many. You can usually obtain at least some foreign-language brochures,

RIGHT ATTITUDE

Whenever you arrive and wherever you go, one thing to bring along is the right attitude—bad attitude, strangely enough, being a particular problem among American travelers (including Californians) visiting California. One reason visitors become annoyed and obnoxious is because, often without realizing it, they started their trip with high, sometimes fantasy-based expectations—akin, perhaps, to being magically cured of all limitations at a Lourdes-like way station along life's freeway—and, once arrived in California, reality disappoints. Even the Golden State has traffic jams, parking problems, rude service people, and lowlifes only too happy to make off with a good time by stealing one's pocketbook—or car. Be prepared.

Visitors also bring along no-fun baggage when they go to new places and compare whatever they find with what they left behind "back home." This is disrespectful. The surest way to enjoy California is to remain open-minded about whatever you may see, hear, do, or otherwise experience. It's fine to laugh (to one's self) at California's contradictions and cultural self-consciousness—even Californians do it—but try to view new places, from laid-back yet sophisticated Los Angeles to the most isolated and economically depressed desert backwater, from the perspective of the people who live and work there. Better yet, strike up conversations with locals and ask questions whenever possible. These experiences invariably become the best surprises of all—because people, places, and things in California are often not quite what they first appear to be.

maps, and other information from city visitor centers and popular tourist destinations. (If this is a major concern, inquire in advance.)

Californians are generally casual, in dress as well as etiquette. If any standard applies in most situations, it's common courtesy—still in style, generally speaking, even in California. Though "anything goes" just about anywhere, elegant restaurants usually require appropriately dressy attire for women, jacket and tie for men. (Shirts and shoes—pants or skirt too, usually—are required in any California restaurant.)

By law, public buildings in California are wheelchair-accessible, or at least partially so. The same is true of most major hotels and tourist attractions, which may offer both rooms and restrooms with complete wheelchair accessibility; some also have wheelchairs, walkers, and other mobility aids available for temporary use. Even national and state parks, increasingly, are attempting to make some sights and campgrounds more accessible for those with physical disabilities; to make special arrangements, inquire in advance. But private buildings, from restaurants to bed-and-breakfasts, may not be so accommodating. Those with special needs should definitely ask specific questions in advance.

Conduct and Custom: Tipping

For services rendered in the service trade, a tip is usually expected. Some say the word is derived from the Latin *stips,* for stipend or gift. Some say it's an 18th-century English acronym for "to ensure promptness," though "to ensure personal service" seems more to the point in these times. In expensive restaurants or for large groups, an automatic tip or gratuity may be included in the bill—an accepted practice in many countries but a source of irritation for many U.S. diners, who would prefer to personally evaluate the quality of service received. Otherwise 15–20 percent of the before-tax total tab is the standard gratuity, and 10 percent the minimal acknowledgment, for those in the service trade—waitresses and waiters, barbers, hairdressers, and taxi drivers. In fine dining circumstances, wine stewards should be acknowledged personally, at the rate of $2–5 per bottle, and the maître d' as well, with $5 or $10. In very casual buffet-style joints, leave $1 each for the people who clear the dishes and pour your coffee after the meal. In bars, leave $1 per drink, or 15 percent of the bill if you run a tab. At airports, tip skycaps $1 per bag (more if they transport your baggage any distance); tip more generously for extra assistance, such as helping wheelchair passengers or mothers with infants and small children to their gates.

At hotels, a desk clerk or concierge does not require a tip unless that person fulfills a specific request, such as snagging tickets for a sold-out concert or theater performance, in which case generosity is certainly appropriate. For baggage handlers curbside, $1 tip is adequate; a tip of at least $1 per bag is appropriate for bell staff transporting luggage from the lobby to your room or from your room to the lobby. For valet parking, tip the attendant $2–3. Tip the hotel doorman if he helps with baggage or hails a cab for you. And tip swimming pool or health club personnel as appropriate for extra personal service. Unless one stays in a hotel or motel for several days, the standard practice is not to tip the housekeeper, though you can if you wish; some guests leave $1–2 each morning for the housekeeper and $1 each evening for turn-down service.

Theme Parks and Diversions

Southern California is noted for its whiz-bang theme parks, some most famous for their hair-raising rides, others for their family-friendly diversions or movie-related special effects. Increasingly, for visitors and residents alike, theme parks take the place of engagement with the broader culture. Yet Southern California offers much more than theme parks, including exceptional art, cultural, and natural history museums, engaging zoos, and eccentric community events. Do the theme parks, by all means—but for a proper introduction to Southern California, be sure to do at least some of the rest—options detailed at some length in this book. See also Playing Here: Outdoor Recreation, below, and subsequent information on national parks, national forests, and state parks.

Entertainment, Events, Holidays

Not even the sky's the limit on entertainment in California. From air shows to harvest fairs and rodeos, from symphony to opera, from rock 'n' roll to avant-garde clubs and theater, from strip shows (male and female) to ringside seats at ladies' mud-wrestling contests, from high-stakes bingo games to horse-racing—anything goes in the Golden State. Most communities offer a wide variety of special, often quite unusual, annual events; many of these are listed by region or city elsewhere in this guide.

WHAT TO BRING

Generally speaking, bring what you'll really need—but as little of it as possible. A good rule of thumb: select everything absolutely necessary for your travels, then take along only half. Remember, you'll be bringing back all sorts of interesting tokens of your trip, so leave space. Remember, too, that camera equipment is heavy; bring only what you'll really use. (Try carrying your packed luggage around for 15 or 20 minutes if you need motivation to lighten the load.) Standard luggage is adequate for most travelers, especially those traveling by bus or car. For those planning to be without personal wheels, and therefore destined to cover more ground on foot, a backpack—or convertible backpack-suitcase—may be more useful, since you can also carry the load on your back as needed. For any traveler, a daypack may also come in handy, for use on day hikes and outings and as an extra bag for toting home travel trinkets.

In characteristically casual California, clothing should be sensible and comfortable. Natural fibers are preferable because they "breathe" in California's variable climate. Cotton is the most fundamental California fiber—quite versatile, too, when layered to meet one's changing needs. Shorts, jeans, T-shirts, and sandals or sport shoes are the standard tourist uniform (swimming suits at the beach). Dark or bright colors, knits, and durable clothing will keep you presentable longer than more frivolous fashions, though laundry services and coin-operated Laundromats are widely available. Even for summer travel—and even in Southern California—always bring a sweater or light jacket, since summer fog can cool daytime temperatures near popular coastal destinations, and evenings can be cool in coastal or foothill areas. A heavier jacket is advisable even for summers in the mountains—and for winters in the desert, particularly in the Mojave Desert, which gets snowfall at higher elevations. Winter weather in mountainous regions also can be quite severe (though in spring sometimes even downhill skiers wear shorts on the slopes), so pack accordingly. Those planning to participate in California-style high life should pack dress clothes, of course, but the most universally necessary thing to bring is a decent (preferably broken-in) pair of walking shoes.

Official holidays, especially during the warm-weather travel season and the Thanksgiving-Christmas-New Year holiday season, are often the most congested and popular (read: more expensive) times to travel or stay in California. Yet this is not always true; great holiday-season bargains in accommodations are sometimes available at swank hotels that primarily cater to business people. Though most tourist destinations are usually jumping, banks and many businesses close on the following major holidays: New Year's Day (January 1); Martin Luther King, Jr.'s Birthday (January 15, usually observed on the following Monday); Presidents' Day (the third Monday in February); Memorial Day (the last Monday in May); Independence Day (July 4); Labor Day (the first Monday in September); Veterans Day (November 11); Thanksgiving (the fourth Thursday in November); and Christmas (December 25). California's newest state holiday is César E. Chávez Day, in honor of the late leader of the United Farm Workers (UFW), signed into law in August 2000 and celebrated each year on the Friday or Monday closest to March 31, Chávez's birthday. In honor of the nation's most famous Latino civil rights leader, all state offices close but banks and other businesses may not.

Shopping Standards
Most stores are open during standard business hours (weekdays 8 A.M.–5 P.M. or 9 A.M.–5 P.M.) and often longer, sometimes seven days a week, because of the trend toward two-income families and ever-reduced leisure time. This trend is particularly noticeable in cities, where shops and department stores are often open until 9 P.M. or later, and where many grocery stores are open 24 hours.

Shopping malls—almost self-sustaining cities in California, with everything from clothing and major appliances to restaurants and entertainment—are the standard California trend, but cities large and small with viable downtown shopping districts often offer greater variety and uniqueness in goods and services offered. Also particularly popular in California are flea markets and arts-and-crafts fairs, the former usually held on weekends, the latter best for hand-crafted items and often associated with the Thanksgiving-through-Christmas shopping season and/or festivals and special events. California assesses a 7 percent state sales tax on all nonfood items sold in the state, and many municipalities levy additional sales tax.

PLAYING HERE: OUTDOOR RECREATION

With its tremendous natural diversity, recreationally California offers something for just about everyone. Popular spring-summer-fall activities include hiking and backpacking; all water sports, from pleasure boating and water-sking to sailing, windsurfing, and swimming; whitewater rafting, canoeing, and kayaking; mountain and rock-climbing; even hang gliding and hunting. In most years, winter activities popular in Northern California can also be enjoyed in Southern California, at least to a certain extent, these including both Alpine and Nordic skiing, snowshoe hiking, sledding and tobogganing, and just plain snow play. Also high on the "most popular" list of outdoor California sports: bicycling, walking and running, and coastal diversions from beachcombing to surfing. The most likely places to enjoy these and other outdoor activities are mentioned throughout this book.

And where do people go to re-create themselves in Southern California's great outdoors? Fewer places than in the recent past, since wide-open spaces are fast disappearing in Southern California. In Los Angeles, San Diego, and other southstate coastal areas, outdoor recreation has long centered on local beaches and swimming, sunning, and surfing, beachcombing and pier fishing. Life at the beach is not as carefree as it once was, however, because of too many people, too many cars, and, in some places, too much pollution—the southstate in microcosm, in other words. Yet Southern California still offers a number of nice local and regional parks as well as state parks and beaches, national forests—unbelievably congested in summer—and national parks, most notably those included in the vast expanse of the state's deserts.

For more information on the national parks, national forests, and other state and federal lands (including Bureau of Land Management wilderness areas) mentioned in this book, contact each directly.

National Parks Information and Fees

For those planning to travel extensively in national parks in California and elsewhere in the United States, a one-year Golden Eagle Passport provides unlimited park access (not counting camping fees) for the holder and family, for the new price of $50. Though the Golden Eagle pass has recently doubled in price, it can still be worth it in California, where fees at certain national parks have recently increased; admission to Death Valley is now $10 (for up to a one-week stay) and Yosemite is $20. Those age 62 or older qualify for the $10 Golden Age Passport, which provides free access to national parks, monuments, and recreation areas, and a 50 percent discount on RV fees. Disabled travelers are eligible for the $10 Golden Access Passport, with the same privileges. You can buy all three special passes at individual national parks or obtain them in advance, along with visitor information, from: **U.S. National Park Service,** National Public Inquiries Office, U.S. Department of the Interior, 1849 C St., P.O. Box 37127, Washington, DC 20013, www.nps.gov. For regional national parks information covering California, Nevada, and Arizona, contact: **Western Region Information Office,** U.S. National Park Service, Fort Mason, Bldg. 201, San Francisco, CA 94123, 415/556-0560 (recorded) or 415/556-0561.

Campgrounds in some national parks in California—including Channel Islands, Death Valley, Joshua Tree, and Sequoia-Kings Canyon in the southern Sierra Nevada just north of Los Angeles—can be reserved (with MasterCard or Visa) through the **National Park Reservation Service,** www.reservations.nps.gov, or by calling toll-free 800/365-2267 (365-CAMP) at least eight weeks in advance. The total cost includes both the actual camping fee plus a $8–9 reservations fee. From California, call 7 A.M.–7 P.M. (10 A.M.–10 P.M. Eastern time). If you're also heading to **Yosemite,** make campground reservations via the Internet (see address above) or by calling toll-free 800/436-7275 (436-PARK). And to cancel your reservations, call toll-free 800/388-2733. To make national park camping reservations from outside the United States, call 619/452-8787.

To support the protection of U.S. national parks and their natural heritage, contact the non-profit **National Parks and Conservation Asso-**ciation (NPCA), 1776 Massachusetts Ave. NW, Washington, DC 20036, 202/223-6722, fax 202/659-0650, www.npca.org/home/npca. Both as a public service and fund-raiser, the NPCA publishes a number of comprehensive regional "overview" guides to U.S. national parks—Alaska, the Pacific, the Pacific Northwest, Southwest included—that cost less than $10 each, plus shipping and handling. To order one or more titles, call toll-free 800/395-7275.

National Forests and Other Federal Lands

For general information about U.S. national forests, including wilderness areas and campgrounds in Southern California, contact: **U.S. Forest Service,** U.S. Department of Agriculture, Publications, P.O. Box 96090, Washington, DC 20090, 202/205-1760. For a wealth of information via the Internet, try www.fs.fed.us. For information specifically concerning national forests and wilderness areas in California, and for maps, contact: **U.S. Forest Service, Pacific Southwest Region,** 630 Sansome St., San Francisco, CA 94111, 415/705-2870. Additional Southern California regional offices are mentioned elsewhere in this guide.

Some U.S. Forest Service and Army Corps of Engineers campgrounds in California can be reserved through ReserveAmerica's **National Recreation Reservation Service** (with MasterCard or Visa) at www.reserveusa .com, or call toll-free 877/444-6777 (TDD: 877/833-6777), a service available 5 A.M.–9 P.M. (8 A.M.–midnight Eastern time) from April 1 through Labor Day and otherwise 7 A.M.–4 P.M. (10 A.M.–7 P.M. Eastern time). From outside the United States, call 518/885-3639. Reservations for individual campsites can be made up to eight months in advance, and for group camps up to 360 days in advance. Along with the actual costs of camping, expect to pay a per-reservation service fee of $8–9 for individual campsites (more for group sites). In addition to its first-come, first-camped campgrounds, in some areas the U.S. Forest Service offers the opportunity for "dispersed camping," meaning that you can set up minimal-impact campsites in various undeveloped areas. For detailed current recreation, camping, and other information, contact specific national forests mentioned elsewhere in this book.

Anyone planning to camp extensively in national forest campgrounds should consider buying U.S. Forest Service "camp stamps" (at national forest headquarters or at ranger district stations) in denominations of 50 cents, $1, $2, $3, $5, and $10. These prepaid camping coupons amount to a 15 percent discount on the going rate. (Many national forest campgrounds are first-come, first-camped; without a reserved campsite, even camp stamps won't guarantee one.) Senior adults, disabled people, and those with national Golden Age and Golden Access recreation passports—see "National Parks Information and Fees," above—pay only half the standard fee at any campground and can buy camp stamps at half the regular rate as well.

For wannabe archaeologists, the U.S. Forest Service offers the opportunity to volunteer on archaeological digs through its **Passport in Time** program—certainly one way to make up for stingy federal budgets. To receive the project's newsletter, which announces upcoming projects in various national forests, contact: Passport in Time Clearinghouse, P.O. Box 31805, Tucson, AZ 85751.

Some Northern California public lands and vast expanses of Southern California are managed by the **U.S. Bureau of Land Management** (BLM). For general information, contact: U.S. Bureau of Land Management, Public Affairs Office, 1849 C St. NW, LS 406, Washington, DC 20240, 202/452-5125; www.blm.gov. For information specifically related to California, contact: **California BLM,** 2800 Cottage Way, Room W1824, Sacramento, CA 95825, 916/978-4400; www.ca.blm.gov. If you plan to camp on BLM lands, be sure to request a current *California Visitor Map,* which includes campgrounds and other features; the BLM also allows "dispersed camping" in some areas (ask for details). For detailed information on all 69 of the BLM's new desert wildernesses, contact the BLM's **California Desert District Office,** 6221 Box Springs Rd., Riverside, CA 92507, 909/697-5200 or toll-free 800/446-6743; www.ca.blm.gov/cdd.

For information on national wildlife reserves and other protected federal lands, contact: **U.S. Fish and Wildlife Service,** Division of Refuges, 4401 N. Fairfax Dr., Room 640, Arlington, VA 22203, toll-free 800/344-9453; www.fws.gov.

California State Parks

California's 275 beloved state parks, which include beaches, wilderness areas, and historic homes, have recently been going through bad times—the unfortunate result of increasing public use combined with budget cuts. That trend was dramatically reversed in 2000, as Governor Gray Davis decided to share with the state parks—and, indirectly, the public—some of the revenue wealth generated by booming economic times. State park support has increased, park day-use fees cut in half, and camping fees reduced.

Day-use fees for admission to California state parks now range from free (rare) to $2 or $3 per vehicle, with extra fees charged for dogs (if allowed), extra vehicles, and other circumstances. In highly congested areas, state parks charge no day-use fee but do charge a parking fee—making it more attractive to park elsewhere and walk or take a bus. For information on special assistance available for individuals with disabilities or other special needs, contact individual parks—which make every effort to be accommodating, in most cases.

Annual passes (nontransferable), which you can buy at most state parks and at the State Parks Store in Sacramento (see below), are $35 for day use. Golden Bear passes, for seniors age 62 and older with limited incomes and for certain others who receive public assistance, are $5 per year and allow day-use access to all state parks and off-road vehicle areas except Hearst/San Simeon, Sutter's Fort, and the California State Railroad Museum. For details on income eligibility and other requirements, call 916/653-4000. "Limited use" Golden Bear passes, for seniors age 62 and older, allow free parking at state parks during the nonpeak park season (usually Labor Day through Memorial Day) and are $20 per year; they can be purchased in person at most state parks. Senior discounts for state park day use ($1 off) and camping ($2 off, but only if the discount is requested while making reservations) are also offered. Special state park discounts and passes are also offered for the disabled and disabled veterans/POWs (prisoners of war). For more information, contact state park headquarters (see below).

Detailed information about California's state parks, beaches, and recreation areas is scattered throughout this guide. To obtain a complete parks listing, including available facilities, campground reservation forms, and other information, contact: **California State Parks,** Public Information, P.O. Box 942896, Sacramento, CA 94296, 916/653-6995 (recorded, with an endless multiple-choice menu); www.cal-parks .ca.gov.

State park publications include the *Official Guide to California State Parks* map and facilities listing, which includes all campgrounds, available free with admission to most state parks but available by mail, at last report, for $2; send check or money order to the attention of the Publications Section. Also available, and free: a complete parks and recreation publications list (which includes a mail order form). Other publications include the annual magazines *Events and Programs at California State Parks,* chock-full of educational and entertaining things to do, and *California Escapes,* a reasonably detailed regional rundown on all state parks.

For information about the state parks' Junior Ranger Program—many parks offer individual programs emphasizing both the state's natural and cultural heritage—call individual state parks. For general information, call 916/653-8959. Also available through the state parks department is an annually updated "Sno-Park" guide to parking without penalty while cross-country skiing or otherwise playing in the snow; for a current Sno-Park listing, write in care of the program at the state parks' address listed above or call 916/324-1222 (automated hotline). Sno-Park permits (required) cost $3 per day or $20 for the entire season, Nov. 1–May 30; you can also buy them at REI and other sporting goods stores and at any American Automobile Association (AAA) office in California. Another winter-season resource, free to AAA members, is the annual *Winter Sports Guide* for California, which lists prices and other current information for all downhill and cross-country ski areas.

California state parks offer excellent campgrounds. In addition to developed "family" campsites, which usually include a table, fire ring or outdoor stove, plus running water, flush toilets, and hot showers (RV hookups, if available, are extra), some state campgrounds also offer more primitive "walk-in" or environmental campgrounds and very simple hiker/biker campsites. Group campgrounds are also available (and reservable) at many state parks. If you plan to camp over the Memorial or Labor Day weekends, or the July 4th holiday, be sure to make reservations as early as possible.

Make campground reservations at California state parks (with MasterCard or Visa) through **ReserveAmerica,** www.reserveamerica.com, or call toll-free 800/444-7275 (444-PARK) weekdays 8 A.M.–5 P.M. For TDD reservations, call toll-free 800/274-7275 (274-PARK). And to cancel state park campground reservations, from the United States call toll-free 800/695-2269. To make reservations from Canada or elsewhere outside the United States, call 619/638-5883. As in other camping situations, before calling to make reservations, know the park and campground name, how you'll be camping (tent or RV), how many nights, and how many people and vehicles. In addition to reductions in the actual camping fee, which can vary from $5–6 for more primitive campsites (without showers and/or flush toilets) to $8–12 for developed campsites, there is no longer a nonrefundable reservations fee. Sites with hookups cost $6 more. You can make camping reservations up to seven months in advance. Certain campsites, including some primitive environmental and hiker/biker sites (now just $1) can be reserved only through the relevant state park.

To support the state's park system, contact the nonprofit **California State Parks Foundation,** 800 College Ave., P.O. Box 548, Kentfield, CA 94914, 415/258-9975, fax (415) 258-9930; www.calparks.org. Through memberships and contributions, the foundation has financed about $100 million in park preservation and improvement projects in the past several decades. Volunteers are welcome to contribute sweat equity too.

Other State Recreation Resources

For general information and fishing and hunting regulations, usually also available at sporting goods stores and bait shops where licenses and permits are sold, call the **California Department of Fish and Game** in Sacramento at

916/653-7664; for license information, call 916/227-2244; www.dfg.ca.gov. For additional sportfishing information, call toll-free 800/275-3474 (800/ASK-FISH).

For environmental and recreational netheads, the California Resources Agency's CERES website, aka the California Environmental Resources Evaluation System at ceres.ca.gov, offers an immense amount of additional information, from reports and updates on rare and endangered species to current boating regulations. The database is composed of federal, state, regional, and local agency information as well as a multitude of data and details from state and national environmental organizations—from REINAS, or the Real-time Environmental Information Network and Analysis System at the University of California at Santa Cruz, The Nature Conservancy, and NASA's Imaging Radar Home Page. Check it out.

Worth it for inveterate wildlife voyeurs is the recently revised *California Wildlife Viewing Guide* (Falcon Press, 1997), produced in conjunction with 15 state, federal, and local agencies in addition to Ducks Unlimited and the Wetlands Action Alliance. About 200 wildlife viewing sites are listed—most of these not in Southern California, however. Look for the *California Wildlife Viewing Guide* at local bookstores, or order a copy by calling toll-free 800/582-2665. With the sale of each book, $1 is contributed to California Watchable Wildlife Project nature tourism programs.

To support California's beleaguered native plant life, join, volunteer with, and otherwise contribute to the **California Native Plant Society** (CNPS), 1722 J St., Ste. 17, Sacramento, CA 95814, 916/447-2677, fax 916/447-2727, www .cnps.org. In various areas of the state, local CNPS chapters sponsor plant and habitat restoration projects. The organization also publishes some excellent books. Groups including the **Sierra Club, Audubon Society,** and **The Nature Conservancy** also sponsor hikes, backpack trips, bird-watching treks, backcountry excursions, and volunteer "working weekends" in all areas of California; call local or regional contact numbers (in the telephone book) or watch local newspapers for activity announcements.

STAYING—AND EATING— IN THE GOLDEN STATE

Camping Out
Because of many recent years of drought, and painful lessons learned about extreme fire danger near suburban and urban areas, all California national forests, most national parks, and many state parks now ban all backcountry fires—with the exception of controlled burns (under park supervision), increasingly used to thin understory vegetation to prevent uncontrollable wildfires. Some areas even prohibit portable camp stoves, so be sure to check current conditions and all camping and hiking or backpacking regulations before setting out.

To increase your odds of landing a campsite where and when you want one, make reservations. For details on reserving campsites at both national and state parks in Southern California, see relevant listings under Playing Here: Outdoor Recreation, immediately above. Without reservations, seek out "low-profile" campgrounds during the peak camping season—summer as well as spring and fall weekends in most parts of Southern California, late fall through early spring in desert areas—or plan for off-season camping. Some areas also offer undeveloped, environmental, or dispersed "open camping" not requiring reservations; contact relevant jurisdictions above for information and regulations.

Private campgrounds are also available throughout Southern California, some of these included in the current *Campbook for California and Nevada*, available at no charge to members of the American Automobile Association (AAA), which lists (by city or locale) a wide variety of private, state, and federal campgrounds. Far more comprehensive is Tom Stienstra's *Foghorn Outdoors: California Camping—The Complete Guide to More Than 1,500 Campgrounds in the Golden State.* (Foghorn Outdoors), available in most California bookstores. Or contact **California Travel Parks Association,** 530/823-1076, fax 530/823-5883, www.campgrounds.com/ctpa, which features a great online campground directory. Request a complimentary copy of the association's annual

California RV and Campground Guide from any member campground, or order one by mail—send $4 if you live in the United States, $7 if outside the United States—by writing to: ESG Mail Service, P.O. Box 5578, Auburn, CA 95604.

For a Cheap Stay:
Hostels, YMCAs, YWCAs
Among the best bargains around, for travelers of all ages, are the **Hostelling International– American Youth Hostels** (HI-AYH) scattered throughout and near Southern California—in the desert, in major urban areas, including various spots along the coast, and along the eastern slopes of the Sierra Nevada. Most are listed separately throughout this guide but the list continually expands (and contracts); the annual HI-AYH *Hostelling North America* guide, available free with membership or for $6.95 plus tax at most hostels, includes updated listings. Most affiliated hostels offer separate dormitory-style accommodations for men and women (and private couple or family rooms, if available), communal kitchens or low-cost food service, and/or other common facilities. Some provide storage lockers, loaner bikes, even hot tubs. At most hostels, the maximum stay is three nights; most are also closed during the day, which forces hostelers to get out and about and see the sights. Fees are typically $10–16 for HI-AYH members, usually several dollars more for nonmembers. Since most hostels are quite popular, especially during summer, reservations—usually secured with one night's advance payment—are essential. Contact individual hostels for details (or see listings elsewhere in this book), since reservations requirements vary. Guests are expected to bring sleeping bags, sleepsacks, or sheets, though sheets or sleepsacks are sometimes available; mattresses, pillows, and blankets are provided.

For membership details and more information about hostelling in the United States and abroad, contact: Hostelling International–American Youth Hostels, 733 15th St. NW, Ste. 840, Washington, DC 20005, 202/783-6161, fax 202/783-6171, www.hiayh.org. For details about Southern California hostels, contact the **HI-AYH Los Angeles Council,** 1434 Second St., Santa Monica, CA 90401, 310/393-6263, fax 310/393-1769, www.hostelweb.com/losangeles, headquartered at the Santa Monica hostel, and the **HI-AYH San Diego Council,** 437 J St., Ste. 301, San Diego, CA 92101, 619/338-9981, fax 619/525-1533, www.hostelweb.com/ sandiego, newly located in downtown's historic Gaslamp Quarter. For more information on Northern California hostels, contact the **HI-AYH Golden Gate Council,** 425 Divisadero St., Ste. 307, San Francisco, CA 94117, 415/863-1444 or 415/701-1320, fax 415/863-3865; www.norcalhostels.org, and the **HI-AYH Central California Council,** P.O. Box 3645, Merced, CA 95344, 209/383-0686; www .hostelweb.com/centralcalifornia.

You'll find other reputable hostels in California, some independent and some affiliated with other hostel "chains" or umbrella organizations (such as the Banana Bungalow group, now well represented in Southern California). For current comprehensive U.S. listings of these private hostels, contact: **BakPak Travelers Guide,** 670 West End Ave., Ste. 1B, New York, NY 10025, 718/626-1988, fax 718/626-2132, bakpakguide .com, and **Hostel Handbook of the U.S. and Canada,** c/o Jim Williams, 722 St. Nicholas Ave., New York, NY 10031. Copies of both these guides are also usually available at affiliated hostels.

Particularly in urban areas, the **Young Men's Christian Association** (YMCA) often offers housing, showers, and other facilities for young men (over age 18 only in some areas, if unaccompanied by parent or guardian), sometimes also for women and families. **Young Women's Christian Association** (YWCA) institutions offer housing for women only. Life being what it is these days, though, many of these institutions are primarily shelters for the destitute and the homeless; don't steal their beds unless absolutely necessary. For more information, contact: **Y's Way International,** 224 E 47th St., New York, NY 10017, 212/308-2899 (Mon.– Fri. 9 A.M.–5 P.M.), or contact local YMCA outposts in both Hollywood and San Diego. Another low-cost alternative in summer is on-campus housing at state colleges and universities; for current information, contact individual campuses (the student housing office) in areas you'll be visiting.

Modern "Motor Hotels":
Motels and Hotels

California, the spiritual home of highway and freeway living, is also the birthplace of the motel, the word a contraction for "motor hotels." Motels have been here longer than anywhere else, so they've had plenty of time to clone themselves. As a general precaution, when checking into a truly cheap motel, ask to see the room before signing in (and paying); some places look much more appealing from the outside than from the inside. Midrange and high-priced motels and hotels are generally okay, however. In addition to the standard California sales tax, many cities and counties—particularly near major tourism destinations—add a "bed tax" of 5–18 percent (or higher). To find out the actual price you'll be paying, ask before making reservations or signing in. Unless otherwise stated, rates listed in this guide do not include state sales tax or local bed taxes.

Predictably reliable on the cheaper end of the accommodations scale, though there can be considerable variation in quality and service from place to place, are a variety of budget chains fairly common throughout California. Particularly popular is **Motel 6,** a perennial budget favorite. To receive a copy of the current motel directory, from the United States and Canada call toll-free 800/466-8356, which is also Motel 6's central reservations service, or try the website at www.motel6.com. (To make central reservations from outside the United States, call 817/355-5502; reserve by fax from Europe and the United Kingdom at 32-2-753-5858.) You can also make reservations, by phone or fax, at individual motels, some listed elsewhere in this book. Other inexpensive to moderately priced motels are often found clustered in the general vicinity of Motel 6, these including **Comfort Inn,** toll-free 800/228-5150, www.comfortinn.com; **Days Inn,** toll-free 800/329-7466, www.daysinn.com; **Econo Lodge,** toll-free 800/553-2666, www.econolodge.com; **Rodeway Inn,** toll-free 800/228-2000; www.rodewayinn.com; and **Super 8 Motels,** toll-free 800/800-8000, www.super8.com. You can also pick up a current accommodations directory at any affiliated motel.

You'll find endless other motel and hotel chains in California, most of these more expensive—but not always, given seasonal bargain rates and special discounts offered to seniors, AAA members, and other groups. "Kids stay free," free breakfast for families, and other special promotions can also make more expensive accommodations competitive. Always reliable for quality, but with considerable variation in price and level of luxury, are **Best Western** motel and hotel affiliates, toll-free 800/780-7234 in the United States; www.bestwestern.com. Each is independently owned and managed, and some are listed in this guide. Though there are many upmarket hotels and chains in California—the gold rush is over, but the West's amenities rush is in full swing—the **Four Seasons,** www.fshr.com, and **Ritz-Carlton,** www.ritzcarlton.com, hotel and resort chains top most people's "all-time favorite" lists of luxurious places to stay in California if money is no object.

For members of the American Automobile Association (AAA), the current *Tourbook for California and Nevada* (free) includes an impressive number of rated motels, hotels, and resorts, from inexpensive to top of the line, sometimes also recommended restaurants, for nearly every community and city in both Southern and Northern California. Nationwide, AAA members can also benefit from the association's reservations service, toll-free 800/272-2155; with one call, you can also request tour books and attractions information. Other travel groups or associations offer good deals and useful services too.

Bargain Room Rates and
Bed-and-Breakfasts

Even if you don't belong to a special group or association, you can still benefit from "bulk-buying" power, particularly in large cities—which is a special boon if you're making last-minute plans or are otherwise having little luck on your own. Various room brokers or "consolidators" buy up blocks of rooms from hoteliers at greatly discounted rates and then broker them through their own reservations services. In many cases, brokers still have bargain-priced rooms available—at rates 40–65 percent below standard rack rates—when popular hotels are otherwise sold out. For great hotel deals, try **Hotel Discounts,** toll-free 800/715-7666; www.hoteldiscount.com. Particularly helpful for online reservations is the discounted **USA Hotel Guide,** toll-free 888/729-7705; www.usahotelguide.com.

For other bargain hotel prices in Los Angeles, San Diego, and sometimes also Santa Barbara and Palm Springs, contact **Hotel Reservations Network,** toll-free 800/715-7666; www.180096hotel.com, and **Room Exchange,** toll-free 800/846-7000; www.hotelrooms.com. If you're willing to bid for a hotel bargain, try **Revelex;** www.revelex.com.

Another hot trend in California is the bed-and-breakfast phenomenon, though it has yet to catch fire in Southern California, with the exception of Santa Barbara and vicinity, Big Bear, Palm Springs, and other popular resort destinations. Many bed-and-breakfast guides and listings are available in bookstores, and some recommended B&Bs are listed in this book. Unlike the European tradition, with bed and breakfasts a low-cost yet comfortable lodging alternative, in California these inns are actually a burgeoning small-business phenomenon—usually quite pricey, in the $100–150-and-up range (sometimes less expensive), often more of a "special weekend getaway" for exhausted city people than a mainstream accommodations option. In some areas, though, where motel and hotel rooms are on the high end, bed-and-breakfasts can be quite competitive.

For more information on what's available in all parts of California, including private home stays, contact **Bed and Breakfast California,** P.O. Box 282910, San Francisco, CA 94128, 650/696-1690 or toll-free 800/872-4500, fax 650/696-1699; www.bbintl.com, affiliated with Bed and Breakfast International, the longest-running bed-and-breakfast reservation service in the United States. Or contact the **California Association of Bed and Breakfast Inns,** 2715 Porter St., Soquel, CA 95073, 831/462-9191, fax 831/462-0402; www.cabbi.com.

The Land of Fruits and Nuts and California Cuisine

One of the best things about traveling in California is the food: they don't call the Golden State the land of fruits and nuts for nothing. In Southern California's increasingly rare agricultural and rural areas, local "farm trails" or winery guides are still available—ask at local chambers of commerce and visitor centers—and following the seasonal produce trails offers visitors the unique pleasure of gathering (some-times picking your own) fresh fruits, nuts, and vegetables direct from the growers.

This fresher, direct-to-you produce phenomenon is also quite common in most urban areas, where regular farmers' markets are *the* place to go for fresh, organic, often exotic local produce and farm products. Some popular Southern California farmers' markets are listed elsewhere in this book—but ask around wherever you are, since new ones pop up constantly. For a reasonably comprehensive current listing of California Certified Farmers' Markets (meaning certified as locally grown), contact: **California Federation of Certified Farmers' Markets,** P.O. Box 1813, Davis, CA 95617, 530/753-9999, fax 530/756-1858; farmersmarket.ucdavis.edu.

Threaded with freeways and accessible on-ramp, off-ramp commercial strips, Southern California has more than its fair share of fast-food eateries and all-night quik-stop outlets. (Since they're so easy to find, few are listed in this guide.) Most cities and communities also have

ROBERT HOLMES/CALIFORNIA DIVISION OF TOURISM

Poppies are California's state flower.

locally popular cafés and fairly inexpensive restaurants worth seeking out; many are listed here but also ask around. Genuinely inexpensive eateries often refuse to take credit cards, so always bring some cash along just in case.

The southstate is also famous for its "California cuisine," which once typically meant consuming tastebud-tantalizing, very expensive food in very small portions—almost a cliché—while oohing and ahhing over the presentation throughout the meal. But the fiscally frugal 1990s restrained some of Southern California's excesses, and even the best restaurants now offer less pretentious menus and slimmed-down prices. The region's culinary creativity is quite real, and worth pursuing (sans pretense) in many areas. Talented chefs, who have migrated throughout Southern California from Los Angeles and San Francisco as well as from France and Italy, usually prefer locally grown produce, dairy products, meats, and herbs and spices as basic ingredients. To really "do" the cuisine scene, wash it all down with some fine California wine.

OTHER DETAILS

Visas for Foreign Visitors

A foreign visitor to the United States is required to carry a current passport and a visitor's visa plus proof of intent to leave (usually a return airplane ticket is adequate). Also, it's wise to carry proof of one's citizenship, such as a driver's license and/or birth certificate. To be on the safe side, photocopy your legal documents and carry the photocopies separately from the originals. To obtain a U.S. visa (most visitors qualify for a B-2 or "pleasure tourist" visa, valid for up to six months), contact the nearest U.S. embassy or consulate. Should you lose the Form I-94 (proof of arrival/departure) attached to your visa, contact the nearest local U.S. **Immigration and Naturalization Service** (INS) office or contact headquarters: 4420 N. Fairfax Dr., Arlington, VA 22203, 703/235-4055. Contact the INS also for a visa extension (good for a maximum of six months). To work or study in the United States, special visas are required; contact the nearest U.S. embassy or consulate for current information. To replace a passport lost while in the United States, contact the nearest embassy for

your country. Canadian citizens entering the United States from Canada or Mexico do not need either a passport or visa, nor do Mexican citizens possessing a Form I-186. (Canadians under age 18 do need to carry written consent from a parent or guardian.)

Time

California, within the Pacific time zone (two hours behind Chicago, three hours behind New York) is on daylight saving time (a helps-with-harvest agricultural holdover), which means clocks are set ahead one hour from the first Sunday in April until the last Sunday in October. Without this seasonal time adustment, when it's noon in California it's 10 A.M. in Hawaii, 8 P.M. in London, midnight in Moscow, and 4 A.M. (the next day) in Hong Kong.

Business Hours, Banking, Money

Standard business hours in California (holidays excepted) are Monday through Friday 9 A.M.–5 P.M., though many businesses open at 8 A.M. or 10 A.M. and/or stay open until 6 P.M. or later. Traditional banking hours—10 A.M. until 3 P.M.—are not necessarily the rule in California these days. Particularly in cities, banks may open at 9 A.M. and stay open until 5 or 6 P.M., and may offer extended walk-up or drive-up window hours. Many banks and savings and loans also offer Saturday hours (usually 9 A.M.–1 P.M.) as well as 24-hour automated teller machine (ATM) service; you'll even find ATMs at most theme parks and, increasingly, inside most grocery stores. Before traveling in California, contact your bank for a list of California branches or affiliated institutions.

For the most part, traveling in California is expensive. Depending on your plans, figure out how much money you'll need—then bring more. Most banks will not cash checks (or issue cash via automatic tellers) for anyone without an account (or an account with some affiliated institution). Major credit cards (especially Visa and MasterCard) are almost universally accepted in California, except at inexpensive motels and restaurants. Credit cards have become a travel essential, since they are often mandatory for renting cars or as a "security deposit" on bicycle, outdoor equipment, and other rentals. The safest way to bring cash is by carrying traveler's checks.

American Express traveler's checks are the most widely recognized and accepted.

Domestic (U.S.) travelers who run short of money, and who are without credit lines on their credit cards, can ask family or friends to send a postal money order (buyable and cashable at any U.S. Postal Service post office); ask your bank to wire money to an affiliated California bank (probably for a slight fee); or have money wired office-to-office via Western Union, toll-free 800/325-6000 (800/225-5227 for credit-card money transfers; 800/325-4045 for assistance in Spanish). Use the local phone book to find Western Union offices. In each case, the surcharge depends upon the amount sent.

International travelers, avoid the necessity of wiring for money if at all possible. With a Visa, MasterCard, or American Express card, cash advances are easily available; get details about affiliated U.S. banks before leaving home, however. If you must arrange for cash to be sent from home, a cable tranfer from your bank (check on corresponding California banks before leaving), a Western Union money wire, or a bank draft or international money order are all possible. Make sure you (and your sender) know the accurate address for the recipient bank, to avoid obvious nightmarish complications. In a pinch, consulates may intervene and request money from home (or your home bank) at your request—deducting their cost from funds received.

Measurements, Mail, Communications

Despite persistent efforts to wean Americans from the old ways, California and the rest of the union still abide by the British system of weights and measures (see measurements chart in the back of this book). Electrical outlets in California (and the rest of the United States) carry current at 117 volts, 60 cycles (Hertz) A.C.; foreign electrical appliances require a converter and plug adapter.

Even without a full-fledged post office, even most outback California communities have at least some official outpost of the U.S. Postal Service, usually open weekdays 8 A.M.–5 P.M., for sending letters and packages and for receiving general delivery mail. At last report, basic postal rates within the United States, which seem to be steadily on the increase, were 21 cents for postcards, 34 cents for letter mail (the first ounce). Rates for international mail from the United States were 50 cents for postcards, 80 cents for letters (the first half-ounce), and 70 cents for aerogrammes; to most other destinations, 70 cents for both postcards and aerogrammes, and 80 cents for airmail letters. The postal code for any address in California is CA. For mail sent and received within the United States, knowing and using the relevant five- or nine-digit zip code is important. Mail can be directed to any particular post office c/o "General Delivery," but the correct address and zip code for the post office receiving such mail is important—especially in cities, where there are multiple post offices. (For zip codes and associated post office information, refer to the local phone book, call toll-free 800/332-9631, or go to www .usps.com.) To claim general delivery mail, current photo identification is required; unclaimed mail will be returned to the sender after languishing for two to four weeks. At larger post offices, **International Express Mail** is available, with delivery to major world cities in 48–72 hours.

Telephone communication is easy in California (always carry change in your pocket in case you need to make an emergency call). Local calls are often free (or inexpensive) from many motel and hotel rooms, but long-distance calls will cost you. Some hotels add a per-call surcharge even to direct-dialed or credit card calls, however, due and payable when you check out. And the anything-goes aspect of deregulation has also resulted in a spate of for-profit "telephone companies" that generate most of their income through exorbitant rates charged through the hotels, motels, and miscellaneous pay telephones they serve. Using your own long-distance carrier (usually with a personal phone card) is typically a better deal. If in doubt about what long-distance services are available on a given phone system, what rates they charge, and whether a hotel or motel surcharge will be added to your bill, ask *before* making your phone call(s). Collect and person-to-person operator-assisted calls are usually more expensive than direct-dial and telephone company (such as AT&T or Sprint) credit-card calls, but in some cases they could save you a bundle.

Telephone communication in California has been further complicated, almost overnight, by a mushrooming number of area codes, those three-digit parenthetical regional prefixes preceding seven-digit local telephone numbers. This chaotic change in California, as elsewhere, is directly related to the proliferating numbers of people, phones, fax machines, pagers, and online computer connections. In the past decade, every telephone area code has "split" (usually into two, the previous code plus a new one) at least once, and some more than once. This book has made every effort to keep up with area code changes, and has noted upcoming changes that were known at the time of publication. But during the useful life of this guide, it's likely that a few new area codes will present themselves nonetheless, or that area codes and/or phone numbers associated with areas outside this book's immediate scope will change. So—when in doubt, call the local operator and check it out.

IN THE KNOW: SERVICES AND INFORMATION

Services

Except for some very lonely areas of the California desert, even backwater areas of Southern California aren't particularly primitive. Gasoline, at least basic groceries, laundries of some sort, even video rentals are available just about anywhere. Outback areas are not likely to have parts for exotic sports cars, however, or 24-hour pharmacies, hospitals, and garages, or natural foods stores or full-service supermarkets, so you should take care of any special needs or problems before leaving the cities. It's often cheaper, too, to stock up on most supplies, including outdoor equipment and groceries, in urban areas.

General Information

Visitors can receive free California travel-planning information by writing the **California Division of Tourism,** P.O. Box 1499, Dept. 61, Sacramento, CA 95812-1499, or by calling toll-free 800/462-2543, ext. 61. Or try the Internet site, gocalif.ca.gov, which also includes an accommodations reservation service. California's tourism office publishes a veritable gold rush of useful travel information, including the annual *California Official State Visitors Guide* and *California Celebrations.* Particularly useful for outdoor enthusiasts is the new 16-page *California Outdoor Recreation* guide. The quarterly *California Travel Ideas* magazine is distributed free at agricultural inspection stations at the state's borders. For travel industry professionals, the *California Travel and Incentive Planner's Guide* is also available.

Most of these California tourism publications, in addition to regional and local publications, are also available at the various roadside volunteer-staffed **California Welcome Centers,** a burgeoning trend. The first official welcome center was unveiled in 1995 in Kingsburg, in the San Joaquin Valley, and the next four—in Rohnert Park, just south of Santa Rosa; in Anderson, just south of Redding; in Oakhurst in the gold country, on the way to Yosemite National Park; and at Pier 39 on San Francisco's Fisherman's Wharf—were also in Northern California. There are others in Northern California, too, including the fairly new one in Arcata. Yet there are also several in Southern California, including the **Ontario Mills/American Wilderness Experience** near Ontario and the **Tanger Factory Outlet Center** at the junction of I-40 and I-15 in Barstow, both in San Bernardino County. Eventually the network will include virtually all areas of California; watch for signs announcing new welcome centers along major highways and freeways.

Most major cities and visitor destinations in Southern California also have very good visitor information bureaus and visitor centers, listed elsewhere in this book. Many offer accommodations reservations and other services; some offer information and maps in foreign languages. Chambers of commerce can be useful too. In less populated areas, chambers of commerce are something of a hit-or-miss proposition, since office hours may be minimal; the best bet is calling ahead for information. Asking locals—people at gas stations, cafés, grocery stores, and official government outposts—is often the best way to get information about where to go, why, when, and how. Slick city magazines, good daily newspapers, and California-style weekly news and entertainment tabloids are other good sources of information.

Special Information: For the Disabled

Twin Peaks Press, P.O. Box 129, Vancouver, WA 98666, 206/694-2462, or toll-free 800/637-2256 for orders only, publishes particularly helpful books, including *Wheelchair Vagabond, Travel for the Disabled,* and *Directory of Travel Agencies for the Disabled.* Also useful is the *Travelin' Talk Directory* put out by **Travelin' Talk,** P.O. Box 3534, Clarksville, TN 37043, 615/552-6670, a network of disabled people available "to help travelers in any way they can." Membership is only $10, a bargain by any standard, since by joining up you suddenly have a vast network of allies in otherwise strange places who are all too happy to tell you what's what. Also helpful: **Mobility International USA,** P.O. Box 10767, Eugene, OR 97440, tel. and TDD 541/343-1284, fax 541/343-6812, www.miusa.org, which provides two-way international leadership exchanges. Disabled people who want to go to Europe to study theater, for example, or British citizens who want to come to California for Elderhostel programs—anything beyond traditional leisure travel—should call here first. The annual membership fee is $25 for individuals, $35 for organizations.

Special Information for Seniors

Senior adults can benefit from a great many bargains and discounts. A good source of information is the *Travel Tips for Older Americans* pamphlet published by the U.S. Government Printing Office, 202/275-3648, www.gpo.gov, available for $1.25. (Order it online at www.pueblo.gsa.gov/travel.) The federal government's Golden Age Passport offers free admission to national parks and monuments and half-price discounts for federal campsites and other recreational services; state parks also offer senior discounts. (For detailed information, see appropriate recreation listings under Playing Here: Outdoor Recreation, above.) Discounts are also frequently offered to seniors at major tourist attractions and sights as well as for many arts, cultural, and entertainment destinations and events in Southern California. Another benefit of experience is eligibility for the international **Elderhostel** program, 75 Federal St., Boston, MA 02110, 617/426-7788 or toll-free 877/426-8056, www.elderhostel.org, which offers a variety of fairly reasonable one-week residential programs in California.

For information on travel discounts, trip planning, tours, and other membership benefits of the U.S.'s largest senior citizen organization, contact the **American Association of Retired Persons** (AARP), 601 E St. NW, Washington, DC 20049, 202/434-2277 or toll-free 800/424-3410, www.aarp.org. Despite the name, anyone age 50 and older—retired or not—is eligible for membership. Other membership-benefit programs for seniors include the **National Council of Senior Citizens,** 8403 Colesville Rd., Ste. 1200, Silver Springs, MD 20910, 301/578-8800, fax 301/578-8999; www.ncscinc.org.

Not Getting Lost: Good Maps

For more information about AAA membership and services in Southern California, contact the **Automobile Club of Southern California,** 2601 S. Figueroa St., Los Angeles, CA 90007, 213/741-3686, www.aaa-calif.com, but there are also regional offices throughout the southstate. Members can also order maps, tour books, and other services online. If you'll also be visiting Northern California, the AAA affiliate there is known as the **California State Automobile Association,** and the main office address is 150 Van Ness Ave., P.O. Box 1860, San Francisco, CA 94101-1860, 415/565-2012 or 415/565-2468; www.csaa.org. For AAA membership information, from anywhere in the U.S. call toll-free 800/222-4357, or try www.aaa.com.

The best maps money can buy, excellent for general and very detailed travel in California, are the **Thomas Bros. Maps,** typically referred to as "Thomas guides." For the big picture, particularly useful is the *California Road Atlas & Driver's Guide,* but various other, very detailed spiral-bound book-style maps in the Thomas guide street atlas series—San Francisco, Monterey County, Los Angeles, Orange County, San Diego—are the standard block-by-block references, continually updated since 1915. Thomas guides are available at any decent travel-oriented bookstore, or contact the company directly. In Southern California, you'll find a major Thomas Bros. Maps store at 603 W. Seventh St., Los Angeles, CA 90017, 213/627-4018; the map factory and other store is in Orange County, at 17731 Cowan in Irvine, 949/863-1984, fax 949/852-9189. In Northern California, stop by Thomas Bros. Maps, 550 Jackson St., San Francisco, CA 94133, 415/981-7520. Or order any map by calling, from anywhere in California, toll-free 800/899-6277—or by trying, from anywhere in the world; www.thomas.com.

When it comes to backcountry travel—where maps quickly become either your best friend or archenemy—the going isn't nearly as easy. U.S. Geological Survey quadrangle maps in most cases are reliable for showing the contours of the terrain, but U.S. Forest Service and wilderness maps—supposedly the maps of record for finding one's way through the woods and the wilds—are often woefully out of date, with new and old logging roads (as well as disappearing or changed trail routes) confusing the situation considerably. In California, losing oneself in the wilderness is a very real, literal possibility. In addition to topo maps (carry a compass to orient yourself by landforms if all else fails) and official U.S. maps, backcountry travelers would be wise to invest in privately published guidebooks and current route or trail guides for wilderness areas; the Sierra Club and Wilderness Press publish both. Before setting out, compare all available maps and other information to spot any possible route discrepancies, then ask national forest or parks personnel for clarification. If you're lucky, you'll find someone who knows what's going on where you want to go.

Aside from well-stocked outdoor stores, the primary California source for quad maps is: **U.S. Geological Survey** (USGS), 345 Middlefield Rd., Menlo Park, CA 94025, 650/853-8300 (ask for the mapping division); an index and catalog of published California maps is available upon request. Or try the USGS website, www.usgs.gov, or call toll-free 888/275-8747. Also contact the U.S. Forest Service and U.S. National Park Service (see Playing Here: Outdoor Recreation, above). The best bet for wilderness maps and guides is **Wilderness Press,** 1200 Fifth St., Berkeley, CA 94710, 510/558-1666 or toll-free 800/443-7227 (for orders), fax 510/558-1696; www.wildernesspress.com. Most Wilderness Press titles are available in California bookstores.

Not necessarily practical for travelers are the beautiful yet utilitarian maps produced by **Raven Maps & Images,** 34 N. Central, P.O. Box 850, Medford, OR 97501, 541/773-1436, or (for credit-card orders) toll-free 800/237-0798; www.raven-maps.com. These beauties are big, and—unless you buy one for the wall and one for the road—

you'll never want to fold them. Based on U.S. Geological Survey maps, these shaded relief maps are "computer-enhanced" for a three-dimensional topographical feel and incredible clarity—perfect for planning outdoor adventures. Raven's *California* map measures 42 by 64 inches, and *Yosemite and the Central Sierra* is 34 by 37 inches. Wonderful for any California-lover's wall is the three-dimensional, five-color *California, Nevada, and the Pacific Ocean Floor* digital landform map, which offers three aerial oblique views: now, five million years ago, and five million years in the future. Fabulous. All Raven maps are printed in fade-resistant inks on fine quality 70-pound paper and are also available in vinyl laminated versions suitable for framing.

SURVIVING: HEALTH AND SAFETY

Emergencies, Medical Care, and General Health

In most places in Southern California, call 911 in any emergency; in medical emergencies, life-support personnel and ambulances will be dispatched. To make sure health-care services will be readily provided, health insurance coverage is almost mandatory; carry proof of coverage while traveling in California. In urban areas and in many rural areas, 24-hour walk-in health care services are readily available, though hospital emergency rooms are the place to go in case of life-threatening circumstances.

To avoid most health and medical problems, use common sense. Eat sensibly, avoid unsafe drinking water, bring along any necessary prescription pills—and pack an extra pair of glasses or contacts, just in case. Sunglasses, especially for those unaccustomed to sunshine, and sunscreen and a broad-brimmed hat, can help prevent sunburn, sunstroke, and heat prostration. Drink plenty of liquids, too, especially in hot weather.

No vaccinations are usually necessary for traveling in California, though here as elsewhere very young children and seniors should obtain vaccinations against annually variable forms of the flu virus; exposure, especially in crowded urban areas and especially during the winter disease season, is a likelihood.

As in other areas of the United States, the AIDS (Acquired Immune Deficiency Syndrome) virus and other sexually transmitted diseases are a concern. In mythic "anything goes" California, avoiding promiscuous or unprotected sex is the best way to avoid the danger of AIDS and venereal disease—though AIDS has also been proven to be transmitted via shared drug needles and contaminated blood transfusions. (All medical blood supplies in California are screened for evidence of the virus.) Sexually speaking, "safe sex" is the preventive key phrase, under any circumstances beyond the strictly monogamous. This means always using condoms in sexual intercourse; oral sex only with some sort of barrier precaution; and no sharing sex toys.

City Safety

Though California's wilderness once posed a major threat to human survival, in most respects the backcountry is safer than the urban jungle of modern cities. Tourism officials don't talk about it much, but crimes against persons and property are a reality in California (though the state's overall crime rate has dropped sharply in recent years). To avoid harm, bring along your streetsmarts. The best overall personal crime prevention includes carrying only small amounts of cash (inconspicuously, in a money belt or against-the-body money pouch); labeling (and locking) all luggage; keeping valuables under lock and key (and, in automobiles, out of sight); being aware of people and events, and knowing where you are, at all times; and avoiding dangerous, lonely, and unlighted areas after daylight, particularly late at night and when traveling alone. (If you're not sure what neighborhoods are considered dangerous or unsafe, ask locals or hotel or motel personnel—or at the police station, if necessary.)

Women traveling alone—not generally advisable, because of the unfortunate fact of misogyny in the modern world—need to take special care to avoid harm. For any independent traveler, self-defense classes (and/or a training course for carrying and using Mace) might be a worthwhile investment, if only to increase one's sense of personal power in case of a confrontation with criminals. Being assertive and confident, and acting as if you know where you are going (even when you don't), are also among the best deter-

rents to predators. Carry enough money for a phone call—or bus or taxi ride—and a whistle. When in doubt, don't hesitate to use it, and to yell and scream for help.

General Outdoor Safety

The most basic rule is: know what you're doing and where you're going. Next most basic: whatever you do—from swimming or surfing to hiking and backpacking—don't do it alone. For any outdoor activity, be prepared. Check with local park or national forest service officials on weather, trail, and general conditions before setting out. Correct, properly functioning equipment is as important in backpacking as it is in hang gliding, mountain climbing, mountain biking, and sailing. (When in doubt, check it out.)

Among the basics to bring along for almost any outdoor activity: a hat, sunscreen, and lip balm (to protect against the sun in summer, against heat loss, reflective sun, and the elements in winter); a whistle, compass, and Mylar "space blanket" in case you become lost or stranded; insect repellent; a butane lighter or waterproof matches; a multipurpose Swiss Army-type knife; nylon rope; a flashlight; and a basic first-aid kit (including bandages, ointments and salves, antiseptics, pain relievers such as aspirin, and any necessary prescription medicines). Hikers and backpackers and other outdoor adventurers should bring plenty of water—or water purification tablets or pump-style water purifiers for long trips—at least minimal fishing gear, good hiking shoes or boots, extra socks and shoelaces, "layerable" clothing adequate for all temperatures, and a waterproof poncho or large plastic garbage bag. (Even if thunderstorms are unlikely, any sort of packable and wearable plastic bag can keep you dry until you reach shelter.) The necessity for other outdoor equipment, from camp stoves to sleeping bags and tents, depends on where you'll be going and what you'll be doing.

Poison Oak

Poison oak (actually a shrublike sumac) is a perennial trailside hazard, especially in lowland foothill areas and mixed forests; it exudes oily chemicals that cause a strong allergic reaction in many people, even with only brief contact. (Always be careful what you're burning around the campfire too; smoke from poison oak, when inhaled, can inflame the lungs and create a life-threatening situation in no time flat.) The best way to avoid the painful, itchy, often long-lasting rashes associated with poison oak is to avoid contact with the plant—in all seasons—and to immediately wash one's skin or clothes if you even suspect a brush with it. (Its leaves a bright, glossy green in spring and summer, red or yellow in fall, poison oak can be a problem even in winter—when this mean-spirited deciduous shrub loses its leaves.) Learn to identify it during any time of year.

Once afflicted with poison oak, never scratch, because the oozing sores just spread the rash. Very good new products on the market include Tecnu's **Poison Oak-n-Ivy Armor** "pre-exposure lotion," produced by Tec Laboratories, Inc., of Albany, Oregon, toll-free 800/482-4464 (ITCHING). Apply it before potential exposure to protect yourself. Another excellent product, quite helpful if you do tangle with poison oak, is Tecnu's **Poison Oak-n-Ivy Cleanser,** the idea being to get the toxic oils off your skin as soon as possible, within hours of initial exposure or just after the rash appears. The cleanser also helps eliminate the itching remarkably well. (But do *not* apply after oozing begins.) Various drying, cortisone-based lotions, oatmeal baths, and other treatments can help control discomfort if the rash progresses to the oozing stage, but the rash itself goes away only in its own good time.

Lyme Disease and Ticks

Even if you favor shorts for summer hiking, you had better plan on long pants, long-sleeved shirts, even insect repellent. The weather may be mild, but there's an increasing risk—particularly in California coastal and foothill areas, as in other states—that you'll contract Lyme disease, transmitted by ticks that thrive in moist lowland climates.

A new ailment on the West Coast, Lyme disease is named after the place of its 1975 discovery in Old Lyme, Connecticut. Already the most common vector-transmitted disease in the nation, Lyme is caused by spirochetes transmitted through blood, urine, and other body fluids. Research indicates it has often been wrongly diagnosed; sufferers were thought to have afflictions such as rheumatoid arthri-

tis. Temporary paralysis, arthritic pains in the hands or arm and leg joints, swollen hands, fever, fatigue, nausea, headaches, swollen glands, and heart palpitations are among the typical symptoms. Sometimes an unusually circular red rash appears first, between three and 30 days after the tick bite. Untreated, Lyme disease can mean a lifetime of suffering, even danger to unborn children. Treatment, once Lyme disease is discovered through blood tests, is simple and 100 percent effective if recognized early: tetracycline and other drugs halt the arthritic degeneration and most symptoms. Long-delayed treatment, even with extremely high doses of antibiotics, is only about 50 percent effective.

Outdoor prudence, coupled with an awareness of possible Lyme symptoms even months later, are the watchwords when it comes to Lyme disease. Take precautions against tick bites: the sooner ticks are found and removed, the better your chances of avoiding the disease. Tuck your pants into your boots, wear long-sleeved shirts, and use insect repellent around all clothing openings as well as on your neck and all exposed skin. Run a full-body "tick check" daily, especially checking hidden areas such as the hair and scalp. Consider leaving dogs at home if heading for Lyme country; ticks they pick up can spread the disease through your human family.

Use gloves and tweezers to remove ticks from yourself or your animals—never crush the critters with your fingers!—and wash your hands and the bitten area afterward. Better yet, smother imbedded ticks with petroleum jelly first; deprived of oxygen, they start to pull out of the skin in about a half hour, making it easy to pluck them off without tearing them in two and leaving the head imbedded.

GETTING HERE, GETTING AROUND

By Bicycle

Most parts of Southern California are not much fun for cyclists. Let's face it. This is car country. Cycling on public roadways here usually means frightening car traffic; brightly colored bicycle clothing and accessories, reflective tape, good lights, and other safety precautions are mandatory. And always wear a helmet. Only the brave would pick this part of the world—or at least the urban part of this world—for bicycle touring, though some do, most wisely with help from books such as *Bicycling the Pacific Coast* (The Mountaineers) by Tom Kirkendall and Vicky Spring. Yet there are less congested areas, and good local bike paths here and there, for more timid recreational bikers; rental bike shops abound, particularly in beach areas. For those who hanker after a little two-wheel backroads sightseeing, some areas of San Diego and Santa Barbara Counties are still sublime. Many national parks—including Santa Monica Mountains National Recreation Area, Joshua Tree, and Death Valley—have become mountain biking meccas, as are some of Southern California's national forests and BLM areas. On available BLM lands, however, cyclists sometimes compete for turf with four-wheelers and off-road vehicle enthusiasts.

Various good regional cycling guides are available, though serious local bike shops—those frequented by cycling enthusiasts, not just sales outlets—and bike clubs are probably the best local information sources for local and regional rides as well as special cycling events. For upcoming events, other germane information, and referrals on good publications, contact: **California Association of Bicycling Organizations** (CABO), P.O. Box 26864, Dublin, CA 94568. The **Adventure Cycling Association,** P.O. Box 8308, Missoula, MT 59807, 406/721-1776 or toll-free 800/755-2453, fax 406/721-8754, www.adv-cycling.org, is a nonprofit national organization that researches long-distance bike routes and organizes tours for members. Its maps, guidebooks, route suggestions, and *Cyclist's Yellow Pages* can be helpful. For mountain biking information via the Internet, also try the **International Mountain Bicycling Association** at www.greatoutdoors.com/imba.

By Bus

Most destinations in Southern California are reachable by bus, either by major carrier, by "alternative" carrier, or in various combinations of long-distance and local bus lines. (For information on local bus lines, see relevant chapters below.) And if you can't get *exactly* where you want to go by bus, you can usually get close.

Greyhound is the universal bus service. Obtain a current U.S. route map by mail (see below), but check with local Greyhound offices for more detailed local route information and for information about "casino service" to Las Vegas and other local specials. Greyhound offers discounts for senior adults and disabled travelers, and children under age 12 ride free when accompanied by a fare-paying adult (one child per adult, half fare for additional children). The **Ameripass** offers unlimited travel with on-off stops for various periods of time, but it is usually more economical for long-distance trips with few stopovers. International travelers should inquire about the **International Ameripass.** For more information, in the United States contact Greyhound Bus Lines, Inc., at toll-free 800/232-2222; www.greyhound.com.

Then there are alternative bus options, most notably **Green Tortoise,** the hippest trip on wheels for budget travelers, combining long-distance travel with communal sightseeing. Sign on for a westbound cross-country tour to get to California, an eastbound trip to get away—seeing some of the most spectacular sights in the United States along the languid, looping way. As the motto emblazoned on the back of the bus says: "Arrive inspired, not dog tired." Unlike your typical bus ride, on Green Tortoise trips you bring your sleeping bag—the buses are converted sleeping coaches, and the booths and couches convert into beds come nightfall. And you won't need to stop for meals, since healthy gourmet fare (at a cost of about $10 a day) is usually included in the freight; sometimes the food charge is optional, meaning you can bring your own. But Green Tortoise also offers a weekly three-day **California Coast Tour,** with departures from both Los Angeles and San Francisco, making it easy—and fairly entertaining—to get from one end of the state to the other. From San Francisco, you can also get to Southern California on the Green Tortoise **Death Valley National Park** tour; drop-offs can be arranged in either Bakersfield or Mojave, and Greyhound can get you to Los Angeles. For more information, contact: Green Tortoise Adventure Travel, 494 Broadway, San Francisco, CA 94133, 415/956-7500 or, from anywhere in the United States and Canada, toll-free 800/867-8647; www.greentortoise.com.

By Train

An unusually enjoyable way to travel the length of the West Coast to California, or to arrive here after a trip west over the Sierra Nevada or across the great desert, is by train. Travel the California coastline on Amtrak's immensely popular and recently spiffed up **Coast Starlight,** which now features more comfortable tilt-back seats, a parlor car with library and games, and California-style fare in its dining cars. (From San Diego, the two-way route continues north to Oakland, across the bay from San Francisco, and eventually all the way to Seattle.) Departing from grand Union Station near downtown L.A., head east to New Orleans on the **Sunset Limited,** to San Antonio on the **Texas Eagle,** and to Chicago on the **Desert Wind** and the **Southwest Chief.** Regional trains operated by Amtrak within California include the **Pacific Surfliner** (formerly the San Diegans) along the state's central and south coasts. With Southern California's Metrorail and Metrolink mass transit system, it's now possible to fill in many gaps via commuter train; for information, see the Greater Los Angeles chapter below. Various historic and recreational train routes also operate in California.

For **Amtrak** train travel routes (including some jogs between cities in California by Amtrak bus), current price information, and reservations, contact a travel agent or call Amtrak at toll-free 800/872-7245 (USA RAIL), www.amtrak.com or amtrakwest.com. For the hearing impaired, Amtrak's toll-free TTY number is 800/523-6590 or 523-6591.

By Automobile

This being California, almost everyone gets around by car. There are exceptions even in Southern California, however, where Metrorail and Metrolink and Metropolitan Transportation Authority (MTA) buses get at least a few people off the freeways. Urban freeway driving in California, because of congestion and Californians' no-nonsense get-on-with-it driving styles, can inspire panic even in nonlocal native drivers. If this is a problem, plan your trip to skirt the worst congestion—by taking back roads and older highways, if possible, or by trying neighborhood routes (but only if you know something about the neighborhoods). Alternatively, plan to arrive

---

AMTRAK'S CALIFORNIA PASSES

New in the new millennium is Amtrak's **California Rail Pass,** patterned after Europe's popular Eurail Pass. The California Rail Pass, $159 for adults and $80 for children ages two–15, allows unlimited Amtrak travel within the state on any seven days within a given 21-day period. The pass is valid on the California portion of the *Coast Starlight* route connecting Los Angeles to Seattle and on "local" Amtrak trains, too, including the *Capitol* trains between Sacramento and San Francisco and the *Pacific Surfliner* route between San Diego and San Luis Obispo.

Similar passes excluding *Coast Starlight* travel are available for regional travel in Northern and Southern California, respectively, and allow five days of unlimited travel within a given seven-day period. The Northern California Pass is valid as far south as Santa Barbara, and the Southern California Pass extends north to San Luis Obispo. The price for either the Northern or Southern California Pass is $99 adult and $50 children.

Amtrak California passes can be purchased at staffed Amtrak stations, from your travel agent, or by calling Amtrak at toll-free 800/872-7245 (USA-RAIL). Get more information online at www.amtrak.com or www.amtrakcalifornia.com.

---

in Southern California after the day's peak freeway commute traffic, usually any time after 7 or 8 P.M.

A good investment for anyone traveling for any length of time in California is a membership in the American Automobile Association (see In the Know: Services and Information, above) since—among many other benefits, including excellent maps and trip planning assistance—a AAA card entitles the bearer to no-cost emergency roadside service, including five gallons of free gas or at least limited towing, if necessary.

Gasoline in California is typically more expensive than elsewhere in the United States, up to 40 cents per gallon more, only in part because of California's new cleaner-burning "reformulated" fuels, the world's cleanest gasoline. The effect of using the new gasoline is roughly equivalent to the effect of taking 3.5 million cars off the road on any given day—or sucking about three million pounds of toxins and particulate matter out of the air. The clean fuels are designed to reduce vehicle emissions and improve air quality, which seems to be working, but a new concern is that clean fuel residues are polluting California's water. The Golden State's pollution solutions are, clearly, ideas that still need work.

To check on current **California road conditions** before setting out—always a good idea in a state with so much ongoing road construction and such variable regional weather—call **Caltrans** (California Department of Transportation) from anywhere in California at toll-free 800/427-7623, and from outside California at 916/445-7623. The road-condition phone numbers are accessible from touch-tone and pay phones as well as cellular phones. Or check road conditions for your entire trip route on the regularly updated Caltrans website; www.dot.ca.gov.

Though every municipality has its own peculiar laws about everything from parking to skateboarding or roller skating on sidewalks, there are basic rules everyone is expected to know and follow—especially drivers. Get a complete set of regulations from the state motor vehicles department, which has an office in all major cities and many medium-sized ones. Or contact **California Department of Motor Vehicles** (DMV), 2415 First Ave., P.O. Box 942869, Sacramento, CA 94269; www.dmv.ca.gov. Foreign visitors planning to drive should obtain an International Driver's License before leaving home (they're

GETTING ORIENTED:
LOS ANGELES AS THEME PARK

Because Los Angeles is such a private place—and such a vast and inexplicably complicated place—it can be as intimidating to plan a visit as to actually make the trip. While Los Angeles is not just Disneyland anymore, thinking of L.A. as one huge theme park somehow makes an upcoming stay seem much more manageable. Simply plan your trip as if parceling out available time and resources between L.A.'s various "lands." The following chapters on greater Los Angeles are organized to help you do just that. Starting with this book as your general guide, don't hesitate to venture off the well-trodden tourist track. Historic home and walking tours, mural excursions, beach walks and nature hikes, serious museum exploration, even club- and movie theater-hopping—these are *not* the things most visitors do when they come to Los Angeles. Many are so mesmerized by the region's well-known theme parks—Disneyland, Knott's Berry Farm, Sea World, Six Flags Magic Mountain, Universal Studios—or by the shopping malls that they rarely go any farther. They rarely visit *Los Angeles*. Don't make that mistake. Do what Angelenos do while you're here—and see and do Los Angeles.

Yet be forewarned. Even imagined as a theme park, the Los Angeles experience can be overwhelming. The English novelist Christopher Isherwood, a longtime L.A. resident, had this advice to offer:

To live sanely in Los Angeles, you have to cultivate the art of staying awake. You must learn to resist (firmly but not tensely) the unceasing hypnotic suggestions of the radio, the billboards, the movies and the newspapers; those demon voices which are forever whispering in your ear . . . what you should think and do and be.

So, see and do L.A.—and stay awake.

Touring "L.A. Land"
If Los Angeles were one huge theme park—and if this guidebook were used to navigate among its many competing attractions—**High Cultureland** would be represented by the Pasadena and Vicinity chapter immediately following, since that region of greater L.A. is largely defined, still, by its cultural golden age. Most famous for its annual Tournament of Roses Parade, Pasadena features some excellent museums, intriguing architecture, and other impressive cultural attractions well worth any visitor's time. Come anytime but avoid summer if at all possible, since Pasadena's heat-related smog can be quite menacing.

not available here); licensed U.S. drivers from other states can legally drive in California for 30 consecutive days without having to obtain a California driver's license. Disabled travelers heading for California can get special handicapped-space parking permits, good for 90 days, by requesting applications in advance from the DMV and having them signed by their doctors (there is an application fee). If you'll be renting a car, ask the rental car agency to forward a form to you when you make reservations.

Among driving rules, the most basic is observing the posted speed limit. Though many California drivers ignore any and all speed limits, it's at their own peril should the California Highway Patrol be anywhere in the vicinity. The statewide speed limit for open highway driving varies, typically posted as somewhere between 55 and 70 miles per hour; freeway speeds can vary at different points along the same route. Speed limits for cities and residential neighborhoods are substantially slower. Another avoidable traffic ticket: not indulging in what is colloquially known as the "California stop," slowing down and then rolling right through full-stop intersections without first making a complete stop.

Once arrived at your destination, pay attention to parking notices, tow-away warnings, and the color of the curb: red means no parking under any circumstances; yellow means limited stops only (usually for freight delivery); green means very limited parking; and blue means parking

---

Cultureland proper would have to be this book's Downtown and Around chapter, with its concentration of contemporary museums and theaters and other cultural attractions. More significantly, the otherwise corporate downtown area offers visitors the best up-close opportunity to appreciate Los Angeles as a multiethnic culture, what with El Pueblo de Los Angeles, Chinatown, Little Tokyo, East L.A., and Koreatown in such close proximity.

A Los Angeles **Movieland** would cover the territory included under Hollywood and Vicinity. Though much of mythic Hollywood Boulevard is fairly seedy and sad these days—not at all what visitors expect —historic Hollywood, adjacent West Hollywood, and the nearby San Fernando Valley still successfully tell the story of L.A.'s astonishing self-creation as the world's entertainment capital.

In many ways, Movieland also describes swank Beverly Hills and environs. But since Beverly Hills was built largely with entertainment industry wealth, **Richland** is actually more appropriate. The Beverly Hills and Vicinity chapter also includes Century City and Westwood near the University of California at Los Angeles (UCLA) campus, as well as Brentwood, home of the grand new Getty Center and the Skirball Center, all communities that prefer to think of themselves as part of L.A.'s tony "Westside."

Farther west is the sophisticated beach town of Santa Monica. If there were a **Beachland** in Los Angeles, this book's The Los Angeles Coast chapter would cover it, including Santa Monica and the territory both north and south—west, at least as far as Santa Catalina Island.

As a sad commentary on our times and on the reality, not the rhetoric, of America's current cultural values, much of what would have to be called **Poorland**—some of the most poverty-stricken ghettos in the United States, generally situated between downtown Los Angeles and Long Beach—is not covered in this book. Except for the most street-savvy travelers, visiting these areas without a knowledgeable local escort would be very unwise, actually downright dangerous, because of the very real possibilities of predation and the general local terror created by gangs and gang violence. Yet gangs are mobile—everyone in Los Angeles has a car—and poverty is ubiquitous; gangsters live in almost all areas of Los Angeles, so reasonable caution is wise anywhere in the L.A. region.

Areas many people think of as part and parcel of Los Angeles are more appropriately considered Greater Southern California—let's call it **Escape from L.A. Land.** Immediately south of Los Angeles, along the coast and inland, is Orange County, home to Disneyland and other major attractions. Next south is San Diego County, which includes the city of San Diego, other coastal cities, and parts of the county's inland desert. Also in Greater Southern California are Palm Springs and the vast California deserts; the "Inland Empire" region represented by Riverside and San Bernardino; and Santa Barbara along with other destinations along the coast north of Los Angeles. Some destinations in Escape from L.A. Land are listed in this book's Near Los Angeles chapter.

for the disabled only. In hill areas of Southern California, always turn your front wheels into the curb (to keep your car from becoming a roll-away runaway) and set the emergency brake.

Driving while under the influence of alcohol or drugs is a very serious offense in California—aside from being a danger to one's own health and safety, not to mention those of innocent fellow drivers. Don't drink (or drug) and drive.

By Rental Car

Renting a car—or a recreational vehicle—in California usually won't come cheap. Rates have been accelerating, so to speak, in recent years, especially when consumers put the kibosh on mileage caps. Turns out people really liked the idea of unlimited "free" mileage. So now the average car rental price is just above $50 a day (lower for subcompacts, higher for road hogs). Still, bargains are sometimes available through small local agencies. Among national agencies, National and Alamo often offer the lowest prices. But in many cases, with weekly rentals and various group-association (AAA, AARP, etc.) and credit card discounts ranging from 10–40 per-cent, you'll usually do just as well with other major car rental agencies. According to the *Consumer Reports* June 1996 national reader quality survey, Hertz, Avis, and National were rated highest by customers for clean cars, quick and courteous service, and speedy checkout.

Beware of the increasingly intense pressure, once you arrive to pick up your rental car, to persuade you to buy additional insurance coverage. In some companies, rental car agents receive a commission for every insurance policy they sell, needed or not, which is why the person on the other side of the counter is so motivated (sometimes pushy and downright intimidating). Feel free to complain to management if you dislike such treatment—and to take your business elsewhere. This highly touted insurance coverage is coverage you probably don't need, from collision damage waivers—now outlawed in some states, but not in California—to liability insurance, which you probably don't need unless you have no car insurance at all (in which case it's illegal to drive in California). Some people do carry additional rental-car collision or liability insurance on their personal insurance policies—

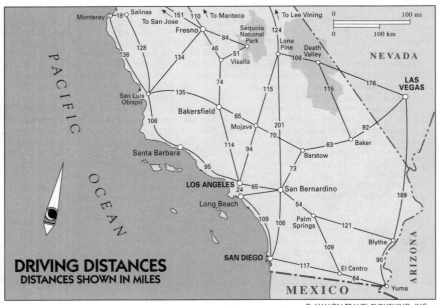

DRIVING DISTANCES
DISTANCES SHOWN IN MILES

UNIVERSAL STUDIOS, HOLLYWOOD

Travel & tourism is a major industry in California. Universal Studios is the third most popular tourist attraction in the United States, behind Disneyland and Disneyworld.

talk to your agent about this—but even that is already covered, at least domestically, if you pay for your rental car with a gold MasterCard or Visa. The same is true for American Express for domestic travelers, though American Express recently rescinded such coverage on overseas car rentals; it's possible that Visa and Master-Card will soon follow suit. (Check your personal insurance and credit card coverage before dealing with the rental car agencies.) And bring personal proof of car insurance, though you'll rarely be asked for it. In short—buyer beware.

For current information on options and prices for rental cars in Southern California, Northern California, and elsewhere in the United States, contact **Alamo,** toll-free 800/327-9633, www.alamo.com.; **Avis,** toll-free 800/831-2847, www.avis.com; **Budget,** toll-free worldwide 800/527-0700, www.budget.com; **Dollar,** toll-free 800/800-4000, www.dollar.com; **Enterprise,** toll-free 800/736-8222, www.enterprise.com; **Hertz,** toll-free worldwide 800/654-3131, www.hertz.com; **National,** toll-free 800/227-7368, www.nationalcar.com; and **Thrifty,** toll-free 800/847-4389, www.thrifty.com. You can also make rental car arrangements online, either directly through individual home pages or through virtual travel agencies and reservations systems such as **Travelocity,** www.travelocity.com, and **The Trip,** www.thetrip.com.

Though some rental agencies also handle recreational vehicle (RV) rentals—heck, in Beverly Hills you can even rent a Rolls Royce—travelers may be able to get better deals by renting directly from local RV dealers. For suggestions, contact area visitor bureaus—and consult the local telephone book.

By Airplane
Airfares change and bargains come and go so quickly in competitive California that the best way to keep abreast of the situation is through a travel agent. Or via the Internet, where major U.S. airlines regularly offer great deals—discounts of up to 90 percent (typically not *quite* that good). Popular home pages include **American Airlines,** www.aa.com; **Continental,** www.flycontinental.com; **Delta,** www.delta-air.com; **Northwest,** www.nwa.com; **TWA,** www.twa.com; **United,** www.ual.com; and **US Airways,** www.usairways.com. Also look up the people's favorite, **Southwest,** at www.iflyswa.com. Have your credit card handy. To find additional websites, know your computer—or call any airline's toll-free "800" number and ask. Fueling travel agents' fears that online airline ticket sales will doom them (and independent online agencies) is the news that five airlines—American, Continental, Delta, Northwest, and United—plan to launch their own "independent" online travel service, **Orbitz.**

But the online agencies may be able to fight back: **Travelzoo,** www.travelzoo.com, searches the 20 major airline websites for the deep-discounted fares and posts them, so you don't have to spend hours looking for the best deals. Relative newcomer **Hotwire,** www.hotwire.com, offers airline tickets at a 40 percent discount (though with limited consumer routing control), as well as hotel rooms and rental car discounts. For possibly great deals on last-minute departures, try **Savvio;** www.savvio.com.

Another good information source for domestic and international flight fares: the travel advertisements in the weekend travel sections of major urban newspapers. Super Saver fares (booked well in advance) can save fliers up to 30–70 percent and more. Peak travel times in and out of California being the summer and the midwinter holiday season, book flights well in advance for June–August and December travel. The best bargains in airfares are usually available from January to early May.

Bargain airfares are often available for international travelers, especially in spring and autumn. Charter flights are also good bargains, the only disadvantage usually being inflexible departure and return-flight dates. Most flights from Europe to the United States arrive in New York; from there, other transcontinental travel options are available. Reduced-fare flights on major airlines from Europe abound.

Keep in mind, too, if you're flying, that airlines are getting increasingly strict about how much baggage you're allowed to bring with you. They mean business with those prominent "sizer boxes" now on display in every airport. Only two pieces of carry-on luggage are allowed on most carriers—some now allow only one—and each must fit in the box. Most airlines allow three pieces of luggage total per passenger. (Fortunately for parents, diaper bags, fold-up strollers, and—at least sometimes—infant carrier seats don't count.) So if you are philosophically opposed to the concept of traveling light, bring two massive suitcases—and check them through —in addition to your carry-on. Some airlines, including American, charge extra for more than two checked bags per person. Contact each airline directly for current baggage guidelines.

GREATER LOS ANGELES

INTRODUCTION: GREATER LOS ANGELES

Apocalypse City, Angel City

Scribes and small-screen prognosticators love to announce the death of Los Angeles. With every new disaster they do it again. Recently the L.A. experiment seemed all but assassinated by the latest Los Angeles Police Department (LAPD) corruption and bad-guy frame-up scandal. Previously L.A. was declared dead because of the nasty Northridge earthquake of 1994. In addition to demolishing entire neighborhoods and killing dozens of people, the quake snapped off major freeways, thereby desecrating the city's most cherished cultural symbol—spokes in the sacred wheel of Southern California life. Just months before that, Los Angeles seemed doomed because of raging wildfires and the winter mudslides that came in their wake. Before that the city was decimated by the demise of California's defense industry, coupled with the economic and social challenge of absorbing a seemingly endless stream of illegal immigrants. Not to mention riots related to the Rodney King police brutality case, and the Watts riots almost 30 years before that. Not to mention the smog.

The apocalyptic tendencies of Los Angeles—more accurately, our collective determination to place Los Angeles at the center of our fascinations with disaster and futuristic despair—are as well represented in literature as in real life. Consider the nuclear holocaust in Thomas Pynchon's *Gravity's Rainbow*. The earthquake in *The Last Tycoon*. The riot in *The Day of the Locust*. And little-known classics such as Marie Corelli's strange 1921 romance *Secret Power*, in which L.A. is decimated by an atomic explosion, along with Ward Moore's hilarious 1947 *Greener Than You Think*, in which the city is done in by Bermuda grass. Movies have also made their contribution to the cult of L.A. Apocalypse, of course, *Blade Runner* most memorably, though the recent list also includes *Independence Day* and *Escape from L.A.*

Even so, in recent years L.A. has suffered from entirely too much dystopia, entirely too much rumination on the subject of utopia gone wrong. Entirely too much *reality*. And reality has never been the point here. Los Angeles, after

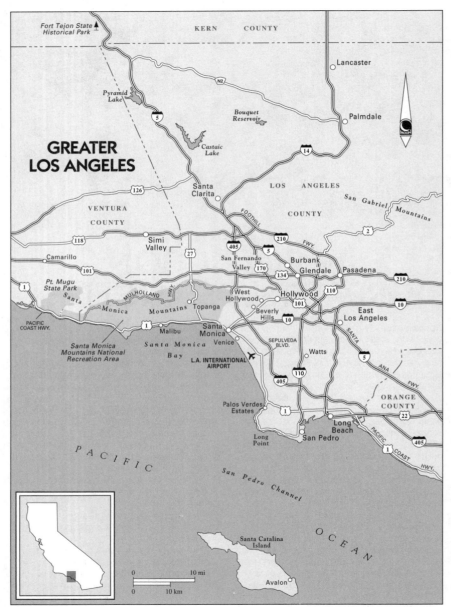

GREATER
LOS ANGELES

all, is both the world's foremost fantasy factory and psychic playground for America's most child-like narcissisms.

The lesson of Los Angeles is the lesson of the movies. Big faces on the big screen reassure us that "individual lives have scope and grandeur," in the words of California writer Richard Rodriguez. "The attention L.A. lavishes on a single face is as generous a metaphor as I can find for the love of God."

From a strictly secular point of view, the sun is also generous. In Los Angeles the sun always shines, on the degenerate and deserving alike. At last report this was still true.

LOS ANGELES AS IDEA

CITY OF DREAMS AND DREAMERS

That Los Angeles is both "city of angels" and favored social demon-hold of modern literature and cinema is, here, an acceptable contradiction. Contrast, contradiction, and irony are the life-blood of Los Angeles. Yet it wasn't always thus. In its younger years, Los Angeles seemed in-spired by the idealistic, almost innocent ideas that directed its growth. Utopia preceded dystopia, at least officially.

Since its humble beginnings, Los Angeles has been a city of dreams and dreamers. The first settlers hailed from Mexico, then a colony of Spain; *vecinos pobladores* or village people were lured by government promises of free land and free cattle. In fairly rapid historical succession, the conquest known as California passed from Spain to Mexico and then to the United States. New dreamers and dreams kept coming, yet for another century Los Angeles remained a remote cowtown linked to the rest of California by dirt roads, remnants of the land-grant ranchos, and memories of the missions' cultural heyday.

With the arrival of the railroads in the 1870s and 1880s, the world rushed in. To lure new cit-izens, sell real estate, and support business growth, civic boosters promoted the southstate's sunshine, healthful climate, and glorious gar-dens and orange groves—and the chance to start over, to imagine a new, healthier life, a life of unlimited possibilities.

In the pursuit of unlimited possibility, Los Ange-les has largely succeeded in breaking even nat-ural laws. Starting with no water, no port, and no substantial population, Los Angeles promoted itself—its idea of itself—into existence.

But the symbols of the dream—the Southern California dream, the California dream, the American dream of a limitless future—con-stantly change. A fetching señorita with a Spanish fan, looking out over herds of long-horned cattle, was the ideal of Southern Cali-fornia immigrants during the days of the Span-ish (then Mexican) ranchos. It was oranges and winter-blooming roses during the era of California's yeoman farmers, and fields of oil derricks during the southstate's rush to reap black gold. It was overnight fame and fortune during Hollywood's moviemaking heyday. After World War II came worship of the new in the form of real estate—and endless social mobil-ity, symbolized by the private passenger car and unprecedented numbers of new freeways and highways. As families laid claim to new homes on newly developed land, waves of suburban sameness rolled out in all directions, away from the terrifying unpredictability of war. Then came the southstate's defense and aero-space industries, part of the Cold War dream of reaching past the ends of the earth to defend hearth and home.

Now that frontiers are measured more accu-rately in cyberspace than space, the Los Ange-les dream seems to require personal comput-ers, Internet access, cellular phones, pagers, and other technological accessories of the good life. And the quest for life everlasting—unlimited life—goes on, given Southern California's obses-sion with health, fitness, and at least the appear-ance of eternal youth.

Yet the dream itself remains remarkably con-stant. People come to Los Angeles for the sun-shine, the mild climate, the palm trees, the beach, the endless expanse of sky and sea—that sense of unlimited personal freedom—and to reimagine and reinvent themselves. The Los Angeles of myth is the land of happy endings. Like Disneyland.

"REAL" LOS ANGELES

Outsiders' interpretations of Los Angeles—what everyone thinks they know about the place—are often seriously mistaken. For all its casual friendliness, Los Angeles is actually an aloof city, self-protective. One certainly experiences that truth on the freeways—so many millions of people, so oblivious to each other, every person moving through life in a freewheeling, independent world. For all its fabled flamboyance and sometimes shameless public shenanigans, Los Angeles is in real life a very private place. "Real" L.A. is a private, not a public, domain—which is why finding it can be such a challenge for visitors who even attempt the task. When L.A. isn't performing on its varied public stages—and L.A. in all its guises works long, hard hours—the city stays home with family and friends, or goes out to play, privately. Los Angeles tolerates its tourists as revenue enhancements—"tourist" a term that was invented here—but rarely invites them home or out on the town. Traditionally the supremacy of individuality and the need for privacy follow Angelenos everywhere.

For all its vastness, or perhaps because of it, L.A. is also parochial and self-absorbed. "Family values" matter here because immediate family is almost all there is to anchor people in such a fast-paced society. Even political battles in Los Angeles are largely fought on the neighborhood level. Yet such self-absorption has its price. While Southern California can't muster the political will to properly finance its public schools, libraries, and health-care services, Los Angeles is number one in the nation for plastic surgery: breast enhancements, liposuction, facelifts, nose and eyelid jobs. Fitness centers are also central to Southern California culture, as are psychiatrists and psychologists and sometimes out-there spiritual advisers.

For all its wealth, Los Angeles largely lacks the memorable monuments to grand ideas and idealism so typical of European and other American cities, be they cathedrals, museums, or public libraries. While exceptions to this rule can still be found downtown and in affluent communities such as Beverly Hills and Pasadena, the most striking architecture in Los Angeles is private, not public. Rather than invest its billions of dollars in old-fashioned public betterment and enlightenment, L.A. spends its money on private pleasures—on great walled mansions and estates and, on a more modest scale out in the suburbs, on backyard barbecues, swimming pools, and all the other accoutrements of middle-class family living.

Parochial Los Angeles does seem improbable, given the city's social and cultural perch at the edge of both Mexico and the Pacific Rim. Yet even L.A.'s recent arrivals tend to settle into particular neighborhoods. Because of its insularity, until quite recently Los Angeles could imagine itself untouched by the multiethnic chaos that now defines it.

Rather than a melting pot, L.A. is a multicultural anthology in which every recent ethnic arrival has its own page, if not an entire separate chapter. Immigrants from more than 140 different nations live within Los Angeles County, including the largest populations of Armenians, Filipinos, and Koreans outside their respective nations, and the largest U.S. populations of Cambodians, Iranians, and Japanese. Latin American immigrants—Guatemalans, Mexicans, and Salvadorans—dominate many chapters, as do third- and fourth-generation migrants from the U.S. Midwest. Still, the story lines rarely intersect.

This, says writer Richard Rodriguez, is as it has always been in Los Angeles—and in America. Thanks to Protestantism, he says, "The immigrant country of the nineteenth century became a country of tribes and neighborhoods more truly than a nation of solitary individuals. Then, as today, Americans trusted diversity, not uniformity. Americans trusted the space between us more than we liked any notion of an American melting pot that might turn us into one another." Yet, according to Rodriguez, "any immigrant kid could tell you that America exists. There *is* a culture. There is a shared accent, a shared defiance of authority, a shared skepticism about community." By extension, there is also a shared culture in Los Angeles.

While it's true that Los Angeles is home to anything, everything, and everybody, the city's endless possibilities are still more possible for some than for others. For all its current social, political, and economic turmoil, L.A. is a strikingly tolerant city. And it's a lively city.

National trendsetter in popular entertainment, lifestyle, fashion, and vocabulary, Los Angeles boasts more university graduates per capita than any other U.S. city. There are more colleges and universities here, a total of 176 at last count, than in the entire state of Massachusetts. But culture here doesn't always come with a university degree. Los Angeles is also the mural capital of the world, with a "collection" of more than 1,500 outdoor wall paintings displayed on store-fronts (and sides), street corners, and alleyways throughout the county. Long characterized as culturally and intellectually vapid, Los Angeles is home to more actors, artists, dancers, filmmakers, musicians, and writers than any other city—at any time in the history of civilization.

After taking a good look around, even visitors soon realize that Los Angeles is not just Disneyland anymore.

LOS ANGELES AS PLACE

As defined by the U.S. Census Bureau, the greater Los Angeles metropolitan area encompasses Los Angeles County, including the city of Los Angeles, and urban areas of adjacent Orange, Riverside, San Bernardino, and Ventura Counties. The total population of the five-county L.A. area—16.4 million according to the 2000 census, and counting—exceeds the population of every state in the union except California, New York, and Texas. Taking in a total of 34,149 square miles, greater Los Angeles—with its abundance of computers, fax machines, and cellular phones—has more telephone area codes than any other region of the country.

Even Los Angeles proper is difficult to locate precisely. Its geographical boundaries are puzzling even to people who live here, which is why Angelenos have fairly vague notions of official local lines of demarcation. The writer Dorothy Parker once observed that Los Angeles amounted to "seventy-two suburbs in search of a city." She was correct, historically. In the latter years of the 19th century, small cities sprang up throughout Los Angeles County, typically at the end of the city's famed trolley lines. Then came freeways and two-car garages and the dominance of L.A.'s automobile, trends that soon filled in the spaces between communities. Shortly after World War II, the present-day tendency toward sprawl was well established, with boundaries between L.A. the city and L.A. the county almost hopelessly blurred by exponential growth.

For the record, the present-day city of Los Angeles takes in 467 square miles, or almost one-tenth of Los Angeles County's 4,083-square-mile area; the city includes many apparently separate communities or districts such as Hollywood. Aside from the city of Los Angeles, there are numerous unincorporated areas known as Los Angeles—and 87 other incorporated cities within the county's borders—all of which are still considered "L.A." in a general sense.

Yet even the terms traditionally used to define L.A.'s relationship with itself—such as "city" or "downtown" or "suburbs"—have been largely abandoned by urban planners, who now conceive of L.A. as a series of "constellations" or urban villages comprising a metropolitan "galaxy."

Even if Los Angeles is an urban universe unto itself, there are still natural borders and boundaries to contend with.

LAND OF EAST-WEST MOUNTAINS

If one gets started early, on a pleasant winter's day in Los Angeles it's possible to walk on the beach and swim or surf in the ocean, snow ski down pine-scented alpine slopes, and sunbathe poolside in the Palm Springs desert. The variety of terrain and climate zones in and around Los Angeles is fairly astonishing.

For all its expansiveness, Los Angeles as place is nonetheless quite insular. Bordered on the west by the Pacific Ocean, greater Los Angeles is bounded on the north by the Santa Monica, San Gabriel, and San Bernardino Mountains. Notable segments of the unusual east-west-trending Transverse Ranges that separate the southstate from the rest of California, L.A.'s northern mountain peaks reach to 10,000 feet. To the east lies the vast California desert, to the southeast the San Jacinto Mountains, and to the southwest the Santa Ana Mountains. What remains is the vast Los Angeles Basin—the endless expanse of open space upon which the city, county, and fellow entities have constructed themselves.

The common conception of the L.A. Basin as one vast, desolate natural desert needing only water—water from the Owens Valley, from the Colorado River, from the Feather River—to burst into civilized bloom is being thoroughly debunked. Always a winning argument when used to convince Los Angeles voters to finance major water engineering construction projects, the fact is that in the early 1800s the vast plains south and west of downtown, all the way to the ocean, were forested marshlands. Water-loving alders, sycamores, and willows stretched all the way to the waterfront in Santa Monica and Wilmington, kept alive by the fact that the Los Angeles River bogged down in ponds and marshes and rarely reached the ocean. The massive floods of the 1820s and 1830s finally created a river channel to the sea, draining L.A.'s vast wetlands and vanquishing its native flatland forest. In addition, the entire Los Angeles Basin sits atop what were once immense artesian pools, a high-pressure underground water supply that provided most of the water for California's citrus and avocado groves. Except during periods of extended drought—not all that unusual during the longer marches of time across Los Angeles—the area was never a desert, despite the region's relatively low average annual rainfall. To experience that environment, head east into the Mojave and Colorado Deserts.

New Kid on the Block

As measured on a geologic scale, Los Angeles is something of a new kid on the tectonic block, first rising out of the ocean 100–160 million years ago and then slipping back under water before bursting forth to stay with the help of massive

A RIVERBED RUNS THROUGH IT

The Los Angeles River, originally the main attraction of downtown Los Angeles, is dry most of the year. With more than 90 percent of L.A.'s water now "imported" from elsewhere via aqueduct, the city's namesake river has become little more than a concrete-sealed drainage ditch and illegal sewage and trash dump popular also with skateboarders, daredevil cyclists, and rookie bus drivers in training.

Yet some in Los Angeles have other plans for the city's central 58-mile-long river. In 1994, for example, the Washington-based American Rivers conservation group added the Los Angeles River to its list of top 30 endangered and threatened U.S. rivers.

And rather than go along with the U.S. Army Corps of Engineers' original plans to augment the L.A. River's flood-control capacity by adding two- to eight-foot-tall cement flood walls to 20 miles of the river and its Compton Creek and Rio Hondo tributaries, Friends of the Los Angeles River decided to fight. The group has gained support for its more environmentally sensitive "natural" alternatives, which, some say, are also more effective and cost-effective.

But in January of 1995 came torrential rains—14 days and 14 nights of rain, causing severe flooding, neighborhood evacuations, and an official $53 million in damages. Angelenos couldn't cope—and politicians seemed unwilling to tolerate any further delays. As the Corps and L.A. County public works workers were poised to begin pouring concrete for the Los Angeles County Drainage Area project (LACDA), Friends of the Los Angeles River, Heal the Bay, and TreePeople filed suit to stop them. While settlement talks progressed, the Federal Emergency Management Agency (FEMA) threatened to levy punishing insurance rates if flood-control construction didn't begin. Friends settled its lawsuit in March of 1996 when the county agreed to fund a 25-member task force to study alternatives. But the river talks ran aground again in April of 1996, when the county's public works director stated that no elements of the plan would change, no matter what the task force concluded.

To publicize the river's plight, in September of 1996 the group sponsored the Great Los Angeles River Canoe Race along an unchanneled section of the river in the Sepulveda Dam Recreation Area. Here, the river has a sandy natural bottom, and trees and other thick vegetation still line its banks. Yet that media performance, starring actor Ed Begley, Jr., among the environmentalist canoe crews, still wasn't igneous extrusions. The present-day landscape is of more recent origin, since even six million years ago the Palos Verdes Peninsula was still an island in the Channel Islands chain and the ocean lapped the shores of Glendale. Geologists estimate the Pacific and Northwest tectonic plates, which still shape L.A., move at the rate of about 1.75 inches per year—about as fast as fingernails grow in the same period—except when earthquakes speed things up substantially. By this reckoning, Palos Verdes inches toward Pasadena at the rate of about one-third inch each year, and Los Angeles City Hall is 10 feet closer to San Francisco than when it was built in 1924.

The prehistoric species unearthed from the ooze at the La Brea pits, and which collectively provided Los Angeles with its later oil wealth, lived from 9,000 to 40,000 years ago. About 40 percent of the larger La Brea mammal species, from ancient horses, camels, and llamas to mastodons, have been extinct for about 11,000 years, though many of the smaller mammal, bird, and aquatic species found in this prehistoric depository survive.

Standing on Slippery, Soggy, or Tinder-Dry Ground

In addition to earthquakes, years of unrestrained real estate speculation and development have served to increase local insecurities—and local disaster potential—still more. Consider the consequence of becoming too comfortable with the "average" low levels of rainfall: Los Angeles and other areas have built willy-nilly throughout coastal and other floodplain areas. Then there's Southern California's habit of building some of its most exclusive homes on higher ground. In years of exceptionally high rainfall—which happens at least once every 15 years, with the arrival of El Niño—major flooding results in many areas. So do major mudslides, particularly in areas where

---

enough to change minds on the Los Angeles County Board of Supervisors, which had been heavily lobbied for 100-year flood control protection by Downey and six other affected cities. (The cities of Los Angeles and Santa Monica have long opposed the plan.) Members voted 4-1 to accept the controversial environmental impact report on the increased concrete channeling of the river. Yet supervisors also agreed to establish a group to study alternatives, the 28-member Los Angeles River Watershed Management Task Force.

As evidence mounted that many ideas proposed by Friends of the Los Angeles River, the task force, and other groups were indeed viable—even national Corps policy now supports restoring channeled rivers whenever possible—the political tide began to turn.

Flood-wall construction will progress in places along the L.A. River but—with any luck at all, and with adequate funding—other flood-control and river restoration work will also go forward; in 1997 the county selected environmental consultants Simons Li & Associates to study current proposals.

Alternative flood-control ideas include improving communications between dams along the L.A. and San Gabriel Rivers to synchronize water flow; using gravel pits and/or area parks for underground water storage; and widening some sections of the river to accommodate heavy runoff. L.A.'s political leaders have not yet decided to return sections of the Los Angeles River to a natural state, which would require removing concrete and replacing it with "soft bottom" and vegetation.

According to Arthur Golding, chair of the Los Angeles River Task Force of the American Institute of Architects, Los Angeles Chapter, there are good reasons for L.A. citizens and visitors alike to care about the fate of the Los Angeles River. "Though it is no longer a principal source of water sustaining the city, a living river would be an emblem of responsible water management in a dry climate and a symbol of sustainable development," Golding says. "To deny the river is to deny the origin of the city. To rethink the river is to discover a unique opportunity to define urban places, join neighborhoods and communities together, and reconnect us to our landscape and our history."

For current information about the Los Angeles River, including guided public walks, bird-watching opportunities, and scheduled restoration work days, contact: **Friends of the Los Angeles River** (FoLAR), 570 W. Ave. 26 #250, Los Angeles, CA 90065, 323/0585 or toll-free 800/527-4837 (LA RIVER); www.folar.org. The website offers abundant links to related endeavors and organizations.

SHAKY GROUND

In many ways Los Angeles has challenged the very laws of nature and still lives to brag about it. Building itself upon a swarming underground snake pit of earthquake faults is L.A.'s first act of hubris, however unintentional. Though the San Andreas Fault is perhaps the world's most famous, Southern California actually features countless earthquake faults. More than 200 of these are capable of producing earthquakes of a magnitude greater than 6.0 on the Richter scale—two major new faults were recently discovered beneath downtown's high-rises—and no spot in Los Angeles County is more than 30 miles away from at least one of them. While Los Angeles has experienced more than 200,000 earthquakes in the past 100 years, only a handful have shaken things up enough to make the news.

As do other Californians, Angelenos live with a fairly constant if unacknowledged anxiety that the predicted "big one"—a massive earthquake, perhaps measuring 8.0 or 9.0 on the Richter scale—will hit here at some time within the next 50–100 years, causing death and destruction on an unimaginable scale. The Northridge earthquake, which struck in the early morning of January 17, 1994, a fortunate fact of timing that no doubt helped minimize the loss of human life, measured 6.7 on the Richter scale and brought down sections of nearby freeways and crippled large parts of the San Fernando Valley. To visualize what the "big one" might be like, keep in mind that the intensity of earthquakes increases by a factor of ten for every measured point—meaning that an 8.0 earthquake is 10 times more powerful than a 7.0 quake, for example.

While earthquake safety construction standards are taken seriously in California, and while "earthquake retrofitting" of older buildings, bridges, and freeways has been under way for quite some time, with every serious quake it becomes increasingly obvious that no amount of public earthquake and emergency preparedness will help much in a massive earthquake—an event that would disrupt communication, transportation, and water and electrical power supplies for lengthy periods. Even most Los Angeles residents, like people in the San Francisco Bay Area and other areas of quake-prone California, live in a state of denial about this fact. Few take even the most basic steps to safeguard their family's well-being in case of a major quake, such as setting aside functioning battery-operated flashlights and radios, extra blankets, and emergency water, food, and first aid supplies. Of those who are prepared, some also pack such provisions in their cars—since one never knows where or when an earthquake will hit.

homes have been built on steep, slippery, fairly unstable slopes, as in Malibu and other coastal areas. Mudslides are predictably worse after major wildfires, which denude hillsides. Yet fire is a fairly common natural occurrence, since native plantife is fire adapted.

LAND OF ENDLESS SUNSHINE

Its early promoters used the Southern California climate as a major selling point, a historical trend that has never ended. And the sun is fairly constant in Southern California, which boasts an average of 329 sunny days each year. Of course, not every year is "average."

About every 15 years Southern California experiences El Niño, an offshore ocean warming that yanks the West Coast's stormy weather and rainfall sharply south. After an El Niño in wild-weather 1982, another arrived in the winter of 1997–98—drenching Southern California with 31 inches of rain. In an average year, L.A. receives 14–15 inches of rain. Despite the fairly low annual rainfall, Los Angeles is not a desert. Its proper climatic classification is "Mediterranean," matching the characteristics of places such as Athens, Rome, and the French Riviera.

No one here brags about this fact, but when it rains in Los Angeles it "acid rains," a phenomenon related to the region's high smog levels. Los Angeles has some of the world's worst acid rain—two to three times higher than elsewhere in the United States, as acidic as vinegar in the mountains near San Bernardino (300 times more acidic than "normal"). And the problem is not limited to greater Los Angeles. Acid rains generated by Los Angeles smog are acidifying previously pristine areas in the higher reaches of the Sierra Nevada. More common locally, however, is Southern California "acid fog," a serious problem for asthmatics.

Except for temperature extremes encountered in the desert and the mountains, both summer and winter temperatures in Southern California are mild. As the L.A. visitor bureau says, "There are no unpleasant seasons in Los Angeles." Greater Los Angeles is characterized by balmy temperatures year-round, with summer highs in the 80°F range and winter highs in the upper 60s. Though inland areas of Los Angeles can get quite hot in summer—and smoggy, as the heat and inversion layer captures local air pollution and holds it close to the ground— coastal areas are typically air-conditioned, naturally, by cooled ocean breezes. Coastal fog is cooler yet.

The L.A. Curse: Smog

Mix some of L.A.'s endless sunshine with moist air and the combustible fuel wastes from millions of cars and you get "smog," a contraction combining "smoke" with "fog"—that dirty brown haze on every horizon, and a painful, health-damaging breathing experience. Despite L.A.'s fame for its smog, and despite increasing numbers of cars on the road, local air quality—as measured in the number and severity of smog alerts—has actually improved since the 1970s, when Southern California first got serious about cleaning up its act. Typically worst for summer smog is the eastern San Gabriel Valley, Pasadena, and points east. Locals who can manage often plan their annual get-out-of-town getaways during July and August, when the air quality is at its most insufferable—

good enough reason for tourists to avoid the area then, if at all possible. The San Fernando Valley and areas in and around downtown can also be horrendous.

FLORA AND FAUNA: PALM TREES AND FERAL PARAKEETS

Much of the exotic lushness of Southern California is as native as pink plastic lawn flamingos. Before people began planting them here, Los Angeles had no palm trees, for example. Both the official city flower, the bird of paradise, and the official city tree, the Erythrina palm, are exotic imports. Except in rare areas, native plant species have long since lost out to domesticated plants in Los Angeles. Increasingly native animal species that manage to survive in and around Los Angeles are forced to compete with humans and feral dogs and cats—even feral parakeets and parrots—for limited territory and food supplies.

Native Species under Siege

Since Southern California in general, and urban Los Angeles in particular, have yet to acknowledge any final limits to human population growth and urban/suburban sprawl, most other native species here exist precariously. The massive loss of natural biodiversity in Southern California is rivaled in the United States only by the losses in Florida, Hawaii, and southern Appalachia—a

In January 1886, an extraordinary two days of rain flooded Los Angeles, which had no drainage system or ditches. The flood drowned four people and washed away 25 houses and a new railway station.

fact that has stimulated recent discussion of focusing the nation's efforts to protect endangered species primarily in these locations.

More than 100 Los Angeles County species—among them 41 species of plants—are listed by the U.S. government as "proposed endangered" or "proposed threatened." Now, in addition to one fish, four insect, and one plant species, six local birds are officially listed as endangered: the bald eagle, the American peregrine falcon, the peregrine falcon, the brown pelican, the California least tern, and the least Bell's vireo. Eleven species once found in Los Angeles, including the California condor and the Guadalupe fur seal, are extinct in the region. Six types of whales that migrate off California's shoreline, including the blue, humpback, and sperm whales, are listed as endangered species; four sea turtle species are listed as threatened or endangered.

Among the more common animal species still spotted in suburbia—and sometimes in the city, or on or near freeways—are deer, coyotes, raccoons, foxes, skunks, opossums, squirrels, ground squirrels, and various species of rats, mice, and other rodents. Mountain lions are rare, but increasingly common in more remote foothill and mountain areas; even deer are forced to graze on people's lawns, trees, and shrubbery, and drink from swimming pools and fountains, as human housing subdivisions invade their previous territories. Coyotes are still bolder, all too happy to dine out of people's garbage cans. Domesticated ducks and geese, sometimes accompanied by migrating wild cousins, are common in L.A.'s ponds and other decorative water oases—in swimming pools during drought years—and even residential areas have their hummingbirds and songbirds. Yet rare areas offer abundant bird-watching opportunities or native wildlife observation to any significant degree. Nature in Southern Cal-

ifornia is under relentless pressure from the forces of civilization.

At the edges of sprawl, encounters with predators—coyotes and mountain lions—are sometimes a problem, which is why "edge" residents have learned to keep pets indoors at night, and why small children are often not allowed on hiking trails in open space preserves. Intersecting parks and open-space preserves are managed primarily as migration corridors for struggling yet still surviving wildlife populations.

Creating a New Ecology

In many ways Los Angeles has created, and is still creating, a new ecology, one dominated by introduced species of both plants and animals. Prominent among local plant immigrants are L.A.'s palm trees, none of which grow here naturally, though native palms do grow near Palm Springs and elsewhere in the low desert. Though here as elsewhere in California native grasses were long ago replaced by introduced European species, the L.A. landscape's native oaks, sycamores, alders, and shrubs are now far outnumbered by introduced species—camellias, azaleas, ferns, and exotic tropical and semitropical tree and shrub varieties—that thrive in the mild Mediterranean climate. Most vividly illustrating L.A.'s re-creation of itself as urban tropical forest in the animal kingdom are the impressive flocks of feral parakeets, representing several species and all domestic escapees or their descendants, which thrive throughout fruitful Los Angeles. Local ornithologists also estimate that at least 2,000 feral parrots are at home in Los Angeles, 1,000 in and around Pasadena alone. A flock of about 400 red-crowned parrots was spotted in 1995 in the San Gabriel Valley, for example, and red-crowned and lilac-crowned parrots have been spotted in the San Fernando Valley.

LOS ANGELES AS STORY

DUSTY PUEBLO DAYS

In the beginning there was "Los Angeles man," a mysterious area resident whose skeleton, unearthed in 1936, has been dated as 7,000 years old. In more recent times, from Malibu north lived the Chumash, a fairly sophisticated seafaring people who fished and traded along the coast and throughout the Channel Islands. But the first-known residents of Los Angeles proper were the native Gabrieleño people, who had been pushed west by more aggressive Shoshonean peoples who dominated territories to the east. Sometimes known as the Yang-Na, the name of their village near what is downtown Los Angeles, the total local population has been estimated at about 5,000, scattered throughout the region in communities as large as 1,000 people. The Gabrieleño were here to welcome the first explorers to the Bahia de los Fumos or "Bay of the Fires" (or "Smokes"), so named by Portuguese explorer Juan Rodríguez Cabrillo from offshore in 1542. The "smokes" here were the Indian fires that created the landscape's notable and lingering brown haze—L.A.'s earliest smog.

But the first explorer to arrive in Los Angeles was Gaspar de Portolá, the Spanish governor of the Californias, while on his discovery mission of 1769–70. It would be 10 years before the Spanish availed themselves of the Gabrieleño's prime cottonwood- and alder-sheltered location along the riverbank, one of the few spots where the Los Angeles River flowed year-round.

Los Angeles as place was officially founded in 1781, established by the Spanish as a supply center for Alta California and named after the L.A. River, which in turn was originally named after the festival of the Virgin corresponding to its date of discovery: El Pueblo de Nuestra Señora la Reina de los Angeles de Porciúncula, or "Town of Our Lady Queen of the Angels of Porciúncula." In the beginning Los Angeles was a dusty little pueblo of modest adobes scattered near the river. The city's first settlers were 44 villagers from the Spanish territory that later became the Mexican states of Sonora and Sinaloa—an entourage of blacks, Indians, and mestizos (people of mixed black, Indian, and Spanish ancestry) accompanied by two Spaniards. More than half of the new arrivals were children.

Though Los Angeles served as the capital of Mexican California briefly, in 1845, for the most part even the transfers of power between Spain and Mexico after Mexican independence and between Mexico and the United States after the Mexican-American War had little impact here. The Los Angeles area boasted vast ranchos and an early version of landed gentry, yet most of the Spanish missions and associated cultural enclaves were established elsewhere—along the coast, the region's primary transportation corridor. The 1849 discovery of gold near Sacramento in the north, and San Francisco's subsequent debut as California's center of wealth and power, created a temporary boom market for southstate beef but otherwise left Los Angeles to languish as a lawless frontier border town best known for murder, mayhem, and general anarchy.

In the devastating drought years of the 1860s, the Spanish land grants came under American ownership, thanks to the U.S. judicial system, and cattle gave way to sheep, thanks to the great demand for wool during the Civil War era. Sheep gradually gave way to wheat and then orchards and vineyards and endless other agricultural crops as farmers discovered the profit potential of such a salubrious climate.

DAYS OF ORANGES AND ROSES

The coming of the railroads—first linking Los Angeles to San Francisco in 1871, and then directly to the rest of the United States via transcontinental railroad in 1876—set the stage for L.A.'s first, and subsequently unrelenting, boom years. As boosters and boosterism promoted the benefits to personal health and wealth offered by Southern California, the mass migration began.

orange grove

TOM MYERS PHOTOGRAPHY

There was a central idea behind the U.S. migration to Southern California—the idea that simple, healthful living amid gardens, orange groves, and the fellowship of good friends and neighbors could save civilization from the dehumanization and mindlessness of the industrial era. Earlier in the 20th century, Pasadena, Riverside, and countless other Southern California communities shaped themselves from such ideals. That idea came to be symbolized throughout the United States by the humble orange, and by Southern California's endless orange groves.

As a symbol of the Southern California dream, a regional variation of the American dream—particularly "middle-class America's desire for a home and happy marriage and healthy children," according to historian Kevin Starr—in the late 1800s the orange as icon of the good life was crated for wholesale consumption throughout the United States by advertising executives employed by the California Fruit Growers Exchange (known for its trademark "Sunkist" brand). Real estate sales campaigns in general, promoted by early L.A. power brokers and landowners—railroad barons such as Henry E. Huntington and Charles Nordhuff, and newspaper publishers such as Harrison Gray Otis of the *Los Angeles Times*—often emphasized the same theme, though the boosters' general credo was: "Big is Good, Bigger is Better, Biggest is Best." In parts of the country where winter meant blinding blizzards rather than blooming roses, the campaign wasn't a terribly hard sell.

All but obscured today by subsequent urban and suburban growth in Riverside is the "parent tree" for much of the world's supply of seedless oranges now known as Washington navels, named for the characteristic "belly button." Mother of California's orange industry—and, in a sense, mother of the Southern California myth—was Eliza Tibbets, who in 1873 planted the first two U.S. "bud sports" (mutant bud stock) of the Selecta orange that originated in Bahia, Brazil. That the fruit was clearly superior to any other commercial orange variety of the day—in size, appearance, texture, and flavor—and the fact that navel oranges were also seedless further enhanced their prospects as popular table fruit. In no time at all, Riverside was the most affluent community in all of Southern California.

Yet Pasadena, in the San Gabriel Valley just east of downtown Los Angeles, would reap the richest rewards of California's orange era. Described by acclaimed turn-of-the-century astronomer George Ellery Hale as the "Athens of the West," Pasadena took root thanks to the San Gabriel Valley Orange Association in 1875 and then grew its own golden age of arts and sciences. The arrival of the railroad in 1885 brought bushels of well-heeled easterners eager to escape to a kinder climate—the beginning of Pasadena's long-running reputation as a choice West Coast winter vacation destination. Many of Pasadena's wealthy winterers decided to stay on year-round, to soak up a full measure of sun and the scent of orange blossoms, and they soon built grand homes on the city's wide, wandering streets.

Thanks to the humble orange, the arts and all aspects of culture, not just horticulture, flourished in Pasadena, which made California's greatest contributions to the Arts and Crafts movement. Pasadena's craftsman architecture—most popular from 1900 to 1940, and also fairly common elsewhere throughout Southern California—relied on an uncluttered, woodsy, nature-oriented approach that combined the sensibilities of a Swiss chalet with Japanese (sometimes Chinese) and Tudor touches. Emphasizing simplicity and harmony with nature, they stood as repudiation of all things Victorian.

Pasadena was in step with the march of progress throughout Southern California in other ways as well—most particularly with its annual Tournament of Roses Parade, the ultimate boosteristic beacon of the California good life. Where else, after all, could one find *roses* on New Year's Day?

WATER, OIL, AND AUTOS EVERYWHERE

Yet Southern California's endless self-promotion was limited by the landscape's semiarid nature. No matter how grand the gardens grew in Southern California, nothing could grow for long without water. And with the arrival of hordes of migrants, water was increasingly scarce. Just as Los Angeles was beginning to grow into a recognizable city, the severe Southern California drought of 1892–1904 threatened the city's fragile foothold at the edge of its own dream.

Enter William Mulholland, an Irish immigrant who came to America in 1878, a self-educated man who began his career in Los Angeles as a ditchdigger and ended it as the city's chief water engineer. As superintendent of the Los Angeles City Water Company, Mulholland was a conscientious steward of L.A.'s limited liquid resources, but even concerted conservation was not enough. By 1903 it was clear that L.A. would either have to stop growing altogether—certainly an unacceptable conclusion among L.A.'s well-invested business boosters—or find more water.

So Mulholland and his good friend Fred Eaton, former mayor of Los Angeles, set out to find more water—in the Owens Valley on the eastern side of the Sierra Nevada about 250 miles north of Los Angeles. Mulholland quickly figured that the Owens River could supply enough water to support a city of two million souls instead of 200,000. Thus the Los Angeles Aqueduct, "the most gigantic and difficult engineering project undertaken by any American city," was born—and William Mulholland became an overnight celebrity among the engineers of academe, self-educated Americans, and civic boosters everywhere.

When in 1913 sweet Owens Valley water finally started flowing into the San Fernando Valley from Mulholland's ditch, an event for which 30,000–40,000 residents and a parade of dignitaries turned out, Mulholland said to the multitude: "There it is—take it." And take it they did. They took it to transform the drought-parched landscape into a lush garden of palm trees, fruit trees, and roses that soon welcomed Hollywood—and which Hollywood soon shared with the world via the movies, attracting hundreds of thousands of new residents.

The landscape also sprouted oil wells. In 1892 Edward Doheny discovered oil at "Greasy Gulch," near what is now MacArthur Park. By 1897 there were more than 500 oil wells in and around downtown alone, although oil discoveries fanned out in all directions, including Orange County. Almost overnight California became the third-largest oil producing state in the nation.

Wide open spaces and abundant local fuel supplies made far-flung Los Angeles a perfect testing ground for America's latest invention—the horseless carriage. Automobiles first took to the Los Angeles streets in 1897; by 1915 about 55,000 cars populated area roadways, and by 1927 L.A. was considered a "completely motorized civilization." Ever-inventive Los Angeles established the world's first gas station in 1912; built the world's first freeway in 1939, the Pasadena Freeway (110) from Pasadena into downtown; and installed the world's first parking meter in 1942.

HOLLYWOOD'S HEYDAY

To imagine Hollywood as a pious, prohibitionist utopia is more than even modern Hollywood mythmakers could manage. Yet so it was, until moviemaking came to town. Technically the southstate's moving picture industry began in 1907 in Los Angeles, which Selig Studios chose for filming the outdoor scenes for *The Count of Monte Cristo*. But the distinction between Los Angeles and Hollywood as a film location was moot by 1911, in a sense, since in 1910 the small L.A. suburb of Hollywood surrendered its charter and became part of Los Angeles. In that same year David Wark Griffith, leading director of New York's Biograph film company, came west to Los Angeles with his wife, Linda, and his film troupe, including 17-year-old Mary Pickford, and installed them in the Hollywood Inn on Hollywood Boulevard for the winter-spring shooting season. Between January 20 and April 6, Griffith's troupe produced 21 films in distinct southstate settings—the first films shot entirely *in* Southern California—including *The Thread of Destiny* at Mission San Gabriel and *Ramona* in

THE RAIN OF WALLETS

That summer our fathers left,
when the Angels played
at home,
and the river was dry,
we'd ride past the factories
and body shops
to the cement-frosted shore
of the Santa Ana.
Locking our bikes to chainlink,
we'd scuff down sandbags through
weeds papier-mâchéd by diversions,
leap waste-clotted ponds,
and stretch out on the cool, moongray bed
to watch the lit coliseum
on the Coast of Anaheim,
keeping score by the organ and roars.
Nightly, we'd dream of a ball lifted
by big Don Baylor
out of the lights, over
the train tracks, the freeway,
a record-breaking ball, thought
lost to the world, to history,
but for our hearing its splash
in the thick dark water.

Mornings,
we'd step across green sands
sprouting twisted shirts, retreads,
and chickenwire. In pools beneath
concrete waterfalls
we'd hunt floating crawdads and crappies,

or gather nailshot driftwood
for shoring the sides
of the damp pit we'd dug
in evershade
below the lumbering gridlock
our fathers bumpered each day to L.A.

Noontime, eyes
to the vacation sun,
we'd lie in the dugout
and wait for the wallets
to fall,
gutted by pickpockets and worse,
tossed from windows
off I-5 North
into the wide white nowhere
that was ours.

As the rain began,
we'd step into the sun
and gather the leather quarry,
never with the cash or plastic inside
that could prove our integrity,
only the names, birthdates, and faces
of victims
who'd suspect our phone calls
and who never once, in a long summer,
rewarded two boys
for giving back to them
everything they could.

—Michael Sigalas

Ventura County. Griffith's disciple Mack Sennett arrived in 1912 to begin his Keystone comedies, star vehicles for the English vaudevillian Charlie Chaplin.

Still, Hollywood resisted Southern California's growing general affinity for film. But before the community could mobilize much protest against the carousing, notoriously carefree movie people, they had already arrived. Within five years about 35 movie studios had relocated from the East and Midwest, creating overnight chaos on Hollywood's sleepy unpaved streets. But concerns about Hollywood's moral corruption proved to be no match for movie industry money, and by the Roaring '20s, Hollywood's stars glittered as national and international idols.

During the 1920s and '30s the stretch of Hollywood Boulevard between La Brea Avenue and Vine Street glittered with glitz, boasting magnificent movie theaters, notorious nightclubs (Hollywood invented the Flapper style), notoriously good restaurants, chic shops, and stylish hotels. By the mid-1920s the Hollywood movie business was the fifth-largest industry in the United States, generating 90 percent of the world's films and grossing about $1.5 billion per year.

But the emerging West Coast film industry reached far beyond Hollywood, right into the heart and mind of heartland America and, quite quickly, the world. Movies appealed to the elemental and universal human experience; to get the drift of the story lines, one did not need an Ivy League education. Soon Hollywood–Los Angeles– both created and interpreted national aspirations, and modern mass culture was born.

BARBIES AND BOMBERS:
LOS ANGELES AFTER WORLD WAR II

For all of Southern California's earlier, more innocent glories, the modern middle-class myth of Los Angeles is largely the creation of the post–World War II era. And L.A. had rallied for the war effort in a big way, turning its entrepreneurial spirit to the task of building bigger and better aircraft and weaponry—the beginnings of Southern California's centrality to the U.S. defense and space technology industries. It's not by accident that Hughes Aircraft, McDonnell Douglas, Northrup, and Lockheed are practically neighborhood names in Los Angeles. Though the regional aerospace industry actually got its start in the World War I, during World War II Southern California produced one-third of America's warplanes. Military bases were also a growth industry in and around Los Angeles; after passing through on the way to war in the Pacific theater, many soldiers decided to come back to L.A. to stay—a decision that fueled massive postwar suburban growth.

Yet for all their success in putting Los Angeles on the military-industrial map, the war years wrote particularly shameful chapters of American history, including the mass incarceration of L.A.'s Japanese-American citizens and Japanese immigrants in relocation camps–an event that disenfranchised and shattered entire families and communities. Also infamous were the "zoot suit riots" of 1943, during which uniformed U.S. servicemen took it upon themselves to beat bloody any young Mexican-American, black, or Filipino males they found in the general vicinity of downtown—a rampage successfully stopped only by special order of the U.S. State Department.

Los Angeles in the 1950s and 1960s was, officially, a happy, homogenized, and sunny suburban existence, birthplace of the Barbie doll, the DC-3, and the Internet. Yet certain postwar chapters of L.A. history were also dark and frightening, early shadows cast by the Cold War, including local activities of the House Un-American Activities Committee. Such events successfully launched the national political career of young Richard Nixon, born and raised in Orange County just south of Los Angeles, but ended the careers of many actors, artists, and writers as a direct result of the Hollywood blacklist.

LOS ANGELES IN THE NEW AGE

Like the rest of the nation, most of Los Angeles remained fairly comatose, culturally speaking, throughout the 1950s. But that all changed in the 1960s as Southern California established itself as a high-tech and industrial center and the world's entertainment industry capital. In the 1960s, messengers from L.A.'s ever-present spiritual fringe—rogue philosophers, faith healers, and miscellaneous other true believers well established here since the city's early days of alternative cures for consumption (tuberculosis)—stepped forward to help create California's New Age along with wild-haired surfers, dope-smoking students, and fad-happy hipsters of all socioeconomic stripes.

But L.A.'s new age was not just dope and VW vans. Los Angeles awoke to sober new truths about itself in the 1960s, following the Watts riots of 1965—a firestorm of long-repressed racial rage ignited over a seemingly insignificant event—a six-day "incident" in which 34 people died. Sadly for Watts, the riots served primarily to end outside economic and social investment in some of L.A.'s poorest neighborhoods. In a sense, the incipient political messages of the 1960s weren't fully realized in Los Angeles until the 1970s, along with the next social sea change—the news that whites or "Anglos" were again a demographic minority in Los Angeles for the first time since the mid-1800s. Absorbing the full impact of this new reality, politically and socially, is proving to be a major challenge for Los Angeles.

The 1980s were watershed years for most of Los Angeles, especially in the period leading up to and immediately following the 1984 Olympic Games. (Los Angeles is the only city in the world to have hosted the Olympics twice; the first time was in 1932.) Suddenly Los Angeles, not New York, was the place to be—and continued to be that place, thanks to the city's newly vibrant architecture, arts, movie, music, and theater. That Los Angeles also came of age in a culinary sense, becoming one of the world's foremost destinations for fine food aficionados, also elevated the city's sense of itself.

Yet Los Angeles cannot forever evade its shadows, racism and poverty among the disenfranchised, a truth that emerged again in the 1990s. Natural disasters grabbed their share of the headlines in these years—the Northridge earthquake, massive fires, mudslides—but social disasters had the most lasting impact. The racial rage that first ignited the Watts riots, having simmered almost silently for three decades, erupted again full force when the videotape of Rodney King being "subdued" by Los Angeles Police Department officers was broadcast around the world. After the original acquittal of the officers, full-scale rioting ensued—throughout downtown L.A., Koreatown, Hollywood, and coming perilously close to Beverly Hills and other affluent Westside addresses. The riots again proved counterproductive, setting off racial backlash and sinking affected neighborhoods into deeper poverty. The acquittal of O.J. Simpson in the subsequent racially tinged murder case reinforced a self-righteous backlash, a development that also offers little hope for more enlightened relations between the races.

Yet racial tension is not a black-and-white issue in Los Angeles. The question is much more complicated than that, given the vast numbers of African, Middle Eastern, Eastern European, South American, and Asian immigrants now at home in the region. For example, many segments of the white, black, and even Latino communities are outspoken these days against the social and economic impacts of ongoing illegal immigration—and illegal immigrants themselves—on Los Angeles, which demonstrates what a racially and culturally loaded issue immigration has become.

As California writer Richard Rodriguez says, the birth of a new society—any birth—is traumatic. And L.A. is just now, at the beginning of the 21st century, being born. Now that the city has lost its "suburban innocence," that development certainly an improvement over past obliviousness, Los Angeles is beginning to create itself. While this new Los Angeles is "forming within the terror and suspicion and fear that people have of one another," as Rodriguez says, it's "better not to like one another than not to know the stranger exists."

THE NEXT LOS ANGELES— BACK TO THE FUTURE?

In the 1990s, two California historians shaped the popular public debate over whether L.A.'s cup is now half-full or half-empty. Mike Davis, author of *City of Quartz: Excavating the Future in Los Angeles,* views the bleak L.A. landscape of gang warfare, racial strife, and mindless mass middle-class culture through a Marxist lens, as an endless capitalist struggle with clear classes of winners and losers. Decent jobs for the working class, he says, have all but disappeared in L.A., plunging major sections of the population into the poverty that breeds despair and violence. Kevin Starr, now California's state librarian and author of *Material Dreams: Southern California Through the 1900s,* among other titles in his history series, sees L.A. as "the Great Gatsby of American cities," a land still perfumed by the memory of orange blossoms, rose gardens, and tile-roofed bungalows. Utopian Los Angeles would return, he says, if "you banish violent crime from L.A."

But both agree that the only hope for a feasible future in Los Angeles is a vigorous defense of public life and public space—libraries and parks and social institutions—and an end to the city's tendency to wall itself off from itself within private estates and gated communities.

To the extent that Los Angeles succeeds in reinventing itself, in reincarnating itself as a new and inclusive city, it will be by heading "back to the future"—toward a community-oriented sensibility that somehow got left behind in L.A.'s mad pursuit of personal dreams.

GOVERNING THE UNGOVERNABLE

The present-day politics of Los Angeles are heading "back to the future," but so far in ways that are difficult to define. Symbolizing the trend is Los Angeles Mayor Richard Riordan, first elected in 1993 and reelected in 1997 after the long-running reign of black Democrat Tom Bradley. Riordan is a wealthy, white, Republican businessman on the shady side of 50—not at all whom one would expect to represent contemporary L.A., given the city's increasingly nonwhite, non-Republican demographics.

Some suggest that Riordan's mayoral victory is a victory for fear—perhaps anxiety—though it also expresses people's heartfelt desire, no matter how futile, to return to a more familiar, more predictable society. Conservative politicians, always a clear preference in L.A.'s earlier days of all-out boosterism, now represent some regional sociopolitical peculiarities. Chief among them is Southern California's backlash against the impacts of illegal immigration—a backlash that resulted in the successful statewide passage of Proposition 187, a package of laws that, until declared unconstitutional in 1998, denied nearly all publicly funded services to illegal immigrants.

Riordan supporters, however, say that the city's pro-business mayor was elected not by the usual reactionaries but by an immigrant/ urban economic growth coalition concerned about increasing both overall economic opportunities and wages.

To the extent that L.A.'s "new" politics turn out to be the Republican politics of the past, they are not destined to last. That true was amply demonstrated by the 2000 presidential election, in which L.A.'s vote was decidedly Democratic. The city's ethnic enclaves had long since started to find their political voices. In 1949, Edward Royal from East L.A. became the first Latino elected to the Los Angeles City Council; in 1962, both Roybal and black Assemblymember Augustus Hawkins were elected to the U.S. Congress. Police officer Tom Bradley—destined to become L.A.'s first black mayor, a five-term, 20-year reign—was first elected to the city council in 1963, one of the first three African Americans elected. In 1982, Los Angeles sent three Latinos and three African Americans to Congress—more nonwhites than any other metropolitan area. In subsequent years, L.A.'s multiethnic representation at all levels of government has been reasonably high.

Yet the politics of Southern California would be radically different if all elements of its various communities were proportionately represented among voters. And they aren't. As elsewhere in the United States, voter registration tends to be highest among middle-aged, middle-class white voters and lowest among the poor of all ethnicities.

Facing Up to "Electoral Apartheid"

According to Jorge G. Castañeda, political scientist at the National Autonomous University of Mexico and author of *The Mexican Shock,* California's current culture shock has rallied around "misguided" political attempts to punish, if not banish, illegal immigrants who have swarmed into Los Angeles from Mexico to fill the seemingly endless demand for inexpensive labor. No longer hidden away in the dusty small towns of California's San Joaquin, Sacramento, and Imperial Valleys, Mexico's illegal immigrants now throng the sidewalks of L.A.'s once-uptown Broadway theater district; they compete with blacks, Chicanos, and other ethnic minorities for urban housing and jobs.

"The influence Mexico is bringing to bear on the society of its northwestern neighbor lies here: urban and different, unassimilable, and obtrusive," Castañeda says. "Mexico's presence is still felt in the orchards and fields of the Central Valley, but it is more prevalent in the parking lots, restaurants, and gardens of Los Angeles. . . . At a time when so few Americans still subscribe to the principle of redistribution of wealth and the need to actively reduce inequality in society, the very fact that the white, suburban, middle-aged middle class should be paying taxes to provide services to Mexicans—that is, to the brown, Catholic, Spanish-speaking poor—became anathema. Pile on the California recession of the early '90s and the undeniable growth of the sheer numbers [of immigrants] involved, and Proposition 187 becomes explainable, if not understandable."

The result in California—and particularly in Los Angeles—has been a clear political and social distinction between "those who work and those who vote," according to historian Mike Davis, author of *City of Quartz.* "Thus," in Castañeda's view, "immigration from Mexico in its undocumented, politically maimed form is directly linked to the 'dedemocratization' of California society," a situation some consider "electoral apartheid."

"The people of Los Angeles did not elect Riordan, the voters did," Castañeda says, "and the people and the voters are not the same thing."

Less is Less

But whoever may govern Los Angeles, conservative, liberal, or undecided, faces almost unimaginable social, political, and economic challenges and complexities. A de facto megacity, Los Angeles and surrounding counties are politically subdivided into countless incorporated cities, special districts, and miscellaneous regional governing boards under local, state, and federal mandates. Getting all affected entities to focus on the same sociopolitical chapter, let alone the same page, is something no one has yet managed successfully, at least not for long. All politics are local in Los Angeles, and the region's separate communities and neighborhoods have different concerns. Clearly shared problems—air and water quality, violent crime, and obtaining equitable financing for public schools, police and fire protection, and other essential public services—are precisely those most difficult to solve within such a fragmented governmental structure.

While demand for public services is high in greater Los Angeles, generating the resources to provide them is an increasing impossibility because of vast discrepancies in available local revenues and taxation limits imposed by Proposition 13 and subsequent "taxpayer rights" measures. The most striking public symbol of L.A.'s straits is the massive downtown jail, the 4,000-bed Twin Towers Correctional Center, completed in 1995. It cost $373 million to build. Los Angeles County, which had already closed three jails because it lacked operating funds, couldn't afford to hire the additional 513 deputies and 222 civilian employees needed to operate Twin Towers—so the new jail stood empty while jail overcrowding throughout Los Angeles forced the early release of countless convicted criminals. Meanwhile, in 1996, doctors at the Martin Luther King Jr./Drew Medical Center held a news conference to propose "bullet rationing" throughout L.A. to cut down on the number of gunshot victims at inner-city hospitals.

BIG BUCKS: L.A.'S WORLD-CLASS ECONOMY

If Los Angeles County were a separate nation, it would boast the world's 19th-largest gross domestic product, about $282 billion in 1997. The five-county Los Angeles region is the world's 12th-largest economy, with a 1997 gross product of some $473 billion. The Southern California economy now rolls along at warp speed after some shockingly slow years in the early 1990s—that decline the direct effect of U.S. defense cutbacks and the indirect effect of overinflated property values.

It's nonetheless true that the region's vast wealth is parceled out fairly unevenly. An estimated 95,000 households in Los Angeles County earn more than $150,000 per year—sometimes much more—and about 600,000 households earn less than $15,000 per year. The vast majority of L.A. area households fall somewhere in the middle, of course, but 1.3 million people—about 16 percent of the county's population, including one child in five—live below the federal poverty line. As many as 236,000 people are homeless, including 42,000 children.

In 1994 the Los Angeles Customs District became national leader in "two-way trade value." By 1998 the district's total import-export trade had grown to $180.6 billion. Japan is Southern California's leading international trading partner. The number one import in Los Angeles—no real surprise—is passenger cars, though even many imports were first imagined here, since L.A. is a major domestic and international automobile design center. The number one export? Integrated electronic circuits, also a major import, and "microassemblies." But with aerospace a significant regional employer, it's no surprise that aircraft, spacecraft, and associated parts are also high on the list. Current expansions and improvements at both the Port of Los Angeles and the Port of Long Beach, along with the $1.8 billion Alameda Corridor project, aim to make Los Angeles an undisputed leader in world trade.

With California the dominant "entertainment" producer in the world, Los Angeles County is the world's entertainment industry capital. In fact, film, music, television, amusement parks, computer games, themed restaurants, and retail entertainment sectors are growing so fast that UCLA economists predict that more people in California will work in "The Industry" by 2010 than in electronics and aerospace combined.

The vast majority of the state's movie and television production employees, more than 131,000 of about 138,900, live and work in Los Angeles. More than 47,500 members of the Screen Actors Guild, more than half the total membership, also call L.A. home. An average of 150 movies or TV productions are shot on any given day in L.A.

As entertaining as such facts are, the five leading businesses in Los Angeles are, in descending order of significance, business and management services, tourism, health services (including medical manufacturing), wholesale trade—California Mart and the Produce Mart in downtown L.A. are the largest apparel and produce centers, respectively, in the nation—and direct international trade. The retail trade keeps things hopping too. For most visitors, shopping is the number one reason to come to L.A., which helps explain why the Los Angeles region is the largest retail sales market in the United States, the second largest internationally.

Yet in many respects, Los Angeles is just a massively overgrown small town, chock-full of mom-and-pop restaurants and other businesses. The number of minority-owned businesses has grown dramatically in recent years, making Southern California number one in the nation for businesses owned by Asians, African Americans, and Latinos. The Los Angeles–Long Beach area boasts the largest number of businesses in the nation owned by women.

LOS ANGELES AS DIVERSION

Unless one refuses to participate in the ongoing circus that is Los Angeles, it's almost impossible to avoid diversion here—starting with the family-focused theme parks scattered throughout the region, covered in relevant chapters below. But L.A. offers much more to see and do, from exceptional museums to classic movie theaters, from live theater and concert performances to endlessly cool dance clubs. And the impressive Los Angeles parade of festivals and special community events could keep anyone entertained for a lifetime.

There are two primary approaches for experiencing Los Angeles arts and entertainment. The first is placing a major arts or entertainment performance (or community event) at the

center of one's travel plans, and then planning everything else—where you'll stay and eat, what else you'll see and do—accordingly. The other is to grab a local newspaper—the *L.A. Weekly* or *New Times,* say, *Los Angeles Magazine,* or the Thursday or Sunday calendar sections of the *Los Angeles Times*—and see what strikes your fancy at the moment, a style of "planning" most Angelenos exercise frequently. Or, at least for major goings-on, call the **Los Angeles Convention and Visitors Bureau** 24-hour events line at 213/689-8822; a touch-tone menu allows callers to select from a five-language access menu, with events information available in English, French, German, Japanese, and Spanish.

THE ARTS IN LOS ANGELES

For most of its short life, Los Angeles has suffered a massive cultural inferiority complex. Helped along over the years by Johnny Carson's favorite late-night joke—"The difference between Los Angeles and yogurt is that yogurt has an active, living culture"—wags from New York and other points north and east have long enjoyed perpetuating it. One of the most cutting slurs came from the lips of architect Frank Lloyd Wright: "It's as if you tipped the United States up, so that all the commonplace people slid down there to Southern California."

But these days, vibrant and vital Los Angeles isn't listening to its detractors. With the city's growing wealth and sophistication and its large, diverse population has come exponential growth in both traditional and avant-garde arts. And in many areas the local arts scene is inextricably entwined with L.A.'s new cutting-edge seat at the nation's culinary table, with stylish eateries an easy stroll or shuttle hop from major theaters and other performance venues.

Most of the city's major theaters and music venues are downtown, and most of its arts and cultural museums are either downtown or quite nearby; see that chapter, below, for details. Pasadena is another major cultural destination; look to that chapter for more detailed suggestions. "The Westside," including Santa Monica, Beverly Hills, and adjacent chi-chi sections of West Hollywood, is noted in particular for its impressive array of art galleries, though there are also a few don't-miss museums and other arts attractions; for more details, see those chapters.

Los Angeles Concerts

The undisputed entertainment capital of the world, Los Angeles often poses as the world's live entertainment capital as well. One of the most famous concert venues in Los Angeles is the open-air **Hollywood Bowl** amphitheater in the Hollywood Hills, 323/850-2000, a popular venue for the Los Angeles Philharmonic Orchestra but most famous for its summer pops concerts; for detailed information, see Hollywood and Vicinity, below. The **John Anson Ford Theater** nearby, 323/461-3673, is famous for its summer Shakespeare as well as a variety of free summer concerts. Also immensely popular: the **Greek Theatre,** 323/665-1927.

Downtown, the Performing Arts Center's (formerly the Music Center's) **Dorothy Chandler Pavilion,** 213/972-7211, is home base for both the **Los Angeles Philharmonic Orchestra** and the immensely popular **Los Angeles Music Center Opera,** though other concerts and performances are often scheduled. Just south of town is the famed **Shrine Auditorium,** just west of Figueroa on W. Jefferson, 213/749-5123, where the annual Academy Awards ceremony is usually staged; it's also a popular concert venue.

Other major regional venues include the **Universal Amphitheatre** at Universal Studios, 818/777-3931; the **Santa Monica Civic Auditorium,** 310/458-8551; and the **Pasadena Civic Auditorium,** 626/793-2122.

Popular for big-deal yet intimate concerts and performances, from Sting to the Joffrey Ballet, is the grandly refurbished art-deco **Wiltern Theater,** 3790 Wilshire Boulevard, 213/388-1400. The most stylish place around for musicals is Hollywood's art deco **Pantages Theater** on Hollywood Boulevard, 323/468-1770, also a smaller concert venue.

Local universities, particularly the University of California at Los Angeles and its **UCLA Center for the Performing Arts,** and even community colleges are other prime arts venues. The primary venue for UCLA is the **Wadsworth Theatre,** 310/825-2101, north of Wilshire Boulevard and just west of the San Diego (405) Freeway on the grounds of the U.S. Veterans Administration complex in Westwood. UCLA's **Royce Hall,** a venerable on-campus venue, stages most major concerts and performances.

Los Angeles Theater

Not quite ready to rival New York as an international theater destination, Los Angeles is nonetheless an increasingly serious U.S. contender. Greater L.A. stages about 1,100 theatrical productions annually, with an average of 21 openings each week. Particularly hot for alternative and "new" small theater productions these days is the greater Hollywood area—Hollywood (Hoho), West Hollywood (Weho), and North Hollywood (Noho)—though lively theatrical performances are staged all over town. Theater tickets are available through individual box offices, and also often through TicketMaster in L.A. at 213/365-3500 or Telecharge, toll-free 800/233-3123.

Starting with major-league theater, the **Performing Arts Center** on Grand Avenue downtown, formerly known as the Music Center, 213/972-7211, is the uptown theatrical showcase. The **Ahmanson Theatre** is the main stage for mainstream productions, and the trendsetting theater-in-the-round **Mark Taper Forum** is lauded for launching such original hits as *Angels in America, Children of a Lesser God,* and *Jelly's Last Jam.*

The **Shubert Theatre** in Century City, 310/201-1500 for tickets, is popular for musicals and long-running major productions such as *Sunset Boulevard,* which got its international start there. The onetime Westwood Playhouse on Le Conte Avenue in Westwood is now UCLA's **Geffen Playhouse,** 310/208-6500 or 310/208-5454 for the box office, most famous as the place Jason Robards and Nick Nolte got their respective show-biz starts; call for current program information. The historic **Pasadena Playhouse,** 626/792-8672 for information, 626/356-7529 or toll-free 800/233-3123 for tickets, features imports from New York as well as original local productions. Other popular theaters include the **Stella Adler Theater,** 6773 Hollywood Blvd., 323/655-8587 for tickets. Garnering many bouquets in recent years, on various local stages, is L.A.'s **Center Theatre Group.**

For summer-run weekend Shakespeare and such on a downhome neighborhood scale, head to Topanga Canyon and Will Geer's **Theatricum Botanicum,** 310/455-3723. Award-winning small or "alternative" theaters in Hollywood include actor-director Tim Robbins's equity-waiver **Actors' Gang,** 323/465-0566; the **Hudson Backstage Theater,** 1110 N. Hudson Ave., 323/769-5674; **Matrix Theater,** 7657 Melrose Ave., 323/852-1445; and West Hollywood's **Coast Playhouse,** 323/650-8507. Best bets farther west include the 99-seat **Santa Monica Playhouse,** 310/394-9779. For almost-sure-to-shock-mom-and-dad performance art, the place is **Highways** in Santa Monica, 310/453-1755, a venue so popular that potential performers must apply a year or more in advance.

Los Angeles also boasts a respectable number of ethnic theater venues, including the **Japan American Theatre** in Little Tokyo, 213/680-3700, which presents contemporary Japanese-American productions along with traditional Japanese theater, and the **Vision Complex** in Leimert Park, 323/295-9685, owned and operated by actress Marla Gibbs and affiliated with her Crossroads Arts Academy.

ENTERTAINING LOS ANGELES

The distinction between "art" and "entertainment" can be fuzzy, particularly in eclectic Los Angeles—which is why you'll find entertainment celebrities on display in bookstores, and poetry readings in neighborhood coffeehouses. (For a rundown on regional poetry events, pick up a copy of *Poetry Flash,* a monthly newspaper well-established in the San Francisco area before it headed south to include Los Angeles.) And while most of America considers movies mere entertainment, in L.A. filmmaking is an art form. Mysterious movie "sneak previews," often grandly advertised in the pages of the *Los Angeles Times* entertainment section, can be fun for last-minute movie diversion. And sometimes you'll get an extra $10 or so if you agree to stay after and share your opinions in an impromptu studio focus group. Much to the chagrin of directors, producers, and sometimes actors, public opinion may change the film's final cut—and alter a movie's ending, beginning, love scenes, and so on. For a rundown on what's playing where while you're in town, call the *Los Angeles Times* "MovieFone" at 777-3456, from various local area codes (213, 310, 714, etc.).

Los Angeles Nightlife: The Bar Scene

Whatever your bar-scene pleasure, be it grunge bar or elegant jazz lounge, L.A.'s got it—somewhere. Hollywood is famous for its lively nightlife. For a slice of Hollywood's hip underside, the place is the **Lava Lounge** in a minimall at 1533 N. La Brea Ave., 323/876-6612. A tad more fame-conscious is the incredibly cool **Good Luck Bar** nearby in Los Feliz at 1514 Hillhurst Ave., 323/666-3524. The ultimate well-heeled entertainment industry hangout—Are you cool enough? Stylishly dressed?—is the **Bar Marmont** at the

Château Marmont, 8171 Sunset Blvd., 323/650-0575. Still among the best jazz lounges in town is the historic **Cinegrill** at the Hollywood Roosevelt Hotel, 7000 Hollywood Blvd. (across from Mann's Chinese), 323/466-7000. Shows usually start at 8 P.M. and 10:30 P.M. (cover); slip in earlier just for a drink.

But there is life—even nightlife—beyond Hollywood. Always fun in Santa Monica is **Ye Olde King's Head,** 116 Santa Monica Blvd., 310/451-1402, where you can get Guinness on tap along with darts. You'll also find plenty of tame and trendy possibilities along Santa Monica's Main Street, and just blocks from the Third Street promenade is the Euro-style **West End,** 1301 Fifth St. (at Arizona), 310/313-3293. Most of L.A.'s elegant hotels offer stylish lounges, but none quite as comfortably stylish as the bar at the **Regent Beverly Wilshire Hotel,** 9500 Wilshire Blvd., 310/275-5200.

Other notable watering holes are mentioned in the following chapters. If bars are a personal priority, find an area of town that feels comfortable and then ask around for suggestions.

Los Angeles Nightlife: Clubs, Comedy Clubs

Los Angeles offers an immense, immensely complex, and constantly evolving nightclub scene, from Johnny Depp's too-cool **Viper Room** and the **Roxy** on the Sunset Strip to neighboring 1960s' classics, including **The Troubador** and **Whisky a Go-Go.** Salsa clubs are increasingly popular throughout the city. Especially cutting-edge in and around Hollywood are "multi" clubs—one venue will dress itself in a number of separate identities, the music and the mood determined by separate promoters, depending on which night you arrive—and after-hours clubs. In recent history, a handful of after-hours clubs took the place of L.A.'s all-night "raves," now extinct in most of the city because of gangs, violence, and bad drugs; at last report ravers had retreated to the suburbs.

If dance or music clubs aren't quite what you're looking for, there's always comedy. Always a hoot, for example, is the **Groundlings Theatre,** 7307 Melrose Ave. (at Pointsettia) in West Hollywood, 323/934-9700, home base for an established if evolving comedy troupe whose membership has included Pee Wee Herman, the

vamp vampire Elvira, and *Saturday Night Live* stars Phil Hartman and Julia Sweeney. Main Groundlings shows, which change at least several times each year and are staged on Friday and Saturday nights, are theatrically wrapped around a theme—*Groundlings and the Tijuana Brass,* for example, and *Days of Wine and Groundlings*—and then decorated with a little improv. Also often fun in West Hollywood: Budd Friedman's **The Improvisation,** 8162 Melrose, 323/651-2583, the West Coast's incarnation of New York's The Improv and the likeliest place to see the likes of Brett Butler and Ray Romano, and **The Comedy Store,** 8433 W. Sunset Blvd., 323/656-6225. The laugh house in Pasadena is **The Ice House,** 626/577-1894, where Steve Martin, Lily Tomlin, and Robin Williams got their starts. A best bet on the Westside: the **Comedy & Magic Club** in Hermosa Beach at 1018 Hermosa Ave., 310/372-1193.

Speaking of magic, to get into Hollywood's famed **Magic Castle,** 7001 Franklin Ave., 323/851-3314, a members-only showcase for top-drawer magicians, you'll need to go as someone's guest. If you successfully finagle an invite, rest assured the effort will be worth it. But if you can't, there's always **Wizardz** at CityWalk outside Universal Studios, 818/506-0066, where magic shows come packaged with dinner. For psychic readings, there's Vizionz; for fortune telling, Spiritz. And you can always drown your Magic Castle disappointment in the peculiar cocktails served at Wizardz's Magic Potionz bar.

ENTERTAINING TOURS

Los Angeles is a sprawling, spread-out place, a city that seems to extend beyond all landward horizons. Basic issues—like deciding what to see and do in this expansive world of possibilities, and figuring out how to get there—tend to confound first-time visitors. One perfectly legitimate way to "do" L.A., then, is by signing up for guided tours, thereby delegating the details to the hired help.

Guided Tours by Hearse, Trolley, Bus, and MTA

To tour the lives and lifestyles of L.A.'s rich and notorious, you can always stop for the latest editions of various "Maps to the Stars' Homes" hawked by Beverly Hills area entrepreneurs. Always more fun, though, was the **Grave Line Tours** guided postmortem tour of local fame, an enterprise launched in 1987. "Mourners" climbed into the Cadillac hearse and cruised the streets of Hollywood, Beverly Hills, and other Los Angeles neighborhoods to find out how, when, where, and sometimes why celebrities died. Since 1999 the classic Grave Line hearse tour has been offered by **Tourland,** 323/782-9652; www.tourlandusa.com. Tourland's **Oh Heavenly Tour** revisits the sometimes tawdry and twisted pasts of local celebrities by reservation only, though standby seating is sometimes available. Tours, which run about two and a half hours, depart daily at 10 A.M. and 1 P.M. from the front of Ubon restaurant on the first floor of the Beverly Center on Beverly Boulevard. In addition, Tourland offers an evening **Haunted Hearse Tour,** which visits locales reportedly haunted by celebrities. The fee for each tour is $40 per person. For more conventional sightseeing, **Trollywood Tours,** 323/469-8184, offers one-hour Hollywood tours on a historic trolley car.

Architours promotes "architecture, art, and design as a cultural resource." Tours and special events emphasize culture, history, residential and public architecture, gardens and plazas, public and private art, and furniture and graphic design. For current details and reservations, contact: Architours, P.O. Box 8057, Los Angeles, CA 90008, 323/294-5821 or toll-free 888/627-2448, fax 323/294-5825; www.architours.com. Or try a quirky trip with **Googie Tours,** named for a defunct local coffee-shop chain, which specializes in Southern California's fast-disappearing vernacular architecture. Tour stars include bowling alleys, cocktail lounges, coffee shops, motels, and fine-dining destinations such as the giant drive-through Donut Hole doughnut shop in La Puente. For information, contact Googie Tours, P.O. Box 34787, Los Angeles, CA 90034, 323/980-3480.

Due to lack of funding, at last report the Social and Public Art Resource Center (SPARC) in Venice was no longer offering its immensely popular mural bus tours, which once roamed all over Los Angeles—but it's still possible to organize private group tours through SPARC

($200/hour, two-hour minimum) with at least two months' advance notice. For details, contact SPARC, 310/822-9560; www.sparcmurals.org. Still going but with a limited bus tour schedule ($25 per person, by advance reservation) is the **Mural Conservancy of Los Angeles** (MCLA), 818/487-0416 or 323/257-4544, www.lamurals.org. The website—still partially constructed, at last report—will one day include maps to most L.A. mural sites, for you do-it-yourselfers, in addition to its existing indexes of murals and muralists.

Some of the neon lighting, dating to the 1920s, that made Los Angeles one of the world's flashiest cities is now on display at the Museum of Neon Art (MONA) downtown; you can appreciate much of the rest at CityWalk outside Universal Studios, and still more abundantly along certain city streets. To see some of L.A.'s historic local lights in their neo-natural neon environments, sign on for the museum's after-dark **Neon Cruise** guided double-deck bus tour, an event usually offered every month for a fee of $45 per person. For current information, call the **Museum of Neon Art** at 213/489-9918, or check the museum's website, at www.neonmona.org, for a tour schedule.

Guided Tours on Foot, by Bike, via Skateboard

Guided walking tours are available in most areas of Los Angeles; contact visitor centers for current details. Now a long-running local institution, the **Los Angeles Conservancy** offers inexpensive and informative walking tours designed to interpret L.A.'s past, present, and future. The group offers 12 regular tours—in addition to occasional special tours—emphasizing historic areas and structures. These include **Little Tokyo, Pershing Square,** and **El Pueblo de Los Angeles** as well as **Union Station, City Hall,** and other landmark buildings. The **Broadway Theaters** tour, which allows visitors inside some of L.A.'s grand old movie theaters, is one of the Conservancy's most popular. The usual Conservancy tour fee is $8. All tours, typically one or two hours, start Saturday at 10 A.M. Reservations are required; you can reserve by phone or online. The Art Deco, Broadway Theaters, and Pershing Square tours are offered every Saturday. Others —including The Biltmore Hotel, Union Station,

Little Tokyo, Terra Cotta, Palaces of Finance, and Angelino Heights, in addition to miscellaneous special tours—are offered on a regular rotating schedule. No tours are offered on Thanksgiving, Christmas, or New Year's Day. For more information or reservations, contact **Los Angeles Conservancy Tours,** 523 W. Sixth St., Ste. 1216, Los Angeles, CA 90014, 213/623-2489; www.laconservancy.org.

Combining a walking tour with quick trips on the city's metro system and unique funicular railway, historian Greg Fischer's two-hour **Angel City Tours,** 310/470-4463, offer a facts-versusfiction historical introduction to downtown L.A.

But why walk when you can run? **Off 'N Running Tours,** toll-free 800/523-8687, offers threeto eight-mile courses for fitness walkers and runners in Santa Monica, Beverly Hills, and downtown L.A.; the $45 per person fee includes a runner's breakfast and—for L.A. memorabilia—a T-shirt.

You can also bike it. The actor-guides of **L.A. Bike Tours, LLC,** 323/658-5890 or toll-free 888/775-2453, www.labiketours.com, whose motto is: Tour Buses Are for Couch Potatoes. Tours include mountain bike tours of Hollywood, Beverly Hills, Venice Beach/Santa Monica, and the Getty Center—bikes, helmets, lunches, snacks, and water included in the $20– 55 per person price. For a little extra adventure, sign on for the two-day **Santa Barbara Coastal Adventure.** Or try a two- to four-hour tour of Santa Monica, Venice, and Marina del Rey by bicycle or roller blades, both offered by **Perry's Beach Café and Rentals,** 310/372-3138.

Spectator-sports fans, how 'bout a behindthe-scenes baseball history tour? Dodger blue is on display at guided **Dodger Stadium Tours,** 323/224-1400 (tickets also available at the stadium gift shop), which include the clubhouse, press box, bullpen, dugout, and the new 8,000-square-foot museum.

EVENTFUL LOS ANGELES

When it comes to finding something to do, there's something for everyone in Southern California—a fact reflected in the amazing array of events held annually in Lotusland. Los Angeles celebrates about 170 ethnic festivals alone, for example, and other reasons to celebrate pop up all the time. The following listings are far from complete; other events are mentioned in the L.A. chapters following. To select from the overwhelming array of local possibilities, pick up local newspapers and magazines while you're in town.

January: Days of Football and Roses
After the city survives New Year's Eve bashes of every imaginable inspiration, every new year kicks off with Pasadena's **Tournament of Roses Parade** on January 1—that historic winter flower festival on wheels that convinced so many California migrants to shovel out of their snow-covered hovels for good and head west. The big parade, which turns dignified Pasadena into a circus, is followed by the **Rose Bowl,** the "big game" for winners of the PAC 10 and Big Ten college contests. Alternatively, see the Shogun Santa on parade during the **Japanese New Year Celebration** in Little Tokyo, a festival featuring traditional Japanese song and dance. Or do **Disney on Ice** at the Los Angeles Sports Arena, a family-fun extravaganza that usually runs for the first two weeks in January. Or head for Long Beach and the **Martin Luther King Parade,** which runs down Alameda and Seventh Streets and ends with a party in Martin Luther King Park.

January is also peak season for **whale-watching** along the coast—see coastal chapters for local details—and sometimes prime time for snow skiing in the mountains. (If conditions here are less than perfect, head north from the desert along the eastern slope of the Sierra Nevada to Mammoth and vicinity, Southern California's favorite ski area.) Or head to the desert for golf, sand traps, sand, and sun.

February: Dragons, Magic, and Valentines
Watch the Golden Dragon Parade in Chinatown downtown to usher in the **Chinese New Year,** a festival of traditional song and dance plus flower market and street fair, the crowning of Miss L.A. Chinatown, and the Firecracker 5K/10K run. **Mardis Gras** is celebrated at the Farmers Market (Third and Fairfax), and also at the Santa Monica Pier. Also intriguing: the annual **Brazil Carnaval,** usually held at the Hollywood Palladium, and the annual **California**

International Antiquarian Book Fair. And if the latter seems too highbrow, consider the **Los Angeles Comic Book and Science Fiction Convention.**

February is also Black History Month, and the **Pan African Film Festival** held at the Magic Johnson Theaters in Baldwin Hills is an impressive showcase on the subject (various children's films too). Other major events include **Black Cultural Fest** in Inglewood, the **African American Heritage Celebration** downtown, and **Ragga Muffins–Bob Marley Day** in Long Beach, a celebration of Bob Marley's birthday and "roots, rock, and reggae."

But don't forget **Valentine's Day,** which in L.A. might include include poetry readings, themed dance reviews and performance art (ribald and otherwise), and **Valentine's Day Erotica Night** at Beyond Baroque in Venice, 310/822-3006. If you still can't get a date, head for the desert and Indio's **National Date Festival.** And if that doesn't work, try the **Kennel Club of Beverly Hills Dog Show** at the L.A. Sports Arena.

March: Movie Madness, Music, and Many Blooms

Come March, film fans and fanatics around the world wait with bated breath for the ceremonious annual **Academy Awards** announcements. (And in L.A., miscellaneous celebratory spoofs of Hollywood's favorite self-celebration add to the movie madness.) But some Angelenos are on the road. The **Los Angeles Marathon** in early March, 310/444-5544 or www.lamarathon.com, draws about 30,000 runners, cyclists, and wheelchair competitors. High-tech and trendy even in its sports events, L.A. was the first marathon to introduce chip-timing in 1995. Or celebrate spring with high-flying anarchy, at the **Santa Monica Pier Spring Kite Festival,** ideal for those who don't like fees, rules, or competition. Just show up—and bring your kite.

Other community parties include the city of Santa Clarita's annual **Cowboy Poetry and Music Festival,** complete with dances and a Chuck Wagon food concession serving "authentic cowboy breakfasts" and other meals. Also in March: the **Catalina Country Music Celebration.** Most livestock, though, along with snakes, spaniels, and sweet tweety birds, head for the

annual **Blessing of the Animals** on Olvera Street at El Pueblo de Los Angeles downtown. Whether it falls in March or April, count your own blessings at the **Easter Sunrise Service** at the Hollywood Bowl. Sometimes in need of post-celebration salvation are **St. Patrick's Day** revelers throughout Los Angeles. Memorable festivities include the **Beverly Hills St. Patrick's Day Parade** on Rodeo Drive, a party typically rich with celebrities. The town even rolls out a green carpet.

If people are a little green in spring, so are plants. By March, many are in glorious bloom, including more than 2,000 varieties on display at the L.A. County Arboretum's **Camellia Show** in Arcadia. And from there it's a short freeway drive to tour the 100,000-plus camellias at **Descanso Gardens** in La Cañada Flintridge. Then there's the **Sierra Madre Wisteria Festival,** when the world's largest wisteria vine—with more than one million blossoms—is in bloom and accessible to the public. And March is usually prime time for appreciating desert wildflowers. Or wait until April and head to Lancaster for the **California Poppy Festival.**

April: Hot Cars, Historic Fantasies, Great Books

Spectator sports fans line Shoreline Drive for the **Toyota Grand Prix of Long Beach,** an internationally renowned formula-one auto race. A bit more participatory is the **Renaissance Pleasure Faire,** staged near San Bernardino on weekends from April into June—perfect chance to transport the family to Elizabethan times (for a price). Or visit a romantic version of old California, at the historic annual outdoor **Ramona Pageant** in Hemet, 35 miles southeast of Riverside.

Celebrate the love of reading and literacy at the *Los Angeles Times* Festival of Books, featuring authors, books, bookstores, publishers, and special children's events. Or celebrate the earth and its continued existence. Special L.A. Earth Day events include the **Arroyo Seco Earth Walk and Festival,** starting at Brookside Park in Pasadena; **La Gran Limpieza** L.A. River cleanup, which hauls out tons of trash and recyclables; and the two-day **Eco Maya** celebration at Barnsdall Art Park.

May: Cinco De Mayo and Cherry Blossoms

Celebrating **Cinco de Mayo** on Olvera Street is a long-running local tradition. But Los Angeles also hosts the biggest Cinco de Mayo block party in the nation—**L.A. Fiesta Broadway** downtown, between First St. and Olympic Blvd. The party stars major Latino music acts, ethnic foods, and goods galore. (Cinco de Mayo is celebrated elsewhere around town too.) Also a big deal downtown: the **Little Tokyo Spring Festival,** a monthlong series of events including the **Arigato Bazaar,** the **Cherry Blossom Festival,** the **Children's Day Celebration,** and the Japanese American National Museum's **Community Celebration,** among others.

Also come in May for the **Los Angeles Cuban Cultural Festival,** the **Aloha Expo,** the **Pacific Islander Festival,** the **L.A. Jewish Festival,** and the **Belize Caye Festival.**

Smaller-scale May celebrations include **National Tap Dance Day** at Occidental College in Eagle Rock, the **Topanga Days Country Fair** in Topanga Canyon, the annual **Insect Fair** at the Los Angeles County Arboretum, and the **Claremont Spring Folk Festival.** For music in May also consider **Starfest** in Pomona, a four-day country music extravaganza, the **UCLA Jazz and Reggae Festival,** and the **Long Beach Bach Festival.**

May is also the month for the annual **Venice Art Walk,** the major fund-raising event for the Venice Family Clinic. The walk itself is a self-guided Sunday stroll through artists' studios and gallery exhibits. If you have plenty of extra cash on hand, come for the champagne reception on the preceding Friday, or sign on for guided docent tours and gourmet lunches, art fair, or auction.

June: Jazz, Junior Athletes, and Just Plain Sun

People say that the annual **Playboy Jazz Festival** at the Hollywood Bowl, ain't what it used to be, since it tries too hard to be all things to all people. Be that as it may, people still show up in droves to hear the likes of the Thelonious Monk Institute Jazz Ambassadors, Eddie Palmieri, Dianne Reeves, and Gladys Knight. Alternatively, there's always the annual **Southern California Cajun and Zydeco Festival** in Long Beach. Also traditional in June is the **All Sport**

L.A. Watts Summer Games at Cal State Dominguez Hills, the largest high-school athletic competition in the nation.

Head for Calabasas and Soka University for the **Summer Solstice Folk Music, Dance, and Storytelling Festival,** sponsored by the California Traditional Music Society. Also traditional fun in L.A.: the **Highland Gathering and Games** Scottish festival, and the **Great American Irish Fair and Music Festival** at Santa Anita Racetrack.

Pay homage to the creator of Barnsdall Art Park at the annual **Frank Lloyd Wright Birthday** bash. Or head to North Hollywood and the **NoHo Performing Arts Festival,** staging live performances at more than 25 theaters. The **Los Angeles Gay and Lesbian Pride Celebration,** is also center stage in June, attracting about 40,000 people to West Hollywood.

And by mid-June the L.A. beach scene is fully alive for another summer season—something to at least look at while you drive by, since parking is all but impossible in some areas.

July: Flag-waving, Fireworks, and Freewaves

Los Angeles is big on flag-waving and fireworks, as one would expect in an economy traditionally dependent on U.S. defense industry dollars. Some of the bigger shows are at Dodger Stadium, the Hollywood Bowl (complete with concert), the Rose Bowl, the *Queen Mary,* at the Santa Monica Pier (held at sunrise), and at Catalina Island's Avalon Bay. Cal State Northridge also puts on a grand pyrotechnics show, plus a family-oriented festival. In addition to various concerts and community barbecues and picnics, the Fourth also delivers special events such as **Mr. and Ms. Muscle Beach Venice Physique Contest** at Venice Beach and the **Fourth of July Country Fair** at Rancho Palos Verdes. Check local publications for current details.

Los Angeles likes fireworks, but it loves—*loves*—its cars, which is why the annual **Blessing of the Cars** at Verdugo Park in Glendale isn't really all that weird. Hot rods, custom jobs, and classic cars, more than 1,000, are the stars here, but they graciously share the spotlight with bands—blues, rock, rockabilly—snazzy car detailers, and the bedazzled general public. **Cruise Night** and a free concert follow.

But don't miss performances of the **Shakespeare Festival/L.A.** at the U.S. Veteran's Administration Grounds in Westwood, staged in July and August. If you can't pay the price of admission, the cash cost is free with a canned-food donation. Also staged (and broadcast) in July and August: **L.A. Freewaves Video Festival.** There's also **Outfest—the Los Angeles Gay and Lesbian Film Festival,** showing more than 200 films and videos during its 10-day run at the Directors Guild of America in Hollywood.

Other local cultural celebrations in July include the **Big Time Blues Festival** in Long Beach, **Our Nori (Our Song) Korean-American Celebration** at the John Anson Ford Theater in the Hollywood Hills, and the **Los Angeles Lotus Festival** in Echo Park, 213/485-1310.

Midsummer is also time for the Japanese **O-bon Festival** in West L.A., as well as **Festa Italia** at the Third Street Promenade in Santa Monica and the annual **Malibu Art Festival.** Not to mention the **Catalina Dixieland Jazz Jamboree** in late July or early August, which actually begins aboard the boats departing from either San Pedro or Newport Beach and continues, parade-style, to Avalon's Casino.

August: Hot Festivities and Festivals

The **Nisei Week Japanese Festival** in Little Tokyo celebrates the traditional and contemporary cultural heritage of Japanese Americans—from arts and crafts to tea ceremonies, from a parade and crowning of the annual queen to a 5K run. And don't miss the Tofu Festival. Other August cultural festivals include the annual **Los Angeles African Marketplace and Cultural Faire** at Rancho Cienega Park, the annual **Hungarian Festival** at Alpine Village in Torrance, and the annual **City Birthday Bar-B-Que and Western Dance** in San Dimas. And there's always **Old Miner's Days** at Big Bear Lake, with parades and burro races, and the **San Bernardino County Fair** in Victorville, with crafts, gem and minerals exhibits, carnival, livestock auction, and rodeo.

For something much hipper, head for the annual **Sunset Junction Street Fair** in Silver Lake, a community party featuring bizarre bazaar booths, great ethnic food stands, crazy carnival, and disco dancing (really). But for most people the homemade music's the thing, in a good

year featuring everyone from the Trailer Park Casanovas and Sluts for Hire to Earlimart. Be there or be square. Street fair proceeds benefit the neighborhood's Youth at Risk program. Silver Lake also hosts the annual avant-garde **Beyond Baroque Music Performance Benefit.**

Los Angeles also boasts a number of more predictable music festivals in August, from the **Long Beach Jazz Festival** to the **Los Angeles Blues Festival.** But also hit the beach—actually, various local beaches—for the **International Surf Championship and Festival** held throughout the South Bay, and head to Santa Monica for the annual **Sand Castle Festival** next to the pier. If you're lucky enough to get tickets, make a day on the Westside truly bizarre by attending the annual **Performance Art Olympics** at Highways in Santa Monica. Devotees of the stinking rose won't want to miss the annual **L.A. Garlic Festival** in Westwood, sponsored by everyone from the *L.A. Weekly* to the makers of Clorets. Noted L.A. chefs and restaurateurs whip up their wonders for the sweet-breathed crowds, who also enjoy live jazz and other entertainment.

September: Sunshine and Super Fairs

Untraditional Los Angeles holds the largest *traditional* county fair in the entire U.S. of A. And what a lineup. The **Los Angeles County Fair,** held throughout September in Pomona, includes a carnival with sideshows and whiz-bang rides, livestock competitions and exhibits, exhibition butter churning and horseshoeing, techies and high-tech gadgets on parade, wine-tasting, great food, and bad (as in bad for you) food. Some people particularly like the old-fashioned pie- and cake-baking contests, or the canning and quilting competitions. You name it, you can find it at this fair.

Or head to CityWalk outside Universal Studios and the annual **International Street Performers Festival,** where you can expect everyone from the Red Elvises—Russian rock 'n' rollers—to the Butterfly Man and the Dancing Caballeros.

Other September revels are more modest but in many ways more fun—more "real L.A."—including the **Abbott Kinney Boulevard Festival** in Venice, a very popular non-yup event that benefits various community organizations.

Mexican Independence Day at Olvera Street in El Pueblo de Los Angeles downtown, scheduled on or around September 16, is a traditional family-style festival with plenty of music and good eats. (Attention, gringos: Do not confuse Mexico's Independence Day with Cinco de Mayo, a historic tendency that tends to irritate California's Chicanos; the latter event commemorates Mexico's victory in the Battle of Puebla.) **Thai Cultural Day** at Barnsdall Art Park in Hollywood features traditional dance, classical and folk music, great Thai food and carved vegetables, children's folk games, even demonstrations of Thai boxing and Thai headdress making. Then there's **Oktoberfest** at the Alpine Village in Torrance, which of course starts in September. Inspired by the faux European ambience here, hundreds get sauced, eat schnitzel, and do the chicken dance with genuine gusto.

Also in September: the annual **Chinese Moon Festival** in Chinatown downtown; the **Festival of Philippine Arts and Culture** in San Pedro; downtown's **Latin American Heritage Festival;** the **Leimert Park Jazz Festival;** the **Watts Towers Day of the Drum Festival**—an international drumming extravaganza—and the annual **Simon Rodia Watts Towers Festival,** an all-day jazz, gospel, and rhythm and blues festival.

October: Halloween and Wild Things

The annual **Halloween** revel is probably wilder in West Hollywood than anywhere else in town, but there are other best bets for a frightfully good time—including, believe it or not, Knott's Berry Farm in Orange County, which becomes **Knott's Scary Farm** just for the occasion. (Immensely popular, so get tickets well in advance.) Or take a stroll with the Art Deco Society of Los Angeles on the annual **Hollywood Cemetery Walking Tour.** For costume ideas, consider Pasadena's annual **Halloween Howl Dog Costume Contest.** Various movie theaters around town also sponsor a variety of frightening films; even Beyond Baroque sponsors an annual program of **Spooky and Rare Old Films.** Be in L.A., and be scared.

Hot Halloween-season music festivals include the **International Salsa Festival** at the Universal Amphitheatre and the **Catalina Island Jazz Trax Festival.**

RED WIND

Wherever you find yourself in the Los Angeles universe, things change when the Santa Ana winds blow from the northeast off the desert, typically between November and January. The atmosphere here becomes hot and dry and unbelievably irritating. The way Raymond Chandler described it in his short story "Red Wind," the dusty, desiccating Santa Ana winds "come down through the mountain passes and curl your hair and make your nerves jump and your skin itch. On nights like that every booze party ends in a fight. Meek little wives feel the edge of the carving knife and study the backs of their husbands' necks." This notable Southern California weather phenomenon, which reverses the usual cool west-to-east airflow off the ocean, also increases the danger of late fall wildfires and plays havoc with people's allergies. But don't let a blustery Santa Ana season put you off. Desert winds do have the beneficial effect of scrubbing the air clean throughout the entire Los Angeles Basin—which is why a December or January day can offer the most glorious scenic vistas in Southern California.

October has its share of cultural celebrations, too, from the annual **Scandinavian Festival** in Santa Monica to the **Watts Third World Arts Festival.** Always fun, for film aficionados, is the American Film Institute's **Los Angeles International Film Festival,** the world's largest, two weeks' worth of some of the year's most significant films. The **Women in Film Festival** also comes in October.

Other October events include the annual **Open Studio Tours** of the Brewery Art Colony downtown, and the hip-hopping **Lowrider Classic Tour** at the Los Angeles Sports Arena, including the *Latinpalooza* stage show.

November: Days of the Dead, Days of Thanks

El Dia de los Muertos (Day of the Dead) is a Mexican folk festival based on the pre-Columbian belief that one's ancestors come back to visit us, in spirit form, every November 1. So Day of the Dead festivities pay homage to the spirits of everyone's forebears. Events around Los Angeles include Aztec dancers and children's workshops at the Andres Pico Adobe in Mission Hills; happenin' music, theater, and performance art at Self-Help Graphics in East L.A.; and puppet theater, clowns, and family-friendly fun on Olvera Street in El Pueblo de Los Angeles downtown. Look for more Day of the Dead events at the new Latin American Art Museum in Long Beach. Midmonth brings the annual **Los Angeles Mariachi Festival** downtown.

Also in November is the annual **Plein Air Painters of America Festival** on Catalina Island, a working celebration of "open-air" painting. Definitely wacky, toward the end of the month, is the demented annual **Occasional Doo Dah Parade** in Pasadena. This now infamous spoof of the annual Rose Parade stars such folks as the chanting Benzedrine Monks and the Marching Toilets and Precision Potty Drill Team, the parade itself followed by a local pub crawl. (If you crawl, don't drive.) This parade has no theme, no rules, and no noticeable organization; though it attracts fewer fans than the Rose Parade, the crowds get bigger every year.

Then Los Angeles gives thanks for friends, for family—and for having made it through another year. The huge annual **Hollywood Christmas Parade,** with the usual slew of celebrities and Disney characters, is held the Sunday after Thanksgiving, starting at Sunset and Hollywood Boulevards. (You can watch without crowds on local TV.) East L.A. holds another Christmas parade, a community celebration that draws about 200,000 people.

December: Dickens and Downtown Tree Lighting

Though Los Angeles is far from strictly Christian, Christmas is the most publicly celebrated winter religious festival—next to consumerism, of course, which is strictly observed during the holiday season throughout Los Angeles. The annual **Downtown Tree-Lighting Ceremony** at Citicorp Plaza, during the first week in December, includes Santa and his elves, carolers, and orchestral Christmas music. At noon throughout December carolers sing forth from Arco Plaza for the **Dickens Downtown Christmas Celebration.**

Celebrate Christmas Mexican style, starting on Olvera Street at El Pueblo de Los Angeles downtown with **Las Posadas,** a weeklong series of evening processions that reenact the journey of Mary and Joseph to Bethlehem; on the final night, baby Jesus shows up too. Most coastal harbor areas offer variations on the **Harbor Parade of Lights** theme, with light-bedecked boats dazzling the crowds in the weeks leading up to Christmas.

Kwanzaa is seriously celebrated in some quarters of the African-American community in Los Angeles, partly because this contemporary celebration of African heritage was invented by a professor at Long Beach State. An annual three-day **Kwanzaa Festival** is celebrated in Leimert Park after Christmas; music, dance, poetry readings, and other events are scheduled elsewhere.

SPORTING LOS ANGELES

Los Angeles Spectator Sports

The news in 1997 that **Los Angeles Dodgers** owner Peter O'Malley sold the city's National League baseball team to international media mogul Rupert Murdoch sent the entire region into fits of athletic apoplexy. Yet young boys and their fathers (and young girls and their mothers) still flock to Dodger Stadium in Chávez Ravine downtown, just off the Pasadena Freeway in Elysian Park, for the summer ritual of dugouts and Dodger 'dogs. For current info and tickets, call the Dodgers at 323/224-1400. For the latest news about the team, in five different languages no less, try www.dodgers.com. For American League ball, head for Anaheim in Orange County and the **Anaheim Angels,** formerly the California Angels, 714/634-2000.

Big news in Los Angeles is downtown's new **Staples Center,** 1111 S. Figueroa St., toll-free 877/305-1111 for general information or 213/742-7340 for tickets; www.staplescenter.com. Among the teams now calling the Staples Center home are the NBA's **Los Angeles Lakers,** a team still synonymous with Earvin "Magic" Johnson and Shaquille O'Neal, and the **Los Angeles Clippers.** The National Hockey League's **Los Angeles Kings** also get down at the Staples Center.

The oddest thing about Los Angeles sports is that the region lacks a national football franchise, since both the Los Angeles Rams and the Los Angeles Raiders (previously and subsequently the Oakland Raiders) packed up and left town in 1995. What to do? Since Los Angeles has always lived by the "If We Build It, They Will Come" sports philosophy, local discussion now centers on where to build a new stadium—to lure a new football franchise. Local and regional boosters are salivating over the prospect of landing "the big one" for their own neighborhoods. Given the success of the Disney Company in regional sports—Disney's Mighty Ducks have made quite a splash in hockey at The Pond in Anaheim, and Disney is now part owner of the Anaheim Angels—some local wags think a new NFL expansion team could be called the Lion Kings, perhaps housed in The Den.

While you wait for the return of the NFL, whenever and wherever that may be, there's always collegiate football. The mythic L.A. teams are the **University of California at Los Angeles (UCLA) Bruins,** 310/825-2101, and the **University of Southern California (USC) Trojans,** 213/740-2311.

Other spectator sports abound throughout the region, from golf, tennis, beach volleyball, and surfing tournaments to thoroughbred racing; consult local newspapers for current offerings.

Los Angeles Recreation and Participatory Sports

Los Angeles is a playful city. People play at just about everything. In-line skating and skateboarding are fairly recent rages—roller skating was invented in Los Angeles, after all, in the 19th century—but surfing, body surfing, and "boogie boarding" take better advantage of the ocean, along with swimming (usually safe where you find lifeguards), sailboarding, sailing, and ocean kayaking. Beach volleyball is another serious pursuit in the land of sand and sun, as are beach walking, jogging, bicycling, golf, and tennis. Pier fishing is popular all along the coast—even adults can fish freely without a license—and, for those who can afford a boat or boat fare, ocean fishing is also a local passion. The truly "big ones" in these waters always get away, fortunately, which is why whale-watching is an endlessly popular winter pursuit, both by land and by sea. Head for the crowded nearby mountains for hiking, backpacking, mountain biking, mountaineering, and rock-climbing in summer

(also in winter in the Santa Monica Mountains), and both cross-country and downhill skiing.

Indoor recreation is also popular in Los Angeles—health and fitness clubs in particular. Many walkers and joggers have abandoned the uncertainties of public streets for the recreational treadmill. And bowling is new again, a retro passion. Places such as **Hollywood Star Lanes,** 5227 Santa Monica Blvd. in down-at-the-heels Hollywood, 323/665-4111, offer the thrill of a strike 24 hours a day. Pool halls, sometimes dignified by the phrase "billiards parlor," abound, and video game parlors are absolutely ubiquitous.

SHOP 'TIL YOU DROP

Shopping is a serious pursuit in Los Angeles, perhaps one reason L.A. is so popular with international travelers. For 88 percent of visitors from other lands, according to the U.S. Travel and Tourism Association, shopping is the preferred activity in the United States. But the region's sprawling malls, the magnets of local consumerism, are an outgrowth of Southern California car culture—the local preference for absolute mobility.

If you're doing the malls, seven-acre **Beverly Center** is centrally located just east of Beverly Hills and south of West Hollywood at 8500 Beverly Blvd., 310/854-0070, recognizable to movie addicts as the setting of the 1991 Woody Allen/Bette Midler movie *Scenes from a Mall* and home to a collection of more than 200 upscale shops and associated parking. Just across La Cienega is the **Beverly Connection,** another possibility, where the **Rexall Drugs** is locally known as the "drugstore to the stars." Then there's the **Century City Shopping Center** along Santa Monica Boulevard in Century City, 310/553-5300, a pleasant outdoor mall, and the glass-enclosed **Westside Pavilion** at Pico and Overland Boulevards in West L.A, 310/474-6255. Downtown offers the **Seventh Street Marketplace,** on S. Figueroa Street near the Hilton hotel, 213/955-7150. The most famous malls in L.A. proper—inspiration for Frank and Moon Unit Zappa's 1980s spoof *Valley Girls*—are in the San Fernando Valley, and include the **Glendale Galleria** in Glendale, 818/240-9481 and **Sherman Oaks Galleria** in Sherman Oaks, which ironically had to close due to lack of customers (it will reopen as a business center). The granddaddy of them all, though, is actually in Orange County—**South Coast Plaza,** 714/435-2000, just off the San Diego Freeway (the 405) in Costa Mesa.

Increasingly, however, even Southern Californians are rejecting the malls—a fact of local life that sends various shopping centers into periodic fits of re-creation and remodeling on a more intimate scale. Shopping areas and districts are all the rage these days, at least among L.A.'s more affluent citizens, and you'll find dozens of these throughout greater Los Angeles. **Rodeo Drive** in Beverly Hills is L.A.'s most famous shopping destination, with stores so expensive and exclusive that they seem increasingly ridiculous even by local standards; most residents, after all, shop along Beverly Drive and nearby Beverly Boulevard. Or on Melrose.

Now nearly as famous as Rodeo Drive, **Melrose Avenue** started as a fairly avant-garde youth-oriented rebellion against mass consumerism, in what was once a low-rent district just south of West Hollywood. Now Melrose, still hip but increasingly mainstream, is among the city's most commercial districts—though it still has its eccentricities. "Melrose" was originally defined as the mile and a half of Melrose between La Brea and Crescent Heights, but now it extends into high-rent West Hollywood, its trendiness spreading south along **Robertson Boulevard,** the "decorator's row" of Beverly Hills, and also spilling south onto L.A.'s **Beverly Boulevard** and **W. Third Street.** And intersect-

ing sections of both North and South **La Brea Avenue** also hold increasing local appeal for shopping and dining.

But trendier by far than Melrose—and at last report still L.A.'s post-hip, post-postmodern hangout and shopping destination—is **Vermont Avenue** in nearby Silver Lake, a fairly rough neighborhood on the eastern edge of Hollywood.

Other popular L.A. "destination streets," considerably more comfortable for most visitors and middle-class families, include **Old Pasadena** in downtown Pasadena and, in Santa Monica, the **Third Street Promenade, Main Street** near Venice, and **Montana Avenue.** Still up-and-coming and always surprising is **Abbott Kinney Boulevard** in Venice, a neighborhood still more neighborhood—albeit rough in surrounding areas—than tourist attraction.

The shopping experience at **CityWalk** outside Universal Studios is, sadly, probably a snapshot of our shared future—in L.A. and elsewhere—as the fear-driven middle class increasingly seeks entertainment, dining, and shopping opportunities in an absolutely safe, sanitized, and insular urban environment, the commercial equivalent of gated communities.

Most of L.A.'s unique and individual shops can be found in or near the shopping destinations and districts just mentioned; a few are specifically mentioned in the following chapters. But while poking around town in search of beautiful, odd, or unusual L.A. items to take home for family and friends, keep in mind that local museums boast some of the best general gift shops around. And museum shopping offers the added benefit of supporting local arts and cultural attractions.

LOS ANGELES AS DESTINATION

GETTING SETTLED

A visitor's first priority in Los Angeles should be settling in—feeling comfortable, as if one actually belongs here. For most people this means first checking into appropriate accommodations and then becoming familiar with the general surroundings, including finding nearby restaurants and other essential resources. If you arrive without much thought as to where you'll be going or why—not likely, since you have this book—then your first outing, once settled, should be to one of L.A.'s two primary visitor information centers (see Getting Informed, below). A quick information stop can be prudent anyway, since all kinds of special admission discounts and coupons are typically available; scoop them up and save some money.

Some forethought will definitely make any trip more enjoyable. Given the distances involved in Los Angeles travel, and given people's varying comfort levels with the intensity of L.A. freeway driving, the most critical decision is where you'll be staying. Some people would rather unpack just once, finding the perfect accommodation—someplace with a kitchen, say, or a large swimming pool to exhaust the children before nightfall—and then striking out in all directions, freeway map firmly in hand, on daily sight-seeing excursions. Others prefer an area-by-area approach, sampling accommodations and restaurants situated near relevant general destinations; for obvious reasons, this is the way to go if you have no car or would prefer not to drive much. Either approach works just fine, so long as you think it out ahead of time.

Where to Stay
From a strictly fiscal point of view, Los Angeles offers a wide range of accommodation options. If money is no object, of course, finding appropriate lodgings is fairly simple: Just find the line of limos and flash that gold card. Los Angeles boasts a generous supply of elegant, stylish, and expensive hotels, in Pasadena and downtown, in Beverly Hills and West Hollywood, and at the beach. Most offer every imaginable amenity—often including children's activity programs, so Mom and Dad (or Grandma and Grandpa) can easily get off alone once in awhile. Fairly good news for luxury-loving travelers of more modest means: Many high-end hotels cater largely to the entertainment industry and other business people with generous expense accounts. On off-season weekends and during the holiday season, great deals are available for the rest of us.

Midrange options abound, particularly motels but also converted apartments with full kitchens. Los Angeles has few bed-and-breakfasts, however, because with some notable exceptions—particularly Santa Barbara up the coast—Southern California is just not big on B&Bs. The anonymity and absolute privacy offered by hotels and motels suit the local personality much better.

As always, finding truly inexpensive yet decent and safe accommodations is the real challenge. Fortunately for budget travelers, Los Angeles features some (a few) inexpensive hotels and motels. It also offers a number of very nice hostels, most featuring private family or couples rooms; if it matters, reserve well in advance to make sure you land one. Better yet, many hostels are at or very near the beach. Camping is also a low-end option, along the coast in places, at state parks and national forests, and at various private establishments.

Increasingly, Californians and visitors to California define themselves—and make travel plans—in terms of desired experience more than absolute economics. Translated into practical choices for travelers of middle-class means, this might mean opting to stay two or three days at an inexpensive beach hostel and another two days at a midrange motel and then splurging on a special weekend at a five-star hotel. And why not? The ultimate goal, after all, is experiencing as much of Los Angeles as possible while staying within one's total budget.

For specifics on lodgings in greater Los Angeles, refer to the following chapters. Along with sights and area restaurants, accommodations in all price ranges are listed by locale.

Where to Eat

Los Angeles restaurants are among the region's genuine treasures, a tangible tribute to the astonishing multiethnic, multicultural experiment now well under way. In addition to the area's famed upscale restaurants—many of these almost affordable now, their revamped menus more in keeping with the budget-conscious times—greater Los Angeles is beloved for its burger joints, its mom-and-pop barbecue stands and café, and its almost endless variety in ethnic eateries.

To eat as Angelenos do—"Hey! Let's go to East L.A. for a burrito!"—may require driving across the entire L.A. Basin and back just for one meal. But visitors can modify that approach within a smaller geographic area and still sample an amazing selection of culinary traditions. It's worth making the effort, since eating out in Los Angeles is an experience like no other, definitely satisfying what writer Richard Rodriguez calls "the hunger in the American soul for foods that violate borders and lead us far from American loneliness." Even international visitors tend to gravitate toward what's familiar: Mexicans eating Mexican, Japanese eating Japanese, Italians eating Italian. Yet to limit oneself to what is known and predictable somehow misses the entire point of Los Angeles.

GETTING THERE: BY FREEWAY

One self-guided Los Angeles tour that few visitors ever take, at least not intentionally, is a tour of local freeways—*every* local freeway. It wouldn't take all that long, either, if one drove a few miles on each. Depending upon local traffic, of course.

No, though Angelenos love their freeways they use them strictly to get wherever they're going. They've been doing it ever since 1940. And once visitors arrive by freeway, in either their personal or rental cars, they join in the same transportation rite.

Los Angeles is connected to itself and to the rest of the world by more freeways than any other city in America—a total of 16 major freeways and a large handful of lesser ones. Life on a Los Angeles freeway—any freeway—is life in the fast lane, a very fast lane.

Noteworthy as the first freeway in Los Angeles, also the first freeway in the West, is the Pasadena Freeway, the 8.2-mile stretch of narrow-laned roadway still connecting Pasadena to downtown through the Arroyo Seco. The freeway's first five miles opened for business on December 30, 1940, designed for cars traveling about 45 miles per hour. Of course no one called it a freeway in those days, though people did sometimes call it a "free way." One proposed name for L.A.'s first ode to automobility, which was known as the Arroyo Seco Parkway, was "stopless motorway," a phrase that somehow failed to seize the public's imagination.

But freeways themselves did.

Many Los Angeles freeway routes actually follow old footpaths once used by deer and native peoples; the paths later became mission roads, stagecoach routes to the beach, paved roads, streetcar lines, and finally freeways. With the impressive tangle of roadway today—Los Angeles features 27 freeways, weaving in and out of each other like the strands of a giant, if loose, concrete yarn ball—it's almost impossible to imagine a footpath climbing sleepily up Sepulveda Pass, which the San Diego Freeway dominates today.

The newest freeway in Los Angeles—most likely its last—is the 17-mile, eight-lane, east-west **Century Freeway,** also known as Interstate 105 or the Glenn Anderson Freeway, that stretches between Norwalk and El Segundo near LAX. The Century parallels the Santa Monica (10) and Artesia (91) Freeways, and connects four major north-south routes: the San Diego (405), Harbor (110), Long Beach (710), and San Gabriel River (605) Freeways. An alternate route from downtown to LAX, the Century's notable features include the elevated Green Line trolley tracks down the center median, traffic sensors, closed-circuit TV cameras (so Caltrans can see why traffic has slowed), and metered on-ramps.

Also quite modern is the new elevated section—the "transitway," for buses and carpoolers only—of the Harbor Freeway (I-110) near downtown, just a few miles long but a harbinger of roadways to come, as Los Angeles builds and rebuilds its freeways to manage ever-increasing levels of traffic.

Yet other concerns tend to weave their way into local freeway lore. The area's shortest freeway—the Marina Freeway (90), not even two miles long—was originally known as the Richard M. Nixon Freeway, for example, so named in 1971 by the California Assembly. But after the Watergate debacle, the state Senate stripped Nixon of his freeway title in 1976.

Speeding toward Freedom

The posted freeway speed in most areas of Los Angeles is 65 or 70 miles per hour (mph), sometimes faster, sometimes slower, depending upon local conditions. But speed is everything in L.A., another local metaphor for unlimited personal freedom. Even when 55 mph was the official speed limit here, almost no one paid any attention. And for newcomers and visitors, this can be a nerve-wracking fact of freeway life. Los Angeles drivers are typically good drivers, but people here drive fast—*very* fast, at least 70 or 75 mph when things are moving along well, though it's not uncommon for neophytes to be passed by locals zipping along at 80, 85, or 90. One must either "go with the flow," at least to an extent, to avoid the ire of fellow drivers—and to avoid becoming a traffic hazard or accident oneself—or stay in the right-hand lanes, stubbornly going the speed limit and contending with the constant distraction of cars jockeying for position as they merge on and off the freeway. Fast

drivers have no problem with L.A.'s addiction to speed, but cautious drivers and slowpokes may be unnerved.

Beating the Rush

For years a local truism held that the Ventura Freeway (Hwy. 101) through the San Fernando Valley was the world's busiest roadway, and L.A.'s busiest freeway. But this was never true, it turns out, despite what the *Guinness Book of World Records* says. Because car-counting meters on the Santa Monica (I-10) and San Diego (I-405) Freeways—the actual record-breakers—were broken for almost five years, the entire world was misinformed. Most nightmarish of all is the junction of the San Diego and Santa Monica, not far north of Los Angeles International Airport.

To avoid getting stuck in L.A.'s slow (but rarely stopped dead) rush-hour freeway traffic, on weekdays avoid being on the road between peak commute hours, 6–10 A.M. and 3–7 P.M. Plan to set out on your sightseeing excursions mid-morning, enjoying lunch and dinner in the same general vicinity before getting back on the freeways. On weekends, avoid going in the same direction as "escape" and "return" traffic—leaving L.A. in all directions on Friday afternoons or evenings and returning late in the day on Sunday. Otherwise, get going early on weekends, and avoid stadiums and sports arenas before and after big games.

an omnipresent landmark of Los Angeles: the freeway

MICHELLE & TOM GRIMM/LOS ANGELES CVB

STAY OUT OF THE WAY IN L.A.: SOME RULES OF THE ROAD

People in Los Angeles measure distance not in miles but in minutes—meaning minutes by freeway, or drive time. Angelenos also chronically underestimate drive times. This peculiar form of bragging rights ultimately implies that a *true* Angeleno could actually get from Pasadena to Santa Monica in 15 minutes, though you'll soon realize that you won't. (Angelenos also typically blame traffic when they're late—an excuse almost everyone will accept.) When taking directions from locals, then, visitors would be wise to generously pad the alleged drive time—or to double-check it, with the aid of a good map.

In keeping with their underestimation of average drive times, Los Angeles drivers also grossly underestimate their travel speed. If the posted speed limit is 65 miles per hour, most Angelenos will drive 80 or 85—and actually believe themselves when they tell the California Highway Patrol officer they were only going 60.

Angelenos typically refer to local freeways by name, not number—which can be mighty confusing for neophytes, since the Hollywood Freeway (101) is also the Ventura Freeway, the Santa Monica Freeway (I-10) is also the San Bernardino Freeway, the Golden State Freeway (I-5) is also the Santa Ana Freeway, and the faithful north-south San Diego Freeway (405) never actually arrives in San Diego (not until after it's become I-5). When Angelenos *do* mention freeway numbers instead of names they use "the" as a fairly pointless modifier, as in "the 405" and "the 110," so when you hear such phrases you'll at least know that the topic of freeways is under discussion. Fortunately for visitors, most maps list both freeway names and numbers.

Then there are those unique L.A. words or phrases that make no sense whatsoever to innocent tourists, such as "Sigalert," even if they are listed in the *Oxford English Dictionary*. A Sigalert, according to the *OED*, is "a message broadcast on the radio giving warning of traffic congestion; a traffic jam," though technically Sigalerts apply only to tie-ups of 30 minutes or more. The word itself pays homage to L.A. radio broadcaster Loyd Sigmon, whose breaking traffic-jam bulletins of the 1950s are the stuff of local legend.

More important than local lingo, however, is a clear understanding of the local rules of the road. Los Angeles drivers never signal their intention to change lanes on the freeway, for example—a sure mark of a tourist—because doing so only allows others an opportunity to fill that particular spot of road first. Yet if someone honks, rudely cuts you off—which probably wouldn't have happened if you hadn't signaled—or tailgates for revenge, do remain calm. Don't allow that middle finger to leave the steering wheel, either, since no amount of rude driving is worth getting rammed at 70 miles per hour (or worse).

Also, never drive in front of a BMW or behind a Volvo.

Be particularly generous to L.A. drivers—give them a wide berth—if it's "pouring down rain" (as measured in actual precipitation, a tenth of an inch or less) because most Angelenos have never seen rain. Those who have tend to use wet roadways as yet another technique to increase their overall speed, through the miracle of hydroplaning. Most L.A. drivers don't know the difference between headlight high beams and low beams, either, so don't bother trying to explain the concept. In Los Angeles, headlights are either on or off. Be grateful, when it's dark outside, if the car coming toward you has them on.

Avoiding traffic jams—knowing when to switch freeways, and when to exit freeways and take surface-street or connector road shortcuts—is something of an art in Los Angeles. Yet even visitors can play the game with the aid of a tutor, such as the popular *L.A. Shortcuts: The Guidebook for Drivers Who Hate to Wait*. For those who prefer to avoid freeways altogether—it's possible to do that, even in Los Angeles—guides such as *Freeway Alternates* can help you do just that.

Don't ever misplace your map. Even native Los Angeles residents constantly refer to them, particularly the excellent, very detailed Thomas Bros. maps. Almost every car in Los Angeles has a Thomas Bros. guide to Los Angeles or Los Angeles/Orange County, if not San Diego or Riverside/San Bernardino, right there in the glove compartment, easily available when the need arises. And the need *will* arise, the minute you miss your first freeway change and need to figure out if there's another way to get where you're going without doubling back (sometimes there isn't). But such detailed maps cost money, not typically worth the investment if you'll only be here a week or two. If you're a AAA member, stock up on California, Southern California, and L.A. city or regional maps either before you come or as soon as you arrive. Or buy good road maps at local visitor bureaus and travel-oriented bookstores.

Basic Freeway Facts—and Safety

Despite increasingly congested freeways, the idea of carpooling didn't really begin to catch on in L.A. until the 1990s, when "carpool only" lanes —High-Occupancy Vehicle (HOV) or "diamond lanes"—began to appear on local freeways, and when area employers started offering financial incentives to get people out of their cars. Even now, most vehicles on the road carry an average of one person. But HOV lanes, which require at least two occupants, are starting to work in Los Angeles—speeding up trip time in the diamond lane (usually the number one lane, closest to the freeway median) as well as the general flow of traffic. If you're driving solo on L.A.'s freeways, frustrated by a traffic slowdown, don't be tempted to dart into a diamond lane and cheat the system. Fines are stiff—close to $300, sometimes higher—and in the age of cellular phones, don't think an angry Angeleno stuck in traffic won't think of turning you in. Once you're pulled over by the California Highway Patrol (CHP), no excuse will get you off.

Given Los Angeles drivers' lust for speed, slower drivers—people going only 70 miles per hour, say—should stay in the center or center-right lanes if at all possible, allowing faster drivers plenty of room to move as they race toward their destinies. If you'll be traveling only a short distance on a particular freeway, and if traffic is

---

THE FREEWAY MAZE: UNTANGLING THE CONCRETE YARN BALL

Antelope Valley Freeway	Hwy. 14
Artesia Freeway	Hwy. 91
Corona del Mar Freeway	Hwy. 73
Foothill Freeway	I-210
Garden Grove Freeway	Hwy. 22
Gardena Freeway	Hwy. 91
Glendale Freeway	Hwy. 2
Golden State Freeway	I-5
Harbor Freeway	I-110 ("the 110")
Hollywood Freeway	Hwy. 101 and Hwy. 170
Long Beach Freeway	I-710 ("the 710")
Marina Freeway	Hwy. 90
Orange Freeway	Hwy. 57
Pasadena Freeway	I-110 ("the 110")
Pomona Freeway	Hwy. 60
Riverside Freeway	Hwy. 91
Ronald Reagan Freeway	Hwy. 118
San Bernardino Freeway	I-10 ("the 10")
San Diego Freeway	I-405 ("the 405")
San Gabriel River Freeway	I-605
Santa Ana Freeway	I-5 and Hwy. 101
Santa Monica Freeway	I-10
Terminal Island Freeway	Hwy. 47
Ventura Freeway	Hwy. 101 and Hwy. 134

---

heavy, stay in the freeway's right-hand lanes and avoid the frustration of maneuvering between lanes—assuming your upcoming exit will be to the right, of course. That's usually the case, particularly on L.A.'s newer freeways and interchanges, but some freeways feature surprising (surprising if you don't know about them) left-hand exits or traffic "splits." So study your road map carefully before setting off into unfamiliar territory—the Thomas Bros. guides include handy freeway entry and exit maps—and watch freeway signs carefully. If you're paying attention, you'll usually have plenty of time to prepare even for left exits. Familiarizing yourself with route maps ahead of time will also help in planning an instant emergency strategy, should you miss a key exit at some point. Also allow yourself extra travel time to avoid feeling pressured, a factor that may affect your concentration.

Most traffic congestion in Los Angeles is caused by "traffic incidents," not accidents, these varying from unexpected breakdowns to flat tires. To avoid being an incident, make sure your vehicle is road-ready before setting out. But should the unexpected occur, pull off to the right to park if at all possible, turn on your emergency blinkers or "flashers," and call for help from the nearest call box. Numbered call boxes (yet another L.A. invention), no more than a mile apart (often closer) on the right shoulder of every area freeway, are not telephones; they can be used only for automobile emergencies. Once you explain your problem and your location (relative to the box), the operator will dispatch towing assistance—a service sometimes offered free by local authorities, but AAA or other towing service coverage is always handy.

GETTING THERE: BY BUS, BOAT, TRAIN, AND PLANE

By Bus, Boat, and Train
Greyhound, toll-free 800/231-2222, www.greyhound.com, is the primary commercial bus service into greater Los Angeles. Routes come from all directions—certainly wherever there's a freeway—and can deliver travelers, if not to the desired city, then at least as close as the nearest major transit center. The main Greyhound bus terminal is downtown. If no one can meet you, simply catch a local bus and complete the trip via the available mass-transit system. (Call to clarify local connections, using relevant chapters below, once you devise your main bus route.) Alternative bus companies, including San Francisco-based **Green Tortoise,** toll-free 800/867-8647, can also deliver travelers to Los Angeles.

Always a pleasure these days—harking back to Hollywood's golden era—is coming and going by train, a service provided by **Amtrak,** 800/872-7245; www.amtrak.com. Stepping out into grand Union Station near downtown Los Angeles, where one can also make intercity train connections, is a delight even for the most jaded traveler. From Los Angeles, trains run to Santa Barbara and points farther north—a lovely trip, often following the coastline—as well as east across the desert. For more information on bus and train travel, see this book's Introduction.

More unusual, but not *that* unusual, is arriving in Los Angeles by boat. Most major cruise ships dock at **Los Angeles Harbor** in San Pedro, or in adjacent Long Beach. Contact your travel agent to arrange a cruise-ship cruise to Los Angeles.

By Airplane
Most visitors, if they don't arrive by car, come by air. The largest airport in the region is **Los Angeles International Airport,** most commonly known by its unfortunately suggestive international handle, "LAX" (pronounced "EL-AY-EX," however), 310/646-5252, located near the coast just south of Marina del Rey and north of El Segundo, just west of the San Diego Freeway (I-405). This is the airport everybody loves to hate. But few hate it enough to try another airport, which is why traffic can be so nightmarish in the general vicinity.

To avoid the crush at LAX, even locals often use other regional airports, including the **John Wayne Airport** in Orange County, 949/252-5006; the **Burbank/Pasadena/Glendale Airport,** 818/840-8847, in the San Fernando Valley but convenient to Hollywood, Pasadena, and downtown; and the surprisingly busy **Ontario Airport** serving San Bernardino and Riverside, 909/937-2700.

Los Angeles International Airport
As writer Pico Iyer has observed, airports are "the new epicenters and paradigms of our dawning post-national age—not just the bus terminals of the global village but the prototypes, in some sense, for our polyglot, multicolored, user-friendly future." That's as good a general description as any for LAX, but Iyer points out that the airport is also a metaphor for L.A. itself, "a flat, spaced-out desert kind of place, highly automotive, not deeply hospitable, with little reading matter and no organizing principle."

What a welcome to L.A. Served by about 80 major airlines, Los Angeles International Airport handles about 54 million passengers each year, making this the fourth-busiest airport in the world. And while the idea seems insane, airport officials and some local politicians are pushing to expand airport business by about 60 percent by the year 2015—a possibility none too popular with surrounding residents already beset by horrendous traffic, air pollution, and airplane noise. Since surrounding land is scarce, proposed new runways would be built out into Santa Monica Bay with an assist from massive landfill construction projects. If the idea of an endlessly bigger LAX, a $12 billion project, seems less than appealing, the only effective way travelers can express that opinion is by taking their business elsewhere—for a listing of other area airports, see above—and by further making that point in letters and phone calls to local officials. International visitors are almost destined to disembark here, however.

Even an unexpanded LAX can't help inventing and reinventing itself. These days LAX is busy improving itself yet again—adding a space-age veneer—including spiffing up its food service. The airport's Jetsonsesque "theme building" has become the otherworldly **L.A. Encounter** café, redesigned by Disney Imagineering and complete with lava lamps, a robotic maître d', and waiters in space suits. The futuristic menu, designed by local chefs John Sedlar and Patrick Glennon, includes "chocolate planetary orbs with Saturn rings" as the house dessert. But pay no attention to the restaurant's flight status video monitors—strictly fictitious, unless you're headed to Mars. Reasonably healthy food, from bran muffins to green salads and other vegetables, is available everywhere. Look for a variety of international cuisines in the International Terminal.

As in most monstrously large airports, once you arrive you follow airport signs to find parking, rental car agencies, and terminals—and pray you'll get to the right places on time. Pray, too, that no one breaks into your car if you leave it in the lots here. Because rates of vandalism tend to be high in the airport's far-flung B and C parking lots—though they are patrolled regularly by security guards—LAX users often opt for one of the many private guarded lots just west of the San Diego Freeway (the 405) along Century Boulevard; various airport-area hotels also offer nonguest parking, for a price. That price—and the level of service provided—can vary greatly among private parking lots, so it pays to check out available options thoroughly.

All in all, it's much simpler to forget about driving and parking, if at all possible, and get a ride with **Super Shuttle**, www.supershuttle.com, 323/775-6600, 310/782-6600, or toll-free 800/258-3826 in Los Angeles County; 714/517-6600 in Orange County; 818/556-6600 or toll-free 800/660-6042 in the San Fernando Valley; 626/443-6600 in Pasadena and the rest of the San Gabriel Valley; and 909/467-9600 or 909/

428-6600 in the Inland Empire. There are many, many other shuttle services, of course—even flashier limo service, as well as regular cab service—so pick a carrier licensed by the Los Angeles Dept. of Airports. Some shuttles offer discounts for senior citizens and AAA members and on prepaid round trips. Always make shuttle reservations at least 24 hours in advance. To check a given shuttle's safety record, call the state Public Utilities Commission toll-free at 800/366-4782. Many higher-end area hotels also offer airport shuttle service, either free or low-cost. **Airport Bus**, toll-free 800/772-5299, also provides airport service—even to John Wayne Airport—from area hotels. For current LAX transit information, including public transit connections, from Southern California call toll-free 800/310-5465.

LAX has eight domestic terminals and one international terminal, all of them connected by free shuttle buses. Restrooms, nursery rooms, basic business services, lockers, gift shops, restaurants, and bar/lounges are available in every terminal. For computerized visitor assistance in various languages, head to one of the airport's "QuickAID" touch-screen video terminals. Even better is LAX Traveler's Aid, which features a foreign language translation "link." To get away from the airport's bustle, head for the theme building or the palm-lined oasis in Terminal 5.

GETTING AROUND

Most visitors come to Los Angeles by car, or climb into a rental car immediately after arrival, and get around the way most Angelenos do—via the vast web of local freeways. Once you get here by freeway you're already getting around by freeway, so for a detailed introduction to that adventure see Getting There: By Freeway, above.

By MTA
The Los Angeles Metropolitan Transit Authority provides public bus service throughout Los Angeles County, with some routes more generously staffed—and more useful to visitors—than others. The city's MTA buses are the only reliable form of mass transit for city residents without cars, including large segments of L.A.'s

working poor population and the elderly. When MTA raised bus fares in the mid-1990s, protests erupted in so many quarters, particularly from various public-interest groups and community organizations, that the preexisting general fare of $1.35 (90 cents with prepaid tokens) was reinstated. On some bus routes, off-peak individual fares are just 75 cents. Monthly MTA passes also available.

For information on MTA routes and fares, call 213/626-4455 or toll-free 800/266-6883 or check www.mta.net. Sometimes it seems as if no one will ever answer the phone, however, so for detailed regional bus route and schedule information, it's typically easier to try the website, which also offers online links to most other Southern California transit systems. Or stop by local **MTA Customer Centers,** at various locations, for schedules and to buy passes. Downtown, stop by Level C of the Arco Plaza, 515 S. Flower St., open Mon.–Fri. 7:30 A.M.–3:30 P.M., or the Union Station/Gateway Center (at the East Portal), open weekdays 6 A.M.–6:30 P.M. Along Wilshire, there's a customer center at 5301 Wilshire Blvd., open weekdays 9 A.M.–5 P.M.; in East L.A., at 4501 Whittier Blvd., Ste. B (on Ford north of Whittier), open Tues.–Sat. 10 A.M.–6 P.M.; and in Baldwin Hills at 3650 Martin Luther King Jr. Blvd., also open Tues.–Sat. 10 A.M.–6 P.M. You'll also find MTA centers in Hollywood, at 6249 Hollywood Blvd., open Mon.–Fri. 10 A.M.–6 P.M., and in the San Fernando Valley (Van Nuys) at 14435 Sherman Way, Ste. 107, open Mon.–Fri. 9 A.M.–5 P.M. All MTA offices are closed on weekends.

A variety of other local transit systems also serve greater Los Angeles; for current information on public transportation in Pasadena, Hollywood, Santa Monica, Long Beach, and other areas, see relevant chapters below or contact local visitors bureaus.

By Metrorail and Metrolink

Los Angeles once boasted one of the world's most far-flung and efficient public transportation systems—the Pacific Electric Red Car electric trolley system that connected nearly every suburban or coastal L.A. community with each other and with downtown. The Red Cars, in fact, were largely responsible for L.A.'s sprawling growth pattern—more so than freeways, which came much later—since trolley transport made it con-

venient for people to get around even without cars. When the last of the Red Car trolley system was dismantled in 1961, L.A.'s congestion and smog problems quickly reached crisis proportions.

Los Angeles is once again looking to masstransit trains and trolleys to solve its traffic problems, though at this point things aren't working quite as well as the old Red Cars did.

Operated by the Metropolitan Transit Authority (MTA) and built with generous amounts of federal funding, the new and multifaceted Los Angeles Metrorail system serves fairly limited areas of L.A. and Southern California, though original plans called for substantial regional expansion. Designed primarily for Los Angeles commuters of the professional class, it would seem, the system has suffered from cost overruns, dramatic construction delays, and the local and national humiliations of fraud and kickback allegations, federal investigations, and substantial recent funding cuts. Los Angeles itself seems almost evenly divided on the question of whether its modern mass-transit system has been worth it—and whether it will make any real difference in eliminating area traffic congestion. (Metrorail's ongoing disasters were publicly symbolized, in the mid-1990s, by the giant construction-related cave-in and sinkhole along Hollywood Boulevard.) A recent poll determined that, by a narrow majority, Los Angeles residents oppose the city's new subway system, including further construction, and doubt that it will ever serve parts of the city that most need it.

Metrorail's most vocal critics point out that the system was designed primarily for the convenience of more affluent commuters, that its range is too limited to serve most residents, and that the money spent on Metrorail would have been better spent on improving the local bus system.

The MTA's **Red Line,** the city's subway, serves Union Station, downtown L.A., a short section of Wilshire Boulevard, and Hollywood and North Hollywood (as far as Universal Studios). The MTA's **Blue Line** electric trolleys run 22 miles between Long Beach and downtown L.A., passing Watts Towers and other rarely-seen-by-tourists neighborhoods along the way. The Blue Line is linked to the east-west **Green Line** that connects Norwalk to El Segundo (but not nearby LAX; you'll have to lug your luggage onto an airport bus for that trip). For that utilitarian lapse in particular—and since El Segundo is no longer a major aerospace employment hub, thanks to U.S defense downsizing—the Green Line has been dubbed the "train to nowhere" in the local press. Scoring at least one point for convenience, however, the Blue Line stops just one block from the transit mall in downtown Long Beach.

The MTA's Metrolink commuter rail system is the fastest-growing commuter rail system in the nation. Metrolink includes 404 miles of track that link cities such as San Bernardino, Riverside, Lancaster, Oxnard, and Oceanside to Los Angeles. The fares are quite pricey (for example, a one-way downtown to Oxnard ticket will set you back $8.75), but there's a 25 percent discount for off-peak travel.

Though the entire system is far from entirely useful even for visitors, both Metrorail and Metrolink do offer the opportunity for unusual car-free day trips and around-town excursions.

Fares for the Metrorail system are the same as for MTA buses; for details, see By MTA, immediately above. Fares for Metrolink trains vary according to distance traveled. For route and other information on the Metrorail Red, Blue, and Green Lines, contact MTA at 213/626-4455 or toll-free 800/266-6883, www.mta.net. For route and fare information for the Metrolink regional commuter trains, call 800/371-5465.

GETTING INFORMED

To receive a comprehensive and current visitors guide, the glossy *Destination Los Angeles,* and other information before coming to Los Angeles, write to: **Los Angeles Convention and Visitors Bureau (LACVB),** 633 W. Fifth St., Ste. 6000, Los Angeles, CA 90071, 213/689-8822 or toll-free in the U.S. and Canada 800/228-2452 (24 hours a day); www.lacvb.com. Visitors can also make hotel and rental car reservations through the LACVB's toll-free number. Other publications include a variety of popular "pocket guides" and the annual magazine-style *Festivals of Los Angeles* guide. To find out what else is going on around town, call the bureau's 24-hour events hotline at 213/689-8822; with a touch-tone phone, dial up current events information in English, French, German, Japanese, and Spanish.

Los Angeles also sponsors two separate walk-in visitor centers, both of which provide region-wide information—maps, brochures, calendars, information on foreign-language tours, shopping, dining, even listings of upcoming television tapings—much of it available in six languages, as well as multilingual personal assistance. The LACVB's **Downtown Visitor Information Center,** 685 S. Figueroa St. (between Wilshire Blvd. and Seventh St.), 213/689-8822, is open Mon.–Fri. 8 A.M.–5 P.M., and Saturday 8:30 A.M.– 5 P.M. The satellite **Hollywood Visitor Information Center** is inside the historic Janes House at Janes Square, 6541 Hollywood Blvd. in Hollywood, 213/689-8822, and is open Mon.–Sat. 9 A.M.–5 P.M.

Local chambers of commerce and visitor information bureaus also abound throughout greater Los Angeles; all can be quite helpful. Various local or regional information sources are listed in the following chapters; contact any of them for visitor information in advance of, or during, your visit.

Local publications can be particularly helpful in introducing oneself to the wonders of Los Angeles. The local newspaper of record—California's newspaper of record, really—is the *Los Angeles Times,* distributed everywhere. Pick it up if only for the Sunday "Calendar" section, which lays out just about everything going on in town in the week ahead. The Thursday edition of the *Times* includes its "Calendar Weekend" pull-out section. Various cities also have local daily and/or weekly newspapers. Among magazines, *Los Angeles* is the slick "lifestyle" publication.

But to find out what's really hip and happenin', pick up alternative publications such as the *L.A. Weekly* or *New Times,* not to mention countless 'zines that come and go faster than freeway traffic, available in coffeehouses, neighborhood restaurants, bookstores, and other popular hangouts. Particularly good, wherever you might find them: *Poetry Flash* and *Art issues.*

Otherwise, the best local source of visitor information is the local telephone book, particularly if you seek a particular product or service. Pick the closest place with the right product and/or right price, since distances in Los Angeles can turn a simple errand into an all-day adventure.

COURTESY AISLINN RACE

PASADENA AND VICINITY

Enthroned above an oak-studded arroyo in the shadow of the San Gabriel Mountains, Pasadena the place is actually an *idea*—the idea that simple, healthful living amid gardens, orange groves, and the fellowship of good neighbors can save civilization from the mass-production mindset of the industrial era. Pasadena represents the central idea that created Southern California. Described by acclaimed turn-of-the-20th-century astronomer George Ellery Hale as the "Athens of the West," Pasadena took root in agriculture and then grew its own golden age of arts and sciences.

CROWNED BY AGRICULTURE— AND CULTURE

In the beginning there was Indiana, where the winters were cold and brutal. After the particularly harsh winter of 1872–73, a like-minded group of Indiana farmers sent schoolteacher and journalist Daniel M. Berry west by train to scout out a Southern California site for an agricultural paradise. Berry's choice was the western San Gabriel Valley, where Ivy League-educated farmers already cultivated vineyards, orange groves, and roses in the sunshine and salubrious fresh air.

Berry and his fellows, who came to be known as the Indiana Colony, bought a 4,000-acre section of the San Pasqual Ranch, at the price of $6.31 per acre. The Indianans established themselves as the San Gabriel Orange Grove Association in 1875. They called their community Pasadena, a Chippewa word purported to mean "Crown of the Valley," and set about cultivating the good life.

Crowned by Upper-Crust Culture

Like the rest of Southern California, Pasadena grew rapidly during the real estate boom of the 1880s. In the wake of the settlers, the arrival of the railroad in 1885 brought bushels of well-heeled easterners eager to escape to a kinder climate—the beginning of Pasadena's long-running reputation as a choice West Coast winter vacation destination.

Many of Pasadena's wealthy winterers decided to stay on year-round, to soak up a full measure of sun and the scent of orange blossoms. They soon built grand homes on the city's wide, wandering streets. Business tycoons and the heirs of industry included Adolphus Busch of St. Louis, Chicago's William J. Wrigley, and Henry E. Huntington. Prominent new citizens also included Mrs. James Garfield, widow of the

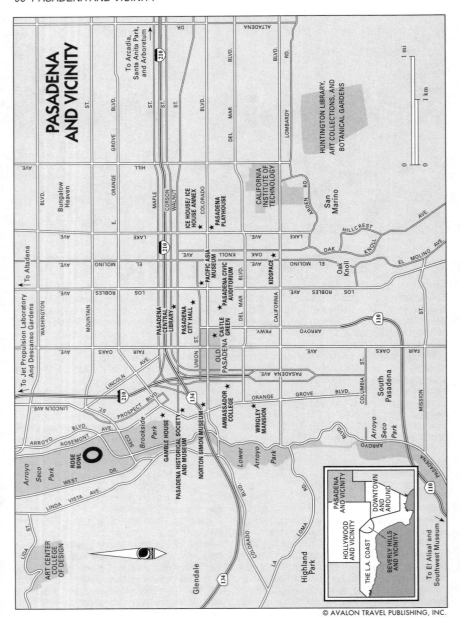

© AVALON TRAVEL PUBLISHING, INC.

assassinated president, and the children of John Brown, abolitionist martyr. Feminist writer Charlotte Perkins Gilman, once freed from the insanity behind "The Yellow Wallpaper," made her last home in Pasadena.

For writers and artists, Pasadena was a good choice. The arts and all aspects of culture, not just agriculture and horticulture, flourished. Pasadena's genteel pursuit of history, literature, poetry, music, art, and the artistic aspects of horticulture created a heaven on earth for the upper middle-class liberal Protestants who made it their home.

THE CRAFTSMAN CROWN

By 1900 Pasadena's population was 10,000; within seven years it reached 30,000. The design and decorative demands of the city's well-to-do residents meant steady work for the country's finest artists and architects. It was no accident, then, that Pasadena soon became an architectural showcase. Many of its treasures still stand.

Most "Pasadena" of them all, ultimately, was the impact of the Arts and Crafts movement, inspired by John Ruskin and William Morris in England but popularized throughout the United States by German immigrant Gustav Stickley, publisher of *The Craftsman* magazine and himself a craftsman-style furniture designer.

Craftsman architecture was inspired by the nature-oriented style of summerhouses built in British colonial India—an uncluttered, outdoorsy design that seemed to combine Japanese (sometimes Chinese) sensibilities with Tudor touches and the broad, sweeping eaves of a Swiss chalet. In Pasadena these distinctive homes were sided with shakes or shingles, usually redwood, and built upon a foundation of boulders brought up from the Arroyo Seco; prominent chimneys also were built of arroyo stone. With wide porches supported by heavy tie beams, craftsman houses typically featured roof supports that extended beyond the gable. Many included sleeping porches, to take full advantage of Southern California's mild weather.

Most important, though, the craftsman approach was a repudiation of all things Victorian, including architecture and furnishings that were ornate, overly fussy, overstuffed. The Arts and

BUNGALOW HEAVEN

Always satisfying is a stroll through Pasadena's Bungalow Heaven neighborhood north of the Foothill Freeway (I-210), the area between Lake and Hill Avenues bordered on the north by Washington Boulevard and on the south by Orange Grove. Officially recognized as a local landmark district since 1989, here you'll find block after block of middle-class takes on the craftsman theme. These "Model T's" of home design, some available by mail-order catalog, were marketable symbols of the California good life. A two-bedroom Pasadena bungalow that cost $2,000 in 1910 would set you back about $350,000 today, however. So the best way to appreciate the impressive interior workmanship is to take the annual neighborhood home tour, held on the last Sunday in April. For tickets and information, call the **Bungalow Heaven Neighborhood Association** at 626/585-2172.

Crafts movement instead emphasized simplicity and harmony with nature—integrating every element of interior design, including light and air, with the world outside, down to the last landscaping detail.

The Brothers Greene and Greene

The architectural achievements of brothers Charles Sumner Greene and Henry Mather Greene in Pasadena came to epitomize America's Arts and Crafts movement—pragmatic, functional design with aesthetic sensibility, a social statement made through architecture. "I seek till I find what is truly useful, and then I try to make it beautiful," Charles Greene once said.

The Greenes' oft-imitated style was reserved not just for a home's architecture. Greene and Greene also shared their design vision with talented craftspeople who created Tiffany stained-glass lamps, leaded-glass windows, furniture, light fixtures, rugs, and other interior and exterior items.

Yet Greene and Greene reserved their talents for the wealthy, contradicting core Arts and Crafts ideals. As historian Kevin Starr comments, a notable characteristic of a Greene and Greene home is its "cunning concealment" of servant staircases and other service features.

Bungalows Hold Court

The Greene brothers' unstinting commitment to quality workmanship—and their hope that their own work, though reserved for the rich, would set new, higher standards in housing for the masses—carried through in Pasadena's middle-class craze for craftsman bungalows. Known for both quality construction and innovative style, the craftsman represents Pasadena's most popular approach to domestic architecture.

Other popular area architects of the time included Alfred and Arthur Heineman, Sylvanus Marston, Louis B. Easton, and Frederick Louis Roehrig. Heineman, Heineman, and Marston were influential in the development of bungalow courts, many of which remain today. The bungalow court, originally designed to accommodate tourists, first appeared about 1910. The concept soon evolved into a fashionable form of apartment life, one combining the social benefits of group living with the privacy of single-family residences.

Also particularly influential during Pasadena's Arts and Crafts epoch was Ernest Batchelder, whose hand-carved tiles with almost medieval Southern California nature motifs can still be found in original local craftsman homes. Batchelder's tiles were primarily used for fireplaces, rendered in earthy tones and left unglazed or finished with a very soft matte effect. Formerly, you could see Batchelder's work on public display in downtown Pasadena's Santa Fe Railroad Passenger Station, now closed.

JACKIE ROBINSON: FROM SEGREGATION TO INTEGRATION

Pasadena's own Jackie Robinson faced insults and racism when he broke the color barrier and integrated major league baseball in 1947. He played his way into baseball's Hall of Fame and helped the Brooklyn Dodgers win five league championships and a World Series. His success, however, never dulled his memory of the first time he faced racial troubles. Robinson had learned about racism when he was a child growing up on Pepper Street in Pasadena.

His mother, three older brothers, and sister had moved from Georgia to Southern California when Robinson was an infant. One day when he was about eight years old, he was sweeping the sidewalk when a little neighbor girl shouted at him: "Nigger, nigger, nigger."

Within minutes, Robinson, the little girl, and her father were throwing rocks at each other. The girl's mother broke up the fight, but it was all part of a pattern that Robinson faced throughout his life. The all-white neighborhood was soon circulating a petition to force the Robinsons to move. The neighbors would call police and complain about noise. But the family remained united, and Robinson's mother told the neighbors that they did not frighten her. Robinson later credited his mother with teaching him strength in the face of adversity.

Sports became Robinson's outlet for his aggressiveness and his desire for competition. At John Muir Technical School, he earned letters in baseball, basketball, football, and track. As quarterback, he led Pasadena Junior College to a perfect 11–0 season. At UCLA, he became the first athlete to earn letters in four sports.

After serving in World War II, Robinson was signed to a major league contract in the fall of 1945. But leading white players and baseball commentators called the signing a publicity stunt and claimed that no African American was good enough to play professional baseball with whites.

After the signing, the *Los Angeles Times* called Robinson the best all-around athlete of "his race" in Southern California. But Southern California's black newspaper, the crusading *California Eagle,* knew better. It called Robinson the best all-around athlete of any race in the nation. In 1947, Robinson was named Rookie of the Year and helped Brooklyn to the National League pennant.

During his 10-year career, Robinson saw hundreds of black players signed to major league teams. He had paved the way for integration of America's most popular game. Along the way he endured taunts from fans, jeers from fellow players, and constant mistreatment because his skin was black.

Throughout it all, he remained calm and yet was known as a fiery competitor. Instead of throwing rocks at his tormentors, he let his dignity and great skills fight the hatred spawned by racism.

CROWNED BY PROGRESS: PRESENT-DAY PASADENA

Since its earliest settlement, Pasadena was considered a "progressive" community, sometimes even bohemian, albeit a bit blue-nosed bohemian. Born from late 19th-century ideals, Pasadena still somehow avoided a direct answer to the main philosophical question posed by its own idealism and experience: Is the good life aristocratic or democratic?

The easy answer is that Pasadena opted for its own variation of landed aristocracy—thus today the city is known for its architectural heritage, lush landscapes, affluent and aesthetic family neighborhoods, world-class art collections, and top-drawer educational institutions. Pasadena also betrays a hint of aristocratic attitude. To traditional Pasadenans the big money, fine homes, and culinary innovation of L.A.'s Westside, for example, represent the dubious currency of the nouveau riche. Westsiders have square footage, Pasadenans have *architecture*.

The more complicated answer is that Pasadena was never just for the rich. Early on, its genteel aspirations married Southern California's fundamentally middle-class mores. The point of Pasadena was to be "Beautiful, Clean, Cultured, Moral, and Esthetic," according to a 1907 editorial in the *Pasadena Daily News*. Local architecture bolsters this perspective—most particularly, the spectacular Greene and Greene Gamble House and abundant local variations on the craftsman theme, not to mention exquisite public buildings, all of which speak volumes about the human value of workmanship and worthwhile work in service to some higher purpose, the process as well as the product.

The city's tendency toward social senescence and snobbishness is not really about money at all. Pasadena simply reserves the right to make moral distinctions about who and what is worthy. The local list of worthies includes the people Pasadena has attracted over the years, including, in the sciences, Albert Einstein and at least 21 Nobel Prize winners, and in the arts, every decade's world-class performers. But the city is most proud of those it has reared, including writer Upton Sinclair and sculptor Alexander Calder, baseball great Jackie Robinson and the revered and feared World War II–era Gen. George Patton.

Life in Pasadena is changing. The city still supports a thriving community of writers, artists, craftspeople, and actors, but that community can't afford to live here, finding nearby Highland Park and Mt. Washington more affordable and hospitable. No longer an enclave of white Protestant propriety with a hidden black and brown servant class, Pasadena is fast becoming a "majority minority" city, with almost 30 percent of its population Latino, 20 percent black, and 10 percent Asian.

As elsewhere in California, the test for modern-day Pasadena will be whether its conception of moral and social worth will stretch to include everyone.

SEEING AND DOING PASADENA

Surprisingly appealing, this self-satisfied city is so sure of its essential worth that it sees little need to primp and pimp for the almighty tourist dollar. Most famous as hometown for the annual New Year's Day Tournament of Roses Parade downtown and the afternoon Rose Bowl post-season college football game, Pasadena is otherwise low-key about its attractions, which are legion. Southern California boosterism played its part in Pasadena's past, but these days heavy-handed hype is notably absent. Pasadena simply *allows* one to enjoy its fairly civilized pleasures. And what a pleasure that is.

OLD PASADENA

The rudely reversed adage, in Angeleno lore, is that Pasadena is a nice place to live, but no one would want to *visit* there. The reinvigoration of Old Pasadena has changed all that. (The correct current promotional term, by the way, is "Old Pasadena," not "Old Town" or "Old Town Pasadena," a distinction largely lost even on native Pasadenans.) Once given over to harmless derelicts, pawn shops, and X-rated entertainment venues, Old Pasadena is now one of the liveliest street scenes in all of Southern California—a destination in its own right for tony trendsetters and throngs of wannabes who stroll the streets in search of something new, something old, or something old that's been made new.

Central to this ambitious downtown renovation is the foundation upon which it is being built—block after block of attractive, high-ceilinged brick buildings dating from the late 1800s. The city's stringent architectural preservation standards have meant slow going for some renovation projects. But no one visiting here seems to mind. As it is there is no shortage of restaurants, coffeehouses, clubs, antique stores, galleries, and gift and specialty shops.

Old Pasadena's "center" lies at the intersection of Colorado Boulevard and Fair Oaks Avenue, with most of the action on Colorado. The roughly 14-block district—defined by East Holly and Union Streets to the north, Green Street to the south, Pasadena Avenue to the west, and Arroyo Parkway to the east—keeps growing. The southern reach of Old Pasadena is fast approaching Del Mar, for example, with parking meters already in place.

People try to tour Old Pasadena by car—ridiculous—and horse-drawn carriage rides are available, but the best way to experience it all is on foot. Quite a kick are the scramble crossings at key intersections along Colorado Boulevard. An X marks the spots where pedestrians are permitted to cross intersections diagonally, from one corner to another. Like crowd-crazy Beverly Hills and Las Vegas, Pasadena seeks to solve the problem of too many people with a 1940 Denver, Colorado, foot-traffic control innovation.

Since Old Pasadena is literally filled to its old-brick rafters with good restaurants and other diversions, definitely plan to do more than window shop and scurry from block to block when the lights change. For specific suggestions, see "Eating in Pasadena," below, as well as "Shopping As Entertainment" and "Artful, Entertaining Pasadena."

To truly appreciate what's here, historically speaking, take a **Saturday morning walking tour** offered on the second Saturday of each month by Pasadena Heritage, $5 per person. For current information and reservations (required), call 626/441-6333, or check out www .pasadenaheritage.org.

PASADENA OVERVIEW

For a very contemporary introduction, start with Old Pasadena, the astonishingly successful shopping, entertainment, and restaurant district downtown, fruit of Pasadena's very careful cultivation of its past.

Next, tour at least some of the attractions in and near Pasadena's Arroyo Seco, the deep ravine on Pasadena's west side. Here you'll find Cal Tech's Jet Propulsion Laboratory, the Rose Bowl stadium, and the fabled Gamble House and other Greene and Greene craftsman-era accomplishments, concentrated in Little Switzerland and Prospect Park.

After a stop at the nearby headquarters of the Pasadena Historical Society, a continuing architectural tour leads down South Orange Grove Boulevard, though only the restored mansions at Ambassador College and the Wrigley Mansion (now office space for the Tournament of Roses) are open for tours.

Other particularly striking neighborhoods, architecturally speaking, include the Oak Knoll area, with the historic Ritz-Carlton, Huntington Hotel as centerpiece, nearby Lombardy Road, and, north of downtown, Bungalow Heaven, Pasadena's largest neighborhood of craftsman bungalows.

This introductory exploration comes full circle downtown at the California Institute of Technology (Cal Tech) and a look at still more architectural and cultural gems, including the city's noteworthy art museums, the Norton Simon Museum and the Pacific Asia Museum.

For an appreciation of both the aristocratic and democratic ideals woven into the Pasadena idea, mandatory side trips include the nearby Huntington Library, Art Collections, and Botanical Gardens in San Marino and, back toward Los Angeles in Highland Park, El Alisal and the Southwest Museum. If there's time, take in Descanso Gardens, with the world's largest camellia collection, the Los Angeles State and County Arboretum, and maybe even a thoroughbred race at Santa Anita Park.

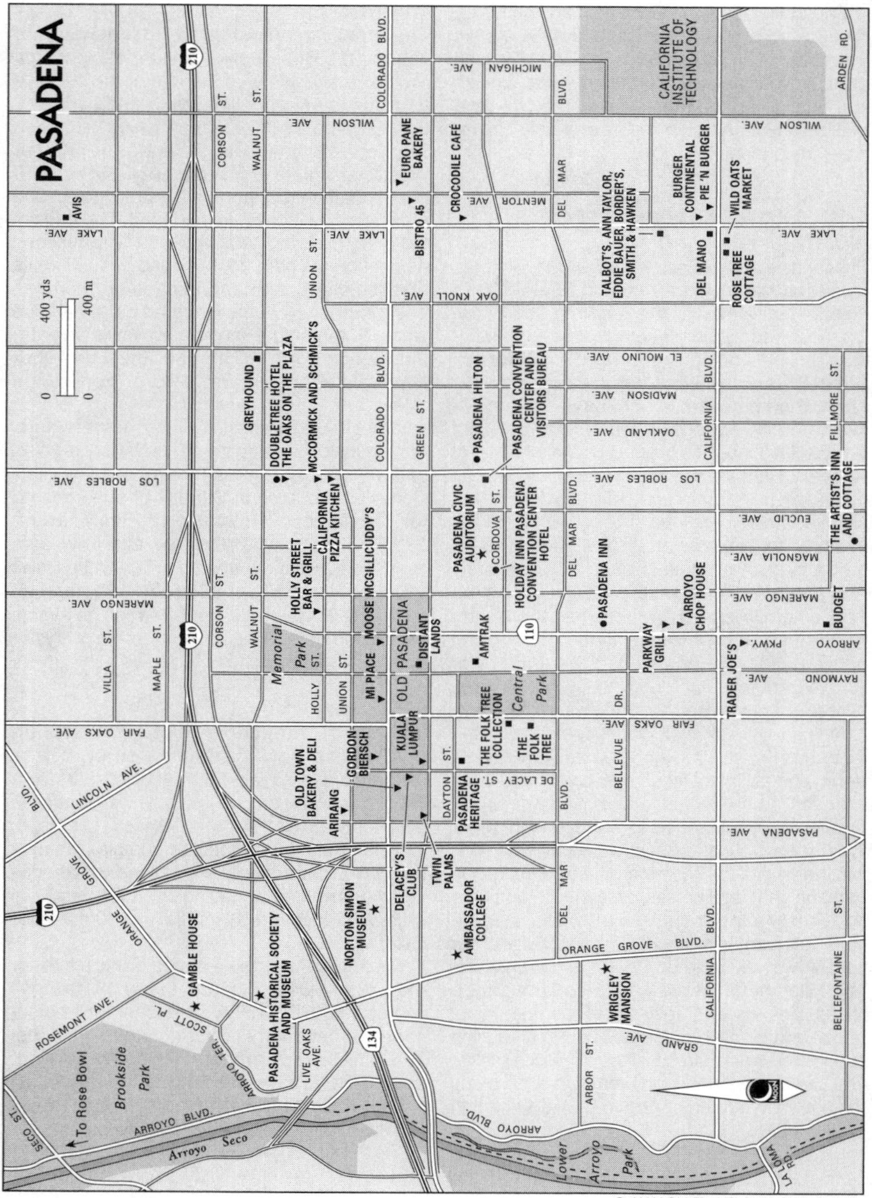

PASADENA

AVIS

210

AVIS

LAKE AVE.

CALIFORNIA INSTITUTE OF TECHNOLOGY

ARDEN RD.

COLORADO BLVD.

MICHIGAN AVE.

WILSON AVE.

WILSON AVE.

CORSON ST.

WALNUT ST.

EURO PANE BAKERY

CROCODILE CAFÉ

MENTOR AVE.

DEL MAR

BURGER CONTINENTAL

PIE 'N BURGER

WILD OATS MARKET

BISTRO 45

LAKE AVE.

OAK KNOLL AVE.

TALBOT'S, ANN TAYLOR, EDDIE BAUER, BORDER'S, SMITH & HAWKEN

DEL MANO

ROSE TREE COTTAGE

LAKE AVE.

400 yds

400 m

GREYHOUND

DOUBLETREE HOTEL, THE OAKS ON THE PLAZA

McCORMICK AND SCHMICK'S

COLORADO BLVD.

GREEN ST.

PASADENA HILTON

PASADENA CONVENTION CENTER AND VISITORS BUREAU

EL MOLINO AVE.

MADISON AVE.

OAKLAND AVE.

CALIFORNIA AVE.

FILLMORE ST.

LOS ROBLES AVE.

HOLLY STREET BAR & GRILL

CALIFORNIA PIZZA KITCHEN

MOOSE McGILLICUDDY'S

PASADENA CIVIC AUDITORIUM

CORDOVA ST.

HOLIDAY INN PASADENA CONVENTION CENTER HOTEL

DEL MAR BLVD.

LOS ROBLES AVE.

THE ARTIST'S INN AND COTTAGE

EUCLID AVE.

MARENGO AVE.

VILLA ST.

MAPLE ST.

210

CORSON ST.

WALNUT ST.

Memorial Park

HOLLY ST.

UNION ST.

MI PIACE

OLD PASADENA

DISTANT LANDS

AMTRAK

110

PASADENA INN

PARKWAY GRILL

ARROYO CHOP HOUSE

MAGNOLIA AVE.

MARENGO AVE.

BUDGET

ARROYO PKWY.

RAYMOND AVE.

TRADER JOE'S

FAIR OAKS AVE.

LINCOLN AVE.

OLD TOWN BAKERY & DELI

GORDON BIERSCH

ARIRANG

KUALA LUMPUR

DAYTON ST.

PASADENA HERITAGE

THE FOLK TREE COLLECTION

THE FOLK TREE

DE LACEY ST.

Central Park

BELLEVUE DR.

FAIR OAKS AVE.

DEL MAR BLVD.

PASADENA AVE.

GROVE BLVD.

210

134

GAMBLE HOUSE

PASADENA HISTORICAL SOCIETY AND MUSEUM

ROSEMONT AVE.

SCOTT PL.

ARROYO TER.

Brookside Park

To Rose Bowl

NORTON SIMON MUSEUM

DELACEY'S CLUB

TWIN PALMS

AMBASSADOR COLLEGE

LIVE OAKS AVE.

ARROYO BLVD.

Arroyo Seco

ORANGE GROVE BLVD.

WRIGLEY MANSION

DEL MAR BLVD.

CALIFORNIA BLVD.

ARBOR ST.

GRAND AVE.

BELLEFONTAINE ST.

Lower Arroyo Park

ARROYO BLVD.

LA LOMA RD.

SECO ST.

N

© AVALON TRAVEL PUBLISHING, INC.

Especially during the lunch hour and on Friday and Saturday nights, street parking is almost impossible to find in Old Pasadena. And if you do bulldoze your way into a metered space, the fee is a quarter per quarter-hour, with a two-hour total time limit. A better bet: reasonably convenient city parking lots.

THE ARROYO SECO

Pasadena's Arroyo Seco ("Dry River") is a steep-sided natural ravine stretching from the San Gabriel Mountains all the way into Los Angeles. Spanned by the recently restored, dramatically arched, and oddly curving 1913 **Colorado Street Bridge,** the arroyo has invited grand presence since early settlement days. Nearby, at 125 S. Grand Avenue, is the original Vista del Arroyo Hotel, now the Ninth U.S. Circuit Court of Appeals. Farthest north, actually in La Cañada Flintridge, is the Cal Tech–affiliated Jet Propulsion Laboratory, the lead U.S. center for robotic exploration of the solar system, managed for NASA by the California Institute of Technology. Across the arroyo, adjacent to Glendale, is the Art Center College of Design. Then there's the Rose Bowl, a landmark amid the surrounding public parklands, Brookside Park and Lower Arroyo Park, popular for hiking, biking, running, horseback riding, golfing, and swimming.

One arroyo park is no longer here, however— Adolphus Busch's privately owned **Busch Gardens,** one of California's "most celebrated landscapes," as the local Cultural Heritage Commission puts it, opened to the public in 1906. What started out as a 30-acre steep-sloped slide into the arroyo, then commonly used for dumping garbage and dead horses, gardener Robert Gordon Fraser transformed into a pre-Disney fairyland with themed statuary (Snow White and her seven dwarves, Little Bo Peep, Hansel and Gretel). Miles of pathways wandered through terraced grounds with flower gardens, fountains, pools, and fanciful buildings. Though a housing subdivision has taken the place of "Busch's folly," you can find remnants and reminders still along the southern stretch of Arroyo Boulevard, north of Laguna Road.

The Rose Bowl

The most famous sight in Pasadena is, of course, the Rose Bowl stadium, designed by Myron Hunt. This was the site of the nation's first post-season collegiate football championship game, in 1902. After Michigan stomped Stanford 49–0, it took 14 years for another West Coast team to agree to play. But by 1919 the contest was so popular—attracting 30,000 fans—that a stadium was needed. The original stadium, built in 1922, was open-ended and horseshoe-shaped. It was closed in 1928 for its first reconstruction and expansion, and has been expanded and renovated several times since. For the most impressive view of the stadium, look north from either the Foothill or Glendale Freeway just before the Orange Grove exit.

The UCLA Bruins play their home games here, traditionally, and the Rose Bowl also hosts various special events throughout the year. Come on the second Sunday of every month for the famous **Rose Bowl Flea Market,** 323/560-7469, where astute antiquers can almost always find a treasure. The Rose Bowl, 991 Rosemont Blvd., 626/577-3100, is open Mon.–Fri. 9 A.M.–4 P.M. For $2–when no events are under way–come in through the Chrysler Court of Champions for a look-see.

Brookside Park

In 1990 the **Amateur Athletic Foundation (AAF) Rose Bowl Aquatics Center,** 360 N. Arroyo Blvd., 626/564-0330, opened in 61-acre Brookside Park, an addition built with funds left over from the 1984 Olympic Games in Los Angeles. This stunning competition complex features two Olympic-size pools, championship high-diving platform, and a wading pool. Recreational swimming fees are $1 adults and 50 cents for children.

Brookside Park also features picnic tables for more than 6,000 people; a pricey 18-hole golf course, 626/796-0178; lighted tennis and horseshoe courts; badminton and handball courts; and facilities for archery and lawn bowling. **Jackie Robinson Stadium** is the regulation baseball diamond, seating 4,200, though Brookside also has two lighted softball fields.

The Art Center College of Design

The Art Center College of Design, across the Arroyo Seco at 1700 Lida St., 626/396-2200, established in Los Angeles in 1930, is an internationally renowned arts and design school emphasizing the practical—the most basic practical consideration being post-college employment. The college's nine majors include advertising, illustration, environmental design, and graphic design as well as packaging, photography, and filmmaking. Architect Craig Ellwood designed the college's current digs in 1977. The sleek, black, steel-and-glass rectangular box sits on a chaparral-covered hill and spans an adjacent ravine. The fine sculpture garden and striking views of the city still don't outshine the student work on display here. Galleries also feature revolving exhibits of national and internationally known artists and designers, working in various media. The **Williamson Gallery** is open to the public Tues.–Sun. noon–5 P.M., until 9 P.M. on Thursday, closed Monday and holidays. Free campus tours are offered daily. To get here: Take Colorado Boulevard west to the Colorado Street Bridge. Turn right at San Rafael, which turns into Linda Vista. Follow Linda Vista north to Lida, turn left, and follow the signs.

THE GAMBLE HOUSE AND VICINITY

The Gamble House

If there's time for nothing else while in Pasadena, do visit the Gamble House. Pasadena's premiere architectural showpiece, this is one of the finest examples of the finest moment in American domestic design—justifiably designated both a state and national historic landmark.

Architects Charles and Henry Greene designed this Japanese-influenced craftsman as a winter home for David and Mary Gamble of Cincinnati, heirs to the Procter & Gamble fortune. No expense was spared in constructing this richly detailed 1908–1909 ode to simplicity. At a time when $5,000 would buy a very spacious house on a view lot, the Gambles spent $50,000 for this shingle-sided home graced with exotic hand-rubbed woods and inlays, leaded-glass windows, and the home's trademark oak-motif Louis Tiffany stained-glass door.

Now managed by the University of Southern California's School of Architecture, the Gamble House is meticulously maintained. Most astonishing, almost all of the original Greene and Greene furnishings and design details are still here. Except for the rugs, everything was manufactured in the Greenes' own Pasadena studios.

The Gamble House, 4 Westmoreland Place (three blocks north of Colorado Blvd.), 626/793-3334, www.gamblehouse.org, is open for docentled tours Thurs.–Sun. from noon to 3 P.M. (closed on major holidays). Tours begin every 15 minutes and typically last one hour. Admission is $5 for adults, $4 for seniors, $3 for students (with valid ID), and free for children 12 and under. Call to arrange group tours, offered by arrangement only. For something special, come during the Christmas season, when the house is decked out for the holidays—the only time visitors can take self-guided tours. Whenever you come, don't skip the Gamble House Bookstore in the onetime garage.

Gamboling near the Gamble House

The Gamble House neighborhood is an enclave of Greene and Greene homes colloquially known as **Little Switzerland.** Most are not open to the public, but the area is well worth an impromptu walking tour. If you're lucky you may be able to sign up for an organized walking tour with the Pasadena Heritage, which offers a home tour in the spring and a craftsman weekend tour in the fall. For current details, call 626/441-6333, or check www.pasadenaheritage.org.

Next door to the Gamble House, at 2 Westmoreland Place, is **Cole House** (1907), a Greene and Greene that's now a Unitarian Neighborhood Church office. The lovely grounds here are open to the public.

Ranney House (1907) at 440 Arroyo Terrace (at the corner of N. Orange Grove Boulevard) belonged to Mary L. Ranney, one of the Greenes' design assistants, who did most of the architectural work here on her own.

F. W. Hawks House (1906) at 408 Arroyo Terrace is a characteristic Greene and Greene use of fieldstone. The **Van Rosem–Neill House**

(1903) at 400 Arroyo Terrace features a boulder-based wall of "clinker brick" protecting the front terrace. Carefully restored, this home appears much as it did when featured in a 1915 issue of *The Craftsman* magazine.

The **White Sisters House,** (1903), 370 Arroyo Terrace, was designed for the three sisters-in-law of Charles Greene. The original brown shingles were replaced with stucco.

Next door at 368 Arroyo Terrace is one of the architects' own, the **Charles Sumner Greene House** (1902), using favorites fieldstone and clinker brick in a design with projecting rafters and low-pitched roof.

One of the most striking Greene and Greene homes in the area is the **Duncan-Irwin House** (1901, 1906) at 240 N. Grand Ave., originally a small, one-story bungalow until an addition and remodel in 1906 expanded it to 6,000 square feet with six bedrooms, six bathrooms, and six fireplaces. Banks of windows offer views of Arroyo Seco and the San Gabriels.

Across the street, at 235 N. Grand Ave., the only Greene and Greene remnants of the **James A. Culbertson House** (1902, 1906–15) are the bay window, Tiffany glass-paneled front door, pergola, and retaining wall. Most famous for its grand interior, with hand-carved art nouveau panels designed by Charles Greene, the original home was all but destroyed by a fire in 1902.

While in the area, take a drive up **Prospect Boulevard,** a fine old neighborhood shaded by camphor trees. Of special interest is **Hindry House** (1909) at 781 Prospect Blvd., a massive mission-style mansion by brothers Arthur and Alfred Heineman, noted Pasadena architects. **Bentz House** (1906) at 657 Prospect is a well-preserved Greene and Greene. Note, too, the stone and wrought iron entrance gates at Orange Grove and Prospect, also designed by the brothers Greene.

Near the Gamble House:
Feynes Mansion

The **Pasadena Historical Society and Museum** is right in the neighborhood, inside the 1905 neoclassical Feynes Mansion, 470 W. Walnut St. (at N. Orange Grove Blvd.), 626/577-1660. Once home to the Finnish consul, the 18-room museum displays original 15th- and 16th-century European antiques alongside American paintings. In many ways the basement is more intriguing, with exhibits of historical photographs and memorabilia. The historical society's gift shop is also here–doing its part to assist the $2 million fund-raising campaign for construction of the Pasadena History Center.

In a separate building on this lush four-acre estate is the **Finnish Folk Art Museum,** a replica of a 17th-century Finnish smokehouse and living room with antiquities from the collection of former Finnish Consul Y. A. Paloheimo.

The Pasadena Historical Society museums are open Thur.–Sun. 1–4 P.M. for self-guided tours, $4 adults, $3 seniors and students, free for children under 12.

South from the Gamble House:
Millionaires' Row

In the early 1900s, Orange Grove Boulevard was known as Millionaires' Row, a showplace neighborhood of winter homes of the wealthy. Along what was often referred to as Pasadena's "Fifth Avenue," the palatial homes and gardens here included the eccentric Bavarian hunting lodge–style stone mansion of Adolphus Busch, second-generation heir of the St. Louis beer brewing dynasty, whose original Pasadena Busch Gardens became a major Southern California tourist attraction. Other prominent citizens included heirs to the Liggett-Myers tobacco and Standard Oil fortunes.

Few of the ostentatious old Orange Grove estates survived the conversion of this high-priced real estate into more contemporary homes, condos, and apartment complexes. The former home of J. W. Robinson, founder of the Southern California department store, was demolished by William Wrigley to make way for his rose garden, for example.

Ambassador College is a four-year liberal arts college and headquarters of the Worldwide Church of God, publisher of *Plain Truth* magazine. At home on onetime Millionaires' Row, 300 W. Green St. (at the corner of S. Orange Grove), the college campus includes four fully-restored mansions open to the public. Campus tours are available; for information and reservations, call 626/304-6123.

The **Wrigley Mansion,** 391 S. Orange Grove Blvd. (near Del Mar Blvd.), 626/449-4100, was winter home for chewing gum magnate and

Chicago Cubs owner William J. Wrigley Jr. Now **Tournament House and Wrigley Gardens,** headquarters for the Pasadena Tournament of Roses Association, the mansion exhibits memorabilia from past parades and football games. Guided tours are offered only during Tournament of Roses downtime, February through August, Thursday only, 2–4 P.M., but the surrounding rose gardens are open daily except December 31 and January 1.

THE OAK KNOLL AREA

The Oak Knoll area, with its meandering oak-shaded streets, was developed in the 1800s to attract the same wealth as that on Orange Grove Boulevard. The money to construct fine homes and estates in turn attracted fine architects, which is why the area is worth a wander. To reach the Oak Knoll area, follow Orange Grove Boulevard south to California Boulevard, turn left, continue to Oak Knoll, then turn right.

The **O'Brien House** (1912) at 1327 S. Oak Knoll Ave. is a fine craftsman with notable Oriental details, designed by Arthur and Alfred Heineman. Next on the tour, crowning Oak Knoll's original oak knoll, is the recent reincarnation of the historic Huntington Hotel, now the Ritz-Carlton, Huntington Hotel, 1401 S. Oak Knoll Ave.— well worth exploring even if you can't afford an overnight. After wandering through the hotel's public areas and touring the grounds, continue the Oak Knoll tour by making a quick left turn onto Hillcrest Avenue.

The Huntington Hotel

Albert Einstein once stayed here. So did Theodore Roosevelt, Prince Philip and Princess Anne, even cosmetics queen Elizabeth Arden.

First known as the Wentworth Hotel, the Huntington was named by Civil War general M. C. Wentworth, who built it in 1906. The earliest days of this Oak Knoll landmark were difficult. Even during Pasadena's resort hotel heyday, it closed within months of opening, still unfinished. Henry E. Huntington bought it in 1911, completed construction, and hired William Hertrich, who landscaped his San Marino estate, to design the 23-acre grounds—including the still-thriving Horseshoe and Japanese gardens—before the

hotel reopened for business in 1914. Despite fairly frequent changes in ownership over the years, it's been the Huntington Hotel ever since.

Highlight of a garden tour is the **Picture Bridge,** a covered footbridge crossing the arroyo to the hotel's cottages. The simple post-and-rail design features 39 triangular oil paintings of California scenes by artist Frank M. Moore, framed by the ceiling cross-supports.

That the Huntington Hotel, the last of Pasadena's grand resorts, exists at all today is something of a miracle. Most of the hotel was closed in the 1980s because of seismic safety concerns, and it looked as if the grand old lady of Pasadena had presided over her last society gala. Then came the endlessly patient and persistent Ritz-Carlton people, who first tried to satisfy local preservationists' demands for total historic preservation. That was not possible, as it turned out, since the main hotel building was structurally unsound. Ritz-Carlton delivered the next best thing—an astonishingly accurate new version of the hotel's turn-of-the-20th-century self with every conceivable modern amenity somehow incorporated, open for business since 1991.

Southern Californians love the Huntington Hotel—a statement on par with observing that the sun sets over the Pacific Ocean. If one's pocketbook permits, this stunning hotel is *the* place to stay in Pasadena.

On Hillcrest Avenue

Highlights of a neighborhood drive include **Landreth House** (1918) at 1385 Hillcrest, an American classical revival by Reginald D. Johnson, and **Spinks House** (1909) at 1344 Hillcrest, a Swiss chalet-styled craftsman by Greene and Greene. **Freeman House** (1913) at 1330 Hillcrest, designed by Arthur S. Heineman, is a craftsman known for its Batchelder tile work. At 1311 Hillcrest is **Prindle House** (1926, 1928), a Spanish colonial revival by George Washington Smith.

Elliott House (1925) at 1290 Hillcrest Ave. is a spectacular if subtle example of the Spanish colonial revival style by Wallace Neff, heir to the Rand-McNally fortune and Southern California "artist in adobe," who was also responsible for building homes for Fredric March and Groucho Marx and for renovating Pickfair for Douglas Fairbanks and Mary Pickford. **Griffith House**

(1924) at 1275 Hillcrest is an exploration in the same genre by Johnson, Kaufman, and Coate. **Hurshler House** (1950) at 1200 Hillcrest is a change-up, done in international style by Ain, Johnson, and Day.

Last but not least, two more Greene and Greene homes: the **Cordelia Culbertson House** (1911) at 1188 Hillcrest Place, with gunite walls, striking green-tiled roof, oriental accents, and the **Robert R. Blacker House** (1907) at 1177 Hillcrest Ave., which the Greene brothers considered their finest achievement. This stunning craftsman "bungalow" cost more than $100,000 to build at the turn of the 20th century, despite the fact that Blacker was in the lumber business. The home was the center of major local controversy—and the impetus for serious Pasadena heritage protection laws—in the mid-1980s, when a Texan bought it and began selling off the original Greene and Greene accoutrements.

If you're not yet tired of nosing around in rich people's neighborhoods, east from the Oak Knoll area via California Boulevard and then Arden Road (to the south) is **Lombardy Road,** which borders San Marino a block north of the old Huntington estate. The stretch between Arden and Chaucer Roads is packed with architectural noteworthies, many in revivals of Spanish colonial, Mediterranean, and Monterey styles.

DOWNTOWN AGAIN

The California Institute of Technology
The original **Throop University,** founded in 1891, was at the corner of Fair Oaks and Green, still standing as part of the Castle Green. The four-year college evolved into the **Throop Polytechnic Institute** and emphasized training in the manual arts for all grades, heavily influenced by the Arts and Crafts movement philosophy. Polytechnic eventually split into two schools, the Hunt and Grey–designed craftsman **Polytechnic School** preparatory at 1030 E. California Blvd. and the now world-renowned **California Institute of Technology** ("Cal Tech") at 1201 E. California Blvd., noted for its physics, engineering, and astronomy departments. This is the place Albert Einstein changed his mind about the nature of the cosmos, and where Carl Ander-

son discovered the positron. Cal Tech is the most selective undergraduate school in the nation, with 22 Nobel Prize laureates among its faculty and alumni.

Cal Tech's original campus plan and Spanish and Italian Renaissance–style buildings were designed by architects Hunt and Grey, and constructed from 1928 to 1939 by Bertram Grosvenor Goodhue and Associates. Most notable is the faculty club, the **Athenaeum,** U-shaped and built around a courtyard heavy with wisteria. Designed by Gordon B. Kaufmann and completed in 1930, the Athenaeum didn't open until 1931, its grand opening postponed for the formal dinner honoring Albert Einstein's arrival for a three-month stay. Only faculty and guests can dine here, but you can see this astonishing dining hall on the campus architectural tour.

Regular campus tours, geared toward students and prospective students, are offered during the school year Mon.–Fri. at 2 P.M., except during winter break or when it's raining. Even better is the free Cal Tech campus architectural tour, offered Sept.–Nov. and Jan.–June on the fourth Thursday of the month. For information, call campus public relations at 626/395-6327. Also worth a stop: Cal Tech's well-known seismology facility, the **Earthquake and Media Center** and, during special events, the Cal Tech–affiliated **Jet Propulsion Laboratory,** specializing in National Aeronautics and Space Administration (NASA) research.

Castle Green
Another Pasadena noteworthy, included on the National Register of Historic Places, Castle Green is all that remains of one of America's most prestigious resort hotels, **Hotel Green.** Built with the fortune Col. G. G. Green made by hawking patent medicines, Castle Green, 50 East Green St. (at Raymond), is the second of two hotel buildings once connected by the **Bridge of Sighs** promenade over Raymond Avenue, the most desirable place in town from which to view the Rose Parade. (President Taft once stood here.) The first hotel building, originally the Hotel Webster, was built in 1890 and torn down in 1924, so now the promenade ends a bit abruptly.

The remaining six-story "castle," an apartment cooperative since 1926, was the original hotel's annex, constructed in 1899. Its architecture is an eccentric and extravagant interpretation of then-popular Spanish, Moorish, and Classical styles, with red-tiled roofs and turrets, towers, balconies, and verandas done in olive green, gold, and orange. The public rooms downstairs—the entry, main salon, card room, Moorish room, and downstairs ballroom—look much as they did originally and are rented out for special events and the occasional film crew.

Pasadena Civic Center
Inspired by the City Beautiful movement, Pasadena's regal beaux-arts civic center is an intentionally striking symbol of civic pride, built in the 1920s. The three dominant public buildings are surrounded by a host of neoclassical commercial buildings downtown, all completed before the Great Depression.

Most striking is **Pasadena City Hall,** 100 N. Garfield Ave., with its crownlike dome and Italian Renaissance courtyard design, by John Bakewell, Jr. and Arthur Brown, Jr., who also created San Francisco's City Hall. The formal Italian/ Spanish vernacular **Pasadena Central Library,** 285 E. Walnut St., 626/744-4052, was designed by Pasadena architect Myron Hunt, more famous for the Huntington estate in San Marino.

Now effectively cut off from the rest of the Civic Center by the Plaza Pasadena, the **Pasadena Civic Auditorium,** 300 E. Green St., 626/449-7360, is an Italian Renaissance palace, known for its Pompeian revival interiors by artist Giovanni Smeraldi. It's a worthy venue for performers, including Ray Charles and Placido Domingo, and television's annual Emmy Awards have been held here.

The Pasadena Playhouse
The Spanish revival–style Pasadena Playhouse, the State Theater of California since 1938, was founded by Gilmor Brown, who merged a traveling troupe with local amateur actors. Host to touring plays and musicals, and historic training ground for new Hollywood acting talent–including Conrad Bain, Katherine Helmond, Stacy Keach, and Stephanie Zim-

City Hall

PASADENA CONVENTION AND VISITORS BUREAU

balist–the playhouse was central to Los Angeles cultural life until the 1960s, when financial problems forced its closure. Another local star on the National Register of Historic Places, the 1924 Pasadena Playhouse was refinanced, carefully restored, and reopened in 1986.

Two theaters are on the premises, the main 700-seat auditorium and a smaller 99-seat house for Equity-waiver performances. The Pasadena Playhouse is downtown at 39 S. El Molino Ave. (between Colorado and Green). For information, call 626/792-8672; for tickets, call the box office at 626/356-7529 or toll-free 800/233-3123. Members of the **Pasadena Playhouse Alumni and Associates** offer behind-the-scenes tours, by appointment only. Special group tours can also be arranged.

ARTFUL, ENTERTAINING PASADENA

MUSEUM-QUALITY PASADENA

Norton Simon Museum

Norton Simon (1907-1993) was an immensely successful and charismatic corporate leader, a one-time candidate for the U.S. Senate, and the husband of actress Jennifer Jones. He was also "an art collector of genius," his personal collection representing 2,000 years of Western and Asian art. Tough times for the Pasadena Museum of Modern Art coincided, rather fortuitously, with Norton Simon's desperate need to find a home for his burgeoning collection; in 1974 Simon began creating one of the world's foremost public art collections. When you spot Rodin's *The Thinker* out on the lawn, you know what's inside has got to be good. There's more Rodin, of course, but the Norton Simon collection is richest in Picassos, Rembrandts—including *The Bearded Man in the Wide Brimmed Hat, Self-Portrait,* and *Titus*—and Goyas. An entire gallery of Degas, both paintings and sculptures, lines the curving staircase. The Impressionist collection is vast, including also Cézanne, Matisse, Monet, Renoir, Lautrec, and van Gogh. Also here: Renaissance works by Raphael, Rubens, and Brueghel, ancient ivory, bronze, and stone sculptures from India and Southeast Asia. Don't miss the museum shop, with an exceptional selection of books, prints, and cards.

The Norton Simon Museum is near the Colorado Street Bridge at 411 W. Colorado Blvd., 626/449-6840, www.nortonsimon.org, and is open Thurs.–Sun. noon–6 P.M. Admission is $6 adults, $3 students and seniors, children under 12 free.

Pacific Asia Museum

Designed in 1924 by architects Mayberry, Marston, and Van Pelt as both gallery and home for Grace Nicholson, aficionada of Asian art, Pasadena's own northern Chinese Imperial Palace—included on the National Register of Historic Places—features a green tile roof, ceramic guard dogs to ward off evil spirits, and a peaceful central courtyard complete with bubbling brook and koi. (The garden is one of two authentic Chinese gardens in the United States.) Though the Pacific Asia Museum is the only Southern California museum specializing in the arts and crafts of Asia and the Pacific, most exhibits here are on loan from other museums or private collections. The bookstore/gift shop is worth a wander. Free lectures and workshops on Asian arts and culture are offered on the third

The Norton Simon Museum houses a rich collection of Picassos, Rembrandts, and Impressionist works.

Saturday of every month. The Pacific Asia Museum, 46 N. Los Robles Ave. (at Colorado), 626/449-2742, www.pacificasiamuseum.org, is a block south of the Doubletree Hotel and is open Wed.–Sun., 10 A.M.–5 P.M. Admission is $5 adults, $3 seniors and students, children under 12 free.

Kidspace Museum
Kidspace is a children's museum founded by the Junior League of Pasadena in 1979 to encourage hands-on exploration by children–the perfect antidote after touring all the hands-off attractions in town. Housed in the onetime gymnasium of a former elementary school (now a continuation high school), Kidspace offers abundant opportunities for creative play without too many of the gee-whiz technoid special effects becoming so popular at children's museums. Exhibits include a child-size TV and radio station, talking robots, real uniforms to try on, and a hospital room with a soft-sculpture doll (complete with removable organs). Summer workshops are offered, and special events are held throughout the year at Kidspace, 390 S. El Molino (at California Blvd.), 626/449-9143. During the regular school year Kidspace is open only Wednesday 2–5 P.M. and on weekends 12:30–5 P.M.; in summer and during school vacations, Mon.–Fri. 1–5 P.M. Admission is $5 for adults and children over age 2, $3.50 for seniors.

ENTERTAINING PASADENA

Theatrical Pasadena
Pasadena is a serious theater and concert city, attracting major regional, national, and international performers. The city's most prominent venue is the 1931 **Pasadena Civic Auditorium,** downtown at 300 E. Green St., where Natalie Cole's "Unforgettable" concert was filmed for PBS's *Great Performances*. Home to the **Pasadena Symphony** and former home of the annual Emmy Awards ceremony, the 2,961-seat Civic hosts performers such as Ray Charles, the American Ballet Theatre, and the Vienna Philharmonic. For current events information, call 626/793-2122. For tickets, call the box office at 626/449-7360.

Performances at Pasadena's most beloved theater, **Pasadena Playhouse,** tend toward the contemporary, with recent world premieres including "Same Time, Another Year" and "In the Moonlight." The season typically runs from September to July, with ticket prices $12–40. For tickets, call 626/356-7529 or TicketMaster in Los Angeles, 213/365-3500.

Now that Pasadena's acoustically perfect Ambassador Auditorium at Ambassador College has closed shop, other schools are increasingly called upon to help fill the venue void. Concerts, dance performances, lectures, plays, and films are regularly scheduled at **Beckman Auditorium** and **Ramo Auditorium** on the Cal Tech campus. For information and tickets, call Cal Tech's Office of Public Events, 626/395-4652. To find out what's going on at **Pasadena City College,** call 626/585-7123.

Comedy: The Ice House
The fun and funny Ice House, 24 N. Mentor Ave., 626/577-1894, is a fairly famous comedy club, where since opening night in 1960 the likes of Jay Leno, David Letterman, Steve Martin, Pat Paulsen, Lily Tomlin, and Robin Williams have made names for themselves. The **Ice House Annex** next door offers music acts, improv theater, and "one person" theater acts. Cover charge is $8.50 Sun.–Thurs. nights $11.50–12.50 on Friday and Saturday nights.

Making the Scene
Kevin Costner was once a major draw at the **Twin Palms** restaurant and nightclub, 101 W. Green St., 626/577-2567. After the divorce, Costner's ex-wife, Cindy, got sole custody of the place. While the Twin Palms has lost some of its movie star cachet, it's still quite glamorous. The restaurant fare is good, though some people come here to make the scene. Stars of the large patio bar are the–hey!–*twin palms*. Live music is on tap nightly after 9 P.M., except Monday, when comics take the stage. Cover charge varies.

Count on finding the more settled crowd mixed in with traveling business types at the **Ritz-Carlton, Huntington Hotel Lobby Lounge,** 1401 S. Oak Knoll Ave., 626/577-2867, an elegant bar featuring live entertainment. On Saturday, count on show tunes 8–9 P.M., swing tunes 9 P.M.–midnight.

Otherwise, best bars include **Delacey's Club 41,** 41 S. DeLacey (between Colorado and Green), 626/795-4141, a 1920s-style saloon that's enjoyable for drinks and conversation if you can snag one of the high-walled booths. **McCormick and Schmick's Seafood Restaurant,** 111 N. Los Robles (at Union), 626/405-0064, is noted for its gorgeous Arts and Crafts interiors but is more famous for its happy hour, serving excellent appetizers to well-dressed professionals and the not-so-well-dressed crowd from City Hall. The nearby **Holly Street Bar & Grill,** 175 E. Holly (at Arroyo Pkwy), 626/440-1421, offers a quiet, grown-up atmosphere for a similar crowd. Not feeling grown up? Then the place is **Moose McGillicuddy's** at 119 E. Colorado Blvd. (at Arroyo Pkwy), 626/304-9955, providing *Northern Exposure* atmosphere, cheap well drinks, $2 beers, and theme nights for those in college or those who wish they still were. The food menu here leans heavily toward burgers.

Coffee and Conversation
For good coffee and quiet conversation, there's always ubiquitous **Starbucks,** the Seattle coffee chain that has colonized much of California and the rest of the nation. Pasadena has three locations, at 556 S. Fair Oaks Ave, 1000 Fair Oaks Ave., and 3429 E. Foothill Blvd.

Or if you have already been to **Starbucks** many times and you're looking for a good cuppa java in a hipper world-beat atmosphere, try **Equator,** 22 Mills Place, 626/564-8656, a small alley on the south side of Colorado near Fair Oaks, for coffee drinks so good some consider them dessert.

The Cinema Scene
The two movie houses in Old Pasadena are close enough to spy on each other. The **AMC Old Pasadena** on Union, just west of Fair Oaks in the One Colorado complex, 626/585-8900, has eight first-run movie theaters, underground. Across the street is the six-screen **United Artists Pasadena Marketplace,** 64 W. Colorado, 626/795-1386. For bargain flicks, try the **Academy 6 Theaters,** 1003 E. Colorado, 626/229-9400, where all seats are $5, and $3 for children, seniors, and matinee shows. For historic movie-theater ambience, head to South Pasadena (see below) and its **Rialto Theater** on Fair Oaks, 626/799-9567.

EVENTFUL PASADENA

In addition to its other accomplishments, Pasadena is still crowned by its pronounced cultural contradictions—best illustrated by the coexistence of the very traditional, straitlaced, family-oriented Tournament of Roses Parade and Rose Bowl on New Year's Day and the notoriously weird, wacky, these-people-should-be-in-strait-jackets Pasadena Doo Dah Parade, originally a January Rose Parade spoof now held in November. For a full roster of Pasadena events,

Rose Parade

ROBERT HOLMES/CALIFORNIA DIVISION OF TOURISM

WACKINESS ON PARADE:
THE OCCASIONAL DOO DAH PARADE

It seems that for every action in California there's a reaction. Such is the case with Pasadena's Occasional Doo Dah Parade, which began in the 1970s as an almost spontaneous spoof of the city's long-running Tournament of Roses Parade. With no rules, no theme, and no beauty queens—but at least a few drag queens, not to mention other unusual personas—the Doo Dah is the antithesis of the sober, sunny, all-American image at the heart of the Tournament of Roses. An all-time favorite at the Doo Dah Parade, for example, is the stiffly starched and suited Synchronized Briefcase Drill Team, though the West Hollywood Cheerleaders are also immensely popular. Another recent entry: the Snake Sisters' Frida Kahlo Dreadfully Painful Memorial Art Walk in Homage to her Creative Genius and Superfluous Hair.

Among musical entries, the beloved Lounge Lizards don reptile costumes to croon Frank Sinatra tunes. For the big band sound, count on Snotty Scotty and the Hankies; Dred Zeppelin does Led Zeppelin to a reggae beat. The almost memorable Boring Men's Club, now de-funct, was a past crowd pleaser, but the BBQ and Hibachi Marching Grill Team has since filled in admirably.

As fun and funny as the Doo Dah Parade is, its atmosphere is irreverent, almost intentionally tasteless, slightly unwholesome, and a bit wild. If you're concerned about your children being exposed to such raw and rough-edged community creativity, don't bring them—and don't allow them access to a Southern California television set on parade day. Like the Rose Parade, the Doo Dah has become so popular that it's now televised.

Originally staged as a January 1 alternative to the Tournament of Roses, the Occasional Doo Dah Parade is now scheduled for the Sunday before Thanksgiving; the parade route winds through Old Pasadena.

For more information about the Occasional Doo Dah Parade and to submit proposed entries, call **The Light-Bringer Project,** at 626/440-7379. The Light-Bringer Project, an umbrella community arts organization, sponsors a variety of other intriguing events throughout the year.

---

contact the visitors bureau (see Getting Oriented, Getting Around, below).

Boosterism on Parade:
The Tournament of Roses

The only social artifact of Pasadena's past boosterism is now an international event. Every year on January 1 Pasadena struts its stuff for the multitudes assembled along Colorado Boulevard and for a worldwide television audience of about 450 million. New Year's Day is the only time Pasadena as a destination is nearly impossible.

The **Tournament of Roses Parade** has been held here since 1890, when it was prosaically known as the "Battle of the Flowers" and featured Ben Hur–style chariot races, these followed in short order by ostrich races and (only once, in 1913) elephant and camel races.

Despite its fame, there's still something downhome and folksy about the Tournament of Roses Parade, with its high school marching bands and mounted sheriff's posses. But the real fascination is the fact that only "fresh plant material" can be used to decorate its fantastic floats. In the beginning, Pasadena loaded its horse-drawn creations with bushels and bushels of its own winter-grown roses–a scene undeniably appealing to snowbound easterners, making the event a major boon to local real estate sales. The scene is unbelievably sophisticated these days, with dedicated teams–led by "floral directors" –creating mobile art using a palette of flowers, fresh greenery, vegetables, fruit rinds, beans, rice, seed pods, and dried tree bark. Since the flower artists can use no artificial chemicals or dyes, they make the most difficult colors (red, for instance) by resorting to exotic blends of spices.

In 1902 the first **Rose Bowl** post-season college football game was added to the day's festivities. Michigan stomped Stanford 49–0, and that West Coast humiliation was enough to retire football from the day's rosy agenda for 16 years. But football was a major passion by 1922, when the venerable Rose Bowl stadium was constructed; now the afternoon PAC 10 championship game finishes Southern California's celebration of the new year.

The only drawback to Pasadena's annual Tournament of Roses celebration is the chaos created by the relentless crowds—hundreds of thousands of parade-goers stretched out along Colorado Boulevard. Most of these fanatics camp out the night before to assure a vantage point, sometimes uncomfortably cold, even in Southern California. So if the prospect of parade day seems daunting, consider coming in December to see the floats under construction and to enjoy other pre-New Year's events.

For information on the Tournament of Roses Parade, the Rose Bowl, and associated before-and-after events, call 626/449-4100 or 626/449-7673 (ROSE), or check www.rosebowl.com. If you do come for the big day and want to book hotel rooms—at least a year in advance, and prices will be sky high—remember that when Jan. 1 falls on a Sunday, both the Rose Parade and Rose Bowl are scheduled for Jan. 2. This is Pasadena, after all, rooted in the Midwestern belief that it's a sin to so much as mow the lawn on a Sunday.

SHOPPING AS ENTERTAINMENT

Shopping Old Pasadena

Inveterate shoppers find historic Old Pasadena quite appealing these days, with city blocks full of antique and specialty stores, art galleries, restaurants, and coffeehouses. The district's centerpiece is the **One Colorado** complex at the corner of Colorado Boulevard and Fair Oaks Avenue, 626/564-6601, a courtyard style complex featuring national retailers, specialty shops, entertainment centers and nightclubs.

Del Mano, 517 S. Lake Ave. (near California Blvd.) 626/793-6648, offers some of the finest American-made arts and crafts, jewelry, and textiles you'll ever see.

Distant Lands, 62 S. Raymond Ave., 626/449-3220, is a specialty bookstore stocking a wide selection of books and videotapes about travel,

---

---

domestic and international, and an impressively well-informed proprietor.

A bit off the boulevard along Fair Oaks but well worth finding is **The Folk Tree,** 217 S. Fair Oaks Ave., 626/795-8733, a small shop filled with reasonably priced folk art, clothing, and religious artifacts from Mexico and Central America. To the rear is an excellent contemporary folk art gallery. Next door is **The Folk Tree Collection,** 199 S. Fair Oaks, 626/793-4828, with furnishings, folk art, clothing, textiles, beads, and slightly more expensive artifacts from around the globe.

Old Pasadena Antiquities

The largest one-stop antique shop is the **Pasadena Antique Center,** 480 S. Fair Oaks, 626/449-7706, with more than 130 vendors under one roof. Also worth exploring in the neighborhood: **Bruce Graney and Company,** in the Cal-Fair Plaza at 1 W. California Blvd., 626/449-9547, possibly the best dealer in town for 18th- and 19th-century English furnishings, with an emphasis on fine carved pine.

Many, many fine antique shops are scattered throughout Old Pasadena, including **Jay's Antiques,** 330 S. Fair Oaks, 626/792-0485, noted for mission-style furnishings, oriental rugs, and American Indian crafts, and the **Jack Moore-Nexus Gallery,** 1419 N. Lake Ave., 626/577-7746, featuring Arts and Crafts period furnishings and folk art.

For still more antique venues, see South Pasadena, below.

Shopping South Lake

Since the departure of The Gap and Banana Republic for hipper digs in Old Pasadena, the bankruptcy of the neighborhood's I. Magnin

BARGAIN SHOPPERS' BONANZA: RESALE GLAD RAGS

Fueled by consumer desires to save money on high-end, quality clothing, an increasingly popular trend in Pasadena's glad rags trade is resale or "gently worn" clothing shops for women, and, to a lesser degree, men and children. Well-to-do women who buy designer couture or upscale sportswear to attend various charity functions can't be seen in the same outfit too often, after all. Just plain folks can benefit from this social fact of life by buying top-quality but used clothing at a fraction of the original price.

Several resale boutiques in Old Pasadena, all within easy walking distance of each other, sell not just fancy ball gowns but casual clothing and accessories as well: **Clothes Heaven,** 110 E. Union, 626/440-0929; **Bailey's Designer Resale for Men,** 109 Union, Pasadena, 626/449-0201, and **Bailey's Backstreet for Women,** 93 E. Union, Pasadena, 626/449-4101; and **Silent Partners,** 99 E. Union, Pasadena, 626/793-6877.

former cachet, however, and are making headway. Anchoring the South Lake shopping district is a 250,000-square-foot Macy's and several smaller but well-known stores, including **Talbot's, Ann Taylor, Eddie Bauer, Smith & Hawken,** and the enormous **Borders Books and Music Store,** which took over the long vacant I. Magnin building.

At the south end of the district is the **Rose Tree Cottage,** 828 E. California Blvd. (at Lake), 626/793-3337, a Tudor-style bungalow court that has been converted into several shops. Stop for tea and scones and shop for English imports. Wander through other cottages to find antiques, herbal body treats, and needlepoint.

Next door is **Wild Oats Market,** 824 E. California Blvd. (at Lake), 626/792-1778, an excellent full-service natural/organic foods grocery store, including a juice bar, an oil bar, and deli. This squeaky-clean store also stocks an extensive selection of books, homeopathic herbs and vitamins, and natural beauty products. You can even get a massage here.

department store, and the arrival of Ross Dress for Less, Pasadena's upscale old-money South Lake shopping district has been suffering an identity crisis. Local merchants are fighting the good fight to win back their

PRACTICAL PASADENA

STAYING IN PASADENA

The Ritz-Carlton, Huntington Hotel

Pulling up to the Ritz-Carlton, Huntington Hotel is like arriving at the Huntington family's estate for the weekend, or so one can imagine. Touches of a 19th-century sensibility are everywhere, including fresh flowers, oriental carpets, and British hunt club–era artwork. The staid but plush guest rooms feature fine furnishings and overstuffed armchairs, large closets, refrigerated honor bars, and three telephones, with the modern distraction of television discreetly tucked away in the armoire. The all-marble bathrooms are similarly sedate yet up to date, with hair dryers and thick terrycloth robes.

Once arrived at the Huntington, you might be tempted never to leave. Aside from the Olympic-

size pool—the original and California's first—the hotel offers tennis courts, a fine fitness and exercise center, even spa and salon services. The hotel's restaurants are also enticing, from the formal signature restaurant, **The Georgian Room,** and men's-clubbish **The Grill,** to more relaxed **The Cafe and Terrace** (wonderful Sunday brunch). Especially popular with traditional Pasadenans is the **Lobby Lounge,** for afternoon tea.

With its convenient central Southern California location, just minutes by freeway to downtown L.A. or the San Fernando Valley film and TV studios, the Huntington does a brisk convention and "business" business—typically great news for pleasure travelers, since weekend packages and Christmas-season rates here can be a bargain. Another plus is the exceptional service. Stop at the concierge desk, for example, to

If you dream of putting on the ritz, the ritzy Ritz-Carlton, Huntington Hotel is the place to do it.

request the Ritz-Carlton's very helpful "how to get there" cards, which cover every imaginable southstate destination. For more information contact: **The Ritz-Carlton, Huntington Hotel,** 1401 S. Oak Knoll Ave., 626/568-3900. To make reservations, in the United States call toll-free 800/241-3333; www.ritzcarlton.com. Room rates: $310–410, suites $495–2,500.

The Doubletree Hotel–Pasadena

If the Ritz is just a bit too ritzy, try the 12-story **Doubletree Hotel** downtown at 191 N. Los Robles (at Walnut), 626/792-2727 or toll-free reservations 800/222-8733, www.doubletree.com, which is located in the heart of downtown Pasadena. Within walking distance of Old Pasadena, great restaurants, and downtown arts and entertainment, the Doubletree features 360 very attractive rooms and suites, airy and contemporary, complete with wood-shuttered windows. Also here: an on-site restaurant (a *feast* for Sunday brunch) plus heated pool, sauna and whirlpool, complete fitness center. Airport van service is provided. If you drive, valet parking is optional. To park yourself–and avoid the occasional traffic jam at the entrance–drive around the corner and cruise into the shared hotel/public parking lot (underground); once parked, find the

elevator that pops up in the hotel's lobby. As elsewhere, suites are substantially more expensive than rooms. Rates: $139 –179.

Other Downtown Hotels

Popular with conventioneers, of course, is the **Holiday Inn Pasadena Convention Center Hotel** downtown, 303 E. Cordova St., 626/449-4000 or toll-free for reservations 800/238-8000. It's two blocks south of Colorado via Marengo, adjacent to the Pasadena Convention Center and Civic Auditorium and across the street from the Plaza Pasadena shopping mall. The usual, plus pool and tennis courts. Rates: $79–139.

Nearby is the **Pasadena Hilton,** a high-rise near the Pasadena Convention Center at 150 S. Los Robles, 626/577-1000, www.hilton.com, also especially amenable for business travelers. For reservations at this and other Hilton hotels, call toll-free 800/445-8667 (AAA members, call 800/916-2221). Rates: $109 –139.

The Artists' Inn and Cottage

Near South Pasadena's Mission West antiques district, on Magnolia Street between Meridian and Fairview, The Artists' Inn is an 1895 Midwestern Victorian, once centerpiece of a poultry

ABOUT SMOG AND SUMMER WEATHER

The dazzling fresh air which drew early settlers, many of whom suffered respiratory ailments, is long gone. Given the lay of the land, otherwise welcome ocean breezes blow nearly all of L.A.'s smog east, smack dab into these foothills. The problem is particularly acute in summer. Trapped in the valley under a heat-induced inversion layer, the summer smog all but obliterates any view, even close up, of the neighboring San Gabriel Mountains. The simple act of opening one's eyes, not to mention breathing, can be mighty unpleasant during August, September, and sometimes October. Consider coming some other time.

farm. The place is now dressed in more artistic ambience, reminiscent of a visit to the Huntington or the Norton Simon Museum. Each room reflects either an artistic period or an artist's work—the soft colors of the "Impressionist," for example, the three-dimensional replication of "Van Gogh's Bedroom," and the works by Gainsborough, Reynolds, and Constable in "Eighteenth Century English." In addition to the four rooms in the main house, there are five suites in the cottage, most with fireplaces and hot tubs. All have private baths. Breakfast, everything homemade, is up to you—either full breakfast or something light. For more information and to make reservations, contact: The Artists' Inn, 1038 Magnolia St., 626/799-5668 or toll-free 888/799-5668; www.artistsinns.com. Rates: $110–205.

More Moderate Accommodations
Lower-priced accommodations are farther away from downtown—though keep in mind that all area room rates typically skyrocket around Jan. 1, when the Tournament of Roses is in full bloom.

Among better motel bets is the **Best Western Pasadena Royale,** 3600 E. Colorado Blvd. (two blocks west of Rosemead Blvd.), 626/793-0950, near Pasadena City College and just about as close to the Huntington Library, et al. as to downtown Pasadena. All rooms have cable TV, free movies, refrigerators; amenities include swimming pool, sauna, and whirlpool. Minisuites and

suites are also available. Rates: $65–129. Nearby is the **Best Western Pasadena Inn,** with similar amenities and rates, 3570 E. Colorado Blvd. (just west of Rosemead), 626/796-9100. Both offer free continental breakfast and free local calls. For reservations at either–or at the similarly priced **Best Western Colorado Inn** at 2156 E. Colorado Blvd., 626/793-9339–call toll-free 800/528-1234. And ask about special discounts. There's also a quite nice **Quality Inn** in the same general vicinity at 3321 E. Colorado (at Madre), 626/796-9291, with basic rooms from $69, deluxe rooms with hot tubs from $129.

For good family lodging elsewhere, try the **Pasadena Inn,** 400 S. Arroyo Pkwy. (near California), 626/795-8401, a clean 62-unit motel with reasonable rates and recently renovated. There's a pool here, plus a Thai seafood restaurant. Rates: $65–119.

EATING IN PASADENA

It's difficult to get a bad meal in Pasadena. The city boasts more than 250 restaurants, many of these concentrated in the Old Pasadena and Lake Avenue shopping districts. While Pasadena is not yet as trendy as West Hollywood or L.A.'s Westside, it's working on it. By the time you arrive, some newer restaurants may be long gone, like so many tumbleweeds tossed aside by the Santa Ana winds. Most eateries listed here have passed the test of time, but call first or otherwise scout out the scene to avoid disappointment.

Cheaper Eats: Lake Avenue and Vicinity
Tiny **Euro Pane Bakery,** 950 E. Colorado Blvd., 626/577-1828, is a beloved local bakery with just several tables—*the* place for scrumptious cinnamon rolls, scones, croissants, specialty breads, and some wicked desserts (like those lemon bars). For lunch, stop by for simple yet stylish sandwiches.

Brought to you by the Parkway Grill people (see below), the **Crocodile Café,** 140 S. Lake Ave. (near Green), 626/449-9900, is something of a "people's Spago." Low-rent foodies congregate here for salads, pastas, pizzas from wood-burning ovens, and oakwood-grilled seafood, chicken, and other entrées, all in a crazed California-casual atmosphere. (Snag a spot out on the much quieter patio if at all possible.) Pizzas and pastas are always good; the grilled chicken sandwich is excellent. Get here early, though, because it's always crowded (no reservations) and there's almost always a wait—maddening when you're weak from hunger and it all smells so *good*. Service can be uneven. Another Crocodile Café is in Old Pasadena, 626/568-9310. To wrestle other Crocodiles, head for Burbank or Santa Monica.

Burger Continental, 538 S. Lake Ave. (near California), 626/792-6634, is a zany hole-in-the-wall burger joint and student hangout, just the place for a bargain-basement meal after upscale shopping. Owner Harry Hindoyan has presided over this Pasadena institution for more than 30 years. The extensive menu features Armenian specialties like kebabs and rice pilaf and just about everything else you can imagine, including American standards; if you can't decide, Harry's happy to make suggestions.

Just off Lake Ave. is **Pie 'N Burger,** 913 E. California Blvd. (at Lake), 626/795-1123, another place socialites and Cal Tech students are destined to blend—as American as pecan pie, though the burgers, fries, and milkshakes are the aristocrats here.

Cheaper Eats: Old Pasadena and Vicinity
South Pasadena's Trader Joe's—the first and original—has closed, but in Pasadena proper you can still easily pull together an instant picnic or replenish the road food stash. **Trader Joe's,** 613 S. Arroyo Pkwy., 626/568-9254, is a bargain gourmet store designed to "cater to the over-educated and the underpaid," in the words of the successful chain's founder Joe Coulombe. If that category fits, seek and find cheese, nuts, coffees, fresh juices, baked goods, selected wines and beer, plus a host of all-natural quick foods and assorted oddball essentials.

A best bet for breakfast is the **Old Town Bakery & Deli,** 166 W. Colorado Blvd. (near S. Pasadena Ave.), 626/793-2993. If you consider breakfast a variation on dessert, here you can choose hazelnut meringue cake with caramel filling.

For astonishing Malaysian specialties, such as spicy sweet *sambal* shrimp, curried eggplant filets, *asam laksa* noodles, and *rojak,* travel to **Kuala Lumpur,** 69 W. Green (near Pasadena), 626/577-5175, a clean, well-lighted, unassuming place. Closed Mondays.

If you've seen it and done it in Northern California, you'll know what to expect at the **Gordon Biersch** brewpub, One Colorado (41 Hugus Alley), 626/449-0052. The upscale brew is the real draw, so most customers care less about the beer-hall fare, not bad at all—and not that expensive—if you stick to what's simplest. Well-selected appetizers or salad with soup of the day might get you out the door with some change to spare.

Near the Civic Center
A hot spot for Sunday brunch is indoor-outdoor **The Oaks on the Plaza** at the Doubletree Hotel, 191 N. Los Robles (at Walnut), 626/792-2727, where a shamelessly generous buffet spread—10 stations in all, offering French pastries and omelettes, prime rib and sushi—includes champagne.

For something a bit lighter, look for **California Pizza Kitchen** nearby, at 99 N. Robles (at Union), 626/585-9020, with trademark eclectic toppings. In between is a branch of **McCormick & Schmick's,** 111 N. Los Robles (at Union), 626/405-0064, specializing in seafood but most noteworthy for its painstaking interior design, paying homage to Pasadena's craftsman craftsmanship.

The people's choice for seafood, by the way, is family-run "always boneless" **Cameron's,** out toward Pasadena City College at 1978 E. Colorado Blvd. (at Berkeley), 626/793-3474. At a gawdawful early hour every day the proprietors set out for Long Beach/San Pedro, where they eyeball the day's catch before personally toting the best back to the Crown City. Fish doesn't get much fresher than that.

Fine and Fashionable
Always-packed **Mi Piace** is a chic New York–style café in Old Pasadena, 25 E. Colorado Blvd. (near Raymond), 626/795-3131, an Italian eatery as popular for its making-the-scene scene as its pizzas, pastas, fine pastries, and tiramisu. With Ol' Blue Eyes belting out some boisterous tunes, it's a good choice for late supper or after-theater dessert and cappuccino.

If you want something different, check out **Arirang,** an upscale authentic Korean barbecue in Old Pasadena, 114 W. Union (at Delacey), 626/577-8885, where patrons sizzle exotic variations on the themes of chicken, beef, and shrimp on the tabletop *hwaro.*

Looking for red meat in Pasadena? Try the **Arroyo Chop House,** 536 S. Arroyo Parkway, 626/577-7463, which serves thick slabs of USDA prime-cut Midwestern aged beef steaks, big martinis, and big cigars (the latter only on the patio). Chow down, too, on the best Texas-style chili—better than the legendary chili at L.A.'s legendary Chasen's ever was—and other steakhouse selections. Prices are high, but portions are generous.

Very Fine and Fashionable
In the let's-do-the-town department, for Pasadenans the **Parkway Grill** 510 S. Arroyo Pkwy. (at California), 626/795-1001, the best restaurant in town—very California. Even after a successful decade-long run, the Parkway still serves fresh, cutting-edge fare, beautifully presented. Sometimes called "Spago of the East" for its similar open-kitchen approach and specialty oak-grilled pizzas and applewood-smoked free-range chicken (from Sonoma, no less), the Parkway is actually better—easier to get into, for one thing, and less expensive to boot. Graceful wood, brick, and stained-glass decor and exceptional, friendly service make the best even better. Open for lunch and dinner daily (semiformal attire at dinner). Sunday brunch is quite the treat too. Excellent wine list. Reservations advisable.

The art-deco **Bistro 45** near the Pasadena Playhouse at 45 S. Mentor Ave., 626/795-2478, is one of the classiest kids in town, a Californian with a French accent. If dishes such as panroasted New Zealand elk with syrah-garlic sauce and pearl onion-apple compote or free-range veals with herbs, bacon, and sun-dried cherry sauce neither frighten nor offend you, this is the place.

Cornered in an unlikely minimall in a mostly residential district is **Derek's Bistro,** 181 E. Glenarm (at Marengo), 626/799-5252, where the menu changes frequently to include the freshest available ingredients. A fixed-price four-course dinner features appetizer, entrée, chef's selection of cheese and fruit, and dessert. One day's entrée selection might include Thai shrimp cakes on spicy Asian slaw with a savory caramel sauce, rack of lamb, venison in red pepper sauce, or superbly grilled fish. Cozy rooms, patio dining, and elegant service add appeal to this gem.

GETTING ORIENTED, GETTING AROUND

Getting More Information
The best all-around source for current information on what to see and do in and around Pasadena is the very helpful **Pasadena Convention and Visitors Bureau,** 171 S. Los Robles Ave., Pasadena, 626/795-9311; www.pasadenavisitor.org. For pamphlets, guides, and other information related to local architecture and historic preservation efforts, contact **Pasadena Heritage,** 80 W. Dayton St., 626/793-0617; www.pasadenaheritage.org. Pasadena Heritage also sponsors a variety of walking tours and intriguing special events throughout the year.

The *Pasadena Star-News,* www.pasadenastarnews.com, is the city's paper of record, with its free weekly "Cheers" entertainment section available throughout Old Pasadena. The free *Pasadena Weekly,* www.pasadenaweekly.com, also provides arts, entertainment, and restaurant listings.

Getting Here by Freeway
Freeways converge on Pasadena. The main drag coming from the east or west is the **Foothill Freeway** (I-210), with exits gracefully dumping people right downtown. Coming in from the San Fernando Valley is the **Ventura Freeway** (Hwy. 134). The **Pasadena Freeway** ("the 110") rolls up out of Los Angeles and into South Pasadena via the somewhat narrow Arroyo Seco roadway. Yet another local piece of history and California's first freeway, the Pasadena was originally known as the Arroyo Seco Parkway and completed in 1941.

A major local battle for several generations has been the attempt to stop CalTrans from extending the **Long Beach Freeway** (I-710) through South Pasadena to connect the Foothill and San Bernardino Freeways—an "improvement" that will doom about 1,000 historic homes and cut into South Pasadena once again. Cities such as Sierra Madre want the link-up to improve foothill traffic flow; South Pasadenans and most Pasadenans, naturally enough, think one freeway dissection per community is more than enough. Even if locals manage to beat the freeway-building bureaucracy over this one—and they have managed to so far, for well over 40 years, partially because of the fact that South Pasadena is home to so many lawyers—Cal-Trans long ago acquired the project right-of-way, alas, so most of the buildings standing in the way of progress have been all but destroyed by intentional neglect.

Getting Here Other than by Car

Just 20 minutes away from downtown Pasadena is the **Burbank/Glendale/Pasadena Airport,** served by commuter lines at least from most major West Coast carriers, and it's a much more attractive alternative, budget-wise, to LAX now that it's served by Southwest Airlines. Though major hotels and some motels provide free shuttle service to and from the airport, **SuperShuttle,** 310/782-6600, serves this and all other major southstate airports. **Airport Bus,** 714/938-8900 or toll-free 800/772-5299, offers nonstop service from LAX and John Wayne Airport to Pasadena hotels, but not the Burbank airport. If your travel plans are complicated, **Prime Time Shuttle,** toll-free 800/262-7433,

connects Pasadena to the local airport and LAX, with connections also to cruise ships and Amtrak. Approximate fares to Pasadena airports are $16 from hotels, $25 from residences (or $20 for AAA members).

Glendale, about seven miles from Pasadena, has **Amtrak** service, with two trains daily. For ticket information and reservations, call Amtrak toll-free at 800/872-7245 or try www.amtrak .com. Though everyone will wait until at least 2010 for the **Blue Line** Metrorail commuter train to open its Pasadena line, major-league mass transit is coming.

To come and go by bus, the **Greyhound** station is downtown at 645 E. Walnut St., 626/792-5116.

Rent cars at **Avis,** 570 N. Lake Ave., 626/449-6122. Of the two local **Budget** car rental agencies, 626/449-0226 or toll-free 800/527-0700, the 750 S. Arroyo Pkwy. office is closest to downtown.

Getting Around: Public Transit

The **MTA** bus system, which services Pasadena, has headquarters at 1 Gateway Plaza, Los Angeles; call 213/626-4455 or toll-free 800/266-6883, or try www.mta.net, for current route and fare information. In addition, Old Pasadena and the South Lake shopping district are linked by the visitor-friendly Pasadena ARTS Bus shuttle system.

NEAR PASADENA

Due north, bordering Pasadena, is **Altadena,** most noted for its dramatic **Christmas Tree Lane**—Santa Rosa Avenue, between Woodbury Road and Altadena Drive—with impressive deodar cedars lit up to the heavens during the holiday season. The popularity of "making the tour" during the holidays, a tradition since 1920, led to the lane's status as a state historical landmark, this one recognizing the unique social convergence of botany, electric lights, and automobiles.

Another Altadena attraction is the "members-only" storefront **International Banana Museum,** 2524 N. El Molino Ave., 626/798-2272, www .bananaclub.com, an astonishing collection of bananamania—banana golf putters, banana umbrellas, banana toothpaste, and banana yo-yos. Lifetime membership in the Banana Club is $15. The museum is open only by appointment.

West of Altadena is **La Cañada Flintridge,** most famous for its Descanso Gardens. From here, turn onto Highway 2 to wind up into the San Gabriel Mountains and Angeles National Forest.

Downtown **Sierra Madre,** east of Altadena, will seem familiar to science-fiction film fanatics, since the tiny triangular town center here was the central "pod" distribution point in the original 1956 *Invasion of the Body Snatchers.* Whether that movie was actually a metaphorical warning against the anti-Communist McCarthy-era mindset then inflicted upon Hollywood's artistic community is still a matter of some debate— but well worth debating.

Farther east are suburbs and shopping malls created largely by L.A.'s burgeoning middle-class car culture, including **Arcadia,** home of the Arboretum of Los Angeles County, the one-time estate of eccentric Elias J. "Lucky" Baldwin, and the Santa Anita Park horse racing complex (detailed information below).

Follow Foothill Boulevard east from here and you're on historic **Route 66**—not a very inspiring trip, really, given the roadside poverty en route, until you encounter near-deserted old desert towns.

Immediately south of Pasadena proper are

the area's most exclusive zip codes, the small cities of **South Pasadena** and **San Marino.** Though neither resembles a tourist town, both have their attractions—the most noteworthy being The Huntington Library, Art Collections, and Botanical Gardens in San Marino. Anyone exploring the Huntington's cultural vision, however, needs to sample the bohemian Arroyo Seco philosophy. Fortunately, the opportunity is quite close. Just a few miles away, back toward Los Angeles via the Pasadena Freeway, is the downslope crown of Pasadena's arroyo-culture creation. The all-but-forgotten El Alisal, the craggy craftsman-style home of eccentric early Pasadena resident Charles Lummis, serves as headquarters for the Los Angeles County Historical Society. The Southwest Museum, founded by Lummis, is just up the hill. Aside from some good, very cheap Mexican restaurants, also in the neighborhood is Heritage Square, where the Los Angeles Cultural Heritage Board continues its desperate attempt to save at least some classic California buildings from a head-on collision with progress—in this case, by collecting them from elsewhere and installing them here in an architectural zoo.

For more information on these and other sights near Pasadena, read on.

SOUTH PASADENA

South Pasadena is *very* Pasadena, but separate, a tightly knit small town with fine homes, wide and well-shaded streets, and one of the best public school systems in Southern California. South Pasadena is also a favored setting for the film industry, often a stand-in for Midwestern suburbs. No wonder it's one of the region's most desirable residential neighborhoods, even on TV and in the movies. The Spielberg-produced *Little Giants* was filmed here, for example, along with *thirtysomething* and countless other TV shows and made-for-TV movies.

Not being a typical tourist destination makes South Pasadena that much more appealing for exploration. The **Rialto Theater,** 1023 Fair Oaks,

626/799-9567, is one of the few cavernous old movie theaters not yet ruined by modern subdivision into miniplexdom. Stop in to see first-run art films as they were meant to be seen, on a *big* screen. All very appealing to the casual but well-to-do artistic community that lives in the area. **Mission West,** which takes in the 900- and 1000-numbered blocks along Mission Street, is an unusually appealing historic shopping district featuring antique and specialty stores, an art gallery, and beloved **Buster's Ice Cream & Coffee Stop,** 1006 Mission (at Meridian), 626/441-0744.

Eating and Drinking in South Pasadena
South Pasadena's most popular fast foodery is **Señor Fish,** 618 Mission Rd. (at Orange Grove), 626/403-0145, where cheap and tasty fish tacos and wonderful ceviche tostadas top the "catch of the day" list.

Popular for other reasons is **Bristol Farms,** 606 S. Fair Oaks (just off the 110 Freeway), 626/441-5450, the best gourmet food market in Southern California. Here you'll find an in-house butcher shop, sushi chef, bakery, and deli. The produce department includes specialty items you won't find anywhere else. Bristol Farms' reasonably priced ready-made gourmet dinners are a hit with busy working families. Next door is the Bristol Farms **Cook 'n' Things,** a cookware store overflowing with fine linens, flatware, kitchen gadgets, and gift items.

Serving French/Japanese cuisine, **Shiro,** 1505 Mission St. (near Fair Oaks), 626/799-4774, is one of the best restaurants in Southern California, a quirky 1950s' place where the food is allowed to be the main attraction. Chef Hideo Yamashiro's changing menu is the foodies' holy grail, so make reservations at least one week in advance. Most diners opt for the delectable catfish, which is garlanded with cilantro and served in a light Ponzu sauce.

SAN MARINO AND "THE HUNTINGTON"

San Marino is an exceptionally high-rent residential area hacked from the holdings of famed local robber baron—ahem, railroad and real estate baron—Henry E. Huntington in the 1920s and 1930s. San Marino is so exclusive that it lives by its own lights. People here, for example, take a dim view of reckless behavior such as allowing motorists to make right turns after stopping at red lights downtown—otherwise legal in California. So in San Marino it's against the law; you'll get a ticket if you're caught. San Marino has also outlawed all bars.

Understated opulence, at least the appearance of California-style "old money," is the community's keynote. To observe still more staid, serene, wealthy Californians—their homes, at least—explore the neighborhoods surrounding what remains of the original Huntington Estate. Cruising well-lit **St. Albans Road** during the somewhat ostentatious Christmas season is almost the ultimate in reverse slumming.

For ladies who lunch, of particular note in San Marino is **Julienne,** 2649 Mission St. (at Los Robles), 626/441-2299, a favorite of Julia Child whenever she's in town. It's also a real gem for breakfast. Or, at the adjacent takeout store, pick up everything a food lover could want for a seat-of-the-pants picnic. The Huntington doesn't permit picnics, alas; the best picnicking place close by is **Lacy Park,** 1485 Virginia Rd, $3 entrance fee for nonresidents. Call city hall for information and reservations at 626/300-0700.

The Huntingtons Create a Legacy
Henry Huntington kept marriage, as well as money, within the family. He first married the sister of his uncle's adopted daughter; after a divorce, he married his Aunt Arabella.

The mysterious past of imperious Arabella included at least two illicit liaisons—the second with Collis Huntington, who eventually married her—and a son born out of wedlock. But there was little hint of scandal during her lifetime. By 1900, when her husband died, Arabella Duval Huntington was one of the richest women in the world. Her greatest pleasure was spending money—particularly on international art.

Though Henry loved the San Marino Ranch he bought in 1903 just south of genteel Pasadena, his Aunt Arabella preferred the social whirl of Paris. (Rumor had it that after their marriage, Arabella extracted two weeks in Paris for every week she spent in California.) To lure her to the

RAILROAD AND REAL ESTATE SPECULATION: THE HUNTINGTON FORTUNE

Nephew of Collis P. Huntington—he, president of the Southern Pacific Railroad and one of the "Big Four" credited with linking California to the rest of the nation by rail—Henry Edwards Huntington failed, upon his uncle's death in 1900, in his bid to become chief engineer of the family's railroad empire. But the younger Huntington soon made his own fortune by linking Los Angeles-area mass transit with real estate speculation, a career move capitalized by the sale of his Southern Pacific stock.

Starting with the failed remnants of the Los Angeles and Pasadena Railroad electric trolley system, Huntington's new **Pacific Electric Company** got its big red trolleys rolling in 1901. By 1910, when Huntington stepped down as the company's chief engineer and, ironically, Southern Pacific took over, the Pacific Electric had successfully connected down-town Los Angeles to more than 50 far-flung communities throughout Southern California, the first step toward suburbanization—a development that tripled the region's population. Huntington also succeeded in making an obscene profit, since he typically ran new trolley lines only into areas owned by his real estate partnerships. (One fellow land speculator was Harrison Gray Otis, then-publisher of the *Los Angeles Times*. It was really no surprise, then, to see trolley-related home developments praised in the pages of the *Times*.)

Henry Huntington inherited about $40 million upon his uncle's death in 1900 and earned another $30 million through his own railroad and real estate deals. When in 1913 he married his uncle's widow and only other heir, Arabella, he further compounded his fortune—though some would argue that she had compounded hers.

Southern California wilderness, according to historian Kevin Starr, "Henry Huntington set out to transform his estate into a utopia of high culture." The Huntington Library, Art Collections, and Botanical Gardens stand as the legacy of that endeavor.

The Huntington Library

One of the world's great research libraries, the Huntington emphasizes British and American history, literature, and art from the 11th century to modern times. Collected here are about 3.1 million manuscripts, 357,000 rare books, 321,000 reference volumes, and thousands of prints, photographs, and miscellany.

Inside the **Library Exhibition Hall,** open to the general public, are some of the Huntington's treasures, including John James Audubon's *The Birds of America,* an exceptional collection of early editions of Shakespeare, a Gutenberg Bible (circa 1450–55), and the illuminated Ellesmere manuscript of Chaucer's *The Canterbury Tales* (circa 1410). Popular favorites include letters and works from early American leaders such as Benjamin Franklin, Thomas Jefferson, George Washington, and Abraham Lincoln, along with first editions and manuscripts of Thoreau, Twain, Blake, Shelley, Wordsworth, and other literary lights. In addition to the permanent display, several changing exhibits from the collection are presented every year.

Technically part of the Huntington's impressive art array, the four galleries of the **Arabella D. Huntington Memorial Collection** are housed in the library's west wing—with Renaissance paintings and 18th-century French sculpture, tapestries, furniture, and sundry accessories of the era's cultured life.

Huntington Art Collection: Huntington Gallery

Housed in the baronial beaux-arts residence designed for the family in 1910 by Myron Hunt and Elmer Grey, the Huntington Gallery is dedicated largely to 18th- and early 19th-century British art. The collection's most famous paintings are in the Main Gallery: the 1770 *Blue Boy,* by William Gainsborough, and, facing, the 1794 *Pinkie,* a portrait of young Sarah Barrett Moulton by Thomas Lawrence. (Pinkie died of tuberculosis within months of the portrait's completion; her brother, who owned the painting, grew up to become Elizabeth Barrett Browning's father.) Beyond the abundant displays of historic portraiture there is much more to see, including the exquisite 1782 bronze sculpture *Diana* by Jean-Antoine Houdon and Wedgwood ceramics.

Changing exhibits in the Huntington Gallery typically feature a thematic twist on more obscure treasures, be they Rembrandt etchings or the wild, wild visions of William Blake.

Huntington Art Collection: Scott Gallery

If more fascinated by American adventures in arts and crafts, allocate extra time for the Virginia Steele Scott Gallery of American Art north of the Huntington Gallery (just beyond the Shakespeare garden). Most of the painting collection spans the two centuries from the 1730s. Gilbert Stuart's *George Washington* is surely the most familiar face in the Portrait Gallery. Don't miss the stunning *Breakfast in Bed* by Philadelphia-born Mary Cassatt, in the Nineteenth-Century Gallery, and, in the Twentieth-Century Gallery, *Reflections* by Frank Benson, along with Walt Kuhn's *The Top Man.* The Main Gallery offers a brief historical overview of American art.

A fairly recent addition—well worth your time—is the impressive exhibit honoring Pasadena's part in the turn-of-the-century revolution in home design and woodworking craftsmanship, particularly the contributions of architects Charles and Henry Greene (discussed in depth in this chapter's introductory section).

Included here are a meticulous re-creation of the Henry M. Robinson House dining room, with its astounding adjustable-height stained-glass chandelier, all-original furnishings, and reassembled stairway from the Arthur A. Libbey House. The exhibit's Main Gallery demonstrates the evolution of the Greenes' design genius, starting with Mission Oak styles, continuing into ash, Port Orford cedar and Honduras mahogany crafted with increasingly Chinese sensibilities, and culminating in masterworks of very rare hand-rubbed oil-finished woods with exquisite joinery and inlays. Also included here: art-glass and leaded-glass light fixtures, tables, chairs, rugs, hardware, picture frames, even garden pottery, along with samples of the brothers' later independent designs.

The **Greene & Greene Center for the Study of the Arts and Crafts Movement in America,** in the Dorothy Collins Brown wing of the Steele Gallery, includes both the exhibit and the Greene & Greene Library, originally established by the Gamble House and University of Southern California in 1968. The library is open by appointment only; for information call 626/405-2225.

The Huntington Botanical Gardens

The impression is that of a public park, with people wandering throughout these 120 landscaped acres in aimless but thorough appreciation. Though the expansive, eclectic gardens are themed—Australian, Japanese, jungle, subtropical, palm, rose, camellia—the overall idea is still the acquisitiveness of empire-building, since Henry Huntington was first and foremost a pragmatist. Most of the 14,000 species collected here, including the Chilean wine palm, represent plant families Huntington believed would further boost Southern California real estate and agricultural development. Since Huntington's day, however, the emphasis has changed. International species preservation—protecting endangered plants from Madagascar, for example—is now a high priority.

Visitor favorites include the Rose Garden, with 1,800–2,000 species, the meditative Japanese and Zen Gardens, and the spectacularly exotic Desert Garden—the largest outdoor grouping of mature cacti and succulents in the United States, about 4,000 species—that does not resemble any desert landscape.

The Huntington Bookstore

Though the fourth central aspect of the Huntington is actually its international research program, most visitors will be more attracted to the bookstore in the entrance pavilion. The Huntington is Southern California's oldest book publisher; the scholarly list is available here. Also for sale—proceeds help finance the Huntington and its programs—are general-interest books, guides, cards and postcards, and high-quality reproductions.

Huntington Practicalities

Admission to the Huntington is free, by decree of Henry E. Huntington himself. Since the Huntington needs to generate substantial private funding to keep the institution up and running, however, a "voluntary donation" of $8.50 for adults, $7 seniors, and $5 for children and students is suggested (children under 12 admitted free).

The Huntington, 1151 Oxford Road (between Orlando and Euston) in San Marino, is open Tues.–Fri. noon–4:30 P.M. and 10:30 A.M.–4:30 P.M. on weekends. In the summer months of June through August, hours are 10:30 A.M.–4:30 P.M. Tues.–Sun. The museum is closed Mondays and major holidays. For current information, call 626/405-2141 or check www.huntington.org; to arrange a school group tour, call 626/405-2127.

Videotaping and informal still photography are permitted throughout, but tripods and flash bulbs/flash attachments are not allowed inside the buildings.

With the exception of the Japanese Garden—where, incidentally, the famous "red bridge" is no longer red—all gardens and buildings are wheelchair-accessible. Docent-guided garden tours are offered daily at 1 P.M., and at other times as posted. To arrange a guided group tour of the gardens during nonpublic hours, call 626/405-2127. An introductory slide program runs continuously; self-guided tour pamphlets (small fee) are also helpful.

A surprising array of lectures and performances are scheduled year-round, free to the public. Special activities—moonlight hikes, birdwatching, and plant sales, luncheons, dinners, tours, and special screenings of movies filmed at the Huntington—are available only for members. For information on joining, call 626/405-2290.

Picnics are not permitted on the grounds, but food and refreshments are available at the **Rose Garden Cafe and Tea Room.** The café menu is contemporary and imaginative, with offerings such as tequila lime fajitas with black beans and corn, but also includes kid-friendly fare—all quite good and fairly reasonable. As is traditional at the Huntington, afternoon tea in the adjacent Tea Room (once Huntington's private bowling alley) is quite nice. Reservations are advised; call 626/683-8131.

HIGHLAND PARK: EL ALISAL ET ALIA

To fully appreciate the contrast between the aristocratic and democratic visions of the Golden State's golden age, if you tour the Huntington you also must visit Arroyo Seco. Visitable remnants of Pasadena's arroyo-culture roots are cultivated in Highland Park, an aging dream garden made that much more romantic by the surrounding area's poverty. Latino gang turf in recent years, Highland Park near the following attractions is typically safe for tourists during daylight.

In contrast to the Huntingtons' approach—the acquisition of European and East Coast perspective and style—arroyo culture found beauty in its own backyard, truth in transformative life lived at the edge of the vanishing western wilderness. In and around Pasadena's Arroyo Seco, a nativistic variant of the Arts and Crafts philosophy took root and flourished—the genesis of the Greene brothers' architectural creations for local gentry.

But arroyo culture did not concern itself with traditional notions of the genteel. Gentility, here, was a work in progress—"the spiritualization of daily life through an aestheticism tied to crafts and local materials," in the words of historian Kevin Starr, and "of pure, simple, democratic art," according to transplanted English preacher George Wharton James.

Arroyo Seco's aesthetic was most strikingly rendered in untamed, distinctly Southern California-style craftsmanship in woodworking, metallurgy, and stone masonry, tile, pottery, and jewelry making. The Arroyo Seco's hands-on idealism was such a powerful philosophical influence in turn-of-the-20th-century California that both the local Throop Polytechnic Institute (forerunner of the much more theory-based California Institute of Technology) and Stanford University near San Francisco included crafts instruction as curriculum basics.

Bookishness, though, was more important, literature being the Arroyo Seco's most democratic art. Literary lights published by Charles Fletcher Lummis in his *Land of Sunshine* magazine included Jack London, Frank Norris, Robinson Jeffers, and Mary Austin—all of whom had moved on by the time Lummis died of a brain tumor here in 1929, clutching the page proofs of *Flowers of Our Lost Romance,* his "best of" collection of essays.

El Alisal

Sliding downslope toward L.A. via the Pasadena Freeway, your first Arroyo Seco stop along the ravine's lower reaches is El Alisal, striking arroyo-stone home of Charles Fletcher Lummis. Described by Kevin Starr as the Arroyo Seco's "prophet of place," the Harvard-educated writer and editor Lummis branched out to embrace a self-consciously Southwestern sense of style, with Native American basketry and blankets as necessary accessories. Both blatant booster and provincial protector of the Southern California good life, Lummis landscaped fortresslike El Alisal with palms, succulents, and other desert plant life. Also here: original and period furnishings, historical displays, photographs, publications. Note the fireplace, designed by Mount Rushmore sculptor Gutzon Borglum.

Since the building also serves as headquarters of the **Historical Society of Southern California,** Lummis House docents are quite helpful, as are the books, periodicals, and pamphlets available here. El Alisal, 200 E. Ave. 43 (at Carlota Blvd.), 323/222-0546, is open only Fri.– Sun. noon–4 P.M. Free, though donations are greatly appreciated. Group tours are scheduled on Friday, by reservation only. To get here, from the Pasadena (110) Freeway exit at Ave. 43, head east, and turn onto Carlota. Off-street parking is available near the entrance.

The Southwest Museum

Halfway up Mt. Washington, whose upper reaches are still home to a community of writers and artists, is another of Charles Fletcher Lummis's pet projects—the striking mission revival-style Southwest Museum. Opened in 1914, the Southwest is Southern California's finest collection of Native Americana, with art and artifacts presented in galleries on California, the Southwest, the Pacific Northwest, the Great Plains, and Northern Mexico. Though many aspects of the museum are renowned nationally and internationally, the Southwest's California basketry collection is particularly astonishing —the more so now that this art is all but lost. Proceeds from the gift shop help support the museum, its programs, and the maintenance of its treasures.

The Southwest Museum is just up the hill from El Alisal at 234 Museum Drive, 323/221-2164, open Tues.–Sun. 10 A.M.–5 P.M. (closed on major holidays). Admission is $5 adults, $3 seniors and students, $2 children ages 7–17 (under 7 free).

Casa de Adobe, operated under Southwest's auspices in Sycamore Grove Park, 4605 N. Figueroa Street, 323/225-8653, was designed by Theodore Eisen and built in 1917, Eisen's imaginative representation of a Mexican-era rancho. At press time the museum was closed for seismic retrofitting—call for current hours.

If so much southwestern exposure makes you hungry for a Mexican meal, been-there-forever **La Abeja** near the museum at 3700 Figueroa, 323/221-0474, serves the real thing, real cheap.

Heritage Square

If you do save historic structures from the wrecking ball of progress in Los Angeles, then the buildings have to go *somewhere.* One of those places is here in Heritage Square, just across the freeway from El Alisal et al. at 3800 Homer St. (off Avenue 43), where vanishing architectural species from the years 1865–1914 are penned up inside chain-link fencing. Most instantly impressive is the 1885 **Hale House,** with its wildly authentic color schemes. To get an idea of the ingenuity and determination it takes to move a building across the Los Angeles basin, study the **Palms Depot** photo documentary. Heritage Square is open to the public 11:30 A.M.–4:30 P.M. on Saturday, Sunday, and most holidays, with tours typically offered every 45 minutes. Park inside the chain-link fence. Admission is $5 adults, $3 seniors and children 13–17, $2 children 7–12. But kick in more, if you can, because the Cultural Heritage Foundation of Southern California, Inc., 626/449-0193, can use all the help it can get.

DESCANSO GARDENS

To Pasadena's northwest, on the way to Glendale and the film industry's true home in the San Fernando Valley, is La Cañada Flintridge and 165-acre Descanso Gardens, onetime Rancho del Descanso ("Ranch of Rest")—the estate of *Los Angeles Daily News* owner and publisher E. Manchester Boddy.

Most famous here are the camellias, more than 100,000 plants representing about 600 species—the largest cultivated collection in the world. After building his 22-room Georgian colonial home in the oak forest here, Boddy was dismayed to discover that not much would grow on the grounds because of the soil's high acidity. Consultations with horticulturist J. Howard Asper convinced Boddy to try growing camellias, which thrived under similar conditions in eastern Asia's mountain valleys. The rest, as they say, is history. To fully appreciate the camellia bloom, plan to come from January into March.

New is Descanso's five-acre International Rosarium, with 5,000–7,000 rose species and varieties arranged by "theme," these including the fascinating historic rose specimens of the California Mission Garden and the interplanted wonders of the White Garden. These displays are most impressive in spring and summer. Descanso Gardens also features a bird observation station, built in conjunction with the Audubon Society.

Descanso Gardens is just south of Foothill Blvd. at 1418 Descanso Dr., 818/952-4400, www.descanso.com, open daily (except Christmas) 9 A.M.–5 P.M. Admission is $5 adults, $3 seniors and students, $1 for children ages 5–12 (under 5 free). Call for current information on guided tram tours ($2).

MISSION SAN GABRIEL

Just south of San Marino is the city of San Gabriel, site of Mission San Gabriel Arcángel, Spain's earliest outpost in the valley. Devastatingly damaged in the 1987 Whittier Narrows earthquake, the church was forced to close for the first time since construction in the 1790s. Delicately carved beams and entire sections of adobe parted company; the landmark bell tower cracked. After extensive reconstruction, including restoration of the painted ceiling, Mission San Gabriel reopened in September 1993—just in time for another shakedown, the 1994 Northridge quake. This time only the museum and the old adobe rectory were affected. The museum has reopened in a long, narrow 1804 adobe addition and features Franciscan artifacts, early California furnishings, and the most extensive and important collection of paintings of all the missions (many of these also restored). Elsewhere, explore the requisite mission kitchen

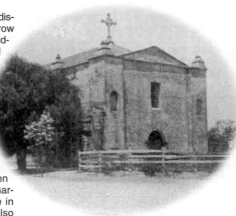

Mission San Gabriel Arcángel, built in the 1790s, has suffered two earthquakes in recent years.

circa the early 1800s, other implements of early California industry, and the mission itself.

Mission San Gabriel Arcángel, 537 W. Mission Dr. in San Gabriel, 626/457-3035, is open daily 9 A.M.–4:30 P.M. Admission is $4 adults, $1 children ages 6–12.

THE ARBORETUM OF LOS ANGELES COUNTY

The Arboretum of Los Angeles County is the 127-acre remnant of Elias J. "Lucky" Baldwin's original 46,000 acres, bought in 1875, which soon became "Arcadia," a speculative real estate venture that rivaled any of land barons Henry Huntington and Harry Chandler. Chandler, in fact, bought and developed Baldwin's estate in 1936, minus this parcel.

Though the smog here is sometimes so thick one wonders how any plants survive, they do— and most of the 4,000 species represented seem to thrive. Historic on-site buildings include the 1840 Hugo Reid Adobe and the old Santa Anita Depot, a transportation boon that made millions for Lucky Baldwin. Baldwin's personal flamboyance lives on, too, in this patch of Arcadia, most notably in the fine frilly white Queen Anne "cottage" and outbuildings designed by architect A.

A. Bennett, more famous for the state Capitol in Sacramento and Riverside's Mission Inn.

The Arboretum of Los Angeles County is just off the Foothill Freeway (I-210) in Arcadia, at 301 N. Baldwin Avenue. Admission is $5 adults, $1 children ages 5–12 (under 5 free). Tram service is $2 per person until 3 P.M. For information on current hours and upcoming special events, call 626/821-3222; www.arboretum.org.

SANTA ANITA PARK

Horse ranching was once big business in these parts, so stumbling upon the illustrious Santa Anita racetrack out in the suburbs really isn't so strange. The original track, near here, was built by Lucky Baldwin in 1907, but Santa Anita as a public event got its start in 1934 as the vision of onetime minor league second baseman and credit dentist Charles H. "Doc" Strub. Snubbed by San Francisco, Strub sent his dream south. He gained the support of movie producer Hal Roach and, at a time when a loaf of bread cost a nickel, Strub spent the shocking sum of $1 million to build the grandest horse-racing palace of them all. He stunned the racing world again by announcing Santa Anita's first-day $100,000 handicap. From the start, Santa Anita attracted the best horses and riders, along with socialites, movie stars, and Depression-fatigued families, transforming the grifter's game into something respectable.

Santa Anita is still quite the scene, despite endless competition for Southern California's attention. The elite meet and greet in the private Turf Club upstairs. Best bet for just plain folks to fully appreciate horse racing's star qualities is near the valet parking booth, listening to the announcer rattle off the names of the rich and famous as their limos jockey for position. But even from the cheap seats, you'll get a full-on view of the astonishing shadow-sculpted Sierra Madre just beyond the track.

Thoroughbred horse racing is a year-round event in California, the season at each track dictated both by climate and tradition. The race crowd is typically "back to the track" at Santa Anita by Christmas, and the season runs through April. The Oak Tree Racing Association also sponsors a monthlong meet from early October into November. Admission is $4 (free for children under 17), parking $3. Post time is usually 12:30 or 1 P.M.

If at all possible, do take a "backstage" tour, offered on weekends during the racing season starting at 8 A.M. and leaving every 20 minutes until 9:30 A.M.—it's a rare chance to explore and peek into the complicated community of 2,000 horses and the owners, trainers, jockeys, grooms, stable hands, hot walkers, and horsey hangers-on who populate this secretive stable city. (Tours are offered only during racing season, and cancelled if it's raining.) You can attend morning track workouts for free.

Santa Anita Park is just off the Foothill Freeway (I-210) between Baldwin Ave. and Colorado Place (off Colorado St.); the entrance is at 285 W. Huntington Dr. at Colorado, in Arcadia. For more information, call the affiliated **Los Angeles Turf Club** at 626/574-7223; www.santaanita.com.

ELSEWHERE IN THE SAN GABRIEL VALLEY

North, east, and south of the Los Angeles suburb of Pasadena are Pasadena's own suburbs. A riverbed runs through it all, the seasonal San Gabriel River. Once rural and agricultural, during and after World War II the valley industrialized, to a large degree in service to the Pentagon. Social trauma arrived along with the impending end of the region's economic dependence on defense-related work. In many ways the once-stolid San Gabriel Valley has become a transition zone—for inner-city residents and immigrants moving up the socioeconomic ladder and for the once well-employed moving down.

Monrovia is most noted for its historic downtown district, **Duarte** for its **City of Hope** hospital. The wealthy residential areas of **Bradbury** are in stark contrast to industrial **Azusa**—the name purported to be an acronym for "A to Z in the U.S.A."—which has earned the dubious distinction of having California's highest per capita murder rate. **San Dimas**, almost classic 1950s' suburbia, is home to a **Raging Waters** amusement park.

The area's real gem is **Claremont**, home to the noted private **Claremont Colleges**, just off

Foothill Boulevard (the old Route 66) near the Riverside County line. The six colleges in Claremont—**Pomona, Harvey Mudd, Scripps, McKenna, Pitzer,** and the **Claremont Graduate University**—share some facilities but otherwise possess very distinct identities. Scripps, for example, is one of the few all-women's colleges in the West; Harvey Mudd is a highly respected science and engineering school.

If you've got time, explore the colleges and the community. Wandering the campus and the adjacent **Village,** a downtown shopping district where the street names memorialize the nation's finest East Coast universities—Harvard, Yale, Dartmouth—is an unexpected pleasure.

South of Claremont is **Pomona,** where the Foothill Freeway and the San Bernardino, Orange, and Corona Freeways converge. Once a major citrus-producing region—despite the "apple" identification suggested by the name—Pomona today is best known as home to one of California's polytechnic universities, **Cal Poly Pomona.**

INTO THE MOUNTAINS: ANGELES NATIONAL FOREST

Where the Glendale Freeway ends in La Cañada Flintridge is where the **Angeles Crest Highway** (Hwy. 2) begins, snaking its way into Angeles National Forest up a busy residential boulevard, then up through scrubby foothills, and finally up into pines, firs, and brisk, truly blue skies.

If you drive strictly to get somewhere, after about 50 miles you'll end up in **Wrightwood,** a cabin-clustered resort area on the other side of the mountains. If you're heading into the woods for a respite, bring lunch and/or camping gear. Picnic areas and first-come, first-served public campgrounds abound, albeit packed in summer. (On peak weekends, when the forest is literally overwhelmed by families fleeing city heat, officials block key roadways at 11 A.M. or earlier to avoid absolute gridlock.) About 28 miles from La Cañada Flintridge is the **Chilao Visi-**

tor Center, 626/796-5541, open daily, a worthwhile stop to gather both information and environmental insight.

Avoid the crowds and come in later fall, winter, or early spring, when the air is cleaner and the dry hills exchange their warm-weather straw for a green coat capped by snow. In many areas of Angeles National Forest hiking and backpacking are best in late winter and early spring, a time when the Sierra Nevada and other major West Coast mountain ranges are still snowed in. But if you're looking for snow play in winter, you'll find it here—if you can find a place to park —along with nearly everyone else in Southern California. Small, family-friendly ski areas are here: **Mount Waterman, Kratka Ridge,** with its quaint single-seat chairlift to reach more challenging runs, and **Ski Sunrise,** with its spectacular desert views.

Road conditions permitting, essential is the five-mile detour to the **Mount Wilson Observatory,** 626/440-1136, owned by the Carnegie Institution of Washington. The observatory was established here in 1904, and by 1917 became the center of the world's astronomical universe with the help of both a 60-inch and 100-inch telescope and galaxies of great scientists. Since World War II after-dark Los Angeles has become one gigantic night-light, so Mount Wilson's view of the heavens has dimmed somewhat. Important astrophysical research continues, however, solar astronomy in particular. The museum is open weekends from 10 A.M.–4 P.M., free admission. Tours are available weekends at 1 P.M. There are no restaurants at the observatory, so you might want to pack a picnic lunch.

For more information on the area, including locations of ranger stations and district offices, campgrounds, picnic areas, hiking trails, and other forest attractions, contact: **Angeles National Forest Headquarters,** 701 N. Santa Anita Ave., Arcadia, CA 91006, 626/574-5200; www.r5.fs.fed.us/angeles. Day-use fees are now charged throughout the forest, so inquire if you plan to do anything other than drive through.

COURTESY AISLINN RACE

DOWNTOWN AND AROUND

With all due respect to Dorothy Parker and her historic quip about Los Angeles being "seventy-two suburbs in search of a city," these days there *is* a city here, even a downtown. Skyscrapers and a maze of frantic freeways have all but overshadowed its humble origins. Downtown Los Angeles was all of Los Angeles in the late 18th century, when this scruffy adobe outpost of Spanish empire was plopped down along the banks of the lazy Los Angeles River. Downtown Los Angeles today has that contemporary American look, with its dark, windy canyons of glass and steel surrounded, and intruded upon, by abject poverty. On weekdays scores of suits scurry along sidewalks going about the business of business. On weekends and after closing time, corporations close up shop and the heart of L.A. beats faster with the more exciting rhythms of performance art and panhandling.

Downtown Then: Dusty Pueblo
Los Angeles began here in 1781, established by the Spanish as a supply center for Alta California and named after the L.A. River, which in turn was originally named after the festival of the Virgin corresponding to its date of discovery: **El Pueblo de Nuestra Señora la Reina de los Angeles de Porciúncula,** or "Town of Our Lady Queen of the Angels of Porciúncula." In the beginning Los Angeles was a dusty little pueblo of modest adobes scattered near the river, its dirt streets criss-crossed by crude irrigation ditches and populated by more chickens and goats than people. The city's first settlers were 44 villagers from the Spanish territory that later became Mexico's Sonora and Sinaloa Provinces—an entourage of blacks, Indians, and "mestizos" (people of mixed ancestry) accompanied by two Spaniards. In 1791 there were 29 adobes in Los Angeles and 139 settlers; by 1830 the population had mushroomed to 650. Even with American occupation and statehood, little changed here. The 1849 discovery of gold near Sacramento in the north—and San Francisco's subsequent debut as the center of California's wealth and power—left Los Angeles to languish as a lawless frontier border town beset by murder and mayhem, described in the

1854 diaries of the Reverend James Woods, a Presbyterian from Massachusetts, as no heavenly city of angels but a heathen hellhole beset by "sin" such as public horse racing on Sunday. Strait-laced Protestants were out of place in Los Angeles until much later in the city's history.

Downtown Now: City sans Suburbia

Except during the corporate workweek, strait-laced Protestants are still out of place in downtown Los Angeles. An island of commerce just over four square miles and surrounded on all sides by freeways, downtown L.A. is the center of the city's civic and corporate affairs—the sometimes squalid hub of a regional economy exceeding $380 billion. As the skyscrapers went up, downtown's residential population skipped town, fleeing to the suburbs throughout the 1950s. Most streets are bustling by day and deserted by night, a trend in middle-class abandonment civic leaders have tried to challenge through concerted redevelopment efforts.

The city's long-running effort to revitalize downtown, to lure Angelenos back to this self-consciously contemporary "urban village" designed for shopping and other entertainments, has resulted in new luxury apartments and condominiums, trendy shops, new movie theaters, and restaurants. Residential buildings near the freeways boast signs of the times: "If You Lived Here You Would Be Home Now." But if you really lived in downtown Los Angeles, you'd most likely either be homeless or a hopeless workaholic. In fact, in the shadows of towering office buildings, a group of 21 10-foot by 10-foot fiberglass domes that resemble golf balls make up **Dome Village,** providing transitional housing for the homeless outside the confines of traditional shelters and unsightly encampments.

A notable redevelopment focal point for visitors is 133-acre Bunker Hill, a once-funky neighborhood of grand but faded Victorians that were home to the urban poor before the houses were bulldozed to make way for upscale apartments and interconnected cultural attractions that now form an identifiable metropolitan center for Los Angeles. Pedestrian-friendly stairways, walkways, and the newly refurbished Angel's Flight

RAILWAY TO HEAVEN

Care for some hands-on historical education with your downtown tour? The time-honored Bunker Hill **Angel's Flight** represents Old Los Angeles reborn. This soaring L.A. landmark—the city's most famous railway, an inclined funicular cable car system dating to 1901—recently flew back from the past. ("Funicular" refers to the fact that the two cars, one ascending and one descending, counterbalance each other along the three-track, 298-foot route.) In early 1996, Angel's Flight was officially resurrected, connecting the Red Line's Pershing Square subway station—the Fourth and Hill Street entrance—to the Water Court at California Plaza.

The original Angel's Flight, aptly called "the shortest railway in the world," departed from Third Street to connect the Hill Street business district with the once-fashionable Bunker Hill neighborhood. Dismantled and removed in 1969 for Bunker Hill redevelopment, the railway has been painstakingly refurbished and reconstructed. Included in the restoration project were the two orange and black cable cars—the Olivet and the Sinai, twin parallelograms with stair-stepped interiors—and the original beaux arts classical revival station house and arched entryway.

Angel's Flight is downtown—at 351 Hill St., on Hill between Third and Fourth Sts.—and operates daily 6:30 A.M.–10 P.M. Railway fare for the one-minute (one-way) ride is 25 cents per person. Ticket books (valid for one person only) are $1 for five rides. Official souvenirs are available at the top of the hill on Saturday and Sunday 10 A.M.–4 P.M. For current information, contact: **Angel's Flight Railway Foundation,** P.O. Box 712345, Los Angeles, CA 90071, 213/626-1901. For additional information—or to request a mail-order merchandise catalog—call 213/487-3716.

Last-Minute 2001 Update: On February 1, 2001, one of the two Angel's Flight cars broke loose and smashed into the other car in a freak accident, one in which one rider was killed and seven were injured. Preliminary investigation revealed that the railway's cable came off a spool, though what caused this to happen wasn't immediately clear. At last report the railway was closed pending necessary repairs, and planned to reopen.

railway link major destinations, the city's Central Library, the Museum of Contemporary Art, the Biltmore Hotel, and Pershing Square Park among them. Just blocks away are more local landmarks, including the Bradbury Building and the grand Grand Central Market.

Discovering Downtown

Downtown's slice of L.A. life is defined by tangled freeway angles and a jumble of zeros and ones—an area triangling both south and east from the junction of the Hollywood/Santa Ana Freeway (Hwy. 101) and the Harbor/Pasadena Freeway (the 110) in the north and, in the west, east from the junction of the Santa Monica (I-10) and the Harbor Freeways. As downtown trails off vaguely into a vast, seemingly abandoned warehouse district, its eastern "border" is established absolutely by the Los Angeles River, the unofficial boundary with East L.A., but perhaps more realistically by the railroad tracks along Alameda Street.

Most downtown attractions are concentrated in a much smaller area, however, within walking distance of the Los Angeles Civic Center—the largest government center outside Washington, D.C., they say—and the three-theater Performing Arts Center of L.A. County, formerly known as the Music Center. To the southwest, right next to the Museum of Contemporary Art (MOCA), is the new campus of the Colburn School of Performing Arts, a 55,000-square-foot facility complete with 420-seat chamber music hall. Other major downtown attractions include MOCA, the affiliated "Temporary Contemporary"—now a reasonably permanent fixture known as The Geffen Contemporary at MOCA—and the Museum of Neon Art.

Other notable landmarks beneath downtown's canopy of skyscrapers include the Los Angeles Public Library, also known as the Central Library; Los Angeles City Hall (aka *The Daily Planet* headquarters in the *Superman* TV series); the Bradbury Building; and Broadway's historic movie theaters. Broadway itself has become an attraction, the busiest Latino shopping district west of Chicago.

Well east of Broadway, near Third Street and Central Avenue, is Little Tokyo, a busy Japanese-American cultural and shopping district. Other commercial downtown attractions include the

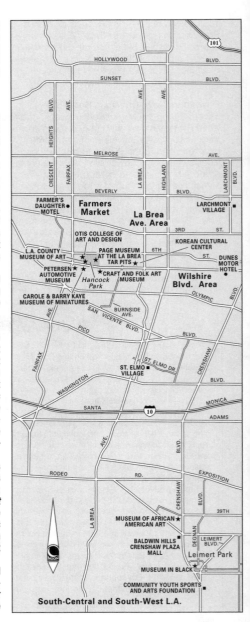

South-Central and South-West L.A.

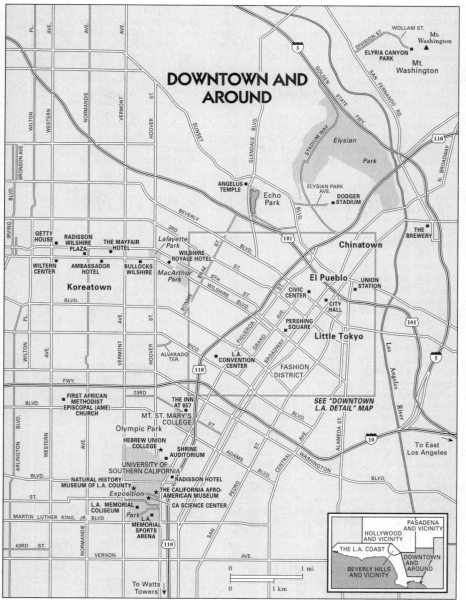

DOWNTOWN AND AROUND

Mt. Washington

WOLLAM ST.

DIVISION ST.

ELYRIA CANYON PARK

Mt. Washington

GOLDEN STATE FWY.

SAN FERNANDO RD.

STADIUM WAY

Elysian Park

GLENDALE BLVD.

SUNSET

ELYSIAN PARK AVE.

ANGELUS TEMPLE

Echo Park

DODGER STADIUM

BEVERLY

Chinatown

THE BREWERY

GETTY HOUSE

RADISSON WILSHIRE PLAZA

THE MAYFAIR HOTEL

Lafayette Park

WILSHIRE ROYALE HOTEL

N. BROADWAY

El Pueblo

UNION STATION

WILTERN CENTER

AMBASSADOR HOTEL

BULLOCKS WILSHIRE

MacArthur Park

BRAE

6TH

Koreatown

BLVD.

WILSHIRE BLVD.

CIVIC CENTER

CITY HALL

FIGUEROA

GRAND

PERSHING SQUARE

BROADWAY

Little Tokyo

Los Angeles River

PICO

ALVARADO TER.

L.A. CONVENTION CENTER

FASHION DISTRICT

FWY.

FIRST AFRICAN METHODIST EPISCOPAL (AME) CHURCH

23RD

THE INN AT 657

MT. ST. MARY'S COLLEGE

SEE "DOWNTOWN L.A. DETAIL" MAP

Olympic Park

HEBREW UNION COLLEGE

SHRINE AUDITORIUM

ALAMEDA ST.

To East Los Angeles

UNIVERSITY OF SOUTHERN CALIFORNIA

NATURAL HISTORY MUSEUM OF L.A. COUNTY

RADISSON HOTEL

THE CALIFORNIA AFRO-AMERICAN MUSEUM

Exposition Park

CA SCIENCE CENTER

L.A. MEMORIAL COLISEUM

MARTIN LUTHER KING, JR. BLVD

L.A. MEMORIAL SPORTS ARENA

43RD ST.

VERNON

AVE.

To Watts Towers

0   1 mi

0   1 km

PASADENA AND VICINITY

HOLLYWOOD AND VICINITY

THE L.A. COAST

DOWNTOWN AND AROUND

BEVERLY HILLS AND VICINITY

© AVALON TRAVEL PUBLISHING, INC.

Grand Central Market, the Flower Market (one of the nation's largest wholesale outlets), and the equally impressive Fashion District (formerly known as the Garment District). And if you're in town for a major convention—possibly anational political convention—the odds are you'll soon know your way around the ever-growing Los Angeles Convention Center, just off the Harbor Freeway north of the Santa Monica Freeway. Brand new downtown, on Figueroa adjacent to the convention center, is the Staples Center, home court to the L.A. Lakers and L.A. Clippers NBA teams, the L.A. Kings ice hockey franchise, and the L.A. Avengers Arena Football League team.

But the historic heart and soul of Los Angeles is just north of the downtown stretch of the Santa Ana Freeway (Hwy. 101)—in tourist-friendly El Pueblo de Los Angeles, a historic district commemorating the city's official birth in 1781. Just east of El Pueblo is Union Station, L.A.'s grand art deco train station and new central metropolitan transportation hub. Just north of El Pueblo is "New" Chinatown—as opposed, historically, to Old Chinatown, which was razed in the 1930s to make way for Union Station. Farther north—beyond the 110—is Elysian Park and beloved Dodger Stadium, where the L.A. Dodgers still star as the local boys of summer.

SEEING AND DOING DOWNTOWN

EL PUEBLO DE LOS ANGELES

Commemorating the city's humble beginnings at the junction of several worlds, **El Pueblo de Los Angeles Historic Monument** is bordered by Alameda, Arcadia, Ord, and Spring Streets, and is situated somewhere near the city's birthplace. (The original 1781 pueblo was lost in 1815 to floods, which forced settlers to scramble to higher ground northwest of town.) Included within this 44-acre historic district are some of the oldest buildings in Los Angeles. The city's namesake church, finally completed by the Franciscans in 1822 and known today as the Old Plaza Church, still holds court on the northern edge of the plaza, on N. Main Street. But the real action is along Olvera Street, a bright and bustling open-air 1930s-vintage marketplace dotted with historic adobes—one of the city's most popular tourist attractions. Though it wasn't always thus, these days the cultural color is fairly authentic, a particular draw on weekends for L.A.'s large Mexican-American community. The area's historic features, alas, are all but overwhelmed by commerce and the chaos of contemporary life. For a deeper appreciation, take a guided walking tour.

Special Olvera Street events include the **Blessing of the Animals** held every year on the Saturday before Easter, an event allowing hamsters to horses to get the nod from God; the weeklong **Cinco de Mayo** celebration held

DOWNTOWN'S DASHING DASH

If planning an impromptu self-guided tour, keep in mind that getting around downtown sans car is fairly easy, at least during the day, thanks to the city's Downtown Area Shuttle Hop or **DASH minibuses**, 213/808-2273 or toll-free 800/266-6883, www.ladottransit.com. On weekends these magenta and silver buses loop through the area and stop every two or three blocks, connecting the Flower Market and Fashion District with the Financial District, Exposition Park, and various Metrorail stations. Looping north, DASH runs from the Central Library to the Grand Central Market, Little Tokyo, City Hall, Union Station, Olvera Street, Chinatown, and the Music Center. Fare is 25 cents per "hop," no matter how far it takes you, which is a great deal no matter how you add it up. Weekday routes are different. Call or see the website for current route details.

And L.A.'s DASH shuttles now roam considerably farther afield—to Hollywood, Northridge, even Venice (summer only). For details, try the website or call 213, 310, 323, or 818/ 808-2273.

the week of May 5; and the pre-Christmas **Las Posadas** procession staged nightly from December 16 through Christmas Eve. This Mexican Christmas celebration, held over nine consecutive nights, reenacts the search by Mary and

AMÉRICA TROPICAL

In summer of 1932, Mexican muralist David Alfaro Siqueiros began to paint a mural on the south side of Olvera Street's Italian Hall, a work he called *América Tropical*. Now undergoing a painstakingly restoration by art conservators from L.A.'s Getty Conservation Institute, *América Tropical* depicts a tangle of ominously luxuriant vegetation surrounding a stylized pre-Columbian pyramid and totemic sculptures. But the artist's dramatic design finale—a crucified Indian lashed to a Christian cross clutched in the talons of an American eagle, and, just to the right, armed peasant revolutionaries posed on a rooftop as they take eagle-eyed aim at the predator—so outraged Depression-era L.A. civic leaders that this part of the mural was soon obliterated with white paint; within years the entire work was whitewashed.

Siqueiros, who found himself in Los Angeles during a period of California immigrant bashing, was soon deported from the United States.

Despite Siqueiros's less than rousing L.A. welcome, the artist is now considered one of *los tres grandes* among Mexico's muralists, keeping posthumous company with José Clemente Orozco and Diego Riviera. And, in one of those rich historical ironies, it turns out that L.A.'s early censorship greatly assisted his artistic legacy. Without the protection provided by such thick coats of white paint, *América Tropical* would have faded into absolute oblivion long ago. Just when restoration will be complete—and when the public will once again be able to view the mural—is uncertain, given the decades already committed to revivifying *América Tropical*.

Joseph for room at the inn. On Christmas Eve the procession finally arrives at the Avila Adobe, where the baby Jesus joins the party. Afterward, children celebrate by gleefully attacking piñatas filled with candy.

For more information, contact: El Pueblo de Los Angeles Historic Monument, Sepulveda House Visitor Center, 622 N. Main St., 213/628-1274. The Sepulveda House Visitor Center (and museum) is open Mon.–Sat. 10 A.M.–3 P.M. (closed Christmas Day), but Olvera Street is open daily 10 A.M.–8 P.M.; in summer, some shops stay open even later. Call for current tour schedules of various historic buildings and for information on free guided walking tours. At last report El Pueblo tours were offered Tues.–Sat. at 10 A.M., 11 A.M., noon, and 1 P.M. (excluding Thanksgiving and Christmas).

Olvera Street and Vicinity

One of L.A.'s most popular attractions, Olvera Street was originally a "typical Mexican marketplace" developed in 1929 from the somewhat whimsical historical ideas of the city's social elites. Yet the Old Mexico City–style street scene that unfolds here on weekends is no typical tourist trap. Vendors hawk handicrafts and tasty treats from stalls, or *puestos*, along winding pathways of Spanish tile and brick. A very real L.A. scene, Olvera's **Old Plaza** is the place to perch under a huge Moreton Bay fig tree, inhale burri-

tos, and hum and sway to mariachi tunes tapped forth from the *kiosko*, the hexagonal bandstand. Presiding over all is the **Old Plaza Church**, still centerpiece of an active parish and more formally known as La Iglesia de la Reina de Los Angeles de Porciúncula. The church, unveiled in 1818, was originally a simple adobe built by Franciscan padres with Indian labor; its more ambitious rebuilding took another 40 years.

At 17 Olvera St. is **Pelanconi House** (1855), the first brick building ever built in Los Angeles. The huge wine cellar of this onetime private home has housed La Golondrina restaurant almost forever. More intriguing, though, is what's on the walls of the nearby 1908 **Italian Hall.** For more details see the special topic, "América Tropical."

Farther north, at 622 N. Main, is **Sepulveda House,** built in 1887 by Eloisa Martínez de Sepulveda for use as a hotel/boarding house—a rare example of a commercial structure designed in Eastlake Victorian style. Walking down the east side of Olvera, look for the path of *zanja madre* or "mother ditch"—now marked by diagonal brick inlays—built in 1783 to funnel water from the Los Angeles River to the plaza.

At 14 Olvera is the **Avila Adobe,** the oldest building in Los Angeles, built in 1818 by onetime pueblo Mayor Don Francisco Avila. The simple one-story structure, now a museum displaying furnishings typical of the period, was once the town's most luxurious home. The museum is open for tours Mon.–Sat. 9 A.M.–5 P.M. (free).

On the southeast corner of the Old Plaza is the city's first fire station, the **Old Firehouse,** a modest two-story brick building built in 1884 and now a museum featuring early fire-fighting equipment. Just south is the restored **Garnier Block,** a brick and sandstone structure built by Phillippe Garnier in 1890 as storefronts and apartments for Chinese businessmen. The south end of the building was torn down when the Santa Ana Freeway was built in the 1950s.

The first L.A. **Masonic Temple** (1858), 416 N. Main St., was built in Italian Renaissance style. Just south, at 420 N. Main, is the **Merced Theater** (1870), the city's first—a 400-seat auditorium designed by Ezra F. Kysor in lavish Italianate style, abandoned eight years after completion when the neighborhood went into decline. Early Chinese immigrants used secret passageways beneath the Masonic Temple and the Merced as opium dens. Architect Kysor also built the adjoining **Pico House,** the first three-story masonry structure in Los Angeles. This handsome Italianate building—at one time considered the finest south of San Jose—was commissioned as a hotel by the last Mexican governor of California, Pio Pico. The luxurious amenities of Pico House did indeed attract the carriage trade.

Union Station

This spectacular art deco transportation palace, directly east of El Pueblo at 800 N. Alameda St. (at César E. Chávez Ave.), was built on the site of L.A.'s original Chinatown. The last of the grand American train stations, Union Station was built in 1939 by the Southern Pacific, Union Pacific, and Santa Fe Railroads. Its Spanish colonial revival style, the work of architects John and Donald Parkinson, blends Moorish influences with streamline moderne. Stepping inside the grand waiting room, where the wood-beamed ceiling rises to a dramatic 52 feet above polished marble floors, is like traveling back in time. Giant decorative archways at each end lead to serene courtyards landscaped with oaks, figs, and jacarandas along with Mexican fan palms and birds of paradise—a public embodiment of Southern California's private garden style, which

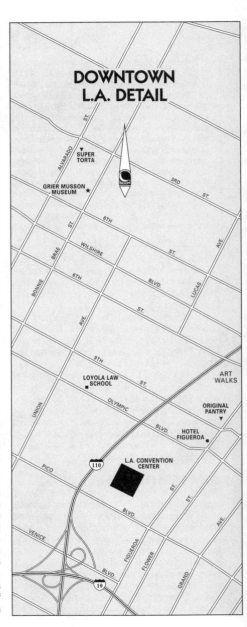

DOWNTOWN L.A. DETAIL

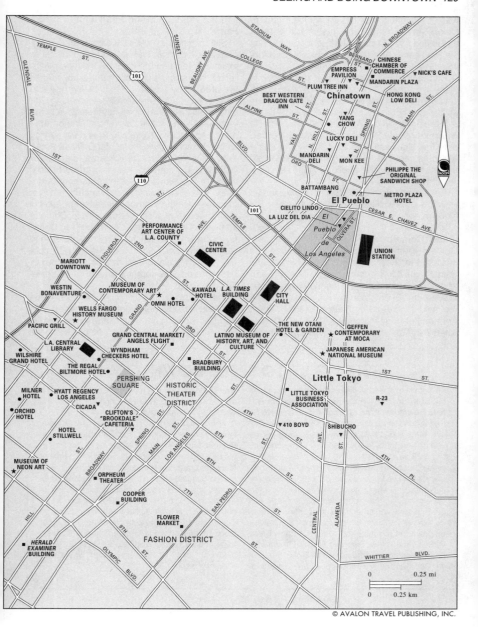

© AVALON TRAVEL PUBLISHING, INC.

was still inventing itself in the 1930s. Many of Union Station's original furnishings are intact and in fine form. Striking art deco signs still point the way; heavy wooden chairs still offer travelers comfort and privacy.

Understandably, Union Station has starred in many films, these including *Union Station* (set in Chicago), *The Way We Were, Blade Runner,* and *Bugsy.* Yet L.A.'s grandest grande dame still presides over L.A. rail travel as home to **Amtrak** and, at the adjacent **Gateway Center,** both the **Metrorail Red Line** subway and the **Metrolink** regional commuter service. Well worth a peek: the impressive public art in the new transit center.

For the complete Union Station story, sign up for a Saturday walking tour with the Los Angeles Conservancy.

"New" Chinatown

Chinatown in Los Angeles certainly won't be mistaken for San Francisco's, but beyond the tourist traps it has authentic appeal—most particularly in the markets and the restaurants lining the streets. Events can be fun, too, including the major **Chinese New Year** celebration in late February or early March, the **Miss L.A. Chinatown Pageant,** the **Golden Dragon Parade,** and the **Chinese Moon Festival and Street Fair.**

Still considered "new" Chinatown, since L.A.'s original Chinatown was razed in the 1930s to make way for Union Station, the main drag here is N. Broadway; the district's general boundaries are created by César E. Chávez Avenue and Spring, Yale, and Bernard Streets. Making Chinatown still more fascinating these days is the fact that it's not just a reinvented Canton anymore. Home to 15,000 residents and still serving as the de facto cultural center for Chinese Americans living throughout the L.A. area—particularly in East L.A.'s popular "Asian restaurant cities" south of Pasadena, including Alhambra, Monterey Park, San Gabriel, and very affluent San Marino—the neighborhood increasingly reflects the influence of more recent ethnic Chinese immigrants from Southeast Asia, the "Teo Chew" collectively known by longtime neighborhood residents as the Chiu Chou. Signs in Cambodian, Lao, Thai, and Vietnamese add to neighborhood business competition and communication confusion.

The 600 block of N. Spring St., originally home to Mexican immigrants from Sonora, housed the neighborhood's earliest Chinese residents, beginning in the 1930s; the 700 block of New

GETTING UP TO SPEED DOWNTOWN

To get up to speed downtown, stop by or contact the **Los Angeles Convention and Visitors Bureau Downtown Visitor Center,** 685 S. Figueroa St. (between Wilshire Blvd. and 7th St.), 213/689-8822 or toll-free 800/228-2452, www.lacvb.com, open for walk-in assistance weekdays 8 A.M.–5 P.M. and Saturdays 8:30 A.M.–5 P.M.

Another help in understanding what's up downtown is the Los Angeles Conservancy, www.laconservancy.org, which offers inexpensive and informative walking tours designed to interpret L.A.'s past, present, and future. The group offers 11 regular tours—in addition to occasional special tours—emphasizing historic areas and structures. These include **Little Tokyo, Pershing Square Landmarks,** and **Angeleno Heights** as well as **Union Station, Art Deco,** and other landmark buildings. The **Broad-**

way Theaters tour, which allows visitors inside some of L.A.'s grand old movie theaters, is one of the Conservancy's most popular.

The general Conservancy tour fee is $8. All tours, typically one or two hours, start Saturday at 10 A.M. Reservations are required. The Art Deco, Broadway Theaters, and Pershing Square Landmarks tours are offered every Saturday. Others—including the Biltmore Hotel, Union Station, Little Tokyo, Terra Cotta, and Palaces of Finance, in addition to miscellaneous special tours—are offered on a regular rotating schedule. No tours are offered on Thanksgiving, Christmas, or New Year's Day. For more information, contact: **Los Angeles Conservancy Tours,** 523 W. Sixth St., Ste. 1216, 213/623-2489 or 213/430-4211 (event hotline); www.laconservancy .org.

High St. is also long established. But Chinatown's main action centers along the 700–1000 blocks of N. Broadway—the CityWalk of the late 1930s, almost a Hollywood-style version of Shanghai streets—where new Chinatown blended into earlier Italian neighborhoods. The streets are lined with movie theaters and restaurants; Chinatown's architecture is even more dramatic at night, lit by miles of neon. The most lavish Chinese ornamention, complete with totemic rooftop animals, lines **Gin Ling Way,** a pedestrian walk connecting Broadway and Hill Street. Concentrated along the 700 block of N. Broadway are fresh herb and produce shops and markets aflutter with live fish and poultry, including long-running **Superior Poultry,** 750 N. Broadway (between Ord and Alpine Streets), 213/628-7645. Step inside always-crowded **Phoenix Bakery,** 969 N. Broadway, 213/628-4642, Chinatown's oldest and largest bakery, for famous whipped cream cakes topped with fresh strawberries. Or sample dim sum from one of the shops across the way at **Mandarin Plaza,** 970 N. Broadway. North Broadway near Bernard is considered **Association Row** for its concentration of Cantonese family and fraternal organizations.

While wandering the neighborhood in search of fresh produce, spices, gifts, and dim sum, also note local **murals,** including *Party at Lan-T'Ing,* on the W. College St. side of the Los Angeles Public Library branch at 850 Yale St., and the three tiled Chinese scenes at 913 N. Broadway. The former is believed to be the largest mural of its kind outside China.

For more information about area attractions and businesses, contact: **Chinese Chamber of Commerce,** 977 N. Broadway, Ste. E, Los Angeles, 213/617-0396, www.lachinesechamber.org, which largely represents established Cantonese establishments.

Los Angeles Children's Museum

Strictly kids' stuff, this downtown museum offers hands-on arts, humanities, and science education for children aged two to 10. In **Club Eco,** kids create masterpieces from recyclables. In the **Recording Studio,** they become recording stars; in the **Video Zone,** TV news anchors. In **The Cave** they commune with lifelike dinosaur holograms. A huge pillow-filled room allows children to shed excess energy before settling down to focus on the kids-only exhibits here.

Los Angeles Children's Museum is located inside the Los Angeles Mall at 310 N. Main St. (at Los Angeles St.), 213/687-8800; www.lacm.org. (The museum is looking for a new home, so be sure to call for current info before setting out.) During the school year, the museum caters to classroom groups and is open to the general public on weekends only, 10 A.M.–5 P.M. (closed Thanksgiving, Christmas, and New Year's Day). In summer, it's open to the public also Tues.–Fri. 11:30 A.M.–4 P.M., Sat.–Sun. 10 A.M.–5 P.M. Admission is $5, under age 2 free.

OTHER DOWNTOWN CULTURAL ATTRACTIONS

Los Angeles City Hall and the Civic Center

Now dwarfed by downtown high-rises, Los Angeles City Hall (1926–28) was until 1966 the tallest building in downtown L.A., the grand symbol of the city. Before 1957, earthquake building standards forbade all structures taller than 13 stories. The city's most notable exception, 27-story City Hall—designed by architects John C. Austin, John and Donald Parkinson, and Albert C. Martin, Sr., its interiors by Austin Whittlesey—was allowed only after L.A. voters approved its specific exception. And if you wonder why L.A.'s City Hall seems so *familiar,* the building was featured in the opening scenes of the popular 1950s TV series *Dragnet.* In addition to many other movie and TV roles, it also served as headquarters for *The Daily Planet* fictional news organization in the *Superman* television series.

The builders made great effort to use only California materials in the construction of City Hall. Its façade features California granite; the mortar used throughout contains sand from each county in the state, cement from each California cement mill, and water from each of the 21 Spanish colonial missions. And the building's bronze ceremonial doors are cast from California ores.

Los Angeles City Hall is part of the Los Angeles Civic Center north of First St., at 200 N. Spring St. (between First and Temple), 213/485-2121, its "tourability" affected by ongoing restoration and budget-breaking seismic safety reconstruction. But do see the recently restored rotunda, featuring 23 spectacular ceramic tile panels. And take in the view from the top floor observation deck, which—despite subsequent skyscrapers—still presents a commanding view of downtown. Free 45-minute tours of City Hall are offered by reservation only (sometimes cancelled due to construction), weekdays at 11 A.M. and noon, or sign on for a guided Los Angeles Conservancy tour (see Getting up to Speed Downtown above).

Latino Museum of History, Art, and Culture

A onetime Bank of America building on a dispirited stretch of Main Street one block south of City Hall at 112 S. Main St. (between First and Second Sts.), 213/626-7600; www.latinomuseum.org, is now home to one of L.A.'s newest museums—the long-promised Latino Museum of History, Art, and Culture, which opened in May 1998 after more than a decade of searching for a home and adequate funding. The museum celebrates Latino artistic, cultural, and historic achievements not just in Los Angeles but throughout the United States, the Americas, and the world. Beyond traditional exhibits, the museum also hosts art symposia, film festivals, and special cultural, educational, and other events. Recent exhibitions included *César E. Chávez: An American Leader* and *Dia de los Santos—Dia de los Muertos (Day of the Saints—Day of the Dead).* The museum is open daily 10 A.M.–4 P.M. except major holidays. Admission is free.

Travelers heading toward L.A.'s Westside shouldn't miss the **Museum of Latin American Art** in Long Beach, which opened its first wing in November 1996.

COMING SOON: DOWNTOWN DISNEY

Stalled for a decade in the planning and fund-raising stages, construction of the **Walt Disney Concert Hall** in downtown Los Angeles began in December 1999—something of a new beginning. Construction of the concert hall's underground parking garage began in December 1992, but halted abruptly two years later due to cost overruns. Subsequent fundraising, earnest since 1996, raised almost 95 percent of monies needed for the $255 million venue. Future home of the Los Angeles Philharmonic, downtown's Disney memorial is scheduled to open in time for the 2002–2003 performance season.

The Disney Concert Hall, a long-awaited downtown landmark designed by L.A architect Frank O. Gehry and situated atop Bunker Hill adjacent to the Performing Arts Center, has been through dozens of revisions since Gehry won the commission in 1988. The current design resembles sterling silver nun's cap caught in a tornado or perhaps, as the project's construction manager Jack Burnell has suggested, "the crash of a 747." But according to *Los Angeles Times* architecture critic Nicolai Ouroussoff, the new Gehry creation represents "a substantial victory against the commonplace and the mediocre." According to Ouroussoff, "The potential success of the project can be seen as a turning point in the city's cultural growth."

Recent additions to construction plans include administrative offices for the L.A. Philharmonic and a 200-seat performance space for the California Institute of the Arts. These new elements allowed Gehry to reconfigure the concert hall's design. The hall's curved exterior surfaces have been simplified, for one thing. The building's bowed façade now leans out over the curb line, providing a pedestrian canopy and a stronger presence along the street's main access. On the outside, the hall will have a flowerlike "wrapper" of limestone and stainless steel, everything surrounded by public gardens.

The hall's interiors promise to be equally dramatic. Gehry has pulled the building's exterior "skin" away from the concert hall's interior, for example, creating a double-wall design with multilevel foyers in between. Audiences will scan the heavens through thin bands of skylights above, and natural light will illuminate the main lobby during daytime concerts. Acoustics are expected to be superb.

For more information about the Walt Disney Concert Hall and to see current architectural representations, visit the official website: www.disneyhall.org.

—Karen Pollock and Kim Weir

Los Angeles Times Building

The *Los Angeles Times* Building, 202 W. First St. (between Spring and Broadway), 213/237-5000, www.latimes.com, is easily identified by its stately clock tower. The Times-Mirror Corp. outgrew the original structure designed by Gordon Kaufmann in 1935, and the impressive moderne-style limestone structure was intermeshed in 1973 with a modern steel and glass addition by William Pereira and Associates—an interesting architectural hodgepodge, at any rate. Stop by the lobby to read the history of Los Angeles in headlines or take a free tour to peek in on the making of a great, if historically conservative, newspaper, from the newsroom to pressroom. The paper offers two different guided walk-through tours on weekdays—a free 45-minute stroll for individuals, couples, and school-age children through the "old plant" editorial offices (no reservations required, call for current time), and a group-oriented, reservations-only 45-minute tour of the new plant and its pressroom (times vary). Children must be over age 10 for either tour. Free parking is available at 213 S. Spring Street. Make tour reservations at least a week in advance.

Los Angeles Central Library

Still L.A.'s most astonishing public building even after two 1986 arson fires and subsequent reconstructive surgery, the beloved and strange Los Angeles Central Library is the 1926 masterwork of architect Bertram Goodhue, with an assist from Carleton M. Winslow, Sr. Centerpiece of this beaux arts-inspired landmark is the central book tower, topped by a pyramid of tiled mosaic sunbursts and, at the apex, a hand-held torch of knowledge. The search for knowledge is represented by the sphinx, and by the bright rotunda, illuminated with a stunning globelike chandelier. Everywhere around, Goodhue's vision renders the ordinary quite extraordinary, an inventive adventure in art, history, religion, and portentous philosophy that is, architecturally, by turns Byzantine, Egyptian, and Spanish. Inimitably American, though, is the official beneficence and optimism suffusing Dean Cornwell's 1932 rotunda mural cycle, which depicts a fairy-tale version of California's colonization and multi-ethnic mixing. (For a decidedly different point of view, head to Olvera Street for a peek at David

Siqueiros's surprising *América Tropical,* painted in the same year—and quickly painted over by outraged civic leaders. See above.) Also to be appreciated: the library's restored fountains and gardens, the largest of the latter complete with restaurant. Not to mention the library's new "modernist beaux arts" east wing—rather boring in comparison to Goodhue's contribution—designed by Hardy Holzman Pfeiffer Associates and named for former L.A. Mayor Tom Bradley. Bradley is also honored, if unofficially, by the three towering skyscrapers that now dwarf the Central Library, a clumsy collective homage to the chummy redevelopment relationships that financed library improvements.

The Los Angeles Public Library's Central Library, 630 W. Fifth St. (between Flower and Grand), 213/228-7000, is open Mon.–Thurs. 10 A.M.–8P.M., Fri.–Sat. 10 A.M.–6 P.M., and Sunday 1–5 P.M. Free guided tours are offered Mon.–Fri. at 12:30 P.M., Saturday at 11 A.M. and 2 P.M., and Sunday at 2 P.M. For library events information, call 213/228-7040, or check the library's website at www.lapl.org.

Pershing Square

The only park in downtown Los Angeles, Pershing Square was established in 1866 on a five-acre remnant of the original pueblo land grant. Bounded by Fifth, Sixth, Hill, and Olive Streets and originally bordered by white picket fences, Pershing Square was once lush with banana trees, palms, and birds of paradise. By the 1930s it also accommodated evangelists, socialists, and other Angelenos sounding forth from figurative soapboxes.

This local free-speech tradition withered in the 1950s when the park was razed to plant, instead, an underground parking garage. The bleak urban badlands that quickly sprouted atop the garage soon became home to the homeless and, more insidiously, drug dealers and other shady characters. The destruction of Pershing Square by short-sighted civic leaders is not among L.A.'s finest accomplishments.

Yet in California even cities reserve the right to reinvent themselves—thus the latest "new" and newly improved Pershing Square. The first rush to clean it up came in 1984, when the Olympics came to town. That and subsequent efforts failed to thrive. But after a two-year, $14.7 million re-creation, the new Pershing Square was unveiled in February of 1994. Its style suggesting a European plaza more than the wide-open urban grassland of American tradition, Pershing Square has distinct open-air "rooms," from performance area and statue garden park to stylized tidepool. Its bold colors and sleek contemporary whimsy—purple carillon tower, rose-colored walkways, canary yellow walls, even a faux earthquake faultline—seem strong enough to bridge the vast cultural gap, and the tiny geographical gap, between downtown's Latino and Anglo identities. To date, nothing else in Los Angeles has been that powerful.

The Biltmore Hotel

Backing up to Pershing Square is the Biltmore Hotel, the grandest of the grand old hotels in Southern California, designed by architects Schultze and Weaver and completed in 1923. Designated a Los Angeles Historical Cultural Landmark in 1969, the Biltmore had gotten a bit dowdy over the years. So Angelenos were understandably ecstatic about the grande dame's $40 million makeover in the late 1970s, a restoration that lovingly polished the hotel's marble, garish gold gilt, and crystal chandeliers. The Biltmore's magnificent painted ceilings were redone more recently. The hotel's wonders are abundant. Secret details include the private elevator in the Presidential Suite—John F. Kennedy planned his successful 1960 presidential campaign from the Biltmore's lobby—and the baby grand piano in the Music Suite. Considerably more accessible for most of us are the stunning gold-gilt ceilings in the Galeria, adjoining the lobby, where Italian artist Giovanni Smeraldi symbolically recreated the city. Fans of the once popular *Murder, She Wrote* TV series will recognize the Biltmore's lobby, with an elaborate skylight and hand-painted carved wood ceilings, as a stand-in for miscellaneous ritzy hotels around the world. The lobby also starred in the movie *The Poseidon Adventure*.

The public areas and restaurants of the Biltmore Hotel, 506 S. Grand Ave. (Grand at Fifth), Los Angeles, 213/624-1011 or toll-free 800/245-8673 for reservations, www.thebiltmore.com, are open to the public during reasonable business hours for impromptu self-guided tours. To truly appreciate what you're seeing, though, sign on

for a Saturday tour with the Los Angeles Conservancy, 213/623-2489.

Wells Fargo History Museum

Inside the Wells Fargo Building, 333 Grand Ave., 213/253-7166, L.A.'s Wells Fargo Museum recalls well over a century of the company's rough-and-tumble history at the edge of the wild, wild West. In the days when the trip from St. Louis, Missouri, took three weeks by stagecoach rather than three hours by airplane, the trip was no picnic—a fact you'll appreciate once you climb aboard the historic stagecoach, always a favorite with the kids. But there's more to explore, since the museum here boasts one of the most extensive collections of authentic Western memorabilia in Southern California. Admission is free, and it's open Mon.–Fri. 9 A.M.–5 P.M.

On Broadway

In fairly recent history, Broadway between First and Ninth Streets has become the city's main Latino shopping district, one that offers considerably more—cheap stereos, bridal fashions, even immigration lawyers—than El Pueblo's tourist-oriented entertainment. Strolling this lively boulevard, studying the shop signs and listening in on passing conversations, may convince you that you've suddenly arrived in Mexico City, a fact that gives rise to the overall Angeleno tendency to describe the area as "third world." Stop at downtown's Grand Central Market, 317 S. Market St. (described in more detail below) for a fascinating selection of authentic ethnic food and other wares.

Beyond—actually, above—the confusion of ongoing cultural collision are Broadway's historic buildings. Within this significant Los Angeles historical district stand many 1900s' survivors of L.A.'s free-swinging wrecking ball. Broadway between Third and Ninth is the first and largest **Historic Theater District** listed on the National Register of Historic Places. Broadway's 12 movie palaces, now showing Spanish-language and some triple-X-rated films, were built between 1910 and 1931. Guided theater district tours, offering access to many of these grand old entertainment palaces, are offered by the Los Angeles Conservancy, 213/623-2489. But as long as you behave yourself (absolute quiet, please!), on Saturday at 10 A.M. you can slip into the 1925

Orpheum Theater, 842 S. Broadway (at Ninth St.), to sit in on the weekly practice session of the **Los Angeles Organ Society,** which gives the magnificent Wurlitzer pipe organ a weekly workout.

Bradbury Building

This is one of L.A.'s notable architectural jewels, designed and built with guidance from a Ouija board, so be sure to stop by just to appreciate its sparkle. The modest five-story brick exterior of the 1893 Bradbury Building, 304 S. Broadway (at Third St.), 213/626-1893, gives no hint of the fantastic art-nouveau vision inside. The focal point of architectural draftsman George Herbert Wyman's inspiration is the small, open interior courtyard, almost frilly with elaborate wrought-iron grillwork yet grounded with rich, dark oak walls, old brick, and marble and tile floors. Balconies and open-cage elevators reach upward into a stunning glass atrium that fills the building with magical light. Modern movie buffs have seen this place before, as a rainy-day interior set in *Blade Runner.* The breathtaking first impression is well worth the trip. The Bradbury Building is open to the public (up to the first floor landing) daily 9 A.M.–5 P.M.

Herald Examiner Building

Of particular interest to students of architecture, the Herald Examiner Building, 1111 S. Broadway (at 11th St.), was commissioned in 1912 by William Randolph Hearst. Julia Morgan, Hearst's architectural sidekick, designed this Spanish-style building to house Hearst's publishing empire. Hearst was so pleased with the results of their first collaboration that he hired Morgan to help create their joint masterpiece, the byzantine castle at Hearst's San Simeon "ranch."

Little Tokyo

Just east of the Civic Center, along First Street between Main and Alameda, is the heart of Little Tokyo, cultural center for L.A.'s Japanese American community. Japanese immigrants first settled in the Los Angeles area more than 100 years ago, but the local community was devastated, overnight, when Japanese Americans were forcibly divested of their businesses, farms, homes, and neighborhoods and "relocated" in World War II–era internment camps throughout

the West. After the war, many L.A.-area citizens of Japanese descent moved to the suburbs. But Little Tokyo rebounded; it remains a thriving—and growing—area cultural center. East First Street between Central Avenue and San Pedro Street, listed on the National Register of Historic Places, is now protected as a National Historic Landmark.

The Japanese American National Museum is a new star in downtown's vital Little Tokyo district, a neighborhood where mom-and-pop stores thrive alongside chic boutiques, luxury hotels, and fine restaurants. Other area attractions include the Geffen Contemporary at MOCA (see Museum of Contemporary Art, below) and its galaxy of nearby galleries, the Japan America Theatre at Noguchi Plaza, the Japanese Village Plaza north of Noguchi Plaza, and attractive Weller Court adjacent to the New Otani Hotel. Popular neighborhood Japanese gardens include the rooftop retreat at the New Otani and the lovely James Irvine Garden behind the Japanese American Cultural and Community Center on San Pedro Street. The center itself sponsors many cultural activities in conjunction with Japanese festivals.

For more information about the area, contact the **Little Tokyo Business Association,** 244 S. Pedro St., Ste. 303, Los Angeles, 213/620-0570. For tours of Little Tokyo, call 213/628-8268.

Japanese American National Museum

A fairly recent museum exhibit here, *America's Concentration Camps: Remembering the Japanese American Experience,* reminded Americans about a chapter of U.S. history most would prefer to forget. But the World War II–era executive order that banished Japanese Americans living on the West Coast—the majority of them U.S. citizens—to military relocation camps has not been forgotten in Southern California. Many California families so detained lost everything as a result—their homes, their land, their neighbors, their businesses and jobs—and have been struggling to rebuild their lives, and to understand, ever since.

The Japanese American National Museum, housed in a former Buddhist temple, emphasizes the history of Japanese in America in both permanent and special exhibits. The museum's newest feature is the 85,000-square-foot Pavilion of the Japanese American National Museum, adjacent, opened in early 1999. The most visible aspect of a $45 million expansion, designed by architect Gyo Obata, the new sandstone, granite, steel, and glass pavilion features interior cherrywood paneling, a grand staircase, and galleries with natural lighting. Don't miss the 90-foot-long "wall of water" in the garden.

The Japanese American National Museum, 369 E. First St. (at Central Ave.), Los Angeles, 213/625-0414 or toll-free 800/461-5266, www .lausd.k12.ca.us/janm/, is open Tues.–Sun. 10 A.M.–5 P.M., with last admission at 4:30, but Thursday 10 A.M.–8 P.M. (closed Thanksgiving, Christmas, and New Year's Day). Admission is $6 adults and $5 seniors, $3 college students with ID, and children ages 6–17. Free on Thursday 5–8 P.M. and all day on the third Thursday of every month. Call for current exhibit information.

South of Little Tokyo

Self-guided tourists with a natural tendency to end up in scary neighborhoods should keep an eye out for the **Coca-Cola Bottling Plant,** 1334 S. Central Ave. (at 14th St.), 213/746-5555, one of L.A.'s most famous temples of the secular vernacular. (Should you try to get here on purpose, head south on Central from First Street near Little Tokyo; the plant is just over two blocks north of the I-10 underpass.) It was remodeled in 1936 by Robert V. Derrah in a moderne-era transportation theme—the theme in this case, "big boat." Coca-Cola's landlubbing white-plaster ocean liner features rounded corners, porthole-style windows, and black wainscoting with a red stripe to mark the waterline. Anchoring the scene, at the street corners, are two giant coke bottles. Very classy commercial act.

ARTFUL DOWNTOWN L.A.

Though downtown's arty arts community of the 1970s and '80s has all but abandoned its semi-industrial neighborhood aesthetic, a trend accelerated by the 1992 riots, the cultural attractions still here are worth the price of parking. Downtown Los Angeles provides the foundation for much of L.A.'s more formal arts community, its

KOREAN CULTURAL MUSEUMS

Though Koreatown is still recovering from Metrorail construction down Wilshire to Western—and from the ill-will so violently expressed during the 1992 Rodney King-related riots—well worth a stop for a general orientation is the **Korean American Museum,** located in a suite within the Wiltern Theatre building at 3780 Wilshire Blvd. (at Western), 213/388-4229; www. kamuseum.org. The Korean American Museum is dedicated to preserving Korean-American culture through educational activities and changing exhibitions (donations appreciated). There is no permanent collection, but exhibitions range from Korean family stories and malodorous kim chee to interactive exhibitions on Korean small businesses.

Another worthwhile stop is the **Korean Cultural Center,** 5505 Wilshire Blvd., 323/936-7141, www.kccla.org, open weekdays 9 A.M.–5 P.M. and Saturday 10 A.M.–1 p.m, closed Sundays and holidays. Through its various programs, the Korean Cultural Center introduces and supports Korean arts, history, and culture in America. Museum displays emphasize the Korean arts, from traditional to more contemporary forms. Of equal fascination, though, is the focus on the Korean immigrant experience—through photographs, letters, historical documents, and artifacts provided in large part by Susan Ahn, daughter of Chang Ho Ahn, who came to California in 1902 to lead an international movement to free Korea from Japanese rule. The museum is closed on all major U.S. holidays and on selective Korean national holidays; if in doubt, call ahead.

notable institutions including the Performing Arts Center, the Museum of Contemporary Art (MOCA), and the Geffen Contemporary at MOCA in Little Tokyo (intended to be temporary, staying open only until MOCA's debut in the 1980s, thus originally known as the Temporary Contemporary). An offbeat downtown standard, the avant-garde Los Angeles Contemporary Exhibitions (LACE), is now at home in Hollywood. Another is still going strong, however—L.A.'s Museum of Neon Art (MONA), the only permanent neon-art museum in the world, relocated from the warehouse district in 1996.

NEON~L.A.'S SIGNATURE FLASH

If imitation is the sincerest form of flattery, just imagine how flattered Los Angeles is by the existence of Las Vegas and all that flashy neon.

The **Museum of Neon Art (MONA)** in L.A., open at its new downtown location since February of 1996, celebrates the city's love affair with neon lighting—a commercial art form that once decorated countless L.A. storefronts, theater marquees, and roof lines. The original fuel for L.A.'s signature flash was neon itself, a colorless, odorless gas that glows orangey-red when zapped by electricity, a fact of nature first discovered in France in 1898. (Other colors are created by other gases.) America's first neon signs, manufactured in France, were installed in 1923 at an L.A. Packard dealership.

Some of L.A.'s original tubular light show still shines, lighting up **Broadway** downtown, sections of **Wilshire Boulevard, Western Avenue** between Wilshire and Third Street, **Alvarado Street** flanking MacArthur Park, and countless other streets.

MONA, the glowing logo of the Museum of Neon Art, was created by Lili Kakich in 1981.

MUSEUM OF NEON ART

(For a fairly comprehensive map of restored Los Angeles neon, see the "neon map" on city's Department of Cultural Affairs website: www.culturela.org.) Other areas, such as **Melrose Avenue,** are at the forefront of the city's neo-neon renaissance, thanks in large part to citywide consciousness-raising credited to MONA and its founding artist Lili Lakich.

Downtown on the first floor of the Renaissance Tower, in Grand Hope Park on W. Olympic, the Museum of Neon Art (MONA) is the only permanent neon museum in the world. A stunning and electrically enigmatic likeness of the Mona Lisa—the museum's logo, designed by Lakich—marks the spot. The permanent collection at MONA includes an impressive array of classic L.A. neon and electric signs, dating from the 1920s. Changing exhibits—such as the museum's opening 1996 exhibition, *Electric Muse: A Spectrum of Neon, Electric, and Kinetic Sculpture*—emphasize neon as a contemporary art form. Head to **CityWalk** outside Universal Studios to appreciate more of the MONA collection, which includes the Richfield Eagle and the Melrose Theater sign.

For a still flashier appreciation of local lights, sign on for the museum's after-dark "Neon Cruise" L.A. bus tour, offered at least monthly, $40 per person. In addition to its neon tours, the museum offers introductory classes in neon design and technique four times each year.

The Museum of Neon Art is open Wed.–Sat. 11 A.M.–5 P.M. and Sunday noon–5 P.M. (closed Monday, Tuesday, and major holidays). On the second Thursday of every month, the museum is also open 5–8 P.M.—and at that time admission is free to all. Otherwise admission is $5 adults, $3.50 seniors and students (children age 12 and under free). Call for current information on docent-led tours, current exhibits, neon art classes, and "Neon Cruise" tours. The museum's entrance is on Hope (at Olympic); during regular museum hours, free parking is available in the Renaissance Tower's garage on Grand just south of Ninth Street.

For current exhibit and other information, and to make reservations for MONA's Neon Tours, contact: Museum of Neon Art (MONA), Renaissance Tower, 501 W. Olympic Blvd., 213/489-9918, fax 213/489-9932; www.neonmona.org.

Those with the wherewithal to tote home personal art collections should keep in mind that private galleries gather near the art museums. Most noteworthy as the territory of working artists is near Little Tokyo in downtown's **Arts District,** an area bracketed by both the 10 and 110 Freeways and unofficially bordered by Alameda Street on the west and the L.A. River on the east. Another unusual arts destination, if you're lucky enough to be in the area when an open house or other public event is scheduled, is **The Brewery** northeast of downtown proper at 2020 N. Main St., 323/222-3007, an isolated 20-acre complex near I-5 that once manufactured Pabst Blue Ribbon Beer. These days, an intoxicating mix of artists, artisans, architects, and designers create their masterpieces all day and night, unperturbed by noise or crime at what has become one of the nation's largest working arts centers.

Yet one of downtown's almost unsung wonders is the simple fact that, here, even the absolutely penniless can possess a wealth of art—public art, displayed out and about in sometimes surprising places. Many public art projects have been financed by developer fees associated with downtown's domineering high-rises, giving people on the ground something more entertaining to look at. Thus 30-foot-tall air raid alarms abandoned at Cold War's end have been transformed into giant yellow daffodils; even bike racks and office-building windows have become raw materials for artistic expression.

Art Walks: Public Art in the Streets

The corner of Seventh and Figueroa Streets sits on poetry, at least if you're looking at one of the granite benches. Among the miscellaneous Robert Creeley poems seated along Seventh, accompanied by James Surls's etching of a rocking chair: "If I sit here/long enough/all will pass me by/one way or another." Another features five sets of eyes, with the words: "Human eyes/are lights to me/seated/in this stone"—all part of the **Poets' Walk Project** at Citicorp Plaza. But don't miss *Corporate Head* by sculptor Terry Allen, on the southeast corner of Seventh and Figueroa. More than a few confused corporados have no doubt tried to offer aid and emergency assistance to this stranded bronze suit, his head hopelessly lost in the building itself.

At Eighth and Figueroa is Andrew Leicester's sculpted futuristic courtyard with bat-wing gates, *Zanja Madre,* most famous in Hollywood circles as the subject of the artist's copyright infringement lawsuit against Warner Bros. over its use of the sculpture as a set design centerpiece for Gotham City in the film *Batman Forever.* Public art isn't necessarily *that* public.

Also worth a look downtown, before diving into the subway galleries: the 63-foot-tall *Four Arches* by Alexander Calder, 333 S. Hope St.; *Source Figure* by Robert Graham, atop the Bunker Hill steps; and Jonathan Borofsky's *Hammering Man,* on Ninth between Main and Los Angeles Streets, and his *Molecule Man,* 255 E. Temple.

Though corporations sometimes work directly with individual artists on downtown public arts projects, the city's Cultural Affairs Department and downtown's Community Redevelopment Agency are the primary agents of artistic change.

ROBERT HOLMES/CALIFORNIA DIVISION OF TOURISM

skyscraper with part of Alexander Calder's Four Arches

Art Rides: Public Art on the Subway

The **Metropolitan Transportation Authority** (MTA) is a fairly new star in L.A.'s public arts cosmos, with artistic reflection on view at Metrorail stations along the Red, Blue, and Green Lines reflecting city history and culture. And you can see it all for $5, the price of an all-day fare.

Red Line: For a tour starting downtown, start at **Union Station** and Metrorail's Red Line subway. At the western entrance is Cynthia Carlson's *City of Angels* mural, wings above the L.A. coast. To the east is Terry Schoonhoven's *Traveler,* a mural-style timeline marching forward from the days of the Spanish conquistadores. Starring at the next stop, the **Civic Center Station,** are the suspended fiberglass beings of Jonathan Borofsky's *I Dreamed I Could Fly.* At **Pershing Square Station,** appreciate Steven Antonakos's geometric *Neons for Pershing Station.* The Los Angeles obsession with Hollywoodesque imagery gets attention at the **Seventh Street/Metro Center Station** with Joyce Kozloff's tiled sequences of film characters and scenes in both *The Movies: Fantasies* and *The Movies: Spectacles.*

At the Red Line's **Westlake/MacArthur Park Station** beneath Wilshire, the reality of many L.A. residents' lives is more accurately reflected by Francisco Letelier's *El Sol* and *La Luna* (The Sun and The Moon) stoop-labor murals. Also here: Therman Statom's mirrored ladder sculpture, *Into the Light.* Above the entrance at the next stop, the **Wilshire/Vermont Station,** is Peter Shire's industrial-object sculpture series, *Los Angeles Seen.* At the **Wilshire/Normandie Station,** Frank Romero's *Festival of Masks Parade* commemorates the annual public-disguise fest sponsored annually by the Craft and Folk Art Museum. And at the **Wilshire/Western Station,** Richard Wyatt's dual 50-foot murals, *People Coming* and *People Going,* "monumentalize" downtown denizens.

Blue Line: Start an art tour of the Metro Blue Line, which runs from downtown to Long Beach on the Westside via Watts and Compton, at downtown's **Pico Station,** S. Flower St. and W. Pico Blvd. It's a cosmic kickoff, considering Robin Brailsford's awning theme; the green metal square represents a turtle, the yellow one is earth, and orange is the entire universe. Sample

intriguing people's art along the way—California history tiles by East Los Streetscapers at the **Slauson Station,** for example, and the long-running winner for best en route graffiti (as of early 1997), the **Firestone Station**—then Long Beach offerings near the end of the line. Starring at the **First Street Station,** for example, is Paul Tzanetopoulos's collection of disks decorated with abstract designs and Native Americana; at the **Pacific Station,** June Edmonds's pre-Columbian figures.

Green Line: Highlights of the route from Norwalk to Manhattan Beach include Meg Cranston's bees (inspired by the Sejat Indians' name for the area, Suka, meaning "Place of the Bees") in Norwalk; Sally Weber's interpretation of the Chumash "Celestial Chance" legend (about a confrontation between Sun and Coyote) in Lynwood; Daniel Martinez's paper airplane/aerospace theme in El Segundo; and Carl Cheng's "ocean blue" theme (you'll know you've finally arrived at the beach) in Manhattan Beach.

For more complete Metro arts information, or to take a guided tour, call 213/922-4278. For directions to the various Metro stations by car, bus, or train, call toll-free 800/266-6883 or try www.mta.net.

Museum of Contemporary Art

Los Angeles is an international mecca for contemporary art and artists, with the post-World War II art world here defined, uniquely, by exposure to and creation of popular culture and the entertainment industry. The phenomenon is difficult to accommodate within museum walls, yet L.A. tries. Along with the 20th and 21st-century collections and exhibits at the Los Angeles County Museum of Art's Anderson Building, downtown's Museum of Contemporary Art (MOCA) on Grand Avenue at California Plaza is central to L.A.'s centrality on the world's easel.

When it opened in December 1986, already a celebrity among downtown redevelopment projects, MOCA was hailed as the tonic to revivify Los Angeles the cultural wasteland. Designed by acclaimed Japanese architect Irata Isozaki, the seven-level building—98,000 square feet of red sandstone and grand pyramidal skylights—takes an elegant and impressive (if all but underground) stand against downtown's skyline. Isozaki's first major U.S. work is a work of art in its own right, architecturally abstract but grounded in geometry and Eastern tradition.

What's inside, though, is predominantly Western. The museum's permanent collection boasts important works by Diane Arbus, Sam Francis, Franz Kline, Louise Nevelson, Claes Oldenburg, Jackson Pollock, Robert Raushenberg, Mark Rothko, Andy Warhol, and others. Both the museum's permanent collection and special exhibits showcase works created since the 1940s, including painting and sculpture, mixed media, environmental pieces, and performance art. Increasingly, MOCA's changing shows tend toward the hip and flashy L.A. art *event*, pop-culture and entertainment-industry shows Hollywood and the Westside will dress up and drive for. More cerebral topics, such as early 1997's "The Power of Suggestion: Narrative and Notation in Contemporary Drawing," also slip through the doors from time to time. MOCA's collection was bolstered in 1997 by a gift of 105 postwar artworks from the Lannan Foundation, greatly enriching the museum's 4,000-piece holding of postwar art.

In 1983, during early MOCA construction, a temporary museum outpost known as the Temporary Contemporary (or "TC") parked itself in an old police department garage near Little Tokyo at 152 N. Central Avenue. The TC has since become a seemingly permanent museum adjunct known as the **Geffen Contemporary at MOCA** (one same-day admission gets you into both) known for its adventuresome shows and performances.

For current exhibits, box office and other information, or to request a map and brochure by mail, contact: the Museum of Contemporary Art, 250 S. Grand Ave. (just south of First St.), 213/626-6222; www.moca.org. The museum is open Tues.–Sun. 11 A.M.–5 P.M. (until 8 P.M. on Thursday), closed Thanksgiving, Christmas, and New Year's Day. Admission is $6 adults, $4 seniors (over age 65) and students with ID, free for children under age 12. On Thursday evening, 5–8 P.M., admission is free. For parking, try the Performing Arts Center lot.

Performance Arts Center of L.A. County

This imposing performing arts center atop downtown's Bunker Hill—formerly known as the Music Center—is L.A.'s own Lincoln Center, comprised of three separate theaters. The **Dorothy Chandler Pavilion,** named for the philanthropist wife of late *Los Angeles Times* publisher Otis Chandler, is the largest of the three, with seating for 3,250. The Chandler Pavilion's enormous marble lobby, lit with gigantic crystal chandeliers, has provided a glamorous photo-op backdrop for many Academy Awards ceremonies. The pavilion is also a more permanent home for the L.A. Philharmonic, the Performing Arts Center Opera, and other worthies.

The **Ahmanson Theatre** is a 2,100-seat venue for popular performances, musicals, and plays, including L.A.'s run of *Phantom of the Opera* and *Kiss of the Spider Woman.* (Just in case you don't get a good seat, bring binoculars.)

The Center's **Mark Taper Forum** is an intimate 750-seat theater known for its adventurous and contemporary pre-Broadway premieres. *Zoot Suit, Children of a Lesser God, Jelly's Last Jam,* and *Angels in America* are among the hundreds of experimental productions that have established the Taper as a renowned innovative playhouse.

One day soon, the long-awaited Walt Disney Concert Hall will take wing here. Designed by architect Frank Gehry to dominate a full city block just west of the Dorothy Chandler Pavilion at First Street and Grand Avenue, the Walt Disney Concert Hall has long been stalled by cost overruns (anyone with an extra $50 million in pocket change, deposit it here).

For show and ticket information, call the Performing Arts Center, 135 N. Grand Avenue (at the corner of First St.), 213/972-7211, or check the website at www.performingartscenterla.com.

DOWNTOWN MARKETS

Grand Central Market

Here's the L.A. that defies the urban-cool stereotype. Yet the colorful Grand Central Market is so cool that everybody comes here, at least once in awhile. At lunchtime the goal is strictly satiation. Row after row of neon-lit food stalls feature some of the city's most authentic and least expensive Mexican food alongside endless other ethnic selections. Deciding what to

Grand Central Market

buy and where to buy it, is something of a challenge; the best approach for first-timers is just to follow your nose as you shuffle through the sawdust. But you can find just about anything here—fresh produce, meat, and seafood, exotic herbs and spices. The Grand Central Market, 317 S. Market St. (between Broadway and Hill St. and Third and Fourth Sts.), 213/624-2378, is open daily 9 A.M.–6 P.M., closed Thanksgiving and Christmas.

Fashion District

Until recently known as the Garment District, L.A.'s Fashion District is a major center for garment manufacturing—both legal shops and sweatshops—and is a natural magnet for bargain shoppers. The district itself is generally defined as the area east of Main and west of San Pedro between Seventh and Eleventh Streets. Serious shoppers will find the highest concentration of outlet stores on S. Los Angeles Street between Seventh and Ninth. Best bets include the **Cooper Building,** 860 S. Los Angeles St.

(between Eighth and Ninth Sts.), 213/627-3754, multiple floors and more than 80 stores filled with designer clothing, shoes, and linens offered at bargain-basement prices. Or try the **CaliforniaMart,** 110 East Ninth St. (at Main), 213/630-3710, the largest wholesale apparel center in the nation. Be prepared to pay for parking.

Other Wholesale Markets

Extremely early risers and night owls will enjoy the **Wholesale Flower Market,** at 742 Maple Ave. (between Seventh and Eighth Sts.), 213/627-2482, where the action begins daily at 3 A.M. as flower merchants begin picking through the colorful, fragrant bounty. Flowers and potted plants are available to the general public at a considerable discount. Other possibilities for truly adventurous shoppers: the city's **Jewelry District,** just south of Pershing Square and north of Seventh Street (many outlets wholesale only), and the **Wholesale Toy District** in the midst of Skid Row just south of Little Tokyo and west of San Pedro Street.

MID-WILSHIRE AND THE MIRACLE MILE

Wilshire Boulevard is among L.A.'s most historic thoroughfares. It predates even concrete, though not necessarily asphalt. This is the path native Shoshone peoples took to reach the sea—Spanish colonialists called it Camino Viejo, or "Old Road"—and to reach the now-famous La Brea Tar Pits, where they scooped up the sticky, petroleum-rich tar to caulk and waterproof their homes.

Though 16-mile Wilshire Boulevard continues west to the ocean—becoming a grand promenade through Beverly Hills and the Los Angeles Country Club before veering near UCLA and then jogging to Santa Monica—the following section covers the "mid-Wilshire" district, between the Harbor (110) Freeway on the east and opulent Beverly Hills on the west.

WANDERING WEST ON WILSHIRE

At the edge of downtown, on Wilshire Boulevard between Figueroa and Beaudry, is a particularly good spot to view downtown L.A.'s oft-mentioned **four-level freeway interchange**—look north—and certainly a great photo opportunity for those who propose replacing the poppy as California's state flower with the concrete cloverleaf. For an intriguing side trip, just south and west is the **Loyola Law School,** 1441 Olympic Blvd., where the conversion from dreary warehouse to architectural phenomenon–cum-art collection was supervised by L.A.'s famed architect Frank Gehry.

Reconnect with Wilshire by heading north on **S. Bonnie Brae,** a residential neighborhood built during L.A.'s 1880s' real estate boom and home to some of the city's finest Victorians. Among these is the **Grier Musser Museum,** 403 S. Bonnie Brae, 213/413-1814, which houses an impressive collection of Victorian-era antiques. Anna Grier Musser and her descendants amassed such a huge collection of Victoriana that they purchased and refurbished a 13-room Queen Anne-style mansion to handle their overflow. The museum, open to the public only by appointment or on special occasions, was founded as a tribute to Musser, a Pennsylvania antique dealer who hosted the 1950s television show *Know Your Antiques.* The 800 block of Bonnie Brae boasts a broad cross section of the most fashionable American styles of affluence in that era: colonial revival, Gothic, Moorish, and Queen Anne. Nearby is another prestigious turn-of-the-20th-century neighborhood—**Alvarado Terrace** between Pico and Hoover, once the most desirable neighborhood in the city and still relatively unperturbed by progress—a curving street of terraced lawns and stately mansions built in large part by architect Pomeroy Powers.

MacArthur Park, on Wilshire between Alvarado and Park View, is 32 acres of rare plants and trees with lake and well-trodden children's play areas—yet not a particularly safe place for tourists, decidedly dangerous after dark. But on the weekends neighborhood vendors sell crafts, sundries, and jewelry made in Mexico from brightly colored wood-lacquered carts. Known as Westlake Park when the one-

---

PUTTING WILSHIRE ON THE MAP

Wilshire Boulevard, which meanders west from downtown to the Pacific Ocean, was named for H. Gaylord Wilshire (1861–1927), a somewhat eccentric socialist millionaire who meandered west to L.A. from Ohio to win (and lose) fortunes as a farmer, inventor, gold miner, and real estate developer. Considering renewed popular interest in healing magnets, keep in mind that Wilshire the man financed Wilshire the real estate venture with profits generated from an invention he called the I-on-a-co—a magnetic horse collar alleged to cure any ailment (including gray hair) by "magnetizing" the iron in the bloodstream. But it was the discovery of oil—vast underground pools of black gold—that put Wilshire Boulevard on the map. Edward Doheny was the first to strike it rich, accidentally digging into his own oil field with a garden shovel.

time marsh was claimed for the gentry in 1890, the park was renamed during World War II for General Douglas MacArthur. A statue of Mac-Arthur stands at the park's southeast corner—and a statue of *Los Angeles Times* founder Harrison Gray Otis stands to the southwest, near Park View. The prestigious **Otis College of Art and Design**—originally the Otis Art Institute, long established at the north end of the park—is at least indirectly responsible for various contemporary artworks scattered throughout the park. *Clock Tower: A Monument to the Unknown,* fabricated from rusty found objects by George Herms, is dedicated to the old men who once played chess here. These days, though, Otis College is but a neighborhood memory. The school moved on, finding safer, more spacious digs elsewhere. The Los Angeles Board of Education hopes to transform the abandoned Otis campus into a much-needed elementary school, and the city planning commission may turn one of its dorms into a 400-bed correctional facility for minor offenders on work furlough.

As recently as 1980 no lesser authority than the *Los Angeles Times* could boast that the two-mile stretch of Wilshire between MacArthur Park and Wilton Place was "Los Angeles' Champs Elysées." Those days are long gone. Most of the boulevard's art-deco icons are boarded up or otherwise gone for good, with only the homeless enjoying the fading historic scenery after dark. What large-scale corporate flight and drastically changing neighborhood demographics couldn't destroy, rioting looters in 1992 did—using the original Rodney King police-brutality verdicts as their excuse. (Given the well-publicized racial overtones of that case—and equally well-publicized tensions between the black and Korean communities, a subject given major play in the pages of the *Los Angeles Times*—perhaps it should have been no surprise that Koreatown businesses bore the brunt of the rampage. But it was still a surprise.) After tearing up this section of Wilshire for the Metrorail subway, endlessly disruptive construction that put many surviving small businesses out of business, the city then decided to route the remainder of the rail line to the Westside from Western Avenue along Pico instead—virtually guaranteeing moribund future prospects for Wilshire.

Bullocks Wilshire, just east of Vermont Avenue (between Wilshire Place and Westmoreland) at 3050 Wilshire Blvd., was the city's premiere department store during L.A.'s art deco golden age. Known as I. Magnin Bullocks Wilshire before closing shop in 1993, this five-story masterpiece topped by a signature zigzag moderne copper-clad tower was L.A.'s initial link between cars and consumers. When it opened for business in 1929, Bullocks Wilshire was the first to successfully lure wealthy shoppers in shiny new cars out to the bean fields (literally) from fashionable downtown. The building is now owned by the Southwestern University School of Law, and the private law library and university offices now housed here are decked out in Bullocks Wilshire's original deco glory.

In the center of mid-Wilshire's Wilshire Center neighborhood, with its high-rises and immigrant-crowded housing, stands the old **Ambassador Hotel** at 3400 Wilshire—L.A.'s first grand resort hotel when it opened in 1921. The Ambassador reached stellar social heights during the heyday of Hollywood stars. The low point came in 1968, when presidential candidate Robert F. Kennedy was assassinated near the restaurant's kitchen. The aging hotel remained open for business until 1987, and preservationists have battled plans to demolish it—be the perpetrator developer Donald Trump or the city Board of Education—ever since. For information on the hotel's status, contact the Los Angeles Conservancy, 213/623-2489; www.laconservancy.org.

Other art deco icons have been successfully saved, including the classic Pellissier Building at the southeast corner of Wilshire and Western, now the stunning **Wiltern Center** with a 12-story tower and the lovingly restored **Wiltern Theatre.** Its deep turquoise terra-cotta façade embellished with dazzling zigzag moderne-style copper, the 2,300-seat Wiltern had been badly damaged by vandals before the building's restoration.

Just one block north of Wilshire at 605 S. Irving Blvd. (at Sixth St.) is the **Getty House,** built in 1921 in English half-timber style and the official residence of L.A.'s mayors—at least former Mayor Tom Bradley, who lived here for 16 years —since the home was donated to the city by the Getty Oil Company. Recently restored with $1.2 million in private contributions and the endless volunteer hours of L.A.-area designers, the Getty House now hosts foreign dignitaries, fundraising events, and official city functions, since Bradley's successor, Mayor Richard Riordan, has preferred living at his Brentwood estate.

Stretching from Wilshire to Beverly Boulevard and bounded on the east and west by Bronson and Highland Avenues, respectively, is the rest of the leafy residential neighborhood of **Hancock Park,** one of the last elegant residential tracts developed in the Wilshire area and still home to respectable quantities of L.A.'s old and new money. Henry Hancock, who bought Rancho La Brea in 1860, discovered oil—the fluid foundation of the family's subsequent fortune—and in 1910 his son laid out subdivisions around the Wilshire Country Club. These mansion-rich neighborhoods housed the Crocker, Doheny, Huntington, and Van Nuys families, to name just a few of

MID-WILSHIRE OVERVIEW

As with Sunset Boulevard, following Wilshire west makes a fascinating linear tour of Los Angeles. Reaching out from downtown along and around Wilshire are neighborhoods of recently arrived immigrants from Central America and Mexico. Between Vermont and Western Avenues lies Koreatown, home to the largest population of Koreans outside of Korea. High-rises line the business district from Lafayette Park to La Brea Avenue; Larchmont Village in the wealthy Hancock Park neighborhood is a fashionable neighborhood shopping and dining district. The historic Miracle Mile shopping district stretches between La Brea and Fairfax Avenues, roughly coinciding with the city's premier museum district, which begins in Hancock Park (the park, not to be confused with the same-named neighborhood).

New—or new again—along Wilshire Boulevard are the flashing rooftop neon signs that once served as real-life beacons for Raymond Chandler's fictional private eye Philip Marlowe. How fitting. And how international. Though the French invented neon lights—and, indirectly, L.A.'s signature public flash—two British scientists named the gas they discovered in 1898 after the Greek word for "new."

L.A.'s most prominent. Tours of area homes and buildings designed by Paul Revere Williams, the first African-American fellow of the American Institute of Architects, are typically offered in February—during Black History Month—by the Los Angeles Conservancy. (For more information on Conservancy tours, see Getting up to Speed Downtown, above). Charming **Larchmont Village,** situated primarily on Larchmont Boulevard on a four-block stretch between First Street and Beverly Boulevard, is the neighborhood's shopping district.

Wilshire's **Miracle Mile,** between La Brea and Fairfax Avenues, a somewhat self-promotional designation for the car-oriented 1920s' shopping district built by A. W. Ross, is fast regaining its former glory. Between La Brea and Burnside, a historic district included on the National Register of Historic Places, are 19 elegant streamline and zigzag moderne survivors. Wilshire's expansive museum district—a must-do destination—begins here in Hancock Park (the park, not the neighborhood) at the redundantly known La Brea Tar Pits (*la brea* means the tar) and associated George C. Page Museum. Next door is the Los Angeles County Museum of Art (LACMA), offering impressive collections, special shows, and endlessly popular Friday Night Jazz. Across the street is the fascinating Craft and Folk Art Museum. Fairly new to the neighborhood: the Carole and Barry Kaye Museum of Miniatures and the très-L.A. Petersen Automotive Museum.

Bullocks Wilshire
(Southwestern University)

Just east of Vermont Avenue at 3050 Wilshire, Bullocks Wilshire was aptly described as a "cathedral of commerce" when it first opened in 1929. Now included on the National Register of Historic Places and a fascination for architecture fans and social historians alike, Bullocks Wilshire—known as I. Magnin Bullocks Wilshire when it closed its department store doors in 1993—was built when travel still seemed the privileged domain of the privileged few yet everyone was on the move. The transportation tribute here is a natural, starting with the Herman Sachs mural at the entrance and continuing throughout with images of ships, trains, and airplanes linking the elegant fixtures, furnishings, rich wood veneers, and artful collages of the old-money shopping salons.

A cultural preservation scandal was averted in late 1993 when the R. H. Macy Co. agreed to return most of the exquisite historic fixtures and furniture it had stripped from the building—miscellaneous sconces, marble-topped tables, mantel clocks, fireplace screens, antique salon-style divans and chairs, even the men's-clubbish chrome and leather chairs. Missing are the stunning Lalique crystal chandeliers, designed to impersonate streamline-moderne skyscrapers, which had been moved here in 1972 from downtown's Oviatt Building; they remain in a San Francisco I. Magnin.

The Bullocks Wilshire Building, owned by the **Southwestern University School of Law,** is now a private law library and university office space. At last report Southwestern offered guided tours; for current information, call the university's Public Affairs office at 213/738-6731.

La Brea Avenue

La Brea between Wilshire and Santa Monica Boulevards could be classified as Melrose for the More Settled Set. (Since the two streets intersect, once you've taken the wild ride along mad, mad Melrose you can leap off here. Or vice versa.) During its heyday this wide, car-accommodating street overflowed with stylish car dealerships. Many of these neglected 1930s art deco and Spanish-revival car palaces are flourishing in the neighborhood's rebirth as an upscale artsy enclave. Neighborhood attractions include good vintage clothing stores, unusual furniture and furnishings shops, and art and photography galleries. Best of all, La Brea boasts some of the city's most popular restaurants (reservations often mandatory) and one of L.A.'s best bakeries.

For glad rags, first stop is **American Rag Cie,** 150 S. La Brea Ave. (on the east side of La Brea, at First), tel. 323/935-3154. American Rag's original claim to fame was retro clothing, both new and "gently used." And this is still one of L.A.'s best vintage clothing shops; the warehouselike hall is divided into eras, making it easier to search for that 1950s' crinoline dress, '40s tuxedo, or psychedelic tie. Everything's clean and in good repair. Now the glad-rag gallery has expanded to include a chic shoe emporium, styl-

ish European fashions and accessories (for both men and women), and, best of all, home furnishings. All five shops are united by the stars and stripes of American Rag. Just a few doors down is the terrific **Golyester,** 136 S. La Brea (between First and Second), 323/931-1339, with an outstanding collection of vintage and couture clothing from the 1930s and '40s plus antique textiles, all museum quality and offered at very reasonable prices. For hats, try **Drea Kadilak,** 463 S. La Brea (at Sixth St.), 323/931-2051. If you've always hankered after one of those only-in-L.A. poured-on latex dresses, the place to look is **Syren,** just west of La Brea at 7225 Beverly Blvd. (near Formosa), 323/936-6693, which supplied the full-body rubber suits in the movie **Batman.**

Stylish antique and furniture shops—particularly near Sixth Street. and Beverly Boulevard—and art and photography galleries round out the neighborhood's shopping options. Check out **Mortise & Tenon,** 446 S. La Brea (one and a half blocks north of Wilshire), 323/937-7654, for its stylish handmade furniture, lighting, and accessories. Though you'll want to get out of your car and walk the neighborhood, just to see what's where, art-wise, be sure to poke into the **Jan Baum** and other collected galleries at 170 S. La Brea (between First and Second), 323/932-0170, a favorite Angeleno destination. Venturing north you'll find, among others, the respected **Fahey/Klein Gallery,** 148 N. La Brea (near Beverly Blvd.), 323/934-2250, and the **Jan Kesner Gallery,** 164 N. La Brea (at Beverly Blvd.), 323/938-6834, two of L.A.'s best for photography. Also worth a look: **Couterier Gallery** at 166 N. La Brea.

Hungry yet? Stop at the **La Brea Bakery,** 624 S. La Brea (near Sixth St.), 323/939-6813, for the city's best breads and baked goods—such things as hearty whole-grain, walnut, and rye-currant bread, not to mention the scones, *fougassa,* and delectable pastries and desserts. Every morning well-heeled Angelenos join the "bread line" here quite happily, partaking in a local foodie tradition that gets particularly dramatic on weekends and before major holidays. If you can't get by the tiny bakery, don't worry. Celebrity bread chef Nancy Silverton ships millions of loaves to Trader Joe's and high-end grocery chains throughout Southern California (and beyond); just look for the La Brea Bakery label. For fine sit-down fare at breakfast, lunch, and dinner, the very popular California-style Mediterranean **Campanile** restaurant is right here, too, which Silverton helps to oversee with her co-owner/husband/chef Mark Peel. Campanile is one of L.A.'s best restaurants, a relaxed bastion of well-being.

Quite good, at the more modest end of the expense spectrum, is **Flora Kitchen,** 460 S. La Brea, 323/931-9900, a casual café serving great salads, sandwiches, and specials. Half of the café seating is inside **Rita Flora** flower shop, where the aroma and arrangements are arresting. Immensely popular for Northern Italian is **Ca'Brea,** 346 S. La Brea (between Third and Fourth Sts.), 323/938-2863, along with too-hip **Farfalla La Brea,** 143 N. La Brea (between First and Second Sts.), 323/938-2504. For French-Vietnamese, the place is **Mandalay,** 611 N. La Brea (north of Beverly Blvd. near Melrose, at Clinton), 323/933-0717. For more on where to eat in this and other Wilshire-area neighborhoods, see Practical Downtown (and Around), below.

Page Museum at the La Brea Tar Pits

The main attractions here are the Pleistocene fossils—bones of sloths, saber-toothed cats, dire wolves, woolly mammoths, and prehistoric condors—plucked from L.A.'s famous La Brea Tar Pits, the largest fossil concentration ever discovered. Some of the pits are still open for active exploration, an urban aesthetic oddity complete with ersatz Ice Age mascots just outside the museum.

About 35,000–40,000 years ago, right here along what is now Wilshire Boulevard, oil deposits rose from the earth's depths and collected in pools on the surface. The crude oil gradually thickened into sticky asphalt; when prehistoric California critters ambled down to this watering hole, the goo got them. The remains of such unlucky animals—prey and predators alike—were first discovered in the early 1900s, and the bone harvest has continued ever since. Well over 100 tons of Ice Age fossils, more than 1.5 million vertebrate and another 2.5 million invertebrate fossils, have been recovered to date, representing more than 140 plant species and 420 species of animals, not counting birds and insects.

What was collected, and how, is the story told by the museum, which is hunkered down into the earth like a bunker; only the entrance and a frieze depicting life in prehistoric times are visible from the street. Exhibits include fossil reconstructions—whole skeletons of prehistoric mammoths, wolves, sloths, and birds—along with a glassed-in working paleontology lab (affectionately known as the "fishbowl") and short documentary films. Always the biggest hit with the kids: the "La Brea Woman" hologram, allowing bones to magically become flesh.

La Brea Tar Pits

TOM MYERS PHOTOGRAPHY

If you have time on your hands, incidentally, La Brea's pits are actively excavated still—in July and August, when summer heat softens the asphalt in Pit 91 and everywhere else around town. Serious volunteers are welcome to share the workload, as always, at the George C. Page Museum, but even intrigued bystanders can enjoy the show.

Page Museum at the La Brea Tar Pits is in Hancock Park at 5801 Wilshire Blvd. (on the north side of the street, at Curson), 323/934-7243; www.tarpits.org. The museum is open Mon.–Fri. 9:30 A.M.–5 P.M., Sat.–Sun. 10 A.M.–5 P.M., closed major holidays. Two free tours are offered Wed.–Sun.; the first, at 1 P.M., explores Hancock Park, and the museum tour begins at 2 P.M. (To arrange tours for nonschool groups—reservations are required–call 323-857-6306.) Admission is $6 adults, $3.50 seniors and students with ID, $2 for children ages 5–10 (under 5 free), but free for everyone on the second Tuesday of every month. All-day parking in the museum lot is $5 with museum validation, otherwise $7.50. Metered street parking is nearby, most feasible north of the park.

Los Angeles County Museum of Art

The well-endowed Los Angeles County Museum of Art in Hancock Park is typically known by its less than poetic abbreviation: LACMA. The largest county museum, LACMA is a collection of rather unremarkable buildings—"shopping mall architecture" one critic sniffed when it opened in 1965—surrounding a central courtyard. Yet neither the awkward acronym nor the architecture succeeds in keeping people away.

The remarkable art collected here will keep even a reluctant visitor busy for at least a half-day. The **Pavilion for Japanese Art** features the famed Shin'enkan painting collection as well as sculpture and ceramics. Galleries in the **Hammer Building,** home to often notable special exhibits, emphasize photography, drawings, and prints. The focus of the **Anderson Building** is contemporary sculpture, painting, and special exhibits.

Do save time for the **Ahmanson Building,** home to most of the museum's eclectic but impressive collection—classical paintings, home furnishings and decorations, textiles, costumes, mosaics, silver, and ancient glass. Among its other treasures: the world's largest collection of Indian, Nepalese, and Tibetan art. The **Carter Gallery,** subdivided into four smaller rooms, successfully showcases 17th-century French paintings—one of the finest American collections, including *Magdalen with the Smoking Flame* by Georges de La Tour—English ceramics and European porcelain, 18th-century Italian sculpture and paintings, and 18th-century French paintings. The **Leo S. Bing Center** contains the 500-seat Bing Theater, venue for many film series, concerts, and public lectures. The museum also offers an art rental gallery, extensive art research library, and an excellent museum shop and on-site café.

The Los Angeles Museum of Art also includes the adjacent 1940s May Company building at Wilshire and Fairfax—the best example of streamline moderne architecture, a post-art-deco phenomenon, remaining in Southern California. Now known as **LACMA West,** since its $3 million renovation, the onetime department store is home to blockbuster exhibits such as *Van Gogh's Van Goghs.* Also intriguing at LACMA West is the satellite gallery space for L.A.'s venerable **Southwest Museum,** 323/933-4510, $6 admission, where exhibitions such as *Common Threads: Pueblo and Navajo Textiles* are always worth the time. (For more information on the Southwest Museum and its collection and programs, see Near Pasadena.)

Beyond its numerous special exhibits and events, the museum itself has become an event—thanks to its free **Friday Night Jazz** program, which showcases L.A.'s best jazz artists in its ever-changing musical lineup. Be it bebop, swing, or some strange sonic experiment, jazz that represents the art form—not necessarily popular entertainment—is served to patrons, along with cocktails, soft drinks, and simple restaurant fare. And free popcorn. In good weather, which means most of the time, Friday Night Jazz is staged outside on the museum's central plaza 5:30–8:30 P.M.; in the summer hundreds, if not thousands, of people show up. If it's raining or unusually cold out—and unless the program has been curtailed during winter—the musicians sound forth indoors. Occasional Sunday afternoon big-band concerts are also popular in summer.

The Los Angeles County Museum of Art is west of the Page Museum at the La Brea Tar

Pits in Hancock Park, 5905 Wilshire Blvd. (at Ogden Dr.), 323/857-6000; www.lacma.org. The museum is open Monday, Tuesday, and Thursday noon–8 P.M.; Friday noon–9 P.M.; and on weekends 11 A.M.–8 P.M. (closed on Wednesdays and major holidays). For tour information, call 323/857-6000. Admission is $7 adults, $5 seniors and students with ID, and $1 children ages 6–17 (age 5 and under free). On the second Tuesday of each month, admission is free for everyone. Call 323/857-6010 for information on current and upcoming special exhibits, events, and jazz programs.

Craft and Folk Art Museum

Across the street from the Page Museum, the Craft and Folk Art Museum features changing exhibits of ethnic, historic, and contemporary folk arts and crafts from around the world. Recent exhibitions included *Carnivale,* featuring carnival photographs and costumes; *Girls' Lowrider Bicycles;* and *Victoriana,* a look at both the romance and darker side of the 19th century. And, as one might imagine, the museum shop here is marvelous.

L.A.'s Craft and Folk Art Museum, 5814 Wilshire Blvd. (on the south side of Wilshire between Curson and Stanley Avenues) 323/937-4230, is open Tues.–Sun. 11 A.M.–5 P.M. (until 9 P.M. on Thursday). Admission is $3.50 adults, $2.50 seniors and students (age 12 and under free).

Carole & Barry Kaye Museum of Miniatures

Unless you're generally inspired by dollhouses, dollhouse-size furniture, and dollhouse-size scenes—poker-playing dogs, for example, a diorama of the O.J. Simpson trial, or a pint-size Louis Armstrong performing at the Hollywood Bowl—L.A.'s miniatures museum won't be as worthwhile as the art and science enlightenment available just across the street in Hancock Park. One notable exception is the museum's **Eugene and Henry Kupjack Gallery,** displaying some of the finest examples of the genre. Eugene Kupjack, father of Henry, is most famous for his work on the **Thorne Rooms,** a 1930s project now part of the permanent collection at the Art Institute of Chicago.

The Museum of Miniatures is directly across from LACMA at 5900 Wilshire Blvd., 323/937-

7766, www.museumofminiatures.com. The museum is open Tues.–Sat. 10 A.M.–5 P.M., Sunday 11 A.M.–5 P.M., closed major holidays. Admission is $7.50 adults, $6.50 seniors (60 and older), $5 ages 12–21, and $3 ages 3–11. Half-price validated parking is available directly below the museum every day but Sunday.

Petersen Automotive Museum

California couldn't live without the automobile, Americans assume. Los Angeles residents in particular live and breathe—or don't breathe—for their cars, it is also assumed. Cars in L.A. are like clothes in New York—the essential ingredient in presenting one's attitude and status to the world. Yet Californians actually own fewer vehicles, use less fuel, and drive fewer miles than the national average. Californians *do* love their cars, however, and the myth of unfettered geographic and social mobility that powers them. And L.A. *is* the only major U.S. city designed of, by, and for car culture.

Thus the appeal of the Petersen Museum, named after Robert Peterson, publisher of *Hot Rod* and **Motor Trend** magazines. This poparty paean to southstate automobility is not just another parking lot for antique cars. The Petersen, instead, acknowledges and incorporates almost every aspect of L.A.'s car culture—from its oddball architecture and old gas stations to drive-in diners, L-shaped strip malls (an L.A. first), and freeways. Upstairs are various cars presented as historical icons—including Greta Garbo's 1925 Lincoln—and works of art. It's all exceptionally well done. Past shows have included *The Lowriding Tradition,* examining L.A.'s lowrider culture as mobile folk art, and a feature on "woodies" and surf culture.

The Petersen Automotive Museum, 6060 Wilshire Blvd. (at Fairfax), 323/930-2277, www.petersen.org, is open Tues.–Sun. and Mondays that are holidays 10 A.M.–6 P.M., closed major holidays. Admission is $7 adults, $5 seniors (over age 62) and students with ID, $3 children ages 5–12 (under 5 free). To arrange guided tours, call 323/964-6346.

Farmers Market

An L.A. landmark since 1934, the Farmers Market ain't what it used to be. During the Depression, farmers paid 50 cents each day for the privilege of hawking produce from beat-up old trucks parked here. These days it's quite citified; vendors sell their wares from permanent stalls inside. But it's still casual, colorful, lively, and loud—one of those places kids can visit without constantly apologizing for themselves. You can find just about anything here—specialty foods, flowers, arts and crafts, clothing, jewelry—yet the food stands are the real draw. The **Kokomo** café, open at breakfast and lunch, is quite popular with show-biz types since CBS Studios' Television City is right next door. This is just the place to power down breakfast basics, hearty but hip burgers, and the best BLTs in town while waiting for some celebrity or pseudo-celeb to stroll by. Also here is the **Gumbo Pot,** a real deal for Cajun, serving the cheapest and best gumbo, jambalaya, and blackened redfish around.

The Farmers Market, 6333 W. Third St. (at Fairfax), 323/933-9211, is open Mon.–Sat. 9 A.M.–6:30 P.M. and Sunday 10 A.M.–5 P.M. (until later in summer) except on major holidays.

Nearby on Fairfax

Fairfax between Beverly Boulevard and Melrose Avenue, particularly between Oakwood and Rosewood Avenues, is the traditional cultural center of L.A.'s Russian-Jewish immigrant community. In addition to Russian restaurants, this has long been the place to look for kosher groceries, shops, and delis—including well-known and colorful 24-hour **Canter's Deli,** 419 N. Fairfax Ave. (at Melrose), 323/651-2030, where the hot pastrami sandwich is king. Other items are quite popular too. On the back of the menu is a rough tally, pointing out that (at last report) Canter's had served more than 24 million bowls of chicken soup, 20 million bagels, and 10 million matzo balls. This is the place if you're missing New York, seeking verbal abuse from a cranky waitress, or hoping to catch a celebrity in a late-night nosh.

Canter's is also *cool.* On almost any night the music scene at the adjacent **Kibitz Room,** gets *down,* especially after midnight or at Tuesday's jam session, which takes over even the dining room. Actually the entire neighborhood is becoming suspiciously hip. As younger Orthodox Jewish families migrate north to North Hollywood and west of Fairfax to the Pico-Robertson region, the hipsters have been moving in. Other trendy late-night hangouts include the cosmic **Nova Express Café,** at 2042 N. Fairfax Ave., 323/651-4421, and super-cool **Max's Bar and Lounge,** 426 N. Fairfax Ave., 323/658-7533.

TOM MYERS PHOTOGRAPHY

Farmers Market

St. Elmo Village

For a taste of contemporary L.A.'s urban folk art, stop by St. Elmo Village in the general vicinity of Wilshire at 4830 St. Elmo Dr. (in the Mid-City neighborhood, off La Brea just south of Venice Blvd.), 323/931-3409, where artist Roderick Sykes and friends transformed a neglected cluster of bungalows into a garden of vivid, imaginative color with little more than endless ingenuity, "found objects," and bright paint. On the walls here are faces of every color and ethnicity along with hopeful messages, images, and sculpture promoting brotherhood and peace. This official L.A. cultural landmark now serves as an innovative children's art center.

AROUND DOWNTOWN

TO EXPOSITION PARK

Directly southwest of downtown proper—via Figueroa St., for the freeway-phobic—is Exposition Park, originally a 19th-century fairground and present-day home to several of the city's fine museums. Along the way are other urban attractions.

Intriguing for students of historic architecture is the downtown campus of **Mt. St. Mary's College,** 213/746-0450, where incorporated **Chester Place** between 23rd St. and W. Adams Blvd. exemplifies gracious L.A. living at the turn of the 20th century. This 20-acre site was originally developed by Judge Charles S. Silent in 1895 as a residential park for 13 mansions. The **Doheny Mansion,** 8 Chester Place, is considered the finest on the block. Designed by Theodore Eisen and Sumner Hunt, this Spanish-style Gothic chateau was bought from the original owner by oil baron Edward Doheny shortly after construction in 1900. These onetime homes, with modernized interiors, are now used as classroom and administrative office space and are not open for public tours. But you can "walk the block" from 23rd to W. Adams—and, for a vigorous, eye-opening stroll, continue west on Adams almost all the way to Crenshaw for many more examples of well-preserved historic L.A.

West of Figueroa the **Shrine Auditorium** at 665 W. Jefferson (at Royal), 213/749-5123, was the largest theater in the world when it was built in 1925. Architects John C. Austin, A. M. Edelman, and G. A. Landsbery are responsible for this Hollywood version of Islamic architecture. The auditorium is well known as venue for the Academy Awards and other entertaining affairs.

Nearby and bordering the University of Southern California is **Hebrew Union College,** 3077 University Ave., 213/749-3424, open here since 1954. Until recently the impressive collection of Judaica displayed at the Skirball Museum here was a major public attraction, but the museum has moved to the Westside and rededicated itself as the Skirball Cultural Center. For additional information, see Beverly Hills and Vicinity.

University of Southern California

Just south of the Shrine Auditorium, between Jefferson and Exposition Boulevards and Vermont Avenue and Figueroa, is the USC campus, known locally as simply "SC," the oldest private coeducational university of significant size on the West Coast. With 191 buildings on its 152 acres, USC was founded in 1880 with 53 students. Current enrollment approaches 30,000. Despite encroaching poverty from surrounding neighborhoods, the campus itself—with its red brick and ivy—often stars in movies and TV shows. Some of its most memorable buildings include the **Doheny Memorial Library** and the wood-frame **Widney Hall,** which dates from 1880. Famous for its good football players, the school boasts 100 or so All-Americans and Heisman Trophy winners; "Fight on!" is the long-running rallying cry. (Most USC games are played at the nearby Memorial Coliseum in Exposition Park.) The university is also noted for outstanding professional schools in architecture, law, medicine, and cinema. In 1929 USC established the first university film studies program in the United States. Famous alumni include George Lucas and Steven Spielberg, who have endowed a state-of-the-art film production facility here. Free tours of the campus are offered Mon.–Fri. and depart hourly between 10 A.M. and 3 P.M. For information, call 213/740-6605.

EXPOSITION PARK

Directly south of USC but otherwise not in the most inviting of neighborhoods is Exposition Park, originally an agriculture-oriented fairground established in 1872. The Southern California Agricultural Society organized fairs, carnivals, and eventually horse races here; but once gambling began, in the 1890s, saloons and houses of ill-repute soon followed. The 114-acre park was reclaimed for use by respectable people at the behest of Judge William Miller Bowen, who hoped to create a "landmark of worthwhile cultural significance." After the city and county of Los Angeles and the state of California jointly bought the land in 1910, work began on the park's first museum—the Natural History Museum of Los Angeles County.

But Judge Bowen's dream wasn't fully realized until 1932, when Los Angeles hosted the Olympics in Exposition Park, which explains the existence here of the Los Angeles Memorial Sports Arena and the Los Angeles Memorial Coliseum. (Many events were also held here during L.A.'s 1984 Olympics.) The Coliseum, seriously damaged in the 1994 Northridge earthquake, was recently home to the L.A. Raiders football team—repaired just in time for the Raiders' announcement that the football franchise was moving back to Oakland. Also still standing—and open, in summer, for public swimming—is the stunning Olympics-era **McDonald's Swim Stadium**, 213/740-8480, very carefully built out of beach sand. Impressive in peak season is the sunken **Exposition Park Rose Garden** at the park's north end at 900 Exposition Blvd., 213/763-3466, a popular site for weddings, with more than 20,000 rosebushes in at least 190 varieties. In Southern California, roses bloom from March to November. The garden is open daily 7 A.M.–5 P.M. Free.

Much more exposition than park even today, Exposition Park buildings house the jazzy new California Science Center, complete with new seven-story Imax theater; the venerable Natural History Museum of Los Angeles County; and the very attractive California Afro-American Museum, with its emphasis on both art and history, opened in time for the 1984 Olympics.

Exposition Park is just south of USC, between Exposition and Martin Luther King Jr. Boulevards and Figueroa Street and Menlo Avenue. State Drive, with access to public parking lots, passes between the rose garden and the museums; take N. Coliseum Drive to reach Memorial Coliseum, W. Coliseum Drive to reach the Sports Arena. Entrance to the park is free, though fees are charged for parking and admission to some attractions.

California Science Center

Centerpiece of a $300 million master plan to spiff up Exposition Park, the dazzling new California Science Center is a 245,000-square-foot facility providing scientific "edutainment" for jaded Southern California kids already mesmerized by television, video games, and theme parks. Consider Tess, the 50-foot-tall animatronic "woman" whose bones, muscles, organs, and blood vessels are exposed to explain how the body works. More than 125 hands-on activities are included within the "World of Life," a contemporary biology expo, and the "Creative World," a technological exploration of computer technology, digital imaging, and other innovations. Here children can experience a simulated earthquake; strap themselves into a space docking simulator to retrieve a damaged satellite in zero gravity; watch you-are-there videotape of heart surgery as projected onto a dummy patient; simulate the experience of driving a car sober and then drunk; and watch anti-smoking videos while sitting in a coughing chair made of cigarette butts. There's plenty more, and plans for expansion are already in the works. It's fun and educational for the whole family and—with the exception of the 3-D movies in the new seven-story Imax theater—the California Science Center is free.

The California Science Center, 700 State Dr. in Exposition Park, 213/744-7400, www.casciencectr.org, is open daily 10 A.M.–5 P.M. (closed major holidays). Museum admission is free. Parking is $5. Imax admission is $7.50 adults, $6 students with ID, $5.50 seniors, and $4.75 children ages 4–12; theater times vary. Call the center's main number for current exhibit and Imax information.

Natural History Museum of Los Angeles County

This is the largest and most popular museum in California, housed in a graceful 1913 Spanish Renaissance building boasting more than 30 galleries and halls. The museum collection includes more than 35 million specimens and artifacts, most of which come out of storage only for temporary exhibition. But what *is* on display can easily keep you occupied for an entire day–the uncannily real North American and African dioramas (veritable taxidermy theses), the prehistoric fossil and dinosaur exhibits, the rare "Megamouth" shark, the gem stones, the Times-Mirror Hall of Native American Cultures. A real hit with the kids is the museum's **Ralph M. Parsons Insect Zoo,** which comes complete with a "bioscanner" video camera for an up-close view of the "zoo" animals. A refrigerator door opens to reveal the critters' favorite foods— accompanied by a recorded kazoo rendition of "The worms crawl in, the worms crawl out." (Keep an eye on the family fridge once you get home.) There is always at least one special museum exhibit under way, too, such as *The Great Russian Dinosaurs* fossil show, *Pavilion of Wings* butterfly experience, and *Robot Zoo* exhibition on biomechanics.

For current special exhibit information, call the Natural History Museum, 900 Exposition Blvd., 213/763-3466; www.nhm.org. The museum offers a free guided tour daily at 1 P.M. June–Sept., weekends only Oct.–May. The museum is open daily on weekdays 9:30 A.M.–5 P.M. and on weekends 10 A.M.–5 P.M. (closed major holidays). Admission is $8 adults, $5.50 seniors

The collection at the Natural History Museum includes more than 35 million specimens and artifacts.

and students with ID, and $2 children ages 5–12. Group tour discounts available. Admission is free on the first Tuesday of every month.

The California Afro-American Museum

Opened just in time for the 1984 Olympics and the Olympic Art Festival, the California Afro-American Museum is one of the loveliest buildings in Exposition Park, with airy galleries and a glass-roofed sculpture patio. Originally "dedicated to Afro-American achievements in politics, education, athletics, and the arts," the museum's ongoing emphasis is on the arts and art history—sculpture, paintings, photography, and multimedia exhibits. Recent shows have included a multimedia tribute to jazz genius Duke Ellington and an exhibit on black music in Los Angeles in the 1960s. Free admission. The museum is open Tues.–Sun. 10 A.M.–5 P.M. For current schedule and other information, contact: California Afro-American Museum, 600 State Dr., 213/ 744-7432; www .caam.ca.gov.

Los Angeles Memorial Coliseum and Sports Arena

Built in 1923, the L.A. Memorial Coliseum, 3911 S. Figueroa St., 213/ 748-6131, seats 91,000. It gained fame as a central venue for the 1932 Olympic Games, and took a bow again in the 1984 Olympics. While visiting the Coliseum, take note of Robert Graham's *Olympic Arch,* a work that created quite a stir when it was unveiled in 1984. The massive sculpture is topped with two headless bronze nudes—one male, one female—as symbolic representations of all athletes.

The Coliseum hosts USC football games, soccer games, and other sports and special events. Should L.A. lure another National Football League franchise to town, it probably won't settle in here since the cost to outfit the Coliseum with sky

RACHEL TAYLOR

boxes and other accoutrements of corporate sports is considered astronomical. The indoor **Los Angeles Sports Arena**, 3939 S. Figueroa St., 213/748-6131, built in 1958 as a companion to the Coliseum, seats 16,000. The Sports Arena regularly hosts USC basketball, conventions, car shows, an occasional concert, and the like.

SOUTH-CENTRAL AND SOUTHWEST LOS ANGELES

Imagine John M. Deutch, then-director of the U.S. Central Intelligence Agency (CIA), America's most secretive government bureaucracy, showing up in November of 1996 at Locke High School in the unincorporated South-Central Los Angeles community of Watts. Imagine further that the purpose of the Deutch drop-in was to deny that his agency's laxity was even indirectly responsible for the Nicaraguan Contra crack cocaine trafficking that funneled cheap street drugs into L.A.'s black community. Such was the furor here over reports first published in the *San Jose Mercury News* that suggested such a connection. No matter what evidence subsequent investigations produce—or fail to produce—a government conspiracy to introduce drugs and related gangland violence into South-Central Los Angeles is already established, here, as fact. Given the reality of past Jim Crow laws and early U.S. Supreme Court decisions; unpunished Ku Klux Klan lynchings and other violent attacks against blacks; documented spying by the Federal Bureau of Investigation (FBI) against the Reverend Martin Luther King, Jr. and Malcolm X; and that agency's active covert campaign against the Black Panther Party just decades ago, skepticism in the face of even the most sincere denials is understandable. And Los Angeles has its own Jim Crow history—and its own history of rage in the face of genuine injustice, including the Watts Riots of 1965 and the similarly destructive 1992 riots ("the uprising," here) that erupted after the round-one acquittal of two Los Angeles Police Department officers in the Rodney King police brutality case.

Yet to focus on such facts alone would be to miss the point entirely, because South-Central and southwest Los Angeles feature—and have always featured—some of L.A.'s most vibrant cultural attractions.

Residents lament the long-gone heyday of the historic 1928 **Dunbar Hotel** south of downtown on S. Central Ave. (just east of Vernon), luxurious digs for prominent black L.A. visitors from the 1930s into the '50s, though the Dunbar was recently refurbished and reincarnated as a residential hotel and museum. Gone, too, are the famous Central Avenue blues and jazz clubs of the 1930s and '40s, a period captured vividly in writer Walter Mosley's evocative contemporary novels. But also long vanished are the days when blacks in L.A. were forced by law to live in restricted areas, which explains why so many of what would otherwise be considered "black community attractions"—clubs, restaurants, art galleries, museums, and stars' homes—have migrated to the west and elsewhere throughout Los Angeles.

Most of South-Central/southwest L.A.'s most accessible attractions are concentrated in and around affluent Baldwin Hills and, just to the east, Leimert Park, soul of a thriving local arts community. Nearby highlights include the **First African Methodist Episcopal (AME) Church,** 2270 S. Harvard Blvd., 323/730-9180, designed by noted L.A. architect Paul Williams. The church is gospel music heaven—guests welcome on Sunday for 8 A.M., 10 a.m, and noon services—founded in downtown L.A. by former slave Biddy Mason in 1872 and moved here in 1969. Not to mention the **Community Youth Sports and Arts Foundation,** 4828 Crenshaw Blvd., 323/294-8320, founded by Chilton Alphonse in 1983 to provide teenagers a constructive alternative to gangs and drugs, and the *Los Angeles Sentinel,* 3800 Crenshaw Blvd., 323/299-3800, one of the largest black-owned newspapers in the nation. And both Dulan's Restaurant on Crenshaw, something of a de facto community center famous for its Southern-style soul food, and elegant Harold & Belle's on Jefferson, known for its Cajun, Creole, and other specialties long before such fare became fashionable.

Various local tour companies can include other destinations on their itineraries, such as, farther east, the renowned **Watts Towers** and the adjacent **Watts Towers Art Center,** 1727 E. 107th St., 213/847-4646, the latter famous for its exceptional community arts workshops.

Watts Towers

TOM MYERS PHOTOGRAPHY

For cultural and historical tours of South-Central and southwest Los Angeles, custom tours, special-interest tours—to enjoy gospel music, say, or blues and jazz and other community arts—and tours combining other areas of the city, contact local companies. Valerie Holton's **Black L.A. Tours,** 3450 W. 43rd St., Ste. 108, Los Angeles, 323/750-9267, specializes in historical and cultural tours, including tapings of popular TV shows. Her custom itineraries cover many of the places mentioned above and below —and then some. She can accommodate both small and large groups. **H. Weeks Tours,** 1421 S. Temple Ave., Compton, 310/ 603-2987, is another good bet. Hersley Weeks happily accommodates with custom-designed local tours, and he can also arrange longer bus tours to major L.A. tourist sights or to Las Vegas, the Grand Canyon, and various destinations en route. (For more suggestions, contact the L.A. Convention and Visitors Bureau.) In addition, during Black History Month in February, the local **Our Authors Study Club,** 323/758-4520, offers a major annual tour of L.A.'s black historical sights—an entourage of eight or more buses— in addition to sponsoring other community events throughout the year.

Baldwin Hills, Leimert Park, and Vicinity

The opening of Magic Johnson's dazzling **Magic Theatres,** 323/290-5900, 12-screen movie complex was big news in 1995 at the previously ailing **Baldwin Hills Crenshaw Plaza Mall**—the first first-run movie venture in the Crenshaw district, gratefully hailed by the community as both major cultural and economic investment by the famous former L.A. Lakers basketball star and his business partner Sony Pictures. Another major attraction at the mall itself, home to many black-owned small businesses, is the free **Museum of African American Art** on the third floor of the Robinson's May building, 4005 S. Crenshaw Blvd. (at Martin Luther King, Jr. Blvd.), 323/294-7071. A large part of the museum's permanent collection comprises the art, art collection, and archives of noted Harlem Renaissance artist Palmer Hayden. Dedicated to preserving and promoting art by and about people of African descent, the museum sponsors several special exhibits each year; call for current show information. The museum is open Thurs.–Sat. 11 A.M.–6 P.M., Sunday noon–5 P.M. Admission is free, but donations are appreciated.

Especially on weekends, the most intriguing place around is relaxed Leimert (le-MURT) Park, a neighborhood of black professionals just east of Baldwin Hills. Among the homes here is the longtime residence of **Ralph J. Bunche,** the first African American to win a Nobel Peace Prize. Leimert Park's Spanish-style homes, bungalows, and apartment buildings were designed in the late 1920s by Olmsted & Olmsted—an architectural firm headed by the sons of Frederick Law Olmsted, New York's Central Park

"OUR TOWN" AND A TOWERING IMAGINATION

One of the world's finest folk art shrines, the elaborate walled complex known as **Watts Towers** at 1765 E. 107th St. in South-Central L.A., was built by Italian immigrant Simon Rodia. Working without helpers—without formal plans, for that matter, and without scaffolding, machinery, rivets, or bolts—from 1921 until 1954 Rodia labored in his free time to build what he called Nuestro Pueblo, or "Our Town." His walled town first consisted of his small home, a gazebo, a fountain, a fireplace, and a barbecue—all framed from discarded steel (old pipes and bedframes), slathered with cement, then decorated with broken bottle glass, seashells, and bits of broken tiles and dishes. Then Rodia expanded, adding the three eccentric Gothic-style spires, more fountains, a fishpond, birdbaths, even a covered porch—everything woven together with patterned pathways and elaborate arches.

Simon Rodia was not without detractors. During World War II, for example, some thought the towers were secret radio transmitters designed to aid the Japanese. Others believed the elaborate compound was a secret burial site for his wife. But Rodia's town was actually a monument to historic adventurers and explorers. One tower, for example, represents Marco Polo's ship.

Rodia, who earned his living as a mason and tilesetter, abandoned his masterpiece almost as soon as it was completed. He deeded the property to a neighbor and then vanished from the neighborhood without telling a soul why he was inspired to build his "town," or why he was leaving. Years later, Rodia was found living in Martinez, near San Francisco. He finally told at least part of the story. "I wanted to do something for the United States," he said. "Because I was raised here, you understand, because there are nice people in this country." Rodia's monument to the vastness of human potential is now a National Historic Landmark.

The Watts Towers sustained an estimated $2 million damage in the 1994 Northridge earthquake, and repairs were funded by the Federal Emergency Management Agency and a generous grant from American Express. Public tours of Watts Towers were suspended for years because of ongoing renovation and restoration work, but were scheduled to begin again in January 2001. Restoration is now expected to be completed in 2003. For current tour information, call the community-based **Watts Towers Art Center** next door to the towers, 213/847-4646. For additional information, contact: **Watts Towers of Simon Rodia State Historic Park,** c/o City of Los Angeles Department of Cultural Affairs, 1727 E. 107th St., Los Angeles, CA 90002; www.culturela.com. The Watts Towers complex is accessible by Metrorail's Blue Line; get off at the 103rd St. stop.

---

planner. The neighborhood was named, prosaically, after developer Walter H. Leimert.

Leimert Park's "village" or commercial district—including the tiny triangular public park facing 43rd Place, where impromptu conversations and performances convene—is centered along the one-block section of Degnan Boulevard between 43rd Street and 43rd Place, several blocks east of Crenshaw Boulevard and just north of Vernon. To get here: If coming from Exposition Park or the Harbor Freeway (I-10), head west via Martin Luther King Jr. Boulevard past Vermont and Western and then head southwest on Leimert Boulevard; turn right onto either 43rd (street or place). From the Santa Monica Freeway (I-10), head south on Crenshaw, past Exposition and Martin Luther King Jr. for about 15 blocks, and then turn left onto either 43rd.

From the west and the San Diego Freeway (I-405), exit east at the Marina Freeway (Hwy. 90) onto Slauson Boulevard, continue east for almost two miles, and then head north into the Baldwin Hills via Stocker Street; four blocks past Crenshaw, turn right onto Degnan.

Food for the Soul

After seeing the Museum of African American Art at the mall (see above), the next tour stop should be Brian Breyé's free back-room **Museum in Black,** 4331 Degnan Blvd. (at Crenshaw Blvd.), 323/292-9528, with its gruesome collection of racist American memorabilia—thousands of horrifying mementos, from genuine baby shackles and slave manifests to "darkie" salt and pepper shakers—and, for sale up front, considerably more appealing African and African

American crafts. (Call ahead for shop hours.) For more arts, crafts, and gift items, also well worth a stop is **Gallery Plus** next door at 4333 Degnan, 323/296-2398. Look for other fascinating shops in the immediate vicinity, including the **Dawah Book Shop and Fragrance Warehouse,** 4801 Crenshaw (near 48th St.), 323/299-0335, perhaps the most aromatic bookstore in the universe, featuring body oils and lotions, soaps, shampoos, and incense in addition to shelves stocked with history, science, and religion. Hot for jam sessions and poetry readings—and particularly popular with the hip-hop crowd, is the online **KAOS Network** coffeehouse and multimedia art scene at 4343 Leimert Blvd., 323/296-5717.

Food for the Body
Even when the soul is sated, sooner or later one must minister to the stomach. A knockout for takeout—definitely not for vegetarians—is **Phillips Bar-B-Que,** 4307 Leimert Blvd. (two blocks east of Crenshaw Blvd.), 323/292-7613, where those in the know call in their orders to avoid the wait for delectable smoky pork ribs. For Southern-style soul food and community schmoozing, the place is **Dulan's** 4859 Crenshaw Blvd., 323/296-3034—a relative of Marina del Rey's **Aunt Kizzy's Kitchen**—and famous for its fried catfish, chicken and dumplings, and other specialties. Open for meals on Sunday only.

Farther north, **Harold & Belle's,** 2920 W. Jefferson Blvd. (between Crenshaw and Arlington), 323/735-9023, offers the most upscale soul food in L.A. at both lunch and dinner. Since almost forever, Harold & Belle's has served gargantuan portions of Creole and Cajun cuisine, great gumbo and shrimp Creole, platters of Louisiana-style hot links, fried catfish, and breaded oysters—everything accompanied by huge quantities of potato salad and corn on the cob. The place is always packed, so make reservations, park in the guarded lot, and plan to eat leftovers for a day or two.

Another area favorite, now relocated some distance south, is the genuine Jamaican **Coley's Place,** 310 E. Florence (near La Brea) in Inglewood, 310/ 672-7474, where the fine fare includes shrimp St. James and other sumptuous seafood, peppered beef and shrimp patties, and goat curry—actor Wesley Snipes's favorite, they say—on a menu also including fry bread, peach cobbler, and ginger beer. Open for lunch and dinner daily, and for brunch on Sunday.

EAST LOS ANGELES: EL BARRIO

As poignantly depicted in the film *My Family (Mi Familia),* the Los Angeles River has long been the traditional boundary between downtown and East L.A.'s Mexican-American community, El Barrio (The Neighborhood). But before L.A.'s downtown industrial expansion, from World War I through the 1920s, the city's Latino families rarely migrated far from their traditional "Sonoratown" neighborhoods surrounding El Pueblo's plaza. As Mexican Americans were shoved out of the city, they largely moved north toward Elysian Park and across the river to the east and southeast, into Boyle Heights, Lincoln Heights, and Belvedere. Largely dependent on the city's original Pacific Electric trolley system, the earliest Latino citizens—who called themselves Mexicanos, or Mexicans, "Mexican American" being a post-World War II term—also migrated to areas served by public transit, including Watts, Long Beach, and Pasadena. But El Barrio in the undesirable lowlands of East L.A. was ultimately the preferred destination, since for a time at least families could establish homes, neighborhoods, and businesses without suffering segregation and the other forms of social ostracism that met them elsewhere in L.A.

It's not surprising that El Barrio has also been home to some of the Mexican-American community's most tragic cultural clashes with broader L.A. society.

One of the first came in the 1930s, during the Great Depression—when unemployment was high everywhere yet nowhere higher than in El Barrio. Since even the U.S.-born of Mexican descent were viewed as temporary residents, belonging in L.A. only as a cheap labor source, the Los Angeles Chamber of Commerce quickly abandoned its "Americanization" campaign and instead urged U.S. immigration officials to undertake an aggressive "deportation drive"—even offering to pay the cost, which turned out to be

$14.70 per person when shipped out on Southern Pacific railroad cattle cars. Despite the fact that many of the deportees were American-born and most of the rest had committed no crimes nor entered the U.S. illegally, more than a half million left L.A. in the 1930s—some abandoning their communities voluntarily, out of fear. So successful was the Chamber of Commerce campaign that journalist Carey McWilliams observed sardonically that the chamber was "forced to issue a statement assuring the Mexican authorities that the community is in no sense unfriendly to Mexican labor and that repatriation is a policy designed solely for the relief of the destitute."

World War II changed everything for the better—at least initially. By 1942 almost every home in El Barrio proudly displayed a flag in the window, signaling that at least one member of the family was in uniform. (In the war's body count, Mexican Americans accounted for one-fifth of total L.A.-area casualties, though at that time they comprised only one-tenth of the population.) Others were actively engaged in the extraordinary industrial effort in support of the war, underway throughout L.A. Yet such immense wartime commitment was not enough to overcome the rampant racism that erupted in the Zoot Suit Riots of 1943.

Jarred by the suddenly clear social contradictions between mass World War II heroism abroad and shameful treatment at home, postwar East L.A. began, albeit slowly, to organize itself to combat cultural and political abuse—a process undeterred by violent police attacks during East L.A.'s 1970 anti-Vietnam War march in Laguna Park, and still in progress today.

Yet the overcrowded housing conditions and abject poverty in areas of downtown and East L.A. now beset by gang violence are not necessarily direct descendants of historically poor treatment of Mexican Americans and other Latinos in L.A. Certainly not entirely. The astonishing rates of recent Latino immigration into the community—both legal and illegal immigration— have created intense social and economic strains between "Americans" and "foreigners."

Touring East L.A.

East L.A. is one of the many separate "cities" that make up the whole of Los Angeles—this one the de facto Latin American capital of the United States, its total estimated Latino population exceeded only by those of Guadalajara and Mexico City.

César E. Chávez Avenue, the eastern extension of Macy Street formerly known as Brooklyn Avenue, leads to "Little Mexico" and its restaurants and shops, though the flashiest introduction

---

WARTIME WAKE-UP CALL: THE ZOOT SUIT RIOTS

Despite East L.A.'s immense commitment to World War II—almost every family sent at least one of its members into battle—not everyone got with the program, particularly rebellious second-generation "Chulos" too poorly educated to serve in the military and sometimes in trouble with the law—pool-hall hoodlums and "zoot suiters" to the police and draft dodgers in the opinion of Navy and Marine recruits stationed near Chávez Ravine.

Unhappy relations with the authorities quickly worsened after August 1942, when 22 Chulo gang members were arrested in the suspected murder of a man found near a popular neighborhood swimming hole. (The actual cause of death was never established.) Only five defendants were acquitted; the rest were sentenced to prison or jail terms. The convictions were appealed—and ultimately overturned. Yet throughout the city tensions continued,

particularly between Chulos and U.S. servicemen; a series of skirmishes ultimately erupted in the disgraceful "zoot suit riots" of June 1943. The first altercation was outside a dance hall in Venice, when soldiers looking for a fight attacked several Chulos. On subsequent nights the rumor that the Mexican Americans had started it brought out mobs of uniformed sailors and Marines and civilians. Thousands swooped into downtown L.A., El Barrio, and other parts of the city to hunt for zoot suiters, strip off their clothes, and beat them bloody. (Blacks and Filipinos were also attacked with abandon.) Since Los Angeles officials failed to intervene, the "riots" stopped only when the U.S. State Department—under pressure from the Mexican government and embarrassing international press coverage—stepped in to place downtown L.A. and El Barrio off-limits to U.S. servicemen.

to East L.A. is via **Whittier Boulevard.** Or visit **El Mercado,** 3425 E. First St., 323/268-3451, a three-story marketplace overflowing with inexpensive pottery and glassware, clothing, produce, food stands, and mariachi music, open daily 10 A.M.–8 P.M. (until later on weekends). Yet these days "East L.A." also includes many areas west of the Los Angeles River, which explains why downtown's **Grand Central Market** is so popular with Latino shoppers. Another best bet is **Huntington Park** southeast of downtown, where **Pacific Boulevard** between Randolph and Florence has become a colorful, family-oriented Latino marketplace, particularly lively on weekends (free off-street parking provided in city lots).

But East L.A. is most famous for its vibrant murals—splashing color and culture as well as personal and political statements on available wall space—and for its South American and Mexican restaurants.

Striking out beyond the main drags, the markets, and the murals, try an eating tour. In L.A. even the most WASPish Westsiders take particular pride in knowing the best ethnic restaurants and cheap-eats places in town—which is why people from all over head to East L.A. for Mexican food. **El Tepayac Cafe,** 812 N. Evergreen Ave. (near César E. Chávez Ave.), 323/268-1960, is famous for its burritos—the biggest and the best, stuffed with various meat fillings, chile sauce, rice, beans, and guacamole. One makes a meal. Open daily 6 A.M.–9:45 P.M., on Friday and Saturday until 11 P.M. Another possibility, beloved for its *taquitos,* is simple stucco **Ciro's,** 705 N. Evergreen Ave., 323/269-5104. A car-culture classic in East L.A.: **King Taco,** a 1950s-style drive-in at 2400 César E. Chávez (at Soto), 323/264-3940.

Pretty **La Parrilla,** 2126 César E. Chávez (at Chicago), 323/262-3434, is famous for its housemade tamales (fresh on the weekends) but most famous for its astonishingly fresh seafood. It's open daily for breakfast, lunch, and dinner.

Top of the mark for foodies, though, is **La Serenata de Garibaldi,** 1842 E. First St., 323/265-2887, open for lunch and dinner and a dazzling Sunday brunch. Try *gorditas* or fresh soup (served with rice and beans) at lunch. Seafood stars at dinner. Closed Monday.

NORTH-CENTRAL LOS ANGELES

Just north of downtown are two geographic islands separated from downtown by L.A.'s "four-level interchange," where the San Bernardino, Pasadena, and Hollywood Freeways intertwine themselves like thick concrete shoelaces. Tucked into long, deep ravines just beyond the freeways is an area rich with history, most easily separated into the Echo Park/Elysian Park and Highland Park/Eagle Rock neighborhoods. Home to L.A.'s first suburb and first public park, these gentle hills were originally the domain of native peoples who lived and hunted small game near the hillside springs. The area still has an almost rural feel, surprising so close to downtown. Small wood-frame homes from the late 1800s line the hillsides, the winding roads connecting them fringed by huge eucalyptus trees. The population is largely blue-collar Latino, although there is also a thriving artists' community drawn by both the affordable rents and the quaint, usually quiet surroundings.

Angelino Heights
The first suburb in Los Angeles, Angelino Heights just west of Dodger Stadium, was built as a neighborhood for professionals, its stylish Victorian homes connected to downtown by a mile-long Pacific Electric trolley line. The homes here were built during California's real estate boom of the 1880s, when railroad passage from Kansas City dropped to as low as $1. Thousands of hopeful new residents soon arrived in sunny Southern California but, though they could afford passage, many could not sustain themselves once here. The big boom went bust and Angelino Heights, surrounded by less expensive homes, gradually deteriorated.

But in the 1970s residents of the 1300 block of **Carroll Avenue** decided to open their homes for annual tours—to raise money to restore the neighborhood to its former splendor. Eleven structures on this block (and others) are designated by the city of Los Angeles as cultural historical landmarks. Tours of Angelino Heights ($8 per person) begin at 10 A.M. on the first Saturday of every month, reservations required; call the Los Angeles Conservancy, 213/623-2489; www.laconservancy.org.

Echo Park

The disturbing film *Mi Vida Loca,* about teenage girl gangsters and guns, takes place in the bullet-riddled streets of Echo Park the neighborhood, just west of Angelino Heights. Echo Park the park, on Bellevue Avenue in the shadow of the Hollywood Freeway (Hwy. 101) between Glendale Boulevard and Echo Park Avenue, is mostly placid lake with lily pads, tiny palm-fringed islands, and rental boats—a hot spot for area families on weekends though somewhat infamous, too, for drug dealers and sometimes unsavory situations. At the northwest end of the park, at 1100 Glendale, is the **Angelus Temple,** a striking circular building modeled after the Mormon Tabernacle in Salt Lake City and constructed in 1923 for the congregation of legendary evangelist Aimee Semple McPherson.

Elysian Park and Dodger Stadium

Elysian Park was set aside for public use when Los Angeles was founded in 1781. The second-largest city park in L.A., 600-acre Elysian retains much of its natural chaparral, a landscape crisscrossed with hiking trails. At the central picnic area along Stadium Way are barbecue pits, a small man-made lake, and children's play area. The **Chávez Ravine Arboretum** protects 10 acres of rare trees. A recreation center offers basketball courts and volleyball. Despite the presence here of the **Los Angeles Police Academy** and shooting range—and the academy's cafeteria-style restaurant, open to the public—solo hikes into the more isolated areas of the park are not recommended. And after dark, forget it.

Hugging the slopes of Chávez Ravine is Dodger Stadium, 1900 Elysian Park Ave., 323/224-1400, www.dodgers.com, reached via the Pasadena Freeway (the 110) and then Stadium Way. Dodger Stadium, home to the **Los Angeles Dodgers** since the team moved west from Brooklyn in 1958, offers 56,000 seats and almost as many parking spaces. Washing a few Dodger

dogs down with cold beer on a summer afternoon has long been a form of high culture in L.A.—some sort of authentic culture, anyway, one that crosses all the city's usually well-drawn economic and ethnic lines.

Highland Park and Vicinity

The neighborhood atop **Mt. Washington,** most easily reached via the tiny twisting streets above El Alisal and the Southwest Museum, has long been a haven for artists and artsy types. A surprise here is the **Elyria Canyon Park** nature preserve on the tiny mountain's southwest slope, at the end of Wollam Street (reached via San Fernando Rd. and then Division St.); an easy two-mile trail leads to and through the preserve.

Follow San Fernando Road northwest to Verdugo Road and then Eagle Rock Boulevard to the university community of **Eagle Rock** on the other side of the mountain, adjacent to Glendale.

Charles Fletcher Lummis, the Harvard-educated journalist who coined the term "southland" to describe Southern California, walked to L.A. from Cincinnati, Ohio, on assignment for the *Los Angeles Times* in 1885. Lummis, who ultimately settled here, founded the renowned Highland Park **Southwest Museum** collection of Native American and Southwestern art and artifacts. **Casa de Adobe** just down the hill, built in 1918 by the Hispanic Society of California, was donated to the museum in 1925. Over the course of 13 years, Lummis built his own Arroyo Seco home **El Alisal** ("The Sycamore") nearby. Across the freeway—also reached via the Avenue 43 exit from the Pasadena Freeway—is **Heritage Square,** an interesting collection of historic L.A. buildings rescued from the wrecker's ball.

For more information about these attractions and about Charles Fletcher Lummis and the Arroyo Seco culture he helped create, see the Pasadena chapter. **Pasadena,** historic centerpiece of California's Arts and Crafts movement just up the freeway, is where much of the Southern California myth was crafted.

PRACTICAL DOWNTOWN (AND AROUND)

STAYING DOWNTOWN

Though Angelenos dash into downtown for the theater, musical performances, or the latest contemporary art show, the area is not typically on locals' lists of favorite destinations—largely because the social and economic gulf between affluence and abject poverty is so obvious, and so startling. Most people prefer to avoid having to notice. But for those unafraid of the downtown experience, quite decent inexpensive and moderately priced lodgings aren't difficult to find amid downtown's dour towers. In addition to glass-and-glamour accommodations, downtown also boasts one of Southern California's grandest old hotels. All high-end stays can be genuine bargains come weekends, when the suits depart, at least in the absence of major conventions. But inquire about hotel parking prices, which in some cases are exorbitant.

Less Expensive Accommodations
Best bets for budget travelers include the friendly and safe 250-room **Hotel Stillwell** opposite Chase Plaza at 838 S. Grand Ave. (between Eighth and Ninth Sts.), 213/627-1151 or toll-free 800/553-4774; www.stillwell-la.com. Rooms are quite basic but clean, with color TV, phone, air conditioning, and private baths. East Indian and Asian art prints decorate the hallways and large lobby. Added bonuses: the Tandoori breads, meat dishes, shrimp curry, vegetarian selections, and other specialties served at **Gill's Cuisine of India,** 213/623-1050, the restaurant in the back of the lobby (open for lunch and dinner, closed Sunday), as well as **Hank's American Grill,** the in-house bar and grill. Rooms $49–59, suites $75–95.

Also a bargain downtown: the **Orchid Hotel,** 819 S. Flower St., 213/624-5855. This 1920s' flower, a real find, features clean, modern, quite basic rooms with in-house laundry and public parking nearby. Weekly rates available. Rates: $38 double, $200 weekly. Right next door and

also fairly friendly to the pocketbook is the **Milner Hotel,** 813 S. Flower St., 213/627-6981, where rates include breakfast. Rates: $70–85.

Moderate Accommodations
A best bet in Chinatown is the 50-room **Best Western Dragon Gate Inn,** 818 N. Hill St. (at Alpine), Los Angeles, 213/617-3077, toll-free 800/282-9999, www.dragongateinn.com, with all the usual plus in-room refrigerators, cable TV, free movies, and tea makers, not to mention the inexpensive on-site restaurants, Chinese herbalist shop and pharmacy, secured underground parking, and elevator to rooms. Children under 18 stay free. Rates: $79–99. Also in Chinatown but adjacent to El Pueblo's Olvera Street and just a half-block from Union Station (and Metrorail) is the 82-room **Metro Plaza Hotel,** 711 N. Main St. (at Cesar E. Chavez Ave.), 213/680-0200 or toll-free 800/223-2223; www.metroplazahotel .com, a comfortable motel featuring extras such as satellite TV (free movies), in-room refrigerators and microwaves, and phones in both the bedroom and bathroom. Rooms $69–85, suites $139–158.

More Expensive Accommodations
For an upscale yet reasonably cost-conscious European-style stay, consider the **Kawada Hotel** near the Civic Center at 200 S. Hill St., tel. 213/621-4455 or toll-free 800/752-9232; www .kawadahotel.com. Central to most of downtown's attractions yet popular with business types, the Kawada's rooms feature two phones, TV with VCR, and in-room refrigerators. Fun for those unafraid of earthquakes is the **Epicentre** quake-themed California-style restaurant downstairs, 213/625-0000, which serves lunch on weekdays, dinner nightly. The **Shockwave Café** is also a treat. Rates $109–129 (weekend rates as low as $79).

The bloom may be off the neighborhood but not so 295-room **The Mayfair Hotel,** now a gracefully aging Best Western just west of most downtown action (and the Harbor Fwy.) at

1256 W. Seventh St., between Figueroa and Union, 213/484-9789 or toll-free 800) 528-1234. The Mayfair gathered bouquets for its Georgian grandeur in 1927 from *Architectural Digest,* and more recently received the community's Rose Award for Historic Preservation. The Mayfair is also an occasional movie star, boasting scenes in Arnold Schwarzenegger's *True Lies,* for example. Best of all, though, The Mayfair is a reliable downtown stay with clean, comfortable rooms, on-site continental restaurant, and conference and exercise facilities. Rates $70–280.

Downtown's most "L.A." midrange stay, though, is still the 285-room 1927 **Hotel Figueroa** across the street from the Staples Sports Arena and near the Convention Center at 939 S. Figueroa St. (south of Ninth), 213/627-8971 or toll-free 800/421-9092; www.figueroahotel.com. Along with reasonable prices, the vaguely Spanish style here is much of the attraction—an appeal translated into a terra-cotta color scheme, hand-painted furniture in the very large guest rooms, tiled bathrooms, and ceiling fans almost everywhere. The lovely tiled lobby features a hand-painted ceiling but the balmy palm courtyard is more central, with graceful pool, spa, and bar. Two on-site restaurants add to the Figueroa's convenience. Rates $98–165.

Luxury Accommodations

Grandest of the grand old Los Angeles landmark hotels, thanks to a $40 million facelift and a more recent makeover, **The Regal Biltmore Hotel** on S. Grand at Fifth has been restored to its stylish 1923 supremacy. Details such as the stunning beamed ceiling—hand-painted by Italian artist Giovanni Smeraldi and now the oversoul of the hotel's new lounge—help create an ambience of classical luxury. So do imported Italian marble, plum velvet, **Bernard's** restaurant, and the Romanesque health spa. Even the pool is unbelievably beautiful, an elegant indoor art deco ingenue that stole scenes in the movie *Bugsy.* For appetizing casual Italian, try in-house **Smeraldi's** restaurant. Downstairs is **Sai Sai,** for authentic Japanese. Attractive and modern if somewhat small rooms, done in pastels and French furnishings, can be almost reasonable on some weekends and at off times, so do inquire

about special rates, promotions, and packages. For extra luxury, sign on for the hotel's Club floor, with extras including private library, big screen TV, breakfast, cocktails, hors d'oeuvres, and personal valet.

For more information or to make reservations, contact: The Regal Biltmore Hotel, 506 S. Grand Ave., 213/624-1011 or toll-free 800/245-8673; www.thebiltmore.com. Rates: $169–199, suites $300 and up.

Across from the Biltmore, two stone sailing ships, the *Mayflower* and the *Santa Maria,* are chiseled into the stone façade of downtown's **Wyndham Checkers Hotel**—an elegant architectural reminder of its original 1927 incarnation as the Mayflower Hotel. To transform the Mayflower's tattered timbers into the luxurious 188-room Checkers boutique hotel took about $49 million, for starters. Now a boutique version of the Biltmore, the Checkers Hotel imported intimate European ambience to downtown with fine art, exotic fabrics, and elegant antiques, everything polished with marble. But the Old World elegance is offset by every imaginable modern amenity, including business center, in-house laundry service, dry cleaning, and 24-hour room service, rooftop lap pool, steam room, saunas, whirlpool, and fitness/massage facilities. The hotel's restaurant, **Checkers,** is noted for its exceptional California cuisine. For more information and reservations, contact: Wyndham Checkers Hotel, 535 S. Grand Ave. (at Fifth), 213/624-0000 or toll-free 800/996-3426; www.wyndham.com. Rates: $179–300, suites $400 and up.

Then there's the 35-story, 1,368-room **Westin Bonaventure,** John Portman's 1978 landmark hotel, the Buck Rogers-style futuristic fantasy with five mirrored cylindrical towers and multiple glass elevators that you've seen featured in so many movies. Particularly popular with conventioneers, the Bonaventure has comfortable rooms that are just part of this virtual city, with its five acres of ponds and waterfalls, endless shops, 20-restaurant food court, and obligatory sky-high revolving lounge. For a fee, guests can work out in the 85,000-square-foot health club next door. Inquire about specials and packages. For more information and reservations, contact: Westin Bonaventure, 404 S. Figueroa (between Fourth and Fifth Sts.), 213/624-1000 or toll-free

800/228-3000; www.westin.com. Rates: $175–215, suites $200 and up.

Another sign that L.A. has arrived: the world-class **Omni Hotel** near downtown's Museum of Contemporary Art at 251 S. Olive St., 213/617-3300 or toll-free 800/442-5251, www.omnihotels.com, formerly an Inter-Continental and remembered by international media hounds as home-away-from-home for the jury in the original O. J. Simpson murder trial. Those everyday citizens, sequestered here for nearly a year, no doubt missed their families and friends—but, given the luxurious surroundings, they didn't miss much else. Contemporary rooms are perfectly plush, with cable TV, free and pay-per-view movies, refrigerators, and honor bars. In addition to conference rooms, various business services, the availability of child care (extra fee), and the in-house **Grand Cafe,** the hotel offers a workout room, heated swimming pool, steam room, and saunas. Rates: $175–210, suites $475 and up.

More Luxury Accommodations

The New Otani Hotel, star of downtown's Little Tokyo, blends elegant Japanese style with an all-American emphasis on convenience. In-room amenities include refrigerator, color TV, and kimono. For the ultimate Zen experience, book a tatami suite with futon beds, *ofuro* baths, and first-class pampering—or show up for any of the regular arts and culture courses, from flower arranging to shiatsu massage. The hotel's rooftop **Garden in the Sky** offers a half-acre of Shinto serenity. Other Otani attractions: the exceptional **A Thousand Cranes** restaurant, a long-running star of L.A.'s cuisine scene; the American **Azalea Restaurant** and bar; and the convenience of on-site upscale shopping. For more information or to make reservations, contact: The New Otani Hotel, 120 S. Los Angeles St. (at First), 213/629-1200 or toll-free 800/252-0197; www.newotani.com. Rates: $185–210, suites $475 and up.

Formerly the Los Angeles Hilton, and then the Omni Los Angeles Hotel and Centre, the 900-room **Wilshire Grand Hotel,** near the Convention Center at 930 Wilshire Blvd. (at Figueroa), 213/688-7777 or toll-free 888/773-2888; www.thewilshiregrand.com, is a financial district hotel catering to business travelers and conventioneers. The best rooms with a view are in the Towers, of course, but international shops also offer an eyeful. Rates: $189–239, suites $375 and up.

Check out the deluxe and surprisingly intimate 469-room **Marriott Downtown,** at 333 S. Figueroa St. (near Sixth St.), 213/617-1133 or toll-free 800/228-9297; www.marriott.com, where 14 stories of mirrored glass reflect upon four acres of landscaped grounds. Large guest rooms feature sofas, minibars, and marble baths, two-line phones, and morning newspapers and coffee. Other amenities: exercise facilities and heated pool, health club (fee), and the contemporary **Three Thirty Three** and other in-house restaurants. Also a plus: the never-crowded Laemmle fourplex movie theater right next door. Rates: $179–209, suites $249–350.

The sleek, glossy, and recently redone **Hyatt Regency Los Angeles,** 711 S. Hope St. (at Seventh St.), 213/683-1234 or toll-free 800/233-1234, www.hyatt.com, in the heart of the financial district, also largely caters to business travelers—which makes it a best bet for weekenders. Aside from the tasteful underground lobby, which adjoins the Broadway Plaza shopping complex, every room offers a full wall of city views. Two floors of suites, known as The Regency Club, feature a private lounge, library, and VIP spa. Rates: $175–225, suites $250 and up. Weekend rates available.

STAYING AROUND DOWNTOWN

Staying South of Downtown

Best bet for an uptown hotel-style stay near the University of Southern California (USC) and Exposition Park is the 243-room **Radisson Hotel,** 3540 S. Figueroa St. (just west of the 110), 213/748-4141 or toll-free 800/244-7331; www.raddisson.com. Rates: $115–175.

More intriguing alternatives nearby include bed and breakfasts. Five-room **The Inn at 657** is just a half-block west of Figueroa at 657 W. 23rd St., 213/741-2200 or toll-free 800/347-7512; www.patsysinn657.com. Suites at this tiny one-time 1948 home-cum-apartment complex include all the comforts of home. Among them: delightful and roomy rooms (three feature two bedrooms), color TV with VCR and cable, free local phone calls, stocked kitchens (in the four apartment-style units), free parking, even an outdoor spa. Full breakfast is served in the morning, snacks in the afternoon. The Inn at 657 is equally convenient to the Convention Center and downtown, too, just a dash away from the Downtown Area Short Hop (DASH) minibus stop. Rates: $110–125.

Staying on and along Wilshire

If you're doing Wilshire's museum row and can absorb Westside sticker shock, staying in West Hollywood or Beverly Hills is certainly convenient. But the area offers affordable options, including the **Dunes Motor Hotel** two blocks west of Crenshaw at 4300 Wilshire Blvd. 323/938-3616, toll-free 800/443-8637 in California, or toll-free 800/452-3863 from elsewhere in the United States. Rates: $59–79. A good bet closer to the museum action is the **Farmer's Daughter Motel** across from the Farmers Market at 115 S. Fairfax Ave. (near Beverly), 323/937-3930. Summer rates of $71–95 (lower at other times).

For still more "real L.A." atmosphere, try the well-maintained 1924 **Chancellor Hotel** in Koreatown at 3191 W. Seventh St., 213/383-1183. Primarily a residential hotel popular with young professionals and students, the Chancellor accommodates travelers on a space-available basis. The rates are a real deal since breakfast and dinner are included. Rates: $45.50–54. Another art deco classic even closer to downtown, near once-inviting MacArthur Park, is the Howard Johnson **Wilshire Royale Hotel,** 2619 Wilshire Blvd. (at Rampart), 213/387-5311, recently refurbished in contemporary style. Rates: $89–119. Still more stylish, though, is the **Oxford Palace Hotel** in Koreatown, six blocks south of Wilshire at 745 S. Oxford Ave. (between Seventh and Eighth Sts.), 213/389-8000. Basic amenities include in-room refrigerators, VCRs and movies, and breakfast. High-season rates $175, off-season rates $159. Inquire about specials and discounts.

EATING DOWNTOWN

Like accommodations, dining in downtown L.A. reflects the diversity of the population. Free meals for the skid row homeless are served within blocks of some of the most expensive meals in town. Gourmands can sample fine French, Italian, Californian, and nouvelle cuisine in the financial district—and Chinese (and Vietnamese) in Chinatown, Japanese in Little Tokyo, Mexican in El Pueblo, and working-class and ethnic American near the market districts.

People's Eats: El Pueblo and Vicinity

In honor of L.A.'s beginnings as El Pueblo de Los Angeles, if you find yourself anywhere near El Pueblo's Olvera Street stop for a sit-down meal at surprisingly good, surprisingly authentic **La Luz del Dia** ("The Light of Day"), 1 W. Olvera St., 213/628-7495, where specialties include

El Pueblo's Olvera Street

piccadillo tacos, *carnitas,* and fresh cactus salad. (You can also find real Mexican in East L.A. and, downtown, at the **Grand Central Public Market** on S. Broadway.) Best bet for *taquitos* is **Cielito Lindo,** on Olvera at Cesar E. Chavez, 213/687-4391, the little shack next to the horse trough. Time-honored in this neighborhood, too, is **Casa la Golondrina** inside Pelanconi House, 17 W. Olvera, 213/628-4349, the setting definitely part of the appeal.

A classic one block north of Union Station is **Philippe the Original Sandwich Shop,** 1001 N. Alameda St. (at Ord), 213/628-3781, more than a place to grab a quick bite. Philippe's is a sociological phenomenon, a fragment of downtown history frozen in time. Most famous as the originator of the French-dipped sandwich—according to local lore, Philippe himself accidentally dropped a sandwich into gravy—Philippe's is also noted as home of the 10-cent cup of coffee. But be warned: during periods of rising coffee prices, a cup of Joe sometimes goes for 11 cents. The cavernous café is barnlike and basic, with sawdust floors and row upon row of shared chest-high tables and stools. Philippe's regular clientele includes escapees from downtown's glass canyons, fans and baseball players refortifying after a game at Dodger Stadium, and folks perennially down on their luck. No passing trend, Philippe's. At the end of a busy day, even the servers look as if they've been on their feet since the establishment first opened in 1908. So decide what you want, be it a beef, lamb, or pork dip, before you belly up to the endless counter, and be quick about it. Thousands are lining up behind you every day, hungry for a hit of Philippe's rip-snorting house mustard. After you're served, though, take your time. This is a perfect place for savoring a slice of L.A. life—and a slice of that cream pie. Philippe's is open daily 6 A.M.–10 P.M.

With a sophisticated style and spirit inspired by its landmark location, **Traxx** at Union Station brings fine dining back to L.A.'s dazzling Spanish colonial art-deco train station. Both restaurant and bar, Traxx recaptures the glamour and excitement of the golden age of train travel while serving unmistakably contemporary and elegant meals. Chef Tara Thomas, formerly of 410 Boyd, specializes in new twists on classic cuisine. The eclectic menu features "small plates," such as ahi tuna Napoleon with crispy wonton, wasabi caviar, and sesame soy dressing, for example, and "full plates," such as house-cured double-cut pork loin chop with prosciutto and rosemary or crisped whitefish on a bed of fennel, capers, niçoise olives, and tangerines. Traxx, on the main concourse of Union Station, 800 N. Alameda St., 213/625-1999, is particularly popular with local artists, downtown executives, and time-starved commuters who plug their laptops in at the bar.

People's Eats: Chinatown

In a sense, even L.A.'s "new" (post-1930s) Chinatown is no longer new. The contemporary Chinese migration is out toward the suburbs—to the clustered East L.A. cities of Alhambra, Monterey Park, Rosemead, and (for the very wealthy) San Marino and South Pasadena. Some of the best Chinese dim sum anywhere, for example, is served in East L.A. at well-known establishments that include the **Empress Pavilion, NBC Seafood Restaurant,** and the **Ocean Star Seafood Restaurant.**

Be that as it may, remnants of Chinatown's past culinary glory *do* survive in Chinatown—starting with the beef curry pies, shrimp dumplings, coconut sweet buns, and other delectable takeout available at **Hong Kong Low Deli,** 408 Bamboo Ln., 213/680-9827, a distant relative tucked into the alley behind the World War II–era Cantonese dining palace of the same name. (To find the place, look for the line of hungry customers.) You'll have to eat your meal elsewhere, but here you can easily gather up enough to gorge yourself for little more than pocket change. Hong Kong Low is open daily 7:30 A.M.–5 P.M. For the best Cantonese roast duck around, head for **Lucky Deli,** 706 N. Broadway (at Ord St.), 213/625-7847.

Another best bet for a quick bite in Chinatown is **Mandarin Deli,** 727 N. Broadway, 213/623-6054 (between Alpine and Ord Sts.), an inexpensive, clean, and popular place serving traditional noodle and dumpling dishes. Order the "handmade" noodles, and don't miss the marvelous fish dumplings. The Mandarin is open daily for lunch and dinner. There's another, more uptown Mandarin in Monterey Park at 728 S. Atlantic Blvd., 626/289-2891; you'll find them elsewhere around L.A., too. But this spartan noodle palace is the first and original.

For seafood, best bet is **Mon Kee,** 679 N. Spring St. (at Ord St.), 213/628-6717, serving the best Cantonese seafood in Chinatown at lunch and dinner daily. The food here is so good nobody cares about the minimal ambience. People's favorites include the crab in black bean sauce and chicken with scallops and snow peas. Expect to wait for a table. **Yang Chow,** 819 N. Broadway (between Alpine and College), 213/625-0811, is another best bet—in this case for Szechuan specialties, from slippery shrimp and *kung pao* chicken to *mu shu* anything. Another possibility, considerably more stylish and stylized, is the **Plum Tree Inn,** 937 N. Hill St. (at College), 213/613-1819, serving both Mandarin and Szechwan cuisine. Spicy Plum Tree beef and sweet and pungent shrimp are among the house favorites. If you like your food spicy, ask to order from the Chinese menu.

Then there's **Empress Pavilion,** 988 N. Hill St., Ste. 201 (at the mall on N. Hill between College and Bernard), 213/617-9898, pastel dim sum palace extraordinaire, open daily 9 A.M.–10 P.M., perfect for breakfast. If the kids have never been to Hong Kong, this huge Chinatown palace will give them the general idea. The Empress offers an astonishing number of items to choose from—you can't miss with a "gourmet selection" or specialty—but the dim sum selections, all quite good, are a great place to start. Or go for the seafood, something of a house specialty and usually perfectly prepared, such as the Maine lobster, Dungeness crab, and prawns with glazed walnuts. Killer crispy duck, too.

"New" new Chinatown is represented by some impressive places, including cuisine from other countries. For Cambodian, try **Battambang,** 648 New High St. (at Ord St.), 213/620-9015. And for more culinary surprises, wander the neighborhood.

People's Eats: Little Tokyo

The most enjoyable way to sample Little Tokyo is to wander rather aimlessly, if hungrily, through the various food courts. One possibility is **Japanese Village Plaza** between First and Second Streets. Another: **Weller Court,** 123 S. Ellison at Onizuka St., where you'll find everything from Japanese fast food to very elegant entrées.

One of the best and most elegant sushi bars around is **Shibucho** in Yaohan Plaza on the top floor, 333 S. Alameda St., 213/626-1184, which can also be quite reasonable. It's open for lunch Monday–Saturday, dinner daily. Hardly a people's palace but exceptional and surprising nonetheless: **A Thousand Cranes** at the New Otani Hotel, 120 S. Los Angeles St., 213/629-1200, where East and West blend deliciously at Sunday brunch.

Though the heyday has passed for the avant-garde restaurant and artsy club scene surrounding Little Tokyo—an era that boasted Gorky's, a hip Russian café, and café/clubs such as Troy—the neighborhoods bordering Little Tokyo are still a best bet for seeking outposts of the alternative, since they do pop up from time to time. Another of L.A.'s best sushi bars, **R-23** is an off-the-beaten-path Japanese restaurant that has remained one of the Loft District's best secrets for five years. Housed in a stunning industrial building minimally decorated with exposed brick and beams, vertical wood columns, and chairs made from cardboard, R-23 features a small menu and à la carte sushi. Best for a quick lunch: assorted *chirashi,* various high-quality sashimi resting atop a bowl of rice, with ginger and wasabi. If you can find your way here, you'll find yourself doing lunch with escapees from City Hall and the hip Fashion District. L.A.-speak for "restaurant between Second and Third," R-23 is at 923 E. Third (at Alameda), 213/687-7178.

Other stylish alternatives to skid row have successfully taken root, too, such as **410 Boyd,** 410 Boyd St., 213/617-2491, beloved for its lobster club sandwich and lunch specials, and particularly popular with downtown loft-dwellers. Great place, but the neighborhood is definitely not recommended for the timid. Open for lunch Monday–Friday, for both lunch and dinner Tuesday–Friday; secure parking.

People's Eats: Downtown and Around

Always reasonable—and always fun, given the setting—is sawdust-floored **Maddalena's Cucina** at downtown's own **San Antonio Winery,** 737 Lamar St. (off N. Main, just east of the L.A. River), 323/223-1401, open daily 10 A.M.–5 P.M.—the culinary outlet for a working winery in business here since 1916. Though it's a challenge to picture it these days, once—when L.A. boasted 20 wineries—this neighborhood was solidly Italian. The vineyards have long since been paved over, of course, and the San Antonio is the era's sole survivor. (The Riboli family now produces wines from grapes trucked in from elsewhere in California.) Take the tour, sample the wares. For downtown L.A., it's all a big surprise.

For coffee shop fans there's an L.A. classic nearby, tucked in among the railroad yards. Ham is the thing at **Nick's Cafe,** 1300 N. Spring St., 323/222-1450, famous for its ham and eggs breakfasts, ham omelettes, ham sandwiches, and just plain slabs o' ham. Sure, it's a working stiffs' breakfast and lunch stop—open from before dawn to 5 P.M. on weekdays, to 11:30 A.M. on Saturday—but it's meat and potatoes done right, cooked from scratch on the premises. Nick's is near the Police Academy, which explains all those regulation haircuts.

Another place most people are surprised to find in L.A., given the city's much-hyped hedonism, is **Clifton's "Brookdale" Cafeteria** downtown at 648 S. Broadway, 213/627-1673, built by Christian philanthropist Clifford E. Clifton. Throughout the Depression, Clifton's "Golden Rule Cafeterias" served ample portions of good, wholesome food to customers who paid what they could afford. But Clifton did more than feed the hungry huddled masses. He also attempted to elevate their spirituality and spirits—by building this strange six-level oasis, an ersatz redwood forest complete with babbling brook and waterfall. Clifton's is easy to find; just look for the street evangelists out front. One can't judge the effectiveness of their sidewalk proselytizing—for years, one regular wore a sandwich board demanding NO SEX—but it's all certainly *different.* And the food is cheap and good. On a chilly day, enjoy a hearty bowl of soup or chili with a side of cornbread.

Also très traditional downtown: the **Original Pantry,** 877 S. Figueroa St. (at Ninth), 213/972-9279. Mayor Richard Riordan is the current owner of the restaurant and he and his circle of top L.A. business people are often in residence. The Original has been open 24 hours a day, every day, since 1924—except for one much-publicized, politically scandalous day in November 1997, when the place was cited for health code violations and closed for a thorough cleaning. Even that event didn't dent the patient line of patrons outside on the sidewalk, waiting to get in

—24 hours a day, every day, since 1924. Generous portions of good old-fashioned Americana—steaks, roast chicken, even macaroni and cheese—are the Original Pantry's specialties. Hearty bacon and egg breakfasts, accompanied by the best hash browns in town, propel Angelenos to get in line for more. The **Original Pantry Cafe,** now open next door, serves terrific hamburgers, sandwiches, and pastries from the Pantry's own bakery. You can expect an enormous meal.

Not to be missed if you're heading east toward Wilshire's museums is very purple **Super Torta** just north of MacArthur Park in a strip mall at 360 S. Alvarado St. (at Maryland), 213/413-7953, which serves a sumptuous Americanized version of the Mexican sandwich—your choice of meat with beans, guacamole, mayo, and jalapeños on the side—and even *horchata,* a sweet, rice-based drink, to wash it all down. If you're craving something from other locales, head for Koreatown and C & K Importing, the best-known ethnic market (Greek) in Los Angeles. Inside is **Papa Cristo's Taverna,** 2771 W. Pico (off Normandy), 323/737-2970, offering fab Greek grilled goodies—beef, lamb, or fish—served with creamy fried potatoes, a traditional salad, and pita bread. The garlicky *loukaniko* sausage, flavored with orange peel and simmered in wine, comes highly recommended. Eat in or take out.

And if hunger assaults you somewhere south of Wilshire, the traditional USC student destination for Mexican food and margaritas is **El Cholo,** 1121 S. Western Ave. (between Pico and Olympic), 323/734-2773, open here since 1927. The taco tray delivers a do-it-yourself meal of tortillas, meats, beans, and sauces, though feel free to try anything. It's all good. In season—traditionally June to September—best bets include the green corn tamales and the salsa *verde* crab enchiladas.

More Uptown Downtown

If you're contemplating the Museum of Contemporary Art, also contemplate a scrumptious lunch or a light Thursday evening supper at Joachim Splichal's California-French **Patinette,** inside the museum at 250 S. Grand Ave. (near Second St.), 213/626-1178, serving surprising sandwiches and pasta salads, wine by the glass, and espresso.

Kissing cousin to the Contemporary's Patinette is **Café Pinot** in the garden near the Central Library at 700 W. Fifth St. (at Flower), 213/239-6500. One of downtown's best eating events, Café Pinot is a sibling to Pinot Bistro in Studio City, Pinot Hollywood, and Pinot at the Chronicle in Pasadena—conceptual descendants, all, of Patina on Melrose, one of the city's best restaurants. What that pedigree brings you here is a Paris-style garden bistro serving wonderful roast chicken and other unforgettables at dinner—on Thursday, the herb-crusted turkey breast is the thing—and wonderful lunch specials and specialties. Ask for a seat on the comfortable patio near the Central Library's fountains and surrounding gardens. As lovely as it is here for lunch, the real drama comes in the evening, when surrounding skyscrapers shimmer with light, and sometimes moonlight. This place is perfect for a pre-theater meal, too, if you can get in by 6 P.M. Pinot is open weekdays only for lunch, 11:30 A.M.–2:30 P.M., and for dinner nightly from either 5 or 5:30 P.M., depending on the day (closed major holidays).

Uptown **Pacific Grill,** inside the Sanwa Bank building at 601 S. Figueroa St. (between Sixth St. and Wilshire), 213/485-0927, serves contemporary American fare of all ethnic persuasions. Pacific Grill is open only for lunch on Mon.–Fri. 11 A.M.–2 P.M.

The Oviatt Building, an ersatz 1930s' luxury ocean liner awash in rich woods, black marble, and burgundy velvet armchairs, is home to glamorous **Cicada,** at 617 S. Olive Street (between Sixth and Seventh Sts.), 213/488-9488, which took over the helm here, so to speak, when Rex, Il Ristorante closed following proprietor Mauro Vincenti's death. Owned by Stephanie and Bernie Taupin (he, Elton John's longtime songwriting partner), Cicada is Northern Italian and expensive. Free shuttle service to the music center makes this a popular pre-theatre dinner spot.

For contemporary American on the company expense account, the place is **Bernard's** at the Biltmore Hotel, 506 S. Grand Ave. (at Fifth), 213/612-1580, where the exquisite no-nonsense fare includes New York steak and chicken, lamb, and duck. Bernard's is open Tues.–Sat. for dinner.

Additional options for uptown dining downtown are mentioned under upscale hotel listings in Staying Downtown, above.

EATING AROUND WILSHIRE

Ethnic foodies, take note: Korean restaurants and shops abound in Koreatown, which skirts Wilshire Boulevard close to downtown. L.A.'s Korean community is half a million strong, which brings to mid-Wilshire an astonishing array of Korean bars, coffeehouses, restaurants, cafés, noodle houses, and elegant dining rooms. South of Wilshire along Pico and Olympic, stretching from downtown west to Fairfax Avenue, are other surprising and distinct ethnic areas—Thai, Vietnamese, Taiwanese, Japanese, and Indonesian—blending at the edges with Central American and Mexican neighborhoods. Exploring along Eighth and Ninth Streets is L.A.'s ultimate multicultural culinary adventure. Another dining destination, Fairfax Avenue between Pico and Wilshire, is becoming known for its Ethiopian restaurants. Kosher country begins just west of Fairfax, where Pico is becoming a Jewish "restaurant row." But Fairfax north of Wilshire, particularly between Beverly Boulevard and Melrose, marks the Fairfax district—L.A.'s traditional, now transitional, Russian-Jewish neighborhood, known for its Russian restaurants and kosher shops, groceries, and delis, including the famous 24-hour Canter's. Also in the neighborhood, at Third Street, is the Farmers Market, where dozens of food stalls and simple restaurants attract all kinds of Angelenos (and buses of tourists). Prime-time for people watching.

Korean People's Eats

Los Angeles food writer Jonathan Gold describes a bowl of Korean bean-curd stew like this: "Soon tofu looks less like food than a special effect from a Wes Craven movie, a heaving, bright-red mass in a superheated black cauldron that spurts geysers, spits like a lake of volcanic lava, and broadcasts a fine, red mist of chile and broth that tints anything within six inches a pale, lustrous pink. A network of bubbles forms on the surface of the stew and amalgamates into a throbbing, blood-colored froth that occasionally opens up like a cinematic portal to doom, revealing glistening white chunks bobbing within." If a close approximation of that experience appeals to you, **Beverly Soon Tofu** 2717 W. Olympic Blvd., 213/380-1113, is the place to get it. Or try other Korean specialties—*mandoo* dumplings, for instance, both crispy fried or boiled versions—at **Ddo-Wa**, 3542 W. Third St., 213/387-1288. At **Shin Chon** 244 S. Oxford Ave., 213/384-2663, Korean beef soup *(sol-long-tang)* is the only thing on the menu. The bowl is bottomless. More upscale is **Sa Rit Gol** at 3189 W. Olympic Blvd., 213/387-0909, famous for pork barbecue, thin loin strips marinated in red chile sauce and then cooked on a tabletop grill. Intrigued but not quite willing to risk a full-fledged meal? Then consider **Sool In Nun Ma-Ool**, 2500 W. Eighth St., 213/380-3346, an elegant drinking establishment that serves minimeals such as leeks and oysters fried in egg batter, crisp mungbean pancakes, and steamed tendon with scallion salad. The house specialty is something you won't find just anywhere—whole octopus, rubbed with chile paste and then grilled. To serve it, the waitress lifts the 'pus off the platter with tongs and then snips off pieces of tentacle with scissors.

Other People's Eats

If you're low on cash after doing museum row, head for the **Farmers Market**, 6333 W. Third St., on the north side of W. Third Street at Fairfax. The excellent **Gumbo Pot,** 323/933-0358, is among the choices here; the Cajun/Creole fare is almost a steal. The namesake gumbo is a mainstay, along with jambalaya, meat loaf, muffulettas, and catfish, chicken, shrimp, and oyster po' boys. Everything's available for takeout, too, so stop by to pack an unusual picnic. (For a Sierra Nevada or other brew, head to the beer bar nearby.) The Gumbo Pot is open Mon.–Sat. 8:30 A.M.–6:30 P.M., Sunday 10 A.M.–5 P.M., closed major holidays. Particularly entertaining at breakfast, because of its tendency to draw execs and even the occasional celeb from nearby CBS Television City, is the Farmers Market's **Kokomo,** 323/933-0773, a hip and happenin' café where such things as grilled cheese sandwiches and sweet-potato French fries manage to pass for health food. Those in the know say

Kokomo also has the best BLT in town. Selections $6–9. Dinner served too.

A real find nearby is **Fiddler's Bistro** at the Park Plaza Lodge motel, 6009 W. Third St. (at Martel), 323/931-8167, a coffee shop with Middle Eastern flair where the Greek fare is the best bet—and a low-budget opportunity to be a voyeur within the everydayness of the Hollywood scene. Entrées quite reasonable.

For kosher, try 24-hour **Canter's Delicatessen**, 419 N. Fairfax (between Beverly Blvd. and Melrose), 323/651-2030, a neighborhood fixture almost since time began. The food's just decent and the service often downright rude, but some folks also eat that up.

More People's Eats

Maurice's Snack 'n' Chat is an L.A. icon, this one south of Wilshire at 5549 W. Pico Blvd., 323/930-1795. A place frequented from time to time by Quincy Jones, Danny Glover, Whoopi Goldberg, and other celebs, this lively restaurant serves unpretentious soul food that gets there when it gets there—so you can chat even before you snack. The fare here is *not* what the doctor ordered—fried chicken, short ribs, black-eyed peas, yams, spoon bread, and downhome desserts, including peach cobbler and coconut cake—but it's tasty and the place is fun, so what the heck. Make a reservation, BYOB, and plan on staying awhile. It's open for lunch and dinner daily. For a mid-Wilshire burger experience, head for **Mo' Better Meatty Meat Burger**, 5855 W. Pico Blvd., 323/938-6558. Some L.A. burger fanatics rate Mo' Better's best, but service can be slow—always a consideration if the kids are hungry and cranky. There's another Mo' Better on Melrose.

For real-thing Thai—and the choices are multiple in this neighborhood—try **Alisa**, 2810 W. Ninth St., 213/384-7049, which is undistinguished except for the surprise Northern Thai "restaurant within a restaurant" **Chao Nue,** a rare find in L.A. Bring everyone you know, request "northern food," and order everything.

If hunger strikes while you're gallery-hopping along La Brea, one possibility is **Pink's Hot Dogs** north of Melrose at 711 N. La Brea, 323/931-4223 (no phone orders), justifiably famous for its chili dogs but increasingly popular for such things as chicken fajita burritos and chili-drenched tamales. Or stop by the cherubic and clean **Divine Pasta Co.,** 615 N. La Brea, 323/939-1148, where you can sit down to some of the city's best fresh pasta and sauce (served with salad). And if you're doing La Brea in the morning, line up with everyone else at the famed **La Brea Bakery,** 624 S. La Brea, 323/939-6813, for breakfast pastries to go or a bag full of specialty breads, including the wonderful sourdough black-olive.

Fancier Fare on and near La Brea

The La Brea Avenue area north of Wilshire sports more than its fair share of great midrange-and-more restaurants. For starters, try the **Authentic Cafe,** 7605 Beverly Blvd. (between Fairfax and La Brea), 323/939-4626, open daily for lunch and dinner. Tiny and terrifically popular, the Authentic Cafe is best known for tamales, nachos, new renditions of Mexican standards, and somewhat Southwestern pastas and pizzas. Seemingly unrelated items appear on the menu, too, such as Chinese dumplings, other Asian dishes, and eclectic miscellany—which makes the Authentic Cafe as authentically Los Angeles as anyplace around. It's got a cappuccino bar too. No reservations, so be prepared to wait.

Now that the semi-industrial City Restaurant at 180 S. La Brea has been recycled, **The Original Sonora Cafe,** 323/857-1800, has transplanted its pretty pricey Southwestern self from downtown into that impressive space. It's open for lunch Mon.–Sat., for dinner daily.

But don't miss **Ca'Brea,** 346 S. La Brea (between Third and Fourth), 323/938-2863. One of the most reasonably priced Northern Italian restaurants in Los Angeles, casual, stylish, and wildly popular Ca'Brea serves such things as baby-back ribs and beans, crab cakes, seafood pastas, and a wonderful fresh mozzarella salad. Daily specials bring new surprises, but count on fresh fish, pastas, soups, and salads. Ca'Brea is open weekdays only for lunch, Mon.–Sat. for dinner. Reservations always advisable. To meet a more uptown member of the same culinary family, frequently rated as L.A.'s best Italian, try **Locanda Veneta,** close to West Hollywood and Beverly Hills at 8638 W. Third St., 310/274-1893.

Hancock Park's Larchmont area also features some nice neighborhood eateries, these including an outpost of **Chan Dara,** 310 N. Larchmont Blvd., 323/467-1052, serving sophisticated Thai, and **Girasole Cucina Italiana,** 225$1/2$ Larchmont, 323/464-6978, offering rustic, authentic Venetian cuisine (BYO alcoholic beverage).

Campanile

The ultimate neighborhood culinary destination is Campanile, 624 S. La Brea (between Wilshire and Sixth St.), 323/938-1447. This onetime massage parlor, auto dealership, and Charlie Chaplin office building, a Moorish art deco beauty complete with bell tower, has gone postmodern. Not the most expensive restaurant in Los Angeles nor the trendiest, Campanile is quite possibly the best. The fare here, from grilled chicken, lobster, and fresh fish dishes to sumptuous salads, is fairly simple yet superb, the atmosphere airy and unassuming, the prices quite reasonable. The real deal is breakfast—quite leisurely on a weekday, and always fortified by fresh baked goods from the associated and equally acclaimed La Brea Bakery, adjacent. Campanile is open daily for breakfast, weekdays only for lunch, and Mon.–Sat. for dinner (closed Thanksgiving and Christmas). Reservations are necessary for dinner.

COURTESY AISLINN RACE

HOLLYWOOD AND VICINITY

THE TRAPPINGS OF TINSELTOWN

"Strip away the phony tinsel in Hollywood and you'll find the real tinsel underneath," Oscar Levant once said of the world's supreme dream machine. Since then the phony tinsel has been stripped away, along with most of what might have been real. For a while it seemed the last few strands of authentic memorabilia had been all but thrashed by trash and trashy attractions.

Film aficionados flock here, pilgrims to a movieland mecca. Lured by the recollected romance of big-screen stars such as Marilyn Monroe and Lana Turner and the he-man heroism of the John Wayne western, people stumble off the tour bus onto the Hollywood Walk of Fame these days only to confront the gritty and grimy hard-eyed human conflagration of prostitution, porn palaces, and unapologetic poverty that is, now, Hollywood. Worldly wits foretold this turn of events. "It's hard to know where Hollywood ends and the DT's begin," W. C. Fields

once said. Ditto for Oscar Wilde's general observation: "All of us are in the gutter, but some of us are looking up at the stars."

Tinseltown: The Place and the Idea
First and foremost, Hollywood is a place—a place that began its decline shortly after the peak of its prominence, during the Great Depression. During the past decades Hollywood successfully substituted one reel of illusion for another, dumping glued-on glamour for disaffection, desperation, and despair, right in step with the modern psyche.

But Hollywood is also an idea. If you prefer visiting the idea, a Hollywood Boulevard where everyone is clean-cut, courteous, and hopelessly happy, you can. You can go to Florida, for example. The Disney-MGM Studios theme park in Orlando features "Hollywood Boulevard as you've always imagined it to be." *That* Hollywood Boulevard features actors, animatronic actors, adoring crowds, various other artificial sights and sounds, and an admission price of well over $30. (On the other hand, the real Hollywood Boulevard is absolutely free and authentically eccentric, its gutters overflowing with the unambiguous angst of modern life.) Or you can visit CityWalk at Universal Studios, just up the hill. In the immediate vicinity, Hollywood the idea extends beyond Cahuenga Pass into the San Fernando Valley and, from the Hollywood flatlands, west into the fairly new city of West Hollywood. Coming soon: Hollywood's next installment, near the shores of the Pacific Ocean on L.A.'s Westside.

Tinseltown II: The Sequel

Hollywood is changing yet again—cleaning up its act, albeit laboriously, and getting ready for a new performance. In 1986 the Los Angeles City Council decided to help its Hollywood district, once referred to even by residents as a "Club Med for crime," glue some of its glamour back on with a 30-year, $922 million facelift affecting more than 1,000 acres—a project second only in scope to the massive downtown Bunker Hill redevelopment. Included in the price tag: housing for teenage runaways and otherwise homeless street people. In addition, a Hollywood Entertainment District was created in 1996, with property assessment funds earmarked for local security patrols, ongoing cleanup, and other civic improvements.

Symbolizing this snazzy, cleaned-up Hollywood is the Metro Red Line's new subway station, opened in 1999, a way station for the ride that whisks people between downtown and Hollywood and Vine in minutes. Symbols of Hollywood abound at the station. Bus shelters were constructed to look like cartoons of Mann's Chinese Theatre, a limousine, and the Brown Derby restaurant. Inside, stylized Southern California palm trees serve as columns and old film reels cover the ceiling.

HOLLYWOOD CITYPASS

For those planning to seriously see the sights in and around Hollywood, the local CityPass ticket book might be worth the investment. The Hollywood CityPass includes admission tickets to eight attractions—Universal Studios, the Egyptian Theater, the Hollywood Entertainment Museum, the Museum of Television and Radio, the Petersen Automotive Museum, the Autry Museum of Western Heritage, the Museum of Tolerance, and the Reagan Presidential Library and Museum—and at last report cost $49.75 for an adult, $38 for children (age 3–11). Sure, that sounds steep—but in 2000 admission to Universal Studios alone was $41 for adults and $31 for children.

Conveniently for vacation planners, the Hollywood CityPass ticket book is undated and can be bought in advance. (Tickets are invalid, however, if removed in advance from the booklet.) The only limitation is, the CityPass is good for 30 days, beginning with the first day of use.

For current information and to buy ticket books online, go to www.citypass.net or www.universalstudios.com. For recorded information, call (707) 256-0490. You can also buy the Hollywood Citypass at the admission gates at Universal Studios Hollywood.

Helping things along considerably is the fact that boom times are back—even in Hollywood—thanks to burgeoning international demand for entertainment industry "product." With total annual receipts in excess of $19 billion, Hollywood's export trade runs to at least $6 billion annually.

Most modern movie corporations abandoned Hollywood's first wave of building sites years ago, of course, but the new studios aren't all that far away. These days Tinseltown's true territory has vast but vague borders, starting somewhere on the far side of the Hollywood Hills in the sprawling San Fernando Valley. Hollywood's second wave includes the Disney, Warner Bros., and NBC studios in Burbank and the fairly new Manhattan Beach Studios in Manhattan Beach, entertainment industry outposts all undergoing major expansions. The tourist-oriented Universal Studios, on the cusp between old and new Hollywood in the Hollywood Hills, plans to double its size within the next few decades.

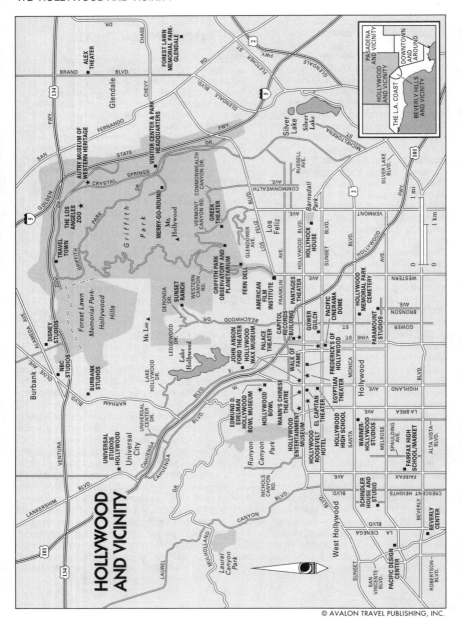

TINSELTOWN THEN: MAKING THE MYTH

Pious Prohibition

To imagine Hollywood as a god-fearing, prohibitionist utopia is more than even modern Hollywood mythmakers can manage. Yet—long ago and far away—once the native Cahuenga people were dispensed with, so went the Cahuenga Valley. Scattered sheep ranches, small vegetable farms, and a few citrus groves defined the landscape in late 1887. That year, just before L.A.'s 1880s' real estate boom went bust, Horace Henderson Wilcox and his wife, Daeida, bought up the area for a future subdivision. Daeida Wilcox originally favored the name "Figwood" for their fig and apricot ranch but named it "Hollywood" instead, after the summer home of a woman she met on the train coming to California.

Active prohibitionists with utopian Midwestern ideals, the Wilcoxes cut the theoretical town from their own cloth—banning saloons and liquor stores and offering free land for church construction. The boom busted by 1889; Horace died soon after, and the widow Wilcox married another paragon of puritanical virtue. Together they continued their quest for a properly churched community.

Hollywood had become home to about 500 residents by the early 1900s. The electric trolley regularly rumbled into town loaded with tourists destined for the De Longpre gallery and gardens, the Glen-Holly Hotel, and the Hollywood Hotel. In 1903, the city incorporated and established a high school. In 1904, Sunset Boulevard was completed, linking Hollywood to Los Angeles, at long last. Until 1911, then, the L.A. suburb of Hollywood developed in the predictable Southern California pattern.

The First Picture Shows

Hollywood's stolid sobriety was soon shattered, forever—because moviemaking came to town. In the beginning it was something of a bootleg business, in defiance of fees, royalties, and other efforts by Thomas Alva Edison and the Edison Company to control the new industry through the Motion Pictures Patents Company (known as "the Trust").

Technically the southstate moving picture industry began in 1907 in Los Angeles, which Selig Studios chose for filming the outdoor scenes for *The Count of Monte Cristo*. The first film companies to establish permanent Southern California studios selected Los Angeles, Santa Monica, and Santa Barbara—locations that shared the advantage of being close to Mexico, where film companies and crews could escape the Trust's attorneys, process servers, and thugs.

The distinction between Los Angeles and Hollywood as a film location was moot by 1911, in a sense, since in 1910 the small suburb surrendered its charter and became part of Los Angeles. In that same year David Wark Griffith, leading director of New York's Biograph film company, came west to Los Angeles with his wife, Linda, and his film troupe, including 17-year-old Mary Pickford, and installed them in the Hollywood Inn on Hollywood Boulevard for the winter-spring shooting season. Between January 20 and April 6, Griffith's troupe produced 21 films in distinct southstate settings—the first shot entirely *in* Southern California—including *The Thread of Destiny* at Mission San Gabriel and *Ramona* in Ventura County.

D. W. Griffith would return for equally productive filmmaking forays during the next few winters and, intentionally or not, established the unmatched utility of Los Angeles and Hollywood. As historian Kevin Starr puts it, here Griffith discovered "an environment, social and scenic, that was composed of fragments available for eclectic use"—the near-perfect weather and light, and the astonishing geographic variety: the ocean and coast, mountains and forests, valleys and prairies, and the desolation of desert. Here were farms and ranches and sunny new cities with endless architectural variety. And here was a society still searching for an original identity—the perfect place for the infant film industry to define itself.

Griffith's disciple Mack Sennett arrived in 1912 to begin his Keystone comedies, star vehicles for the English vaudevillian Charlie Chaplin. Sennett—a heavy-drinking, cigar-smoking womanizer credited with inventing Hollywood's infamous "casting couch"—explored and celebrated Los Angeles in film as no other American city, before or since. So appealing was the then-fresh Southern California landscape, as revealed in movie theaters throughout the nation, that the region's population grew to over one million within just a few years.

Cleaning Up the Neighborhood

Hollywood resisted Southern California's growing general affinity for film. Before local morality mavens could mobilize much protest, however, those carousing carefree movie people had arrived. In a sense, Hollywood's blue-nosed attitudes caused the bohemian invasion. If Prohibitionists hadn't closed down the Blondeau Tavern at Sunset and Gower, for example, New Jersey's Nestor Film Company would never have found its permanent Hollywood niche in 1911.

Within five years about 35 movie studios had relocated from the East and Midwest, creating overnight chaos on Hollywood's sleepy unpaved streets. Movie cowboys didn't all abandon their roles at the end of the workday; heavy-drinking heathens on horseback charged through neighborhoods, brandishing pistols and trampling flower beds. Without warning or permission, entire production crews encamped on private front lawns to shoot their next scheduled scene. And the behavior of actors and actresses hardly dispelled the notion of moral depravity. Not surprisingly, Hollywood boarding houses shunned movie people. The Hollywood Hotel posted a "No Dogs or Actors" sign—a snub that reportedly caused actress Gloria Swanson to snarl: "We didn't even get top billing!" Los Angeles in general looked askance at Hollywood's glittery gypsies, shunning them socially. The Los Angeles Country Club was notorious for refusing membership to any and all actors. A classic Hollywood story features Victor Mature pulling bad reviews out of his pocket and telling club officials: "I'm no actor, and I can prove it."

Hollywood's "Conscientious Citizens" were indeed conscientious and petitioned the city to run film companies out of town. But moral concerns proved to be no match for movie industry money. By the Roaring '20s, Hollywood's stars glittered as national and international idols. Abundant cash and employment opportunity also changed the community's mind about the merits of the movies. They also changed the commu-

nity; starry-eyed young people rushed the gates of Hollywood's Babylon, dreaming of stardom but settling for almost anything.

Accidental Purist: Cecil B. DeMille

Flamboyant director Cecil B. DeMille created the Hollywood of myth—almost an accidental result of his collaboration with fellow New Yorkers Jesse Lasky and Lasky's brother-in-law, Samuel Goldfish (later, Goldwyn), in the Jesse L. Lasky Feature Play Company. DeMille's directorial debut also resulted in Hollywood's first full-length film, *The Squaw Man,* more or less made in their studio—a barn—and adjacent orange grove at the dirt-road juncture of Selma and Vine. Cast and crew commuted to other locations in a two-ton flatbed Ford truck.

If DeMille was almost an accidental director, Hollywood was his accidental destination. When C.B. (as he was called) set out from New York, he planned to shoot *The Squaw Man* in Flagstaff, Arizona. A dust storm foiled his filming schedule, so DeMille and company got back on the train and continued west. They ended up in Hollywood.

One could argue also that DeMille became

BOB RACE

Even an assassination attempt didn't stop C.B. DeMille from founding the Hollywood of myth.

Hollywood's accidental purist. Dogged by "accidents," disasters, threats, and at least one assassination attempt—"The first critic of a DeMille picture," the filmmaker reportedly quipped, while attributing such sabotage to the Trust—DeMille ultimately completed the film, a phenomenal six-reel success that led to many more.

DeMille also played a starring role in early Hollywood's cinematic subculture, becoming an enduring Southern California symbol—the heroic director all done up in jodhpurs, leather boots (to prevent rattlesnake bites), even holster and pistol. Others in DeMille's entourage exuded exuberance and creative extravagance, including Ina Claire, Geraldine Farrar, and Gloria Swanson, Wallace Berry, and Walt Disney.

Film critics have blamed DeMille, father of the film spectacle *(The Ten Commandments,* *Madame Satan, King of Kings),* for demeaning and derailing the American film industry in its infancy. DeMille certainly did relish cinematic excess, the vulgarity of showmanship. But entertainment, not art, made money at the box office, and DeMille was the first to figure that out. So the year 1914, when Cecil B. DeMille decided to settle permanently in this sleepy L.A. suburb, "must be considered both the actual and symbolic founding of Hollywood," according to Kevin Starr.

The Glory Years

During the 1920s and '30s the stretch of Hollywood Boulevard between La Brea Avenue and Vine Street glittered with glitz, boasting magnificent movie theaters, notorious nightclubs (Hollywood invented the Flapper style), notoriously

AMERICAN FILM INSTITUTE

Before the Sisters of Immaculate Heart of Mary bought the grounds in the early 1900s to build a school, the mythic California bandit Joaquin Murrieta buried his loot here, according to L.A. lore. So the sisters were besieged by treasure hunters for more than 50 years—until 1957, when said hill was thoroughly excavated for construction. No treasure. And, finally, no more treasure hunters, unless you count the legions of starry-eyed film folk who attend classes at the American Film Institute (AFI), which bought the property in 1980.

The institute, 2021 N. Western Ave., was founded in 1965 with President Lyndon B. Johnson's signature on the National Foundation of the Arts and Humanities Act. The AFI's multiple mission includes preserving film and television heritage, identifying and training new talent, and increasing public recognition and understanding of "the moving image as art." Programs established to achieve these ends include AFI's **National Center for Film and Video Preservation,** its **Center for Advanced Film and Television Studies,** the **Louis B. Mayer Library,** and world-class film festivals held each year in New York, Washington, D.C., and (of course) Los Angeles. One of the largest and most prestigious film festivals in the country, the **Los Angeles International Film Festival** is scheduled during the last two weeks of October, screening almost 100 films at various venues throughout the city and drawing more than 40,000 participants. For current information, call 323/856-7707.

Though new industry buzz emerges here all the time, according to AFI's television special *One Hundred Years—One Hundred Movies,* the top 10 of the top 100 films of all time are (drumroll): *Citizen Kane, Casablanca, The Godfather, Gone with the Wind, Lawrence of Arabia, Wizard of Oz, The Graduate, On the Waterfront, Schindler's List,* and *Singing in the Rain.*

Recipients of the American Film Institute's coveted **Life Achievement Award** include director Martin Scorsese, Clint Eastwood, Steven Spielberg, Jack Nicholson, Elizabeth Taylor, and Sidney Poitier. The list reaches well into Hollywood's past, too, including also Frank Capra, Alfred Hitchcock, John Huston, and Orson Welles.

But much of the institute's work involves finding—and assisting—new talent, through its programs for minority filmmakers and production training, its directing workshops for women, and ongoing outreach efforts. Advanced technology classes and seminars—typically offered on nights and weekends and open to the general public—cover everything from the art and craft of animation and digital film technologies to acting, directing, and screenwriting.

For more information about AFI and its programs, call 323/856-7707 or point your browswer to www.afionline.org.

good restaurants, chic shops, and stylish hotels. By the mid-1920s the Hollywood movie business was the fifth-largest industry in the United States, generating 90 percent of the world's films and grossing about $1.5 billion per year.

Hollywood's prosperity and social ascendance coincided with the rise of the West Coast studio system. Fox, First National, Metro, Goldwyn (the latter two later becoming Metro-Goldwyn-Mayer), Paramount, Universal, Warner Bros.—all stepped forward to vanquish the pioneering East Coast film companies, finally busting the Trust and creating their own tightly controlled monopolies in its stead. Artists and directors as well as bankers and businessmen got into the act. In 1919 Charlie Chaplin, Douglas Fairbanks, and Mary Pickford joined forces with D. W. Griffith to form United Artists, a company owned and directed by directors and movie stars. "So the lunatics have taken charge of the asylum," said Metro's Richard Rowland.

But the democratic impulse ran much deeper. The emerging West Coast film industry reached far beyond Hollywood, right into the heart and mind of heartland America and, quite quickly, the world. Movies appealed to the elemental and universal human experience, both mirroring and creating public and private dreams. To get the drift, one didn't need an Ivy League education. Hollywood's mass appeal soon obliterated the culturally more sophisticated East Coast film companies, with their classic artistic aims and highbrow Greek and Latin names. Instead, film stars—by and large, ordinary, everyday people who achieved social transcendence as entertainers—both interpreted and inspired national aspirations.

The Gory Years

With the overnight advent of a national entertainment industry and a nationwide mass culture came the rather loud suggestion that it was all rather insidious and un-American. Anti-Semitism fueled the anti-Hollywood uproar. Of the loosely affiliated Jewish Americans who soon dominated the industry—Harry Cohn, Samuel Goldfish (Goldwyn when he later took the name of his film company), William Fox, Carl Laemmle, Jesse Lasky, Marcus Loew, Adolph Zukor, all four Warner brothers—many were foreign-born, refugees from New York's Lower East Side glove, garment, and fur trades who still spoke thickly accented English.

So early in its history Hollywood became head cheerleader for patriotism in general and, in particular, a rather limited definition of the American way—serving the national myth but also narrowing it. What Kevin Starr describes as Southern California's "aggressively patriotic sensibility" is still much in evidence today. The rabid beast of Southern California superpatriotism has viciously bitten itself—and the rest of us—on various occasions.

Hollywood virtually invented the present-day "attack ad" political campaign, for example, in its all-out 1934 campaign against writer Upton Sinclair, then a socialist candidate for California governor. Sinclair's primary sin? As part of his End Poverty in California election platform—immensely popular in Depression-era days—Sinclair proposed tax hikes for the studios and casually mentioned the possibility of a state-run film industry. Irving Thalberg at MGM Studios coordinated the public disinformation campaign against Sinclair, enlisting Carey Wilson (scriptwriter for *Mutiny on the Bounty)* to write several "California Election News" shorts broadcast in movie theaters throughout California. The most effective "documented" Californians' worst fears—that if Sinclair were elected, scores of bums and other communist or criminal undesirables would swarm into the state to take advantage of promised benefits.

But just over a decade later, Hollywood's dirty tricks boomeranged with a vengeance. With encouragement from homeboy Richard M. Nixon, Southern California happily helped ferret out suspected Hollywood communists and "comm symps" (communist sympathizers) during U.S. Senator Joseph McCarthy's 1947 House Un-American Activity Committee hearings.

As McCarthy's red-baiting campaigns increased in ferocity, they entranced even Hollywood's national audience. But the infamous "Hollywood blacklist," which ruined lives and careers throughout the entertainment industry, endured even after McCarthy's fear mongering came to an appropriately ignoble end.

Though it took years to truly hit its mark, Sen. Margaret Chase Smith of Maine fired the first effective volley against McCarthy's all-American witch-hunt when she took the Senate floor in

AISLINN RACE

HOLLYWOOD

THE HOLLYWOOD SIGN

The huge "Hollywood" sign looming over the landscape from atop scrubby Mount Lee is the city's universal symbol. While wandering among the stars' stars along the Hollywood Walk of Fame, keep in mind that the best pedestrian view is from Hollywood and Vine, looking north past the landmark Capitol Records Building. For a close-up look (legally possible only from public streets), head north into the Hollywood Hills' Beachwood Canyon via Beachwood (accessible from Franklin). Continue through the stone gateway; turn left onto Ledgewood, follow it up the hill to Deronda, then turn right and continue to its end. (Do not disturb the neighborhood.)

These fifty-foot-tall letters, fabricated from white sheet metal and originally outlined in 4,000 lights, advertised *Los Angeles Times* publisher Harry Chandler's adjacent 500-acre real estate development, a gated tract complete with castle towers, Black Forest cottages, and Ruritanian hunting lodges dubbed "Hollywoodland." (The caretaker charged with changing the light bulbs lived in a tiny cabin tucked behind an L.) But even then Hollywood's glitz was deceptive. In 1932, for example, 24-year-old actress Peg Entwistle—despondent when RKO Studios declined to sign her to a long-term contract—leaped to her death from the top of H, the sign's only recorded suicide but enough of a shock that locals soon considered the 13-letter sign an omen of bad luck. The following year audiences at the nearby Hollywood Bowl, finally fed up with the sign's rude glare, started stealing its light bulbs and shattering them with BB guns.

The sign's maintenance was increasingly erratic, abandoned altogether by 1939. The final bad-luck blow came in 1949 when the dilapidated "land" section tore loose and slid downhill to its doom. That same year, the Hollywood sign was deeded to the Hollywood Chamber of Commerce for the purposes of civic promotion.

This being Hollywood, the entire town eventually realized that a cosmetic makeover was long overdue. To raise the necessary cash to rebuild the sign, in 1978 local celebrities came to the rescue, donating $27,700 per letter. Hugh Hefner, for example, held a benefit at the Playboy Mansion for the sake of Y; Gene Autry paid for an L; and rocker Alice Cooper bought the last O in memory of Groucho Marx. But facelifts beget more facelifts. Thus in 1999, on QVC's *Extreme Shopping: Hollywood* show, an anonymous sponsor contributed another $100,000 to the Hollywood Sign Trust.

Hollywood's Hollywood sign is a magnet for merry pranksters. In keeping with Hollywood's original Christian mission, in long-gone days the sign was altered to read "Holywood" whenever evangelist Aimee Semple McPherson came to town. Since then it's been "Dollywood" to promote Dolly Parton, "Hollyweed" to memorialize marijuana, and "Perotwood" to honor the rebel yell of American presidential politics. Perhaps to recognize the entertainment value of Lieutenant Ollie North's testimony during the Iran-Contra hearings, the sign was altered during Ronald Reagan's presidency to read "Ollywood." And fans of the movie *Grand Canyon* will remember Kevin Kline's dream version, "Hullo Mack." Displaying substantially less imagination, Southern California collegians regularly drape the sign with "UCLA," "USC," "Cal Tech," "Go Navy," and other such banners, just before the big game.

1950 to deliver what she later described as a "declaration of conscience."

Without ever mentioning McCarthy, Nixon, or others by name, she observed that the U.S. Congress had been "debased to the level of a forum of hate and character assassination sheltered by the shield of congressional immunity. . . . I speak as a Republican. I speak as a

woman. I speak as a United States senator. I don't want to see the Republican Party ride to victory on the four horsemen of calumny—fear, ignorance, bigotry, and smear."

Whether or not a direct result of McCarthyism, present-day political sympathies in Hollywood run counter to prevailing Southern California conservatism, with studio executives and stars alike much more likely to work their fund-raising magic on behalf of Democratic, if not necessarily liberal, candidates.

Hollywood Babylon:
The Inmates and the Asylum

For other reasons, Hollywood has always been an easy target for those uneasy about its phenomenal influence. One such history-making period arrived during the 1920s, when Hollywood's dream factories otherwise could do no wrong.

The great success of the Hollywood star system, which transformed everyday people into icons of idolatry, also proved to be a vulnerability. The mass migrations of potential stars included ordinary people with all-too-human foibles and, sometimes, shady characters escaping complicated pasts. Actors and actresses, typically young, single, and a bit sybaritic in social and sexual conduct, found Hollywood of the 1920s a perfect playground. But a well-publicized series of scandals involving drugs, drink, sex, murder, and suicide both titillated and terrified Hollywood's largely unsympathetic audience, which soon discovered the power of public disapproval to end stars' careers.

Other scandals were more successfully squashed—including the bizarre death of producer Thomas Ince aboard William Randolph Hearst's yacht the *Oneida* in 1924. Officially Ince died of a heart attack. According to Hollywood lore, the jealous Hearst suspected his girlfriend Marion Davies of carrying on with Charlie Chaplin. That night on the *Oneida,* Hearst reportedly burst into his mistress's stateroom and shot "Chaplin"—discovering too late that it was, instead, Ince. The enduring monument to this tawdry tale is the Church of Scientology's Chateau Elysee mansion at Franklin and Bronson, supposedly a secret payoff to the widow Ince.

So Hollywood learned, quickly, to manage its affairs, often enlisting its own moviemaking magic to buff up its tarnished image. The Academy of Motion Picture Arts and Sciences and its annual Oscar awards, brainchildren of Louis B. Mayer, were created largely to elevate industry respectability. Promotional entertainment programs on TV continue the job today, undeterred by the occasional scandal-mongering blockbuster such as the 1991 book *You'll Never Eat in This Town Again* by former movie producer Julia Phillips and the 1996 *Hit and Run: How Jon Peters and Peter Guber Took Sony for a Ride in Hollywood* by Nancy Griffin and Kim Masters.

TINSELTOWN NOW:
TOURING HOLLYWOOD

Hollywood proper is a not a city but a neighborhood district within the city of Los Angeles, further subdivided into two geographical areas: the flatlands and the hills. An industrial and residential hodgepodge inhabits the flats. Studios, soundstages, and businesses catering to the entertainment industry cluster along Hollywood, Sunset, and Santa Monica Boulevards in central Hollywood, along with rundown bungalows and small apartment buildings now home to recent immigrants from the Americas, Asia, and the Middle East. The neighborhood's cultural diversity is best reflected by the student population at Hollywood High School, where dozens of different native languages are spoken.

Some of Hollywood's fabled star quality not only survives but thrives in residential areas of the Hollywood Hills, particularly along the narrow streets of Nichols Canyon and Laurel Canyon. The eclectic cultural collection here is largely architectural, with the high-priced real estate mixing Moorish castles and Spanish-style haciendas, modest vine-covered cottages, and ultramodern experiments in exhibitionism. Farther up in the hills, you can't miss Madonna's onetime home, a wildly striped maroon and yellow mansion not far from the Hollywood sign.

To get oriented to area attractions and Los Angeles in general, stop by the **Hollywood Visitors Bureau** inside the Janes House, 6541 Hollywood Blvd. (on the north side of the street, between Wilcox and Hudson), 323/461-9520. The tiny Victorian house, once a school attended by the children of Douglas Fairbanks, Charlie Chaplin, and other Hollywood heavies, is appropriately stranded in a minimall.

HOLLYWOOD BOULEVARD AND VICINITY

Most people start their Hollywood exploration at or near the mythic intersection of Hollywood and Vine (see below). Alternatively, if coming from West Hollywood, start at the district's western boundary, at La Brea Avenue and the **Hollywood La Brea Gateway.** A public art installation, *Gateway* has been described by *Vogue* magazine as "a pop homage to Hollywood's Golden Age" and "simultaneously heartwarming and high camp." It makes part of its new-wave neon point by mocking the polished metallic maleness of the Academy Awards "Oscar" statuette. The 30-foot-tall Hollywood gazebo is supported, instead, by four glittery female shapes: Dorothy Dandridge, Dolores Del Rio, Mae West, and Anna May Wong, four dreamers and doers described by one filmmaker as "Hollywood's women of steel."

Like it or not, once you spot the Hollywood La Brea Gateway on the boulevard, you'll know you've just arrived in (or just left) historic Tinseltown.

Vicinity of Hollywood and Vine

Look north into the hills from the intersection of Hollywood and Vine for the best downtown view of the landmark **Hollywood Sign,** the city's most famous symbol. (For more on the sign itself, see The Hollywood Sign.) In the foreground sits the landmark **Capitol Records Building,** 1750 N. Vine. In 1954, Nat King Cole and Johnny Mercer of Capitol Records proposed that the company's new headquarters be designed to resemble a giant stack of records with a stylus on top. So it was—and there it is, the world's first circular office building, by Welton Becket. Though now it looks like just another Holiday Inn, when it opened in 1956 this was avant-garde L.A. In a sense it still is; the red beacon atop the 87-foot stylus/spire incessantly flashes the letters H-O-L-L-Y-W-O-O-D in Morse code, and Capitol's website—hollywoodandvine.com—is one of the coolest around. Things may get even cooler, since a multimillion-dollar renovation and expansion of the Capitol Records complex is in the works. Across the street, at 1735 N. Vine, is the **Palace Theater,** once home to *This Is Your Life,* Bing Crosby's *Hollywood Palace* show, and, later, *The Merv Griffin Show.*

Look east to spot the spectacular 1929 **Pantages Theater,** 6233 Hollywood Blvd. (between Vine and Argyle Avenue), 323/468-1770, the first art deco movie house in America. Glistening black marble sets the stage for a dazzling drama of interior design, the lobby and the women's powder room in particular. When Howard Hughes owned the theater in the 1950s, the Academy Awards were staged here. The well-preserved, 2,900-seat Pantages, is now a prominent venue for Broadway-style musicals.

The Pantages also serves as artistic anchor for the neighborhood's thriving small theater district, also starring the **Henry Fonda Theater** at Hollywood and Gower. More famous, though, is the **James A. Doolittle Theater,** 1615 Vine, once the CBS Playhouse Theater and home to Cecil B. DeMille's "Lux Radio Theater" broadcasts in the 1930s and '40s. Staking out the intersection of Hollywood and Argyle are both the small **Stella Adler** and **West Coast Ensemble** theaters. Look for the **Theatre Theater,** 1715 Cahuenga, and the **Ivar,** 1605 Ivar Avenue. Also in the neighborhood, near Pantages Theater: another real-Hollywood remnant, **Collectors Bookstore,** 6225 Hollywood Blvd., 323/467-3296, always a worthwhile stop for posters, photos, memorabilia, and books.

Hollywood Walk of Fame

Americans prefer their heroes and heroines down to earth, and Hollywood has been more than accommodating when it comes to memorializing movie stars and assorted other special species. Here, you look down on them. You can even wipe your feet on fame, all along Hollywood Boulevard.

Hollywood Boulevard had been in decline almost since the beginning, certainly since the 1930s and the Great Depression, when studios and stars started leaving town. To recapture some of the glitz and glamour of bygone days, in the late 1950s the Hollywood Improvement Association launched the promotional Hollywood Walk of Fame—a total of 2,518 coral-colored terrazzo stars outlined in brass and surrounded by squares of gray terrazzo. Walk of Fame stars extend one block north, south, and east from the intersection of Hollywood and Vine, but the dominant constellation shoots west about 12 blocks along both sides of the boulevard.

Just how celebrities make the final Walk of Fame cut, a decision made by the Hollywood Chamber of Commerce's screening committee, is still one of those arcane mysteries—almost as puzzling as Academy Award winners. Why, for example, did hero dog Rin Tin Tin make the team but not King Kong? Why Mickey Mouse but not Donald Duck? Why the Beach Boys but not the Beatles? Why not Richard Burton, Madonna, or Peter Sellers? The process is otherwise quite straightforward. Assuming celebrities fit into one of Hollywood's stardom categories—theater, motion pictures, television, radio, recording—and otherwise pass muster, they fork over $15,000 to get their names walked on by the public.

TOURING MOVIELAND

Spending time in Los Angeles includes the pleasure of unexpected celebrity sightings—at gas stations or drugstores, in restaurants and clubs, on the freeway or along a sidewalk in West Hollywood or Beverly Hills—and the sudden surprise of stumbling upon a film shoot. During on-location moviemaking, normal life in Los Angeles comes to a halt. Traffic is rerouted, landmark buildings "renamed," and entire neighborhoods redecorated and repopulated, if only for a few hours or days. For Angelenos, it's all such a common occurrence that few pay much attention.

To increase your odds of discovering movieland on location, you need to know where to go. One possible spot on shoot-season weekdays is Paramount Ranch in Agoura Hills, famous for the repertoire of westerns shot here over the years—where *Dr. Quinn, Medicine Woman* was filmed—and now part of the Santa Monica Mountains National Recreation Area. Otherwise, the best plan of action is to make a plan. Find out what is being filmed, and where, on any given day at the **Los Angeles Film and Video Permit Office,** 7083 Hollywood Blvd., Fifth Fl. in Hollywood, 323/957-1000, www.eidc.com, open weekdays 8 A.M.–6 P.M. The office provides a free "shoot sheet" for the day, and you can also download shoot sheets from the website. The shooting information includes the exact address of each filming location, along with the name of the production company, the movie or TV show, and the hours reserved for the shoot. Since you won't be allowed on private property, look for movies or TV shows (sometimes just scenes) being shot in public places. Even with plan in hand, don't be too disappointed if, upon your arrival, nothing's going on. Overnight the shoot may have been canceled, delayed until another date, or rescripted for another location. It happens. That's Hollywood.

You can also get someone else to show you around. **Hollywood Heritage** offers walking tours of historic Hollywood and its surviving monuments on the second Saturday of every month (at other times by reservation). For information, call 323/874-4005. Though a bit ghoulish for some tastes, the informative and highly entertaining **Oh Heavenly Tour** offer some sense of real-life Hollywood with a hearse ride through Movieland's past—particularly the places where movie stars and Hollywood movers and shakers have died. For current information and reservations (essential), call 323/782-9652.

For a close-up look at the workings of present-day Hollywood, head for the studios. In addition to the ongoing parade of possibilities that has transformed **Universal Studios** into a tourist diversion, several offer very informative public tours. And you can also sign on for a stint in the studio audience during the tapings of various TV shows.

Warner Bros. Studios VIP Tour

As almost the only tour, for decades Warner Bros. offered the best moviemaking tour in Hollywood. It still does. The two-hour Warner Bros. walkabout—through soundstages, prop rooms, set construction sites, and other peculiar places in the hardly glamorous backstage world of film—is quite good, the real deal. Unlike the Universal Studios tour, the VIP tour is far more personal, so expect to be educated and entertained. You'll most likely sit in on a live film shoot to boot.

Another reason to take the tour is the chance to visit the excellent new **Warner Bros. Museum,** well worth some extra time. (The museum is "doable" only on the tour.) On display here is an impressive selection of memorabilia and artifacts from the studio's animation and filmmaking history—everything from *Casablanca*'s piano, the real Maltese Falcon, and John Wayne's saddle to Jack Warner's personal address book. And find out just how little James Dean and his fellow actors were paid for their work in *Giant*.

To take the Warner Bros. VIP Tour, head for The Burbank Studios, 4000 Warner Blvd. in Bur-

The original eight honorees, installed at Hollywood Boulevard and Highland Avenue in 1960, were all film personalities—Oliver Borden, Ronald Coleman, Louise Fazenda, Preston Foster, Burt Lancaster, Edward Sedgwick, Ernest Torrence, and Joanne Woodward. Puzzling over some of these stars suggests a portable Walk of Fame truism, equally useful elsewhere:

Even when it's engraved in stone, fame doesn't necessarily endure.

It doesn't necessarily fade either. Among the almost mythic characters encountered while shuffling along on the Walk of Fame: Louis Armstrong, Charlie Chaplin, James Dean, Cecil B. DeMille, Marlene Dietrich, W. C. Fields, Greta Garbo, Clark Gable, Judy Garland, Groucho

---

bank. For information and reservations—necessary at least a week in advance during the summer high season—call 818/954-1744. No tours are offered on Thanksgiving, Christmas, New Year's Day, or, usually, on other holidays that fall on a weekday. Golf-cart tours—with plenty of walking, so wear comfy shoes—are scheduled on the hour on weekdays, 9 A.M.–3 P.M. (last departure); in summer, tours are scheduled on the half hour 9 A.M.–4 P.M. often also offered on Saturday at 10 A.M. and 2 P.M. (call to verify). The per-person fee is $32, Visa and MasterCard accepted; no children under age 10 are allowed on studio tours. Free parking.

For free tickets to all Warner Bros. live audience TV shows, call Audiences Unlimited at 818/753-3470.

NBC Television Studios
Compared to the Warner Bros. tour, NBC's 70-minute tour isn't quite as much to write home about, but it is cheaper. You do get to poke into just about everything backstage, including *The Tonight Show* set. More fun for true TV junkies is lining up to land tickets for NBC shows taped before a live studio audience. The tour price is $7 adults, $3.75 for children ages 6–12, children under 5 free. Admission to live-audience NBC shows is free (advance tickets required). For information, call NBC at 818/840-3537 or 818/840-4444. NBC Studios, 3000 W. Alameda Ave. in Burbank, are closed on Thanksgiving, Chistmas, and New Year's Day.

Paramount Studios
Head to Paramount Studios to tour the last major studio still in Hollywood. The tour involves two hours of walking (with no trams or golf carts), so be sure to wear comfortable shoes and bring a bottle of water. Adults and children ages 10 and older can take the guided Paramount Studios tour, scheduled every hour from 9 A.M. to 2 P.M. on weekdays only, for $15 per person (first-come basis). Tours start at the main gate, 5555 Melrose Ave.

(nearby parking available). For current information, call 323/956-4385 or 323/956-3036. Or opt to help populate the studio audience for popular TV shows, including *Frasier.*

Sony Pictures Studios
Once Columbia Pictures and MGM, Sony Pictures Studios in Culver City also offers a movieland walking working-studio tour of its past, present, and future—from *The Wizard of Oz* to *Men in Black* and beyond. The two-hour tour, $20 per person, wanders through soundstages and show sets, wardrobe departments, and "backdrop" artists' studios. There's a gift shop, of course, and you can even eat at the studio commissary. Sony Pictures is located at 10202 W. Washington Blvd. in Culver City. For tour reservations, call 323/520-8687.

Other Movieland Adventures
If you're poking around Hollywood's mean streets, be sure to stop at the **Hollywood Entertainment Museum,** 7021 Hollywood Blvd., 323/465-7900. To understand Hollywood's foundations, the place is the **Frederick's of Hollywood Lingerie Museum,** 6608 Hollywood Blvd., 323/466-8506.

As entertainment capital of the world, Hollywood is more than just the movies. The fascinating **Museum of Television and Radio** at 465 N. Beverly Dr. in Beverly Hills, 310/786-1000, is an unbelievably comprehensive collection of classic TV and radio programming—popular with researchers, of course, but well worth some time for popular media fans. For radio aficionados seeking more than entertainment, try the **Pacifica Radio Archives** at KPFK Radio, 3729 Cahuenga Blvd. W. in North Hollywood, 818/506-1077, the oldest collection of public radio programming in the nation, with more than 40,000 documentary and historical tapes. For library access through the Internet: www.pacifica .org.

For more information on most of these attractions, see separate listings elsewhere in this chapter.

Marx, Marilyn Monroe, Elvis Presley, John Wayne, and Rudolph Valentino.

New celebrities are regularly inducted into this earthy hall of fame, to great public fanfare. To find out who's next, and when, contact the **Hollywood Chamber of Commerce,** 7018 Hollywood Blvd., 323/469-8311; www.hollywood-coc.org.

Frederick's of Hollywood
Lingerie Museum

This, the original Frederick's of Hollywood, was started in 1946 by Frederick Mellinger, inspired by the popularity of the World War II–era Betty Grable pin-up. Unless you're underwear shopping, skip the crotchless panties and other merchandise displays and skip upstairs to the lingerie museum, starring undergarments of the rich, famous, and sometimes voluptuous—Jayne Mansfield, Marilyn Monroe, and Mae West, Madonna, and Cher. (Though Madonna's black and gold bustier was ripped off during L.A.'s 1992 riot rampage, it later miraculously reappeared.) Drag queens, don't despair: unmentionables worn by Tony Curtis and Jack Lemmon in *Some Like It Hot* are also on display.

Frederick's, 6608 Hollywood Blvd., 323/466-8506, is free and open Mon.–Sat., 10 A.M.–6 p.m and Sunday, noon–5 P.M.

Farther West on the Bull

The north side of Hollywood Boulevard between Cahuenga and Highland is known as **Booksellers' Row,** best bet for finding unusual and out-of-print books at a fair price. Most famous among the storefronts here is **Larry Edmonds Cinema Bookshop,** 6644 Hollywood Blvd. (three blocks east of Highland at Cherokee), 323/463-3273, open daily 10 A.M.–6 P.M. (closed on major holidays). A popular place even within "the industry," Larry Edmonds specializes in new and out-of-print books on film and theater—the world's largest collection—as well as movie memorabilia. The Marilyn Monroe and James Dean posters are always big sellers.

Musso & Frank Grill across the way at 6667 Hollywood Blvd., 323/467-7788, is another Hollywood classic—the oldest restaurant in town, established in 1919. This was the rendezvous of William Faulkner, F. Scott Fitzgerald, Ernest Hemingway, and other literati when they were in Hollywood trolling for studio cash. Famous for its martinis, chicken pot pie, and old-school restaurant atmosphere, these days this Raymond Chandleresque establishment is hip all over again.

Egyptian Theatre

Predecessor to Sid Grauman's more famous Chinese Theatre, the 1921 Egyptian Theatre hosted Hollywood's first movie premiere—the original 1922 screening of *Robin Hood.* Designed by architects Meyer and Holler in Egyptian revival style—all the rage in the 1920s, when King Tut's tomb was first unveiled—the aptly named Egyptian was once a stunning sight, a pre-Disneyland Disneyland fantasy. To enter, moviegoers wound through a courtyard bazaar lined with mummy cases, huge vases, banana palms, caged wild animals, and shops selling exotic wares. On opening night, a spear-carrying soldier paced the roofline; usherettes masqueraded as Cleopatra's handmaidens.

The historic Egyptian Theatre, 6712 Hollywood Blvd., 323/466-3456, is back—saved at long last from its long, slow destruction from modernization and from instantaneous damage inflicted by the 1994 Northridge earthquake. Restored to its original gaudy grandeur by American Cinematheque's determined $14.2 million campaign, this Hollywood landmark's "new" look includes a revivified 150-foot-deep exterior courtyard (sans caged animals) and a state-of-the-art 650-seat auditorium that retains the ornate sunburst patterned ceiling. Other notable features here, or soon to be here: an 83-seat screening room, a restored and enlarged lobby, Egyptian murals and reliefs, a neon blade sign and period marquee, on-site restaurants and gift shop, and a 1922 Wurlitzer organ to accompany silent film presentations.

The Egyptian Theatre is permanent home and headquarters of American Cinematheque, a nonprofit film center that presents classic, rare, and unusual works, including new and experimental works. The theater is also open to the public for tours. For more information about the theater and about American Cinematheque, call the phone number listed above or try the group's website: www.americancinematheque.com.

Hollywood Kitsch Museums

Unless you possess an insatiable appetite for California kitsch, lots of time, and a whole lot of extra cash, Hollywood Boulevard's trio of tourist-kitsch museums is missable. Should any or all of the above describe your circumstances, the **Hollywood Wax Museum,** 6767 Hollywood Blvd., 323/462-8860, is always popular. Some likenesses are too tired to be recognizable, though generally speaking stars' heads and hands go into storage whenever stardom dims. (Only the heads and hands are fashioned from wax; bodies are fiberglass, more or less interchangeable.) The museum is open Thurs.–Sun., 10 A.M.-midnight, Fri.–Sat. 10 A.M.–2 A.M. Admission is $9.95 adults, $6.95 children, free for kids under age five.

As if the free Hollywood sidewalk sideshow weren't entertaining enough, across the street is **Ripley's Believe It Or Not! Odditorium,** 6780 Hollywood Blvd., 323/466-6335, starring freaks, geeks, and original works such as the full-size portrait of Hollywood cowboy John Wayne fashioned from dryer lint. (To find this place, look for the large Tyrannosaurus rex on the roof.) The odditorium is open daily 10 A.M.–11 P.M. Admission is $8.95 adults, $5.95 children, free for kids under age five. The **Hollywood Guinness World Of Records Museum,** 6764 Hollywood Blvd., 323/463-6433, showcases fanaticism in general and world-class fanatics in particular. Replicas and videos document a variety of feats. For others, just tap into the computer system here. The World of Records is open Sun.–Thurs. 10 A.M.–midnight, until 2 A.M. on weekend nights, closed Monday. Admission is $14.95 adults, $8.95 children, free for kids under age five.

El Capitan Theatre

First opened in 1927 as a "legitimate" theater (for stage productions), El Capitan Theatre, 6838 Hollywood Blvd. (a half-block west of Highland), 323/467-7674, was purchased in 1941 by Paramount Pictures, transformed into a movie venue, and renamed the Paramount Theater. Its present-day reincarnation as El Capitan, with dazzlingly authentic interiors, made this the new debut theater for Walt Disney Productions. In addition to modern improvements such as earthquake safety features, bigger and better bathrooms, and access for the

---

MUSEUM OF DEATH

With the recent opening of the Museum of Death in Hollywood, following its move from San Diego's Gas Lamp Quarter, the aversion that Los Angeles has traditionally exhibited in the face of mortality seems to have, well, *died.* Or at least swooned into a temporary coma. Death is on the way to becoming cool in L.A. Even here, it's fair to assume that the actual act of bidding adieu to life on earth is not notably more popular than it ever was. Yet as the museum's popularity testifies, the accessories and memorabilia of death and dying exert considerable fascination.

Among items in the extensive collection on display here are such treasures as letters and paintings by serial killers, graphic crime scene photos, and a baseball signed by Charles Manson, Mr. Helter-Skelter himself. The museum collection was inspired, in fact, by artworks requested by the owners from imprisoned serial killers. There's more, though, much more, from the working guillotine, embalming table, and vintage Vincent Price shrunken-head apple-sculpture kit to Tibetan funerary skulls and the Heaven's Gate diorama.

For those interested in communing with mementos of life's ultimate transition, stop by the Museum of Death, 6340 Hollywood Blvd., Ste. 2 (entrance on Ivar), 323/466-8011, open daily noon–8 P.M. Admission is $7. For an introduction to an interesting but unrelated L.A. enterprise, visit www.citymorguegiftshop.com, where you can visit the online Cemetery of the Stars.

---

disabled, El Capitan's recently restored glories include its outdoor box office, original lobby murals, fabulously intricate ceiling, and quaint opera boxes. Worth a G or PG rest stop, no matter what's playing. And the "bargain matinees"—the first two shows of the day—make it almost a bargain.

Mann's Chinese Theatre and Vicinity

Most famous of all the famous Hollywood theaters, Mann's Chinese Theatre, 6925 Hollywood Blvd., 323/464-8111, was originally known as **Grauman's Chinese Theatre,** after owner-showman Sid Grauman. Grauman commissioned architects Meyer and Holler to construct

MONUMENTS TO THE MOVIES

Los Angeles is the best place in the world to go to the movies. Anyone anywhere can *get* movies—at the neighborhood multiplex, say, or at the video store. But L.A. is the land of grand movie theaters, single big-screen theaters that transform mundane human experience into myth in the larger-than-life Hollywood tradition. Though Los Angeles has been notably lax in saving its heritage—happily tearing down the past to make way for a more profitable future—many of its historic movie palaces survive. And a few relative newcomers expand the possibilities for movie fans and fanatics.

Visitors tend to think "Hollywood" when searching for a place-related synonym for the movies in L.A., but downtown Los Angeles is actually the city's movie theater capital. Or was. Broadway between Third and Ninth Streets is the largest registered district of historic movie theaters in the nation, the center of L.A.'s public cinematic display in the early 20th century. Many of the grandest grand old palaces on historic Broadway have become nightclubs, including the Mayan and the El Rey, and others have been converted into swap-meet venues, including the Arcade, the Cameo, and the Roxy. Other downtown movie icons have been bulldozed, the California and the Paramount among them; others, including the Million Dollar and United Artists, have become churches. The old Warner at Seventh and Spring is now a jewelry market, and these days the spectacular Los Angeles is used as a set for film shoots and private parties.

But some are still open for business. Most notable among these is the lovingly restored 1911 French Renaissance **Orpheum**, 842 S. Broadway, the city's oldest operating movie theater—not to slight the rococo **Palace**, 630 S. Broadway, and the Spanish Renaissance **State**, 703 S. Broadway. Sadly for their determined owners, the neighborhood's changing character tends to discourage most moviegoers, particularly those from suburbia and the Westside. Another way to appreciate Broadway's movie places is on a walking tour with the nonprofit **Los Angeles Conservancy,** 213/623-2489, or www.laconservancy.org, which also sponsors a monthlong classic movie series, "The Last Remaining Seats," in various downtown theaters every June.

Mann's Chinese Theatre

Long after Broadway is finally bulldozed for a new crop of corporate skyscrapers, the famous Chinese Theatre in Hollywood will abide. Originally known as Grauman's Chinese Theatre, after owner and showman Sid Grauman, this elaborate impression of a Chinese temple was unveiled in 1927 with the premiere of Cecil B. DeMille's *King of Kings.* A 30-foot-tall dragon guards the huge pagoda-like entrance. Inside are more dragons and other Chinese motifs. The red lobby and auditorium are remarkably well preserved, just one reason why this is still one of L.A.'s best theaters. But if you do a movie here, be sure to see what's playing in the *main* theater, behind the courtyard, not in the two added-on shoeboxes—so you can see the theater. You can't miss Mann's Chinese Theatre at 6925 Hollywood Blvd. (near Highland Ave.) in Hollywood, 323/464-6266.

El Capitan Theatre

First opened in 1927 as a "legitimate" theater (for stage productions), El Capitan Theatre, 6838 Hollywood Blvd. (near Highland Ave.), 323/467-7674, was bought in 1941 by Paramount Pictures, transformed into a movie venue, and renamed the Paramount Theater. Its dazzling present-day reincarnation as the color-crazy El Capitan—dare we say reimagineered restoration?—financed by the Walt Disney Company, also made this the new Los Angeles debut theater for Walt Disney Productions. When it reopened for business in 1991, welcome improvements at El Capitan included bigger and better bathrooms as well as disabled access. But much of the glory here is pure grace, from El Capitan's outdoor box office, original lobby murals, and fabulously intricate ceiling to quaint opera boxes.

Egyptian Theatre

Restored to its original gaudy grandeur by the film organization American Cinematheque, the 1922 Egyptian Theatre, 6712 Hollywood Blvd., 323/466-3456, hosts a film series of classic, rare and unusual films, including a 55-minute documentary *Forever Hollywood,* which screens daily. The Egyptian, predecessor to Sid Grauman's more famous Chinese

Theater, hosted Hollywood's first movie premiere—the original 1922 screening of *Robin Hood*. Now that renovation is complete moviegoers are again be able to wind their way to the theater through an exotic courtyard lined with banana palms, mummy cases, and other stylistic oddities.

Vista Theater

Something of a faded monument to Hollywood's glory, the Vista at 4473 Sunset Dr. (at Hollywood Blvd.) in East Hollywood, 323/660-6639, is a beloved neighborhood movie house—constructed on the site of Charlie Chaplin's very first movie studio, no less. And before the Egyptian reopened, the Vista's sphinxes were the only notable emblems of that particular movie-theater era. Every other row of seats has been removed, too, freeing extra legroom for enjoying French-language and other arty films as well as stellar Hollywood blockbusters. If the neighborhood makes you nervous, come for a matinee.

Showcase Theater

Hollywood also boasts the Showcase at 614 N. La Brea Ave. (one half block south of Melrose Ave.), 323/934-2944, once the Gordon Theater, preserved as a single-screen theater when it was rehabilitated in the 1980s. Famous for its Woody Allen premieres and similar fare, the Showcase also benefits from the fact that Pink's (as in hotdogs) is just a block away.

Silent Movie Showcase

Hollywood's eccentric, locally famous Silent Movie Showcase, 611 N. Fairfax Ave. (one half block south of Melrose Ave.), 323/655-2520, has been silent movie fans' (reportedly including Johnny Depp) holy grail since 1947. Now reopened following the tragic murder of its former proprietor, it is the only place to see the classics, with live organ accompaniment, almost any time.

Fine Arts Theater

Cecchi Gori got out the big Beverly Hills checkbook to finance a gloriously garish facelift for the art-deco Fine Arts Theater, 8556 Wilshire Blvd., 310/652-1330. Every bit as gaudy as Disney's El Capitan, the theater is a standout tribute to Hollywood even if the bill of fare shown here isn't always.

Bruin and Village Theatres

Westwood is still one of Southern California's favorite destinations for moviegoers, with both large- and small-screen theater stars. Dominating the big-screen department, historically speaking, are the neighboring Bruin and Village Theatres. The Bruin, at 948 Broxton Ave. (at Wayburn), 310/208-8998, is fairly modest by moderne standards but the Village, at 961 Broxton (at Wayburn), 310/208-5576, with its landmark neon-lit tower, is one of L.A.'s great theaters—popular still for major movie premieres. A respected remnant of the Fox theater chain, slightly less foxy inside than out, the 1931 Spanish moderne Village is distinguished by its 70-foot screen and a superb sound system. Notice, too, the gold rush–themed frieze. To appreciate this theater in its totality, the best view is from the balcony—if it's open.

Crest Theater

Another find in Westwood, just south of Wilshire Boulevard, is the art-deco Crest Theater, 1262 Westwood Blvd., 310/474-7866, reborn in recent years as an intimate and stylish venue for first-run and other films. Hollywood buffs in particular will appreciate the interior murals, showcasing street scenes from L.A.'s moviemaking golden age.

Other Fine Movie Houses

Still the artsy movie house in West Los Angeles, the **Nuart Theater,** 11272 Santa Monica Blvd. (one block west of the 405 freeway), 310/478-6379, screens the likes of *Antonio Gaudi* and *Woman in the Dunes*. But nothing beats the show down the coast at the weekends-only **Old Town Music Hall** revival house at 140 Richmond St. in downtown El Segundo, 310/322-2592, also a concert house. The after-show singalongs and fluorescent-painted pipe organ alone are worth the price of admission.

If you find yourself near Pasadena, the place for first-run art films on the big screen is the slightly fading **Rialto Theater** in South Pasadena at 1023 Fair Oaks Ave., 626/799-9567. And if you make the short trip west across the big water to Catalina, keep in mind that the spectacular art-deco **Casino** in Avalon, 310/510-0179, is another L.A. classic—the world's first theater designed specifically for "talking pictures," in fact.

Mann's Chinese Theatre

TOM MYERS PHOTOGRAPHY

this elaborate impression of a Chinese temple, unveiled in 1927 with the premiere of Cecil B. DeMille's *King of Kings*. The huge pagoda-like entrance is guarded by a 30-foot-tall dragon. Inside, more dragons and other Chinese motifs populate the red lobby and the carpets, seats, walls, and ceilings of the auditorium. The original Chinese Theater is surprisingly well preserved, and still one of the best movie palaces in greater Los Angeles. (The whale mural on the east side, part of Laguna Beach artist Robert Wyland's personal campaign to save the whales, is quite recent.) But if you do see a movie here, for the genuine experience make sure the show is playing in the main theater behind the courtyard, not in the added-on shoeboxes up front.

A bigger draw than the theater itself is the courtyard. More than two million people come to mill around and study celebrity footprints in the concrete each year—the inspiration, no doubt, for the later Walk of Fame. The impressions here, though, are highly individual—an imprint of Betty Grable's "million dollar legs"; the horseshoe prints of Trigger, Roy Rogers's legendary palomino steed; Jimmy Durante's schnozzola; Harpo Marx's harp; Donald Duck's webbed feet; and robotic treadmarks from both R2D2 and C-3PO of *Star Wars* fame. More than 150 stars have left their marks here. Since fame is indeed fleeting, rumor has it that concrete squares featuring less stellar performers are chiseled out and then stored in the basement to make room for new stars.

How the footprint tradition was etched into Hollywood history is a story with multiple-choice endings (choose one). According to the most romantic version, one day actress Norma Talmadge accidentally stepped in wet concrete. According to another, impressario Grauman himself made the first impression. The supposed true story—does anyone in Hollywood tell any other kind?—is that Grauman happened by when a French stonemason, completing the courtyard, left his handprint in the concrete for posterity, as his forebears had done when building the cathedral at Notre Dame. Immediately grasping the promotional potential, Grauman invited Talmadge, Mary Pickford, and Douglas Fairbanks to leave their marks on Hollywood history. When the press coverage was inadequate, he made all three stars come back the next day and do it again.

Next door is the site of Hollywood's most visible redevelopment project, an open-air, four-story complex strategically located above the new Metrorail Red Line station linking Hollywood with both downtown Los Angeles and Universal Studios. When completed, this shopping and entertainment complex will include 300,000 square feet of broadcast and music studios, entertainment venues, shops, and restaurants, with a grand staircase framing a view of the Hollywood sign. Also here: a 3,300-seat auditorium that will soon bring the annual Academy Awards ceremony—and all those Oscars—back to Hollywood.

Hollywood Roosevelt Hotel

As tightly woven into the fabric of local history as the Chinese Theatre across the street, the lovely Spanish colonial Hollywood Roosevelt Hotel, 7000 Hollywood Blvd., is definitely worth a stop. In the glory days of the 1930s, the Roosevelt was *the* place to stay, but then Hollywood Boulevard slid straight downhill and took this dignified grande dame along for the ride. After a $35 million facelift and much fanfare, the Hollywood Roosevelt reopened in 1985. Site of the somewhat disastrous first Academy Awards ceremony in 1927, Douglas Fairbanks presiding, this is also where Bill "Bojangles" Robinson taught Shirley Temple how to tap dance up the stairs and where Montgomery Clift, in town for the filming of *From Here to Eternity,* discovered the bugle—and the pleasure of blowing his horn throughout the hotel at all hours. If you're planning a stay, try Room 928, reportedly haunted by Clift's spirit, said to be still angry about a 1957 car accident that scarred his face.

An impromptu tour starts in the stunning art-deco lobby, where piped-in vintage jazz accompanies you to the "museum" of movie memorabilia on the mezzanine. The Roosevelt's in-house supper club, **Cinegrill,** was a favorite of Marilyn Monroe, said to have favored the dark booth in the northwest corner. Don't miss the hotel's celebrated Olympic-size swimming pool in the courtyard, with a custom blue-squiggle bottom paint job by artist David Hockney. (When someone dives in, the entire pool shimmers.) Also well worth it: the courtyard's **Tropicana Bar.**

Hollywood Entertainment Museum

Just a few blocks west of Mann's Chinese Theatre, until the 1980s the intersection of Hollywood and Sycamore was dominated by Hollywood's four-story Garden Court Apartments, a lavish luxury complex inhabited by the likes of John Barrymore, Lillian Gish, and Rudolph Valentino. After a far from genteel decline, the vacated residential hotel became known as "Hotel Hell," hosting only transients and runaways. After preservationists battled but failed to save the landmark building, the Garden Court was razed in 1985—making way for a museum dedicated to memorializing lost Hollywood.

The 33,000-square-foot **Hollywood Entertainment Museum** at 7021 Hollywood Blvd. (at Sycamore), 323/465-7900, www.hollywoodmuseum.com, actually pays homage to both old and new Hollywood, its timeline starting with silent films and film stars and ending with authentic *Star Trek* and *Cheers* sets.

The 15-foot-tall Goddess of Entertainment presides over the clean and stylish central gallery, cradling all of the entertainment arts—radio, television, film, and sound—in her arms. Every half-hour the big screen flashes the very entertaining six-minute high-speed retrospective *The Stuff That Dreams Are Made Of.* Also worth a look: the World War II–era minimodel of Hollywood.

Don't miss remnants of Hollywood's now-defunct **Max Factor Museum of Beauty,** included here as part of the rotating Max Factor Collection. If beauty is only skin deep, then this is the place for some in-depth study of said skin. Russian immigrant Max Factor worked in L.A. for years as a downtown barber, selling on the side concoctions such as his own Kill 'Em Quick Shampoo (for head lice) and theatrical makeup. But traditional greasepaint, quite thick, cracked under the heat of stagelights—a particularly gruesome problem in movie production, since filming halted whenever facial overhauls became necessary. So Factor set out to solve that problem, and in 1914 created a flexible greasepaint, Panchromatic Make-up ("pancake" makeup), that literally changed the face of the film industry. The rest, as they say, is history. In addition to bits of beauty lore and hairpieces worn by movie stars, two truly bizarre pieces of Max Factor machinery deserve special attention whenever they're on display—the curved metal-and-clamps Beauty Calibrator, used by makeup artists to determine facial imperfections, and the 1939 Kissing Machine. The latter—actually a replica of Max Factor's original, designed to test lipstick indelibility—forces two sets of soft rubber lips together under 10 pounds of pressure. The museum's makeup arts display also includes video demonstrations of human beings transformed by makeup into movie stars.

On another wall is the museum's "Dream Merchants" audio exhibit, in which Walt Disney talks about animation, Tina Turner discusses sex appeal, and Orson Welles opines on the always troublesome artistic subject of money.

In the museum's west wing, beyond the "Back Lot" hodgepodge of props, costumes, and other movie memorabilia, is an authentic set from the original *Star Trek* TV series. After sitting in Captain Kirk's chair you can examine Klingon masks and try to pass Trekkie trivia tests on video. Next stop is *Cheers,* or someplace that looks just like it, and then it's on to the gift shop.

Before spending your dinner money on still more stuff to carry home, spend some time in the museum's education center, which includes an electronic archive and library (complete with entertainment industry job bank, always useful), a recording studio, and editing suite. Endlessly fun, if the Foley Room sound-effects suite is available, is making the sounds—footsteps and so forth—for the short film *The Chicken Detectives* (or whatever else may be cued up).

The Hollywood Entertainment Museum is open daily 11 A.M.–6 P.M., closed Wednesday. Admission is $7.50 adults, $4.50 seniors and students, $4 children ages 5–12 (under 5 free). Parking is $2 with validation in the basement parking garage.

Also worth a stop for peeking into Hollywood's past—but open only on weekends—is the **Hollywood Studio Museum** near the Hollywood Bowl (see below), housed in Cecil B. DeMille's original moviemaking barn.

BEYOND THE BULL: GOWER GULCH, WHERE IT ALL BEGAN

The most famous remains of Hollywood's glamorous past cluster around Hollywood Boulevard, but the area known as "Gower Gulch"—the Gower Street area bounded by Sunset Boulevard, Vine Street, and Selma Avenue—is where the Hollywood of America's imagination actually sprang to life. Since almost all historical evidence has vanished, abundant imagination is necessary for this particular tour.

Start one long block south of Hollywood Boulevard at the intersection of Vine and Selma—where, on the southeast corner, Tinseltown's first full-length feature film, Cecil B. DeMille's *The Squaw Man,* was produced. The associated movie venture, the Jesse L. Lasky Feature Play Company, later merged with Adolph Zukor's

Famous Players, an enterprise that thrived here, eventually taking over the entire block; as Paramount Studios, it became even larger. The original studios here, though, were razed to make way for NBC's Radio City. Since 1964, a parking lot, office building, and bank have marked the spot.

Another block south, then east on Sunset Boulevard, stands the 1940s big-band hot spot—the still-happening **Hollywood Palladium,** 6215 Sunset, noteworthy in the 1950s for the big-bubble sound of *The Lawrence Welk Show.* Across the street, at 6230 Sunset, is the **Aquarius Theater,** now called the Star Search Theatre and used for talent shows. The Doors often played at this venue, which in their time was also called Hullabaloo and Kaleidoscope.

Historically, though, Gower Gulch proper extended north and south from Sunset, a cinematic skid row ("Poverty Row") crowded with low-budget B-movie studios that cranked out cheap cowboy movies by the spittoon-full. Notable in the neighborhood these days is the CBS **Columbia Square** complex at 6121 Sunset, 323/460-3000, home base for George Burns and Gracie Allen as well as Edgar Bergen and Charlie McCarthy during radio's prime time. Originally here: Hollywood's first "studio," the old Blondeau Tavern rented by the Nestor Film Company. Columbia Studios, king of Poverty Row, long reigned from what is now **Sunset-Gower Studios** across the intersection at 1438 N. Gower, 323/467-1001. Taking over the original California Studios in 1927, the Cohn brothers assembled their Columbia empire by acquiring other Poverty Row players. Among the classic films created here: Frank Capra's *It's a Wonderful Life.*

MORE HOLLYWOOD

Paramount Studios and Vicinity

Mae West once described herself as "the girl who works at Paramount all day and Fox all night." Paramount Studios, 5555 Melrose Ave., 323/956-4385, last of the major studios remaining in Hollywood, is at home on the city's longest-running movie lot, built in 1917 for Peralta Studios. Paramount took over in 1926. These days the complex includes the onetime

RKO Studios, first owned by Joseph P. Kennedy and then by Howard Hughes. Lucille Ball bought it in 1957 and built her **Desilu Studios** here. Memorable RKO films include *King Kong* (1933) and *Citizen Kane* (1941), not to mention classics starring Fred Astaire and Ginger Rogers and the Marx Brothers.

Thousands of films have been produced at Paramount, which traces its heritage to *The Squaw Man* and the Jesse L. Lasky Feature Play Company—making this *the* time-honored Hollywood institution. Thus, according to Hollywood lore, for good luck aspiring actors and actresses must hug the historic iron gate at Bronson and Marathon while chanting the Norma Desmond (Gloria Swanson) line: "I'm ready for my close-up, Mr. DeMille" and otherwise unloading some of the pathos of the 1950 *Sunset Boulevard,* filmed here. (Hug and chant at your own risk.) More pedestrian, by far, is the low-key two-hour Paramount Studios walking tour scheduled every hour from 9 A.M. to 2 P.M. on weekdays only, $15 per person (first-come basis). Children under 10 not admitted. Tours start at the main gate, 5555 Melrose Ave. (nearby parking available). Or opt to help populate the studio audience for popular TV shows, including *Frasier.* For current information call 323/956-4385 or 323/956-3036.

For details on other Tinseltown studio tours, see Touring Movieland elsewhere in this chapter.

The Movies on Melrose

Across the street from Paramount at 5536 Melrose is **Lucy's El Adobe Cafe,** 323/462-9421, popular with former Governor Jerry Brown and his then-companion Linda

Ronstadt during California's olden days of liberal Democratic governors. Otherwise this stretch of Melrose Avenue and vicinity, which marks the southern boundary of L.A.'s Hollywood district, offers a peek into Tinseltown as gritty industrial factory—the surviving sound stages and affiliated film and sound businesses so essential to creating the illusion of reality. To the southwest, at 650 N. Bronson, is **Raleigh Studios,** dating from 1914 and Adolph Zukor's film *The Girl from Yesterday,* starring Mary Pickford. In 1915 came Douglas Fairbanks in *The Mark of Zorro.* Memories of Ronald Reagan as host of the *Death Valley Days* TV series also linger here. The old Technicolor Building, 6311 Romaine Street, is now the **UCLA Film Archives** —not open to the public, though parts of the archival collection are shown around town during festivals, revivals, and seminar lectures. The **Hollywood Center Studios** rental lot, off Romaine at 1040 N. Las Palmas, is the current incarnation of Francis Ford Coppola's ill-fated **Zoetrope Studios,** founded here in 1980 upon the success of *The Godfather.*

Hollywood Memorial Park Cemetery

Since perennial youth and beauty are Southern California's essential social standards, here the concept of eternal life takes on a strangely stagey, theatrical edge. It's no coincidence that the southstate boasts what Peter Theroux has called "the happiest cemeteries in the world," lushly landscaped afterlife theme parks. It's probably also no coincidence that most of them are near Hollywood.

A time-honored gem of the genre is right downtown—65-acre Hollywood Memorial Park Cemetery just north of Paramount Studios and east of Gower at 6000 Santa Monica Blvd. (south side), 323/469-1181, open daily 8 A.M.–5 P.M. (If you call and someone answers "Hollywood Forever," you've dialed the right number.) Here some of Hollywood's immortals have taken their final rest. A map/guide to the gravestones is available at the gate.

Most spectacular of the stars' graves is that of **Douglas Fairbanks,** right next to the studio, with a view of the Hollywood sign. Inside the entryway, the Fairbanks tomb is just beyond the lily pond. The sarcophagus, fronting a portrait portico and dramatic columns, is inscribed "Good Night Sweet Prince, and Flights of Angels Sing Thee to Thy Rest." Nearby is **Tyrone Power's** grave, a useful marble bench inscribed with the same "Sweet Prince" sentiment plus a few more thoughts from Shakespeare's *Hamlet.* Adjacent is the mausoleum of **Marion Davies,** William Randolph Hearst's mistress, inscribed "DOVRAS." Nearby is **Jayne Mansfield's** memorial of pink granite. (Mansfield was famous for driving around town in her pink Cadillac.) Perhaps most peculiar is the full-size Atlas rocket replica marking the grave of **Carl Morgan Bigsby,** "symbolic of his pioneering work in graphic arts."

Most infamous over the years, though, has been **Rudolph Valentino's** final rest, in unpretentious crypt No. 1205 inside the Cathedral Mausoleum—intended to be a temporary stay until a suitably dramatic personal monument could be constructed. Fancy digs or no, for many years a mysterious "Lady in Black," presumably a grieving love, appeared each year on the anniversary of Valentino's death to lay flowers at his grave—one of Hollywood's best post-career publicity stunts. Exposed, the lady visits no more.

Laid to rest in the cemetery's original Jewish section along with Las Vegas gangster **Bugsy Siegel** and actor/director **John Huston** is **Mel Blanc,** original voice for an astonishing array of Hollywood cartoon characters. His cemetery sign-off? That old Warner Bros. standard: "That's all, folks!" Across the way are two *Our Gang* child stars, **Carl "Alfalfa" Switzer** and **Darla Hood.**

Not to miss: the stunning **Otis-Chandler** spectacle at the center of Hollywood Memorial, honoring the founders of the non-union *Los Angeles Times* newspaper and its related family real estate dynasty. Memorialized here are **Harry Chandler, Marian Otis Chandler,** and **Eliza S. Otis,** wife of Harrison Gray Otis. The fourth monument, "Our Martyred Men," honors 20 employees killed during a union-organizing-era bombing of the Times Mirror Building in 1910.

And if just the idea of a cemetery tour appeals to you, be advised that you can also do it in cyberspace. Bone up locally with a visit to the darkly humorous Grim Society website at www .grimsociety.com. Created by a group of Hollywood animators with a macabre appreciation for the morbid, the Grim Society's site is filled with ghoulish trivia, obituaries, and detailed maps of Los Angeles cemeteries.

More on Santa Monica Boulevard

Other sights along Santa Monica Boulevard include the walls surrounding **Warner-Hollywood Studios** at Formosa Avenue, historically home base for **United Artists** and, later, **Goldwyn Studios.** Across the street, at 7156 Santa Monica (two blocks west of La Brea), is the old **Formosa Cafe,** 323/850-9050, a traditional industry hangout and a virtual museum of on-the-walls movie memorabilia saved from progress only after a loud local fight.

At 1150 Highland Ave., just off Santa Monica, is one of L.A.'s great used-music stores, **Aron's Records,** 323/469-4700, specializing in used LPs and CDs but also carrying a vast selection of new CDs.

More on Sunset Boulevard

An experiment in 1950s futurism is the **Pacific Cinerama Dome,** impersonating a humongous golf ball at 6360 Sunset (near Vine), 323/466-3401. Once known as the best place in town to see "big movies" (70 mm blockbusters) on the theater's wrap-around wide screen, in the age of virtual reality and home video the Cinerama Dome here—the sole survivor of its era—no longer projects a viable vision of the future. Which is why the owner is turning it into yet another money-making multiplex. Fortunately, the city's preservation board has granted the Cinerama Dome's exterior "landmark" historic status. Just down the street, the **Hollywood Athletic Club,** at 6525 Sunset, once featured a pool, weight room, and gym where stars such as Rudolph Valentino and Charlie Chaplin would work out and hide out with the all-male membership. It's now a public bar and grill (with billiards and snooker).

In the onetime headquarters of the long-running *Hollywood Reporter,* 6715 Sunset, are the fairly new offices of the ***L.A. Weekly,*** the Los Angeles-area's most noted arts, entertainment, and alternative news weekly. Leonard N. Stern, owner of the Hartz Mountain pet products empire, bought the *Weekly* in late 1994; he also owns *The Village Voice* in New York.

The landmark **Hollywood High School,** 1521 Highland Ave., boasts dozens of graduates who later graduated to some notable role within "the industry," among them Lana Turner, Carol Burnett, Lawrence Fishburne, Judy Garland, Linda

Evans, and John Ritter. These days most of the school's students are recent immigrants; like many public schools in Los Angeles—more than 80 native languages are spoken by the system's students—this school is a multilingual crazy-quilt of cultures representing almost every spot on the globe.

At Hollywood's end, at 1416 N. La Brea just south of Sunset, is **A&M Recording Studios,** once Charlie Chaplin's movie lot.

The most famous stretch of Sunset Boulevard, the "Sunset Strip," begins in West Hollywood (see below).

SILVER LAKE, LOS FELIZ, AND VICINITY

Like the city of West Hollywood, Silver Lake is noted for its gay-ity. But the population here is actually quite diverse, with gays, lesbians, and a wide variety of cultural eccentrics sharing neighborhoods with residents of various ethnic persuasions—Guatemalan, Salvadoran, Honduran, Mexican—and a respectable number of well-rooted retirees. A low-rent refuge for punk rockers and other cultural misfits since the 1970s, the area's cultural fusion today is nearly impossible to categorize. Or describe. You'll have to experience it to understand it—or begin to understand it. In the view of many here, the fact that postcool, post-Westside artistic L.A. shares general territory with gangsters just makes it all that more cutting edge. Occasional nighttime gunplay keeps the Westside wimps away.

The district was named for Herman Silver, the city water and power commissioner who authorized the construction of namesake Silver Lake (west of Glendale Boulevard) in 1906. Hollywood arrived by the 1920s and '30s, when film stars including Fatty Arbuckle, Clark Gable, Judy Garland, and Gloria Swanson called the area home. Architects Rudolf Schindler and Richard Neutra took a shine to the neighborhood, too, which explains the impressive number of homes here that bear their architectural signatures. Over the years the beautiful people migrated west to Beverly Hills, Brentwood, and other Westside beauty spots, but their classy buildings still stand. One remaining Silver Lake star: the steep outdoor stairway featured in

1932's *The Music Box*, Stan Laurel and Oliver Hardy's Academy Award–winning comedy short, as well as in their 1927 *Hats Off.*

Aside from the ghosts of Laurel and Hardy, area attractions include Frank Lloyd Wright's spectacular Hollyhock House in Barnsdall Park; other architectural icons by Wright, Richard Neutra, Rudolph Schindler, and others; the posthip Vermont Avenue business district; and L.A.'s beloved Rockaway Records. Not to mention the wild nightclubs.

The Vermont Avenue and Silver Lake Scenes

Vermont Avenue forms the unofficial boundary between the Hollywood and Silver Lake districts, stretching north into Los Feliz. The stretch of Vermont between Hollywood Boulevard and Russell Street is also cutting-edge, commercially cool Los Angeles—an L.A. not created or interpreted by marketing directors, money managers, and the media. Proudly dubbed the "anti-Melrose" by its denizens—though the Melrose mayhem could be just around the corner, figuratively as well as literally—Vermont Avenue's quirky business district includes shops such as the **Dresden Room,** 1769 N. Vermont (near Hollywood Blvd.), 323/665-4294 and **¿Y Qué? (So What?)** 1770 N. Vermont, 323/664-0021, locally famous for its vintage toys and eccentric collection of cultural remainders—such as "Welcome Back Kotter" dolls and Sharon Tate posters. Just down the street is also-out-there **Mondo Video A Go Go** 1724 N. Vermont, 323/953-8896. Worth seeking out between tattoo and body-piercing shops is the **Skylight Bookstore,** local literary locus at 1818 North Vermont Ave., 323/660-1175, at the at the onetime Chatterton's, the beloved neighborhood bookstore that closed when owner William Koki Iwamoto died.

But there's more to the Los Feliz/Silver Lake scene than Vermont Avenue, including L.A.'s long-running independent **Rockaway Records,** 2395 Glendale Blvd. (near Fletcher), 323/664-3232, the playlist includes an impressive selection of used CDs. In "downtown" Silver Lake, generally defined as the odd stretch just east of Vermont where Hollywood and Sunset Boulevards both funnel into Sunset, the center of the scene is **Ozzie Dots** vintage clothing at 4637

Hollywood Blvd., 323/663-2867 and, next door, **Soap Plant** 4633 Hollywood Blvd., 323/663-0122.

Hollyhock House and Barnsdall Park

In 1917 Aline Barnsdall, a 35-year-old oil heiress from Chicago, deserted her husband and headed west to Los Angeles, determined to start an artists' colony. Barnsdall commissioned architect Frank Lloyd Wright to assist with the colony's aesthetic foundation—to design and construct her personal home, an experimental theater, and both studios and apartments for visiting artists on the 36-acre knoll she planted with olives (Olive Hill) in eastern Hollywood. The combination clicked, perhaps partly because Wright was also in the throes of personal trauma—a domestic disaster that could have been scripted in Hollywood's movie mills.

The American Institute of Architects recently designated the Hollyhock House as one of the most significant structures of the 20th century—an official federal designation. It's well worth a stop to see why, though Hollyhock House is closed to the public until spring 2003 for extensive renovation and restoration. Completed in 1921, this 6,200-square-foot Mayan temple of concrete and stucco, done in Wright's California Romanza style, is adorned inside and out with a stylized hollyhock motif (the hollyhock being Aline Barnsdall's favorite flower). The astonishing living room, redone to reflect its original, highly unusual craftsman concept, includes Wright's symmetrical oak sofas. Essentially room dividers fashioned into sofas with attached tables and then crowned by Arts and Crafts-style sculpture, the sofas surround the fireplace and its water-filled moat.

Wright had completed the main house and only two of the guest cottages when Barnsdall called a halt to the project; in 1923 she donated what is now Barnsdall Park to the city of Los Angeles. It wasn't until 1956 that L.A. finally recognized the significance of Hollyhock House. By that time the home had shed several different owners, most of its original furnishings, and much of its structural integrity. Serious restoration began in the 1970s. Designated a historic cultural monument in 1963, Hollyhock House and the surrounding "arts park" are now operated by L.A.'s Department of Cultural Affairs.

Barnsdall Park includes several arts venues: the **Municipal Art Gallery and Theater,** exhibiting the work of Southern California artists and craftspeople; the **Junior Arts Center,** which offers studio arts classes for young people (ages 4–18) and exhibitions geared to younger audiences; and the **Barnsdall Arts and Crafts Center,** housed in one of Frank Lloyd Wright's guest cottages, which offers art classes for adults.

Hollyhock House is in Barnsdall Park, on the south side of Hollywood Boulevard between Edgemont Street and Vermont Avenue. **Note:** Due to major earthquake damage, Hollyhock House is closed to the public until spring 2003 to undergo extensive renovation and restoration. For current information, call 323/913-4157.

Other Area Architecture

Frank Lloyd Wright continued to refine his concepts and style with the **Ennis-Brown House** (1924) at 2607 Glendower Ave., another well-located and massive Mayan temple (private) overlooking Los Angeles.

The finest example of international-style architecture in Los Angeles, according to those who know about such things, is Richard Neutra's **Lovell House** (1929) at 4616 Dundee Dr. (off Commonwealth Canyon north of Los Feliz Blvd. but best viewed from Aberdeen Ave. below), also a private residence. The experimental construction and design—using only concrete, glass, and steel—marked a turning point in Neutra's career, one that helped create a futuristic look for Southern California and revolutionized world architecture.

Neutra's own international dwelling, **Neutra House,** 2300 Silver Lake Blvd. (private), built in 1933, is another modern architectural landmark. Here he intended to prove that the "new architecture" wasn't merely a passing fad but a stylistic trend capable of delighting succeeding generations. Damaged by fire in 1963, the house was rebuilt in similar style using steel, stucco, and glass.

For a comprehensive look at Neutra's later architectural vision, here overlooking the reservoir awaits an entire neighborhood to explore. As elsewhere, these are private homes, so do not disturb the residents. Immediate neighbors include **Yew House,** 2226 Silver Lake Blvd. (1957); **Kambara House,** 2232 Silver Lake

(1960); **Ivandomi House,** 2238 Silver Lake (1960); **Sokal House,** 2242 Silver Lake (1948); and **Treweek House,** 2250 Silver Lake (1948). Of interest just behind: **Reunion House,** 2440 Earl St. (1949); **Flavin House,** 2218 Argent (1958); **O'Hara House,** 2210 Argent (1961); and **Aki House,** 2200 Argent (1962).

Silver Lake's upper Micheltorena Street, an elusive residential route on the reservoir's west side, is a neighborhood of small houses designed by big international-style architects: **Daniel House,** 1856 Micheltorena (Gregory Ain, 1939); **Lautner House,** 2007 Micheltorena (John Lautner, 1939); **Silvertop,** 2138 Micheltorena Street (Lautner again, 1957); **Oliver House,** 2236 Micheltorena (Rudolph Schindler, 1933); **Alexander House,** 2265 Micheltorena (Harwell Harris, 1940); **Tierman House,** 2323 Micheltorena (Ain, 1940); and **Orans House,** 2404 Micheltorena (Ain, 1941).

GRIFFITH PARK

Most famous for its main attractions, the Los Angeles Zoo and the Griffith Observatory and Planetarium, Griffith Park is a wonder—at 4,000 acres, the largest city park in the United States. The park was donated to the city of Los Angeles in 1896 by mining magnate Griffith J. Griffith (no relation to D. W. Griffith of Hollywood lore). Griffith had big plans for the park early on—including construction of the observatory, which came in the 1930s—but Los Angeles was reluctant to accept more of his largesse, at least during his lifetime, because of lingering scandal over Griffith's conviction and jail time for trying to murder his wife.

The park's sylvan attractions include hiking and horseback trails (stables too), golf courses, tennis courts, soccer fields, a swimming pool, and a seemingly endless supply of picnic areas. Among the prettiest places for picnicking is the aptly named **Fern Dell,** a shady glade along a spring-fed stream; small pathways wind around sparkling pools, waterfalls, and thousands of ferns.

Main attractions with kid appeal include the observatory, the zoo, and pony, stagecoach, and miniature train rides. The **merry-go-round** here is a piece of national history, complete with original organ and dazzling wooden horses with real horsehair tails—a 1926 Stillman Company carousel, one of the last ever built and one of the few still in operation. If younger kids need to run, climb, scream, and otherwise let off steam, head for the park's free Travel Town (see below), with tons and tons of kid-safe and climbable transport.

Though kids also like the Disneyfied exhibits at the fine Autry Museum of Western Heritage (see below), so do thinking adults. And even confirmed city slickers can take steeds out on leisurely trail rides from picturesque **Sunset Ranch** stables, on the park's eastern edge at 3400 N. Beachwood Drive, 323/469-5450. Popular even with Angelenos, Friday night "moonlight rides" climb up into the surrounding San Gabriel Mountains for breathtaking views of the sparkling lights (and smog) below. Also fun: special performances at the park's intimate **Greek Theater,** 2700 N. Vermont, 323/665-1927. An outdoor amphitheater nesting in the foothills, it hosts rock, pop, jazz, blues, country-western, and more from June through October. Pack a picnic along to put the tables outside to good use; just beyond the Doric columns you can buy box suppers as well as beer and wine or you can bring your own.

The park's steeper slopes have been left undeveloped except for hiking and horseback riding trials, making this one of the few L.A. places where one can still explore the nearly natural chaparral—the native landscape before Mulholland's aqueducts transformed the region with imported water.

To stretch car-cramped legs, take the fairly challenging six-mile round-trip hike to the top of **Mount Hollywood**—only for those willing to exert themselves in exchange for a panoramic view of the Los Angeles basin. (Hiking in Griffith Park is best in late winter or early spring, when the grass is green, temperatures mild, and air most transparent.) Though other hikes are possible, this particular route follows a combination of roads and park trails to the summit of Mount Hollywood, continues east along the ridge top, then meanders down through Fern Canyon. Near the end of the official Mount Hollywood Trail is **Dante's View,** an east-facing garden viewpoint built by Dante Orgolini in the 1960s

and personally tended until his death in 1978. *The* sunrise view.

Get oriented to the park's attractions and trails at the visitor center (free maps available). The park is technically open daily 5:30 A.M.–10 P.M. —the late hour to accommodate stargazers at the observatory—but roads and bridles are open only during daylight. Park admission is free, though various attractions and events within its boundaries charge separate admission. Griffith Park is just north of the Hollywood Freeway (Hwy. 101) and south of the Ventura Freeway (Hwy. 134), just west of the Golden State Freeway (I-5). The park's main entry (at Crystal Springs Drive, which becomes Griffith Park Drive) is reached from the south via Los Feliz Boulevard, just off I-5, though you can also enter from Los Feliz at either Fern Dell Drive or Vermont Avenue. For more information, contact the ranger station at 323/913-4688.

Griffith Observatory and Planetarium

The recently restored Griffith Observatory and Planetarium, a moderne classic poised just above the smoggy Los Angeles basin, was designed in 1935 by architects John C. Austin and F. M. Ashley. James Dean slashed it out here in *Rebel without a Cause.* Even on a bad day, when smog-shrouded sights seem surreal, the view from the decks and walkways outside is impressive. On a clear day you really can see forever.

Exhibits in the **Hall of Science** include a seismograph that monitors Southern California's nearly constant earthquake activity. On clear nights (try winter) you can actually see something when you peek into the heavens through the observatory's twin refracting telescope, one of the world's largest. Particularly popular at the observatory's **Planetarium Theater** are the **Laserium** laser light shows, though informative astronomy programs are also offered. Since it's a rare smog-free night that allows much of a celestial view, the main planetarium shows dazzle the audience with various ersatz versions and other earth-science programs—a theme park for the universe where the entertainment changes regularly.

*Griffith Observatory
and Planetarium*

The observatory is open Tues.–Fri., 2–10 P.M., weekends, 12:30–10 P.M.. In the summer months of June through September, the observatory is open every day from 12:30–10 P.M. Admission to Hall of Science exhibits (including the telescope) is free. The observatory's 12-inch telescope is available for night-sky viewing Tues.–Sun., 7–9:45 P.M.,. On clear days when the observatory is open, images from solar telescopes in the west dome are projected down to viewers on the main floor exhibit area. Children under age 5 aren't allowed to attend regular planetarium programs, but a special kids' show is scheduled every afternoon. Planetarium Theater admission is $4 adults, $3 seniors, and $2 children ages 5–12. Laserium admission is $9 adults, $8 seniors and children ages 5–12. The observatory sits in the heart of the park at 2800 Observatory Road (long and winding); enter the park from Vermont Avenue. For current observatory program information, call 323/664-1191 or look up www.griffithobs.org. For Laserium information, call 818/997-3624.

The Los Angeles Zoo

After a troubled decade, things are finally improving at the 113-acre Los Angeles Zoo, one of the nation's most prominent. In the 1980s federal inspectors criticized the zoo's fundamentals—exhibit size and quality, sanitation, drainage, food storage—but it wasn't until the threatened loss of national accreditation in 1995 that Los Angeles got serious about solving such problems. Things had devolved to the point that a penguin exhibit was decimated by disease and wily coyotes broke into the zoo to prey upon captive birds. In 1998 L.A. voters approved proposition CC, a $47.6 million city of Los Angeles bond measure to repair and improve the zoo—so life for the corraled animals here is getting better by the day.

Home to more than 2,000 animals in 75 simulated habitats, the L.A. Zoo includes exhibits arranged by general geographical region: North and South Americas, Africa, Australia, and Eurasia. At **Tiger Falls** the big cats lounge around near convincing but fake waterfalls and pools. The zoo's $4.5 million **chimpanzee exhibit** is the first phase of the much more ambitious **Great Ape Forest.** Other highlights: the **walk-through aviary** exhibiting about 50 exotic birds and Australia's **Koala House,** where the koalas on exhibit seem happy to hang out in the eucalyptus. In other animal pens, "food toys" and other playthings help entertain animals who have yet to benefit much from zoo improvements.

A terrific state-of-the-art children's zoo, **Adventure Island,** opened in 1989. Touch-and-explore exhibits teach children about animals, their habits, and their natural habitats. At the prairie dog exhibit, poke your head up from "underground" holes to see what the prairie dog sees; likewise, to see like a bee, try out the "bee head." Various gentle creatures tolerate petting, and the animal nursery allows human babies and their parents to coo over other species' new arrivals.

Not so accessible to the general public are the zoo's ongoing captive breeding programs and other efforts to preserve the world's endangered species, these including white tigers and koalas.

The entrance to the Los Angeles Zoo is at 5333 Zoo Drive in Griffith Park. The zoo is open daily 10 A.M.–5 P.M., open until 6 P.M. in summer (July 1 to Sept. 4). Closed Christmas Day, General admission is $8.25 adults, $5.25 seniors, $3.25 children ages 2–12 (under 2 free). Walking the zoo's 113 acres can be exhausting, so take advantage of the tram if it's an issue—or get oriented on the **Safari Shuttle Tour.** Strollers and other special services are also available. For more information, call 323/644-6400 or 323/644-4200 or check www.lazoo.org.

Autry Museum of Western Heritage

America's legendary "singing cowboy" Gene Autry ("Back in the Saddle," "Bells of Capistrano") founded the Autry Museum, a fascinating collection of cowboy memorabilia. Credit Walt Disney Imagineering for museum exhibits scoring high in both content and entertainment value. Even the museum's guided-tour cassette is incredibly cool, narrated by hip cowboy crooner Willie Nelson. Autry's namesake is a very well-done general introduction to the colorful yet confusing heritage of the American West—sufficiently high-tech to hold the attention of generations raised by television sets yet thoughtful enough to be worth the electricity.

Sharing a parking lot with the Los Angeles Zoo, this fairly new addition to Griffith Park is dedicated to preserving the culture of the Old West—both real and imagined. **The Spirit of Imagination** exhibit, for example, allows the kids to view themselves (via video monitor) on horseback, being chased by cowboys while hearing the William Tell Overture. Video presentations explore various Western filmmaking topics. Related exhibits feature costumes and props from movie and TV shows along with their mass-marketed product spin-offs—such collectibles as Tom Mix's secret manuals, Zorro's masks, and Davy Crockett's coonskin caps.

Central to **The Spirit of Romance** is film footage of William F. ("Buffalo Bill") Cody performing in a 1902 Wild West Show. Even city slickers can appreciate the exquisite workmanship on handtooled silver-studded celebrity saddles, Annie Oakley's gold pistol, the Lone Ranger's spurs, and other examples of hifalutin cowboy high art. The real-life hardships of leaving home for a new life in the West is brought home by **The Spirit of Opportunity.**

The museum's **Western Heritage Theater** screens westerns and documentaries, and sometimes presents live performances; stop at the information desk for theater schedules. Also on the premises: a family-friendly restaurant and an engaging gift shop. Where else in Los Angeles are you likely to find such a classy collection of cowboy hats and boots, traditional and nontraditional western garb, unusual jewelry, amusing gifts, and thoughtful educational items? The largest collection of Autry Museum cowboy collectibles is available by mail-order catalog (call for information) or on the museum's website: www.autry-museum.org.

The museum is open Tues.–Sun. 10 A.M.–5 P.M. (also on most Monday holidays), Thursday 10 A.M.–8 P.M. The second Tuesday of every month is free. Admission is $7.50 adults, $5 seniors and students with ID, and $3 for children ages 2–12. Free parking. Free guided tours are offered only by reservation. For information on current and upcoming curated shows and special events, contact: Autry Museum of Western Heritage, 4700 Western Heritage Way, 323/667-2000; www.autry-museum.org.

Travel Town

At the north end of the park, at 5200 Zoo Dr., is Travel Town, 323/662-5874, an open-air museum dedicated to well-traveled transportation—and kids' inclination to climb all over same and *drive.* Unlike typical museums, here the displays—antique trains, planes, and automobiles—are designed to be used. Indoors, fire trucks, a circus animal wagon, and other vehicles beckon. Travel Town is open weekdays 10 A.M.–4 P.M., 10 A.M.–5 P.M. on weekends.

Though recent MTA transport proposals may threaten this tradition, each Sunday members of the **Los Angeles Live Steamers** club show up with their handmade miniature steam locomotives, which run on seven-inch-wide tracks, to give kids free train rides through miniature tunnels and towns at a site just northeast of Travel Town. At last report rides were offered between 11 A.M. and 3 P.M. For more information, call 323/669-9729.

THE HOLLYWOOD BOWL AND VICINITY

Like almost every other star in town, this Hollywood landmark has had an expensive facelift—and now it's undergoing something of a "bottom lift," focusing this time on upgrading bathrooms and other fundamentals. No one complains—a rare thing in this city—because Los Angeles loves its Hollywood Bowl.

Hollywood Bowl: From Perfect to Near-Perfect

One of the world's most famous amphitheaters, the Hollywood Bowl in 1919 was known as Daisy Dell—simply a rough-cut stage set up in a natural "bowl" blessed with perfect acoustics, a venue popular for religious plays.

Along came progress, alas. Determined to bend nature to its own design, soon thereafter L.A. County dynamited the area to make room for a new stage and 17,619 poured-concrete seats. The original sound quality was obliterated as a result; efforts to engineer a solution have never fully succeeded. Using materials salvaged from *Robin Hood* movie sets, in 1926 Lloyd Wright (son of Frank Lloyd Wright) took just 10 days to design and build a Mayan-inspired pyramid-shaped band shell, which was excellent acoustically but fairly hideous to look at. Wright tried again in 1928 but his second attempt was ruined by rain. In 1929 Allied Architects designed the current stage. Architect Frank Gehry added the floating spheres above the stage in 1980 in another attempt to improve the acoustics.

Perfect acoustics or no, this is one of L.A.'s favorite places, perfect for evening concerts—jazz, rock, pop, and classical. Though this is the summer home of the Los Angeles Philharmonic Orchestra, the Grateful Dead mounted the stage here, too, as did Bob Dylan, the Beatles, Mel Tormé, and Benny Goodman. And Miles Davis, Duke Ellington, Ella Fitzgerald, and Billie Holiday. And Aaron Copland, Vladimir Horowitz, Sergei Rachmaninoff, and Igor Stravinsky.

The cheap seats offer some of the best views (bring seat cushions). The local concert custom is to come early and picnic; many L.A. restaurants and delis offer Bowl-season picnic specials, made to order with one day's notice. Even for viewing the suppertime antics of socialites, the cheap seats are best (bring binoculars too). Boxes at the Hollywood Bowl are so precious they are bequeathed in wills—which only partially explains the fine china, silver candlesticks, and other picnic finery carted along by the high-society set.

Edmund D. Edelman Hollywood Bowl Museum

For historical perspective on the Hollywood Bowl, stop by the Edmund D. Edelman Hollywood Bowl Museum, fresh from a complete renovation and major expansion. A new multimedia exhibit in the main gallery, downstairs, tells the Bowl story. The 10-minute "home movie," created from film archive material, is a gem, along with the first recording ever made in the Hollywood Bowl—the Adagio from *Sleeping Beauty,* with Eugene Goosens conducting the L.A. Philharmonic in 1928. And it's amusing to discover that teen idol Frank Sinatra's performance in 1943 provoked considerable controversy. Also on display: the original Lloyd Wright drawings and prototypes. The upstairs gallery hosts rotating special exhibits. The museum is open year-round, Tues.–Sat. 10 A.M. until showtime when there's entertainment at the bowl, 10 A.M.–4:30 P.M. otherwise. Admission is free. For more information, call 323/850-2058.

Practical Hollywood Bowl

Here's something only Angelenos typically know: Anyone can show up on most summer mornings at 9 or 9:30 A.M. to attend rehearsals for that evening's performance—free. No crowds, no parking headaches, and no problem grabbing the great seats. Bring your own coffee and croissants.

The Hollywood Bowl sits at the "intersection" of Highland Avenue (Hwy. 170) and the Hollywood Freeway (Hwy. 101). The regular concert calendar starts in early July and runs through mid-September, but the grounds and picnic areas are open year-round (closed Christmas), sunrise to sunset. Access to the grounds is free, since this is a public park. Parking is free in the off-season, and, during concert season, free before 4 P.M. Since parking at the Bowl during performances is otherwise expensive and inconvenient, take one of the park-and-ride shuttles from around town. Call for current performance information and ticket sales. For more information: Hollywood Bowl, 2301 N. Highland Ave., 323/850-2000; www.hollywoodbowl.org.

Hollywood Studio Museum

Across bustling Highland Avenue from the Hollywood Bowl is the unassuming yellow barn that served as headquarters for Cecil B. DeMille during shooting for *The Squaw Man*—Hollywood's oldest existing studio building. DeMille rented the barn, known simply as the DeMille Barn or "the Barn" in these parts, and part of the surrounding orange grove for $25 per month. Later moved to what is now Paramount Studios, the decrepit old barn gathered cobwebs on Paramount's back lot until 1979. When the Hollywood Chamber of Commerce failed to put it to good use, Hollywood Heritage came to the rescue—restoring the barn and moving it to its present site.

Museum displays emphasize artifacts from the silent-movie era: historic motion-picture

---

SOME CLASSIC L.A. DRIVES

The Stars-to-Sea Highway

If you have an adventurous spirit and time to spare, the classic L.A. "view" tour is the "Stars-to-Sea Highway," 25-mile **Mulholland Drive** heading west from the Hollywood Freeway (the 101) near Cahuenga Pass in the Hollywood Hills to Woodland Hills. For truly intrepid scenery seekers, the route continues out of the Santa Monica Mountains to the Pacific Ocean at Leo Carrillo State Beach and the Pacific Coast Highway (Hwy. 1) just east of the Ventura County line. (To do the entire route, which includes a fairly rugged unpaved section through Topanga State Park just southeast of Woodland Hills and other rough spots, a four-wheel-drive or other reasonably reliable, destruction-proof vehicle is advised.) Alternatively, take just half the trip by exiting in either direction from the San Diego Freeway (the 405) north of Brentwood near Sepulveda Pass.

Notable just east of the Hollywood Freeway is the lovely mission-style concrete "castle wall" and moat known as **Hollywood Reservoir**. Originally named Mulholland Dam when it was formally dedicated in 1925—to honor L.A.'s premier water engineer, William Mulholland, architect of the Los Angeles Aqueduct—the reservoir was quietly renamed after the St. Francis Dam disaster that soon doomed Mulholland's career and reputation. Yet Mulholland's namesake street remains unchanged.

Heading east to west, Mulholland Drive snakes west along the ridge tops above Hollywood, offering both close-ups of some spectacular homes and breathtaking panoramas of the endless L.A. basin and the San Fernando Valley. At night, it's all absolutely dazzling, particularly from the **Mt. Olympus Overlook** about one mile west of the **Hollywood Bowl Overlook** (at Runyon Canyon Park's northern entrance). Both daytime and nighttime views are typically better—and, in a sense, less "breathtaking"—in winter and early spring, when the smog level is low.

At the junction of Mulholland Drive and Topanga Canyon Boulevard, Mulholland Drive becomes "Highway" but otherwise continues to slither west across the twisting spine of the Santa Monica Mountains, slicing through suburban sprawl and wilderness along the way. Most scenic is the eight-mile "outback" section between **Las Virgenes** and **Kanan Dume Roads,** which has starred as Australia, England, and other imaginary movie locales. Following the route all the way west eventually leads to the Pacific Ocean. Plan to pack a picnic lunch (or dinner) and head for remote, picturesque **Nicholas Canyon County Beach** south of Leo Carrillo State Beach.

Cheap Thrills

Another way to start a Mulholland Drive sojourn—definitely a cheap thrill—is to begin your trip on **Dixie Canyon Avenue** just off Ventura Boulevard to the north in Sherman Oaks. At Dixie Canyon's suburban end, the road is wide and civilized, at least for a few blocks. But it soon descends wildly—hey, great views!—trying to decide, as its ruts, rattles, and rolls down the mountainside, whether it's merely a twisted equipment and props dating from 1913 to the 1950s, a movie camera once belonging to Charlie Chaplin, and Cleopatra's 40-pound shield from the 1934 movie. Also here: a re-creation of Cecil B. DeMille's original office and miscellaneous furnishings from the Egyptian Theatre.

In 1996 the DeMille barn suffered a disastrous fire. Fortunately the building has been restored in the years since, and in 1999 Hollywood Heritage reopened the museum on a limited basis. At last report the Hollywood Studio Museum, 2100 N. Highland Ave., 323/874-BARN, was open 11 A.M.–3:30 P.M. on weekends and at other times only by appointment. Admission is $4 adults, $2 seniors and children ages 5–12, children under 5 free. For the muse-

um's current status, call Hollywood Heritage at 323/874-4005.

John Anson Ford Theater

Across the Hollywood Freeway (the 101) from the Hollywood Bowl, the John Anson Ford Theater, 2580 Cahuenga Blvd., 323/461-3673, is a much smaller Hollywood Hills amphitheater. The 1,300-seat venue hosts Shakespeare, free jazz, and other summer performances. This is also the site of an infamous Southern California church-versus-state battle. The original open-air theater here, the Pilgrimage Theater, was built in 1920 by Pittsburg Paint heiress Christine Wetherell Stevenson (also an early mover and shaker in the construction of the Hollywood

---

and treacherous one-lane dirt road or a coyote path. (Not recommended for street cars, but definitely a possibility for off-roaders. And experienced mountain bikers.) The prospect of civilized transport, *paved road,* again presents itself at the intersection with Mulholland Drive.

Another cheap thrill starts in the Silver Lake neighborhood. From Glendale Boulevard, head north on Alvarado into the hills above Echo Park to **Fargo Street**—L.A.'s steepest up-and-down thoroughfare—and create your own amusement ride. (Good brakes and steady nerves mandatory.) Adjacent **Baxter** is also good for a few gasps.

Urban adventurers with a preference for flatland might instead prefer the more thought-provoking sociological thrills associated with taking **Santa Monica Boulevard, Sunset Boulevard,** or **Wilshire Boulevard** west from downtown.

On the Beach

By and large the Southern California coastal driving experience will not mirror any of those appealing escapist images used by TV car commercials to brainwash consumers. The success of the cars-are-freedom sales pitch is reflected, instead, in bumper-to-bumper traffic and the occasional sun- or celebrity-drunk yahoo determined to run others off the road. But a drive along L.A.'s stretch of the famed **Pacific Coast Highway** ("PCH," or Hwy. 1) can be a pleasure—especially on a nonsummer weekday—if you get out and about *early,* before the crazy people are out of bed.

But the point of driving PCH is not to escape the horrors of overpopulated urban life. The point is to immerse, wallow, or *drown* yourself in them. Since

parking will be all but impossible in many coastal areas, you'll have plenty of time to work on it.

For a lightweight beach tour, begin amid the boat-groupie culture of **Marina del Rey,** the world's largest man-made harbor with associated upscale hotels and restaurants, and then work your way north through the tortured seaside eccentricities and spruced-up canals of **Venice** to open-minded **Santa Monica,** where at last report the middle-class still coexisted with the rich and famous and the occasional poor person. Heading north past **Pacific Palisades** and its swell seaside jogging park eventually leads to **Malibu,** where movie stars and other shy, affluent types apparently don't mind paying millions and millions of dollars for exclusive homes that periodically burn up in wildfires or, after the torrential rains that follow, slide down into the sea. Your reward, if you continue north to near **Ventura County,** is access to some of L.A.'s best "getaway" beaches.

A more serious—but more complicated—tour of the L.A. coastline starts in Long Beach far to the south, detouring from PCH to take in the heavy-industrial byways of sister port cities Wilmington and San Pedro on the way to the pleasant serenity of the Palos Verdes Peninsula. Once you roll down out of Rolling Hills, again stick to coastal roadways to tour the South Bay beaches and beach towns of Redondo Beach, Hermosa Beach, Manhattan Beach, and El Segundo, some quite semi-industrial. (Miniature oil derricks, even in people's backyards, are not particularly uncommon in this neck of the woods.) From El Segundo on into Playa del Rey, you can enjoy the endless aerial traffic coming and going from LAX.

Bowl) to stage her pageant about the life and times of Jesus Christ, "The Pilgrimage Play." Stevenson died in 1922; a year later friends and admirers honored her by planting a 34-foot-tall illuminated cross on the hill above the theater (usually lit up only at Easter and during the play's summer run). Brush fires destroyed the original theater in 1929, though it was rebuilt in 1931 in "classic Judaic style" and renamed—after a former county supervisor—in 1941, when the property was donated to Los Angeles County. "Pilgrimage" performances continued here until 1964, when the first legal skirmish over religious use of a publicly funded facility ended the tradition. After years of neglect and vandalism, the cross finally fell in 1984. But it was resurrected and relit—as a universal symbol of peace—in 1994 through the efforts of local crusaders and Hollywood Heritage, which bought the site from the county.

Into the Hollywood Hills

Prestige addresses, protected by high walls and state-of-the-art security systems, have always been up in the hills. Meander your own makeshift tour route along **Mulholland Drive,** which eventually leads to the Pacific Ocean (see Some Classic L.A. Drives elsewhere in this chapter), or stretch your legs on a vigorous three-mile foothill loop through **Runyon Canyon Park** and the

onetime San Patrizio estate, also known as The Pines. Known originally as No Man's Canyon, Runyon Canyon was bought in 1929 by actor John McCormick after his hit movie *Song of My Heart*. His mansion was called San Patrizio (St. Patrick) but renamed The Pines by millionaire Huntington Hartford, who bought the property in 1942 with the idea of building an ambitious futuristic hotel designed by Lloyd Wright (son of Frank Lloyd Wright). Nothing ever came of that dream—nor the development dreams of subsequent owners. A city park since 1984, Runyon Canyon is accessible from Mulholland but the main trailhead, at The Pines gate, is usually approached from Fuller Avenue (north of Franklin). For still more exercise, hike north through adjacent **Wattles Gardens Park,** just west.

Assuming no smog alerts, *the* place to go jogging in Hollywood is around the surprisingly lovely **Lake Hollywood** reservoir, open daily at 6:30 A.M., closing before dusk, and reached via either Weidlake or Lake Hollywood Drives. If you're lucky you can eavesdrop on the earnest and/or inane conversations of actual entertainment industry people. For information, call 323/463-0830. No dogs are allowed. If you do have Fido along, head instead for **Laurel Canyon** and the fenced dog park there—a place where dogs run free.

PRACTICAL HOLLYWOOD

STAYING IN HOLLYWOOD

"Living in Hollywood is like living in a lit cigar butt," irascible comic Phyllis Diller observed in the 1970s. Staying in Tinseltown a few days isn't so bad though. Some areas are a bit dicey, true, and others astronomically expensive, but staying somewhere in or near Hollywood is feasible for just about everyone. The belly of the beast—Hollywood proper—features hostel options, definitely a boon for streetwise budget travelers. Even motel rooms here are more reasonably priced than those in more glamorous locales. (Just steer clear of any establishment advertising hourly rates.) A number of good midrange motels are also available in the San Fernando Valley.

If you're in the market for upscale lodgings head to West Hollywood, which doesn't offer much else. In addition to the upmarket hotels listed below, consider also Beverly Hills and vicinity—quite nearby, adjacent to West Hollywood—and other Westside possibilities. Since during the workweek swankier places often cater to business types with entertainment-industry expense accounts, weekend rates and special packages can be great deals.

Budget Bonanza: The Hollywood Hostels

Sure, Hollywood Boulevard has seen better days. And sure, the streets in the neighborhood are more than a bit unsavory, especially after dark. But for low cost and central location—right on the Hollywood Walk of Fame, close to West

Hollywood and the club scene, reasonably close to Hollywood's little theater action—the **Hollywood International Hostel,** 6820 Hollywood Blvd. (between High and La Brea Avenues), 323/463-0797 or toll-free 800/750-6561, www.hollywoodhostel.com, can't be beat. Now in a safer location, next to El Capitan Theatre and across from Mann's Chinese, the Hollywood International offers 40 rooms. Shared dorm space is the norm, two to four beds to a room, but private rooms are also available. Also here: a full kitchen, common areas (with game room, library, and TV with cable, satellite, and videos), laundry and storage facilities, even a sundeck and shuttle service (airport, bus, and train pickups, plus rides to the beach and major amusement parks). Free linens. Especially in summer, students and out-of-state travelers get priority, so bring a passport and/or photo ID. Rates: $40 private room (maximum of two people), $15 dorm rooms. Breakfast included.

Fun and definitely above the Hollywood fray, the pleasant 250-bed **Banana Bungalow Hollywood Hotel and Hostel** features both private rooms (some with private bath) plus cheaper hostel-style accommodations. Facilities include full kitchen, laundry, library, weight room, arcade, basketball courts, pool, and sundeck, plus a store and café/restaurant. And color TV in every room. Free linens, breakfast, and parking. Free shuttle service to the beach, Disneyland, and Universal Studios, plus airport, train depot, and bus station pickup. Passport required (even for American travelers); international guests get dorm priority. Reservations advisable in summer. Dorm accommodations (four to six beds per bungalow) are $15–20. Private rooms start at $55. Banana Bungalow is near the Hollywood Bowl (on the way to Universal Studios) in the Hollywood Hills, next to the Hollywood Freeway, about one mile north of Franklin Avenue. For more information, contact: Banana Bungalow Hollywood Hotel and Hostel, 2775 Cahuenga Blvd. West in Los Angeles, 323/851-1129 or toll-free 800/446-7835; www .bananabungalow.com.

**Moderate to Expensive Hollywood Stays:
Off the Tourist Trail**
The best bets for a midpriced overnight are motels a bit off the tourist trail, including smaller

(cheaper) rooms at **Days Inn Hollywood,** 7023 Sunset Blvd. (just east of La Brea), 323/464-8344 or toll-free 800/346-7723. Rates: $105 and up. Not in the best neighborhood but closer to Griffith Park and within reasonable reach of Universal Studios is the recently renovated and quite comfortable **Ramada Limited Hollywood,** 1160 N. Vermont Ave., 323/660-1788 or toll-free 800/272-6232. In addition to standard rooms ($99 and up), suites with microwaves, refrigerators, and coffeemakers ($129 and up) can be a sweet deal for families or groups. Then there's the quite nice, similarly priced **Best Western Hollywood Hills** right off the Hollywood Freeway at 6141 Franklin Ave. (east of Vine), 323/464-5181, where many of the rooms come with microwaves. And there's always the on-site **Hollywood Hills Coffee Shop,** which shared some fame by association when its "Last Cappuccino Before 101" sign starred in *The Brady Brunch Movie.* Rates: $79 and up (lower in the off-season). This being California, all of the above come accompanied with a heated swimming pool and at least a few extra amenities.

**Moderate to Expensive Hollywood Stays:
In the Heart of Hollyweird**
Also a pretty sweet deal for families or groups—if you don't mind the Hollyweird scene, and especially if you'll be staying awhile—is the **Hollywood Orchid Suites Hotel** near Mann's Chinese Theatre, just north of Hollywood Blvd. at 1753 N. Orchid Ave., 323/874-9678 or toll-free 800/537-3052. Suites here include kitchens, so you can cook (and eat) in. Rates: $79–109. Also in the heart of Hollyweird is the **Holiday Inn Hollywood,** 1755 N. Highland Ave, 323/850-5811 or toll-free 800/465-4329—but not for the faint of heart because the neighborhood is well, eccentric. The comfort level is fairly high, the decor decent standard-Holiday-Inn style, but the main attraction is the **Windows on Hollywood** revolving restaurant (dinner only) on the 23rd floor, which offers standard American cuisine and a view all the way to the San Bernardino Mountains on a clear night. Without a special discount standard, high-season rates can be a bit stiff, though, so this isn't a midrange bargain unless you score a good weekend deal (sometimes possible). Rates: $129–229.

Not in such an interesting setting but quite

comfortable—and usually a much better deal—is the **Best Western Hollywood Plaza Inn** near the Hollywood Freeway, a half-mile north of Hollywood Boulevard at 2011 N. Highland Ave., 323/851-1800, or toll-free 800/445-4353. Rates: $89–119 (rates lower in the off-season).

Clarion Hollywood Roosevelt Hotel

This updated Hollywood classic holds revered rank in movie-industry mythology. On Hollywood Boulevard across the street from Mann's Chinese Theater, the Hollywood Roosevelt was the setting of the first Academy Awards ceremony in 1927 (Douglas Fairbanks presiding) and the place Bill "Bojangles" Robinson taught Shirley Temple how to dance up the stairs. (Movie memorabilia and industry artifacts are on display on the mezzanine.) Meticulously restored to its original splendor after a $35 million facelift, the Hollywood Roosevelt is still Old Hollywood but hipper—with 40 movie-star "theme" suites and 65 ever-popular "cabana" bungalow-style suites surrounding the pool. The Olympic-size pool is itself a cultural landmark, painted by artist David Hockney. Do pop into the **Cinegrill** supper club here, one of Marilyn Monroe's favorite Old Hollywood haunts. Most rooms here are small but quite charming—and surprisingly reasonable, all things considered. Rates: $143–269.

For more information, contact: Clarion Hollywood Roosevelt Hotel, 7000 Hollywood Blvd., 323/466-7000, or toll-free 800/950-7667 for reservations; www.hollywoodroosevelt.com.

EATING IN HOLLYWOOD

The best post-dinner destination in all of Los Angeles is **Yamashiro**, the "castle on the hill" at 1999 N. Sycamore Ave. (off Franklin), 323/466-5125, a beautifully detailed 1913 Japanese mountain palace built by Asian art importers, the brothers Adolph and Eugene Bernheimer. A mansion surrounded by seven acres of glorious gardens, complete with 600-year-old pagoda, this was a star-happy club in Hollywood's golden age and is now a stylish restaurant and bar. On a warm L.A. night, ask for a spot on the stunning indoor-outdoor garden patio to enjoy a drink—then drink in the most spectacular nighttime view of Los Angeles. Other

good spots to drink in that Old Hollywood ambience include the **Formosa Cafe,** 7156 Santa Monica Blvd. (just west of La Brea), 323/850-9050, and the Raymond Chandleresque **Musso & Frank Grill,** 6667 Hollywood Blvd. (at Las Palmas Ave.), 323/467-7788 (for more information, see below).

Also "very Hollywood" for natural food folks is the weekly **Hollywood Farmers Market** (certified), where produce, baked goods, and food stalls are accompanied by arts and crafts. The market is held Sunday 8:30 A.M.–2 P.M. at Ivar and Selma. Also try the **Melrose Weekend Market** at Fairfax High School (on the corner of Melrose and Fairfax), open Sunday 9 A.M.–5 P.M., small admission fee.

In restaurants as in nightclubs, many trendy "Hollywood" stars these days are actually in or near West Hollywood (see below) or just starting to constellate in and around North Hollywood—which is not to suggest that you'll starve in Hollywood proper, famous for being all over the map in all ways. Local favorites include all-American cheap-eats dives, classy hole-in-the-wall ethnic eateries, and very classy supper clubs.

People's Favorites: Burgers and Such

Tommy's Original World Famous Hamburgers in Silver Lake at 2575 Beverly Blvd. (at Rampart), 213/389-9060, open 24 hours, is L.A.'s original Tommy's, yet another Tinseltown star. Tommy's serves "the world's only true chiliburger"—a meal that can stay with you for days, and a very spicy version at that. But a true Tommy burger can leave telltale grease stains on your clothes, a problem easy to avoid if you follow traditional Tommy burger etiquette. Simply prop yourself up against the convenient exterior counter (no seating) to catch the drippings. Posted rolls of industrial-strength paper towels come in handy too.

It's probably fitting that a Tommy's defector started **Jay's Jayburgers,** 4481 Santa Monica Blvd. (at Virgil), 323/666-5204, an immensely popular takeout shop serving much more civilized chiliburgers—restrained creations that won't wake you up at 2 A.M. Not only that, you can wash it down with genuine California sunshine—fresh-squeezed lemonade.

Pink's Hot Dogs, 709 N. La Brea (at Melrose), 323/931-4223, is another fast-food chili icon.

People, including the occasional Hollywood celebrity, happily ignore the unhappy neighborhood to line up for the all-beef dogs drowning in all-beef chili.

People's Favorites: Ethnic Eats

Thai is big in these parts. The General's Noodle Soup—named for the very officially dressed fellow directing traffic in the lot on weekend afternoons—is one reason people throng around **Sanamluang Cafe,** 5176 Hollywood Blvd. (at Kingsley), 323/660-8006, open for late supper until 4 A.M. and everybody's favorite Thai noodle shop. Wonderful for sit-down Thai at both lunch and dinner—at least before 9 P.M., when it becomes a noisier nightclub venue—is **Kruang Tedd,** 5151 Hollywood Blvd. (at Winona), 323/663-9988.

Jitlada is an established local Thai star, a cozy family-run restaurant housed in a grungy minimall, 5233½ Sunset Blvd. (at Howard), 323/667-9809, serving some of L.A.'s best—hot stuff. If you aren't familiar with spicy Thai food, let the staff guide your selection. Always recommended: the spring rolls; the traditional *mee krob* (a sticky, sweet, and crisp noodle appetizer studded with chicken, shrimp, and coriander); the hot and sour soup with shellfish; and the shrimp specialties.

One of L.A.'s all-time favorites for Thai, still, is the original **Chan Dara** in Hollywood at 1511 N. Cahuenga Blvd. (at Sunset), 323/464-8585, open for dinner nightly, lunch on weekdays only. Everything here is done very well, from the satays to flaming barbecued chicken, pad Thai noodles, and panang curries. Another Chan Dara is just south at 310 N. Larchmont (near Hancock Park), 323/467-1052, yet another in West L.A. at 11940 W. Pico (between Bundy and Barrington), 310/479-4461.

For takeout, don't miss serene **Chamika Catering Sri Lankan Restaurant,** inside the onetime Big Weenies Are Better hot-dog stand at 1717 N. Wilcox (at Hollywood Blvd.), 323/466-8960, famous for its coconut-rich dishes and curries, unbelievable hot "deviled shrimp," and banana delight. (There are a few tables, if you prefer eating here.) To pack an international picnic basket, you could also start with an Armenian-style roast chicken to go from **Zankou Chicken,** 5065 Sunset Blvd. (at Normandy),

323/665-7842, which serves garlicky spit-roasted Armenian-Lebanese-style whole chickens. Or try popular **Moun of Tunis,** 7445½ Sunset Blvd. (at Gardner, four blocks west of La Brea), 323/874-3333, where people line up to weep over the wickedly hot *harissa* and other Moroccan delicacies while sitting on floor cushions in exceptionally exotic surroundings.

People's Favorites: Melrose Avenue

For a taste of "historic" Melrose, try **Tommy Tang's,** a local favorite since 1982, at 7313 Melrose (near Fuller), 323/937-5733. There may be better Thai/sushi bars in L.A., but not many. And few could serve such theater. The crowd here is new-wave Fellini; on Tuesday nights the waiters do it in drag. Tang's is open daily for lunch and dinner.

Among the worthiest neighborhood newcomers is the **Vienna Cafe,** 7356 Melrose (at Fuller), 323/651-3822, with a full Mediterranean café menu at breakfast, lunch, and dinner, and marvelous sandwiches, vegetarian selections, and bakery goods to go.

Chianti, 7383 Melrose Ave. (between La Brea and Fairfax), 323/653-8333, is a very dark and romantic old-world Northern Italian place with a knack for discretion even in seating arrangements (booths). More affordable, well-lit, and catering to a younger crowd is little sister **Chianti Cucina** adjacent (same address and phone), where the pastas and risottos are served with stylish simplicity.

Upscale Café Fare

Most of Hollywood's most stylish restaurants lie near Paramount and NBC Studios, within easy reach of folks with ready cash. Not all are horribly expensive, though, especially at breakfast or lunch. **Boxer,** 7615 Beverly Blvd. at Stanley (between Fairfax and La Brea), 323/932-6178, is a trendy storefront café serving box-shaped innovations to enthusiastic foodies—such things as tomato, beet, and avocado salad, and crusty pizza with caramelized onions, niçoise olives, roasted peppers, and garlic.

Long-running **Angeli Caffè,** 7274 Melrose Ave. (between Fairfax and La Brea), 323/936-9086, is a noisy, modern, and minimalist pizza and pasta joint catering to the hip and hungry at lunch and dinner. Though pizza popped fresh from wood-burning ovens is hardly culinary news in California, here they do it quite well—topping the pies with new twists on authentic Italian themes. Folks also rave over the antipasto dishes, frittatas, and panini. Still très cool for hanging out with the latest crop of young Hollywood stars and fashion models, at last report, was the inexpensive Italian **Caffè Luna,** 7463 Melrose Ave. (between Vista and Gardner), 323/655-8647. It's open until all hours, and always a good stop for a leisurely latte.

The French bistro **Les Deux Cafés,** 1638 N. Las Palmas Ave. (between Hollywood Blvd. and Selma Ave.), 323/465-0509, is/are one of those only-in-Hollywood kind of places, an exquisite and exquisitely relaxed fine foodery fashioned from a quaint onetime crack house attached, mid-parking lot, to the adjoining kitchen via an oddly lovely outdoor garden. Even the grease-pencil-and-Mylar dining room menu is designed to change constantly, to take full advantage of the best and freshest produce, fish, and meats. Très L.A., très cool. It's open daily for breakfast and lunch, Tues.–Sun. for dinner. Another possibility is the peaceful little oasis **Off Vine,** 6263 Leland (near Vine parallel to Sunset, one block south), 323/962-1900, (lunch and dinner only), housed in a charming cottage with a romantic patio.

The stylish but casual French **Pinot Hollywood** bistro and its associated **Martini Lounge** and **Patinette** on-site bakery at 1448 N. Gower St. (at Sunset), 323/461-8800, are kissin' cousins to Joachim Splichal's other "Pinot"s—and to his acclaimed **Patina** (listed below). Some foodies consider Pinot Hollywood the Musso & Frank of the new century, what with its fatal attraction for Gower Gulch movie people and studio execs. The bakery opens at 7 A.M. for coffee, muffins, and such. The restaurant, patio, and sofa-stuffed lounge open for dinner Mon.–Sat., for lunch on weekdays.

Roscoe's House of Chicken and Waffles

Everybody loves this place, a mainstay of L.A.'s R&B crowd right in the heart of Hollywood at 1514 N. Gower St. (between Sunset and Hollywood Blvds.), 323/466-7453. Roscoe's is one of those classic Los Angeles dining experiences—a funky place in a funky neighborhood that manages to defy all trends, attracting L.A.'s

upper crust, lower crust, and every kind of crust in between. The place delivers just what it promises, from morning till midnight—great Southern fried chicken with perfect waffles on the side. If you need vegetables, order some greens. Roscoe's also has places in the Mid-Wilshire district at 5006 W. Pico and at 106 W. Manchester in South-Central L.A.

Old Hollywood: Musso & Frank Grill

Musso & Frank, 6667 Hollywood Blvd. (three blocks west of Cahuenga Blvd.), 323/467-7788, is the last survivor of Old Hollywood, now that the original Chasen's is gone. William Faulkner, F. Scott Fitzgerald, Ernest Hemingway, and other literati hung out here while in town slumming for studio cash. But this is also a remnant of Raymond Chandler's imaginary Hollywood, a dark men's-clubby place outfitted with polished wood, red leather booths, and other stylish details circa 1919. Critics have described the cuisine as "simple food done well." Best bets: the grilled chops, famous chicken pot pie, and perennial breakfast menu. Not to mention the best martinis in town. It's open daily 11 A.M.–11 P.M., closed Christmas, Thanksgiving, and New Year's Day.

New Hollywood: Patina

Joachim Splichal's flagship French Californian at 5955 Melrose (between Highland and Vine), 323/467-1108, is one of L.A.'s best—famous for its imaginative yet substantial fare, starting with endless variations on the potato theme and ending with flawless desserts. Choosing one of the "tasting menus" eliminates the problem of what to order for an entrée. Premium. But children under age 10 eat here for free, so don't hesitate to bring the family if you're planning a truly special meal. Patina serves dinner nightly, lunch Tues.–Fri. only.

New Hollywood: Citrus

Chef Michel Richard started his L.A. sojourn with a wonderful West Hollywood pastry shop and catering biz—and though he no longer owns it, Michel Richard on S. Robertson Blvd. is still going strong, serving breads, cakes, and simple café fare, from omelettes and quiche to salads. But Richard's cheery Citrus, 6703 Melrose Ave. (at Citrus, a block west of Highland), 323/857-0034, is a bustling big-city French bistro included on all of L.A.'s "best restaurant" lists. Such things as crab cole slaw, Thai-spiced lobster, mesquite-smoked salmon, and superb desserts keep everyone coming back for more at both lunch (weekdays only) and dinner (every night but Sunday). Citrus is also quite expensive, however, so foodies on a budget will greatly appreciate the associated **Bar Bistro**.

EATING IN SILVER LAKE

Stylin' It in Silver Lake

Ever-popular **Cha Cha Cha**, 656 N. Virgil Ave.(just south of Melrose), 323/664-7723, is one of those places where the chi-chi go slumming. This terrific little Caribbean café, casual and cheery though in a fairly dicey neighborhood, is beloved for its empañadas, jerked chicken, Caribbean shrimp, and unusual pizzas. Reservations advisable at dinner. Valet parking suggested, to make sure your car's still around when you're ready to go.

Dinner-only **Vida**, 1930 Hillhurst Ave. (near Franklin), 323/660-4445, was named for owner Fred Eric's mother. His original title—"..."—was too elliptical, too darned abstract, and way too hard to pronounce. But just contemplating the very punny and fairly pricey entrées, such as "Okra Winfrey Creole Gumbo" and "Ty Cobb Salad," makes people smile well before the fabulous food arrives. A neighborhood sibling, **Fred 62**, 1850 N. Vermont (at Franklin), 323/667-0062, serves 24-hour diner fare to a hip Silver Lake crowd.

Elegant dinner-only **Mexico City**, 2121 Hillhurst Ave. (near Los Feliz Blvd.) in Los Feliz, 323/661-7227, serves fine Mexican fare too few Americans have ever tasted, such as marinated pork or red snapper in a garlic and capers sauce. It serves many vegetarian options, too, including sweet green corn tamales and other appetizers, spinach enchiladas, and calabacitas poblanas (zucchini with cheese and chiles). Some say the area's best Mexican restaurant is long-running and romantic **El Chavo**, 4441 Sunset Blvd. (near Vermont) in Silver Lake, 323/664-0871, famous for its Sonora chicken and chicken mole.

Silver Lake's gay foodies tend to gravitate toward the **Cobalt Cantina**, 4326 Sunset Blvd. (at Fountain), 323/953-9991, with a local following lining up at the "shack"—originally home to the original L.A. Nicola—for the good soups and salads, roasted half-chickens, meat loaf, and corn tamales with sweet potatoes. The popular **Martini Lounge** is next door.

People's Favorites

At Silver Lake's **Back Door Bakery**, 1710 Silver Lake Blvd., 323/662-7927, everybody loves the inner beauty of the Apple Ugly (a popular muffin here). A tad fancier for baked goods—and lunch and dinner—is **La Belle Epoque**, 2128 Hillhurst Ave. (one block south of Los Feliz Blvd.) in Los Feliz, 323/669-7640, the place for a sit-down coffee break complete with apricot custard, rum-almond croissants, or mousse cake.

Netty's deli and café, 1700 Silver Lake Blvd., 323/662-8655, is the place for enjoying unusual Cajun, Californian, and Latin fusion. **El Conchinito** diner, 3508 W. Sunset Blvd., 323/668-0737, serves Mexican with West Indies flair. **Yuca's Hut**, 2056 N. Hillhurst in Los Feliz, 323/662-1214, is beloved for its burritos, carnitas, and such (closed Sunday).

For too-cool Japanese fare in Silver Lake, the place is **Mako**, 1820 N. Vermont Ave. (no phone, and no name out front). Also cool is the **Armitage** restaurant, 1767 N. Vermont, 323/664-5467. Also try **Millie's** for hip but home-style coffee-shop fare, 3524 W. Sunset Blvd., 323/664-0404, and the 24-hour **Astro Family Restaurant**, 2300 Fletcher Dr. (off Glendale Blvd., near I-5), 323/663-9241.

TINSELTOWN TRANSPORTATION AND INFORMATION

Arriving in Tinseltown by Metrorail and by Car

The Metrorail is a bit of a sore subject in L.A., as construction has been plagued by cost overruns, delays, and disasters. But progress is taking place: today the MTA's underground **Metrorail Red Line** provides connections between downtown and the communities of Hollywood, Long Beach, Redondo Beach, and Norwalk. The rail line now runs through (beneath) the Hollywood Hills to emerge in North Hollywood near Universal Studios. One-way tickets go for $1.35 and are available from coin-operated machines at rail stations.

For Metrorail information, call 800/266-6883 within L.A. County or check www.mta.net.

From downtown L.A. and the Westside, it's reasonably easy to get to Hollywood and West Hollywood by car via surface streets, **Wilshire, Santa Monica,** and **Sunset Boulevards** being the most obvious routes across the territory. But this being L.A., most people get around by freeway. As elsewhere throughout Southern California, the best freeway strategy on weekdays is to avoid peak commuter times if at all possible, setting out for a day's exploration at 9 or 10 A.M. and returning by 3 P.M.—or staying put until 7 P.M. or later, perhaps enjoying a leisurely evening meal while everyone else is stuck in traffic. Except at freeway bottlenecks and near major attractions (such as Universal Studios), weekend traffic is less horrifying.

From downtown, the **Hollywood Freeway (Hwy. 101)** quickly arrives in the heart of Hollywood and passes Universal Studios before descending into the San Fernando Valley, where it becomes the **Ventura Freeway (Hwy. 101)** heading west and the **Hollywood Freeway (Hwy. 170)** continuing north through North Hollywood. The **Golden State Freeway (I-5)** skirts Hollywood east of Silver Lake and Griffith Park and slides down into the San Fernando Valley, traversing Glendale, Burbank, and Sun Valley before joining Highway 170. The massive L.A. traffic funnel manifests just north of the San Fernando Valley proper, as first I-405 (the San Diego Freeway) and then I-5 and I-210 (the Foothill Freeway) converge for the journey up and over the Tehachapis.

Something of a backdoor route into Hollywood is provided by the **Glendale Freeway (Hwy. 2),** which meanders south from I-210 near La Cañada Flintridge to intersect the Ventura Freeway (Hwy. 134 here) before pouring out onto Glendale Boulevard in Silver Lake. (Hwy. 2 resurrects itself as Santa Monica Blvd., nearby.) The dominant—and notably congested—thoroughfare traversing the territory from east to west is the **Ventura Freeway,** Highway 134 from Pasadena, which becomes Highway 101 near North Hollywood and Universal Studios.

Tinseltown by Air: The Burbank/ Pasadena/Glendale Airport

Lockheed, where Rosie the Riveter cranked out so many of World War II's warbirds, is gone now, run off to Marietta, Georgia, dragging its corporate toolbox behind it. But the legacy of a small factory hidden away by that big corporation lives on at the airport—the bomber hangar and tiny airport workshops at Burbank's top-secret "Skunk Works," where the Cold War's U-2 spy plane, the Mach 3-plus SR-71 Blackbird, and the F-117 "Stealth" fighter were born. Known officially as the Advanced Development Co., the Skunk Works (named for Al Capp's "Li'l Abner" comic strip) is now in the desert, in Antelope Valley's Palmdale 50 miles to the north. Who knew that Burbank's mild-mannered regional airport had such a mysterious past?

Growing fast between the Golden State and Hollywood Freeways and now officially known as the **Burbank/Pasadena/Glendale Airport,** 818/840-8847, this regional airport is popular with Angelenos, business travelers, and tourists trying to avoid the craziness at LAX. In addition to its multiple commuter services, its major carriers include Alaska, American, Southwest, and United Airlines.

Tinseltown Information

If you find yourself in the general vicinity anyway, Hollywood is a good general stop for Los Angeles visitor information. An outpost of the L.A. visitor bureau, the **Hollywood Visitor Information Center,** 6541 Hollywood Blvd., 213/689-8822, is open Mon.–Sat. 9 A.M.–5 P.M. For information with a strictly local emphasis, and to find out when and where the next star will fall to earth along the Hollywood Walk of Fame, contact: **Hollywood Chamber of Commerce,** 7018 Hollywood Blvd., 323/469-8311. Every month Hollywood's chamber unveils a new Walk of Fame star (typically on the third Wednesday, at noon), making this one of those sure celebrity-spotting bets if you really *must* see a star—and if almost any star will do.

TINSELTOWN NOW: TOURING WEST HOLLYWOOD

The distinction is largely lost on most visitors, but the hippest parts of "Hollywood"—the clubs, the famous bookstores, the best restaurants and hotels for spotting celebrities—are actually in West Hollywood. Affectionately called WeHo by its residents, West Hollywood is part of L.A.'s rather amorphous and affluent "Westside" but still a bit scruffy by Beverly Hills standards. If they're not hiding out in Beverly Hills, Bel-Air, or the Santa Monica area, some of the stars who star on West Hollywood's bold Sunset Strip billboards hang out with other tony industry trendoids in its hotels, power-lunch ghettos, designer shops, and fitness centers.

An unincorporated area of Los Angeles until cityhood was approved in late 1984, West Hollywood elected the nation's first predominantly gay city council—not too surprising since much of the motivation for cityhood grew out of alleged harassment toward the gay community by the Los Angeles Police Department (LAPD). One of the new mayor's first official acts was to ceremoniously remove the newly illegal "Fagots Stay Out" sign that had been hanging over the bar in Barney's Beanery for about 20 years. (In Hollywood mythology Barney's is best known as the place Janis Joplin beaned The Doors' Jim Morrison over the head with a bottle of Southern Comfort.) But West Hollywood's fantasy of becoming a "gay Camelot," which attracted international media attention, was, to a certain extent, delusional. The first disappointment came early, when the city's first mayor resigned after a $7,000 embezzlement conviction—and the city's gay coalition lost its majority on the city council. Soon thereafter the scourge of AIDS decimated the local community of gay activists. Though West Hollywood was among the first cities in the United States to extend health benefits to city employees' "domestic partners," two-thirds of city voters aren't gay.

Shaped cartographically like a handgun pointed due east down Santa Monica Blvd., West Hollywood covers just under two square miles and supports the highest population density of any city west of the Mississippi River. Families with children, the mainstay of most towns, make up a miniscule proportion of West Hollywood's population; about 75 percent of households here are "nonfamily." About 70 percent of residents are renters, which perhaps explains why rent control was also an early city council agenda item.

Show up on Memorial Day weekend for the annual **Chalk It Up** street mural festival, the world's largest, usually held in West Hollywood Park across from the Pacific Design Center. But West Hollywood's biggest and best party occurs on **Halloween,** an official city holiday here (along with Yom Kippur). Other major festivities include

---

COMING ATTRACTIONS: WEST HOLLYWOOD

Centered along L.A.'s famous Sunset Strip, still renowned for its nightlife, West Hollywood boasts a lively street scene during daylight, too, when patrons pack coffeehouses, sidewalk cafés, bookstores, boutiques, and music shops. West Hollywood also teems with movie producers, music and publishing industry people, and agents—not to mention Warner Hollywood Studios, Geffen Records, and the Writers Guild of America West—which helps explain the Strip's two-mile stretch of bold "vanity billboards," some of the most overwhelming, far-out outdoor advertising you'll see anywhere. Other West Hollywood highlights include the monumental Pacific Design Center, its surrounding upscale designer district, and the gay business district along Santa Monica Avenue. West Hollywood's stylish eccentricities also extend east into L.A. along Melrose Avenue, a once cutting-edge cultural destination that's now a notable commercial success. In the nearby Little Muscovy neighborhood, where a large population of Soviet Jews live, is the Schindler House and Studio, one of L.A.'s architectural landmarks.

the two-day **Gay and Lesbian Pride Celebration** (with parade) in June and the **Gay & Lesbian Film & Video Festival** in July.

For information about the city of West Hollywood, contact: **West Hollywood Convention and Visitors Bureau,** 8687 Melrose Ave. (at the Pacific Design Center) in West Hollywood, 310/289-2525.

SUNSET STRIP

From its intersection with poverty downtown near Olvera Street, where the City of Angels was born, Sunset Boulevard winds northwest and then west for almost 25 miles, reaching land's end at the comfortable community of Pacific Palisades. Along the way it connects many of L.A.'s famously segregated social extremes: illegal immigrants begging for work on street corners, teenage runaways trolling for tricks, the wealthy shoppers of Beverly Hills and Bel-Air.

Midway down the Boulevard, in West Hollywood, is Sunset's most historic stretch—the mythic "Sunset Strip," less than two miles long and running along the base of the Hollywood Hills between Crescent Heights Boulevard to the east and Beverly Hills to the west. The Strip was known for its illicit casinos, gangsters, speakeasies, slumming movie stars, and general licentiousness in the 1930s and '40s; its clubs in those days included hot spots such as the Trocadero, Mocambo, and Ciro's. By the 1950s Las Vegas, with more neon and deeper pockets, was siphoning off the Strip's glitzy glamour and biggest talent, but the myth was maintained during the decline by Ed "Kookie" Byrnes and the faux freewheeling *77 Sunset Strip* TV show. In the 1960s flower children, bikers, and straight-ahead rock 'n' roll clubs invaded the Strip. So well established was the Sunset Strip's reputation as a refuge from social norms that it made sense, in the 1970s, when gays began arriving in the general neighborhood—as did former Soviet citizens, then still moving into the fairly new ethnic enclave of Little Muscovy. But the Sunset Strip's final resurrection was financed by migrating music, television, and movie production companies and the upscale amenities they attracted.

These days the Strip's club scene is strong once again. Venerable venues such as the **Troubador,** the **Roxy,** and **Whisky A Go Go** still pack in the crowds, along with relative newcomers such as the **House of Blues,** a link in the Dan Akroyd–related chain, and Johnny Depp's **Viper Room.**

If you're not clubbin' it, consider strollin' it, especially easy to manage with a little help from West Hollywood's public **Sunset Shuttle,** 310/858-8000. As you drive east to west into the sea of celebrity faces magnified by vanity billboards—one-of-a-kind image enhancements masquerading as the pinnacle of Hollywood success—attractions include the 1927 **Château Marmont,** 8221 Sunset, famous "hideout" hotel for stumped screenwriters and movie stars. Errol Flynn, Greta Garbo, Jean Harlow, even Howard Hughes first made the place famous, though it is now somewhat infamous as the site of comedian John Belushi's death by drug overdose. Other notable hotels include the striking art deco **Argyle,** 8358 Sunset, the onetime St. James's Club private hotel and men's club known to Raymond Chandler fans as the Sunset Towers; the exclusive and hip **Sunset Marquis** just off Sunset at 1200 N. Alta Loma, popular with rock stars only in part because of the private recording studio; and **Wyndham Bel Age,** 1020 N. San Vicente.

Known more for its nightclubs, restaurants, and hotels, the Sunset Strip isn't so famous as a shopping destination. A few of particular interest in the neighborhood: **Book Soup,** 8818 Sunset Blvd. (between Laraby and Horn), 310/659-3110, a venerable locally owned L.A. bookstore and bistro specializing in literature and books on the entertainment industry, also famous for its international magazine and newspaper selection (and a best bet for book signings and celebrity spotting, some say); **Tower Records,** across the street at 8801 Sunset, popular PR venue for music celebs promoting new products (for classical music and videos, head for the annex across the street); and the **Virgin Megastore,** just beyond the Strip at 8000 Sunset (in Crescent Heights), 323/650-8666, where Hollywood's historic old Schwab's Drugstore once stood.

AISLINN RACE

Buyers will find more than 200 top designer showrooms in 1.25 million square feet at the Pacific Design Center.

PACIFIC DESIGN CENTER

Despite apparently antithetical politics, West Hollywood is the place people from Beverly Hills and Bel-Air go to shop, dine, and otherwise divert themselves—a perfect locale for L.A.'s design district, the largest concentration of stylish showrooms in the country outside New York City. At its heart is the Pacific Design Center (PDC), a glossy beast affectionately known as the Blue Whale, with its colored-glass sidekick, the Green Hornet. (The third creature in the series—the red one, perhaps destined to be the Red Fox, Red Snapper, or Red-Tailed Hawk—has yet to be born. Or hatched.) Surrounded by a triangle of style-slick streets—La Cienega, Santa Monica, and Beverly Boulevards—the PDC boasts more than 200 top designer showrooms and 1.25 million square feet of spacious style. Once proudly aloof, exclusive, and open only to the trade, in recent years even the PDC has felt some pressure to open its doors to the bourgeoisie (and "discounted markup" retail sales). The result? A PDC somewhat friendlier to the more ordinary affluent and still trying to get in step with at-large L.A. The change hasn't revolutionized showroom admissions policies, but it is reflected in the overall atmosphere, with public exhibits, events, and tours now offered in addition to people-friendly businesses such as cappuccino bars and cafés.

Most furnishings, fabrics, and art available at the PDC's private showrooms are for sale only to "the trade" (professional interior designers), though some shops do welcome interested amateurs for both browsing and buying. To get some idea of who has what and where it might be, public PDC tours are offered (weekdays at 10 A.M., at last report, arranged through the concierge). For more information, contact the Pacific Design Center, 8687 Melrose Ave. (at San Vicente Blvd.), 310/657-0800. For extra help, shops such as **L.A. Design Concepts,** 8811 Alden Dr., 310/276-2109, can negotiate purchases at PDC trade-only outlets for about 15 percent above list price.

Near the Pacific Design Center

If touring the PDC seems less than exciting, then tour the neighborhood. From the Whale and Hornet, "avenues of design" fan out in all directions. Both Robertson and La Cienega are famous for their art galleries and showrooms. Quite pleasant for window shopping is Robertson between Beverly Boulevard and Melrose—particularly appealing for an after-dinner stroll, when window displays shine forth.

Heading south on Robertson you'll find even more attractions—including marvelous **Storyopolis,** 116 N. Robertson Blvd., Plaza A (across from The Ivy restaurant), 310/358-2500 or toll-free 800/958-2537, just the place to take the kids if they tire of the usual tourism grind. Storyopolis is a multimedia event with a storytelling emphasis—a combination kid's bookstore, entertainment service, and art gallery featuring illustrations by folks such as Maurice Sendak and Sara Midda. The bookshop part, with more than 5,000 children's books, is spacious and relaxed, with comfy chairs—even a computer for consuming stories on CD-ROM. Book signings here are more like story time, usually featuring prominent authors of children's literature reading their own work. And once a month there's a craft and storytelling hour (fee). Other bookstores are big in the neighborhood, too, some of the best including **The Cook's Library,** 8373 W. Third St. (between Orlando and King's Rd.), 323/655-3141, and the **Traveler's Bookcase** next door at 8375 W. Third, 323/655-0575.

Just south of the city limits, on San Vicente, is the bustling **Beverly Center,** with its mainstream mall shopping, 200 more specialized shops, and **Hard Rock Café.** Nearby, at 330 S. La Cienega, is a **Borders Books and Music,** 310/659-4045.

In the same general vicinity and always popular—reportedly a favorite of entertainer Dolly Parton—is **Trashy Lingerie,** 402 N. La Cienega, 310/652-4543. For more trashy lingerie, leather, high-end European and designer fashions, and other miscellaneous galleries, shops, clubs, and restaurants, there's also Melrose.

MELROSE AVENUE AND AROUND

Melrose Avenue is très L.A. Imagine Venice Beach with a generous trust fund. Or Hollywood if it were backed up by a Beverly Hills bank account—casual and cheeky but unbelievably costly. Fashionably cheap. That's Melrose Avenue. This eclectic and entertaining neighborhood is prime time for people watching. Coffeehouses, restaurants, and clubs abound. Shops sell antiques, used books, and vintage clothes, high-end arts, homewares, and L.A.-designer wear. Melrose seems too successful, too self-consciously cool, to be truly avant garde. But in L.A. one truth doesn't necessarily cancel out another. Judge for yourself.

To "do Melrose" right, wear good walking shoes and otherwise prepare to explore. Melrose Avenue is prominent in West Hollywood

proper and extends east to Silver Lake, but "real Melrose" traditionally covers the distance between N. La Brea and Fairfax Avenues. This hipster heaven extends its reach all the time—to several blocks west of Crescent Heights Boulevard, for example, and to the east as well—but what most people consider coolest are the 7200–7700 addresses, the nine-block stretch between Alta Vista Boulevard and Spaulding Avenue.

Whatever its actual boundaries, Melrose Avenue made a name for itself by attracting people with purple hair, pierced body parts, and a passion for antifashion fashion. But these days, especially on weekends, the first and original Melrosians are outnumbered by throngs of trendy shoppers and tourists with excess cash, everyone hunting the same thing—radical recycled clothing, leather wear, and arty, high-concept accessories hiding out in the endlessly colorful "see me" shops.

The emphasis at **Retail Slut** 7308 Melrose, 323/934-1339, is vivid fashion for the young and the young at heart, from body-hugging knits to bold non-wallflower floral prints. The motto is: "If you don't know what it is, go ask your big sister." Another Melrose standout is **Fred Segal,** 8118 Melrose, 323/651-1935, a trendy mini-department store and purveyor of very chic high-end merchandise arranged as a series of boutiques. Prices are high, but once a year look for Fred Segal's half-off blowout sale. (Snob alert: If you aren't famous or rich, as many clients here are, or capable of generating that illusion, salespeople may ignore you.) More welcoming Melrose shops include **Aardvark's Odd Ark,** 7579 Melrose (at Carson), 323/655-6769, a recycled clothing store of long standing, just the place for finding the perfectly pitched loud Hawaiian shirt and 1950s' bowling attire, and **Maya Jewelry,** 7452 Melrose (at Vista), for an unbelievable selection of unusual yet affordable earrings and other items.

Though **l.a. eyeworks,** 7407 Melrose, 323/653-8255, is clearly cutting edge—cool enough to lowercase itself—here eyeglasses, including Southern California's ubiquitous sunglasses, are elevated to conceptual art with international appeal. High quality, higher prices.

For "antiques and weird stuff" try **Off the Wall,** 7325 Melrose, 323/930-1185, an assortment of cool finds like life-sized plastic cows and egg chairs. Always popular, too, is the **Wound and Wound Toy Co.,** 7374 Melrose, 323/653-6703, with a wonderful collection of—you guessed it—wind-up toys, music boxes, and more.

Just off the trodden tourist path is the **Out of the Closet Thrift Store,** 360 N. Fairfax Ave. (between Beverly Blvd. and Melrose), 323/934-1956, and at least a half-dozen other L.A. locations. Los Angeles has thrift stores all over town. But Out of the Closet is a thrift store with a conscience, since proceeds support both the medical and hospice care programs of the AIDS Healthcare Foundation. Just about everything you can imagine buying is available here—clothes and accessories, CDs, TVs, appliances, and used furniture—and just about anything you no longer need is accepted as a tax-deductible contribution.

A fairly famous avenue resident is farther "uptown" on Melrose—**The Bodhi Tree** bookstore, 8585 Melrose, 310/659-1733, where actress Shirley MacLaine began her literary path to spiritual enlightenment among the New Age meditation, psychology, astrology, and music books.

Being a public thoroughfare Melrose Avenue is always "open," though some of the more out-there Melrose neighborhoods are downright unappealing and/or unsafe after dark. Should you arrive on a Sunday before the shops open, stop off at the **Melrose Weekend Market** at Fairfax High School (on the corner of Melrose and Fairfax), for flea market finds including vintage 1940s-style Hawaiian shirts, California pottery, and cool records. This one has food and music too. Open 9 A.M.–5 P.M., small admission fee.

SCHINDLER HOUSE AND STUDIO

West Hollywood's only notable noncommercial attraction, this world-renowned modernist monument was designed by architect and Austrian immigrant Rudolf Schindler—a disciple of Frank Lloyd Wright—and built in 1921. And thanks to the largesse of Vienna's Museumangewandtekunst (MAK), or Museum of Applied Arts, the house has been renovated and preserved as a study center for experimental architecture. For all his brilliance, Rudolf Schindler was largely unappreciated—and underemployed—by Los Angeles. Most of his modest work can be seen in and around Silver Lake.

Inspired by the idea of airy North African desert camps, Rudolf Schindler built this radically modern two-family home at very low cost, using concrete, redwood, canvas walls, and floor-to-ceiling glass. The shared kitchen at the center served as the "pin" from which the minimalist pinwheel design spun outward into the outdoors. An Arts and Crafts innovation—sleeping porches—here evolved into open-air "baskets" on the roof. Revolutionary in construction as well as concept, Schindler's innovations included bare slab-tilt concrete wall panels and individual indoor "studios" in lieu of conventional living and dining rooms; the "living rooms," complete with fireplace, were outdoors.

The Schindler House and Studio, now open under the auspices of the MAK Center for Art and Architecture, is north of Melrose Ave. at 835 N. Kings Rd., 323/651-1510, www.makcenter .com, and open to the public Wed.–Sun. 11 A.M.–6 P.M., $5 admission. Guided tours are available Saturday and Sunday at 11:30 A.M. and at 12:30, 1:30, and 2:30 P.M.

PRACTICAL WEST HOLLYWOOD

STAYING IN WEST HOLLYWOOD

Travelers looking to save money while looking here for L.A. design, art, and style trends may find better accommodations deals in Beverly Hills, believe it or not. But it's not true that only rock stars or music and movie execs can afford to stay in West Hollywood.

Consider the very nice **Best Western Sunset Plaza Hotel** at 8400 Sunset Blvd., 323/654-0750, 323/656-4158, or toll-free 800/252-0645 in California, 800/421-3652 in the United States and Canada. Also a motel, the Sunset Plaza offers some apartment-style kitchen units. Plus it's within a crawdad's throw of the House of Blues, and boasts a heated swimming pool. Rooms and suites go for $135–$225.

Another reasonably priced option—by local standards—is the **Ramada Plaza Hotel** (formerly the Ramada West Hollywood), 8585 Santa Monica Blvd. (just west of La Cienega), 310/652-6400 or toll-free 800/845-8585. The place is right in step with the rest of West Hollywood too (if you were worried), with even the postmodern exterior screaming "Hey, we're in style!" The futuristic sensibility travels from lobby into the guest rooms—the two-story "lofts" are coolest—without letting on that this is actually a stylish reincarnation of Hollywood's infamous Tropicana Motel, long beloved by degenerate rockers and L.A.'s artistic intelligentsia. Now that everything's spiffed up, expect to pay $145 and up for rooms, and $225 and up for suites. You'll find an affiliated fitness center across the street and an on-site food court—grab Starbucks coffee or a smoothie and fresh bagels or eggrolls to go—but don't forget that many of L.A.'s great restaurants are just a stroll away.

Good value is what you get at pleasant three-story **Grafton on Sunset,** a three-story boutique hotel just east of La Cienega at 8462 Sunset Blvd., 323/654-6470, which offers a galaxy of executive perks like VIP access to area clubs, same day laundry and dry cleaning service, and an outdoor Mediterranean garden. Rooms are $135–$175, while suites start at $200.

Otherwise, inquire about lower weekend rates and seasonal special packages at pricier places.

Château Marmont

All but out-shouted by the billboards and general chaos of the Sunset Strip, this serene French Normandy "château" has been famous as a haven for Hollywood celebrities since it first opened in 1929. Once a residential castle for the likes of Errol Flynn, Greta Garbo, and Jean Harlow, and the place studios sent writers to "hole up" to finish movie scripts, in more recent years the Château Marmont gained unwelcome notoriety as the place John Belushi met his maker while on speedballs, that toxic concoction of cocaine and heroin. Still the best Hollywood-area choice for absolute privacy, and still a popular celebrity hideout, the Château Marmont specializes in reclusive luxury. The most coveted, and more expensive, are the bungalows near the pool. Child care, complimentary cell phones, full fitness center, and room service are available, though the understated dining room and **Bar Marmont** offer real Hollywood atmosphere. Rooms are $220–$280, suites start at $335. For information and reservations, contact: Château Marmont, 8221 W. Sunset Blvd., 323/656-1010, or toll-free 800/242-8328.

The Argyle

Until fairly recently the private St. James's Club, a British expatriate refuge renovated and refurbished in grand style in the 1980s at a cost of over $40 million, the Argyle is a 1931 art deco masterpiece now listed on the National Register of Historic Places—but it's a destination better known to mystery fans, and to Raymond Chandler's literary private eye, Philip Marlowe, as the **Sunset Towers.** Though rooms are a tad small by contemporary standards, they are stunning, with handcrafted Italian furniture (some feature gondola beds) and endless deco details. The Argyle includes all the usual comforts and deluxe amenities—including in-room safes and fax hookups and a spectacular rooftop pool, outdoor lounge, and spa/fitness center. And what views! Up here on top of the Hollywood world you can pretend to be a Hollywood player, which may explain why the Argyle starred in the film version of *The Player,* that slightly cynical Hollywood morality tale. Other main attractions: the hotel's Hollywood portrait collection, a wonderful book and video library (including all films ever shot here, quite a list), and the celebrated California-style French restaurant **fenix**. Its phonetically correct yet modest lower-cased presentation belies its reputation—and its classy Old Hollywood supper-club style. Expect to shell out $220–$270 for a room, $300 and up for a suite.

For more information, contact: The Argyle, 8358 Sunset Blvd., 323/654-7100 or toll-free 800/225-2637 for reservations; www.argylehotel.com.

Hotel Mondrian

Los Angeles is abuzz over the Mondrian all over again since a makeover by owner Ian Schrager (formerly of New York's Studio 54) and owner of New York's Royalton. The wildly playful exterior paint job, echoing namesake painter Piet Mondrian's geometric work, is long gone. Can a name change be far behind? The hotel's new stark sensibility was imported to Hollywood by French architect Philippe Starck; the result is self-consciously stylish and theatrical, the new Mondrian something of an outsiders' stagey reinterpretation of Hollywood's mythic see-and-be-seen scene. Enamored critics have lent the new Mondrian subtitles such as "Hotel Surreal," for its intentional distortions of scale—five-foot clay pots dwarf the outdoor dining area and free-standing 30-foot-tall "doors" marking the entrance also make visitors seem small—and its semi-futuristic obsession with white, light, and cool exhibitionistic *space.* Less laudatory reviews take a more Orwellian turn, pointing to the Mondrian's very un-Hollywood absence of excess and its scary sign-speak ("dream" over the beds, "think" by the desks, "health" at the exercise facilities, "pleasure" at the gift shop). The swimming pool—actually the "Water Salon"—is designed for lounging around, not swimming; there's even an underwater sound system.

In short, this is not Tinseltown's idea of itself, not the kind of place Hollywood types would choose to unwind. But corporate types like it—and the Mondrian *is* right across the street from the House of Blues, itself a hip and high-concept outsiders' reinterpretation of a tin-roofed shack in the Louisiana bayou—so it fits right into the neighborhood, a happening corner of the Sunset Strip. Rooms here are surprisingly inviting, with eat-in kitchens (harking back to its original incarnation as an apartment building) and all the comforts served up with some spectacular city views. The Sky Bar here is the ultimate see-and-be-seen scene. Rooms start at $240, and suites go all the way up to $2,600. For more information and reservations, contact: Mondrian Hotel, 8440 Sunset Blvd., 323/650-8999 or toll-free 800/525-8029; www.mondrianhotel.com.

Sunset Marquis Hotel and Villas

This is where aging rock stars, sundry celebrities and pseudo celebs, music and movie industry execs, and other "real Hollywood" people stay, along with anyone else who can afford the freight. Just off the Sunset Strip in a quiet residential neighborhood, this onetime apartment building and surrounding "villas" (a collection of onetime bungalows and homes) offer peace and privacy with California-style Mediterranean charm in both suites and villas, mixed up here and there with '60s style. There's a $600,000 in-house recording studio here too. The grounds have a flowing grace, with abundant greenery and exotic birds, swimming pools, sauna and health spa, hot tub, a koi pond, waterfall, and outdoor café, but the real sightseeing takes place in the **Whiskey Bar,** *the* star-watching watering hole. Suites start at $305, villas at $600.

For more information, contact: Sunset Marquis Hotel and Villas, 1200 N. Alta Loma Rd., 310/657-1333, or toll-free 800/858-9758.

Wyndham Bel Age Hotel

Another onetime West Hollywood apartment building transformed into an elegant all-suites hotel, the recently renovated Bel Age just off the Sunset Strip is French provincial in style, classical in attitude—with carefully appointed suites, classical music, classy international fine art, and exquisite French-Russian fare in the acclaimed on-site **Diaghilev** restaurant here. For classic jazz and more casual continental fare, head to the hotel's **Club Brasserie**. Up on the roof you'll find a pool, garden, and hot tub. Suites are $240–$500. For more information, contact: Wyndham

Bel Age Hotel, 1020 N. San Vicente Blvd., 310/854-1111. For reservations, in the U.S. and Canada call toll-free 800/996-3426.

"Le" Hotels

At one time six West Hollywood hotels sported "Le" in their titles to identify them as intimate upscale siblings of the L'Ermitage Hotel Group, onetime apartment buildings in quiet residential areas refashioned into elite retreats. Le Bel Age Hotel de Grande Classe is now a Wyndham hotel (see above), Le Mondrian Hotel de Grande Classe is now the Mondrian Hotel (see above), and Le Dufy is now a sophisticated Summerfield Suites (see below). Not usually inexpensive, these business-oriented hotels *can* be great bargains—with rates as low as $99—during the November-December holiday season and at other "off" business times.

The recently renovated all-suites **Le Montrose** (originally Le Valadon) near Beverly Hills, just south of Sunset Boulevard and east of Doheny at 900 Hammond St. (at Cynthia), 310/855-1115 or toll-free 800/776-0666, www.lemontrose.com, offers art-nouveau ambience, ample comforts, extras such as mountain bikes and maps for neighborhood touring. Suites are $290–$460. Nearby is four-story **Le Rêve**, 8822 Cynthia St. (at Larrabe), 310/854-1114 or toll-free 800/835-7997, with country French demi-suites, junior suites, and executive suites, stunning rooftop "view" pool, and spa. Suites are $139–$265. Also popular with entertainment industry execs is the all-suites **Le Parc**, 733 Westknoll Dr., 310/855-8888 or toll-free 800/578-4837, www.leparcsuites.com, where each suite features a sunken living room, fireplace, kitchenette, wetbar, and separate bedrooms. Also here: a guests-only restaurant, tennis court (up on the roof), basketball hoops, workout room, pool, spa, and sundeck. Suites are $300–$400.

Sophisticated, recently renovated **Summerfield Suites Hotel,** formerly Le Dufy, 1000 Westmount Dr. (south of Sunset Blvd. near La Cienega and Santa Monica), 310/657-7400 or toll-free 800/833-4353, no longer features that French Impressionist air. Understated contemporary style is accompanied by sunken living rooms, fireplaces, and kitchens or kitchenettes. Heated pool. Rates are $258–$315.

Facing the Beverly Center at the edge of West Hollywood proper is the ten-story California-style country French **Hotel Sofitel,** formerly Ma Maison Sofitel, 8555 Beverly Blvd., 310/278-5444, or toll-free 800/521-7772, www.sofitel.com, with pool, workout, and spa facilities, casual café, nice restaurant, every other imaginable amenity. Rack rates are $349–$795, but inquire about specials.

EATING IN WEST HOLLYWOOD

West Hollywood is a must-do destination for dedicated international foodies—a mythic L.A. restaurant locale. Long-running local restaurant celebrities include see-and-be-seen icons such as Diaghilev, Eclipse, fenix at the Argyle, and The Ivy. And L'Orangerie. And Morton's. You get the idea. In and around West Hollywood famous and/or great restaurants outnumber parking spaces. At the hippest of the hip places, sometimes the stars and star-makers outnumber parking spaces.

WeHo People's Eats

West Hollywood's most famous diner these days is scruffy **Barney's Beanery,** 8447 Santa Monica Blvd. (one block east of La Cienega), 323/654-2287, infamous for its "celebrities out slumming" associations. Barney's offers a vast array of burgers and hot dogs, sandwiches, and omelettes, but most people come to play pool and to sample the impressive beer selection.

Cowboys and cowgirls are back in style at the countrified **Saddle Ranch Chop House,** 8371 Sunset Blvd., 323/822-3850, a nightclub and restaurant with an awesome mechanical bull. Munch on a plate of ribs or a hamburger, or order from the late night menu until 1:15 A.M. The bar is an interesting place to stop for a soda or a shot of whisky from a boot-shaped glass (the latter recommended if you'll be riding the bull later). The restaurant is usually packed.

Other popular and reasonably low-rent restaurants in West Hollywood include long-running **Jacopo's,** 8166 Sunset Blvd., 323/650-8128, which makes a good New York-style pizza (and delivers); **Poquito Más** for Mexican, 8555 Sunset Blvd. (at La Cienega), 310/652-7008; and that "vernacular architecture" L.A. landmark **Tail

o' the Pup, 329 N. San Vicente Blvd., 310/652-4517, for hot dogs and such.

Rockin' Restaurants
It must confuse the tourists, what with the Hard Rock Café near soft-rock Beverly Hills in de facto West Hollywood and Planet Hollywood actually in Beverly Hills. But people find the way nonetheless. The **Hard Rock Café** at the Beverly Center, 8600 Beverly Blvd. (at La Cienega), 310/276-7605, is an entertaining and loud place to take the kids, but only if you don't mind paying almost $10 for a burger—not to mention the cost of T-shirts, the local signature Hard Rock lapel pin, and other tie-in merchandise. The hard-driving rock 'n' roll is the real draw, plus the wacky memorabilia and theme decor. The museum-quality exhibits here and elsewhere around the globe inspired Andy Warhol to call the Hard Rock the "Smithsonian of Rock 'n' Roll"; movie memorabilia rounds out the displays. The Hard Rock Café uses no food additives, preservatives, or polystyrene and recycles everything else—including leftover food, which is donated to local homeless charities. It's open daily 11:30 A.M.–midnight, until 12:30 A.M. on Friday and Saturday nights, and closed Thanksgiving and Christmas. In Southern California, there's another Hard Rock in Newport Beach, yet another in Universal City.

The rusty old tin shack just up the hill from Sunset Boulevard isn't typical in L.A., at least not in West Hollywood. But once you've valet-parked the car at the **House of Blues,** 8439 Sunset Blvd. (one block east of La Cienega), 323/848-5100, pretend you've stepped off into the bayou—whatever gets you in the mood for blues, bluesy rock, jazz, gospel, reggae, zydeco, and more. The Tinseltown link in the chain forged by Hard Rock founder Isaac Tigrett and "Blues Brother" Dan Ackroyd, Hollywood's House of Blues also serves "international peasant fare" at lunch, dinner, and Sunday brunch—Southern fried catfish, down-home barbecue, wood-fired peasant pizza, even Indian and Thai fare. For dessert, try the bourbon bread pudding.

Especially at dinner and at the immensely popular Sunday Gospel Brunch, reserving a table is the best way to get good seats. Nightly show times vary, depending on single or double billings and/or early and late shows. The high-energy gospel brunch (reservations required) is scheduled on Sundays and features fried catfish nuggets, smoked chicken with andouille potato hash, and cornbread. Call ahead for show times.

Like the Hard Rock Café, the House of Blues exists for a higher purpose than just making beaucoup bucks from its clubs and tours and related sales of art, books, music, clothing, and gift items. Its motto—"On a Mission from God"—refers in part to the nonprofit House of Blues Foundation, dedicated to promoting racial harmony and furthering both multicultural and music education.

Casual Café Fare
Where to go near Beverly Hills and West Hollywood that's not celebrated, celebrity-hyped, and hyper-expensive? One place is **Kings Road Cafe,** 8361 Beverly Blvd. (at Kings Rd.), 323/655-9044. Tasty thin-crust pizzas and simple pastas are mainstays at this Italian-style café, but breakfast is also quite imaginative—at least 10 different egg dishes, such as eggs baked with goat cheese (served with toast made from house-baked bread) plus potato selections, oatmeal, risotto, scones and pastries, even fresh fruit. And the menu here keeps expanding, now that Kings Road has a full kitchen. It's open daily for breakfast, lunch, and dinner, closed major holidays.

The bustling sidewalk café credited with starting L.A.'s dim sum craze is **Chin Chin,** 8618 Sunset Blvd. (near La Cienega), 310/652-1818. It's open for lunch and dinner daily, late supper on weekends.

Best bet for an imaginary and affordable trip to the Left Bank is **Le Petit Bistro,** 631 N. La Cienega (one block north of Melrose), 310/289-9797, where the simple fare—dishes such as roast chicken or eggplant and tomato tarts—is quite popular with people actually *from* France. It's open for lunch on weekdays only, for dinner nightly. Fancier, pricier, but also quite fun: the internationalist and romantic **Café La Bohème,** 8400 Santa Monica Blvd. (at Orlando), 323/848-2360. For Asian-French in the same price range, amazingly popular these days is relative newcomer **Jozu,** 8360 Melrose Ave. (at King's Rd.), 323/655-5600, serving such things as sautéed scallops with green curry sauce and crab-shrimp cakes with green papaya salad. Complimentary sake is served.

As elsewhere across America, the people's place to savor Wolfgang Puck's signature wood-fired pizzas and such is at the local **Wolfgang Puck Café,** 8000 Sunset Blvd. (near Crescent Heights), 323/650-7300.

More West Hollywood Fun
Long popular with the local gay crowd is the festive and hip **Marix Tex Mex Cafe,** 1108 N. Las Flores Drive (at Santa Monica), 323/656-8800, known for its killer margaritas, superb fajitas, New Mexico-style chimichangas, chalupas, and chilaquiles. There's always a wait here, at lunch, dinner, or weekend brunch. There's another Marix near the beach in Santa Monica, but you'll wait there, too.

The Palm, 9001 Santa Monica Blvd. (between Robertson and Doheny), 310/550-8811, is a pricey California branch of the New York surf and turf joint. The sometimes boisterous men's club sensibility here is punctuated, on the walls, with caricatures of the famous and infamous who have enjoyed the Palm's huge steaks (with cottage fries), gigantic lobsters, and Maryland crab. Noted for noise, rude waiters, and an industry clientele.

For something considerably more romantic at dinner, try the often overlooked old **Trocadero,** 8280 Sunset Blvd. (near Harper), 323/656-7161, an emblem of Hollywood's Golden Age all jazzed up into an art deco beauty boasting both California cuisine and big band sounds. Or try quite reasonable **Talesai,** 9043 Sunset Blvd. (at Doheny), 310/275-9724, for elegant, upscale Thai conveniently close to the clubs. One of L.A.'s best.

Celebrity-Spotting Hot Spots
Regular folks can get short shrift at **The Ivy,** 113 N. Robertson Blvd. (between Third and Beverly), 310/274-8303, a popular spotlight-on-the-celebrities spot serving a West Hollywood version of American Cajun and Creole fare. It all seems casual enough—down to the intentionally tired upholstery—but appearances can be deceiving. "Power tables" are out on the garden patio and inside next to the fireplace. Once you turn your attention to the food here, you'll appre-

ciate that the crab cakes, Caesar salads, and Cajun prime rib generally get rave reviews.

Social centerpiece of Hollywood power-brokers is **Morton's,** a grown-up's star venue brought to you by Hard Rock Café cofounder Peter Morton. Now in minimalist digs at 8764 Melrose Ave. (at Robertson), 310/276-5205, Morton's showcases Hollywood ego-size T-bone steaks along with grilled veal chops, lamb, and swordfish and such. And Morton's famous lime-grilled chicken. It's open for lunch weekdays, for dinner every night but Sunday. On Monday nights, the stars really shine.

At **Ago,** 8478 Melrose Ave., (at La Cienega), 323/655-6333, the owners—Robert De Niro, Tony and Ridley Scott, and Harvey and Bob Weinstein—are Hollywood stars of equal stature with the celebrity clientele. With help from restaurateur Agostino "Ago" Scinadri, here Hollywood serves up incredibly authentic Italian, and with none of the usual industry snobbery. This popular and not-too-pricey hot spot is beloved for its fine food, friendly service (no matter who you are), and lovely decor.

Other spots to spot at least the occasional star, star-to-be, or star wannabe include the swank French-Chinese **Chaya Brasserie,** 8741 Alden Dr. (near Robertson), 310/859-8833; the French-Vietnamese **Le Colonial,** 8783 Beverly Blvd. (at Robertson), 310/289-0660; the Italian **Madeo,** 8897 Beverly Blvd. (near Doheny), 310/859-4903; **Pane e Vino,** 8265 Beverly (at Switzer), 323/651-4600; and the inventive Chinese **Yujean Kang's,** sibling to Pasadena's acclaimed same, 8826 Melrose Ave. (between Robertson and Doheny), 310/288-0806.

Fine Dining with or without Celebrities
Now back in the hands of original owners Gerard and Virginie Ferry, **L'Orangerie,** 903 N. La Cienega Blvd. (between Melrose and Santa Monica), 310/652-9770, is more than maintaining its reputation as one of L.A.'s best for French nouvelle cuisine—and as L.A.'s most romantic dining destination. The baby vegetable stew is always a hit. Like taking a quick trip to Versailles, L'Orangerie is very chic and très expensive. It's open Tues.–Fri. for lunch—power-lunching, usually—and Mon.–Sat. for dinner.

Le Chardonnay, 8284 Melrose Ave. (at Switzer), 323/655-8880, is also one of L.A.'s renowned beauties, a two-level art-nouveau dining room with mirrored walls, carved rosewood, and etched glass. Reflections from the glassed-in rotisserie make everything glow at this California-style French bistro—including the patrons. And they really light up when the food arrives, be it the grilled half-chicken with crispy pommes frites or Louisiana crab cakes. It's open weekdays only for lunch, Mon.–Sat. for dinner.

Named after Sergey Diaghilev, the 1920s Ballets Russes impressario, very elegant, very expensive dinner-only **Diaghilev** at the Wyndham Bel Age Hotel, 1020 N. San Vicente Blvd. (at Sunset), 310/854-1111, serves almost nou-velle Franco-Russian romance in grand style—with cozy loveseat-style seating, long-stemmed roses, and balalaika performances, caviar, flavored vodka cocktails, and chicken Kiev. And venison shish kebab. And tournedos Igor Stravinsky. And hazelnut-chestnut cake.

Formerly of the former La Toque, chef Ken Frank seems to have found a fitting new home for his inspired California cuisine at the Argyle's art-deco **fenix at the Argyle,** 8358 Sunset Blvd. (near La Cienega), 323/654-7100, where the stars include seafood, fish, and steak with a Jack Daniels and pepper sauce. It's open Mon.–Sat. for breakfast, lunch, and dinner, for brunch on Sunday.

BEYOND HOLLYWOOD: TOURING THE VALLEY

Though the third wave of Southern California cinema seems destined to wash ashore near the Pacific Ocean on L.A.'s Westside, the San Fernando Valley is the present-day destination of Hollywood the idea. This is where most of Southern California's movie and television studios came, after all, when they abandoned Hollywood the place—to Burbank, Glendale, San Fernando, and a sea of stucco, shopping malls, and superheated summer smog.

Few people, even Angelenos, think of the Valley as "Los Angeles," but it is. It's been the entire suburban sector of the city since William Mulholland's earliest water engineering feats. This is where the modern concept of suburbia began, in fact, with swarms of affordable government-subsidized housing developments constructed here and in Long Island's Nassau County to meet post–World War II demand. The concept of suburbia as middle-class escape from urban ills may end here, too, since subsequent decades have witnessed high-rises, ethnic and social segregation (gated communities and homelessness), along with increasingly extreme income disparities, pollution, and gridlock. By all reasonable modern measures, the San Fernando Valley is now a city—a crazy-quilt patchwork of cities and citylike communities—boasting 45 percent of L.A.'s land area and one-third of its population. If it were one unified city, politically speaking, it would be the second largest in the state.

Valley culture has been widely characterized, even locally, by Frank and Moon Unit Zappa's satirical 1982 "Valley Girl"—an ode to suburban shopping-mall speak in general, "Like, fer sure, totally," and to the Sherman Oaks Galleria in particular—but such white-bread social stereotypes no longer fit the San Fernando Valley. So it should come as no surprise that in 1999 the Galleria itself closed up shop for an ambitious two-year renovation that transformed the media-hyped mother of all malls into an office complex with movie theaters and sit-down restaurants. With the Sherman Oaks Galleria essentially gone for good, Valley culture is increasingly defined by the Latino, Asian, and other ethnic and immigrant populations, largely shoehorned into "inner city areas," which make up half the population. Regional cultural events include Glendale's annual only-in-L.A. **Blessing of the Cars,** during which a local priest anoints cars and prays for the safety of their drivers, and the equally unusual **Love Ride** motorcycle party, an annual muscular dystrophy benefit attracting more than 20,000 bikers. Much tamer: the very down-home **Grana-**

da Hills Christmas Parade down Chatsworth Street. A bit more high-brow: the prestigious Padua Hills Playwrights Festival and Workshop.

Distanced from downtown L.A. politics and disaffected by overburdened schools, stand-still freeways, and other inadequate services, the San Fernando Valley loudly threatens secession. How that would work is a mystery, since L.A.'s Department of Water and Power controls the water, lifeblood of Southern California's seemingly endless growth. But in the wake of the 1994 Northridge earthquake centered here—the most destructive urban quake in U.S. history—reconstruction, recovery, and retrofitting, not water, are primary local political concerns.

UNIVERSAL STUDIOS HOLLYWOOD

The third most popular tourist attraction in the United States, trailing only Disneyland and Disney World, Universal Studios Hollywood does have a certain universal appeal. This is especially true if visitors seek the abbreviated version of Hollywood and its historic impact—a family-friendly theme park focused on Hollywood themes. Universal Studios is also a genuine studio, however, established in 1915 by Carl Laemmle at this onetime chicken ranch. In the days before the "talkies," Laemmle let the public in to watch—cheering and jeering from nearby bleachers—and profited from it by charging a quarter admission and selling fresh eggs at all

COMING ATTRACTIONS: THE VALLEY

When the San Fernando Valley voted to include itself within the city of Los Angeles in 1915, only Burbank, Glendale, and San Fernando on the valley's east side held back. Burbank gained dubious national fame as the "beautiful downtown Burbank" of comedian Johnny Carson and Rowan and Martin's *Laugh-In* but has certainly had the last laugh since establishing itself as the nation's new entertainment industry headquarters. Beyond the TV and movie studios, Burbank boasts the most historic Bob's Big Boy drive-in, though the famous fast-food chain was founded next door, in Glendale. Long known for its jacaranda trees, Ozzie Nelson–style family values, and occasional outbreaks of Ku Klux Klan activity, Glendale is most famous, internationally, for its Forest Lawn Memorial Park, in the words of founder Dr. Hubert L. Eaton "as unlike other cemeteries as sunshine is like darkness, as eternal life is unlike death."

East toward the San Gabriel Valley and Pasadena lies the fairly isolated community of Eagle Rock. Adjacent to Glendale but north are Sun Valley, San Fernando, and Sylmar, neighborhoods historically considered the "rust belt" surrounding Burbank and Van Nuys, where General Motors and Lockheed once ruled the valley's economy. Van Nuys also boasts the last surviving outdoor movie theater in the San Fernando Valley: Pacific's Van Nuys Drive-In. Surprisingly lovely for a sewage treatment plant is the six-acre Japanese Garden at the Donald C. Tillman Water Reclamation Plant in Van Nuys,

where a healthy population of gnats, mosquitoes, and dragonflies now attracts some of the swallows that are supposed to return to Mission San Juan Capistrano in spring.

Rather than touring the valley's first towns, most visitors stop first at Universal City and its Universal Studios Hollywood theme park—L.A. County's most popular attraction. Next door is North Hollywood, along with Van Nuys considered the core of the urbanized San Fernando Valley's "inner city." Yet North Hollywood is also home to the trendifying NoHo Arts District and big-time urban renewal, given the arrival of the city's Metrorail. North Hollywood also features the longest mural in the world—the 2,435-foot-long Great Wall of Los Angeles (on Coldwater Canyon Blvd. between Oxnard St. and Burbank Blvd.), a colorful cultural history of Los Angeles painted on a Tujunga Wash flood control reservoir.

The San Fernando Valley's "main street" is Ventura Boulevard, which runs west from Universal City to Woodland Hills along the Santa Monica Mountains' north flank, roughly paralleling the Ventura Freeway. En route to the ocean both roadways weave through some of the valley's most established and "upscale" communities: Sherman Oaks, Encino, Tarzana—named after the book *Tarzan,* written by former resident Edgar Rice Burroughs—Woodland Hills, and beyond. This busy corridor also offers backdoor access to the fragmented Santa Monica Mountains National Recreation Area, crethe exits. The end of the silent-picture era also ended public access, but in 1964 Universal Studios dusted off the tradition by offering its original "back lot" tram tour. Admission prices and cinematic sophistication have been increasing ever since, and Universal Studios the movie theme park just keeps growing. **Universal City**'s commercial "urbanopolis" spreads across 413 acres and already includes the **Universal Amphitheater,** an 18-screen **Cineplex** movie theater, hotels, multiple restaurants, and office space, everything linked by an abbreviated, commercialized collection of Los Angeles themes known as **CityWalk.**

Plenty else is here to see and do, but kids and childlike adults race first to the "rides." At least one major attraction is unveiled every two to three years. Without special privileges—see admission options below—to get the most out of your entertainment investment arrive as early as possible then *go* when the gates open, heading first to the most popular rides and other priority destinations. Lines get longer as the day goes on. Alternatively, in summer, head for popular attractions during the dinner hour. Summer is in some ways the worst time to come—huge crowds, long lines—but in other ways it's the best, since some shows and

---

ated in an attempt to protect large sections of the coastal Santa Monica Mountains from development. Other highlights along the way include the five-acre Los Encinos State Historic Park in Encino, near the site of a major accidental archaeological find in the 1980s, and the awesome swirl of business towers and shopping centers at the Warner Center, just north of the freeway near Woodland Hills. The valley's influence now extends into adjacent Ventura County—through Calabasas, Agoura Hills, and Thousand Oaks via the Ventura Freeway—which makes Oxnard, on the coast, the San Fernando Valley's de facto seaport.

Heading east along the valley's northern corridor leads to Simi Valley, home of the Ronald Reagan Presidential Library and the folk-art wonder of Grandma Prisbey's Bottle Village. Like Santa Clarita to the north, Simi Valley is a white-flight suburb home to disproportionate numbers of LAPD officers and their families.

Star of the northern San Fernando Valley is its lovely 1797 namesake, Mission San Fernando Rey de España in Mission Hills (not to be confused with gang-troubled North Hills nearby). Adjacent to Granada Hills is Northridge, ground zero for L.A.'s most recent earth-shaking (1994) and home to California State University Northridge. Founded in 1958 as San Fernando Valley State College and now boasting an enrollment of about 28,000, CSU Northridge is a commuter college best known for its engineering and computer science programs. Neighboring Chatsworth, famous for its cowboy-country sensibilities and the "faces" in the hills

above, has been described by L.A. social historian Mike Davis as an "exopolis" and "urbanizing suburb," something of a social segue between the valley's urban center and the amorphous "Super Valley" to the north and west. South of Chatsworth is Canoga Park, where inside the library at the Sutter Middle School (Winnetka Ave. and Sherman Way) a hidden treasure abides—the massive mural *The First Spring,* considered the career masterpiece of Kay Nielsen. The Danish-born artist died in poverty but gained fame as an illustrator of children's books—including the 1914 *East of the Sun and West of the Moon,* and 1924 *Hans Christian Andersen's Fairy Tales*—and as art director for the "Night on Bald Mountain" sequence of Disney's *Fantasia.* More or less between Canoga Park and Reseda, "home of the Karate Kid," is one of L.A.'s smallest communities—the onetime utopian chicken farm of Winnetka, totaling 18 city blocks.

At the edge of the valley, plan a stop at the Nethercutt Collection at San Sylmar, an impressive collection of some of the best cars that money can buy. Head north from the valley, via I-405 or I-5, to reach the mammoth Six Flags Magic Mountain amusement park and—to stretch your legs a bit—several worthwhile parks, including Placerita Canyon Park and the William S. Hart Museum and Regional Park. Beyond, on the long climb over the Tehachapi Mountains, are Castaic Lake and Pyramid Lake. Near the Grapevine Grade summit, as I-5 begins its long slide into the San Joaquin Valley, is Fort Tejon State Historic Park.

programs are seasonal, staged daily and/or frequently only in summer and on weekends.

The Rides

Always a must-do attraction is the **Studio Tour,** a 45-minute ride that takes you behind the scenes of the movie-making scene. The tram—now roomier and redesigned, with state-of-the-art audio and video technology—winds through 35 settings, from the Mummy's Tomb and the prehistoric jungle of *Lost World: Jurassic Park* to the Bates Motel featured in Alfred Hitchcock's *Psycho.* The fictional locations of popular TV shows are here too, from *Murder, She Wrote,* **Kojak,** and **Quantum Leap** to classics such as **McHale's Navy** and **Leave It to Beaver.** What you'll see when you're there depends on which sets are currently in use for filming.

Remember when James Cameron, Oscar-winning director of the Hollywood megahit *Titanic,* climbed up there on stage at the Academy Awards and declared himself King of the World? Well, the king has come down off his throne, at least long enough to create a major new attraction at Universal Studios. Cameron's futuristic film-based virtual adventure **Terminator 2: 3D,** a virtual sequel to *Terminator 2: Judgement Day,* is a 12-minute "giant format" combo of digital imaging technology and live action stunts.

In 1993, the Steven Spielberg-enhanced **Back to the Future—The Ride** made its debut. And it's no disappointment even now—a white-knuckle DeLorean ride from Doc Brown's Institute of Future Technology that blasts through the space-time continuum into futuristic Hill Valley and then snaps back into the Ice Age, free-falls into volcanoes, and faces off with dinosaurs. Then there's the tamer **E.T. the Extraterrestrial Adventure,** which takes star-bound bicyclists "home" with E.T. No doubt the hottest attraction is **Backdraft,** a simulated but very explosive warehouse fire.

Still the best thing going, though, is **Jurassic Park—The Ride.** Universal Studios celebrated its 30th anniversary as a genuine theme park in 1994 with "Jurassic Park—Behind the Scenes," a demonstration of the technological wonders that went into making the movie. But Universal's real thrill actually lumbered out of the manufactured jungle in 1996, when **The Ride** opened its gates. After five years of work and more than $100 million, monstrously popular Jurassic Park adds the you-are-there element to some of the scarier scenes in Michael Crichton's novel and subsequent smash-hit movie. Sir Richard Attenborough, who played the park's creator in the movie, welcomes visitors via video at the gates of this Jurassic Park before guests climb onto river rafts and shove off for a tour. Early encounters with peaceable plant-eating dinosaurs in Herbivore Country offer no preparation for the demolished Land Rover later discovered dangling from a guardrail or the hole in the velociraptors' electrified fence. Or the terrifying Tyrannosaurus rex. Or for rafts suddenly careening over a waterfall, out of control, and plunging into nothingness at about 50 miles per hour. The finale of the 5.5-minute ride is so scary, in fact, that expectant mothers and people with cardiac conditions are advised to avoid Jurassic Park altogether. Parents and non-tall people, please note that riders must be at least 46 inches tall.

Beyond the Rides

Curious George Goes to Town is a new interactive playground, this one awash with water play. Live shows are also an integral part of the Universal Studios lineup, including the **Rugrats Magic Adventure!** (new in 2000). TV- and movie-related revues don't always enjoy a long run, but action adventure does, including the always macho lineup of the **Wild, Wild, Wild West Stunt Show,** and the **Waterworld** live-action show, providing action and water bound hijinks.

The **World of Cinemagic** is a comparatively cerebral demonstration of movie-making magic—from the special effects in *Harry and the Hendersons* and *Back to the Future* to "The Magic of Alfred Hitchcock," which demonstrates just how the shower scene in *Psycho,* the "fall" from the Statue of Liberty in *Saboteur,* and other famously terrifying Alfred Hitchcock scenes were created.

Universal CityWalk:
One-Stop Los Angeles

"What to do when you don't know what to do" is how CityWalk promotes itself these days. Perhaps it's the place to go when you don't know where else to go—L.A.'s L.A.-themed refuge from itself. Such was the consternation of critics when CityWalk first opened in 1993 as L.A.'s "idealized reality," a miniature mall-style Los Angeles concentrating simulated local culture into a few commercialized "city" blocks.

CityWalk's very creation suggested an underlying belief that it's not possible to fix the old city of Los Angeles—to make it a prosperous, safe, and welcoming place—so here's a facsimile, a sanitized version of the real thing. A one-stop Orwellian Los Angeles that celebrates Hollywood by leaving behind the lost souls now wandering its streets, that memorializes L.A.'s historic architecture by transplanting it from the poverty of its actual neighborhoods. An L.A. culture that shops on Melrose Avenue and goes clubbing in Silver Lake without worrying about dodging bullets or car thieves, or that spends the day at Venice Beach or Santa Monica without having to endure panhandlers and "Will Work for Food" signs. CityWalk is urban living without the possibility of unpleasantness, a place designed to exploit people's desire to feel good about all they've come to fear.

Before CityWalk opened its doors for business—the year after L.A.'s Rodney King–related riots—historian Kevin Starr, now state librarian, sounded the alarm about what it symbolized. "This sounds like the end of L.A. history," he said. "Los Angeles finally gives up on itself and creates an idealized version. Have we so lost L.A. as a real city that we need this level of social control for anything resembling the urban experience?"

But as much as critics decried CityWalk as plastic and pointless, it never entirely lived down to expectations. No matter how good the pizza, it was smarmy to see a low-rent version of Wolfgang Puck's Spago, prototype for the **Wolfgang Puck Cafe** chain established here and everywhere else in Southern California. And it's horrifying to contemplate the potential future represented by the mechanically reproduced "waves" at CityWalk's "beach." But this poverty-free promenade did—and does—have a "real L.A." feel, however, understandably attractive to Angelenos battle-fatigued by the extra effort it takes just to live here. Among CityWalk's notable and worthwhile successes: the historic neon signage displayed by L.A.'s **Museum of Neon Art,** which now has its own real-city museum in downtown L.A; the 350-seat **B.B. King Blues Club,** a genuinely good nightclub that serves up major-league blues artists and gospel breakfasts; and cultural oddities such as **Wizardz Magic Club and Dinner Theater,** where you can see a magic show, dine on a three-course meal, and have your fortune told. Not to mention outlets of **Benitas Frites, Jody Maroni's Sausage Kingdom,** and **Tommy's World Famous Hamburgers.** Among other results of CityWalk's recent expansion, nostalgia buffs really dig **Retro Rad,** with its impressive selection of retro-styled clothing and accessories, **The Wound & Wound Toy Co.,** and rockin' **Jillian's Hi Life Lanes** bowling alley.

So, you decide. Is this Los Angeles better than the real thing?

CityWalk is open daily, 11 A.M.–11 P.M. weekdays, 11 A.M.–midnight weekends, though some restaurants and nightspots stay open later. Admission is free. For current information, call 818/622-4455.

Practical Universal Studios

Universal Studios Hollywood is open 8 A.M.–10 P.M. in summer (box office: 7 A.M.–5 P.M.) and 9 A.M.–7 P.M. at other times (box office: 8 A.M.–4:30 P.M.). Strollers, wheelchairs, and other special services and facilities are available.

Regular admission prices tend to increase regularly but at last report were $41 adults, $36 seniors (age 60 and older), $31 children (ages 3–11, under 3 free)—plus 2 percent L.A. municipal tax. The **Celebrity Annual Pass** is $49, good for 333 days of admission (restricted dates); the **Director's Pass** is $69, with front-of-line privileges and reserved show seating; and the **Producer's Pass** is $99, with front-of-line privileges, reserved show seating, personalized walking tour, and a behind-the-scenes look at the Wild West Stunt Show. Another option is the all-day **VIP Experience,** $125, which includes access to the VIP Lounge, private tram with exclusive personalized tours of the back lot (including prop warehouse) and theme park, front-of-line privileges, and reserved show seating. In addition, the **Southern California Value Pass,** $75, includes admission to Sea World San Diego, and the **Hollywood CityPass,** $49.75 adults, $38 children, includes admission to seven other Hollywood area attractions. Cash and credit cards with ID (no personal checks) are accepted. Parking is extra: $7 for most vehicles, $10 for RVs.

For information on attractions, rides, and basic practicalities, contact: Universal Studios Hollywood, 100 Universal City Plaza in Universal City, 818/622-3801 (recorded message, in English and Spanish); www.universalstudios.com. To book Universal Studios "Hollywood vacation packages," call toll-free 877/223-4855 or see the website.

To get here: From the Hollywood Freeway (Hwy. 101) between Hollywood and the San Fernando Valley take either the Universal Center Drive or Lankershim Boulevard exits and go with the flow. From the Ventura Freeway (Hwy. 134), exit at Cahuenga Boulevard and proceed south to the Lankershim Boulevard entrance.

NORTH HOLLYWOOD AND THE NOHO ARTS DISTRICT

Right next door to Universal Studios and City-Walk is a slice of the real-life city both were created to avoid—North Hollywood. These days, however, the neighborhood is undergoing a transformation, what with the arrival of the new Metrorail Red Line station on Lankershim Blvd. (at Chandler). Another shining neighborhood star is the new headquarters for the **Academy of Television Arts and Sciences** on Lankershim Blvd. (at Magnolia), featuring a 28-foot winged muse flying up from its outdoor fountain. Bohemian attitude got here first, though, with Lankershim Blvd. leading the way and Magnolia Ave. playing a supporting role in the development of the **NoHo Arts District.**

For information about Tinseltown north and the NoHo Arts District and vicinity, contact: **Universal City/North Hollywood Chamber of Commerce,** 5019 Lankershim Blvd. in North Hollywood, 818/508-5155.

Seeing and Doing NoHo
Despite television's august organizational presence, live theater is *lively* in and around the NoHo neighborhood—at almost two dozen venues including **Actors Forum Theatre, American Renegade Theater, The Bitter Truth Theatre,** and **Deaf West Theatre,** not to mention

the Equity playhouse performances at the historic **El Portal Theater** or the municipally owned **Lankershim Arts Center.**

Local night spots include the seriously cramped but seriously fun **Blue Saloon,** 4657 Lankershim Blvd. (near Riverside), 818/766-4644, a straight-ahead beer hall known for ear-blasting blues, rock, rockabilly, and country, and the small **Baked Potato,** 3787 Cahuenga Blvd., 818/980-1615, which serves up vintage jazz with a menu of 21 varieties of baked potato.

There's plenty more to explore in the neighborhood, too, including vintage clothing shops, coffeehouses, and ethnic eateries, as well as book and music stores. **Iliad Bookshop,** 4820 Vineland Ave. (at Camarillo), 818/509-2665, is among the best gently used bookstores around.

If you're overhauling the house and looking for a few unusual touches—Gothic gargoyles, old Arts and Crafts tile work, original Victorian doors and windows, antique light fixtures, chandeliers, and fireplace mantels—head for **Scavenger's Paradise,** in a glorious onetime church at 5453 Satsuma Ave., 323/877-7945. Paradise helps reincarnate at least the spirit of old L.A. buildings that failed to dodge progress.

Or perhaps you're overhauling yourself and looking for something unique. At the **Western Costume Company Outlet Store,** 11041 Vanowen St., 818/760-0902, "it doesn't cost much to dress like a star." There's no telling what you might find at this retail sales outlet for Hollywood's largest TV and movie wardrobe supplier. You can walk away with an evening gown worn by your favorite soap opera star, a faux fur stole, a spacesuit, genuine Hollywood cowboy boots, or a bouncing *Baywatch* T-shirt. If you're lucky, you may even find something left over from **Nudie's Rodeo Tailors Inc.**—responsible for Roy Rogers's first fringed rhinestone-studded cowboy suit and Robert Redford's gaudy flash in *The Electric Horseman*—which closed its famous Lankershim shop in the mid-nineties.

BEAUTIFUL DOWNTOWN BURBANK

Burbank's city seal features both a film frame and an airplane—symbols of Burbank's predominant industries, movie and TV production

THE VALLEY'S CELEBRITY CEMETERIES

It's not your typical burial plot. **Forest Lawn Memorial Park** is more like a religious theme park—one that deals with the subject of death by avoiding it almost entirely, similar to youth-worshiping Los Angeles itself. Inspiration for both Jessica Mitford's book *The American Way of Death* and Evelyn Waugh's fictional country club for the dead in *The Loved One,* Forest Lawn is the final resting place of many southstate celebrities—Gracie Allen, George Burns, Nat King Cole, Walt Disney, W. C. Fields, Errol Flynn, Clark Gable, and Carole Lombard among them. Forest Lawn is also famous for its statuary and art replicas—in particular, dramatic presentations of a stained-glass *Last Supper,* and *Crucifixion* and *Resurrection* oil paintings. For more, stop in at the Forest Lawn Museum next to the Hall of Crucifixion-Resurrection. The self-guided tour brochure and map will show you around.

Forest Lawn Memorial Park, 1712 S. Glendale Ave., 323/254-3131 or 818/241-4151, is open daily 8 A.M.–6 P.M.

A second Forest Lawn cemetery and park is just 10 minutes away by freeway in the Hollywood Hills west of Griffith Park, 323/254-7251 or 818/984-1711, this one with an "American liberty" statuary theme. There are at least three others—in **Covina Hills** to the east and in **Cypress** and **Sunnyside** farther south.

To truly tour the San Fernando Valley's cemetery scene, don't miss the **Los Angeles Pet Memorial Park** farther west in Calabasas at 5068 N. Old Scandia Ln., 818/591-7037, known as the "Happier Hunting Ground" in Waugh's *The Loved One.* Among celebrity pets buried there: Pete the ring-eyed pooch from "Our Gang," Humphrey Bogart's dog Droopy, Charlie Chaplin's cat Boots, Tonto's faithful steed Scout from *The Lone Ranger,* and Hopalong Cassidy's horse Topper.

---

and Lockheed Aeronautical Systems, Inc. One of these days it may drop the airplane, since Lockheed moved its operations lock, stock, and fuel barrel to Marietta, Georgia. But the city once proud to crown doe-eyed Debbie Reynolds "Miss Burbank" in 1948 is still going strong. Business is booming at the city's major studios—at the Walt Disney and Warner Bros. Studios, at the National Broadcasting Company (NBC), and at Universal Studios Hollywood overlooking Burbank—with major expansions in the works just about everywhere. Still the big news in Glendale, just to the east, is the Mediterranean-style DreamWorks SKG animation studio complex—the 12-acre dream of Steven Spielberg, Jeffrey Katzenberg, and David Geffen.

Seeing and Doing the Studios

Business *is* business, and most TV and movie production facilities aren't tourist attractions. But that fact doesn't stop visitors from admiring the cartoonish architectural kitsch of the **Walt Disney Company** corporate headquarters at Alameda Avenue and Buena Vista Street, where the 20-foot-tall Seven Dwarfs hold up the roof with their bare hands. Also visually fantastic (but also no visitors): Roy Disney's **Feature Animation**

Building across the street, decked out in wild colors and a sky-high version of Mickey Mouse's apprentice wizard's hat from *Fantasia.*

There *are* industry sight-seeing opportunities, beyond the staged presentations up the hill at Universal Studios. Among the best: Burbank's very worthwhile **Warner Bros. Studios VIP Tour,** which now includes a wander through the studio's wonderful **Warner Bros. Museum,** and the **NBC Television Studios Tour** and free show tapings. For information, see Touring Movieland elsewhere in this chapter.

Seeing and Doing Other Things

For a taste of local culture—the San Fernando Valley's good ol' days—head to the oldest Bob's in the country, the **Original Bob's Big Boy '49** in Burbank at 4211 Riverside Blvd., 818/843-9334, and load up on "original Double Deck Hamburgers" with the help of genuine carhops on Saturday and Sunday nights. For the record, though, the *original* Original Bob's went up in Glendale but bit the dust (with the help of a bulldozer) to make way for a minimall.

The local art-deco classic is the **Burbank City Hall** at 275 E. Olive Ave. (at Third St.), a Depression-era Works Project Administration project.

AMERICA'S HOMETOWN: GLENDALE AND BEYOND

This Midwestern L.A. enclave has long since said good-bye to its orchards and row crops, and to the Gladding, McBean, and Company factory that produced so much of Southern California's "look" with its art and mosaic tiles, roofing tiles, terra cotta ornamentation, and pottery products. These days Glendale is starting to say hello to a more multicultural norm, a change that's apparent even at the **Glendale Galleria.** But Glendale invented itself as America's hometown along Brand Boulevard, where the 1922 Greco-Egyptian **Alex Theater,** 216 N. Brand, 818/243-7700, included on the National Register of Historic Places, is grand once again after a $6.1 million restoration that transformed it into a performing arts center.

Equally theatrical, though, is **Forest Lawn Memorial Park,** a Southern California cemetery that has become Glendale's most famous contribution to L.A. culture. To sample other contributions, stop at the palatial, vaguely East Indian **El Mirador** mansion in the northwestern foothills, stunning home to the **Brand Library and Art Galleries,** a park, and picnic grounds at 1601 W. Mountain St., 818/548-2051. Here you can also enjoy one of the world's largest CD collections, changing gallery shows, and thousands of art books. Or tour northeast Glendale for a look at several of Frank Lloyd Wright's 1920s creations (private homes): **Derby House,** 2535 Chevy Chase Dr., **Calori House,** 3021 E. Chevy Chase, and **Lewis House,** 2948 Graceland Way.

M*A*S*H AND MALIBU CREEK STATE PARK

Fans of the M*A*S*H television series, filmed at Malibu Creek State Park, will recognize the scenery —and enjoy posing for impromptu photos inside the junked jeep and ambulance parked in weeds along the Crags Road trail route. Much of the land now included in the park, more than 4,000 acres, was owned by Twentieth Century Fox until the mid-1970s, so, naturally, many TV shows and movies have been filmed here over the years—and at adjacent Paramount Ranch. The house from the Cary Grant film Mr. Blandings Builds His Dream House still stands, and if you use your imagination you can also picture Pleasantville here. In addition to TV and movie musings, free and technical rock-climbing are also popular.

Yet trails are the real draw. The short one-mile hike to Century Lake is an easy trek for the kids. (The old M*A*S*H set is one mile farther.) Starting at the parking lot, head west on Crags Road to Malibu Creek. Head right at the fork to reach the visitor center, for basic information and orientation. Cross the bridge here and continue up the road; at the crest, descend to the left. Man-made Century Lake, now something of a freshwater marsh, is quite inviting to ducks and other waterfowl. If the kids are still willing, backtrack toward the bridge and then take the Gorge Trail south to Rock Pool—yet another one of those Southern California sights that seems vaguely familiar since you may have seen it before—in movies such as Swiss Family Robinson.

Six miles of the Backbone Trail also traverse the park. For inveterate hikers, Malibu Creek State Park also offers trail access to the city of Calabasas's **Lost Hills Park.** Other visitor draws include pleasant picnicking, a large campground, and the regional state park headquarters. The land's main claim to fame, however, is as the southernmost natural habitat of California's valley oak.

Parking lot hours are 8 A.M.–sunset, though the park itself is open 24 hours except in extreme fire danger or other emergency. Parking is $2 per vehicle. The visitor center is open limited hours, on weekends only. Call for information on nature walks and special activities. To reserve park campsites, contact **ReserveAmerica,** toll-free 800/444-7275; www.reservamerica.com. To get here: From the Ventura Freeway (the 101) in Calabasas, head south on Las Virgenes Road three miles to the Mulholland Highway intersection. Continue south on Las Virgenes/Malibu Canyon Road another quarter-mile to the park's entrance. From Pacific Coast Highway (Hwy. 1), head north almost six miles on Malibu Canyon Road to the park entrance. For more information, contact: Malibu Creek State Park, 1925 Las Virgenes Rd. in Calabasas, 818/880-0367 or 818/880-0350.

MAJOR MASS: EARLY CALIFORNIA HIGH ART

The standard story about California mission culture goes something like this: With reinforcements provided by Spanish military garrisons, a few hardy Franciscan priests arrived in the wilds of California to establish some semblance of civilization. They enlisted the aid of local native peoples—willing and otherwise, largely otherwise—to build the mission buildings, tend the cattle herds and crops, and otherwise eke out a marginal life in the wilds of California. Not counting the native arts and cultures that were soon all but lost, only with substantial American settlement a century later did "the arts" and "culture" take root, imported from Europe and the East Coast.

But contrary to the popular myth, early California mission life was as dedicated to the high arts as it was to the survival arts—and to musical performances in particular. And California's most important early cultural legacy came not from pioneers pushing west but from those heading north.

Major excitement has been generated in the music world by the recent rediscovery, at Mission San Fernando Rey de España, of three masses written by the Italian-born composer Ignacio de Jerusalem, Mexico City Cathedral choirmaster in the mid-1700s. Found in 1992 inside a plain metal locker in the mission archives, the mass manuscripts suggest a far more sophisticated level of New World artistic creation and performance than previously imagined. Based on reports by early California travelers, the current speculation is that entire Native American orchestras and choirs had already been formed at some of the missions by 1804, the year the Jerusalem masses arrived—an accomplishment far surpassing the simple church psalms of the American East during the same era.

To appreciate the complexity and depth of early California music, seek out the 1993 CD *Mexican Baroque* by the San Francisco choral group Chanticleer, which includes parts of Jerusalem's "Polychoral Mass in D."

Eagle Rock

Eagle Rock the town is best known for the very selective and ethnically diverse Occidental College, a private liberal arts school. But just as Hollywood has its sign, Eagle Rock has its rock. East of Glendale, west of Pasadena, and perched on the north-facing slopes of Mount Washington, the town is named for Eagle Rock—a huge sandstone boulder that resembles an eagle in flight (in the right light). It's visible from the eastbound Ventura Freeway. The town's totem has the same significance to L.A. as Mount Rushmore has to South Dakota, so no one here complained when the city bought it for $700,000 in 1995 to prevent its desecration by an apartment complex.

MID-VALLEY AND WEST

Mission San Fernando Rey de España

Why not use a little movie lore to lure the kids into a hands-on California history lesson? Some of Steve Martin's *L.A. Story* was filmed here, after all, as were dozens of other movies and *Dragnet*

and *Gunsmoke* episodes. With four-foot-thick walls and named for King Ferdinand III of Spain, the 1797 Mission San Fernando is the largest adobe building in the United States. As elsewhere in California, early mission life was dedicated to agricultural enterprise and the arts and crafts of survival; the small museum here tells the story. But mission life was also dedicated to the arts. Aside from surviving recent earthquakes, the mission generated major excitement among art and music historians with the recent discovery of three sophisticated masses written by the Italian-born composer Ignacio de Jerusalem, Mexico City Cathedral choirmaster in the mid-1700s. Some of the artifacts excavated from the "Lost Village of Encino" are also now at home here.

Mission San Fernando Rey de España, 15151 San Fernando Mission Blvd. in Mission Hills (two blocks east of Sepulveda Blvd.), 818/361-0186, is open daily 9 A.M.–4:30 P.M., closed Thanksgiving and Christmas. Admission is $4 adults, $3 seniors, and $3 children ages 7–15 (under 7 free).

Ronald Reagan Presidential Library

Here's one won for the Gipper—an allusion better appreciated once you tour museum exhibits on Ronald Reagan's Hollywood days. Fans of former President Ronald Reagan—including "new" Republicans hoping to rewrite the U.S. Constitution, for whom the affable Ronald Reagan is founding father of America's resurrection —tend to love this place. Those who aren't Reagan enthusiasts, including those who view him as the Forrest Gump of modern American politics, may find the self-ovations on display here a bit excessive. In any case, you can't help being saddened by the news that the most glorious memories of one of L.A.'s own, America's 40th president, are increasingly lost to him as Alzheimer's disease takes its relentless toll.

"Dutch" Reagan was born in Tampico, Illinois, and grew up in the white-clapboard town of Dixon. Once arrived in Tinseltown, he starred in an impressive string of B movies, from *Desperate Journey* and *Little Queen of Montana* to the chimp classic, *Bedtime for Bonzo*. But those were the Democratic years, when Reagan was a member of the Screen Actors Guild. Ronald Reagan became a Republican "in name as well as thought" at the age of 51. His surprisingly easy ascent to America's political summit began in 1960 when he campaigned for Richard M. Nixon; in 1964, he backed Barry Goldwater's presidential campaign. After a two-term dash through the California governorship, Reagan arrived at the White House as 40th president of the United States. Most permanent exhibits here cover those years, including a section of the Berlin Wall, a replica of the Oval Office, and a re-creation of the White House Cabinet Room. Don't even bother to ask about the Iran-Contra exhibit. There isn't one.

For more information, including current special exhibits and programs, contact: Ronald Reagan Presidential Library, 40 Presidential Dr., Simi Valley, 805/522-8444; www.reagan.utexas.edu. Admission is $5 adults, $3 seniors, free for those under age 15. The library is open 10 A.M.–5 P.M., closed Thanksgiving, Christmas, and New Year's Day. To get here: From I-5 or 405, exit at Highway 118—the Ronald Reagan Freeway—and head west. From the 118, exit at Madera Road South and continue three miles to Presidential Drive; turn right. A Marie Callendar's restaurant is now on site, open 10 A.M.–5 P.M.

Los Encinos State Historic Park

If coming or going along the valley's southern edge, this is a place to stop for some peace or a picnic if the stop-and-go flow of the Ventura Freeway starts making you crazy. This quiet five-acre park, named for its live oaks ("los encinos"), commemorates Gaspar de Portolá's expedition through the neighborhood in 1769. The history of the land, which was once the heart of Vicente de la Osa's 4,460-acre Rancho del Encino, is told by a docent-led tour of period

Ronald Reagan, America's
40th president, is still the star
at the presidential library.

KIM WEIR

exhibits in the original nine-room "linear" adobe house here—a onetime "hospitality stop" along El Camino Real—and a self-guided tour of the grounds. The two-story French provincial Garnier House, now a visitor center and small museum, was built of native limestone by two Basque brothers who owned the ranch in 1872.

Historians had long puzzled over the fate of the "Lost Village of Encino" described in detail by Father Juan Crespi in his 1769 Portolá expedition diaries. The mystery of the Gabrieleño village was solved in July of 1984, when demolition of a restaurant on the southeast corner of the Balboa/Ventura Boulevard intersection—a half-mile from Los Encinos State Historic Park—unearthed the first of more than two million artifacts: arrowheads, stone tools, seashell beadwork, and Spanish glass beads. The first catalogued discoveries were released by archaeologists in 1994; some will eventually be displayed at Garnier House.

Los Encinos State Historic Park, 16756 Moorpark St. in Encino, 818/784-4849, is open Wed.–Sun. (except major holidays) 10 A.M.–5 P.M. Admission is free. Reservations are required for picnicking on weekends. Call for current guided tour schedule (small fee). To get here: From the Ventura Freeway (101), exit at Balboa Boulevard and head south; turn east (left) onto Moorpark.

Leonis Adobe Museum and Plummer House

Despite the popularity of Spanish names for cities, streets, and chi-chi shopping districts, in Southern California it's difficult to find authentic remnants of California's rich history as part of Spain and Mexico. The Leonis Adobe is one such survivor, a humble early 19th-century mud-brick building remodeled into a gracious two-story Monterey-style home in 1879. For more Old California sensibility, explore the barn and barnyard and then compare and contrast the totality with the adjacent Plummer House Victorian and the Victorian garden on the other side of the restaurant. **Calabasas Creek Park** is also operated under

GRANDMA PRISBREY'S BOTTLE VILLAGE

Tressa "Grandma" Prisbrey started collecting her first cobalt-blue Milk of Magnesia bottles in 1956. But by the mid-1970s she had transformed thousands of them, along with car license plates, doll's heads, and old TVs, into an eccentric folk-art "village" including curving walls, wishing wells, the Shrine to All Faiths, Cleopatra's Bedroom, and the Pencil House. A wonder in the annals of American folk art, this particular creation represents the most time-involved art creation by any female in all of recorded history, according to Bottle Village enthusiasts. Grandma Prisbrey died in 1988, and years of neglect and vandalism took their toll even before the 1994 Northridge quake shook down and damaged more of Grandma Prisbrey's meandering masterpiece. Until recently Grandma Prisbrey's Bottle Village, quite close to the Reagan museum, was scheduled for restoration with funds from a federal grant. But local Republican Rep. Elton Gallegly declared preservation of the bottle empire a taxpayer boondoggle and successfully campaigned in early 1997 to cut off federal funds, suggesting instead that Grandma Prisbrey's be bulldozed. The pro-Bottle Village people appealed the funding cut to no avail.

But all is not lost. As of late 1999 some $25,000 in grant funds had been received for minor repairs, and certain private parties have expressed an interest in helping with the estimated $500,000-plus pricetag for total restoration. (The small Preserve Bottle Village Committee is a 501(c) 3 nonprofit organization; large and small donations are appreciated. Grantwriting assistance will also help.) Pending restoration,, Grandma Prisbrey's Bottle Village is viewable from the street at 4595 Cochran St. in Simi Valley. It's open to visitors for guided tours by appointment only (small donation requested); for $5, get your souvenir copy of Grandma Prisbrey's own 1960 book about her project. For current information and visitor reservations, call Grandma Prisbrey's Bottle Village at 805/583-1627.

museum auspices. For more information, contact: Leonis Adobe Museum, 23537 Calabasas Rd. in Calabasas, 818/222-6511, open Wed.–Sun. 1–4 P.M., closed Thanksgiving, Christmas, and New Year's Day.

Another respite, and vestige of the region's rural past, **Orcutt Ranch Horticultural Center** is a 25-acre outdoor "museum" in West Hills at 23600 Roscoe Blvd., 818/883-6641. The center is abloom with antique farm machinery and citrus orchards, roses, and other seasonal delights. For more outdoor access, head to Agoura and the **Peter Strauss Ranch**, 818/597-1036, or, for longer hiking trails, the Santa Mon-ica Mountains National Recreation Area's **Paramount Ranch** in **Agoura Hills**, 818/597-9192, where the TV show *Dr. Quinn, Medicine Woman* was filmed.

PRACTICAL VALLEY

STAYING IN THE VALLEY

The San Fernando Valley features the predictable tourist-type hotels—most noticeably the large and pricey **Sheraton Universal Hotel** at Universal Studios, 333 Universal Terrace Pkwy., 818/980-1212 or toll-free 800/325-3535 (internationally) for reservations, with regular rates starting at $279, and the more business-oriented **Universal City Hilton and Towers**, 555 Universal Terrace Pkwy., 818/506-2500 or toll-free 800/445-8667, with standard room rates of $150–185. Much more affordable options include the **Banana Bungalow** Hollywood hostel just down the hill near the Hollywood Bowl (see Staying in Hollywood, above). More interesting choices include those listed separately below.

Other good accommodation options are scattered throughout the San Fernando Valley; motels line lengthy stretches of Ventura Boulevard as it meanders west toward Calabasas. If you end up anywhere near Calabasas—while coming or going from Paramount Ranch in Agoura Hills or various other Santa Monica Mountains outings, for example—a perennial best bet is the **Country Inn** motel at 23637 Calabasas Rd., 818/222-5300 or toll-free 800/456-4000, where the amenities include breakfast. Weekend rates are $119, weekday rates $109. In Mission Hills, you won't go wrong at the **Best Western Mission Hills Inn** at 106 Sepulveda Blvd., 818/891-1771 or toll-free 800/352-5670, what with free breakfast and newspaper come morning—$73 double, with weekly rates available. In Burbank, consider the fun **Safari Motel** (see listing below). Less expensive stays in Glendale, where motels tend to line the length of Colorado Street (east and west), include **The Chariot Inn**, 818/507-9600 or toll-free 800/458-4080, and the **Econo Lodge**, 818/246-8367 or toll-free 800/553-2666 (central reservations). Both are in the $45–70 range.

Sportsmen's Lodge Hotel

In general, a family-friendly alternative to the towering tourist hotels at Universal Studios is the nearby Sportsmen's Lodge motel on Ventura Boulevard just a mile south of the Hollywood Freeway. Part of the appeal of this contemporary English-themed hostelry is strictly outdoors—particularly the expansive, lushly landscaped pines-and-palm-trees grounds complete with footbridges, waterfalls, and swans in the lagoon. The place also tries to live up to its country-manor image indoors, particularly at the semiformal **Caribou at the Lodge** wild game restaurant. Also here—great little on-site coffee shop, Olympic-size courtyard pool, spa, fitness center. Rooms are large yet simple, decked out in country pine, earthbound colors, and the usual amenities. Free parking. Child-care services and monthly rates are available, along with free shuttle service to and from Universal Studios and the Burbank Airport. Standard rooms are $134, pool view rooms $172, and suites are $187–$290. Discounts and packages can lower the tariff considerably, particularly in the off-season.

For more information, contact: Sportsmen's Lodge Hotel, 12825 Ventura Blvd. in Studio City, 818/769-4700; www.slhotel.com. For reservations, call toll-free 800/821-8511.

The Safari Inn

This spirited and spunky motel, conveniently close to Warner Bros. Studios, is a favorite of entertainment industry people without big bucks or studio expense accounts. And it should be a favorite of just plain folks who find themselves in Burbank for whatever reason. Rooms are contemporary and quirky if otherwise fairly basic—

the older rooms, in the original motel section, are the cheapest—and there's a good restaurant here too. Free parking. The Safari is just over a mile southwest of the Golden State Freeway (I-5) via Olive Avenue. Standard rooms are $89–109, deluxe rooms $109–$129, and suites $129–$159. For more information, contact: The Safari Inn, 1911 W. Olive Ave. in Burbank, 818/845-8586. For reservations, call toll-free 800/782-4373.

EATING IN THE VALLEY

Eating in and around Universal Studios
Of course you'll end up at Universal Studios. CityWalk outside the gates offers the best eats. **Jody Maroni's,** 818/622-5639, serves sausages, about a dozen kinds including Italian and Mexican jalapeño. Then there's the **Hard Rock Café,** 818/622-7626, and the **Wolfgang Puck Café,** 818/985-9653, both serving the usual at lunch and dinner. And a couple dozen other possibilities.

Many worthwhile choices are reasonably close to Universal Studios. For an early-morning breakfast in Studio City, **DuPar's** coffee shop, 12036 Ventura Blvd. (at Laurel Canyon), 818/766-4437, is the hippest place around, what with the number of genuine Tinseltown action, actors, and actresses it attracts. (People have to get to work—early, in Hollywood—and they have to eat *somewhere* close to the studios.) A best bet in the casual-and-quite-good eclectic category for lunch or dinner is the immensely popular (and crowded) **Out Take Cafe,** 12159 Ventura Blvd. (near Laurel Canyon), 818/760-1111. Try the vareniki, or potato-filled ravioli, served with sour cream and caramelized onions. Or the chicken Vesuvio. Another good bet is **Art's Deli,** 12224 Ventura Blvd. (at Laurel Canyon), 818/762-1221, beloved for its pastrami sandwiches. Or try the Valley's own **Killer Shrimp,** 4000 Colfax (at Ventura), 818/508-1570, serving only huge Gulf shrimp in simmered Cajun sauce—always best with the French bread cubes for dunking.

People's Eats in Burbank and Glendale
Barron's coffee shop, 4130 W. Burbank Blvd. (at Evergreen) in Burbank, 818/846-0043, is a local mainstay—a best bet for breakfast. Then there's circa-1946 **Chili John's,** 2018 Burbank Blvd., 818/846-3611, with its genuine U-shaped counter—a 24-seater—and famous groundsteak and chicken chilis. Not that you can't find more upscale style, especially near the Media Center—or up the hill to Studio City—like, for instance, **Au Bon Pain: Baker, Sandwich Maker,** 350 San Fernando Rd., 818/843-8946.

For inexpensive espresso, cappuccino, guava pastries, seafood sandwiches, and hot meat pies, the place is **Porto's Cuban Bakery** in Glendale at 315 N. Brand Blvd., 818/956-5996. For neighborhood Thai at either lunch or dinner, try **Indra,** 517 S. Verdugo Rd. (at Maple), 818/247-3176. If you're headed east to Pasadena—or just hungry for down-home Polish food at Warsaw prices—dance on into **Polka** just beyond Glendale at 4112 Verdugo Rd. (at York) in Eagle Rock, 323/255-7887, beloved for its kielbasa, kotlet, golabki, and gulasz. Polka is open daily for lunch and dinner.

People's Eats Elsewhere
North Hollywood's **Swasdee** in a strip mall across from the Thai Buddhist Temple, 8234 N. Coldwater Canyon Blvd., 818/997-9624, serves sizzling curries and other red-hot tastes of the real thing. And some folks say the best thin-crust pizza in L.A. is served forth from **Joe Peep's Pizzeria** near North Hollywood at 12460 Magnolia Blvd. in Valley Village, 818/506-4133.

But don't miss **Dr. Hogly Wogly's Tyler Texas Bar-B-Que,** 8136 N. Sepulveda Blvd. in Van Nuys, 818/780-6701, another mythic southstate dining destination—the kind of place people go hours out of their way to find. This funky Formica-clad café serves unforgettable ribs, beef brisket, Texas hot links, and chicken, everything smoked right here. No one walks away hungry at dinner, which comes with cole slaw (token vegetable), baked beans, macaroni salad, and a half-loaf of fresh-baked bread. Don't forget the pecan pie.

For hot dogs the place is **Rubin's Red Hot,** 15322 Ventura Blvd. (at Sepulveda) in Sherman Oaks, 818/905-6515, a Chicago-style drive-through and sit-down notable, too, for its El-track architecture. (You really can't miss it.) Not counting Joe Peep's fans, the general consensus is that the best around comes from **Paoli's Pizzeria** in Woodland Hills, 21020 Ventura Blvd., 818/883-4136, famous for its white-sauce and sausage pizzas.

Dining Destinations
Better restaurants aren't necessarily expensive. Witness the French **Café Bizou** in Sherman Oaks, 14016 Ventura Blvd. (between Hazeltine and Woodman), 818/788-3536. And the Venetian **Ca' del Sole** in North Hollywood, 410 Cahuenga Blvd., 818/985-4669, sibling to Ca' Brea, where even vegetarians leave with a satisfied smile. Don't forget the valley's colorful Caribbean **Cha Cha Cha,** 17499 Ventura Blvd. in Encino, 818/789-3600.

But cuisine can be quite dear. **Pinot Bistro,** 12969 Ventura Blvd. in Studio City, 818/990-0500, the first "concept" spin-off from Joachim Splichal's California-French Hollywood star Patina, was quickly dubbed the valley's best by the *Los Angeles Times,* and "best new restaurant" by *Esquire* magazine. The concept is classy French bistro—checkered floor, dark wood, and fireplace—and the content is Parisian, too, featuring onion soup, pastas, and fish.

Saddle Peak Lodge between Calabasas and Malibu at 419 Cold Canyon Dr., 818/222-3888, is still the valley's special-event destination, a one-time mountain lodge with a rustic but elegant wilderness ambience. Saddle Peak is noted for serving perfectly prepared fresh American game—fish, fowl, and venison—and lots of it. Sunday brunch is a special treat. With such things as wild mushroom and onion pie on the appetizer menu, fixed-price entrées include crab cakes, the chef's omelette, fresh fish plate, and farm-style steak and eggs. Weather permitting, sit outside and take in the scenery too. It's open daily for dinner and for brunch on Sunday. Reservations required. The lodge is on Cold Canyon Drive at Paiuma Road (nearest major intersection: Las Virgenes Rd. and Mulholland).

NORTH FROM TINSELTOWN

ESCAPE FROM L.A.

At the north end of the San Fernando Valley the San Diego, Golden State, Hollywood, and Foothill Freeways all flow together to become I-5, a galloping freeway designed to funnel traffic up and out of the Los Angeles basin, over the Tehachapi Mountains, and eventually out into the arid San Joaquin Valley. Just north of this great convergence, the Antelope Valley Freeway (Hwy. 14) branches east toward Lancaster and Palmdale, the latter a technology and aeronautics oasis in the high desert where housing subdivisions have displaced most of the original Joshua trees. En route are some worthwhile parks—William S. Hart, Placerita Canyon, and Vasquez Rocks—and *The Birds* star Tippi Hedren's private Soledad Canyon Shambala Preserve, a haven for unwanted zoo animals and more than 70 lions, tigers, and other big African and Asian cats born in captivity but otherwise abandoned to fate (tours offered twice monthly).

Dominant in Valencia on I-5 is Six Flags Magic Mountain, a theme park most appreciated for its thrill-a-minute rides. Usually overlooked in the neighborhood is the California Institute of the Arts, or CalArts, an integrated arts college founded by Walt Disney. The five major departments here—art, music, film-video, dance, and theater—are well integrated, but CalArts is still most famous for its animation artists.

Farther north at Castaic Junction, as I-5 thunders on, Highway 126 heads west toward Ventura on the coast, passing Piru, Fillmore, the quaint Victorian town of Santa Paula, and the remaining citrus orchards responsible for Valencia's name and this valley's original wealth. From Highway 126 just west of I-5, head north to reach the unusual town of Val Verde, one of California's few truly integrated communities, established in the 1920s as a vacation haven for L.A.'s blacks. Many of the original summer cottages have since become homes for United Farm Workers (UFW) organizers and field hands; about one-third of the population is white.

Back on I-5, attractions beyond Castaic Junction include Castaic Lake and Pyramid Lake

SIX FLAGS CALIFORNIA

Some people love roller coasters—people such as poet Peter Schjeldahl, who described in the pages of *Harper's* at least one spiritual benefit of his relationship with his Coney Island favorite: "It's important to ride the Cyclone many times, to comb out the distraction of terror—which gradually yields to the accumulating evidence that you are not dead."

Hard to improve on the profundity of such a recommendation. And it's hard to miss, even from I-5, the mammoth Time Warner–affiliated **Six Flags Magic Mountain** and **Six Flags Hurricane Harbor** amusement parks, about 30 miles north of downtown L.A. Magic Mountain, the first and original star here, specializes in not-so-cheap thrills—including 12 coasters and more than 100 rides in this 260-acre park. The latest addition is **Goliath**, which takes guests on a three-minute white-knuckle ride beginning with a near vertical 61 degree first drop and heading into a series of intense turns. Somewhere among it all, you'll experience huge spiral curves and "zero gravity" drops.

Riddler's Revenge is purported to be the world's tallest and fastest stand-up roller coaster. This ride's twist: riders stand, rather than sit, as they race 65 mph through vertical loops, barrel rolls, and a drop of 146 feet. **Superman the Escape,** launches from a 415-foot tower to reach speeds of 100 miles per hour. The looping two-minute **Batman The Ride,** is in semi-industrial "Gotham City" along with the similarly themed circular **Acme Atom Smasher** and centrifugal-force **Gordon Gearworks** (look for the bathrooms at the Acme Atom Smasher Coolant Pump Facility). Other favorites include the three-looped, 188-foot-tall **Viper,** the **Ninja** with its enclosed, suspended train cars (the track is *above* you), **Flashback,** the dual-track **Colossus,** and the classic wooden **Psyclone.**

If none of that proves that you're not dead, there are other possibilities, including the **Dive Devil** skydiving bungee jump. Thrill-seekers fling themselves from atop 150-foot "flight deck" towers, free-fall for 50 feet, and reach speeds of up to 60 miles per hour before—from just six feet above the ground—arching back 100 feet in the opposite direction.

The faux tropical landscape and lagoons of Hurricane Harbor feature remnants of a lost civilization —could it be Los Angeles?—and more than a dozen water-play attractions, such as a wave pool, both tube and speed slides, and a pirate-themed kiddie play area.

Though closing hours vary, Six Flags California on Magic Mountain Parkway is open daily in summer at 10 A.M. (on weekends only during much of the year); call for current schedule information. At last report, admission was $40.99 adults, $20.50 seniors, and $20.50 for children under 48 inches tall (free for age 2 and younger). Parking $7. There's an additional charge for some attractions, such as the Dive Devil. For current information, contact: Six Flags California, 818/367-5965 and 661/255-4849 (show and entertainment hotline), or 661/255-4136; www.sixflags.com.

state recreation areas, and Fort Tejon State Historic Park.

Nethercutt Collection at San Sylmar

Imagine the face of wealth, as accumulated by Dorothy and J. B. Nethercutt, he the former CEO of Merle Norman Cosmetics. The Nethercutts' "total immersion in beauty" has resulted in this collection of wonders—from Duesenbergs, Packards, and Pierce-Arrows (parked on an Italian marble floor) to elegant musical instruments, clocks, and fine furnishings. Free two-hour tours are offered Tues.–Sat. at 10 A.M. and 1:30 P.M. (reservations required, limited to 12 people). If you come, remember that "San Sylmar is a house of beauty" so "please dress accordingly." For more information, contact: The Nethercutt Collection at San Sylmar, 15200 Bledsoe St., Sylmar, 818/367-2251.

William S. Hart Museum and Regional Park

Amid all the usual signs of progress in the Santa Clarita Valley is this 253-acre Old West oasis, remnant of the vast rural acreage once owned by movie cowboy William S. Hart. Perfect for picnicking and family play, the park includes Hart's magnificent 1920s home, now the William S. Hart Museum, open for docent-guided tours. Classics of cowboy style collected here include Navajo rugs and works by Remington and Russell.

The park is open daily 7 A.M.–sunset. The house, affiliated with the Los Angeles County Museum of Natural History, is open for 30-minute tours Wed.–Fri. 10 A.M.–12:30 P.M. and on weekends 11 A.M.–3:30 P.M. The museum is closed Thanksgiving, Christmas, and New Year's Day. For more information, contact: William S. Hart Museum and Regional Park, 24151 N. San Fernando Rd., Newhall, 661/254-4584. To get here from I-5, head east via Highway 126; from the Antelope Valley Freeway (Hwy. 14), head northwest via Highway 126.

Placerita Canyon Park
The first gold discovered in California came out of Placerita Canyon, just north of L.A., in 1842, six years before James Marshall's much more famous find at Sutter's Mill in the Sierra Nevada foothills. According to the romantic version of the tale, vaquero Francisco Lopez was rounding up stray horses when he decided to siesta under an oak tree here. He slept, and he dreamed—about gold, gold everywhere around him. When he awoke, he remembered the dream. He also remembered that his aunt had asked him to bring home some wild onions. So he pulled up nearby onions and discovered flecks of gold among the roots. The "Oak of the Golden Dream" still stands, near the nature center. The park also features a pleasant picnic area, short self-guided nature trail, and a longer hiking route that highlights the lasting damage done by hydraulic mining technology. Placerita Canyon is most pleasant when it's green, in winter and spring. To get here: From I-5 exit at the Antelope Valley Freeway (Hwy. 14, the route to Palmdale), continue several miles to Placerita Canyon Road, then turn right. It's open daily 9 A.M.–5 P.M., closed Christmas. Free parking. For more information, contact: Placerita Canyon State and County Park, 19152 W. Placerita Canyon Rd., Newhall, 661/259-7721.

Vasquez Rocks County Park
In the 1870s California's "Mexican Robin Hood," the bandit Tiburcio Vasquez, made a name for himself here—and finished making a name for himself here, after a shootout and chase with sheriff's deputies. (Vasquez escaped but was later captured and hanged.) In more recent history, these twisted and surreal sandstone formations have starred in countless TV shows, westerns, and movies, including sci-fi spectaculars such as *Star Wars* in 1977, the 1979 *Star*

Trek flick, and countless *Star Trek* TV episodes. L.A.'s Vasquez Rocks park is halfway to Palmdale near Agua Dulce on Escondido Road north of Highway 14, 661/268-0840, and is open daily dusk to dawn.

Santa Clarita Woodlands Park
The site of Chevron Oil's first well in the Newhall Oil Field is now included within one of L.A.'s newest parks, a lush and lovely "bridge" between the coastal Santa Monica Mountains (north slope of the Santa Susana Mountains) and the inland San Gabriel Mountains. Here migrating wildlife are granted at least the possibility of safe passage through one of L.A.'s fastest growing regions. Over 3,000 acres in total size, the park includes Rice, Wiley, and Towsley canyons, and the onetime oil town of Mentryville. Multiple hiking trails traverse the territory. The main entry to Santa Clarita Woodlands Park is at Towsley Canyon's Ed Davis Park, though all park trails are accessible from the Old Road, just off I-5. The park is open daily for day use only, from dawn to dusk. Starting at noon on the first and third Sunday of every month, docents show up at Mentryville to share the area's history.

For more information, contact **Ed Davis Park,** 661/255-2974, or the **Santa Monica Mountains Conservancy,** 310/589-3200.

Northeast from Santa Clarita and Valencia
If you can ignore the shocking sprawl of Santa Clarita and "Canyon Country," interesting and historic territory lies to the north. Midway between **Bouquet Canyon** and **Elizabeth Lake** is **San Francisquito Canyon** ("Little St. Francis Canyon") and site of the doomed **St. Francis Dam,** the largest arch support dam in the world when it was built in the 1920s. (To get here, from Saugus take San Francisquito Canyon Road.) The tragic midnight dam collapse of 1928 killed more than 500 people asleep in the valleys below—the rampaging water roaring through even Santa Paula—in one of the worst natural disasters in U.S. history. To his dying day, L.A. water engineer William Mulholland believed (with good reason) that the dam's destruction was the work of saboteurs and dynamite, though he himself was ultimately blamed (the real-life drama inspired the film *Chinatown*). The road route today

BOB RACE

No individual has had a more lasting impact of Los Angeles than William Mullholland. His epic engineering feat, the Los Angeles Aqueduct, still works today. However, he is perhaps better known for his responsibility in the St. Francis Dam tragedy (which collapsed in 1928 and sent 12 billion gallons of water straight through San Francisquito Canyon all the way into the ocean between Ventura and Oxnard).

follows the general path of the first of L.A.'s aqueducts, the **Los Angeles Owens River Aqueduct** originating near Mono Lake along the eastern slopes of the Sierra Nevada.

Continue on San Francisquito Canyon Road to reach the outskirts of Lancaster and the **Antelope Valley Poppy Reserve** (for more details see The Deserts chapter). Or, by taking the winding side road to **Green Valley** and **Bouquet Reservoir,** create a loop route that returns through the typically parched, sparsely wooded landscape—prettiest in winter and early spring—to Saugus via Bouquet Canyon Road. At upper elevations, near the reservoir, public campground and picnic areas are scattered along the roadway.

Pyramid Lake State Recreation Area

This surprisingly pretty lake just off the interstate is popular for fishing, boating, and camping. In places the "shoreline" seems almost vertical—the onetime canyon walls of Piru Creek Gorge, still reaching skyward. Pyramid Lake is part of the massive California State Water Project. Thanks to modern California water engineering, the water collected here comes from the Feather River watershed some 450 miles farther north; from here it continues south to Lake Perris, end of the line. To get an idea of the size and scope of California's immense commitment to moving northstate water south, stop by the water project's **Vista del Lago Visitor Center** here.

Pyramid Lake State Recreation Area is in the Tehachapi Mountains 50 miles north of Los Angeles, just off I-5 in Gorman, 661/257-2892. Day use is $3 per vehicle ($6 for vehicles with trailers), but touring the visitor center is free. Camping is also available, 661/248-6575. The recreation area is open for day use 7 A.M.–5 P.M. in winter, 6 A.M.–8:30 P.M. in summer.

The Vista del Lago Visitor Center (take the Vista del Lago exit), 661/294-0219, is open daily 9 A.M.–5 P.M., closed Thanksgiving, Christmas, and New Year's Day. The California State Water Project's Feather River water is pumped up and over the Tehachapis—with massive 450-ton pumps and 14-foot-diameter pipes—beginning at the **A. D. Edmonston Pumping Plant** in the San Joaquin Valley.

Closer to L.A. but also popular for sailing, swimming, fishing, and picnicking is **Castaic Lake State Recreation Area,** operated by L.A. County, which also offers limited RV and tent camping. For information, call 661/257-4050.

Fort Tejon State Historic Park

A pleasant respite from I-5, which actually runs right over the original site of Fort Tejon (te-HON) in Grapevine Canyon, the remnants of the 1850s fort represent the early days of California statehood. The military post here was established in 1854 by Edward F. Beale, the U.S. Commissioner of Indian Affairs for California and Nevada, for the stated purpose of protecting the Indians at the San Sebastian Reservation in Tulare Valley, 20 miles north, and the government reservation itself, including horses and livestock. The location here was deemed ideal for two reasons. One, horse and cattle rustlers heading through this pass on the way to L.A. could literally be cut off at the pass, and two, this route, unlike the deserts, offered water. Fort Tejon soon became regimental headquarters for the First U.S. Dragoons and for Jefferson Davis's U.S. Army Camel Corps, a successful desert transport experiment discontinued with the outbreak of the Civil War and the arrival of transcontinental railroads. When the U.S. government abandoned the post in 1864, Beale incorporated it into his vast surrounding Tejon Ranch (*tejón* or badger being the name of Ignacio del Valle's original Mexican land grant here). Land donated by and bought from the Tejon Ranch Corporation assisted in the fort's restoration, a project begun in 1949.

These days Fort Tejon State Historic Park, on the west side of I-5 about 75 miles north of Los Angeles and 35 miles south of Bakersfield, open daily 10 A.M.–5 P.M., is most popular as a traveler's rest and picnic stop—some fantastic grizzled valley oaks—though **Living History Days** held on the first Sunday of each month and **Civil War Reenactment** festivities attract a more interesting crowd. At one time more than 20 adobe buildings stood here but today only a few remain, including one restored barracks and officers' quarters. The visitor center/museum tells the story. For information, call 661/248-6692.

COURTESY AISLINN RACE

BEVERLY HILLS AND VICINITY

Beverly Hills—or "BH," as irreverent Angelenos abbreviate it—is sister city to Cannes, France, which may help explain the astonishing number of French street names and other Old-World affectations. Beverly Hills specializes in the retail sales of European, continental, and world-renowned everything. Despite its small-town suburban soul, BH is serious about maintaining its worldly image. Cachet saves the day in BH. When prestigious PaceWildenstein was getting ready to open its doors here in 1995, establishing the city's new identity as L.A.'s high-end art center, 10 massive sculptures by Henry Moore were begged and borrowed from around the globe to celebrate the occasion and temporarily installed on the front lawn of Beverly Hills City Hall. But BH being BH—and considering the 15 obese Fernando Botero sculptures subsequently exhibited in Beverly Gardens Park—some wags couldn't resist observing that, *here* of all places, so many fat people so publicly displayed must surely be against the law.

BEFORE BEVERLY HILLS

Tucked into the wooded hillsides above Sunset Boulevard are some of L.A.'s priciest houses, home to "movie people" and others on the roster of Southern California's wealthiest citizens. This was not always the case. The area north of Wilshire Boulevard was once known as the Rancho Rodeo de las Aguas, or "Gathering of Waters," where a few impoverished farmworkers lived in tumbledown shacks and tended to the 4,500 acres of lima bean fields owned by Doña Maria Rita Valdez, a soldier's widow who used her inheritance to buy the ranch in 1810.

The neighborhood ambience began to change shortly after the turn of the century when oil was discovered in what is now West Hollywood. Three speculative businessmen, Charles Canfield, Burton Green, and Max Whittier, bought Rancho Rodeo de las Aguas for $670,000 in hopes of finding exploitable oil deposits. After drilling more than 30 wells but finding very little oil, the three formed the Rodeo Land and Water Company and converted their investment into a real estate development known as Beverly Hills—named after the Massachusetts town of Beverly Farms where, as the story goes, Presi-

dent Taft had recently been vacationing.

Wilbur Cook was hired to plan the L.A. region's newest city; he started with a triangular business district north of Wilshire Boulevard and with wide residential streets north of Santa Mon-

WELCOME TO THE WESTSIDE

The various cities and residential enclaves that comprise L.A. County's Westside—Beverly Hills, Bel-Air, Brentwood, Westwood, West L.A., Malibu, Pacific Palisades, Santa Monica, and Venice, for starters—are sometimes known, in more culturally diverse areas of town, as the "white-bread Westside."

This phrase refers to middle- and upper-class mores more than eating habits, of course, since health-conscious Westsiders typically prefer natural foods and whole grains. Relatively short on historical points of interest and big-time tourist attractions, the Westside compensates with great restaurants, art galleries, and shopping districts. (If it's hip, it's here.) A few fine museums, including the world-class Getty Center. Beaches for swimming, surfing, and seeing and being seen. Pleasant public parks and promenades. And hiking trails into what remains of L.A.'s coastal mountain wilderness.

According to the Westside myth, in Beverly Hills the streets are paved with jewels and jewelry stores. Exclusive Bel-Air, Brentwood, and Pacific Palisades are the toniest of the Westside's tony suburbs. The offspring of L.A.'s remarkably affluent live in Westwood, a collegiate metropolis adjacent to the University of California at Los Angeles (UCLA). In Malibu, celebrities and artsy eccentrics live on the beach and in the sylvan enclaves of Topanga Canyon. Then there's adjacent Santa Monica, beach city extraordinaire, where well-to-do-homeowners, retirees, young families, and the homeless coexist peaceably—and where everyone else on the Westside comes to play. Next south is Venice, home to aging bohemians, young hipsters, street performers, and Muscle Beach. Less colorful but quieter West L.A. is a middle-class suburb packed with small single-family homes and condominiums.

Westside reality, however, is considerably more complicated. Long gone is the area's cherished cachet of semirural, small-town living. Population pressure—including the near impossibility of finding a parking space—is intense, and increasing. As liberal Santa Monica becomes increasingly intolerant of homelessness and the cutting-edge

architecture of Venice a backdrop for gangsters, the indigent, and the elderly, inner-city teenagers have discovered the pleasures of hanging out in once-tony Westwood. Increased population has also increased the dangers of "natural disasters"—raging wildfires, mudslides, and earthquakes. Geologically speaking the area's bedrock is, at best, precarious. When the Really Really Big One hits on the Westside, the land beneath it will essentially liquefy.

Complicating the question of Westside identity still more is the fact that people don't agree on what is and isn't "Westside." Historically the divide between L.A.'s Eastside and Westside was established by the Los Angeles River. Yet according to the Los Angeles Police Department, L.A.'s Air Quality Management District, and public utilities such as Pacific Bell, the actual east-west border is La Cienega Boulevard, a north-south thoroughfare that slices through West Hollywood and the far eastern section of Beverly Hills. Westside consumers, always on the lookout for stylish shopping opportunities, sometimes extend their neighborhood farther east, to increasingly fashionable La Brea Avenue.

Whatever the Westside's essential boundaries may be, the advent of the automobile made possible its mass settlement. The car also connects Westside communities with their most valuable assets: sunshine, balmy temperatures, and fresh air. The sun shines on everyone in L.A., rich and poor. But clean air—"air quality"—and the milder coastal climate come with a premium price tag. People on the Westside are united by their collective willingness to breathe deep while Pacific Ocean breezes suck up the smog—much of it generated here—and blow it inland to befoul foothill neighborhoods.

"Westside," then, is more state of mind than particular place. This is the Los Angeles of L.A.'s hedonistic imagination—a mental landscape of postcard-pretty palm trees, sporty convertibles, and luxurious private retreats close to crashing surf and white-sand beaches.

ica Boulevard. The Rodeo Land and Water Company then built a handful of model homes on one-acre properties along Sunset Boulevard, in the "hills" of Beverly Hills, which sold for $800 to $1,000 each, and smaller homes on smaller lots near Santa Monica Boulevard, in the Beverly Hills "flats," priced at $300 to $400. By 1914 Beverly Hills—population 250—had become comfortable with its upscale suburban image and incorporated as an independent city.

In 1920, when the population had mushroomed to 634, Beverly Hills was reborn as myth —and as international upscale destination. That year, film star Douglas Fairbanks, Sr. bought a hunting lodge in the foothills behind the Beverly Hills Hotel and grandly remodeled it for his bride, actress Mary Pickford, who named the 14-acre estate and Tudor-style home Pickfair. Fellow celebrities Charlie Chaplin, Will Rogers, and Gloria Swanson soon moved into the neighborhood to take advantage of the countrylike setting such a short distance from their jobs at Hollywood's studios and to escape the snobbery and discrimination so apparent in L.A.'s "society neighborhoods." Soon Beverly Hills became *the* pre-

ferred home for "movie people." The local population increased from 634 to 17,428 in the decade between 1920 and 1930. Beverly Hills further, and finally, defined itself as separate from L.A. in 1923, during the hard-fought local battle against annexation, in which the stars themselves actively campaigned to protect their fairly bohemian way of life from the disapproving judgments of larger L.A.

So it is more than somewhat ironic that the snobbish evils once exemplified by "L.A. society" have now made this their permanent address. Today the main business of Beverly Hills is accumulating and maintaining its wealth—and its glamorous international image. More gardeners, maids, and other servants are employed per capita than anywhere else in L.A. Each of its 51 perfectly pedicured streets boasts its own tree species. In addition to the astonishing number of Rolls-Royce, Mercedes-Benz, Jaguar, and Ferrari automobiles registered at private Beverly Hills addresses, local car rental agencies have extras on hand. Long before it became the law of the land in California, Beverly Hills banned smoking in its restaurants. The city also bans fast-food franchises.

SEEING AND DOING BEVERLY HILLS

Tourists are not exactly encouraged to drive around to stare, slack-jawed and speechless, at the city's most noted attractions: the splendid hillside palaces and mansions of the incredibly rich and sometimes famous. But you can—either on a tour, or on your own, after buying one of those cheesy "Maps to the Stars' Homes" hawked from street corners. Do be aware, however, that driving aimlessly through rich people's neighborhoods, especially in a derelict or dangerous-looking car, will bring you to the attention of squads of private security guards and sometimes the local police. Beverly Hills, all six square miles of it, is a thoroughly policed and protected city.

For many, shopping is the other main BH attraction. Rodeo Drive is most famous, but most residents of Beverly Hills and Brentwood are more likely to shop almost-affordable Beverly Drive (one block east of Rodeo Drive) and genuinely cutting-edge Beverly Boulevard. Other

BH attractions include the Robinson Mansion and Gardens, the fabulous and fairly new Beverly Hills Public Library at the city's civic center, the Roxbury Park children's playground on Olympic Boulevard, and, for strolling, two-mile-long Beverly Gardens Park along Santa Monica Boulevard. A reasonably new draw is the Beverly Hills branch of the Museum of Television and Radio. Also well worth a visit in the general vicinity: the timely Museum of Tolerance, and both the new Getty Center and Skirball Cultural Center atop Sepulveda Pass.

For more information, and for assistance with hotel reservations and other practical matters, contact: **Beverly Hills Visitors Bureau,** 239 S. Beverly Dr., Beverly Hills, CA 90210, 310/248-1015 or toll-free 800/345-2210 (in California only), www.bhvb.org. If you'll be here only briefly, hop aboard the **Beverly Hills Trolley** for a 40-minute "Golden Triangle" tour of architecture and affluence. Tours leave on the hour between noon and 4 P.M., Tues.–Sat. in the off-season with extended hours in summer; meet at the corner of Rodeo Drive and Dayton Way. For more information, call the City of Beverly Hills at 310/285-2438.

BASIC BEVERLY HILLS

The Golden Triangle
The triangular 20-block retail core of BH, north of Wilshire Boulevard and south of the intersection of Santa Monica Boulevard and Rexford Drive, is promoted as the "Golden Triangle." The visitor bureau's walking-tour brochure guides the hale and hearty past the major sights. You can also get a quickie overview via the Beverly Hills Trolley Tour.

Starting from the Beverly Hills Visitor Bureau on S. Beverly Drive, Golden Triangle highlights include the Spanish colonial **Artists and Writers Building,** 9501 Santa Monica Blvd. (at Rodeo Dr.), founded by Will Rogers and built in 1924 for use by Hollywood's writers, artists, and set designers—still in use today. Several blocks east on Little Santa Monica is the Litton Building at 375 N. Crescent Avenue. Onetime **Music Corporation of America (MCA)** headquarters, the building is a striking example of American federal revival architecture, designed by noted L.A. architect Paul Williams and built in 1937. The east-end pillars are survivors of Marion Davies's famous "Beach House," which also served as part-time residence of William Randolph Hearst. Across Little Santa Monica is a more contemporary local landmark—the 1950s' space-age neon-lit **Unocal Gas Station,** 427 N. Crescent Dr., preserved against the ravages of progress. The soaring cantilevered three-cornered canopy, a brilliant beacon in the night, harks back to a time when America was as excited about the freedoms gained via cars (and gasoline) as it was about space travel.

Next stop is the impressive **Beverly Hills Civic Center** across Little Santa Monica on N. Crescent, where the stunning, recently restored 1932 Spanish Renaissance **Beverly Hills City Hall,** designed by architects William J. Gage and Harry Koerner, has long been the main attraction. The predominantly two-story floor plan forms an H, and at the center is a third story

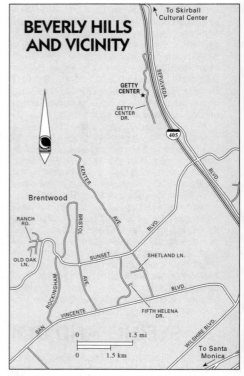

with an ornate eight-story tower and tiled dome. (The tower symbolizes business as it rises successfully from a solid government foundation—blasphemy these days but a popular theme during the Great Depression.) The center's more contemporary additions, designed by architect Charles Moore and his Urban Innovations Group, include three oval courtyards that connect city hall with a new fire department and police headquarters, public library, and parking garage—a "people friendly" place for shoppers and other pedestrians.

Particularly wonderful at the civic center—and a tribute to the civic generosity of Beverly Hills—is the new mansionlike, vaguely Spanish baroque **Beverly Hills Public Library,** 444 N. Rexford Dr., 310/288-2220, spacious and splendid. The library's 92,000 square feet are filled with marble countertops from Thailand,

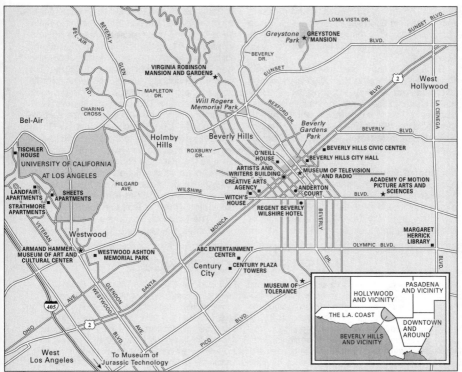

© AVALON TRAVEL PUBLISHING, INC.

mahogany bookshelves, brass light fixtures and other art deco touches, even a deluxe kid-scale children's reading area and theater. And books, about 300,000 of them. The $25 million library, completely computerized, is stuffed with other information-age conveniences, including a public auditorium. Also a draw, for low-income Angelenos and book lovers alike, are the library's two low-cost used bookstores—an impressive selection of community castoffs. Unlike other California libraries, ravaged by declining civic budgets, the Beverly Hills Public Library is open even on weekends, when working people are free to use it.

Another impressive public building, this one from another age, is the **Beverly Hills Post Office** on Santa Monica between Crescent and Cañon, a spectacular Italian Renaissance creation of terra-cotta and brick ablaze inside with murals and tiled mosaics. Then wander awhile along two-mile **Beverly Gardens Park.** Just north, at 507 N. Rodeo Dr., is the **O'Neill House,** an Antonio Gaudi-inspired (some BHers pronounce it "gaudy") art nouveau gem from the 1980s. Originally only the pavilion and guest house on the alley were decked out with such exuberance. But after Don O'Neill, owner of an art deco specialty shop, died some years back, his wife tore down their sedate Spanish-style bungalow and built this home as a memorial. Then there's the **Witch's House,** also known as the Spadena House, 516 N. Walden Dr. (at Carmelita), designed by Henry Oliver in 1921, when fairy-tale architecture was all the rage. The fairy tale here dips into the psyche's dark side, what with the steeply pitched shingled roof, small helter-skelter windows and shutters, gabled "witch's broom" entrance, and surrounding moat.

Originally used as office space and dressing rooms for Irvin C. Willat Productions, a movie studio in Culver City, the house was moved to its Beverly Hills location in 1931 and is now a private residence.

Back on Wilshire, east from Merv Griffin's Beverly Hilton Hotel, is the I. M. Pei–designed **Creative Arts Agency,** 9830 Wilshire Blvd., a major player in the highly competitive "agents" business. The neighborhood showstopper, though, is the 1928 Italian Renaissance **Regent Beverly Wilshire Hotel,** 9500 Wilshire Boulevard.

Museum of Television and Radio

"One Museum, Two Locations" is the way the Museum of Television and Radio in Beverly Hills explains its transcontinental kinship with its New York twin, originally known as the Museum of Broadcasting and founded in 1973 by William S. Paley. Designed by architect Richard Meier and open since March of 1996, the three-story, white steel-and-glass museum houses the total (duplicate) television and radio programming collection—about 100,000 programs spanning more than 75 years of broadcast history. Two theaters continuously screen miscellaneous TV programs and commercials, and an all-day radio show is available. The entire collection is available in a vast computerized library, so it's possible to view any TV program—from a *Rocky and Bulwinkle* episode to the pilot for *Charlie's Angels*—or listen to any radio show simply by keying a request into a computerized kiosk. Also quite accessible: the museum's industry-related gallery exhibits. A sample from the museum's first-year schedule: **Stand-up Comedians on Television, Rock 'n' Roll and Radio,** and **Star Trek: The Tradition Continues,** a gallery exhibit of costumes, makeup, and "facial appliances."

MUSEUM OF TOLERANCE

Appropriate for children old enough to understand the historical depths of man's inhumanity, the Museum of Tolerance adopts a hands-on, high-tech approach in confronting bigotry and racism. The experience begins with a semiformal tour. You know you're in for something different right from the start, when each group of visitors meets the Host Provocateur—a 10-foot-tall stack of video monitors—and must choose between two entry doors, one marked "Prejudiced," the other "Unprejudiced." The museum's very imaginative "Tolerancenter" engages visitors with more than 30 interactive displays, including "The Other America," a hate-group primer in the form of a wall map. Visitors move on to, and into, World War II's Holocaust, carrying photo passports of individual children affected by the Nazi reign of terror. As the tour continues—passing through a prewar Berlin café scene, through German discussions of "the final solution," and into the Hall of Testimony—the passports are updated. By the end you'll know what happened to that one child whose passport you carry. If the children ended up in the gas chambers, you'll also be able to imagine the horror of their last moments.

The Museum of Tolerance is just beyond Beverly Hills proper in Simon Wiesenthal Plaza, 9786 W. Pico Blvd. (at Roxbury Dr.), 310/553-8403; www.wiesenthal.com. The tour typically takes about two and a half hours, but visitors are encouraged to stay longer, to see other exhibits. At last report the museum was open for tours on weekdays starting at 10 A.M. with the last tour at 4 P.M., and on Sunday at 11 A.M. with the last tour at 5 P.M. The museum is closed Thanksgiving, Christmas, and all Jewish holidays. On Fridays from April through October, the last tour begins at 3 P.M.; from November through March, at 1 P.M. Advance tickets are available through the museum or through TicketMaster. Tour tickets are $8.50 adults, $6.50 seniors (62 and older), $5.50 students with ID, and $3.50 children ages 3–12. Wheelchair accessible. Foreign-language tours available. Below-street parking (accessible from Pico) is free.

Special security note: The Museum of Tolerance is very serious about security. All visitors pass through metal detectors and rigorous security checks; the contents of backpacks and handbags are carefully scrutinized for anything that might be used as a weapon to do bodily harm or as a tool to inflict property damage. Even seemingly innocuous items, such as ever-handy Swiss Army knives, are confiscated (returned at the end of your tour by security guards).

Museum of Television and Radio

Sponsored by the museum and scheduled in early March is the annual two-week **William S. Paley Television Festival,** the World Series of TV series—featuring a dozen or more "tributes" to various programs, including clips and one complete episode, and then an audience-participation question-and-answer session with TV stars and other principals. The screenings are usually held elsewhere, and separate admission is charged for each tribute; call for current information.

The museum is within BH's "Golden Triangle," 465 N. Beverly Dr. (at Little Santa Monica Blvd.), 310/786-1025, www.mtr.org. The museum is open Wed.–Sun. noon–5 P.M. (noon–9 P.M. on Thursday) and closed July 4, Thanksgiving, Christmas, and New Year's Day. Suggested donation is $6 adults, $4 students and seniors, and $3 children (age 12 and under). Free validation parking (two hours) is available in the museum's underground garage.

Academy of Motion Picture Arts and Sciences

Still without the equivalent of a Museum of Television and Radio to celebrate their arm of the entertainment industry, at least movie people have an uptown address. And the Academy of Motion Picture Arts and Sciences does more than just haul out all that glitz, glitter, and glib banter for the annual Academy Awards ceremony. It also has a swell theater at its headquarters here in Beverly Hills—the **Samuel Goldwyn Auditorium,** sometimes available for public screenings. Though this is not a museum, lobby exhibits are often worth a looksee. Prominently on display here in years past, for example, was Clark Gable's best-actor Oscar for the 1934 film *It Happened One Night,* auctioned off by Christie's for the sum of $607,500 despite the Academy's strenuous legal objections. But the gold statuette's "anonymous" new owner turned out to be Hollywood golden boy Steven Spielberg, who bought it for the express purpose of returning it to its rightful artistic place. (Now *that's* a movie with a happy ending.) Also a pleasure: the **Margaret Herrick Library of the Academy of Motion Picture Arts and Sciences** on S. La Cienega, an incredible library of film-related books, magazines, scripts, photos, and press clippings (open to the public, no lending allowed). The Academy of Motion Picture Arts and Sciences is east of the Regent Beverly Wilshire Hotel at 8948 Wilshire Blvd., 310/247-3000.

The Greystone Park and Mansion

The largest and most extravagant house in Beverly Hills has a scandalous history. The 46,000-square-foot Greystone Mansion was built by oil millionaire Edward L. Doheny, Sr., implicated in the Teapot Dome scandal of the early 1920s after he contributed $100,000 to the private cause of Secretary of the Interior Albert Fall in exchange for secret leases to public-owned government oil reserves.

Doheny prospered nonetheless, and the gray limestone-and-slate mansion was completed in 1928 at a 1920s' price tag of more than $4 million. Doheny never lived in the mansion himself —he preferred his Victorian home on Chester Place—so Greystone became a gift to his son, Edward L. Doheny, Jr., married man and father of five. But the younger Doheny had lived there less than a year when he and his secretary, Hugh Plunkett, were found dead in Doheny's bedroom. The family released a vague statement that Plunkett was "highly excited and nervous" and Doheny was trying to convince him to retire. But according to the gossip of the day, Doheny and Plunkett were lovers and, rather than risk the disgrace of public exposure, Doheny killed Plunkett and then turned the gun on himself.

Doheny's widow occupied the mansion until 1955, and eventually the city of Beverly Hills bought the mansion and adjacent hillside to build a reservoir, which now provides 50 percent of the city's water supply. The mansion, 905 Loma Vista Dr., 310/550-4654, is closed to the public, though the glorious 16-acre grounds are perfect for picnics (free) and open daily 10 A.M.–6 P.M.

Also fun for garden aficionados is the beaux arts-style **Virginia Robinson Mansion and Gardens,** 1008 Elden Way, 310/276-5367, tours available by appointment only, $7 ($4 seniors and students). Make your reservations at least one week in advance.

Rodeo Drive and Beverly Hills Shopping

If one's voyeuristic appetite for affluence can't be satisfied by touring well-manicured BH lawns and well-barred security gates—see Bopping Around Beverly Hills: Celebrity Sights, below— try upscale shopping. Or upscale window-shopping. For BH's most ostentatious displays, the time-honored destination is Rodeo Drive (pronounced ro-DAY-o, a deliberately correct, if somewhat affected, bow to proper Spanish pronunciation), particularly the stretch between Santa Monica and Wilshire Boulevards. For most people, the appeal is strictly vicarious—simply the desire to see where mythic star wardrobes were born. Especially in summer and on weekends, the streets are packed with camera-toting tourists just waiting for a chance to immortalize a frightful fashion mistake—spandex worn with fur, say—or document some major or minor star on film. What celebrities you do see in the neighborhood won't be visible for long. They tend to come early or at odd times, dash into exclusive shops, then dive back into their waiting limos (there's often a line of 'em, snaking around the block). Rather than schlep up and down Rodeo Drive dodging tourists, most people living in and around Beverly Hills are much more likely to shop along **Beverly Drive** just one block east of Rodeo, or ultrahip **Beverly Boulevard,** which segues into West Hollywood and similar great shopping along **Robertson Boulevard.**

But if you must "do" Rodeo: For window shopping, nighttime is the best time, when windows

Bring lots of cash if you plan to do any shopping in the area around Rodeo Drive.

are lit and the glitz even more glittery. Among notable Rodeo Drive destinations: **Cartier,** 220 N. Rodeo Dr., 310/275-5155, one of the world's big names in jewelry, with many pieces still designed from original Louis Cartier drawings. For classic chic, the classic hit with monied tourists is **Chanel,** 400 N. Rodeo, 310/278-5500, the L.A. branch of the French designer studio.

Almost always more fascinating than the rest of the neighborhood is the elegant **Regent Beverly Wilshire Hotel** on Wilshire Boulevard at the foot of Rodeo, the regal and recently refurbished Italian Renaissance hotel that starred with Julia Roberts in the film *Pretty Woman.*

Serious shopping distractions nearby, along BH's "department store row" on Wilshire between Santa Monica Boulevard and Beverly Drive, include **Saks Fifth Avenue, Neiman Marcus, Robinson's May,** and the neo-Mediterranean **Barneys New York.** (Look for **Bloomingdale's** in the Beverly Center on Beverly Boulevard.) The onetime Gump's on Wilshire at Camden Drive is now the West Coast home of **Pace-Wildenstein Gallery,** 310/205-5522, the world's largest blue-chip art dealership, this one designed by Charles Gwathmey and catering to an affluent entertainment industry clientele interested in works by contemporary and Impressionist artists as well as Old Masters. But BH also has a **Sotheby's,** on Wilshire at Bedford, 310/274-0401, expanded to handle jewelry and print auctions, and a sibling of New York's **Gagosian Gallery,** at 456 N. Camden, 310/271-9400, designed by Richard Meier.

BOPPING AROUND BEVERLY HILLS: CELEBRITY SIGHTS

Beverly Hills is L.A.'s most beloved tourist destination. Most people come here to see movie stars, which explains the hundreds and hundreds of outdated and inaccurate maps to the stars' homes sold each week. Real estate changes hands fast in this town, propelled in part by stars' rapidly changing fortunes. The only way to find out for sure who lives where is to research local property records—sometimes little help, in the case of corporate or otherwise hidden ownership—or the extremely inadvisable technique of knocking on doors to ask for autographs. (According to this theory, if the maid or butler says you need to contact such-and-such agency, assume you've got the right address. And if you're told so-and-so doesn't live there, that's probably the truth.)

But intentionally bothering people at home is always rude. The best way to see and appreciate movie and TV stars is to seek them out in their natural social habitats—at the restaurants, galleries, and clubs they're most likely to visit. Beverly Hills, West Hollywood, and nearby L.A. neighborhoods are thick with such places.

If you must peer at the well-protected homes of power and privilege, don't be obnoxious about it. Stay off people's lawns, don't climb through their trees, shrubs, and garbage cans, and resist poking your camera or camcorder lens in strangers' faces.

One way to warm up to the challenge of *civil* celebrity sight-seeing is to visit noncelebrity structures first. In Beverly Hills proper, consider **Anderton Court,** 328 N. Rodeo Dr., one of the few commercial buildings ever designed by Frank Lloyd Wright. Designed in the 1950s, near the end of Wright's career, Anderton Court is three stories of knees and elbows—sharp angles formed by roofline and balconies—topped with a spiky *Jetsons*-style tower.

Touring Celebrity: Beverly Hills

Beverly Hills neighborhoods near triangular Will Rogers Memorial Park are star-studded. At 730 N. Bedford Dr. is the former **Lana Turner** home, where Turner's daughter stabbed her mother's lover Johnny Stompanato to death with a kitchen knife—a notorious Hollywood scandal ultimately judged as "justifiable homicide." Just west is Roxbury Drive, where the star roster includes the late **Jimmy Stewart** (918 Roxbury), **Lucille Ball** (1000 Roxbury, where she lived until her death in 1989), and **Peter Falk** (1004 Roxbury).

Pickfair, 1143 Summit Dr., the onetime mansion of **Mary Pickford** and **Douglas Fairbanks, Sr.,** where Beverly Hills celebrity got its geographical start, was all but razed when **Pia Zadora** bought the place, tearing down all but one original room. Other onetime celebrity addresses include the retreat of silent screen cowboy **Tom Mix,** 1018 Summit, and **Charlie Chaplin's** place, 1085 Summit.

Benedict Canyon is something of a bad-luck neighborhood. At 10048 Cielo Dr. (then numbered 10050), is the home where the followers of **Charlie Manson** murdered actress **Sharon Tate** and others during their helter-skelter 1969 killing spree. Just off Cielo at 1436 Bella Dr. is **Rudolph Valentino**'s onetime home, Falcon Lair, which he bought to escape his unrelenting fame and fawning fans. Valentino enjoyed his privacy for only a year before he died here in 1926. Down the hill at 1579 Benedict Canyon is original Superman **George Reeve**'s suicide site.

In the hills east of the canyons are the homes of Trousdale Estates, remnants of the old Doheny empire. **Elvis Presley**'s onetime mansion, at 1174 Hillcrest Dr., is a tourist favorite, as is Villa Rosa, 1187 Hillcrest, the **Danny Thomas** mansion where talk show host **Phil Donahue** and **Marlo Thomas** were married.

At 1011 N. Beverly Dr. is the onetime home of **Marion Davies,** mistress of **William Randolph Hearst** (Hearst died here in 1951). Other famous BH addresses include **Fred Astaire**'s onetime home, 1155 San Ysidro, and **John Barrymore**'s, 1400 Seabright Drive.

Touring Celebrity: Bel-Air

Alfonzo Bell, who first made millions in oil, subsequently turned his attentions to yet another Southern California money-making enterprise—real estate. Just two years after Douglas Fairbanks, Sr. moved into Pickfair in Beverly Hills, drawing the world's attention, Bell offered the first lots for sale in his nearby Bel-Air—"Beautiful Place," as translated crudely from the French, but also an ego-boosting play on Bell's last name. Advertisements announced that Bel-Air would be the "crowning achievement of suburban development."

Bell's 200-acre tract of land north of Sunset Boulevard and west of Beverly Glen, just north of what is now the UCLA campus, was divided into multiple lots of several acres each. The subdivision included tennis courts, an 18-hole golf course, polo fields, stables, and bridle paths. At Bel-Air's entrance Bell erected two imposing gateways of wrought iron and stone staffed by uniformed guards. A private police force protected the neighborhood and escorted invited guests to their hosts' estates.

But all was not beautiful in Bel-Air. Bell blatantly discriminated against Jews, blacks, and Asians as well as the supreme social scourge of Southern California—movie people. Such exclusionary practices and policies worked well for Bell during Southern California's 1920s' oil and real estate boom. But when the Great Depression arrived in the 1930s, only movie people could afford neighborhood prices. By the 1940s, Hollywood's glamour days, Bel-Air was teeming with movie stars—a turn of events that served only to enhance Bel-Air's reputation. Today Bel-Air's bottom line is still green, and property is sold to anyone who can afford it, regardless of race, nationality, occupation, or former occupation.

Even more exclusive than Bel-Air is **Holmby Hills,** adjacent to Beverly Hills, a neighborhood of mansions and estates just north of Sunset Boulevard and just east of the Bel-Air East Gate. Lush landscaping, tall fences, and well-secured gates protect most of these estates from the prying eyes of the public.

Among Bel-Air's more recognizable addresses is 750 Bel-Air Rd., where Jed, Granny, and the rest of the Clampett clan assembled to shoot episodes of the *Beverly Hillbillies* TV series. **Howard Hughes** once lived at 1001 Bel-Air Rd., property subsequently owned by **Zsa Zsa Gabor.** Famous residents of St. Cloud Road have included former **U.S. President Ronald** and **Nancy Reagan**—but only, according to local lore, after Nancy raised hell with the U.S. post office insisting that the original "666" street address be changed.

Notable addresses in the Holmby Hills include **Jayne Mansfield**'s Pink Palace, 10100 Sunset Blvd., more recently owned by **Engelbert Humperdinck.** Look for **Hugh Hefner**'s infamous Playboy Mansion at 10236 Charing Cross Road. The former **Bing Crosby** family home, 594 S. Mapleton, is just blocks from the onetime home of **Humphrey Bogart** and **Lauren Bacall,** 232 S. Mapleton.

Touring Celebrity: Brentwood

Brentwood is a sleepy upper-crust enclave between Pacific Palisades on the west and the San Diego Freeway and Bel-Air on the east. Most recently famous as the home of the new Getty Center, Brentwood is also home to Loyola

Marymount University. Less prestigious than neighboring Bel-Air or Beverly Hills, Brentwood nonetheless has its share of lush estates and celebrity residents. Picturesque San Vicente Boulevard, which eventually ends at Palisades Park in the west, defines Brentwood. With its green, tree-shaded median—a freeway for joggers—San Vicente, along both sides, is also Brentwood's central shopping district. North of San Vicente are large, elegant homes occupied by predominantly white corporados driving Volvos and BMWs; those neighborhoods are also accessible from Sunset Boulevard. South of San Vicente Boulevard are densely populated neighborhoods of apartments and condominiums, havens for singles and young married couples.

Notorious as the neighborhood where **O. J. Simpson**'s ex-wife **Nicole Brown Simpson** and **Ron Goldman** were murdered, Brentwood has attracted the media spotlight many times before. The unpretentious home at 12305 Fifth Helena Dr., for example, is where **Marilyn Monroe** died. Just around the corner and up the block, at 12216 Shetland Ln., is the house where **Raymond Chandler** lived and wrote detective

novels during the 1940s. And in the 1930s and '40s actress **Joan Crawford** lived with her daughter Christina—who lived to tell about it in *Mommie Dearest*—at 426 N. Bristol. The childhood home of child star **Shirley Temple** is the European-style farmhouse at 231 N. Rockingham Road.

Well worth a shopping stop in the neighborhood is **Del Mano Gallery,** 11981 San Vicente Blvd., 310/476-8508, featuring an exceptional collection of contemporary crafts by American artisans—jewelry, pottery, glassware, quilts, woodwork, clothing, handbags, and textiles. **Dutton's Books** nearby at 11975 San Vicente (near Montana), 310/476-6263, is a small, well-rounded bookstore (new and used) with a strong selection of fiction, nonfiction, and children's books. For trendy fashions and healthy fast food—day-to-day Westside culture—head for the **Brentwood Gardens** minimall, 11677 San Vicente.

CENTURY CITY: MOVIE CITY

Formerly the back lot for Twentieth Century Fox Studios, Century City did not exist before 1961. In the late 1920s, Twentieth Century Fox was one of the most successful movie studios around, but by the mid-'50s television was cutting into the movie industry's audience. That fact, coupled with a series of box-office flops, shoved the studio into serious financial trouble. Desperate for money to keep the studio in business, executives realized that "location shooting" was the wave of the future in movie-making—and that they could save their cinematic empire by developing the land upon which it stood. About 260 acres between Beverly Hills and West L.A. that once served as the back lot for Twentieth Century, some of the choicest real estate in Los Angeles, thus became Century City. Architect Welton Becket signed on to plan and design the glittery futuristic "city."

Now an upscale enclave of millions of square feet of office and commercial space, Century City is a very prestigious L.A. address—and still central to the film business, the place top entertainment-industry executives, accountants, and lawyers hang their hats. A 13-story triangular tower designed in 1975 by architect Minoru Yamasaki anchors the city at each end—the **ABC Entertainment Center** and **Century Plaza**

OF ARCHITECTURAL NOTE: CLIFF MAY

In the 1930s, architect Cliff May and other California architects began to combine elements of the craftsman-inspired bungalow and the look of early California ranchos—experimentation that resulted in the California ranch-style home. More than any other individual, May is credited with popularizing the California ranch style, characterized by low-pitched overhanging shake roofs and long, often L-shaped, one-story wings sometimes wrapped around a central courtyard. Add large panes of glass looking out onto lush landscaping and there it is—the embodiment of the Southern California good life. By the southstate's building boom in the 1950s, a majority of California tract houses were ranch-style adaptations.

You can see Cliff May's office at 13151 Sunset Blvd. in Brentwood, at the entrance to a neighborhood of May houses on the 13000 blocks of Riviera Ranch and Old Oak Roads.

Towers. Century City's future was clearly envisioned even at the opening of the first tower, in 1961. Actress Mitzi Gaynor snipped film footage, rather than the customary ribbon, at the dedication ceremony.

Between the towers is a below-street-level concourse of theaters, restaurants, and shops. The **Shubert Theatre,** 2020 Avenue of the Stars, 310/201-1500, is L.A.'s home for many Broadway plays and long-running musicals. Glenn Close had a very successful run here with *Sunset Boulevard.*

Another Century City draw is **Harry's Bar and American Grill,** 2020 Avenue of the Stars, 310/277-2333, an exact replica of Harry's Bar in Florence, Italy, made famous by Ernest Hemingway. Truly entertaining every year is the bar's festive **Imitation Hemingway Competition,** typically judged in March (grappa toasts included). Earnest entries from around the world, each including an obligatory promotional reference to Harry's, are judged by a dozen or so of L.A.'s most respected and most Hemingway-literate writers.

In L.A., the land of megamalls, the **Century City Shopping Center and Marketplace** along Santa Monica Blvd., 310/553-5300, is one of the most attractive and pleasant outdoor shopping malls around. **Bullocks** and **Bloomingdale's** anchor the mall; highlights of the dozens and dozens of boutique-style shops include **Ann Taylor** for women's clothing, the **Pottery Barn** and **Crate & Barrel** for well-designed and fairly affordable housewares, and the **Metropolitan Museum of Art** gift shop. Also here: **Brentano's,** one of L.A.'s most popular bookstores. For chi-chi fast food, head for the mall's **Marketplace,** an indoor/outdoor food court. Here you'll find outposts of **Johnny Rockets, Houston's,** and New York's popular **The Stage Deli** along with the yellow-and-blue remains of Steven Spielberg's yellow submarine-themed **Dive!** restaurant.

WESTWOOD VILLAGE: COLLEGIATE METROPOLIS

Westwood began as a section of the 1840 Rancho San Jose de Buenos Ayres land grant. The property changed hands many times before 1922, when the Janss Investment Company offered the Regents of the University of California a 200-acre parcel at a substantial discount. In 1929 the University of California at Los Angeles (UCLA)—then known simply as the Southern Branch of the University of California—opened its doors to students. And the Janss Company's surrounding development, charming Mediterranean-style Westwood Village, began to prosper.

The community partnership of UCLA and Westwood has been so successful that today Westwood boasts some of the most horrific traffic in Los Angeles; Westwood Boulevard at Wilshire is the busiest intersection in all of L.A. Apartment buildings constructed to accommodate UCLA's record enrollment and high-rise residential and office complexes along Wilshire have pushed area "carrying capacity" to the breaking point.

Much of Westwood's original "village" charm has been lost to congestion and escalating land values that encourage, instead, high-volume chain stores, fast-food restaurants, and new banks and other quick-cash ATM outlets. Westwood's new appeal for inner-city teenagers looking for a late-night hangout has also challenged its long-running reputation as mild-mannered, middle-class cultural haven.

Yet Westwood still boasts the highest concentration of first-run movie theaters in the world. Beyond Hollywood Boulevard, this is L.A.'s most inviting—and exciting—place to do the movies. Blockbusters are premiered here regularly to take advantage of Westwood's huge old big-screen theaters with state-of-the-art sound systems—places such as **Village Theatre,** 961 Broxton Ave., 310/208-5576. For a genuine Southern California adventure, attend a movie in Westwood on opening night. About one-quarter of a premiere audience are people either involved in the production or special guests of the studio, while the rest are "real people" required to gauge audience reaction. Most premieres are scheduled for either Friday or Saturday night, when streets are blocked off to encourage a strolling fashion show amid the classic building façades.

In and around Westwood

Most people come to Westwood to see movies

and just hang out, the primary purpose of students who live on campus or who cram themselves into apartment complexes south of campus. But Westwood also has its shops, including ever-popular and ever-growing **Rhino Records,** 1720 Westwood Blvd. (at Massachussets), 310/474-8685, one of L.A.'s best for reggae, bluegrass, blues, rock, and jazz, whether mainstream or independent, domestic and imported, new or used. Rhino carries vinyl and an intriguing selection of anthologies manufactured under its own label. Knowledgeable staff.

For die-hard shoppers there's the flashy postmodern **Westside Pavilion** at Westwood and W. Pico Blvds., 310/474-6255, anchored by the giant clock tower of **Nordstrom.** Trendy stores within are lit by a central glass atrium.

Westwood's winding streets are lined with lovely old homes—and some unusual homes and apartments. The 1949 **Tischler House,** 175 S. Greenfield Ave., a glass-prowed ship anchored on the hillside, was designed by Rudolph Schindler. The clean, simple international-style **Strathmore Apartments,** 11005 Strathmore Dr., designed in 1938 by Richard Neutra, are constructed of wood and stucco; the eight rectangular units, reached by a central stairway, climb a steep hillside. (Orson Welles and Clifford Odets are among noted former tenants.) Richard Neutra is also responsible for the **Landfair Apartments,** also constructed in 1938, at 10940– 54 Ophir Dr. between Landfair and Glenrock Aves., a flat-roofed, two-story building of stucco and glass now owned by UCLA. Interesting here, too, are the landmark 1949 John Lautner-designed **Sheets Apartments,** 10919 Strathmore, where huge stucco platforms emerge from the hillside to serve either as foundations or roofs for the four huge redwood cylinders that house residents—like a fleet of hot tubs ready for space launch. A miniature forest, complete with waterfall, accompanies them.

If not for the presence of **Marilyn Monroe** in the tiny **Westwood Memorial Park,** a small cemetery south of Wilshire and east of Glendon, this area too might have been snapped up for apartment construction. Marilyn's crypt, in the Corridor of Memories, is marked by a small plaque. For 20 years her former husband Joe

DiMaggio had six red roses placed on her crypt three times a week. Actress **Natalie Wood** is also buried here, along with *Playboy* playmate **Dorothy Stratten** and child-star **Heather O'Rourke** (from *Poltergeist*).

UCLA: Berkeley's "Southern Branch"

It's ironic that the University of California at Los Angeles (UCLA) campus, 310/825-4321, www.ucla.edu, stood in for the UC Berkeley campus in the film *The Graduate*. When UCLA held its first classes as the "southern branch" of the original University of California campus at Berkeley, the 419-acre campus had just four buildings and 280 students. Today UCLA has grown to about 160 buildings and more than 35,000 students, the largest enrollment of any UC campus. Considered one of the finest research universities in the nation, UCLA is also lauded for its fine academic programs and as a major West Coast center for arts, culture, and cinema.

Bounded by Sunset Boulevard on the north, LeConte Avenue on the south, Hilgard Avenue on the east, and Gayley and Veteran Avenues on the west, UCLA still boasts its original four Italian Romanesque buildings from the late 1920s: **Powell, Royce, Haines** and **Kinsey Halls.** Powell is home to the Department of Film and Television's **Archive Research and Study Center,** where more than 25,000 films and TV episodes are preserved. (UCLA's **Melnitz Hall** often opens its doors for free screenings of the film school's collection.) Just across the well-manicured quadrangle from Powell is the campus symbol, Royce Hall, which includes a 1,850-seat performing-arts auditorium. Adjacent to Royce is the **Fowler Museum of Cultural History,** 310/825-4361, with permanent and changing exhibits on non-Western cultures. It's open Weds.–Sun. noon–5 P.M., Thursday until 8 P.M. Admission is $5 adult, $3 for seniors and students.

Among the loveliest places on campus is the **Franklin D. Murphy Sculpture Garden,** with five acres of lush landscaping and sculptures by Joan Miró, Henri Matisse, Henry Moore, and Auguste Rodin. Adjacent is the **Wight Art Gallery,** featuring contemporary and classics on display, and the **Grunwald Center for the Graphic Arts,** where the "works on paper" collection exceeds 35,000.

For sports fans—particularly Bruins fans—the **Morgan Center Hall of Fame** is a must-do destination. **Pauley Pavilion,** designed by Welton Becket and Associates, seats 12,545 and hosts UCLA Bruins basketball and various cultural events. Before big games, pick up ever-popular UCLA sweatshirts and other "Bearwear" selections at the **Ackerman Student Union** bookstore. The adjacent Gothic **Kerckhoff Hall,** home to student government offices and *The Daily Bruin* student newspaper, was designed by Royce Hall architects Allison and Allison in 1933 as a U.S. version of King Edward VII's Westminster chapel.

The **Center for Health Sciences** dominates the southern end of the UCLA campus—this the largest medical complex in the United States, home to the highly regarded **Schools of Medicine, Nursing, Dentistry, and Public Health.** Among the many health research institutes also housed here: the world-renowned **Jules Stein Eye Institute,** the **Jerry Lewis Center for Muscular Dystrophy,** and the **Neuropsychiatric Institute.**

Once you're done with a UCLA tour, the eight-acre **Mildred Mathias Botanical Gardens** on the southeastern edge of campus, with hundreds of species of trees and shrubs, make a pleasant escape.

UCLA Tours: The Bruin's-Eye View
To see what's where at UCLA, pick up a self-guided tour brochure at the on-campus **visitor center** or at the various campus entry kiosks. UCLA's **Campus Shuttle,** 310/206-2908, can get you around. Or sign up for a guided tour (reservations required), up to two hours long and scheduled on weekdays at 10:15 A.M. and 2:15 P.M., and on Saturdays during regular semester session at 10:15 A.M. only. For more information, contact: **UCLA Campus Tours,** 310/825-8764. Then, assuming you've been able to find a place to park, spend some time poking into the shops and coffeehouses of Westwood, adjacent to the campus.

Armand Hammer Museum of Art and Cultural Center
One of L.A.'s newer museums, the Armand Hammer Museum at 10899 Wilshire Blvd. (at Westwood), 310/443-7000, is built from the pre-viously private collection of the increasingly controversial industrialist—a subject people here won't be inclined to discuss. Armand Hammer, former chair of Occidental Petroleum, was widely vilified throughout the L.A. art world when he reneged on his promise to leave his collection to the Los Angeles County Museum of Art. His namesake museum was hammered again in 1994, on a grander scale, when it decided to sell its Codex Hammer—Hammer's most prized possession, previously known as the Codex Leicester collection of original Leonardo da Vinci technical manuscripts—at auction, to the highest bidder. Microsoft's Bill Gates bought it, for $30.8 million.

Though the museum collection may expand dramatically someday, now that the Codex is gone "the Hammer" is noted for its thousands of Honoré Daumier sculptures and lithographs. The other real draw is the Hammer's world-class traveling exhibits. (Call for current shows.) The Hammer is open Tues.–Sat. 11 A.M.–7 P.M. (until 9 P.M. on Thursday) and Sunday 11 A.M.–5 P.M., closed July 4, Thanksgiving, and Christmas. Admission is $4.50 adults, $3 students and seniors, $1 for UCLA students, and free for children under age 17. Parking is available at a discounted rate in the museum's underground parking garage.

CITIES ON A HILL~ THE GETTY AND VICINITY

Two new "cities" recently risen on the hills overlooking Sepulveda Pass, just off the San Diego Freeway north of Brentwood and Bel-Air, are among L.A.'s most striking new cultural attractions. The $800 million Getty Center, one of the world's most remarkable arts facilities, finally opened its doors to the public in December 1997. Not far north of the Getty is the impressive $65 million Skirball Cultural Center, a three-winged modernist monument of pink granite, green slate, and curving stainless steel with visitor-friendly facilities including the extraordinary Skirball Museum of Jewish History and a children's Discovery Center. The two institutions occasionally offer joint colaborative exhibits, such as *Sigmund Freud: Conflict & Culture* in 2000.

The Getty as Phenomenon

Originally envisioned as a second location for Malibu's renowned J. Paul Getty Museum, "the Getty" has become considerably more—starting with six huge stone building complexes and gorgeous central garden on 110 terraced acres with panoramic views of the city, the sea, and surrounding mountains.

The Getty is L.A.'s latest astonishment—architect Richard Meier's contemporary yet classic arts enclave, a 25-acre complex built of imported Italian travertine marble rising like a medieval castle above both city and sea on a ridge near Brentwood. "If God had the money," observed L.A. design critic Sam Hall Kaplan years before the Getty Center even opened its doors, "this is perhaps what he would do." The architectural statement, in his view, is that "this is a cultural institution here for the ages, not a passing indulgence, not a deconstructionist exercise by yet another narcissistic architect."

Whether God and other architects like it or not, and whatever else the Getty Center accomplishes, it has successfully carved out and created space—lots of it, nearly one million square feet—to make art appreciation more central to Los Angeles life. (Situated right next to the San Diego Freeway, how much more accessible could an L.A. art museum be?) It has also built the most formidable private arts program in the world, thanks in large part to the $4.1 billion J. Paul Getty Trust, an accumulation of cash now more than triple the oil baron's original bequest in 1976.

In addition to its stunning new museum and ever-expanding museum collection, Getty Trust projects now housed at the Getty Center include its international arts conservation and restoration institute, its high-tech art history information institute, its research institute fellowships in art history and the humanities, and its education, grant, and museum management programs. Getty Center highlights also include a 450-seat auditorium, a 750,000-volume library with reading areas and a small exhibit area, and a restaurant, a cafeteria, and two cafés. Visitors can also pack a picnic and just enjoy the facilities—for free.

The Getty as Museum

The Getty Center's centerpiece is its museum.

Inside the two-story circular lobby are two small theaters for visitor orientation and a book and gift shop. Surrounding a central garden courtyard are the five museum pavilions—vast galleries that allow display of much more of the J. Paul Getty Museum's collection, including European sculptures, illuminated manuscripts from the Middle Ages and the Renaissance, and previously unseen photographs from its collection of more than 60,000. Galleries are also highly interactive, with audio guides, multimedia computer stations, and expanded special-audience educational programs.

Prominently on display, in the sophisticated natural light of second-floor galleries, are stars of the Getty's growing Impressionist and post-Impressionist painting galaxy, including Vincent van Gogh's *Irises* and Claude Monet's *Morning, Snow Effect* and *Wheatstacks*. Visitors may also see fairly new Renaissance acquisitions—including Michelangelo's 1530 chalk-and-ink drawing *The Holy Family with the Infant Baptist on the Rest on the Flight into Egypt,* bought in 1993 for $6.27 million, and Fra Bartolommeo's *The Holy Family with the Infant St. John,* painted in 1509 and bought in 1996 for $22.5 million.

The museum's 15-room decorative arts section is a study in opulence. Here, exquisitely tarted-up rooms—with damask walls, faux marble, mirrors, and elaborately carved and painted panels—authentically exhibit the Getty's French furniture, tapestries, and other elegant domestic wares from baroque, neoclassical, *régence,* rococo, and other stylistic periods.

The previous showcase of the J. Paul Getty Trust was the original J. Paul Getty Museum in Malibu, an exact replica of a Roman villa. Now the museum's second campus, the Getty Villa has closed for renovation and reconfiguration, and is scheduled to reopen in the year 2002 as both the Getty Trust's museum of Greek and Roman antiquities and its "center for the display, conservation, and interpretation of ancient art in the broadest sense." The Getty Villa will also promote "a deeper understanding of, and critical appreciation for, comparative archaeology and cultures." Special exhibits of the ancient art and artifacts of Asia, Africa, Latin America, the Near East, and Eastern Europe will also be featured at the Getty Villa.

The Practical Getty

More than a million visitors commune with the Old Masters and other elements of the Getty's art world here each year. They arrive at the hilltop palace after a five-minute electric monorail-style tram ride up the hill from the six-story underground parking garage at the west end of Getty Center Drive, just off the San Diego Freeway (the 405) and N. Sepulveda Boulevard. The Getty Center is open to the public Tuesday and Wednesday 11 A.M.–7 P.M., Thursday and Friday 11 A.M.–9 P.M., and Saturday and Sunday 10 A.M.–6 or 7 P.M. (closed on Monday and on major holidays). Admission is free, though there is a $5 parking fee. Advance parking reservations are required—except for college students with valid ID and for anyone arriving for the Getty's "reservation-free" evenings, Thursday and Fri-

day after 4 P.M. Visitors arriving by bike, bus (MTA and Santa Monica buses serve the museum), or taxi also need no reservations. People planning to arrive by car and park elsewhere in nearby Brentwood are strongly discouraged, since this practice has caused considerable tension in the neighborhood. No pets are allowed, with the exception of trained guide and service animals.

Once arrived, Getty guests can take a detailed self-guided tour with the museum's hand-held CD-ROM audio guide, available in both English and Spanish, for a small rental fee. The audio guide features a special "family track" to assist with meaningful arts discussions between children and adults. Another resource is the Getty Center's staffed Family Room, on the courtyard near the East Pavilion, with its multitude of hands-on activities, games, puzzles, books, and CDs to connect kids with what they'll see in the galleries. Fun for older, computer-savvy kids and adults is the Getty's Digital Experience—a cornucopia of user-friendly information on Los Angeles arts and culture served up via CDs, videos, and online computers.

For further information on special programs, current exhibits, and advance reservations, contact: Getty Center, 1200 Getty Center Dr., Los Angeles, CA 90049, 310/440-7300; www .getty.edu.

ROBERT IRWIN'S CENTRAL GARDEN

Another Getty Center attraction is the 134,000-square-foot Central Garden near the museum, designed by "real-world" L.A. artist Robert Irwin—an intentionally self-conscious human-crafted garden reflecting upon the natural world as humanity has made it. Like a sculptor using both geometric and photosynthetic elements as "clay," Irwin has created a garden shaped like a huge handheld mirror, the overall image a severe and architectural landscape in winter yet soft, scented, and sensuous in summer. The mirror's "handle," roughly paralleled by a pathway, is created by an echo-chambered stream flanked by flowering plants and a canopy of trees. At stream's end, within a circular "natural" amphitheater, the stream becomes a shallow pool with a geometric maze of flowering azaleas—images of nature that seem to float on the water's surface. Irwin's garden won't be in full flower for at least a decade, since it will take at least that many years for the two main tree plantings—the sensuous crape myrtles and the London plane trees that will one day form a carefully clipped canopy above the stream—to achieve their intended effects. So in the meantime, just pull up one of the French café chairs and sit a spell. And enjoy.

Beyond the Getty:
Skirball Cultural Center

About two miles north of the Getty Center is the splendidly simple four-story Skirball Cultural Center, designed by Boston-based architect Moshe Safdie and named after Jack Skirball, a rabbi and producer of Alfred Hitchcock films. Various other museums and cultural monuments document the Jewish experience, but this one celebrates Jewish life—and Jewish-American life—in an effort to explain Jewish traditions, values, and vision. Yet the new Skirball center is dedicated to full participation in L.A.'s efforts to "create a new paradigm for its cultural institutions." Part of the point here is interpreting the American-Jewish experience as it translates to the experience of all immigrants—an effort to strengthen the fabric of American society and its institutions.

The center itself is some institution—including the Skirball Museum of Jewish History, the hands-on children's Discovery Center, an education center with classrooms, plus auditorium, conference facilities, and a large outdoor courtyard for concerts and other events, altogether 125,000 square feet of buildings on a 15-acre site.

The 15,000-square-foot museum covers 4,000 years of Jewish history throughout the world, celebrating in particular the American-Jewish experience. (An earlier, much smaller incarnation of the museum was, until recently, housed at Hebrew Union College just south of downtown L.A.) The core permanent exhibit—*Visions and Values: Jewish Life from Antiquity to America*—includes artifacts and art from ancient Israel and around the world, an ancient mosaic from Tiberias, recreated ruins of a sixth-century synagogue, and gallery exhibits on beliefs and celebrations. Then visitors "cross the big ocean," accompanied by sounds of the sea, beginning the American-Jewish experience. Particularly evocative here: the huge replica of the Statue of Liberty's torch and original benches from Ellis Island. After more American-Jewish history—including a reminder of the first Jewish arrivals in North America, who came from Brazil in the mid-1600s—exhibits integrate American-Jewish accomplishments and experience with the Holocaust and the rise of present-day Israel.

For information on current museum exhibits and other details, contact: Skirball Cultural Center, 2701 N. Sepulveda Blvd., 310/440-4500; www.skirball.org. The center is on N. Sepulveda Boulevard, on the west side of the San Diego Freeway just south of Mulholland Drive; from the 405, take the Skirball Center Drive/Mulholland Drive exit and follow the signs, crossing Sepulveda Drive into the center's south entrance. The museum is open Tues.–Sat. noon–5 P.M., Sunday 11 A.M.–5 P.M. (closed Monday). The Skirball is closed Thanksgiving, Christmas, and New Year's Day; call for other holiday closings. Admission is $8 adults, $6 seniors and students, free for children under age 12.

Changing exhibits, which regularly include art and history retrospectives, also spotlight very contemporary themes; call the general number listed above or see the website for current exhibit information. Free public tours are available daily,

no reservations required. To arrange private group tours (10 or more), special guided tours for the blind or visually impaired, or tours conducted in Hebrew, Yiddish, Spanish, French, German, or Italian, call 310/440-4573. The Skirball Cultural Center is wheelchair accessible, and wheelchairs are available upon request. Facilities include **Zeidler's Cafe** (call 310/440-4515 for reservations) and the equally impressive **Audrey's Museum Store,** 310/440-4505.

WILDERNESS CITY: THE SANTA MONICA MOUNTAINS

One of the few east-west-trending mountain ranges in the United States, the Santa Monica Mountains extend upward from the sea as part of the Channel Islands and then eastward from Pacific Ocean beaches and tidepools to Mount Hollywood in Griffith Park on the mainland, creating the geographical divide between the Los Angeles Basin and the San Fernando Valley.

The Santa Monica Mountains National Recreation Area, a 70,000-acre parkland pastiche created by Congress in 1978, protects much of the remaining open space in the Santa Monica Mountains—city, county, state, federal, private, and once-private lands and beaches—within a unified identity. Yet within that unity is great diversity. Maintaining separate boundaries are parks of long standing, including Malibu Creek State Park, Topanga State Park, and Will Rogers State Historic Park, various public beaches, and attractions such as Paramount Ranch, Peter Strauss Ranch, and the fairly new Streisand Center for Conservancy Studies. Thanks to the Santa Monica Mountains Conservancy and other groups and individuals, land acquisitions continue to expand this national park—and the boundaries of individual parks within it—while extending the recreation area's trail system, popular with hikers, mountain bikers, and horseback riders. At last report, hikers, bikers, and equestrians were still battling over the issue of increasing mountain bike access to back-country trails—to some an issue of overuse and abuse of trails as well as "machine-age encroachment," to others a question of equal rights for cyclists.

At the beaches, summer is prime time, but the off-seasons offer at least the opportunity for solitude (and better beachcombing). Winter and spring, when the sky is blue and the hills are green, are the best seasons for exploring the mountains, which boast about 860 species of flowering plants in environments varying from grasslands, oak woodlands, and riparian sycamore and fern glades to coastal chaparral and craggy red-rock canyons. The only Mediterranean ecosystem protected by the National Park Service, the Santa Monicas have posed for TV and movie crews as Greece, Italy, France, Korea, the Wild West, and the antebellum South. Some areas are absolutely otherworldly; interplanetary film possibilities have yet to be fully explored here.

But because so much of the area is urban, surrounded by millions of people and bordered by two of the world's busiest freeways, and its attractions far-flung, finding one's way around in the Santa Monica Mountains can get complicated. To get oriented, stop by or contact the national park's visitor center and associated bookstore, open daily 9 A.M.–5 P.M. (closed Thanksgiving, Christmas, and New Year's Day). Along with maps and other helpful publications, the office offers a wonderful quarterly calendar of guided walks and other events, *Outdoors in the Santa Monica Mountains National Recreation Area,* also available online.

For more information, contact: **Santa Monica Mountains National Recreation Area Visitor Center,** 401 W. Hillcrest Dr., Thousand Oaks, CA 91360, 805/370-2301; www.nps .gov/samo. To get there from the Ventura Freeway (Hwy. 101), exit at Lynn Road and continue north; turn east on Hillcrest; then turn left onto McCloud. The visitor center is the first driveway on the right. For information on area state parks, contact **California State Parks,** 1925 Las Virgenes Rd., Calabasas, CA 91302, 818/880-0350. Though associated state parks and beaches charge at least a nominal day-use or parking fee, general access to national parks land is free. (For information on relevant state parks, see listings below. For state and county beaches, see The Los Angeles Coast chapter.) Access hours also vary. Wildfires are a major threat to the park and its urban and suburban neighbors, so no fires are allowed within most park areas. Permission to explore environmentally sensitive areas, including **Cold Creek Canyon Preserve** near Topanga State Park, are by permit only, so docent-led hikes are usually the best way to go.

Will Rogers State Historic Park

"The more you read about politics," laureate Will Rogers once observed, "you got to admit that each party is worse than the other." America's favorite cowboy commentator, originally a rodeo trick roper, was still making a name for himself in 1928 when he and his family settled at this ranch in then-rural Pacific Palisades, just north of Santa Monica.

The unassuming 31-room home features mission-style furniture, eclectic Western decor, and some eye-catching oddities—including a stuffed calf Rogers regularly used for indoor roping practice. Museum exhibits tell the Will Rogers story, up to and including his tragic death in 1935. To make a day of it, enjoy the picnic grounds and the national park's hiking trails—including very popular Backbone Trail, now open to mountain bikers. Otherwise, the big weekend draw is the equestrian action—polo matches, a continuation of the tradition started by Rogers himself, open to the public. There's also a roping and training area for horses.

For more information, contact: Will Rogers State Historic Park, 1501 Will Rogers State Park Rd., 310/454-8212, fax 310/459-2031. The park is open daily 8 A.M.–7 P.M. in summer, 8 A.M.–6 P.M. in other seasons. The Rogers home/ museum is open daily 10:30 A.M.–5 P.M. for tours (closed Thanksgiving, Christmas, and New Year's Day). Tours run every hour on the half-hour, starting at 10:30 A.M., with the last tour at 4:30 P.M. Weather permitting, polo matches are scheduled on Saturday at 2 P.M. and Sunday at 10 A.M. Park admission is free, technically, but parking is $2 per vehicle.

Topanga State Park

Native peoples called this canyon "Topanga," meaning "the place where the mountains meet the sea." And so it is. One of the world's largest urban wildlands, Topanga State Park's 11,000-plus acres, preserved as open space, are almost all within L.A.'s city limits. Topanga is a hiker's and equestrian's park, with most fire roads now also open to mountain bikers. Most trailheads start at the old Trippet Ranch at the park's official entrance, with pleasant picnic area and self-guided nature trail. The eastern section of the aptly named Backbone Trail ambles along ridge tops and then down toward the sea, ending at Will Rogers State Historic Park—and offering, en route, some dazzling views of the Pacific Ocean and Santa Monica Bay.

To reach the park entrance, head south from the Ventura Freeway (the 101) or north from Pacific Coast Highway (Hwy. 1), exit at Topanga Canyon Boulevard and turn east onto Entrada Road. Hikers can also reach the park from Will Rogers State Historic Park. The park is open daily 8 A.M.–sunset (parking lot hours), but Topanga is actually never closed except during extreme fire danger or other emergency. Technically park admission is free, but parking is $2. No dogs are allowed. Campgrounds here are first-come, first-camped. For more information, contact: Topanga State Park, 20825 Entrada Rd., 310/454-8212 or 818/880-0350. For the spring wildflower report, call 818/768-3533.

Paramount Ranch

The primary set for filming the popular television series *Dr. Quinn, Medicine Woman,* Western Town at Paramount Ranch boasts an illustrious Hollywood-western history. A remnant of 2,700 acres of Rancho Las Virgenes bought by Paramount Studios in 1927, the ranch also served as studio set for *The Rifleman* and *Have Gun Will Travel* episodes, not to mention *Bat Masterson* and *The Cisco Kid.*

When the kids are done poking through the façades of Western Town, why not take a hike? Just behind Western Town is half-mile Coyote Canyon Trail. In early spring the route leads up through the wildflowers and oak woodlands to some possible picnic sites—and a good eagle's-eye view of Western Town below—before circling back down. For a more ambitious hike, set out on the park's Run Trail. A recent 320-acre addition to Paramount Ranch adds still more trail.

On weekdays, Western Town is often used for film shoots. During filming the public is wel-

come to observe but not to wander through the sets. The Old West sets are open to the public every weekend and on weekdays when no filming is under way. Filming or no, the ranch is open to the public daily for picnicking and hiking, 8 A.M.–sunset. Most educational, however, are the monthly Saturday-morning guided hikes (free, call for scheduled dates).

To get here: From the Ventura Freeway (the 101), exit at Kanan Road and continue south for about three-fourths of a mile. Turn left at the "Cornell Way" sign and then go to the right (Cornell Way becomes Cornell Road). The ranch entrance is another 2.5 miles on the right.

Celebrity Spreads: Streisand and Strauss

Wonderful as a respite from San Fernando Valley gridlock is the **Peter Strauss Ranch** near Agoura, where you can picnic on the lawn or stretch your legs on a mile-long stroll. Among newer park acquisitions is the Barbra Streisand Center for Conservancy Studies. Actress, songstress, and movie producer Barbra Streisand donated her exclusive 22.5-acre, $15 million Malibu spread to the state in late 1993, and it's now known as **Ramirez Canyon Park,** operated by the Santa Monica Mountains Conservancy. An environmental think tank, the Streisand Center for Conservancy Studies offers occasional public tours of the center's architectural, botanical, and historical features, including two of four homes here. For both of these celebrity spreads, call the national park office for current information.

Point Mugu State Park

Here, about 10 miles south of Oxnard in Ventura County, the Santa Monica Mountains meet the sea. Many hillside areas were seriously burned in Southern California's raging 1993 wildfires, as was much of Malibu's mountainous backdrop, but the coastal chaparral and woodlands are rapidly regenerating. The rugged Boney Mountain Wilderness, a section of the Backbone Trail, and the ocean-view La Jolla Canyon Loop Trail are hiking highlights of this 15,000-acre park. To enjoy the beach—a five-mile stretch of ocean frontage is included here—try Sycamore Cove or Thornhill Broome (the latter backed by campsites). Inquire about swimming safety. Adjacent to Point Mugu, in the north, is the national park's Rancho Sierra Vista and Satwiwa Native American Natural Area. Adjoining on the southeast is the recreation area's Circle X Ranch.

Visitor facilities include developed woodland campsites (less wooded now) at Big Sycamore Creek Campground and primitive campsites at the beach, picnic areas, restrooms, dump station, and trails for horses, hikers, and mountain bikers. Day use is $2. For campsite reservations, especially during the peak April—Sept. season (and weekends), contact ReserveAmerica, toll-free 800/444-7275; www.reservamerica.com. For other visitor information, contact Point Mugu State Park, 9000 W. Pacific Coast Hwy. in Malibu, 818/880-0350, 805/488-5223 (recorded), or 805/488-1827.

Palo Comado Canyon and Other Recent Acquisitions
In 1993, the Santa Monica Mountains Conservancy acquired about 1,600 acres owned by entertainer Bob Hope in Palo Comado Canyon next to the Ventura County line; the deal was part of a complicated land transaction involving the Ahmanson Ranch development in the works northeast of Calabasas in nearby Las Virgenes Canyon. (Runkle Ranch, more than 4,000 acres near Simi Valley now open to the public as Rocky Peak Park, and 339-acre Corral Canyon near Malibu, have also been acquired as part of a complicated land exchange connected to the Ahmanson Ranch housing development.) The hiking high point of Palo Comado is 750 acres of oaks, meadows, and old movie sets at **China Flat.**

Another long-standing park priority is acquiring parcels to eventually extend popular **Backbone Trail** the entire 65-mile distance between Will Rogers State Historic Park and Point Mugu State Park. Fairly new sections of trail include **Fossil Ridge** and **Hondo Canyon,** both accessible from Mulholland Highway. The acquisition of **Zuma and Trancas Canyons,** between Mulholland Highway/Encinal Canyon Road and PCH, is also a step in that direction.

The Santa Monica Mountains Conservancy and the recreation area are in the process of acquiring other new acreage. For current information on acquisitions open to the public, contact the national parks office.

STAYING IN AND AROUND BEVERLY HILLS

Bankrolled by entertainment-industry wealth, together Beverly Hills and adjacent West Hollywood comprise L.A.'s premier hotel district; nearby Westwood and Bel-Air also offer uptown contenders, including the Hotel Bel-Air, one of the nation's most beloved luxury hotels. Yet serene Beverly Hills still has its surprises—including the fact that it can be less expensive to stay here than in wilder West Hollywood. (Besides, BH is that much closer to the beach.) Also look for reasonably priced accommodations in neighboring Westwood. As in other areas attractive to business travelers, inquire about discounts and holiday, seasonal, and/or weekend specials, which here can sometimes transform a pricey luxury stay into an unbelievable bargain.

BEVERLY HILLS STAYS

Reasonably Reasonable in BH
Not everything in Beverly Hills is outrageously expensive. One popular option is the **Beverly Terrace Motor Hotel** near the Pacific Design Center, one block from Melrose Avenue at 469 N. Doheny Dr. (near Santa Monica Blvd.), 310/274-8141. The 39 standard motel-style rooms are typically booked months in advance. Beyond the basics, enjoy the small pool, sundeck, free parking, and continental breakfast. Rates are $105–$125. Another best bet in Beverly Hills is the brick colonial **Maison 140,** 140 S. Lasky Dr. (near Santa Monica Blvd.), 310/271-2145 or toll-free 800/432-5444, a small, friendly hotel with European style and little extras such as continental breakfast and free parking. Who cares if the bathrooms are a bit small? Rooms are $140–$180, a relative bargain. If you *must* have opulence, just stroll through the neighborhood and eyeball the Peninsula Beverly Hills around the corner (and see other luxury hotel listings, below).

Possible Beverly Hills Deals
Once the Beverly Crest Hotel, the four-story,

48-room **Beverly Hills Inn,** 125 S. Spalding Dr., 310/278-0303 or, for reservations, toll-free 800/537-8483, isn't flashy yet is quite comfortable and convenient. Amenities include cable TV, free movies, in-room refrigerators, laundry and exercise facilities, saunas, pool, and coffee shop. Continental breakfast and parking included. Rates are $155–$225.

Even standard-brand stays are not entirely standard in and around Beverly Hills. The friendly, recently renovated **Holiday Inn Select Beverly Hills** just north of Pico Blvd. at 1150 S. Beverly Dr., 310/553-6561 or toll-free 800/465-4329 (worldwide), once a Ramada Inn, can still offer vacation value at a very convenient uptown address. All rooms feature coffeemakers and VCRs, color TVs, and both free and "fee" movies (making it easier to catch up on Tinseltown's tinsel while you're here). Beyond the usual motel amenities and the pool, a stay here includes free shuttle service and free use of a nearby fitness center. Rates run $149–190 for rooms, $300 for suites.

Bargains are sometimes available at **Merv Griffin's Beverly Hilton Hotel,** fast becoming more than just another Hilton. Merv's Hilton, located at 9876 Wilshire Blvd. (at Santa Monica Blvd.), 310/274-7777 or toll-free 800/445-8667, is a pretty classy joint. Long gone are the dreary guest cubicles—in their stead are large, elegant rooms with terraces, color TVs, cable, movies, in-room coffeemakers, and honor bars. The elegant rooftop L'Escoffier restaurant is gone, but a spiffed-up **Trader Vic's** remains. **Griff's,** the new poolside restaurant, is a best bet for Sunday brunch. Rooms are $230–280 double, from $300 suite.

If you've always fantasized about staying *on* Rodeo Drive, the 86-room **Luxe Hotel Rodeo Drive,** 360 N. Rodeo Dr., 310/273-0300 or toll-free 800/421-0545, recently renovated, attractive rooms and the street's only sidewalk café—perfect for people watching. Breakfast and free parking included, with substantial discount rates for AAA members. Rates are $255 and up.

Particularly Good Value in BH

Some of the best BH stays lie just beyond the city limits. A bargain by Beverly Hills standards is the ever-popular **Beverly Plaza Hotel,** two blocks east of La Cienega at 8384 W. Third St.,323/658-6600 or toll-free 800/624-6835, www.beverlyplazahotel.com, just blocks away from the Beverly Center and otherwise well-situated for serious shopping. (The $10 per day taxi voucher helps, too.) Not to be confused with the Beverly Hills Plaza Hotel in nearby Westwood, the five-story, 98-room Beverly Plaza features simple, traditional, and tastefully decorated rooms amply stuffed with amenities. Standard here: cable TV, honor bars, and in-room refrigerators, plus exercise facilities, sauna, and pool. The wonderful Spanish-Mediterranean restaurant **Cava,** complete with tapas bar, is another draw. Rates: $149 and up, but inquire about discounts.

The **Carlyle Inn,** near the design district one block south of Olympic Blvd. at 1119 S. Robertson Blvd., 310/275-4445 or toll-free 800/322-7595, www.carlyle-inn.com, appears to be a nondescript four-story stucco bunker. Yet inside hides a gracious little boutique hoThe 32-room Carlyle features an interior courtyard, graceful lobby, lovely rooms, restaurant, fitness facilities, hot tub, and sundeck. Enjoy a full buffet breakfast, afternoon tea, wine in the evenings, and special extras—such as free shuttle service 6 A.M.–9 P.M. within a five-mile reach. All rooms have in-room coffeemakers, safes, and data ports as well as color TVs with cable. Rates of $130–165.

The **Renaissance Beverly Hills** nearby, 1224 S. Beverwil Dr., 310/277-2800 or toll-free 800/ 421-3212, is the contemporary reincarnation of the old Beverly Hillcrest Hotel, once known for its 1960s' kitsch. This Beverly has had a facelift in addition to a name change, and recently acquired a clever sophistication, making this one of the more affordable, attractive, and appealing "new" luxury hotels in town. All rooms at this 12-story beauty are large, with balconies, views, and the usual comforts. Other pluses here: pool, full fitness facilities, business suites with in-room faxes, good on-site restaurant, and around-town shuttle service. Rates: $198 and up, with special rates available.

Another possibility: **The Radisson Beverly Pavilion,** 9360 Wilshire Blvd., 310/273-1400 or toll-free 800/441-5050, a small boutique-style hotel within walking distance of prime Beverly Hills shopping. Known for good service, its excellent on-site restaurant **Earth,** and stylish rooms—upper-floor rooms facing west come with sunset views—the Beverly Pavilion also provides a rooftop pool, sundeck, and the usual luxury amenities, including in-room refrigerators and hair dryers. Rates are $159–219.

Beverly Hills Hotel

Even staid Beverly Hills was silly with excitement in the mid-1990s with the news that the mythic mission revival-style "Pink Palace" was ready to reopen after a $100 million renovation. Star of the original 1937 *A Star is Born* and of more recent films including *The Way We Were, California Suite,* and *American Gigolo,* for all its on-screen glory the Beverly Hills had needed some very basic rebuilding—to improve its antique electrical wiring and sputtering old plumbing system and to install such necessities as central air-conditioning. Built in 1912, when most of the area was still one big lima bean field—its original address was "halfway between Los Angeles and the sea"—the 194-room Beverly Hills Hotel is now owned by the Sultan of Brunei, Hassanal Bolkiah, and once again a favorite playground—no, elaborate stage set—for the rich, famous, and celebrity-conscious.

Recently enlarged rooms and historic bungalows on the 12-acre grounds feature every imaginable comfort, including Ralph Lauren linens, computers, fax machines and copiers, VCRs and color TVs, CD players, telephones with private direct lines, even butler-service buttons, not to mention the possibility of in-room massage and other spa services. Now—huge bathrooms include double sinks of Grecian marble, more media—telephones and TVs—even motorized draperies. Special features of the Beverly Hills Hotel include those private cabanas near the pool area, which is still something of a see-and-be-seen celebrity standard in these parts; the cabanas are also populated with phones and business paraphernalia. Most famous for phones, though, is the **Polo Lounge,** long renowned for its "power booths," favored uptown digs for Hollywood deal-making and once again fully plugged in. Also back in business: the **Fountain Coffee Shop,** still decked out in the hotel's trademark banana-leaf wallpaper. For romance, one of the best choices around is the art-deco ambience of the elegant California-style French **Polo Grill.**

The landmark pink stucco Beverly Hills Hotel is grandly situated on Sunset Boulevard above triangular Will Rogers Memorial Park (at Rodeo Drive), 9641 Sunset Blvd., 310/276-2251 or toll-free 800/283-8885; www.beverlyhillshotel .com. Historic bungalows and rooms are more expensive. Standard rooms start at a budget-breaking $325, while elaborate bungalows and suites top out at about $4,000. That's right—per night.

Regent Beverly Wilshire

In Beverly Hills, one can also opt for Old-World opulence. A good choice in that category, one of the city's finest hotels, is the Regent Beverly Wilshire, a posh circa-1928 Wilshire Boulevard landmark.

Start exploring in the lobby, a stunning display of antiques and elegant wood, glass, and marble, and soak up still more ambience in the **Lobby Lounge**—just the place for afternoon tea—**The Bar,** usually overflowing with agents and other entertainment industry types, and either the café or the elegant **Regent Dining Room.** Don't miss the lovely pool area, either, or the spa; the full gym is on the second floor. The Beverly Wilshire's lavish $4,000-a-night presidential suite has hosted Elvis Presley and the late Japanese Emperor Hirohito, among many other international luminaries, though it's much more famous as home base for the cynical-businessman-meets-hooker-with-a-heart-of-gold movie romance *Pretty Woman.*

The grand older rooms are in the Beverly Wilshire's **Wilshire Wing;** newer rooms are in the **Beverly Wing** tower and offer balconies overlooking the pool. All rooms are large, with double-glazed windows to minimize street noise, period furnishings, and gigantic marble bathrooms—complete with deep, wide bathtubs, separate showers, and large vanities. All the usual amenities, too, from cable TVs and movies to in-room safes and honor bars. A special welcoming touch upon arrival: fresh raspberries and cream delivered to your room. Complete business services are available; contemporary executive suites feature a separate living room.

The Regent Beverly Wilshire sits at the foot of Rodeo Drive at 9500 Wilshire Blvd., 310/275-5200; for reservations within California, call toll-free 800/421-4354. "Standard" room rates are $365–540; suites range from $520 to a whopping $4,500. Here as elsewhere the tab is somewhat fluid, so ask about weekend specials.

Four Seasons Hotel Los Angeles

One of L.A.'s best hotels—and one of its most attractive—the 16-story Four Seasons is another jewel in the impressive Canadian chain. This 285-room hotel features large rooms amply outfitted for either business or pleasure, with two

The Regent Beverly Hills Wilshire Hotel presides over Rodeo Drive.

TVs (one in the bathroom), two two-line telephones (and free mobile phones), a well-stocked honor bar, plus hair dryer, sumptuous terry robes, and other little luxuries. The inviting pool, exercise facilities, spa, and sundeck are on the fourth floor. Head for the lobby bar to be an entertainment industry social voyeur, to the café or swank **Gardens** restaurant for more substantial fare. Located in a quiet residential neighborhood. Room rates are $325–395, suites from $650, with various discounts usually available. For more information or reservations, contact: Four Seasons Los Angeles, 300 S. Doheny Dr. (at Burton Way), 310/273-2222, www .fourseasons.com; for Four Seasons' central reservations service, call toll-free 800/332-3442.

Peninsula Beverly Hills
The Peninsula Beverly Hills is the epitome of discretion. Tucked into a quiet residential neighborhood, the contemporary French Renaissance palace and two-story villas serve as home-away-from-home for the classically, cautiously wealthy. Tasteful yet opulent rooms and suites feature marble floors, antique furnishings, fine fabrics, telephones with voice mail, TVs with VCRs, and down comforters; refrigerators and minibars are discreetly tucked away behind French doors. Suites and villas come with individual security systems, fax machines, and CD players; some feature fireplaces, spa baths, and private patios. Full fitness and spa facilities, including rooftop pool, steam room, and saunas, and complete business services are also available. Since the Peninsula Beverly Hills is sister to the Palace Hotel in Beijing and the Peninsula and the Kowloon in Hong Kong, it seems only fitting that the **Belvedere** here serves fine, formal French with Asian touches, though you can enjoy more casual fare at the lobby piano lounge. And if you need a lift somewhere, one of the hotel's Rolls-Royce fleet can drop you off.

For more information and reservations, contact: Peninsula Beverly Hills, 9882 Little Santa Monica Blvd., 310/273-4888 or toll-free 800/462-7899; www.peninsula.com. Deluxe rooms are $375–450, suites also available.

L'Ermitage Beverly Hills
This luxury hotel is one of L.A.'s best, and it's also a darling of tech execs and entertainment people, who appreciate the state-of-the-art electronic amenities. Spacious guest rooms are appointed with guest cell phones that work as far away as San Diego and Palm Springs, high-speed Internet access and WEB TV, and "intelligent" in-room lighting and climate control systems that adapt to an individual guest's preferences. Other luxuries include L.A.'s largest rooftop pool, fitness facilities with a view, library, and tea lounge, not to mention free limousine service around Beverly Hills. Rooms are $330–475, suites $600 and up. For more information or reservations, contact: L'Ermitage Beverly Hills, 9291 Burton Way, 310/278-3344 or toll-free 800/800-2113; www .lermitagehotel .com.

Le Meridien at Beverly Hills
The contemporary seven-story Le Meridien is another excellent L.A. accommodation, catering to business travelers and offering Asian style. Nondescript on the outside yet sleek, sophisticated, and charming inside, Le Meridien features a stylish Pacific Rim restaurant, **Pangaea,** fitness facilities, saunas, pool, and abundant all-business amenities. Generous rooms include sliding screens, fascinating desks, fully equipped phones, fax machines, in-room coffeemakers, refrigerators and honor bars, and complete entertainment setups: TV, VCR, CD player. Techies will appreciate the bedside electronic "command center." Large bathrooms feature Japanese soaking tubs. Rooms start at $300, and suites are $345–1,800. Free or valet parking.

For more information, contact: Le Meridien, 465 S. La Cienega, 310/247-0400; www .nikkohotel.com. For reservations, call toll-free 800/645-5624 or 800/645-5687.

BEL-AIR AND BRENTWOOD STAYS

Hotel Bel-Air
Beverly Hills and vicinity boasts glitzier and more ostentatious luxury hotels, but the Hotel Bel-Air is a world-class act—a stunningly beautiful 11-acre country château complete with creek, tiny lake with swans ("Swan Lake"), forested gardens, bougainvillea, birds of paradise, and the luxury of

absolute serenity and solitude. This celebrated hideout for celebrities, royalty, and the reclusive rich, a hidden Mediterranean village with 92 tile-roofed bungalows, is also an immensely popular Southern California getaway for honeymoons, anniversaries, and other special occasions. (Here, affluence doesn't invariably translate into snobbery—a marvelous feature.) In the 1920s the hotel's main buildings were the real estate sales offices for the original Bel-Air development; hotel conversion came in the 1940s, with later buildings continuing the original style.

And the style here—terra-cotta tile floors, wood-burning fireplaces, handmade rugs, private patios and gardens, and endless understated luxuries—has attracted celebrities such as Grace Kelly and Gary Cooper, Howard Hughes, the Rockefellers, and the Kennedys. Marilyn Monroe's favorite bungalow has been converted into the Bel-Air's new health spa. More popular destinations, though, include the exceptional California-French restaurant, the Swan Lake dining terrace, and the fabulous pool (reserve a spot early). Rooms are $380–580, suites start at $650.

For more information or reservations, contact: Hotel Bel-Air, 701 Stone Canyon Rd., 310/472-1211 or toll-free 800/648-4097, www .hotelbelair.com.

Brentwood Stays

Near the San Diego Freeway, particularly convenient for business travelers, is the **Summit Hotel Bel-Air** in Brentwood, just west of the San Diego Freeway at 11461 Sunset Blvd., 310/476-6571 or toll-free 800/468-3541. Formerly a Radisson, this attractive two-story garden oasis features contemporary California style; large rooms with color TVs and VCRs, in-room coffeemakers, refrigerators, and honor bars; and tennis court, pool, and exercise facilities. Rooms are $139–165.

Quite reasonable in Brentwood is the 20-room **Brentwood Motor Hotel** one mile west of the San Diego Freeway at 12200 W. Sunset Blvd., 310/476-9981 or toll-free 800/840-3808, www.bmhotel.com, where recently renovated and redecorated rooms feature cable TV, free movies, refrigerators, and coffeemakers. Rooms are $99–124.

WESTWOOD AND CENTURY CITY STAYS

W Los Angeles

This elegant all-suites hotel, adjacent to UCLA and just a limo-stretch away from Beverly Hills, doesn't make a dazzling first impression. But the entertainment industry and other corporate client types are unperturbed, since the cold 15-story concrete façade is transformed, once inside, into warm and contemporary California suites featuring the usual luxuries, plus ethernet laptop connections and AVEDA toiletries. Not to mention two swimming pools, complete spa, and the outstanding **Mojo** restaurant. For more information or reservations, contact: W Los Angeles, 930 Hilgard Ave. (three blocks north of Wilshire Blvd.), 310/208-8765 toll-free 800/421-2317; www.whotels.com. Rates in this all-suites property start as $239 for suites and $325 for penthouse suites.

Other Westwood Stays

A more affordable alternative across the street from the Westwood Marquis is three-story **Hilgard House,** 927 Hilgard Ave., 310/208-3945 or toll-free 800/826-3934; www.hilgardhouse .com. This small (47-room) European-style hotel on the eastern edge of UCLA offers quaint rooms with Queen Anne–style furnishings, window seats, refrigerators, color TVs with cable, and Jacuzzi bathtubs (first floor rooms only), breakfast and parking included. Room rates are $119–129, with special rates sometimes available. From here it's an easy stroll to Westwood Village restaurants and movie theaters and 10 minutes by van to the Getty Center.

Also quite comfortable and even more affordable: the quiet four-story, 80-room **Hotel del Capri** surrounded by high-rises at 10587 Wilshire Blvd., Los Angeles 90024, 310/474-3511 or toll-free 800/444-6835; www.hoteldelcapri.com. Most of the 80 rooms feature fully equipped kitchenettes, whirlpool tubs, and color TVs with cable and free movies. Rooms are $100–110, suites $125–135. Free parking, pool, lovely gardens.

Then there's the **Beverly Hills Plaza Hotel,** 10300 Wilshire Blvd., 310/275-5575 or toll-free 800/800-1234, formerly the Beverly Hills Ritz

Hotel and, before that, the Beverly Hills Comstock HoThe hotel is a snazzy and contemporary onetime apartment complex built around a central courtyard and pool; every suite, except the studio suites, features living room and kitchen, bathroom, and bedrooms—a very inviting setup for a longer stay. Rates start at $165 for a junior suite and soar to $495 for the penthouse suite.

The 99-room **Century Wilshire Hotel,** 10776 Wilshire Blvd., 310/474-4506 or toll-free 800/421-7223, www.centurywilshirehotel.com, is another apartment building converted to a hotel, this one particularly popular with Europeans. Each suite features a fully equipped kitchenette, tiled bathroom, and English-style decor; extras include free parking, pool, and continental breakfast. Daily standard room rates are $95–115, suites $125–275, with weekly and monthly rates available.

Other possible Westwood stays include the **Royal Palace Westwood** just north of Wilshire Blvd. at 1052 Tiverton Ave., 310/208-6677, www.royalpalacewestwood.com, a 36-unit apartment-style motel popular with visiting professors and featuring just the basics plus kitchenettes (rooms $80–125), and the upscale 296-room **Doubletree Hotel** (formerly the Holiday Inn Westwood Plaza) close to UCLA and Westwood Village at 10740 Wilshire Blvd., 310/475-8711 or toll-free 800/472-8556 (rooms $185–219, with lower weekend and promotional rates).

Best bets for a motel-style stay near Westwood include the **Best Western Westwood Pacific Hotel** a block west of the San Diego Freeway at 11250 Santa Monica Blvd. (at Sawtelle Blvd.), 310/478-1400 or toll-free 800/528-1234. Room rates are $89–109. Expensive. And the all-suite **Best Western Royal Palace Inn and Suites** also near the freeway, just south of Pico Boulevard at 2528 S. Sepulveda Blvd., 310/477-9066 or toll-free 800/528-1234, where the basics include kitchenette and queen-size sleeper sofa (in addition to the bed). Rates are $85–105.

Westin Century Plaza Hotel

This is where Ronald Reagan usually stayed when he visited Los Angeles during his presidency. In fact, every president since Lyndon Baines Johnson has stayed here—as have miscellaneous international royalty—since the rooftop helipad is a major boon for the incessantly security-conscious. Designed in the mid-1960s by Minoru Yamasaki, the main body of this vast 20-story hotel has 724 rooms, each with three telephones, private wall vaults, stocked bars, and private balconies. Major benefits and other social events often whirl throughout the hoMost people are more entertained by the good restaurants here, the **Cafe Plaza,** the trendy **Breeze** restaurant, and the **Lobby Court** cocktail lounge. Room rates are $229–375, but this being a business-oriented hotel, look for specials and packages on weekends.

For more information or reservations, contact: Westin Century Plaza Hotel and Tower, 2025 Avenue of the Stars, 310/277-2000 or 551-3300, toll-free 800/228-3000.

Other Century City Stays

Also nice in the neighborhood: the **Park Hyatt Los Angeles at Century City,** 2151 Avenue of the Stars, 310/277-1234; for central reservations call toll-free 800/233-1234. This 367-room luxury hotel is big with business, thus the in-room fax machines and expanded business center. Comfortable rooms feature gigantic bathrooms and the usual generous amenities; for voyeurs of moviemaking, some rooms overlook the Twentieth Century Fox back lot. A major on-site attraction is the fitness complex, featuring indoor and outdoor heated pools, saunas, steam rooms, and whirlpool spas. Standard room rates hover around $299, suites start at $359.

Less pricey choices include the **Courtyard by Marriott** just east of Beverly Glen at 10320 W. Olympic Blvd., 310/556-2777 or toll-free 800/321-2211 (regular rooms $169 during the week, $129 on weekends; and the **Holiday Inn Express at Century City** next door at 10330 W. Olympic Blvd., 310/553-1000 or toll-free 800/553-1005, with in-room coffeemakers and microwaves, bathrooms with whirlpool tubs (rooms $119–139).

EATING IN AND AROUND BEVERLY HILLS

FAIRLY AFFORDABLE FARE

People's Eats in BH: Burgers and Such

Sooner or later everyone goes to **Hamburger Hamlet,** 122 S. Beverly Dr. (at Wilshire Blvd.), 310/274-0191, famous for its bacon cheeseburgers. The original Hamlet, on Bonner Drive in West Hollywood, 310/278-4924, is now well past 50 years old, vinyl booths and all, but has had a facelift. For burgers and such served with self-conscious 1950s-style kitsch—and milkshakes made with Dreyer's ice cream—the place is campy **Ed Debevic's** diner, 134 N. La Cienega Blvd., 310/659-1952, open daily for lunch and dinner. For better 1950s' fare, in this case with unmistakable New Wave flair (dig that fondue), even veggie options, the place is the new, improved **Cadillac Cafe** back again at 359 N. La Cienega Blvd., 310/657-6591, where it originally parked in the 1980s. For more predictable retro, there's always smallish **Johnny Rockets,** 474 N. Beverly Dr., 310/271-2222, where the fare runs to good malts, fries, juicy burgers, and general jocularity.

People's Eats in BH: Beyond Burgers

The place for fresh-baked bagels and other fundamentals is **The Nosh of Beverly Hills,** 9689 S. Santa Monica Blvd., 310/271-3730. But for sit-down breakfast consider the **Beverly Hills Breakfast Club** tucked into department store row at 9671 Wilshire Blvd. (at Roxbury Dr.), 310/271-8903, serving good French toast and omelettes or salads and sandwiches and open daily for breakfast and lunch.

Want to really save money for shopping Rodeo Drive? Then stop by the popular chain **Baja Fresh,** here situated across the street from Johnny Rockets at 475 N. Beverly Dr., 310/858-6690, and saluted for its freshly grilled healthy Mexican fare. Very inexpensive, tasty, and fresh.

Inexpensive Asian fare isn't easy to come by in Beverly Hills, but one possibility is **ABC Szechwan Chinese Restaurant,** 9036 Burton Way (at Doheny), 310/288-2182, where a four-course lunch will set you back less than $10. It's open for lunch Mon.–Sat., for dinner daily. Also unusual is the Japanese **Curry House,** 163 N. La Cienega Blvd. (one block north of Wilshire Blvd.), 310/854-4959, just a few doors down from the much more famous (and much, much more expensive) Matsuhisa. What's served here is an Americanized version of Japan's favorite curried dishes, as translated from the Indian originals through the English, including breaded pork cutlets, chicken, and battered shrimp, not to mention a number of other well-prepared entrées quite popular in Japan. Stay for coffee and dessert—particularly the tofu cheesecake. Takeout available. Validated parking in the adjacent lot.

For pizza, some say the best in town comes from actress Cathy "Raging Bull" Moriarty's **Mulberry Street Pizzeria,** 347 N. Cañon Dr. (at Dayton), 310/247-8998, famous for its thin-crust New York-style. For authenticity's sake, even the water used for making the pizza dough is shipped in from New York—the mineral content is different—and the crust is cooked on stone, instead of steel, at 650° F for the perfect crunch. Another people's favorite is tiny **Jacopo's,** 490 N. Beverly Dr. (at Little Santa Monica Blvd.), 310/858-6446, serving its own cheese-rich New York-style pizza (popular for takeout, but Jacopo's delivers too). **California Pizza Kitchen,** 207 S. Beverly Dr. (one block south of Wilshire Blvd.), 310/275-1101, colloquially known as the poor man's Spago, is another best bet. Wood-fired pizzas are the thing here, served up in exotic displays such as BLT or Thai chicken and in less unusual combos including tomato, garlic, and basil.

Richer People's Fare

Where you eat, more than what you eat, establishes social status in Beverly Hills. So many major movers and shakers frequent **Nate 'n' Al's,** 414 N. Beverly Dr. (near Little Santa Monica Blvd.), 310/274-0101, that you can almost make the BH scene—the Hollywood deal-making scene—just by strolling through the door of this, the world's largest deli. Nothing fancy about the food, though—just the basics: decent sandwiches, cheese blintzes, and such, reasonably inexpensive.

Quite wonderful for takeout—definitely an eat-in dinner option if you've got a microwave or kitchenette handy—is stylish **Porta Via,** 424 N. Cañon Dr. (at Little Santa Monica Blvd.), 310/274-6534, where you can order everything from spectacular salads and wild mushroom-and-spinach lasagna to Italian sandwiches on house-made focaccia (seasonally changing menu). Offered in the A.M.: fresh-baked apple coffeecake, pear tarts, muffins, scones, and such.

At home in a former hardware store, **The Farm of Beverly Hills,** 439 N. Beverly Drive (near Little Santa Monica Blvd.), 310/273-5578, is now a chic café whose chef is Ben Ford, son of Harrison. Though there hasn't been much agricultural activity in Beverly Hills for many a blue moon, the walls here are decorated with antique farm tools in keeping with the theme. Wonderful sandwiches, salads, and desserts make this a great stop, after shopping or otherwise.

And there's always ever-popular **Il Fornaio,** 310 N. Beverly Dr. (at Dayton Wy.), 310/550-8330, open daily for breakfast, lunch, and dinner, where you can keep it fairly affordable by ordering carefully. You'll find plenty to choose from—fresh-baked breads, sandwiches, salads, pastas, rotisserie-roasted chicken, or just coffee and treats from the espresso bar. Even better, though, for a simple yet superb meal is **Il Pastaio,** 400 N. Cañon Dr. (at Brighton), 310/205-5444, a casual sibling to Santa Monica's famous Drago. Though the fresh pastas are the main attraction, the many distractions are worthy.

Stylish and catapulted to local stardom by the Silver Lake bohemian set is the elegant and colorful Indian **Bombay Palace,** 8690 Wilshire Blvd. (two blocks east of Robertson), 310/659-9944, where the buffet lunch is a real deal. Vegetarians can have a fun, flavorful time, but Bombay Palace has something for everyone.

Not in Beverly Hills proper but close enough is **Versailles,** 1415 S. La Cienega Blvd. (at Pico Blvd.), 310/289-0392, a hip and relaxed joint serving L.A.'s best Cuban food. The star here is the roast chicken, served whole or half, mari-nated in citrus vinegar, topped with raw onions, and stuffed with garlic cloves—crisp on the out-side, juicy and flavorful on the inside—and served with fried plantains with black beans and white rice. If you're meandering south and then toward the coast, the original Versailles is south of Century City—and the Santa Monica Free-way—in Culver City at 10319 Venice Blvd. (just west of Motor Ave.), 310/558-3168.

STYLISH AND EXPENSIVE FARE

Stylish, Somewhat Expensive Cafés

Fabulous for smoked fish, served as an accompaniment to eggs or as appetizers or presented as unusual sandwiches, is the chic **Barney Greengrass** café on the fifth floor of Barneys New York department store at 9570 Wilshire Blvd. (at Camden), 310/777-5877. This designer deli features a vodka and caviar bar, and is a popular power-breakfasting spot for industry agents working nearby. Also open for lunch and early dinner. Another place to spy on the beautiful people is the **Armani Cafe** on the third floor of Emporio Armani, 9533 Brighton Way, 310/271-9940, where light Northern Italian is the style.

Also quite pretty at lunch and dinner: the pricey Italian **Il Cielo,** 9018 Burton Way, 310/276-9990, one of the most romantic restaurants in Los Angeles.

But if you're pursuing great food more than style, the place is warm and welcoming **Trattoria Amici** at the Beverly Terrace Motor Hotel, 469 N. Doheny Dr., 310/858-0271, serving heaps of rustic Italian, from pizzas and pasta to grilled chicken. It's open for lunch Mon.–Fri., for dinner Mon.–Saturday. Also fun for Italian: hip yet refreshingly relaxed **Prego,** 362 N. Camden Dr. (a half block north of Wilshire Blvd.), 310/277-7346, a trattoria serving authentic Northern Italian, grilled specialties, sizzling pizzas hot out of the wood-fired oven, and pastas and salads.

For a stylish change-up, elegant **Gaylord,** 50 N. La Cienega (just north of Wilshire), 310/652-3838, serves traditional Indian fare carefully prepared by chefs trained at the original Gaylord in New Delhi. You can't miss with the nan bread and dishes such as mulligatawny soup and tandoori chicken—everything top drawer.

Stylish, Somewhat Expensive Steakhouses and Such

For die-hard carnivores, BH's link in the New Orleans-based **Ruth's Chris Steak House** chain is a prominent presence. This restaurant, at 224 S. Beverly Dr. (between Olympic and Wilshire Blvds.), 310/859-8744, is particularly attractive for the genre, with posh semicircular leather booths and frosted-glass fixtures. But a steakhouse it is, the place for porterhouse, New York strip, and rib-eye served with shoestring potatoes or extra crispy cottage fries.

Men's-clubbish **The Grill on the Alley**, 9560 Dayton Way, 310/276-0615, is Southern California's original "Grill"—and proud papa of the Daily Grill chain. What you'd expect at such a manly restaurant is what you get: steaks, chops, fish, crab Louie, corn chowder, Hollywood's own Cobb salad, and pecan pie. The Grill is open Mon.–Sat for both lunch and dinner.

Salmon, anyone? Something like a steakhouse for seafood, **McCormick and Schmick's**, 206 N. Rodeo Dr. (at Wilshire Blvd.), 310/859-0434, serves football-player portions of well-prepared seafood and fish in an attractive, relaxed setting. It's open daily for lunch and dinner. **Lawry's The Prime Rib,** 100 N. La Cienega Blvd. (just north of Wilshire Blvd.), 310/652-2827, is the place for—you guessed it—prime rib, tender and cut to order. It's open daily for dinner only.

Always fun after dinner is open-late **Kate Mantilini,** a painfully hip steakhouse at 9109 Wilshire Blvd. (at Doheny), 310/278-3699, named after a 1940s female boxing promoter, where the doomsday architecture and the boisterous bar scene are often equally entertaining. Open daily for breakfast, lunch, and dinner until 2 A.M., which is when you are most likely to spot a celeb.

Still More Stylish, Still More Expensive

The new **Spago Beverly Hills,** 176 N. Cañon Dr., 310/385-0880, offers something considerably more elegant, and more expensive, than fans of the original Spago in West Hollywood might expect. Now that Puck's signature wood-fire baked pizzas and other favorites are widely available through the Wolfgang Puck Café and Wolfgang Puck Express chains—and now that Spago itself is becoming a nationwide chain—

perhaps it was inevitable that Spago would restyle itself into something more uptown. At home on the former site of the Bistro Garden, the restaurant has been redesigned to accent natural lighting and to allow the indoor dining room to flow more gracefully into the garden setting. The new Spago is open for both lunch and dinner.

Lauded for its exceptional weekday happy hour, multilevel **Maple Drive,** 345 N. Maple Dr., 310/274-9800, is the rich person's idea of a neighborhood restaurant. Sampling the fare here, a selection of contemporary Mediterranean with California flair, is one way to see Beverly Hills through its own eyes. The tall-backed booths are where the celebs and the let's-make-a-dealers converge, but some prefer hovering around the maple bar. Maple Drive is open weekdays only for lunch—with happy hour 4–7 P.M., at last report, with all free drinks served along with wonderful free fare—and Mon.–Sat. for dinner.

Another local magnet for the Hollywood power-lunch bunch is the Japanese-influenced **Matsuhisa,** 129 N. La Cienega Blvd., 310/659-9639, where the sushi is a unique art form and exotic seafood dishes are the other main attraction. It's open weekdays for lunch, nightly for dinner.

The Belvedere at The Peninsula Beverly Hills Hotel, 9882 Little Santa Monica Blvd. (at Wilshire), 310/788-2306, is another Hollywood power-breakfast mecca. At other times expect sumptuous California Asian cuisine served to gorgeous diners in an equally gorgeous dining room. The menu includes low-calorie "spa" dishes, too.

EATING IN BEL-AIR AND BRENTWOOD

Bel-Air Fare

For a friendly, inexpensive meal, the place in Bel-Air is tiny **Graziella** in the Glen Center at 2964 Beverly Glen Blvd., 310/475-7404, a best bet for light pastas and salads. Quite expensive and exceptional in the same general neighborhood is the ultra-romantic French **Four Oaks Restaurant,** a onetime speakeasy tucked away at 2181 N. Beverly Glen Blvd. (two lights north of Sunset Blvd.), 310/470-2265, open for Sunday brunch, for lunch Tues.–Sun., and for dinner every night. Patio dining, too, weather permitting. And while we're discussing amore, the expensive and considerably more famous California-French fare at the **Hotel Bel-Air,** 701 Stone Canyon Rd., 310/472-1211, is without a doubt the neighborhood's most powerful draw. One of the most romantic places in L.A. for dinner, this is also an unforgettable choice at breakfast—try the lemon pancakes—and lunch. Reservations are always wise. Wander the lovingly tended grounds while you're here; the Hotel Bel-Air offers a civilized and sophisticated escape from L.A.'s harsher landscapes.

Brentwood Fare

The surfers' favorite South Bay takeout chicken joint now has an outlet in Brentwood—the wonderful Peruvian **El Pollo Inka,** a little piece of Machu Picchu at home in a faux-'50s diner in a strip mall at 11701 Wilshire Blvd. (at Barrington), 310/571-3334. El Pollo Inka is as famous for its green chile *aji* sauce as for its imaginative potatoes, wood fire-roasted chicken, and ice-cold Cuzquena beer. It's open daily for lunch and dinner, offering live music on weekends. A real deal.

Generally more "Brentwood" in style, though, is **A Votre Santé,** 13016 San Vicente Blvd. (at 26th St.), 310/451-1813, serving vegetarian and macrobiotic fare—a haven for those who don't do dairy or oil or sugar. A small eat-in area is filled with shiny people in spandex and sweats, but takeout is big business too. Beyond the veggie burgers and wraps, the tabbouleh and hummus, dairyless corn chowder, salads, garden pastas, and fresh steamed vegetable dishes come highly recommended. It's open daily for breakfast, lunch, and dinner.

The **Brentwood Gardens** minimall, 11677 San Vicente Blvd., 310/820-7646, is a best bet for something quick and reasonably good—from trendy restaurants such as the **Daily Grill,** 310/442-0044 to **California Pizza Kitchen,** 310/826-3573.

Fine dining in Brentwood is the bustling Italian **Toscana,** 11633 San Vicente Blvd. (one block east of Barrington), 310/820-2448, where the fine fare dances from pizza to steaks and game. It's a very popular industry hangout, so make reservations well in advance. Toscana is open for dinner daily, for lunch every day but Sunday.

Good for celebrity-spotting—but every customer is treated like a star.

EATING IN CENTURY CITY

Family Fare

For affordable family fare—especially if those in your family have wildly different tastes—cruise the restaurant offerings the Century City Marketplace, 10250 Santa Monica Blvd. (between Beverly Glen and Avenue of the Stars), the likes of New York style **The Stage Deli** and **Houston's,** to retro burger joint **Johnny Rockets.** An intriguing choice is the **Tacone** stand, featuring a specialty devised here by Joachim Splichal of Patina—something like a handheld, cone-shaped taco shell. Ethnic-flavored fillings include such things as jerked shrimp with rice and black beans with shredded beef and rice.

Fancier Fare

Harry's Bar and American Grill inside the ABC Entertainment Center at 2020 Avenue of the Stars, 310/277-2333, is like a theme bar for expatriate Hemingway wannabes—an exact replica of the Harry's in Florence, Italy, a classy hideout of dark wood and brass. Appropriately, each spring Harry's sponsors the International Hemingway Competition; whoever crafts the best parody gets an all-expense paid trip to the European Harry's. Year-round, though, right after work, the bar scene here oozes with entertainment execs, lawyers, and other schmoozing professionals—also a good show. It's also the place to go before seeing a show at the Shubert. Harry's also serves good lunch, dinner, and after-theater fare—all-American burgers and steaks and Northern Italian specialties.

For fine dining, best bets beyond the Century City Plaza in Century City include the elegant yet relaxed French-Italian supper club **Lunaria,** 10351 Santa Monica Blvd., 310/282-8870, open for lunch on weekdays only, for dinner and jazz on Tues.–Sat. nights. **La Cachette,** 10506 Santa Monica, 310/470-4992, is a cozy romantic "hideaway." Owner/chef Jean-François Meteigner, formerly of the outstanding L'Orangerie, prepares classic French dishes with a California twist.

EATING IN AND AROUND WESTWOOD

Westwood is jammed with bars and restaurants, some quite memorable. On Westwood Boulevard south from Wilshire is L.A.'s "Little Persia," with an abundance of Iranian and other authentic bakeries, cafés, groceries, and shops. Good restaurants abound in nearby residential neighborhoods of West L.A., too, some of which are included in this section.

For good frozen nonfat yogurt, the place in Westwood is the **Bigg Chill,** 10850 W. Olympic Blvd., 310/475-1070. For connoisseur's coffee one possibility is **City Bean,** a "microroaster" at 10911 Lindbrook Dr., 310/208-0108.

People's Eats: Westwood and Vicinity

Definitely an L.A. classic, the **Apple Pan,** 10801 W. Pico Blvd. (at Glendon Ave., one block east of Westwood Blvd. in the shadow of the Westwood Pavilion), 310/475-3585, makes one ponder the existential meaning of "fast food." Historians can—and will—quibble about the facts, but we know fast food was a Southern California creation, whether derived from the original McDonald Brothers restaurant in San Bernardino, precursor to a worldwide chain of golden arches, or from West L.A.'s own tiny classic, the Apple Pan restaurant, a hectic home away from home complete with plaid wallpaper and cramped counter area. The pace here is impressively frenetic—the food flung in all directions from the U-shaped counter, faster than you can blink—while the near-perfect burgers, cheeseburgers (topped with melted Tillamook cheddar), and thin-sliced Virginia ham sandwiches beg to be savored. Save room for the apple pie, the Apple Pan's claim to fame, though some people would kill for the banana cream—made with fresh bananas—or the chocolate, boysenberry, or pecan. No credit cards. It's open daily 11 A.M.–midnight, closed major holdiays. If the Apple Pan is just too packed, other possibilities include classic **Marty's Hamburgers,** 10558 W. Pico Blvd., 310/836-6944, famous for its all-meat chiliburgers and foot-long hot dogs.

Another people's attraction along Pico is tiny **John O'Groats,** 10628 W. Pico Blvd. (a block west of Beverly Glen), 310/204-0692, a popular diner serving one of L.A.'s best inexpensive breakfasts and Scots-style specialties, including fish and chips, soups, and homemade biscuits. It's open daily for breakfast and lunch, Thurs.–Sat. only for dinner.

A popular collegiate hangout, complete with checkered tablecloths and Italian-style kitsch, **Lamonica's N.Y. Pizza,** 1066 Gayley Ave. (just off Wilshire), 310/208-8671, is designed to resemble a subway station and serves very good New York–style pizza by the slice.

For people's noodles, a best bet here is **Noodle Planet,** 1118 Westwood Blvd. (near Kinross), 310/208-0777, where first-rate pad Thai, yellow curry, Thai barbecue chicken, Vietnamese hand roll, and such things as sticky rice with mango are all made with fresh, unprocessed ingredients. Head to West L.A. for inexpensive Japanese soul food, including **Ashai Ramen,** 2027 Sawtelle Blvd., 310/479-2231, beloved for noodles, dumplings, and pork pot stickers (closed Thursday). For some of L.A.'s best Japanese noodles, try **Yokohama Ramen,** 11600 Gateway Blvd. (at Barrington Ave.), 310/479-2321.

The most popular Mexican around is **La Salsa,** 11075 W. Pico Blvd. (at Sepulveda), 310/479-0919, famous for burritos and soft tacos and plenty of salsa choices. Wonderful for Iranian: **Shahrezad,** 1422 Westwood Blvd. (at Ohio), 310/470-3242. Other exotic possibilities include the more expensive dinner-only Moroccan **Koutoubia,** 2116 Westwood Blvd., 310/475-0729.

Fancier Fare

The pursuit of fancier fare in and around Westwood takes foodies on an international neighborhood journey, certainly appropriate given UCLA's worldly stature. The Italian **La Bruschetta,** 1621 Westwood Blvd. (at Massachussets), 310/477-1052, was named after bread—Italian bread rubbed with garlic and olive oil and then grilled. This terrific neighborhood restaurant serves imaginative, reasonably priced pastas and exquisite seafood. It's open weekdays for lunch, Mon.–Sat. for dinner.

The Nuevo Latino **Mojo** at the W Hotel, 930 Hilgard Ave., 310/208-8765, is a complete turnaround from the stuffy Dynasty restaurant that once occupied this space. Things have lightened up all the way around now that local chef David Slatkin has taken over the space and turned it into a lively, younger scene. Sidle up to one of two bars—one drenched in red light, one in blue—and order a Cuban mojito (white rum, fresh mint, and lime mixed with sugar and crushed ice) or a Cuba libre. Signature dishes include beer-roasted clams, conch croquettes, and ropa vieja duck tamale. Reservations advisable.

COURTESY AISLINN RACE

THE LOS ANGELES COAST

Beverly Hills may have the swank shopping districts and Brentwood the Getty Center, but coastal Los Angeles—the rest of L.A.'s Westsides—has the sand. In some ways the only thing that connects the diverse communities of coastal L.A. is the beach, miles and miles of dazzling white sand, one of the most enduring symbols of the Southern California good life.

Santa Monica is L.A.'s beach city extraordinaire, where everyone else on the Westside comes to play. Just north is the strung-out stretch of beach known as Malibu, where celebrities and artsy eccentrics live both on the beach and in the sylvan enclaves of Topanga Canyon. Immediately south of Santa Monica is Venice,

home to aging bohemians, young hipsters, and street performers. Less colorful but quieter West L.A. is a middle-class suburb packed with small single-family homes and condominiums. On L.A.'s sociopolitical map the coastal Westside also includes Marina del Rey, Playa del Rey, the South Bay's stylish Palos Verdes Peninsula, and the very western working-port cities of Long Beach and San Pedro. A short boat ride west leads to fabled Santa Catalina Island and the tiny tourist town of Avalon. Also visible offshore on a clear day, seeming to bob in the blue Pacific Ocean like massive pieces of driftwood, are the lonely, lovely islands of Channel Islands National Park.

SANTA MONICA AND VICINITY

Santa Monica is the quintessential L.A. beach town, a distinction held since the early 1900s when the original Looff "pleasure pier" was the bayside beacon for long days of Southern California–style fun in the sun. But unlike other popular L.A. tourist destinations, Santa Monica is much more than just a pretty face and a good time on the weekends—despite its place in L.A. literature as the barely disguised 1930s' "Bay

City" in Raymond Chandler's *Farewell My Lovely*. These days the city is considered politically "progressive," a rarity in Southern California. That tendency has translated into rent control—recently abolished, after significant local damage in the Northridge earthquake—and a trend toward liberal politicians that's still going strong. Until 2000, when he "termed out" (left office due to mandatory term limits), Santa Monica's own

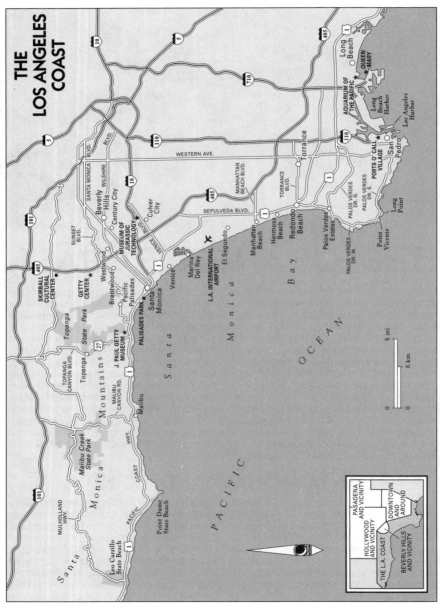

THE
LOS ANGELES
COAST

© AVALON TRAVEL PUBLISHING, INC.

state senator was Tom Hayden, a thoughtful politico better known as an anti-Vietnam War activist, one of the original Chicago Seven, ex-husband of actress and fitness enthusiast Jane Fonda. (The fact that Hayden ran unsuccessfully against Richard Riordan for L.A. mayor in 1997 hasn't diminished his stature here—or diminished his taste for city politics. In June 2001 he faced election again, this time for the Fifth District seat on the Los Angeles City Council.) And Santa Monica's state Assembly member Sheila Kuehl—better known in some circles as the character Zelda Gilroy from *The Many Lives of Dobie Gillis* 1960s TV series—is California's first openly gay legislator, a Harvard Law School grad who was elected to the Assembly in 1994 and the first woman in California history to be named as speaker pro tem. The city's political tendencies have spawned, particularly among local landlords, the disparaging nickname of "People's Republic of Santa Monica"—not nearly as marketable as "The Zenith City by the Sunset Sea" of the late 19th century or the present "A Fortunate People in a Fortunate Land." By Southern California standards the community is also atypical socially—movie stars and the just plain wealthy blended with a large expatriate British population, senior citizens, middle-class and low-income families, and poverty-stricken activists, artists, and street people. As odd as it seems in these days of escalating public intolerance, most everyone here gets along most of the time.

Most of Santa Monica's initial attractions are front and center, along or near the edge of Santa Monica Bay—the bay implied in the title of that insipid yet notoriously popular TV show *Baywatch,* which moved on to Hawaii before it was cancelled in 2001. The city's own strand of sand is Santa Monica State Beach. On weekends and in summer an equal draw is the associated Santa Monica Pier—now including a 1922 carousel and a carnival of fun rides. But Santa Monica offers much, much more, including the nearby pleasures of Malibu, Venice, the Santa Monica Mountains National Recreation Area, and Will Rogers State Historic Park, wacky and world-class art galleries, imaginative shopping, and an unusual range of good accommodations and great restaurants—in every price category. Beach town or no, Santa Monica has it all.

Most people arrive via the Santa Monica Freeway (I-10), though one of the city's claims to fame is its location at the Pacific Ocean end of the original Route 66. Once here, it's easy to get around via the city's Big Blue Bus. (If you're driving, bring pockets full of quarters. Local parking meters, particularly near the beach, have voracious appetites.) For current information about "Bay City," contact: **Santa Monica Visitor Center,** 1400 Ocean Ave., Santa Monica 90401, 310/393-7593, www.santamonica.com, which is in Palisades Park and open for drop-in assistance daily 10 A.M.–4 P.M. (until 5 P.M. in summer). Watch L.A.-area newspapers for Santa Monica special events, major ones scheduled on weekends and/or summer evenings, or call Santa Monica's 24-hour "Funshine Line," 310/393-7593.

Earlier People, Earlier Republics

Gaspar de Portolá claimed what is now Santa Monica for Spain in 1769. According to local legend, Franciscan Father Juan Crespi selected the name—choosing St. Monica because the area's natural springs reminded him of the tears she shed when her son, Augustine, destined to become a saint himself, turned to Christianity. But the grassy mesa was still unoccupied in 1822, when nascent Mexico rousted the Spanish. A three-way tussle over its ownership because of conflicting land-grant titles was resolved only in 1851, after California statehood: Don Francisco Sepulveda received 30,000-acre Rancho San Vicente y Santa Monica, while Ysidro Reyes and Francisco Marquez jointly gained the 6,600-acre Boca de Santa Monica, which included Santa Monica Canyon and much of the bayside coastline.

In 1872 cattleman Colonel R. S. Baker bought the Sepulveda spread and much of the Reyes-Marquez property. Just two years later Baker sold three-fourths of his land wealth to the British-born millionaire John P. Jones, the junior U.S. senator from Nevada. Jones had big ideas. Together he and Baker planned the new town of Santa Monica, which would include a wharf and interconnected trans-California railroad—to serve Jones's Nevada silver mines and other future industry. Some in Los Angeles detected a threat to their own potential prosperity and attacked the planned city of Santa Monica as an intended

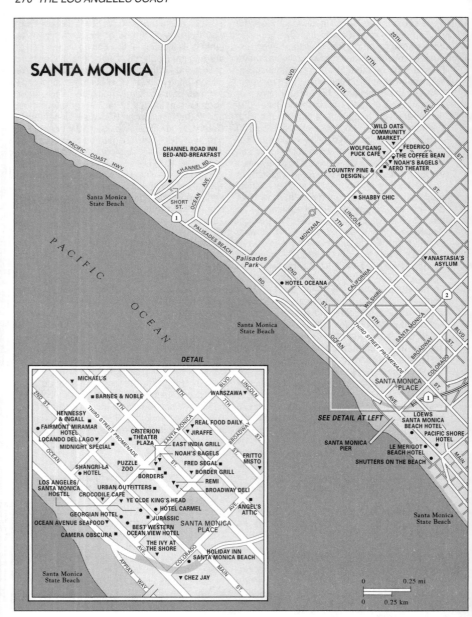

SANTA MONICA

PACIFIC COAST HWY.

CHANNEL ROAD INN
BED-AND-BREAKFAST

CHANNEL RD.

Santa Monica
State Beach

SHORT
ST.

OCEAN AVE.

PALISADES BEACH RD.

PACIFIC OCEAN

Palisades
Park

■ HOTEL OCEANA

Santa Monica
State Beach

BLVD.

14TH

17TH

20TH

AVE.

ST.

WILD OATS
COMMUNITY
MARKET
WOLFGANG   ▼ FEDERICO
PUCK CAFE ▼   ▼ THE COFFEE BEAN
               ▼ NOAH'S BAGELS
COUNTRY PINE &   AERO THEATER
DESIGN

■ SHABBY CHIC

MONTANA

2ND

ST.

7TH

CALIFORNIA

LINCOLN

WILSHIRE

4TH

SANTA MONICA

BROADWAY

COLORADO

▼ ANASTASIA'S
ASYLUM

2

BLVD.

ST.

OCEAN

THIRD STREET PROMENADE

SANTA MONICA
PLACE

SEE DETAIL AT LEFT

1

LOEWS
SANTA MONICA
BEACH HOTEL

SANTA MONICA
PIER

LE MERIGOT
BEACH HOTEL

SHUTTERS ON THE BEACH

PACIFIC SHORE
HOTEL

MAIN

Santa Monica
State Beach

DETAIL

▼ MICHAEL'S

■ BARNES & NOBLE

2ND ST.

THIRD STREET PROMENADE

2ND

6TH

BLVD.

LINCOLN

ST.

WARSZAWA ▼

HENNESSY
& INGALL ■
● FAIRMONT MIRAMAR
HOTEL
LOCANDO DEL LAGO ▼
MIDNIGHT SPECIAL ■

SANTA MONICA

▼ REAL FOOD DAILY
▼ JIRAFFE
● EAST INDIA GRILL
▼ NOAH'S BAGELS
▼ FRED SEGAL ■

BROADWAY

ST.

CRITERION
THEATER
PLAZA

PUZZLE
ZOO
■
● BORDERS

SHANGRI-LA ●
HOTEL

LOS ANGELES/
SANTA MONICA
HOSTEL ●
CROCODILE CAFE ●
URBAN OUTFITTERS ■
▼ YE OLDE KING'S HEAD
● HÔTEL CARMEL
▼ JURASSIC
GEORGIAN HOTEL ●
BEST WESTERN
OCEAN AVENUE SEAFOOD ▼
OCEAN VIEW HOTEL
● CAMERA OBSCURA ■
THE IVY AT
THE SHORE

OCEAN

APPIAN WAY

AVE.

2ND

ST.

ST.

FRITTO
MISTO ■

▼ BORDER GRILL
▼ REMI
▼ BROADWAY DELI

ANGEL'S
ATTIC ●

SANTA MONICA
PLACE

AVE.

HOLIDAY INN
SANTA MONICA BEACH

MAIN

▼ CHEZ JAY

COLORADO
ST.

Santa Monica
State Beach

0   0.25 mi

0   0.25 km

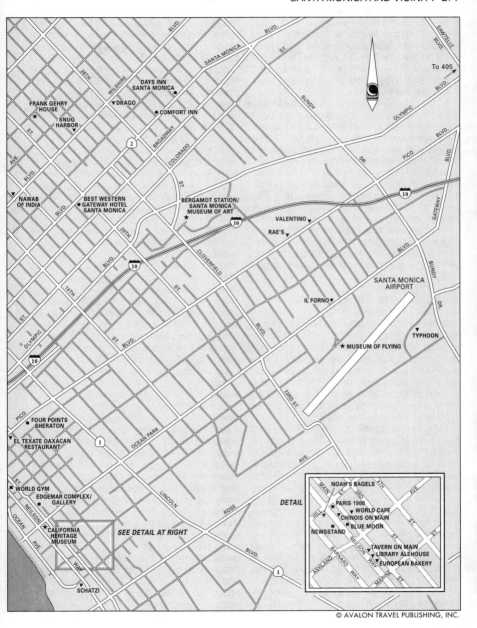

BLVD.

BLVD.

ST.

SANTA MONICA

BLVD.

SAWTELLE
BLVD.

To 405

BLVD.

OLYMPIC

BUNDY

28TH

WILSHIRE

DAYS INN
SANTA MONICA

▼ DRAGO

FRANK GEHRY
HOUSE
★

SNUG
HARBOR
▼

● COMFORT INN

2

BROADWAY

COLORADO

ST.

DR.

PICO

BLVD.

10

NAWAB
OF INDIA

BEST WESTERN
● GATEWAY HOTEL
SANTA MONICA

BLVD.

20TH

BERGAMOT STATION/
SANTA MONICA
MUSEUM OF ART
★

10

VALENTINO ▼

RAE'S ▼

CLOVERFIELD
ST.

BLVD.

GATEWAY

BUNDY

DR.

SANTA MONICA
AIRPORT

10

14TH

ST.

IL FORNO ▼

BLVD.

OLYMPIC

10

ST.

23RD ST.

★ MUSEUM OF FLYING

TYPHOON
▼

PICO

● FOUR POINTS
SHERATON

▼ EL TEXATE OAXACAN
RESTAURANT

1

OCEAN PARK

LINCOLN

ROSE

AVE.

■ WORLD GYM

EDGEMAR COMPLEX/
GALLERY

NELSON

OCEAN

AVE.

★ CALIFORNIA
HERITAGE
MUSEUM

WAY

SEE DETAIL AT RIGHT

BLVD.

1

SCHATZI

DETAIL

NOAH'S BAGELS

MAIN ST.

3RD

4TH

ST.

AVE.

ST.

HILL

● PARIS 1900
▼ WORLD CAFE
▼ CHINOIS ON MAIN

■ BLUE MOON

NEWSSTAND

NELSON
WAY

ASHLAND

BARNARD

WAY

MARINE
ST.

▼ TAVERN ON MAIN
▼ LIBRARY ALEHOUSE
▼ EUROPEAN BAKERY

© AVALON TRAVEL PUBLISHING, INC.

rival. But others lined up eagerly in 1885 to buy the city's first lots. Within months Santa Monica was booming, boasting more than 150 homes, 75 or so "tent" or temporary homes, and 1,000 citizens. With the wharf open for business and the railroad under construction, a prosperous future seemed assured.

In 1877 the city's first resort, the Santa Monica Bath House, opened for business. A full day's stagecoach ride from downtown Los Angeles, Santa Monica nonetheless beckoned as a balmy respite while the rest of L.A. scorched in the summer heat. Vacationers could enjoy the cool ocean breezes from tents pitched in Santa Monica Canyon. Hotels, restaurants, and shops soon followed; summer residents began to stay year-round. In 1887 Santa Monica voted to incorporate and become an independent city.

Yet Santa Monica's success would be some time coming. Jones lost most of his fortune—and his railroad—when silver prices plummeted. His wharf was condemned and quickly demolished.

Losing the Port but Finding No "Pier" in Tourism

The earliest incarnation of Santa Monica's pier was known in the early 1870s as "Shoo-Fly Landing," the point of departure for asphalt tar from Hancock Park's La Brea Ranch that was destined to become paved streets in San Francisco. Then came John Jones's 1875 Los Angeles and Independence railroad, its wharf and depot allowing steamers to deliver goods destined for Los Angeles via railway.

In the late 1880s the Los Angeles "port war" began. Collis Huntington, owner of Southern Pacific Railroad, wanted L.A.'s official harbor to be in Santa Monica—where he, coincidentally, owned most everything. Those who feared Huntington's monopoly in the Santa Monica area and elsewhere fought hard against his plans. Nonetheless determined that the Port of Los Angeles would be in Santa Monica, Huntington upped the ante by building California's most massive pier; his finished Santa Monica Pier measured 4,720 feet long and 130 feet wide when it opened for business in 1902. Yet Huntington lost the war, and San Pedro to the south became L.A.'s primary port city. All Santa Monica shipping stopped by 1910, and raging surf ravaged Huntington's grand pier.

But if Santa Monica failed as a center of commerce and trade, it succeeded as one of the region's preferred recreation destinations. Santa Monica's grand Arcadia Hotel, the North Beach Bath House, and the Deauville Beach Club soon signaled the city's arrival among L.A.'s monied minions. And the city's final incarnation of its earlier dreams, the Santa Monica Municipal Pier, arrived in 1912, quickly followed by the adjoining Looff "pleasure pier" in 1916. The Looff pier featured a trademark carousel, other amusements, and the enormous Blue Streak roller coaster. In July of 1924 the La Monica Ballroom opened at pier's end; it was the largest ballroom in the world, host to crowds of up to 10,000. Rather than a rough industrial port, Santa Monica became instead a sleepy seaside retreat—a serene small town largely unperturbed by progress until the 1960s and the completion of the Santa Monica Freeway, when it became easier for the world to get here.

Yet illicit entertainment did arrive, symbolized in the 1920s by offshore gambling ships. These 24-hour floating casinos were careful to remain at least three miles from shore, just beyond the state's legal jurisdiction. Water taxis ferried customers from the pier to the *Tango, Texas, Showboat,* and *Rex,* ships that could host up to 1,900 guests at a time. Offshore gambling flourished here until 1939, when the California Supreme Court declared the area between Point Dume and Point Vicente as "bay," not open sea, and therefore subject to state regulation.

The beachfront running south of the Santa Monica Pier to Venice Beach was Chandler's mythic if slightly sleazy "Bay City." Stretching along the pearly sand north of the pier was early L.A.'s notorious "Gold Coast," where sumptuous spreads included the fabulous beach homes of Marion Davies (mistress of William Randolph Hearst) and others of Hollywood's party-hearty set. Almost all that remains of that era is the Sand and Sea Club at 415 PCH, once servants' quarters for the Davies mansion. A few surviving Gold Coast–era mansions have been similarly reincarnated, or walled off from public view. Other old-timers hang on, or try to. Santa Monica's landmark 1926 Breakers Beach Club—more recently reborn as the Sea Castle Apartments, then vacated because of severe damage inflicted by the 1994 Northridge earthquake and miscellaneous fires—was gutted by fire in 1996. Now the Sea Castle has been reincarnated yet again as a complex of 178 luxury apartments.

AT THE BEACH

Chances are good that you'll recognize **Palisades Park,** even if you've never been there. Most people have seen it hundreds of times on TV and in the movies—the classic leisurely-L.A.-at-the-beach setting, where lovers stroll at sunset against a backdrop of swaying palms and rustling eucalyptus, and everybody's grandparents walk the poodle or gather on park benches to gossip and play friendly games of chess. This popular film location, a narrow 14-block-long strip of lawn, benches, and trees perched atop steep, eroding bluffs overlooking the Santa Monica Pier, the beach, and the Pacific Ocean, is often visitors' first stop, given the convenient location of the Santa Monica Visitor Center here. At the Senior Recreation Center, nearby at 1450 Ocean Ave., 310/458-8644, is Santa Monica's own **Camera Obscura,** a tourist attraction more popular in the 18th- and 19th-century United States than today. Perhaps the optical "illusion" created by a camera obscura—rendering reality so clearly—is simply too real in these days of virtual reality. (Ask for the key and see for yourself. Small fee.) An oddity that dates to Leonardo da Vinci's notebooks and 11th-century Arab scholarship, the Camera Obscura is composed of prisms, lenses, and mirrors installed in a dark-

ened chamber that allows light in through an opening no larger than a pinhole. The camera then projects a reversed (upside-down) image of the outside world (in this case, a swath of the coastline) onto a white circular disk along the chamber's opposite wall.

Once reality has been virtually established, head for the beach. The good news is, the wide strand of dazzling white sand at **Santa Monica State Beach** is one of the busiest beaches around in summer—which is bad news if you're looking for privacy. It's also bad news if the ocean is temporarily off-limits because of pollution, an ongoing storm-drain and urban-waste disposal problem generated throughout L.A. and an issue that raises the ire of residents around Santa Monica Bay. (For the possibility of wide open spaces at the beach, head north beyond Malibu or south to the world-famous weirdness of Venice Beach, where most of the action is along the Boardwalk. For general beach information and a bay pollution update, see Life's a Beach.) A day at the beach includes the usual seeing-and-being-seen scene, sometimes a rousing round of beach volleyball, and performance artists—California clowns. Not to mention those overgrown lifeguard chairs-cum-musical instruments—let's call them "wind" instruments—installed as public art projects between the pier and Pico Boulevard. On a breezy day the aluminum pipes atop artist Douglas Hollis's 18-foot-tall *Singing Beach Chairs* catch the wind and make odd tunes.

Palisades Park covers more than 26 acres overlooking the Pacific Ocean; the original park was dedicated in 1892.

DONNA CARROLL

Santa Monica Pier and Pacific Park

Santa Monica's mild-mannered municipal pier and pleasure pier survived the usual ups and downs of tourist-town life largely unscathed until the 1970s, when civic warfare raged over the fate of the dilapidated piers, then slated for demolition by the Santa Monica City Council. The slow work of rebuilding the past began—an effort slowed still further by 1983's disastrous storms, which dismembered major sections of the pier. Work on the municipal pier was completed in 1990, including restoration of the two-story **Hippodrome** (with its 1922 Looff carousel, featured in *The Sting* and other films), the original arcades, and the old bumper cars. Much of the rest of the pier is lined with restaurants, fast food-eries, and curio shops. Fishing, once a favorite recreational activity at the pier, is no longer recommended because of bay pollution. Special events, including weekend **music concerts,** annual **Cirque du Soleil** performances, and multiple new amusements, now attract the crowds.

At the foot of the rebuilt and expanded pier complex is the new **children's playground** designed by Moore, Rubell, and Yudell, featuring an assortment of kiddie-style carnival rides and

LIFE'S A BEACH

Along with the cult of celebrity, palm trees, and fancy freeways lined with bright shiny cars, the beach is among L.A.'s most universal symbols. The beach—as in The Beach, the youthful social creation of 1950s Los Angeles—is all about sun-bleached attitude, arcane sports, superficial sexuality, and saltwater-scented steel guitar. And The Beach lives on today, with each youthful summer's new toast-brown crop happily packed into the stucco sameness of beachfront sardine cans. Pale imitations turn up in places such as Florida and Australia, but Los Angeles invented The Beach.

And so the slang phrase "Life's a Beach" takes on genuine meaning in Los Angeles County, where the sunny sands of L.A. lore now suffer a relentless assault of urban ills, all related to the southstate's relentless population growth. Too much traffic and too little parking. Garbage. Graffiti. Alcohol-and gang-related violence. Water pollution. Still a localized problem, ocean water pollution levels are generally decreasing because of improved sewage treatment facilities and greater citizen awareness about the effects of dumping toxic substances into sewers and storm drains. Yet if pollution is disappearing, in some places so is the sand—in a natural southward drift exacerbated by the construction of breakwaters and harbors and, inland, by damming the rivers and streams—and associated sediment flow—that would otherwise replenish the sand supply. These days, maintaining the bay's wide white beaches is additional engineering work.

Fun in the Sun

Santa Monica Bay, the shallow white sand-fringed coastal indentation harboring most of L.A. County's beaches, was once one of the world's richest fishing areas. Those days are long gone, after a half-century's relentless flow of industrial chemicals and other toxic wastes from land to sea. But the bay is slowly getting cleaner—clean enough that, in the 1990s, even porpoises returned. According to L.A.'s **Heal the Bay,** to swim safely avoid obvious pollution "problem areas" (usually posted as no-swim areas), steer clear of all storm drains (most of which are *not* signed or otherwise identified, so heads up), and don't swim for at least three days after a rainstorm. For the latest information on the environmental health of Santa Monica Bay's beaches, contact: Heal the Bay, 2701 Ocean Park Blvd., Ste. 150, Santa Monica, CA 90405, 310/581-4188, fax 310/581-4195; www.healthebay.org. A nonprofit coalition working to achieve fishable, swimmable, and surfable coastal waters—with pollution levels within standards set by the federal Clean Water Act—Heal the Bay publishes an **Annual Beach Report Card** for L.A. County's beaches, also available on the website, complete with maps and charts of both dry (summer) and wet weather pollution measurements. To support its work, Heal the Bay sponsors occasional fund-raisers and community events and also sells T-shirts, sweatshirts, and other items. Go ahead and buy one. It's a very good cause.

But if alcohol—even beer or wine—is a central cause in your life, forget about enjoying it at the beach. It is illegal to drink alcohol on public beaches (and at city and county parks), a zero-tolerance a huge dragon's head carved from river-washed granite that "snorts" a soothing, safe mist (water). Santa Monica's new pier extension is Pacific Park, 310/260-8744; www.pacpark.com. Pacific Park harks back to the good ol' days of California amusement piers, until now an extinct species on the West Coast. Major new attractions here include an ocean-view roller coaster—the five-story-tall **Santa Monica West Coaster**—and California's only giant Ferris wheel, the **Pacific Wheel.** In addition to more pedestrian rides for the kids, a thrill for adults is the **Sig Alert** bumper-car adventure.

Other new pier attractions include the **UCLA Ocean Discovery Center,** 310/393-6149, an interactive aquarium-style education center with tidepool and "under the pier" marine life exhibits.

Admission to both the municipal pier and Pacific Park is free, but there is a charge for various attractions. Prices for most of the new Pacific Park amusement rides are in the $1–3 range, for example. The amusement park is open daily 10 A.M.–10 P.M. in summer, with an abbreviated schedule in winter.

---

policy that can get you booted off the beach and cost you $50 to boot if you're cited. The get-tough beach booze policy is in response to astronomical increases in alcohol-related assaults, drownings, and post-beach car wrecks. (And what lifeguards say is law at the beach. Unless you want to leave the beach earlier than planned, think twice before defying them.)

You can sunbathe, though. And swim, fairly safely where lifeguards are on duty. And surf, body surf, and boogie-board. And play very competitive beach volleyball. And picnic. Particularly north of Malibu and near the Palos Verdes Peninsula you can tidepool. Pier and surf fishing are permitted at most piers and many public beaches. Catches include spotfin and yellowfin croakers, corbina, and barred and walleyed perch. And you can run with the grunion, which come ashore to spawn on certain nights in March, June, July, and August. When the annual grunion runs are announced in local media, hundreds of people suddenly arrive after dark, flashlights in hand, ready to gather the slippery silver fish by hand—or try to. (For more on the annual grunion run, see Grunion Run Free, So Why Can't We? in the Orange County chapter.) Or you can watch sunsets, often spectacularly colorful given L.A.'s polluted air.

Deep-sea fishing expeditions—in search of barracuda, kelp bass, bonito, halibut, mackerel, rockfish, and sheepshead—and winter whale-watching excursions depart from Paradise Cove, Santa Monica, Marina del Rey, Redondo Beach, San Pedro, Long Beach and other spots along the coast. Contact local visitor bureaus and chambers of commerce for excursion-boat suggestions.

Practical Considerations

Beach curfews are fairly standard, with beaches usually closed to the public midnight–6 A.M.; some parking lots also close at midnight, though others close at sunset. No parking is allowed on most stretches of Pacific Coast Highway (PCH) 10 P.M.–6 A.M.; PCH parking is free, where you can find it. In public parking lots, available at many beaches, weekday rates range from $2 to $7 per day (rates usually higher on weekends). *Pay close attention to signs regarding parking restrictions* to avoid the unhappy experience of returning from a blissful day at the beach only to find that your car has been locked up for the night or, worse yet, towed and impounded. It'll be mighty expensive to get it out of car jail.

For general beach information, stop by or call the **Los Angeles County Department of Beaches and Harbors Visitor Information Center,** 4701 Admiralty Way in Marina del Rey, 310/305-9546 or 310/305-9546, fax 310/822-0119; http://beaches.co.la.ca.us. For questions about specific beaches, call **L.A. County Lifeguard Headquarters** at 310/577-5700. (Be patient if you're put on hold; rescues and other beach emergencies take precedence. And these folks do get busy, particularly in summer and on balmy weekends.) For general beach weather and tides (recorded), call 310/457-9701. For a beach-by-beach surf report, updated three times daily by L.A. County lifeguards (this is a revenue-generating service), call (900) 844-9283. Make reservations for state park and beach campgrounds along the L.A. County coast, mentioned elsewhere in this chapter, through ReserveAmerica at toll-free 800/446-7275.

MUSEUMS, ARTS, ARTSY SHOPS

Extremely hip Santa Monica claims its share of attractions from yesteryear, including the **Angel's Attic** museum of antique dollhouse miniatures, toys, trains, and dolls housed in a beautifully restored 19th-century Victorian at 516 Colorado Ave., 310/394-8331, open Thurs.–Sun. 12:30–4:30 P.M. Admission is $6.50 adults, $4 seniors, and $3.50 children under age 12. With reservations, you can enjoy tea, lemonade, and cookies on the veranda (for an additional $7.50 per person). The **California Heritage Museum,** 2612 Main St., 310/392-8537, open Wed.– Sun. 11 A.M.–4 P.M., is housed in an 1894 American colonial revival mansion designed by Sumner P. Hunt and later moved to the unlikely intersection of Ocean Park Avenue and Main. The home once belonged to Roy Jones, son of city founder John Jones. The first floor has been restored and furnished in typical Santa Monica style of three eras: the 1890s, the 1910s, and the 1920s. The second floor serves as a gallery for historical exhibits and shows by contemporary local artists. The city's archives are also housed here. General admission is $3, students and seniors $2.

Museum of Flying

Airplane fans and fanatics will enjoy this colorful museum, starring the *New Orleans,* the first plane to fly around the world—one of two open-cockpit Douglas World Cruisers that made the trip in 1924. Douglas Aircraft Company planes are well represented throughout, in fact, which is only fitting since the museum sits on the site of the original Douglas Aircraft Company, precursor to McDonnell Douglas. (Don't miss the original Donald Douglas boardroom on the second floor —a fabulous 22-seat round table with a built-in

illuminated globe as its centerpiece.) Almost all planes here have been meticulously restored and are still flight-ready, including the red-and-yellow checkerboard *Harvard II* T-6 trainer and the *Dago Red* P-51 Mustang, the world-record speeder clocked at 570 miles per hour in 1983. Video kiosks on the first floor, where most planes are displayed, show most of the planes in action. More history of flight awaits on the second floor, largely dedicated to Donald Douglas memorabilia. The museum's theater, film and video archives, and the Donald Douglas library are on the third floor. The museum also boasts a great little book and gift shop. While you're in the general neighborhood, tour architect Gregory Ain's **Mar Vista** futuristic housing subdivisions, built for Douglas Aircraft workers in the late 1940s, on the 3500 blocks of Meier, Moore, and Beethoven Streets. Like Douglas aircraft, some houses have survived in near-original condition.

For lunch and dinner, the adjacent, very good **DC3 Restaurant,** 310/399-2323, serves upscale food with an ethnic twist: menu options include inventive appetizers like DC3 seafood wontons, soups, salads, and entrées like blackened swordfish or Napoleon of salmon filet.

The Museum of Flying is at home in a hangar at 2772 Donald Douglas Loop N, on the north side of the Santa Monica Airport, one block south of Ocean Park Boulevard via 28th Street. The museum is open Wed.–Sun. 10 A.M.–5 P.M. At last report admission was $7 adults, $5 seniors and students with ID, and $3 for children ages 3–17. For more information, call 310/392-8822 or check www.museumofflying.org.

Santa Monica Museum of Art

Santa Monica cool extends to its arts scene, which succeeds in being as cutting edge—or just "edge," as they say in these parts—as any in L.A. To start your personal search for edge art, try the Santa Monica Art Museum, 310/586-6488, previously at home in the Edgemar complex along Main Street and in new digs among various local edge galleries at Bergamot Station, 2525 Michigan Ave., Bldg. G-1. Also surrounded by architect's offices and working artists' studios, the museum exhibits modern and contemporary sculpture and painting by relatively unknown artists and also presents performance

and video art. Call for information on current shows and events. At last report the museum was open Tues.–Sat. 11 A.M.–6 P.M. and for Friday night "salons," closed Sunday and Monday and also Thanksgiving, Christmas, and New Year's Day. But call to verify hours, as well as current exhibit information, because the schedule is somewhat fluid. Admission is by suggested donation—$3 for most folks, $1 for artists.

Bergamot Station
Near the freeway and the intersection of 26th Street and Olympic Boulevard, Bergamot Station—named for the old Red Car trolley station that stood here until the 1950s—is the city's latest cutting-edge arts locale. Situated at 2525 Michigan Ave., building G-2, 310/829-5854, is the city's latest contemporary but still fairly low-rent conglomeration of more than 40 fine-arts galleries features almost six acres of "arts space." Not to mention new digs for the Santa Monica Museum of Art and the **Gallery Café.**

Most galleries at Bergamot Station are open Tues.-Sat. 10 A.M.–6 P.M.; special events are scheduled at various times. For a more comprehensive listing of local galleries, check the website at www.bergamotstation.com, inquire at the visitor center—and pick up a current copy of the *L.A. Weekly.*

Frank Gehry House, Other Local Architecture
Speaking of art and artists: In what sort of home would an acclaimed local architect live? Take a drive by 1002 22nd Street (at Washington) and see for yourself. Noted for his innovative designs, Santa Monica's own Frank O. Gehry transformed this house, once a small Dutch-style cottage, into a highly unusual example of the architectural arts. Using low-cost materials such as sheet metal and chain-link fencing for which Gehry has become famous, his domestic creation was included in a *Los Angeles Magazine* article titled "Nightmare Neighbors." The Gehry House so enraged one local architecture critic that he encouraged his dog to do his "duty" on Gehry's lawn, making his own symbolic statement.

For a traditionally pleasing local architectural tour, take a look at local **John Byers** homes. A prolific architect of the late 1920s, Byers built an enclave of attractive Spanish colonial houses on lovely La Mesa Drive, just off San Vicente, in the shade of gigantic Moreton Bay fig trees planted by Santa Monica's earliest residents. Look for some of Byers's homes at 2021, 2034, 2101, 2153 and 2210 La Mesa Drive, and for his onetime office nearby at 246 26th Street.

Third Street Promenade
When you're done with the public parade on and around the pier, try this one. Santa Monica's

Architect Frank Gehry's house, adorned with sheet metal and chain-link fence, outraged some of his more conservative neighbors.

BOB RACE

Third Street Promenade has become one of L.A.'s hottest "destination streets," an easygoing shopping and entertainment district just blocks from the beach. A pedestrian-only adventure, Third Street between Wilshire and Broadway is an intriguing mix of old and new Santa Monica, of kitsch and chic and chain stores, all decked out with palm trees, topiary sculpture, pushcart vendors, and street entertainers. Beyond the boutiques and funky stores here, diversions and entertainment along these three blocks include great bookstores, galleries, multiplex movie theaters, coffeehouses, and good restaurants.

Start with the bookstores. Long-running **Midnight Special,** 1318 Third St. (between Arizona and Santa Monica), 310/393-2923, specializes in books and magazines and literature, politics, and poetry (regular readings scheduled). Equally revered **Hennessy & Ingall,** 1254 Third (just north of Arizona), 310/458-9074, is *the* stop for books and publications on architecture, art, and design. The chains are here too. The neighborhood boasts a **Barnes & Noble,** 1201 Third (at Wilshire), 310/260-9110, and a **Borders** bookshop, music store, and café at 1415 Third (between Santa Monica and Broadway), 310/393-9290.

Equally fun, though, are the oddities for sale at some of the truly eccentric shops—assuming they haven't been displaced by the chain-sponsored commerce rapidly increasing here. Always entertaining: the **Urban Outfitters** warehouse at 1440 Third, 310/394-1404, stark in its ersatz post-apocalypse decor and specializing in consumer goods for nonconsumers and **Jurassic's** museum-grade fossils at 131 Broadway (at Second). One of the most intriguing toy stores around is **Puzzle Zoo,** 1413 Third, 310/393-9201, where you might find the limited edition Goddess of the Sun Barbie and the Kasparov electronic chess partner.

Then try the eateries—**Johnny Rockets** 310/394-6362, for burgers; the more uptown **Broadway Deli** on the promenade, 310/451-0616; and exceptional Italian **Remi,** 310/393-6545, sibling to New York's Remi. And the ubiquitous **Starbucks.**

At the south end of the promenade, just across Broadway, is **Santa Monica Place,** for still more shopping. This three-story enclosed Frank Gehry-designed mall has an open, breezy feel, thanks to its ocean-facing windows and skylights. Among other claims to fame—including **Ann Taylor's** classic women's clothing, **Williams-Sonoma** housewares, and **The Body Shop's** soaps and lotions—Santa Monica Place starred in Arnold Schwarzenegger's *Terminator 2.*

Just north of the Third Street action is **Fred Segal,** 500 Broadway (at Fifth), 310/393-2322, the hippest of hip department stores, companion to the original store on Melrose. Divided into a series of stylish boutiques for men, women, and children, this is a great people-watching place even if you'll never afford the freight. Fred Segal seems to attract affluent and hip teens and people who look like recording artists (and may well be). Look for the spectacular half-price sales each September—though even then Fred Segal is quite expensive.

Best for Third Street Promenade parking, by the way, are the various public lots along Fourth, reasonably inexpensive. But if you're just here for a quick stroll, the parking lot at Santa Monica Place is free for a stay under three hours (small flat fee in the evening).

Montana Avenue

Long considered one of Santa Monica's most stylish shopping streets, Montana Avenue between Lincoln Boulevard and 17th Street (near Brentwood north of Wilshire) is *very* Westside, an expensive blend of chic shops and nosh stops. **Federico,** 1522 Montana, 310/458-4134, is a long-running local favorite, selling Native American, Mexican, and silver jewelry. **Country Pine & Design,** 1318 Montana, 310/451-0317, is famous for its unique items for the home. **Shabby Chic,** 930 Montana, 310/453-0985, is a popular local furnishings shop. Stop at **The Coffee Bean** at 1426 Montana, 310/453-2093, for delicious coffee and baked goods. Or try the casual **Wolfgang Puck Café** at 1323 Montana Ave. (at 14th), 310/393-0290. And while you're in the neighborhood, see what's playing at the independent **Aero** theater, 1328 Montana, 310/395-4990, which starred in the movie *Get Shorty.*

Strolling Main Street

A stroll along Main always affords an intriguing introduction to the real Santa Monica and its unique cultural combination of chi-chi and cheap. Though Main stretches south from Pico Boulevard on the north to Rose Avenue in Venice Beach, particularly popular for shopping and dining is the area between Ocean Park and Rose, where the classic old-brick buildings attract both the trendy and the traditional. You'll know you've gone too far, and drifted south into eccentric Venice, once you see sculptor Jonathan Borofsky's clownish three-story-tall "ballerino" looming above Main like the crazed stage creation of some mad puppeteer—a huge ballerina's body, en pointe, crowned by a sad clown face complete with five-o'clock shadow.

Most famous along Main are some of Santa Monica's most famous restaurants, including Arnold Schwarzenegger's **Schatzi,** 3100 Main St., 310/399-4800, and Wolfgang Puck's **Chinois on Main,** 2709 Main St., 310/392-9025. But the many other main attractions include Joe Gold's **World Gym,** 2210 Main, 310/450-0080, where Arnold Schwarzenegger got serious about working out (he still drops by occasionally) and where the clients include a list of big and bulky world champs as long as your arm.

To really find out what's going on, try **Newsstand,** 2726 Main St., 310/396-7722, boasting L.A.'s best selection of magazines and newspapers. Another hit is **Blue Moon,** 2717 Main, 310/450-7075, something of a French-styled *parfumerie* selling sunglasses on the side. **Paris 1900,** 2703 Main St., 310/396-0405, recycles the glad rags of the rich circa 1900-1930. Just down the way is cybersoul sister to Almost Paradise in Long Beach and Cyber Java in nearby Venice Beach, Santa Monica's own worldly **World Cafe,** 2820 Main, 310/392-1661 (www.worldcafela.com), where neon-lit hieroglyphics, Captain Nemo dining-room decor, and Mexican patio umbrellas set the stage for sophisticated drinks, snacks, and cyberchat.

Until recently home to the Santa Monica Museum of Art, the **Edgemar** complex along the 2400 block of Main was designed by Santa Monica architect Frank O. Gehry (Mr. Chain-Link-and-Sheet-Metal himself) and built on the site of the old Edgemar Egg Company. Poke around here to find more galleries and shops and eateries.

VENICE: WESTSIDE BOHEMIA

Abbott Kinney had a dream. That dream became a vision, a utopian plan, then an obsession. What was Abbott Kinney's dream? He built an exotic seaside resort here, patterned after the great Italian city (complete with canals), and he expected the grandeur of his creation to spark an early 20th-century American cultural renaissance and create an international image of Los Angeles as sophisticated Mediterranean city. Kinney's plans never quite succeeded. But in recent decades his vision has been revisited, as Venice has become one of L.A.'s avant-garde outposts of the arts and architecture. Yet, as in Kinney's day, the hedonistic eccentricities of Venice Beach and along its two-mile Ocean Front Walk are still the community's main attractions.

For some local events and referral information, call the **Venice Area Chamber of Commerce** at 310/396-7016. For current visitor information, check out www.venice.net/chamber, or contact the L.A. visitor bureau at (213) 689-8822; www.lacvb.com.

Abbott Kinney's Dream

After making his millions selling Sweet Caporal cigarettes, Abbott Kinney came to California to build his personal Venice. In 1904 Kinney bought 160 acres of marshland just south of Santa Monica for his "Venice of America" seaside resort. He drained the marsh, re-creating it as a canal-laced landscape, and then hired architect Norman F. Marsh to design Venice, patterned after its namesake Italian city. The first phase of Kinney's dream included an elaborate Italianate business district, its first first-class hotel—the St. Mark Hotel, patterned after St. Mark's Cathedral in Venice, Italy—and a grand 2,500-seat public auditorium out on the new pier.

The city's three-day opening gala, a veritable circus of enthusiasms, began on July 4, 1905. More than 40,000 potential buyers toured Venice's 19 miles of 40-foot-wide canals in gondolas imported for the occasion, like their gondoliers, from Italy. Others paraded down city streets on the backs of camels. In the auditorium out on the pier, Sarah Bernhardt performed *Camille* during a black-tie performance, backed by the Chicago Symphony Orchestra. Enthralled tourists came and went, and many bought property. Hundreds of lots at the beach along Venice's new canals were sold, some for the then-astronomical price of $2,700 each—twice the going price of Beverly Hills real estate. Yet construction was slow. A number of modest craftsman-style homes were built along Venice's canals, but not the grand rococo palaces that Kinney had envisioned.

Abbott Kinney soon concluded that most people were more interested in the pleasures of sun and surf than in high culture, and in 1907 he built a grand casino. Buoyed by that success, Venice soon featured the world's largest amusement park, with 10-cent camel rides, two roller coasters—including the famous Race through the Clouds—and a dance pavilion. He imported the Ferris wheel from Chicago's 1893 Columbian Exposition. He built an Arabian-style bathhouse with hot salt water, and a bowling alley, a skating rink, a shooting gallery, and an aquacade. Abbott

swimmers at Venice Beach

ROBERT HOLMES/CALIFORNIA DIVISION OF TOURISM

Kinney's Venice became a metaphor for what L.A. would become—a unique combination of popular and classical cultures.

Yet for all its successes, large and small, Abbott Kinney's dream seemed to depend on him, personally, for its continuing existence. After he died in 1920, Venice soon hit the skids—largely because of the demise of L.A.'s electric trolley system and the increasing popularity of the automobile. (Venice's location, far from a major thoroughfare, put the resort at a competitive disadvantage for the tourist trade.) Then small oil wells and derricks dotted the landscape throughout Venice, petroleum-based goo blackened the canals and beaches, and the remaining tourists left town. Kinney's dream became a nightmare. Soon plagued by storms, fires, and political scandals, Venice residents voted in the 1920s to annex themselves to the city of Los Angeles. Most of the city's increasingly murky canals were filled in because of public health concerns. Abbott Kinney's dream died.

Of Arts and Eccentricities

In a style Abbott Kinney could never have imagined, the dream of Venice as cultural mecca did revive. Drawn to the community's relatively low rents and unique, vaguely European style—including the arched bridges over the canals—in the 1950s beatniks and other bohemians arrived to establish L.A.'s latest avant-garde enclave, quickly followed in the 1960s by Summer of Love devotees and in the 1970s by working artists. Many well-known L.A. artists have studios in Venice, lured by the (once) affordable rents, eccentric ambience, and proximity to the beach. In the 1980s Venice—certain parts of Venice—became a chi-chi address for cool-conscious Westsiders. The latter turn of events has spawned some interesting architectural styles as well. Since building codes here are more lenient than in adjacent beach towns, architects solved the problem of postage stamp-size lots by building multilevel structures—and then sometimes finishing them with intentionally shabby exteriors to discourage burglars. Though beset in recent years by seemingly uncontrollable gang violence and other urban ills, Venice still proudly parades its eccentricities. A community where million-dollar homes stand next to run-down shanties, Venice has even cleaned up its canals.

Trouble in Bohemia

Venice has had its share of troubles in recent years. Black vs. Latino gang wars over the crack-cocaine trade broke out throughout the region—in Oakwood, Santa Monica, Mar Vista, and Culver City—in 1994, and 17 people, many of them innocent bystanders, were cut down in the crossfire. Outraged Venetians pushed for a greater L.A. police presence and protection—and got it, at least during the day, when tourists were afoot. But chaos still reigned at night. In a well-planned fit of vigilante justice, early one morning a group of ski-masked residents wielding sledge hammers demolished four permanent concrete picnic tables that had consistently attracted a bad element to the Boardwalk during the wee hours. Awakened by the racket, watching from their windows, the neighbors cheered. Subsequently, almost all of Los Angeles cheered.

Despite Venice's considerable bad press, most neighborhoods here are vital, with genuine and genuinely strong cross-cultural community connections. Most of the community is united against gangster violence. For haven't-got-a-clue visitors and tourists, however, recent local history suggests due caution. If at all in doubt about one's street savvy, stick to the well-trodden tourist path along the Venice Boardwalk—and plan to blow this pop stand well before nightfall. The after-dark scene can get mighty unsavory, not just here but elsewhere along the L.A. coast where major boulevards or freeway exit/on-ramp routes dead-end at the beach. Such strategic spots tend to attract gangsters with an eye to making a quick getaway, as necessary.

Ocean Front Walk and Venice Beach

Abbott Kinney's gaudy amusement park, the Coney Island of the West for two decades, is long gone. But its spirit lives on. Unless the kids have led a truly sheltered suburban life—or perhaps especially if they have—they'll probably enjoy the human zoo that Venice's Ocean Front Walk, known locally as the Venice Boardwalk, has exhibited in recent years. Watch 'em watch Rastafarians and bikini-clad babes on in-line skates blithely dodge bicyclists, baby strollers, and bug-eyed tourists. Robert Gruenberg, the Venice Boardwalk's famous chainsaw juggler, hung up his gas-powered Sears Craftsman in

Street performer Harry Perry rocks and rolls down Venice streets.

MICHELLE & TOM GRIMM/LOS ANGELES CONVENTION AND VISITORS BUREAU

1994, alas. But there's plenty more circus available here—roller-skating swamis, fire-eaters, palmists, and tarot card readers along with dancers, singers, and comedians. Sidewalk merchants sell T-shirts, sunglasses, hats, clothing, jewelry, crystals, and posters along the Venice Boardwalk, which stretches for two miles along Ocean Front Walk between Ozone Avenue and Washington Street. Venice's oceanfront promenade and pier have been undergoing major renovations adding new entertainment areas, lighting, and even pagodas.

Once the kids are satiated with the street performance, nudge them on to Muscle Beach, "the pit" where muscle people get pumped on open-air weight lifting. (This Muscle Beach is no real relation to the original Muscle Beach of Jack LaLanne fame, just south of the Santa Monica Pier; old-timers say it was originally known as Mussel Beach—after those well-muscled bivalves.) Among the endless snack stands, best bet for meat lovers is **Jody Maroni's Sausage Kingdom,** 2011 Ocean Walk, 310/306-1995, famous throughout L.A. for its fabulous all-natural links—from sweet Italian to Yucatán chicken. But if the Boardwalk's crowded sidewalk cafés seem just too crowded, beat a retreat to the **Rose Cafe,** 220 Rose Ave., 310/399-0711, Venice's coolest coffeehouse, bakery, deli, and neighborhood café since almost forever. While in the neighborhood, die-hard shoppers should stop by **DNA Clothing Company,** 411 Rose, 310/399-0341, one of L.A.'s best outlet shopping spots, featuring top-drawer clothing and jeans for women and men at bargain-basement prices.

Then do the beach, which doesn't get nearly the attention—or crowds—as do the Venice Boardwalk or Santa Monica State Beach just north. Venice Beach is a *beautiful* beach, a broad belt of palm-dotted white sand stretching up coast and down and out into the surf. The huge concrete **Venice Pier** at the foot of Washington Boulevard—open again after lengthy reconstruction—isn't all that romantic but is quite pop-ular with skaters and pier fishers. Open daily 8 A.M.–10 P.M., the pier also features public restrooms. Parking in the lot (Washington and Ocean Walk) is $5 weekdays, $6.50 weekends.

Other Venice Sights

Like Abbott Kinney, start with the canals and then move on to the arts. The **Venice Canals**—six survive—are just minutes east of the busy beach scene, in a fairly upscale neighborhood bordered on the south by Washington Street, on the north by S. Venice Boulevard, on the west by Pacific Avenue, and on the east by Ocean Avenue. After decades of political battles, the surviving canals were restored in 1993. **Grand** and **Eastern** Canals run north-south, and **Carroll, Linnie, Howland,** and **Sherman** Canals run east-west. Since the neighborhood's transportation system is largely dependent on canal and footpath, only the Grand Canal—along Pacific Avenue—can be reached by road.

VIEW FROM THE EDGE:
THE MUSEUM OF JURASSIC TECHNOLOGY

If you bring the kids, prepare for possible whining. Prepare for the fact that they'll think you tricked them. They'll think you offered an afternoon in Jurassic Park (as in *Jurassic Park*—The Ride) when instead, you offered them something equally amazing from "real life"—a view of the world as seen from the edge of science.

The motto of West L.A.'s strange Museum of Jurassic Technology is "nature as metaphor." This particular metaphorical interpretation of the natural world is most intriguing. Half the exhibits are real—or seem to be—and the others are highly unlikely, from the mounted horns, spore-eating ants, and fruit-stone carvings to the superstitions exhibit. An enormous hit in 1996 was the exhibit of "microminiature" creations by Soviet-Armenian violinist Hagop Sandaldjian, including likenesses of Disney's Goofy and Snow White and the Seven Dwarfs, even Pope John Paul II, all mounted on sewing needles and visible only through microscopes. Some of Sandaldjian's works are still on display in the Churchy Marrin Annex, where at last report the main exhibit was **Garden of Eden on Wheels: Selected Collections from Los Angeles Area Mobile Home and Trailer Parks.** On exhibit in the Coolidge Pavilion, opened in September 1999, is **The World is Bound with Secret Knots: The Life and Works of Athanasius Kircher, S.J., 1602–1680.**

In the opinion of Lawrence Weschler, author of *Mr. Wilson's Cabinet of Wonder,* the Jurassic rekindles one's sense of wonder while undermining "the sense of the authoritative" normally extended to museums. But the museum's curator suggests you leave even that preconception at home. Wonder is as wonder does—metaphorically speaking.

The Museum of Jurassic Technology, in a nondescript storefront in Culver City's historic Palms District, on Venice Blvd. four blocks west of Robertson Blvd. (directly across from Bagley), is open Thursday 2–8 P.M. (sometimes from noon) and Fri.–Sun. noon–6 P.M. (closed major holidays and the first Thursday in May). Suggested donation is $4 adults, $2.50 children (under age 12 free), students, and seniors). For more information, contact: Museum of Jurassic Technology, 9341 Venice Blvd., Culver City, CA 90232, 310/836-6131, fax 310/287-2267; www.mjt.org.

The **Grand Lagoon,** or where it once was, can be found at Windward Avenue and Main Street. Now a concrete traffic circle, this originally was where all of the canals met. A few of the original **Venice arcades,** patterned after those surrounding the Piazza San Marco in Venice, Italy, remain at St. Mark's Place, 67–71 Windward.

Yet don't wander too far. Not many blocks from the canals is the now-notorious neighborhood known as **Oakwood.** Plagued with drug and gang activity, Oakwood is known locally as the Demilitarized Zone or DMZ. While living in this neighborhood, according to L.A. artistic lore, actor Dennis Hopper was inspired to direct the film *Colors.*

More inspiring for most people are local arts venues. The **Beyond Baroque Literary Arts Center** is housed in Venice's onetime city hall, 681 Venice Blvd., 310/822-3006. Both small-press-oriented bookstore and library, this is also the place for poetry readings and other local literary events. Next door, in the 1923 art-deco old Venice Police Station, is the **Social and Public Art Resource Center (SPARC),** 685 Venice Blvd., 310/822-9560, www.sparcmurals.com, where a block of jail cells has been converted into an art gallery. Yet SPARC is considerably more famous for its work in preserving and promoting mural art projects throughout Los Angeles. Stop by for some local suggestions; SPARC knows everything about public murals, and there are endless people's-art displays throughout the area, some dating to the 1960s.

Come in May and meet local artists during the popular annual **Venice Art Walk,** an open studios–style arts event and silent auction that's also a primary fundraiser for the Venice Family Clinic. The Venice Art Walk is usually scheduled for the fourth Sunday in May. Or shop for art anytime. Long-running local galleries include **L.A. Louver,** 45 N. Venice Blvd., 310/822-4955, famous for its representation of artists Wallace Berman, David Hockney, and Edward Kienholz, among many others.

More affordable for most folks are the arts, crafts, and antique shops along the 1200–1500 blocks of **Abbott Kinney Boulevard**—until 1990 known as W. Washington Boulevard, a source of endless confusion, what with Washington Blvd. and Washington St., too. Now it's one of L.A.'s relaxed new "destination" streets. To get started, try **Toni's Arte,** 1426 Abbott Kinney Blvd., 310/399-2122. For pizza, stop by **Abbott's Pizza Company,** 1407 Abbott Kinney Blvd., 310/396-7334, famous for its funky atmosphere and killer pizzas. Abbott's even offers breakfast and dessert pizzas. Right next door is **Abbott's Habit** coffeehouse, 310/399-1171, serving the real thing by the mug or by the pound, along with bakery items.

Marina del Rey, Playa del Rey, and Playa Vista

Undeveloped coastal wetlands until 1968, when the county of Los Angeles set about the business of draining one of the coast's last remaining wetlands and building the largest man-made small-craft harbor in the world, Marina del Rey is largely boat harbor—and boats, boats, boats. When row after row of life-at-the-beach-themed apartment houses and condominiums were built here in the late 1960s and early '70s it was only natural, given the area's proximity to LAX, that planeloads of stewardesses, stewards, and other unattached airline employees would move in to share the neighborhood with the retirees and yachties—which won Marina del Rey its reputation as preferred port for swinging singles. Redevelopment plans—allowing 22-story high-rise "residential towers," apartment buildings, and hotels while ignoring the need for new parks and other genuine public access—will likely change the character of the neighborhood yet again.

Marina del Rey offers few attractions beyond upscale hotels (including a Ritz-Carlton) and fairly corporate entertainments. For tourist kitsch, there's always **Fisherman's Village,** 13755 Fiji Way, 310/823-5411, an odd replication of a New England fishing village featuring gift shops, restaurants, South Seas foliage, and a view of the Marina channel. From here, you can sign on for a dinner cruise with **Hornblower Dining Yachts,** 310/301-6000, or sportfishing and winter whale-watching tours with **Marina del Rey Sportfishing,** 310/822-3625.

According to the annual "beach pollution report card" issued by Heal the Bay, always-popular **Mother's Beach** on Palawan Way within the marina is not recommended for swimming—especially for kids—because of continuing harbor pollution. A better bet by far is **Dockweiler State Beach,** sometimes known locally as Playa del Rey, below the bluffs along the harbor's face, with little at-the-beach clutter but clean restrooms, lifeguards, and some grassy picnic areas. Dockweiler stretches from Venice south to the mouth of the harbor and beyond, on the harbor's south side. Water quality is generally good at Dockweiler, except near storm drain outlets and, south of the harbor, near the outfall for the Hyperion sewage treatment plant.

For more information about the area, contact **Los Angeles County Dept. of Beaches and Harbors,** Visitor Information Center, 4701 Admiralty Way, Marina del Rey, 310/305-9546; www.beaches.co.la.ca.us.

Just south of Marina del Rey and east of the beach, surrounding the intersection of Lincoln and Jefferson Boulevards, is a surviving 1,000-acre section of the once-wildlife-rich **Ballona Wetlands,** owned at one time by eccentric billionaire Howard Hughes, who built his famous *Spruce Goose* here. The fate of the Ballona Wetlands—how much should be preserved or restored, how, and where—is an ongoing battle in one of L.A.'s latest development wars. **Playa Vista,** as this new city along the Westchester bluffs will be called, was slated to become the city's latest "Hollywood" if the new **Dreamworks SKG** film studio and other proposed commercial and residential developments proceeded as planned. However, progress on the project was delayed when environmentalists protested the destruction of the area's wetlands. Dreamworks subsequently pulled out of the project.

STAYING IN SANTA MONICA AND VICINITY

Santa Monica and other coastal enclaves are typically well booked and most expensive on weekends, though midweek and seasonal specials are possible. More significant, for true budget travelers and families, is the fact that in addition to the ubiquitous luxury options, Santa Monica and other coastal communities feature a variety of hostels and other inexpensive and midrange motel options.

LOW-RENT SANTA MONICA STAYS

The best bargain around is the 200-bed Hostelling International–American Youth Hostels **Los Angeles/Santa Monica Hostel,** 1436 Second St. (between Santa Monica Blvd. and Broadway), Santa Monica, 310/393-9913; www.hiayh .org or www.hostelweb.com/losangeles. This is a budget traveler's bonanza, even though prices here are a bit higher than in other area hostels. What you get for the difference is an exceptional value, just two blocks from the beach and pier and, in the other direction, one block from the lively Third Street Promenade. The Santa Monica International is at home in a four-story one-time town hall, an aged brick and dark wood building complete with historic common room (once a saloon), full-service travel store, laundry and kitchen, library, TV room, large open-air courtyard, bicycle storage, and lockers. Most of the rooms are dormitory style with two or four beds per room (linen rental, small extra fee), though private rooms are available for couples. Bathrooms are shared. Free airport shuttle service and organized area tours (extra) are also offered. This hostel is understandably popular, so make reservations (by phone, fax, or mail, with credit card confirmation) well in advance.

Venice, just blocks south of Santa Monica, offers other hostel-style accommodations. Also inquire at the visitor center for lower rent suggestions.

MIDRANGE SANTA MONICA STAYS

As elsewhere, midrange accommodations in Santa Monica comprise a somewhat confusing category. Most of the options listed here offer "moderate" prices throughout the year. Yet during the off season or in slow years, and/or with the right discount or package deal, some of Santa Monica's "classic" and high-rent offerings can become quite affordable (see other listings below). It often pays to inquire. Many of the following offer student, senior citizen, AAA, and/or other discounts or specials.

Notable near the Beach

A notable deal by Santa Monica standards is the **Hotel Carmel** near the HI-AYH hostel at 201 Broadway (at Second St.), 310/451-2469 or toll-free 800/445-8695. This is one of Santa Monica's grande dames, well preserved and still quite attractive after all these years, with lovely lobby and basic rooms with ceiling fans—a best bet for budget-conscious families bound for the beach. The Hotel Carmel is also a jump away from the Third Street Promenade's premier people watching and shops, movie theaters, and

Affordable stays are just blocks away from the beach in Santa Monica.

restaurants. Though this is largely a families-and-couples kind of place, from mid-September through May the Hotel Carmel offers college students (with IDs) a hefty rate discount. Rates: $80–155.

Up on a hill three blocks inland from the ocean is the very comfortable 309-room **Four Points Sheraton** 530 Pico Blvd., 310/399-9344 or toll-free 888/627-8532 for central reservations, www.fourpoints.com, featuring two heated pools, in-room coffeemakers and the usual comforts, even free airport shuttle service. Rates: $139–175, sometimes dropping in the off-season. For a similar deal close to the beach and pier, try the **Holiday Inn Santa Monica Beach,** 120 Colorado Blvd., 310/451-0676 or toll-free 800/465-4329 for central reservations, www.holidayinn.com, with swimming pool and the usual amenities. Rates: $159–239.

Other possibilities include the **Best Western Ocean View Hotel,** 1447 Ocean Ave., 310/458-4888 or toll-free 800/452-4888. Rates: $139–259, but often less expensive in the off-season. And the 168-room **Pacific Shore Hotel** near both the beach and Main Street at 1819 Ocean Ave., 310/451-8711 or toll-free 800/622-8711, which features an exercise room, pool, sauna, hot tub, and sundeck. Some rooms have ocean views. Rates: $109–169.

Not near the Beach

Well away from the beach but fairly affordable—particularly in the off-season—and quite comfortable is the **Best Western Gateway Hotel Santa Monica,** 1920 Santa Monica Blvd., 310/829-9100 or toll-free 800/528-1234 (central reservations), www.bestwestern.com, which offers free beach shuttle service, full fitness facilities, and in-room video games among its many amenities. Rates: $109–139. Other possibilities in the same vicinity include the **Comfort Inn,** 2815 Santa Monica Blvd., 310/828-5517 or toll-free 800/228-5150; www.comfortinn.com, where a stay includes free morning newspaper and breakfast and amenities include in-room coffeemakers and refrigerators plus family-size heated pool, and the **Days Inn Santa Monica,** 3007 Santa Monica Blvd., 310/829-6333 or toll-free 800/591-5995; www.daysinn.com. Both are $87–150.

CLASSIC SANTA MONICA STAYS

Shangri-La Hotel
Santa Monica's 1939 Shangri-La Hotel, 1301 Ocean Ave. (at Arizona Ave.), 310/394-2791 or toll-free 800/345-7829, www.shangrila -hotel.com, is a local favorite, an art deco ocean liner of a building looming large from a corner berth. Popular with writers and more eccentric movie stars, the Shangri-La has no pool and no bar, but this small 55-room hotel does offer evocative elegance overlooking Palisades Park, a nice continental breakfast and free morning newspaper, and afternoon tea. Most of the tasteful rooms—successfully restored to their original deco glory, but with color TVs and cable—feature full kitchens and sundecks; most have ocean views. Rates:$145–420.

Georgian Hotel
Another art deco gem, the historic eight-story Georgian near the pier at 1415 Ocean Ave., 310/395-9945 or toll-free 800/538-8147, www.georgianhotel.com, was lovingly restored to its 1933 ambience in 1993. Most of the 84 rooms and suites offer ocean views, along with contemporary comforts including coffeemakers, refrigerators, honor bars, and cable TV (free movies); some have microwaves. No air-conditioning, usually unnecessary here. Breakfast is served in the dining room every morning, afternoon tea and cocktails on the veranda. Lunch and dinner are also available. Rates: $210–475.

Hotel Oceana
Another likely spot to spot the occasional off-duty celebrity is the very cool Hotel Oceana a few blocks north of Wilshire at 849 Ocean Ave. (between Montana and Idaho Aves.), 310/393-0486 or toll-free 800/777-0758; www.hoteloceana.com. Tasteful rooms overlook the courtyard pool; others offer ocean views. Basic amenities include kitchens, in-room coffeemakers, microwaves, cable TV (free movies). Air-conditioning is rarely needed this close to the ocean, so the Oceana doesn't have it. Though technically this is a pretty high-rent class act, if you opt for one of the few studio apartments—and if you come in the dead of the off-season, say, Febru-ary—a stay here might be almost affordable, about half the usual tab; rates are higher but still more reasonable in spring and fall ($250–600). Continental breakfast included.

Channel Road Inn Bed-and-Breakfast
A real find for B&B fans, the Channel Road Inn just east of Pacific Coast Highway is merely a mile or so north of the Santa Monica Pier and Third Street Promenade. The inn is an inviting shingle-sided 1910 colonial revival period piece moved to this site in the 1960s and then transformed into a 14-room inn in the late 1980s. Most rooms and suites offer ocean views, some feature fireplaces, and all have private baths. Just a block from the beach, technically just beyond Santa Monica city limits, the inn also offers a friendly introduction to neighborhood life. Bikes are available if you feel like exploring, or soak up the ambience from the bayview hot tub. A good deal including full breakfast with home-baked muffins. For more information or reservations, contact: Channel Road Inn, 219 W. Channel Rd., 310/459-1920; www.channel-roadinn.com. Rates: $150–325.

MORE HIGH-RENT SANTA MONICA STAYS

Fairmont Miramar Hotel
Santa Monica's classic classy hotel is downtown's historic Miramar, "where Wilshire meets the sea," now a Fairmont, 101 Wilshire Blvd., 310/576-7777 or toll-free 800/325-3535; www.fairmont.com. Onetime private mansion and Santa Monica playground for Hollywood stars including Humphrey Bogart, Greta Garbo, and Betty Grable, the Miramar still requires an entrance; visitors drive in through impressive wrought-iron gates and circle the huge Moreton Bay fig. Time and a $33 million restoration continue to transform the Miramar. The once-palatial grounds have been subdivided by progress, and the hotel's fabled courtyard bungalows, surrounding the lush jungle, pool, and patio just beyond the bright and spacious lobby, have been replaced with 31 snazzy new ones. Yet the Miramar abides, with a sophisticated international atmosphere both rarified and relaxed. The hotel's his-

toric charms are most apparent in the older brick Palisades wing, overlooking Palisades Park, yet rooms in the more contemporary Ocean Tower come with almost aerial views. Amenities abound, including in-room safes, coffeemakers, and honor bars, color TVs with cable (free movies), countless little luxuries, a wonderful on-site restaurant, and full fitness facilities. Rates $249 and up.

Le Merigot Beach Hotel

Santa Monica's newest upscale hotel, just a block from the beach at 1740 Ocean Ave., Le Merigot is a contemporary take on the city's art-deco sensibilities, from the potted palms and blond woods in the lobby to the day-at-the-beach pastel colors and artful furnishings in the 175 guest rooms—some with views. Yet the attitude here is European—so L.A.—and extends to the hotel's **Cézanne** restaurant, **Café Promenade,** and **Le Troquet** bar. For more information or reservations, call 310/395-9700 or toll-free 877/ 637-4468; www.lemerigotbeachhotel.com. Rates: $279–459.

Loews Santa Monica Beach Hotel

Before Shutters opened its shutters onto the Santa Monica sands, the Loews Santa Monica Beach Hotel, 1700 Ocean Ave. (between Pico and Colorado), 310/458-6700 or toll-free 800/235-6397 (central reservations), www.loewshotels.com, had the notable distinction of being L.A.'s only beachfront hotel. Though this hotel isn't exactly *on* the beach, it's certainly close enough. The stunning contemporary lobby, colored in soft tones of seafoam green, peach, and sand and accented by potted palms and bold wrought-iron grillwork and glass, somehow evokes L.A.'s most intriguing Victorian-era architecture, downtown L.A.'s famed Bradbury Building. The same general idea—inspiring skylit enclosures—carries over to the indoor-outdoor pool area overlooking the beach. Many of the hotel's 350 rooms and 35 one- and two-bedroom suites, luxuriantly decked out and featuring the usual amenities, overlook the beach. Other attractions include complete fitness facilities (personal trainers available), the adult-supervised Splash Club for vacationing families, the sophisticated French Provincial **Lavande** restaurant, 310/576-3181, and the casual **Ocean Cafe.** Rates: $310 and up.

Shutters on the Beach

Definitely on the beach, Shutters on the Beach, 1 Pico Blvd. (just off Ocean Ave.), 310/458-0030 or toll-free 800/334-9000, www.shutterson the-beach.com, looms over the sand like an overgrown beachhouse—shutters and all—by design. Shutters, with its 198 rooms and suites right on the beach, was designed in the spirit of Southern California beach homes and resorts of the 1920s and 1930s. Otherwise, everything is cutting-edge contemporary, light, open, and vaguely reminiscent of plein-air watercolors. Rooms are small but attractive—note that some "partial view" rooms barely spy the sea—with the usual luxury amenities, marble bathrooms, and large Jacuzzi tubs. Sliding shutter doors open onto private patios or balconies, providing the "shutters" of the hotel's name. Other pluses include two good on-site restaurants, the outstanding **One Pico,** 310/587-1717, and the casual café **Pedals,** both the **HandleBar** and an attractive lobby lounge, large pool and patio areas, spa, full fitness facilities—even a rental service for Santa Monica essentials, from bikes, in-line skates, and volleyball nets to swim fins and children's beach toys. Unfortunately for determined ocean swimmers, the hotel's beach sits at the mouth of the Pico-Kenter storm drain, with its attendant bacterial "danger" signs from time to time—so heads up if you actually brave the waters. Rates: $340 and up.

STAYING IN VENICE AND VICINITY

People's Stays: Venice Hostels

The **Cadillac Hotel,** 401 Ocean Front Walk (at Dudley), 310/399-8876, isn't the Cadillac of hotels. Venice isn't the Cadillac of beach towns, for that matter, and not a totally comfortable area after dark. But if the wild and wacky rush of Southern California humanity is your scene— people watching from sidewalk cafés, dodging the in-line skaters and cheap trinket stalls on the way to the wide, wide expanse of white sand—then the art deco Cadillac Hotel is one place to park yourself come nightfall. Most of the rooms (30) are private (just the basics), some with private bathrooms. Rates: $69–120. The remainder offer hostel-style dorm accommodations, with four beds to a room and bathrooms down the hall. Other features: sundeck, sauna, gym, laundry and storage facilities, even a pool table. Free airport shuttle service.

Other nearby hostels run by InterClub include the **Venice Beach Hotel,** 25 Windward Ave., 310/392-3376, and the **Airport Hostel,** 2221 Lincoln Blvd., 310/305-0250, both of which offer dormitory-style and private rooms.

Venice Beach House

The Venice Beach House is an L.A. rarity—a bed-and-breakfast. This one is a rarity among rarities, however, since this lovely, early 20th-century home also happens to be a graceful craftsman bungalow just steps from the beach and a block from the Venice Canals. North of Washington Boulevard and west of Pacific Boulevard on one of Venice's "walk streets" (onetime canals, long since filled in), the Venice Beach House features nine well-appointed period rooms with antiques and wicker. The Pier Suite comes with a sitting room, fireplace, king-size bed, and ocean view; smaller, less expensive garden-view rooms share bathrooms. For reservations, contact Venice Beach House, 15 30th Ave., Venice 90291, 310/823-1966.

Other Venice Stays

Quite nice in Venice's motel category is the **Inn at Venice Beach** (formerly the Mansion Inn) just two blocks from the beach at 327 Washington Blvd., 310/821-2557 or toll-free 800/828-0688; www.mansioninn.com. Rates: $99–149.

Fun and funky in Venice, with spacious and attractive rooms, is the **Marina Pacific Hotel and Suites** just a block from the beach and otherwise smack-dab in the middle of everything at 1697 Pacific Ave., 310/452-1111 or toll-free 800/421-8151; www.mphotel.com. Rates: $119–169.

Staying in Marina del Ray

Reigning monarch of the South Bay hotel scene is **The Ritz-Carlton, Marina del Rey,** 4375 Admiralty Way, Marina del Rey, 310/823-1700 or toll-free 800/241-3333, www.ritzcarlton.com, which here serves as scenic backdrop for yachts and yachters. The usual ritzy amenities abound, thick terrycloth robes and every other imaginable comfort, plus full fitness and business facilities. The crisp, classic decor includes French doors in most rooms, opening out onto balconies overlooking the boat harbor. Dining options include the excellent **Terrace Restaurant** and the less formal **Pool Café.**

More fun and much more affordable for most people, though, is the **Best Western Jamaica Bay Inn** on Mother's Beach at 4175 Admiralty Way, 310/823-5333 or toll-free 888/823-5333, www.bestwestern-jamaicabay.com, the only place around actually on the beach. (Because of harbor pollution, however, ocean swimming here is not advisable.) Rooms are large, with either terraces or balconies, and bathrooms are a bit small. Pleasant beachfront café. Rates: $89–189.

EATING IN SANTA MONICA AND VICINITY

PEOPLE'S EATS

People's Eats: Farmers' Markets
If you time things right, load up on fresh fruits, vegetables, fabulous flowers, and other essentials at the big-deal **Santa Monica Certified Farmers' Market,** held year-round at Arizona Avenue between Second and Third Streets on Wednesday 9:30 A.M.–2 P.M. (bring quarters for area parking meters) and on Saturday 8:30 A.M.–1 P.M. Also on Saturday, there's an open-air Farmers' Market at the intersection of **Pico Boulevard and Cloverfield,** 8 A.M.–1 P.M. On Sunday there's still another, at **Victorian Heritage Square** at Ocean Park Boulevard and Main Street, scheduled 9:30 A.M.–1 P.M., the fun here including pony rides and other kid's stuff.

Otherwise, for natural foods, cosmetics, and such, there's always the **Wild Oats Community Market,** 1425 Montana Ave. (at 15th St.), 310/576-4707, a link in the chain that genuine co-ops tend to disdain.

People's Eats near the Pier
A real deal for authentic Mexican is colorful **El Texate Oaxacan Restaurant,** 316 Pico Blvd. (at Fourth St.), 310/399-1115, which at first glance looks something like a surfer bar. The treasure here is the wide selection of rich mole sauces, blends of roasted chiles, seeds, nuts, and spices so perfect with chicken (start with the *coloradito,* or "little red"). Entrées include enchiladas, *chiles rellenos, empañadas,* and pizzalike *clayudas* and *memelas.* If you're not in the mood for margaritas or beer, wash everything down with *tejate*—the traditional summer drink created from cornmeal, chocolate, and walnuts. El Texate is open daily 9 A.M.–11:30 P.M. Also always a people's favorite: the colorful **Crocodile Cafe,** 101 Santa Monica Blvd. (at Ocean), 310/394-4783, the onetime site of Santa Monica's dignified old-school French Belle-Vue restaurant. The terribly hip Crocodile is so popular that it's not the best choice if you'll need to be

somewhere soon. Otherwise, the fare is usually worth the wait—especially for the money. Some appetizers, such as the chicken tacos, make a meal. Or order the grilled romaine salad, dressed with yogurt and spicy pecans. Or the Santa Fe or "almost cheeseless" pizzas. And anything for dessert. It's open daily for lunch and dinner (until midnight). Full bar.

For an extreme stylistic alternative, a good bet for families, head for **Ye Olde King's Head Restaurant and Pub,** 116 Santa Monica Blvd. (between Ocean and Second St.), 310/451-1402, which has been serving English specialties for more than 25 years—everything from fish and chips and bangers and mash to royal tea. Entertainment provided by warm beer and darts. It's open for lunch and dinner daily, for high tea weekdays only.

Numerous people's possibilities lie along the Third Street Promenade, an easy stroll from the beach. For an array of dining options, check out the food court at the **Criterion Theater Plaza,** 1315 Third St., where nothing on any menu is more than $12 (most choices are much less). Among the star here is **Wolfgang Puck Express,** 310/576-4770, for fast reasonably priced pastas, pizzas, and salads. This and other fast fooderies here are open daily 11 A.M.–11 P.M.

People's Eats Not near the Pier
For a very good, very inexpensive bagel breakfast, the place is ubiquitous **Noah's New York Bagels,** 1426 Santa Monica Blvd. (between 14th and 15th Sts.), 310/587-9103; there is another Noah's at 2710 Main St. (near Hill), 310/396-4339. A best bet for vegetarians, with the kitchen open into the wee hours seven days a week, is **Anastasia's Asylum,** 1028 Wilshire Blvd. (at 11th St.), 310/394-7113, a fun and funky art gallery/coffeehouse/restaurant serving tofu lasagna along with open-poetry nights. For organic vegetarian food, the place is **Real Food Daily,** 514 Santa Monica Blvd., 310/451-7544, fresh and unusually good, from *seitan* fajitas to vegetable sushi and eggless Caesar and Peru-

vian quinoa salads. Good desserts too. It's open Mon.–Sat. for lunch and dinner. Exceptional vegetarian fare is available at **Nawab of India,** 1621 Wilshire Blvd. (at 17th St.), 310/829-1106, noted for its home-style Northern Indian lunch buffets (brunch buffet on weekends).

One of the best for all-American breakfast is **Rae's,** 2901 Pico Blvd. (at 29th St.), 310/828-7937, a real-deal 1950s diner where, most weekends, people are only too happy to line up and wait. (No credit cards.) Rae's is open daily for breakfast, lunch, and dinner. Or head to breakfast-anytime **Snug Harbor,** 2323 Wilshire Blvd. (between 23rd and 24th Streets), 310/828-2991, where diner standards, including the dinner salad, are more sophisticated than you'd expect. Omelettes star at breakfast—available anytime—along with fresh-squeezed orange and grapefruit juices. Snug Harbor is open for breakfast, lunch, and dinner on weekdays, for breakfast and lunch only on weekends.

Given the endless possibilities along Main, one of the better choices is among the least expensive—attractive **Tavern on Main,** 2907 Main St. (at Ashland Ave.), 310/392-2772, serving contemporary ($5) takes on all-American standards in nouveau 1930s style. If you've been frugal while wandering Main, blow a few bucks at local sweets and dessert shops, including the nearby chocoholic shrine **European Bakery,** 2915 Main, 310/581-3525, famous for creating wonderful brownie biscotti, luscious cakes, and almost everything else in sight from Valrhona chocolate. For some after-dinner cheer, the **Library Alehouse,** 2911 Main, 310/314-4855, is a veritable library of Pacific Northwest microbrews on tap, where the various "taster specials" allow you to sample five three-ounce samples. (You can also "read" on the patio.) Some might prefer splurging on a Salty Dog—grapefruit juice and vodka served margarita style in a salt-rimmed glass. The place to get 'em is the **Galley,** 2442 Main, 310/452-1934, Santa Monica's oldest surviving dark bar and surf-and-turf restaurant.

A bit fancy for cheap-eats freaks but quite affordable for the genre is Italian **Il Forno,** 2901 Ocean Park Blvd. (between 29th and 30th Sts.), 310/450-1241, a best bet for antipasti, pastas, and pizza. It's noisy, friendly, reliable, and open weekdays only for lunch, Mon.–Sat. for dinner.

And there's a fabulous new Italian in town—**Fritto Misto,** 601 Colorado Ave. (at Sixth St.), 310/458-2829, busy, unbelievably reasonable, and well worth the long waits. Owner Robert Kerr makes his own pasta, ravioli, and sausages fresh daily. House specialties include such things as "Atomic" pasta—two seared Cajun-seasoned chicken breasts served on a bed of chile linguine and tossed with peppers and onions in a chipotle cream sauce. Not to mention some marvelous vegetarian selections. Here, you can also create your own specialty by selecting pasta, sauce, and favorite add-ins. The wine list includes boutique wines listed at half the price other restaurants charge. Such a deal! Don't miss the delectable desserts. Open for lunch and dinner.

RICHER PEOPLE'S EATS

Richer People's Eats near the Pier

Santa Monica's legendary high-class diner and sawdust-floored dive is **Chez Jay,** 1657 Ocean Ave. (between Pico and Colorado), 310/395-1741, once a favorite coastal hangout for regulars Ava Gardner, Vivien Leigh, Frank Sinatra, and Willie Shoemaker. The private booth in back is sometimes called the Kissinger Room, because Henry Kissinger often hid out there with his dates. According to local lore, this is also the place Daniel Ellsberg—working next door at the Rand Corporation think tank—passed the Vietnam War-era *Pentagon Papers* to a reporter. Things are a bit less exciting these days. Continental Chez Jay, the name alone an uncanny spoof on L.A. food snobbery, serves such things as exceptional steaks, lobster thermidor, steamed clams, and shrimp curry, most everything accompanied by the restaurant's famous side dish—baked potatoes, bananas, and sour cream. Dessert is "nonfattening homemade organic cheesecake." Chez Jay is open for lunch on weekdays, dinner nightly.

Almost always worth the dent in the pocketbook: **Ocean Avenue Seafood,** 1401 Ocean Ave. (at Santa Monica Blvd.), 310/394-5669, a stylish yet classic oyster bar and seafood restaurant featuring modern art, pastel walls, dark wood paneling, and an indoor-outdoor bar. Classics such as the New England clam chowder, crab cakes, and blackened catfish are always available—but the ever-changing list of fish and fish dishes, usually offering more than two dozen choices on any given day, keeps everyone surprised. It's open daily for lunch and dinner (brunch on Sunday).

Even more expensive is **The Ivy at the Shore,** almost facing the pier from 1541 Ocean Ave. (at Colorado), 310/393-3113. This fashionable faux beach shack, complete with bamboo, breezy patio seating (glassed-in and heated on nippy evenings), and tropical-themed bar, is notable along palm-lined Ocean. Like its stylish older sibling near West Hollywood, this Ivy specializes in California-style adaptations of no-nonsense regional Americana—crab cakes, shrimp, and other seafood specialties, Cajun prime rib, Louisiana meatloaf, pizzas, and pastas. Simpler at lunch are the sandwiches and salads (don't forget the Maui onion rings). The Ivy's Caesar salad is famous throughout Los Angeles. Almost equally famous: delectable desserts. Ivy's is open daily for lunch and dinner (brunch on Sunday); closed major holidays.

Richer People's Eats near the Promenade

Start searching for possibilities where almost everyone else does, along the Third Street Promenade. Prime for people watching—one of those only-in-L.A. places—is the spacious, light, and airy **Broadway Deli,** 1457 Third St. (at Broadway), 310/451-0616, where the proprietors don't do a particularly good job with traditional New York deli standards. (But hey, this is California.) The Broadway does just about everything else, though, from superb French bistro fare to reinvented American comfort food, including macaroni and cheese and killer burgers. (Not necessarily impressive: the blintzes, pastrami sandwiches, lox, and other Jewish deli standards, though they are served here.) Put together an unforgettable picnic lunch or dinner by ordering takeout from the deli counter. Or settle into a booth, and order just about anything your heart desires—from blueberry pancakes and French toast to Caesar salad, beef stew, chicken pot pie, pizza, mushroom barley soup, and tapioca crème brûlée. This is a fairly pricey place, but if you order judiciously you'll still be able to afford the gas—or plane fare—to get home. Espresso bar, fresh-baked breads and bagels, delightful desserts. Astonishing foodie shop, too, which you'll get to know well while you wait (no reservations). The Broadway Deli is open daily 7 A.M.–midnight, 8 A.M. until 1 A.M. on Friday and Saturday nights.

But don't overlook dignified yet relaxed **Remi** also near Broadway, at 1451 Third St. (near Broadway), 310/393-6545. Though cousin to New York's Remi, this restaurant's influences come all the way from Venice—the one in Italy, not the eccentric upstart just down the beach. The jaunty nautical theme here launches all kinds of classics, such as grilled quail, roasted stuffed pork chops, rack of lamb, and some stunning seafood pastas. The perfect finish for a perfect meal: the house-made tiramisu. Remi is open daily for lunch and dinner (closed Christmas and New Year's Day). If Remi's not possible, other choices include **Locando del Lago,** 231 Arizona Ave. (between Second and Third Sts.), 310/451-3525, noted for dishes from Lombardy. The patio is also a plus.

One block east of the Promenade and well worth the detour is the flamboyant dinners-only **Border Grill,** 1444 Fourth St. (near Broadway), 310/451-1655. The bizarre and bright faux folk art-splashed walls serve as apt accompaniment to the stunning food served here—everything the creation of chefs Mary Sue Milliken and Susan Feniger, who apply their formal training in classical French cooking to the bold flavors of coastal Mexico and Central America. You can make a meal of the appetizers, the green corn tamales, the *panuchos* and *platano empañadas* stuffed with cheese and black beans, thereby keeping the total tab almost reasonable. Then again, you'd miss the entrées—such things as grilled skirt steak marinated with garlic, cilantro, and cracked pepper, served with moros, avocado-corn relish and Roma tomatoes, sautéed rock shrimp with toasted *ancho* chiles, and marinated breast of chicken served with onion-orange salsa. And for dessert, how about a slice of Oaxacan chocolate cake? Full bar. The Border Grill is open nightly for dinner (closed major holidays).

Richer People's Eats Elsewhere

Culinary stars at the Santa Monica Airport include stylish California-style **DC-3** at the Museum of

Flying, 2800 Donald Douglas Loop N. (just off 28th St., south of Ocean Park Blvd.), 310/399-2323, which serves grilled seafood, chicken, and such, along with a hip and lively singles bar scene during happy hour and on weekends; live jazz some nights. The romantic runway views at sunset are thrown in for free. During the week, DC-3 provides a valuable public service for parents. While adults sit down to peaceful fixed-price dinners on Tuesday, Wednesday, and Thursday nights, the kids are whisked away, stuffed with pizza, and otherwise entertained on their own supervised museum tour. Another high-flyer at the airport is the exotic Pacific Rim **Typhoon,** 3221 Donald Douglas Loop S. (at Airport Ave.), 310/390-6565, where the "pilot's pillar" showcases the pilot's licenses of some of the famous and infamous who have flown in for the pan-Asian fare. Universal favorites include Thai coconut chicken curry, Indonesian stir-fry, and fried catfish. Up on the roof, weather permitting, is the Asian beer garden.

Main Street has its own stars, including sophisticated California-style **Röckenwaggner** inside the Edgemar complex at 2435 Main (near Pico), 310/399-6504, the perfect choice for a special weekend brunch. The marinated mushroom salad is one of Chef Hans Röckenwaggner's signature dishes, along with the smoked salmon "short stack" and other exceptional fish and seafood. Röckenwaggner's is open for weekend brunch, lunch Tues.–Fri., and dinner daily.

Warszawa, 1414 Lincoln Blvd. (between Santa Monica Blvd. and Broadway), 310/393-8831, is the only Polish restaurant in town—and a very good one. In a onetime private home, Warszawa serves hearty dinners in four cozy lace-curtained rooms. Favorite dishes here include the thick pea soup with smoked ham, roast duckling stuffed with herbs, and hunter's stew with sausage, sauerkraut, beef, bacon, and dumplings. For dessert, try the cheesecake with brown sugar crust, the rum torte, or the chocolate cream walnut cake. Warszawa is open Tues.–Sun. for dinner.

Rich People's Eats

Known for its fine California cuisine, **JiRaffe,** 502 Santa Monica Blvd. (at Fifth St.), 310/917-6671, is one of the Westside's most innovative and popular restaurants. The culinary creation of two talented L.A. chefs, Josiah Citrin and Raphael Lunetta, formerly of Jackson's in West Hollywood, JiRaffe serves such things as grilled smoked pork chops with wild rice, smoked bacon, apple chutney, and cider sauce, and whitefish with zucchini and artichokes, fava beans, and sugar snap peas.

Though there's plenty of competition these days, **Chinois on Main,** 2709 Main St. (between Hill and Ashland), 310/392-9025, is still one of L.A.'s best, and most popular, restaurants. One of the oldest L.A. offspring of celebrity chef Wolfgang Puck and his partner Barbara Lazaroff, Chinois as environment reflects the China of Lazaroff's childhood imagination as painted in celadon green, fuschia, and black, with chinoiserie cranes and dragon on the walls. Carved window frames open onto an orchid garden. Chinois as eatery was originally invented by Puck in partnership with chef Kazuto Matsusaka; most of the "Chinois Classics" are still here, including the fried catfish with ginger, the tuna tempura sashimi, and the Szechuan pancakes with stir-fried duck, mushrooms, and cilantro. But the menu has also evolved under the guidance of new chef Makoto Tanaka into something simpler and lighter, with lovely vegetable-rich lo mein with soy, honey, and black bean sauce (lunch only) and seared scallops with a sauce of red onions, red wine, cream, and butter. Chinois is noisy, expensive, and sometimes a challenge for reservations—if it's important, try weeks in advance—but it's still one of the best shows in town.

If you can't get reservations at Chinois, then try **Valentino,** 3115 W. Pico Blvd. (west of Bundy Dr.), 310/829-4313, the best Italian restaurant in L.A.; respectable restaurant critics say it's the best in the entire country. This casual, chic dining destination stars lobster cannelloni and other surprising pastas, osso buco, and fish, lamb, rabbit, and veal entrées. As important as the spectacular food is Valentino's wine list, one of the best anywhere—though it did suffer something of a setback when about 20,000 bottles of wine shattered in the 1994 Northridge earthquake. Valentino is open for dinner only, Mon.– Saturday. Very expensive. Reservations mandatory.

Drago, 2628 Wilshire Blvd. (at 26th St.), 310/828-1585, is Santa Monica's other dashing, elegant Italian, showcasing variations on Sicilian country fare—pastas and risottos, grilled fish and roasted quail. Excellent wine list. It's open for lunch on weekdays, for dinner every night. Reservations required.

Michael's, 1147 Third St. (just beyond the Promenade), 310/451-0843, was Santa Monica's—and one of L.A.'s—original California cuisine scenes. Owner Michael McCarty, a Cordon Bleu chef, opened his restaurant here in 1979 at the brash age of 26—quickly "blowing L.A.'s mind" with his modern American cuisine. So many of L.A.'s great chefs and restaurant owners worked here at one time or another that in 1995 Michael's hosted a celebrity-chef reunion as a benefit for local museums—an immense success, with L.A.'s best manning personal cooking stations for the benefit of the assembled masses. The snob appeal of a meal at Michael's no longer sells as well as it once did, even in L.A., and the astronomical prices have dropped by a third. (Still very expensive.) But the patio still beckons as one of the prettiest dining destinations in the city, and McCarty's personal contemporary art collection still enlivens the restaurant's walls. Michael's is open Mon.–Fri. for lunch, Mon.–Sat. for dinner. Reservations wise. There's another **Michael's** in New York City.

For other fine dining possibilities, consider Santa Monica's upscale hotels.

EATING IN VENICE AND VICINITY

Eating In Venice
For all practical purposes the unincorporated Venice district of L.A. is the southern extension of Santa Monica—quite convenient if you've got wheels and typically safe to explore if you stick to the main drags and don't hang out too late after nightfall.

If you're in or around Venice, the premier local people's place is the **Rose Cafe,** 220 Rose Ave. (at Main St.), 310/399-0711. Not the best restaurant in town and not one of the trendy beachfront venues, in many ways the Rose Cafe *is* Venice. This is where true Venetians hang out, along with an inordinate number of movie people

at times and young execs. The style here is beach bohemian, coffee and pastries being the staff of life. For lunch and dinner, consider a salad or simple sandwich. The patio is the place to be.

Figtree's Cafe, right on the Venice Boardwalk at 429 Ocean Front Walk, 310/392-4937, is another locals' favorite for breakfast. (Get there early on weekends, by 9 A.M., and expect slow service; regulars are liable to nurse their cappuccinos and read the Sunday paper for hours.) Vegetarian dishes are a specialty. Try the wonderful polenta, the hearty French toast on thick-sliced raisin nut bread, or the satisfying Santa Fe omelette. Lunch and dinner fare includes pastas, burritos, tostadas, veggie stir-fry, and fresh fish. Figtree's is open daily for breakfast, lunch, and dinner.

A best bet among more expensive Venetian venues lives with Jonathan Borofsky's Emmett Kelly–faced dancer, the sad *Ballerina Clown en pointe* above the intersection of Rose and Main. Trendy **Chaya Venice,** 110 Navy St. (at Main), 310/396-1179, stars art-deco Asian decor, eclectic Franco-Japanese-California fare, and seafood—curried crab soup, spring rolls, even a sushi bar. It's open weekdays for lunch, Sunday for brunch, nightly for dinner. Even better, though, and a real find for frugal foodies, is **Joe's,** 1023 Abbott Kinney Blvd. (between Westminster and Broadway), 310/399-5811, where the California-French seafood stars at lunch (Tues.–Fri. only), Sunday brunch, and dinner. One of L.A.'s best restaurants, serving one of L.A.'s best Sunday brunches. Also fairly inexpensive and quite good for Thai is romantic **Siamese Garden** right on Venice's Grand Canal at 301 Washington Blvd. (near Strongs Dr.), 310/821-0098, open for lunch weekdays only, for dinner nightly.

Eating in Marina del Rey
Aunt Kizzy's Back Porch in the Villa Marina Shopping Center at 4325 Glencoe Ave. (between Washington Blvd. and Mindanao Way), 310/578-1005, is not exactly what you'd expect in a Marina del Rey minimall. Aunt Kizzy's is a fantastic country-style soul food café serving hefty portions of crispy fried chicken, catfish, ribs, pork chops, and jambalaya, along with rice and red

beans and Southern-style vegetables. Everything here is so good that people are willing to wait and wait to get in—and they do, with nary a complaint. Aunt Kizzy's is open daily for lunch 11 A.M.–4 P.M., for dinner 4–10 P.M. (closed Thanksgiving and Christmas).

If you just can't wait, another possibility is **Benny's Barbecue,** 4077 Lincoln Blvd. (near Washington), 310/821-6939, a takeout stand in the marina that's locally famous for dishing out fiery barbecued ribs, lamb shanks, L.A.'s best hot links, beans, and excellent coleslaw. Also beloved in these parts: **Killer Shrimp,** 523 Washington St. (at Ocean), 310/578-2293. You like the name? You'll like the place. An unassuming storefront in an ugly minimall that serves one item only: killer shrimp, flown in fresh daily from Louisiana, prepared in a lively sauce of beer, butter, garlic, secret herbs and spices, and served with crusty French bread just made for dipping.

Considerably more stylish and expensive is the California-style **Cafe del Rey,** 4551 Admiralty Way (at Bali Way), 310/823-6395, where the eclectic international fare runs from the very simple—pizzas, tasty burgers, niçoise salad—to the surprisingly imaginative. The café is open daily for lunch and dinner, also a good choice for Sunday brunch. Another fine-dining choice, especially if you're en route to LAX, is dinner-only **The Library** at the Los Angeles Renaissance Hotel, 9620 Airport Blvd. in Inglewood, 310/337-2800, famous for its exceptionally well-prepared seafood. For a dining *experience,* the place is **The Dining Room** at the Ritz-Carlton, 4375 Admiralty Way, 310/823-1700.

UP THE COAST:
NORTH OF SANTA MONICA

Heading north from Santa Monica via the Pacific Coast Highway (PCH, or Hwy. 1) leads to the pleasures of Ventura, Santa Barbara, and San Luis Obispo Counties and, eventually, the famous Big Sur coast. Well worth exploring on this side of the L.A. County line are some of L.A.'s favorite residential hideouts—Pacific Palisades, Topanga Canyon, and Malibu—and some of its best beaches. Seeming almost as vast as the Pacific Ocean it looms above is the Santa Monica Mountains National Recreation Area, a crazy quilt of wilderness areas and preserves interspersed with outposts of suburbia. Many recreation area highlights, detailed in Wilderness City: The Santa Monica Mountains in the Beverly Hills chapter, are easily accessible from PCH north of Santa Monica.

PACIFIC PALISADES:
AN OPTIMIST'S PARADISE

Like sections of Santa Monica and Malibu, Pacific Palisades perches atop high cliffs (palisades) overlooking the Pacific Ocean. The cliffs are famous for giving way during heavy rains, encouraging expensive homes to slip off their moorings and entire hillsides to slide away to sea—mudslides that inconveniently block the Pacific Coast Highway below. Otherwise the main event in this amazingly upmarket neighborhood just north of Santa Monica is the annual **Fourth of July parade**—an event in which members of the community's long-running **Optimist Club** march down the street, in close-order drill, in their underwear. The existence of the Optimists is still central to community life, as is Swarthmore Avenue, center of the low-key local business district. But Will Rogers State Historic Park is usually more celebrated—as are Gelson's grocery, a best bet for spotting local celebrities, and Mort's restaurant, *the* place to eat (celebs primarily hang on the wall). Celebrities are legion in Pacific Palisades. Ron and Nancy Reagan lived here before they moved to the White House in 1984, for example, and past mayors of Pacific Palisades include Chevy Chase, Dom DeLuise, Ted Knight, and Rita Moreno.

For current information on the area, contact: **Pacific Palisades Chamber of Commerce,** 15330 Antioch St., Pacific Palisades, 310/459-7963.

UPLIFTING L.A.

Harry Haldeman—grandfather of H. R. (Bob) Haldeman, a key player in ex-President Richard Nixon's infamous Watergate debacle—was a jovial plumbing supply businessman originally from Chicago, a man as passionate about hard liquor and Cuban cigars as conservative politics. Inspired by the example of San Francisco's exclusive Bohemian Club, in 1913 Haldeman and like-minded revelers recruited from the still-prestigious Los Angeles Athletic Club established the Uplifters Club—the name "The Lofty and Exalted Order of Uplifters" contributed by *The Wizard of Oz* author L. Frank Baum. Though the group's official motto was "to uplift art and promote good fellowship," the ability to lift up one's glass was also crucial. After Prohibition's nationwide alcohol ban went into effect in 1919, the group bought 120 acres of redwoods and eucalyptus groves in Rustic Canyon (below what would later become the Will Rogers ranch) and founded the Uplifters Ranch—a private retreat where captains of industry and a select group of talented friends could protect their sybaritic revelry from the long arm of the law.

The Uplifters' social centerpiece was its clubhouse, now part of the eight-acre **Rustic Canyon Recreation Center** and park on Latimer Road, 310/454-5734, open to the public. In its hard-drinking heyday the Spanish colonial revival clubhouse featured drinking halls, a grand ballroom, and a "library" (actually a poker parlor). Uplifting the grounds were tennis courts, a swimming pool, polo field, trapshooting range, outdoor amphitheater, and dormitories, all part of the wooded playground enjoyed by Walt Disney, Busby Berkeley, Harold Lloyd, Daryl F. Zanuck, and others among L.A.'s most privileged ranks. In 1922 members began to build rustic weekend and summer cabins on land leased from the Uplifters; many of these structures remain. The Uplifters Club dissolved more than 50 years ago but artists, writers, and actual and spiritual descendants of the Uplifters continue to live here.

To reach Rustic Canyon Recreation Center—and to take a respectful peek at this part of the Pacific Palisades past—head south from Sunset Boulevard via Brooktree Road, which follows a tree-lined brook, to the old clubhouse at 600-700 Latimer Road. (Allow plenty of time to get lost. Both Latimer and Haldeman Roads, the Uplifters' main thoroughfares, are narrow, with no curbs or gutters, and largely unlighted at night.) A handful of cabins and lodges—all private residences, so don't trespass or otherwise be obnoxious—still stand, among them 31, 32, 34, 35, and 38 Haldeman and 1, 3, and 8 Latimer. The Marco Hellman cabin at 38 Haldeman was transplanted from *The Courtship of Miles Standish* 1923 movie set. Earl Warren, former California governor and U.S. Supreme Court justice, summered here during the 1940s and '50s.

Methodists, Artists, and Optimists on Parade

Pacific Palisades began its official community life as a movie studio back lot built by Thomas Ince at the end of Sunset Boulevard in the early 1900s. The area was more thoroughly settled in the 1920s by members of the Methodist Episcopal Church who hoped to establish a western Chautauqua here. The Chautauqua was a cultural, educational, moral, and philosophical program with communal overtones, a social movement started in New York in the late 1870s. Summer Chautauqua events featuring artists, writers, and other philosophers were held in Pacific Palisades during these early years—which helps explain why local streets are largely named for former Methodist bishops, religious schools, and scholars. But interest in the Chautauqua movement soon faded, and the Methodist movers and shakers here lost their land grant in 1928.

Artists, writers, and movie stars soon arrived in their stead, a trend that lasted for two solid decades. Some of them, including Aldous Huxley, Elsa Lancaster, Charles Laughton, and Thomas Mann, emigrated to escape the threat of Nazi Germany. (Pacific Palisades reminded them of the French Riviera, it was said.) By the 1940s the community was well established as an L.A. center for art and architecture, though affluence is the primary criterion for residence nowadays.

Seeing and Doing Pacific Palisades

The most popular local attraction lies well east along Sunset, near Brentwood—**Will Rogers**

State Historic Park, 1501 Will Rogers State Park Rd. (just north of Sunset Blvd.), 310/454-8212. This 187-acre ranch estate is where noted cowboy humorist and philosopher Will Rogers lived from 1924 until his death in 1935. Rogers's ranch-style home, open daily for public tours, is also a museum; don't fail to appreciate the wrap-around shower on the second floor. (For more information on the Rogers park and the adjacent Topanga State Park wilderness, see Wilderness City: The Santa Monica Mountains in the Beverly Hills chapter.) The lush lawns and landscaped grounds, where the horsey set still plays polo matches on weekends, are also perfect for picnics, Frisbee, and sunbathing.

Near the ocean end of Sunset is the **Self-Realization Fellowship Lake Shrine,** 17190 Sunset Blvd., 310/454-4114, which was used as a movie location before Paramahansa Yogananda, author of *Autobiography of a Yogi,* bought the 10-acre site in 1950. At the center of the shrine, dedicated to the universality of all religions and the exaltation of nature, is the picturesque, luxuriantly landscaped spring-fed lake. A small chapel shaped like a Dutch windmill, a golden-domed archway, a houseboat, and gazebos frame lake views and provide good photo ops. The shrine is open to the public for peaceful walks and meditation. Call for information.

Other Pacific Palisades sights are architectural. Most of the significant area architecture was influenced by John Entenza, editor and publisher of the trendsetting *Arts and Architecture* magazine, and his **Case Study House Project,** which encouraged prominent Southern California architects to experiment with new materials and styles. Noted "case study" houses include the landmark international-style **Eames House and Studio,** 203 Chautauqua Blvd., something like a three-dimensional Mondrian painting set in a meadow, designed by Charles Eames in 1947-49; the similar **Entenza House,** 205 Chautauqua Blvd., designed by Charles Eames and Eero Saarinen in 1949; and the international redwood-and-brick **Bailey House,** 219 Chautauqua, designed by Richard J. Neutra in 1946-48. Pacific Palisades features many other architectural gems, most of which are not visible from public streets.

Quite accessible, however, are the **Castellammare Stairways,** reached from Sunset Boulevard via Castellammare Drive, which leads up to this enclave of million-dollar homes overlooking the Pacific Ocean. Among the vertical hiking possibilities here (near Castellammare): the stairway just off Posetano Road that climbs to Revello Drive, and the stairway from Breve Way to Porto Marina. For sheer popularity, however, stop on the way back into Santa Monica for a run up the 200-step **Adelaide Stairway** (promoted as L.A.'s Ultimate Stairway in myriad magazine "lifestyle" articles), which starts, on the uphill end, at Fourth Street and Adelaide Drive and winds down to E. Channel Road. Come during the week to avoid the hordes of fitness fanatics who turn the stairway into a human freeway on weekends.

MALIBU: SURFING CELEBRITY

Aside from an appreciation for Malibu's clean beaches, good surf, and aquamarine waters, the one thing that unites Malibu residents is the Pacific Coast Highway, which here is a tenuous lifeline. Celebrated for its surfing, its celebrities, and its chic coastal cachet, Malibu most often makes it into the news as a disaster area for its almost predictable "natural" disasters, created by human incursions into an unstable, fire-adapted ecosystem. Whether or not wildfires have finished their occasional summer and fall wind sprints to the sea, the rains begin—and the mudslides, which may carry houses, carports, landscaped yards, sometimes streets and entire hillsides with them. If the Pacific Coast Highway is closed for days at a time, be it from behemoth bouncing boulders or mudslides, people here take it in stride. Building more houses here—and continually rebuilding them—is not particularly intelligent.

Yet try telling that to people in Malibu, who moved here to get away from it all. The fact that "it" had already arrived, in the forms of crushing urban crowds and nightmarish traffic, was a prime motivating factor for Malibu's incorporation in 1990. During his one-year term as the city's "honorary mayor," actor Martin Sheen declared Malibu a nuclear-free zone and a refuge for the homeless. But since incorporation, residents have drawn battle lines over growth-related issues.

Despite the definitive dot on most maps, Malibu as place has always been difficult to find. Though the star-studded Malibu Colony, the Malibu Pier, and several Malibu beaches have served as unofficial community signposts, in most people's minds "Malibu" was a rather vague regional appellation taking in the 20-plus miles of Los Angeles County coastline between Topanga Canyon and Ventura County. But now Malibu has definite city limits, and an official 20-square-mile territory, stretching north from Topanga Canyon to Leo Carrillo State Beach at the Ventura County line.

The main attractions are Malibu's beaches—more than 20 miles of them. The beaches along the Malibu coastline are still reasonably clean, despite heavy recreational use and some local pollution problems, and provide some of the best surfing and ocean swimming in Southern California. Traffic on a summer day along the Pacific Coast Highway can be brutal and parking nearly impossible, however. Plan to arrive before the noontime "rush hour"—say, by 11 A.M., if not earlier—while parking places are still available. A second highway rush usually occurs between 4 and 5 P.M., when most people head home for dinner. If you're well supplied and willing to while away some time, the good news is that sunsets are fairly unpopulated and peaceful. Better yet, come in the off season—spring, fall, and winter —when beaches can be quite balmy and pleasant yet much less crowded. The weather is moderate year-round. Barring the occasional storm, some of the finest beach days come in winter—though some spots are crowded on weekends during whale-watching season.

For current information about the area, contact: **Malibu Chamber of Commerce,** 23805 Stuart Ranch Rd., Ste. 100, Malibu, 310/456-9025; www.malibu.org.

Landing on Malibu

Though the ocean here draws the soul, the land is more highly valued. After the native Chumash people were dispatched to nearby Franciscan missions, Malibu's history became an endless tangle of land and road-building disputes.

José Bartólome Tapía traveled to California from Sonora, Mexico, in 1775 with the de Anza expedition. In 1805 Spain granted Tapía, a farmer and the eldest of nine children, the Topanga Malibu Sequit ranch, named for three

area Indian villages. The ranch thrived until Tapía died in 1824, though his wife, Doña Maria, kept it until 1848. After the death of her eldest son, Doña Maria sold the ranch, for 400 pesos, to a granddaughter's husband, Leon Victor Prudhomme, a 26-year-old Frenchman. But in the transition from Mexican to American rule in 1850, records detailing the early Spanish land grant to Tapía were lost. After a long legal dispute with the California Land Commission, Prudhomme sold the ranch in 1857 to Matthew Keller, an Irishman who took advantage of the defective title and the Panic of 1857 to buy it for the outrageously low price of 10 cents per acre, or a total of less than $1,400. Keller gained undisputed legal title in 1863 and presided over the ranch's 13,300-plus acres, which produced some of California's first wines, until his death in 1881. Son Henry Keller sold the land in 1887 for $10 an acre.

Frederick Hastings Rindge, son of a Massachusetts wool merchant, inherited a $2 million estate in 1883 at the age of 26. A Harvard graduate, Rindge established a city hall, public library, a boys' school, and children's sanitarium in Cambridge before he and his wife, May, bought the Malibu rancho and moved to California. The change, Rindge believed, would improve his health. The family built a home on Ocean Avenue in Santa Monica—a day's journey by wagon from Malibu, where the primitive dirt road could be crossed only at low tide—and began to improve the isolated ranch. As detailed in Rindge's book, *Happy Days in Southern California,* published in 1898, the family built a lovely, landscaped home east of Malibu Creek, added a barn, corrals, and bunkhouses, and planted grain and lemon groves. Most of the land was set aside for cattle grazing, though. The Rindge family eventually owned the entire 24-mile stretch of coastline north of Las Flores Canyon.

The happiest days ended in 1903 thanks to the worst fire in Malibu's recorded history, probably started by squatters. Fanned by hot Santa Ana winds, the wildfire rapidly torched the entire ranch. Along with most everything else the family home was destroyed, which forced the Rindges to move into Los Angeles. Two years later Frederick Rindge died.

When Frederick Rindge died in 1905, his widow, May, began fighting what became an endless series of turf battles to protect the land from trespasses large and small—from home-steaders, squatters, railroads, and the state of California's highway-building plans. When armed guards, high fences, and dynamiting her own roads failed to stop progress, May Rindge resorted to the courts. She appealed California's plan to condemn part of her property, to build the Pacific Coast Highway, all the way to the U.S. Supreme Court—and lost.

Celebrities and Surfing

In the midst of the daunting financial problems generated by her war against the Pacific Coast Highway, the "Queen of Malibu" May Rindge decided to lease out beachfront property, at Malibu La Costa and between Carbon Canyon and the Malibu Pier. Actress Anna Q. Nilsson signed the first lease, and the area was quickly established as a residential colony for publicity-shunning movie people. Among Malibu's first wave of celluloid celebrities were Clara Bow, Ronald Colman, Dolores Del Rio, John Gilbert, Barbara Stanwyck, and Jack Warner. Later, Escondido, Trancas, and Zuma Beaches were opened to development, and still more movie stars moved to the area. The celebs have been coming ever

THE QUEEN OF MALIBU

After the disastrous Malibu fire of 1903 and the death of Frederick Rindge in 1905, Malibu's most determined settlement family kept on. Frederick's widow, May Rindge, decided to keep the Malibu ranch—and keep it intact—and to do that, she fought battle after battle for more than 30 years.

Local newpapers named May Rindge the "Queen of Malibu" when she built her own railway to fend off encroachment by the Southern Pacific Railroad. May Rindge—president of The Hueneme and Malibu and Port of Los Angeles Railroad, which she used to ship grain and hides to market—convinced the Interstate Commerce Commission that her railroad was sufficient for public convenience and necessity.

But even the Queen of Malibu was daunted by her battles against the state of California's highway plans. That war began in 1908. May Rindge spent many years and hundreds of thousands of dollars to fight the planned course of Pacific Coast Highway through her Malibu property.

The war's final battles were fought in court—in four cases brought before the California Supreme Court and two before the U.S. Supreme Court. But during almost two decades of legal skirmishes, May Rindge constructed high fences along the edges of her property. She hired armed guards to ride the range in an attempt to keep out surveyors, squatters, and other trespassers. Riding sidesaddle, she often joined the patrol, though as the years wore on she resorted to horse-and-buggy patrols and, later, automobile missions. Even after the courts established the state's right of eminent domain with regard to the Malibu property in 1923, state engineers and their sheriff deputy escorts were barred by hired guns brandishing pistols. Then, on October 14, 1925,

Superior Court Judge Frederick Valentine granted the state a right-of-way through the Malibu ranch for construction of the Pacific Coast Highway—and May Rindge was awarded only $109,289 of the $9.18 million in compensatory damages she requested.

In the midst of her war against the highway, May Rindge was rebuilding the family home—this time, a 40-room Mediterranean-style mansion high on a hill. To produce the vast quantities of decorative ceramic tiles used in the home, she brought Italian tile-makers to Malibu and thereby founded the Malibu Tile Company.

But after expensive years of litigation—and after spending $500,000 on mansion construction—May Rindge's money finally ran out. The spectacular hilltop mansion was never completed. Later sold to the Franciscans for $50,000, the Rindge mansion was used as a retreat center until it burned to the ground in a late 1960s wildfire—but remnants of the era remain at Malibu's Serra Retreat, which still welcomes frazzled real-worlders for spiritual resuscitation (see "Staying North of Santa Monica"). You can also see exquisite examples of the Malibu Tile Company's 1920s tile work at the Adamson House just west of the Malibu Pier.

To hold on to the ranch, in the 1920s May Rindge leased sections of Malibu's exclusive waterfront to movie stars—the beginnings of the famed Malibu Colony—and in the 1930s took advantage of Depression-era corporate reorganization. But to no avail. The entire Rancho Topanga Malibu Sequit Rancho was put up for sale in December of 1940. Almost a pauper, the hard-fighting Queen of Malibu died two months later, at age 75, in her home in L.A.'s West Adams District.

since, their presence now central to the Malibu mystique. (Less celebrated citizens try not to stare but still get a thrill from spotting movie stars stopping for basic supplies at Trancas Market and other local shopping hot spots.) Luminaries of current or recent history include Johnny Carson, Ted Danson, Larry Hagman, Dustin Hoffman, Madonna, Burgess Meredith, Carroll O'Connor, Robert Redford, Steven Spielberg, and Sylvester Stallone. And Danny DeVito and Rhea Perlman, Bruce Willis and Demi Moore, and John McEnroe and Tatum O'Neal. To name a few. And not counting the colony's large numbers of artists, writers, and other talented citizens.

Malibu is also famous for its surfers, who cherish access to the coast's best breaks and beaches as much as Malibu's movie stars cherish absolute privacy—a continuing source of social tension that somehow adds to the peculiar ambience. Here, throughout the Malibu Colony, megamillion-dollar beachfront bungalows and baronial estates adopt a sober street-side decorum that rarely hints of the glass-walled glories on the private side. Building such exclusive homes in the style of townhouses—with little or no space in between to discourage both snooping and beach access—somehow just encourages public curiosity, making people ever more determined to find the few available access walkways (follow the surfers). Malibu Road along the waterfront is a classic example.

Malibu Pier
Start exploring Malibu at the 700-foot Malibu Pier, opened to the public with great fanfare and fireworks on July 4, 1945. The present-day pier replaced the 400-foot-long Rindge Pier, built here in 1903 so supplies could be delivered to the ranch by boat. Rindge's pier was later damaged by storms and then intentionally demolished in 1943. The pier area is particularly popular for fishing (tackle and bait available) and watching both surfers and sunsets. Surrounding the pier is Malibu Lagoon State Beach, which includes the Malibu estuary, the historic Adamson House and associated museum, and **Malibu Surfrider Beach**, one of the West Coast's most famous surfing beaches. Largely east of the pier (it feels "south") though the best breaks are to the west ("north"), Malibu Surfrider Beach has been celebrated in countless Frankie Avalon, Annette

Funicello, and *Gidget* movies. More significantly, according to local lore, Surfrider is California's 1926 surfing birthplace. In summer perfect waves roll to shore at Surfrider day after day—an accident of ocean currents, upwellings, and winds that creates heaven for surfers, kayakers, and windsurfers but hell for those who dislike overcrowded beaches. Swimming and surfing aren't recommended here, since Heal the Bay regularly "flunks" Surfrider and adjacent beaches in its annual water quality survey. But surfers still come, since they have to go where the waves are. If you want to watch, the pier offers ringside railings for surfing voyeurs.

If you hunger for a bracing after-beach breakfast, head for the **PierView Cafe and Cantina**, 310/456-6962, on the beach just east of the pier. Or head for local shopping malls. Best bets for breakfast or weekend brunch—and later meals—include **Marmalade** in the Cross Creek Plaza, 310/317-4242, and, at Malibu Colony Plaza, both casual **Coogie's**, 310/317-1444, and uptown **Granita**, 310/456-0488, the latter sea-themed culinary adventure established by Wolfgang Puck and Barbara Lazaroff.

Malibu Lagoon State Beach
Malibu Lagoon offers an opportunity for impromptu bird-watching and nature appreciation, right off the highway. One of only two estuaries remaining within the boundaries of Santa Monica Mountains National Recreation Area, this small patch of marsh at the mouth of Malibu Creek serves as a natural fish nursery—and bountiful buffet for neighborhood and migrating shorebirds. (While visiting, stay on the boardwalks.) More than 200 species of birds use Malibu Lagoon as a migratory stopover. Nearby beach areas are popular for swimming, though water at the mouth of Malibu Creek is polluted—twice monthly, the lagoon is drained—and swimming is not recommended on those days. With its offshore reefs and kelp beds, the area is also popular with skin and scuba divers.

Also well worth exploring: the adjoining **Malibu Lagoon Museum** and the grand **Adamson House.** Chances are you'll never see the inside of local movie stars' homes, so amuse yourself, while touring Adamson House, with the knowledge that most celebrities would kill to own a place like this. Former home of Rhoda and

Merritt Adamson—daughter and son-in law of Frederick and May Rindge, who owned the vast Malibu Ranch in the early 1900s—this 1929 Spanish-Moorish beach house was designed by architect Stiles O. Clements, who took full advantage of the Rindge-owned Malibu Tile Company's exceptional craftsmanship. The stunning Adamson House, listed on the National Register of Historic Places, is rich with handcrafted teak, graceful wrought-iron work, and leaded-glass windows. But, inside and out, it is primarily a tile-setter's fantasy—a real-life museum-quality display of 1920s' California tile work, richly colored geometric and animal-motif patterns worked into the walkways, walls, and lavish fountains. There's even a tiled outdoor dog shower. The museum adjacent, at home in the home's seven-car garage, chronicles area history with memorabilia, art, artifacts, and photographs.

Malibu Lagoon State Beach adjoins the Malibu Pier and includes famous Malibu Surfrider Beach (see above). Adamson House and the Malibu Lagoon Museum, 23200 Pacific Coast Hwy. (Hwy. 1), are one-quarter mile west of the Malibu Pier and 13 miles west of Santa Monica. The lagoon and Adamson House grounds are technically open 24 hours, though the adjacent county parking lot ($5 fee), shared with Surfrider Beach, is open daily 8 A.M.–5 P.M. only (side-street parking available early morning and evening). Another parking lot ($6) is one block north at Cross Creek Road. Beach, lagoon, and museum access are free; small fee for Adamson House tours. The Adamson House is open only for tours (one hour), usually offered Wed.–Sat. 11 A.M.–3 P.M. (last tour at 2 P.M.); the museum is open during the same hours. Reservations are required for groups of 12 or more and the museum closes on days with moderate to heavy rain—call ahead. For more information, call 310/456-8432.

MALIBU: THE COASTLINE

Beaches North of Malibu Colony

Last stop before the Ventura County line in the north is **Leo Carrillo State Beach,** typically much less crowded than the "city beaches" closer to Malibu Colony, Santa Monica, and

urban points south. Named for the actor who played Pancho in *The Cisco Kid* TV series, 1,600-acre Leo Carrillo features 1.5 miles of stupendous craggy coastline and both rocky and sandy beaches—the totality perfect for surfing, sailboarding, swimming, and, at low tide, tidepooling. A popular whale-watching spot in winter, Leo Carrillo is also good for scuba diving. (Riptides are a danger occasionally.) Inland, ranger-guided hikes are regularly scheduled, and, in summer, campfire programs. Pleasant picnicking, too (there's a store here). A pretty campground, across the highway, is set among the sycamores back from the beach, and there's another nearby at North Beach. For a spectacular ocean view with minimal effort, take the short trail up the hill from near the booth at the campground entrance. Leo Carrillo State Beach, 35000 Pacific Coast Hwy. (Hwy. 1), is 25 miles west of Santa Monica and about 15 miles from "downtown" Malibu. Leo Carrillo's main entrance is just east of Mulholland Highway's intersection with the highway—a great drive, if you're out exploring. Day-use parking is $3 per vehicle; call for camping fees, which vary for developed, RV (self-contained), and hike/bike sites. The beach is open daily 8 A.M.–midnight. The visitor center is open daily in summer. For more information, call 805/488-5223. For camping reservations, a must in summer and on most weekends, call ReserveAmerica toll-free at 800/444-7275.

Next east is one of L.A.'s best-kept secrets, rumored to be the preferred beach escape for L.A.'s lifeguards on their days off—picturesque, pristine, and remote **Nicholas Canyon County Beach,** 34000 Pacific Coast Highway. Nicholas, a graceful quarter moon of sand curving around a small bay, is well protected from highway noise and has no skate rentals, no snack stands—none of the usual L.A. beach chaos and clutter. Just peace, quiet, and a few kayakers and surfers. (And lifeguards and restrooms.) The **Robert H. Meyer Memorial State Beach,** next east at 33000 Pacific Coast Hwy., is actually a string of smaller state beaches tucked into a residential area: **El Pescador, La Piedra,** and **El Matador,** the lovely latter beach the most popular. As many as 10 episodes of *Baywatch* were once filmed here each year, but most people come for the dramatic cliffs, rock formations, and caves along the sandy beach. (No lifeguards but picnic tables and portable toilets. Parking lot open 8 A.M.–sunset, $2 fee.) Nearby is **El Sol State Beach,** difficult to find.

Trancas Beach at PCH and Guernsey Avenue is another residential-area beach, most accessible by walking from **Zuma Beach.** Zuma, 30000 Pacific Coast Hwy., was the location for a multitude of 1950s and 1960s surfing movies— the likes of *Deadman's Curve, Beach Blanket Bingo,* and *Back to the Beach*—but gathered even more fame in the 1970s, thanks to singer/ songwriter Neil Young's album *Zuma.* Postcard-pretty if hardly private, Zuma's appeal is as fundamental as its endless expanse of white sand, rowdy beach volleyball, and children's playground. Popular with the rowdy surfing set. For all the fun and frolic, though, think safety. Riptides here have been known to drag up to 20 people at a time straight out to sea—keeping the lifeguards plenty busy. Access to the beach, open sunrise to sunset, is free but there is a fee to park in the *huge* lot. Locals avoid even that by jockeying for highway and street parking. Full services are available (lifeguards, restrooms, snack bars, and rental shops). Just below often-packed Zuma is clean, sandy, and equally popular **Westward Beach,** reached from Pacific Coast Highway via Westward Beach Road (limited free parking along the beach road). Or, park at Zuma and walk along the beach.

Continue on Westward Beach Road to reach the parking lot for busy **Point Dume State Beach,** whose sand neatly segues into Westward's. Point Dume once featured a vertical "point"—a rocky peak—in addition to its seaward point, until the former was flattened for a housing development. Reaching Point Dume's secluded series of sandy pocket beaches and rocky shores, scattered below impressive cliffs, requires a little walking. Small caves and tide pools abound throughout the 35-acre **Point Dume Natural Preserve,** where the rocky west face is popular with technical climbers. A stairway and hiking trail start at Westward Beach and climb to the headlands and the **Point Dume Whale Watch,** a popular series of sites for watching the midwinter migration of California gray whales—good for views any time. Look for California brown pelicans, California sea lions, and harbor seals on offshore rocks. Though it's

not condoned as a nude beach officially, historically beach-in-the-buff enthusiasts have always hiked around the point or down the stairway from the headlands to the rocky north end of **Pirate's Cove** and its stunning beach, but winter storms often block access. Point Dume is a good swimming, sunbathing, and diving beach (for experienced divers), only fair for surfing; lifeguards, very clean restrooms, outdoor showers, and a soft drink vending machine provided. Parking at Point Dume is $3.

Point Dume adjoins pretty, private **Paradise Cove Beach.** But unless you're absolutely desperate to find a place to toss down the beach towel, the parking fee alone—$15—is enough to discourage most people from trying this tiny beach near the pier on Paradise Cove Road. (If you park on PCH and walk in, it'll cost you only $5. And the Sandcastle Restaurant validates parking.) But it is a quiet, family-friendly beach with rocky bluffs, caves, and tide pools to explore. At Pacific Coast Highway and Escondido Road is coastal access (highway parking only) for residential-area **Escondido Beach,** narrow, sandy, and empty, indeed fairly well hidden. Look for the Coastal Access signs. Actual "access" begins at a gate on the ocean side of the highway, which is unlocked 6:30 A.M.–6:30 P.M. daily, just north of Geoffrey's Restaurant in the 27400 "block" of the Pacific Coast Highway; the beach path starts at a stairwell between two houses. No lifeguard, no services.

Then there's very narrow **Dan Blocker State Beach,** named for the big, brawny actor better known as affable Hoss Cartwright on TV's long-running *Bonanza.* Dan Blocker extends from Malibu Road (at Pacific Coast Hwy.) to Corral Canyon Road. Most people head for the sandier southeast end, which can be packed; beach fans can find more privacy toward the less accessible, rockier end near the mouth of Corral Creek. Highway parking only, easy beach access. Popular for surf fishing and swimmers; lifeguards in summer and on busy weekends.

For those willing to brave the movie-star-beachhouse obstacles along Malibu Road, back in Malibu Colony both **Puerco Beach** and **Amarillo Beach** beckon (no lifeguards, bathrooms, or other services). Park on the north end of Malibu Road, where it meets the highway, or from the highway take Webb Way south to Malibu

Road, praying all the while for a parking spot. To reach Amarillo and points east, it's easiest to walk from Puerco.

Along the coast are a few decent stops for a meal with a view, including the **Paradise Cove Beach Café** at Paradise Cove, 310/457-2503, and **Geoffrey's** near Point Dume, 310/457-1519. If your beach explorations lead you far afield, don't forget the ever-popular **Neptune's Net** on PCH about a mile north of the Ventura County line, 310/457-3095, beloved for its down-home, no-frills funk. Best bet at lunch or dinner is the steamed shellfish. Pick your own lobsters or crabs right out of the fish tanks.

Beaches South of Malibu Colony

Beyond Malibu Lagoon State Beach and Malibu Surfrider Beach near the pier (see Malibu Pier and Malibu Lagoon listings above) is a string of difficult-to-reach residential-area sandy spots: **Carbon Beach,** 22200 Pacific Coast Hwy., just west of Carbon Canyon Road; **La Costa Beach,** 21400 PCH; **Las Flores Beach,** 20900 PCH; and **Big Rock Beach** (look for the big rock), 20600 PCH, just north of Carbon Canyon Road. The best way to reach all of these beaches—and watch the tides, so you don't get stranded—is by walking east from Malibu Surfrider Beach or west from Las Tunas. By contrast, rocky **Las Tunas Beach** next east, right on the highway, is very easy to reach but not all that pleasant because of the din of traffic. It's most popular with surf fishers and scuba divers; lifeguards in season, portable toilets. Bring water.

Topanga State Beach, easy to find along the 18700 "block" of Pacific Coast Highway, a quarter-mile west of the J. Paul Getty Museum and a quarter-mile east of Topanga Canyon Boulevard., is popular for swimming (if you don't mind dodging a few ocean rocks) and sunny picnics. On a clear day, from the bluffs here you can see Catalina Island. Sometimes you can also see dolphins just offshore, or passing whales. Mostly what you'll see at Topanga, though, are surfers and sailboats. The swells here are second only to those at Malibu Surfrider. The water quality is usually good, too, so in summer the beach can be quite crowded. The small parking lot ($2 fee) is usually full by 11 A.M., or try to find a spot along the highway. Lifeguards, full services. Another good possibility is **Castle Rock**

Beach across the highway from the Getty Museum, a pleasant sandy beach with easy access, parking lot ($6), portable toilets, lifeguards.

Will Rogers State Beach seems to stretch forever beneath the unstable palisades of Pacific Palisades—and this strand of sand does go on some distance, since from here to Redondo Beach it is interrupted only by the boat harbor at Marina del Rey. An excellent swimming beach—particularly toward the north, where water quality is usually best—Will Rogers is uncrowded, at least compared to teeming Santa Monica State Beach just south, because of limited parking. Surfing is fair. Facilities include playgrounds, picnic tables, volleyball nets, lifeguards, restrooms, the works.

BEYOND THE BEACHES

The Getty Villa: J. Paul Getty Museum

Beyond the surf and the stars, the community's most famous attraction is now the second location for the renowned J. Paul Getty Museum, 17985 Pacific Coast Hwy. (between Sunset and Topanga Canyon Boulevards), Malibu, www .gett.edu—still closed at last report, though after remodeling it is expected to reopen in 2002 as the Getty Center's classical antiquities exhibit and restoration center. (If you can't wait, head to Brentwood and the glorious new Getty Center, 310/440-7300; see Cities on a Hill in the Beverly Hills chapter.) The museum's collection of European paintings and drawings—Goya, Cézanne, van Gogh, Rembrandt, Renoir—along with illuminated manuscripts, American and European photography, home furnishings fit for French royalty, and European sculpture, bronzes, ceramics, and glass, are now installed at the Getty Center.

The 38-gallery Getty Villa is, and will be, perfect for the Getty classics, one of the finest U.S. collections of ancient Greek and Roman art and artifacts—sculptures and figurines, vases, mosaics, and paintings. When the museum reopens, expect special exhibits of ancient Asian and Eastern European art as well.

The Getty Villa is also a classic—a re-creation of the Villa dei Papiri, an ancient Roman country house with a view of the Bay of Naples.

TOPANGA CANYON

The equally indefinable inland and upland neighbor to Malibu is the laid-back burg of Topanga in mountainous Topanga Canyon, reached from PCH via Topanga Canyon Boulevard (Hwy. 27), increasingly a high-speed commuter thoroughfare. (The tailgaters' apparent message: Pull over or die.) Beyond the highway, the artsy community sprawls off in all directions—up tortured hillsides, down one-lane roads—within the canyon's 21-acre watershed. Famous for its mudslides, Topanga Canyon does shed water after heavy winter rains—which certainly explains the Chumash name, Topanga, roughly translated as "Mountains that Run into the Sea." Here, they often do. When hillsides aren't preoccupied with slip-sliding away, rustic cabins, lodges, standard-brand ranch homes, and more ambitious architectural adventures provide both physical and spiritual home for Topanga's people, predominantly actors, artists, musicians, poets, writers, and screenwriters. Topanga thrives on its artistic ambience and its community eccentricities—the roadside crystal stands and such—many of which hark back to the earliest inklings of the Age of Aquarius. Yet given the region's increasing suburban popularity, back-to-the-landers without 30-year-old roots would be financially challenged to plant themselves here today.

Most of Topanga the town is strung out along the highway about halfway between the San Fernando Valley and the Pacific Ocean. A popular stop for breakfast and lunch is **Willows,** 137 S. Topanga Canyon Blvd., 310/455-8788. You can also stop locally for supplies and deli sandwiches at places such as **Fernwood Market,** 446 S. Topanga Canyon Blvd., 310/455-2412, and **Froggy's Topanga Fresh Fish Market** (also a good restaurant), 1105 N. Topanga Canyon Blvd., 310/455-1728.

Some classic Topanga neighborhoods and destinations, including the **Inn of the Seventh Ray** natural-foods restaurant, 310/455-1311, are tucked in among the creekside oaks and sycamores alongside Old Topanga Canyon Rd., which eventually intersects scenic Mulholland Highway. For books about the area and basic New Age supplies, stop by **The Spiral Staircase** next to the Inn of the Seventh Ray at 128 Old Topanga Canyon, 310/455-3370.

Another wonder in Topanga is **The Will Geer Theatricum Botanicum,** 1419 N. Topanga Canyon Blvd., 310/455-3723, a small, woodsy outdoor theater that remains part of the legacy of actor/philosopher Will Geer. The classically trained Geer eventually became one of the world's most beloved actors—baby boomers will remember him as Grandpa Walton on The Waltons TV series—yet his professional and personal lives were all but undone in the 1950s by his refusal to cooperate with the communist-hunting House Committee on Un-American Activities. "Blacklisted," or barred from working in Hollywood, Geer moved his family to Topanga Canyon and established a Shakespearean theater to showcase the talents of other blacklisted Hollywood talent. Along with theater tickets, he and his family also sold their homegrown vegetables. Will Geer's daughter, Ellen, has served as the theater's artistic director since 1979, the year after the actor's death. Call for current program information or check the theater's website at www.theatricum.com.

Easily accessible from Topanga is **Topanga State Park,** prime for hiking—in the absence of major storms and mudslides—especially in "the green months" of winter and early spring. For more information, see Wilderness City: The Santa Monica Mountains in the Beverly Hills chapter.

Even the Getty gardens, the trees, shrubs, and flowers, the statuary and outdoor wall paintings, represent those at the original villa of 2,000 years ago. Villa dei Papiri, thought to have belonged to Julius Caesar's father-in-law, was buried by the volcanic rubble of Mount Vesuvius when the mountain erupted in A.D. 79. Discovered by treasure hunters and excavated during the 18th century, the reborn villa inspired Getty; the Getty Villa, completed in 1974, was constructed from excavation drawings.

Other Malibu Attractions

Other attractions include the prestigious private **Pepperdine University** campus, 24255 Pacific Coast Hwy., 310/456-4000, a nondenominational four-year liberal arts college established in 1973 by George Pepperdine, founder of Western Auto Supply. The attractive 819-acre campus, on a hill overlooking the ocean, was designed by architect William Pereira. These days Pepperdine is particularly noted for its postgraduate law and business schools. The men's volleyball team is typically one of the best in the country—which isn't that surprising, given the number of beach volleyball nets strung up all along the Malibu coast. Pepperdine's popularity among Southern California surfers was lampooned in Garry Trudeau's *Doonesbury* cartoon strip in 1997, when it was announced that Whitewater special prosecutor Kenneth Starr would soon join the faculty here. Bigger news in most years: summer's **Malibu Strawberry Creek Music Festival** and other special performances and events held here.

Then there's the vast expanse of **Santa Monica Mountains National Recreation Area,** which dips its chaparral-covered toes into the sea all along the Malibu coastline. Many mountainous areas were severely scorched during Malibu's 1993 wildfires; the fire-adapted ecosystem is quickly recovering, but fire scars are still apparent in many areas. For more information about parks and other destinations reasonably accessible from near Malibu, see Wilderness City: Santa Monica Mountains in the Beverly Hills chapter.

Charmlee Regional County Park is a little-known but charming park overlooking the Pacific—460 acres of meadows, oak woodlands, and chaparral on bluffs up to 1,300 feet above sea level. Charmlee is stunning for spring wildflowers and a perfect spot for watching the winter migration of the gray whales, just offshore. The undeveloped park is also ideal for a simple get-off-the-highway picnic, or for hiking on trails and fire roads. It's open during daylight hours, year-round. To get here, take Encinal Canyon Road from Pacific Coast Highway north of Malibu.

STAYING NORTH OF SANTA MONICA

Malibu offers the main accommodation action north of Santa Monica. And Malibu is a bit short on inexpensive places to stay—on places to stay, period—which is just the way Malibu likes it. Beyond the area's state park campsites, the 30 fairly quaint but clean 1920s-vintage cabins of the **Topanga Ranch Motel** south of central Malibu, right across from the beach at 18711 Pacific Coast Hwy. (PCH), 310/456-5486, are among

the area's more affordable options. Some units have kitchens; a few boast two bedrooms. Rates: $60–85. The attractive 21-room **Casa Malibu Inn** right on the beach in "downtown" Malibu, 22752 PCH, 310/456-2219, features an inviting central courtyard, some rooms with kitchens and balconies. Rates: $95–329. Another possibility is the decent 16-room **Malibu Country Inn** motel north of Malibu proper at 6506 Westward Beach Rd. (at PCH), 310/457-9622, with a small swimming pool, in-room refrigerators and coffeemakers. Rates: $125–250, but somewhat less expensive in the off-season.

Since 1990, Malibu has boasted a seriously stylish small hotel right on the beach, complete with tile work and Berber carpets—the **Malibu Beach Inn,** in the pink and snuggled onto a strip of beachfront near the pier at 22878 Pacific Coast Hwy., 310/456-6444 or toll-free 800/462-5428; www.malibubeachinn.com. Space here is too tight for so much as a swimming pool—but who needs a pool when the wide blue Pacific Ocean is in your front yard? Rooms are reasonably spacious, with the usual luxury amenities, small private balconies, and gas fireplaces (most rooms). Perfect for just hanging out: the motel's friendly Mediterranean-style terra-cotta-tiled patio hanging out over the rocky shore. Two-night minimum stay on weekends from May through October. Rates: $169–249.

For a still quieter, still more serene weekend stay, room to retreat is often available for individuals at the Franciscan **Serra Retreat Center,** 3401 Serra Rd., P.O. Box 127, Malibu, CA 90265, 310/456-6631, or www.sbfranciscans.org, which offers regular group retreats at this scenic remnant of the original Topanga Malibu Sequit ranch, the spot where "Queen of Malibu" May Rindge started but never completed her hilltop mansion. Suggested per-day donation, $90–140, which includes three substantial meals.

EATING NORTH OF SANTA MONICA

Just north of Santa Monica in Pacific Palisades, **Gladstone's 4 Fish,** 17300 Pacific Coast Hwy. (at Sunset Blvd.), 310/454-3474, has always been one of the most popular restaurants on the Westside—not because the food was so great but because, for singles, it's such a terrific place for trolling. (After a close call in 1997, when it looked as if Gladstone's might lose its prime beachfront locale, the lease was renewed for another long run.) The wait is always long, the crowd is always noisy. But even if you eat elsewhere, have a tropical drink on the patio at sunset just to watch the attractive beach buns and bunnies.

Dinner-only **Modo Mio,** 15200 Sunset Blvd. (enter on La Cruz), 310/459-0979, is the place for dinner, a stylish yet cozy neighborhood favorite serving rustic Tuscan fare. The incredible selection of specials keeps everyone surprised. For less expensive reservations-required fare, closer to Santa Monica, *the* place is the popular Italian **Caffe Delfini,** 147 W. Channel Rd. (at Pacific Coast Highway), 310/459-8823, where seafood and pastas star—Delfini's famous seafood soup and such things as broiled shrimp with fresh tomato and basil and homemade ravioli. The restaurant also has a regular celebrity clientele. Less expensive still, perfect for pizza, is the friendly neighborhood dinner-only **Vittorio!,** 16646 Marquez Ave. (at Sunset), 310/459-3755. Inexpensive just off Pacific Coast Highway is **Marix Tex Mex Playa,** 118 Entrada Dr., 310/459-8596, the coastal cousin of West Hollywood's happiest Tex-Mex joint, famous for its fajitas. This place is open daily for breakfast, lunch, and dinner.

Not to be missed in Topanga Canyon: **Froggy's Topanga Fresh Fish Market,** 1105 N. Topanga Canyon Blvd. (Hwy. 27), 310/455-1728. Malibu's chi-chi crowd may do fish at some swank place near the beach, but everybody else comes here. This fun and funky fish palace, a Topanga Canyon classic, doesn't get by on looks or general eccentricity. The fish is the thing, and here it's done quite well. Open for dinners, Froggy's is noteworthy for its rotisserie chicken and salads but famous for chowder, shrimp, lobster, and just about anything else that's fresh and on the menu. It's open 5 P.M.–9:30 P.M., until 10 P.M. on Friday and Saturday nights, closed Thanksgiving and Christmas. This place is easiest to find when navigating by local landmarks. With that proviso, Froggy's is on Topanga Canyon Boulevard (Hwy. 27) on the San Fernando

Valley side of the post office but on the Pacific Coast Highway side of Theatricum Botanicum, the very cool community theater. Also locally famous, for vegetarian and some meatier entrées: the hip and hippie-friendly **Inn of the Seventh Ray** in Topanga Canyon at 128 Old Topanga Rd., 310/455-1311, famous for its homemade bread and Sunday brunch. The inn is open daily for lunch and dinner.

Eating in Malibu

Top of the food chain in Malibu proper is gloriously garish **Granita** in the Malibu Colony Plaza mall at 23725 W. Malibu Rd., 310/456-0488, another of Wolfgang Puck and Barbara Lazaroff's progeny, sometimes puckishly referred to as Spago-by-the-Sea. The interior, with the trademark open kitchen and equally typical high decibel levels, was designed to resemble an underwater sea cave inhabited by eclectic fishlike creatures—no wilder than the imaginative California-style Mediterranean fare. Yet it almost seems barbaric to dive into so much fish and seafood, no matter how delectable, while they're watching. Usually clotted with celebrities, Granita makes it challenging for regular people to get in, particularly on weekends. Try reservations—and coming for lunch during the week. It's very expensive and open for lunch Wed.–Fri., for brunch on Saturday and Sunday, for dinner every night.

Another fine-dining destination—if you find yourself in the vicinity of Malibu and in the mood for a drive—is exquisite **Saddle Peak Lodge,** a onetime hunting lodge in the Santa Monica Mountains near Calabasas, 818/222-3888.

For fish tacos and such, surfers and like-minded souls roll in to the fun and funky **Reel Inn,** 18661 Pacific Coast Hwy. (at Topanga Canyon Blvd.), 310/456-8221. More sophisticated and stylish, quite good for simpler fare and takeout, is **Marmalade,** 3894 S. Cross Creek Rd. (at PCH), 310/317-4242, a simple deli cafe featuring fresh bakery items (with or without marmalade), good salads, soups, and such things as chicken pot pie. (There's another Marmalade in Santa Monica, on Montana Avenue, and one in Westlake Village.) Pricier but unpretentious is Italian **Allegria,** 22821 Pacific Coast Hwy. (just south of Cross Creek Rd.), 310/456-3132, a lively trattoria serving authentic Venetian-style pastas and pizza. Another celeb-watching hot spot, open daily for lunch and dinner. To linger over a homey Italian meal, the place is **Tra di Noi,** 3835 Cross Creek Rd., 310/456-0169.

DOWN THE COAST: THE SOUTH BAY

SOUTH BAY BEACH CITIES

The strands of sand and beach towns south of Los Angeles International Airport (LAX) comprise L.A.'s "South Bay," the southern Santa Monica Bay. This is where the Beach Boys came of age—in Manhattan Beach—and where, in nearby Hermosa Beach and Redondo Beach, Southern California's middle-American surf culture got its biggest sendoff in the 1950s and '60s. But it all started in 1907 when George Freeth, billed as "the man who could walk on water," was imported to Redondo Beach by that ceaseless land-sales promoter Henry Huntington for a special "prove it" performance. Walking the offshore waves with the help of an eight-foot, 200-pound wooden surfboard, Freeth introduced the ancient Polynesian sport of kings to the neighborhood. You can tour the entire area from a bicycle seat, thanks to the 20-mile **South Bay Bike Trail** that runs from Will Rogers State Beach (north of Santa Monica) to Torrance Beach in the south. Or you can drive. Huge public parking lots abound along the South Bay's beaches.

Rising above the southernmost reach of Santa Monica Bay is the Palos Verdes Peninsula, a collection of affluent residential enclaves that separate L.A.'s surf cities and their semi-industrial inland neighbors from San Pedro and the Port of Los Angeles, next south, and Long Beach, home port of the RMS *Queen Mary,* the new Long Beach Aquarium of the Pacific, and other attractions. Next stop south of Long Beach is Orange County.

El Segundo and Manhattan Beach

El Segundo is sometimes also described as L.A.'s own Mayberry, U.S.A., for its insular Midwestern mores. Before the end of the Cold War and the rapid decline of Southern California's defense industry, no one much minded comments about "El Stinko," a reference to Playa del Rey's 144-acre Hyperion Waste Treatment Plant and its downwind influence here. And no one complained about the huge circa-1911 Chevron oil refinery just south. (The town was named for it. El Segundo means "The Second [One]" in Spanish, since Standard Oil's first refinery—this plant was Standard before it was Chevron—opened in Richmond, near San Francisco.) And no one seemed to hear the ear-rending racket from LAX jet traffic overhead. Everyone was too busy working—at Aerospace Corp., Hughes Aircraft, Northrop, Rockwell, and TRW. Not to mention Mattel Toys. Some of those jobs have disappeared, in L.A.'s new post-defense economy, but others have taken their place. These days El Segundo—conveniently near LAX, after all—is getting serious about attracting new industry and, closer to the beach, trendier and tourism-related businesses.

Chic Manhattan Beach, just south, already riding the latter wave, doesn't have such problems—which is why restaurants and businesses along the El Segundo side of the bustling, increasingly chi-chi Rosecrans Avenue corridor shamelessly advertise their address as "Manhattan Beach." At the beach—Manhattan State Beach, a continuation of the nearly seamless broad bay strand that starts north of Santa Monica—you'll find excellent swimming, lifeguards, both clean water and sand, the works. If you're driving, you'll find free parking along Vista del Mar to Highland, metered parking along most streets, and public lots close to attractive "downtown," at both 11th and 13th Streets. There's also a metered lot at 43rd Street. For fishing, try 900-foot **Manhattan Beach Pier** at the foot of Manhattan Beach Boulevard. You can also stroll **The Strand,** which here wanders past beachfront homes as it meanders south to Hermosa Beach.

For more information about the area, contact the **City of El Segundo,** 310/607-2249, www.elsegundo.org, and the **City of Manhattan Beach,** 310/802-5000; www.ci.manhattan-beach.ca.us.

Redondo Beach and Hermosa Beach

Redondo State Beach is the hot-weather hot spot in these parts, though nothing like this old resort town's turn-of-the-20th-century heyday. Still, at times it's almost as difficult to park your beach towel as it is your car. As elsewhere along L.A.'s South Bay, the two miles of beach here are wide and sandy. The **Redondo Beach Pier,** at the foot of Torrance Boulevard, marks the beach's northern reaches. In 1988 storms and subsequent fires ravaged the 60-year-old wooden horseshoe-shaped pier, the most recent of many local pier incarnations—and the city rebuilt in grand style. Designed by Edward Beall, the new, nautically themed $11 million Redondo Beach Pier—complete with sail-like awnings—is a sturdy yet wondrous concrete creation, complete with 1,800 life-size etchings of marine life, including sharks, scuba divers, and whales. (Water quality near the pier is less than perfect though.) **King Harbor** just north, along Harbor Drive between Horondo and Beryl Streets, is the result of a massive redevelopment that cost Redondo Beach its historic downtown, replacing it with 50 acres of high-rise apartment buildings. King Harbor has its own piers, with restaurants, shops, and such, and also offers harbor cruises, sportfishing and winter whale-watching charters, and bike and other sports equipment rentals. Not to take a back seat to Long Beach, Redondo Beach even offers gondola rides at King Harbor, through **Gondola Amore,** 310/376-6977. The best surfing is just north, at Hermosa Beach, and well south of Redondo at Torrance Beach. Be that as it may, come to Redondo in August for the annual **Surf Festival.**

Head north from Redondo to Hermosa Beach, most famous as L.A.'s best for beach volleyball, site of numerous competitions and championship matches. Hermosa Beach also features row upon row of at-the-beach apartments and the **Hermosa Beach Pier,** historically a fishing pier, which along with lower Pier Ave. had a $1.5 million facelift in early 1997 to create another L.A. "destination street." **The Strand** stroll here is quite pleasant, passing beach homes, restaurants, and shops. Not to be missed in the neighborhood is the independent **Nations! Travelstore,** 500-504 Pier Ave., 310/318-9915 or toll-free 800/546-8060, www.nationstravelmall.com, a combination bookstore, map and supply stop,

SOUTH BAY BICYCLE TRAIL

What better way to see the beach, and the Los Angeles beach scene, than by bike? The South Bay Bicycle Trail, accessible at any point along the route, runs south from the white sand of Will Rogers State Beach along local beaches to Torrance, with a strategic inland detour only to bypass the harbor at Marina del Rey. Highlights along the way include the dazzling Santa Monica beach scene, wild and wacky Venice Beach, complete with in-line skaters run amok and muscle-bound Muscle Beach, and the tony trendiness of Marina del Rey's boating brigade. And the swaying palms, sun, sand, and fresh ocean air. Oh sure, a few ecstasy-assassinating intrusions await along the way, especially toward the South Bay, where the L.A. Department of Water and Power's power plant smokestacks and incessant LAX jet traffic detract from an otherwise postcard-perfect setting. But you can pull over to rest your angst at municipal piers and other key attractions, including Marina del Rey's boat harbor and the shop-happy King Harbor at the north end of Redondo Beach.

Since most people in greater Los Angeles don't make it to the beach until close to noon, early morning is a great time for a bike ride. (This being the beach side of a very urban area, avoid being on the bike path after dark.) The paved bike path runs a total distance of approximately 20 miles; even a biking beginner can make the one-way trip in two hours or less. Start early and stop for breakfast before heading back. Bike rental establishments are available all along the beachfront bike path.

and travel agency beloved for its exceptional product selection and customer service.

Head south from Redondo to Torrance Beach and then, for top-notch surfing, stroll to Malaga Cove below the bluffs. It's easier to get to the cove from the Palos Verdes Peninsula (see below).

For more information about the area, contact: **Redondo Beach Visitors Bureau,** 200 N. Pacific Coast Hwy., 310/374-2171 or toll-free 800/282-0333, www.redondo.org, and the **Torrance Visitors Bureau,** 3400 Torrance Blvd., 310/792-2343; www.torrnet.com.

PALOS VERDES PENINSULA

If you lived in paradise, wouldn't you want to keep it that way? The upper-class and upper-middle-class communities atop Palos Verdes Peninsula are fairly exclusive, and largely proud of it—a sense of entitlement that, unfortunately, sometimes extends to local beaches. Demonstrating an international surfing phenomenon known as "localism," the feared Bay Boys of Palos Verdes—"trust-fund babies," according to a *Surfer* magazine editor—have long made it their business to keep nonlocals out of primo surf spots such as Lunada Bay, a stance that has led to verbal assaults and worse on more than one occasion, and an attitude that has led to significant lawsuits against Palos Verdes Estates. Whatever the absolute truth underlying such conflicts, it's clear that no one here wants the now-common California beach overcrowding problems and related traumas—trash, graffiti, violence—that are increasing all along the coast, particularly at the best surfing beaches.

Few such troubles perturb the Palos Verdes Peninsula, which eons ago was one of the Channel Islands. Serious social problems here include the challenge of dodging horses and riders on public streets (equestrians have the right-of-way) and coping with the noise and effluence of the wild peacock flocks in Rolling Hills Estates and Palos Verdes Estates. The peninsula is home to several of L.A.'s most affluent communities—Rolling Hills is, officially, the wealthiest town in America, and its neighbors are also at the top of the list—and what its people value most is their privacy. Yet despite ongoing surf-turf wars the peninsula's parks, other public facilities, and businesses generally welcome visitors.

Though you must meander the peninsula's winding interior roads to get a close-up view of life here, most people are satisfied with a leisurely coastal drive. And, on a clear day, the views are spectacular. Starting in the north, from Pacific Coast Highway (Hwy. 1) head southwest on Palos Verdes Boulevard, which soon becomes Palos Verdes Drive W., then, at Hawthorne Boulevard, Palos Verdes Drive S.; heading north on Palos Verdes Drive E. eventually leads to east-west Palos Verdes Drive N., completing the blufftop "perimeter" drive. But a true coastal tour would continue east along 25th Street into San Pedro, perhaps jogging south to Paseo del Mar and then east again to the Cabrillo Marine Aquarium.

To explore local features and natural history in detail, sign on for one of the monthly guided hikes offered through the **Palos Verdes Peninsula Land Conservancy,** 310/541-7613; www.pvplc.org. For more information about the area, contact: **Palos Verdes Peninsula Chamber of Commerce,** 310/377-8111; www.palosverdes.com/pvpcc.

Touring the Palos Verdes Peninsula

First stop along the peninsula coast tour is in town, actually, in Palos Verdes Estates. The **Neptune Fountain** at the **Malaga Cove Plaza** was inspired by the architecture of Italy's Sorrentine Peninsula. (When in the 1960s King Neptune's anatomy was somehow dismembered, locals rallied and replaced the notable lost part with a strategic fig leaf.) Elsewhere throughout this area are architectural reminders of what the Palos Verdes Peninsula might have been, if plans made in the 1920s by banker Frank A. Vanderlip, architect Myron Hunt, and the similarly talented sons of landscape architect Frederick Law Olmsted had been fully realized. To appreciate the Olmsteds's local heritage, head to **La Venta Inn,** 796 Via del Monte, 310/373-0123, then it's off to **Malaga Cove** proper, accessible from Paseo del Mar (east of Via Arroyo), an inspiring side trip in its own right. Also known as **RAT Beach** (short for "Right After Torrance" Beach, not an urban wildlife reference), this top-notch surfing beach is equally popular for rock and shell collecting and tide-pool exploration.

From Malaga Cove the truly adventurous can scrabble south over the rocks to the shale-cliffed scenery of **Bluff Cove,** also popular with surfers, and on to the famous surf-turf battleground of **Lunada Bay,** a six-mile round-trip. This adventure is recommended only during pacific (that is, peaceful) surf—and only at low tide, when the tide's heading out. Notable near Lunada is the 1961 wreckage of the Greek freighter *Dominator,* which failed to dominate these treacherous shores.

Back on the main road, continue south to one of L.A.'s premier winter whale-watching sights—the **Point Vicente Interpretive Center** at 31501

Palos Verdes Dr. W., 310/377-5370, where the second-floor gallery is packed with California gray whale voyeurs from mid-December into March each year. Any time—at least on a clear day—the center offers an impressive view of Santa Catalina Island and a worthwhile introduction to area natural history. Open daily, except major holidays. Small fee.

The historic 1926 **Point Vicente Lighthouse** perches on a cliff farther down the coast at 31550 Palos Verdes Dr. W., 310/541-0334. The 67-foot-tall lighthouse is powered by a two-million-candlepower bulb, and visitors can climb the 74 steps to the top to check out the handcrafted Fresnel lens that produces the long light beam. Tours are held every second Saturday 9 A.M.–3 P.M. and by appointment for groups.

Next south is the peninsula's rather notorious **Portuguese Bend** area, where in the 1950s massive landslides doomed more than 100 homes. Things are still plenty unstable today. One of this neighborhood's most popular attractions is the small but stunning **Wayfarers Chapel,** 5755 Palos Verdes Dr. S., 310/377-1650, designed by Lloyd Wright (son of Frank Lloyd Wright) and built of glass, redwood, and Palos Verdes stone. Except during special events—weddings are understandably popular here, typically scheduled on weekends between 1 and 3 P.M.—this Swedenborgian Church chapel and lovely grounds are open daily for meditation.

For some prime-time picnicking, try nearby **Abalone Cove Shoreline Park and Ecological Preserve,** a federal reserve near Portuguese Point at 5970 Palos Verdes Dr. S., 310/377-1222, where the grassy lawn offers easy access to the rocky beach below—and to tide pools teeming with these precious, and protected, ocean creatures. Best time for abalone voyeurism is in December and January. Parking $5. Nearby **Smuggler's Cove** is a long-popular nude beach, unofficially, so a subject of local conflict.

If you're making a day of it, the best bet in Southern California for dahlia and fuchsia displays is the **South Coast Botanic Garden,** a onetime landfill at 26300 Crenshaw Blvd., 310/544-6815, where the peak dahlia bloom comes in mid-August. Also here: plant collections representing every continent except Antarc-

tica (organized by color), some 1,600 roses, and the "Garden of the Senses."

San Pedro

With its hilly streets, ocean fog, views, and military installations, San Pedro is, some local wags say, L.A.'s own little San Francisco, complete with a miniature, but much friendlier, Mission District, along Pacific Street. (It's san PEE-dro, by the way, despite California's predilection elsewhere for correct Spanish pronunciation.) That perspective is a hard sell even in this semi-industrial port city, however.

If people find themselves in San Pedro, most head to the shops, restaurants, and other tourist diversions of **Ports O' Call Village** at the end of Sixth Street, 310/831-0287, a shopping mall in the style of a New England seaside village. But San Pedro has more intriguing features—including the **Port of Los Angeles** itself, which was created at a cost of $60 million between 1920 and 1940. The best way to get the big picture is on guided boat tours ($6–10) with **Spirit Cruises,** 310/548-8080, which depart from Ports O' Call. From the **World Cruise Terminal** and **Catalina Terminal** here, travelers depart on sea journeys near and far. A particularly impressive sight is soaring **Vincent Thomas Bridge,** which from the Harbor Freeway (the 110) connects San Pedro (via Hwy. 47) to Terminal Island— Southern California's largest suspension bridge, built in 1963 (small toll on the return trip). **Terminal Island,** once known as Rattlesnake Island, was a vibrant resort destination earlier in this century, L.A.'s own Brighton Beach, complete with pleasure pier. Starting in 1906, it was also home to a close-knit village of Japanese-American fishermen and their families—an idyllic life ended forever with World War II–era Japanese internment in 1942. Terminal Island today, an uninviting diesel-scented jungle of canneries, loading cranes, and old warships, also includes a federal penitentiary.

Other significant San Pedro attractions include two seaworthy museums: the **Los Angeles Maritime Museum** at Berth 84 (at the foot of Sixth St.), 310/548-7618, and the **S.S. Lane Victory Ship Museum** at Berth 94 (near the World Cruise Terminal), 310/519-9545, a onetime ammunition carrier, now a national historic landmark. Well worth a stop in nearby **Wilmington**

Ports O' Call Village,
San Pedro

TOM MYERS PHOTOGRAPHY

are the **Banning Residence Museum,** 401 E. M St., 310/548-7777, the restored 1864 Greek revival mansion of General Phineas Banning and a major interpretive center for 19th-century L.A. history, and the **Drum Barracks Civil War Museum,** 1052 Banning Blvd., 310/548-7509, the only remaining structure from the Civil War–era Camp Drum, where 7,000 troops were based. Both museums are open only for guided tours (call for times); donations greatly appreciated.

Definitely worth a stop, especially with tots in tow, is the **Cabrillo Marine Aquarium and Museum,** 3720 Stephen White Dr., 310/548-7562, open Tues.–Fri. noon–5 P.M. and on weekends 10 A.M.–5 P.M. (open on some "holiday" Mondays, closed Thanksgiving, Christmas). It's free—suggested donation is $2 adults, $1 children, and parking is $6.50—and full of educational opportunity, thus quite popular with school groups. But anyone can be a kid here. Housed in a contemporary Frank Gehry–designed building, the Cabrillo features 38 tanks now home to an abundance of Southern California sea life. Among the most popular exhibits: the "tidal tank," a veritable room with a view of a wave, and the shark tank. Other exhibits include a "touch tank" filled with sea anemones and starfish, and a whalebone graveyard. The aquarium also offers seasonal whale-watching tours and "grunion run" programs; call for current information. From

here, set out for both **Cabrillo Beach** and 1200-foot **Cabrillo Pier,** just inside the breakwater. Also worth a stop (though not open to the public) **Point Fermin Lighthouse** at the end of the breakwater at 807 Paseo del Mar—the only remaining wooden lighthouse on the Pacific Coast, shining forth here since 1874.

Budget travelers, keep in mind that San Pedro's **Point Fermin Park,** back toward the Palos Verdes Peninsula on S. Paseo del Mar, includes the **HI-AYH Los Angeles/South Bay Hostel,** 3601 S. Gaffey St., Bldg. 613, 310/831-2836. Next to Point Fermin Park is San Pedro's own "sunken city." In 1929 an entire neighborhood of exclusive homes started slipping to sea here—at the rate of 12 inches per day—and was quickly relocated to more solid ground. But the ground kept slipping, and keeps slipping. The jumble of old pavement and palm trees is a slightly surreal sight. If you get hungry and enjoy biker bars, *the* place locally is **Walker's Cafe,** almost on the sunken-city spot at 700 S. Paseo Del Mar, 310/833-3623.

The best beach around for scuba diving and pleasant scenery is San Pedro's rocky **Royal Palms State Beach** on the Palos Verdes Peninsula at the south end of Western Avenue.

For more information about the area, contact: **San Pedro Peninsula Chamber of Commerce,** 390 W. Seventh St., 310/832-7272; www.sanpedrochamber.com.

PRACTICAL SOUTH BAY

Accommodation options south of Santa Monica range from very inexpensive at-the-beach hostels to midrange motels and five-star luxury hotels.

Close to both beach and LAX is ever-popular **Barnabey's Hotel,** 3501 Sepulveda Blvd. (a half block south of Rosecrans), Manhattan Beach, 310/545-8466 or toll-free 800/552-5285. Three-story Barnabey's is a real surprise—an ersatz 19th-century English inn with four-poster beds and an antique-rich ambience yet all the modern conveniences, including in-room coffeemakers and data ports, on-site pub, pool, and hot tub. Rates: $130–200.

For other places to stay in Redondo Beach, Torrance, and elsewhere in the South Bay, contact local visitor bureaus and chambers of commerce.

To find what's new and sometimes the best in South Bay dining, explore on and around piers and coastal areas. Less expensive possibilities in Manhattan Beach include the popular Americanized Mexican **Pancho's,** 3615 Highland Ave. (at Rosecrans Ave.), 310/545-6670. Look for the **Wolfgang Puck Café,** 310/607-9653, and other trendy alternatives along the Rosecrans Avenue corridor separating El Segundo and Manhattan Beach. Quite impressive is California-French style **Reed's,** 2640 N. Sepulveda Blvd. (near Marine), 310/546-3299, a shopping-center shining light. Another pricier possibility is California-French **Cafe Pierre,** 317 Manhattan Beach Blvd. (at Highland Ave.), 310/545-5252. This upscale beach café is noted for outstanding bouillabaisse and grilled fish.

Great for vegetarian is **The Spot** in Hermosa Beach at 110 Second St. (at Hermosa Ave.), 310/376-2355, though the Middle Eastern **Habash Cafe,** 233 Pacific Coast Hwy. (between Second and Third Sts.), 310/376-6620, offers some intriguing nonmeat alternatives at breakfast, lunch, and dinner. The onetime Diana's in Hermosa Beach has now been incorporated into the original **Hennessey's Tavern,** 8 Pier Ave., 310/372-5759, a fairly sophisticated beach pub serving suds and sandwiches and live entertainment on weekends. (You'll find Hennessey's all up and down this stretch of L.A. coastline.)

For fast-food seafood in Redondo Beach, check out **The Blue Moon Saloon,** 207 N. Harbor Dr. (near Beryl), 310/374-3411. For something a bit fancier, try popular **Chez Melange,** at the Palos Verdes Inn, 1716 Pacific Coast Hwy. (near Palos Verdes Blvd.), 310/540-1222, a Spago for just plain folks serving everything from Japanese to Cajun, open every night for dinner, on weekdays for breakfast and lunch, and on Sunday for brunch. Chez Melange has spawned two respected spin-offs in the general vicinity, too—**Depot** inside a beautifully restored train depot in Torrance at 1250 Cabrillo Ave. (at Torrance Blvd.), 310/787-7501, and the casual Cal-Asian **Gina Lee's Bistro** in Redondo Beach at 211 Palos Verdes Blvd. (between Pacific Coast Hwy. and Catalina Ave.), 310/375-4462.

Quite good in Torrance for eclectic California cuisine is **Christine,** open for weekday lunches and dinner daily at the Hillside Village, 24530 Hawthorne Blvd., 310/373-1952, but **Aioli,** 1261 Cabrillo Ave. (at Torrance Blvd.), 310/320-9200, offers options beyond the sit-down dining room—including the **Breadstix Bakery** and tapas. Aioli is open for dinner every night, for lunch on weekdays only, and for brunch on Sunday.

LONG BEACH:
IOWA BY THE BAY GOES BIG TIME

Long Beach is the second-largest city in Los Angeles County, dwarfed only by L.A. itself, and the fifth-largest in the state. The city's history follows the fairly predictable Southern California course, from coastal wilderness and rangeland suburb of Spain and Mexico to extensive Midwestern settlement. The population of transplants from Iowa was once so dominant, in fact, that "Iowa picnics" became the most memorable community social gatherings during the Great Depression. Then came turn-of-the-20th-century seaside resort and booming port, regional oil development, and the monumental Long Beach earthquake that flattened downtown in 1933—the indirect impetus for downtown's then-new art deco style. Howard Hughes, the aviator and engineer later famous as the world's most eccentric billionaire, made history here in 1947 when he took his *Spruce Goose*—the world's largest airplane—for its first and only flight.

Downsizing the Military,
Upsizing Tourism

During and since World War II, but before the post-Cold War era of military downsizing, the U.S. Navy was central to Long Beach life, given the presence of the Long Beach Naval Station, Long Beach Naval Ship Yard, and Boeing, McDonnell Douglas, and other aviation and defense-related industry. Symbol of that past was the Iowa-class USS *Missouri,* America's last active battleship, host to Japan's formal surrender at the end of World War II and later recruit for offshore duty in the Persian Gulf during Operation Desert Storm. When "Mighty Mo" was finally decommissioned here in 1992, thousands and thousands turned out for the event. Both the naval station and shipyard have since been shut down. Yet the city is determined to recover from its defense-related economic losses. The Port of Long Beach is the busiest cargo port on the West Coast, doing a brisk Pacific Rim trade,

and promoting downtown and port-side tourism is also a major priority.

Long Beach is an astonishingly diverse community with large immigrant populations, recently gaining national notoriety as the first California city to adopt a uniforms-only public school dress code. Despite the city's pressing social problems, people visit Long Beach primarily because it's still apple-pie appealing, unassuming, and affordable, with clean air and coastal diversions, a spruced-up downtown, and a lively cultural scene. (Many also show up here on business; both the Long Beach Convention and Entertainment Center and the World Trade Center are downtown.) And some say there are more worthy breakfast, burger, and pie shops in Long Beach than anywhere else in L.A. County.

Though bad press from occasional outbreaks of gang warfare is a bane of Long Beach existence, visitors don't need to be overly concerned. (One area at high risk for violent crime is north of downtown, straddling the 710 between Highway 47 and Temple Avenue, south of Pacific Coast Highway and north of Seventh Street; another, well north of downtown, stretches between Long Beach Boulevard and Orange Avenue, south of South Street and north of Del Amo Boulevard.) Reasonable precautions are prudent, of course, as in any urban area.

Special annual events well worth the trip include the **Toyota Grand Prix of Long Beach** in April—an event that transforms Shoreline Drive, Seaside Way, and other downtown streets into an international raceway—the **Cajun and Zydeco Festival** in June, and the long-running **Long Beach Blues Festival** in September.

For more information about Long Beach and its attractions, contact: **Long Beach Convention and Visitors Bureau,** One World Trade Center, Ste. 300, Long Beach 90831, 562/436-3645, or toll-free 800/452-7829, or www.golong-beach.org.

SEEING AND DOING
LONG BEACH

On the Waterfront in Long Beach

The visitor action in Long Beach is downtown and nearby, on the waterfront. The famed **Pike Amusement Park**—where Southern California once entertained itself on the roller coaster and boardwalk, and where W. C. Fields, Buster Keaton, and other early film-industry icons made movies—once stood near the current site of the huge Long Beach Convention and Entertainment Center. Though Hollywood subsequently stole the moviemaking spotlight, later Long Beach films have included *The Creature from the Black Lagoon, Corrina Corrina, Speed,* and the opening scenes to *Lethal Weapon.* And until quite recently TV's *Baywatch* was filmed here, too, at least in part.

Though the new **Long Beach Aquarium of the Pacific,** 562/590-3100, is the city's newest big attraction—and centerpiece of the $650-million Queensbay Bay redevelopment project—the surrounding **Rainbow Harbor** is now home port for the tallship *Californian,* toll-free 800/432-2201, www.californian.org, available for high-seas adventure sails when it's moored in Long Beach. For more boating, take a Venetian-style gondola ride through the Naples Island neighborhood with **Gondola Getaway,** 562/433-9595, where the basket of bread, cheese, and salami is provided—along with the "O Sole Mio"—but you'll have to bring your own vino. Still most famous in Long Beach, though, is the RMS *Queen Mary,* a floating cruise-ship-cum-museum moored on the other side of Queensway Bridge featuring hotel rooms, restaurants, and shops, 562/435-3511 or toll-free 800/437-2934 (hotel reservations); www.queenmary.com. A new, also-tourable companion for the *Queen* is a retired Soviet submarine, Podvodnaya Lodka B-427, also known by the code name *Scorpion,* decommissioned in 1994. The gigantic golf ball-like geodesic dome nearby is the Queen Mary Seaport Dome, onetime home of Howard Hughes's *Spruce Goose,* now a popular movie-making soundstage.

Looking out onto the Queen, from the downtown side of the bay, is the **Shoreline Village** shopping complex at 407 Shoreline Village Dr., 562/435-4093, complete with a 1906 **Charles Looff carousel** for the kiddos.

BIG-TIME TRANSIT OPTIONS

The **Long Beach Freeway,** the 710, a major shipping corridor, delivers residents, visitors, and truckers alike right into downtown and/or the port district. Newcomers, heads up: Should you see a spectacular crash on six-lane **Shoreline Drive** in Long Beach, it's not always necessary to call 911. One of Hollywood's favorite filming sites for "freeway" disasters, Shoreline is regularly shut down for film shoots—20 or more times in an average year. (Don't worry. Actual traffic is routed around the action.) But in Long Beach, it's uniquely possible to get out—and stay out—of your car altogether.

Excellent Long Beach area public transportation includes L.A. Metropolitan Transit Agency's Metrorail **Blue Line** mass transit system, 213/626-4455 (schedules) or 213/922-6235 (information), www.mta.net, which runs 22 miles between Long Beach and downtown L.A. At downtown's **Long Beach Transit Mall** at First Street and the Promenade, riders can connect to 36 different local bus routes and interconnect with other bus systems. For detailed regional bus route and schedule information, stop by the **Long Beach Transit Information Center,** 223 E. First St., or call Long Beach Transit, 562/591-2301; L.A.'s local MTA outpost, 562/626-4455; and the Orange County Transit District, toll-free 714/636-RIDE.

Best yet for visitors is the free **Long Beach Runabout** downtown shuttle, 562/591-2301, which ferries folks around downtown and to and from the *Queen Mary,* Shoreline Village, the convention center, hotels, restaurants, and shopping districts. If you'd prefer to get around by water but left the yacht back home, the 40-foot **Catalina Express** water taxi, toll-free 800/995-4386, connects the aquarium with Shoreline Village, the *Queen Mary,* and with the Catalina Express terminal (for the trip to Catalina Island).

Or head for the wide white sandy beach. Or take a beachfront bike ride. Well worth a stop at the beach is the **Long Beach Museum of Art,** 2300 E. Ocean Blvd., 562/439-2119, www.lbma.org, where you get artistic beach views in addition to an eyeful of contemporary art, photography, and sculpture. The museum opened, following renovation, in September 2000 and is open Tues.–Sun. 11 A.M.–7 P.M. Admission is $5 adults, $4 students/seniors, free for children under age 12.

Bike It or Not: Beach and Bay Overview
The paved **Shoreline Path** introduces bicyclists to Long Beach as both port and "pleasure place," weaving its way from the Los Angeles River and Shoreline Village on the west to Belmont Shore on the east, paralleling Ocean Boulevard—and the beach—for much of the way. The route starts at the port, near Shoreline Village and within view of the venerable RMS *Queen Mary.* The path heads east along the broad, sandy beach—and those enticing semitropical "islands" off-shore, actually dressed-up oil drilling platforms—while sashaying past some stately historic buildings along Ocean Boulevard, including one mansion now home to the **Long Beach Museum of Art.** End of the line is the remarkably congested **Belmont Shore** area, where the "elite retreat" cachet still holds. (One of the best respites in sight here is the Belmont Brewing Company at the foot of tiny **Belmont Pier,** beloved locally for fishing.) Beyond the beach-front homes the bike path becomes a board-

LONG BEACH AQUARIUM OF THE PACIFIC

The latest star—shall we say sea star?—brightening the Long Beach waterfront is the $100 million, 120,000-square-foot Long Beach Aquarium of the Pacific. At least indirectly inspired by the phenomenal success of the Monterey Bay Aquarium, which was the first to examine local ocean ecology in such exquisite, intimate, and technologically enhanced detail, the emphasis here is on the entire Pacific Ocean, the largest body of water on earth.

The Aquarium of the Pacific features 550 species of aquatic life in three major galleries, these corresponding to the ocean's three regions: **Southern California/Baja,** the **Tropical Pacific,** and the **Northern Pacific.** The Great Hall of the Pacific—the size of a football field, to represent the Pacific's vastness—offers an overview and a preview.

The aquarium first dips into the offshore waters of Southern California and the Baja Peninsula, from underwater kelp forests to bird's- and otter's-eye views of seals and sea lions frolicking in a facsimile Catalina Island environment. The interactive Kids' Cove here teaches the kiddos about other families' habits and habitats—in this case, those of marine animal families—and allows them to hike through whale bones, "hatch" bird eggs, and hide out with the hermit crabs. Then it's a quick splash south to Baja's Sea of Cortez and its sea turtles, skates, and rays. The Northern Pacific exhibits begin in the icy Bering Sea, where puffins nest near playful sea otters. This frigid sea shares other

aquatic wealth, from schooling fish to giant octopuses and Japanese spider crabs. First stop in the Tropical Pacific is a peaceful lagoon in Micronesia, which sets the stage for the stunning 35,000-gallon Deep Reef exhibit—the aquarium's largest—with its vivid panorama of tropical sea life. If you time it right, you can watch divers feed the fish. Should you need feeding yourself, dive into the aquarium's **Café Scuba,** overlooking Rainbow Harbor. And to take home some specific memento of the Pacific Ocean, see what's on sale at the **Pacific Collections** gift shop.

The Long Beach Aquarium of the Pacific is centerpiece of the $650-million Queensbay Bay redevelopment project. The largest waterfront development in California history, Queensway Bay also encompasses the Rainbow Harbor resort complex.

Just off Shoreline Drive at 100 Aquarium Way (follow the signs), the Aquarium of the Pacific is open daily 9 A.M.–6 P.M. (closed Christmas). At last report admission was $14.95 adults, $11.95 seniors (age 60 and older), and $7.95 children (ages 3–11). Group rates (for 20 or more) are available with advance reservations. For more information or to purchase advance tickets, call the aquarium at 562/590-3100 or check the website at www.aquariumofpacific.org. The 40-foot **Catalina Express** water taxi, toll-free 800/995-4386, connects the aquarium with Shoreline Village, the *Queen Mary,* and the Catalina Express terminal (for the trip to Catalina Island).

The RMS Queen Mary *is one of the largest passenger ships ever built.*

TOM MYERS PHOTOGRAPHY

walk, for pedestrians only. Only locals get to the beach early, which makes mornings the best time for a bike ride. As is always prudent in L.A., avoid being on the bike trail after dark.

Long Beach is also as good a place as any to begin a more ambitious tour of L.A.'s **Port of Los Angeles** commercial and industrial development, a trek not advisable by bike. San Pedro is L.A.'s cruise ship central as well as departure point for many Catalina ferries and other pleasure craft. Farther west are the placid coastal pleasures of Palos Verdes and vicinity; continue north to explore a few South Bay beach towns. To explore south of Long Beach, follow Second Street in Belmont Shore to Pacific Coast Highway (PCH) and then continue southeast across the San Gabriel River to arrive in Orange County and Seal Beach, Huntington Beach, and Newport Beach along the coast.

RMS *Queen Mary*

If the kids have never been on an ocean liner, a setting right out of old romantic movies, they might enjoy exploring this one. Who knows? If they loved *Titanic* the movie, they might just love this ship. The RMS *Queen Mary,* with its sleek streamline-modern interiors, was first launched in 1936. At 1,019 feet long, this is one of the largest passenger ships ever built. More details—and some insight into luxury travel standards of yesteryear—are revealed in stateroom and other exhibits. The engine room and the bridge offer hands-on perspective on the mechanics of this

massive ship. Also onboard: hotel rooms, restaurants, and shops. The adjacent **Queen Mary Seaport** offers more of Southern California's ubiquitous shopping.

At last report *Queen Mary* admission was $15 adults, $13 seniors (age 55 and older) and active members of the military (with ID), $9 children ages 4–11. Guided one-hour tours cost an additional $7 adults, $4 children. Parking is $8 per day. For more information and hotel and restaurant reservations, call 562/435-3511, or toll-free 800/437-2934 (hotel reservations), or check www.queenmary.com. The *Queen Mary* is open daily 10 A.M.–6 P.M.; last admission is 30 minutes before closing on Saturday, otherwise 90 minutes before closing. The *Queen Mary* is directly across the harbor from the Aquarium of the Pacific at 1126 Queen's Hwy., Pier J. From the end of the Long Beach Freeway (the 710), follow the signs. From downtown, get here via Shoreline Drive and Queensway Bridge.

A new companion for the *Queen* is a retired Soviet submarine once capable of firing low-grade nuclear torpedoes. Commissioned in 1973 by the Soviet government, Podvodnaya Lodka B-427, also known by the code name *Scorpion,* was decommissioned in 1994. Tours of the *Scorpion,* berthed at the bow of the *Queen Mary,* are $10 adults and $9 seniors, military with ID, and children ages 4–11. Hours are 10 A.M.–6 P.M. daily, but last admission is 30–90 minutes before closing (depending on the day). Call 562/435-3511 for current details.

More Long Beach Attractions
The new **Museum of Latin American Art** close to downtown at 628 Alamitos Ave. (the northern extension of Shoreline Dr., south of Seventh St.), 562/437-1689, www.molaa.com, is the only U.S. museum with this exclusive artistic focus. This 1920-vintage 20,000-square-foot building houses the Robert Gumbiner Foundation collection of Latin American art, rotating contemporary exhibits, "La Galeria" gallery and store, and both performance area and research library. The museum is open Tues.–Sat. 11:30 A.M.–7:30 P.M., Sunday noon–6 P.M. Admission is $7 adults, $5 students and seniors, free for children 12 and under. Call for current exhibit information or check the museum website.

Other Long Beach museums include the free **Lifeguard Museum** at the historic Long Beach Marine Stadium, 5255 Appian Way, built for the 1932 Olympics, 562/570-1360, open only 10 A.M.–2 P.M. on the second Saturday of each month. (But call first. Sometimes the lifeguard business gets too busy to indulge even history, especially during summer.) For an introduction to local history, stop by the **Historical Society of Long Beach Gallery and Research Center,** in the Breakers Building, 562/495-1210.

Amateur historians should also explore two small outposts of early Southern California still at home in Long Beach. The seven-acre remnant of **Rancho Los Alamitos,** 6400 E. Bixby Hill Rd., 562/431-3541, offers free tours of the 1800-vintage adobe, later farm buildings, and lovely gardens Wed.–Sun. 1–5 P.M. (last tour starts at 4 P.M.). **Rancho Los Cerritos,** 4600 Virginia Rd., 562/570-1755, offers weekend-only guided tours of this 1844 Monterey-style adobe home and surrounding gardens—once the center of a 27,000-acre sheep ranch—which is also open to the public Wed.–Sun. 1–5 P.M. Admission to both homes is free. Closed on holidays.

Historians of California's future should visit **Little Cambodia** along Anaheim Street, the largest Cambodian settlement outside Phnom Penh. For business, restaurant, and other information, call the **Cambodian Association of America,** 562/426-6002, or the **United Cambodian Community,** 562/433-2490.

Book lovers, don't miss family-run **Acres of Books,** 240 Long Beach Blvd. (at Maple), 562/437-6980, the nation's largest selection of used books, open here since 1934 and reported to be one of writer Ray Bradbury's favorites. Another historic local business is **Bert Grimms Tattoo Studio,** 22 S. Chestnut Pl. (at Ocean), 562/432-9304, where, according to local lore, gangsters Bonnie Parker and Pretty Boy Floyd got their skin ink. Prime-time for shopping is a 15-block stretch of Second Street in Belmont Shore and downtown's Pine Avenue/ Broadway district.

PRACTICAL LONG BEACH

Staying in Long Beach
In the absence of a major downtown convention, and particularly in the off-season, Long Beach-area accommodations can be a relative bargain for families and budget travelers. The best bargain anytime, complete with panoramic ocean views and surrounding sports fields, park, and picnic areas, is the nearby 60-bed HI-AYH **Los Angeles/South Bay Hostel** in Angel's Gate Park in San Pedro at 3601 S. Gaffey St., Bldg. 613, 310/831-8109, www.hostelweb.com, primarily dorm-style accommodations (groups welcome) though private rooms are available. The hostel features on-site kitchen and laundry, library, TV and VCR, and barbecue—and from here it's just a stroll to the beach. Dorm beds are $16 members, $18 nonmembers; private rooms $39 nonmembers, $42 members. Reservations essential in summer.

Other fairly inexpensive accommodations abound in Long Beach along or near Pacific Coast Highway. Here, though, the highway runs through some rough neighborhoods and—if you were expecting oceanfront views—doesn't get close to the coast until it reaches the Orange County line. Be that as it may, best bets include **Motel 6** on Seventh Street near California State University at Long Beach, 562/597-1311 or toll-free 800/466-8356, www.motel6.com, with rates $54 d, and **Super 8** across from the community hospital, 562/597-7701, with rates $66 d and up. Just south of PCH is the **Best Western of Long Beach,** 1725 Long Beach Blvd., 562/599-5555 or toll-free 800/528-1234 (central reservations), www.bestwestern.com, where a plus is the proximity of the Metrorail Blue Line across the street. Rates start at $89 double.

Fairly basic but good choices closer to the beach and just a few blocks from the convention center include the **Inn of Long Beach,** 185 Atlantic Ave., 562/435-3791, innoflongbeach.com, from $79 d, and the nearby **TraveLodge Convention Center,** 80 Atlantic Ave., 562/435-2471 or toll-free 800/578-7878, from $89 d.

Keep in mind that high-end accommodations are sometimes quite reasonable in Long Beach, especially on weekends, during the holiday season, or with AAA, AARP, and other discounts. So inquire about discounts and packages at some of the nicest local hotels, including the **Hyatt Regency Long Beach** at Two World Trade Center (Ocean Ave. and Golden Shore St.), 562/491-1234, with rates $199–299; the **Renaissance Long Beach Hotel,** 111 E. Ocean Blvd. (at Pine), 562/437-5900, with rates $145–165; and the **Westin Long Beach,** 333 E. Ocean Blvd., 562/436-3000, with rates $119–199.

For something definitely different, consider an onboard overnight at the RMS *Queen Mary,* at 1126 Queen's Hwy., Pier J, 562/435-3511 or toll-free 800/437-2934 (reservations) www.queenmary.com, and sleep in a 1936-vintage oceanliner cabin. Special package deals include the Catalina Getaway, Paradise Package, and the Royal Romance Package. Rates are $125–400. For more ship information, see the general travel listing for the *Queen Mary,* above.

Long Beach also offers bed-and-breakfast choices, including the antique-rich **Lord Mayor's Inn Bed & Breakfast,** 435 Cedar Ave. (between Fourth and Fifth Sts.), 562/436-0324, www.lordmayors.com, the onetime home of Long Beach's first mayor, Charles Windham, elected in the early 1900s. Savory cinnamon rolls come with breakfast. Rates are $85–125.

Eating in Long Beach: Downtown
Increasingly stylish dining and shopping star downtown on and near Pine Avenue and along Belmont Shore's Second Street. Popular and good for fresh fish and seafood downtown is the **King's Fish House Pine Avenue,** 100 W. Broadway (at Pine), 562/432-7463, open for lunch and dinner daily, for breakfast on weekends. For classy Northern Italian, the place is grand **L'Opera,** 101 Pine (at First St.), 562/491-0066, open nightly for dinner, weekdays for lunch. Among the many other choices in the

neighborhood: the see-and-be-seen **Alegria Cocina Latina,** 115 Pine (at First), 562/436-3388, where tapas star but gazpacho, sandwiches, salads, and substantial dinners are also on tap. (The deli opens in the morning, too, for pastries and coffee). Live music nightly, and don't miss the flamenco show. For a contemporary culinary escape to the islands of the Caribbean, try **Cha Cha Cha,** 762 Pacific Avenue (near Eighth St.), 562/436-3900, open for lunch and dinner daily.

After dinner downtown, there's entertainment. Among downtown's most popular nightclubs: the **Blue Cafe,** 210 Promenade North (at Broadway), 562/983-7111, famous for its blues acts, billiards, and low ($5–10) cover charge; **Cohiba Club,** 144 Pine (at Broadway), 562/437-7700, for dancing to DJs and live bands; and **Jillian's,** 110 Pine (near Broadway), 562/628-8866, for billiards and dancing in The Vault.

If making the scene isn't your scene, the mellowest coffeehouse around is **The Library,** 3418 E. Broadway (at Redondo Ave.), 562/433-2393, which features plush couches and good paperbacks. Also here: banana-flavored cheesecake and baseball-sized blueberry muffins. And you can always go to the movies, at the large selection of screens downtown provided by AMC's **Pine Square 16,** 562/435-1335, one of Southern California's largest cinema complexes.

Eating in Long Beach:
Near Belmont Shore
A classic Long Beach dining destination is lively **Small Cafe** (formerly Russell's) near Belmont Shore, 5656 E. Second St. (near Westminster), 562/434-0226, one of the southstate's best burger establishments. Some people come strictly for the pies with the mile-high meringues, including banana, chocolate, peanut butter, and sour cream. Another all-American burger destination is **Hof's Hut,** 4828 E. Second St. (at St. Joseph), 562/439-4775, where the Hofburger is the main attraction—not counting the snorkeler's fin dangling from the stuffed shark's mouth. For fancier American-style fare, the place is **Shenandoah Cafe,** 4722 E. Second (at Park), 562/434-3469.

A bit more international is **Provençe Boulangerie,** 191 Park Ave. (at Second St.), 562/433-8281, doing a brisk business in coffee, croissants, baguettes, wonderful breads, soup, and other simple wonders. Best for Italian is genuinely friendly **Christy's Italian Cafe**, 3937 E. Broadway (at Termino Ave.), 562/433-7133. (If you're one of those cigar-sucking trendoids, the **Havana Cigar Club** is right next door.) For fabulous Indian food, the place is **Natraj**, 5262 E. Second St. (near La Verne Ave.), 562/930-0930, where the Mon.–Sat. lunch buffet and the all-you-can-eat Sunday brunch are particularly great deals. But the classic vegetarian hot spot in Belmont Shore is inexpensive **Papa Jon's Natural Market & Cafe**, 5006 E. Second St. (at Argonne Ave.), 562/439-1059, serving a great TLT—tofu, lettuce, and tomato sandwich—as well as broccoli sesame pasta, vegetable shepherd's pie,

spinach lasagne, and veggie and tempeh burgers.

For eats at the beach, try the **Belmont Brewing Company**, 25 39th Pl., near the end of Belmont Pier, 562/433-3891, where good food is served with respectable local brews—including the ever-popular dark Long Beach Crude. Also near the pier, overlooking the beach near the end of Termino (behind Yankee Doodles) is **Ragazzi Ristorante**, 562/438-3773, serving a nice selection of pastas, pizzas, and chicken and fish dishes. For big-time beef eaters, **555 East** at 555 E. Ocean Blvd. (near Atlantic), 562/437-0626, bills itself as an American Steakhouse and is generally considered the best in Long Beach.

CATALINA: 22 MILES ACROSS THE SEA

Thanks to one of those schmaltzy old songs, Santa Catalina Island's original location in the American imagination as "island of romance" was "twenty-six miles across the sea," though it's actually only 22 miles from San Pedro on the mainland. But romantic it was—first famous as the private fiefdom of William Wrigley, Jr., of chewing gum fame, and as onetime spring training camp for his Chicago Cubs. The western pulp writer Zane Grey, whose "pueblo" now serves as a hotel, also loved Catalina. And the roster of movie stars and celebrities who have been here at one time or another, for one reason or another, would practically fill a book. Catalina even has its own movable movie memorabilia—a herd of buffalo, woolly chocolate-colored descendants of beasts originally imported in 1924 for the filming of The Vanishing American.

Yet all is not nostalgic. In its own way, quaint Catalina also walks the cutting edge. To solve its ongoing water supply problems, for example, Catalina started up its own desalination plant to transform seawater into drinking water. Because unrestrained automobile traffic would clearly ruin the town, perhaps even sink the island, few cars are allowed on Catalina. Instead, if not on foot most people get around greater Avalon by golf cart—an appropriate local transportation option. And most of the island is owned, and protected, by private trusts—which means that all but the most innocuous activities, such as eating and

shopping, are strictly regulated. Hiking and biking are allowed only by permit, for example, and camping in the interior is by reservation only.

Present-day Catalina, second largest of the Channel Islands at 48,438 acres, otherwise retains its charms—fresh air and mild climate, rugged open space, a healthy ocean environment—because the island is relatively unpopulated. Avalon, the island's only town, boasts barely 3,000 souls. Southern California's version of a whitewashed Mediterranean hillside village perched above a balmy bay, Avalon is brushed with bright colors and stunning tiles—the most concentrated public and private displays of 1930s' California tile work anywhere. Anchoring Avalon Bay on the north, just beyond the town's tiny bayside commercial district, is the spectacular Moorish Casino, the art-deco masterpiece built by William Wrigley, Jr., to house the first theater specifically designed for movies. Beyond Avalon, the island's other primary visitor destination is remote Two Harbors, snuggled into the isthmus to the northwest.

The official island population may be miniscule but the unofficial head count can be astronomical in summer and on "event" weekends. (Avoid the crazy crowds by coming in spring or in October—on a weekday if at all possible.) If you're a people person, annual events well worth the trip over include the **Silent Film Festival** at the Casino's Avalon Theatre, a benefit for the Catalina

Island Museum Society; the **Fourth of July** gala, including golf cart parade and spectacular fireworks over Avalon Bay; the **Catalina Festival of Art** in late September; the two-weekend **Catalina Jazz Trax Festival** in October; and the glitzy big-band **New Year's Eve Celebration** at the Casino Ballroom.

Crowds or no crowds, most folks manage only a day trip—taking in the ocean wind and waves on the way and then sampling the shops and the island's main "urban" sights before climbing back on the ferry to head home. (For day trips avoid Tuesday and Wednesday, when the cruise ships dock.) One of California's small tragedies is the fact that so few visitors realize that on a longer stay Catalina offers *solitude,* a very rare Southern California commodity, and a wealth of other worthwhile pursuits.

SEEING AND DOING CATALINA

Avalon

Avalon is fringed with palms, olive trees, and tourists. Most of the latter spend most of their time clustered along bayside Crescent Avenue, the city's main commercial strip. While you're still figuring out where else to go, the moment you step off the ferry start your impromptu Avalon "tile tour." The city's eccentric beachfront **plaza** is one huge outdoor installation of decorated geometric tiles. All along the waterfront, watch for Catalina's unique building façades, fountains, and decorative planters. Don't miss **El Encanto Market Place** and, along the beach, the **Serpentine Wall.** If a brisk but brief walk fits the agenda, head uphill to the recently

restored **Wrigley Memorial.** The granddaddy of all tile destinations, though, is on the other end of town—Wrigley's **Casino** at the north end of the bay. Included in the Casino's small museum collection are dishware, pottery, and inlaid tables. Along with other interior and exterior tile work, the Casino's patio is paved with classic Catalina tiles.

Catalina Island's grand Casino was originally William J. Wrigley, Jr.'s Casino, a circular Moorish palace built for dancing (he forbade drinking and gambling) and sedately presiding over the bay since 1929. Wrigley was a stickler for detail. So perfect were the acoustics of the movie theater here—the first designed specifically for "talking pictures"—that in 1931 engineers for New York's Radio City Music Hall came to Catalina for a lesson. But the theater's glories don't stop with the sound. The art-deco murals and spectacular tile work are both by John Gabriel Beckman, onetime art director for Columbia Studios, who also painted Grauman's Chinese Theater in Hollywood. Completely refurbished in 1987, the Casino harbors other attractions—including its original **Page pipe organ,** small **art gallery,** the **Catalina Island Museum** (open daily, small donation), and a grand second-floor **ballroom.** And its view of the bay. Sadly, for impromptu types, the only way to see the entire Casino is on a guided walking tour (see below). Otherwise you can visit the museum and art gallery separately, the ballroom only during special events. For information on the weekly movie—usually well worth it, and one of the few ways to appreciate the fabulous interior of the Casino's **Avalon Theatre**—call 310/510-0179.

BOB RACE

Chewing gum tycoon William Wrigley, Jr. built the art deco Casino to house the first theater specifically designed for movies.

Santa Catalina Harbor

TOM MYERS PHOTOGRAPHY

If time permits, and if Avalon proper loses its appeal, head for the ocean—or the island's interior. Swimming, sunbathing, snorkeling, skin diving, sportfishing, kayaking, golfing, parasailing, sailing, bicycling, hiking, and camping are a few possible diversions. Various tours, by land or by sea, are also quite worthwhile. For suggestions on what else to do, see Catalina Hiking and Biking and Catalina Tours and Diversions, below.

Touring Two Harbors and the Interior
Welcome to The Other Catalina—the one where you really can get away from it all, especially in the winter. The most protected of Two Harbors' "two" is **Catalina Harbor,** on the island's ocean side; **Isthmus Cove,** the other, faces into the channel on Catalina's north side. Once called Union Harbor, this unassuming half-mile-wide isthmus bore witness to much of Catalina's most colorful history, starting with the mysterious temple and rites of the native Gabrieleño Indians reported by the 1602 Vizcaíno expedition. From the island's own fur trader, smuggler, bootlegger, and gold-rush days through late 19th-century tourism, Two Harbors has maintained both its solitude and serenity, a dirt-road refuge remaining the getaway "mooring" of choice for both boaters and campers—and filmmakers. Movies filmed in and around Two Harbors include *Mutiny on the Bounty, Treasure Island, Sea Hawk, The Ten Commandments, The King of Kings, McHale's Navy,* and *MacArthur.*

The sweeping seascape is the main attraction at Two Harbors, about six miles from Catalina's western tip, whether one enjoys it on the beach, on foot, or onboard a kayak. By way of general introduction, take the short hike from the village at Isthmus Cove—where the ferries and shuttles dock—across the isthmus to Catalina Harbor. (Beware of buffalo.) In addition, from Two Harbors hikers can set out on Catalina's most westerly trails. West island campsites, camping tepees, tent cabins, rustic cabins (available mid-October to mid-April only), boat-accessible yurts, the Banning House bed-and-breakfast, kayak and "safari" tours, and scuba and snorkeling trips are all available through a single concessionaire: Two Harbors, 310/510-2800. Also here is the **Catalina Marine Science Center** operated at Big Fisherman's Cove (near Isthmus Cove) by the University of Southern California's Institute for Marine and Coastal Studies, available for group tours by reservation.

Catalina Hiking and Biking
It's possible to tour Catalina Island's hilly backcountry terrain by bus, but, if at all possible, hiking or biking is the better way to go. The sights, sounds, and scents offered by Catalina's unique sea-bound ecosystem, including unusual plant and animal life and some astonishing 360-degree vistas, are so much more savory when discovered in solitude. You can combine almost two dozen trails—some long, some short, some scenic, some less so—to turn an island trip into

a trek. Make it an overnight or multiday trip by camping at Little Harbor Campground and/or Two Harbors Cove Campground—and more remote campsites beyond. But unless you're willing to literally carry the kids, a trans-island trek may be too challenging for youngsters.

The most ambitious island bike ride starts from Avalon and traverses the entire island's hilly terrain, by road, to Two Harbors. You can bring your own bicycles across from the mainland, or by arrangement with Catalina's Express, or rent bikes on the island. Again, the trek is typically too tough for the kiddos; bike rides in and around Avalon are a fun family alternative.

Hiking or biking into Catalina's interior is by permit only; bike permits ($50 per person or $75 per family per year) are required for treks beyond Avalon and vicinity. To obtain permits and other current information, call the **Santa Catalina Island Conservancy** at 310/510-2595.

Guided hikes and other outdoor adventures are available through **Catalina Fitness Company**, 310/510-9255, and other local concerns.

Catalina Tours and Diversions

If hiking and biking seem too *vigorous* and you're without golf cart, consider taking one of Catalina's popular guided tours. Discovery Tours, toll-free 800/626-1496, operated by the island's Santa Catalina Island (SCI) Company, dominates the market—and has since 1894. For a trip to the isthmus for a picnic dinner, take the **Sundown Isthmus Tour,** offered only in the warmer months. Also exciting, also seasonal, are the **Flying Fish** and **Seal Rocks** tours onboard the *Blanche W.* Among the newest tours Discovery offers is the **Undersea Tour.** If you're not a scuba diver or snorkeler, the best way to see the sea— and under the sea—surrounding Catalina Island is from onboard a semisubmersible boat. Both the *Starlight* and *Emerald* cruise the swaying fronds of the offshore kelp forest. Passengers get up close and personal with the fish, crustaceans, and other sea creatures through the large underwater windows. As on glass-bottom-boat tours, on a night cruise you may also see a live ocean light show—the phenomenon of phosphorescence. Or go down all the way (to a depth of about 40 feet) in the two-person **Seamobile Submersible** yellow submarine, toll-free (877) 252-6262, a trip offered June through October.

Discovery Tours for landlubbers, toll-free 800/626-1496, include the very worthwhile **Casino Walking Tour,** which pokes into the Casino Ballroom, the Avalon Theatre, and almost every other cranny of William Wrigley, Jr.'s masterpiece. To see the rest of Avalon without walking up and down all those hills, sign on for the **Avalon Scenic Tour** or the **Avalon Scenic & Botanical Garden Tour.** The **Skyline Drive** tour offers an inland "overview," between Avalon and the Catalina Nature Center at the airport. The 28-mile, half-day **Inland Motor Tour** includes a refreshment stop at William Wrigley, Jr.'s **El Rancho Escondido** Arabian horse ranch. Tour prices start at $9 and range to $35 per person, at last report, with lower rates for children and seniors. "Combo" tours can save a few dollars. For more information or reservations, contact the SCI Company's **Discovery Tours,** 310/510-8687 or toll-free 800/626-1496 (reservations); once on the island, stop by the Discovery Tours center across from the Green Pleasure Pier. For something more adventurous on land, the Santa Catalina Island Conservancy offers **Jeep Eco-Tours,** 310/510-2595.

Other individuals and groups also offer tours and activity-oriented attractions—including ocean rafting, scuba and "shark" diving, sportfishing, and golfing and miniature golfing. For a current list of suggestions, contact the visitor bureau (see below) or, once arrived, poke around the Green Pleasure Pier in Avalon and elsewhere along the waterfront. Or head for Two Harbors (see above), which offers its own diversions.

PRACTICAL CATALINA

Staying on Catalina: Camping

If you'll be here longer than a day, you'll need a place to stay. The most inexpensive option is camping. Avalon's only campground is **Hermit Gulch** just over a mile outside town, 310/510-8368, which features flush toilets and lighted restrooms, coin showers, and both tent cabins and tepees in addition to standard campsites. The most popular place "on the other side" is the large **Two Harbors Campground** at the isthmus, with flush toilets and cold showers. Teepee camping—definitely something different—is also available at Two Harbors, as are rustic cabins (off-season only) and fairly uptown "yurts" at Goat Harbor. Other "out there" developed campgrounds include palm-fringed and protected **Little Harbors Campground,** the only option along the island's south (windward) side; **Black Jack** in the pines atop Mount Black Jack, the only inland choice; and on-the-beach **Parson's Landing** north of Two Harbors. Call 310/510-8368 for reservations at any of these campgrounds. Reservations for various Catalina Island Conservancy primitive boat-in "cove" campsites—including **Starlight Beach** and **Frog Rock Cove,** on the island's leeward side—are available through Two Harbors, 310/510-2800. **Descanso Beach Ocean Sports,** 310/510-1226, offers camping trips—by kayak—to remote island locales.

Staying on Catalina: Hotels and Inns

With the exception of campgrounds, most accommodation options are in Avalon. The local visitor bureau (see below) is quite helpful in arranging hotels and bed-and-breakfast inn reservations—mandatory during the island's summer season—or, request current visitor information well in advance of your trip and go it on your own. (Prices can be "fluid," especially at peak visitor times, so get a firm commitment when you reserve. Two- or three-night minimum stays on weekends, especially in summer, are the rule.) For bargain rates, come in the off-season—the best time to come anyway, in many respects—which generally runs from mid-October through mid-April. Ask about other specials and packages. The visitor bureau can also recommend local home and condominium rental agencies.

"Uptown" in Two Harbors is the **Banning House Lodge,** 310/510-2800, or toll-free 800/785-8425, a most comfortable base camp for backcountry Catalina exploration. This comfortably rustic turn-of-the-20th-century hunting lodge, now an 11-room bed and breakfast overlooking both harbors, has hosted Hollywood celebrities on location and, during World War II, U.S. Coast guard officers. Each room has a view and a historic theme. Warm yourself by the living room fireplace in the evenings, in the company of fellow explorers and the vacant stares of animal-head trophies. Room rates start at $119.

Most elegant in Avalon is the **The Inn on Mt. Ada,** overlooking Avalon Bay from Wrigley Road, 310/510-2030 or toll-free 800/608-7669; www .catalina.com/mtada. One of California's most elegant bed-and-breakfast inns, this onetime summer estate of chewing gum magnate William Wrigley, Jr. and family is a graceful Georgian colonial mansion built in 1921. Now included on the National Register of Historic Places, this six-room bed-and-breakfast still boasts many of its original furnishings and all the accoutrements of upper-class ease. Yet the friendliness of its new identity makes it Southern California's getaway of choice for celebrating special events. (For weddings, anniversary celebrations, and other occasions, you can rent the entire inn.) A stay here is much less expensive—and the island itself is much less crowded—on winter weekdays. High-season rates start at $330 (two-night minimum on weekends). All meals included.

Intriguing choices in town, for different reasons, include the pretty pink **Hotel St. Lauren** on Beacon Street, 310/510-2299 or toll-free 800/ 645-2496, www.stlauren.com, a "modern Victorian" with ample motel-style amenities, rooftop patio, and high-season rates of $142–310, and the actually historic **Zane Grey Pueblo Hotel** at 199 Chimes Tower Rd., 310/510-0966 or toll-free 800/378-3256. Zane Grey, American master of the romantic cowboy adventure novel, started his romance with Catalina Island in the 1920s. The island's healthy herd of bison is one Zane Grey legacy—descendants of the 14 left behind after the 1924 filming of *The Vanishing American.* Avalon's Zane Grey Pueblo is another. A rambling adobe on a hill overlooking Avalon, Grey's former home is now a bed-and-breakfast-style hotel with modern plumbing and private baths but few other concessions to modern times. The Pueblo features rooms named after Zane Grey novels, striking 1920s-style Southwestern decor, even an arrowhead-shaped swimming pool. Rates are a relative bargain at $135–165.

Across from the beach and fairly affordable is the SCI Company's 1950s-style **Pavilion Lodge,** toll-free 800/322-3434, with rates from $109. Popular high-end hotels (motels without cars or parking) along bustling Crescent Avenue that sometimes offer affordable rooms in the off-season or midweek include the romantic Mediterranean-style **Hotel Villa Portofino**, 310/510-0555 or toll-free 800/346-2326, with rates $145–295, and the **Hotel Metropole**, 310/510-1884 or toll-free 800/541-8528, with high-season rates $335–395. Less expensive inland is the Best Western **Catalina Canyon Resort** on Country Club Drive, 310/510-0325 or toll-free 800/253-9361 (shuttle service provided to and from town). High-season rates are $119–350.

For cheaper rates—and a better workout—plan to climb Avalon's hills and/or stay in older small hotels. The remodeled, diver-friendly **Catalina Beach House**, 310/510-1078 or toll-free 800/974-6835, offers high-season weekend rates as low as $95, with discounts during the week and in the off-season. Charming and quaint, also usually best bets for low weekday rates, are the old-Catalina-style housekeeping cottages at **La Paloma**, 310/510-1505 or toll-free 800/310-1505. High-season rates are $89 and up.

Eating in Catalina

When you're hungry, Catalina is happy to feed you. Fast fooderies and restaurants cluster along Avalon's waterfront. For pizza and Italian-style sandwiches in an eclectic college-kid atmosphere, the place is **Antonio's Pizzeria** at 230 Crescent Ave. (at Metropole), 310/510-0008. **Cafe Prego** at 603 Crescent (near Clarissa), 310/510-1218, is friendly and comfortable, a neighborhood bistro facing the bay along Avalon's main drag—just about perfect for escaping the madding crowds at dinner (in summer, lunch too). You won't go wrong with the seafood pastas or the lasagna, but you can also "go American" and get a good steak. Or head for all-American **Rick's Cafe** at 417 Crescent (at the green pier), 310/510-0333. Catalina's classic local breakfast café, also open for lunch, is the

Runway Cafe way out there at the airport at 1 Buffalo Springs Rd., 310/510-2196.

The time-honored choice for fresh fish at lunch or dinner is **Armstrong's Fish Market and Seafood Restaurant** at 306 Crescent Ave., 310/510-0113. For a romantic Italian dinner, the place is **Villa Portofino** at 111 Crescent, 310/510-0508; for continental, **The Channel House** at the Metropole Marketplace, 310/510-1617.

Getting Here, Getting Oriented

For an unforgettable trip over to Catalina, take the helicopter—a 15-minute ride over via **Island Express**, 310/510-2525. Though Catalina boasts a small airport and yacht harbors, most people get here via commercial ferry. **Catalina Express** ferries, 310/519-1212 or toll-free 800/360-1212, depart from San Pedro Harbor and Long Beach. From June into September, the Express also offers a 45-minute coastal shuttle between Avalon and Two Harbors. Catalina Cruises' **Catalina Jet** passenger ships, toll-free 800/228-2546, make daily departures from Long Beach year-round. Another possibility by sea is **Catalina Passenger Service**, 949/673-5245, which sets sail from Newport Beach at the Balboa Pavilion.

For current details on transportation options, tours, special events, accommodations options and packages, and other practical information, contact: **Catalina Island Chamber of Commerce and Visitors Bureau**, P.O. Box 217, Avalon, CA 90704, 310/510-1520; www.catalina .com.

For in-depth information, the best comprehensive guidebook to Santa Catalina Island and environs is *Guide to Catalina and California's Channel Islands* by Chicki Mallan, widely available on the island, around departure points on the mainland, and in California bookstores.

GREATER
SOUTHERN
CALIFORNIA

COURTESY AISLINN RACE

ORANGE COUNTY
THE DIFFERENCE BETWEEN L.A.
AND ORANGE COUNTY

Sun-kissed Southern California rivals, Orange County and Los Angeles argue endlessly about whose neighborhood is most blessed—a full-blown feud evolved into advanced social sport, sometimes nasty, sometimes hilarious.

The differences between the two are difficult to grasp for those just passing through, though. Both feature sunny neighborhoods strung together by shopping centers and stressful freeways. Both have sped through the Southern California boom-bust cycles of agriculture, oil, land development, and aerospace. Both steal their water from elsewhere. Both have sandy beaches, bad neighborhoods, good neighborhoods, all of it high-priced. Both embrace an idealized self-image, disregarding uglier truths. And both believe the other is missing the best of all possible worlds.

Some say the spat started in the late 1800s, when Los Angeles County was almost as large as Ohio. Tired of taxation without representation, and bitter about their second-class status, residents of the Santa Ana Valley—modern-day Orange County—staged their first anti-tax rebellion by seceding from L.A. Though often amicable, the post-breakup bickering continues to this day.

Urbane Angelenos point out that orange trees in Orange County are about as abundant as the seals at Seal Beach. (There are no seals at Seal Beach.) That high culture in Orange County is best represented by the John Wayne statue at the airport. That the entire county, in fact, is more G-rated than a Disney cartoon. That only Orange County could produce the likes of ex-President Richard Nixon, not to mention local politicians prone to stating publicly that men who support abortion rights are "women trapped in men's bodies . . . who are looking for an easy lay" as Rep. Robert K. "B-1 Bob" Dornan of Garden Grove once said. (Dornan since lost his congressional seat to Loretta Sanchez, a subject that still rankles in some circles.) That at its best Orange County exhibits a standard-brand and superficial beauty, at its worst, vapid nouveau-riche snobbery. That the FBI has identified

Orange County as the capital of white-collar crime, and that when Orange County filed for bankruptcy in 1994, it entered the record books with the biggest municipal bankruptcy in U.S. history. That, all things considered, Orange County is little more than an emergency gasoline stop on the road to San Diego.

Indignant Orange County residents counter that people from Los Angeles are self-absorbed cultural elitists who live only to consume the latest fads in food, clothing, and thought. Behind all that anti-Orange posturing, they say, Angelenos are just jealous—because Orange County, not L.A., now represents the quintessential Southern California lifestyle. Orange County has no smog. People in Orange County can still drop the tops on their convertibles and surf the freeways fast enough to get speeding tickets. They can go to the beach without getting caught in gang crossfire. And they aren't social

hypocrites. People in Orange County, where beach-bleached blondes are the societal ideal, don't congratulate themselves on multiculturalism in the light of day and then retreat at night, in the L.A. style, to economically and ethnically segregated neighborhoods.

But according to T. Jefferson Parker in his entertaining essay "Behind the Orange Curtain," only one fundamental difference separates Los Angeles citizens from those who inhabit the Big Orange:

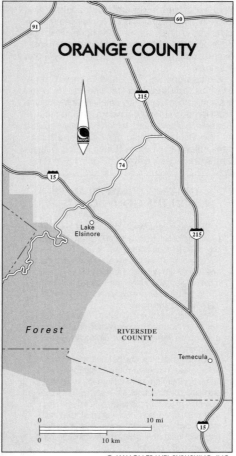

© AVALON TRAVEL PUBLISHING, INC.

L.A. people all want to be someone else. Look at them, and, as Jim Harrison has written, "see the folly whirling in their eyes." The waiters all want to be novelists; the novelists all want to be screenwriters; the screenwriters all want to direct; the directors all want to produce; the producers all want to keep the other guys relegated to net participation and guild minimums.

Now take Orange Countians. We know who we are. The blandly handsome, heavily mortgaged, marathon-running, aerospace department manager, driving to work in his Taurus, does not entertain dreams of movie making. He has weapons to build, a country to defend, a family to provide for. Or take the blond mall rat, age 16, eyes aflame with consumer fever. She doesn't secretly wish to be Michelle Pfeiffer. She actually has never heard of Michelle Pfeiffer. The loose-jawed surfer dude in Huntington Beach entertains not a single thought besides the next south swell, south being to his left, he's pretty sure, if he's facing the gnardical tubes of the Pacific, which he usually is.

People in L.A., Parker explains, "want to be someone else because they're miserable; people in Orange County are content to be who they are because they're happy. It's clear. People in L.A. can't face reality. We can."

Reality is complicated, of course. Orange County is whiter and wealthier than Los Angeles, still, but in 1999, for the first time in 15 years, less than half of registered Orange County voters were Republicans. Besides, L.A. voters also sent Richard Nixon and Ronald Reagan to the White House. Orange County voters are more likely than Angelenos to oppose offshore oil-drilling and to support environmental action, but these days both regions are equally lathered over the issue of illegal immigration. And, all denial aside, Orange County does have smog, as well as nightmarish freeway congestion. But it also has culture with a capital "C," symbolized by the spectacular Performing Arts Center adjacent (you guessed it) to its most famous shopping mall.

Born into endless summer, freed from community by freeways, and taught to believe that here, life can be all things to all people, Orange County and Los Angeles are actually very much alike. But Los Angeles is older, more experienced. Like a village elder trying to atone for the folly of youth, the City of Angels seems more willing to acknowledge the shadow side of the sunny Southern California dream and to struggle to make peace with it.

GETTING ORIENTED TO THE BIG ORANGE

Take a good look at Orange County. According to a 1976 British Broadcasting Corporation (BBC) documentary, Orange County represents "the culmination of the American dream." Those who claim to know such things contend that Orange County is also a picture postcard of America's future, an in-progress postsuburban ode to progress featuring four-star hotels, high-tech and *Fortune* 500 companies, and wave after wave of master-planned communities. Most famous in this latter category is Orange County's overnight city of Irvine (incorporated in 1971, with the slogan "Another Day in Paradise") and its University of California at Irvine campus—both developed on former agricultural holdings by the Irvine Company, the county's largest landowner.

The main feature of this futuristic postcard, though, is the general absence of "downtown," replaced in Orange County's newly developed nether regions by minimalls and, more centrally, a shopping mall cum cultural center—the one-time lima bean field known as South Coast Plaza, among the state's top tourist draws.

Orange trees are rare in Orange County these days. Not so surf and surfers, yachts and yachters, sunny white-sand beaches, and shopping elevated to the status of art. For these attractions head to the coastal cities, which generally offer arts, entertainment, nightlife, better restaurants, and most hotels.

Less well advertised is the fact that Orange County, unlike other vast swaths of suburbanized Southern California, still offers outdoor adventure, including some sublime hikes. Unrelenting development makes the opportunity increasingly rare along the coast—with the reliable exceptions of Crystal Cove State Park and vicinity, and the Upper Newport Bay or "Back Bay"—and slightly less difficult elsewhere.

The Los Angeles-style east-west social divide also applies in Orange County, with citizens here also separated north and south. Ethnic and lower-income neighborhoods are concentrated in older inland cities, largely in the north, while new development—destined for the more affluent—is spreading ever southward, especially along the coast.

Getting oriented to inland Orange County cities makes it easier for first-time visitors to find the amusement parks (invariably near freeways). Most famous among the world's theme parks is Anaheim's Disneyland, which recently debuted its new Disney's California Adventure theme park, adjacent. In nearby Buena Park is Disneyland's predecessor, Knott's Berry Farm (origi-

GETTING COMFORTABLE ON THE GOLD COAST

In the grand century-old tradition of Southern California boosterism, coastal Orange County is promoted as "The Gold Coast," even "The American Riviera." The implication? Affluence, exclusivity, and an excess of excess. Fortunately, most of Orange County hasn't paid much attention to the hype, so people of modest means can still have a grand time.

Megamoney or no, for a less frenetic experience avoid the warm-weather crowds, bad enough on weekends but typically worse in summer.

Weatherwise, expect mild Mediterranean temperatures and sun year-round. Especially in early summer, morning and evening fog is common along the coast, so pack a sweater or light jacket. In winter, at least occasionally you'll need a jacket or coat. Even more occasionally it rains in Orange County—an event so unusual, however, that most local drivers become disconcerted and distracted. Be careful.

nal home of the boysenberry), and a multitude of lesser-known family entertainments.

Inland Orange County can also claim television evangelist and "possibility thinking" enthusiast Reverend Robert Schuller, who started the world's first drive-in ministry, a tradition still honored at the multi-million-dollar Crystal Cathedral in Garden Grove.

Former U.S. President Richard Milhous Nixon was born (and buried) in the northeastern Orange County town of Yorba Linda, site of the Richard Nixon Library and Birthplace.

And where else but in Orange County would the very airport be named after that mythic icon of God-fearing gunfighter capitalism, John Wayne?

The Orange County Appeal

Orange County's 42-mile coastline arches to the southeast like a sliver of moon, from the San Gabriel River and Seal Beach in the north to San Clemente and San Diego County in the south. Seal Beach suns itself on the ocean edge of what once were vast coastal wetlands, spongy salt-grass marshes that provided prime bird habitat. Then came the discovery of oil; the region's oil and housing industries devised new and better land uses. Small oil derricks still dot the landscape, as they have for some time. The major 1920s community celebration in Huntington Beach just to the south, for example, was the Black Gold Days Festival, held over Labor Day weekend. In these times, though, Huntington Beach worships the ocean—specifically, spectacular surf, the draw for international surf competitions and associated tourist trade.

Just south of the Santa Ana River begins Newport Beach, premier yachting port for Southern California since the 1920s. Not so staid these days, now the symbolic center of Orange County's high-rolling, high-living lifestyle, the Newport Beach area embraces an upscale collection of bayside communities including Balboa Island, Lido Isle, and Corona del Mar. The next major city down coast is Laguna Beach, a low-key artists' enclave in the early 1900s but renowned today for its high-rent real estate and highly unusual ode to the arts, the Pageant of the Masters. The coast saunters south past Laguna Niguel, one of Orange County's newest cities, then Dana Point, the small yacht-harbor community named for Richard Henry Dana, Jr., author of *Two Years before he Mast.* Taking leave of Harvard University in the 1830s, in hopes that the sea air might improve his health, Dana and shipmates came ashore here strictly for commerce—to load tanned cattle hides from the nearby mission at San Juan Capistrano. Famous for the expectation that swallows will return (as the song goes) every year on March 19th, the mission is a worthwhile destination any day of the year.

Last stop along the Orange County coast is San Clemente, where the onetime Western White House compound of ex-President Richard M. Nixon is visible from the state beach. For the details of Nixon's astonishing journey from Orange County homeboy to national and international leader, head for northeastern Orange County and the town of Yorba Linda, site of the Richard Nixon Library and Birthplace.

Also inland, in increasingly artsy downtown Santa Ana, is one of Orange County's most surprising and appealing attractions—the Bowers Museum of Cultural Art.

PRACTICAL ORANGE COUNTY

Most cities in Orange County have visitor bureaus and/or chambers of commerce, many of these listed by locale below. Because Anaheim's Disneyland has been the main tourist attraction for decades, it's no accident that the best overall source for travel information is the **Anaheim/ Orange County Visitor and Convention Bureau,** based at the Anaheim Convention Center, 800 W. Katella Ave., 714/765-8888. To request publications, call toll-free 888/598-3200. Call the **Visitor Information Hot Line,** 714/765-8888, ext. 9888, for timely recorded information on attractions, entertainment, and upcoming events. For fax-on-demand information, which requires a touch-tone phone, call the InfoFax number at toll-free 888/440-4405. For information via the Internet, the visitor bureau's address is www.anaheimoc.org. The visitor bureau also sponsors various promotions, these sometimes including special discounts that come in handy (for example, a recent "Family Values" coupon book).

The newspaper of record is the *Orange*

County Register, steadily challenged by the highly competitive *Los Angeles Times,* which prints a special Orange County edition. The local *Daily Pilot,* now owned by the *Times,* is included with the *Times*'s home delivery.

Biggest and hippest of the alternative newspapers regionally has long been the *L.A. Weekly,* available at hip places countywide. In late 1995 the *Weekly* launched its *O.C. Weekly,* surely a sign that Orange County's arts, entertainment, and alternative political scene has come into its own. Other interesting free magazines and newspapers include *Entertainment Today,* and *The Sun* (the latter distributed in Seal Beach and Huntington Beach). The slick-paper lifestyle magazine, written more for residents than people just passing through, is *Orange Coast.*

Transportation by Air

Though LAX is Southern California's main international airport, the smaller regionals—John Wayne, Long Beach, Burbank, and Ontario—generally offer competitive fares and fewer hassles. Depending on where you're headed, regional flights may also let you avoid the freeway trip through L.A.—nightmarish during commute hours.

Inside Orange County's spiffy expanded and remodeled **John Wayne/Orange County Airport,** 949/252-5200, www.ocair.com, John Wayne himself is there to greet you. (You can't miss him.) Along with various commuter services, airlines serving John Wayne include **Alaska, America West, American, Continental, Delta, Northwest, TWA,** and **United.** And it was a big, big deal in 1994 when no-frills **Southwest** added its name to the list.

The John Wayne/Orange County Airport is centrally located, technically in Santa Ana but also practically in Costa Mesa, Irvine, and Newport Beach. Easiest freeway access is from I-405. Also feasible is the Costa Mesa Freeway (Hwy. 55), which connects to I-5, the latter often

EVENTFUL ORANGE COUNTY

Among Orange County's more famous events is the astonishing **Pageant of the Masters** scheduled during July and August in Laguna Beach, with life imitating art imitating life in the form of *tableaux vivants,* or living pictures. The main annual events up the coast in Huntington Beach include the **Gotcha Pro of Surfing,** (formerly known as the OP Pro and the Bluetorch Pro) and the **U.S. Open of Surfing,** the most well known among the multitude of local surfing competitions, both held in July. The **Orange County Fair,** held at the fairgrounds in Costa Mesa, also comes in July.

But there's always something worth doing. Come at other times throughout the year to appreciate surprising aspects of local culture and community.

Whale-watching is a major draw in winter, particularly during January and February, with excursion boats departing from Newport Beach, Dana Point, and other coastal locales. Dana Point's popular **Festival of the Whales,** complete with film festival, street fair, and concert series, is held over several consecutive weekends from mid-February into early March. Unique in February is the **TET Festival** in Westminster's Little Saigon, celebrating the Vietnamese New Year.

According to local legend the swallows return to Mission San Juan Capistrano every year on March 19—thus the annual **Festival de los Golondrinas** or The Swallows Festival in San Juan Capistrano, with **Swallows Day** now typically scheduled for the weekend closest to that mythic date. In late March and early April comes Mission San Juan Capistrano's **Mud Slinging Festival,** during which "children of all ages" (including politicians, appropriately enough) personally participate in renewing the adobe mud façades of the mission's historic buildings.

In April comes the **Spring Garden Tour** in Laguna Beach as well as the annual **Green Scene Garden Show** in Fullerton, and, at the local Sawdust Festival grounds, Laguna's annual **Art Walk.** Another big deal in April is the countywide **Imagination Celebration** for children, teenagers, and families.

Come in early May for the **Orange County Art & Jazz Festival** in Anaheim. Garden Grove's historic **Strawberry Festival** in late May celebrates the bygone days of gardens and groves, when the community was known as the strawberry capital of America. Also scheduled in May: the downtown **Anaheim Children's Festival** and, in Costa Mesa, the annual **Highland Gathering and Festival** or Scottish Festival, celebrating Scottish culture.

a horrendous transition. If traveling Newport Bay area streets, another possibility is MacArthur Boulevard (Hwy. 73) from the coast, which delivers you right to the terminals.

Most car rental agencies have outposts at John Wayne. The cheapest but not most convenient means to and from the airport is public transit, **Orange County Transportation Authority (OCTA)** buses, 714/636-RIDE (636-7433), ext. 10 for route and fare information. If you go this route be sure to leave yourself *plenty* of time. Upmarket hotels (sometimes others) offer free airport shuttles. Next-best bet: a commercial shuttle service such as **SuperShuttle,** toll-free 800/258-3826, www.supershuttle.com, which offers 24-hour door-to-door service.

Transportation by Train
The main Orange County stop for **Amtrak** is in the south, the striking **San Juan Capistrano Depot** in San Juan Capistrano, just west of Camino Capistrano at 26701 Vertugo St., open limited hours. Local OCTA buses (see Transportation by Bus, below) connect to Laguna Beach and San Clemente. Amtrak also stops at the pier in San Clemente—where you can catch Bus 91 south to the last stop, then take Bus 1 north along the coast. Amtrak also stops in Anaheim (Edison International Field), Santa Ana, Fullerton, and Irvine. Call Amtrak toll-free at 800/872-7245 for route, fare, and reservation information, or check www.amtrak.com.

The first Orange County link in the periwinkle-and-white **Metrolink** Southern California mass transit system arrived at Fullerton, where the commuter trains made their debuts in March of 1994. The trains run on weekdays only; for current fare and schedule information, call 714/808-5465 or toll-free 800/371-5465, or check www.metrolinktrains.com.

Transportation by Bus
Cars are king in Orange County, but you can get here and get around reasonably well by bus.

Come in early June for the annual **Orange County Herb Faire,** held at the Fullerton Arboretum. Also on tap in early June is the popular **Temecula Balloon and Wine Festival** nearby, in Riverside County's Temecula Valley. In early June, come to Anaheim's Arrowhead Pond for the annual **Taste of Anaheim,** a daylong indulgence in fine food, wine, and live entertainment. In late June comes **A Taste of Orange County,** at last report held at the Marine Corps Air Station in El Toro, a three-day sampling of local cuisine, wine, and music—blues, reggae, jazz, and country-western.

The high season for Orange County arts arrives in Laguna Beach in late June and early July—the beginning of the summer's continuing events in Laguna Canyon, including the juried **Art-A-Fair** show, the alternative arts **Sawdust Festival,** and the more traditional **Festival of Arts,** which includes the annual Pageant of the Masters performances. Come on Independence Day for the annual **Old Glory Boat Parade** in Newport Beach—or head for Huntington Beach and its huge annual **Independence Day Celebration**—a community parade almost 100 years old, the largest parade of its kind west of the Mississippi—as well as the annual **Surf City Festival** celebration of fine food and art.

Autumn activities include the **Orange International Street Fair** in the city of Orange, the annual

Sand Castle and Sand Sculpture Contest at Corona Del Mar State Beach, and **Taste of Newport** in Newport Beach—all scheduled in September. The big event in October is the ghoulish, ghostly, and frightfully fun **Halloween Haunt** at Knott's Berry Farm—not recommended for children, who would probably prefer much less spooky **Camp Spooky.** Another Halloween season pleasure is the **Pirate Festival** at Mission San Juan Capistrano, a reenactment of the 1818 raid on the mission by Hippolite Bouchard.

The holiday season officially begins in November, with **A Christmas Fantasy Parade** at Disneyland, the **Knott's Berry Farm Christmas Crafts Village,** and other crafts fairs. Traditional favorites in December include the **Christmas Boat Parade** in Newport Harbor, the Huntington Harbor **Cruise of Lights,** and **Roger's Gardens Christmas Fantasy,** a nursery-wide holiday extravaganza that actually begins in October. Also an Orange County tradition is the South Coast Repertory's **La Posada Magica,** a candlelit procession depicting Joseph and Mary's search for shelter.

For more information about these and other events, contact the **Anaheim/Orange County Visitor and Convention Bureau,** 718/765-8888, www.anaheimoc.org, as well as local visitor bureaus.

The **Santa Ana Greyhound Station** is in the transit center just off the Santa Ana Freeway (I-5), 1000 E. Santa Ana Blvd. at Santiago, 714/ 999-1256 or toll-free 800/231-2222; www.greyhound.com. In Santa Ana call 714/542-2215; in Anaheim, 714/999-1256. From Santa Ana, buses connect with L.A., Riverside, and San Diego as well as Santa Barbara, San Luis Obispo, and San Francisco. Greyhound can also get you to and from the coast, with very limited service to Laguna Beach and Huntington Beach. Local public transit expands bus travel options.

Orange County Transportation Authority (OCTA) buses, 714/636-7433 or www.octa.net for current schedule and fares, serve the entire county, albeit on a fairly limited basis. Daily start and end times vary by route, but on weekdays buses are available after 5 or 6 A.M. and run until 7 or 8 P.M. Weekend service starts later and ends earlier. If you're relying on buses, be sure to check current hours.

Transportation by Car
Two freeways—I-405, known as "the 405" or the San Diego Freeway in local vernacular, and I-5, known hereabouts as the Santa Ana Freeway—are Orange County's major north-south thoroughfares. Judicious use of other intersecting freeways will get you almost anywhere. Most Orange County freeways are now undergoing major reconstruction, however, to keep pace with general growth and traffic increases, so allow extra time in key locales (especially during commute hours).

Construction continues at I-5 and Highway 55, the Costa Mesa Freeway; the 55 runs directly into downtown Newport Beach. If coming via the 405, take Highway 73, the Corona del Mar Freeway, *then* the 55. For more road construction headaches, head north to the junction of Highway 55 and Highway 91. The 55 connects Santa Ana, Tustin, and Orange with Highway 91, the Riverside Freeway, which in Orange County runs west-east from La Palma through the Anaheim/Fullerton area and on toward Corona in Riverside County.

The most notorious local freeway construction project has an unofficial title—"the Orange Crush," in the city of Orange at the intersection of I-5, Highway 57, and Highway 22. The Garden Grove Freeway, Highway 22, connects the 405 to the 55 just north of Santa Ana and Tustin as well as the southern end of Highway 57, the Orange Freeway. The Orange runs north through Placentia to intersect Highway 90, the Imperial Highway, which connects Brea with Yorba Linda and Highway 91.

California's Pacific Coast Highway (PCH), or Highway 1, is Orange County's scenic route—running almost the entire length of the coastline before merging with I-5 just east of Dana Point in the south county. A multilane route most of the way, PCH is typically a slog—slowed like everything else in Southern California by too much traffic. And most people here do drive, usually one to a vehicle. To join them on a temporary basis, contact the visitor bureau for a current listing of area car rental agencies.

BOB RACE

SEAL BEACH AND VICINITY

Enticed by more famous Orange County beach towns, tourists tend to miss Seal Beach—a neat-as-a-pin neighborhood with a 1950s' bohemian feel, an attractive downtown, and plenty of pom-pom palms. The beach itself is wide and sandy, offering a view of both ocean and the man-made offshore island featuring California's first off-shore oil well, drilled in 1954.

Enjoy Main Street. The **Book Store,** 213 Main, 562/598-1818, is a classic in the used-book genre, an overwhelming hodgepodge of words in print. (Proprietor Nathan Cohen, a retired merchant seaman, may offer help in navigating the stacks.) With or without book in hand, stop nearby for ice cream or cappuccino; bikini shops and beach-style boutiques offer more expensive distractions. After the beach and a stroll on the pier, to stay longer take in a movie at the landmark **Bay Theatre,** 562/431-9988, known for its eclectic and arty films.

If the beach scene here gets too crowded, just south are **Surfside Beach** and **Sunset Beach,** quieter areas with public beaches and lifeguard towers. (Stroll. Bike it. Take the bus. If driving, park along either North or South Pacific Avenues, parallel to PCH.)

For a fine bike ride, the **bikeway** at Bolsa Chica State Beach, just south, begins at Warner and runs south all the way to Huntington State Beach, about five miles. Heading north by bike is not much fun, with cyclists competing with cars on PCH all the way to Belmont Shores (Long Beach).

For more information about the area, including exact dates for upcoming events, call the **Seal Beach Chamber of Commerce** at 562/799-0179 between 10 A.M. and 2 P.M. on weekdays or check www.sealbeachchamber.com.

The Seal Beach Pier

A prime attraction, right at the end of Main Street, is the Seal Beach Pier, one of the longest along the coast (1,865 feet) and a focal point of local life since its construction in 1906. Popular these days for rock cod fishing (rental rods and bait available) and promenade-style people watching, the Seal Beach Pier boasts a colorful past.

Crown jewel of the "Jewel City" amusement complex, the pier at one time sported 50 giant rainbow-making "scintillator" lamps to enhance night-time ocean swimming. Jewel City itself featured a roller coaster shipped down from San Francisco after the 1915 World's Fair. Movie stars and special events, such as stunt fliers, also attracted the crowds.

Not everyone considered the local goings-on innocent, however. One Orange County preacher called Seal Beach "the plague spot at our doors." In 1916—when ladies were required to wear stockings while bathing in public—the wild women of Seal Beach flagrantly violated the law by painting their legs "to fool the coppers." And in the 1920s and '30s, sailors from Long Beach and bad boys from Los Angeles were known to sneak down to Seal Beach to partake of the more serious sins of illicit gambling and prostitution.

The pier itself has had wild times too. It survived the earthquake in 1933, but not the big breakers of 1935. It survived a hurricane in 1939, but not the disastrous storms of 1983. The most recent incarnation of the Seal Beach Pier opened to the public on January 27, 1985.

Staying in Seal Beach

If you think this laid-back, blast-from-the-past beach town is the perfect place to park yourself permanently, think again. At last report Seal Beach had Orange County's highest rents. And you won't find much here in the way of budget accommodations. (Try Huntington Beach instead.) A possibility for families, though, if you can stand the kids in your room (children under 17 stay free), is the **Radisson Inn,** 600 Marina Dr., 562/493-7501, www.radisson.com, with the usual motel amenities, fitness center, pool, whirlpool, bike rentals, and rates usually $99– 146. And if the 1850s are more your style than the 1950s, consider a stay at the two-story **Seal Beach Inn and Gardens,** a stylish and secluded 23-room bed-and-breakfast close to the beach at 212 Fifth St., 562/493-2416 or toll-free 800/443-3292; www.sealbeachinn.com. Guest rooms, some with kitchens, refrigerators, and whirlpool baths, are furnished with antiques and named after flowers—many of which you'll find here, part of the riot of color blooming forth from every container, cranny, and nook. There's a small swimming pool, too. Rates: $165–350, depending upon type of room.

Eating in Seal Beach

Head to the pier for bomber-size burgers and a view of the oil wells. *The* place forever—or at least since the Seal Beach Grand Old Opry House gave up the ghost—is flashy diner-style **Ruby's** at the end of the pier, 562/431-7829, where you'll find all kinds of patties, including chicken, turkey, and veggie, plus great shakes and other tasty pleasures from the past. Breakfast is a best bet too. And if you miss it here, Ruby's is almost an institution along the coast and elsewhere in Orange County.

The most popular all-around hangout in Seal Beach is **Hennessey's Tavern,** 140 Main, 562/598-4419, one of a small chain of Irish-style pubs serving breakfast, lunch, and dinner in addition to beer, here overflowing with surfers, hippies, country music, and the scent of suntan lotion. Best bet for breakfast, though, is the homey long-running **Harbor House Cafe** on PCH (at Anderson) just south of town in Sunset Beach, 562/592-5404, open 24 hours, famous for its omelettes, almost as famous for the gallery of movie stars on knotty-pine walls.

An unusual local landmark since 1930 and still offering homage to the good ol' stunt flying days is the **Glide 'er Inn,** 1400 PCH, 562/431-3022, where the reference is to aeronautics in general, biplanes in particular. Airplane memorabilia papers the walls, model planes serve as de facto mobiles, and seafood dominates the menu.

If seafood is your passion, though, **Walt's Wharf,** 201 Main, 562/598-4433, offers greater creativity with whatever's in season—such things as oak-grilled Chilean sea bass with roasted macadamia nuts. There's an oyster bar here too, and a good selection of imported beers. Another good choice, for seafood and prime rib, not to mention great breakfasts, is the **Kinda Lahaina Broiler,** 901 Ocean Ave., 562/596-3864.

BOLSA CHICA STATE BEACH

Stretching south three miles from Seal Beach in the north to the Huntington Beach Pier, broad, sandy Bolsa Chica State Beach is in one sense an extension of what you'll find farther south at Huntington State Beach—thousands of paved parking places, restrooms with showers, fire rings, snack stands, and all. The primary differences? This is a better bet for beginning surfers than Huntington Beach. Also, Bolsa Chica offers 50 RV campsites.

The main parking lot entrance is on PCH about 1.5 miles south of Warner Avenue. Day use (parking fee) is $3. For more information about Bolsa Chica, call 714/848-1566. To reserve a campsite—a necessity in summer—call ReserveAmerica toll-free at 800/444-7275 or check www.reserveamerica.com.

Bolsa Chica Ecological Reserve

In many ways more fascinating than the beach is 1100-acre Bolsa Chica Ecological Reserve across PCH. Not exactly pristine, Bolsa Chica is an on-going oilfield restoration project; some areas are not open to the public. Bolsa Chica, one of the county's few remaining wetland tracts, provides seasonal habitat for more than 200 species of waterfowl and shorebirds, including the endangered California least tern. Amigos de Bolsa Chica, a local citizens' group, is responsible for preventing the total loss of Bolsa Chica to another marina and housing development. (The California Coastal Commission decided in November 2000 to allow development to proceed on the upper mesa only—considered a major victory on behalf of the Bolsa Chica reserve.) So shake that sand out of your shoes and stroll along the 1.5-mile loop trail, just to see what a little enlightened citizen action can do. For current information on guided walks, usually offered September through April on the first Saturday of the month starting at 9 A.M., call 714/897-7003.

HUNTINGTON BEACH AND VICINITY

SURF CITY

If you've tried to find Surf City on a California map, put an "X" right here, on the once-grungy blue-collar oil town of Huntington Beach. The city has long called itself "Surfing Capital of the World" and "Surf City." But now it's official. After some public skirmishes with Santa Cruz, that scrappy little surf city up north, Huntington Beach ended up with the Surf City trademark.

Surfers have dominated the local fauna since the 1920s. But surfing didn't become a social phenomenon even in Huntington Beach until the 1960s, when Bruce Brown of nearby Dana Point was knighted the "Fellini of foam" for *Endless Summer*, his classic surfing film, and Dick Dale, "King of the Surf Guitar," rode the same wave to the top of the pop music charts. (Dale's sound was a total Orange County creation, since even his guitar—a Fender Stratocaster—was a local invention, thanks to Leo Fender of Fullerton.) Then came the Beach Boys, who captured the national teenage imagination and catapulted surfing into the category of popular sport. But then came the Beatles. Almost overnight everyone—everyone except serious surfers—tuned into another wavelength, an entirely different cultural wave.

FIVE DAYS AT HUNTINGTON

As dawn sleeps in, I stir
salt-cured in sandy sheets
and know by turns the distant crash
as no semi threading overpass, but
the clap of sea on sea.

The coming sun in the small of my
    back,
at the foam edge of the continent,
the largest body of water on earth
seeps like December between my toes,
stretching farther than I can think,
with room for a million drownings.

Mouth wet for salt, I wade shy,
insultingly late to a family reunion.
I push through
the liquid ice: knee high, crotch, eyes
    low,
nails to chest,
waiting.

The ocean rears clear
to Japan, rises over the moon to

bear-hug me
down: I fall,
frightened, footless,
dependent on mercy, the
almighty Pacific
pausing a moment from all it does
to wrestle me as a son.

I suck breath, go down,
and down again,
slam head to sand,
feel for earth,
dive for sky—
and learn a reflex so deeply
that sixteen years on
the pre-dawn thunder
of a truck through a valley town
will find me eyes to ceiling,
breathing fiercely
to remember my place
in the cold birthing of the day.

—MICHAEL SIGALAS

According to local lore, surfing was imported to Huntington Beach from Hawaii in 1907. In those days surfers were all but alone in the Orange County surf, riding 100-pound homemade redwood boards. But wood has long since given way to polyurethane, plain canvas swim trunks to neoprene wetsuits. And "mellow" has lost out to "aggro" (aggressive attitude, in the lingo) now that conditions are crowded and surfing is a multibillion-dollar international sports and fashion industry.

THE NEW SURF CITY

About seven million people do Huntington Beach every year, most just day tripping. It's tough to find the skurfy surf-rat bar scenes and seedy low-rent storefronts of yore, though. They're all but gone—replaced in the 1980s and '90s by a strategically redeveloped business and tourism district with a crisp California-Mediterranean style. Huntington Beach figured that spiffing up the neighborhood might attract a different crowd—people inclined to spend more money than surfers typically do, thereby increasing sales tax revenues. Subsequent downtown redevelopment involved razing seven of nine city blocks and ponying up large public subsidies for developers—investments that haven't entirely paid off yet.

From the point of view of history-minded surfers, there went the neighborhood.

But even with redevelopment, surfing is still the main event in Huntington Beach. Annual competitions include the **The Bluetorch Pro of Surfing** (formerly the OP Pro), usually held in late July, a famed stop on the Association of Surfing Professionals world tour and the largest surfing event on the U.S. mainland. But Bluetorch qualifier events are just the prelude to August's **U.S. Open of Surfing,** part of the World Surfing

THE SURFRIDERS: SURFING GOES GREEN

You'd never guess it, to watch competitive young surfers duke it out for ocean elbow room, but surfing has *traditions,* concerns much more lasting than who gets there first, fastest, or with the most finesse.

One surfing tradition is caring about coastal waters and fighting environmental decline, whether from oil and sewage spills or impending development. Surfing is increasingly an endangered species, a development directly related to human activity as well as human efforts to correct the problem. Flood-control dams upriver, for example, prevent sand from flowing to sea to replenish beaches. The coastal breakwaters and jetties built to trap existing sand have the unfortunate side effect of aggravating sand erosion—the ocean continues to suck it out to sea—while destroying waves.

But even surfers were shocked in February of 1990 when the British Petroleum-chartered oil tanker *American Trader* impaled itself on its own anchor about a mile offshore. About 400,000 gallons of oil spilled, much of it scooped up or dispersed at sea but a substantial amount washing ashore to foul 15 miles of beaches and wetlands and kill seabirds from Anaheim Bay in L.A. County to the Newport Beach peninsula. In one of those ironies of fate—since Huntington Beach is still Orange County's main oil producer—most of the oil came ashore near Bolsa Chica and Huntington Beach. Along with the professional crews, hundreds of Orange County volunteers turned out to stop the oil and then to clean things up.

Since 1984 the Surfrider Foundation, which began in surf-happy Huntington Beach, has been on the front lines of the battle to protect the oceans and the coastline. Originally a handful of long-haired locals—the group began educating the public by spray painting storm drains with the message "Drains to Ocean," and it is still famous for its guerrilla theater—the Surfrider Foundation is now a national organization.

In addition to some notable national victories—including restoring natural dune habitat on the Outer Banks in North Carolina and, in Hawaii, successfully suing Honolulu for dumping raw sewage into Kailua Bay—the foundation is still at the forefront of the long-running local battle to forestall a housing subdivision at the Bolsa Chica wetlands.

For more information about the organization, or to join, contact: **Surfrider Foundation,** 122 S. El Camino Real #67, San Clemente, CA 92672, 949/492-8170, fax 949/492-8142; www.surfrider.org.

Championship tour. If battling the seriously surf-crazed crowds during big-time competition is an unappealing option, you'll find many smaller, more neighborly surfing events staged throughout the year.

For more information about Huntington Beach, contact: **Huntington Beach Conference and Visitors Bureau,** 417 Main Street, 714/969-3492 or toll-free 800/729-6232 (SAY-OCEAN), fax 714/969-5592; www.hbvisit.com.

HUNTINGTON BEACH BEACHES

The city beach or **"Main Beach"** starts in the north at Goldenwest, saunters past the Huntington Beach Pier—itself a seaward extension of Main Street—and then meanders south, merging at Beach Boulevard (south of Main) with **Huntington State Beach.** The state beach stretches south another two miles to just beyond Brookhurst, at the Santa Ana River and Newport Beach border.

The pier area is Huntington's most famous and challenging surfing zone, but the state beach is the stuff of surfing movies—one of the widest, whitest expanses of sand you'll see this side of the Colorado Desert. A five-acre preserve along the river protects nesting sites for the California least tern. Across PCH from the state beach is 114-acre **Huntington Beach Wetlands,** a small preserve under the jurisdiction of the California Department of Fish and Game.

In summer, and on almost any hot-weather weekend, plan to arrive quite early to stake out territory for your beach towel. Aside from sunbathing, swimming, surfing, and just bummin' around, beaches around here are known for very serious volleyball. They're also popular for picnicking and the peaceable pursuit of surf fishing and cycling. Facilities include countless paved parking spaces, wheelchair access, restrooms with cold showers and dressing rooms, picnic tables, stores and snack stands, even fire rings for after-dark beach parties—the happening scene, especially near the pier. And the lifeguards mean it when they tell you to quit doing whatever you're doing.

For beach parties, be aware that the curfew is 11 P.M. No camping is allowed. The parking fee for the city beach is $6, for the state beach is

$3 (avoidable altogether if you walk). Parking lots are accessible from PCH at Magnolia, Newland, Huntington, and Main. For more beach information, call 714/848-1566.

For surfing lessons, contact local surf shops. Most offer beginner and intermediate lessons, if not advanced. **Huntington Surf & Sport,** for example, at PCH and Warner, 714/841-4000, offers a half-day private lesson for $125, board and wetsuit included. Lessons are available daily (typically in the morning, when the surf's best), but call at least a week or two in advance for reservations.

The Huntington Beach Pier

In 1904 the city was officially christened Huntington Beach after Henry Huntington, the fellow responsible for extending the Pacific Electric Railroad out this way. But the first pier here was built in 1903, when Huntington Beach was still called Pacific City and still hoping to become the West Coast rival to Atlantic City. In 1914 the original was replaced with a concrete pier, the first ever built in the United States—bearing some resemblance to the brand-new pier you'll see today, opened to great public fanfare in 1992.

The Huntington Beach Pier has been torn up, by both hellacious waves and earthquakes, and then rebuilt so often that even locals get fuzzy on the history. But pier problems peaked in the 1980s. Big winter waves in early 1983 battered the end of the pier, and the End Cafe, so the pier's end was removed, rebuilt, and the whole thing reopened in 1985. January storms in 1988 finally brought the end of The End, however, when it dropped into the ocean—along with plenty of the pier itself—some 10 minutes after the proprietor closed up shop. The pier was closed, demolished, and completely rebuilt at a cost of $10.2 million.

The new, improved, pedestrian-friendly Huntington Beach Pier, 12 feet taller than the original and 1,856 feet long, is still the place for watching sunsets and daring surfers. Pier fishing is a strong local tradition. Another link in the Ruby's dining chain also sits out here. For other dining and diversions, head across PCH to Main Street.

Dwight's Snack Bar, 714/536-8083, on the beach just south of the pier, is the place to go for almost any kind of rental, including beach chairs, boogie boards, bikes, and in-line skates. (For rentals, bring a driver's license.) Just north of the pier is the **Kite Connection,** 714/536-3630, which sells and rents "sport kites." Rentals run $8–12 an hour; lessons are free. Call for information about the local **Kite Festival,** held here every spring.

SEEING SURF CITY

The International Surfing Museum
Mandatory for any serious study of local history is a visit to Huntington Beach's International Surfing Museum, 411 Olive Ave., 714/960-3483. The spruced-up 1930s' building itself offers hidden cultural history as the onetime location of Sam Lanni's acclaimed **Safari Sam's** nightclub —*the* local club scene until 1985, when Sam sauntered off to hunt new challenges.

Among the oldies but goodies collected inside are vintage surfboards, of course, including Batman's board from the original movie. Also here: the cornerstone from the original 1903 pier, and the bust of Duke Kahanamoku once on display at the foot of the pier. Famed Hawaiian swimmer and four-time Olympic winner, Kahanamoku was 20 years old in 1911 when he and his friend George Freeth surfed local beaches—introducing the sport to California, according to local lore —on the way to the 1912 Olympic games.

Especially fun among regular exhibits is the 1960s display, a rollicking reminiscence on surfdom's lasting cultural impact. Special exhibits rotate about every three months, with themes such as "Music, Music, Music"—an amazing array of surf music albums—and "Women in Surfing," which coincided with the debut of *Wahine,* the first women's surfing magazine. The museum is open noon–5 P.M., daily in summer and Wed.-Sun. in winter. Admission is $2 adults, $1 students, children under 6 free.

Other Huntington Beach Attractions
There *was* life before surfing, even in Huntington Beach. The best place to explore that life is the **Newland House** at 19820 Beach Blvd. (at Adams Ave.), 714/962-5777, a Victorian farmhouse included on the National Register of Historic Places. The house and gardens have been meticulously refurbished; many of the 19th-cen-

tury furnishings are original family pieces. And anyone who thinks recorded music began with compact discs should be sure to check out the working Victrola here. The Newland House is open Wednesday and Thursday 2–4:30 P.M., and on weekends noon–4 P.M. Friendly, informative guides are available for tours. Small admission.

Also worth a stop, if something special's going on, is the cultural focal point of local redevelopment—the **Huntington Beach Art Center,** 538 Main, 714/374-1650, which offers gallery shows, traveling exhibitions, and studio space for artists-in-residence programs, plus sponsors a multitude of community arts education programs. Gallery admission is $3.

Unlike other Orange County beach towns, at last report Huntington Beach didn't offer commercial whale-watching excursions. But you can embark from here on a **Sail Catalina** trip, 714/568-9650, the first sailing passenger service to and from Catalina Island since the late 1800s. The boat motors over in the morning, shoving off from Peters Landing, then sails back. Sunset cruises and off-season charters are also available.

STAYING IN SURF CITY

Best bet for budget travelers is the very clean **Colonial Inn Youth Hostel,** housed in a circa-1903 three-story colonial at 421 Eighth St., 714/536-3315. Opt for a bed in one of three communal rooms ($16) or, for more privacy, check into one of 14 double rooms with twin beds ($18 per person). Curfew here is 11 P.M., but you can rent a late key.

In other options, Huntington Beach offers more reasonably priced choices than most beach towns, but most of the better motel deals are inland along Beach Boulevard. Settle in at the **Comfort Suites,** for example, 16301 Beach Blvd. (at McDonald, one block west of I-405), 714/841-1812 or toll-free 800/714-4040, $59 d.

Comfortable, reasonable, and right across the highway from the beach is the small **Sun 'n' Sands Motel,** 1102 PCH (five blocks north of the pier, between Main and Goldenwest), 714/536-2543, with the basics plus pool and free movies, cable TV. Rates: $59 and up in the summer season, from $45 otherwise (kids under 12 free).

For a different beach ambience, try the neat and neighborly **Sunset Bed and Breakfast,** 16401 PCH (at 25th St.), 562/592-1666. Summer rates $45–95, winter rates $45–85.

A central feature of downtown redevelopment is the upscale **Waterfront Hilton Beach Resort,** 21000 PCH, 714/960-7873 or toll-free 800/822-7873. Beyond the stunning lobby, with its waterfalls and tropical plants, the Mediterranean-style complex offers 12 stories of ocean-view rooms across from the beach and balmy palm landscaping, pretty pool area, tennis courts, and more. Rates: $135 and up in summer, otherwise $115 and up, but ask about special discounts and packages.

EATING IN SURF CITY

Locals' Favorites

Some of the local surf scene's most beloved hangouts survive, much to everyone's post-redevelopment relief. **The Sugar Shack,** 714/536-0355, still stands, for example, a funky little café at 213 1/2 Main, the place *everybody* goes, for more than 25 years. The Shack serves surfer-sized breakfast starting at 6 A.M., juicy burgers and such at lunch and early dinner. If it's crowded, add your name to the waiting list—cleverly attached to the tree out front. Also everybody's favorite, wherever you find it in Orange County, along the southern L.A. coast, and elsewhere, is **Wahoo's Fish Tacos,** 120 Main St., 714/536-2050. A Wahoo's Fish of the Day or Banzai Burrito will fill you up just fine—and deliciously—for under $5.

For healthy vegetarian, the place is **Mother's Market and Kitchen** next to the Newland House at 19770 Beach Blvd., 714/963-6667, where breakfast, lunch, and dinner are served daily, 9 A.M.–9:30 P.M. The market here is well worth a wander, too, selling fresh produce, kitchen gadgets, and natural cosmetics.

Popular with college students and the young local surf set, is boisterous, cool, and casual **Huntington Beach Beer Company,** 201 Main (at Walnut), 714/960-5343, where the specialty is pizza baked in a wood-fired oven. Sandwiches and salads are also on tap, everything washed down by brewskies such as Huntington Beach Blonde and Brick Shot Red. Quite the scene on Friday and Saturday nights.

A popular locals' choice is the **Park Bench Cafe** in Huntington Central Park, 17732 Goldenwest (at Slater), 714/842-0775, especially enjoyable on a glorious sunny day—and most famous recently for the addition of its special Canine Cuisine menu, a bone tossed to patrons also visiting the neighborhood "bark park." Doggie selections include the Hot Diggity Dog (hot dog on a bun) and the Wrangler Roundup (ground turkey patty). Humans shouldn't fear that the place has gone to the dogs, however. Dogs and their people dine only on the perimeter of the patio, on the lawn. Breakfast and lunch are served daily except Monday (closed). Another good bet here: **Breakfast in the Park,** 714/848-0690. Huntington Central Park is on both sides of Goldenwest, between Edwards and Gothard.

But don't miss **Tosh's Mediterranean Cuisine and Bakery,** 16871 Beach Blvd., 714/842-3315, where you can pack a special picnic basket or sit down for marvelous Greek and Turkish fare at either lunch or dinner (seafood and vegetarian selections also available). Very good value if you're ravenous, since bread, soup, and salad are served with meals. For good sushi and such, try **Matsu Japanese Restaurant, Steakhouse, and Sushi Bar** across from the Friendship Inn at 18035 Beach Blvd. (at Talbert), 714/848-4404.

Locals' Favorites: Fancier Fare

Immensely popular for hip seafood and Southwestern favorites is David Wilhelm's **Chimayo at the Beach,** 315 Pacific Coast Highway, 714/374-7273. The tequila choices alone are enough to make your head spin.

Another possibility for casual dining is the **Studio Café,** 300 PCH, 714/536-8775, specializing in seafood and sea views. Other local restaurants get more attention. **Baci,** 18748 Beach Blvd. (at Ellis), 714/965-1194, is quite good—some say the best, locally—for Italian, and reasonably priced as well. The very good continental **Palm Court** restaurant at the Waterfront Hilton, 714/960-7873, is also quite popular—casual during the day but dress-up dining with a view come nightfall.

Eventful, Entertaining Huntington Beach

In addition to annual surfing competitions, major events in Huntington Beach include the annual **Fourth of July Parade and Fireworks Show** and the **Pier Fest** in August. At Christmas, consider coming for the annual **Huntington Harbour "Cruise of Lights"** tour of outdoor holiday decor. Something is going on almost all the time, however; stop by the visitor center for a complete listing.

As for entertainment, if you're lucky you'll arrive when Dick Dale and the Deltones are playing paeans to the surf, somewhere in Orange County. If not, rock out on weekends at **Out of Bounds** at 21022 Brookhurst St. (at Atlanta), 714/968-9800, or head for the long-running **Longboard Restaurant and Pub,** 217 Main, 714/960-1896, to sample the bar scene. Otherwise, nightlife here has never entirely recovered since the famous Golden Bear was bulldozed into oblivion and Safari Sam's closed shop. Nearby, though, for rock 'n' dinner, there's the **Galaxy Theater,** 3503 S. Harbor in Santa Ana (just off the 405), 714/957-0600. Well worth the trip south is **The Coach House** in a semi-industrial complex off the freeway in San Juan Capistrano. (For details, see San Juan Capistrano, below.) And Newport Beach, just south of Huntington, offers nightlife galore.

For local community theater, see what's playing at the **Huntington Beach Playhouse,** 21141 Strathmore Ln., 714/375-0696.

NEWPORT BEACH AND VICINITY

Postsuburbia seems to require constant investment in the supremacy of the new. In most parts of Southern California, for example, tradition dictates that at the first sign of aging either a bulldozer or cosmetic surgeon be called in. That said, even Orange County has history. And Newport Beach is a good place to start looking for it.

History of La Puerta Nueva

After native peoples were safely corraled at the missions, the land now known as Newport Beach was originally included in the Rancho Santiago de Santa Ana, granted by the Spanish government in 1810 to Juan Peralta and José Antonio Yorba. In 1837 the Mexican government gave the land to José Sepulveda as part of his 47,000-acre Rancho San Joaquin. On early maps the upper reaches of what is now Newport Bay were identified as Bolsa de San Joaquin (Pocket or Bay of San Joaquin) or Bolsa de Guigara (Bay with High Banks). The as-yet-unformed harbor area was poetically described as Cienega de los Ranos (Frog Swamp) and Cienega de San Joaquin (San Joaquin Swamp). The modern name, La Puerta Nueva (The New Port) came in the 1870s, with the construction of a livestock/supply-loading chute, wharf, and warehouse.

Now a nouveau-riche niche with a nautical theme, in the 1920s and '30s Newport Beach was the preferred seaside escape for the old-money minions from Los Angeles. (In California "old money," like all other things, is relative.) Henry E. Huntington made it all possible with the extension of the Pacific Electric Railroad to Newport Bay. And close-to-home adventure continued outward from Newport, the cat's meow being the ferryboat day trip to Catalina Island. Once the shallow harbor was dredged, landfill islands, yachting marinas, and summer homes starting popping up all over the place.

Modern Newport Beach

Famous former residents include John Wayne, Shirley Temple, even George Burns and Gracie Allen, Roy Rogers and Dale Evans. Celebrities come and go, though. In the end the truly astounding thing about Newport Beach is the price paid here for social status, reflected most obviously in the value of both real estate and boat slips. A million or two will buy little more than a modest beach bungalow with no yard, no parking, and no rest from the daily summer struggle with nightmarish tourist traffic. Some of the luxury yachts on display in Newport Harbor carry equally phenomenal price tags. And some people would sell their very souls just for the chance to drop anchor in one of the 10,000 slips here, *the* high-price, high-prestige California yacht harbor.

Go figure.

Of course the *weather* is quite nice, year-round.

For those who track the ever-changing local identity of California's Highway 1, or Pacific Coast Highway, as it slides south along the coast, here it's called West Coast Highway until it crosses the channel on the west side of the harbor at lower Newport Bay, and East Coast Highway on the east side. For more information on the area, contact the **Newport Beach Conference and Visitors Bureau,** 3300 W. Coast Hwy. in Newport Beach, 949/722-1611 or toll-free 800/942-6278 (94-COAST) in the United States and Canada, fax 949/722-1612. To explore Newport on the Web, go to www.newport-beach-cvb.com. For information on adjacent Costa Mesa, contact the **Costa Mesa Tourism and Promotions Council,** P.O. Box 5071, Costa Mesa, CA 92628, 714/435-2109, fax 714/435-8522; www.costamesa.ca.com.

SEEING NEWPORT BEACH

Despite its high-priced harbor and hotels, keep in mind that Newport Beach is still more residential area than tourist destination. The unmistakable aroma of money, money, money is often aloft on the sea breeze, but just plain folks still find plenty to do here. Newport Beach is just so darned *pleasant.*

Hold that thought when you're trapped in traffic on Pacific Coast Highway or desperately trying to snare a parking place.

Parking is such a nightmare, particularly near the college-student scene at Newport Pier, that touring the area on foot is truly a stress-reducing alternative. If hiking long urban distances isn't feasible, cycling might be—so bring bikes if you've got them, or plan to rent.

Exploring Newport Harbor from its watery underside isn't all that pleasurable, given the sheer numbers of boats and people. The exception to the rule is Corona del Mar State Beach, with offshore reefs worth exploring. Even better is Crystal Cove State Park between Newport and Laguna Beach, an underwater marine sanctuary with good diving. Laguna Beach is actually closer to Crystal Cove, but if you're based in Newport rent snorkeling or scuba gear (certification required for divers) at the **Aquatic Center,** 4537 W. Coast Hwy. (at Balboa), 949/650-5440.

The best way to tour Newport Harbor is by boat. Unusual is a one-hour gondola tour with **Gondola Company of Newport,** headquarters at Lido Marina Village, 3404 Via Oporto, Suite 102B, 714/675-1212.

For the classic harbor cruise—during which you'll find out just which celebrities lived where, et cetera—try **Catalina Passenger Service (CPS)** and its *Pavilion Queen,* an ersatz river boat, and *Pavilion Paddy,* both docked at the Balboa Pavilion. In addition, CPS offers trips to and from Catalina Island as well as whale-watching tours. For current information call 949/673-5245 or toll-free 800/830-7744.

Most whale-watching and sportfishing tours also shove off from the pavilion. **Bongos Sportfishing Charters,** 2140 Newport Blvd., 949/673-2810, offers whale trips from just after Christmas through March and sportfishing year-round, as does **Newport Landing Sportfishing,** 309 Palm St., 949/675-0550. For information on private exclusive yacht charters, for total privacy and/or to accommodate large groups, contact the visitors bureau for referrals.

ON THE BALBOA PENINSULA

First and often last stop on a people's tour is the Balboa Peninsula, a long, arthritic finger of sand pointing south from **Newport Boulevard,** the seaward end of the line for the Costa Mesa (55) Freeway. You can also get here from the Coast Highway and **Balboa Boulevard.** Humanity is so well established here, the entire harbor so sheltered from sea-driven storms, it's a surprise to discover that the peninsula is a geological newborn. The Balboa Peninsula didn't begin to exist until after 1825, a year of massive flooding that caused the Santa Ana River to suddenly change course and deposit sand and sediments in the harbor.

Newport Pier and Vicinity
The Newport Pier—about a half-mile past the highway at the ocean end of McFadden Place, between 20th and 21st Streets—was originally McFadden's Wharf, built in 1888 to accommodate the train from Santa Ana delivering produce and steamship passengers. **Newport Beach** —the actual beach by that name—

stretches both west and east from the pier (this one constructed in the 1940s), which serves as madding-crowd central in summer and on most weekends.

The most historic attraction at the Newport Pier is the **Newport Dory Fishing Fleet** adjacent. Hard at it since 1891, this is the only surviving dory fleet on the West Coast. Arrive by 10 A.M. to scoop up some of the day's catch, marketed in open-air stalls. For more information on the fleet and other aspects of Newport's harbor history, stop by the **Newport Beach Nautical Museum** at its new location in the Reuben E. Lee "river barge," 151 E. Coast Hwy., 949/673-7863, open Tues.–Sun. 10 A.M.–5 P.M.

To try your hand at the landlubber's version of the dorymen's life, consider pier fishing. **Baldy's Tackle,** 100 McFadden, has been around almost as long as the dorymen; stop by to rent fishing tackle as well as bikes. It's a five-minute walk to the end of the pier.

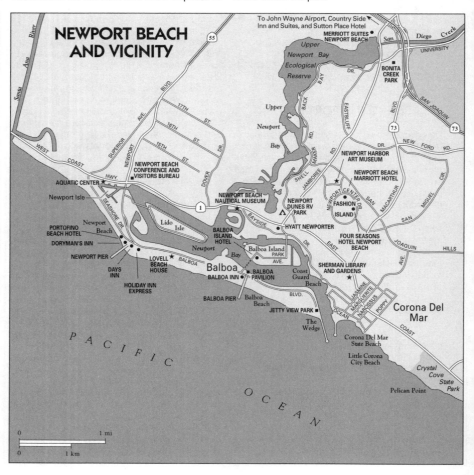

Balboa Pier and Vicinity

A stroll to the Balboa Pier, which juts into the ocean from Balboa's Main Street, two miles to the east, takes considerably longer—especially if you dawdle along the concrete boardwalk. Accompanied by landscaped lawn, bandstand, and palm trees, the Balboa Pier is the focal point for more placid pursuits. On most days **Balboa Beach** is relatively lonely and quiet, especially on the stretch toward the jetty. Even the ocean is quieter here, since the sandy beach falls away steeply and the waves seem to arrive from nowhere.

Downcoast is the jetty, a rocky chin protecting the harbor mouth as it inhales and exhales sailboats. The angle formed between Balboa Beach and the jetty is known as **The Wedge,** internationally famous for its stupendous shore breaks, locally infamous for bone-breaking bodysurfing, surfing, and swimming. (It's dangerous. No joke.) To get the big picture, head out to **Jetty View Park** at the tip of the peninsula.

Balboa Proper

Both the pier and the **Balboa Pavilion** at 400 Main St.—originally a bathhouse cum boathouse, now de facto loading dock for boat tours—were built in 1905 by Southern California developers working overtime to attract home buyers to this otherwise desolate sand spit. (Encouraged by a generous cash donation and free railroad right-of-way, Henry E. Huntington aided their cause on July 4, 1906, when the first of his electric trolleys to Newport Beach delivered potential buyers from Los Angeles.) In the 1940s the pavilion was a big-band bandstand—home of the "Balboa" dance craze—though the nearby Rendezvous Ballroom, long gone, was the more famous venue.

Not to be missed amid the surrounding shops and schlock is the reconstructed Balboa **Fun Zone** promenade along the bay, one of the few places left anywhere with genuine arcade-era pinball machines, skee ball, and such. For electronics addicts, video games are available.

Adjacent to the pavilion is the three-car Balboa Ferry, for the trip to and from Balboa Island.

Also worth appreciating is the lovely 1930 Spanish colonial **Balboa Inn** at the foot of the pier, a hotel designed by architect Walter Hagedohn, more famous for his Union Station in Los Angeles.

A still grander presence presides at W. Ocean Front and 13th Street, back toward the Newport Pier—the concrete **Lovell Beach House.** Considered one of the finest American examples of early modern architecture, it was designed in 1926 by Rudolph M. Schindler for health enthusiast Dr. Lovell. The house is suspended above the beach by columns and cantilevers, actually five poured-concrete frames. The ground level is an outdoor living area combining a fireplace with

Balboa Beach

ROBERT HOLMES/CALIFORNIA DIVISION OF TOURISM

the necessities of parking, play, and washing up. The main living area above (two stories) ponders the Pacific. Sleeping balconies, once alfresco, are now enclosed—surely in recognition of the fog-chill factor—and the roof features a sunken sunbathing deck. But Bauhaus is not *your* house, so don't bother the residents.

OFF THE BALBOA PENINSULA

Balboa Island and Vicinity
Not to be confused with Balboa Peninsula is Balboa Island just off the mainland, a buffed neighborhood of beach bungalows reached by car from W. Coast Highway and Marine Avenue.

If you drive, though, you won't see much, because you'll never find a place to park. A better option—and much more fun—is coming over as a pedestrian on the nearly perpetual **Balboa Island Ferries,** 949/673-1070, a service shuttling people and automobiles (maximum capacity, three cars at a time) back and forth daily since the early 1900s. The ferries ($1 fare) run daily—from 6:30 A.M. to midnight Sun.–Thurs., until 2 A.M. on Friday and Saturday nights—between Palm Avenue on the peninsula and Agate Avenue on the island.

"Agate," by the way, indicates another island oddity. Most cross streets are named for gems and stones—Jade, Topaz, Garnet, and Emerald.

Marine Avenue is the village boutiquery and business district, where one can also pursue

simple pleasures—such as a world-famous "Balboa bar" (vanilla ice cream bars dipped in chocolate) from **Dad's,** or a frozen chocolate-dipped banana from **Sugar 'n' Spice.** *The* restaurant on Balboa Island is **Amelia's,** 311 Marine Ave., 949/673-6580, known for seafood, Italian specialties, and family-run atmosphere.

To eyeball James Cagney's onetime island estate, head west. That's it, just offshore at the end of Park—**Collins Isle,** sticking out from the west side of Balboa Island like a sandy little toe.

Like other private landfill islands scattered around the bay, **Lido Isle** to the harbor's far west—reached from the peninsula via Newport Boulevard and Via Lido—is an elite and elegant residential enclave where potentially public lawn areas are designated "private" community parks.

Corona Del Mar and Vicinity
Gardeners enjoy the **Sherman Library and Gardens** in Corona del Mar. Here they get a thorough education in just what will grow, and grow well, in the onetime desert of Southern California. Just south of the harbor on the mainland at 2647 E. Coast Hwy. (at MacArthur Blvd.), 949/673-2261, the Sherman honors the "Pacific Southwest" in its specialized library and two-acre garden of desert and tropical plants. More tropicals, and a koi pond, are in the modern conservatory. Also here: a wheelchair-accessible "discovery garden" for the seeing-impaired. The gardens are open 10:30 A.M.–4 P.M. daily except major holidays, the library on weekdays only.

RENDEZVOUS AT BALBOA

"Where was I when Dick Dale blew
for sunburned surfers at the Rendezvous?"
I've asked that. When the dancefloor ashed,
I was two,
and fifteen years from sun when
my freckled mom
served shrimp-in-a-cup
to Lou Costello in the Fun Zone.
I never saw Weissmuller waxing his fleet,
   or John Wayne setting glass to bar
   to crush a hand at Dillman's.
"Why couldn't I pop Hamm's in the sandy
   lot
as the Beach Boys opened
for the Belairs?" "Why must the Chantays
   play
and Mar-kets stomp
only in black and white,
and I,
never in the crewcut crowd,
always holding the frame?"

I stand on this loud corner at twenty-nine
and hear, in a Miata sliding past,
the primal thump of my successors' youth.
Now even the girls in lime mohawks
and eye-lined rockabillies
wheel their Vespas in ghostly turns
around flappers, dorymen, and WACs, as
   pierside, Stan Kenton looks down from
   the gazebo
over a plaid-blanket sea,
snaps thrice,
and ignites his Fabulous Horns.
Crackling strains billow into
the fog-bleached night and
damn!

   I sit at seventeen with Stacey White
   —since Berryed, divorced, Wilsoned, with
   kids—
   beside an orange fire, puckering black.
   Where does he look? Mistward, for wor-

thier dates.
Why blind to her own thrown shadow,
a black tombstone angel
twitching on footpocked sand?
Stace White, retainer in hand,
of a hundred pages in a journal long-
boxed,
as gravity-fettered,
as suitable for framing,
as queer-lipped Miss Balboa, 1910.

Again,

   twenty,
   he walks the pier
   with, but not of,
   gawky Cress Delahanty
   wedged beneath his arm,
   ignoring the Hmong fishermen
   for the straw hats cast
   in his mind;

I try to look away

   at twenty-five,
   three drinks deep, trying to glare
   a black-marker obscenity from the wall
   of the Balboa Inn,
   imagining a time before graffitti,

and blink as Kenton's fog
rounds a corner and rolls
down Balboa Boulevard at me,
bleaching every step
I've taken but

   a moment back,
   on this corner,
   a Miata pounding past

this,
rearing only at the curb,
at my toes, at the edge
of my last breath,
held back only as long

(continued on next page)

RENDEZVOUS AT BALBOA
(cont'd)

as I keep breathing.

The horns stop, have stopped. Now,
now,
I hear every exhalation as
an interlude
a low-pitched, tremulous run
stalling those Fabulous Horns,
in time to the pale parade
I must review: sweater girls,

punks, and doggers,
Stacey White, Tarzan, The Duke,
Miss Balboa 1910, '11, '12,
my mother and Lou Costello,
stalk in the gutters, blades drawn
to usher
each ashen-faced fool I was
to the Rendezvous.

—MICHAEL SIGALAS

Small admission. The Tea Garden restaurant here serves light lunch fare, pastries, beverages, but is open to the public only on Saturday, Sunday, and Monday 11 A.M.–3 P.M.

Besides shops and shopping, the star attraction of Corona del Mar is half-mile-long **Corona Del Mar State Beach** at the mouth of Newport Harbor, operated by the city and framed by cliffs and the rocky jetty at the eastern harbor entrance. Offshore is crystal-clear azure ocean; underfoot, warm white sand; everywhere around, lush landscaping—the classic California postcard. It would be wonderful, too, if everyone else in Southern California weren't so determined to be here. To reach the parking lot and day-use facilities for the main beach, from the Coast Highway take Jasmine Street to Ocean Boulevard. Day use (parking) is $3, but for the privilege of paying it, be sure to get here early. For more information, call the visitor bureau, 949/722-1611.

Also hardly a secret is **Big Corona Beach** off Marguerite Avenue, where one can just sit and watch the boats pass. The secluded cove at **Little Corona Beach**, with its **tide pool reserve** (visit at low tide), is reached via Ocean Boulevard (at Poppy).

Other Newport Beaches

Back in Newport is the only "secret" beach around, the small **Coast Guard Beach** at the Harbor Master Coast Guard Station. Here you'll find a relatively peaceful stretch of sand, safe swimming, volleyball nets (bring your own ball),

and picnic tables. Park on the street. The Coast Guard Beach is off the 1900 block of Bayside Drive. To get here from the highway, take Jamboree toward Balboa Island and then turn left onto Bayside.

"Bay beaches" include just about any accessible patches of sand fringing Newport Bay. One with lifeguards, volleyball nets, restrooms, showers, and some wind protection is on the peninsula's Bay Avenue between 18th and 19th Streets. Look for others at Montero and 10th Streets, and at the end of every street on Balboa Island.

UPPER NEWPORT BAY
ECOLOGICAL RESERVE

Visitors quickly appreciate why the Spanish called this place "Frog Swamp," since the Upper Newport Bay Ecological Reserve or "Back Bay" is a brackish salt- and fresh-water marsh complete with cattails, pickleweed, and aromatic mudflats. The most frightening fact is that this very small preserve is the largest remaining unengineered estuary in Southern California.

The Back Bay may be small but it is a marvel —an ecologically rich Pacific Flyway sanctuary that provides shelter to about 200 bird species and 20,000-30,000 birds during the year. Two endangered species, the light-footed clapper rail and Belding's savanna sparrow (found only in Southern California), can be spotted here, along with the California brown pelican, the California least tern, and the peregrine falcon.

SOUTH COAST PLAZA: SHOPPING
AS THE CENTER OF EVERYTHING

Consumerism as Culture

Think of it as a theme park for consumerism, this one attracting more than 20 million visitors each year and, in 1999, raking in an estimated $12.4 billion. The most notable diversion at Orange County's South Coast Plaza megamall in Costa Mesa is the mall itself. Unique in the neighborhood, though, are the sociocultural segues between art, commerce, entertainment, finance, and fine dining—Orange County's foremost foray into the culture of consumerism and consumerism as culture.

This being one of the largest-grossing retail centers in the United States, going to South Coast Plaza typically involves spending money. But rest assured that here commerce is not crass. The preferred promotional etiquette at South Coast Plaza is to refer the mall itself as a "retail center," its shoppers as "guests."

All in all, it's hard to imagine the landscape a few short decades ago, when it was just another Orange County lima bean field.

A New South Coast Plaza

As in other theme parks, the territory here is geographically subdivided. The center is three-story **South Coast Plaza at Bristol,** 3333 Bristol Street (between the 405 and Sunflower), 714/435-2000, www.southcoastplaza.com, with its multistory atriums and elegant decor and a surprising variety of shops anchored by Bullock's, Nordstrom, Macy's, Sears, and Robinsons-May. On the west end is **Jewel Court,** Orange County's version of Rodeo Drive, with upscale shops including Tiffany & Co., Emporio Armani, Louis Vuitton, Cartier, and Chanel. Centerpiece of **Carousel Court** on the mall's east end is—you guessed it—a turn-of-the-20th-century carousel, a fitting enticement for the Sesame Street General Store, Disney Store, GapKids, FAO Schwarz, and other attractions aimed at the younger set.

Then there's the single-level **South Coast Plaza Village** just east of the main mall at Sunflower and Bear Streets, where the Edwards Cinema complex is one notable diversion. Once known as Crystal Court, **South Coast Plaza at Bear,** north of the main mall at 3333 Bear Street, includes an eclectic array, from Abercrombie & Fitch and Adrienne Vittadini to Victoria's Secret. There's also a kiddie carousel here, a new feature, this one with a King Arthur theme.

South of South Coast Plaza and Bristol is the **South Coast Plaza Town Center,** sometimes referred to as The Offices, an area bisected by Anton Boulevard and Town Center Drive—a shimmering 96-acre orchard of bank and business office towers, visual and performing-arts venues, multiplex movie theaters, and inviting eateries.

Major changes at the mall in 1999 and 2000, announced as A New South Coast Plaza, include two new anchors for South Coast Plaza at Bear—a 42,000-square-foot Crate & Barrel Home Store, the chain's West Coast flagship, and a Macy's Home store. Also new is an elevated pedestrian walkway to connect the Bear and Bristol malls. At the main mall, Robinsons-May is expanding by 50,000 square feet. And a new 300,000-square-foot symphony hall designed by renowned architect Cesar Pelli, the **Segerstrom Center for the Arts** to be located next to South Coast Repertory, is coming soon.

Consuming Culture and "California Scenario"

The neighborhood's main action may be trafficking in commerce and consumer goods, but the main attraction is art—most of it in Town Center.

Almost perfectly hidden, wedged into the courtyard created by two black-glass business towers and the adjacent public parking lot, is an understated yet powerful exploration of the California myth—*California Scenario* by the late Isamu Noguchi. This expansive "sculpture garden" offers much more than the term typically implies, staging separate but unified California themes with stunning directness and native-son humor. *Land Use,* for example, is a long, narrow chunk of concrete-colored granite dominating the crest of a landscaped knoll. A meandering stream flows from the tall *Water Source,* past *Desert Land,* to squat, stylized *Water Use.* Funniest of all, though, is *Spirit of the Lima Bean,* 15 dignified desert-colored boulders of decomposed granite piled up to honor South Coast Plaza's primary developers and benefactors, the Segerstrom family—perhaps only incidentally paying homage to the land's previous purpose.

(continued on next page)

SOUTH COAST PLAZA: SHOPPING AS THE CENTER OF EVERYTHING
(cont'd)

California Scenario is tucked away behind the Great Western Bank Building, 3200 Park Center Drive (off Anton Blvd.); parking is available in the adjacent public lot. The courtyard is open daily 8 A.M.–midnight. Appreciating Noguchi's art is absolutely free. For more information, call 714/435-2100.

Various other public sculptures—by **Henry Moore, Joan Miró, Alexander Calder, Claire Falkenstein,** and others—are scattered throughout the Town Center area, indoors and out. If you're too rushed to see them all after doing the mall, walk over to the performing arts center on Town Center Drive—take the pedestrian bridge that spans Bristol—for the stunning first-time impact of Richard Lippold's 60-foot-tall *Fire Bird,* a spectacular vision any time but especially after dark.

Also worthwhile in the arts department is the gallery inside **Bank of America,** 555 Anton. At South Coast Plaza proper, the **Laguna Art Museum** hosts a satellite gallery inside its shop at the mall's east end. Both are free.

Consuming Culture: Performance Arts

The striking, contemporary **Orange County Performing Arts Center** counts among its artistic partners the Pacific Symphony Orchestra, the Philharmonic Society of Orange County, Opera Pacific, Pacific Chorale, and the William Hall Master Chorale. The center also hosts the Los Angeles Philharmonic and touring companies, including the American Ballet Theatre, the Joffrey Ballet, and the New York City Ballet, though classical music, jazz, cabaret, and Broadway musicals predominate. Near-perfect acoustics are the hallmark of the center's 3,000-seat Segerstrom Hall. Incidentally, the center's $74 million construction tab was picked up entirely through private donations—a trend that continues with the current capital campaign for the eventual **Segerstrom Center for the Arts,** which will include a 2,000-seat concert hall and a 500-seat music theater. The Orange County Performing Arts Center is on Town Center Drive at Avenue of the Arts. Call 714/556-2787 for current performance and ticket information (recorded) or 714/556-2121 (administration). Or try the website, www.ocpac.org. Buy

tickets for most performances through Ticketmaster, 714/740-7878, though day-of-performance seats are often available.

Physically but not artistically overshadowed by the performing arts center is the Tony award-winning **South Coast Repertory Theater,** 714/708-5500 (administration); www.scr.org. For tickets, call the box office at 714/708-5555. Started decades ago as a seat-of-the-pants repertory troupe, critical acclaim came along for South Coast Repertory with the brave decision to produce works by new playwrights, though not everything presented is avant-garde. The Mainstage Theater here seats 507, the smaller Second Stage just 161, so call well in advance for current show schedule and reservations; last-minute tickets are scarce. Best bet for spur-of-the-moment attendance: matinees and midweek performances. **The Next Stage:** Major changes are in the works for South Coast Repertory, which plans to add a third, 336-seat proscenium theater designed by Cesar Pelli, office space, dressing rooms, and a sweeping new façade. Groundbreaking is scheduled for the fall of 2001 and construction is expected to take a year. renovation of the existing building will begin after the 2001-02 season. The completely redone South Coast Repertory will debut for the 2002-03 season—with new names for all three theaters.

Consuming Food: Eating at South Coast Plaza

There are dozens of dining options at and near South Coast Plaza. For a change of pace head south to the Southwestern **El Torito Grill** in Town Center at 633 Anton Blvd. (at Bristol), 714/662-2672, where specialties such as red snapper fajitas keep the crowds coming back for more.

Inside South Coast Plaza at Bristol, a best bet for families is the local **Ruby's** burgers-and-shakes outpost (first floor), 714/662-7829. Between Bullock's and the Bullock's men's store is the **Wolfgang Puck Cafe,** 714/546-9653, a stylish but casual California café serving reasonably priced renditions of trademark Puck-style pizzas, pastas, and salads. In the Sears wing is the **Rainforest Café,** 714/424-

9200, where the casual fare comes with the ultimate in faux-environment dining. Near Nordstrom is **Troquet,** 714/708-6865, fabulous for contemporary French bistro fare.

Justifiably popular in the South Coast Plaza Village is the casual **Gustaf Anders Back Pocket,** 714/668-1737, affiliated with the landmark **Gustaf Anders,** famous for Swedish continental cuisine. **Morton's of Chicago,** at Sunflower and Bear, 714/444-4834, plans to move across the street into the renovated, onetime Planet Hollywood site sometime in late 2001. For fine Persian cuisine, the place is **Darya** on Plaza Drive, 714/557-6600.

For upper-crust pizza at lunch or before a show, try **Scott's Seafood Grill and Bar** at 3300 Bristol (at Anton), 714/979-2400. A Southern California link in the popular San Francisco-based chain, Scott's is considerably more famous for its seafood, its generous Sunday brunch, and its fixed-price pretheater menu.

Popular with patrons of the arts is David Wilhelm's dramatically elegant **Diva** near the performing arts center, 600 Anton (at Bristol), 714/754-0600, serving a contemporary California menu so exciting its audience keeps coming back for encores. The signature "ahi towers" here are meant to mimic neighborhood architecture. It's open for lunch weekdays only, for dinner nightly. Jazz several nights each week. Also drawing the stylish crowds these days is **Pinot Provence,** at the Westin South Coast Plaza Hotel, 686 Anton, 714/444-5900, a slice of upscale Mediterranean life and Joachim Splichal's first Orange County restaurant.

Consuming Peace: Staying at South Coast Plaza

The **Westin South Coast Plaza Hotel** across from South Coast Plaza and just steps from the performing arts center at 686 Anton Blvd., 714/540-2500 or toll-free 800/228-3000, fax 714/662-6695, www.westin.com, is the neighborhood's swank stay, with luxury rooms and all the amenities— including **The Spa** and Joachim Splichal's **Pinot Provence** restaurant. The nearby **Wyndham Garden Hotel,** 714/751-5100, fax 714/751-0129, offers similar comforts and Expensive–Premium rates. Both are popular with business types. Another possibility is the **Costa Mesa Marriott Suites,** 714/957-1100. For other options not too far afield, see this chapter's Newport Beach and Vicinity.

Practical South Coast Plaza

South Coast Plaza offers a multitude of "concierge services," including stroller and wheelchair loans, package checking, valet parking, and dinner or theater reservations. For assistance, stop by the concierge desk on the mall's first level, in the center near the carousel, or call 714/435-8571 or toll-free 800/782-8888. To find your way around, pick up a current South Coast Plaza Directory. Also request the mall's Address Book brochure and map. For other South Coast Plaza information, try the website: www.southcoastplaza.com.

Many area hotels offer free shuttle service to and from South Coast Plaza. If yours doesn't, a commercial shuttle bus service connects the three main shopping complexes—stops are shown in the directory and listed on the website—and the **Orange County Connection** "speed shuttle" makes the rounds between South Coast Plaza and Anaheim area (Disneyland), Long Beach area, and other hotels on a daily basis. Call 714/435-2000 or toll-free 800/782-8888 for current prices and schedules.

Cut off by the Coast Highway on the west and otherwise surrounded by view homes perched high on the earthy diatomaceous cliffs, the Back Bay is best appreciated on foot or by bike—bike trails span the northern stretches and follow San Diego Creek—though you can see most of it by car. Auto tour access (one-way only) is off lower Jamboree Road; turn onto Backbay Drive at the Hyatt Newporter and keep going. Parking areas are scattered along the route—so even if you're driving, pick a spot, park, and get out to see the sights in person.

No matter how you go, stop first at the **Newport Bay Naturalists office** on Shellmaker Island (600 Shellmaker Dr., just off Backbay Dr.), 949/640-6746, or check www.newport-bay.org for maps, bird and plant checklists, and historical background.

Naturalists offer free two-hour guided **discovery walks** every Saturday and Sunday, starting at Shellmaker Island at 1 P.M. Also offered on weekends throughout the year: canoe and kayak tours, twilight cruises, an evening "owl prowl," and family campfire programs. For more information, contact the office on Shellmaker Island (see above).

From October through March, Newport Bay enthusiasts also offer free walking tours, starting in the preserve's southeast corner near the intersection of Backbay and Eastbluff Drives. For more information, call Newport Bay Naturalists at 949/640-6746.

For restrooms and a pleasant picnic after a Back Bay adventure, head to **Bonita Creek Park** on University Drive, just one block east of the Jamboree-Eastcliff intersection.

The Back Bay is also accessible from the north. The heavily eroded, star-thistly perimeter is less aesthetic (this is, after all, primarily a judiciously preserved wetlands area) but otherwise wonderful for a meditative stroll up and down the bluffs. To get here from Highway 73: Exit at Irvine Avenue and head west about 1.5 miles, then turn left onto University Drive. Parking (street) is usually available on University.

ARTFUL, ENTERTAINING, AND EVENTFUL NEWPORT

Newport Area Arts

Marooned in a business park near Fashion Island is the **Orange County Museum of Art,** originally known as the Newport Harbor Art Museum, 850 San Clemente Dr., 949/759-1122, www.ocma.net, nationally acclaimed in the late 1980s for its contemporary California art collection and cutting-edge special exhibits. One of its recent achievements was the traveling Anne Frank exhibit, with over 600 photographs. And recently the museum's fortunes received a boost when it was announced that the Irvine Company was donating an adjoining library building for a proposed expansion project.

Particularly striking outside are this museum's red "gem," a sculpture by Jonathan Borofsky, a rusting six-foot iron cube protruding from the building, and the outdoor sculptures. Particularly striking inside are the rotating exhibits— and here, even the permanent collection rotates. The museum is open Tues.–Sun. 10 A.M.–5 P.M. (closed Monday). Admission is $5 adults, $4 students/seniors, free for children under 16.

For classic or limited-run films, the place is the **Edwards Lido Cinema,** 3459 Via Lido,

949/673-8350, cozy one-screen theatre with comfortable seating. Matinee prices are $3.75 on showings before 6 P.M.

Newport Area Entertainment

To avoid the making-the-scene scene, a comfortable alternative is a coffeehouse. Something of a surprise on the peninsula is the **Alta Cafe Warehouse and Roasting Co., 506 31st St.** (off Newport Blvd.), 949/675-0233. The fare is simple but wholesome at breakfast, lunch, and dinner, the atmosphere relaxed and moody, the coffee blends strong and witty. (The Frank Sumatra, for example, is distinguished by its "good personality.") For entertainment, blues, jazz, and folk music are on the menu. Alta Cafe is typically open 7 A.M.–11:30 P.M., until 12:30 A.M. on Friday and Saturday nights.

Best bet for jazz, though, is the **Studio Cafe** near the Balboa Pier, 100 Main St. (at Balboa), 949/675-7760, with top-flight blues or jazz on tap nightly. It also offers a dining room and full bar, so you could do worse than to just park yourself here once the sun sets. The Sunday afternoon jam session is worth a special trip.

And if you find yourself washed ashore anywhere near the Fashion Island mall, rocking out in the mall's parking lot is Orange County's outpost of the **Hard Rock Cafe,** 451 Newport Center Dr. (at San Miguel), 949/640-8844. The usual burgers and such are served, along with hygienic exposure to rock 'n' roll memorabilia as suitable for young rockers as for aging hipster parents. People also stop by to collect T-shirts and the local variation of Hard Rock's glam-rock guitar lapel pin.

Otherwise, Newport Beach is somewhat notorious as a making-the-scene scene. Hot clubs include **The Warehouse,** at 3450 Via Oporto, 949/673-4700, with dancing Thursday, Friday, and Saturday nights. On weekends there's a DJ upstairs, live band downstairs. If you eat dinner here (seafood) the dancing's free; otherwise, there's a $5 cover.

The View on the 16th floor of the Marriott in Fashion Island, 900 Newport Center, 949/640-4000, offers live jazz and dancing on Friday and Saturday nights. Overlooking the Balboa Peninsula, this is also the place to drink in the view over drinks.

Newport Area Events

The most famous local event is the annual **Newport Harbor Christmas Boat Parade** wherein more sporting members of the local yachting crowd decorate their boats in lights and sometimes outlandish decorations and then cruise the harbor. During the week before Christmas, typically, the parade circumnavigates the harbor from 6:30–8:30 P.M.—beginning and ending at Collins Island—putting on quite a show for the folks assembled in restaurants and along public beaches. (Also fun at Christmas: the outrageously beautiful—and outrageously expensive—Christmas decorations at **Roger's Gardens,** 2301 San Joaquin Hills Rd., 949-640-5800.) Expect similar silliness at the theme-oriented **Character Boat Parade,** usually held in mid- to late July. The 10-day **Newport Seafest,** which includes seafaring fun as well as **A Taste of Newport,** usually begins in mid-September. Contact the visitor bureau at toll-free 800/942-6278, www.newport-beach-cvb.com, for more information on these and other events.

STAYING IN NEWPORT BEACH

Newport Camping

It's not cheap and the ambience leaves room for improvement, but **Newport Dunes RV Park** just off Jamboree Road at 1131 Back Bay Dr., 949/729-3863 or toll-free 800/288-0770, is close to the harbor action. It's also practically in the Back Bay, if you're hankering for a hike. It even has a small marina (rental boats available) and children's playground. But if you're going to play here, you'll pay: RVers and intrepid tent campers unpack themselves onto small concrete slabs—like sardines into a can—and pay $25 and up. Alternatives include state park campgrounds up and down the coast.

Lower Rent Newport Accommodations

In Newport Beach and elsewhere along the coast, you'll pay a premium for seaside location and ocean views. Ritzier hotels cluster near the airport and area malls. It's certainly no crime if travelers in search of more modest accommodation retreat to Costa Mesa, just inland from Newport.

One particularly pleasant motel on northbound Newport Boulevard (where it becomes a one-way paralleling the 55 Freeway) is less than a mile from the harbor and reasonably close to everything else—most notably the shops and restaurants at the Triangle Square complex, which is within easy walking distance. Rooms at the **Holiday Inn Express,** 2070 Newport Blvd., between 21st and Bay Ave., 949/631-6000, feature all the basics; some have microwaves and refrigerators. With the ocean so close by, who cares that it doesn't have a pool? Standard rates start at $99, $89 with AAA or AARP membership. The **Days Inn** adjacent, 2100 Newport Blvd., 949/642-2670, $59–89, has a pool.

One of the best deals in the entire county is just off the 405 Freeway—the **Country Inn and Suites,** 325 S. Bristol St. in Costa Mesa (on South Bristol at Red Hill Ave., on the west side of the street), 714/549-0300 or toll-free 800/322-9992; www.countrysuites.com. This well-appointed modern motel, within easy reach of the coast and all other major Orange County attractions, has country French bed-and-breakfast style. Amenities include in-room refrigerators and color TV with videocassette players. Some rooms and studio suites feature microwaves and whirlpools. Extras include full buffet breakfast and morning newspapers, plus two swimming pools, whirlpools, exercise facilities, coin laundry. Since the Country Inn here does substantial "business" business, weekend rates are lowest—a real boon for pleasure travelers—starting at $89. Weekday rates are substantially higher, but with big discounts for AAA and AARP members. Weekly and monthly rates are also available.

Higher Rent Newport Accommodations

The area's upmarket and luxury hotels generally do double-duty as both business and pleasure destinations, thus their locations—within easy reach of corporate business parks, major malls, and John Wayne Airport. Official rates are high; ask about specials and packages, especially for off-season weekends.

Top of the mark is the 19-story **Four Seasons Hotel Newport Beach** near Fashion Island, 690 Newport Center, 949/759-0808 or toll-free 800/332-3442, www.fourseasons.com, rated in 1994 by *Condé Nast Traveler* readers as one of the world's finest hotels. From the outside it looks like yet another too-tall, bewindowed box. Inside, though, it's elegant yet airy, all sand-beige and pastels. And those windows let in some grand views. Along with luxury in-room amenities, facilities here include tennis courts, a huge pool, complete fitness center, and guaranteed tee times and weekend golf packages at nearby courses. The Four Seasons even offers free mountain bikes—the better to explore the Bay. Among the several restaurants here is **Pavilion,** where people dress up for the California-style American. The Four Seasons also boasts a complete business center, not to mention full conference facilities. Rates: $235–475.

Overlooking the Back Bay, **Marriott Suites Newport Beach,** 500 Bayview Circle (at Jamboree Rd.), 949/854-4500 or toll-free 800/228-9290, www.marriott.com, is primarily an upscale business-oriented hotel, quite welcoming on weekends for pleasure travelers. Pool, saunas, fitness facilities, and rental bikes make a weekend stay more than pleasant. And don't miss **The View** sushi bar. Standard in-room amenities are almost too much, from two color TVs and two phones (with call waiting) to wet bar and refrigerator. Rates: $139–199 (children 18 and under free).

From the outside the **Sutton Place Hotel** (formerly Le Meridien Newport Beach), 4500 MacArthur Blvd., 949/476-2001 or toll-free 800/243-4141, www.suttonplace.com, looks something like a squared-off cruise ship, this one with big windows on every deck. Inside, it's very contemporary, very Southern California, with all the expected amenities, including tennis courts, pool, and business center. Most beloved at Sutton Place is its French restaurant **Antoine,** one of Orange County's best in any category. Rates: $118–185. While Sutton Place is technically in Newport Beach, for all practical purposes it's a South Coast Plaza/John Wayne Airport hoStay here to take advantage of weekend South Coast Repertory theater and/or Pageant of the Masters packages.

More convenient to Newport Harbor is the **Hyatt Newporter,** 1107 Jamboree Rd., 949/729-1234 or toll-free 800/233-1234, www.hyattnewporter.com, with spacious resort-style grounds and an amazing array of sports and fitness facilities—including access to the John Wayne Tennis Club. Rates: $169 and up. Lush, too, but less outdoorsy is the **Newport Beach Marriott Hotel and Tennis Club** near Fashion Island, 900 Newport Center Dr., 714/640-4000 or toll-free 800/228-9290; www.marriot.com. The "tennis club" refers to eight lighted tennis courts (extra). Golf is also available. Rates: $169 and up.

Anyone opting for a street-side room at the appealing 1930s' Spanish-style **Balboa Inn,** by the Balboa Pier and Balboa Beach at 105 Main St., 714/675-3412, www.balboainn.com, also receives a free nightly live-jazz serenade from the Studio Cafe just across the way. The decor here is flowery country French. Each of the 34 rooms and 14 suites boasts a view of some sort (not necessarily the ocean), though the most pacifying peek at the Pacific is from the pool area. Seven rooms include an in-room spa, 10 have a fireplace. Continental breakfast is served in the lobby. Rates from $169, from $145 in the off-season. P.S. Kareem Abdul-Jabbar once owned the place, which explains the oversized doorways and furniture in Room 220.

Newport Bed-and-Breakfast Inns

Newport Beach bed-and-breakfast inns deliver the most ocean ambience. Probably the best bet for romance—and not all that pricey if you opt for a cheaper room—is the two-story **Portofino Beach Hotel** on Balboa Peninsula just north of the pier, 2306 W. Ocean Front (at 23rd St.), 949/673-7030, www.portofinobeachhotel.com, with 15 rooms, four villas, and a "casa" that sleeps 10. The style here is upscale European, with decor running to antiques, armoires, and brass beds. Some rooms and three villas look out over the ocean; some feature skylights, fireplaces, and in-room whirlpool tubs. Rates: $159–279 (weekly rates available), and children 16 and under stay free. Breakfast is included; there's also a restaurant on the premises.

For Victorian romance with frills, flounces, and French and American antiques, try the **Doryman's Inn** nearby, a dignified 1891 brick beauty across from the Newport Pier at 2102 W. Ocean Front, 949/675-7300. Every room features a fireplace and sunken marble Jacuzzi tub, some have a four-poster bed with mirrored headboard.

Besides breakfast, other goodies include a bottle of wine or champagne upon arrival, butter cookies and chocolates in the evening, a patio with a view, even a rooftop sundeck. Rates: $175–325.

The only place to stay out on Balboa Island (adults only) is the down-home 1925 **Balboa Island Hotel,** convenient to the ferry at 127 Agate Ave., 949/675-3613. The three rooms here, two with a queen bed, one with a twin, share bathrooms. For breakfast, count on fresh fruit, muffins, and coffee. Rates: $85 in the high season, $65 otherwise.

EATING IN NEWPORT BEACH

Casual at Breakfast

You'll find no shortage of coffee-and-pastry stops in and around Newport Beach. For atmosphere à la Berkeley on Balboa Peninsula, try the **Alta Cafe Warehouse and Roasting Co.,** 506 31st St. (off Newport Blvd.), 949/675-0233. For croissants and great coffee, try **C'est Si Bon,** off the highway in Newport Beach at 149 Riverside, 949/645-0447, also in Corona del Mar at 3444 E. Coast Hwy., 949/675-0994.

As beloved in Orange County as Peet's is in Berkeley, **Diedrich's** is the native java hot spot. The closest Newport location for most folks is actually in Costa Mesa at 474 E. 17th St. (the extension of Westcliff Dr., near Irvine Ave.), 949/646-0323. There's another in Newport Beach proper, at 3601 Jamboree Rd., 949/833-9143, more convenient if you're heading out to the Back Bay. Seattle-based **Starbucks Coffee** is also established here, tucked into a little shopping center at 1128 Irvine Ave., 949/650-0369, and no doubt many more places by now, but the minimalist atmosphere is more conducive to takeout than hangout.

Funky for classic American breakfast is laid-back, low-key **Cappy's Cafe,** 5930 W. Coast Hwy. in Newport Beach, 949/646-4202. If you find yourself out out on Balboa Island early in the day, try **Wilma's Patio,** 225 Marine, 949/675-5542. On the peninsula, consider **Britta's Cafe**

two blocks from the Balboa Pavilion at 205 Main, 949/675-8146, though **Ruby's** at the end of the Balboa Pier has its charms. (For more on Ruby's, see below.)

Consider any of the area's upscale hotels for something more elegant in the morning.

Local Classics

The 1940s-style **Ruby's** out on Balboa Pier, 949/675-7829, is the first and original in this popular chain of boogying burger joints done in red, white, and polished chrome. Sitting on the roof for alfresco breakfast is a real treat at this one. The original Ruby's is still going strong, but now there are Ruby's outposts all over Southern California.

But the best bet for *fast* fast food—fresh burgers sans ambience—is **In-N-Out Burger,** closest here at 594 19th St. in Costa Mesa, toll-free 800/786-1000, where snap-to service comes with the employee profit-sharing plan.

Food snobs pooh-pooh the place, but for inexpensive and decent seafood *everybody* goes to **The Crab Cooker,** a lobster-red presence on the peninsula at 2200 Newport Blvd., 949/673-0100. Lunch and dinner specialties include Man-

hattan-style clam chowder, mesquite-grilled seafood and, yes, crab. As you can tell from a glance at the shuffling crowd on the sidewalk outside, no reservations are taken here (no credit cards either); add your name to the list and then join the line. Once you land a table, appreciate the ambience. A shark chained to the ceiling presides over the close-quarters decor: Formica tables with quaint plastic breadstick and condiment containers, paper plates and placemats, even disposable silverware. At last report copies of the proprietor's 45 rpm single, "I Know Why The Fishes Cry," were still available for $1. There's another Crab Cooker in Tustin, 17260 E. 17th St., 714/573-1077.

Sabatino's Sausage Company

Virtually immune to tourist traffic is Sabatino's Lido Shipyard Sausage Company, 949/723-0645, tucked in among the boat shops and warehouses at 251 Shipyard Way, Cabin D on the Lido Peninsula—itself an opposable thumb on Balboa Peninsula, accessible via Lido Park Dr. just off Lafayette Ave. in Newport Beach.

Sabatino's is open daily for lunch and dinner. Eat cafe-style outdoors, weather permitting, to fully appreciate the semi-industrial shipyard ambience, or indoors, where the atmosphere is also relaxed. Sandwiches and salads dominate the lunch menu; you can't go wrong with any Sabatino's sausage sandwich or a Caesar salad, but the Sizzling Sausage Platter is a star attraction, served with pasta and bread (best with the giardinera, or Italian-style olive relish). The wonderful Sicilian sausages here date from an 1864 Sabatino family innovation, in which fat is removed from the meat and special goat's-milk cheese added in its stead. The result? Sausages, either mild or spicy, that are quite moist and incredibly tasty. Especially at dinner Sabatino's is also popular for its pasta specialties and other traditional Italian dishes—chicken, fresh fish, and veal selections, not to mention a superb rack of lamb. But unless you're religious about vegetarianism, do *not* leave this place without taking along at least one selection from the sausage counter.

Finding Sabatino's is a bit tricky, though certainly worth the effort. From downtown Newport Beach, head south on Newport Boulevard. After crossing the Coast Highway, turn left onto Via Lido (at the first light). Turn right onto Lafayette, then left at Lido Park Drive. There's a stop sign and "Lido Peninsula" sign, though it looks as if you're driving into a residential area. Continue to the next stop sign, at Shipyard, and turn right.

Also Imaginative and Affordable
JACKshrimp, 2400 W. Coast Hwy. (near Tustin Ave.), 949/650-5577, is hot stuff, a jammin' jambalaya joint serving secret-recipe jambalaya and Louisiana-style shrimp specialties in a very casual atmosphere. Lunch is served only on Friday, 11:30 A.M.–2:30 P.M. Dinner is served nightly, Mon.–Thurs. 5:30–10 P.M., Friday and Saturday until 11, on Sunday starting at 3:30 P.M. For healthy Mexican, the place is **La Fogata** near the Port Theater in Corona del Mar, 3025 E. Coast Hwy., 949/673-2211.

One of the area's best bets for Chinese is in Costa Mesa. The long-running **Mandarin Gourmet,** 1500 Adams Ave., 714/540-1937, is beloved for its traditional Peking duck, seafood dishes, and almost endless menu.

For exceptional French picnic fixings, try the **Pascal Epicerie,** 949/261-9041, adjacent to the famed restaurant of the same name on Bristol Street. For more information, see Fine Dining, below.

Higher-Priced Spreads
The Golden Truffle, 1767 Newport Blvd. (between 17th and 18th, just before the 55 Freeway begins in Costa Mesa), 949/645-9858, is as unassuming as it is exceptional, a French-Caribbean bistro serving specialties such as chianti braised lamb shank with noodles and Caribbean prime Angus skirt steak with soul slaw and fries. The Jamaican jerk chicken salad is nothing to shake a stick at either. The menu changes seasonally, featuring 15–20 specials every night. It's open Tues.–Sat. for lunch and dinner. Fabulous for French is **Pescadou Bistro,** 3325 Newport Blvd., 949/675-6990, with a surprisingly reasonable fixed-price menu.

Immensely popular for Northern Italian is lively, dinner-only **Issay Restaurant,** 485 N. Newport Blvd., 949/722-2992. Another impressive Italian is family-run **Mama Rose** in nearby Costa Mesa at 2346 Newport Blvd., 949/650-1949, open Tues.–Sat. for dinner only. Well worth it for relaxed yet pricey Indian fare is **Mayur,** 2931 E. Coast Hwy., 949/675-6622, featuring seafood and other specialties, such as shrimp Vindaloo, shrimp Tandoori, and chicken tikka Masala.

The tony New England-style **Yankee Tavern,** 333 Bayside Dr. in Newport Beach, 949/675-5333, adds dressed-down East Coast airs. Highlights include a traditional New England boiled dinner. The rest of the menu runs to beer-battered fish and chips, turkey meat loaf, and Yankee pot roast.

Tonier but most appreciated for its spectacular seafood is **21 Ocean Front** overlooking Newport Pier at 21 Ocean Front, 949/675-2566. One of the best bets around, though, is surprisingly relaxed **Bistro 201,** 3333 W. Pacific Coast Hwy., 949/631-1551.

Fine Dining, Dressed Up and Dressed Down

Genuine gastronomic adventure awaits in Newport Beach. Head to the south of France, for example, via one of Orange County's best restaurants. Serving Provençal in a rose garden of a bistro, **Pascal** in a shopping center just off the Del Mar Freeway at 1000 N. Bristol Ave. (near Jamboree), 949/752-0107, is just about everyone's favorite unstuffy French restaurant. Specialties include seared salmon filet with watercress sauce and baby lamb rack with sweet garlic. Reservations definitely advised. Men: jacket required. You can also try Pascal to go—thanks to the dandy little take-out shop adjacent, 949/261-9041, which offers baguette sandwiches and such things as eggplant caviar, unusual salads, whole cooked chickens, and French ham and cheeses.

Another contender for favorite French restaurant is **Aubergine** on the Balboa Peninsula at 508 29th St., 949/723-4150, open Tues.–Sat. from 6 P.M. (reservations a must). Fine dining doesn't get finer than this, at a Cal-French restaurant still one of the brightest stars on the southstate's dining scene. Set in a beachside cottage, the restaurant recently reopened after a complete renovation with a stylishly understated new decor. Choice of three fixed-price menus: three course, $55; five course, $75; and the chef's nine-course tasting menu for $90. And the atmosphere is unusually warm, only in part due to the neighborhood setting.

For stylish pan-Asian fare and impressive sushi bar, the place is **Aysia 101,** 2901 W. Coast Hwy., 949/722-4128. Also a hit in Orange County is **Kitayama,** south of Jamboree Rd. at 101 Bay View Pl., 949/725-0777, open for lunch weekdays only, for dinner nightly. For impressive California-style Japanese, try **Abe Restaurant,** 2900 Newport Blvd., 949/675-1739, open for lunch and dinner.

Quite special for Sunday brunch and fancy-dress California cuisine at dinner, the **The Pavilion** at the Four Seasons Hotel near Fashion Island at 690 Newport Center Dr. (at Santa Cruz), 949/760-4920, is hard to beat. Orange County's most popular dress-up dining spot, though, seems to be Fashion Island's **The Ritz,** 880 Newport Center Dr. (at Santa Barbara), 949/720-

---

A NEWPORT ROMANCE: VILLA NOVA

A Newport Beach favorite since the 1930s for romantic dress-up dining along the waterfront is Villa Nova, 3131 W. Pacific Coast Hwy. (near Newport Blvd.), 949/642-7880. This is the place, after all, where Joe DiMaggio took Marilyn Monroe on a blind date, and where Vincent Minelli proposed to Judy Garland. And how many places do you know that still have a piano bar?

Now open at a new location, since the original building perished in a fire a few years back, the very Italian Villa Nova is famous for its vast menu. Choosing is the hard part—from endless house-made pastas and gnocchi served with secret-recipe 1920s' sauces "imported" from Abuzzi, Italy, to seafood, chicken, steak, veal, and various house specialties. Children's menu, too, and an impressive list of Californian, Italian, and French wines. Reservations definitely advisable.

1800, where you can expect traditional continental fare.

To dent the bankroll on behalf of the beef-eater tradition, hoof it over to **Five Crowns,** 3801 E. Coast Hwy. (at Poppy) in Corona del Mar, 949/760-0331. This ersatz English manor is beloved by tourists and locals alike for its humongous portions of prime rib and other specialties. The filet mignon is excellent, tender enough to slice with a spoon.

DOWN THE COAST: CRYSTAL COVE STATE PARK

South along the coast toward Laguna Beach is one of Orange County's genuine gems, Crystal Cove State Park, the largest remaining patch of coastal land still open to the general public. And what a patch it is—tide pools and sandy coves along more than three miles of shoreline, plus, on the other side of the highway, once-wooded El Moro Canyon in the San Joaquin Hills, a total of 2,791 acres owned until 1979 by the Irvine Company.

The beach here, open daily from 6 A.M. to sunset, is usually one of the loneliest around—a real draw when you've had enough of Orange County crowds. Offshore, to a depth of 120 feet, is one of the state's official "underwater parks," a prime scuba- and skin-diving locale. For more pedestrian aquatic explorations, study local tide tables and head for the tide pools. This low-tide adventure (don't touch) is usually better in winter, when the tides are more extreme because of the gravitational pull of both sun and moon. Access points to beach parking and facilities are at El Moro Canyon, Reef Point, Los Trancos, and Pelican Point.

Inland, some 23 miles of trails wind through the hills of El Moro Canyon, which is heaven for mountain bikers, hikers, and pikers on horseback. Climb on up, at least for the ocean views, or come along on park-sponsored interpretive walks or backcountry hikes—the latter often to places not otherwise open to the public.

Also fascinating is the *town* of **Crystal Cove,** seemingly unchanged since the 1920s and now included on the National Register of Historic Places. The 46 beachfront bungalows, originally built to house Irvine Company ranch hands, are scheduled to be made available for rent one day soon—a process delayed by the fact that current residents are (understandably) reluctant to leave their cheap oceanfront digs, and the fact that there has been some controversy over state park plans to "rehab" the town as a swank beach resort. Other park facilities are currently available, including fairly unobtrusive picnic areas and restrooms with showers.

The day-use fee at Crystal Cove is $3. For other park information, including if and when the cabins and campground will be available, contact: Crystal Cove State Park, 8471 Pacific Coast Hwy., Crystal Cove, 949/494-3539 or 492-0802.

LAGUNA BEACH AND VICINITY

THE ARTS, ARTISTS, AND ASSORTED OTHERS

Unlike most beach towns, laid-back Laguna Beach has tried to put a lid on the booming business of T-shirteries and other standards of the tourism trade—to little avail. It's hard to believe that this village of just under 30,000 attracts about three million tourists each year. Why do they come? Because Laguna Beach is lovely, for one thing, with a woodsy, small-town feel, white-sand beaches, and craggy coastal coves and outcroppings vaguely reminiscent of Big Sur. For another, because this artsy onetime artists colony has a quirky creative character.

Built on land never included within a land-grant rancho, since the days of early settlement Laguna Beach has gone its own way. And the town still cultivates its eccentricities. Chief among them is the odd and oddly compelling annual Pageant of the Masters presentation of *tableaux vivants,* "living pictures" allowing life to imitate art imitating life. Other oddities persist. Even in this uncharitable bottom-line age, for example, affluent Laguna Beach still tries to find room for artists, oddballs, and assorted others who don't fit the mass-produced American mold. Nonetheless, having money is almost a necessity here. Worthy civic intentions notwithstanding, bohemians have all but been replaced by BMWs and beach resorts.

Even this latest Laguna Beach lifestyle is threatened by success. The city's population has more than doubled in the past 10 years. With the arrival of tourist season every summer, the population doubles again. On summer weekends in particular, traffic can become hopelessly snarled—in town, and up and down the highway—with parking spaces nearly as precious as local real estate. And more people are on the way. Like waves from an inland sea, new residential developments roll toward Laguna Beach from the north, south, and east.

Artistic Laguna Beach

In the 1930s Laguna Beach was hardly the typical California tourist destination. The real appeal was the possibility of escaping, from Los Angeles and vicinity in particular. Big-screen stars fleeing their own celebrity, including Charlie Chaplin and Bette Davis, and a galaxy of lesser-

known artists populated little Laguna Beach. For
the most part, this tiny artists' enclave was close
enough to L.A. for convenience yet far enough
away to avoid public curiosity and scrutiny. That
trend continued over the years, even as cultural
celebs became more beat, then countercultural.
In the 1960s, for example, Timothy Leary was a
common local sighting.

These days the Laguna Beach arts scene is
populated in part by members of the city's large
gay and lesbian community, responsible for new
public housing and other support for AIDS
patients. Financial pressures for local artists—
those still here—are immense, however, since
most are quickly being priced out of the market
for both living and studio space.

PAGEANT OF THE MASTERS AND FESTIVAL OF THE ARTS

Especially on a first-time trip to Laguna Beach,
seeing the sights should be synonymous with
attending the town's simultaneous Festival of
the Arts and Pageant of the Masters, held
together in July and August.

The fine arts and crafts on display—all strictly
local, displayed by artists and craftspeople from
up and down the Orange County coast—*are*
fine, the variety great: handmade musical instruments, furniture, sculpture, and scrimshaw.
There's even a "junior art" division.

But the pageant is unlike anything you're likely
to encounter anywhere else on earth—a living,
breathing tribute to the art world's old masters
and ancient treasures, a carefully staged two-
hour magic show that's been tickling everyone's
fancy since the 1930s.

The Pageant of the Masters

The pageant's *tableaux vivants,* or living pictures, are large-scale sleight of hand or trompe
l'oeil, literally, "fooling the eye." Whether the
oversized artwork on display is Leonardo da
Vinci's *Last Supper* (a pageant favorite), Renoir's
Grape Pickers at Lunch, or Monet's *Women in
the Garden,* on cue the costumed participants
come on stage and freeze into the background
frieze. Then—after the house goes dark and the
stage lights come on—the entire audience gasps.
Because there on stage, 50 times larger than

GREETERS CORNER

While wandering toward Main Beach, take note
of Greeters Corner in **Main Beach Park** at the
end of Forest Avenue. The statue in front of
the **Greeters Corner Restaurant,** 329 S. Coast
Hwy., 949/494-0361, commemorates the town's
long tradition of greeters—and, in particular,
Eiler Larsen. A Danish immigrant and World
War I veteran, Larsen arrived in Laguna Beach
in the 1930s to serve as "the Laguna greeter," a
title (and unpaid job) he held for 30 years. An
organized attempt to silence Larsen failed in
1959, once a local survey established that almost 90 percent of the citizenry wanted him to
stay—and to continue waving and bellowing at
passing cars.

Someone has served in the role of local greeter
since the late 19th century, when Laguna Beach
was known as Lagona—a variation of "Lagonas,"
a coastal territory named in the 1500s by local native peoples. In the 1880s, for example, Portuguese fisherman Joe Lucas would holler at
passing stagecoaches. At last report, the town's
greeting duties fall to a fellow by the name of
Number One Archer.

life, is an uncanny reproduction of the real thing.

So there's really no need to traipse across
the country to the Metropolitan, or cross oceans
to the Louvre or Uffizi, when you can come to
Laguna Beach.

It's not all high art, though. In the process of
dazzling the crowds with impersonations of two-
and three-dimensional reality, pageanteers also
pose as sculptures, California orange-crate
labels, hair combs and other jewelry, even
postage stamps.

It takes endless volunteer effort—not to mention 100 gallons of makeup, 75 gallons of paint,
1000 yards of fabric, and a budget of about
$800,000—to pull off this elaborate charade.
Annual pageant proceeds, usually in excess of
$200,000, support scholarships for high school
and college students.

Practical Pageant and Festival

The annual arts festival and pageant take place
in July and August at Irvine Bowl Park, also
known as the Festival of the Arts Pageant

Grounds, 650 Laguna Canyon Road. The theater is the Irvine Bowl itself, a 2500-seat theater nestled into the canyon hillside.

More than 250,000 people typically attend these events, so also plan for lodgings. If you're staying in town, walk to the festival; it's only a few blocks from Main Beach. If you're here just for the day and driving, once parked, stay parked—then, if you're also heading downtown, walk. To find a parking place, arrive very early in the day. A shuttle bus service (small fee) runs between the area's summer festivals and the parking lots along Laguna Canyon Road.

Admission to the festival itself is $5. Pageant tickets start at $10 each and are generally sold out months in advance, but if you're lucky there may be cancellations on an appropriate performance night. For current information contact: **Festival of the Arts/Pageant of the Masters,** 650 Laguna Canyon Rd., Laguna Beach, 949/497-6582 for general information, toll-free 800/487-3378 to order tickets, or check www.pageanttickets.com.

The Sawdust Festival and Art-A-Fair
Since the 1960s the Sawdust Festival has been the "alternative" Laguna Beach arts celebration, now a major-league crafts fair held more or less concurrently across the road at 935 Laguna Canyon Rd., 949/494-3030; www.sawdustartfestival.org. These days it's an "Auld Tyme Faire," in the ever-popular Renaissance style, with mimes, strolling minstrels, and plenty of ale. Also going on every summer: the juried Art-A-Fair festivities at 777 Laguna Canyon Rd., 949/494-4514, or check www.art-a-fair.com.

OTHER LAGUNA BEACH ARTS

More Arts Festivals
If slogging through the summer crowds seems unappealing, come some other time. Arts and crafts fairs of some sort are scheduled year-round, including the April **Art Walk Lunch** at the festival grounds (eat, then meet the artists) and the Sawdust Festival's **Winter Fantasy** from mid-November into December. During the rest of the year, crafts fairs are typically scheduled at least twice each month; call the visitors bureau at 949/497-9229 for information.

The Laguna Art Museum
These days Laguna Beach is hardly recognizable as "SoHo by the Sea." But at the turn of the 20th century, scores of American artists

LAGUNA BEACH INFO AND TRAVEL TIPS

Famous Laguna Beach arts festivals make the sun-loving summer beach scene that much more congested. Anyone phobic about personal space (and parking space) might consider coming for the arts festivals as a day trip—staying elsewhere—and returning at some other time for more thorough exploration.

For more information about local attractions, contact the **Laguna Beach Visitor Bureau and Chamber of Commerce,** 252 Broadway, Laguna Beach, 949/497-9229 or toll-free 800/877-1115 (prerecorded), fax 949/376-0558; www.lagunabeachinfo.org.

Traffic Safety, Getting Oriented, Parking
If you plan to come or go from the east via Laguna Canyon Road (Hwy. 133), which connects Laguna Beach to the 405 inland—be extra cautious. This narrow two-lane highway has become Orange County's blood alley, its high accident rate attrib-

uted to too many people in too much of a hurry. The same caution holds for the alternative route inland, Laguna Canyon Road to El Toro Road to I-5. Aside from the coast highway, there are no other routes into Laguna Beach.

Once here, you'll need to orient yourself to Pacific Coast Highway. Laguna Beach highway addresses north of Broadway are designated "North Coast Highway"; those south of town to Crown Valley Parkway, "South Coast Highway."

Unless your vehicle is safely stored at a local motel or hotel, parking is a challenge. Metered parking (bring lots of quarters) is available on many streets. There are also various lots (try Ocean) where all-day parking runs around $8–10. If you're coming just for the Pageant of the Masters and associated arts festivals, come early, park in the large lots along Laguna Canyon Road, and shuttle back and forth to town. Arrive by 10 A.M. and there should be no problem.

MADAME MODJESKA *IN AMERICA*

Susan Sontag's recent novel *In America* was inspired by Orange County's own Helena Modjeska, the noted 19th-century actress who renounced her European stage career and emigrated from Poland to the United States to start a utopian farming venture with her husband. In its fictionalized facts, the book parallels Modjeska's story. A star of the Warsaw stage married to the aristocratic Count Bozenta—in revolt against his family and dreaming of his own agricultural eden—in 1876 Modjeska and her husband arrived in California with an accomplished entourage that included Henryk Sienkiewicz, who later won the Nobel Prize for literature.

In the book, as in real life, they all settled down in what was then the Wild West of Orange County—European overlords determined to wring both civilization and crops out of the wily Mexican-American wilderness.

And in the book, as in the course of actual events, none of the privileged Poles knew beans about farming. As Modjeska would later recall in her autobiography: "The most alarming feature of this bucolic fancy was the rapid disappearance of cash and the absence of even a shadow of income."

So Helena Modjeska resumed her career—and soon became one of the most accomplished actresses on the American stage during the golden age of theater.

"It felt like, an escapade; like leaving home; like telling lies—and she would tell many lies," reflects Sontag's protagonist as she arrives in San Francisco. "She was beginning again; she was rejoining her destiny, which conferred on her the rich sensation that she had never gone astray."

As Modjeska's star ascended in America, she crisscrossed the country in her own private railroad car and eventually played opposite Edwin Booth and Maurice Barrymore, the greatest actors of the day. She became Camille, and Ophelia. She was Nora in the premiere of Ibsen's *A Doll's House.* Yet her most famous role was Rosalind in Shakespeare's *As You Like It.*

Equally adept at besting the twists and turns of fate, in the 1880s the now wealthy Madame Modjeska and Count Bozenta returned to Orange County to build a more theatrical version of their earlier dream. The grand rambling home they built here, complete with a small stage extending out into the garden, was called Arden, as Modjeska later wrote, "because, like the Forest of Arden in *As You Like it,* everything that Shakespeare speaks of was on the spot—oak trees, running brooks, palms, snakes, even lions." She and the count lived here for 18 happy years, from 1888 to 1906.

Mountain lions still roam the Santa Ana Mountains, though they are not so common these days. And Modjeska's home still stands in a live oak grove on the banks of Santiago Creek, its original Forest of Arden—English yews, palms, white lilac, and crown of thorns—still thriving. Now a National Historic Landmark known as **Modjeska House Historical Park,** 25151 Serrano Rd. in Modjeska Canyon, about 10 miles east of Lake Forest via Santiago Canyon Road, the estate is owned by the county of Orange. The home and gardens are open to the public only for docent-guided tours—the canyon road is narrow, the area residential, and gawkers are discouraged—which at last report were offered by advance reservation only at 10 A.M. on the second and fourth Saturday of the month. Tour fee is $5. For more information and reservations, call 949/855-2028.

---

arrived here determined to paint in the open air *(en plein air)* like the French impressionists and Hudson River School. The legacy of artists of The Plein Air School, including Joseph Kleitsch, William Griffith, and Frank Cuprien, has been lasting. Which explains the fact that, while other high school football teams identify themselves as "cougars" or "chargers," for example, the big bruisers here are known as the Laguna Beach High Artists—surely enough to strike fear into the heart of any opponent.

The hot pink Laguna Art Museum, 307 Cliff Dr. (at Coast Hwy.), 949/494-6531, www.lagunaartmuseum.org, has earned renown as the only Southern California art museum to focus exclusively on American art—contemporary California art in particular, along with avant-garde special shows. After a short-lived merger with the Orange County Museum of Art, the Laguna Art Museum is once again a local institution. At last report the museum was open Tues.–Sun. 11 A.M.–5 P.M., and until 9 P.M. the first Thursday of the month (with free admission). Regular admission: $5 adults, $4 students, $3 children.

The Laguna Playhouse

Another local pleasure is the Laguna Playhouse, featuring a fine local repertory program. The playhouse, 606 Laguna Canyon Rd., 949/497-ARTS, www.lagunaplayhouse.com, often presents original work by local playwrights, sometimes as community fund-raisers.

The Ballet Pacifica

Ballet Pacifica's office burned down in the 1993 Laguna Beach fire, thus the official relocation to Irvine. As far as locals are concerned, though, it's still a Laguna Beach phenomenon. The children's concert series is still staged here, at the Festival Forum Theater, 650 Laguna Canyon Rd., in September or October and in February, March, and April. Ballet Pacifica's Christmas *Nutcracker* and three other performances (October, March, and May) are staged at Irvine's Barclay Theater. For current information, call 949/851-9930.

ART OF SHOPPING

Laguna Beach Galleries

Shopping is a serious local pastime, a primary local attraction. Laguna Beach is chock-full of shops, where you'll find the tackiest of tourist

---

SHOPPING ORANGE COUNTY

Shopping in Orange County has almost achieved the status of art in other times, other places. To fully experience this particular cult of culture, a good place to start is **Newport Beach** and vicinity. Newport Beach as a city reaches beyond the beach inland, its borders entwined with sister cities **Costa Mesa** and **Irvine,** the entire area encompassing more business parks, neighborhood shopping districts, and both major-league and minimalls than anyone can count.

The premier destination, of course, is **South Coast Plaza** in Costa Mesa, the county's de facto city center, covered in detail under Shopping as the Center of Everything, elsewhere in this chapter. As if to suggest that a backlash against consumerism is conceivable even in Orange County, a clever approach is **The Lab,** a.k.a. "The Anti-Mall," at 2930 Bristol St. in Costa Mesa, about a mile from South Coast Plaza. A scaled-down variation of Santa Monica's Third Street Promenade theme, The Anti-Mall is a no-frills 40,000-square-foot, two-warehouse adventure in marketing sincerity—decked out to attract Gen Xers otherwise too cool to shop. Anti-Mall decor is classic post-apocalypse, with rusted sheet metal on the walls, exposed ceiling beams, concrete floors, and shipping pallets nailed to the walls for merchandise display. A scene right out of a documentary on toxic waste dumps—rusted oil barrels artfully leaking—stands in as the mall's restful fountain. The recycled look furnishes "the living room" (pool hall) at **Urban Outfitters,** which otherwise offers flannel shirts and high-priced trendy household items perfect for the upscale homeless. **Empire Sports** specializes in skateboard and snowboard apparel, as well as essential sport "hardware." For more boardware, flow into **Department of Water and Power.** For coffee and a place to read, dive into the nouveau bohemian **Gypsy Den. Music X** specializes in acid jazz, independent labels, and imports. **Collectors Library** sells underground comics. Still, style counts. **Na Na** sells Doc Marten-style shoes, **Stateside,** vintage clothing, **Habit,** shoes and clothes. For theater, show up at **Trilogy Playhouse.** Pretty great for a Cuban-style meal is **Habana,** 714/556-0176. For more information about The Lab, call 714/966-6660 or try www.antimall.com.

Predominant in the Newport Beach area, though, is unapologetic shopping. Pretty hip is Costa Mesa's **Triangle Square** at the ocean end of the 55 Fwy. (Newport Blvd.), 949/722-1600; www.trianglesquare.com. One Triangle star is the mega-music **Virgin Megastore,** 1875 Newport Blvd., 949/645-9906. Or you can just do it at **Nike Town,** 949/642-6363, aided by floor upon floor of sportswear, shoes, and equipment. Or **The North Face,** 949/646-0909, for the ultimate in outdoor gear. Also here: a **Barnes & Noble** bookstore, 949/631-0614; an eight-screen **Edwards movie theater, 949/574-7755; and the** Whole Foods Market, 949/574-3800.

Open-air **Fashion Island,** most directly reached via Newport Center Dr. from the Coast Hwy., is the Newport area's original megamall, seriously challenged in recent years by the international success of South Coast Plaza. Encircled by Newport Center Dr. and surrounded by a sea of high-rise business parks, Fashion Island is anchored by Neiman Marcus, Bloomingdale's, Robinsons-May, and Macy's bric-a-brac and fine art and jewelry. Laguna Beach boasts 60–70 art galleries. Unlike special exhibits and collection displays at the local art museum, however, much of the gallery fare is far from cutting edge, in California or elsewhere. To be sure you're buying local art—to support the health and welfare of artists still managing to survive in high-rent Orange County—attend local arts and craft fairs, mentioned above. And when in doubt, don't hesitate to ask. Otherwise, to find out what's what and where it might be, pick up the current *Local Arts* guide, available in most shops.

For an introduction to Laguna Beach's Plein Air School, stop by **Redfern Gallery**, 1540 S. Coast Hwy., 949/497-3356. That's the specialty. **The Vladimir Solokov Studio Gallery** in the same complex, 714/494-3633, is a working studio specializing in bright-colored abstract and mixed media paintings. Nearby, at 1390 S. Coast, is the **Esther Wells Collection**, 949/494-2497, noted for its impressionistic watercolors (always some local art on display) as well as sculpture and jewelry.

To appreciate just how much disposable income some people have, stop by the **Sherwood Gallery**, 460 S. Coast Hwy., 949/497-2668, with its contemporary and pop art, sculpture (some kinetic), jewelry, and unusual furnishings. The

---

Women's. Focal point is the three-story **Atrium Court**, with its pricey farmers market, intriguing food court—from Blueberry Hill Gourmet Hamburger—to Veg a Go Go—and about 200 shopping stops, as various as **Anthropologie** and **Betsey Johnson, Modern Romance** and **Timberland** (inside At Ease). Kids, though, are usually more interested in the mall's "dancing fountains." For information, call 949/721-2000 or toll-free 800/495-4753. Dozens of restaurants, a cinema complex, nice hotels, and the **Newport Harbor Art Museum** round out the neighborhood.

You'll find at least one shopping enclave in every Newport nook. Beyond downtown-style districts mentioned elsewhere, there's **Mariner's Mile** along W. Coast Hwy. (also home port to the Balboa Bay Club) and **Lido Marina Village** on the peninsula along Via Oporto.

And if you tire of Newport Beach and vicinity, try the **MainPlace** mall in Santa Ana, 714/547-7000, www.mainplacesantaana.com, with major department store anchors—Macy's, Nordstrom, and Robinsons-May—plus an abundance of unusual small shops, from **Crate and Barrel** and **Eddie Bauer** to **Retro, Retro.** For movies, try the MainPlace Theaters. There's an abundance of restaurant choices, too, from **Café Sbarro** to the **Paradise Bakery and Café.** MainPlace even offers shuttle service.

In nearby Tustin is the **Tustin Marketplace**, 714/730-4124, with an immensely popular **Ikea** store, even an **In-N-Out Burger.** For something a little more wholesome, try the wonderful **Corner Bakery Café.** Quite recently Tustin Marketplace "exploded" across the street into a matching mall on the other side—the **Irvine Marketplace**—so now you can truly shop 'til you drop. If you don't drop, move on to Orange. **The City Shopping Center** on City Blvd. and the **Brea Mall** just off the Orange Fwy. (Hwy. 57 at Imperial Hwy.) are both in the city of Orange, though **Old Towne Orange,** "the antique capital of California," is immensely popular. The big news these days is *The Block at Orange,* 1 City Blvd. W., 714/769-4001, www.theblockatorange.com, a stylish mix of shops and cool restaurants—these including **Café Tu Tu Tango, Left at Albuquerque,** and the **Wolfgang Puck Grand Café**—and abundant entertainment venues. Diversions include **Borders Books, Dave & Buster's, Gameworks, Mars Music, Vans Skate Park,** a **Virgin Megastore,** and a 30-screen **AMC Theatres** complex.

You can also shop on the cheap. If you're near Disneyland with some time on your hands, lose yourself inside 133,000-square-foot **Anaheim Indoor Marketplace,** 714/999-0888, which offers more than 200 outlets offering name-brand goods at 50-70 percent below retail. The Anaheim Marketplace also offers free shuttle service to area hotels. If heading north from Disneyland into Los Angeles, plan a stop at the **Citadel Factory Stores** looming next to I-5, 323/888-1724, www.citadelfactorystores.com, with more than 40 outlets, from Anne Taylor and Geoffrey Beene to Eddie Bauer and Benetton.

For that funky, old-fashioned, flea-market atmosphere, head to the Orange County Fair Grounds in Costa Mesa for the **Orange County Market Place,** held weekends only, 7 A.M.-4 P.M.

For more information about shopping in Orange County, contact the **Anaheim/Orange County Visitor and Convention Bureau** at 714/765-8888; www.anaheimoc.org.

colorful "Seven Stack Suitcase Dresser" spotted on one stroll, for example, cost a mere $5,400, the "Law & Order Chess Set," $3,200.

Other Shops

Thee Foxes' Trot, 264 Forest Ave., 949/494-4997, is a good stop for bath and homewares and a limited selection of unusual women's clothing. Also good for gifts and homewares is **Areo,** 207 Ocean Ave., 949/376-0535, where some of the vases, candles, candlesticks, and jewelry are locally made (ask).

Kyber Pass, 1970 S. Coast Hwy., 949/494-5021, specializes in jewelry, clothing, and art from Afghanistan. In the this-is-kitschy category, trail's end might be **Trails West Galleries,** 1476 S. Pacific Coast Hwy., 949/494-7888, where you can find Western art (paintings and sculpture) and such things as cowhide-covered pianos. Try **Tippecanoes,** 648 S. Coast Hwy., 949/494-1200, for antique oddities and vintage clothing.

In the next block is **Laguna Village,** 577 S. Coast Hwy., with various arts and crafts booths—a good bet for finding local work—plus the **Laguna Village Cafe,** 949/494-6344, a good bet for a beer-and-breakers break, out on the patio overlooking the ocean. To get up to speed on local writers, almost as numerous in this town as painters and potters, stop by **Upchurch-Brown Booksellers,** 949/497-8373, in the Lumberyard Village.

ART OF THE OUTDOORS: LAGUNA BEACH BEACHES AND PARKS

Main Beach and Vicinity

Main Beach is, well, the city's main beach, dominating the ocean side of downtown between the Laguna Art Museum and Hotel Laguna near Park Avenue. You'll know you've arrived when you spot the imposing glassed-in lifeguard tower, something of a local landmark. Most of the year you also can't miss the pickup basketball players, almost as competitive as the volleyballers. A wooden boardwalk snakes along the beach, with its youngsters, oldsters, and in-line skaters. At this intriguing if tamer version of Muscle Beach in Venice, everybody and everything hangs out.

South of Main Beach, overseen by high-priced real estate, are Laguna's "street beaches." Sections of this slim one-mile strand of sand are known by the names of intersecting streets, from **Sleepy Hollow Lane** and **Thalia** to **Oak** and **Brooks.** Farther south still is half-mile **Arch Cove,** popular for sunbathing, its section again named after relevant streets (Bluebird Canyon, Agate, Pearl, etc.).

Since the coast (actually, the beach) is clear between Laguna Beach and South Laguna, you might find a completely private cove if you're willing to walk, surf-dodge, and rock-hop the distance—not advisable at high tide. For more on what you'll find if you're crazy enough to try it, see South Laguna Beaches and Aliso Pier, below.

More Laguna Beach Beaches

North of Main Beach, atop the bluffs along Cliff Drive, is the **Heisler Park** promenade, a fine place for lolling on the lawn, picnicking, and people watching (public restrooms are here too). Down below are two rocky coves with nice tide pools, **Picnic Beach** at the end of Myrtle St. and **Rockpile Beach** at the end of Jasmine.

Nearby are three inlets that manage to combine the best of the beach scene with the best of beach scenery: **Shaw's Cove, Fisherman's Cove,** and **Diver's Cove.** Needless to say, the area is beloved by locals and often crowded. The path down to Shaw's Cove is on Cliff Drive at the end of Fairview; entrances to Fisherman's and Diver's coves are close together on Cliff, in the 600 block.

Half-moon **Crescent Bay Beach** (entrance at Cliff and Circle Dr.) is quite enticing, and usually offers some privacy for sunning, swimming, and skin diving. To reach **Crescent Bay Point Park** (great views) from Cliff Drive, turn left onto the highway and left again onto Crescent Bay Drive.

Special Beaches and a "Bark Park"

Popular for bodysurfing yet quite private by Laguna Beach standards, **Victoria Beach** is a local favorite. To get here, take Victoria Drive from the highway and then turn right onto Dumond. Tiny fan-shaped **Moss Beach** at the end of Moss Street is one of the best around, well protected for swimming, also popular for scuba diving. The three rocky fingers of **Wood's Cove** have helped create the pocket beaches here, plus providing a pounding-surf sideshow, great swimming, good scuba diving. (To get here, take the steps down from the intersection of Ocean Way and Diamond Street.) None of these beaches have public restrooms—the price of privacy—but at last report lifeguards were on duty, at least in summer.

If you bring Fido or Fifi along on this trip, you'll soon discover that dogs are not welcome at the beach (not to mention most other places). Laguna Beach offers some consolation, though. The city's Dog Park out on Laguna Canyon Road, known by locals as the Bark Park, is one of very few public areas in Orange County where people can legally let their dogs run free. (Free in this case means "loose"; it actually costs $2 to use this well-fenced pooch park.) And if you're sans beast but bored, come out to the Bark Park anyway. Watching dogs and their people at play is cheap entertainment. Laguna Beach's Bark Park is sponsored by RUFF, "Rescuing Unwanted Furry Friends."

South Laguna Beaches and Aliso Pier
Several miles south of Laguna Beach proper is the area aptly known as South Laguna. The main attraction here is **Aliso Creek Beach Park** at the mouth of Aliso Creek. In the late 1800s Helena Modjeska—the Shakespearean actress for whom Orange County's Modjeska Canyon was named—camped out with her entourage here in the coastal wilderness to beat the summer heat. Though houses are now the dominant feature of the surrounding landscape, the first thing you'll really notice is the Aliso Pier, which looks like a gargantuan arrow about to be shot out to sea. But take time to explore the small sandy coves here and the rocky tidepools beyond. For relative privacy, head south; to commune with the college-age crowd, head north.

Short, diamond-headed Aliso Pier is one of California's newest, constructed in 1972. It's also one of the state's most striking, awarded "outstanding design" status by the American Institute of Interior Designers. Only 620 feet long, the pier platform is concrete, perched atop pairs of hexagonal concrete pilings, with a upward-rising angle to help deflect the destructive force of the wild wave action that comes with heavy storms. Even the banisters are unusual (if not exactly politically correct), made of the very hard, scratch-resistant tropical wood *apatung.* And the platform's diamond shape requires extra banister—by design, to allow more elbow room for fisherfolk. At the foot of the pier is a hexagonal concession building, last stop for tackle, snacks, and a trip to the restroom.

STAYING IN LAGUNA BEACH

"Inexpensive" and "expensive" are relative terms, but it's safe to say that nothing in Laguna Beach is truly inexpensive. Here, and down the coast at the Ritz-Carlton, expensive really is expensive. If a low-rent stay is a must, hang your hat in Huntington Beach, or, if heading south, try camping or a cheap motel in Dana Point or the hostel in San Clemente.

Most Laguna Beach lodging rates go up for "the season" either in mid-June or on July 1—just in time for the local arts festivals—and then dive again in mid-September. If you're willing to miss the summer arts pageantry and attendant crowds, come in early June (it can be foggy) or just about any other time. For better value, look for establishments "close to" (not on) the beach and "near" (not in) town, and request a room at the lower end of the options range.

Less Expensive Laguna Options
Both Best Westerns offer good value even in summer, better value in the off-season. To make toll-free telephone reservations at any Best Western, call 800/780-7234 (United States and Canada). Closest to town is the **Best Western Laguna Brisas Spa Hotel,** 1600 S. Coast Hwy., 949/497-7272 or toll-free 800/624-4442, www .bestwestern.com, "just 58 steps from the beach." Half the rooms have an ocean view. All rooms include huge in-room whirlpools, cable TV, free movies, and refrigerators (the latter upon request). Continental breakfast is served. You'll find a coin laundry on the premises, along with heated pool, spa, and sundeck. Rates: $149 and up from June into early September, $129 and up otherwise, kids under 12 stay free (in your room). Senior and AAA discounts avail-

able. The attractive **Best Western Laguna Reef Inn** south of town at 30806 S. Coast Hwy., 949/499-2227, is a straight $99 in the summer for one person ($10 for each extra person, kids 10 and under free), otherwise $69 and up in the off-season. Some units have kitchens, $15 extra. Continental breakfast.

In the motel category, you also can't go too far wrong at the 22-room **Best Inn**, 1404 N. Coast Hwy., 949/494-6464 or toll-free 800/221-2222 for reservations. Rates: $99 and up from mid-June through mid-September, otherwise $79 and up). And check www.bestinn.com for special discounts for seniors, government, and the military.

More Expensive, More Ambience
There's something quite comforting about the predictability of motels, but other styles of accommodation offer more *romance*. Or something.

Two moderately expensive hotels offer both beach-town ambience and convenient central location. The former Hotel San Maarten is now the **Holiday Inn Laguna Beach** across from the beach at 696 S. Coast Hwy., 949/494-1001 or toll-free 800/228-5691; www.holiday-inn.com. Breezy French Caribbean style enlivens the lobby—note the hand-painted ceiling, verdant nature scenes of birds, plants, and flowers—and the tropical courtyard, with its patio and pool. Rooms don't necessarily court the same flash but are reliably "Holiday Inn." Regular rooms run $129–159 on weekdays in summer and $179–199 on weekends; rates are $109–139 at other times, continental breakfast included. Suites with kitchenettes and microwaves (some have in-room spas) are available. Also here, a restaurant and bar, plus free parking.

The local grande dame—and the only place around with a private beach—is the recently redone landmark **Hotel Laguna,** practically on Main Beach at 425 S. Coast Hwy., 949/494-1151 or toll-free 800/524-2927 (in California only); www.hotellaguna.com. Most rooms are modern, with ceiling fans and the basics, and some afford ocean views. Since the Hotel Laguna was Humphrey Bogart's favorite Laguna Beach hideaway, two suites—the **Bogart Suite** and **Bacall Suite**—get special treatment, complete with canopy beds. Room rates run $110–250 in summer, $85-225 and up at other times,

with free valet parking. On-site you'll find a spectacularly good seafood restaurant, **Claes Seafood, Etc.,** and **Le Bar,** for an ocean view with your cocktails.

Laguna Beach Bed-and-Breakfast Inns
Local bed-and-breakfast establishments also offer nonmotel ambience. The **Carriage House Inn,** 1322 Catalina St., 949/494-8945, www.carriagehouse.com, is the historic colonial home once owned by film czar Cecil B. DeMille. In a residential neighborhood and all done up New Orleans style, the two-story Carriage House features a lushly landscaped brick courtyard and six one- and two-bedroom guest suites. All include a living room and private bathroom; all but one feature kitchens and refrigerators; some have in-room coffeemakers. Basic rates year-round are $125–165 ($20 per additional person for the two-bedroom suites), weekly rates available. To get here: About one mile south of Laguna Beach turn east onto Cress Street, go two blocks to Catalina, then turn left.

A long-running local favorite is the Mediterranean-style **Casa Laguna Inn** bed-and-breakfast at 2510 S. Coast Hwy., 949/494-2996 or toll-free 800/233-0449, www.casalaguna.com, an updated ode to 1930s' California. Paths wander past the bell tower and courtyard and throughout the terraced gardens, connecting rooms and suites. Also here are a one-bedroom cottage with private ocean view, fireplace, and full kitchen, and the two-bedroom Mission House. Rooms are small, suites are spacious; some have views; and all are tastefully furnished with antiques and overhead fans. The pool has a view. Head to the library in the morning for continental breakfast; tea is served in the afternoon, wine and hors d'oeuvres in the evening. In July and August there's a two-night minimum on weekends. Peak weekend rates are $135–250, weekday rates $105–225. During the rest of the year, when rates run $105 and up (higher, again, on weekends), modest rooms here can be a best bet for budget romance.

Family-Friendly Aliso Creek Inn
A nice setup for families or traveling homebodies—and a good deal for just about anybody in the off-season—is the lovely **Aliso Creek Inn** in South Laguna at 31106 S. Coast Hwy., 949/

499-2271 or toll-free 800/223-3309; www.alisocreek .com. Just a few hundred yards from the beach yet nestled into a steep-walled canyon, this relaxed 80-acre condo-style motel and resort complex offers a good selection of housekeeping units, from studios to one- and two-bedroom suites, all with kitchens, patios, sitting areas, color TV, free movies. Amenities include a pool, whirlpool, even a wading pool for the kids, not to mention the nine-hole golf course, restaurant, and bar. For those predictable practical family emergencies, there's a coin laundry. Free bonus: Aliso Creek itself, which meanders through the resort grounds on its way to the ocean. From July 1 through Labor Day rates run $155– 328. Otherwise, expect to pay $112–297. Meeting rooms are available.

High-End Hotels

If money is absolutely no object, consider heading south a short distance to Dana Point and the **Ritz-Carlton Laguna Niguel**, the south-state's most luxurious hotel resort. For information, see Dana Point and Vicinity, below.

Otherwise, if you plan to park yourself at the beach and don't care what it costs, *the* place in Laguna Beach is the light and airy **Surf & Sand Hotel** right on the beach south of town at 1555 S. Coast Hwy. (at Bluebird Canyon Dr.), 949/497-4477 or toll-free 800/524-8621 for reservations; www.jcresorts.com. Rooms in the nine-story tower have the most breathtaking views, of course, but you won't go wrong elsewhere, of here, since most rooms are within 30 feet of the beach and include a private balcony looking out over the surf, surfers, and heated pool. Decor is tastefully understated in a day-at-the-beach palette, with sand-colored walls and raw-silk upholstery, shuttered windows and naked wood. The fun indoor-outdoor **Splashes** restaurant sits right on the beach. The art deco lounge is a choice spot for cocktails at sunset. Rates run $310–425 from Memorial Day through October, with a two-night minimum stay in July and on June and September weekends, and a three-day minimum in August. In other seasons prices start at $260, but if business is off you may be able to do better. Ask about specials and packages.

High-end hotels in Laguna Beach also include the well-located, yet reasonably secluded **Inn at Laguna Beach** near Main Beach at 211 N. Coast Hwy., 714/497-9722 or toll-free 800/544-4479 for reservations, fax 714/497-9972. Most rooms are fairly small but attractive, with abundant amenities. Many have a view, too, not to mention color TV/cable and VCRs. In-room continental breakfast is provided. High-season rates, from July 1 through Labor Day, run $249–459. The Inn at Laguna Beach is an especially sweet deal in the off-season, when prices are $129 and up.

EATING IN LAGUNA BEACH

Beach Town Breakfast

Locals' choice for artsy minimalist breakfast is the very cool **Cafe Zinc**, 350 Ocean Ave. (at Forest), 949/494-6302, though on weekends be prepared to wait at the counter and to fight for a table. The morning repast here is as simple as a huge hot cappuccino with a muffin. The frittatas are also good, not to mention the huevos rancheros with papaya salsa. If you come late, order a salad and some homemade soup—very good here—and do lunch. No credit cards. Next door is the equally cool **Cafe Zinc Market**, where you can load up on bread and baked goods, salads, cookbooks, even sundry kitchen items.

The **Beach House Inn**, centrally situated between Main Beach and PCH behind Vacation Village at 619 Sleepy Hollow Ln., 949/494-9707, is a Laguna Beach institution. This is the onetime home of Slim Summerstone, one of the original Keystone Cops. The ambience here is quite casual, and every table offers an ocean view—definitely a fine start for any day. The Beach House is best known for its lobster, steamed clams, and fresh fish specials, yet the all-American breakfast is also a best-bet. Beloved locally for breakfast, especially al fresco, is **The Cottage**, 308 N. Coast Hwy., 949/494-3023. Another possibility is the **Laguna Village Cafe**, 577 S. Coast Hwy., 949/494-6344.

For a special see-and-be-seen Sunday brunch right on the beach, head to **Splashes** outside at the Surf & Sand Hotel, 1555 S. Coast Hwy. (at Bluebird Canyon Dr.), 949/497-4477. If it's foggy or cool, the food's just as good when served indoors.

Laguna Lunch

Many of the more upscale eateries around town also serve lunch, often a variation of the dinner menu but with smaller servings at lower prices. See the "Dining Adventure" listings below for possibilities.

Beloved here and elsewhere in Orange County is **Wahoo's Fish Taco,** 1133 S. Coast Hwy. (PCH about a mile south of Main Beach, between Oak and Brook Sts.), 949/497-0033. Also tops in the *very casual* cheap-eats fast-food category is **Taco Loco,** 640 S. Coast Hwy.

"LEXUS LANES" NOT SO SWIFT AFTER ALL?

The foremost land of freeways, Southern California has recently added "payways," or toll roads too. Pointedly called "Lexus lanes" by California Senator Tom Hayden, these privately financed toll roads charge a fee for the privilege of commuting—a change, critics says, that threatens the southstate's fundamental social premise of unfettered mobility for all. All drivers pay taxes and fees to support public transportation systems, they say, and the systems should work—for everyone. Toll-road supporters contend that payways, which attract drivers willing to pay for a faster commute, help alleviate traffic congestion even on public roadways. Recent events suggest that the critics may win at least the first round of this argument.

The nation's first automatic variable-toll highway, a modified **Riverside Freeway** (Hwy. 91) opened in late 1995 with a new 10-mile, three-lane toll road between Anaheim Hills in Orange County and the Riverside County line. In addition to four lanes of "free" traffic in each direction, this section of the Riverside Freeway includes the **91 Express Lanes** hugging the center divider: two "FasTrack" lanes and a "3+ only" lane for carpoolers, the latter free for cars or vans with three or more people.

There are no toll takers on this toll road. To use the 91 Express Lanes, drivers must prepay a private toll account and obtain a "transponder" for their dashboards, something of an electronic debit card. When cars pass the overhead toll device, it automatically deducts the relevant toll—from $.75 to $3.75 one-way, depending on the date, time, and direction of travel. Scofflaws get no slack. Cameras hanging over the roadway record the license plate numbers of any vehicles without transponders; nonpayers are either billed by mail or pulled over and ticketed by California Highway Patrol officers contracted to patrol the private roadway. For current details about using the toll road, call 909/280-9191 (recorded) or see www.91expresslanes.com.

When the 91 Express Lanes opened, using them

shaved an hour off a two-hour commute during peak traffic periods. Then traffic in the FasTrack lanes also became congested, though still faster than the public lanes. Most recently, though, it became obvious that there still weren't enough takers to make the 91 Express Lanes profitable. When the private owner decided to unload the burden—by creating the nonprofit NewTrac company to buy out its interest, with the aid of state bonds—a political fuss soon erupted. It soon became clear that the value of the 91 Express Lanes had been inflated, to about twice the company's initial cost; at that price still higher tolls would have to be charged, which would drive away more payway users and cause more conjestion on the public roadways. Making the situation even dicier was the fact the Caltrans—the state transportation agency, which had supported the deal yet apparently hadn't understood its cozy nature—had agreed *not* to make needed safety improvements to the public portions of Highway 91, apparently concerned that making it easier to use the *public* highway would draw drivers away from the 91 Express Lanes. Thankfully, when state Treasurer Phil Angelides cancelled the bond sale the NewTrac deal was scuttled.

Aside from raising legitimate concerns about publicly-financed corporate skulduggery, the 91 Express Lanes story also suggests the obvious question: Will this ever work? If private toll lanes on the hideously congested Riverside Freeway aren't profitable, will they ever be elsewhere in California?

In affluent areas of Southern California, toll roads still have their fan clubs. Consider the new six-lane **San Joaquin Hills Toll Road,** a north-south thoroughfare between San Juan Capistrano and Newport Beach, the private extension of public Highway 73. After surviving various legal challenges—the new toll road plows right through Laguna Canyon and the Laguna Coast Wilderness Park—the San Joaquin Hills toll road was finally completed. Yet its revenues, too, have fallen short of projections.

(PCH between Cleo and Legion), 949/497-1635, where the ambience is asphalt-meets-the-sea-breeze and surfers scarf down fish tacos—such things as fresh lobster or mahi-mahi on blue corn tortillas—as quickly as possible. Vegetarians, don't despair. Taco Loco also serves a killer tofu burger.

For imaginative pizza, *the* place is **Z Pizza**, the original well south near Aliso Creek, 30902 S. Coast Hwy., 949/499-4949. Of course there's a **Ruby's** here (S. Coast Hwy. at Nyes), 949/497-7829, the nostalgic diner-style choice for burgers, shakes, fries, and all those other things we all know we shouldn't eat. Ditto for **Johnny Rockets,** at 190 S. Coast Hwy, 949/497-7252.

Late in the afternoon or before dinner, stop for a drink at **Las Brisas,** 361 Cliff Dr. (N. Coast Hwy.), 949/497-5434, a place still known among old-timers as the Victor Hugo Inn. The main reason to dawdle here, though, is to drink in the views—while considering the possibility that Orange County promoters haven't overhyped the "Riviera" angle after all.

Dining Adventures, Not That Pricey
For romantic noshing, the Northern Italian **Ti Amo,** 31727 S. Coast Hwy. (near Third St.), 949/499-5350, is the perfect spot, perched as it is on a bluff overlooking the sea. The place has been lavishly decorated with sponge-painted walls and rich drapes. Entrees include paella, homemade pasta, and wonderful seafood. Or, create an appetizing light meal from several selections on the appetizer menu. Reservations wise at dinner. Some people prefer the artier and romantic **Ristorante Rumari** (dinner only) on the highway between Center and Pearl, 1826 S. Coast Hwy., 949/494-0400, specializing in Northern Italian and Sicilian dishes, particularly fish.

Another possibility if you're craving pasta at dinner is the two-story **Sorrento Grille,** 370 Glenneyre St. (near Mermaid), 949/494-8686, an Italian bistro with American airs and "martini bar." Also great for stylish bistro-style Italian is **Romeo Cucina**, 249 Broadway (at Coast Hwy.), 949/497-6627. Another best bet is **Villa Romana Trattoria**, 303 Broadway, Ste. 101, (9490 497-6220.

For fun, very good New American, generously dished up, the place is tiny **Café Zoolu**, 860 Glenneyre St., 949/494-6825. Immensely popular for creative Californian is **Mark's**, 858 S. Coast Hwy., 949/494-6711, where the seriously discounted Monday night dinners inspire great local appreciation.

At 998 S. Coast Hwy. (just south of Thalia) is **Natraj**, 949/497-9197, the best bet for authentic Indian food—for many miles in any direction.

More Fine Dining Adventures
Five Feet refers to Laguna Beach's elevation. But this local hot spot at 328 Glenneyre, on the corner of Forest and Glenneyre, 949/497-4955, is actually more famous for fine nouvelle Chinese served up with pop art and pink neon. A must for first-timers: the catfish. It's open for dinner nightly, for lunch on Fridays only. Tiny, dinner-only **Dexter's Unque Cuisine,** 2892 S. Coast Hwy., 949/497-8912, is the place for creative Pacific Rim fare.

David Wilhelm's fairly pricey **French 75** bistro, 1464 S. Coast Hwy., 949/494-8444, is immensely popular at dinner and Sunday brunch, though for romance and intimate conversation the tiny **Picayo,** 1155 N. Coast Hwy., 949/497-5051, is probably a better choice.

Tops in local hotel dining is **Claes Seafood, Etc.** at the Hotel Laguna, 425 S. Coast Hwy., 949/494-1151. The seafood, of course, is particularly spectacular. (It's also open daily for breakfast and lunch.) Or, drive south to Dana Point and **The Dining Room,** 949/240-2000, at the Ritz-Carlton Laguna Niguel for spectacular food in an equally stunning setting (semiformal attire). The Ritz-Carlton also offers more casual fare at breakfast, lunch, and dinner in its **Terrace** restaurant, 949/240-5008—out on the terrace overlooking the ocean—and **Club Bar and Grill.** For more information, see Dana Point and Vicinity, below.

ENTERTAINING LAGUNA BEACH

To do the movies, there's an **Edwards Cinema,** 162 S. Coast Hwy., 949/497-1711. For live rock 'n' roll, or reggae—sometimes star-quality—try the comfortably seedy **Sandpiper,** 1183 S.

Coast Hwy., 949/494-4694 (cover charge), a place down-home enough to also offer pinball wizardry and dart boards. At last report Monday night was reggae night at the **White House,** 340 S. Coast Hwy., 949/494-8088.

After-hours coffee haunts—such as the **Renaissance Cafe,** 234 Forest, 949/497-5282, and the **Diedrich's** nearby, 949/497-7660, in the onetime Marriner's bookstore—are otherwise the main attractions, along with local bars. For beer lovers, best bets include the lively **Laguna Beach Brewing Company,** 422 S. Coast Hwy., 949/499-2337, serving 10 different handmade brews along with decent salads and pub fare, and the more stylish **Ocean Avenue Brewery,** 237 Ocean, 949/497-3381, noted for its lagers and porters. The prettiest place in town for pounding a few with a view, though, is the **Towers Lounge** atop the Surf & Sand Hotel at 1555 S. Coast, 949/497-4477.

Gay clubs are prominent in Laguna Beach, particularly the **Boom Boom Room** and, upstairs, **Hunky's Video Bar and Grill** at the Coast Inn, 1401 S. Coast Hwy., 949/494-7588, altogether quite lively, with dance floor and two bars. Considerably more sedate is **Main Street,** a piano bar at 1460 S. Coast Hwy., 949/494-0056.

DANA POINT AND VICINITY

BEFORE THE MAST, BEFORE THE HOBIE CAT

Given the modern-day dominance of subdivisions, shopping malls, and rush-hour traffic, one might forget that, before the United States claimed the territory, pioneers from Spain and the new nation of Mexico made their homes in a much quieter California. For a glimpse into that brave old world, pick up a copy of *Two Years before the Mast,* published in 1840 by Richard Henry Dana, Jr. On leave from his studies at Harvard University to recover from measles-related afflictions, Dana put to sea onboard the *Pilgrim,* a small square-rigged Boston brig that delivered East Coast fineries to California in exchange for tanned cowhides carted over from the mission at San Juan Capistrano and other ports. San Juan Cove—now Dana Cove, which includes Dana Point Harbor, all within Capistrano Bay—was the only safe anchorage between San Diego and Santa Barbara. When Dana returned to Boston and an eventual career as a noted maritime attorney, he recalled the cove, with its rocky harbor and striking 200-foot cliffs, as "the only romantic spot in California."

And perhaps it was. "There was grandeur in everything around," Dana said. In those days the ocean surf swept all the way in to dramatic, sculptured cliffs. Huge prehistoric vultures—California condors, carrion eaters now all but extinct, bred in zoos—launched themselves from these

Dana Point: under the mast

cliffs; birds of prey, ravens and herons, perched here as well. And long before swallows discovered the Capistrano mission, they nested in cliff crevices here.

GRUNION RUN FREE, SO WHY CAN'T WE?

It's a live sex show, yet almost innocent, even wholesome—and certainly educational. This particular procreation education usually begins after midnight. Sometimes shining small flashlights to show the way, people suddenly dash onto the beach, giggling and grabbing—for grunion, those silvery Southern California sexpots of the smelt persuasion.

Human voyeurs come down to the beach not only to watch the frenzied fish but also to catch them—literally—in the act. The hunt seems unsporting, since the grunion are, after all, deeply distracted. Without the aid of nets, window screens, kitchen sieves, and other illegal devices, however, grabbing grunion is actually a challenge. Grunion fisherfolk, optimistically armed with buckets as well as flashlights, can use only their bare hands. And grunion are slippery, like long, wriggling bars of soap. They're also rather sly. No matter what tide charts may say, grunion never show up exactly when and where they're predicted, sometimes skipping the days, hours, and locales people expect. Sometimes just a few roll in with the surf, sometimes thousands. Grunion seem to be more patient even than surfers, content to flip and flop around in the water as long as necessary, waiting for the right wave.

For many years the "grunion run," strictly a Southern California phenomenon, was thought to be some form of moonstruck romance. Much to the delight of local romantics, it was commonly believed that the fish swam ashore during spring and summer simply to fin-dance in the moonlight.

Scientists established in 1919, however, that nature was quite purposeful. The way it really works is this: After dark, near both the new and full moons but after high tide has started to recede, wave after wave of grunion surf onto local beaches. Each wave's "dance" takes 30 seconds or less. Females burrow into the sand, dorsal fin-deep, to lay their eggs (about 2,000 each) while the males circle seductively, fertilizing the roe. All parental responsibility thus discharged, the grunion catch the next wave and head back out to sea. About two weeks later, at the next moon-heightened high tide, the young'n' grunion hatch and are washed out into the big, big watery world.

Fairly remote beaches all along the coast, from Santa Barbara south, are good bets for the grunion grab. March through August are peak grunion-running periods. Grabbing grunion is against the law in April and May, however, to allow the species some spawning success. And anyone over age 16 must have a California fishing license—available at most local bait and sporting goods shops, along with tide charts, tall tales, and free advice.

More recently Dana Point has celebrated the grandeur of local surf, surfing, and surf-related innovations. Several times each year, when storms drove classic long-angled 30-foot waves around Dana Point from the west, hard-core surfers from far and wide assembled here to brave the "Killer Dana." Just like the local cattle-hide trade, Killer Danas are history; harbor construction altered the offshore terrain. But to pay homage to those days of yore, stop by **Hobie Sports** in Lantern Bay Village, 24825 Del Prado, 949/496-2366, where rare and historic surfboards from the collection of Hobie Alter—local inventor of the foam-core surfboard and the Hobie Cat catamaran—are on display.

For more complete information about the area, contact: **Dana Point Chamber of Commerce,** 24681 La Plaza, Suite 115 in Dana Point, 949/496-1555, fax 949/496-5321; www.danapoint -chamber.com.

SEEING AND DOING DANA POINT

A city only since 1989, Dana Point today combines boat harbor, beaches, and Boston saltbox condominium developments. This stylistic twist testifies to popular identification with Richard Henry Dana's East Coast origins yet is odd, given the area's more enduring Spanish and Mexican roots. To sample original local architectural styles, explore older streets, including Chula Vista, Ruby Lantern, Blue Lantern, El Camino Capistrano, and Santa Clara.

Dana Point Harbor

The cultural focal point for Dana Point is Dana Point Harbor, 949/496-6177, where breakwater construction began in 1966. Here, about 2500 yachts bob and sway with the tides. The harbor

A NOTE ON "LANTERN" STREETS

This peculiar local street-name phenomenon—naming streets after colored lanterns—is not a recent affectation. In the 1920s, Dana Point's "downtown" was defined by the Spanish-style plaza, and by streets intersecting Pacific Coast Highway—then known as the Roosevelt Coast Highway—which were named for the rainbow collection of ship's lanterns that marked them, the latter inspiration attributed to Anna Walters Walker, Dana Point's first developer. Most of the original copper street lanterns are long gone, but about 15 of the originals light the newly spiffed-up plaza park.

also features a man-made island park—reached via Island Way—an inner breakwater created during the harbor's unusual cofferdam construction.

Though home port is now in Long Beach, Dana Point Harbor is a regular port for the Nautical Heritage Society's speedy topsail schooner *Californian,* the state's official tall ship. The *Californian* is a re-creation of the first U.S. cutter to patrol the Pacific coast during the bad and bawdy gold rush, the 1848 *C. W. Lawrence* (in service to the U.S. Revenue Service, precursor of the U.S. Coast Guard). Since America's revenuers now typically enlist computers instead of ships to track down scofflaws, the *Californian* is free to serve as an international goodwill ambassador—circling the Pacific Rim each year, visiting Canada, Mexico, and closer ports, as well as occasionally (such as during the 1984 Olympics) leading the Tall Ships Festival parade and embarking on other international adventures. Appropriately enough, Queen Calafia, the imagined matriarchal monarch of the island paradise of California, is enthroned as the ship's figurehead. When moored here—see the website for current information—the *Californian* offers day sails to the public and participates in other educational programs. The Nautical Heritage Society also owns the 1913 Q-Class racing sloop *Virginia,* the only yacht on the West Coast included on the National Historic Register, avail-

able for private sailing lessons. For more information, contact the **Nautical Heritage Society,** 1064 Calle Negocio, Unit B, San Clemente, CA 92673, 949/369-6773 or toll-free 800/432-2201; www.californian.org.

Adjacent to the *Californian* is the **Orange County Marine Institute,** 949/496-2274, noted for its educational and other programs, including nighttime "bioluminescence cruises."

Other harbor diversions include kayaking, canoeing, parasailing, fishing, sportfishing, whale-watching (in winter), and tidepooling. **Dana Wharf Sportfishing** on the harbor's eastern edge, 949/496-5794, handles sportfishing trips, whale-watching and other scenic excursions, and parasailing.

Surfin' USA: Doheny State Beach

Just east of the harbor is Doheny State Beach, donated to the state in the 1930s by L.A. oil man Edward Lawrence Doheny in honor of his son, Ned. The local surf made a bigger cultural splash, though, especially when Doheny made it into the lyrics of the Beach Boys' classic "Surfin' USA."

Head to the broad white-sand beach for the usual fun. The rocky area at the harbor end draws divers and anglers. At night beach bonfires are quite popular, if not nearly as wild as they once were (alcohol consumption has been banned). With the exception of surfing, nothing is as popular here as the grunion run, typically good. (See Grunion Run Free, So Why Can't We? earlier in this chapter.) Doheny also features acres of lawn, a cool change when the sand really cooks. Worth a special stop is the **marine life museum** inside the visitor center, with its 3000-gallon native fish aquarium and tide-pool "touch tank."

Bike riding is actually quite feasible in and beyond Dana Point. The **San Juan Creek Bike Trail** starts just north of the beach; dart under PCH and take the trail all the way into San Juan Capistrano. Alternatively, take the Doheny bike path south along the sand to Capistrano Beach Park and, at Beach Road, merge into the PCH bike lanes. You can ride south into San Clemente, or north as far as Laguna Beach.

Developed campsites (hot showers, picnic tables, fire rings, plus RV necessities) are tucked into the landscape; some are more sheltered than others. Day-use facilities lie to the west of San Juan Creek. The entrance to Doheny State Beach is just off PCH at 25300 Dana Point Harbor Drive; follow the signs. Day use is $2. Full-facility camping is available, as are group camps. For more information, call 949/496-6171. To reserve campsites through ReserveAmerica, call 800/444-7275.

Salt Creek Beach and Park

Almost an adjunct to the Ritz-Carlton Laguna Niguel resort, Salt Creek Beach north of Dana Point proper has long been noted for its good surfing. Two of the best "breaks" around, not often personally appreciated by Ritz-Carlton guests, include "The Point" just below the hotel and "The Beach" to the north. On windy days you'll see hang gliders surf the thermals. And on a clear day you'll see Catalina Island.

Though Salt Creek Beach technically stretches both north and south of the Ritz-Carlton, the southern strand is also referred to as **Laguna Niguel Beach.** (Land-use politics in action: Most everyone thought this stretch of coastline would be incorporated into the new city of Laguna Niguel, thus the name of the beach *and* the holnstead, the area was included in the new city of Dana Point.)

Above the beach is a seven-acre bluff-top park, with vast ocean views. Here you'll find picnic tables and barbecue pits, showers, even a basketball court. A natural amphitheater created by the dramatic slope of the lawn provides a popular venue for summer performances.

Salt Point is just off the highway, with access at both Selva Road and Ritz-Carlton Drive.

PRACTICAL DANA POINT

Sleeping before the Mast

To mind the budget, camp at Doheny. (See Surfin' USA: Doheny State Beach, above.) A winner in the cheap-stay basic-motel contest—if you're not autophobic—is the small **Dana Marina Inn Motel,** 34111 Coast Hwy., 949/496-1300, quaintly situated on an island at the apex of local traffic flow (where PCH divides into two one-way thoroughfares, part of what defines "downtown"). Rates: $46 and up. Another pos-

sibility is the **Dana Villa Motel,** 34311 S. Coast Hwy. (Del Obispo and PCH), 949/496-5727. Rates: $55 and up.

For a few more animal comforts, the **Best Western Marina Inn,** 24800 Dana Point Harbor Drive, 949/496-1203 or toll-free 800/255-6843, www.bestwestern.com, is a good deal anytime. Rates: $84–130.

Dana Point offers pricier places, too, including the very pleasant Victorian Cape Cod–style **Marriott's Laguna Cliffs Resort** (the former Dana Point Resort) adjacent to Doheny State Beach, just west of the highway at 25135 Park Lantern, 949/661-5000 or toll-free 800/533-9748; www.marriott.com. The ambience here is refined casual, those rooms with a view clearly the most appealing. "Activity" amenities include two swimming pools, whirlpools, steam rooms, sauna, exercise room, lighted tennis courts, even table tennis. Rates: $155–299, though ask about specials.

Even more charming, in the bed-and-breakfast style, is the 29-room **Blue Lantern Inn,** 34343 Blue Lantern, 949/661-1304, www.foursisters.com, perched on a bluff overlooking Dana Point Harbor. Built in the fashion of a traditional Cape Cod inn, the Blue Lantern is part of a chain of ten luxurious Four Sisters inns along the coast. Each room has a fireplace, sitting area, refrigerator with soft drinks, and in-room whirlpool tub. The tower rooms offer a delicious coastal view almost any time. Full breakfast and afternoon hors d' oeuvres are served in the library. Rates: $150–500, prices roughly correlated with "view" value. Be sure to book well in advance.

Ritz-Carlton Laguna Niguel

Just 10 miles south of Laguna Beach is Orange County's finest resort—a gem for those who can afford the price tag of pure getaway pleasure.

The Ritz-Carlton Laguna Niguel is a long, low château perched grandly on cliffs overlooking the ocean. The northern Monarch Bay Wing faces north toward Salt Creek Beach and an 18-hole par-70 golf course designed by Robert Trent Jones. The Dana Point Wing overlooks ocean, palm trees, and sunset scenery. Amenities here include four outdoor tennis courts, two heated pools with whirlpool jets, and a complete fitness center with exercise rooms, steam room, sauna, and massage.

Once inside the lobby, guests are greeted by raw-silk wall coverings, French tapestries, Chinese horses, and art, art, art. This Ritz boasts an impressive hotel collection of American and British 19th-century art, not to mention crystal chandeliers (even in the elevators). All rooms have small private terraces, and are attractive and comfortable in the somewhat staid Ritz-Carlton style. Amenities include color TV, free movies, in-room honor bars and safes plus, in the bathrooms, hair dryers, an extra telephone, and thick terry bathrobes. As is typical at Ritz-Carlton hotels, 24-hour room service and other services are top drawer.

In the afternoon, take tea in the mahogany-paneled library. Casual meals, breakfast, lunch, and dinner, are served at the Ritz's **Terrace** café restaurant (outside on the terrace, overlooking the ocean). Another possibility is the **Club Grill and Bar,** which also serves live music in the evening. When cost is no object, **The Dining Room** is truly exceptional, one of the best restaurants in Orange County. And though a dressed-down dress code is otherwise strictly enforced in Dana Point and Laguna Beach, the Ritz-Carlton insists on some semblance of formality. Jackets and ties are required even in the bar, semiformal attire in The Dining Room.

Almost more fun than exploring the hotel is traipsing around the grounds. It's not at all unusual to see cottontail rabbits boldly grazing on the lawn amid the asters and shasta daisies. (Complete garden tours are offered, with a $25 lunch attached.) **Salt Creek Beach** stretches to the north and south of the Ritz-Carlton—an easy exploratory stroll, especially from the hotel, with its easy-access ramp. If heading back uphill is daunting, hotel guests can catch a ride on the Ritz's tiny motorized tram.

The Ritz-Carlton Laguna Niguel is just off PCH at 33533 Ritz-Carlton Dr. in Dana Point, 949/240-2000 or toll-free 800/241-3333; www.ritzcarlton.com. Rates: $395–575 per night in summer, from $295 otherwise. Suites start at $650. Ask about specials and packages.

Dining before the Mast
Quite the draw for pricey steakhouse fare with a Southern accent is David Wilhelm's dinner-only **Savannah Chop House** in Laguna Niguel at 32441 Golden Lantern (Ocean Ranch Center

II, at Camino del Avion), 949/493-7107, open nightly for dinner. Another best bet in the dinner-only category is the elegant yet homey Italian **Luciana's,** south of Blue Lantern at 24312 Del Prado, 949/661-6500, most famous for its pastas. The making-the-scene scene prefers the Italian **Brio,** 24050 Camino del Avion, 949/443-1476, where the early dinner specials are a particular plus. For filling all-American fare 24 hours a day, the place is casual **Harbor House Café,** 34156 PCH (near Violet Lantern), 949/496-9270.

Though the Ritz-Carlton is certainly a classier bar scene, more fun is the **Mugs Away Saloon,** 27324 Camino Capistrano in Laguna Niguel, 949/582-9716, the local answer to attitude bars everywhere. In this one, you drink, dance, and admire the bare-behinds photo collection. These Mugs Away "mugs" commemorate the bar's annual "Moon Amtrak" event, wherein patrons drop their drawers to terrorize and/or titillate train travelers.

SAN JUAN CAPISTRANO

The Swallows of Capistrano
A schmaltzy song started it all. The 1939 Leon Rene tune "When the Swallows Come Back to Capistrano" is responsible for the excited flutter here every year on March 19, St. Joseph's Day, when tourists flock to town to welcome the return of the cliff swallows from their annual Argentina migration. Identifiable by their squared-off cleft tails and propensity for nesting under overhangs and in other protected high-altitude spots, the swallows' first official return was in 1776—the year the United States became a nation and the year Father Junípero Serra established the mission. Serra recorded the event in his diary.

Nowadays, though, on March 19 tourists typically far outnumber the swallows, which never did respect that particular day much anyway. (According to ornithologists, the swallows return in the spring, March 19 being close enough to the spring equinox, with "scouts" spotted quite early in March.) Modern life has created confusion for the mission's mythic swallows. Too many people and too much hubbub scare them off, for one thing. Earthquakes, and earthquake repairs, have knocked down hundreds of old swallow nests, for another, and subsequent scaffolding put up to protect the mission has discouraged still more birds. As a result visitors are as likely to see cliff swallows nesting in the high arches of the May Co. store downtown as at the mission.

All that aside, San Juan Capistrano does what it can to help the swallows do their historical duty—by setting out a buffet of ladybugs and green lacewing larvae in the rose garden in March. It also plans most of its **Fiesta de las Golondrinas,** with parade, fun runs, and people dressed up in swallow costumes, for the week framing March 19. Putting local politicians and other volunteers to good use, the festivities culminate later in the month with a "mud-slinging" contest—with the mud and straw slapped onto old adobes to help preserve them. Though there isn't yet a song to serve as a swallow send-off, Capistrano's birds are supposed to depart on St. John's Day, October 23.

For more information on the area, contact: **San Juan Capistrano Chamber of Commerce,** 31781 Camino Capistrano, Ste. 306 in San Juan Capistrano, 949/493-4700, www.sanjuanchamber.com.

Mission San Juan Capistrano

Its crumbling church walls steadied by scaffolding and surrounded by very contemporary New World ambience, Mission San Juan Capistrano is not the most vigorous survivor of California's 21-mission chain. Yet it's impressive nonetheless. The **quadrangle,** with its storerooms and workshops for making clothing, candles, soap, and pottery, was the center of mission life. Today exhibits, a 12-minute film, and museum displays (including the piano on which the famous swallow song was composed) tell the basic story. Most evocative, though—if you can imagine the scaffolding *desaparecido*—are the ruins of the **Great Stone Church,** built in 1797 and destroyed by an earthquake in 1812. To get an exact idea of what the old church looked like, sans the patina of time, visit the Spanish Renaissance **New Church of Mission San Juan Capistrano** on Camino Capistrano, with its stunning interior murals and artwork. Next door— draped in spectacular color when the bougainvillea is in bloom, and still in use after all these years—is the mission's original **Serra Chapel,** the only one remaining in California in which Father Serra said mass. Capistrano's chapel, constructed in 1777, is also the oldest building standing in the Golden State. Quite striking inside is the ornate "golden altar," made of cherry wood more than 300 years ago and brought here from Barcelona, Spain, in 1922. Wander the grounds, with its ancient gardens, ponds, and Native American cemetery, to complete a thoughtful tour of San Juan Capistrano, once considered "the jewel of the missions."

Mission San Juan Capistrano is on Camino Capistrano at Ortega Highway (Hwy. 74) and

interior of Mission San Juan Capistrano

TOM MYERS PHOTOGRAPHY

accessible either from PCH or I-5. Admission is $6 adults, $4 for seniors and children ages 3–12 (under 3 free). It's open daily 8:30 A.M.–5 P.M. Free guided tours are offered on Sunday at 1 P.M. Call 949/248-2048 for current information.

Other Capistrano Sights, Excitements

Across from the mission's new church is another local newcomer—the postmodern mission-style **San Juan Capistrano Regional Library,** 31495 El Camino Real (at Acjachema), 949/493-1752, designed by Princeton University architect Michael Graves. The courtyard and gardens offer peaceful and private retreats for reading. Call for current hours.

Nearby is the **O'Neill Museum,** 31831 Los Rios St., 949/493-8444, a petite 19th-century Victorian with local memorabilia on display. Pick up the local **historic walking tour** map here (and at the chamber office or various area businesses) to discover San Juan Capistrano's remaining adobes and other venerable ancients. The 1894 Spanish revival **Capistrano Depot,** 26701 Verdugo, for example, is a stunning stop for **Amtrak.**

Not everything in the area is ancient. One of Orange County's hippest clubs is here. **The Coach House,** tucked into a warehouse at 33157 Camino Capistrano, 949/496-8930, is known for good—sometimes great—live music acts. For the best seats, make dinner reservations. And if you find yourself near Santa Ana, also well worth tracking down is the Coach House's sister club, **The Galaxy Theater.**

Ronald W. Caspers Wilderness Park

If the balmy beaches become boring, if you crave a little skin-searing summer heat, Caspers Wilderness Park is the place to go hiking on a hot summer's day. Most people, of course, come anytime *but* summer. Spring, when the hillsides are heavy with wildflowers, is especially appealing.

Caspers has had its share of bad press in recent years, mostly due to **mountain lion attacks** on small children. Though adults are also potential victims, the high-pitched voices and quick, preylike movements of children make them particularly vulnerable. Following the last well-publicized attack, Caspers was open only to adults. No one has yet come up with a perfect solution to the problem of how humans and big

cats can safely share a neighborhood, but Caspers is now open again to children—so long as they are under direct adult supervision at all times. Campsites (no hookups) are particularly popular with RVers, since the terrain isn't that friendly to tents (permitted). Day use is $4 on weekends, $2 during the week. Camping is $12 per vehicle. Hikers and campers must obtain a wilderness permit (free), available here.

The entrance to Ronald W. Caspers Regional Park is at 33401 Ortega Highway (Hwy. 74), about eight miles from San Juan Capistrano. For more information, contact Ronald W. Caspers Wilderness Park, 949/728-0235 or 949/728-3420; www.ocparks.com/caspers.

Eating in San Juan Capistrano

Always convenient for a meal is the good, hearty American **Cedar Creek Inn** across from the mission at 26860 Ortega Hwy., 949/240-2229. A bit harder to find—but well worth the effort—is the very reasonable **Ramos House Café,** in the historic district at 31752 Los Rios St. (California's oldest residential street, east of Del Obispo), 949/443-1342, which serves impressive New American with Southwestern and Cajun flavors. Unusually, Ramos House is open only for breakfast and lunch.

SAN CLEMENTE

This isn't much of a tourist town. The people of San Clemente prefer it that way—and you'll be glad, too, if peace and quiet have eluded you elsewhere. The well-guarded solitude of this red-tile-roofed Republican town was its primary appeal for ex-President Richard M. Nixon and his wife, Pat, who retreated here to La Casa Pacifica, the **Western White House,** overlooking the beach. The best view of Nixon's former estate, a palm-shrouded 25-acre compound, is from San Clemente State Beach. Otherwise, the most exciting scene around is at the San Clemente Pier adjoining the city beach, reached via Avenida Del Mar, where crewcut Marines from nearby Camp Pendleton cavort alongside civilians. For more information about the area, contact: **San Clemente Chamber of Commerce,** 1100 N. El Camino Real, 949/492-1131, fax 949/492-3764; www.scchamber.com.

San Clemente State Beach

Backed by craggy white sandstone bluffs and wind-warped coastal chaparral, milelong San Clemente State Beach, with its fine white sand, is still one of the best things in town—comparatively uncrowded when every other beach in the county is overrun. Reached via various trails, the beach is popular for skin diving, surfing, and just plain sunning and swimming. Up on the landscaped bluffs are picnic areas and a developed campground with 157 sites (72 with hookups). Day use (parking) is $3; camping is also available. For camping details and other information, call 949/492-3156 or 949/492-0802. For camping reservations, call ReserveAmerica toll-free at 800/444-7275 or try www.reserveamerica.com.

To get here, from I-5 exit at Avenida Calafia near the south side of town and follow the signs.

Rancho Mission Viejo
Land Conservancy

On this 1200-acre preserve, three typically distinct ecosystems—oak woodlands, grasslands, and coastal sage scrub—come together to create a richly diverse pocket of Southern California's fast-fading natural history. To protect this heritage, the city of San Clemente, Orange County, and the Rancho Mission Viejo Company entered into a conservation agreement allowing only limited public access. Naturalist-led horseback rides (extra fee), Saturday and evening hikes (the latter in summer only), and new-moon "astronomy nights" are typically offered (small fee) by reservation only. For current information, call 949/489-9778, or check www.theconservancy.org.

Staying in San Clemente

For lone travelers, even cheaper than camping (but without the sand-in-your-shoes ambience) is the clean **San Clemente Beach AYH Hostel,** just five blocks from Amtrak and a couple of blocks from the beach in the onetime public library at 233 Avenida Granada, 949/492-2848 or toll-free 800/444-6111; for general AYH info, check www.hiayh.org. For a bed in one of two dorm rooms (there's also a family room) and access to kitchen and laundry, expect to pay $12 (members) or $14 (nonmembers). Groups and families welcome. Otherwise, San Clemente

has a surprising number of decent motels with what are, by Orange County standards, quite reasonable rates. One best bet for the basics is the small **San Clemente Beach Travelodge** close to I-5 but just a block from the state beach at 2441 S. El Camino Real, 949/498-5954 or toll-free 800/843-1704; www.travelodge.com. Rates start at $69 in summer, $45 otherwise. Always a find where you find it is the **Country Inn & Suites,** located west of I-5 behind Pico Plaza at 35 Calle de Industrias, 949/498-8800 or toll-free 800/874-0860; www.countrysuites.com.

Practically on the beach is the tiny, hill-hugging **Casa Tropicana,** right across from the pier at 610 Avenida Victoria, 949/492-1234 or toll-free 800/492-1245; www.casatropicana.com. This beachfront bed-and-breakfast hotel has a festive "tropical paradise" ambience, an attitude also animating the **Tropicana Bar & Grill** downstairs. Rooms are themed—Coral Reef, Key Largo, Out of Africa—and most feature in-room hot tubs. Full breakfast is included, either in your room or downstairs in the restaurant. Also enjoy the loaner beach chairs and umbrellas. High-season rates: $120–280 (weekday and off-season rates much lower). Two-night minimum on summer weekends.

Eating in San Clemente

You won't starve in San Clemente, but in general the eating-out options are less abundant than elsewhere along the coast. The **Beach Garden Cafe** across from the pier at 618½ Avenida Victoria, 949/498-8145, is a best bet for breakfast.

Next door, at Casa Tropicana, is the **Tropicana Bar & Grill,** 610 Avenida Victoria, 949/498-8767, serving burgers, pasta, and salads along with live music on weekend nights. At the foot of the pier is **The Fisherman's Restaurant and Bar,** 611 Avenida Victoria, 949/498-6390, noted for its fresh seafood (changing menu) at both lunch and dinner. Other specialties include the eggplant Parmigiana and grilled vegetable sandwiches.

From San Clemente South

Before freeway traffic slithers south into San Diego County, it all becomes one with I-5. The area near the new city of Lake Forest, once known as El Toro, is where I-5 and the 405 suddenly join, condensing into the I-5 leg of the San Diego Freeway. This traffic nightmare is known as the "El Toro Y." (Heads up.) Just north of San Clemente, Pacific Coast Highway (Hwy. 1) also becomes one with I-5.

Driving south from San Clemente, note the daunting seven-mile freeway barrier marking the center divide—intended to deter illegal aliens heading north on foot from San Diego, as people have been killed all too frequently while dashing across the freeway.

Just across the county border lies **San Onofre State Beach,** part of a larger state park complete with campground. The most imposing coastal neighbor is the **San Onofre Nuclear Power Plant,** looming at the end of the beach. Next is the massive acreage of Camp Pendleton, a fitting introduction to the dominance of military interests and inclinations in San Diego County.

DISNEYLAND:
THE HAPPIEST PLACE ON EARTH

Anyone who has been a child or had a child since Walt Disney first opened his Magic Kingdom in 1955 already knows most everything of import about Disneyland.

In Disneyland, stories have happy endings. And every performer on the 76-acre Disney stage—from Mickey Mouse and Donald Duck to the latest batch of lovable audio-animatronic creations—smiles, waves, and then smiles some more, as a matter of company policy. They don't call this "The Happiest Place on Earth" for nothing. In Disneyland, if the hero doesn't do it single-handedly, then whiz-bang technological wizardry will save the day. In Disneyland, democracy equals capitalism. And capitalism automatically creates social justice.

In other words, Disneyland isn't real, though suburban America desperately wants to believe it is.

Real or not, Disneyland is as good as it gets, if what you're looking for is a clean, well-lighted, life-sized fantasy theater showcasing Mom, Pop, apple pie, and the American flag. It's also one of the few public places in socially subdivided Southern California where families play in public. For the middle class in particular, commercial enterprises such as Disneyland, Universal Studios, and regional malls have all but taken the places of downtown plazas and neighborhood parks.

WALT DISNEY'S
BRAVE NEW WORLD

If California is a myth, the American dream transplanted to the Wild West, then Disneyland tells the modern middle-class version of the story. Seeking appropriate diversions for his young daughters in the 1940s, according to the Disneyland creation story, Walt Disney became disgusted with American amusement-park sleaze. He decided to build a better mouse trap, so to speak, based on the success of his animated cartoons (Mickey Mouse made his debut as a talkie in 1928). It was an idea whose time had come. Opening day in 1955 was a national televised event, carried live from coast to coast. In the next six months alone, more than a million people traipsed through Disney's Magic Kingdom. More than 40 years later, the first and original Mickey Mouse mecca is still California's number one tourist destination.

Disney the Visionary: Imagineering American Innocence

Disneyland's lasting popularity seems connected to the deep desire to recapture, reimagine, and re-create lost American childhood—both an individual and national need, increasingly apparent since shell-shocked veterans returned from World War II battlefields. Of those who can afford the choice, many would rather live in Disneyland, and in Disneyland-like suburbs, than inhabit or otherwise acknowledge a world of escalating alienation and human atrocity.

Walt Disney was clever enough to "imagineer" that new American innocence. He was also clever enough to build walls, large parking lots, and ticket booths around it. In that sense, also, Walt Disney was a visionary. With shops, stores, and restaurants on every street and street corner, from its inception Disney's perfect world also foreshadowed the less-than-laudable modern world culture—one in which only abject poverty allows escape from entertainment product tie-ins and other consumerist conspiracies.

DOING DISNEYLAND

Highfalutin philosophy and cultural critique aside, Disneyland just *is*. And it can be fun, especially with children in tow, since Walt Disney's exquisitely engineered promotion of America's mainstream mythology is as playful and well done as it is commercially cunning and cliched.

To make a conscious journey through this cartoon version of America's collective unconscious, consider Disneyland as an oversized map of psychic symbols. This territory is divided into eight distinct "lands," each with one overall theme but multiple attractions.

Once "shoppe"ed out on **Main Street, U.S.A.,** from the Central Plaza wander straight ahead—through Sleeping Beauty's castle—into **Fantasyland** and then to **Mickey's Toontown,** both of these latter destinations mandatory for younger youngsters. To start exploringelsewhere, turn left to **Adventureland, Frontierland/Rivers of America, Critter Country,** and **New Orleans Square.** Turn right and you'll land in **Tomorrowland.**

Disneyland is also destined to become much, much larger. Though the Walt Disney Company canceled earlier plans to expand Disneyland into an international megaresort—with a Westcot theme park, 4,600 new hotel rooms, new amphitheater, and two humongous parking structures—that goal may be achieved in increments. **Disney's California Adventure,** a separate 55-acre theme park adjacent to Disneyland, opened in February 2001. *This* California showcases

Sleeping Beauty's castle: a fairy tale come true

ROBERT HOLMES/CALIFORNIA DIVISION OF TOURISM

Hollywood and the entertainment industry, the California beach scene, and outdoor California, along with a new hotel and other commercial features. It would be fair to count this as one large new land—Californialand. Related changes include the renaming of West Street, on the western border of Disneyland, which is now—between Ball Road and Katella Avenue—**Disneyland Drive.** This is where visitors will find themselves, after leaving I-5 at the dedicated Disneyland Resort exit. The new freeway exit leads directly into the huge new Disneyland resort parking structure—the largest in the United States, with 10,301 spaces. In addition, on the other side of Disneyland what was once Freeman Way, connecting Harbor Boulevard and Master Street (Anaheim Blvd.) between Ball and Katella, is now **Disney Way.**

With a transformed Anaheim infrastructure in place, Disneyland is already planning yet another expansion for a 78-acre site south of Katella Avenue—a water park and amusement park incorporating the best rides now up and running at Disney ventures in Florida, Paris, and Tokyo. Elements of that "land" may open to the public as soon as 2003.

Main Street, U.S.A.

Inside the gates, the first mythic representation of the American heart and mind is Main Street, U.S.A. Walt Disney believed that religion represented a divisive element in American public life, so one thing you won't see here are churches. (What a visionary Disney actually was; modern-day Republican politicians and the ranks of the self-righteous should take a lesson). In parades and other events staged along Main Street, clean-cut and youthful ambassadors of the Disney philosophy remain cheerful to a fault. Standards of dress and behavior for the Disneyland cast—employees are called "cast members," their workplace the "stage"—mimic the middle-class mores of 1955.

Instead of church steeples, this Victorian-era village showcases stylized storefronts and ride-on vintage vehicles, such as horse-drawn trolleys and horseless carriages offering one-way rides from the Town Square to the Central Plaza. The 45-passenger **Omnibus** was inspired by the 1920 New York City double-decker.

THE DISNEYLAND RESORT FUNDAMENTALS

A very good reason to hang your hat locally is to avoid Disneyland Resort-area driving. If at all possible park the car at your hotel or motel and walk—or hop a shuttle, a service offered by Disneyland hotels and many other local hostelries. This advice is all the more apropos now that traffic flow and other aspects of All Things Disney have changed dramatically. Walking (or shuttling) around is a good way to get a solid sense of how things now work.

When you hand over your passport at the entrance to Disneyland, you'll receive the current *Disneyland Souvenir Guidebook* pamphlet, complete with maps and basic practical information, plus a daily entertainment schedule. Get a geographic introduction to the entire park (or simply cut back on trudging) by taking the train. The round-trip **Disneyland Railroad** departs from the Town Square, just inside the main Disneyland entrance, with regular stops also at New Orleans Square, Mickey's Toon Town, and Tomorrowland. For a more limited but bird's-eye view, Disney's famous **Monorail** zips continuously between the Disneyland hotels and its only other scheduled stop, in Tomorrowland. Also starting from Tomorrow: the one-way **Skyway to Fantasyland.** Tickets for half-day guided Disneyland tour are available at City Hall on Main Street. Subject to availability, foreign language tours are also offered.

The Magic Kingdom is as accommodating as it is clean and wholesome. Most Disneyland attractions are wheelchair accessible, though some require that you be able to leave the chair and also have someone to assist you. In addition to **stroller and wheelchair rentals,** Disneyland also offers pet boarding (for the day only) at the **Kennel Club.** Though the various Disneyland hotels offer babysitting and childcare programs, Disneyland proper does not. But there is a **Baby Care Center** on the east end of Main Street, set up for diaper changing, nursing, and preparing formulas and bottles. A registered nurse is always on duty nearby at the **First Aid Center.** Small **rental storage lockers** are on Main Street near Lost and Found, down the street next to the Cone Shop, and also near the Videopolis amphitheater in Fantasyland.

Similar services are available in Disney's California Adventure. American Express ATMs are available to the right of the Golden Gateway. Foreign currency can be exchanged at Disney's California Adventure Guest Services, nearby. There's a Baby Care Center in the Pacific Wharf area, and—for emergency first aid—registered nurses are on duty at the nearby Lost Children facility.

To inquire about other pertinent visitor information, contact Disneyland directly (see Practical Disneyland). Disneyland fanatics, a copy of the current official *Birnbaum Brings You the Best of Disneyland* (Houghton Mifflin) may be worth buying as a souvenir. In many respects more intriguing, if harder to find, are the unofficial guides, including the irreverent *Unofficial Guide to Disneyland* and the kinder *Mouse Tales: A Behind-the-Ears Look at Disneyland.*

Particularly worthwhile along Main Street—especially for fans of audio-animatronics technology, or electronics combined with robotics and then wired for sound—is **Great Moments with Mr. Lincoln.** One of Disney's ambitious early efforts, this one is several decades old but still uncannily real. While you wait for the next show, browse the glassed-in lobby displays of Walt Disney memorabilia. Film buffs, don't miss the wheelchair-accessible **Main Street Cinema,** where six screens show classic Disney cartoons. A perennial favorite is the 1928 *Steamboat Willie,* in which Mickey and Minnie Mouse made their big-screen debuts.

Stop at **City Hall** for maps, menus, currency exchange, and just about anything else you might need.

Fantasyland and Mickey's Toontown
Then there's the myth of carefree childhood, one of America's fondest fantasies. The quaint characters in Fantasyland, representing the earliest celluloid memories of the baby-boom generation, seem closer to Walt Disney's original purpose than do the technically jazzier new attractions. Who on this globe doesn't instantly recognize **Cinderella's Castle** as a Disney icon? But if tykes have seen classic Disney cartoon movies such as *Alice in Wonderland, Peter Pan,* and *Dumbo the Flying Elephant,* they'll relate to

the rides here, most fairly tame. Still a thrill, though, is the **Matterhorn** bobsled ride. As a feel-good topper, climb aboard **It's a Small World** for an international cruise. (Good luck extracting that song from your head.) There's much more, too.

Mickey's Toontown is a $100 million playground tuned in to the over-amped expectations of the electronic age and inspired by the cartoon/reality confusion of *Who Killed Roger Rabbit?* Adults accompanying their children through this neighborhood will giggle and guffaw, since there are hundreds of sight gags and adult-level double entendres. The hot ride in Toontown is **Roger Rabbit's Car Toon Spin,** a black-light blast. But for most kids the goofy architecture and silly, surreal side attractions are entertainment enough. Still, make sure they meet Mickey himself at **Mickey's House.** (Actually, he's out back in his own private movie barn.) An equal-time visit to **Minnie's House** amounts to a tour of "lovable decorations," what's cooking in the kitchen, and Minnie's makeup room.

Adventureland

The American myth of adventure mimics the European, requiring exotic experience in some clearly foreign, if otherwise indefinite, locale.

So Adventureland generally delivers excursions into some deep, dark, but unidentifiable jungle. Yet its latest attraction, the **Indiana Jones Adventure: Temple of the Forbidden Eye,** takes place in an actual place, India. While here, Indie and company brave it all for a chance to snatch the usual booty: endless wealth, eternal youth, and second sight.

If the gods favor your day in Disneyland, perhaps Indie mania will have subsided somewhat. When this megahyped adventure first opened in 1995, people stood in line four hours for less than four minutes of special-effects lightning bolts, vipers, insects, "bubbling death," and rampaging boulders. (If you take the trip again, chances are it will be different; 27 random computer-selected routes are possible, with 160,000 total possible adventure variations.) The wait here, however, is part of the journey, an extended and entertaining introduction. Scratchy 1930s-style newsreel footage informs adventurers that they have been enticed to the Temple of the Forbidden Eye—but foolishly, since the

rumored magic of Mara, sacred diety of a long-dead people, is as likely to inflict unspeakably hideous death as to grant one's fondest wishes.

And parents, please note: As on other more challenging Disneyland rides, to come along on this particular Jeep ride to doom, adventurers must be over 48 inches tall.

Younger young 'uns will also hound you into **Aladdin's Oasis,** a sit-down restaurant and entertainment revue featuring characters from the movie. (To give in, you'll need reservations.)

Adventureland's tropical **Jungle Cruise** is a Disneyesque interpretation of *The African Queen* trip, complete with audio-animatronic creatures of all persuasions and predictable (and predictably safe) encounters. While you're listening to the guide's spiel, entertain yourself with the knowledge that ex-president Richard Nixon's press secretary, Ron Ziegler, once held this job.

Press people have to keep up with the times. Old-timers may be surprised to discover that the nearby Swiss Family Treehouse (remember Disney's *Swiss Family Robinson?*) is now **Tarzan's Treehouse.** The original 150-ton tree abides, however. Identified as *Disneydendron semperflorens grandis,* or "large everblooming Disney tree," it has steel limbs and 62 concrete roots, though some of its branches and leaves have been refurbished in keeping with the Tarzan theme. Also ever popular is the parrot José, star of the animistic audio-animatronic **Enchanted Tiki Room** and its revue of singing birds, flowers, and Tiki gods.

Frontierland and Rivers of America

Before fairly recent social and political revisions, the myth of Manifest Destiny was the tale of adventurous settlers pushing the Wild West, the American frontier, ever closer to the Pacific Ocean—all the while taking quite seriously the Old Testament injunction to subdue the earth. With the American earth long since soundly subdued—coonskin-capped pioneers, cowboys, guns, trading ships, and riverboat gamblers remain heroes.

Available for diversion in Frontierland and vicinity are the ever-popular **Big Thunder Mountain Railroad** ride, the **Frontierland Shooting Arcade** (with electronic rifles aimed at Boot Hill), the **Mark Twain Riverboat** and **Rafts to Tom Sawyer Island,** the **Sailing Ship Columbia,**

ADVENTURE CITY

The Anaheim area's smallest theme park is an introduction to urban living geared to 2- to 12-year-olds, smaller than Disneyland's Toontown and Knott's Camp Snoopy yet chock-full of clever participatory kid-sized fun. Try the miniature train ride, the 911 ride, the "crazy bus," the airport (wait in the control tower for hot air balloon rides), and "freeway" roller coaster. Most rides accommodate adults. Tamer attractions, including face painting and a petting farm, appeal to all ages.

Located in the Hobby City complex at 1238 S. Beach Blvd. (between Ball & Cerritos), Adventure City is open daily in summer Mon.–Thurs 10 A.M.–5 P.M., Friday until 9 P.M., Saturday 10 A.M.–10 P.M., and Sunday 11 A.M.–8 P.M. In winter the park is open Fri.–Sun. only from 10 or 11 A.M.–8 or 9 P.M. All-day unlimited admission, including all rides, is $11.95 (seniors $8.95). For current information, including detailed directions from various area freeways, call 714/236-9300 or try the website: www.adventure-city.com.

and the **Mike Fink Keelboats.**

Make first-come, first-served reservations when you arrive to take in the corny **Golden Horseshow Jamboree,** the longest-running stage production in the history of show business, according to the *Guinness Book of Records.* To witness the titanic battle between good and evil, starring Mickey Mouse, cruise back to Rivers of America after dark for **Fantasmic!**

Critter Country

In the Disneyland version of life, animals in general (and wild animals in particular) can be appreciated only to the extent that they are like us—nature as defined by the circumscribed experience of city dwellers and suburbanites. Unless we assign human motivations and emotions to other creatures' antics—unless we anthropomorphize to the nth degree—animals offer nothing to love and little else to value. So in forested, frontier-style Critter Country you'll find the animatronic country-western **Country Bear Playhouse** revue, with its "unbearably funny bearitones," **Teddi Barra's Swingin' Arcade** (parents, get ready to hand over the pocket change), and critter-related shops and eateries. The biggest draw, though, is **Splash Mountain.** People happily wait in line for the privilege of climbing into a floating facsimile hollowed-out log to dive 5.5 stories into a briar patch. Tamer but more authentically American is a participatory cruise through Rivers of America in one of **Davy Crockett's Explorer Canoes.**

New Orleans Square

The official American notion is that, after the Civil War, the North and South lived happily ever after. In locales such as New Orleans, according to the myth, former slaves and slave traders alike then turned their attentions to churning out Dixieland jazz, soulful music, and exotic regional cuisine as well as re-creating gracious lifestyles. Best bet for a home tour here is the very well-done **Haunted Mansion,** an artful collection of "999 happy haunts" guaranteed to stupefy small children and amuse adults. The main attraction of New Orleans Square proper is **Pirates of the Caribbean,** the last Disney attraction largely developed by Walt himself, a gee-whiz whirl through what was, in reality, more barbarian brutality than good-hearted debauchery—or at least it was. Nowadays even the pirates are more politically correct; they still pillage and guzzle rum but they no longer chase women. In keeping with American social trends, the prevailing vice is now gluttony. Usually worth a stop is **The Disney Gallery,** both art show and collectors' playground, showcasing original animation cels and lithographs, posters, and books. Most of Disney's New Orleans is dedicated to shopping and eating. An unmarked door leads to the exclusive (members and guests only) **Club 33,** with its private dining rooms and second-story balconies—the only place in Disneyland that serves alcohol.

Tomorrowland

In terms of space allocation alone, Walt Disney made a major investment in Tomorrowland—surely because of that bedrock American belief that the miasma of modern life will come clean in an appropriately technologized future. Lately, though, even what remained of Disney's original 1950s futurism seemed terribly tired, considering the brave new worlds that have come along

DISNEY'S CALIFORNIA ADVENTURE: WHOSE VIRTUAL REALITY IS THIS?

First and foremost, California is a myth. Now it's also a theme park, thanks to Anaheim's high-rolling, theme park-centered renaissance. Along with almost every other aspect of Anaheim's conventioneering, imagineering core, been-there-forever Disneyland has expanded into multifaceted **The Disneyland Resort**—heart of the equally transformed **Anaheim Resort District,** with its redesigned promenades and 15,000 new trees and shrubs.

The central focus of The Disneyland Resort's $1.4 billion expansion is Disney's California Adventure, a separate 55-acre theme park—charging separate, identical admission—located on what was once Disneyland's main parking lot.

With all its technical wizardry, Disney's latest great adventure seems designed to appeal as much to nostalgic baby boomers as to families, what with carnie-style renditions of *Age of Aquarius* and the Beach Boys' *California Girls* piped in over the sound system. Not to mention the ersatz Robert Mondavi Winery (complete with mini-vineyard), the stylish Wolfgang Puck seafood, and the hang-gliding-over-California simulation—definitely the best virtual ride around. If you don't have the desire or time to tour the *real* California, an encounter delivering difficulties as well as delights, then a day spent here lets you pretend.

Whose virtual reality is this, anyway?

Within the limited range of options on offer here, it's yours.

Doing Disney's California

Attractions at Disney's California Adventure are collected under three main themes: **The Golden State** tribute to the state's scenery and culture, the illusion-rich **Hollywood Pictures Backlot,** and the **Paradise Pier** simulation of the California boardwalk and beach scene. One wag has already suggested that Disney's California is just *too* Disney—and to reflect the place accurately it would need to include The Rolling Blackout, the Wild Ride Gridlock, Burning Tire Mountain, and the Drive-By Shooting. But who comes to theme parks for reality?

The shorthand Disney version of The Golden State—as "imagineered" by Disney cast members and crew—stars **Soarin' Over California,** a simulated hang-gliding tour of the Golden Gate Bridge,

Yosemite, Napa Valley, Palm Springs, Lake Tahoe, and other Golden State wonders. This virtual reality, courtesy high-definition Omnimax film technology and an ingenious mechanical lift system, is made all the more virtually real by piped-in scents and breezes. Whatever else you might be tempted to pass on, don't miss this. Also don't miss the original 22-minute *Golden Dreams* film, starring Whoopi Goldberg as various optimistic historical characters—and as the mythic Queen Calafia herself. California's immigrant past—and present—are the film's primary focus. One could quibble over a number of critical omissions, though many "left-out" details are included in the ending photo montage. Yet for such a short film, one with appeal for so many different ages and backgrounds, *Golden Dreams* is fairly remarkable.

Other Golden California attractions include the yes-you'll-get-wet **Grizzly River Run,** a whitewater rafting simulation larger than a similar Disney attraction in Orlando, Florida. A thoroughly delightful Florida import is **It's Tough To Be A Bug,** a down-in-the-ground 3D introduction to the creepy, crawly world of insects. (They save the best for last.) At the **Pacific Wharf** waterfront village, inspired by Monterey's Cannery Row, tour the **Mission Foods** tortilla-making factory (samples available) or stop by **Boudin Bakery** to see how sourdough bread is made (no samples available). At the somewhat disappointing, mission-style Robert Mondavi family **Golden Vines Winery,** sample the wares in the winetasting room—the first alcohol ever served to the public at a Disney venue—try some deli fare, or head upstairs for a fairly pricey California-style meal (lunch and dinner). **California Workplace** exhibits showcasing artisans and craftspeople at work.

Disney California's Hollywood Pictures Backlot celebrates the animation arts and movie-making with Tinseltown-themed diversions, shops, and restaurants along an ersatz Hollywood Boulevard, the classy Broadway-quality **Hyperion Theater,** even a **Superstar Limo** tour satirizing the beautiful people. Other celebrities include Kermit, Miss Piggy, Fozzie Bear, and others at the **Muppet Vision 3D Theater.** At **Disney Animation,** see how the artists and technicians make their magic—and give it a whirl yourself at the **Sorcerer's Workshop** and

Ursula's Grotto. And—not really a big surprise, considering Disney's corporate acquisition of the American Broadcasting Company (ABC)—Disney's Hollywood also includes the **ABC Soap Opera Bistro,** where diners sit down to eat in recreations of soap opera sets (including *General Hospital*'s Kelly's Diner).

Disney's beach-themed Paradise Pier—which looms above a small, wave machine-powered "ocean"—evokes 1900s' midway rides and amusements, with an assist from state-of-the-art technology. That trend is best exemplified by the massive **California Screamin'** wooden roller coaster, the kid-friendly and freeway-themed **Mulholland Madness** mini-roller coaster, the dazzling yet unnerving 150-foot-tall **Sun Wheel,** and the Buck Rogers-style **Golden Zephyr** rocket ship ride. Midway games and wholesome kiddie rides abound. If you can afford the pleasure, consider a meal at Wolfgang Puck's very cool **Avalon Cove** seafood restaurant—where, in the main dining room, seaweed vines up a central pillar and The Little Mermaid and other sea creatures cavort along one wall.

California Adventure

Practical Disney's California Adventure
Park hours are generally the same as for Disneyland; check before coming. At last report park admission was $43 adults (age 10 and older) and $33 achildren (ages three to nine), the same as Disneyland. The new Disney **Resort Flex Passport**three-day passport, $111 adults, $87 children; four-day, $137 adults, $107 children—makes considerable sense, since the passport is good at both parks (but not for admission to both parks on the same day). To hop between parks on any given day, inquire about **Park-Hopper Passports,** available only to guests at the three Disney hotels. For more information, call 714/781-4000. To reserve lodging packages that include park admission, call toll-free 877/700-3476.

For general information, call 714/781-4560; www.disneyland.com.

Doing Downtown Disney
Connecting Disney's California Adventure with Disneyland proper is the vast new Downtown Disney plaza, a 300,000-plus-square-foot shopping opportunity, public promenade, and theme-park entry plaza larger than St. Peter's Square in Rome. Downtown Disney is dedicated to adult-oriented eating, entertainment, shopping, and other commercial diversions—from outposts of the **House of Blues, Ralph Brennan's Jazz Kitchen,** and the **La Brea Bakery** to the **Rainforest Café** and the Latin-themed dining and night club **Y Arriba! Y Arriba!**

For more information about Disney's California Adventure, Downtown Disney, Disney's Grand Californian Hotel, and other Disney hotels, contact the Disneyland Resort, 714/781-4565; www.disneyland.com.

Staying with Disney:
California Adventure Hotels
Also within the new park is the Walt Disney Company's latest hostelry, the first Disney-designed hotel development on the West Coast. The grand, 750-room **Grand Californian Hotel,** fashioned in craftsman style in another hat-tip to California history and culture, comes complete with two heated pools, two spas, a children's pool, the Eureka Springs health club, the excellent Napa Rose restaurant—with Executive Chef Andrew Sutton, previously from the Napa Valley's Auberge du Soleil—and the family-friendly Storytellers Café. Thematically related to Disney's California Adventure is the 502-room beach town-style **Disney's Paradise Pier Hotel,** formerly the Disneyland Pacific Hotel.

since. Tomorrowland has thus undergone major renovation, both a conceptual and technical facelift.

The focus of today's Tomorrowland is more timeless—and fantastic—blending familiarity, or the comforts of the past, with a gee-whiz Jules Verne enthusiasm for high-tech wonders associated with exploration, education, and imagined life in the future. One new feature is the **Astro Orbitor,** inspired by 15th-century artist, futurist, and inventor Leonardo da Vinci. When you orbit as high as you can, you won't see Jupiter or Mars but you will get a great view of Disneyland. **Autotopia** is also a trip, this one especially for tykes.

Other current highlights include the freshened-up R2D2-introduced **Star Tours,** a fantastic voyage into virtual reality with stellar special effects and more than a few interstellar surprises as the inexperienced robot pilot takes fellow travelers for a ride. As in the Indiana Jones Adventure, central to the experience is the entertaining introduction to space travel received while waiting to board this Disney/George Lucas collaboration.

After Star Tours, the fastest action around is **Space Mountain,** though kids might also get a kick out of the dancing **Cosmic Waves** fountain, just outside the entrance, and the **Rocket Rods** ride. But once they get sucked into the futuristic **Starcade** video game palace, you may never see them, or your pocket change, again.

AN ASIDE ON THE PRICE OF HAPPINESS

If it makes you feel any better about how much it costs to buy access to the Happiest Place on Earth, keep in mind that since 1993 even California politicians have had to pay their own ways. State law bars elected officials who accept more than $250 in gifts in any given year from voting on issues affecting the gift giver—a potential impediment to Disneyland expansion plans—so the Magic Kingdom decided to end its traditional generosity (free passes) toward local politicos. An incensed Anaheim city councilmember subsequently called the Fair Political Practices Commission ruling concerning gratis admission a "Mickey Mouse policy."

Maybe you can shrink the temptation by stopping first at the 3-D **Honey, I Shrunk the Audience!** adventure.

Innoventions, hosted by witty audio-animatronic host Tom Morrow, previews new and upcoming technologies focused on information, entertainment, health and sports, home, and transportation—but all in all adds up to little more than self-promotion by companies that have themselves to sell.

Disney Spectaculars

As of October 1996 it was lights out for Disneyland's long-running **Main Street Electrical Parade,** that extravaganza now replaced by an ever-changing lineup. In 2000, for example, **45 Years of Magic** was the theme of Disneyland's celebration parade, which featured Mickey Mouse, Snow White, Simba, and other Disney animation stars. Disney's first and orginal "skytacular," **Believe: There's Magic in the Stars,** also dazzled. More fantastic, as far as slaying mythic dragons, and a long-running Disneyland favorite is the nighttime **Fantasmic!** spectacle rising out of Rivers of America—that battle between good and evil still going, at last report. But there is an ever-changing series of spectacular parades, spectacles, and family-friendly entertainment at Disneyland, day and night. Once arrived, check the daily entertainment schedule to find out what's happening when and where. Before you come, call Guest Relations at 714/781-4560 or try the website.

For a price, these days you can also create your own event at Disneyland, be it a children's birthday party or a wedding ceremony at Sleeping Beauty's Castle. Contact the Disneyland office (see below) for current information.

PRACTICAL DISNEYLAND

There are those who claim the expansion of Disneyland into The Disneyland Resort—a multi-day destination, with the opening of Disney's California Adventure—is simply a marketing conspiracy to separate you from your hard-earned cash. With so much more to see and do, it's probably true that most visitors will be forking out plenty for extra overnight stays, extra meals, extra theme park admission, and extra shopping. If your budget is limited, tighten up those moneybelts and make the best of it.

Though hours are subject to change, in summer the park is open 9 A.M.–midnight Sunday through Friday, until 1 A.M. on Saturday night. Otherwise, Disneyland is typically open 10 A.M.–6 P.M. on weekdays and 9 A.M. to midnight on weekends.

Bring plenty of money—what you'd like to spend and then some. Disneyland prices increased twice in the year 2000 alone. At last report a one-day Disneyland "unlimited passport," covering park admission plus all attractions and rides, was $43 for adults (age 10 and over), with 10-year-olds defined as adults since May 2000, and $33 for children ages 3–9. (Children under age 3 get in free.) Three- and five-day, non-transferable "flex passports" are also available, but must be purchased in advance (try the website). In addition to the two- and three-day tickets available for Disney's California Adenture—same price as Disneyland admission—special "park-hopper" passes, allowing entrance to both parks on the same day, are available to Disney hotel guests.

Disneyland prices typically increase at least slightly every year. Guided tours, annual passes, and special packages are available.

But the price of admission is only the beginning. There's parking, too, ($7 for passenger vehicles, at last report), and Disneyland doesn't allow you to pack in food or beverages, so expect to spend at least $25 per person for two meals and snacks. (The food tab can go much higher.) And the total cost of Mickey Mouse ears, miscellaneous T-shirts, and other Disneyland memorabilia may floor otherwise frugal fun lovers.

And while devil-may-care types arrive in Disneyland on a whim, most people (certainly most people with small children) *plan,* and plan carefully. Considering the investment of time, money, and emotional energy a trip to Disneyland requires—and since it matters what you'll see and do, and whether you'll enjoy it—it pays to make appropriate plans, including hotel or motel reservations, well in advance. A two- or three-day stay will allow you to see and do just about everything, much less stressfully than a whiz-bang one-day whirlwind tour.

If your family can't afford the extra time or expense, do Disneyland in a day by accepting in advance that you won't accomplish everything—then set priorities. Making a whirlwind tour of Disneyland much more feasible is the free **Fastpass system,** available for at least some attractions, which allows you to reserve a particular "window of opportunity" for that attraction, on the spot—cutting the otherwise interminable wait down to just a few minutes, thereby freeing you and yours to do something else (other than stand in line) in the interim.

Though hours are subject to change, in summer the park is open 9 A.M.-midnight Sunday through Friday, until 1 A.M. on Saturday night. Otherwise, Disneyland is typically open 10 A.M.-6 P.M. on weekdays and 9 A.M. to midnight on weekends. Hours at Disney's California Adventure are similar and seasonally changing; contact the resort for current details.

For more information, contact **Disneyland,** 1313 Harbor Blvd., P.O. Box 3232, Anaheim, CA 92803-3232, 714/781-4565, fax 714/781-1341; www.disneyland.com.

Other Survival Strategies

No matter how carefully you've planned your trip and no matter how much cash or credit you pack, be sure to bring along all-American virtues such as patience and persistence—especially if you insist on coming during the summer or on a holiday weekend. In a typical year, peak crowds can be overwhelming, leading to long lines at the most popular attractions and long waits at food concessions. So plan your trip midweek, if at all possible. Better yet, come anytime *but* summer.

Buy passports in advance to avoid an unnecessary wait at the entrance.

Arrive promptly when the park opens.

Once inside, march your troops immediately to the first "must see" attraction. With any luck, before noon you may manage two or three.

Rather than waste time (and good temper) standing in interminably long lines, migrate to other popular rides and attractions during parades and nightly extravaganzas—whenever large numbers of people will be otherwise occupied. (This strategy is more useful if you'll be staying for more than one day.) Better yet, take advantage of the new Fastpass system, where available. See the website for current details.

Eat a big breakfast—or an early breakfast—before arriving, and plan lunch and dinner either before or after peak meal times.

Keep in mind that less popular and/or more labor-intensive attractions (such as the tall ship tours, raft rides, and canoe trips in Frontierland) are offered only during peak visitation periods.

Also keep in mind that pregnant women and people with certain health conditions aren't allowed on most of the more stimulating rides. For safety reasons, height limits also apply.

STAYING NEAR DISNEYLAND

The sheer number of area hotels and motels is astonishing, as one would expect at the gates to California's number one tourist attraction. Some hostelries affect ye olde archways or otherwise resemble castles, or sport flashy neon magic carpets, lanterns, and other exotic or fantasy-inspired emblems. Most offer free shuttle service to and from Disneyland, plus continental or more ambitious free breakfast. Many offer substantial discounts for members of AAA, AARP, and other organizations. Many also offer their own two- or three-night Disneyland packages, sometimes very good deals, so investigate your options before buying admission tickets. The advantage of staying quite near the park is overall convenience, including the opportunity to stroll away when life in Disneyland becomes overwhelming. It's generally less expensive, however, to park one's family—and one's car—at an accommodation farther away and then shuttle back and forth.

For choice accommodations—and to take advantage of most discount offers—reserve well in advance of your planned trip and ask for price verification as well as a written copy of cancellation policies. Keep in mind that "summer rates" may apply to other peak periods—spring break, the Thanksgiving and Christmas seasons, and other holiday weekends. During peak convention periods prices may also suddenly increase.

If you and yours hope to escape from all things Disney come nightfall, consider a stay elsewhere in Orange County.

The city of Anaheim assesses a 15 percent bed tax, not included in the rates below.

For a more complete listing of local accommodations, plus information on special events and current promotions, contact the **Anaheim/Orange County Visitor and Convention Bureau,** 800 W. Katella Ave., Anaheim, CA 92802, 714/765-8888 or toll-free 888/593-3200 (to request publications), fax 714/991-8963; www.anaheimoc.org. To request detailed information by fax, call the toll-free InfoFax line at 888/440-4405 (touch-tone telephone required).

Staying with Disney

As any reasonably privileged child will tell you, *the* Disneyland experience has always included a stay at Disneyland's adjacent 990-room **Disneyland Hotel,** 1150 W. Cerritos Ave. (off Disneyland Dr.) in Anaheim, 714/778-6600, fax 714/956-6597; www.disneyland.com. The hotel's advantages are obvious: quite pleasant rooms (most in sky-high towers, some one- to three-bedroom suites available), various good on-site restaurants—including the **Goofy's Kitchen** breakfast-lunch buffet, where you can meet and greet Mickey Mouse, Donald Duck, or ensembles of other Disney characters—and family-friendly diversions scattered throughout the lush landscape, including tennis courts, swimming pools, playgrounds, and pedal boats. What kid wouldn't love a dip in the 5,000-square-foot **Never Land Pool,** or taking in the nightly **Fantasy Waters Show**? Grown-up attractions include **Hook's Pointe and Wine Cellar** and **Granville's Steakhouse.** To make up for both, there's the **Team Mickey Workout Room.** In summer, a supervised children's program is available. In addition to free tram service, the hotel offers **Disneyland Monorail** transportation to and from the park.

Another snazzy option and "new" since 1996—at least as a Disney hotel—is the adjacent 502-room **Disneyland Paradise Pier Hotel,** previously the Disneyland Pacific Hotel (and the Pan Pacific before that), at 1717 S. Disneyland Dr., 714/999-0990, fax 714/776-5763; www.disneyland.com. With a jazzed-up paint job outside and muted day-at-the-beach tones inside, Paradise Pier bears a striking resemblance to a stylish California oceanfront accommodation, complete with suites and poolside cabanas. Instead of diving into the ocean for a swim, though, here you'll have to head to the Rooftop

Pool and Spa. To get ready for Muscle Beach, work out at **Team Mickey's Workout II Fitness Center.** Cool and contemporary, with abundant comforts, the Paradise Pier also offers guests complete access to all facilities at the Disneyland HoOn-site restaurants include the Japanese **Yamabuki,** featuring both traditional and modern fare, and, in keeping with the beach theme, **Disney's PCH Grill.** Breakfast and brunch here with **Minnie and Friends.**

The newest and grandest accommodation is the 750-room **Disney's Grand Californian Hotel,** actually located within Disney's California Adventure park at 1600 S. Disneyland Dr. in Anaheim, 714/635-2300; www.disneyland.com. Inspired by the craftsman-style architecture first popular in California during the Arts and Crafts era, the swank Grand Californian resembles a grand early 1900s national park hotel—massive beams to set off earthy yet refined beauty, everything updated to cater to contemporary tastes. The upscale **Napa Rose** restaurant and lounge features exquisite California-fresh cuisine and an impressive list of award-winning California wines. Another dining option is the relaxed **Storytellers Café.** Breakfast brunch at the Grand offers the opportunity to meet up with **Chip 'n' Dale.** To make sure you keep pace with your own little chipmunks, work out at the **Eureka Springs Health Club.** Or enjoy the **Redwood Pool,** complete with slide, and the **Fountain Pool,** which offers early morning lap swimming.

The primary advantage of a stay at any Disney hotel is strategic, since guests of the Disney Hotel are allowed to enter the park one hour early—a boon for beating the crowds to the hottest attractions. There are also multiple services available at each, these including the availability of on-site child care or baby-sitters, photo processing, currency exchange, full-service business centers, recreation facilities, and free tram and monorail service; the Disneyland Hotel has a coin-op laundry room. The primary disadvantage, at least for the budget-conscious, is price, with regular room rates in the $200-and-up range, not including parking. Ask about packages, including off-season and AAA, AARP, or other special group discounts. For reservations at any of the three Disneyland hotels, call The Walt Disney Travel Company at toll-free 877/700-3476 (700-DISNEY), reserve at www

.disneyland.com, or contact your travel agent.

With construction of Disney's California Adventure came the demise of Disney-sanctioned camping in Anaheim; the Disney Vacation Campground is no more. Unaffiliated with Disneyland but a best bet, in terms of Disneylike comfort and style, is the **Destiny Vacation Park** near Knott's Berry Farm at 311 N. Beach Blvd., 714/774-2267, 714/821-4311, or toll-free 800/783-3784, www.destinyrv.com, affiliated with the Las Vegas Oasis, among other parks. Duded up to resemble an old Wild West town, Destiny includes abundant amenities such as pool, hot tub, and laundry facilities. Free shuttle service to and from Disneyland is also provided. Destiny features 222 large, level sites with full hookups, shade trees, and grassy lawns and, for tent campers, 7 tent sites. High-season rates are $30–50 per night for RVs (full hookups), $25 for tents. For other RV and camping alternatives, contact the visitors bureau (see below).

Staying near the Convention Center

The astonishing expansion and makeover of the Anaheim Convention Center—now nearly twice its original size, with a sleek new contemporary look, complete with a surrounding "wave" of glass and a main hallway more than a quarter-mile long—has inspired still more transformation. Many area hotels have been refurbished and some new ones have arrived, these including Four Points by Sheraton and TownePlace Suites by Marriott. Most appealing of all is the new Anaheim "look," with palm-lined boulevards and lush public gardens softening the overwhelming impact of so many motel and hotel rooms (and so much concrete).

If you'll be combining a family trip to Disneyland with an Anaheim business convention, and if you'll have any say in the matter, it may be convenient to stay at a hotel catering to conventioneers. Probably best of the bunch is the 14-story **Hilton Anaheim** just south of Katella Ave., next to the Anaheim Convention Center at 777 Convention Way, 714/750-4321 or toll-free 800/916-2221 for central reservations, fax 714/740-4460, www.hilton.com, a virtual city built to accommodate business, fresh from an $18.5 million renovation. This massive hotel, with more than 1,500 rooms, comes complete with atrium, pools, whirlpools, and complete fitness facilities (complete with areobics classics and basketball gym). On-site baby-sitting is available. Regular room rates are expensive, though ask about off-season specials, AAA, and lowest available rates—as low as $79 in November and December, for example, when business travel slacks off. Tower rooms and suites are $149–309 and $650 and up, respectively. On-site restaurants include the continental **Hastings,** Italian **Pavia,** and the **Café Oasis** coffee shop.

A best bet in the same neighborhood is the **Anaheim Marriott Hotel,** 700 W. Convention Way, 714/750-8000 or toll-free 800/267-3983, fax 714/750-9100, http://marriotthotels.com, with regular rates starting at $125. Inviting rooms have a homey feel, with armoires and casual upholstered chairs. On-site eating options include romantic **JW's Steakhouse,** California-style **Café Del Sol,** and **Starbucks/Marketplace.** Inquire about current Disneyland packages and off-season specials. Both the Hilton and Marriott are just two blocks from Disneyland.

Another possibility for a high-rise stay is the 13-story **WestCoast Anaheim Hotel,** on the south side of Katella Ave. at 1855 S. Harbor Blvd., 714/750-1811 or toll-free 800/426-0670, fax 714/971-3626, www.westcoastanaheimhotel.com, near the Convention Center and just a block from Disneyland. Each room features a state-of-the-art telephone system with voice mail and data port, a Sony play station, coffeemaker, iron and ironing board, hair dryer, and remote control cable TV with movies on demand. Standard rates are $159 and up, but drop as low as $79 (subject to availability) for AAA and other discounts. Kids stay free. Extras include the Olympic-size pool, hot tub, popular **Overland Stage Restaurant and Territorial Saloon,** serving steaks, seafood, and down-home spirits, on-site coffee shop, and espresso bar.

Substantially less expensive and a venerable convention favorite is the **Best Western Raffles Inn & Suites,** 2040 S. Harbor Blvd., 714/750-6100 or toll-free 800/654-0196, fax 714/740-0639; www.rimcorp.com. Typically unavailable to tourists during conventions, at other times these refurbished rooms can be a steal—$59 and up in the off season for up to four people. Family theme rooms are available.

Always reasonable but a particularly good deal in the off-season are family suites at the recently renovated **Anaheim Carriage Inn** near the Convention Center at 2125 S. Harbor Blvd. (south of Orangewood), 714/740-1440 or toll-free 800/345-2131 (reservations only) in the United States and Canada, fax 714/971-5330; www.carriage-inn.com. Regular room rates run $80–120, suites $120–220, but are reduced as much as 50 percent for AAA and other discount programs. All rooms and suites feature refrigerators and microwaves, in-room coffeemakers, and color TV with the works; shared amenities include pool, whirlpool spa, and coin laundry. Equally good deals at other moderately priced establishments—such as the nearby **Ramada Limited Suites,** 2141 S. Harbor, 714/971-3553 or toll-free 800/526-9444 for reservations, fax 714/971-4609, www.anaheim-ramadasuites.com, can be found near West, Harbor, Katella, and other streets near the Convention Center. Many are equally convenient to Disneyland.

Staying near Disneyland

Brand new in 2001: the attractive 358-room boutique-style **Annabella Hotel,** located directly across from Disney's California Adventure at 1030 W. Katella Ave. on the site of the previous Golden Forest, Magic Carpet, and Magic Inn & Suites motels. Regular room rates are from $139 and bungalows are from $159, but substantial discounts are sometimes available. In keeping with the area's California-oriented transformation, the Annabella pays stylistic homage to the state's Spanish mission days, starting with the whitewashed-adobe walls and arched entryway. Stylish rooms include refrigerators and coffeemakers, hair dryers, state-of-the-art entertainment systems, two-line phones, and high-speed tele/data access for Internet and email. Not to mention the full granite bathrooms and all the little comforts. Other draws include the lush 7.5-acre grounds, two swimming pools (one for adults), fitness center, and on-site café. For more information and reservations, call 714/905-1050 or toll-free 800/863-4888, fax 714/905-1054, or try www.anabellahotel.com.

Anaheim offers a surprisingly broad selection of very nice moderately priced motels, some mentioned above. Always a best bet near The Happiest Place on Earth is the refurbished **Candy Cane Inn,** 300 yards from Disneyland's main gate at 1747 S. Harbor Blvd., 714/774-

5284 or toll-free 800/345-7057 (for reservations), fax 714/774-1305. If the name sounds cutesy or little-kiddish, you've got the wrong idea. Instead, here you'll find inviting landscaping, an outdoor courtyard with pool, wading pool, and whirlpool, and large, attractive rooms—some with in-room refrigerators, all with two queen beds, down comforters, coffeemakers, and wood shutters. There's TV too, of course, including the Disney Channel. Rates are $79–139 in the high season, lower at other times, generous expanded continental breakfast included. Special packages and tours are available.

Another good choice is the 131-room **Carousel Inn & Suites**, 1530 S. Harbor Blvd., 714/758-0444 or toll-free 800/854-6767, fax 714/772-9960; www.carouselinnandsuites.com. Rooms and suites are $69–149, continental breakfast included, and all feature microwave, refrigerator, coffeemaker, and a hair dryer. There's a heated pool up on the roof. Disneyland packages are available.

If the kids crave a place with a Fantasyland feel, and you want to settle in close to Disneyland, one possibility is the **Castle Inn and Suites**, 1734 S. Harbor, 714/774-8111 or toll-free 888/560-1629 (for reservations), fax 714/956-4736, noted for its faux medieval parapets and palm trees. Amenities include refrigerators and videocassette players in all rooms, plus heated pool, wading pool, hot tub, coin laundry, and one-hour photo service. Regular rates are $78–98 year-round for two people; suites are $92 and up.

Sweet Suite Deals: Moderate and Up
For families and reasonably compatible couples or other small groups traveling together, sweet deals on suites can turn a midrange stay into a budget bargain—one with many conveniences. In most cases, the best rates are available with AAA or senior discounts.

Close to Disneyland's main entrance is **Anaheim Desert Inn & Suites**, 1600 S. Harbor Blvd., 714/772-5050 or toll-free 800/433-5270 for reservations in the United States and Canada, fax 714/778-2754; www.anaheimdesertinn.com. Whether you opt for a room or one of four different suite configurations, the basics here include refrigerator, microwave, TV/video player with HBO, CNN, ESPN, and the Disney Channel,

plus continental breakfast. Best bet for six or fewer people is the "parlor suite," featuring a bedroom with two queen beds plus a separate living area with sofa bed and second TV. In-room spas are available in regular rooms and the small parlor suites. With discounts the parlor (smallest) suites are $89–119 in the high season, $69–89 at other times (spa suites extra). Similar amenities, and options are available at the **Anaheim Desert Palm Inn & Suites** near the Convention Center at 631 W. Katella, 714/535-1133 or toll-free 800/635-5423 for reservations (United States and Canada), fax 714/491-7409; www.anaheimdesertpalm.com.

Hawthorne Suites, Ltd., two blocks from the park at 1752 S. Clementine St., 714/535-7773 or toll-free 800/992-4884 for reservations, fax 714/776-9073, offers a variety of suite configurations from $119 in summer, $89 and up otherwise. Amenities include continental breakfast; in-room coffee, microwave, refrigerator and safe; two TVs with Disney and other movie channels, plus an indoor pool, whirlpool spa, fitness center, coin laundry.

Nearby is the very comfortable **Peacock Suites Hotel at the Park**, 1745 S. Anaheim Blvd., 714/535-8255 or toll-free 800/522-6401 for reservations, fax 714/535-8914, www.peacocksuites.com, with all imaginable amenities (see above) plus hair dryer, iron and ironing board, and three phones (one's in the bathroom). Regular rates are $119 and up (lower with discounts).

Recently renovated **Days Inn Suites Anaheim At Disneyland Park**, 1111 S. Harbor Blvd. (north of Ball Rd.), 714/533-8830 or toll-free 800/654-7503 (United States and Canada) or 800/544-8313, fax 714/758-0573, www.daysinn.com, offers a particularly good deal for frugal families with its one-room "petite suites," which feature a queen bed plus sofa sleeper, refrigerator, microwave, and cable TV/movies. Swimming pool, whirlpool, coin laundry. Basic summer rates are $79 and up, otherwise $69 and up, lower with discounts. Two-room family suites are also available.

Less Costly Accommodations
Reasonably convenient to Disneyland is the HI-AYH-affiliated **Fullerton Hacienda Hostel**. Budget. (For details, see Fullerton: Night and Day

under Beyond Disneyland: Other Cities and Sights, below.) Otherwise, area improvements mean that low-priced accommodations are harder to find.

Budget chains are well represented near Disneyland. **Motel 6** is a few blocks from the park's main gate at 100 Disney Way, 714/520-9696 or toll-free 800/466-8356 (central reservations), fax 714/533-7539, www.motel6.com, and offers rooms for $42–52 double, lower in winter. Two **Super 8** motels are in the park's immediate vicinity. The first, **Super 8 Motel Anaheim/Disneyland Drive,** just north of Ball Rd. (north of Disneyland) at 915 S. West St., 714/778-0350 or toll-free for central reservations 800/248-4400 (United States) or 800/446-6969 (Canada), fax 714/778-3878, www.super8.com, with rates $45–65. The **Super 8 Motel Anaheim/ Disney/Katella Ave.,** 415 W. Katella Ave., 714/778-6900 or toll-free 800/777-7123 for reservations, fax 714/535-5659, www.super8.com, runs $42–59.

EATING NEAR DISNEYLAND

Dining Disney

The quality of food served at Disneyland, Disney's California Adventure, and the new, 300,000-square-foot Downtown Disney shopping and entertainment complex far exceeds the low expectations of food purists. Sure, you can rustle up burgers, fries, milkshakes, hot dogs, pizza, and other high-fat American favorites at food concessions strategically scattered throughout. But healthier fare is widely available, from fresh fruit and nonfat yogurt to low-calorie or vegetarian entrées and sandwiches. The **Blue Bayou Restaurant** in Disneyland's New Orleans Square is a decent sit-down restaurant, for example, specializing in Disney-style Creole food. The three Disney hotels all offer "character dining" (Goofy, Minnie, Chip 'n' Dale) at breakfast and lunch, and at least one coffee shop or café alternative for families. Quite good at the Disneyland Hotel for elegant grown-up dinner is **Hook's Pointe & Wine Cellar,** which serves California-style seafood, steaks, and such; at breakfast and lunch the Captain Hook

and Peter Pan–themed restaurant is more relaxed, equally inviting for families. For traditional and contemporary Japanese, the place is **Yamabuki** at Disneyland's Paradise Pier HoThe new fine-dining Disney star is the **Napa Rose** restaurant at Disney's Grand Californian HoCulinary bright lights at Downtown Disney include representative samples of some of L.A.'s best restaurants—everything from casual **La Brea Bakery** and the **Rainforest Café** to a Joachim Splichal outpost, **Patina Group.** You can also grab a tasty bite at Downtown Disney's music clubs, including the **House of Blues** and **Ralph Rennan's Jazz Kitchen.**

Dining Farther Afield

In the vast tourist ghetto surrounding Disneyland is the usual plethora of all-American family dining choices. There are more interesting options nearby, though, including the great Iranian **Ali Baba** restaurant, 100 S. Brookhurst (at Lincoln), 714/774-5632. As at its various L.A. locations, **El Pollo Inka,** 400 S. Euclid Ave. (at Broadway), 714/772-2263, is the place for intriguing Peruvian. For a Southern California cultural and culinary tour a bit farther afield, head for nearby Westminister and **Little Saigon** for Vietnamese and French fare (see below) or, just across the L.A. County line in Artesia, **Little Bombay,** L.A.'s own East India, where endless great restaurants, sari shops, and markets line Pioneer Boulevard between 178th and 188th Streets.

For a higher-end gustatory retreat at lunch or dinner, a local favorite is the dressy **Anaheim White House Restaurant** at 887 S. Anaheim Blvd., 714/772-1381, a dignified 80-year-old mansion noted for its intimate dining rooms and exceptional seafood and Northern Italian. Reservations advised for dinner. Lunch is a particular bargain. Another higher-end Anaheim favorite is California-style **Mr. Stox** just east of I-5 at 1105 E. Katella Ave., 714/634-2994, serving pastas, mesquite-grilled meats, and such at lunch and dinner.

Orange County communities near Anaheim all boast great restaurants. See other sections of this book's Orange County chapter for some suggestions.

NEAR DISNEYLAND

KNOTT'S BERRY FARM

Just minutes from Disneyland in Buena Park is Knott's Berry Farm, the nation's first theme park. Originally famous for Cordelia Knott's fried chicken dinners and for its fresh berries—in particular Orange County's own boysenberries, a delectable cross between blackberries, raspberries, and loganberries that Walter Knott helped develop during the Depression—Knott's Berry Farm evolved into a family-run, family-friendly monument to America's pioneering spirit. It was only in 1968 that the Knotts decided to fence the park and charge admission, and in 1997 that the family sold the park to Ohio-based Cedar Fair, L.P.

Ghost Town, Indian Trails

Though Knott's Berry Farm is no longer a family enterprise, its wholesomeness endures. Walter Knott's first and original outpost of down-home, old-fashioned Old West fun, Ghost Town was created to entertain and educate chicken-dinner customers otherwise idly waiting in line. Walter Knott actually rescued various original buildings from desert ghost towns and rebuilt them here.

(He also financed the restoration and preservation of Calico, an abandoned mining town in San Bernardino County, creating a popular county park.) On the outskirts of Ghost town is **Indian Trails,** which acknowledges native cultures with a Native American interpretive center; authentic tipis, hogans, and big houses; and native craft making, storytelling, music, and dance.

Ghost Town recreates a California desert mining town circa 1880 (shades of Calico), including shady ladies in the hotels and carousing gunslingers. Highlights of Ghost Town include **Knott's Wild West Stunt Show,** which showcases some tricks of the TV and movie trade; head to the **Calico Saloon** for the famous Can-Can Show. Blacksmiths, wood-carvers, and storytellers demonstrate authentic skills and crafts, and the **Western Museum** offers more settlement history. For a nominal fee, at the **Old Farm Mine** you can even pan for gold.

In many respects Knott's homage to the American West is more genuine, even in its sometimes golly-gee hokiness, than anything Disneyland has yet manufactured. Yet after more than 50 years of service, Ghost Town seemed tame when measured by modern whiz-bang technical standards.

KNOTT'S BERRY FARM

Knott's Berry Farm

All that changed forever with the debut of the thrilling **GhostRider,** one of the world's longest and tallest wooden roller coasters. In 2000, the A&E cable TV channel rated GhostRider number two among the world's Top 10 Wildest Rides. Another classic at Knott's Berry Farm is the **Timber Mountain Log Ride,** much more thrilling than the **Calico Mine Ride** down into the Calico Glory Hole. Watch out for robbers while riding the **Ghost Town Calico Railroad**—last survivor of the state's original narrow-gauge trains—and climb aboard the authentic **Butterfield Stagecoach** for a horse-drawn trip through time.

Fiesta Village

Once you're out of the Old West, things get more confused. Knott's second theme area, Fiesta Village, honors California's Spanish heritage with mariachi music, a classic Dentzel carousel, some commercial outlets and eateries, and rides such as **Tampico Tumbler.** In 1978 came the unforgettable **Montezooma's Revenge,** a real screamer of a ride just outside Camp Snoopy with a 45-foot-tall loop and the guaranteed thrill of accelerating—backward and upside down—to 55 miles per hour in five seconds flat. Still a wild contender in Southern California's ongoing theme park ride competition is Knott's **Jaguar!** This 2,700-foot-long roller coaster doesn't hurtle down the tracks at 70 miles per hour or flip you upside down en route, but Jaguar! does take its prey on a long (three-minute) aerial stalk through the park—a journey threaded even through the loop of infamous Montezooma's Revenge.

The Boardwalk

The long-running Roaring '20s theme area has been transformed into the The Boardwalk, which bills itself as "A Continuous California Beach Party." All those vintage amusements are slowly giving way to beach-themed amusements, though some of the old-timers, including the **Buffalo Nickel Penny Arcade,** remain. The Boardwalk's first feature, unveiled in spring 1996, is the **Hammerhead,** a variation of the European ride known as the Roto-

SPORTING ORANGE COUNTY

Some sort of sports-franchise virus seems to be afflicting Southern California these days. Foreshadowing the Los Angeles loss—or, more appropriately, *return*—of the L.A. Raiders football team to Oakland, in 1995 Orange County lost its **Los Angeles Rams** pro football team to St. Louis. **Edison International Field of Anaheim** (formerly Anaheim Stadium) still hosts **Anaheim Angels** baseball games, however. For Angels ticket information, call 714/663-9000 or visit the Anaheim Angels website at www.angelsbaseball.com. For almost any stadium event, by the way, a popular pre- and post-game stop is **The Catch** restaurant right across the street, 714/978-3700, where fresh fish and Angus steaks are served in lively sports-bar style.

Also notable is the Disney Company's **Mighty Ducks of Anaheim** National Hockey League expansion team, 714/704-2500, part of the new NHL Pacific Division. Though some wags refer to the endeavor as the "Mighty Bucks," the Ducks nest at the area's newest sports stadium, the impressive **Arrowhead Pond of Anaheim** (known affectionately as "The Pond") across the street from the Anaheim Stadium. The Ducks' season begins in early October and runs through April. The Pond also hosts events such as the WWF's **Smackdown, Disney on Ice,** professional bull-riding competitions, concerts from groups such as **U2,** For nonsports fans, right next door to the Pond is the **Stadium Promenade,** an entertainment complex complete with 25-screen movie theater, endless eateries, and a **Penske Racing Center** with full-size, full-motion, interactive Champ car simulators.

Shake inwhich riders spin—upside down and sideways—and then plunge 80 feet toward a grotto guarded by sharks and mermaids. You won't land in the pool, but you will get wet. And if that's not excitement enough, also here is the **Boomerang,** which roller-coasts riders upside down some six times in less than a minute. For a more individual thrill, try the **Supreme Scream.** The newest excitement is the **Perilous Plunge,** a boat ride with a 115-foot drop at a 75-degree angle—quite a splash. The **Boardwalk** amusements, shops, and food concessions offer calmer California fun. Also in the neighborhood is **Charles M. Schulz Theater,** offering holiday and seasonal productions.

Camp Snoopy, Wild Water Wilderness

Camp Snoopy features Charles Schulz's *Peanuts* comic strip characters transplanted to six acres of California's High Sierra, theme-park style. Camp Snoopy's newest educational attraction is the **Thomas A. Edison Inventors Workshop,** an interactive English-Spanish adventure in electrical and magnetic forces. Developed in cooperation with Southern California Edison, this joint scientific adventure also features an original gramophone, early light bulbs, and other genuine Thomas A. Edison artifacts. Among other recent attractions is the **Rocky Road Trucking Company,** where the kids get to try out a preschool-scale 18-wheeler. Other kid-sized rides include the new **Charlie Brown Speedway** stock car racetrack, the **Flying Ace Balloon Ride,** and the **Timberline Twister** roller coaster.

Knott's added its newest major theme area in 1988—Wild Water Wilderness, an artificial river in three acres of artificial wilderness. The main action? Rafting down **Bigfoot Rapids.** (As in real-life whitewater rafting, you *will* get wet.) The main attraction? **Mystery Lodge,** first known as "Spirit Lodge" at the Expo '86 World's Fair in Vancouver, British Columbia. This spirited and educational spiritual retreat, based on traditional beliefs of Northwestern native peoples, features the Old Storyteller and the holographic magic arising from the smoke of his campfire.

Other Attractions

In addition to its theme areas and associated events, Knott's offers other entertainment and extravaganzas, including (since 1998) **Edison International Electric Nights** at Reflection Lake, a nighttime dazzle of lasers and fireworks, and the **Incredible Waterworks Show.** In winter the Berry Farm becomes holiday-season **Knott's Merry Farm,** with **Snoopy's Twelve Days of Christmas on Ice** and other special events. From Thanksgiving through Christmas Eve, Ghost Town becomes **Knott's Christmas Crafts Village,** a stylized Victorian village overflowing with good cheer and artisans selling their wares (admission free to theme park visitors, otherwise small separate fee). Special spring events include April's **Spring Crafts Festival** and **Snoopy's Birthday Blast.** Come in summer for **Extreme Wheels** events. To many, the most

The Parachute Sky Jump takes riders up 20 stories before letting them float back to the ground.

impressive Knott's parties of them all are October's **Halloween Haunt** and **Knott's Scary Farm** (see below). Call Knott's or see the website for current events information.

Right next door to Knott's Berry Farm is warm-weather-only **Knott's Soak City U.S.A.,** a wet and wild water park featuring multiple high-speed slides, tube slides, inner-tube slides, a six-lane speed slide, a wave pool, and other family-friendly attractions. For current information, call Knott's at 714/220-5200 or try www.soakcityusa.com.

Otherwise Knott's most concentrated commercial enterprise is still **California Marketplace** along Grand Avenue near the park's entrance, featuring street-side gift shops and the famous **Mrs. Knott's Chicken Dinner Restaurant,** 714/220-5080, where about 1.5 million chicken dinners are dished out each year. Still more shopping possibilities circle the square to the west. Even nonshoppers should stop for some boysenberry preserves, a tasty souvenir. Knott's no longer grows boysenberries here at the "farm," now that Orange County is essentially urban, but the family did invent them here.

On the east side of Grand Avenue, adjacent to the park and family picnic areas, is Walter Knott's replica of Philadelphia's **Independence Hall**, recently restored and always worth a peek.

Halloween Haunt and Knott's Scary Farm
Locals will tell you there's no better Halloween party *anywhere* than the one hosted each year by Knott's—and if you plan to come, get your tickets for the Halloween Haunt well in advance. On weekend nights throughout October, adults and brave older children—most dressed in ghoulish and grotesque costumes—stroll through the House of Maniacs, cruise the Cavern of Carnage, climb Santa Claws Mountain, and otherwise enjoy the park's terrifying Halloween transformation. New mazes in 2000 included the Carnival of Carnivorous Clowns, the Voodoo Witch Project, and the Gothic Graveyard. Show-stopping celebrities include **Elvira, Mistress of the Dark** and the **Crypt Keeper** from the *Tales From The Crypt* TV show. Very scary, very fun. Children under age 13 not admitted. At last report Halloween Haunt tickets were $35 in advance, $40 at the door, but—with special seasonal coupons, widely available locally—could be purchased for as little as $29. For advance tickets, call the Haunt Line at toll-free 877/858-7234, try the Knott's website (see above), or call any TicketMaster outlet. Haunt parking is $8.

Not nearly as scary is Knott's Scary Farm, strictly kids' stuff. On weekend days from mid-October through Halloween, 10 A.M.–6 P.M., Camp Snoopy becomes "Camp Spooky," a safe, supervised children's costume party hosted by Charlie Brown, Lucy, and other characters from the *Peanuts* gang. Sometimes even the Great Pumpkin shows up. Scary Farm admission for both adults and children is included in general park admission.

Practical Knott's Berry Farm
Knott's Berry Farm is open in summer 9 A.M.–midnight (until 1 A.M. Saturday night) and in winter 10 A.M.–6 P.M. Mon.-Fri., 10 A.M.–10 P.M. on Saturday, and 10 A.M.–7 P.M. Sunday, though holiday hours may differ. The entire park may close during bad weather; if in doubt, call ahead.

At last report park admission was $40 adults and $30 children (ages 3–11), seniors (age 60 and up), nonambulatory, and expectant mothers. Or come after 4 P.M. on any day Knott's is open past 6 P.M. (in summer and on weekends) for just $16.95 (all ages). Annual passes are also available, along with (at last report) substantial admission discounts for Southern California residents. Parking is $7 autos, $10 R–s and buses, though free three-hour parking is available for visitors to the Chicken Dinner Restaurant, Independence Hall, and California Marketplace.

For more information, contact: Knott's Berry Farm, 8039 Beach Blvd., Buena Park, CA 90620, 714/220-5200 (taped information) or 220-5220 for special guest services; www.knotts.com.

To get here, from either I-5 or the Riverside Freeway (Hwy. 91, known as the Artesia Freeway in this neck of the woods) take the Beach Boulevard exit south. To come via surface streets from Disneyland, head west via Ball Road, Katella Avenue, or other major thoroughfare to Beach Boulevard, then drive north on Beach for about five miles, following the signs.

For current information on other nearby attractions and local practicalities, contact: **Buena Park Convention & Visitors Office,** 7711 Beach Blvd., Ste. 100, Buena Park, CA 90620, 714/562-3560, fax 714/562-3569; www.buenapark.com.

NEAR KNOTT'S BERRY FARM

Medieval Times Dinner and Tournament
Family-style amusement is a major industry in Buena Park, with various diversions strung out like Christmas lights along Beach Boulevard. One of the best is Medieval Times, an ersatz trip into the days of sword fights and knights in armor jousting on horseback. The tournament is well choreographed and, especially if the audience is in the mood to participate, reasonably entertaining. But the dressage-trained Andalusian stallions are a draw all by themselves. Admission—$37.95 adults, $24.95 children ages 3–13—includes a four-course dinner of appetizer, vegetable soup, roasted chicken, spare ribs, potato, with pastries and coffee for dessert. (The kids will love the fact that they eat without utensils, in true medieval style.) A beverage is included; cash bar service available. It's also extra if you want to buy the snapshot taken at the door.

Show times at Medieval Times, 7662 Beach Blvd., 714/523-1100, 714/521-4740 (reservations), or toll-free 800/899-6600 for reservations and showtimes, www.medievaltimes.com, vary depending on the day (two shows on Saturday and Sunday), so call for information. Reservations are advisable, since tour groups can pack the place. Try to arrive one hour early.

Wild Bill's Wild West Dinner Extravaganza

Wild Bill's, practically next door at 7600 Beach Blvd., 714/522-4611 or toll-free 800/883-1547 (for reservations and information, toll-free 800-883-1546), offers the same family-oriented dinner-and-entertainment concept but with a country-western twang. All in all this show is probably more appealing to foreign tourists, judging from the busloadswho mosey on in from the parking lot, especially since Wild Bill's serves hefty helpings of apple-pie Americana à la the Hollywood western. But if you and yours hunger for such fare, Wild Bill's offers two hours of well-done specialty acts with cowboys, dance-hall girls, and Indians (Native Americans), not to mention a decent family-style four-course cookhouse meal of chicken and ribs. Admission is $37.95 for adults and $23.95 for children. Group rates are also available. Show times vary, sometimes with the addition of weekend matinee performances, so call for current information. To get a good seat, make reservations and then arrive early.

Museums as Entertainment

If you're one of those people who can't get enough show-biz schmaltz and happen to have extra time on your hands, head for the **Movieland Wax Museum** a block north of Knott's at 7711 Beach Blvd., 714/522-1154, movieland waxmuseum.com, where you can schmooze with likenesses of more than 270 Hollywood stars—such leading men and ladies as John Wayne, Marilyn Monroe, and Kevin Costner. If you're disappointed that Pee-Wee Herman is not enshrined here, it's not because of morals charges. Movieland did try—multiple times—to memorialize Pee-Wee in paraffin, but Herman's alter ego, Paul Reubens, was not pleased by the image. (That's show biz.) But Donny and Marie Osmond will be immortalized here. There's

also a scene from *Titanic* on display—Jack and Rose above it all, out on the ship's prow. Admission is $12.95 adults, $6.95 children. It's open daily except Christmas Mon.– Fri. 10 A.M.–7:30 P.M. and weekends 9 A.M.–8:30 P.M. (schedule subject to change).

The associated **Ripley's Believe It Or Not Museum** or "Odditorium" across the street at 7850 Beach Blvd., 714/522-7045, www.ripleys-believeitornot.com, displays 10,000 square feet of the bizarre, beautiful, and strange things collected by Robert L. Ripley on his world travels. So it's not so strange that people still flock here just to see coiled feather money, the winged warlock helmet, the Fiji mermaid, and the world's tallest man's enormous shoe, size 36D. Jungled-themed items are the latest draw. Admission is $8.95 adults, $6.95 seniors, $5.25 children. Inquire about combination admission if you'll also visit the Wax Museum; at last report the cost for both attractions was $16.90 adults, $13.95 seniors, and $9.75 children. The Odditorium is open daily 11 A.M.–5 P.M. (closed Christmas).

Museums as History

If the history and diversity of dolls intrigues you, then visit the **Hobby City Doll and Toy Museum** beyond the tourist-trod territory at 1238 S. Beach Boulevard, 714/527-2323. Housed in a replica of the White House, this astonishing and eclectic commercial collection includes thousands of dolls—the owner's personal collection, everything from antique dolls to Barbies. It's open daily 10 A.M.–6 P.M. Small museum admission; entrance to the six acres of collector, craft, and hobby shops is free.

Back in Anaheim, presented with considerably less promotional punch than other area attractions is the **Anaheim Museum** housed in the 1908 Carnegie library at 241 S. Anaheim Blvd., 714/778-3301, which tells the story of Anaheim's German immigrant past as both experiment in communal living and early wine-producing region. Changing special exhibits. It's open Wed.–Fri. 10 A.M.–4 P.M., Saturday noon–4 P.M. Admission contribution greatly appreciated. For information on Anaheim's other historic buildings and other area historical information, see the website for the **Anaheim Colony Historic District,** www.anaheimcolony.com.

Crystal Cathedral

ROBERT HOLMES/CALIFORNIA DIVISION OF TOURISM

Crystal Cathedral

Disneyland aside, Orange County's most intriguing contemporary architectural feat is the Crystal Cathedral of the Reformed Church in America, a modern wonder designed by Philip Johnson and John Burgee. The Reverend Robert H. Schuller's "cathedral" is a striking mirrored glass-and-steel theater standing 12 stories tall and shaped like a four-pointed star. Visually inspiring (especially from a distance) but an acoustical nightmare, the church features nine-story-tall sliding glass doors that open to include worshippers sitting in their cars out in the parking lot.

Schuller, who has spread his "Possibility Thinking" message and expanded his ministry nationwide via his *Hour of Power* TV show, got his start preaching from the roof of the snack bar at the Orange Drive-In Theater. In more recent years Schuller's famous drive-in ministry has become noted for its religious-themed theatrics, quite effectively staged in the Crystal Cathedral. The annual **Glory of Easter** production, for example, features a real-life menagerie—including a 350-pound tiger—in the court of Pontius Pilate and human angels (attached to aerial cables) who swoop down to just a few feet above worshipers' heads. The **Glory of Christmas** is also unusually festive.

The Crystal Cathedral is in Garden Grove at 13280 Chapman Ave., 714/971-4000; www.crystalcathedral.org. Guided tours are offered; call for the current schedule. (Donation requested.) For Glory of Easter and Glory of Christmas reservations, call 714/544-5679 (54-GLORY).

BEYOND DISNEYLAND: OTHER CITIES AND SIGHTS

FULLERTON: NIGHT AND DAY

Earlier in this century, Fullerton was a major agricultural and industrial center, the county's second-largest oil producer. A more recent claim to fame is Santa Ana-born Leo Fender—something of a musical revolutionary, the "Thomas Edison of guitars," the spiritual father of technologies now embraced by plugged-in rock 'n' rollers everywhere. A humble radio repairman and big-band enthusiast, Fender figured out how to repair, then improve, electric guitar amplifiers. Then he turned his attention to reinventing the guitar itself, in the 1940s. Fender's legacy has been lasting—a world full of Stratocasters and endless international imitators.

Fullerton, though, is full of nontract neighborhoods and big shade trees, an oddity in these days of hopelessly homogenized Orange County housing developments. Fullerton manages to be a fairly earthy, fairly artsy, almost easy-going middle-class community with an appealing and vital 1920s-vintage downtown district. In other words, Fullerton is as different from Irvine, the county's other university community, as night from day. Come on Fullerton's last day—and night—each year for family-oriented fun, from art strolls and music to fireworks, at the **First Night** New Year's Eve celebration.

For more information about the community, contact the **Fullerton Chamber of Commerce,** 219 E. Commonwealth Ave., Fullerton, CA 92632, 714/871-3100, fax 714/871-2871; www .fullerton.org. For an online downtown shopping guide, try www.shopfullerton.com.

Seeing Fullerton

Fullerton is no tourist town. But there are attractions, including the 26-acre **Fullerton Arboretum,** on the northeast corner of the Cal State Fullerton campus, 1900 Associated Rd. (at Yorba Linda Blvd.), 714/278-3579 for information, http://arboretum.fullerton.edu, complete with lakes and waterfall, refreshing for a meandering stroll. It's open daily except major holidays, small admission. Tour the 1894 **Victorian Heritage House** here on Sunday, 2–4 P.M. Another local gem is the **Muckenthaler Cultural Center,** 1201 W. Malvern Ave., 714/738-6595, www .muckenthaler.org, where the first floor of the 1924 Italian Renaissance villa hosts changing multicultural art exhibits throughout the year. Galleries are open Tues.–Fri. 10 A.M.–4 P.M., and Saturday and Sunday noon–4 P.M. The center also sponsors various performing arts programs and summer dinner theater performances in the outdoor Theater on the Green. In spring the Muckenthaler Motor Car Show of antique and classic cars is the center's major fundraiser.

But to enjoy Fullerton to the fullest, head downtown to **California State University, Fullerton** and the collection of galleries and good restaurants parked on and around State College Boulevard. For university information, call 714/773-2011 or see www.fullerton.edu.

Staying in Fullerton: Fullerton Hacienda Hostel

Though Fullerton offers various decent, reasonably priced motels—contact the chamber of commerce for suggestions—a special bonus for budget travelers is the HI-AYH-affiliated **Fullerton Hacienda Hostel,** 1700 N. Harbor Blvd., Fullerton, CA 92835, 714/738-3721, fax 714/738-0925; www.hostelweb.com. The hostel is three miles north of the Riverside (91) Freeway in Brea Dam Park, easily accessible by OCTD bus. Once here, weary hoofers can bed down in a comfortable Spanish-style home at a onetime dairy farm (three dorm rooms, eight beds each). Amenities include a fireplace, piano, newly remodeled kitchen, free laundry facilities, even recreational Ping Pong. Lockers and baggage/equipment storage is available. Wheelchair accessible. Free parking. Price is $11–13.

Eating in Fullerton

A good place to grab an espresso as well as a vegetarian meal is **Rutabegorz,** 211 N. Pomona, 714/738-9339. *The* place for New Mexican and Southwestern standards, wonderfully heavy on the chiles, is simple, unfussy **Anita's,** 600 S. Harbor (between Orangethorpe and Valencia), 714/525-0977, which is inexpensive to boot. People's favorites include out-of-this-world bean dip and chips, for smaller appetites, and the sopapillas and pork adobado.

Stop by **Steamers Café,** 138 W. Commonwealth Ave., 714/871-8800, for decent food and the best jazz for many miles around.

For sophisticated atmosphere, try **Mulberry Street,** 114 W. Wilshire (near Chapman), 714/525-1056, where the old-brick-and-wood ambience almost as inviting as the contemporary Italian entrées—seafood pomadoro, rack of lamb. Full bar. Immensely popular, so be patient. Another possibility is the upscale Italian **Downtown Bar & Grill,** 102 N. Harbor Blvd., 714/879-7570. Much more entertaining for the kids, given its eclectic style, is **Angelo's and Vinci's Ristorante,** north of Chapman at 550 N. Harbor Blvd., 714/879-4022, where pizza's the thing.

For old-school style and serious, cozy French, the place is dinner-only **The Cellar,** at Villa del Sol, 305 N. Harbor Blvd. (south of Chapman), 714/525-5682. Another possibility is the elegant French **La Vie en Rose,** 240 S. State College Blvd. in nearby Brea, 714/529-8333, serving fish, seafood, veal, and more. Full bar in the turret. Visit the specialty store/pastry shop.

THE RICHARD NIXON LIBRARY: THE COMEBACK KID COMES HOME

After his death in 1994, ex-President Richard Milhous Nixon finally came home—to the **Richard Nixon Library and Birthplace** in Yorba Linda. More than 40,000 people showed up to say good-bye to Orange County's most famous homeboy, including all five living U.S. presidents, heads of state, Watergate warrior G. Gordon Liddy, and immigrant Vietnamese shopkeepers from the Asia Garden Mall in nearby Westminster. For Nixon loyalists, his funeral was a time of genuine grief. For his equally constant foes, the

day was also quite sad—because for all Nixon's brilliance in the political arena in the end he seemed a tragic figure.

The only American president ever forced by impending impeachment to resign from office, Richard M. Nixon personified the dark side of American politics yet never seemed to understand or accept any real responsibility for his fall. Those who knew him best, who were most familiar with the depths of that Nixonian darkness, have tried to understand. Some speculate that too much success, too soon, created a political persona ill prepared to handle defeat, let alone opposition. According to former Secretary of State Henry Kissinger, Richard Nixon was "a strange mixture of calculation, deviousness, idealism, tenderness, tawdriness, courage, and daring" and a man who wanted to be remembered for his idealism. Less widely quoted is another observation from Kissinger: "Think what this man could have done if anyone hadever loved him."

Nixon's World in Nixon's Words: The Nixon Library

Designated a California historical landmark in January 1995, the Richard Nixon Library and Birthplace first opened on July 19, 1990. The pageantry was nothing if not patriotic, with much speechifying, red, white, and blue balloons galore, and tens of thousands of well-wishers.

The $21 million price tag was equally impressive, making this the most expensive monument yet built in honor of presidents past. Unlike other presidential museums, funded at least in part by the government and subject to some degree of federal review, Nixon's is entirely self-supporting—a fact that threatened, early on, to embroil the institution in as much controversy as the ex-president himself. Before the Nixon Library even opened its doors, critics charged that Nixon and his employees would offer only a flattering spin on his life and times.

It's true that the Nixon Library—more accurately, museum—serves primarily to glorify its namesake rather than explain, let alone criticize. (With or without federal funding, the same can be said of all post-presidency memorials, however.) It's also true that the displays here are exceptionally well done, conceptually and technically. Exploring the place for yourself is well worth the side trip into Orange County's suburban hinterlands.

Once inside, after a stroll through engaging displays on Nixon's Orange County past, first stop is the large movie theater. The 25-minute film *Never Give Up: Nixon in the Arena* runs continuously. Here the master campaigner's continuing campaign may prove a bit nauseating even to some who voted for him—so sneak ahead, if you must, but don't turn back. Worthwhile stops lie ahead, including the striking hallway gallery of Nixon *Time* magazine covers just beyond—a chronicle of one man's remarkable march through American history and a chance to count at least some of the "new" Nixon's who made the trip.

Next is documentation of that long journey, starting with a peek at Richard Nixon's early campaigns. His Red-baiting beginnings get short shrift, but included here are both the "pink sheet" with which Nixon smeared Helen Gahagan Douglas and the intriguing Nixon-votes-Commie handbill distributed in response by Douglas's campaign. (For a fascinating account of this period, though not a Nixon Library-sanctioned title, read *Tricky Dick and the Pink Lady—Richard Nixon vs. Helen Gahagan Douglas: Sexual Politics and the Red Scare, 1950,* by Greg Mitchell.) Coverage of the Alger Hiss spy case, Nixon's earliest political point-making in the national arena, is less riveting than the chance—next stop—to watch the infamous "Checkers" speech on TV. (For those who've forgotten, or who have disliked Nixon for other reasons, keep in mind that our 37th president was the first to inflict big-time politics on the populace via the boob tube.) Also fascinating during Nixon's vice-presidential years are the photos, including Nixon's Kitchen Debate with Nikita Khrushchev. Best of all, though, is the 1957 letter from Martin Luther King, Jr., thanking Nixon for his civil rights advocacy.

Coverage of 1960, the year Nixon lost to John F. Kennedy, features political memorabilia, unpublished *Life* magazine photos, and the chance to time-trip in a '60s-style living room watching clips from the four Nixon-Kennedy debates on black and white TV. This first-ever televised debate—with Nixon nixing makeup, and thus, with four-o'-clock shadow, perspiring

profusely—reportedly taught him that "style was more important than substance."

What the museum bills as "the wilderness years"—1963–67—all but disappear here. One would never know that during this time, with President Lyndon B. Johnson radically escalating American military involvement in Vietnam, Richard Nixon was the nation's leading hawk, crying out loud and long for more bombs, more munitions, more troops.

Before studying the museum's rather sad coverage of the Vietnam War, however, enjoy some stunning pomp and circumstance—most particularly, the odd yet awesome "World Leaders" gallery of life-sized bronze heads of state, among them Mao in an easy chair and Winston Churchill chatting up Charles de Gaulle.

Farther along, visitors can revisit Nixon's 1969 "silent majority" speech and at least token testimony about the contentiousness of the times. Anyone who missed the events leading up to the end of the Vietnam War (and the end of Richard Nixon's political career) will get little enlightenment here—and will scarcely understand the disappearance of Nixon's original Watergate-era vice president, Spiro T. Agnew. The Nixon Library explains that Agnew resigned after conviction "on other charges." (For the record, Agnew was allowed to plead guilty to income tax invasion, sidestepping more serious U.S. Justice Department charges that he had accepted more than $100,000 in bribes and kickbacks.)

Next on the itinerary is the "Life in the White House" exhibit, with some fancy dresses and frippery but also evidence of political wife Pat Nixon's genuine warmth, even during the brutal presidential years.

The Lincoln Sitting Room, next, is a cozy replica of Richard Nixon's favorite White House retreat for speech writing. Also here: a display on speech writing and more speeches (the 1973 "I am not a crook" speech not included on the continuous video); a rundown on the president's domestic accomplishments and affairs (no mention of Vice President Ford's full pardon of Nixon); and a rotating collection of some of the 30,000 unusual, often handmade, sometimes hilarious gifts the Nixons received from the public during the White House years.

FROM COMMIE HUNTING TO WATERGATE: A MAN AND HIS MYTH

During his presidency Richard Nixon was known to stroll the beach below the Western White House in San Clemente wearing a coat, tie, and wing tips—proof positive, if history is less certain, that Nixon was from California but not much of a Californian.

California blessed his political career, however. A young Navy veteran fresh from World War II and supported by local kingmakers, including an unquestioning *Los Angeles Times,* Richard Nixon was right in tune with the Red-baiting tenor of the times. In 1946 he won election to the U.S. Congress by labeling incumbent Jerry Voorhis a Communist dupe. While in Congress, Nixon made a name for himself as an active member of the infamous House Un-American Activities Committee chaired by Joseph McCarthy. In 1950 he landed a U.S. Senate seat, smearing his opponent Helen Gahagan Douglas as "the pink lady."

Largely invisible as vice president to Dwight D. Eisenhower after the 1952 and 1956 presidential elections, Nixon's notoriety waned in a decade of disappointment. He lost to John F. Kennedy in the 1960 presidential race. He was defeated again in 1962, losing the California governorship to one of the state's all-time-great glad-handers, Edmund G. "Pat" Brown. The morning after that election, unshaven, haggard, and stiff with rage, Nixon attacked the press with a display of poor sportsmanship and personal rancor that stunned even his supporters. "You won't have Nixon to kick around any more because, gentlemen," he said, "this is my last press conference."

Hardly. Spurned by California, Nixon left for New York, a career as a private attorney, and a calendar of careful personal appearances—quite genial—designed to support a comeback. Rebuilding his political career seemed unlikely, but the assassination of President John Kennedy, followed by Republican Barry Goldwater's disastrous defeat to Lyndon Johnson in 1964, offered the opportunity to grab again for the presidency. And he did. Nixon swept into the White House in 1968 and 1972, supported by America's "silent majority," on his vague promise to end the war in Vietnam. Unfortunately, his graceless, imperious, and vindictive political style returned with him to Washington.

Beyond an approach to politics that earned him the whispered sobriquet "Tricky Dicky" even among fellow Republicans, Richard Nixon's accomplishments as president were difficult to categorize.

He has been widely recognized for reestablishing political ties with China, though the details of those top-secret negotiations—including discussions about ending the Vietnam War and ongoing U.S. and Chinese relations with the Soviet Union—remain classified by the CIA. (Some speculate that complete revelation of who actually said what, and when, would prove embarrassing to the United States and to parties still living.) That this was Nixon's crowning accomplishment is nonetheless ironic. He opened the door to China, but he had dedicated himself to keeping it closed for 20 years.

Nixon is also credited with bombing Cambodia to hurry the end of the Vietnam War, an "incursion" that "set the Khmer Rouge on the road to murdering a million people," in the words of former *Washington Post* columnist Nicholas von Hoffman. In 1973, Nixon did end the Vietnam War—ultimately a botched retreat, in the view of many, followed by the fall of Saigon in 1975.

On the home front, Richard Nixon's signature established the U.S. Environmental Protection Agency and approved the Endangered Species Act (though in watered-down form, since he typically opposed environmental legislation). But even former U.S. Senator George S. McGovern, whom Nixon defeated in the nasty 1972 presidential election, points out that Nixon's domestic policies—including support for federally funded nutrition programs—weren't necessarily conservative, certainly not in the modern mean-spirited sense of the word.

Though he hoped to be remembered as an idealist, most likely Richard Nixon will go down in history as someone much more complicated than that. He was, after all, the man who nearly destroyed the presidency in defense of his own absolute authority.

One core Nixon belief—that "When the President does it, that means it is not illegal"—set the state for his downfall. That end began with "Watergate," an endless saga of deceit, dishonesty, and denials that followed a bungled burglary of Democratic National Committee headquarters in Washington, D.C.'s Watergate HoLow points in that seamy

Richard Nixon   Richard Nixon

USA 32   USA 32

saga of political intrigue included revelations that key Nixon staffers organized and arranged "dirty tricks" financing for the 1972 Committee to Re-Elect the President (CREEP) operation—including, earlier, wiretapping of Democratic campaign phones. Nixon himself was at least aware of the ongoing cover-up. He refused to admit even that truth, however, until congressional impeachment proceedings were well under way—those proceedings begun only after Nixon refused to turn over tapes and transcripts subpoenaed by the Senate Watergate Committee. Nixon was prepared to defy even the U.S. Supreme Court.

Though 18 1/2 minutes of key secretly recorded White House phone conversations were erased mysteriously, an astonished America eventually did hear plenty of the low-brow language typical of the day-to-day Richard Nixon. Also revealed as a result of the Watergate scandal was Nixon's predilection for seeing politics, and people, in black and white terms—a character flaw inspiring his "enemies list," which included even actor Paul Newman (#19),

whose crime was leaving a nasty note for Nixon in a rental car.

Finally defeated by himself, Richard Nixon resigned on August 8, 1974. The next day he left for a lengthy domestic exile at La Casa Pacifica, the onetime Western White House in San Clemente on the Orange County coast.

On September 8 new President Gerald Ford granted Nixon an unconditional pardon for Watergate—part of a prearranged deal by Republicans to speed Nixon's departure, many speculate.

By the 1980s—having once again abandoned California for New York—Richard Nixon was ready to begin his next comeback, reincarnating himself this time around as a respected elder statesman.

Nixon's friends exonerate him. White House Watergate lawyer Leonard Garment, for example, has explained that Nixon had "large ambitions" and "intense hatreds," and was both "perpetrator and recipient of an immense amount of political abuse." Watergate was an exercise in exorcising "the tremendous demons of hatred that had accumulated over the years."

Alexander Butterfield, a top Nixon White House aide, remains unswayed by the Nixon-as-victim school of thought. "Nothing happened that Richard Nixon didn't OK, nothing," he has said, "and it's preposterous that anything of the magnitude of a break-in of the Democratic National Headquarters didn't come from Richard Nixon."

But many people consider Nixon innocent of all charges, no matter what he actually did—an urge, in the words of *Harper's* editor Lewis H. Lapham, arising from our "common wish to declare, now and forever, world without end, our collective innocence. If Nixon is innocent, we are all innocent."

Almost last but not least is the Watergate Gallery, an overwhelming and oppressively busy three-tiered visual display—newspaper headlines, photo montage, plus Nixon's own commentary—accompanied by the chance to hear parts of the infamous Watergate tapes, including a discussion of hush money, the "smoking gun" cover-up conversation with H. R. Haldeman, and the John Dean "cancer on the presidency" chat. Whether one cherishes or despises the memory of Richard Nixon and his Watergate-era antics, there is little here to alter that perspective—or help place its political implications in any larger context. Helpful in that regard is

Stanley Kutler's book, *Abuse of Power: The New Nixon Tapes,* published in late 1997, which offers transcript excerpts from more than 200 hours of Nixon tapes along with devasting revelations about the extent of Nixon's involvement, from the beginning, in the Watergate cover-up.

Last stop is the Presidential Forum, a small theater where visitors "talk" to Richard Nixon. Select touch-screen questions on consoles at the back of the room and then watch the ex-president's videotaped responses on the larger-than-life screen. Skip this part if you're in a hurry, because you can spend a great deal of time listening for news that isn't there. If you ask Nixon if he is "sorry for Watergate" and ready to "apologize," for example, Nixon says: "I can only answer this by stating a fact: There's no way to apologize more than resigning the presidency of the United States. That said it all, and I don't intend to say anymore." You'll want to ask that question again, though, after Nixon "clarifies" Watergate by explaining what it wasn't—"no one was killed, no one profited from it, no election was affected or stolen"—and then dismisses the issue as "simply a political shenanigan, wrong and stupidly handled."

Underground, beneath the lobby and theater, are the Nixon archives, the actual "library" of the institution's title. Unlike other presidential libraries, this one has no collection of original documents from the Nixon presidency. The official, and complete, collection of Nixon presidential papers is preserved by the National Archives in Alexandria, Virginia. In the wake of Watergate, fearing what might happen to tapes and other documents, the U.S. Congress passed the Presidential Recordings and Materials Act requiring all official Nixon presidential materials to remain under government control. In June 2000, a decades-long old legal conflict was finally settled when the U.S. Justice Department agreed to pay $18 million to Nixon's estate for the tapes and papers.

What is here in Yorba Linda, though—available to approved scholars, but incrementally, as the collection is slowly established—is a large archive of Nixoniana. The collection will eventually include copies of Nixon's complete presidential "special files" (minus material withheld for national security reasons as well as whatever Nixon and library staff deemed unimportant), personal White House diaries, manuscripts of books written by the ex-president, and various campaign, congressional, and vice-presidential papers.

The library's Nixon Center for Peace and Freedom was established as a "bipartisan" foreign and domestic policy institute. In 1995, the center's Architect of the New Century Award was presented to Speaker of the House Newt Gingrich.

Don't miss the small gift shop on the way out. This is the authoritative source for respectful versions of Nixon kitsch, including the infamous "President and the King" (Richard Nixon and Elvis Presley) T-shirts, cards, buttons, and refrig-erator magnets. Quite popular is the "Nixon in 1996—Tan, Rested, and Ready" T-shirt released posthumously. Red-white-and-blue memorabilia and copies of books by and about Nixon are also available—including the ex-president's last two books, *Seize the Moment: America's Challenge in a One-Superpower World* and *In The Arena: A Memoir of Victory, Defeat, and Renewal.* To achieve a balanced perspective, pick up an old paperback copy of *The Final Days,* the Pulitzer Prize-winning story about Watergate by *Washington Post* journalists Bob Woodward and Carl Bernstein (not for sale here), or watch Oliver Stone's rather creative film rendition of Nixon's life and times, *Nixon,* a pathos-rich psychopolitical epic (also not for sale here).

The Nixon Birthplace

No matter how humbling his end, Richard Milhous Nixon's beginnings were humble indeed. He was born on January 9, 1913, in this tiny farmhouse built from a Sears Roebuck kit by his father, Frank. His mother, Hannah, named him after the English king Richard Plantagenet, "Richard the Lionhearted." (All the Nixon boys were named after English kings.)

In 1922 Nixon's family abandoned the nine-acre homestead—the soil was too poor for growing lemons—but only after years of trying to make a go of it. (In 1919 Frank went to work as an oil-field roustabout; Hannah, with sons Richard and Harold in tow, packed lemons in a Sunkist plant.) After a move to nearby Whittier, where Frank opened a gas station, Richard went on to become a star student, in 1929 winning the $20 first prize in a *Los Angeles Times* oratorical contest. His speech denounced a "wave of indifference to the Constitution"—an irony only in retrospect.

Restored to its original simplicity at a cost of $400,000, the Nixon birthplace is definitely worth a stop. (On audio tape, Richard Nixon himself will guide you through.) Most of the modest furnishings are original, including the living room piano, little Richard's violin, and the bed in which the future president was born, supplemented by a few period pieces and reproductions. The tiny kitchen comes complete with wood cookstove, Hannah's cookbooks, and sundry everyday implements of domesticity. The attic room upstairs, shared by Richard Nixon and his three brothers, is typically off limits for visitors. But just imagine a barefoot, nine-year-old Richard Nixon scrambling upstairs to practice his accordion.

The First Lady's Garden

"I have sacrificed everything in my life that I consider precious in order to advance the political career of my husband," Pat Nixon once said. But not all was lost. Pat Nixon loved gardening. Most noteworthy on a stroll through the well-tended grounds, near the Nixon family home, is the First Lady's Garden, which pays homage to her love of the White House Rose Garden. (May is the best month for the flower show.) Here favorite floribundas—including the burgundy red "Pat Nixon"—stretch up from beds of perennials and colorful annuals. A pleasant spot to sit and ponder the perplexing paths of human destiny.

Practical Nixon Library

The Nixon Library and Birthplace is at the corner of Yorba Linda Boulevard and Eureka Avenue. For current information (prerecorded), including special exhibits and events, call 714/993-5075 (fax 528-0544), or try the website: www.nixon-foundation.org. Otherwise, for information write: Richard Nixon Library and Birthplace, 18001 Yorba Linda Blvd., Yorba Linda, CA 92686. The museum is open Mon.–Sat. 10 A.M.–5 P.M., Sunday 11 A.M.–5 P.M., closed Thanksgiving and Christmas. Admission is $5.95 adults, $4.95 active military, $3.95 seniors and students with ID, and $2 children ages 8–11 (under 7 free). Free parking. The grounds can also be reserved for weddings, other celebrations, and corporate meetings by special arrangement.

Exhibits and events are not always partisan. A 1990s' favorite was **Rockin' in the White House: From 'Heartbreak Hotel' to Pennsylvania Avenue,** for example; more recent were **Barbie as First Lady: Gowns and Patriotic Costumes of America's Legendary Leading Lady** and **Presidential Ties: Neck and Neck from Jefferson to Clinton.** But sometimes they are stunningly so. In 1992, for example, retired Marine Lieutenant Ollie North was here for a book signing; Dan Quayle has also been a special guest.

The library and birthplace offer no on-site dining. Nearby best bets for lunch and dinner include **Blue Agave** at 18601 Yorba Linda Blvd.

(north side of Yorba Linda between Lake View and Avocado), 714/970-5095, which serves Southwestern and Tex-Mex fare along with jazz and Spanish flamenco on Saturday. For breakfast (no credit cards), head for the **Original Pancake House** at 18453 Yorba Linda Blvd., 714/693-1390. For more information about the area, contact: **Yorba Linda Chamber of Commerce,** 17670 Yorba Linda Blvd., Yorba Linda, CA 92886, 714/993-9537, fax 714/993-7764, www.yorbalindanet.com.

Getting Here: Either Highway 57 (the Orange Freeway) or Highway 91 (the Riverside Freeway) will get you here; both are accessible from I-5. From Newport Beach and nearby coastal areas, the best option is heading inland via Highway 55, which merges into Highway 91 (continue east). From Highway 91, exit at Highway 90 (the Imperial Highway) and head north; exit at Yorba Linda Boulevard and head west to reach the Nixon Library and Birthplace. From Highway 57, exit at Yorba Linda Boulevard and head east.

INTERNATIONAL ORANGE

The city of Orange got its moniker in a poker game, according to local lore. After accepting the land in exchange for unpaid attorney fees, owner A. B. Chapman decided that the original "Richland" wasn't good enough. So in 1875 he and three associates—each representing a possible new agricultural proclivity, Almond, Olive, Lemon, and Orange—clinched the city's fate in a card game.

These days folks flock to downtown Orange, especially **Old Towne Orange Plaza** (listed on the National Register of Historic Places) as much for the area's good restaurants and abundant antique shops as the old-neighborhood California ambience—and this despite the fact that Orange really could do more to dust off its assets. Orange boasts its malls, too, including **The Block at Orange,** the **Stadium Promenade,** and **The Mall of Orange.**

The biggest event of the year is the three-day **Orange International Street Fair,** usually held over the Labor Day weekend at the end of summer and a tradition since 1910, with several hundred thousand people converging to celebrate world culture with folk dancing, food, music, arts and crafts booths, and more. Also come for **Art Walk Orange** tours of Old Towne Orange's art galleries, held the second Thursday of the month from May through Dec., 6–9 P.M.

Orange County's city of Orange is northeast of I-5, south of the Riverside (91) Freeway, north of the Garden Grove (22) Freeway, and bisected by the Costa Mesa (55) Freeway. For more information, contact the **Orange Chamber of Commerce and Visitors Bureau,** 439 E. Chapman Ave., Orange, CA 92866, 714/538-3581 or toll-free 800/938-0073, fax 714/532-1675; www .orangechamber.org.

Historic Orange

History is a scarce commodity in Orange County, where the orange groves are long gone. The city of Orange, though, offers some evidence of life before freeways and shopping malls, with about 1,200 historically noteworthy buildings. Of these, the most significant are highlighted in the local walking tour—including the **Finley Home,** where the 1945 *Fallen Angels* was filmed; the **Ainsworth House,** 415 Chapman Avenue, a community museum (still closed at last report); and **O'Hara's Irish Pub,** 150 N. Glassell, historically the favorite local watering hole for the Fourth Estate. To shop for antiques, head for the shops along **Glassel Street** downtown, a district that also boasts impressive restaurants. Another old-time attraction downtown, on the "Orange Circle," is **Watson Soda Fountain & Lunch Counter,** 116 E. Chapman, 714/633-1050, an other-era drugstore with modern concessions such as sit-down dining outside on the sidewalk—the better to enjoy the unbelievably good burgers.

Orange County Zoo

To see animals in Orange County that aren't cartoon characters or otherwise artificially animated, head to the small Orange County Zoo in Irvine Regional Park, recently expanded to accommodate **Samson the hot-tubbing bear** and other animal additions. Samson earned his 15 minutes of fame in 1994, when he wandered out of the hills—and away from more natural pastimes—first to eat avocados in Monrovia and then to indulge in regular 20-minute dips in someone's backyard pool and spa. Samson's pursuit

of pleasure cost him his freedom, however; the Department of Fish and Game captured him because of neighborhood concerns about the safety of small children and pets. Many of the zoo's other animals, predominantly representing species of the Southwest, are also displaced locals—including brown pelicans that survived the oil spill in Huntington Beach and the two red foxes that delayed the construction of the Costa Mesa (55) Freeway once their den, amid the construction din, was discovered. The Orange County Zoo is located within Orange city limits about five miles east of the Costa Mesa Freeway, at the end of Jamboree off Chapman Avenue, 1 Irvine Park Rd. in Irvine Regional Park, 714/633-2022, www.ocparks.com. Admission to the zoo itself, open daily 10 A.M.–3:30 P.M., is $1, but park admission is $2 per vehicle.

Eating in Orange

Having burgers at Watson's is only the first nibble of edible Orange. Another bright light in Old Towne is **Felix Continental Cafe,** 36 Plaza Square, 714/633-5842, an adventure in old Havana open daily for breakfast, lunch, and dinner. With any luck at all, you'll end up out on the patio, the best possible location for enjoying both the ambience and the authentic Cuban/Spanish fare.

Immensely popular downtown is the **Citrus City Grille,** 122 N. Glassel St., 714/639-9600, beloved for its well-prepared California-style fare. Wonderful **Papa Hassan's Café,** 421 N. Glassell, 714/633-3903, is a Lebanese gem where the *shawerma,* or skewered lamb, drizzled in yogurt sauce, comes highly recommended. For dessert, just order Heaven, an unbelievable custard with pistachios and whipped cream.

Good restaurants abound throughout Orange, also in adjacent Tustin. **Cafe Français** in Orange at 1736 E. Meats Ave., 714/998-6051, isn't the trendiest or most expensive French restaurant around, but it's one of the best. Specialties include seafood, such as sand dabs sauteed in lemon butter and shallots and served in a cream sauce with grapes, and sea scallops sauteed with leeks and apples in a creamy Calvados lemon sauce. It's open for lunch Tues.–Fri. only, for dinner Tues.–Sun.; reservations a must at dinner.

Hidden away in the back of a minimall, hole-in-the-wall and very inexpensive **Tacos Jalisco** in Orange at 480 N. Tustin Ave. (near Walnut), 714/771-5819, serves some of the best authentic Mexican around, including specialties such as the fish soup. Pick your favorite meat or vegetarian taco fillings and they'll be served to order. Then spice them to your liking at the salsa bar. The chile verde and chile colorado burritos are grand, as is just about anything with carnitas.

Eating near Orange

Popular eateries in neighboring Tustin include the charming Mediterranean **Zov's Bistro** and adjacent bakery, just off the Costa Mesa (55) Freeway in the Enderle Center at 17440 E. 17th St., 714/838-8855. You won't go wrong with the angel hair pasta, the lentil soup, or any of the imaginative sandwiches. People drive halfway across the county for the Key lime pie. If at all possible at lunch, grab a patio table. And if the restaurant's impossibly crowded, the bakery out back is quite good, too, for a basic menu, and you can almost always get in there. Zov's is open for lunch Mon.–Sat., for dinner Wed.–Sat. only.

A onetime Orange hot spot, **Caffé Piemonte** burned down some years ago but has been resurrected here in Tustin at Larwin Square, 498 E. First St., 714/544-8072, and is open for lunch and dinner daily. This lively Italian café's wonderful appetizers, surprising specials, and great pastas—everything from linguine pescatore and penne arrabbiata to the pheasant ravioli—keep the crowds coming back. Everything is quite reasonably priced, especially at lunch. At dinner, reservations mandatory.

Not exactly new in Tustin but newly popular is the Mediterranean **Black Sheep Bistro,** downtown at 303 El Camino Real, 714/544-6060, famous for its pastas and paellas. Open Tues.–Sat. for dinner only, though you may also be able to find something interesting at the adjacent market (open same days from 3 P.M.).

Other best bets in Tustin include **Barolo Italian Cafe** in Tustin Plaza at 13771 Newport Ave., Ste. 9, 714/734-8882, serving such specialties as rigatoni salsiccia, and, for Greek, **Christakis,** 13011 Newport, 714/731-1179, famous for its

dolmades and saganaki. The second location of Newport Beach's famed **Crab Cooker** is also in Tustin, at 17260 E. 17th St. (near Yorba), 714/573-1077.

Not so great for dining atmosphere but serving some marvelous Indian fare—immense portions—is the tiny, real-deal **Laxmi Sweets & Spices** grocery at 638 El Camino Real, 714/832-4671. For Chinese Islamic fare, try **Jamillah Garden,** 2512 Walnut St., 714/838-3522.

WESTMINSTER AND LITTLE SAIGON

Most of Westminster is squeezed by Huntington Beach, Fountain Valley, and Garden Grove into the apple-pie wedge created by the Garden Grove Freeway (Hwy. 22) to the north and the San Diego Freeway (I-405) to the southwest. With the largest population of Vietnamese outside Vietnam, Westminster is known for Little Saigon, centered along Bolsa Avenue between Magnolia Street on the east and Ward on the west. A good place to start exploring Little Saigon is **Little Saigon Plaza** (Bolsa at Bushard), with its colorful shops and authentic Asian restaurants. Nearby, on Bolsa between Bushard and Magnolia, is the **Asian Garden Mall.** Come to Little Saigon in February to celebrate the lunar new year during the **Tet Festival,** which attracts upward of 150,000 revelers.

Among restaurants, the roster of Little Saigon worthies includes **Hue Rendezvous,** 15562 Westminster Ave., 714/775-7192, with specialties from Hue, or Central South Vietnam. For fare from Northern Vietnam, head to adjacent Garden Grove and **Ha Noi,** 10528 McFadden Ave., 714/775-1108. For classic Gallic in Garden Grove, sample the specials at French **Lafayette,** 12532 Garden Grove Blvd., 714/537-5011, open weekdays for lunch, Mon.–Sat. for dinner.

For more information about Little Saigon, contact the local **Vietnamese Chamber of Commerce,** 9938 Bolsa Ave., Ste. 216, Westminster, CA 92683, 714/839-2257. For more information about Westminster, contact the **Westminster Chamber of Commerce,** 14491 Beach Blvd., 714/898-9648, fax 714/373-1499.

SANTA ANA, A PLACE FOR ART—AND SCIENCE

Long bad-mouthed in some Orange County circles as down-in-the-heels and derelict, Santa Ana no longer suits its stereotype. In fact Santa Ana is a city well on its way to becoming the safest of its size—between 250,000 and 500,000—in the entire United States, according to FBI crime statistics. As things now stand, only Anaheim—home of The Disneyland Resort—is safer. Which is all the more reason to check out the *new* Santa Ana—in a very vital sense "a place for art." And some science too.

First there are the museums, most of these located within the "triangle" created by Broadway, 17th Street, and the Santa Ana Freeway (I-5). The **Bowers Museum of Cultural Art** at 2002 N. Main (at 20th St.), 714/567-3600, home also to the delectable new **Tangata** restaurant, is a well-established downtown arts presence. Its associated **Kidseum,** just two blocks away at 1802 N. Main, 714/480-1520, is a hands-on cultural art museum for children and their families, with permanent exhibits on masks, musical instruments, and puppets from around the world, among others, and activities including storytelling. On the north side of the Santa Ana Freeway (I-5) is the **Discovery Science Center,** 1500 N. Main, 714/542-2823, an excellent child-oriented science and technology museum. To the south, reached via Broadway, is the **Old Courthouse Museum**—the building itself a work of art, the landmark old county courthouse—at 211 W. Santa Ana Blvd., 714/834-3703, open Mon.–Fri. 9: A.M.–5 P.M., dedicated to local and regional history.

In terms of the contemporary arts, however, the true center of Santa Ana's artistic renaissance is father south—**Artists Village** in the heart of downtown, an attractive district of old-fashioned buildings that until recently had been all but abandoned by suburban flight.

For more on what's up downtown, stop by the **Santa Ana Chamber of Commerce,** in the Museum District at 2020 N. Broadway (Second Floor), 714/541-5353; www.santaana chamber .com.

Bowers Museum of Cultural Art: Preserving World Culture

That the largest museum in Orange County is dedicated to preserving the art and artifacts of the world's indigenous peoples is quite fitting, given the county's increasing cultural diversity.

Easily accessible from Newport Beach and reopened in 1992 after a four-year, $12 million facelift, the Bowers Museum of Cultural Art in Santa Ana is as expansive in scope as it is small in size. The appealing 1932 Spanish mission-style building downtown, complete with courtyard, was not only renovated but expanded, tripling exhibit space to more than 19,000 square feet. But the territory is still too tight for permanent display of the museum's 85,000-piece collection. So the Bowers Museum is known for its imaginative special shows, such as *African Icons of Power, Perú Before the Inca, Art of the Himalayas,* and *River of Gold: Pre-Columbian Treasures from Sitio Conte.* There's always a reason to come back.

Among permanent exhibits are *Arts of Native America*—art and artifacts from various North American cultures, including intricate beadwork from Plains cultures and exquisite Pomo basketry from Northern California—and *Realm of the Ancestors,* representations of the argonaut cultures of Southeast Asia and Pacific Oceania. Ancient stone art and ceramics of pre-Columbian Mexico and Central America are collected in *Vision of the Shaman, Song of the Priest.*

Also permanent is *California Legacies,* both tribute to Orange County's diverse cultural heritage and homage to the museum's humble beginnings as an odd collection of local memorabilia. (The museum's first show—recently repeated—was a collection of dolls donated by children.) Starting in the 1970s the Bowers Museum began to supplement its collection of regional ceramics and orange crate labels in an aggressive acquisitions program emphasizing pre-Columbian and Native American culture.

The museum's special evening and weekend events, such as "Spirits of the Rainforest" and "California Folk Art," are usually well worth the trip.

Family fun at the Bowers Museum centers around the **Kidseum,** an all-kid section opened in 1995 to "promote cultural understanding among the peoples of Africa, the Americas, and the Pacific Rim." Among the Kidseum's unique attractions: the storytelling room, the theater, the art laboratory, and exhibit space for children's art from around the world.

The Bowers Museum "partnership"—the institution is owned by the city of Santa Ana, managed and governed by a private, nonprofit board of governors, and financed with contributions from the private sector—also sponsors an impressive community education program. Unusual, too, is the Bowers's international cultural art travel program (members only).

Plan a stop at the museum shop for its unusually thoughtful array of books, jewelry, and one-of-a-kind art from around the world. Proceeds support the museum and its programs.

Practical Bowers

Do enjoy the Bowers Museum culinary offerings. New at the Bowers in late 2000, replacing David Wilhelm's Southwesternesque Topaz Café as the museum's social centerpiece, is **Tangata,** owned and operated by renowned L.A.-area restaurateurs Joachim and Christine Splichal, of Patina and Pinot fame—exceptional meals and memorable desserts, everything moderately priced. Chef Otto Guerra runs the restaurant and also supervises catering for special museum events. The indoor-outdoor Tangata is open for lunch Tues.–Sat. 11 A.M.–3 P.M. and for buffet brunch on Sunday (same hours)—the latter very popular and highly recommended. Brunch reservations are wise.

The Bowers Museum of Cultural Art, 2002 N. Main St. in Santa Ana (on Main at 20th St.), has free parking available in the adjacent lot (between 19th and 20th). Museum galleries are open Tues.–Fri. 10 A.M.–4 P.M., and Saturday and Sunday 10 A.M.–6 P.M. Kidseum galleries are open Saturday and Sunday 10 A.M.–4 P.M. Admission is $4 adults, $3 seniors/students, and $2 for children ages 5–12 (under 5 free). For general information call the Bowers Museum at 714/567-3600; for membership, 714/567-3688; for tours, 714/567-3680; for museum store information, 714/567-3643. Or check out the website at www.bowers.org. For schedule information and reservations at Tangata, call 714/550-0906.

Though the Orange, Garden Grove, and Costa Mesa Freeways converge quite close to downtown Santa Ana, the easiest way to get to the Bowers Museum from the coast is via the 55 (the Costa Mesa Freeway) then the Santa Ana Freeway (I-5). From I-5 northbound, exit at 17th Street and head west four blocks to Main and turn north (right). If for some reason you're on I-5 southbound, exit at Main and turn right. (Call to verify directions; the details may change once freeway construction in the area is completed.) By bus, OCTA routes 51, 53, and 55 will get you to the Bowers.

Discovery Science Center: Theme Park for the Mind

Definitely an underappreciated Orange County attraction, the 59,000-square-foot, family-oriented **Discovery Science Center** in Santa Ana dedicates itself to the joys of learning about math, science, and technology. Once you get here, plan to stay a while—at least a half day.

To learn about the distribution of body mass, simply lie down on the **Bed of Nails**—3,500 sharp steel nails embedded in a large wooden table—with some confidence that you'll live to tell about it. To practice riding out those predictable California earthquakes, step into the **Shake Shack** quake simulation room, whereyou can choose various intensities: the Newport Beach quake of 1989 (4.7 on the Richter scale); the Santa Barbara shaker of 1978 (5.1); or Long Beach's nightmare of 1933 (6.4). Or sample the **Tornado,** an eight-foot-tall twister visitors can enter, redirect, and dispel altogether. For a real-time study of human motion, saunter into the **Recollections** room, where a hidden camera reflects full-body images onto a screen in an "animated sequence of color and light."

Other exhibits offer the opportunity to understand pulley systems by attempting to lift oneself; experiment with the wind's power to sculpt the landscape; create ascending cloud rings; and "see" the movement of ocean flows and atmospheric air flows with the help of the fantastic Paul Matisse Kalliroscope. Or dance on a musical floor, pilot an airplane, and try the Tennis Ball Launch.

Everything at the Discovery Science Center is designed to foster creative thinking and encourage an understanding of science through an "inquiry-based" approach. Altogether there are some 100 hands-on exhibits, organized into eight areas: Dynamic Earth, Human Performance, Perception, Principles of Flight, Quake Zone, Space Exploration, the Exploration Station, and KidStation (for ages two to five). There's also a 3-D laser theater; at last report *Pathway to the Stars* was showing, a story about a young girl's quest to become an astronaut.

Other onsite facilities include a compuer lab with 22 computers; two classrooms; the Launch Pad Science Store, with educational books, gifts, and toys; and food service provided by science center sponsor Taco Bell and Pizza Hut. The Discovery Science Center is open daily 10 A.M.–5 P.M. (closed Thanksgiving, Christmas, and New Year's Day). Admission is $9.50 adults, $7.50 seniors (age 55 and older) and youths (3–17), free for age 2 and under. Admission to the on-site 3-D Laser Theater is $1. Parking is $3. A wide variety of educational programs—including professional development classes for teachers—are also offered.

The museum, redesigned by the firm Arquitectonica, is located in the onetime Barjer Brothers Furniture Store on Main Street at I-5 in Santa Ana, about halfway between the Bowers Museum of Cultural Art and the MainPlace Shopping Center. (Look for the 108-foot-tall tilting cube, which generates electricity via 464 photovoltaic panels on its southwest face.) For more information, contact: Discovery Science Center, 1500 N. Main St., Santa Ana, CA 92705, 714/542-2823 (542-CUBE), fax 714/542-2828; www.discoverycube.org.

Artists Village

More or less located between First and Fourth Streets and Broadway and Spurgeon Street in downtown Santa Ana—near the civic center and federal courthouse—Artists Village is a creative example of how to revitalize and redevelop a downtown otherwise spurned by middle-class society. The artists now working and living here in these fabulous historic buildings certainly don't mind that most everyone else skipped town, since they enjoy "great space" with affordable rents. Even better, people living and working here have developed an interconnected community dedicated to the arts, performing arts, and artists. To appreciate what's been done—

and what's still being done—to create this community, walk the neighborhood and see what's happening where.

A good place to start a tour of Artists Village is the **Santora Building of the Arts,** 207 N. Broadway, 714/571-4229, an exquisite onetime department store, replete with potted palms and leaded glass, now home to dozens of working artists' galleries—from Firouzeh Karamlou's striking metal sculptures to the Legacy Gallery and School of the Arts. Come on the first Saturday of the month, 7–10 P.M., for the "open studio" Open House—a chance to meet the artists and buy original art. Downstairs, at 209 W. Second St. Mall, is **Morey's Deli and Café,** 714/834-0688, "home of the Betty Bitch cookies," which becomes the Neutral Grounds coffeehouse at night and hosts The Purple Poet Society every Thursday at 8:30 P.M. (sign-ups at 8:15 P.M.).

Just across the Second Street Mall from Morey's is Cal State Fullerton's **Grand Central Art Center,** 125 N. Broadway, 714/567-7233, which features 31 student apartments upstairs and, downstairs, classroom space and the **Grand Central Art Center Rental and Sales Gallery,** 714/567-7236, where art is offered for sale or rent (three-month minimum placement). Open Tues.–Sun. 11 A.M.–4 P.M. Also here is a watermark print-making workshop and, on the corner of Second and Broadway, the casual **Gypsy Den** restaurant and coffeehouse, 714/835-8840.

Performance arts abound, too, including the **Rude Guerrilla Productions** at the intimate Empire Theater, 200 N. Broadway, 714/547-4688, which (at last report) performed its "modern, proactive plays and fresh spins on the classics" Thurs.–Sat. at 8 P.M. and Sunday at 2:30 P.M. Then there's the **The Hunger Artists Theatre Company,** 204E. Fourth St., Ste. I, 714/547-9100; the **Main Street Players,** 600 N. Main St., 714/547-1872; and the **Orange County Crazies** School of Improvisation at the DePietro Performance Center, 809 N. Main St., 714/550-9890.

Just beyond the boundaries of Artists Village is the three-theater **Santa Ana Performing Arts and Events Center** (formerly the Masonic Temple) at 505 N. Sycamore Street. Upstairs is the new, high-end **Aphrodite Restaurant,** exquisitely restored and renovated—a million smackers was spent on the lighting alone—and all gussied up into a 1930s-vintage French salon. Lunch only was served when the restaurant opened in early 2001, with plans to add a dinner menu later. For more information about Artists Village, show up and look around—or see www.aplaceforart.org.

IRVINE: SEND IN THE CLONES

The official press has run to the superlative since the city's founding in the early 1970s, with Irvine oft promoted as the nation's most successful planned community. Attractive neighborhoods are laced together by lovely pathways, lakes, and landscaping; good schools and public services; convenient shopping; and fine dining even in glass-walled business parks. But now that cloned gated communities are destined to dominate Orange County's remaining open space, critics have started to carp—saying, among other things, that socially homogenous cities are unbearably boring, that a too-planned, too-perfect life leaves little room for life at all. Don't entertain such thoughts while visiting Irvine, however. The people who live here like it just fine.

For more information on the Irvine area, contact the **Irvine Chamber of Commerce,** 17755 Sky Park East, Ste. 101, Irvine, CA 92614, 949/660-9112, fax 714/660-0829; www.irvinechamber.com. For current university information, including arts and entertainment events, contact the **University of California, Irvine** (UCI), 949/824-5011; www.uci.edu.

University of California at Irvine

The campus of the University of California at Irvine (UCI), its official entrance at Jamboree Road and Campus Drive South, is internationally renowned for its graduate-level creative writing program, among other distinctions. The entire campus is a virtual tree zoo, with thousands of specimens—the perfect freeway escape for inveterate tree huggers. What most people miss, however, is the **UCI Arboretum,** an eight-acre collection of bulbs and plants predominantly from Southern Africa. Best bloom is from mid-February into mid-March. The gardens, 949/824-5833, are free and open Mon.–Sat., 9 A.M.–3 P.M. If you're interested in carting home some botanical exotica, ask about public plant sales. While you're in the area, find out what's playing at the **Irvine Barclay Theatre** on Campus Dr., 949/854-4646; www.thebarclay.org.

Irvine Museum

Worth a stop, too, is the Irvine Museum, show-

ORANGE COUNTY'S MISSION DAYS

Few reminders remain of the area's first known people, named by conquistadores the "Juañeno" after the mission at San Juan Capistrano. The Juañenos' 10-month combined solar and lunar calendar—unique in California but common among the Pueblo people in the American Southwest—was one remnant of native culture that survived mission influences long enough to be noted.

Today's Orange County travelers navigate by freeway the desert landscape of cactus, sagebrush, and native grass trod by Captain Gaspar de Portolá and the first inland incursion of Spanish in 1769. Padre Fermí Francisco de Lasuén, one of the far-ranging Franciscan fathers, came in 1775 to select a mission site, San Juan Capistrano. Father Juníipero Serra showed up to dedicate the mission in 1776, the same year Juan Bautista de Anza ar-

rived with the region's first livestock. As was their custom elsewhere, missionaries soon planted gardens, orchards, and vineyards, establishing a foundation for the region's very rich agriculture.

Then began the much-romanticized era of the Californios, the California-born descendants of early Spanish and Mexican settlers. Though only one of the 20 original Spanish land grants was located here—the Yorba family's 30,000-acre Santiago de Santa Ana, which included part of the land now incorporated into the cities of Orange, Santa Ana, and Newport Beach—under Mexican rule the region was divided into six major ranchos. The holdings of the Peralta, Sepulveda, and Yorba families would later form the 93,000-acre Irvine Ranch, from which sprouted the cities of Santa Ana and Tustin and, later, the meticulously planned city of Irvine.

case for Joan Irvine Smith's collection of California impressionist landscapes or "plein air" paintings. Joan Irvine Smith is a member of Orange County's Irvine Ranch clan, the area's largest landowners. The family's wealth has derived largely from Irvine Company real estate developments—thus the irony of this fabulous small museum, with rotating exhibits from Smith's extensive private collection of paintings from the 1920s and 1930s. The collection showcases the Southern California landscape of yore, before developers turned row crops into row upon row of houses.

Featured artists include Franz A. Bischoff, Alson Skinner Clark, and Paul De Longpré. New Irvine Museum exhibits are staged every four months. Recent shows have included **Along El Camino Real: The California Missions in Art,** and as of late 2000 a De Longpré retrospective was being planned.

The Irvine Museum is on the 12th floor of the round Tower 17 office building at 18881 Von Karman Ave. (look for the large American flag up top). It's open 11 A.M.–5 P.M. Tues.–Sat., closed Sunday, Monday, major holidays, and on Tuesday after Monday holidays. Admission is free, with free (validated) parking available in the adjacent parking garage. Both the museum building and parking lot are wheelchair accessible. Children under 12 must be accompanied by an adult. Every Thursday at 11:15 A.M., an Irvine Museum docent offers a brief (20- to30-minute) free tour of the current exhibition, no reservations required. Free guided tours for groups of 10 or more are otherwise available by reservation (call, or see the website, for details). To get here from I-405, exit at MacArthur Boulevard and head south, for about one mile. Turn left onto Campus Drive, then left again onto Von Karman. For information, call 949/476-2565 (recorded) or 949/476-0294 (bookstore and offices), or try the website: www.irvinemuseum.org.

Entertaining Irvine

Though Orange County residents who do the club scene think nothing of hitting the freeways and heading into Los Angeles, big-name entertainment acts are staged locally at the open-air **Verizon Wireless Amphitheater** (previously known as Irvine Meadows Amphitheater) just off the 405 at 8808 Irvine Center Dr., 949/855-6111 for information (recorded) or 949/855-8095 (box office).

The **Irvine Spectrum Center** at the junction of the I-5 and I-405 Freeways, 71 Fortune Dr., 949/789-9180, is Orange County's megaentertainment and shopping scene. The 21st screen at the **Edwards Irvine 21 Theaters** megaplex, 949/450-4900—six stories tall and 90 feet wide, accompanied by 80 speakers—is reserved for the **Imax** theater, 714/832-4629, the first 3-D movie theater on the West Coast capable of projecting feature films, like the one at New York's Lincoln Center. Other Irvine Spectrum entertainment possibilities include **GameWorks,** 949/727-1422, www.gameworks.com, the quintessential electronic gamery, as envisioned by Steven Spielberg, DreamWorks SKG, Sega Enterprises, and Universal Studios, Inc.; the **NASCAR Silicon Motor Speedway,** 949/753-8810, www.smsonline.com; and the **Improv Comedy Theater,** 949/854-5455, www.improvclubs.com. **Dave & Buster's,** 949/727-0555, www.daveandbusters.com, is the place for billiards, shuffleboard, and the "Million Dollar Midway" of electronic, simulation, and other games.

Eating in Irvine on a Budget

You'd expect some high-brow restaurants in such a community, and Irvine has them. Also here, though, are quite a few eclectic, atypical cheap-eats stops, such as **Burrell's BBQ and Cafe,** 14962 Sand Canyon Rd., 714/786-0451. Burrell's soul food used to be served from downhome Santa Ana; now that the zip code has gone upscale, just plain folks and people in BMWs still drive halfway across the county for takeout. This is the place for unbelievably good barbecued ribs, not to mention sweet potato pie, black-eyed peas, and collard greens. The Southern breakfast here, or the Sunday brunch, could easily hold you for the entire day.

Quite the deal for decent Indian fare, especially at lunch, is the **Clay Oven** in the Irvine Village Center, 15435 Jeffrey Rd. (at Irvine Center Dr.), 949/552-2851. As might be expected, a best bet for dining bargains is the University Town Center north of the UCI campus. One of the two local **Z Pizza** outlets is here, 4237 Campus Dr., 949/725-9000. Good for pizza in the same complex is the **Trocadero,** 949/854-5599, also serving blues or jazz on weekend nights. To sample Irvine's own microbrews, try **Steelhead Micro Brewery,** 4175 Campus Dr., 949/856-2227.

El Torito Mexican Restaurant and Cantina is ever-popular at two local locations, either 18512 MacArthur Blvd., 949/833-8230, or 18831 Von Karman Ave. (near the Irvine Museum), 949/863-6400. Also a safe bet for family dining is Irvine's branch of L.A.'s **Daily Grill,** 2636 Dupont Dr. (near Jamboree), 949/474-2223.

Eating in Irvine on the Company Credit Card

Not to be missed is stylish **Bistango** inside the Atrium Court building at 19100 Von Karman Ave. (at Martin), 714/752-5222, serving great California-style fare in a jazzy art gallery atmosphere. The menu is always changing, with simpler fare—wonderful crab cakes, unusual pizzas, chicken half-moon ravioli and other pastas—served along with more elaborate entrees. Great wine list. Open weekdays only for lunch, nightly for dinner. Dressy. Reservations advisable.

A local find for Southern Italian is warm and welcoming **Vessia Restaurant,** 3966 Barranca Pkwy. (near Culver Dr.), 949/654-1155. For elegant classic French, the place is **Chanteclair** near the John Wayne Airport, 18912 MacArthur Blvd., 949/752-8001. For stylish New American, the place is **Trilogy,** 18201 Von Karman Ave., 949/955-0757.

Irvine is within convenient reach of South Coast Plaza, too, and not all that far from Newport Beach and the coast, so there are endless possibilities for fine dining in the general vicinity.

FROM ORANGE COUNTY

North, of course, is Los Angeles. South is San Diego. Heading west will land you in the Pacific Ocean. Angling off to the east and southeast leads to worthwhile stops just beyond the Riverside County line, some of these mentioned below. If for some reason you'll be heading still farther east, taking the backdoor route to Palm Springs and vicinity, consider doing it in May when the otherwise unremarkable town of Hemet hosts the unusual Ramona Pageant—California's official state play—as it has done each

year since 1923. For more information, see the Palm Springs chapter.

Glen Ivy Hot Springs and Vicinity

Fun and funky San Juan Hot Springs on Highway 74 is closed these days, and Murrietta Hot Springs near Temecula, bought by the Calvary Chapel, is now a bible college. But there's still "Club Mud," as Glen Ivy Hot Springs is affectionately known—it's the only European-style spa in the state featuring red-clay mud. Established more than a century ago, Glen Ivy features very contemporary facilities—multiple hot mineral water pools, whirlpools, and baths. The family-friendly spa also offers specialized services, such as massage, herbal wraps, and aromatherapy (appointments required). For a budget spa vacation, stay at an area motel and indulge yourself here for a day or two. Basic day use is $29 Fri.–Sun., $24 on other days. Guests must be 16 or older except on three "family days," when children are welcomed: Memorial Day Monday, July 4th, and Labor Day Monday. No reservations are required for day-use admission (only for spa services). Glen Ivy Hot Springs is open daily 9:30 A.M.–6 p.m April 1–Oct. 31, until 5 P.M. in other months. Closed Thanksgiving, Christmas, and New Year's Day. For more information, contact: Glen Ivy Hot Springs Spa, 25000 Glen Ivy Rd., Corona, CA 91719, 909/277-3529 or toll-free 888/258-2683 (CLUB-MUD) for reservations; www.glenivy.com.

To get to Club Mud from Orange County, take the Riverside Freeway (Hwy. 91) east, then I-15 south; after about eight miles exit (turn right) at Temescal Canyon Road. Continue another mile to Glen Ivy Road, turn right, and keep going.

The otherwise desolate community of Corona offers few bright spots for visitors—one of the most notable two outposts of the very pleasant, very reasonable **Country Inn & Suites** bed-and-breakfast-style motel chain. The original, located one block north of the Riverside (91) Freeway (exit at McKinley) at 2260 Griffin Way, 909/734-2140 or toll-free 800/448-8810 (California only) for reservations, fax 909/734-4056, www.countrysuites.com, features four-poster beds and other country French details, along with full buffet breakfast. Small swimming pool, whirlpool, workout facilities. Rates for one or two people start at $89. (For breakfast, take-out, and sit-down salads, sandwiches, and such (children's menu too), the place is casual **Mimi's Cafe** nearby at 2230 Griffin, 714/734-2073.) The second, **Country Inn & Suites Corona West,** decked out in contemporary Southwestern style, is located at 1900 W. Frontage Rd., 909/738-9113 or toll-free 800/676-1363; www.country-suites.com. Rates start at $75. These and other local motels offer special Glen Ivy packages; see the hot springs website for other possibilities.

Lake Elsinore
Reached via Highway 74 is Lake Elsinore, a Shakespearean reference to the shallow lake and the same-named sleepy town that's overnight becoming a bedroom community for

---

HIKING THE BIG ORANGE

Along the coast especially, Orange County offers outdoor activities and diversions, chronicled elsewhere in this chapter. But unlike absolutely urban areas of Southern California, Orange County also offers some great escapes into the great outdoors.

One popular local hike starts at the end of Modjeska Canyon, at **Tucker Wildlife Sanctuary** beyond Tustin, 714/649-2760. Half the fun is getting there, since Modjeska Canyon is one of the last truly rural residential areas in all of Orange County. At the end of the very narrow road is the Tucker Wildlife Sanctuary, a biological study area for California State University, Fullerton (no dogs allowed) surrounded by Cleveland National Forest. For a vigorous outing—about 12 miles round-trip, prettiest in spring—walk up Harding Road (dirt, signed 5S08), continue through the gate, and stay to the right at the fork (about a half-mile along). The road continues for miles, along the ridge separating Harding and Santiago Canyons. At about five miles in, past the landslide, the road bends to avoid a ravine forested with California bay (laurel) trees. A steep goat path to the right leads down to aptly named Laurel Spring. The Tucker Wildlife Sanctuary is open for hiking daily, sunrise to sunset. To get there: From Santiago Canyon Road, turn onto very narrow Modjeska Canyon Road; drive slowly, out of courtesy to canyon residents, and continue to the end. Parking is scarce.

Another adventure into Orange County's other world takes you into **Holy Jim Canyon** in Cleveland National Forest. This fairly easy, heavily wooded hike—about three miles round-trip, loveliest in spring, but tolerable even in summer—leads to Holy Jim Falls, named after a beekeeping settler known not for his holiness but for his lack thereof—"Cussin' Jim." (Cartographers cleaned up his reputation, posthumously.) Once arrived at the trailhead, an adventure in itself, continue up Holy Jim Road on foot about a half-mile to the gate. Pass through and walk another mile; the trail follows the creek. A branch trail to the right leads to the falls; the main trail continues to Santiago Peak. This section of Cleveland National Forest is open daily, sunrise to sunset. No camping, no fires. To get here: From Interstate 5, exit at El Toro Road and continue to Live Oak Canyon Road. Head to the right. About a mile beyond O'Neill Regional Park, turn left into Trabuco Wash—and onto unsigned, rocky, dirt Trabuco Canyon Road. Taking care to avoid turning into someone's private driveway—there are many cabins in these parts—continue four-and-a-half miles, past the volunteer fire station and the signed Holy Jim turnoff (on the left), and then park.

After hiking Holy Jim Canyon, the truly intrepid might head to **Cooks Corner,** 714/858-0266, at the junction of Santiago Canyon, Live Oak Canyon, and El Toro Rds., a locally famous biker bar serving good drink, great burgers, and live country-western every night. (The herd of Harleys outside marks the spot.) A much tamer alternative is the **Trabuco Oaks Canyon Steakhouse** at 20782 Trabuco Oaks Canyon Dr., 714/586-0722, a local institution—"home of the two-pound cowboy steak"—and a favorite of ex-President Richard Nixon.

Limited free public access—for hiking, horseback riding, and mountain biking—is offered in areas of the **Irvine Company Open Space Reserve,** including **Limestone Canyon** near Irvine Lake; **Emerald, Shady,** and **Bommer Canyons** near Laguna Beach; and the **Laguna Coast Wilderness Park.** For information, call 714/832-7478.

For more suggestions about where to hike in Orange County, pick up a copy of *Afoot and Afield in Orange County* by Jerry Schad (Wilderness Press), also the author of useful "afoot and afield" hiking guides to Los Angeles and San Diego Counties. Also quite good: the *Day Hiker's Guide to Southern California,* by John McKinney (Olympus Press).

Orange County. Known by native peoples as "Little Sea" and by the region's early ranchers as Laguna Grande, Lake Elsinore—which rises with abundant rainfall yet blooms with brackish algae or all but disappears after prolonged drought—is most popular with recreational boaters, water-skiers, and fisherfolk. For more information, contact **Lake Elsinore West Marina,** 32700 Riverside Dr., Lake Elsinore, CA 92530, 909/678-1300.

A big draw during the California League baseball season is the **Lake Elsinore Storm,** at home in a wonderful old-style ballpark known as "the Diamond." Tickets are cheap, and they're almost always available. For current information, call the Storm at 909/245-4487 or try the website, www.stormbaseball.com. Major league teams, including the San Diego Padres, sometimes play off-season exhibition ball here. For inveterate shoppers, Lake Elsinore also offers outlet shopping, including Liz Claiborne, Jones New York, Esprit, and Evan Piccone. **Prime Outlets Lake Elsinore,** 17600 Collier Ave., 909/245-4989, is just off I-15; exit at Nichols Road.

For more information about the area, contact: **Lake Elsinore Valley Chamber of Commerce,** 132 W. Graham Ave., Lake Elsinore, CA 92530, 909/245-8848, fax 909/245-9127; www.levcc.org.

TEMECULA AND VICINITY

The best reason to visit Temecula Valley (teh-MEH-cyoo-lah), the area's premier wine-grape-growing region, is to personally sample the fruit of the vine—easily an all-day if not weekend-long task. With a climate similar to that of Southern France, the Temecula region specializes in premium varietals. Most wineries are spread out along Rancho California Road and are small, many offering wine tasting and sales daily but limited tours. Come in May for the annual **Spring Passport Tasting,** in June for the ever-popular **Temecula Valley Balloon and Wine Festival.** The hot air (for the balloon rides) flows almost as fast as the fine wines.

First, though, stop off in **Old Town Temecula.** The false-front buildings here, along Front Street between Moreno and Third, are remnants of the town's dusty days at the edge of the frontier. Founded in 1882, Temecula was a significant stop for the old Butterfield Stage and, later, a railroad station on the route connecting San Diego and San Bernardino. Also stop by the new, 7,200-square-foot Temecula Valley Museum, 28315 Mercedes St., in San Hicks Monument Park, 909/694-6480, open Tues.–Sat. 10 A.M.–5 P.M., Sunday 1–5 P.M. Exhibits chronicle area history, from the mission days to modern times. Free, but a $2 donation is requested.

For area information, contact the **Temecula Valley Chamber of Commerce** office, 27450 Ynez Rd., Ste. 124, Temecula, CA 92591, 909/676-5090, fax 909/694-0201; www.temecula.org. For current winery information, contact the **Temecula Valley Winegrowers Association,** P.O. Box 1601, Temecula, CA 92593, 909/699-3626 or toll-free 800/801-9463, fax 909/699-2353; www.temeculawines.org. Most wineries are closed on Easter Sunday, Thanksgiving, Christmas Day, and New Year's Day.

Temecula Valley Wineries

The small **Thornton Winery,** about four miles east of I-15 at 32575 Rancho California Rd., 909/699-0099, fax 909/699-5536, www.thorntonwine.com, specializes in sparkling wines. For this reason Thornton, previously the John Culbertson Winery, opened an affiliated "champagne bar" that is now a wildly popular, award-winning restaurant, **Cafe Champagne,** 909/699-0088, open daily for lunch and dinner (closed Monday evenings except on holidays). The winery is open daily 11 A.M.–5 P.M. for tasting and sales (closed major holidays). Tours are offered on weekends only, at 12, 2, and 4 P.M. For information on jazz performances and other special events, call Thornton's event line 909/699-3021.

Callaway Vineyard and Winery, a half-mile farther at 32720 Rancho California, 909/676-4001 or toll-free 800/472-2377, fax 909/676-5209, www.callawaywine.com, is the largest local vineyard and winery operation offering a comprehensive tour, on weekends hourly 11 A.M.–4 P.M., on weekdays at 11 A.M., 1 P.M., and 3 P.M. The visitor center is open daily 10:30 A.M.–4:45 P.M. for tasting (fee) and sales. Try the chardonnay and pinot gris, and any of the Coastal Reserve wines. Also here: pleasant picnic area.

Best bet for picnicking, though, if you didn't pack your own is the **Mount Palomar Winery,** 33820 Rancho California, 909/676-5047 or toll-free 800/854-5177, fax 909/694-5688, www.mountpalomar.com, open daily 10 A.M.–5 P.M. (closed most major holidays; call for specifics). The partially shaded picnic area here is particularly appealing after a visit to the winery's Mediterranean-style deli. Of wines you'll want to take home for "medicinal" purposes after tasting (fee) are Mount Palomar's award-winning Castelletto label Italian classics and its Rey Sol label Mediterranean varietals, including Viognier and Roussanne. Group tours by reservation only (at least two weeks in advance).

Another award-winning area winery—and another good stop along Temecula Valley's main wine road—is **Baily Vineyard and Winery,** right across from the Mount Palomar Winery at 33833 Rancho California, 909/676-9463, open daily 10 A.M.–5 P.M. (call for holiday closures). The tasting room is located at 33440 La Serena Way (corner of Rancho California). In addition to the wines—including chardonnay, muscat blanc, "TV White," and "TV Red"—Baily also features **Carol's Deli & Grocery,** 909/676-9243, at the new wine-tasting room and gift shop. After a taste or two (fee), tarry at the picnic area.

The **Maurice Car'rie Vineyard and Winery** another half-mile along, 34225 Rancho California, 909/676-1711, fax 909/676-8397, is just about the only Temecula Valley winery still offering free tastings—so stop by just to express your appreciation. An attractive, contemporary tasting room presides over this 120-acre vineyard, which specializes in white zinfandel, chardonnay, merlot, sauvignon blanc, and cabernet sauvignon, though muscat canelli and the Late Harvest Dessert Wine may also be available for tasting;

the selection of five tasting wines changes each month. It's open daily 10 A.M. to 5 P.M. (closed most major holidays), tours offered for groups only, by reservation (fee).

The **Cilurzo Vineyard and Winery,** 41220 Calle Contento, just off Rancho California, 909/676-5250, is a small, family-run operation specializing in about a dozen varietals; sample six for the $1 tasting fee, refundable with purchase. Cilurzo's 1998 Reserve Petite Sirah won a double gold medal at the 2000 California State Fair Wine competition. Unless the harvest hubbub is in full swing, you can take a self-guided tour (guided tours by appointment only). Picnicking is permitted; bring your own grub. The winery is open daily 10 A.M.–5 P.M. (closed most holidays).

And there are many more wineries to visit—including the new (in 2000) **Falkner Winery** on Calle Contento, 909/676-8231; the **Filsinger Vineyards and Winery** on De Portola Rd., 909/302-6363; the **Hart Winery** on Avenida Biona, 909/676-6300; and the immensely welcoming **Wilson Creek Winery** on Rancho California Rd., 909-693-9463.

The Santa Rosa Plateau Ecological Reserve

Temecula is most appealing during early spring. If possible, plan a leisurely spring wine country cruise, to also allow an appreciation of the Nature Conservancy's 7000-acre preserve near Murrieta. What you'll find, once here, is a complex upland prairie grassland ecosystem, striking volcanic mesas with vernal pools and ephemeral associated species, *tenajas* or creek-fed pools, the world's healthiest population of Engelmann oaks, and some 70 "sensitive species." As an escape from the relentless march of progress, humans thoroughly enjoy the area. The preserve's primary purpose, however, is to protect "wildlife corridors" into Camp Pendleton, Cleveland National Forest, and accessible reservoirs to the east—thereby preserving the health and diversity of wildlife populations.

For the verdant grasses, wildflowers, and refreshing cool air, spring is the best time to come. Trails are extensive, but for now public access is limited to the Santa Rosa Springs area.

For an introduction to the Engelmann oak, take the short **Oak Tree Trail** loop. To appreciate nature's complex interrelationships with water, take the two-mile **Sycamore Trail** (sometimes closed); it follows Cole Creek, habitat for the rare red-legged frog and southwestern pond turtle. The **Vernal Pool Trail,** which starts farther along the road, leads to the preserve's largest vernal pool, a fleeting 25-acre lake with peak wildflower display from mid-March to early April. From here, take the short, very pleasant **Adobe Loop Trail** for an up-close appreciation of Riverside County's oldest surviving buildings. With the help of trail guides, more ambitious hikers can map out a fairly strenuous day-long trek.

Though winter and spring are the best times to come—docent-led nature walks are offered Nov.–May on certain Saturdays—the reserve is open daily sunrise to sunset. Admission is $2 adults, $1 children (over age 12). To get here: From Temecula head north on I-15, exit (west) at Clinton Keith Road, and continue six miles to the reserve's main entrance, marked by a parking area and kiosk where reserve maps are available. You can also get here heading south on I-15 from Lake Elsinore. For more information, call 909/677-6951.

Staying in and near Temecula

Local accommodations rates can increase during peak visitor periods, so request cost verification and cancellation policies when making reservations. The **Butterfield Inn,** 28718 Front St. in Temecula, 909/676-4833, fax 909/676-2019, offers decent and reasonable motel rooms, $49 and up. Some rooms have refrigerators, all have TV, cable, and free movies. Small swimming pool and whirlpool. Less expensive still is **Motel 6,** near Old Town at 41900 Moreno Dr., 909/676-7199 or toll-free 800/466-8356 (central reservations), fax 909/676-2619, www.motel6.com, with the usual amenities and swimming pool. Contact the chamber of commerce (above) for referrals to other area motels.

Wine tasting is fun, but golf and tennis are, too. As much resort as upscale motel, the attractive **Temecula Creek Inn,** 44501 Rainbow Canyon Rd., 909/694-1000 or toll-free 800/439-7529, fax 909/676-3422, www.jcresorts.com, provides 27 holes of golf on a championship course (extra fee), tennis courts, pool, and whirlpool. All rooms have either balcony or patio (most with a golf course view), coffeemakers, honor bars, and

TV. Junior suites have sitting areas. Children stay for free, with parents. Special AAA and other rates available. Lower rates on weekdays. To get here from I-15, exit at Highway 79 south and head east to Pala Road; turn south and continue a quarter-mile.

The Temecula area also boasts a few bed-and-breakfasts, including the contemporary mission-style **Loma Vista Bed and Breakfast** on a hilltop at 33350 La Serena Way, 909/676-7047, fax 909/676-0077, with its six guest rooms named after wine grapes and full champagne breakfast served each morning. Rates are $115 and up.

Rancho Pavoreal east of Temecula's wine country at 43000 Stanley Rd. in Sage, 909/767-3007 or toll-free 800/507-1376 for reservations (U.S.), fax 909/767-0828, is a 2000-acre working cattle ranch once owned by John Wayne. Rancho Pavoreal accommodates serious horseback riding—horses are provided for a fee, or you can bring your own—as well as serious loafing around the Olympic-sized pool. The low-key yet elegant ranch house features five guest rooms, four named after notable movie cowboys—Gene Autry, Andy Devine, Gabby Hayes, and, of course, John Wayne. The food here is wonderful; breakfast is included, and lunch and dinner are available with reservations. Rates: $110 and up. Getting here is a bit tricky, especially if you'll be pulling a horse trailer; ask for directions and suggested routes when you make your reservations.

Eating in and near Temecula

The best restaurant around is **Cafe Champagne** at the Thornton Winery (formerly the John Culbertson Winery), 32575 Rancho California Rd., 909/699-0088, serving very California fare in a very California setting—overlooking the vineyards. But don't overlook the goat cheese hors d'oeuvres and other appetizers here; several make a modest meal. Entrées include chicken dishes, fresh fish, and good pastas. Always a hit: the gourmet burger. Wine only is on the alcohol menu, of course; don't pass on the Thornton champagne. Quite good, too, is the **Temet Grill,** also very "California"—overlooking the golf course—at the Temecula Creek Inn on Rainbow Canyon Rd., 909/676-5631. American fare, full bar.

Better bets for families are downtown, including real-deal **Mexico Chiquito** a block off Front at 41841 Moreno Rd., 909/676-2933, open daily weekdays 11 A.M.–9 P.M., weekends 8 A.M.–9 P.M. Standard weekday breakfasts at "Little Mexico" include huevos rancheros, chorizo and eggs, machaca, and chile chilaquiles; many more choices are available on weekends. à la carte and lunch/dinner entrées include burritos, enchiladas, tacos, tostadas, and some south-of-the-border surprises. A real deal here: the weekly lunch buffet, which is served Mon.–Thurs. 11 A.M.–2 P.M. Children's menu, full bar.

SAN DIEGO COUNTY
NORTHERN SAN DIEGO COUNTY

To discover San Diego County's northern coast-line, exit the freeway and amble along the ocean. You can exit anywhere, of course, but for the longest coastal cruise, start just south of the Orange County border and head south to La Jolla. The street name changes in each community—becoming Carlsbad Boulevard in Carlsbad, for example, and Camino del Mar in Del Mar—so old Highway 101 is also known, prosaically, as County Road S21.

First stop for most people, just after the old highway separates from I-5, is Oceanside, with a nice pier and beach, urban adjunct to the sprawling Camp Pendleton U.S. Marine base. Just inland is Mission San Luis Rey, "King of the Missions." Farther north along the coast, just south of the county line, is San Onofre State Beach (san ON-uh-fray), technically in San Diego County but geopolitically more connected to San Clemente and other Orange County locales. An unavoidable feature of remote San Onofre is its midbeach nuclear power plant, though the area also offers good spots for swimming and surfing.

South of Oceanside is Carlsbad, named after

Karlsbad, Bohemia, for the similar mineral content in the local spring water, most famous these days as the home of Legoland. Next stop is Encinitas—including, technically, the communities of Leucadia, Cardiff-by-the-Sea, and Olive-hain. Encinitas is historically famous for its flower fields—poinsettias in particular—the downtown Self-Realization Fellowship, the Quail Botanical Gardens, San Elijo State Beach (and the area's various locals' beaches), and Leucadia's galleries and shops.

For a full measure of the simpler pleasures, stop in sunny Solana Beach, just north of Del Mar. Known for its celebrities and chic shopping, Del Mar is also home to the Del Mar Thoroughbred Club summer horse races—and the beach here is dandy. Torrey Pines Road leads south from Del Mar to La Jolla. Along the way are the Torrey Pines reserve, beach, and coastal lagoon, technically still part of the city of San Diego.

A thorough exploration of northern San Diego County also includes excursions inland to Escondido and vicinity, best known as home to the

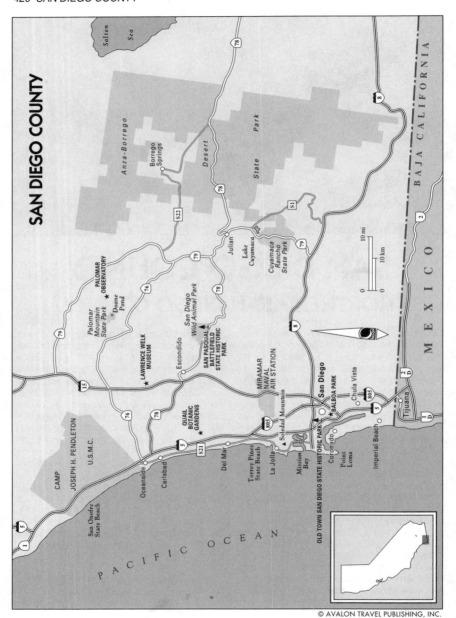

SAN DIEGO COUNTY

San Diego Wild Animal Park; the apple-pie American frontier town of Julian; and fabulous Anza-Borrego Desert State Park, most inviting in early spring.

SOUTH ALONG THE COAST

Oceanside and Vicinity

Immediately north of Carlsbad and almost a suburb of Camp Pendleton is Oceanside, with its own pier, a nice beach with largely crew-cut clientele, and an active, attractive harbor area. A local attraction is the **California Surf Museum,** 760/721-6876, www.surfmuseum.org, an eclectic, almost offhand display of surfboards with themed exhibits and zany gift shop. For more information about the area, call the **Oceanside Visitors and Conference Center** at 760/721-1101, or look them up online at www.oceansidechamber.com.

Historic **Mission San Luis Rey de Francia,** the "King of the Missions" at 4050 Mission Avenue in San Luis Rey, 760/757-3651, was founded in 1798 but not completed until 1815; in 1893 it became a Franciscan seminary. Wander the grounds of San Luis Rey, the state's largest but one of its less visited missions, for an appreciation of early California culture—and the enduring wonder of adobe construction. Museum exhibits and displays reveal the rough reality of mission life. Mission San Luis Rey is four miles east of I-5 via Highway 76 (Mission Ave.) and is open Mon.–Sat. 10 a.m.–4:30 P.M., Sunday noon –4:30 P.M. for self-guided tours, closed major U.S. holidays. Admission is $4 adults, $1 children ages 8–14.

North of Camp Pendleton is **San Onofre State Beach.** The odd detail here is the **San Onofre Nuclear Power Plant,** about five miles south of San Clemente, serving as the Mason-Dixon line between north and south beaches though the two are connected by a public walkway along the seawall. The north is known for excellent surfing, the south for good swimming and body-surfing and its very nice "primitive" campground (for both tents and RVs, no hookups). It's open daily 6 a.m.–sunset. Day-use fee is $3 per vehicle, camping is extra. For more information about the beaches here, call 949/492-4872.

Carlsbad: Bracing for the Big Time

According to local lore, Carlsbad was named after Karlsbad, Bohemia, since its "waters" had a composition identical to the mineral waters of the Ninth Spa in what is now the Czech Republic. Little wonder, then, that the spa trade was also hot here, beginning in the 1880s. The picturesque stone Alt Karlsbad Haus is now home to the stylish **Carlsbad Mineral Water Spa,** 2802 Carlsbad Blvd., 760/434-1887, at the site of the original wells, capped after World War II. Spa services include thearapeutic carbonated mineral water baths, massages, body wraps, aromatherapy, and facials. Carlsbad's famous water, once again being pumped, is also available here and in various area stores.

Present-day Carlsbad is best known as an affluent, family-friendly beach town cum San Diego bedroom community, populated by surfers, eccentrics, entrepreneurs, and high-technology firms. But this genuinely laid-back coastal escape exploded with hustle, bustle, and new business when the 128-acre **Legoland** children's theme park and affiliated resort opened here in 1999. Other local attractions include the National Association of Music Merchants' new, 6,500-square-foot **Museum of Making Music,** 5790 Armada Dr., 760/438-8001 or toll-free 800/ 767-6266, www.namm.com/museum, and the **Gemological Institute of America** (GIA), 5345 Armada Dr., 760/603-4000 or toll-free 800/421-7250, www.gia.edu, where diamonds are a gemology student's best friend. Among other accomplishments, the GIA created the international diamond grading system.

Otherwise Carlsbad wows the crowds with simple joys—every spring in particular, when tourists plow through surrounding **Carlsbad Ranch flower fields** 760/431-0352, best for the ranunculus bloom, early March through late April, and jam into California's largest street fair, the **Carlsbad Village Faire.**

Visitors attracted to homegrown pleasures can sunbathe and swim at the beach, stroll along the seawall (Carlsbad's beach promenade), explore local lagoons, and loll around in coffeehouses and the casual, sometimes eclectic restaurants and shops collected along Carlsbad Boulevard.

Lined with **antique shops** selling heavy silver jewelry, country quilts and estate furniture, the three blocks of State Street between Oak and Beech is an oasis of retro charm. Stroll over to **Aanteek Aavenue Mall,** 2832 State Street, 760/434-8742, for an excellent variety of wares under one roof, including vintage china, glass, and jewelry. Find vintage wares at **Black Roads Antiques,** 2988 State Street, 760/729-3032.

Wind-driven winter waves tend to batter Carlsbad-area beaches, so Carlsbad State Beach and others are typically closed in winter and spring. They're also typically rockier than the southstate stereotype. Of the two local state beaches, **Carlsbad State Beach** is usually the best bet for sandy sunbathing. Farther south on Carlsbad Boulevard (at Poinsettia Lane) is **South Carlsbad State Beach,** popular for ocean swimming as well as its large bluff-top campground (reservations mandatory). Then there are Carlsbad's lagoons. South of Poinsettia along the shore is the quarter-mile interpretive walkway for **Batiquitos Lagoon,** now being revivified and reconnected with the ocean. For more information, call the Batiquitos foundation at 760/943-7583. North of downtown is the **Buena Vista Lagoon,** with an Audubon Society nature center. Call the Audubon Society at 760/439-2473 or look up the Buena Vista chapter on www.audubon.org for information about scheduled birding and other events.

For more information about the community, contact the **Carlsbad Convention and Visitors Bureau** housed in the old Santa Fe Depot on Carlsbad Village Drive, 760/434-6093 or toll-free 800/227-5722. It's open Monday through Friday 9 a.m. to 5 P.M., Saturday and Sunday 10 a.m. to 2 P.M.

Quail Botanical Gardens

Known as "Flower Capital of the World," Encinitas is losing some floral ground to encroaching suburbia. Quail Botanical Gardens, a local horticultural star, is still going strong, however. Here you can wander 30 acres of canyon appreciating thousands of species: tropical and subtropical immigrants from Central and South America, Australia, Africa, and the Himalayas, also drought-resistant native plants.

Quail Botanical Gardens is closed the first Monday of every month, otherwise open daily 9 a.m.–5 P.M. (closed Thanksgiving, Christmas,

LEGOLAND CARLSBAD: A BIG-TIME SMALL WORLD

With over 40 rides, shows, and attractions on 128 acres of appealing parkland, Legoland Carlsbad offers a full and exciting day out for children and their families just 30 miles north of San Diego in Carlsbad.

Opened in 1999, Legoland Carlsbad is the world's second Lego-themed theme park, inspired by the original in Denmark. Like the first Legoland, this one is as expansive in scope as it is small in scale. For starters, there are fantastically detailed Lego models to admire, including 1:20 scale Lego brick reproductions of famous cities like San Francisco, Paris, and New York, each complete with moving vehicles and small-scale people scurrying about the streets. Also quite striking, and fun as educational tools, are replicas of favorite international landmarks; the Sydney Opera House, San Francisco's Alamo Square, New York's Empire State Building, and Mount Rushmore were built using over 30 million Lego bricks.

What sets Legoland apart from other California theme parks is its absence of white-knuckle rides. Rides and attractions here—including a driving school with cars, a gravity coaster, a mini excursion tour, and a DUPLO building area—appeal instead to the two-to—twelve-year-old crowd. Even the food differs from regular theme park fare, with a European twist. Expect fresh fruit, applesauce, salads, and breadsticks along with homemade pizzas, popcorn, and chicken sticks.

Legoland, 1 Lego Dr. (at Cannon Rd.), 760/918-5346, www.legolandca.com, is open daily 10 A.M. to dusk, which translates into 10 A.M.–5 P.M. in winter, 9 A.M.–9 P.M. in summer. Admission is $34 adults, $29 children (ages 3–16). Ask at the gate for special discounts for seniors (over 60). Parking, available in the adjacent lot, is $6. To get here from I-5, take the Canon exit east.

—Pat Reilly

and New Year's Day). It offers general tours (free) every Saturday at 10 a.m. and free children's tours on the first Tuesday of every month. (Group tours are offered only by appointment.) Admission is free on the first Tuesday of every month, otherwise it's $5 adults, $4 seniors, $2 children ages 5–12 (under 5 free). For plant and gift shop purchases, come between 10 a.m. and 4 P.M. daily. Quail Botanical Gardens, 230 Quail Gardens Dr., Encinitas, 760/436-3036, www .qbgardens.com, is approximately 20 miles north of San Diego between Leucadia and Encinitas Boulevards. To get here from I-5, exit at Encinitas Boulevard and head east. Turn left (north) onto Quail Gardens Drive. The gardens are on the left.

Solana Beach

Solana means "sunny spot" in Español, and Solana Beach is still fun and funky in laid-back beach town style yet starting to try on civic phrases such as "chic" and "stylish." To sample the eclectic commercial side of this confusion, stroll the business district, more or less concentrated between Lomas Santa Fe Drive to the north and Via de la Valle to the south, Old Highway 101 to the west, and Cedros Avenue to the east. Still, the beach in Solana Beach is the big thing, though finding a way down to it is something of a challenge. (Hint: Look for the "pillbox.")

STAYING ALONG THE COAST

Budget travelers, head to **Motel 6.** There's one in south Carlsbad at 750 Raintree Dr., 760/431-0745 or toll-free 800/466-8356, fax 760/431-9207. No surprises, and the price is right, $40 single, $46 double. That price gets you basic rooms with color TV and cable, plus swimming pool and proximity to the beach. (If there's no room, there are two other Motel 6 choices in Carlsbad, and another two in adjacent Oceanside.) To get here from I-5: exit west at Poinsettia Lane, turn north on Avenida Encinas, then east (right) onto Raintree.

A decent choice in Oceanside is the **Days Inn,** 3170 Vista Way, 760/757-2200 or toll-free 800/458-6064, fax 760/757-2389. Rooms are nothing fancy but quite pleasant, with color TV, cable, and free movies. Special diversions

include a children's playground, whirlpool, and exercise room plus (for a fee) access to the adjacent 18-hole golf course and lighted tennis courts. The motel is just a few miles from the Carlsbad beach. Rates are $69–79, with weekly and monthly rates available.

In Carlsbad, a best-bet for families is the very attractive, very popular **Best Western Beach View Lodge,** 3180 Carlsbad Blvd., Carlsbad, 760/729-1151 or toll-free 800/535-5588, fax 760/434-5405, where all rooms have refrigerators, some have kitchens or kitchenettes. There's also a heated pool, whirlpool, and sauna, with rates from $80–120. (Monthly rates available in the off-season.) Pricier but right on the beach is the **Best Western Beach Terrace Inn,** on the beach at 2775 Ocean St., 760/729-5951 or toll-free 800/433-5415, fax 760/729-1078. Most rooms have kitchens, many have ocean views. Rates: $119–189. Also popular and pricier still is the **Carlsbad Inn Beach Resort,** 3075 Carlsbad Blvd., 760/434-7020 or toll-free 800/235-3939, where the Old World meets the New World under the palm trees. Rates: $169–239. For the ultimate Carlsbad stay, head for **La Costa Resort and Spa** (see below).

Right next to I-5 but otherwise perfect for a more uptown stay is the **Country Inn,** 1661 Villa Cardiff Dr. in Cardiff-by-the-Sea, 760/944-0427 or toll-free 800/322-9993, fax 760/944-7708, www.countrysuites.com, a stylish Old World–style motel with country French style, a pool, whirlpool, and bed-and-breakfast amenities—full breakfast and morning newspaper, fresh fruit, and afternoon refreshments. A great deal, with rates $82–125.

The **Ocean Inn** in Encinitas at 1444 N. Hwy. 101 (between La Costa Ave. and Leucadia Blvd.), 760/436-1988 or toll-free 800/546-1598, fax 760/436-3921, is a best bet for a base camp, since from here it's just a five-minute walk to the beach. Rooms come with all the motel basics plus in-room refrigerators and microwaves—bring your own cookware and utensils—and color TV, cable, and video players; some feature in-room whirlpool tubs. Other pluses: on-site laundry and rental bikes. Rates start at $69 single, $79 double. Closest to the beach, though, is the relaxed **Moonlight Beach Hotel,** 233 Second St., 760/753-0623 or toll-free 800/323-1259, with large rooms and kitchenettes. Rates: $56–76.

La Costa Resort and Spa

One of California's premier resort retreats, this one is luxurious but relaxed and low-key. Almost a self-contained city, this 400-acre spread comes complete with its own movie theater. Carlsbad's La Costa features world-class spa and fitness facilities, swimming pools, tennis courts, racquetball courts, and two PGA championship 18-hole golf courses. (Inquire about special golf and tennis packages.) To keep it simple, rent bikes here and cruise on down to the beach. Rates: $175–2,300. For more information call 760/438-9111 or toll-free 800/854-5000, fax 760/438-3758, or check out www.lacosta.com. To get here, drive two miles east of I-5 via La Costa Ave., and then continue north for a quarter-mile on El Camino Real.

EATING ALONG THE COAST

As might be expected, Carlsbad is rich with restaurants. Some okay choices: for Southwestern, the **Coyote Bar & Grill** in the Village Faire Shopping Center at 300 Carlsbad Village Dr., 760/729-4695; for Mexican, **Fidel's Norte** near the beach scene at 3003 Carlsbad Blvd., 760/729-0903; for American, the **Pea Soup Andersen's** outpost at the Best Western Andersen's Inn, 850 Palomar Airport Rd., 760/438-7880.

For more bohemian atmosphere you can do better, though, at places such as **Kafana Coffee** at the beach, 3076 Carlsbad Blvd., 760/720-0074 which showcases live music every night in summer and on weekend nights in winter, and the **Pizza Port,** a pizza parlor and surfer hangout at 571 Carlsbad Village Dr., 760/720-7007. For fine dining, the place is casual **Neimans** inside the grand Queen Anne mansion once owned by local "waters" promoter Gerhard Schutte, along the waterfront at 300 Carlsbad Village Dr., 760/729-4131. People come from miles around just for the Sunday brunch.

Rico's Taco Shop in the Target shopping center at 165-L S. El Camino Real in Encinitas, 760/944-7689, is a safe place to bring the kids even after a sand-in-their-shoes day at the beach —quick, casual, and quite good, if what you're looking for is health-conscious Mexican food. At lunch and dinner, the fish tacos and burritos,

carne asada selections, and taquitos are hard to beat. Rico's is open daily 8 a.m.–9 P.M., closed holidays. For fancier fare, wander the **First Street** area in downtown Encinitas to see what's new and appetizing.

Ki's Juice Bar and Restaurant, 2591 S. Hwy. 101 (near Chesterfield) in Cardiff-by-the-Sea, 760/436-5236, is not strictly vegetarian— but if that's what you're looking for, this is where you'll find it. Everything here is fresh and healthy, including organic seven-grain cereal and tofu scramble at breakfast and veggie stir fry, egg salad sandwiches, and Ki's salmon salad at lunch. Expect more of the same at dinner, plus pasta. Juice bar choices include fruit and ice cream smoothies—a chance to try a decent date shake—and fresh juices and blends, including orange and grapefruit, carrot and watermelon. Ki's serves food for the soul, too—live jazz on Friday and Saturday nights (no cover with dinner). It's open Sun.–Thurs. 8 a.m.–9:30 P.M., Fri.–Sat. 8 a.m.-9 P.M., closed holidays. For a totally different take—steak and seafood and such—try the predictably good **Chart House,** nearby at 2588 S. Hwy. 101, 760/436-4044, and **The Beach House,** 2530 S. Hwy. 101, 760/753-1321.

The fare at **Solana Beach Brewery and Pizza Port,** 135 N. Hwy. 101 (at Loma Santa Fe), 760/736-0370, includes good pizza and salads—simple, straightforward flavors intended to complement the local brew. Offerings here include Beacon's Bitter, 101 Nut Brown, Rivermouth Raspberry, and Sharkbite Red Ale. If you can't decide, ask for the "taster"—four four-ounce glasses, a sample of each. While you're sampling, the kids can visit the arcade area. The place is open daily 11 a.m.–12 a.m., closed major holidays. Another possibility: wood-fired pizzas from the **California Pizza Kitchen (CPK)** in the Boardwalk mall, 437 S. Hwy. 1, 858/739-0999. The pizzas are out of the ordinary—popular choices include the BBQ Chicken Pizza with Gouda cheese, onions and barbecue sauce, the Thai Chicken Pizza with spicy peanut-ginger and sesame sauce, and the Vegetarian Pizza with Japanese Eggplant. Open Mon.–Sat. 11:30–10 P.M., Sun. 11:30–9 P.M. CPK also has outposts in La Jolla, 858/675-4424, and Carmel Mountain Ranch, 858/457-4222.

Two-story **Fidel's,** 607 Valley Ave. (near Stevens) in Solana Beach, 858/755-5292, is the place for Mexican food—and lots of it. A combination plate, with rice, beans, and entrées of your choice, should satisfy even the most boisterous beach appetite (children's plates available). If at all possible, grab a table out on the patio. There's another Fidel's on Carlsbad Boulevard in Carlsbad, 760/729-0903. Fidel's is open daily 11 a.m.–9:30 P.M., sometimes later on weekends, and closed Christmas. Reservations taken only for groups of eight or more.

INLAND FROM THE COAST: ESCONDIDO AND VICINITY

Escondido: Wine and Wild Animals
Escondido, which means "hidden" in Spanish, is far from invisible these days. Center of the vast inland territory north of San Diego and its suburbs, Escondido is home to the remarkable San Diego Wild Animal Park—where visitors "visit" Africa and Asia, and exotic animal and plant life in open-air "natural" habitats, via monorail. Adjacent to this world tour of natural history is a monument to the hurried march of local history—the San Pasqual Battlefield State Historic Park. Here in 1846 a small band of "Californios," or California-born Mexican citizens, vanquished legendary scout Kit Carson and U.S. Army troops in one of the more infamous battles of the Mexican-American War. In more recent history Escondido has added high culture to its list of assets, with the $74 million California Center for the Arts, Escondido.

Radiating from Escondido like the spokes of a roughed-up wagon wheel are roads leading to other attractions—including the Lawrence Welk Resort, with its own theater for Broadway-style musical productions. Local vineyards and wineries are also a major draw, most particularly Deer Park Vintage Cars and Wines, famous also for its fabulous array of 1950s kitsch.

From Escondido, intrepid travelers can set out on multiple "loop" day trips—to Palomar Mountain State Park and the Palomar Observatory and then on to Julian, for example, or to Julian via Highway 78, and then on into Anza-Borrego or Rancho Cuyamaca State Parks

before looping back. For more information on both trips, see below.

For more information on the region, contact: **San Diego North County Convention and Visitors Bureau,** 720 N. Broadway, Escondido 92025, 760/745-4741 or toll-free 800/848-3336, fax 760/745-4796; www.sandiegonorth.com.

San Diego Wild Animal Park
The main modern-day attraction in San Pasqual Valley is the 2,200-acre San Diego Wild Animal Park, affiliated with the San Diego Zoo. Here, the collected endangered species are exhibited in their own wide-open spaces, the separate habitats representing Asian plains, Asian marshlands and swamps, North Africa, South Africa, and East Africa. Hikers can hoof it into East Africa on the hilly one-and-three-quarter-mile **Kilimanjaro Safari Walk,** with observation platforms that allow spying on the lions and elephants below. Cages are still cages, of course, no matter how aesthetic, so what you see here is far from "natural," in any meaningful sense. But here people are penned up, too—onboard the **Wgasa Bush Line** monorail, the park's main event. The five-mile monorail ride—sit on the right side if at all possible—traverses the prairies and canyonlands. Especially during summer heat, the best time to hop aboard is early evening, when the park's creatures are up and about and eating. Even better, in summer, are the after-dark treks, when all the park's a stage—lit by sodium-vapor lamps.

The kids will probably insist on extra time at **Nairobi Village,** the center of everything, complete with "petting kraal" (remarkably toddler-tolerant sheep and goats here); the interactive **Mombasa Lagoon** exhibit; the indoor **Hidden Jungle,** with tropical creatures not typically seen; the interactive **Lorikeet Landing,** an Australian rainforest where people can feed the nectar-loving birds all day long; and the long-running **Bird Show Amphitheater,** starring birds of prey and other performers. Exotic gardens here showcase more than 3,000 botanical specimens.

The park's most exotic activity—a must for photographers—is the **photo caravan tour,** which allows shutterbugs to get up close and personal from *inside* the animal compounds, snapping shots from an open-air truck. The tours

ROBERT HOLMES/CALIFORNIA DIVISION OF TOURISM

San Diego Wild Animal Park

run daily, and cost between $85–105, depending on the tour. For information and reservations, call 760/738-5049 or toll-free 800/934-2267. Family-friendly **Roar and Snore overnight campouts** are also offered, seasonally.

The San Diego Wild Animal Park is open daily from 9 a.m., with gates closing at 4 P.M. in winter and 6 P.M. in summer (grounds close an hour later). In summer, Thursday through Sunday evenings are "Swamp Nights," with admission until 8 P.M. and the park itself open until 10 P.M. The park is open for extended hours at other times, too, for special events. At last report admission was $21.95 adults, and $14.95 children ages 3–11 (parking extra). A "combination pass," $38.35 adults, $23.15 children, also covers one day's admission to the San Diego Zoo (to use within five days of purchase). Wheelchairs and strollers are available for rent. To get here: exit I-15 in Escondido at Via Rancho Parkway and

follow the signs east; it's about six miles to the park. From I-5, exit at Highway 78 and head east to I-15; continue south on I-15, then exit east at Via Rancho Parkway. For current information (prerecorded), call the San Diego Wild Animal Park at 760/747-8702, TTY/TDD 760/738-5067, or check out www.sandiegozoo.org.

San Pasqual Battlefield State Historic Park

Near the San Diego Wild Animal Park is the battlefield park, with multiple historic sights and monuments. Even with the nice visitor center here, the social and territorial skirmishes leading to California statehood don't titillate visitors as much as the animal park. The area's roadside produce stands often do, however. Keeping in mind that more than half of the U.S. avocado crop comes from San Diego County, take in more of the area's agricultural riches by meandering north toward Pauma Valley, Pala, or Fallbrook via back roads.

Escondido-Area Wineries

Just north of the Lawrence Welk Resort is **Deer Park Vintage Cars and Wines,** 29013 Champagne Blvd. (old Hwy. 395), 760/749-1666; www.deerparkwinery.com. Adults will enjoy Deer Park's local chardonnay, plus the selection of award-winning red and white wines from its more famous Napa Valley winery. (Try the cabernet.) Also here are a great deli/gourmet market and very pleasant picnic area. Fun for the kids, too, is Deer Park's auto museum—spread throughout various buildings—which includes the world's largest collection of convertibles. Deer Park also displays an amazing antique radio and television collection. To take home some classic Americana, head for the gift shop. One-hour self-guided tours plus tasting are free; admission to the car museum is $6 adults, $4 seniors 55 and older, free for children under age 12. Deer Park is open daily 10 a.m.–5 P.M., until 6 P.M. in summer, closed Thanksgiving, Christmas, and New Year's Day.

The **Ferrara Winery,** 1120 W. 15th Ave. in Escondido, 760/745-7632, is a favorite wine stop. In honor of San Diego County's oldest wine-making and grape-growing family, the Ferrara enterprise has been designated a state his-

CONDOR RIDGE: BORN TO BE WILD

The world can be a dangerous place. And no one, certainly no nonhuman species, can keep all attendant hazards of the civilized world out of their neighborhood. The latest local symbol of this struggle is the California condor *(Gymnogyps californianus)*, the powerful and primal vulture known to Native Americans as the thunderbird. The largest land bird in North America, until 10,000 to 12,000 years ago the California condor flew and foraged across the southern reaches of what is now the United States, from the Pacific to the Atlantic Oceans. Pre-Columbian hunters soon dispatched most of the mammoths and other large animals on whose carcasses the condor fed. By the time of early European exploration the species had retrenched along the North American coastline from British Columbia to Baja California; condors were sometimes observed feeding on beached whales. In more recent California history, the California condor soared inland from the San Rafael Mountains to Sequoia National Park, protected from harm by the land's inaccessibility. Now most of the species' survivors live in protective custody—in "condorminium" cages at California zoos—because the condor's natural environment can no longer assure the bird's survival. Research suggests the precipitous recent decline of the condor was caused by lead shot and bullets, inadvertently consumed by feeding condors, in addition to the increasing incursions of civilization, in the form of power lines, antifreeze, and other hazards.

In 1987 the last wild California condors were captured and packed off as breeders for the captive breeding program, a last, fairly desperate attempt to save the species from extinction. For the coastal Chumash people—haunted by what they were witnessing—the condor roundup suggested the end of the condor, and the end of the condor signaled the end of the world, the "time of purification" when the earth would shake and all life would end then begin again.

Condor Ridge: Engaging Extinction

But the California condor hasn't yet disappeared. Though the species is still teetering on the edge of extinction, captive breeding and some success in releasing the birds into remote areas of their original range offer hope that the end of the world has been postponed. By mid-2000 85 condors had been released into the wild, and 49 were still thriving there.

To get up-close and personal with the California condor—not something likely to happen in nature—stroll through the San Diego Wild Animal Park's new **Condor Ridge** habitat.

A dozen species of rare and endangered North American animals are exhibited here, beginning with the endangered thick-billed parrots once thriving in the pines of Arizona, New Mexico, and northern Mexico. At the base of the pines here, darting among the shrubs, are western greater roadrunners. Next come the grasslands, where northern porcupines accompany the rare, steel-gray aplomado falcons. The prairies habitat is home to endangered black-footed ferrets, desert tortoises, black-tailed prairie dogs, western burrowing owls, American magpies, and western Harris hawks.

At the end of the trail is an observation deck and interpretive center concerning recovery efforts on behalf of the California condor and desert big horn sheep, the latter observed here scrambling around on steep hillsides. Several California condors can also be seen, in their six-story cage.

torical point of interest. Of particular interest to travelers: the wonderful red wines, white wines, dry wines, and dessert wines. The tasting room also features fresh grape juice, wine marinades, and wine vinegars. All Ferrara grape products are crushed, aged and/or brewed, bottled, and sold only on the premises. Self-guided tours (15–20 minutes) and wine tasting are free. The tasting room is open daily 10 a.m.–5 P.M., closed Christmas Day. To get here: From I-15 exit east at Ninth Avenue, turn south onto Upas, then west onto 15th.

Orfila Vineyards and Winery, 13455 San Pasqual Rd., 760/738-6500 or toll-free 800/868-9463, www.orfila.com, formerly Thomas Jaeger Vineyards, is a popular stop on Gray Line and other organized tours. Orfila's wine specialties include cabernet, merlot, chardonnay, and tawny port. The very pleasant picnic area here, overlooking vineyards and valley, is the site of many weddings and other celebrations. Custom gift baskets are available at the gift shop. Tours and tastings are free for individuals; for groups (fee) reservations are required. Orfila is open daily

10 a.m.–6 P.M. One guided tour is offered daily, at 2 P.M., but visitors can take the self-guided tour any time. The winery is closed Thanksgiving, Christmas, and New Year's Day. To get here: exit I-15 at Via Rancho Parkway. Follow the signs toward the San Diego Wild Animal Park, but turn right onto Pasqual Valley Road and continue one mile.

The **Bernardo Winery,** 13330 Paseo del Verano Norte, south of Escondido in the Rancho San Bernardo area, 858/487-1866, www.bernardowinery.com, is one of the oldest continuously operating wineries in Southern California. The wine-tasting room, something of a general store, also features gourmet foods, olive oil, and private-label wines. Self-guided winery tours take about 10 minutes. Lunch is served in the patio dining room daily (except Monday) 11 a.m.–3 P.M. The wine-tasting room is open daily 9 a.m.–5 P.M., gift shops 10 a.m.–5 P.M. (shops closed Monday), and closed major holidays. To get here from I-15: exit at Rancho Bernardo Road, turn north onto Pomerado Road, then east onto Paseo del Verano Norte (just past the Oaks North Golf Club). Continue for 1.5 miles.

LAWRENCE WELK MUSEUM

The Lawrence Welk Resort north of Escondido, just off I-15 at 8860 Lawrence Welk Dr., 760/749-3448, www.welkresort.com, is quite contemporary and well appointed, though in a sense it seems like something straight out of the 1950s. Most of Lawrence Welk's elderly fans come to his namesake resort to golf, swim, play tennis, just loaf, and take in a Broadway-style musical. Featuring stars from the long-running *Lawrence Welk Show,* the **Lawrence Welk Theater's** performance schedules include shows such as *Gotta Sing! Gotta Dance!, George M!, Mame,* and *A Welk Musical Christmas.* For a free look at memorabilia and a short lesson in television history, stop by the free **Lawrence Welk Museum** here. It's open daily 10:30 A.M.–5 P.M.

To get here: from I-15 northbound, exit at Deer Springs/Mountain Meadow Road, turn right on Mountain Meadow, then left onto Champagne Boulevard. From I-15 southbound, exit at Gopher Canyon Road, turn left (it becomes Old Castle Rd.), then right onto Champagne Boulevard.

Palomar Mountain State Park

This mile-high park at the edge of the Cleveland National Forest offers a refreshing pine-scented change from the scrubbier foothills below. Aside from the fine conifers and oaks, the park's easy hikes, meadows, fishing pond, great campground, and just general remoteness are its main attractions. Visitors ascend from Highway 76 east of Pauma Valley via the "Highway to the Stars" (County Rd. S6), built for access to the famous Mount Palomar Observatory, which is just east of the park. The park is open for day use, sunrise to sunset, $2 per car. Campsites available. For more information, contact regional park headquarters: Cuyamaca Rancho State Park, 12551 Hwy. 79 in Descanso, 760/765-0755, www.cuyamaca.statepark.org, or call the park directly at 760/742-3462 (sometimes a recorded information message); www.palomar.statepark.org.

Mount Palomar Observatory

Something of a reluctant tourist attraction, the world-famous Mount Palomar Observatory was built in 1928 to take astronomical advantage of its elevation (6,100 feet), distance from coastal fog, and absence of urban light pollution. No longer boasting the world's largest reflecting telescope, this is still a serious research facility of the California Institute of Technology (Cal Tech) in Pasadena. Visitors can view the 200-inch Hale Telescope and study deep-space photos and other memorabilia. The observatory, 760/742-2119, astro.caltech.edu /observatories/palomar/, is open daily 9 a.m.–4 P.M.

For more excitement, consider taking the **Palomar Plunge,** the lazy person's observatory tour and cycling adventure—all downhill from Mount Palomar. The half-day trek costs $75 per person, including lunch at *the* place to eat on the mountain, the vegetarian **Mother's Kitchen.** If you're not camping, the place to stay in these parts is the **Lazy H Ranch,** down the mountain in Pauma Valley, 760/742-3669. For more information, contact: **Gravity Activated Sports,** 16220 Hwy. 76 in Pauma Valley, toll-free 800/985-4427; www.gasports.com.

Staying and Eating in the Escondido Area

Among inexpensive area stays: **Super 8,** 526 W. Washington Ave. (just west of Centre City Pkwy.), 760/747-3711, rates: $55; and **Motel 6** off the parkway at 900 N. Quince St. (at Mission), 760/745-9252, rates: $52. The very nice **Best Western Escondido,** 1700 Seven Oakes Rd. east of I-15 (exit at El Norte Pkwy.), 760/740-1700, is a very good value, with rooms $79 and up.

The undisputed star of local lodgings is south of town in the Rancho Bernardo area—the **Rancho Bernardo Inn,** 17550 Bernardo Oaks Dr., San Diego, 858/675-8500 or toll-free 800/439-7529, www.jcresorts.com, 265 acres of exquisite tile-roofed rooms, two restaurants, and exceptional resort facilities including a total of 108 holes of golf (45 on site), tennis college, health spa, two swimming pools, rental bikes, the works. Rates are $239 and up. If that's too rich for you, Rancho Bernardo boasts many other nice motels and hotels, most quite reasonably priced.

If you're in a hurry, fast fooderies abound. Freeway flyin' choices concentrate along Centre City Parkway, the I-15 business loop, including the **Fireside Grill & Deli,** 760/745-1931, for steaks and such, and **The Brigantine,** 760/743-4718, for seafood.

If you're looking for finer fare, **Sirino's,** 113 W. Grand Ave. (at Broadway), 760/745-3835, is locally famous for its French classics, quite the find in downtown Escondido. Nowadays Sirino's also offers Italian-style fare: pizzas, pastas, and salads perfect for a lighter meal. Whether you go Italian or French at dinner, be sure to leave room for delectable dessert. It's open for dinner Tues.–Sat., closed major holidays. Also quite good, just across the street, is **150 Grand** (fortunately, at 150 W. Grand), 760/738-6868.

The regional fine dining destination, though, is the elegant French **El Bizcocho** at the Rancho Bernardo Inn (see above), 858/675-8500.

INLAND FROM THE COAST: JULIAN AND VICINITY

The Apple-Pie Old West

This slice of apple-pie Americana, easily reached from either San Diego or Escondido, really does know its apples; small orchards climb the area's hillsides. Julian sprang to life as a hill-country mining town during Southern California's gold rush in the 1890s, and then declined into near ghost-town status until the area's affinity for apple growing was actively cultivated. Since then the town's Wild West character has been spruced up and tamed, as apples (also peaches and pears), fresh-squeezed apple cider, homemade apple pie, and the wistful American desire for simpler times have transformed tiny Julian into a major tourist draw. Bushels of visitors tumble into town during the desert's spring wildflower show, in summer, and for its **Apple Days** and **Fall Harvest Festival** celebrations—also peak seasons for local parking problems. Other main events in the fall include the **Julian Weed Show and Art Mart** and the ever-popular annual **Fiddle, Banjo, Guitar, and Mandolin Contest.**

Main attractions in Julian include the **Julian Pioneer Museum** just over a block south of Main at 2811 Washington St., 760/765-0227, memorializing the hardrock mining and hardscrabble living—as well as the lace curtains and high-button shoes—so prominent in this tiny town's past. It's open from Tues.–Sun. 10 a.m.–4 P.M. from April through November, otherwise open only on weekends and national holidays (same hours) except New Year's Day, Thanksgiving, and Christmas. Admission is $1. The **Eagle Mining Company** is notable at the north end of C St., 760/765-0036—a rare opportunity to tour the inner workings of a gold mine. Dug into a mountainside, the old Eagle Mine and High Peaks Mine ceased commercial operation in 1942, but the mine tunnels and plenty of mining paraphernalia are still in place. Hourly tours are offered daily 10 a.m.–3 P.M., weather permitting, not counting time spent in "rock shop." Come later in the day to dodge school tours. Admission is $7 adults, $3 children ages 6–15, $1 age 5 and under.

Another reason to tarry here—especially for intrepid desert and high-country explorers who prefer a bed to starry nights in a sleeping bag—is the town's proximity to both Anza-Borrego Desert State Park and Cuyamaca Rancho State Park.

For current information about the community, contact the **Julian Chamber of Commerce,** 2129 Main St., 760/765-1857; www.julianca.com.

Anza-Borrego Desert State Park

The largest state park in the contiguous United States, reaching south from the Santa Rosa Mountains almost to the Mexican border, Anza-Borrego Desert State Park consists of 600,000 acres of Colorado Desert. "Anza" refers to Juan Bautista de Anza, the Spanish captain who explored the area in 1774, establishing a viable land route from Mexico to California coastal settlements; "borrego" is Spanish for bighorn sheep. Some sights in this spectacular vastness can be appreciated from the road—the **Borrego Badlands,** the **Carrizo Badlands,** and the **Salton Sea** off in the distance—but other wonders, including **Borrego Palm Canyon, Hellhole Canyon,** and other palm oases, require the effort of a hike. In a good rain year, the park's spring wildflower bloom—usually starting in March, peaking in April—can be spectacular.

An excellent **visitor center** near park headquarters, 760/767-4205, is the best place to start an Anza-Borrego exploration. Call the park's wildflower hot line, 760/767-4684, for peak spring wildflower bloom predictions. The park is open 24 hours and admission is free (except for the Palm Canyon Trail, where hikers are charged a small fee at the gate); the visitor center is open daily 9 a.m.–5 P.M. For additional information—including campground details—contact the local state park headquarters at 200 Palm Canyon Dr., 760/767-5311, or see the website: www.anzaborrego .statepark.org.

Cuyamaca Rancho State Park

A high-country surprise on the edge of the desert east of San Diego, 25,000-acre Cuyamaca Rancho State Park (KWEE-uh-MACK-uh) features both lowland chaparral and fairly lush conifer and oak woodlands. As it's one of the few areas in Southern California with marked seasonal change, come for spring wildflowers, summer thunderstorms, fall colors, and, in winter, snow-dusted mountain peaks. Most of the area is designated as wilderness; camping, nature study, and serious hiking are the park's major attractions.

The park's 110 miles of hiking and horseback riding trails (backcountry camping allowed) lead to **Cuyamaca Peak,** the park's tallest at 6,512 feet, and the less challenging **Stonewall Peak,** with kind switchbacks; they also wind through meadows and oak woodlands. In recent years, mountain lion attacks have become an increasing concern—so hike in groups and otherwise heed all recommended safety precautions.

Also of note: the 1870 **Stonewall Jackson Gold Mine** at the north end of the park, not particularly impressive but providing mute testimony to the area's gold-rush era, and the park museum. Housed, along with park headquarters, in the stone **Ralph M. Dyar Homestead,** the museum emphasizes the culture of the Kumeya'ay Indians who settled the area about 7,000 years ago.

The park is open for day use from sunrise to sunset ($2 per vehicle), and at least one campground is open year-round. Call for camping reservation information (seasonal). For more information, contact: Cuyamaca Rancho State Park, 12551 Hwy. 79 in Descanso, 760/765-0755, or visit www.cuyamaca.statepark.org.

Much of the rest of San Diego County's mountain wilderness is just to the east—the **Mount Laguna Recreation Area** in **Cleveland National Forest,** with still more hiking, camping, and picnicking potential. Though urbanites come east via I-8 and then amble north from Pine Valley via Laguna Mountain Road, the area is also accessible from Julian. Instead of following Highway 79 to Cuyamaca, turn onto the **Sunrise Highway** (County Road S1) just before Lake Cuyamaca, and keep climbing for some of the county's most spectacular desert views.

Staying in and near Julian

Bed-and-breakfasts are the thing in these parts. *The* place since forever—the 1970s, actually—is the fine and funky old-time **Julian Hotel** 2023 Main Street, 760/765-0201, www.julianhotel.com, built during Julian's heyday by Albert and Margaret Robinson, freed slaves. Historical authenticity is the keynote here, since the hotel is listed on the National Register of Historic Places. Most rooms are small, with shared baths, though a one-room cottage, the honeymoon suite, and several rooms do feature private baths. Rates: $72–175 (two-night minimum stay on weekends).

Not part of the town's Wild West heritage but looking the part is the **Julian Lodge,** 2720 C

St. (at Fourth and C, a half-block south of Main), 760/765-1420 or toll-free 800/542-1420. This two-story wood frame hotel boasts modern amenities beneath its 19th-century charm, expressed in attractive period-style rooms (fairly small, as in the good ol' days). All rooms have cable TV but no phone; some have refrigerators and radios. A friendly fireplace beckons from downstairs in the breakfast parlor. And the conference room is not just for conferences—it turns into a good setup for family stays, complete with a Murphy bed and rollaway cots. Rates start at $74. Also new in the neighborhood, quite nice, and substantially more expensive is the **Orchard Hill Country Inn,** 2502 Washington St., 760/765-1700; www.orchardhill.com. Rates are $160–265.

Shadow Mountain Ranch, beyond Julian proper at 2771 Frisius Rd., 760/765-0323, is a onetime cattle ranch and apple orchard refashioned into a country-style bed-and-breakfast inn. Accommodations are available in either the main house—two rooms with fireplaces and antiques—or in the ranch's four cottages, each with particular charms. Grandma's Attic is all wicker and lace, for example, and The Enchanted Cottage—atop a hill—has a potbellied stove and a view of the pines. For couples traveling together, Manzanita Cottage offers two bedrooms with separate entrances, a living room (complete with woodstove), and kitchen. Unique, though, is the Tree House, available only in the summer. Generous ranch-style breakfasts are included. Rates are $90 and up, two-night minimum on weekends.

But if bed-and-breakfasts just aren't your style, plan to camp at either Cuyamaca Rancho or Anza-Borrego Desert State Parks (at least some campsites open year-round). Or beat a high-desert retreat to Borrego Springs in the midst of Anza-Borrego. **La Casa del Zorro** (see below) is the classiest act around, but another good choice is the frontier-style **Palm Canyon Resort** silhouetted against the stunning mountains at 221 Palm Canyon Dr. (near the park visitor center), Borrego Springs, 760/767-5341 or toll-free 800/342-0044 in California. Rooms are spacious and quite attractive in subdued western style, with color TV, cable, and in-room coffeemakers and refrigerators. Also here are a swimming pool, whirlpool, and on-site restaurant and "saloon." Rates start at $85 in the typical fall, winter, and spring travel season, at $60 in torrid summer heat. There's a Good Sam RV park here, too.

La Casa del Zorro Resort Hotel
One of those classic California desert resorts, La Casa del Zorro started out as an adobe ranch house, built in 1937. Since then, whitewashed adobe-style "casitas" have spread out over 32 tree-shaded acres. Rooms here are beautifully decorated and comfortable. Resort amenities include putting green, tennis courts, three swimming pools, rental bikes, and volleyball. (Child care can be arranged.) Two good restaurants are also part of the complex. Mid-season (spring, fall) room rates start at $175 (weekdays), and in the winter high season, $225. The separate two-to four-bedroom "casitas," are $480 and up in winter (substantially lower in summer), with a two-night minimum stay on weekends. For more information: La Casa del Zorro Resort Hotel, 3845 Yaqui Pass Rd. in Borrego Springs, 760/767-5323 or toll-free 800/824-1844; www.lacasadelzorro.com.

Eating in and near Julian
Julian isn't known for its great restaurants. Popular for lunch, though, is **Mom's Apple Pies,** 760/765-2472, and for dinner, the **Julian Grill,** 760/765-0173. Except on weekends and holidays, the dining room at the craftsman-style **Orchard Hill Country Inn** on Washington St. north of Main, 760/765-1420, is open to nonguests (call for reservations).

If a genuinely good meal is mandatory, get ready to drive—all the way to Borrego Springs, in the middle of Anza-Borrego Desert State Park. **La Casa del Zorro Restaurant** at the resort, 3845 Yaqui Pass Rd., 760/767-5323, is the place for dress-up dinners out in the desert, as well as a more casual breakfast and lunch. Dinner entrées include chicken *cordon bleu,* prime rib, scampi, Alaskan salmon, and vegetable curry. Lighter à la carte specials and the changing early-bird specials are the real deals. La Casa del Zorro also offers a feast for the spirit—Old California ambience with candlelit whitewashed walls reminiscent of 1930s' Palm Springs. The restaurant is open daily 7 a.m.–3 P.M., Friday and Saturday 5–10 P.M., and on Sunday 4:30–10 P.M.

But don't miss **Dudley's Bakery,** 30218 Hwy. 78, an area institution near the junction with Highway 79 in Santa Ysabel, 760/765-0488 or toll-free 800/225-3348, open daily 8 a.m.–5 P.M. California history aficionados may stop in Santa Ysabel to peek into **Mission Asistencia de Santa Isabel,** a small 18th-century mission outpost reconstructed in more recent times. But everyone stops at Dudley's across the street before heading into the wilderness or back into the city. This is the place to load up on specialty breads—how about jalapeño loaf?—breakfast pastries, and other goodies. Dudley's offers deli fare, too.

GREATER SAN DIEGO

SAN DIEGO AS DISCOVERY

Captain Juan Rodríguez Cabrillo stepped out onto Point Loma, the tip of what is now San Diego Bay, and claimed the territory for Spain in 1542. His footfall has echoed through contemporary time as California's first and original point of discovery.

The U.S. military discovered San Diego earlier this century and settled in for a long stay, drawn by the area's sublime weather, its fine natural port, and its high-flying wide open spaces.

Despite its straitlaced military tradition, San Diego is no longer a simple social montage of battleship gray and camouflage green, no longer a predictable bastion of conservatism. New people, new high-tech industries, and new ideas have moved in.

Visitors to San Diego discover, and rediscover, a salubrious endless summer of beaches and balmy breezes along with world-class enclaves of culture and equally surprising moderate prices. They discover San Diego's relaxed, casual approach to day-to-day life and find that, here, just about anyone can feel comfortable. The oldest city in California and the state's second largest, San Diego somehow still retains a simpler, small-town sensibility—beyond the freeway traffic, that is.

THE LAY OF THE LAND

Though first-time visitors may see little beyond the harbor and the white-sand beaches of San Diego the city, San Diego the county offers much, much more in terms of diverse land forms.

San Diego's skyline

ROBERT HOLMES/CALIFORNIA DIVISION OF TOURISM

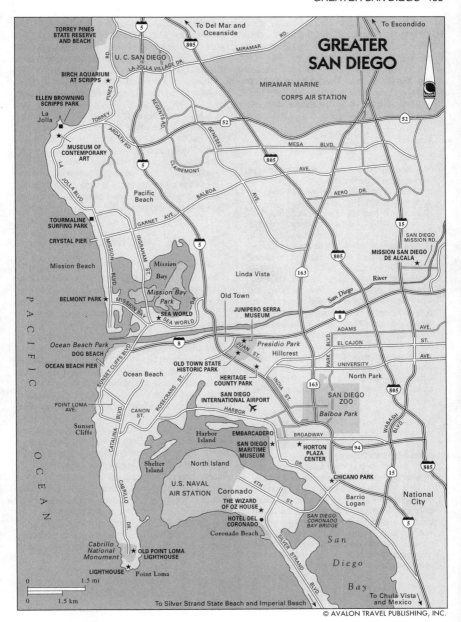

GREATER
SAN DIEGO

To Del Mar and
Oceanside

To Escondido

TORREY PINES
STATE RESERVE
AND BEACH

U. C. SAN DIEGO

MIRAMAR MARINE

CORPS AIR STATION

BIRCH AQUARIUM
AT SCRIPPS

ELLEN BROWNING
SCRIPPS PARK

La Jolla

MUSEUM OF
CONTEMPORARY
ART

Pacific
Beach

TOURMALINE
SURFING PARK

CRYSTAL PIER

Mission Beach

Mission
Bay

Mission Bay
Park

Linda Vista

Old Town

JUNIPERO SERRA
MUSEUM

SAN DIEGO
MISSION RD.

MISSION SAN DIEGO
DE ALCALA

River

BELMONT PARK

SEA WORLD
SEA WORLD

Ocean Beach Park

DOG BEACH

OCEAN BEACH PIER

Ocean Beach

OLD TOWN STATE
HISTORIC PARK

Presidio Park
Hillcrest

HERITAGE
COUNTY PARK

SAN DIEGO
INTERNATIONAL AIRPORT

ADAMS

EL CAJON

UNIVERSITY

North Park

SAN DIEGO
ZOO

Balboa Park

POINT LOMA
AVE.

Sunset
Cliffs

PACIFIC

Harbor
Island

EMBARCADERO

SAN DIEGO
MARITIME
MUSEUM

BROADWAY

HORTON
PLAZA
CENTER

CHICANO PARK

Shelter
Island

North Island

U.S. NAVAL
AIR STATION

Coronado

THE WIZARD
OF OZ HOUSE

HOTEL DEL
CORONADO

Coronado Beach

Barrio
Logan

National
City

SAN DIEGO
CORONADO
BAY BRIDGE

San

OCEAN

Cabrillo
National
Monument

OLD POINT LOMA
LIGHTHOUSE

LIGHTHOUSE

Point Loma

Diego

Bay

To Chula Vista
and Mexico

0   1.5 mi

0   1.5 km

To Silver Strand State Beach and Imperial Beach

Almost one-third of San Diego County is publicly owned and accessible to the public, including 802-square-mile Anza-Borrego Desert State Park, an additional 700-plus square miles of federal land within Cleveland National Forest and federal Bureau of Land Management (BLM) preserves, and numerous county and city parks. Not open to the public but invaluable for creating de facto wildlife sanctuaries and "corridors" on the fringes of urban Southern California is the vast acreage included within U.S. military bases, most notably Camp Pendleton in northern San Diego County.

Inland, or eastward, from the ocean and the beaches, the San Diego landscape becomes one of lowlands and valleys—with the area's only truly "Mediterranean" climate—flanked by the western foothills of the north-south-trending Peninsular Ranges. Most of the county is included, geographically speaking, within the hilly and mountainous Peninsular Ranges, which reaches to just above 6,000 feet in elevation. The range's eastern slope is high desert, rapidly descending toward the low desert of the Salton Sea and surrounding sink.

SAN DIEGO'S "PERFECT" CLIMATE

Just about everyone in San Diego will tell you the climate here is perfect. And so it usually is, if perfection is measured in the 60–70°F range in summer, in the mid-40s to mid-60s in winter. In late summer and fall, however, "Santa Anas" sometimes blow in—several-day events created by inland high pressure; in a reversal of the usual weather pattern, with winds blowing east, or inland, from the cool, moist coastal plain, desiccated desert winds blow west to the ocean. During strong Santa Ana conditions heat-wave mirages shimmer up and down the coastline, with temperatures reaching 100°F or higher; inland, grassland and wilderness wildfire danger becomes extreme. Milder Santa Anas, however, chase away the coastal fog and create wonderful dry weather and temperatures in the mid-80s, often sublime in October and November. What little rainfall there is along the coast and in the foothills—an average of 10–15 inches in a typical year—falls primarily from December into March.

Farther inland, the climate becomes somewhat less predictable. Mild temperatures and low rainfall predominate throughout the foothills in most years, but atop higher Peninsular Range peaks—including Cuyamaca, Laguna, and Palomar—expect cool summer temperatures and substantially more rain, even some snow, in winter. The high-desert climate just beyond the mountains is hot in summer yet cool, sometimes quite cold, in winter. Farther east the low desert begins—an environment isolated from the moderating effects of the ocean, with 100-plus summertime temperatures and mild winters. Though desert rainfall is typically negligible, in some years an astonishingly intense *chabusco* or tropical storm will dump as much as 10–16 inches of rain in a single day.

THE SAN DIEGO STORY

The first known San Diego residents, called the Diegueños by the Spanish, populated the area for thousands of years before European settlement. The Ipai people living north of the San Diego River and the Tapai people to the south shared a linguistic heritage with the Yuma. Foragers who relied on the abundance of the land—particularly the acorn harvest from oak groves and other plant life—the Ipai and Tapai also ate fish, shellfish, and small mammals. They made pottery, unusual in California, for storing both water and food. Well-developed arts included abstract rock art painting, sand painting, and ceramic etching.

Yet the characteristic most noted by the Spanish, in the words of California's first Spanish governor, Pedro Fages, was a "natural and crusty pride," an attitude "absolutely opposed to all rational subjection and full of the spirit of independence." Some historians suggest that if the Ipai and Tapai had possessed any semblance of organized social structure, their resistance to the Spanish *conquistadores* might have succeeded—and might have sent the first explorers packing. Settlement deterred might have meant settlement denied, or at least delayed long enough for England or France to claim California and otherwise radically alter the march of modern history across the New World's western landscape.

Foothold for a Spanish California

Though they repeatedly attacked the local mission and other Spanish outposts, the Diegueños did not succeed in their insurrections. So, officially, California was discovered by Spain. Hernán Cortés spotted the land he called California in 1535, but it was Captain Juan Rodríguez Cabrillo—actually a Portuguese named João Rodrigues Cabrilho—who first sailed the California coast, in search of the mythic Straits of Anian, or the Northwest Passage, to the Spice Islands. On September 28, 1542, Cabrillo stepped out onto "The Point of California," present-day Point Loma, and named the harbor it protected San Miguel, after Saint Michael. Then, on November 10, 1602, the more adequately equipped Sebastián Vizcaíno arrived. He declared Cabrillo's records too sketchy to positively identify the area (and other areas), and two days later, on the feast day of Franciscan San Diego de Acalá, he renamed the bay after the saint and, perhaps incidentally, after his own flagship, the *San Diego*.

Settling Into Spanish California

It would be 167 years before the Spanish returned to San Diego, spurred by the territorial threat of Russians moving south from Alaska. Fearing that the Russian fur traders and settlers might soon control California's harbors, endangering Spain's hold on Mexico, King Charles insisted that royal forces move north from their Mexican bases to formally take possession of—to colonize—California, an enterprise called "The Sacred Expedition of 1769."

Five expedition parties set out, two by land and three by sea. The seafarers fared the worst. One ship never arrived, and the crews of those that did were decimated by scurvy and other diseases. The first overland party set up its bivouac—and de facto hospital for the sickened sailors they found by the bay—in what is now Old Town, thereby locating the city.

The second overland party, led by Gaspár de Portolá, commander of the colonization forces and California's first governor, arrived in late June.

California's First Mission and First City

The ceremonial establishment of San Diego as Spanish colony came on July 16, 1769, when the assembled multitudes ascended the hill above their encampment. The first official European foothold in California, this "Plymouth Rock of the West Coast" was chosen as the site for both California's first mission and its associated military presidio for its commanding views of the valley and the bay. After a solemn mass Father Junípero Serra, the "father president" of California's not-yet-founded mission chain, dedicated the site to the glory of God.

But because of the poor quality of surrounding soils, the mission failed to thrive. The Diegueño people were considered so dangerous that no one was allowed to leave the walled presidio compound surrounding the mission for any purpose without an armed military escort. Native peoples distrusted the military in equal measure, making it difficult for missionaries to attract neophytes—the workforce necessary for both the agricultural success and cultural transformation (some would say genocide) central to California mission society. So in 1774 the mission relocated about five miles up the valley—disastrously, at first, since the unprotected, unfinished mission was soon attacked and burned by 400 or so Diegueño. Things had settled down considerably by 1777, when the new mission complex was consecrated. It soon flourished, with olive, date, and pear orchards, lush gardens, vineyards, and vast herds of sheep, cattle, and horses. Mission life was good, and fairly uneventful—at least until 1812, when a powerful earthquake shattered the mission church. The modern Mission San Diego owes much of its present appearance to the reconstruction work of 1813.

Mission San Diego de Acalá as it appeared at the end of the 19th century

A Sleepy Spanish, Mexican, and American City

Though San Diego was the first Spanish settlement in California, it wasn't the most influential. Monterey to the north soon became California's capital city and cultural center. But after the Mexican revolution, San Diego gained new prestige as de facto capital of both Alta and Baja California because of the personal preference of the governor.

Under Mexican rule, mission days ended and the oft-romanticized era of the ranchos began, supported by brisk Yankee trade for cattle hides, known as "California bank notes." When California was finally included within United States territory after 1848, San Diego barely noticed. With the world's attention focused on booming San Francisco and the Northern California gold rush, San Diego remained a solidly Mexican town, with fiestas and bullfights and other cultural traditions in full flower. U.S. sensibilities established themselves here quite slowly, aided by stagecoach and steamer and the eventual arrival of the railroad. Otherwise business boomed and busted, along with the rest of Southern California, into the 20th century. In 1900, the population of the entire county was 15,000.

The American Military Moves In

San Diego's presence as a major American city coincided with the arrival of the U.S. military, the Navy in particular. The Navy's Pacific Fleet, based in National City, has long been at home on San Diego Bay. The modern military presence began almost unnoticeably, however, with the humble U.S. Naval Coaling Station built in 1907 on the bay side of Point Loma. San Diego's now-famous aircraft and aerospace industries, largely related to defense, started in 1917, with the World War I–era establishment of the North Island U.S. Naval Air Station on Coronado Island—the air base that served as the actual starting point of Charles Lindbergh's famous transatlantic solo flight in 1927. More famous in modern times, the Miramar Naval Air Station just north of San Diego inspired the macho-guy-in-the-sky movie *Top Gun.* Though there have

been other cutbacks and changes, San Diego's most dramatic post-Cold War downsizing denouement came in 1996, when the Navy's Top Gun school moved to Fallon, Nevada, and Miramar became a Marine base. Camp Pendleton, once a Mexican rancho, more recently a U.S. Marine base, still dominates northern San Diego County.

Everyone Else Arrives— Legally and Otherwise

Throughout World War II the local tuna industry was an economic mainstay. In 1950 San Diego was the top fishing port in the United States., producing about $30 million in fish. By 1960, because of stiff competition from Japanese and South American fishing fleets, that chapter in San Diego history was all but over. Maritime markets soon sailed in new directions, however, with increases in port exporting and shipbuilding.

After World War II the aircraft and defense industries also took off, the latter fueled by generous federal government funding. Until economic diversification began, fairly recently, almost 80 percent of local income was derived from defense, both directly and indirectly.

Scientific and technological research facilities also benefited, at least by regional association, along with high-tech industry and academic institutions. But the intelligentsia here is not entirely dedicated to military and industrial pursuits. La Jolla, for example, hosts the internationally renowned Salk Institute and the University of California at San Diego, with its famed Scripps Institution of Oceanography.

CAUTION

Retirees and tourists—both drawn by the sun, the sand, the sea, and the sublime weather—also have a notable presence in and around San Diego.

Not everything is copacetic in San Diego these days, however, and not everyone is welcome. California's current war against illegal immigrants who cross the border from Mexico is fought quite fiercely here—a fact that at first seems ironic, considering San Diego's Spanish and Mexican roots, and odd, considering the community's long-cherished "sister city" relationship with Tijuana, Mexico. Illegal immigration has always occurred here to some degree, yet in recent years San Diego has been literally and figuratively overrun—though that trend has slowed some as the immigrant war has been pushed inland by more successful deterrence here. Residents have been frightened by strangers creeping through their backyards at night, and outraged by "birthing clinics" along the U.S.-Mexico border that cater to women who want their children born as U.S. citizens. And they still fear the increase in wildfires sparked by immigrants' campfires in the tinder-dry backcountry.

BALBOA PARK

BALBOA BACKGROUND AND FOREGROUND

San Diego's cultural heart and soul, home to its renowned zoo, magnificent museums, and much of the city's thriving theater program, Balboa Park is also an architectural and horticultural masterpiece. Unimaginatively known as City Park when its original 1,400 acres of chaparral and scrub brush were set aside by the city in 1868, Balboa Park began to develop its Spanish colonial revival character in preparation for the 1915–1917 Panama-California International Exposition, a massive cultural coming-out party sponsored by the city to celebrate the completion of the Panama Canal.

The elaborate exuberance of the original buildings, intended to be temporary, can be credited to New York architect Bertram G. Goodhue, who personally designed the Fine Arts Building, the California State Building (now the Museum of Man), and the Cabrillo Bridge along El Prado—the formal entrance into the park's beaux arts center. Goodhue also set the stage for other architects.

With the arrival of World War I and San Diego's sudden centrality to the war effort, the exhibition buildings were conscripted for service. In the 1920s, as the military settled into permanent San Diego quarters, the city wisely established the precedent that makes present-day Balboa Park possible—donating the exposition buildings to various nonprofit cultural institutions.

The development of Balboa Park's cultural center continued with construction of the 1935 California-Pacific International Exposition, which added still more buildings, these by architect Richard Requa, with Aztec, Mayan, and Southwestern motifs.

Balboa Park Overview

San Diego's huge central park is lush and inviting, perfect for picnics and aimless ambling. Yet it's almost impossible to *be* aimless, given Balboa Park's astonishing array of attractions. Most visitors start at the San Diego Zoo, at the north end of the park just off Park Boulevard; the zoo can easily become a daylong adventure. Between the zoo and El Prado is the Spanish Village Art Center, studio space for artists and artisans who also sell their wares (open daily 11 a.m.–4 P.M.,

ROBERT HOLMES/CALIFORNIA DIVISION OF TOURISM

Balboa Park

free). At the eastern end of El Prado begins Balboa Park's endless parade of museums. Fairly new ones, such as the Reuben H. Fleet Space Theater and Science Center and the Museum of Photographic Arts, stand beside longtime favorites, including the San Diego Natural History Museum, the San Diego Museum of Art, and the Museum of Man. Adjacent and just north, along Old Globe Way, is the rebuilt Old Globe Theatre—the original Shakespearean venue was torched in a 1978 arson fire—and the other two theaters of the Simon Edison Centre for the Performing Arts. Another don't-miss destination: the 1915 Botanical Building, with its lotus pond and impressive collection of tropical and subtropical plants.

Attractions south of El Prado include the Japanese Friendship Garden and the Spreckels Organ Pavilion with its 1914 Spreckels Organ featuring 4,445 pipes or 72 ranks. (Free concerts are offered year-round on Sunday afternoons at 2 P.M. and, in July and August, on Monday evenings at 8 P.M.) Still more museums farther south include the San Diego Automotive Museum and the excellent San Diego Aerospace Museum, as well as the Centro Cultural de la Raza, "the people's cultural center."

ALONG EL PRADO

Reuben H. Fleet Space Theater and Science Center

Two blocks south of the zoo at 1875 El Prado, just off Park Boulevard near the fountain in Plaza de Balboa, the Reuben H. Fleet Space Theater and Science Center is ever-popular—especially with more precocious kids. The main attraction here is the Omnimax theater, the world's first, which projects movies through a fish-eye lens onto the 76-foot Imax tilted dome. The space theater premieres you-could-be-there space, science, art, nature, and exploration films such as *Eyes on the Universe* and *Titanica*. (Save your neck from cyberstrain by sitting in the back.) Fun even for adults is the 9,500-square-foot science center, with dozens of well-done interactive and hands-on exhibits—such as Chinese res-

FINDING SAN DIEGO'S LATINO HERITAGE

Given the city's Spanish and Mexican cultural roots, San Diego's Latino community is not as visible to visitors as one might expect. The city's phenomenal growth in this century has been fueled primarily by crew-cut U.S. military crews and socially conservative retirees, after all, and most recently by high-tech corporados. The contributions of even San Diego's earliest "Californio" families, rooted here since early mission days, somehow got lost in the fray—including heated community response in recent years to increased illegal immigration from Mexico, San Diego's neighbor to the south. But local appreciation of Latino arts and cultures—and non-WASP culture in general—is increasing. Come in May for the **Old Town Fiesta de Cinco de Mayo,** and in September for the monthlong **Mexican Cultural Festival** and the weeklong **Cabrillo Festival.**

One San Diego arts icon—recently threatened by proposed freeway expansion and reconstruction plans—is **Chicano Park** beneath the San Diego–Coronado Bay Bridge in Barrio Logan. The park is primarily composed of vivid, larger-than-life murals contributed by artists from throughout California, spectacular public art "displayed" on the bridge's concrete supports.

More accessible for most visitors, however, is **El Centro Cultural de la Raza**—"The People's Cultural Center"—in San Diego's Balboa Park, regularly open Wed.–Sun. noon–5 P.M. (free) and at other times for special events. This onetime water tower, a gallery in the round since the 1960s, originally showcased Chicano, or Mexican-American, art as well as theater, dance, and literary productions. In recent years El Centro's focus has expanded to include other Central, South, and Native American cultures. Typically political, El Centro's art exhibits have earned national and international acclaim. An outgrowth of El Centro is the **Border Arts Workshop,** sponsoring art, drama, and music collaborations in venues on both sides of the U.S.-Mexico border.

PRACTICAL BALBOA PARK

If at all possible, spend at least two full days in Balboa Park. Entering the park is free, but the majority of its attractions—the zoo, most museums, the theater program—charge admission. The most economical option for touring the museums, typically, is the multiple-museum ticket—at last report, including admission to nine museums, $25—which is usually a bargain even if you won't be seeing them all. Most museums also offer a "free Tuesday" once each month, with some free on the first Tuesday of the month, others free on the second Tuesday, and so forth. Most museums are open daily from 10 A.M. to at least 4 P.M., but schedules can vary throughout the year; if your time in town is tight, call ahead to verify hours.

For more detailed information on the zoo, museums, and major attractions, see the listings below. For additional information on the park and its current programs and events, contact the very helpful

Balboa Park Information Center in Balboa Park, inside the House of Hospitality at 1549 El Prado, San Diego, 619/239-0512, open daily 9 A.M.–4 P.M.

If you're coming by car, the traditional entrance to Balboa Park is from downtown, heading east via Laurel Street and over the Laurel Street Bridge (the Cabrillo Bridge) spanning Highway 163. Once over the bridge, the street becomes El Prado, which soon becomes the park's primary pedestrian mall. Parking is a particular challenge on summer weekends, so come early in the day; you'll discover that the first lot, at Plaza de Panama, is almost always full. Continue south to find others. The other main route into the park, much more convenient if the zoo is your first or primary destination, is via Park Boulevard. From Highway 163, exit at Park Boulevard; from I-5, exit at Pershing Drive and follow the signs.

---

onant bowls and the Bernoulli Effect beachball. Don't miss the gift shop, with an unusually good selection of books, games, and toys.

Theater admission varies, depending on the movie, but is typically $6.50–11 for adults, $5.50–9 for seniors, and $5–8 for children ages 5–15. Center admission is free on the first Tuesday of every month, otherwise it's $6.50 adults, $5 for kids. The center is open Monday and Tuesday 9:30 a.m.–5 P.M.; Wednesday, Thursday, and Sunday 9:30 a.m.–7 P.M.; and Friday and Saturday 9:30 a.m.–9 P.M. For current movie and other information, call 619/233-1233, or look up www.rhfleet.org.

San Diego Natural History Museum

This imposing museum at 1788 El Prado chronicles the earth's wonders, among them shore ecology, seismography, and local gemstones. Of the "all natural ingredients" on exhibit, kids most savor the live insect displays along with the dinosaur skeletons and other fossils. And just inside the main entrance, swinging from a 43-foot cable, the museum's Foucault Pendulum verifies that the planet is, in fact, rotating on its axis. Special traveling exhibits, films, lectures, and nature outings—including winter whale-watching tours—are also big draws.

Museum admission is $7 adults, $6 seniors and active military, $5 children ages 6–17, free on the first Tuesday of every month. Hours sometimes vary, but the museum is typically open daily 9:30 a.m.–4:30 P.M., closed on Thanksgiving, Christmas, and New Year's Day. The San Diego Natural History Museum is located near the fountain in Plaza de Balboa, just south of the San Diego Zoo and Village Place off Park Boulevard. For more information, call 619/232-3821; www.sdnhm.org.

Museum of Photographic Arts

The Museum of Photographic Arts inside the Casa de Balboa, 1649 El Prado, focuses on both photography as art and the history of photographic arts—showcasing the works of well-known photographers such as Ansel Adams, Edward Weston, and Henri Cartier-Bresson along with those of newer artists. The museum sponsors six to eight special gallery exhibits each year, such as **New York, New York** and **Robert Frank: The Americans,** and a series on marriage, **The Model Wife.** Don't miss the museum store, with fine prints, posters, calendars, cards, and the largest selection of photography books in the western U.S. Admission is $6, free for museum members and children under age 12 accompanied by an adult. It's open daily 10 a.m.–5 P.M., closed on major holidays. For current and upcoming shows and other information, call 619/238-7559; www.mopa.org.

Museum of San Diego History

Another prominent resident of Casa de Balboa at 1649 El Prado, the history museum features rotating thematic exhibits from the San Diego Historical Society's permanent collection plus national traveling exhibits—almost always something of interest, even for the kids. Also take time to take in at least one of the historical society's other local outposts—the **Junípero Serra Museum** in Old Town, for example, or the marvelous **Villa Montezuma/Jesse Shepard House** near the Gaslamp Quarter. The Museum of San Diego History is open Tues.–Sun. 10 a.m.–4:30 P.M., closed Thanksgiving, Christmas, and New Year's Day. Admission is free on the second Tuesday of every month, otherwise $5 for adults; $4 for seniors, students, and active military; and $2 for children ages 6–17. For more information, call 619/232-6203.

San Diego Model Railroad Museum

Down in the Casa de Balboa basement at 1649 El Prado is the San Diego Model Railroad Museum, boasting the world's largest collection of minigauge trains—paradise for toy train lovers. Six separate, and intricate, scale-model exhibits, including the bustling Southern Pacific/Santa Fe route over Tehachapi Pass, come complete with sound effects: bells, whistles, and screeching brakes. With any luck, maybe one of the museum's train buffs will hand over the controls. The museum is open Tues.–Fri.—and the first Tuesday of every month, when admission is free—11 a.m.–4 P.M., and on Saturday and Sunday 11 a.m.–5 P.M. Admission is free for children under age 15, otherwise $4 adults, $3 for students, seniors, and active military. For more information, call 619/696-0199; www.sdmodelrailroadm.com.

Casa de Balboa's **San Diego Hall of Champions Sports Museum,** 619/234-2544, is worth a stop for sports fans particularly interested in local heroes.

San Diego Museum of Art

On the park's Plaza de Panama at 1450 El Prado, the San Diego Museum of Art is best known for its European Renaissance and Baroque paintings, including works by Goya, El Greco, Rubens, and Van Ruisdale. The collection also includes Dalí, Matisse, O'Keeffe, and Toulouse-Lautrec. The cutting-edge contemporary California art in the Frederick R. Weisman Gallery alone is well worth the trip. If the kids are more experienced with computer manipulation than art appreciation, seize the opportunity to expand their horizons—by starting them off at the museum's interactive computer "gallery," the first system of its kind in the United States. Another draw here is the sculpture garden and, for lunch, the **Sculpture Garden Cafe.**

Regular admission is $8 adults; $6 seniors, active military, and students (with ID); $3 children ages 6–17. Free admission on the third Tuesday of every month. It's open Tues.–Sun 10 a.m.–4:30 P.M. For current exhibits and other information, call 619/232-7931; www.sdmart.com.

Timken Museum of Art

Just east of the San Diego Museum of Art at 1500 El Prado, near the Lotus Pond, is the Timken Museum of Art, at home in an attractive building that is Balboa Park's most noticeable architectural anomaly. The collection here is intriguing, dominated by lesser-known works of significant 18th- and 19th-century artists from both Europe and America. It's open Tues.–Sat. 10 a.m.–4:30 P.M., Sunday 1:30–4:30 P.M., closed Monday and the month of September. Admission is free, with free guided tours offered Tues.– Thurs. 10 a.m.–noon. For more information call 619/239-5548 during regular museum hours.

Mingei International Museum of World Folk Art

After two distinguished decades in La Jolla, the marvelous Mingei Museum—where the "art of the people, by the people, and for the people comes to the people"—has made its permanent home in Balboa Park's remodeled House of Charm at 1439 El Prado since the summer of 1996, an arrangement offering six times the museum's original space. Over the years the changing exhibits here have included **Folk Toys** of the World, **Wearable Folk Art,** and **Kindred Spirits: The Eloquence of Function in American Shaker and Japanese Arts of Daily Life.** Call for current exhibit information.

The House of Charm sits on the southwestern corner of the Plaza de Panama. At last report the Mingei was open Tues.–Sun. 10 a.m.–4 P.M., closed on all national holidays. Admission is $5 adults, $2 children. For more information, call 619/239-0003 or check www.mingei.org.

San Diego Museum of Man

The grand Museum of Man, west of the Plaza de Panama at 1350 El Prado, under the California Tower, is striking enough from the outside. The anthropological collection here, one of the finest in the country, made its debut during the 1915 Balboa Park exposition. Expanded and updated over the years, exhibits chronicle human development but emphasize Mexican, Native American (particularly Southwestern), and South American societies. Egyptian artifacts are among recent acquisitions. Equally intriguing, though, is the museum's **Lifestyles and Ceremonies** exhibit, reflecting the dazzling diversity of San Diego's own society.

The San Diego Museum of Man is open daily 10 a.m.–4:30 P.M., closed Thanksgiving, Christmas, and New Year's Day. Admission is $5 adults, $4.50 military and seniors, $3 children ages 6–17, free for children under age 6. It's free for everyone on the third Tuesday of every month. For current program and other information, call 619/239-2001; www.museumofman.org.

BEYOND EL PRADO

San Diego Aerospace Museum and International Aerospace Hall of Fame

These days Balboa Park's exquisite art deco Ford Building—one of the finest remaining examples of its species in the United States, trimmed at night in blue neon—houses an equally impressive and artistic display of aeronautical history makers. Local history is represented by a replica of Charles Lindbergh's *Spirit of St. Louis,* and by a glider on loan from the National Air and Space Museum, first flown in 1883 near San Diego. Especially compelling: the ersatz aircraft carrier flight deck with its World War II–vintage planes. There's much more—about 70 aircraft, with displays arranged artfully and chronologically, accompanied by helpful historical and technical facts. The gift shop here is particularly worthwhile, since proceeds support the museum and its ongoing aircraft assembly and restoration projects.

The San Diego Aerospace Museum is in the southern section of Balboa Park at 2001 Pan American Plaza, most easily reached via Park Boulevard and then President's Way. Admission is free on the fourth Tuesday of the month, otherwise $8 adults, $6 seniors, $3 "juniors" ages 6–17, and free for children under 6 and

---

OLD GLOBE THEATRE AND FRIENDS

First there was San Diego's Old Globe Theatre; dramatic outdoor Shakespeare productions were its original claim to fame. Now joining the 581-seat Old Globe are two more theaters in Balboa Park's performing arts center—the 225-seat **Cassius Carter Centre Stage** and the 612-seat **Lowell Davies Festival Theatre.** The performance calendar for this major-league regional repertory is full almost year-round.

The Old Globe and fellow theaters are in Balboa Park, near the Museum of Man, and reached via Park Boulevard and Old Globe Way. The regular theater season runs from January into June. The **Old Globe Festival,** showcasing Shakespeare, other classics, and modern works, both indoors and out, officially runs from July into September but summer shows can—and usually do—extend through November. No performances are scheduled on major U.S. holidays.

Advance ticket purchases are recommended. Admission varies, in the $23–42 range. For prerecorded ticket information, call 619/239-2255. For bargain same-day tickets to these and other area theaters, as well as to music and dance events, contact the **Times Arts Tix** ticket center at Horton Plaza, 619/497-5000, or check the San Diego Performing Arts League website at www.sandiegoperforms.com.

For more information, contact the **Old Globe Theatre,** 619/231-1941; www.oldglobe.org. Call for current performance schedule and box office hours.

active-duty military. It's open daily 10 a.m.–4:30 P.M., closed Thanksgiving and Christmas Day. For current exhibits and other information, call 619/234-8291 or check www.aerospacemuseum.org.

San Diego Automotive Museum

Nearby, at 2080 Pan American Plaza, this was the Palace of Transportation during Balboa Park's 1935–36 exposition. Car-loving kids of all ages will enjoy this particular garage. About 80 classics and exotics—Hollywood's cars, roadsters, and an exceptional motorcycle collection —make up the permanent collection. Special shows and events—call for current program information—are often quite fun. The gift shop, with unusual and one-of-a-kind items, is a cornucopia for car fanatics.

The San Diego Automotive Museum is open daily 10 a.m.–4:30 P.M. (until 5:30 P.M. in summer), last admission one-half hour before closing. It's closed Thanksgiving, Christmas, and New Year's Day. Admission is free on the fourth Tuesday of every month, otherwise $7 adults, $6 seniors and active military, $3 children ages 6–15, free for children under 6. For current exhibits and other information, call 619/231-2886 or check www.sdautomuseum.org.

SAN DIEGO ZOO

The world-class San Diego Zoo sprang from very humble beginnings. Its original animals were chosen from those left behind by the Panama-California International Exposition. Now famous for its large exotic and endangered animal population and its lush, complex tropical landscape, the 100-acre San Diego Zoo is immensely popular—the city's top visitor draw, attracting more than three million people each year.

Part of the zoo's appeal is the near absence of prison-bar-style cages and pens. Most animals here—the zoo refers to them as "captivating instead of captive"—are kept in naturally landscaped, moated enclosures, very large walk-through aviaries, and other fairly innovative environments. Rarities among the zoo's 4,000 animals (800 species) include Australian koalas–the first exhibited outside Australia–New

---

HIGH-FLYING SAN DIEGO

The development of San Diego has been shaped more by its aerial history—comingled with U.S. military history—than by any other factor.

In the early days of aviation, the industry's pioneers took flight in San Diego to take full advantage of the superb flying weather. **Charles Lindbergh,** the first man to cross the Atlantic Ocean in an airplane, is perhaps the most famous of these fanatical fly boys. In 1927 Lindbergh commissioned San Diegan T. Claude Ryan to build a plane based on Ryan's M-1 design (with wings above the fuselage). Within months, after very few test flights, "Lucky Lindy" left San Diego in his *Spirit of St. Louis*—touching down only briefly on the East Coast before flying off into the history books.

The U.S. military has had a distinguished aerial history in San Diego as well, beginning with test flights made by Glen Curtiss from Coronado's **North Island Naval Station** in 1911. Special air shows and other public events are scheduled at North Island and—at least until its recent move east—at **Miramar Naval Air Station,** the real-life Top Gun, which preceded the movie of the same name.

To get up to speed on San Diego's high-flying history, visit the **San Diego Aerospace Museum** in Balboa Park.

Zealand long-billed kiwis, Sichuan takins from China, wild Mongolian or Przewalski's horses— forerunners of all domesticated horses—and Komodo dragons from Indonesia. Special "guest animals" include two giant pandas on loan from the People's Republic of China, Shi Shi and Bai Yun, who gave birth to a cub, Hua Mei, on August 21, 1999. The San Diego Zoo also boasts the world's largest collection of parrots and parrotlike birds.

The natural habitats—the Polar Bear Plunge, Hippo Beach, Gorilla Tropics, Tiger River, Sun Bear Forest, Pygmy Chimps at Bonobo Road, African Kopje, and Australasia—are most impressive, designed as distinct "bioclimatic zones" with characteristic combinations of plant and animal species.

TO DO THE ZOO, THINK STRATEGICALLY

The zoo is vast and spread out—a moderately challenging four- to five-mile hike if you're in a big hurry and determined to see it all, a potentially tiring stroll even if you're not—so study your zoo map before setting out. The white pathways indicate higher elevations, these shading into gray and then into black, the zoo's lowest elevations. With some forethought, occasional backtracking, and strategic use of the zoo's two central moving staircases, it's possible to do most of your walking on flat ground or heading downhill. The upper mesa levels are less shaded, so see these areas first, particularly during hotter autumn weather.

If all-out zoo trekking is not feasible, take the guided double-decker bus tour for a general introduc-

tion—not a bad idea anyway, considering the valuable overview, informationally, and the great view from the open-air upper deck—then walk only to the must-see attractions on your list. (Spanish-language bus tours are offered daily at noon.) Alternatively, take the Kangaroo Bus, and hop on and off all day for short-distance explorations. Get the big picture on the Skyfari aerial tram, which crosses the zoo just above the treetops, from near the Reptile House to the Horn and Hoof Mesa.

Most zoo animals are most active, and entertaining, in the mornings and late afternoon, so plan to lunch and take in various animal shows—The Wild Ones, for example, and the Wegeforth National Park Sea Lion Show—during midday siesta time.

The San Diego Zoo is also noteworthy for its ongoing research, starting in 1916 with the Zoological Hospital and Biological Research Institute, now known as the Center for Reproduction of Endangered Species (CRES). More than 20 years old, CRES is dedicated to managing species survival—helping endangered and threatened species to mate and produce young successfully, in captivity and in their natural habitats. The California condor captive-breeding program, artificial insemination and other reproductive research, including the "Frozen Zoo" sperm, egg, and embryo bank, and ongoing disease prevention work, are among notable CRES accomplishments.

Since we're all on this big round spaceship together, research done at the San Diego Zoo to save individual animal species, no matter how obscure, may one day save us all.

Polar Bear Plunge

The Polar Bear Plunge is one of the largest polar bear exhibits in the world and a fairly complex arctic kingdom. Chillin' here with the bears are Siberian reindeer, arctic foxes, snowy owls, and a dozen other bird species. The polar bear pond here, near the Skyfari tram station at the zoo's western end, is actually an Olympic-sized pool. The two-level underwater viewing area, with a huge five-inch-thick acrylic window, and other viewing windows allow visitors to watch the bears

play all day. In a necessary concession to climatic reality, the 50-plus species of plants integrated into the environment here are not tundra natives, though these immigrants from around the world look like summertime tundra plant life.

Hippo Beach

Quite the spectacular splash since it opened in the summer of 1995, Hippo Beach is the zoo's hippopotamus habitat. The thrill here is being able to go nose-to-nose with Funani and Jabba—and to get a fish's-eye view of these two-ton herbivores and their astonishing underwater ballets—thanks to the 105-foot-long observation window that flanks the 150,000-gallon pool. The landscape, built to resemble an African marsh, is also home to several fish and bird species. Chances are the kids will be more impressed by the nearby pod of humanized hippos—Lifeguard Mitch, Kahuna Kevin, and Sally the Surfer among the happy hoofers here—sculpted of sand and coated with 30 gallons of Elmer's glue. More fascinating for most adults: the replica of the Egyptian "Tawaret" frieze, depicting the hippo goddess of fertility and child protection.

Tiger River

A complex Asian rainforest with computer-controlled misting and irrigation systems to simulate 100 inches of annual rainfall, Tiger River

was the zoo's first bioclimatic undertaking. Starting near the zoo's Flamingo Lagoon, wander down the ersatz dry riverbed and into the canyon below under a canopy of fig, coral, and orchid trees, flowering ginger, palms, along with 400 other exotic species of bamboo, shrubs, and ferns. First you'll encounter a false gavial, a large crocodile relation, then the slithering ropes of pythons, then the web-footed fishing cats. The reeds and cattails in the marsh are home to pygmy geese, white-breasted kingfishers, and other rainforest birds. Next are the Malayan tapirs, piglike creatures related to both the horse and rhinoceros. Then comes the rainforest royalty, the kings and queens of cats, the tigers—allowed here to play in the ponds or just lounge around in the grass. Rare white tigers and Indochinese tigers alternate in this exhibit. What you won't see is the sophisticated behind-the-scenes scene developed for this aspect of the zoo's ongoing captive-breeding efforts.

Gorilla Tropics

The rainforest extends to Gorilla Tropics, wildly popular since it opened in 1991. The gorillas—four adults and three youngsters, at last count—are central, of course, happily settled onto a hillside planted with figs, bananas, and bamboo. (Here as elsewhere in the San Diego Zoo, the animals eat and otherwise fully enjoy their environment; forests of replacement plants are always on hand.) The jungle sounds, most notable here and throughout nearby aviaries, are provided by a compact disc system with 144 speakers, cleverly camouflaged throughout the landscape.

Scripps Aviary

Just as grand as the gorilla show is a slow stroll through this huge multilevel free-flight aviary, home to hundreds of exotic African birds, including jicanas and the rare Waldrapp ibis. The sound of thunder signals imminent "rain"—in this rainforest it's provided by misting pipes. To

avoid other surprises from the sky, heads up. Smaller aviaries nearby shelter carmine bee-eaters, hornbills, and softbill species.

Pygmy Chimps at Bonobo Road

Not smaller than common chimpanzees yet equally entertaining, the pygmy chimps—also known as "bonobos" in their native Zaire—may be the zoo's most clownish characters, whether playing in the oddly twisted palm forest here or making funny faces at humans on the other side of the glass. These chimps, yet another seriously threatened species, are the first ever exhibited in a U.S. zoo. Also hereabouts are Angolan colobus monkeys and Garnett's galagos, or "bush babies," both arboreal or "treetop" species; rare African crowned eagles, current captive-breeding candidates; and a baboon spider, Africa's largest tarantula.

Sun Bear Forest

In the zoo's central canyon, this ersatz corner of Malaysia is home to playful Malayan sun bears—long-clawed, pigeon-toed tree dwellers that could instead be "moon bears," since the striking gold on their chests is crescent-shaped. The smallest bears in the world, sun bears are hardly cuddly teddy-bear types. Zoologists consider them pound for pound the world's meanest, most aggressive bears. But they're also clownish and quite agile, and willing, like Winnie the Pooh, to do almost anything for honey. Also at home in this particular rainforest are dozens of lion-tailed macaques, a critically endangered species native to India. These arboreal acrobats take advantage of special rubberized monkey-proof "vines" for their impromptu performances. Note the impressive and irreplaceable 40-foot-tall ficus, the only one of its kind at the zoo. Nearby, in a small aviary, are still more exotic birds.

Children's Zoo

Though even the restrooms here are designed for four-year-olds, the Children's Zoo is immensely appealing to "kids" of all ages. Most popular are the two baby animal nurseries, where human babies peer through the glass at animal babies—these rejected by their mothers, injured, or otherwise sickly—as they are bottle-fed and reared by their human caretakers.

At the petting zoo, sheep, goats, and pot-bellied pigs are on parade. Other animals exhibited at the Children's Zoo include exotic birds, spider monkeys, tree kangaroos, small-clawed otters from Asia, lesser pandas, and the always popular—"Ooooh, mom, what's *that?*"—naked molerats. Zookeepers also personally present other animals, from lesser anteaters to meerkats, throughout the day.

Practical San Diego Zoo

The zoo is open daily from 9 a.m. to dusk, which means entrance gates close at 4 P.M. from fall through spring and at 9 P.M. in summer (visitors can stay an hour longer). General admission, which includes admission to the Children's Zoo and all shows, is $18 adults, $8 for children ages 3–11, free for age 2 and under. Deluxe admission, which includes the guided bus tour plus the two-way fare for the Skyfari aerial tram, costs $21 for adults and $11 for children 3–11. Admission is free for everyone on October 3, Founder's Day, and free for children under age 12 during the entire month of October.

Strollers, wheelchairs, and motorized scooters are available for rent on the front plaza next to the clock tower. Film is available at the nearby information booth (as are video camera rentals), but bring your own—more than you think you'll need—since it's expensive here. If you run short of cash, a real possibility if you venture into the zoo's great gift shops, you'll find an ATM in front of the Reptile House. For parking excess baggage, lockers are behind the Reptile House. To save money on meals, pack your own picnic, though snack stands and eateries abound (vegetarian fare available). Best bet for a simple sit-down meal is the **Peacock & Raven** deli just inside the entrance overlooking the peacock lagoon.

For more information, contact the San Diego Zoo, 619/234-3153 (recorded) or 619/231-1515. To study up on the Web, the address is www .sandiegozoo.org. For information on specialty walking and bus tours, call 619/685-3264. For information on the zoo's various education programs, including lectures, workshops, and the popular parent-participation preschooler program, call 619/557-3969. For information about the many benefits of membership in the Zoological Society of San Diego, which operates both the zoo and the San Diego Wild Animal Park near Escondido, call 619/231-0251.

OLD TOWN, DOWNTOWN, AND AROUND

OLD TOWN SAN DIEGO

The old adobe survivors of Old Town San Diego, the state's most popular historic park, are intertwined with—and clearly outnumbered by—a wide variety of minimalls, gift shops, restaurants, and other commercial enterprises that now surround Old Town Plaza.

But modern consumerism didn't doom Old Town's old-timers. It was fate, in the form of a devastating fire in 1872. Most of Old Town's surviving historic buildings, among the earliest outposts of early California settlement history, are clustered in the six-block area bounded by Juan Street on the north, Congress Street on the south, Wallace Street on the west, and Twiggs Street on the east.

Walking Old Town

Highlights of an Old Town history walk include the **Seeley Stables** at Calhoun and Twiggs Streets, 619/220-5442, Old Town San Diego's transportation center until the 20th century, now a museum of horse-and-buggy rolling stock and western memorabilia. (Admission is $2 adults, $1 children.) On Mason at Calhoun is the 1829 **La Casa de Bandini,** center of the young city's social life during Mexican rule, and then after the Yankees arrived, the **Cosmopolitan Hotel.** The ground-floor rooms and walled gardens are now inhabited by a popular Mexican restaurant, **Casa de Bandini,** 619/297-8211, where strolling mariachi bands serenade diners on the patio.

A visit to adobe **La Casa de Estudillo,** 619/220-5422, on Mason St. between Calhoun and San Diego Ave., is a must. (Admission is

$2 adults, $1 children and includes admission to the Seeley museum, and vice versa.) Built in 1827 by Captain José M. Estudillo, commander of the presidio, this was one of the finest homes in Mexican California. Note the leather-tied beams, and the exquisite furnishings, from the Steinway spinet pianos to the blue Duncan Phyfe sofa and elegant oriental rugs. Yet it was the courtyard, with its gardens, well, and outdoor *horno* (bake oven), that served as the center of family life—still serene and meditative, at least on slower days. Family members continued to live here until 1887, after which the home gradually declined. Bought in 1905 by local mover and shaker John D. Spreckels, who restored its grandeur, the house was opened to the public in 1910—promoted as "Ramona's Marriage Place," since the small chapel here reportedly inspired the wedding scene in Helen Hunt Jackson's wildly popular 19th-century novel *Ramona.* The house was eventually deeded to the state; its current restoration began in 1969.

watch tortillas being made in Old Town

Well worth exploring: the 1847 **San Diego Courthouse,** the **Wells Fargo Museum,** the 1865 **Mason Street School,** and the local **Dental Museum.** Inside the tiny **San Diego Union Newspaper Building** is a once-modern marvel of the journalism trade—an ancient Blickensderfer typewriter, complete with wood carrying case.

Just outside Old Town proper is the **Mormon Battalion Visitors Center** at 2510 Juan St., 619/298-3317, free admission, which tells the story of the longest infantry march in history. Also worth a stop for history aficionados is the two-story brick 1857 **Whaley House Museum,** 2482 San Diego Ave., 619/298-2482, one of the few homes in the country ever declared by the U.S. government to be haunted. It served as county courthouse and government center in the 1870s. Artifacts and period memorabilia collected here include one of six "life masks" made of Abraham Lincoln. Admission $4 adults, $2 children.

Practical Old Town

The park itself is free, as is admission to most of its historic buildings, though a few other Old Town-area attractions charge admission. The park's historic buildings are open daily from 10 a.m. to at least 4 P.M., closed Thanksgiving, Christmas, and New Year's Day. Restaurants and some shops have extended hours.

Free Old Town walking tours depart daily at 11 a.m. and 2 P.M. from the state park office, the Robinson-Rose House, 4002 Wallace St., 619/220-5423—also the source for self-guided tour brochures, if you're lucky, as well as special event schedules and other current info. On the first Saturday of each month and every Wednesday, from 10 a.m.–1 P.M. in the Machado y Stewart Adobe, park staff and other local history buffs don period costumes to demonstrate various domestic arts and, next to La Casa de Bandini, the village smithy plies his trade. For more information contact: **Old Town San Diego State Historic Park,** 4002 Wallace St., 619/220-5423.

Old Town San Diego is wedged into the shadows of two major thoroughfares, just east of I-5 and just south of I-8. From I-5, exit at Old Town Avenue. From I-8, exit at Taylor Street, head south, then turn left onto San Diego Avenue. If coming from Point Loma and vicinity, take Rosecrans Avenue east all the way to Old Town.

ROBERT HOLMES/CALIFORNIA DIVISION OF TOURISM

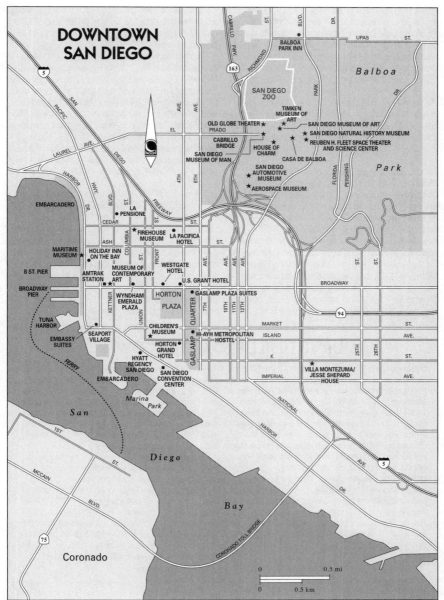

DOWNTOWN SAN DIEGO

Balboa

SAN DIEGO ZOO

BALBOA PARK INN

UPAS ST.

TIMKEN MUSEUM OF ART

OLD GLOBE THEATER ★

SAN DIEGO MUSEUM OF ART

SAN DIEGO NATURAL HISTORY MUSEUM

CABRILLO BRIDGE

HOUSE OF CHARM

REUBEN H. FLEET SPACE THEATER AND SCIENCE CENTER

SAN DIEGO MUSEUM OF MAN

CASA DE BALBOA

Park

SAN DIEGO AUTOMOTIVE MUSEUM ★

AEROSPACE MUSEUM ★

EMBARCADERO

LA PENSIONE

CEDAR

★ FIREHOUSE MUSEUM

LA PACIFICA HOTEL

ASH

MARITIME MUSEUM ★

HOLIDAY INN ON THE BAY

MUSEUM OF CONTEMPORARY ART

WESTGATE HOTEL

B ST. PIER

AMTRAK STATION

U.S. GRANT HOTEL

BROADWAY

BROADWAY PIER

WYNDHAM EMERALD PLAZA

HORTON PLAZA

GASLAMP PLAZA SUITES

TUNA HARBOR

CHILDREN'S MUSEUM

MARKET

EMBASSY SUITES

SEAPORT VILLAGE

HORTON GRAND HOTEL

HI-AYH METROPOLITAN HOSTEL

ISLAND

K

HYATT REGENCY SAN DIEGO

EMBARCADERO

SAN DIEGO CONVENTION CENTER

IMPERIAL

VILLA MONTEZUMA/ JESSE SHEPARD HOUSE ★

Marina Park

San

NATIONAL

Diego

HARBOR

Bay

MCCAIN

BLVD.

75

Coronado

CORONADO TOLL BRIDGE

0   0.5 mi
0   0.5 km

© AVALON TRAVEL PUBLISHING, INC.

Parking can be a nightmare near Old Town, so if you're driving come as early as possible. In 1996 the **San Diego Trolley** extended its routes to include Old Town; taking the trolley is definitely a safe and sane alternative. For a guided get-around—a good general introduction to San Diego, with the option of hopping off at various points and catching a later trolley to continue the tour—try **Old Town Trolley Tours,** headquartered at the tiny Old Town theater on Twiggs Street. These commercial trolley tours leave (and arrive) every 30 minutes between 9 a.m.–4 P.M. Call 619/298-8687 for more information.

To the San Diego Mission
Mission San Diego isn't the most exciting or evocative of California's 21 missions, but it is the first. First founded by Father Junípero Serra in 1769, atop what is now Presidio Hill, the mission was moved to this location in 1774. The new site promised more water and improved agricultural prospects, but it didn't provide peace. Threatened by the mission's territorial incursions, in 1775 native peoples declared war— burning the mission, destroying religious paraphernalia, and killing one priest (Luis Jayme, California's first Catholic martyr, who is honored

here). Wander the garden, stop by the museum, and visit the original chapel—California's first church—for a peek into the mission's past and present lives.

To get to Mission San Diego, 10818 San Diego Mission Rd., from Presidio Park, follow Presidio Drive down the hill and bear right onto Taylor; at the first light, turn left and merge onto I-8 (heading east). Exit at Mission Gorge Road and turn left; turn left again onto San Diego Mission Road. The museum and gardens are open daily 9 a.m.–5 P.M. Admission is $2 adults, $1 seniors (over age 55), and 50 cents for children (under age 12). "Tote-a-tape" tours are available. For more information, call 619/281-8449.

DOWNTOWN SAN DIEGO

Until fairly recently San Diego was known as the city with no downtown, since even residents preferred to be anywhere but. All that has changed after more than two decades of serious redevelopment work that managed to preserve and polish, rather than destroy, what remained of the area's historic character. San Diego now has a lively, people-friendly downtown that

UP THE HILL FROM OLD TOWN

Most notable in **Presidio Park,** just up the hill from Old Town via Taylor Street and Presidio Drive, is the imposing mission revival-style **Junípero Serra Museum,** 2727 Presidio Dr., 619/297-3258, built in 1929, which many visitors mistake for San Diego's mission. Run by the local historical society on behalf of the city, the Serra Museum does mark the hill climbed by Father Serra and his party to lay claim to the territory, and almost marks the site of the Royal Presidio of San Diego and the original mission. Museum exhibits emphasize San Diego's Spanish period, including a fascinating furniture collection and artifacts from presidio excavations. Climb the museum tower for breathtaking panoramic views. The Junípero Serra Museum is open Fri.–Sun. 10 A.M.–4:30 P.M. Admission is $5 adults, $4 seniors, students and military, $2 children 6–17, free for kids age 6 and under.

The entire park, actually, serves as a museum, with various statues, memorials, and the Serra Cross— built in 1913 from presidio floor tiles—telling various parts of the story. The presidio site, directly below the Serra Museum, is a National Historic Landmark, where excavations have been ongoing since 1965. The presidio's chapel, sundry walls, tile floors, and thresholds, even cannonballs, have been discovered.

Presidio Park is perfect for picnics, by the way, but parking is fairly limited, so consider walking up—or come anytime but on a summer weekend.

If you've got the time, worth exploring beyond Old Town proper is **Heritage Park,** 619/291-9784, up Juan Street near Kearney. Here you'll find a collection of brazenly bright Victorians saved from the wrecking ball by the Save Our Heritage Organization (SOHO). One mansion houses a B&B, another an antique store, and yet another a doll shop.

The Mission San Diego de Alcalá was California's first mission.

segues quite neatly into the Embarcadero and the bay.

Downtown San Diego got its start in 1867, the day Alonzo Erastus Horton strolled off a sidewheel steamer onto the "New Town" wharf, at the foot of what is now Fifth Street. Horton saw immediately that San Diego the city should be here, along the bay, not near the Old Town site chosen for security reasons by the Spanish. So Horton soon bought from the city 960 acres of "downtown" land for 27.5 cents an acre–a foolish outlay of $260 for jackrabbits, dust, and fleas, in the minds of lesser civic visionaries.

Nicknamed "Short Block Horton" for the short city blocks he laid out south of Broadway—shorter blocks made for more corner lots, which went for premium prices—Alonzo E. Horton sold so much land so fast he claimed to grow weary from handling all that money, day after day. Yet in the midst of San Diego's first real estate boom, Horton's fatigue failed to stop him. His developments in what was then known as Horton's Addition continued, with a pier, a de facto town hall, and facilities for the railroad, though his grandest accomplishment was the two-story brick Horton House hotel, built for the extravagant sum of $150,000, near the present-day U.S. Grant HoThere seemed to be no end to Horton's success.

Yet it did end, thanks to John D. Spreckels, the sugar magnate associated in local lore with Coronado Island. Building on Horton's original vision, Spreckels built a better pier and started devel-

oping downtown land north of Broadway—soon the most stylish business districts and neighborhoods in town.

Horton's development empire, known today as the Gaslamp Quarter, deteriorated into shabby "Stingaree," named after offshore stingrays and noted for its flophouse hotels, brothels, "prostitution cribs," and general vice (with a capital V). Despite the San Diego Ladies Purity League's determination to clean things up in 1914, in preparation for the Pan-American International Exposition, the neighborhood continued its decline—a trend finally reversed in the 1970s, as San Diego got serious about redevelopment, renovation, and historic preservation.

Horton Plaza

Horton Plaza rises out of old-fashioned downtown San Diego like a Mediterranean or Middle Eastern version of the Emerald City—a jumble of odd open-air plazas, tiled courtyards and fountains, sculptures, stairways, cupolas, and towers all splashed with bold colors and draped in fluttering banners. This architectural marvel, designed by Jon Jerde and presented to the world in 1985, is clearly not your run-of-the-mill shopping mall. Yet as a mall, anchored by Nordstrom, the Broadway, Robinsons-May, and Mervyn's and stuffed to its ramparts with shops, restaurants, and movie theaters, it's a wild success. Particularly good reasons to start your downtown exploration here include the local visitor bureau's helpful **San Diego International Visi-**

tor Center, at 11 Horton Plaza at the corner of First Avenue and F Street, 619/236-1232; the **Horton Plaza Farmers Market,** for uptown picnic fixings, good wines, and wonderful bakery goods; and the impressive **San Diego Repertory Theater Company,** with two stages here.

Horton Plaza inhabits the entire downtown "block" between Broadway and G St. and First and Fourth Avenues. The mall is regularly open Mon.–Fri. 10 a.m.–9 P.M., Saturday 10 a.m.–7 P.M., and Sunday 11 a.m.–6 P.M. (with later Saturday hours in summer and pre-Christmas). Restaurants, theaters, and some shops have extended hours. Walk here or take the trolley or bus, if at all possible, since parking in the underground lot is often nonexistent. For information on what's up, contact: Horton Plaza, 324 Horton Plaza, 619/238-1596 or toll-free 800/214-7467; www.horton-plaza.com.

The Gaslamp Quarter

Most of San Diego's venerable Victorian business buildings, constructed between the Civil War and World War I, are in the city's Gaslamp Quarter, the downtown area just east of Horton Plaza, between Fourth and Sixth Streets and Broadway and L Street. Notorious for "nefarious activity" during decades of decline, the quarter has been undergoing a Renaissance of sorts —with historic hotels, new shops, art galleries, trendy restaurants, and nightclubs at the forefront of this particular downtown revival.

Gaslamp District highlights include the **Horton Grand Hotel,** 619/544-1886, at Island and Third, a Victorian-style creation dating from the 1980s— or the 1880s, if you count original construction dates. The Horton Grand is a re-creation done in the spirit, if not the architectural truth, of two old downtown hotels otherwise doomed by redevelopment—the old Horton Grand Hotel on E Street and the Saddlery Hotel, also known as the Kahle Saddlery and even earlier, when Wyatt Earp stayed there, as the Brooklyn Ho(The bricks and balustrades on Fourth are from the Horton Grand, those on the other side from the Saddlery.) If you don't stay at the Horton Grand, at least wander the lobby areas and visit the small Chinese museum commemorating San Diego's vanished Chinatown.

Other neighborhood landmarks include the baroque revival-style **Louis Bank of Commerce**—known as the Golden Poppy when it served as a whorehouse—on Fifth between E and F Streets, the **Backesto Building** on Fifth at Market, and the Romanesque revival **George J. Keating Building** on F Street at Fifth.

One of Southern California's most popular hip urban events, the annual two-day food and music festival **San Diego Street Scene** takes over the Gaslamp Quarter on two consecutive days in September. To find out about other happenings in the neighborhood, call the **Gaslamp Quarter Association,** 619/233-5227.

For guided and self-guided historic tours, contact the **Gaslamp Quarter Foundation** headquarters, inside the William Heath Davis House at 410 Island (at Fourth), 619/233-4692—the office is open weekdays 10 a.m.–2 P.M., Saturday 10 a.m.–4 P.M., Sunday noon–4 P.M.—or pick up a free brochure/map at area visitor information centers. The foundation's fun self-guided audio tours can be arranged for almost any time, and guided tours leave from the Davis house every Saturday at 11 a.m. A $5 donation is requested for each tour.

Villa Montezuma

After Balboa Park it might be tough convincing the kids they want to do another museum, and, after Horton Plaza, that this old house has entertainment value. But it does. Gaudy and splendid, Villa Montezuma is one of the strangest, most opulent "High Victorians" remaining in California. Built for internationally renowned musician, writer, and spiritualist Jesse Shepard, it's something of a monument to the 1880s' theosophy movement. Shepard and his followers held musical seances and otherwise communed with the spirits here, providing an early—and elegant— example of California's historic fascination with unorthodox spiritual orthodoxy. Villa Montezuma, 1925 K St. (at 20th), is open Saturday and Sunday only, noon–4:30 P.M. Admission is $5, children 6–17 $2, free for children under age 6. For more information, call 619/239-2211.

Children's Museum/Museo de los Niños of San Diego

Since moving downtown from La Jolla in 1994, San Diego's children's museum has gone interactive in an even bigger way—and that's no technological toss-off. The idea here is that children need to "plug in" to the real world, not just virtual ones. Lessons in real life include **Identity/Identidad** and other bilingual exhibits, along with hand-puppet shows and other performances held in conjunction with hands-on workshops. **The Box Show,** a series of boxlike exhibits dedicated to both artistic and educational ends, includes Cora's Rain House, a giant tin building nestled into a recycled-water rainforest.

The children's museum, 200 W. Island Ave. (between Front and Union Sts.), is open Tues.–Sun. 10 a.m.–4 P.M., closed Monday and major holidays. Admission is $6 for adults and children age 3 and older, $3 for seniors. For current programs, events, and other information, call 619/233-5437.

Other Downtown Draws

Across from Horton Plaza's south side at 777 Front St. and adjacent to the haute shopping heaven is the **Paladion** shopping center, 619/232-1685. North of Horton's Plaza, along Broadway at Kettner, is the 1915 **Santa Fe Train Depot,** the city's Amtrak station these days, notably overshadowed by the 34-story **1 American Plaza** office tower. Part of the plaza is the downtown outpost of San Diego's **Museum of Contemporary Art,** 1001 Kettner Blvd. (at Broadway), 619/234-1001, www.mcasandiego.org, the museum's secondary locale housing part of the collection's 3,000 works. For more information on both museums, see La Jolla and Vicinity, below.

Farther east on Broadway, between First and Second Avenues., is the grand old **Spreckels Theater,** 121 Broadway, 619/235-9500, a popular local concert venue. Across the street and one block farther is the 1910 **U.S. Grant Hotel,** 326 Broadway, 619/232-3121, San Diego's most classically elegant hostelry, commissioned by Grant's widow. The U.S. Grant was restored to its original grandeur—do stop to see the lobby—in the 1980s after a painstaking $80 million renovation.

Another time-honored presence a bit farther afield is the **Firehouse Museum,** 1572 Columbia St. (near Cedar), 619/232-3473, with firefighting technology representing handcart and horse-drawn engine eras as well as the earlier ages of internal combustion engines.

AROUND SAN DIEGO BAY

A superlative harbor, San Diego Bay begins at Point Loma, where Cabrillo stepped ashore. Its fairly narrow mouth is created by the "island" city of Coronado, which is connected to San Diego's South Bay area by a narrow isthmus of sand. This seemingly tenuous connection actually forms the long, protected bay.

Starting at Point Loma, major features along the bay's long inland curve include the Cabrillo National Monument, an impressive land's end complete with venerable lighthouse, whale-watching platform, excellent visitor center, bayside trails, even tidepools.

Next come Shelter Island and Harbor Island, not natural islands but onetime shoals built into bayside real estate with the help of harbor dredging.

Fronting San Diego Bay and increasingly integrated with most everyone's idea of "downtown" is the Embarcadero, a bayside walkway along Harbor Drive that winds its way past an armada of vessels—some of them tour boats and cruise ships, others converted into gift shops and restaurants—and other harbor attractions.

Particularly noteworthy in the attractions category is the **San Diego Maritime Museum,** floating the foot of Ash Street. About a half-mile south is the art-deco B Street Pier, also known as the Cruise Ship Pier, local port for major cruise ship lines. Next south is the Broadway Pier, also known as the Excursion Pier, largely dedicated to sportfishing, whale-watching, and harbor tour companies. This is also the place to catch the San Diego–Coronado Ferry to Coronado Island.

Though San Diego's tuna fishing heyday is long gone, the next stop south is **Tuna Harbor,** headquarters for the American Tunaboat Association and also home to the very popular Fish Market restaurant and fresh-fish market. Navy ships may be tied up nearby; if so, on weekends they're usually open for tours.

Usually getting most of the neighborhood attention, though, is **Seaport Village,** a seafaring-themed shopping and restaurant development with turn-of-the-20th-century style. For children and nonshoppers, the best thing here goes 'round and 'round—the 1890 Looff Broadway Flying Horses Carousel, originally stabled at

Coney Island. Worth a stroll nearby is the Embarcadero Marine Park North, a grassy public park angling out into the bay.

Seaport Village ends at the San Diego Marriott Hotel and Marina, though the walkway wanders on. The striking San Diego Convention Center at the foot of Fifth, designed by Arthur Erickson and built by the Port of San Diego, is just beyond the hoWith its fiberglass "sails" and wavelike walls, the convention center could only be confused with a choppy day at the America's Cup. South of the convention center is the Embarcadero Marina Park South and the stunning Coronado Bay Bridge. South of the bridge and east of I-5 begins the region's South Bay.

Cabrillo National Monument

Here's a bit of history with open-air flair. This breathtaking 144-acre vantage point on the ocean edge of San Diego Bay commemorates Cabrillo's exploration of the California coastline in 1542. What actually marks the spot is the Point Loma Lighthouse (no longer in operation but open to the public), a newer lighthouse, various viewpoints, plus a winter whale-watching station, tide pools (explorable at low tide), trails, and a good visitor center. There are no food concessions, however, so bring a picnic or snacks if you'll be staying awhile.

Fully appreciate the breathtaking bay views by hiking the **Bayside Trail,** an asphalt road threading through old World War II military installations, meandering east along the bay. Watch sailboats and ships, not to mention the soaring sea birds—and, on aerially active days, U.S. Navy aircraft taking off from the North Island Naval Air Station across from the trail on Coronado Island. This two-mile round-trip (easy) begins near the lighthouse and typically takes just over one hour.

One of San Diego's best bets for **tidepooling** lies within a stone's throw of San Diego Bay, on the rocky western edge of the Point Loma Peninsula. At low tide, the tide pools near the Coast Guard station teem with ocean creatures tossed ashore at high tide—crabs, sometimes an

---

SAN DIEGO WHALE-WATCHING, BY LAND AND BY SEA

California is one of the world's premier whale-watching locations. The state's long coastline and natural vantage points, good harbors and specialized sportfishing and tour fleets, make whale-watching an immensely popular year-round pursuit for residents and visitors alike.

Most impressive is the annual offshore migration of the California gray whale, until recently an endangered species. In winter, gray whales migrate south along the coast from the frigid Bering Straits to the more tropical climate of Mexico's Baja California. Most boisterous—and most entertaining to watch—is the migration south in January, when mature bulls and breeding cows cruise California waters. Their splashy mating behavior—which often includes "breaching," or leaping up out of the water before slamming back to sea—is a particular thrill on offshore whale-watching tours. By February these newly pregnant females and promiscuous male hangers-on begin their return migration, sometimes passing, en route, southbound stragglers—

juveniles and immature whales of both sexes. In March gray whale cows with newborn calves start north from Mexico, easily visible from land, typically, because of their slow pace and tendency to travel close to shore.

During the summer, blue whales and humpback whales can be observed near southern California's **Channel Islands National Park.**

Sublime and sunny San Diego, with balmy beach weather even in winter, attracts pods and pods of fair-weather whale-watchers. Prime viewpoint in winter is **Cabrillo National Monument** at the mouth of the bay, outfitted with an observation platform. (Since Cabrillo is often crowded, keep in mind that there are many other good locations along the coast.) The **Scripps Institution of Oceanography,** the **San Diego Natural History Museum,** and local **sportfishing and tour companies** all offer ocean-going whale-watching tours. Contact local visitor information centers for current details.

octopus or jellyfish—and also reveal more stationary residents of the rocks, including anemones and starfish. It's okay to look, but not touch, since the tide pools are protected reserves. Ask park rangers about expected low tides. To reach the tide pools, go north from the visitor center. The first road to the left leads to the Coast Guard station and the peninsula's western shore.

Cabrillo National Monument, 1800 Cabrillo Memorial Dr. (the southern end of Cabrillo Memorial Dr., Hwy. 209), is open in winter daily 9 a.m.–5:15 P.M., though the Bayside Trail is open only 9 a.m.–4 P.M. In summer the park is open until sunset, with extended trail hours. Admission is $5 per vehicle, $2 per person entering by bicycle or on foot, and free for seniors with Golden Age Passports, the disabled, and children age 16 and under. For more information, contact: Cabrillo National Monument, 619/557-5450; www.nps.gov/cabr.

Shelter and Harbor Islands

Shelter Island's main claim to fame is as the yacht-harbor home of the America's Cup international sailing competitions, sponsored by the San Diego Yacht Club. But Shelter Island has its charms even without the America's Cup hubbub, most notably a family-friendly fishing pier, yachter's hangouts such as the Fiddler's Green and the Brigantine, and "tiki" resort hotels and restaurants noted for their Polynesian and faux-Polynesian style.

Harbor Island is another yachter's haven, this one close to the San Diego Airport and not coincidentally filled to the gills with waterfront hotels and restaurants.

San Diego Maritime Museum

Star of the show here is the three-masted *Star of India*—the oldest iron-hulled merchant ship still afloat, first launched from the Isle of Man in 1863 as the *Euterpe.* The 1904 *Medea,* a relative youngster hailing from Scotland, was quite a beauty in her day—with imported teak decks and housing, finished inside with quarter-sawn English oak. The museum's gift shop is holed up next door inside the *Berkeley,* an 1898 ferry most famous for serving as rescue ship during the 1906 San Francisco earthquake and fire.

The San Diego Maritime Museum, 1306 N. Harbor Dr., at the foot of Ash Street (the *Star of India* floats at the foot of Grape St.), is open daily 9 a.m.–8 P.M. Admission is $6 adults ($12 for an entire family), $4 seniors and children ages 13–17, $2 children ages 6–12. The museum is supported entirely by private contributions, making this a particularly good place for seafaring history buffs to make an extra donation. For more information, call 619/234-9153 or try www.sdmaritime.com.

The South Bay

National City is known for its **Naval Station San Diego,** aka the 32nd Street Naval Base, home port of the U.S. Pacific Fleet, not to mention the area's shipbuilding yards and the **National City Marine Terminal.**

The South Bay's **Chula Vista** is famous for its **ARCO Training Center** for Olympic athletes, one of only three in the U.S.—the other two dedicated to winter sports—and the **Sweetwater Marsh National Wildlife Refuge.**

Imperial Beach, in the same-named community, stars the **Imperial Beach Pier** and plenty of warm, white sand—the most essential ingredient for its fabulous **U.S. Open Sandcastle Competition** held here each year. Following the sand from Imperial Beach northwest onto the strand leads to **Silver Strand State Beach,** a superb swimming beach on the way to Coronado, justifiably popular with families. For more information on Coronado-area beaches, see Coronado: Crown of the Bay.

Southernmost, adjacent to the U.S.-Mexican border, is **Border Field State Park and Beach.** People avoid the beach here like the plague, since chronic sewage contamination from Tijuana has made swimming unsafe. And beyond the beach this otherwise serene wetlands preserve along the U.S.-Mexican border seems like a war zone, with Border Patrol helicopters slicing the air overhead in search of, and to deter, illegal immigrants. It's difficult to ignore the intensity of this daily San Diego–area drama. The state park is adjacent to the **Tijuana River National Estuarine Sanctuary National Wildlife Refuge,** with visitor center, guided walks and trails, and ongoing research facilities in Imperial Beach.

ROBERT HOLMES/CALIFORNIA DIVISION OF TOURISM

Imperial Beach

BEACH TOWNS AND BEACHES

Beyond downtown, starting north of Point Loma, are the oceanside communities of Ocean Beach, Mission Beach, and Pacific Beach. Still farther north are the fairly exclusive and expensive communities of La Jolla and Del Mar, also included within San Diego's city limits.

Ocean Beach
Strung out along Sunset Cliffs Boulevard just north of Point Loma is Ocean Beach, "O.B." in locals' lingo. Just beyond the western end of the I-8 Freeway, Ocean Beach is San Diego's "farthest out" community—an unusual and unusually settled beach neighborhood with a hip (and hippie) history, an unusual collection of old-timers, surfers, young families, hipsters of all ages, and a smattering of ne'er-do-wells. To get a feel for the place, head for the **Ocean Beach Pier** (though beaches nearest the pier are sometimes unsavory) and stroll the **Newport Avenue** commercial district. Dog lovers, note that Ocean

Beach's **Dog Beach** is one of only three in the county (along with Coronado and Del Mar) where canines can cavort sans leash. (Watch your step.) For more seclusion, head south to the cove beach at **Sunset Cliffs,** on the Point Loma Peninsula—popular with locals and surfers, accessible at low tide and only via slippery sandstone pathways or from the stairways at the feet of Bermuda and Santa Cruz Avenues.

Mission Beach and Mission Bay
Next stop north, beyond the San Diego River, is Mission Beach—about 17 miles of ocean beach and boardwalk plus Mission Bay, onetime wetlands refashioned, in the 1960s, into a faux bay resort area with man-made beaches, hotels, motels, marinas, and condominiums. When passing through in 1542, Cabrillo himself called it a "false bay," since the outlet led straight into the swamp.

Inland, Mission Bay Park is largely undeveloped and "natural"—meaning, in this case, undeveloped—a park popular with San Diegans looking for open space and bracing saltwater breezes for jogging, walking, biking, kite-flying, and water sports. If you're interested in the view from the water but are without your own boat, get around via the **Harbor Hopper,** 858/488-2720, water taxi service or take a sunset cruise on the *Bahia Belle,* 858/488-0551, docked at the Bahia Hotel on West Mission Bay Drive.

Attractions along the ocean include both **South Mission** and **North Mission Beaches,** waterfront walkways, and grassy parks. The **Belmont Park** area, once an abandoned amusement park and boardwalk, now includes shops and shopping in addition to the historic **Giant Dipper** wooden roller coaster and equally venerable **The Plunge** swimming pool.

Sea World
People either love or hate Mission Bay's Sea World, an Anheuser-Busch entertainment park with an ocean animal theme. Those who love Sea World say it offers families the chance to see unusual or endangered sea life up close and personal, a positive experience that increases environmental awareness. Those who hate it point out that with friends such as these—and with an excellent aquarium just north, in La Jolla, not to mention San Diego County's excep-

tional zoos—the beleaguered and endangered creatures of the sea hardly need enemies.

A recent controversy here, for example, involved the Shamu Backstage killer whale exhibit, interactive in the sense that park guests feed, pet, and participate in training Sea World's killer whales. All in all, this is the water-park equivalent of a petting zoo, animal rights activists say. They believe that rather than capturing, breeding, and training whales to perform tricks, Sea World should dedicate its considerable resources to making the real world safe for whales —these captive whales, for starters—and other wild things. Sea World officials respond that whale participation is "voluntary," that whales can swim away—albeit only so far as the next pool—if they wish to avoid their fans.

Of course the traditional star performers of the Sea World show, here and elsewhere, are **Shamu** the killer whale and **Baby Shamu,** actually stage names for a half-dozen or more individual whales. The aforementioned **Shamu Backstage** encounter is adjacent to Shamu Stadium; visitors view the whales through a 70-foot window in the 1.7 million gallon pool while waiting in line to touch them. And if that's not enough Shamu to do, the kids can pose for pictures with an ersatz Shamu and Baby Shamu in two-acre **Shamu's Happy Harbor,** an active—and interactive—playground.

Increasingly, "encounter" and "interactive" are the watchwords at Sea World, because more than anything else, people want to touch—or almost touch—animals they would never see, even at a distance, in real life.

So there's **Shark Encounter,** a three-part exhibit that permits visitors to commune with captive sharks from above, below, and "within" their habitat. A transparent acrylic tunnel allows you to "walk through" the shark tank. At **Penguin Encounter,** a moving sidewalk takes you through a glassed-in Arctic and the hundreds of emperor penguins gliding over glacierlike ice and into the water. At **Rocky Point Preserve,** visitors interact with—feed, pet, and talk to— bottlenose dolphins. Sea World also includes a **California Tide Pool** touch pool and a **Forbidden Reef**—kids love anything that's forbidden— with bat rays and moray eels.

But for those who can afford it, none of the "encounter" exhibits come close to the popularity of Sea World's **interactive dolphin program,** where an extra $125 buys you the chance to don a wetsuit, do a little dolphin training, and then take a dip in the dolphin pool.

There's more to see and do at Sea World, open daily from at least 10 a.m. to dusk, from 9 a.m. in summer (call for current summer schedule). As you might expect, the experience is expensive, with admission $40 adults, $30 children ages 3–11, plus food, high-priced mementos, and parking ($4 motorcycles, $7 cars, and $9 RVs). Behind-the-scenes tours, in addition to other educational activities and the dolphin interaction program, are available by arrangement.

Sea World is in Mission Bay; to get here from I-5, exit at Sea World Drive and follow the signs. For more information, contact Sea World, 1720 S. Shores Rd., 619/226-3901 for recorded information or 619/226-3815.

Pacific Beach

Hippest of all local beach towns these days is Pacific Beach or "P.B." in the local vernacular, where surf, surfers, skates, skaters, hip shops and just hangin' out define local culture. Most of the action is at the beach, at the **Lahaina Beach House** at 710 Oliver, 858/270-3888, at **Garnet Street** shops, and, after dark, at the **Society Billiard Café,** 1051 Garnet Ave., 858/272-7665. Unique here is the **Crystal Pier,** the only pier in California to include a hotel. Social historians and surf scene voyeurs can visit **Tourmaline Surfing Park** (Tourmaline St. at La Jolla Blvd.), the only stretch of local coastline dedicated exclusively to worshipers of the next wave, however grizzled they may be.

LA JOLLA AND VICINITY: SEASIDE SOPHISTICATION

Along the coast just north of Pacific Beach is the village of La Jolla, seven miles of sublime coastline that serves as San Diego's answer to the Riviera—a sophisticated red-tile-roofed Mediterranean image local commerce cultivates quite profitably, and one that attracts old-money minions as well as movie stars.

La Jolla (La HOY-yah, though people here say, simply, "the Village") means "jewel" in Spanish, or, according to local Native American tradition, "hole" or "cave." Both meanings are fitting. Hammered for eons by the relentless surf, the coastal bluffs beneath La Jolla's dazzling real estate are laced with caves, large and small, some explorable by land, some by sea. Other natural attractions are local beaches—including the infamous Windansea Beach, the topnotch but highly territorial surf scene described by Tom Wolfe in *The Pump House Gang*—and area parks, including Torrey Pines State Reserve, sanctuary for about 6,000 very rare pine trees.

Not rare, however, is the human imperative to see, be seen, and make the scene—these, as well as shopping, are major pastimes in and around La Jolla's upmarket downtown. Any and all downtown adventures are best undertaken on foot, since finding a place to park can be all but impossible.

For more information about La Jolla, and for friendly practical assistance from the volunteer staff, contact the **La Jolla Town Council,** 7734 Herschell, La Jolla, 858/454-1444. Since La Jolla is technically part of the city of San Diego, information is also available from the International Visitor Information Center at Horton Plaza in downtown San Diego, 619/236-1232.

Along the Coast: Ellen Browning Scripps Park and Beyond

La Jolla's aqua-blue ocean and adjacent beaches are beautiful but unbelievably popular. If personal space and peace are on your agenda, you won't find either here. Instead, head north along the coast.

Nonetheless, one of La Jolla's jewels is Ellen Browning Scripps Park overlooking La Jolla Cove, a palm-lined promenade where everyone goes to see the sea scene (and be seen). Even children regularly dip into the Scripps legacy; a wonderful local diversion is the **Children's Pool** at the park's south end, with shallow waters and a curved beach protected by a seawall. In recent years, sea lions basking on **Shell Beach** just to the north have provided free entertainment.

South toward Pacific Beach is San Diego's surfing paradise, an area including mythic **Windansea Beach** and **Tourmaline Surfing Park,** neither particularly fun for "outsiders."

North from Children's Pool, starting offshore just south of Point La Jolla, is the **San Diego–La Jolla Underwater Park.** Most popular for skin diving and snorkeling is northern **La Jolla Cove.** Lining La Jolla Bay north of the cove are the town's famed **La Jolla Caves** (small admission), some of them accessible by a stairway starting at the La Jolla Cave and Shell Shop on Coast Boulevard. The best **tide pools** around are along the coast north of the Scripps Pier at the Scripps Institution of Oceanography on La Jolla Shores Drive, the former site of the Scripps aquarium. **La Jolla Shores beaches,** including those below residential areas, are among the best for swimming and sunbathing, along with Torrey Pines State Beach and Del Mar Beach farther north. Between La Jolla Shores and Torrey Pines is an almost inaccessible, unauthorized nude beach known as **Black's Beach,** best reached from Torrey Pines at low tide. For more on that area, see Torrey Pines State Reserve and Beach, below.

THE SCRIPPS LEGACY

Ellen Browning Scripps was half-sister of newspaper publisher Edward Wyllis Scripps, founder of the United Press (UP) newspaper syndicate. A respected journalist too, Ellen Browning Scripps also made millions in real estate—good fortune she shared with Southern California by founding Scripps College in Claremont and by endowing, with her brother, the Scripps Institution of Oceanography in La Jolla. Part of the genteel community of artists, writers, scientists, and just plain wealthy people that settled La Jolla at the turn of the century, she was also a patron of architecture—in particular local architect Irving J. Gill, who designed her 1915 home, now San Diego's Museum of Contemporary Art, and various public buildings here.

In a sense the Scripps family's philanthropic contributions to the community set the stage for present-day La Jolla's cultural influence, with its renowned Salk Institute and the sprawling University of California at San Diego, which now includes the Scripps Institution of Oceanography, the Scripps-affiliated Stephen Birch Aquarium-Museum, and the nationally recognized La Jolla Playhouse theater program.

La Jolla cove

Museum of Contemporary Art

This 1915 Irving Gill original is the primary location of San Diego's Museum of Contemporary Art, 700 Prospect, 858/454-3541; www.mca-sandiego.org. Once home to Ellen Browning Scripps, it reopened in March 1996 after a somewhat controversial two-year, $9.25 million renovation and expansion. Traveling exhibits tend toward the provocative and cutting edge—or, simply, "edge," as they say in L.A.—as do shows from the post-1950s permanent collection. (Call for current program information.) A smaller museum branch in downtown San Diego, on Kettner Boulevard at Broadway, 619/234-1001, is also well worth a stop.

Both museums are open Tues.–Sat. 10 a.m.–5 P.M., Sunday noon–5 P.M., closed Thanksgiving, Christmas, and New Year's Day. The La Jolla museum is also open Wednesday night until 8 P.M. Admission is $4 for adults, $2 for seniors (ages 65 and older), military, and students (ages 12–18), and free for children under age 12. Both museums are free on the first Tuesday and Sunday of every month.

Birch Aquarium at Scripps

The Birch Aquarium at Scripps is the public information center for the University of California's renowned Scripps Institution of Oceanography. Aquarium exhibits include a replica of Scripps Canyon, the underwater valley just off the La Jolla coast, and an abundance of re-created

marine habitats—a kelp forest, for example, and aquatic homes for creatures such as the bioluminescent "flashlight fish." Exhibits in the adjacent building, collected under the banner **Exploring the Blue Planet,** delve into oceanography as science. The simulated submarine dive has major kid appeal. Another fascination: the "ocean supermarket" display of everyday items derived from the ocean.

The Birch Aquarium at Scripps, 2300 Expedition Way, 858/534-3474, is on the edge of the University of California, San Diego campus. The museum is open daily 9 a.m.–5 P.M. (last admission at 4:30 P.M.), closed on Thanksgiving and Christmas. Admission is $8.50 for adults, $7.50 for seniors (age 60 and older), $6 students, $5 for kids (ages 3–17). Parking is $3. Visit the aquarium website at www.aquarium.ucsd.edu.

La Jolla Playhouse

The Tony Award–winning La Jolla Playhouse, 2910 La Jolla Village Dr., 858/550-1010, actually performing at two small theaters at the Mandell Weiss Center for the Performing Arts on the University of California campus, was founded in 1947 by Gregory Peck and like-minded theater buffs. By producing original musicals and plays that subsequently made a name for themselves, such as *Big River, A Walk in the Woods,* The Who's *Tommy,* and various Neil Simon works, the La Jolla Playhouse has established itself in the past decades as one of the most innovative regional theaters in the country. The theater's performance season runs from May through October. Admission varies, but tickets are typically in the $25–40 range. Call for box office hours, which change throughout the year. The Mandell Weiss Center for the Performing Arts is on the University of California campus, La Jolla Village Drive at Revelle College Drive. For current program information, call 858/550-1010, or visit the playhouse website at www.lajollaplayhouse.com.

Also worth a stop on campus, even if you're just passing through, is the **Stuart Collection** of outdoor art. Many of the outdoor pieces stand within an easy walk of the whimsical Theodore Geisel Library, named after the late La Jolla resident better known as Dr. Seuss.

Elsewhere Downtown and Around

Girard Avenue downtown is prime time for La Jolla shopping. Among the multitude of cool shops here—not all of them expensive, by the way—is **Gallery Alexander,** 7850 Girard (between Wall and Silverado), 858/459-9433, with whimsical and unusual items in home furnishings, ceramics, glassware, and jewelry. Also try **Gallery Eight,** 7454 Girard, 858/454-9781.

Poke around elsewhere, too, looking for places such as **John Cole's Book Shop,** in a historic house overlooking the ocean at 780 Prospect (at Eads Ave.), 858/454-4766, and **The Artful Soul,** 1237-C Prospect St. (between Ivanhoe and Cave), 858/459-2009, locally owned and operated and quite casual, showcasing good work by about 20 local artists and artisans. Jewelry is the mainstay, each piece identified by artist, along with small gift items.

To get the big picture of La Jolla and vicinity, head to **Mount Soledad,** reached by following Nautilus Street east. From the summit of this tinder-dry hill, the area's traditional site for outdoor Easter Sunday services, at night the headlights and taillights of the traffic flow below on I-5 seem like endless dazzling strands of diamonds and rubies.

Torrey Pines State Reserve and Beach

Here's a story of endangered species that does not star human beings as the culprits, for a change. Protected in this small preserve are about 10,000 Torrey pines *(Pinus torreyana).*

The rarest pine trees in the United States, these beautifully primeval, strange, and scraggly five-needle pines represent an Ice Age species endangered by too-specific climatic and soil needs. Get oriented at the attractive 1923 adobe-style visitor center, once a private lodge. Short and easy hiking trails wind through the semi-desert forests.

Below the heavily eroded bluffs is Torrey Pines State Beach, one of the most beautiful in San Diego County. Adjacent, technically in Del Mar, is **Los Penasquitos Lagoon,** wetlands that serve as wildlife refuge and bird sanctuary, an area almost destroyed in the 1960s by the construction of the Pacific Coast Highway route here.

Torrey Pines is north of La Jolla Village, just off N. Torrey Pines Road. To reach the preserve from I-5, exit at Genesee Avenue and head west. Turn north (right) onto N. Torrey Pines Road. To reach the beach from I-5, exit at Carmel Valley Road and head west. One parking lot is near the beach, another near the preserve's visitor center. Admission is free, but parking is $2 with a $1 discount for seniors. The beach is open daily, 8 a.m. to sunset; the visitor center is open 9 a.m. to sunset. For more information, contact Torrey Pines State Reserve and Beach, 858/755-2063; www.torreypine.org.

Del Mar: Where the Turf Meets the Surf

For Del Mar's surf, head for **Del Mar Beach.** To watch the sunset, locals and visitors alike gather up top, on the bluffs at the end of 15th Street. For Del Mar's turf, head to the fairgrounds. Del Mar is most famous for its elegant art-deco Spanish colonial **Del Mar Race Track,** "Where the Turf Meets the Surf." Recently reconstructed, the track is the place for some serious thoroughbred racing from late July into mid-September. The show here has always been something of a star-studded affair. The Del Mar Thoroughbred Club was organized in the 1930s by entertainer Bing Crosby and some of his cronies, because Crosby wanted some of the glitz and glitter of glamour racing close to his home in Rancho Santa Fe. Mostly serious gamblers and more sedate business types make up the crowd these days. But you can pony up on the ponies even in the off-season, thanks to the new age of satellite betting. Admission to the Del Mar Race Track,

2260 Jimmy Durante Blvd. (Via de la Valle Rd. at Coast Blvd.), is $4 ($7 for grandstand seats). For more information, call 619/755-1141; www .dmtc.com.

Upscale accommodations and restaurants aren't hard to find in and around Del Mar; there are also some great deals. (For local suggestions, see Staying in San Diego, below.) Shopping opportunities also aren't hard to find, especially in upscale malls such as the Del Mar Plaza. Good deals can be found here, too. For example: relatively inexpensive for earthy natural-fiber women's wear is **Chico's,** 858/792-7080. Stop by the **Del Mar Chamber of Commerce,** 1104 Camino del Mar, 858/755-4844, for more information.

CORONADO: CROWN OF THE BAY

Across from San Diego's Embarcadero is Coronado, an "island" connected to the mainland only by a sandy isthmus and by a sky-skimming arched bridge. A separate city reached from downtown San Diego either by ferry or via the San Diego–Coronado Bay Bridge, Coronado boasts the North Island U.S. Naval Air Station—Charles Lindbergh's departure point for his famous round-the-world flight—and, on the east, the U.S. Naval Amphibious Base, home for the elite Navy SEALS.

Not too surprisingly, the military has, in a sense, created the community here, a culture that revolves around the sound and fury of naval air technology and the needs and interests of retired naval officers and their families. Well-heeled tourists and celebrities are also well attended on Coronado, however, and have been for over a century. The local roll call of fame includes Charles Lindbergh, the Duke and Duchess of Windsor, 14 U.S. presidents, and a dizzying number of stars from both the stage and the silver screen. The list also includes Frank Baum, who wrote *The Wizard of Oz* while living here. **The Wizard of Oz House** still stands, at 1101 Star Park Circle.

For more information about Coronado, contact the very helpful **Coronado Visitor Information** office, 1047 B Ave., Coronado, CA 92118, 619/437-8788, fax 619/437-6006; www.coronado.ca.us.

Hotel del Coronado: The Victorian Heart of Local History

The island's historic centerpiece is the astonishing Hotel del Coronado—known affectionately as the "Hotel Del" or, simply, "the Del"—one of California's grand old hotels, built in 1888, a national historic landmark. When it opened, this sprawling barn-red-and-white Victorian, with its wood shingles, turrets, and cupolas, was the largest structure outside New York City to be lighted with electricity. (Thomas Edison himself officiated at the switch-on ceremony for the hotel's first Christmas tree.) Among other movies, the 1959 comedy *Some Like It Hot,* starring Tony Curtis, Jack Lemmon, and Marilyn Monroe, was filmed at the Hotel Del.

Meander through the lobby and along dark-wood downstairs corridors, where photographs and other mementos tell the hotel's story, and stroll the gorgeous grounds. Fairly recent addi-

When it opened in 1888, the Hotel Del Coronado was the largest building outside New York City to be lighted with electricity.

ROBERT HOLMES/CALIFORNIA DIVISION OF TOURISM

tions include the craftsman-style **Duchess of Windsor Cottage.** Now a meeting hall, the cottage was onetime Coronado home of Wallis Warfield Spencer—the Duchess of Windsor after King Edward abdicated the English throne to marry her.

John D. Spreckels, the sugar-refining millionaire, bought the Coronado Beach Company and its in-progress Hotel del Coronado in 1887—just as San Diego's first boom days were busting. But Spreckels, whose San Diego–area development projects included water engineering, railroads, and Coronado's unique "tent city" resort, survived even the dark days in style. The entire Spreckels family relocated here from San Francisco after the 1906 earthquake and fire; their former home is now the center of Coronado's **Glorietta Bay Inn.**

Guided tours of the Hotel del Coronado, at last report $10 per person, were being offered again starting in June 2000, following the hotel's $50 million restoration of its grand centerpiece, the Victorian building. Call the hotel at 619/435-6611, or try www.hoteldel.com, for details and reservations.

For the entire Coronado story, stop by the free **Coronado Historical Museum** on Loma Ave., 619/435-7242, open Wed.–Sat. 10 a.m.–4 P.M. and Sunday noon–4 P.M.

Seeing and Doing Coronado

Coronado's other present-day pleasures include sun, sand, sailing, windsurfing, 15 miles of shoreline bike paths—you can ride all the way to Imperial Beach—and specialty shopping along downtown Coronado's revitalized **Orange Avenue** and at the Seaport-Village like **Ferry Landing Marketplace.** In addition to its city pool, its 130-acre municipal golf course, its 18 parks, and its 18 public tennis courts, Coronado offers other diversions. **Gondola Cruises,** 619/429-6317, shoves off from the Loews resort on Venetian-style tours of the Coronado Cays canals. Three-hour guided **Navy base tours** of North Island Naval Air Station are offered on Fridays by Old Town Trolley Tours, 619/298-8687. Or take a **Coronado Walking Tour,** 619/435-5892 or 619/435-5993. And you can always see what's playing at the **Coronado Playhouse** on Strand Way, 619/435-4856, or the **Lamb's Players Theatre** on Orange Ave., 619/437-0600.

CORONADO TRIPPING

Getting around Coronado is fun (except on particularly hectic weekends), thanks to its walkable streets lined with trees and bungalows, its paved bike paths, and the **Coronado 904 Shuttle,** 619/233-3004, $1 fare.

Getting to Coronado is even more fun, especially if you take the **Bay Ferry** from the Broadway Pier in San Diego to Coronado's Ferry Landing at First and B Streets. Ferries leave San Diego every hour on the hour 9 A.M.–9 P.M. Sun.–Thurs. (until 10 on weekend nights), and return from Coronado every hour on the half-hour, from 9:30 A.M.–9:30 P.M. Sun.–Thurs.(until 10:30 P.M. on weekend nights). Ferry fare is $2 (pedestrians and bicyclists only), 50 cents extra if you BYOB (bring your own bike). **San Diego Harbor Excursion water taxi,** 619/235-8294, travels to Ferry Landing Marketplace, the Hotel Del, and Le Meridien from Seaport Village on the mainland.

It's also fairly exciting to drive over. It's like riding a rainbow, gliding up and then over the soaring arch of the **San Diego–Coronado Bay Bridge** (Hwy. 75). The toll is $1 heading into Coronado—free with two or more people in the car—and free returning to the mainland.

Coronado also sponsors an almost endless series of special events—from the down-home **Coronado Flower Show** in Spreckels Park every spring and **Art in the Park** on the first and third Sunday of each month to a dazzling **Fourth of July** parade and fireworks. A **Coronado Christmas** is quite eventful, from the tree-lighting ceremonies at the Hotel Del and Santa Claus (sometimes in sunglasses) to caroling, choirs, and—reminiscent of a tradition started locally by Frank Baum—children's story hours. Coronado's Christmas **Parade of Lights,** with every boat in sight decked out in Christmas finery, is usually scheduled for one week in mid-December.

Coronado Beaches

Coronado's spectacular white-sand beaches are almost equally revered. Just oceanward from the Hotel Del is unbelievably broad **Coronado Beach,** typically uncrowded even in summer, since locals prefer beaches just north and south.

COURTESY CORONADO VISITOR INFORMATION

*stopping to smell the
flowers at the Coronado
Flower Show in
Speckels Park*

On the island's bay side are several smaller, more protected beaches.

Silver Strand State Beach, 619/435-5184, extends the entire length of Coronado's sandy isthmus, with beaches on both sides of Silver Strand Blvd. (Hwy. 75), from near Hotel del Coronado to Imperial Beach. This popular family beach, great for swimming, was named for the small silver seashells washed up along the shoreline. Beyond lifeguards, restrooms, and other basic services, facilities here include first-come RV campsites (self-contained only; no hookups); call for current fees. Silver Strand is open daily, 8 a.m.–9 P.M. in summer, until 8 P.M. during the spring, until 7 P.M. during winter. Beach use is free, though there is a parking fee (free from Labor Day through March). For more information about Silver Strand and other area state parks and beaches, contact **California State Parks, San Diego Coast District Headquarters,** 9609 Waples St., Ste. 200, San Diego, CA 92121, 619/642-4200, fax 619/642-4222.

ARTFUL, ENTERTAINING SAN DIEGO

San Diego is renowned for the art museums and other cultural riches collected in Balboa Park, and for both the **Old Globe Shakespeare Festival** and **La Jolla Playhouse** theater programs. The **California Ballet Company, San Diego Opera, San Diego Symphony,** and **San Diego Civic Light Opera** are also center stage on the local arts scene. And the **La Jolla Symphony,** the **La Jolla Chamber Music Society,** and other music groups are still going strong. Touring concerts and other national troupes perform both at downtown venues and at area college and university campuses—the University of California, San Diego, San Diego State University, local community colleges, and private colleges and universities, which are also good bets for guest speakers and eclectic special events. Pick up local newspapers to find out what's going on where. Local papers also publish listings of local art galleries; many are concentrated in the Gaslamp Quarter, in La Jolla, and elsewhere along the coast.

Though Balboa Park's three stages and the La Jolla Playhouse are local theatrical stars, smaller repertory groups and venues abound—including the acclaimed **Blackfriars Theatre** downtown at 121 Broadway, Ste. 203, 619/232-4088; the contemporary **San Diego Repertory Theater,** 79 Horton Plaza, 619/235-8025; and the cabaret-style **Coronado Playhouse,** 1775 Strand Way, 619/435-4856.

For a fairly comprehensive overview of the San Diego arts, including web links to many organizations and institutions, contact **Art & Sol;** www.sandiegoartandsol.com.

Mainstream movie theaters are everywhere; multiple multiplexes cluster at area malls and elsewhere. Often the most challenging cinema is served forth from smaller, sometimes historic theaters. Happening in Hillcrest, for example, is the **Hillcrest Cinemas** multiplex, 3965 Fifth Ave., 619/299-2100, showing foreign and art films. The art-revival house **Ken Cinema** on Adams Ave., 619/283-5909, is brought to you by the same folks. The **Sherwood Auditorium** at the Museum of Contemporary Art in La Jolla, 700 Prospect, 619/454-2594, also screens classic and foreign films.

Entertaining San Diego

San Diego *is* entertaining, from its distinctive neighborhood bar scenes and dance clubs to respectable jazz and rock venues. Again, local newspapers are the best source for what's going on while you're in town. An eclectic around-town club-scene cruise for older hipsters might include, for acoustic jazz, **Croce's** in the Gaslamp Quarter, 802 Fifth Ave., 619/233-4355; the top-flight jazz venue **Chris' Shores Grill** on the top floor of the Summer House Inn in La Jolla, 7955 La Jolla Shores Dr., 858/459-0541; and, for live rock, R&B, reggae, and whatever, the Quonset-hut-chic **Belly Up Tavern** in Solana Beach, 143 S. Cedros Ave., 858/481-9022. And there's always **Planet Hollywood** at Horton Plaza, 619/702-7827, and the also loud **Hard Rock Cafe** in La Jolla, 858/454-5101. If the arthritis and bursitis aren't giving you too much grief, consider headin' out for a country-western stomp at **In Cahootz** in Mission Valley, 5373 Mission Center Rd., 619/291-8635. Otherwise, it's safe to settle in at the bar at the **U.S. Grant Hotel** downtown, 619/232-3121, for great local blues and jazz, or soak up some classy piano-bar comfort at the **Westgate Hotel** downtown, 619/238-1818, and at **Hotel del Coronado** across the water, 619/522-8262.

EVENTFUL SAN DIEGO

With the sublime weather here, it's little wonder that so many San Diego events, among them open-air theater and street festivals, are staged outdoors. Unique or oddball local events can be the most fun, so while you're here ask around and study local newspapers. Museums, colleges, and universities also sponsor a variety of unusual activities.

Mid-December through mid- March is **whale-watching** season, when California gray whales make their northern migration. And in January, catch the **San Diego Marathon** as it winds 26.2 miles down the coast from Carlsbad. The ever-popular international **Festival of Animation,** staged in La Jolla at the Museum of Contemporary Art's Sherwood Auditorium, runs from mid-January through April; the *Sick and Twisted*

FUN NEAR BALBOA: HILLCREST AND VICINITY

Just north of Balboa Park and its fairly traditional ambience is Hillcrest, the one San Diego neighborhood noted for its eccentricities. This conservative city's gay district, centered along Washington and University Avenues between First and Fifth, Hillcrest is also the place to sample the artsy bohemian life, San Diego–style—the small record and bookshops, eclectic art films, small theaters, and good casual restaurants. Redevelopment is the watchword here, though, as elsewhere in San Diego—so hurry, before it all gets too upscale and safely cool.

For music classics and what's new internationally, spin into **Off The Record**, 3849 Fifth Ave. (at University), 619/298-4755. Some of San Diego's best independent bookstores are located in Hillcrest, including **Grounds for Murder**, 3940 Fourth St. (at Washington), 619/299-9500, which provides a vacation's worth of whodunits; **Bountiful Books**, 3834 Fifth Ave. between University and Robinson, 619/491-0664, which boasts more than 20,000 new, used and rare titles; and **Fifth Avenue Books**, 3838 Fifth Ave. between University and Robinson, 619/291-4660, which offers collectible first editions. One of the best bookstores in town, though, is been-there-forever **Blue Door Books**, 3823 Fifth Ave. (at University), 619/298-8610, locally famous for the Lawrence Ferlinghetti poem the poet wrote in honor of the bookstore.

The **Hillcrest Theater**, 3965 Fifth Ave., 619/299-2100, showing artsy independent and foreign films, is prominent at colorful **Village Hillcrest,** a neo-retro-looking contemporary complex at Fifth and Washington. Underground public parking is available here, if you're having little luck elsewhere. For original plays, head over to tiny **Quentin Crisp Theatre**, 3704 Sixth Ave. (at Pennsylvania), 619/688-9210, which stages controversial and quirky plays like *Denial of the Fittest,* a one-woman show written and performed by Judith Sloan.

For coffee and philosophical conversation, *the* place is **The Coffee Bean & Tea Leaf** at 3865 Fifth Ave. (at University), 619/298-5908. Good neighborhood eateries include, for the kids, the faux-'50s **Corvette Diner** at 3946 Fifth Ave. between University and Washington, 619/542-1001, and, more for grown-ups, fun **Kemo Sabe**, 3958 Fifth between University and Washington, 619/220-6802, with its contemporary twists on ethnic favorites. You'll also find Thai food and taco shops on and around University near Fifth.

Farther east along University, at Eighth, is the **Uptown District** complex, another emblem of neighborhood redevelopment. For an eclectic collection of antiqueries, continue east on Washington, north on Park and Mission until it becomes **Adams Avenue.**

---

short-subject collection is screened after midnight. Major San Diego spring events include the **Ocean Beach Kite Festival** in March; the **San Diego Crew Classic,** the **Downtown Art-Walk,** and the **Coronado Flower Show** in April; and the **Pacific Beach Block Party,** the Olympic-caliber **Del Mar National Horseshow,** and Old Town's **Cinco de Mayo** festivities in May.

In June, come for the **San Diego County Fair** at the fairgrounds in Del Mar, the **Mostly Mozart Festival** downtown in the Spreckels Theater, the annual **Ocean Beach Street Fair and Chili Cook-Off,** the **San Diego International Triathlon,** and the **Rock 'n' Roll Marathon.** Also in June, the **Twilight in the Park** summer concert series in Balboa Park begins, continuing through August. In July, the annual **San Diego Lesbian and Gay Pride Parade** is a huge draw, with a rally and festival well into the night. Also in July,

Sand Castle Days at the Imperial Beach Pier is a big hit, fun in the sun along with serious competitive sand-castle construction, along with the **Sizzling Summer Jazz Festival** on Coronado. The **Hillcrest Cityfest Street Fair** comes in August, along with the **Thundertub Regatta** at Mission Bay, part of America's Finest City Week festivities, and the immensely popular **San Diego Comic Convention** happens at the convention center. The convention pays homage to comic books, cartoon and comic art, and comic artists.

The biggest big deal in September is the Gaslamp Quarter's **Street Scene** fall food and music festival (sometimes scheduled in late August), while the **Adams Avenue Street Fair,** a right neighborly neighborhood block party, is much more laid-back. In October, when admission is free for children all month, **Zoo Founder's Day** makes a human zoo out of the San Diego Zoo. All kinds of Halloween fun—including the

Haunted Museum of Man in Balboa Park, and an **Underwater Pumpkin Carving Contest** in La Jolla—round out the year's foremost month of fright. For animals on the march, head to El Cajon with kids in tow in November for the annual **Mother Goose Parade** or to the **Carlsbad Village Faire** in Carlsbad. Magical among the multitude of holiday events in December is **Christmas on El Prado** in Balboa Park and, along the bay downtown, the **San Diego Harbor Parade of Lights.**

OUTDOOR SAN DIEGO

The sun always shines in San Diego County, powerfully enough, most of the time, to dry up even the chance of rain. Since even San Diego's major tourist attractions are out in the open air, it's little wonder then that, here, life is lived outdoors. Recreation and sports are central to local life, which explains the area's endless variety of outdoor activities. Begin with aerial sports—skydiving, sky sailing, aerial barnstorming. Then beachcombing, bicycling, bird-watching, boating—every imaginable type of boat and water sport—and even bocce ball. There's golfing—lots of it, with lush green courses spread out everywhere—and Frisbee golf in Balboa Park. And hiking. Horseback riding. Kayaking. Kite flying. Racquetball. Recreational working-out, at the legion of local health and fitness clubs. Rock climbing. In-line skating. Sportfishing, swimming, surfing, snorkeling, shark diving, scuba diving, sailing, and sailboarding. Tennis. Volleyball at the beaches. Water-skiing. Whale-watching. You name it, chances are San Diego does it—and has at least one outfitter offering the necessary equipment and/or service. For a current listing, contact the local visitor bureau (see Practical San Diego, below).

Recreational San Diego

Inexplicably, nonathletic types sometimes find themselves in San Diego. For them, the local love affair with aerobic exercise, buff bodies, and too-dark tans can be a bit intimidating. For the record, however, you *can* come to San Diego, have a good time, and leave the exercise to someone else. At last report there was no law—no official law, anyway—stating otherwise.

Sign on for a San Diego Bay tour, for example. **Hornblower Cruises** at the Cruise Ship Pier, 1066 N. Harbor, 619/234-8687, www.hornblower .com, offers mainstream one- and two-hour harbor tours, brunch and dinner cruises, even whale-watching trips, with rates $12 and up. The cheapest water trip around, something of a self-designed tour, is the **Coronado Ferry,** which departs from the nearby Broadway Pier, $2 each way (plus 50 cents if you bring a bike), 619/234-4111 for information and schedules. (See Coronado Tripping for more information.) Part with substantially more cash for a sailboat cruise, with outfits such as **Sail U.S.A.,** 619/298-6822.

You can also take a train trip—or a self-designed train-oriented nostalgia trip. Take the **San Diego Trolley** on a 30-mile route around San Diego with more than a dozen stops. Stations include Presidio Park, Balboa Park, San Diego Zoo, Coronado, Gaslamp Quarter, and Horton Plaza. The trolley costs $20 for adults, $8 for children 6–12 (free for children 5 and under), and you can hop off and on again at any point to make the complete loop. The trolley also goes east to old-hometown-style La Mesa, for example, for a visit to the **La Mesa Depot Museum** (open weekends only), 619/595-3030. A more ambitious weekend possibility: the 16-mile round-trip backcountry boogie aboard a vintage steam- or diesel-powered train on the **San Diego & Arizona Railway,** starting at **Campo Depot,** 619/478-9937 (weekends), well east of San Diego in Campo, near the Mexican border.

Or, how 'bout an aerial excursion? **Skysurfer Balloon Company** in Del Mar, toll-free 800/660-6809 or 619/481-6800, for hot-air ballooning, is one good possibility. **Barnstorming Adventures, Ltd.,** toll-free 800/759-5667 or 760/438-7680, www.barnstorming.com, is another, definitely something you can't do every day. Climb into a beautifully restored open-cockpit biplane and go for an easy 20-minute spin or a high-flying "Sunset Snuggler" tour. If you're feeling dangerous, stay out for an hourlong aerial roller-coaster ride with dogfight maneuvers. Vintage plane rides start at $98 per person for 20 minutes. Flights usually depart from either Palomar Airport or Gillespie Field, only as scheduled (reservations required).

Sporting San Diego

Spectator sports are ever popular with San Diego's armchair athletes. For pro baseball, the National League **San Diego Padres** fill the bill at Qualcomm Stadium ("the Q") at 9449 Friars Rd. in Mission Valley (intersection of I-8 and I-805) from mid-April to October. For schedule info, call 619/283-4494; for tickets, 619/29-PADRES. During pro football season, the stadium's stars are the **San Diego Chargers**, 619/280-2111. For Padres and Chargers home games, consider taking the **Express** bus, 619/233-3004, which picks up fans at several locations throughout the city beginning two hours before the game.

The **San Diego Sports Arena** hosts the U.S. International Hockey League **San Diego Gulls**, 619/224-4625 or 619/224-4171, from October through April, and the **San Diego Sockers** professional indoor soccer team, 619/224-GOAL, October–May.

To watch Sunday polo matches from June through October, head to Rancho Santa Fe and the **San Diego Polo Club**, 858/481-9217. In late July through mid-September, you'll find horse-racing action at the **Del Mar Race Track** in Del Mar, 858/755-1141.

SHOPPING SAN DIEGO

You're not looking very hard if you can't find something to buy in San Diego. Major malls are the obvious places to start parting with your hard-earned cash—places such as **Horton Plaza** and the nearby **Paladion** downtown, **Fashion Valley** and the **Mission Valley Center** near Hotel Circle, the huge **University Town Center** in La Jolla's Golden Triangle, and Del Mar's cunningly camouflaged **Del Mar Plaza.** The **San Diego Factory Outlet Center,** 619/690-2999, in San Ysidro, near the Mexican border, is also immensely popular. Savvy shoppers can pick up bargains at **Carlsbad Company Stores,** 760/804-9000, with bargains from Barney's New York, Kenneth Cole and The Gap, among others. The traditional bargain-hunter's bonanza, however, is **Kobey's Swap Meet** at the Sports Arena parking lot, 3500 Sports Arena Blvd., 619/226-0650. Fun and funky, it's open Thurs.–Sun. 7 A.M.–3 P.M. (admission $1).

For specialty items, migrate to the most likely neighborhoods. **Hillcrest**, for example, is a good bet for trendy clothes, gifts, and good bookstores and music shops, as is **La Jolla**, also known for homewares, home fashions, and art galleries. For tourist-grade international arts and crafts and Mexican memorabilia, head for Old Town and **Bazaar del Mundo, La Esplanade,** and **Old Town Mercado.** (Do comparison shop here; some places are substantially less expensive than others.) To hunt down seafaring wares, look around on and near both **Harbor Island** and **Shelter Island.**

STAYING IN SAN DIEGO

A pleasant surprise in San Diego is the range of surprisingly decent accommodation options, from dirt cheap to definitely expensive. You'd expect to find upscale hotels, inns, and resorts along the coast, downtown, and elsewhere, but the surprise is that prime visitor areas also feature hostels, inexpensive hotels, and reasonably priced, pleasant motels. The following suggestions are arranged by general locale. For more choices, contact the local visitors bureau (see Practical San Diego, below, or Coronado: Crown of the Bay, above). For bed-and-breakfast listings, contact the **Bed & Breakfast Guild of San Diego,** 619/523-1300, or the countywide **Bed & Breakfast Directory for San Diego,** 619/297-3130 or toll-free 800/619-7666.

In these increasingly bargain-conscious times, pursue discounts, an effort that pays off particularly well in the September through mid-June "off-season." Why summer is still prime time for vacationers to San Diego, considering the marvelous year-round climate, remains something of a mystery—but don't complain, since everyone else's shortsightedness can save you from the crowds *and* save you money. For summertime bargains, head inland; away from the moderate coastal climate, temperatures soar and prices drop. Larger hotels, resorts, and motel chains almost always offer discounts, with special deals and packages during slow periods. As elsewhere in California and the United States, members of the American Automobile Association (AAA) and the American Association of Retired Persons (AARP) qualify for sometimes substantial discount rates at many accommodations, as do corporate customers. For major deals—savings as much as 50 percent, in some cases—consider booking even resort accommodations through **San Diego Hotel Reservations,** toll-free 800/728-3227. While making travel plans, be aware of the city's all-out conventioneering—and be flexible about trip timing, if at all possible. San Diego's success at attracting major conventions and staging major events is great for the hotel business but bad news for savvy travelers suddenly unable to get a bargain rate.

STAYING IN AND AROUND DOWNTOWN

U.S. Grant Hotel

Downtown's most dignified and time-honored presence, the landmark U.S. Grant Hotel was built in 1910 by Ulysses S. Grant, Jr., son of the former Civil War general and U.S. president. After decades of decline midcentury, the 11-story U.S. Grant reopened in 1985 after an impressive $80 million renovation. The classy classic lobby, with its Palladian columns, marble floors, crystal chandeliers, Old World art, and Chinese porcelain, sets the tone for the guest rooms. Regular rooms are somewhat small but tastefully done in Queen Anne–style mahogany, even the armoire hiding the TV (cable provided; movies available). Marble and tile bathrooms offer other modern comforts, such as terrycloth robes and hand-milled soaps. Official room rates are $185–205 and up but, with reservations at least one month in advance and special discounts (AAA members and others), can go as low as $129. Ask about off-season specials and packages too. One of downtown's best restaurants is the **Grant Grill** here, 619/239-6806, surprisingly reasonable, serving breakfast, lunch, and dinner. Other facilities include exercise room (massage extra), business center, and conference rooms.

The U.S. Grant, downtown at 326 Broadway, inhabits an entire city block. Its formal entrance is directly across from Horton Plaza but, unless on foot, most guests enter the lobby from the parking lot (valet parking). For more information, call 619/232-3121, or check www.grand-heritage.com. For reservations, call toll-free 800/237-5029.

More Uptown Downtown Hotels

The 19-story **Westgate Hotel** is a classic modern American study in contrast—in this case, the contrast between somewhat formal Old World luxury and the ubiquitous, thoroughly modern downtown high-rise in which it hides. The lobby sparkles with Baccarat crystal chandeliers; high tea is served every afternoon. The theme of classical opulence continues through on-site restaurants and into the antique-furnished guest rooms, where bathrooms come with Italian marble and gold-plated fixtures. From the ninth floor up, rooms come with a view too. Rack rates run $184–224, with considerable price flexibility depending on what's going on. Weekends are usually the best deal, with $150 the typical rate. The Westgate is at 1055 Second Ave. (at C St.), 619/238-1818, fax 619/557-3737. For reservations, call toll-free 800/221-3802.

If you prefer more contemporary big-hotel ambience with the usual amenities plus an indoor pool and gym, another good choice downtown is the contemporary **Embassy Suites,** 601 Pacific Hwy. (at N. Harbor Dr.), 619/239-2400 or toll-free 800/362-2779 (EMBASSY). This is a better setup for families, too, since all suites feature a separate bedroom plus conveniences like refrigerators, hairdryers, coffeemakers, and microwaves. All rooms have city or bay views. Full breakfast, as you like it (served in the restaurant), is included, along with free cocktails. Rates run $189–300, with various discounts and specials often available.

The **Wyndham Emerald Plaza,** formerly the Pan Pacific Hotel, also caters to the business trade, but with swimming pool, full fitness facilities, and abundant other extras, it's quite comfortable for tourists who prefer a downtown base. Rates are generally lowest on the weekend, too, sometimes starting at $129; ask about other discounts and specials. And if you're meeting someone, rendezvous under the "emerald" in the lobby. The Wyndham Emerald Plaza is at the Emerald-Shapery Center (between Columbia and State), 400 W. Broadway, 619/239-4500;

www.wyndham.com. For reservations, call toll-free 800/996-3426.

Horton Grand Hotel

Another notable downtown presence is the genteel Horton Grand Hotel in the Gaslamp Quarter, on Island Street between Third and Fourth. The ambience here is historic yet new, a neat trick achieved by building what amounts to a new hotel from the old-brick bones of two time-honored neighborhood hotels otherwise doomed by redevelopment—including the original Horton Grand, which stood in the way of Horton Plaza. Rooms here are cozy, in the Victorian style, with neat touches such as gas fireplaces and TV sets cleverly tucked into the wall (behind a mirror). Rates run $139–219, with various discounts and special packages often available. For more information, contact: Horton Grand Hotel, 311 Island Ave. (at Fourth Ave.), 619/544-1886 or toll-free 800/542-1886 for reservations; www.hortongrand.com.

Downtown Area Bed-and-Breakfasts

The friendly **Balboa Park Inn**, right across the street from Balboa Park, is a stylistic complement to the park's 1915 exposition architecture. All rooms at the inn—actually, four Spanish colonial homes interconnected by courtyards—are tasteful yet simple suites with either one or two bedrooms; fun "specialty" suites include the Paris in the '30s, Nob Hill, and Nouveau Ritz suites. Amenities vary (as does room decor) but include kitchens, fireplaces, patios, in-room whirlpools, and wetbars. Continental breakfast and the morning newspaper are delivered to your door. The inn is on the north end of Balboa Park, and you can walk to park attractions. Rates start at $95 per night. For more information, contact: Balboa Park Inn, 3402 Park Blvd., 619/298-0823 or toll-free 800/938-8181; www.balboaparkinn.com.

Though a summertime stay often requires considerable advance booking, another great deal is the impeccably restored 1913 **Gaslamp Plaza Suites** just a block from Horton Plaza at 520 E St. (corner of 5th Ave.), 619/232-9500 or toll-free 800/874-8770, a time-share condo that also rents out rooms as available. The building itself, with a lovely lobby chiseled from marble and mosaic tiles, is San Diego's first high-rise, circa 1913, and listed on the National Register of Historic Places. The suites—larger ones feature a separate bedroom—are attractive and named famous writers including Shelley, Fitzgerald, and Emerson, with various amenities, some including microwaves, refrigerators, coffeemakers, color TV, the works. Rates are $93–200, depending on room size and amenities, and include continental breakfast—served on the roof, weather permitting. The view is free.

Best Downtown Bets on a Budget

A comfortable downtown budget hotel, on India Street at Date, residential-style **La Pensione** is contemporary and clean. Especially appealing if you'll be staying awhile—the general ambience here, plus on-site laundry, make that an attractive idea—each cozy room (two people maximum) features a private bath, a kitchenette with microwave and refrigerator, and adequate space for spreading out work projects or tourist brochures. Daily rates are $60–80, single or double. Ask about weekly and monthly rates. For more information, contact: La Pensione, 1700 India St., 619/236-8000; www.lapensionehotel.com. For reservations, call toll-free 800/232-4683.

La Pacifica Hotel is another San Diego find—a well-located residential hotel with style, grace, and great rates (daily, weekly, monthly). This gem has a similar setup to La Pensione—private baths, kitchenettes with microwaves and refrigerators, telephone, color TV with cable. Some rooms even have a harbor view. Other pluses: daily maid service, on-site laundry, bicycle storage, and nearby public parking. In summer, rates start at $60 per day. La Pacifica is downtown on Second Avevue, between Beech and Cedar. For more information, contact: La Pacifica Hotel, 1546 Second Ave., 619/236-9292.

Definitely a bargain—one of those places where you'll find a bed even when conventioneers have taken every other place in town—is the landmark **Embassy Hotel** just north of Balboa Park at 3645 Park Blvd., 619/296-3141, these days primarily a residential home for the elderly. Rooms, $54 per night, are fairly basic but quiet and roomy, with private bathrooms and in-room phones. Free laundry facilities. You can even eat with the residents, in the decent cafeteria-style dining room.

HI-AYH Metropolitan Hostel

Affiliated with Hostelling International–American Youth Hostels, the Metropolitan Hostel replaces downtown's Hostel on Broadway. On the corner of Fifth Avenue and Market in the heart of the Gaslamp Quarter, the fully renovated Metropolitan features private and dorm rooms, a laundry, lockers, common kitchen, pool table, and rental bikes. Rates are $17–19 per person. For more information, contact: HI-AYH Metropolitan Hostel, 521 Market St., 619/525-1531. Groups welcome. Children (under age 18) are welcome if accompanied by an adult. Reservations are essential in summer (through September). The office is open daily 7 A.M.–midnight. For information on the Web, the address is www.hiayh .org.

AT THE BAY AND ALONG THE COAST

Near The Embarcadero

Downtown yet on the bay, adjacent to Seaport Village and a stone's throw from the convention center, is the stylish sky-high **Hyatt Regency San Diego** just off Harbor Drive, particularly popular with businessfolk and conventioneers—definitely a great choice if someone else is picking up the tab. All rooms here have an ocean view, but the best look-see of them all is the 360-degree vista from the lounge, especially impressive at sunset. The chic but casual British men's club sensibility here is leavened with bright California sunshine and all-American room to roam, from the health club, pool, and lighted tennis courts to the marina (sailboats available for rent). Regular room rates are $245–290, often lower on weekends. For more information, contact: Hyatt Regency San Diego, One Market Place (at Harbor Dr.), 619/232-1234. For reservations, call toll-free 800/233-1234.

Also along the Embarcadero and almost affordable is the **Holiday Inn on the Bay,** 1355 N. Harbor Drive (at Ash), 619/232-3861 or toll-free 800/465-4329, with large rooms and all the usual amenities. Regular rates run $139–199, but inquire about off-season rates and other specials.

Shelter Island, Harbor Island, and Vicinity

This area naturally attracts the sailing set but also draws wannabe yachters, what with all those pretty, high-priced boats bobbing around everywhere. And the spectacular bay views attract everyone else.

Attractive Hawaii-like tropical landscape and the endless "tiki" on parade is the real appeal of **Humphrey's Half Moon Inn** on Shelter Island, making for comfortable California coastal kitsch complete with in-room refrigerators and coffeemakers. In the midst of San Diego's bustling boat harbor, Humphrey's provides a private boat dock, huge heated pool, and whirlpool spa; for tooling around, rental bikes are available; special events, such as the great outdoor jazz, folk, and easy-rock concerts in summer, keep everyone coming back. (For cool jazz—indoors—during the rest of the year, show up on Sunday and Monday nights.) High-season rates start at $169 or $179 depending on the view, with a two-night minimum on weekends from Memorial Day through Labor Day. For more information, contact: Humphrey's Half Moon Inn and Suites, 2303 Shelter Island Dr., 619/224-3411 or toll-free 800/345-9995; www .halfmooninn.com.

To spend substantially more, head for Harbor Island and the **Sheraton San Diego Hotel and Marina**, 1380 Harbor Island Dr., 619/291-2900 or toll-free 800/325-3535, fax 619/692-2337, www.sheraton.com, originally two separate Sheraton hotels, all recently redone and refashioned into one hoOngoing shuttle bus service connects the two high-rise towers, lower buildings, and various services and programs. Regular rates start at $200.

Along the Coast and Mission Bay

Mission Beach, Mission Bay, and Pacific Beach are filled to the gills with resorts and large hotels, many quite pricey and, in summer, overrun by fellow travelers. But the coastal areas also offer some nice midrange motel-style stays; a motel sitting literally above the surf, on a pier; and several hostels. For more on inexpensive hostel stays, see below.

Mission Bay's classic family getaway is the lush and lovely **San Diego Paradise Point Resort,** a 44-acre island formerly the Princess Resort owned by Princess Cruises. The endless recreation here is the real draw—including paddleboats, water sports, five swimming pools, croquet, and volleyball. Rent bikes and cruise over to the beach, an easy few miles away, with or without the kids; in summer, the organized kids' program gives grown-ups a break too. Rates run $245–290 in summer. For more information, contact: San Diego Paradise Point Resort, 1404 W. Vacation Rd., 858/274-4630 or toll-free 800/344-2626; www.noblehousehotels.com. Also on the upscale end of family-style fun is the 18-acre **San Diego Hilton Beach and Tennis Resort,** 1775 E. Mission Bay Dr., 619/ 276-4010 or toll-free 800/445-8667, www.hilton .com, offering both bungalows and high-rise rooms recently redone in modern mission style. Summer rates are $205–335.

One of the best values around is the **Bahia Resort Hotel,** 998 W. Mission Bay Dr., 858/488-0551 or toll-free 800/576-4229, www.bahiahotel.com, semitropical and attractive, right across the street from a grassy park area and just a stroll from the beach. A bay beach and marina, where the paddlewheeler *Bahia Belle* is berthed (bay cruises, even dinner cruises, available), augment the backyard view from some rooms. Rates are $129 and up, often discounted on a space-available basis. Also reasonable—and a reasonably good family setup, since some rooms feature kitchens or kitchenettes—is the very nice **Pacific Shores Inn** in Pacific Beach at 4802 Mission Blvd., 858/483-6300 or toll-free 800/826-0715 (reservations only), just 100 feet from the broad sandy beach. All rooms have HBO, some have kitchenettes, and continental breakfast is included. Rates run $144–179, lower in the off-season.

The *classic* Pacific Beach stay, though, is right in the middle of the local action—out on the Crystal Pier, at the landmark 1930s **Crystal Pier Hotel,** 4500 Ocean Blvd., 858/483-6983 or toll-free 800/748-5894, actually a pier-long collection of motel-style cottages. The Crystal Pier Hotel features 26 white-and-blue cottages with kitchenettes and surf-view patios—nothing fancy but unique and immensely popular, a fact reflected in the price. Rates: $145–305. Make reservations well in advance for summer (three-day minimum stay in summer, two-night otherwise). Weekly and monthly rates are available in the off-season.

Budget-Travel Bonanza:
Three Coastal Hostels
Most surprisingly, San Diego boasts three hostels at, or very near, the beach. Bright yellow, almost brand-new, and affiliated with the American Association of International Hostels, bustling **Beach Banana Bungalow San Diego** is right at the beach—on Reed Avenue at Mission Boulevard—and right in the middle of the way-cool, way-young Pacific Beach scene. Accommodations are dormitory style, with four to eight beds per room. Rates run $16 for dormitory rooms, $20 for semiprivate rooms. Breakfast and sand volleyball are included; laundry facilities and storage lockers are available. No reservations are taken; show up by 11 A.M. to grab a bed. For more information, contact: Beach Banana Bungalow San Diego, 707 Reed Ave., 858/273-3060 or toll-free 800/546-7835; www.bananabungalow.com.

The newest place around, though, is also the oldest—the **Ocean Beach International Backpacker Hostel,** at home in the historic Hotel Newport in Ocean Beach, on Newport Avenue between Cable and Bacon. This 80-bed hostel is just one block from the beach in San Diego's most laid-back and "local" beach community. Small but private "couples rooms," with two beds and a bathroom, cost $17–19. Most rooms are semiprivate with four or six beds per room; most of these also have private bathrooms. (More bathrooms are in the hallways.) Rates are $15 per person semiprivate, $17 private—including pastries for breakfast. For more information, contact Ocean Beach International Backpacker Hostel, 4961 Newport Ave., 619/223-7873 or toll-free 800/339-7263, email: obihostel@aol .com.

The **Point Loma/Elliott Hostel,** affiliated with Hostelling International–American Youth Hostels, is in a pleasant Point Loma residential neighborhood—close to the ocean but not particularly close to San Diego's other attractions. Yet this 60-bed hostel, on Udall Street, off Voltaire between Warden and Poinsettia, is a reasonably good base for wanderings farther afield. Draws include full kitchen, a travel library, and baggage storage. The basic dormitory rate is $17 for nonmembers, $14 for members. Family rooms are also available. (Children under age 18 are welcome if accompanied by an adult.) Office hours: 8–11 A.M. and 5:30–11 P.M. For more information, contact: Point Loma/Elliott HI-AYH Hostel, 3790 Udall St., 619/223-4778. For information on the Web, see www.hiayh.org.

STAYING IN AND AROUND OLD TOWN

In Old Town

Old Town San Diego offers some of the best lodging bargains around, including the all-suites **Best Western Hacienda Hotel Old Town.** Once a mission-style minimall, it's now a multilevel hillside motel—a quite clever renovation albeit a bit baffling at first, with multiple patios, passageways, stairways, terraces, and elevators to navigate. Wheelchair-accessible rooms are reached via elevators. Once you do find your way around—and find the on-site restaurants and pleasant pool area—you're set for an enjoyable stay. The mood here is San Diego–style Southwestern, with lovely landscaping outside; some rooms open onto terraces, with partially private patios. Inside, most rooms are smallish but quite adequate, with all the usual amenities plus ceiling fans, in-room coffeemakers, microwaves, and refrigerators. Great harbor views at night, especially from upper levels. Rates are $145 and up in summer, somewhat lower at other times, but weekday rates can go as low as $125. Ask about packages and seasonal specials. The Hacienda Hotel Old Town is at 4041 Harney St. (just off Juan), 619/298-4707 or toll-free 800/888-1991; www.bestwestern.com.

Depending on when you're coming—weekdays are usually the best deal any time but summer—other relative bargains in the neighborhood include the **Holiday Inn Hotel Old Town,** $118–189, right next to the freeway at 2435 Jefferson St. (exit I-5 at Old Town Ave.), 619/260-8500 or toll-free 800/433-2131, and the **Ramada Limited Old Town,** 3900 Old Town Ave., 619/299-740 or toll-free 800/451-9846, where rooms are $129–159 and include continental breakfast.

For a quick trip into Victorian San Diego, stay at the gracious two-story **Heritage Park Bed & Breakfast Inn,** the star of Heritage Park just above Old Town, 2470 Heritage Park Row, 619/299-6832; www.heritageparkinn.com. Eight rooms (some share a bath) and one suite make this 1889 Queen Anne most accommodating. Rates: $100–235 (includes breakfast and refreshments), with a two-night minimum on weekends; weekly and monthly rates are available. No smoking, no children under age 14.

Staying near Old Town: Hotel Circle and Mission Valley

"Hotel Circle" refers to the low-priced and mid-range motels that flank I-8 between Old Town and Mission Valley—not a bad location given the instant freeway access, assuming you have a car and don't mind doing the freeways to get around.

Among the cheaper choices in the neighborhood is good old **Motel 6 Hotel Circle,** 2424 Hotel Circle N., 619/296-1612, or, for reservations at any Motel 6 nationwide, toll-free 800/466-8356; www.motel6.com. This one features a swimming pool and the usual basics for $45.99 and up. A remarkable value for sporting types is the 20-acre **Quality Resort Mission Valley,** 875 Hotel Circle S., 619/298-8281 or toll-free 800/362-7871; www.qualityresort.com. Try to land a room away from the freeway noise, and then plunge into any of the three swimming pools (one's heated) or head to the adjacent tennis, racquetball, and health club facilities. Rooms here start at $99 in summer.

If you can't yet swing that trip to Hawaii, consider a stay at the pleasant **Hanalei Hotel,** 2270 Hotel Circle N., 619/297-1101 or toll-free 800/882-0858, www.hanaleihotel.com, yet another of San Diego's Polynesian-themed sleep palaces. Since Hanalei is Hawaiian for "valley of the flowers," the lush tropical foliage fits—as do the extravagant summertime luaus staged in the courtyard and the appealing pool area. Room rates start at $129 in summer, and $109 in the off-season.

Mission Valley's top-drawer digs include the **San Diego Marriott Mission Valley,** a business traveler's hot spot at 8757 Rio San Diego Dr. (exit I-8 at Stadium Way), 619/692-3800 or toll-free 800/228-9290, www.marriott.com, rates: $129–258; and the soundproofed **San Diego Mission Valley Hilton** just off the freeway at 901 Camino del Rio S. (exit I-8 at Mission Center Rd.), 619/543-9000 or toll-free 800/445-8667; www.hilton.com, Rates: $99–199.

STAYING IN LA JOLLA
AND DEL MAR

Affordable in La Jolla

As you'd guess in such exclusive neighborhoods, life can get quite pricey in La Jolla and adjacent Del Mar. Because parking space is also a local luxury, many establishments charge extra for parking; be sure to inquire. **La Jolla Town Council** volunteers, 858/454-1444, can be very helpful if you'd like some personal assistance in making local lodging arrangements.

Low-rent accommodations don't exist in and around upscale, conservative La Jolla. Quite decent midrange motels are available, however, including the **Holiday Inn Express** (previously the La Jolla Palms), 6705 La Jolla Blvd., 858/454-7101 or toll-free 800/451-0358. This place is not in the midst of the local hubbub, but that can be a plus. About five long blocks south of downtown, an easy 20-minute walk, and close to world-famous "locals only" Windansea Beach, the Holiday Inn features large rooms, recently renovated, with all the basics plus a few extras, such as in-room coffeemakers, color TV, cable, and free movies. If you plan to do some home-away-from-home home cooking, some rooms here have full kitchens. Good shopping and great restaurants are a stroll away. Rates: $89–149.

Nothing fancy, **La Jolla Cove Suites** is stylin' it circa the 1950s but still a sweet deal. Quite well situated—right across the street from La Jolla Cove, as advertised—here you'll get the same views as the very rich at a much more reasonable price. You'll also get a full kitchen, so you can eat in anytime you want. Rates run $165 and up in the summer, otherwise $125 and up. Find La Jolla Cove Suites at 1150 Coast Blvd., 858/459-2621 or toll-free 800/248-2683; www.lajollacove.com. And if there's no room here, there may be space at the **Shell Beach Apartment Motel,** 981 Coast Blvd., run by the same folks.

Considerably more expensive but another great deal is the smoke-free **Prospect Park Inn,** a charming contemporary small motel with European hotel style. Squeezed onto a triangular lot at 1110 Prospect next to the grand La Valencia Hotel, it's too easily missed. Nice view from the patio up on the roof. High-season rates are $150

and up for two, continental breakfast included—but ask about off-season specials. For reservations, call 858/454-0133 or toll-free 800/433-1609; www.prospectparkinn.com.

Affordable in Del Mar

A genuine gem in Del Mar, literally *on* the beach, is the minimalist **Del Mar Motel,** close to the racetrack and just a stroll into downtown at 1702 Coast Blvd., 858/755-1534 or toll-free 800/223-8449. Rooms come with refrigerators, color TV, and courtesy coffee; barbecue grills available. Rates from $130 in the high season, starting at $85 otherwise.

Another good deal, between La Jolla and Del Mar, is **The Lodge at Torrey Pines,** 11480 N. Torrey Pines Rd., 858/453-4420 or toll-free 800/995-4507, www.lodgetorreypines.com, boasting one of the best "view" locations around and attractive motel-style rooms. Rates: $95–155, but look for discounts during the off-season.

Upmarket in and around La Jolla

La Jolla's oldest hotel is the still dignified and fairly staid four-story **Grande Colonial,** close to everything downtown at 910 Prospect, 858/454-2181 or toll-free 800/829-1278, www.thegrande-colonial.com, with pool, restaurant, and full bar. Tea is served every afternoon. High-season rates $229–429, low-season rates $179–299. Ocean-view rooms are the more expensive.

Downtown's darling, though, is the historic **La Valencia Hotel,** 1132 Prospect (at Herschel), 858/454-0771 or toll-free 800/451-0772; www .lavalenciahotel.com. Art deco La Valencia, still pretty in pink, was one of those legendary Hollywood celebrity destinations in the 1930s and '40s—*the* place to be, in the classic style of European luxury, as La Jolla began making a name for itself. And it still is, for those who can afford it. Rates run $250 and up, with some of the cheaper rooms not all that stellar. The layout of this Mediterranean-style pleasure palace is stellar, however. "Street level" happens to be the fourth floor, with the floors below on the way down to the ocean, and the others above. Even the elevator—with a human being at the controls!—is straight out of an old classic movie. Three restaurants—one with a 10th-floor view—a swimming pool and gardens terraced into the hillside, and a small spa are also modern classics.

For postmodern comforts, head for La Jolla's "Golden Triangle" east of I-5 and the neoclassical 400-room **Hyatt Regency La Jolla at Aventine,** designed by architect Michael Graves. The rooms here are large and airy—but not nearly as airy as the stunning atrium—and the associated health club is one of San Diego's best. Plenty of restaurants are on-site; it's also an easy stroll from here to the University Town Center, where you'll find more dining. Regular rates run $215 and up, but weekend specials and other discounts can drop prices to $165, based upon availability. For more information, contact: Hyatt Regency La Jolla, 3777 La Jolla Village Dr., 858/ 552-1234 or toll-free 800/233-1234; www.hyatt .com.

Another best bet is the cliff-top **Hilton La Jolla Torrey Pines,** 10950 N. Torrey Pines Rd., 858/ 558-1500 or toll-free 800/774-1500, www .hilton.com, a subtle presence overlooking the ocean, and right next to a great municipal golf course and an excellent health club. Rooms are elegant and generous, with either a terrace or balcony and every imaginable luxury—including free Starbucks coffee, shirt press, and newspaper every morning. Regular rates run $200 and up.

L'Auberge Del Mar Resort and Spa

Right in the middle of everything in Del Mar, this luxury resort with a hillside ocean view graces the site of the famed Hotel Del Mar, a playground for the Hollywood celebrity set from the 1920s through the 1940s. The architecture of this Victorian-style beach house mimics the original, and the lobby still serves as the resort's social center. Guest rooms are country French, with marble bathrooms and the usual luxury amenities. Also here: full European-style spa and fitness facilities—affordable, by separate fee, for just about anyone, if lodging at the hotel is a bit too rich—plus tennis courts, two pools, great restaurants. Best of all, it's only one block to the beach. July, August, and September—race season at the Del Mar Race Track—is the high season, with rates $395 and up. Much lower rates are available at other times. L'Auberge Del Mar Resort and Spa is at 1540 Camino del Mar, 858/ 259-1515 or toll-free 800/553-1336; www .laubergedelmar.com. To get here from I-5, head west on Del Mar Heights Road for one mile, then

turn north onto Camino del Mar. The resort is one mile farther.

Resorts in Rancho Santa Fe

Often a real deal for a special-occasion escape is the **Inn at Rancho Santa Fe,** a San Diego classic with 20 acres of terraced gardens, vine-draped cottages, croquet courses, tennis courts, pool, exercise facilities, and on-site restaurant, with golf and horseback riding available nearby. Another perk here: daytime access to an inn-owned beach cottage in Del Mar. The inn's main building dates from 1923, and was originally built as a guest house for prospective real estate buyers after the Santa Fe Railroad's local experiment with eucalyptus trees failed. (Santa Fe had hoped eucalyptus would produce quality wood for railroad ties; instead, the trees grew up to produce shade for the exclusive residential neighborhoods here.) Quiet and relaxed, it's not particularly oriented toward families though kids are welcome. Rates: $120 and up, AAA discounts and other specials often available. To get here, exit I-5 at Loma Santa Fe Drive (Hwy. 58) and continue east four miles. For more information: Inn at Rancho Santa Fe, 5951 Linea del Cielo (at Paseo), 858/756-1131 or toll-free 800/843-4661; www.theinnatranchosantafe.com.

Privileged sibling to La Jolla's lovely La Valencia Hotel, the contemporary Old California–style **Rancho Valencia Resort,** near Del Mar in Rancho Santa Fe, has it all—red-tiled roofs, bougainvillea-draped walkways, fountains, romantic and luxurious suites tucked into the lush landscape, 18 tennis courts, exercise facilities, championship croquet lawn, pool, hot tubs, and sauna. You'll find an 18-hole golf course next door to this exclusive 40-acre playground. Official rates are $425 and up, but ask about midweek and off-season specials. For more information: Rancho Valencia Resort, 5921 Valencia Circle, 858/756-1123 or toll-free 800/548-3664; www.ranchovalencia.com.

STAYING ON CORONADO

Pricey Stays

If planning to splurge while in the neighborhood, stay at least one night at the historic **Hotel del Coronado,** the city's crowning glory. The legendary and eclectic Queen Anne "Hotel Del" features a classic dark-wood lobby, with a still-functioning birdcage elevator and a spectacular support-free formal dining room, the latter used only on special occasions. Guest rooms in the original wooden section of the hotel, with its marvelous quirky corridors, boast all modern amenities yet a Victorian sensibility—all the more dazzling following the Hotel Del's $50 million renovation, completed in June 2000. Newer hotel units near the beach include the Ocean Towers, the California Cabanas, and the Beach House. And if you aren't sufficiently entertained by the hotel's grandeur, its Olympic-size swimming pool, tennis courts, and pristine white-sand Coronado Beach—beach chairs, umbrellas, towels, even boogie boards provided—then watch the hotel's closed-circuit TV, showing movie after movie filmed at the Hotel Del. Other amenities include wonderful on-site restaurants, from the stunningly Victorian Crown-Coronet dining room, complete with chandeliers designed by *Wizard of Oz* author Frank Baum, to the romantic Prince of Wales Grill and the new Sheerwater (formerly the Ocean Terrace), serving California coastal cuisine. (For very Victorian High Tea, head for the Palm Court on Sunday afternoon.) Not to mention various business services, shopping, complete spa services (extra), and rental bikes, sailboards, and sailboats. Summer room rates begin at $190, with a two-night minimum on weekends, though ask about packages and off-season deals. For more information, contact: Hotel del Coronado, 1500 Orange Ave., 619/435-6611, www.hoteldel.com. For reservations, call toll-free 800/468-3533, fax 619/522-8262, or reserve online.

Another top choice is the 15-acre **Loews Coronado Bay Resort,** 4000 Coronado Bay Rd., 619/424-4000 or toll-free 800/235-6397, fax 619/424-4400, www.loewshotels.com, a lovely contemporary hotel with light and airy view rooms—every room has a view, be it of the ocean, the bay, or the marina (moor your own). All the usual luxuries, on-site restaurants, fitness and business facilities, even a kid's pro-

gram are provided. Rates start at $195, but ask about specials.

Also appealing in the pricier category is the **Coronado Island Marriott Resort,** formerly Le Meridien San Diego, 16 acres fronting the bay directly across from downtown, with lush landscaping, lagoons full of fish and flamingos, tennis courts, pools, health and fitness facilities, business services, and great restaurants. Rooms, suites, and villas, all with a balcony or patio, open onto either a bay or lagoon view. Rates start at $230, but look for off-season specials and packages. The Coronado Island Marriott is at 2000 Second St. (at Glorietta), 619/435-3000 or toll-free 800/228-9290 (central reservations), fax 619/435-3032; www.marriotthotels.com.

Not So Pricey Stays

Thankfully for just plain folks and most families, Coronado also offers budget-friendlier choices, including the **Crown City Inn,** 520 Orange Ave. (between Fifth and Sixth), 619/435-3116 or toll-free 800/422-1173, fax 619/435-6750; www.crowncityinn.com. Every room at this attractive Mediterranean-style motel has a refrigerator, microwave, and coffeemaker, in-room modem hookup, ironing board and iron, plus color TV and cable with free movies. Heated pool, complimentary bikes, on-site laundry facilities. Even better, from here it's just a 10-minute walk to the beach. The **Crown City Bistro** here is open for breakfast, lunch, and dinner and provides impressive room service. Summer rates start at $105 ($85 in the off-season). Ask about discounts and specials.

If there's no room at that inn, **La Avenida Inn,** 1315 Orange, 619/435-3191, fax 619/435-5024, and the **Best Western Suites Coronado Island,** 235 Orange, 619/437-1666 or toll-free 800/528-1234, fax 619/437-0188, are both good alternatives. For more suggestions, contact the very helpful **Coronado Visitor Information** office, 1047 B Ave., Coronado, CA 92118, 619/437-8788, fax 619/437-6006; www.coronado.ca.us.

EATING IN SAN DIEGO

IN AND AROUND DOWNTOWN

Uptown Downtown

Even for those who avoid shopping malls as a matter of principle, the **Panda Inn** at Horton Plaza, 619/233-7800, merits an exception. This wonderful Chinese restaurant is as elegant as it is inclusive, with an impressive list of Mandarin and Szechuan selections. From noodle dishes and twice-cooked pork to fresh seafood, nothing here disappoints. It's open daily 11 A.M.–10 P.M., until 10:30 P.M. on Friday and Saturday, closed Thanksgiving and Christmas.

Just across the street from hustle-bustle Horton Plaza, the **Grant Grill** at the venerable U.S. Grant Hotel, on Broadway between Third and Fourth, 619/239-6806, is a sure bet for escaping the tourist hordes. The hotel's elegant, dignified, and historically correct decor lends a men's club sensibility to the surprisingly good food— from American standards at breakfast and good salads, sandwiches, and specials at lunch to steak and lobster dinners. Full bar. The Grant Grill is open daily 6:30–11 A.M. for breakfast, 11:30 A.M.–2 P.M. for lunch, and 5–10 P.M. for dress-up dinner (until 10:30 P.M. on weekends).

Rainwater's, 1202 Kettner (next door to the Santa Fe Depot), on the second floor, 619/233-5757, is a very uptown downtown establishment and one of the best steakhouses around. Steaks here are huge, side dishes simple but artfully selected. Grilled seafood is also prominent on the menu. If you can manage dessert—and here, that's typically a challenge—locals swear by the hot-fudge sundaes. Rainwater's is also a popular lunchtime rendezvous for the suit-and-tie set. It's open Mon.–Fri. 11:30 A.M.–midnight, on Saturday 5–9 P.M., on Sunday 5–11 P.M. Call for holiday schedules (they vary from year to year).

The Gaslamp Quarter

Fio's, 801 Fifth Ave. (at F St.), 619/234-3467, is tried and true among the Gaslamp Quarter's trendy Fifth Avenue restaurants—a cheery contemporary Italian place looking down on the fray from its seasoned-brick setting. Those with smaller appetites and/or the budget-minded should stick to pastas and salads—or split one of those great pizzas fresh from the wood-fired oven. This a very popular place, so reservations are advisable at dinner. It's open weekdays for lunch 11:30 A.M.–3 P.M., nightly for dinner 5–11 P.M. (until midnight on Friday and Saturday, until 10 P.M. on Sunday). Closed Thanksgiving, Christmas, and New Year's Day. Other excellent choices in the neighborhood: **Bella Luna,** with all those pretty moons, at 748 Fifth Ave. (between F and G), 619/239-3222, open daily for both lunch and dinner, and the stylish Tuscan **Trattoria La Strada,** 702 Fifth Ave. (at G), 619/239-3400, open nightly for dinner, weekdays only for lunch. More casual than its Italian neighbors, bistro-style **Osteria Panevino,** 722 Fifth Ave. (at G), 619/595-7959, open daily for lunch and dinner, serves wonderful vegetable focaccia, spinach ravioli, and pizzas.

Or, try another country. For tapas and other Spanish selections, head to very friendly **Tapas Picasso,** 3923 Fourth Ave. (between Washington and University), 619/294-3061, open nightly for dinner, Tues.–Fri. for lunch. Turn a corner and try yet another country. **Athens Market,** 109 W. F St. (at First Ave.), 619/234-1955, takes you on an ersatz sail through the Aegean—on weekend nights, an experience complete with Greek music, folk dancing, and belly dancers. Perfect for a simple dinner or—to fully sample the tastiest fare, including the specialty sausage— dive into the appetizer menu. Reservations advisable. For coffee and after-dinner sweets, adjourn to the coffeehouse next door (open late). Open daily for lunch and dinner 11:30 A.M.–10 P.M. (no lunch on Sunday), closed Thanksgiving and Christmas, sometimes open only half days on other U.S. holidays.

Another shining light in downtown's Gaslamp Quarter is **Croce's,** 802 Fifth Ave. (at F St.), 619/233-4355, a noted jazz club named in honor of the late singer Jim Croce and operated by his family. The music continues, these days with a pretty jazzy dinner menu, too, on which imaginative international riffs include pastas, salads, and seafood entrees. Best of all, Croce's is open late every night—for dinner, 5 P.M.–midnight. (Closed Thanksgiving and Christmas.) The affiliated **Croce's West** in the same block, 619/233-6945, is another possibility, open every day at 7:30 A.M. for breakfast.

Not that the good ol' U.S. of A. can't be exotic. At the **Bayou Bar and Grill,** 329 Market St. (between Third and Fourth), 619/696-8747, if you didn't know it was San Diego you'd swear you'd somehow stumbled into Louisiana, what with the ceiling fans and color scheme. Once inside, keep it simple. Whether you choose seafood gumbo, another fresh fish dish, or rice and beans accompanied by homemade sausage, do leave room for dessert. Suitably decadent selections include Cajun velvet pie (chocolate and peanut butter) and Creole pecan pie. It's open Mon.–Sat. 11:30 A.M.–3 P.M. and 5–10 P.M. (until 11 P.M. on Friday and Saturday), on Sunday 11:30 A.M.–10 P.M., closed Easter, Thanksgiving, Christmas Eve night, Christmas Day, and New Year's Day.

And there are outposts of down-home Western exotica, such as the gussied-up **Dakota Grill and Spirits,** 901 Fifth (at E St.), 619/234-5554, specializing in "cowboy steak" and other surprises, and **American Buffalo Joe's BBQ Grill and Saloon,** 600 Fifth (at F St.), 619/236-1616, where the 'cue is as good as the country-western.

Eateries on the Way to Hillcrest

Hob Nob Hill, just blocks from Balboa Park at 2271 First Ave. (at Juniper), 619/239-8176, is a long-running neighborhood favorite—serving heaping helpings of all-American favorites, such as pot roast and fried chicken, at very reasonable prices. Breakfast here is one of the best deals in town, and on Sunday everyone shows up (reservations wise).

Also beyond the typical tourist definition of downtown, look for **Little Italy** along India Street, just north of Date. The 1700 block of India is still the center of San Diego's historic Italian district, first settled more than 100 years ago by fishing families. Savory stops here include **Mimmo's Italian Village Deli & Bakery,** 619/239-3710, great for pizza; **Caffe Italia,** 619/234-6767, for sandwiches, coffee, and such; and a number of

good delis and bakeries.

Farther north, in an area overrun with freeway on- and off-ramps, another section of India Street marks the turn-off to Hillcrest, with additional worthy (and inexpensive) eateries. An institution in San Diego, the original "uptown" **El Indio,** 3695 India St. (at Washington), 619/299-0333, is where locals go for Mexican. El Indio claims to have invented the term "taquito," so be sure to try a few. But save space for the killer fish tacos and cheese enchiladas, the burritos, the tostadas. Abundant vegetarian choices, everything inexpensive. And if you're in a hurry, call ahead for takeout. It's open daily 7 A.M.–9 P.M., closed Thanksgiving, Christmas, and New Year's Day. The casual **Banzai Cantina,** 619/296-6388, specializing in imaginative Japanese-Mexican fare at both lunch and dinner, is another neighborhood celebrity. Stop by **Saffron,** 619/574-0177, for takeout.

Hot Stuff in Hillcrest

The **Corvette Diner Bar and Grill** in Hillcrest at 3946 Fifth Ave. (near Washington), 619/542-1001 or 619/542-1476, is one of San Diego's best bets for kids, a raucous rock-out joint complete with DJs and singing wait staff. They'll also like the burgers, shakes, and fries. A rollicking imitation of a 1950s-style diner, the Corvette is known, too, for its meat loaf and other baby-boomer-era comfort foods. Very popular, so expect to wait (no reservations taken). It's open daily Sun.–Thurs. 11 A.M.–11 P.M., until midnight on weekend nights, closed Thanksgiving (and on Christmas if it falls on a weekday). Another hot spot for burgers is **Hamburger Mary's,** 308 University (at Third Ave.), 619/491-0400.

Best bet for pizza is **Pizza Nova** in the Village Hillcrest, 3955 Fifth Ave. (between Washington and University), 619/296-6682. Always cheap and also good is the down-to-earth Japanese **Ichiban** in Hillcrest at 1449 University, 619/299-7203. Another great Italian, this one popular for patio dining, is **Busalacchi's,** 3683 Fifth Ave. (at Pennsylvania), 619/298-0119.

Refreshingly, San Diego still doesn't entirely cotton to the faddish and overly fancy in food, which explains the popularity of casual yet cutting edge **Kemo Sabe,** 3958 Fifth Ave. (between Washington and University), 619/220-6802, with its imaginative and witty Mexican and multiethnic cuisine—"Mad About Moo" enchiladas, for example, starring moo shu pork. Then there's **Montanas,** "an American grill" at 1421 University (between Richmond and Normal), 619/297-0722, fueled by grilled everything and some incredible desserts. More chic in the usual sense is the exceptional **California Cuisine,** 1027 University Ave. (between 10th Ave. and University), 619/543-0790, closed on Monday but otherwise serving lunch on weekdays, dinner nightly.

AT THE BAY AND ALONG THE COAST

Dining by the Bay

A local favorite is the **Fish Market,** 750 N. Harbor Dr. (near Broadway), 619/232-3474. Here, parents can enjoy good seafood—even with young children in tow—along with one of the best waterfront views in town. Most grown-ups go for the mesquite-grilled fish and seafood selections. Most kids are happy with fish and chips, though the children's menu also includes burgers and other American standards. There's a fish market downstairs, plus sushi and shellfish bars and a cocktail lounge. Upstairs is the dressier, more expensive **Top of the Market** dinner restaurant, 619/234-4867, also popular for self-indulgent Sunday brunch. The Fish Market is open daily 11 A.M.–9:30 P.M., until 10 P.M. on Friday and Saturday nights, closed Thanksgiving and Christmas.

Another seafood hot spot is **Anthony's,** a popular local chain. The dress-up destination is **Anthony's Star of the Sea Room,** 1360 N. Harbor (at Ash), 619/232-7408, holding its own bayside with beautiful views and an even grander international seafood selection. A better bet by far, though, is **Sally's** at the Hyatt Regency, One Market Place (at Harbor Dr.), 619/687-6080, where the seafood is served Mediterranean style.

Of course, Coronado Island has its share of bayside bounty—including the elegant French **Chez Loma** 1132 Loma (off Orange Ave.), 619/435-0661, set in an 1889 Victorian cottage and one of San Diego's most romantic restaurants in any category. For other suggestions, see On Coronado, below.

Coastal Cuisine: Ocean Beach, Mission Beach, Pacific Beach

San Diego's classic beach towns have their share of classic burger and taco joints—and a few surprises, such as **Machupicchu** in Ocean Beach, 4755 Voltaire St. (at Sunset Cliffs Dr.), 619/222-2656, which introduces the foods of Peru. The classic appetizer here: the *papas rellenas,* or spicy stuffed potatoes filled with three types of finely chopped meat and vegetables. Among favorite entrées: lamb stew with cilantro sauce, fish with rice and potatoes, the beef sauté (with onions, peppers, and other vegetables), and several wonderful chicken dishes. Other crowd pleasers include the Peruvian clam chowder, the Peruvian *cerviche* (without tomatoes), and pasta with basil sauce. For smaller appetites, try a few appetizers along with the special spinach soup—the latter a big hit with kids, believe it or not. Beer and wine available. It's open Monday and Wed.–Fri. 5:30–9:30 P.M., and Sat.–Sun. 3–9 P.M. (sometimes expanded hours in summer). Closed major holidays.

Also something of a surprise, and an Ocean Beach institution, is **The Belgian Lion,** a very fine dining destination at 2265 Bacon St. (near Lotus St.), 619/223-2700, specializing in traditional French fare and lighter seafood and fresh fish. It's open for dinner only, and only on Thursday, Friday, and Saturday nights. Reservations a must. For German at either lunch or dinner, head for **Kaiserhof,** 2253 Sunset Cliffs Blvd. (at West Point Loma), 619/224-0606 (closed Monday).

IN OLD TOWN

The colorful **Old Town Mexican Cafe,** 2489 San Diego Ave. (at Congress), 619/297-4330, is famous for its humongous portions of just about every Mexican standard and a popular place for locals and tourists alike. And if the kids don't know how tortillas are made, here they can watch. It's open daily for both lunch and dinner.

But **Berta's Latin American Restaurant,** 3928 Twiggs St. (at Congress), 619/295-2343, ranges far beyond predictable Old Town south-of-the-border fare. High points of this Latin American tour include pastas, stews, Peruvian chicken with chiles and feta cheese, and seafood *vat-*

apa from Brazil—all good opportunities for the kids to move beyond tacos and burritos. The wine list is also international. You'll be pleasantly surprised by this friendly respite from the tourist hordes. In balmy weather, the patio is perfect. Berta's is open for lunch and dinner daily, 11 A.M.–10 P.M., closed major holidays.

California-style **Cafe Pacifica,** 2414 San Diego Ave. (between Arista and Linwood), 619/291-6666, a longstanding local choice for uptown dining in Old Town, specializes in seafood. Entrée choices change daily, but count on mesquite-grilled fresh fish selections served with house-made salsa, fruit chutney, or herbed sauces. For smaller appetites: fish tacos, crab cakes, and surprising salads and pastas. It's open for lunch Tues.–Fri. 11:30 A.M.–2 P.M., for dinner nightly 5:30–10 P.M.

IN LA JOLLA AND DEL MAR

Downtown La Jolla Jewels
If you're looking to pack a food-lover's picnic—a basket brimming with garden-fresh produce and fresh fruit—look no farther than **Chino's Vegetable Stand,** 6123 Calzada del Bosque, 858/756-3184. This vegetable stand supplies some of the best restaurants in California, including Berkeley's Chez Panisse. It's open Mon.–Sat. 10 A.M.–4 P.M., on Sunday 10 A.M.–1 P.M., closed Christmas Day.

If you've got teenagers in tow, you won't be able to avoid La Jolla's **Hard Rock Cafe,** 909 Prospect Ave. (at Fay), 858/454-5101, with good burger fare, the usual brain-scrambling blare, and rock memorabilia and mementos. For good coffee and a simple breakfast, the place (packed on weekends) is the coffeehouse-style **Brockton Villa,** 1235 Coast Blvd. (near Prospect), 858/454-7393. Another locals' choice for a casual meal is **SamSon's** deli, 8861 Villa La Jolla Dr., 858/455-1461, where you can count on great omelettes or lox plates at breakfast, great corned beef sandwiches at lunch, stick-to-your-ribs home-style dinners, and celebrity-kitsch decor anytime. It's open daily for breakfast, lunch, and dinner. For something more exotic, try the buffet lunch at the very good **Star of India,** 1000 Prospect (at Gerard), 858/459-3355, a popular place. If you come for dinner, make reservations.

George's at the Cove, 1250 Prospect St. (near Ivanhoe), 858/454-4244, is at the top of La Jolla's seafood food chain, and as beloved for its contemporary American cuisine as for its spectacular local views. You'll have to dress up for the dining room (reservations), but not for either the **Cafe** or the **Terrace,** upstairs, which are more relaxed (no reservations taken, so be prepared for a wait). Simpler fare includes soups, salads, shellfish pastas, fish tacos, even seafood sausages. George's is open daily for lunch 11 A.M.–4 P.M. (until 2 P.M. in the fine dining room), nightly for dinner 5–10 P.M. (until 11 P.M. on Friday and Saturday nights).

For fine dining, French sets the local standard. The excellent, expensive, and somewhat staid **Top o' the Cove,** 1216 Prospect St. (near Ivanhoe), 858/454-7779, a long-running local institution, serves classic French fare and romantic ambience with a view. **The Sky Room,** nearby at La Valencia Hotel, 1132 Prospect (at Herschel), 858/454-0771, is tiny (12 tables) and specializes in contemporary French and spectacular views of both sea and sky. (La Valencia's continental **The Whaling Bar,** open for both lunch and dinner, is another option.)

Inland La Jolla Jewels
Another dine-around destination is La Jolla's "Golden Triangle," rich real estate reared on biotechnology and other high-tech enterprise wedged into the triangle created by I-5, I-805, and Highway 52. The **Hops!** microbrewery at La Jolla's University Town Center (between Broadway and Robinson's May), 4353 La Jolla Village Dr., 858/587-6677, enlivens its shopping-mall setting with high-test homemade beers—Brewer's Blonde, Red Moon Raspberry, Three-Peat Wheat, and Grateful Red ales plus Triangle India Pale Ale and Superstition Stout. The Brewmaster's Special changes. The food's also quite good, imaginative but not too eclectic California-style bistro fare, wood-fired pizza and such, everything under $12. Patio dining available. It's open daily for lunch and dinner 11 A.M.–11 P.M. (until 1 A.M. on Friday and Saturday), closed major holidays.

Other culinary attractions at and near University Town Center include the continental California-style **St. James Bar & Restaurant,** jazzing up a high-rise bank building at 4370 La Jolla

Village Dr. (near Executive Way), 858/453-6650, with a menu including low-fat specialties high on flavor; and the Italian **Tutto Mare,** 4365 Executive Dr. (reached via Town Center Dr., north from Jolla Village Dr.), 858/597-1188, where roasted seafood and seafood pastas star.

Center stage at the theatrical **Aventine Center** nearby, on University Center Lane, are a number of great restaurants, including the very stylish and fairly expensive **Cafe Japengo,** 858/450-3355, offering trendy Pacific Rim cuisine and sushi, and an extensive list of creative desserts.

Best Bets in and around Del Mar
Sbicca's in Del Mar, 215 15th St. (at Camino del Mar), 858/481-1001, is an inventive California bistro serving brunch—crepes, omelettes, *huevos rancheros,* and eggs Benedict—on weekends until 3 P.M. Count on healthy items like the free-range turkey burger, vegetable lasagna, or grilled ahi at lunch. For dinner, consider the salmon au poivre or the Asian-jalapeño flatiron steak. Hours vary, so call ahead.

Other best bets in Del Mar live in the Del Mar Plaza mall at 1555 Camino del Mar (at 15th Street), including the faux-'50s **Johnny Rockets** burger joint on the first floor, 858/755-1954, where burgers, good fries, and malts make the menu. More trendy in the neighborhood, all on the third floor and all serving spectacular ocean views from their outdoor patios: **Epazote,** 858/259-9966, serving California-style Mexican and Southwestern cuisine; ever-popular northern Italian **Il Fornaio,** 858/755-8876; and **Pacifica Del Mar,** 858/792-0476, serving exotic California-style Cajun, Italian, Southwestern, and Pacific Rim fare. All are open daily for lunch and dinner, with dinner reservations advisable.

Downstairs from Pacifica Del Mar, the **Pacifica Breeze Café** serves breakfast, sandwiches, and dinners in the $7–10 range. And the bar draws a fun, trendy crowd on the weekends.

For dress-up dining in nearby Rancho Santa Fe, serving somewhat pricey but casual California-style American fare is **Delicias,** 6106 Paseo Delicias, 858/756-8000, open for lunch and dinner daily except Monday and major holidays. At the top of the local food chain, though, is the fancy French **Mille Fleurs** just a stroll away at 6009 Paseo Delicias, 858/756-3085, open daily for lunch and dinner.

ON CORONADO

For fresh produce and flowers, show up on Tuesday for the **Coronado Certified Farmers' Market,** 619/741-3763, held at the Ferry Market Landing, First Street and B Avenue. Microbrewery fans, you'll find Coronado's own at the **Coronado Brewing Company,** 170 Orange, 619/437-4452. For Pacific Rim–style Southwestern (reservations), the place is the **Chameleon Café,** 1301 Orange Ave., 619/437-6677. Delightful for French bistro fare is **Chez Loma,** near the history museum at 1132 Loma Ave. (at Orange), 619/435-0661.

Generally speaking, though, seafood is the thing in Coronado. For good seafood at lunch and dinner and a chance to appreciate America's Cup memorabilia, head for the **Bay Beach Cafe** at Ferry Market Landing, 619/435-4900. Another best bet for seafood—not to mention the macadamia nut pie—is **Pehoe's,** nearby at 1201 First St., 619/437-4474, with bay views, patio tables, and a good Sunday brunch. For a bit of remodeled history with your seafood and steaks, **The Chart House** is at home in the Hotel del Coronado's onetime boathouse at 1701 Strand Way, 619/435-0155 (casual, children's menu, dinner only, reservations required).

If you're prepared to spend some real money, stars of the local fine dining scene tend to cluster at Coronado's luxury hotels. The elegant **Crown-Coronet Room** at the Hotel del Coronado serves an astonishing, excellent brunch banquet on Sunday—probably enough calories to fuel the entire naval air base for a week—but the hotel also offers more contemporary style, including the **Prince of Wales Grill** and **Sheerwater,** with spacious outside terraces and gigantic fireplaces. For more information or restaurant reservations, call the hotel at 619/435-6611. Other hotel hot spots include **Azzura Point** at Loews Coronado Bay Resort, 619/424-4000, and the charming **L'Escale** brasserie and jazzy **La Provence** at the Coronado Island Marriott, 619/522-3039.

PRACTICAL SAN DIEGO

VISITOR INFORMATION

For current visitor information, contact the multilingual **San Diego International Visitor Information Center,** 11 Horton Plaza in downtown San Diego, 619/236-1212. For information via the Web, the address is www.sandiego.com.

If you're rolling into town on the spur of the moment, stop off at the **Mission Bay Visitor Information Center** on E. Mission Bay Drive (exit I-5 at Clairemont), 619/276-8200, open daily, where you can get enough info to get you around.

The San Diego Union-Tribune is the local newspaper of record but not all that impressive a rag, though even a cursory read will give you some sense of just how conservative this city is. The Thursday "Night and Day" section is useful for figuring out what's going on, but all in all the weekly *San Diego Reader* is a better information source, particularly for entertainment and restaurant listings. Entertaining alternative publications pop up too; look for them in hip bookstores, music shops, and cool coffeehouses.

SAN DIEGO TRANSPORT

Getting Here by Air

Everybody calls it Lindbergh Field, but the official name is the **San Diego International Airport,** three miles northwest of downtown San Diego (closer to Harbor Island) near the bay, just off Harbor Drive. Served by all major U.S. carriers—including **America West, American, Continental, Delta, Northwest, Reno Air, TWA, United,** and including the ever-popular **Southwest Airlines**—the airport is also served by **Aeromexico,** and smaller commuter lines. You can't store anything at the airport (no lockers), but it is open 24 hours, with restaurants, snack stops, and ATMs. For general airport information, call 619/231-2100.

Getting into Town from the Airport

By Bus: San Diego's Metropolitan Transit System (MTS) Route 992 provides service from the airport and downtown San Diego with stops outside each terminal. Buses run every 10 minutes during the week and every 15 minutes on weekends, though if you're traveling on a holiday be sure to check the holiday schedule. Fare is $2; for more information call 619/233-3004.

By Shuttle: One of the easiest ways to get where you're going is via shuttle. The 24-hour **Cloud 9 Shuttle,** 858/278-8877 or toll-free 800/ 9-SHUTTLE, is the most popular shuttle, and charges $6–10 to major points in the city.

By Taxi: Taxis line up outside the terminal and charge $7–10 for the trip downtown, usually a 5–10 minute ride.

Getting Here by Train

In many ways, the most civilized way to get here is by train. San Diego is easily reached by **Amtrak,** 619/239-9021 for recorded information or toll-free 800/872-7245 for reservations and schedules, www.amtrak.com, with daily trains coming and going from Los Angeles, Santa Barbara, and San Luis Obispo; you can also get to Solana Beach and other coastal San Diego County stops on one train or another.

The very attractive **Santa Fe Depot** downtown, 1050 Kettner Blvd. (at Broadway), is open all night; the ticket office is open daily 5 A.M.–9 P.M. The **San Diego Trolley** mass transit lines start here, too, making it quite easy to get around, at least between 5 A.M. and midnight.

Getting Here by Bus

The **Greyhound** bus station, open 24 hours, is downtown, just a few blocks east of the train station at 120 W. Broadway, 619/239-3266 or toll-free 800/231-2222. From here, L.A. is the major destination, though you can also trek east. Since the bus station is in an unsavory neighborhood, by San Diego standards, don't plan to walk the streets late at night—and keep an eye on your luggage. (Lockers are available.)

Getting Here by Car

Most people drive here—a fact quite obvious once you're on the local freeways, where traffic is typically nightmarish. The straight shot into downtown is provided by **I-5,** which dead-ends at the Mexican border; I-5 is also the main thoroughfare for reaching San Diego beach towns, Old Town, and Coronado Island. Inland, **I-15** creates the city's de facto eastern edge; if you follow it north it'll eventually deliver you to Las Vegas. The area's major east-west freeway is **I-8,** which slithers in out of the desert and slides to a stop at Mission Bay (after crossing paths with both I-15 and I-5). Heads up. And good luck, especially when merging—or trying to merge.

Getting Around

San Diego's public **Metropolitan Transit System (MTS),** 619/685-4900 (recorded), www.sdcommute.com (select Public Transit), also provides around-town bus service. Pick up a transit map at the visitor information center at Horton Plaza or call the MTS **Information Line,** 619/233-3004 or TTY/TDD 619/234-5005 (5:30 A.M.–8:30 P.M.), to figure out which bus will get you where. Another resource is the **Transit Store,** downtown at 449 Broadway (at Fifth), 619/234-1060, where you can pick up free brochures, route maps, and schedules. This is also the place to buy a variety of passes: the **Day Tripper** pass, for example, buys all-day access to local buses, the trolley system, and the ferry to Coronado.

More fun by far is the **San Diego Trolley** mass transit system, 619/231-8549 for current route and fare information (recorded). For assistance call 619/233-3004, 619/234-5005 TTY/ TDD. Several lines are now up and running—the **Old Town Line** from the Old Town transit center to the Santa Fe Depot; the **South Line** to the U.S./Mexico border; the **East Line** serving the east-county cities of El Cajon, Lemon Grove, and La Mesa; and the **Bayside Line** through the Gaslamp Quarter and on to the convention center and Seaport Village. The recently completed **Mission Valley** extension extends to Qualcomm Stadium, and is a handy way to get to the park on game days. Trolleys run 5 A.M.–8 P.M. at least every 15 minutes, and every half-hour until midnight, though the schedule varies somewhat from line to line; call for current information, or pick up a schedule at the Transit Store on Broadway (see above). One-way trolley fares run $1–2, depending on how far you're going; before boarding, buy your ticket at the relevant transit center vending machines (carry exact change)—or buy a Day Tripper pass at the Transit Store.

If they didn't drive into town, to get farther faster most people "go local" and rent a car. San Diego is served by the usual car rental agencies—the visitor center can provide you with a current listing—and some allow their cars to be driven into Mexico. If you don't particularly care about appearances, save some money with **Rent-a-Wreck,** 619/223-3300 or toll-free 800/535-1391. Rent-a-Wreck even rents motor homes, along with new and used cars, trucks, and vans. Other options include **Avis,** toll-free 800/331-1212/800/331-2323 TDD, and **Payless Car Rental,** toll-free 800/PAYLESS.

Santa Fe Depot

ROBERT HOLMES/
CALIFORNIA DIVISION OF TOURISM

COURTESY AISLINN RACE

THE DESERTS
LAND OF LOST BORDERS

California's desert is a rugged paint-box panorama of stone-faced mountains and lonely mesas. And sand. Mountains of sand, rivers of sand, valleys of sand, drifting plains of sand scoured white by sun, salt, and wind. Sage and creosote-bush plateaus where tumbleweeds dodge prehistoric rock and rubble. Joshua trees, grizzled high-desert sentries as indifferent to hellish heat and withering winds as to any of humanity's higher hopes. Sweet-water palm oases ripe with songbirds and serpents. The fragile strength of spring wildflowers willing to accept, even celebrate, life in no-man's-land.

California's desert is also space, time, and timelessness, the expansiveness of land without boundaries or any sense of limitation within very limiting natural laws. And air, and open-air attitudes. And sky, an enduring white-hot haze transmuted at dusk into cinnabar, sienna, and old gold. At night, on every horizon, the endless indigo sky contains all else.

In her 1903 *The Land of Little Rain,* California's desert-poet laureate Mary Austin described this "Country of Lost Borders" and the power of its night sky. "For all the toll the desert takes of a man it gives compensations," she wrote, "deep breaths, deep sleep, and the communion of the stars. . . . It is hard to escape the sense of mastery as the stars move in the wide clear heavens to risings and settings unobscured. They look large and near and palpitant; as if they moved on some stately service not needful to declare. Wheeling to their stations in the sky, they make the poor world-fret of no account. Of no account you who lie out there watching, nor the lean coyote that stands off in the scrub from you and howls and howls."

TWO BECOME ONE

California's 25 million acres of desert stretch east from Los Angeles and its edge cities into Nevada and Arizona, south into Mexico, and north to the Sierra Nevada foothills. Yet the Southern California desert is actually two distinct deserts: the low Colorado, which is the vast California extension of Mexico's Sonoran Desert,

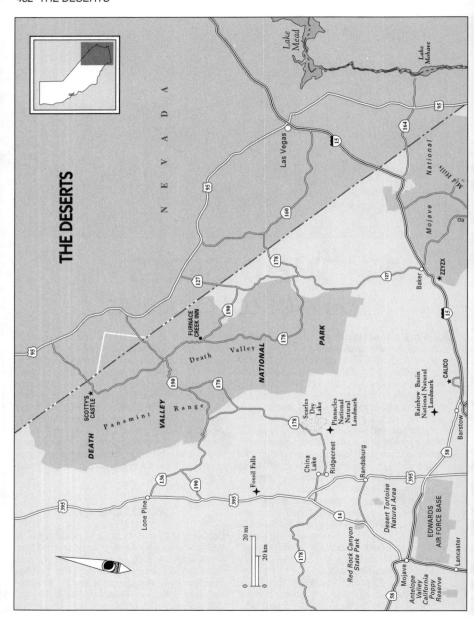

THE DESERTS

NEVADA

Lake Mead

Lake Mohave

Las Vegas

95

160

15

164

95

Mid Hills

Mojave National

RD

178

127

Baker

★ ZZYZX

127

190

FURNACE CREEK INN

15

95

Death Valley

NATIONAL

178

PARK

SCOTTY'S CASTLE ★

190

178

DEATH

VALLEY

Panamint Range

Searles Dry Lake

Pinnacles National Natural Landmark

★

Rainbow Basin National Natural Landmark

✦

CALICO ★

Barstow

178

China Lake

Ridgecrest

Randsburg

58

136

190

395

Fossil Falls ✦

Lone Pine

395

14

Desert Tortoise Natural Area

395

EDWARDS AIR FORCE BASE

178

Red Rock Canyon State Park

Mojave

Lancaster

58

Antelope Valley California Poppy Reserve

20 mi

20 km

0

0

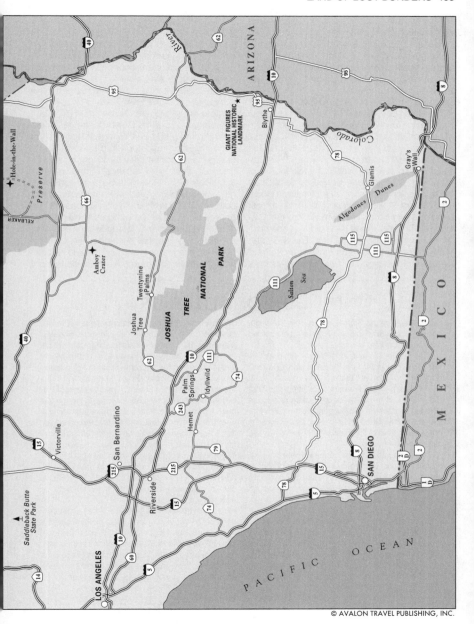

© AVALON TRAVEL PUBLISHING, INC.

and the Mojave or high desert. Travelers heading north along the eastern Sierra Nevada traipse from the Mojave into the far western fringe of California's third desert—the Great Basin, the endless "sagebrush desert" of the West, which spreads into surrounding states from Nevada and extends also into Washington, Wyoming, Colorado, and New Mexico.

The Colorado Desert is desert as most people imagine it: a low-lying landscape of sand, undulating sand dunes, and stark mountains. It is hot in summer—an average of 120°F during the day—and mild and frost free in winter. The Colorado is also very dry, with just a few inches of rain in an average year. For all its dessicated modesty, a secret flamboyance bursts into bloom after winters of above-average rainfall—almost embarrassing botanical excess. Yet the Colorado's plant and animal life is plentiful and quite diverse even during hard times. The two categories of primary Sonoran Desert "indicators" are trees of the legume (pea) family, such as

the smoke tree and green-barked palo verde found in California, and giant cacti, such as the saguaro, that are not (because of insufficient summer rain). Unlike Great Basin flora, which have an evolutionary connection to arctic climates, plants of the Colorado Desert are tropical descendants—jungle plants that learned to live without water.

Most of the Mojave Desert (mo-HAW-vay), spreading north of the Colorado, ranges in elevation from 2,000 to 4,000 feet. It features one characteristic "indicator"—the striking Joshua tree, a giant yucca named by Mormons after the biblical Joshua, since its "arms" turned upward in supplication to heaven—though, in addition to other unique plant species, it shares many with both the Great Basin and Colorado Deserts. The presence or absence of Joshua trees helps determine the vague Colorado-Mojave boundary, an imaginary line that shimmers like a mirage between Indio near Palm Springs and Needles near the Nevada border. The transitional zone

THE LAND OF LITTLE RAIN

East away from the Sierras, south from Panamint and Amargosa, east and south many an uncounted mile, is the Country of Lost Borders.

Ute, Paiute, Mojave, and Shoshone inhabit its frontiers, and as far into the heart of it as a man dare go. Not the law, but the land sets the limit. Desert is the name it wears upon the maps, but the Indian's is the better word. Desert is a loose term to indicate land that supports no man; whether the land can be bitted and broken to that purpose is not proven. Void of life it never is, however dry the air and villainous the soil.

This is the nature of that country. There are hills, rounded, blunt, burned, and squeezed up out of chaos, chrome and vermilion painted, aspiring to the snowline. Between the hills lie high level-looking plains full of intolerable sun glare, or narrow valleys drowned in a blue haze. The hill surface is streaked with ash drift and black, unweathered lava flows. After rains water accumulates in the hollows of small closed valleys, and, evaporating, leaves hard dry levels of pure desertness that get the local name of dry lakes. Where the mountains are steep and the rains heavy, the pool is never quite dry,

but dark and bitter, rimmed about with the efflorescence of alkaline deposits. A thin crust of it lies along the marsh over the vegetating area, which has neither beauty nor freshness. In the broad wastes open to the wind the sand drifts in hummocks about the stubby shrubs, and between them the soil shows saline traces. The sculpture of the hills here is more wind than water work, though the quick storms do sometimes scar them past many a year's redeeming. In all the Western desert edges there are essays in miniature at the famed, terrible Grand Cañon, to which, if you keep on long enough in this country, you will come at last. . . .

The desert floras shame us with their cheerful adaptations to the seasonal limitations. Their whole duty is to flower and fruit, and they do it hardly, or with tropical luxuriance, as the rain admits. It is recorded in the report of the Death Valley expedition that after a year of abundant rains, on the Colorado desert was found a specimen of Amaranthus ten feet high. A year later the same species in the same place matured in the drought at four inches. One hopes the land may breed like qualities in her human offspring, not tritely to "try," but to do. . . .

between the Colorado and Great Basin Deserts, the Mojave borrows seasonal extremes from each—being quite cold (sometimes snow-covered) in the winter, like the Great Basin, and hot in summer, like the Colorado.

For all their differences, the Colorado and the Mojave share a fundamental ecological fragility— a fact that at first strikes many visitors as odd or unbelievable, given the landscape's raw and rugged appearance and the well-honed survival skills of both animals and plants. Yet in such a dry climate with sparse, slow-growing vegetation, both major and seemingly minor disruptions leave lasting scars on the landscape—be they mining pits, off-road vehicle tracks, or old roads (some still marked by wagon-wheel ruts). And desert plants and animals, with so many specialized survival adaptations or requirements and sometimes vast territory needs, can suddenly face extinction with the loss of what might otherwise seem a minimal amount of habitat to housing and mall developments, golf courses, agriculture, and freeways.

Shaking things up still more is the infamous and fairly active San Andreas Fault, California's most famous earthquake fault line, which slithers up through Colorado Desert sand near the Salton Sea, slides northwest past Palm Springs into the Mojave Desert, up into the Transverse Ranges, then slips over Tejon Pass before making a beeline to San Francisco and California's northern coast.

What Relief: Making and Remaking the Desert

California's three deserts are classified as "relief" deserts—meaning that their dry climates result from mountain ranges that intercept most precipitation. Ongoing weather patterns and the continuous work of water, wind, and extreme temperatures maintain and further create the desert—an endlessly interconnected process. For example: hot and cold temperatures fracture and peel away even the hardest granite,

---

There is no special preponderance of self-fertilized or wind-fertilized plants, but everywhere the demand for and the evidence of insect life. Now where there are seeds and insects there will be birds and small mammals and where these are, will come the slinking, sharp-toothed kind that prey on them. Go as far as you dare in the heart of a lonely land, you cannot go so far that life and death are not before you. Painted lizards slip in and out of rock crevices, and pant on the white hot sands. Birds, hummingbirds even, nest in the cactus scrub; woodpeckers befriend the demoniac yuccas; out of the stark, treeless waste rings the music of the night-singing mockingbird. If it be summer and the sun well down, there will be a burrowing owl to call. Strange, furry, tricksy things dart across the open places, or sit motionless in the conning towers of the creosote. The poet may have "named all the birds without a gun," but not the fairy-footed, ground-inhabiting, furtive, small folk of the rainless regions. They are too many and too swift; how many you would not believe without seeing the footprint tracings in the sand. . . .

If one is inclined to wonder at first how so many dwellers came to be in the loneliest land that ever came out of God's hands, what they do there and why stay, one does not wonder so much after having lived there. None other than this long brown land lays such a hold on the affections. The rainbow hills, the tender bluish mists, the luminous radiance of the spring, have the lotus charm. They trick the sense of time, so that once inhabiting there you always mean to go away without quite realizing that you have not done it. . . .

The palpable sense of mystery in the desert air breeds fables, chiefly of lost treasure. Somewhere within its stark borders, if one believes report, is a hill strewn with nuggets; one seamed with virgin silver; an old clayey water-bed where Indians scooped up earth to make cooking pots and shaped them reeking with grains of pure gold. Old miners drifting about the desert edges, weathered into the semblance of the tawny hills, will tell you tales like these convincingly. After a little sojourn in that land you will believe them on their own account. It is a question whether it is not better to be bitten by the little horned snake of the desert that goes sidewise and strikes without coiling, than by the tradition of a lost mine.

Excerpted from The Land of Little Rain, *a collection of essays by Mary Austin, first published in 1903, republished in 1974 by the University of New Mexico Press.*

sculpture work smoothed by wind-blasted sand. Sudden rivers of water—flash floods racing down steep stone canyons—pile boulders, large stones, and gravel into massive alluvial fans. The hot sun, freezing cold, and wild desert thunderstorms pound rocks into sand. The relentless winds pile the sand into dunes. Winds also prune the dead wood from desert trees and shrubs and disperse seeds. Heavy rains cause the seeds to germinate and take root—the new plants slowing wind-blown sand just long enough to start a new dune.

A Landscape Millions of Years in the Making

The popular conception of classical desert as a barren wasteland, some monotonous sea of naked sand baking under a steady sun, does not fit California's complex desert landscape. Its astonishing diversity of landforms and plant and animal life is the direct result of its complex creation story. In brief:

Long, long ago—200 to 600 million years ago—the areas now identifiable as Southern California desert were inundated by ocean, a period "recorded" by rocks (sandstone, limestone) still visible today. Millions of years later these oceanic lands rose out of the sea and erosive forces—sun, rain, ice, and wind—whittled away at them.

Then volcanoes got into the game, creating mountains and depositing mud and ash—a process that continued in the desert until quite recently. Volcanic violence fueled even more ambitious mountain building, however. Some 60 million years ago earthquakes re-created the

Sierra Nevada. Other new mountain ranges—what we know today as the Basin Ranges north of the Great Basin, the Transverse Ranges at the western edge of the Mojave Desert, and the Colorado Desert's Peninsular Ranges—took their places, too, as huge granite blocks popped up through the earth's crust and wild magma flows glued them in place.

Wetter weather conditions soon created a vast region of lakes, streams, and lush vegetation. Time continued to chisel and shape the landscape for the next 25 million years or so, a period of alternating wet and dry cycles during which mountains were created and then crumbled only to be created anew. Fossilization continued. During the next two million years, with the arrival of the Ice Age and the Pleistocene epoch, the region rested.

Then the ice receded, and the land awakened to new possibilities. Rivers of ice-melt sliced through the stony landscape before racing to the sea or pooling into vast inland lakes. Some 10,000 years ago even Death Valley wasn't yet dry. It was a lake—actually, a series of lakes, separated by giant steps in time. But by 6,000 years ago the region's great lakes, including Death Valley's, had become mere puddles, the landscape watered only by streams and sweetwater springs. Some 3,000 years ago the lakes, streams, and springs had vanished; water, and more lakes, came again. But by 2,000 years ago the vast interior was again nearly bone-dry. For its further work, time used wind and intense dry heat.

One day the elements will pound these boulders into desert sand.

KIM WEIR

DESERT SURVIVALISTS: FLORA AND FAUNA

In recent years the California desert has provided evidence that life on land may have existed some 1.2 billion years ago, rather than 500 million years ago as deduced previously. As reported by *Science* in 1994, fossils of microscopic bacteria or blue-green algae filaments discovered in Death Valley and in Arizona suggest that a rich pasture of microbes flourished long before more diverse species began to appear.

That later species diversity is well represented in the California deserts.

More than 2,000 plant species—grasses, annual and perennial wildflowers and herbs, ferns, shrubs, and trees—are at home here, with more than 700 species of flowering plants alone. Half of these plants are common to both the Mojave and Colorado. Yet a high number are endemic to a particular region or isolated area—found nowhere else on earth. Early desert botanical researcher Philip Munz, for example, estimated that one-fourth of the plants in the Mojave Desert are endemic species.

In the desert's animal kingdom are thousands of insect and invertebrate species, more than 300 different resident and migratory birds, countless reptiles (including snakes), and more than 50 different mammals. These include the spectacular but shy desert bighorn sheep—some-

---

DESERT WILDERNESS: NEW NATIONAL PARKS

The California Desert Protection Act—passed by the U.S. Congress on October 8, 1994, and signed into law by President Clinton on October 31 of that year—protects the largest amount of wilderness ever set aside at one time, outside Alaska.

With the addition of 1.3 million acres, the former Death Valley National Monument became **Death Valley National Park**—at 3.3 million acres, the largest national park in the Lower 48 (Yellowstone, 2.2 million acres in Wyoming, is now second largest). The new **Joshua Tree National Park**, also previously a national monument, gained a few acres as well. And the East Mojave National Scenic Area previously managed by the U.S. Bureau of Land Management is now the 1.4 million-acre **Mojave National Preserve**—instead of the East Mojave National Park proposed by environmentalists—but nonetheless managed by the National Park Service.

Within these three new national parks, the California Desert Protection Act designated 39 new federal wilderness areas; 94 percent of Death Valley terrain, for example, is now protected as wilderness. The Act established 69 additional desert wilderness areas, totaling another 3.66 million acres, on nearby federal lands—largely BLM land but also national forests and wildlife refuges.

Aside from obvious turf and name changes, the primary effects of the California Desert Protection Act are philosophical and regulatory—eliminating mining, hunting, target practice, and widespread off-road vehicle use, among other long-running local traditions. (Regulated hunting is still allowed in the Mojave National Preserve and on nonwilderness BLM lands. Off-roading—whether with mountain bikes, dirt bikes, dune buggies, or four-wheel drives—is still permitted on various state and federal lands.) Four-wheel-drive vehicles, motorcycles, and mountain bikes, are still allowed even in national parks, but only on established gravel and dirt roadways. No vehicles are permitted "off-road" or in wilderness areas.

The most remarkable aspect of the California Desert Preservation Act is its emphasis on the cooperative "ecosystem management" of federal lands in the greater Mojave Desert. Altogether, 5.6 million acres of National Park Service lands—in Death Valley and Joshua Tree National Parks and in the Mojave National Preserve—and an additional 4 million acres of BLM wilderness are included in this effort to preserve natural and cultural resources across jurisdictional boundaries.

For detailed information on all 69 of the BLM's new desert wildernesses, contact the California Desert District Office, 6221 Box Springs Rd., Riverside, CA 92507, 909/697-5200; www.ca.blm.gov /cdd. For current information on the national parks, contact Joshua Tree National Park, 74485 National Park Dr., Twentynine Palms, CA 92277, 760/367-5500, www.nps.gov/jotr; Mojave National Preserve, 222 E. Main St., Ste. 202, Barstow, CA 92311, 760/733-4040, (760)326-6322, and 760/928-2572, www.nps.gov/moja; and Death Valley National Park, P.O. Box 579, Death Valley, CA 92328, 760/786-2331; www.nps.gov/deva.

times seen grazing on fairways at Palm Springs –area golf courses—and its primary predator, the mountain lion. Bighorn sheep are still legally hunted as game animals in some desert areas, albeit on a limited, big-ticket lottery basis.

The slow-moving California desert tortoise, a gentle grazer, is among the desert's most endangered animals—crushed by cattle as well as dirt bikes and other off-road vehicles, bulldozed out of the way for subdivisions, captured for food or for life as a backyard pet, and shot for sport. Recent signs suggest that the tortoise is staging a comeback, but many other species are still seriously threatened; they include the desert kit fox, trapped into near extinction for its exquisite fur, and the rare fringe-toed lizard, now protected only at the Nature Conservancy's Coachella Valley Preserve.

Though California desert plants and animals may not survive rapid change wrought by the state's burgeoning human population, in all other ways they are survivors—well-adapted to an inhospitable environment of intense heat (sometimes intense cold), unrelenting sunshine, high winds, very little and infrequent rain, and alkaline soil.

Plant Survival Strategies

Specific plant adaptations to dry desert conditions fall into one of three general categories of "strategy": drought avoidance, drought tolerance, and water storage—the latter a variation of the "save it for a rainy day" philosophy.

The simplest way to avoid a drought is to avoid life in the midst of drought conditions— the strategy of annual herbs and grasses, the desert's famed wildflowers. Desert-adapted annuals produce seeds unusually resistant to the desert's notorious extremes of heat and moisture (or lack thereof), usually with very thick or chemically sensitive seed coats that fail to germinate unless at least one inch of rain falls. Plants that successfully bloom will also set and disperse their seeds, but the seeds of many species will not germinate except under ideal conditions—remaining dormant in the soil, protected by unusually thick seed coats or other adaptions, for years, sometimes decades.

Years of exceptionally heavy, early, and "even" rain—more than five inches, falling at an average of at least one inch per month from November through March—are astonishing years in the desert. Spring puts on an unforgettable show, with the wildflower display usually starting in mid-February or early March and continuing in succession through at least April. Plants and wildflowers that fail to bloom at other times, or showy annuals whose seeds germinate only during rainy years, transform the most desolate and arid desert landscapes—where annuals face little competition from other species—into instant botanical wonderlands. But in any year, at least some of the desert's more ephemeral beauties burst into bloom. The timing can vary considerably from year to year, depending on rain frequency, temperature, and other factors, so before setting out on a spring wildflower tour call various park visitor centers for current information. For an overview of the desert's wildflower season, see also "Wildflowers: The Most Ephemeral Desert Beauty" elsewhere in this chapter.

Desert flora's second survival strategy, drought tolerance, is multifaceted. Trees, most shrubs, and some flowering herbs and grasses have adopted a perennial growth habit, meaning that year after year, during the rainy season, the plant resumes growth or resprouts from its existing root system. Under conditions of extreme stress the plant stops growing, or may die back altogether, only to be born again when the rains return.

Another way to tolerate drought is by minimizing transpiration, therefore conserving precious moisture, through reduced leaf surface area. Under the stress of heat and water loss leaves may become progressively smaller; sometimes they curl or otherwise change shape to minimize exposure to sun and hot air, and sometimes they grow protective hairs or excrete wax- or resinlike sealants. Sometimes leaves, even entire branches, dry up and fall off—all to conserve the plant's root system and its core structure.

Another useful drought-tolerance strategy: vast and extensive root systems. These water-foraging systems may be horizontal, beneath the soil's surface, to immediately capture every available drop of moisture when it does rain; vertical, to take up moisture for a longer time by tapping deeper reserves; or both. Yet another: seasonal color changes. The gray-green desert

DESERT SURVIVAL: BE PREPARED

Human survival in the desert is fairly easy to manage. Yet given the severity of the environment, it's also nothing to take for granted. In any season, never hike, bike, climb, or go four-wheeling alone. Be sure to let someone know where you're going and when you expect to arrive or return—a good idea even on highway trips.

First and foremost, plan your supply stops; beyond Palm Springs, best bets in the desert proper include Barstow and Ridgecrest. Basic readiness for desert travel includes a travel-worthy car—no known engine trouble, good tires and an inflated spare, tire chains, full tank of gas—along with accurate maps, extra water, extra food, extra clothing, blankets or sleeping bags, a fresh first-aid kit, and personal essentials (medications, extra eyeglasses, etc.). Basic emergency supplies include materials for makeshift shade and shelter (tarp or tube tent plus nylon cord), fire-starting and signaling supplies (waterproof matches or lighters, candles, safety flares, flashlight, signal mirrors, whistles), and both salty and high-energy foods.

If you'll be traveling on remote back roads, an extra five-gallon can of gasoline (carried outside the passenger compartment) *and* an emergency five-gallon can of water—beyond what you think you'll need—are also prudent. Also handy: tool kit and car repair manual, extra engine oil, carpet scraps (for traction if you get stuck), spare hoses and clamps, radiator stop-leak, tire repair kit and tire pump, jack pad (to support the tire jack in sandy soils), shovel, electrical tape, and baling or other sturdy wire.

In hot weather stay in the shade during the heat of the day, slow down—avoid overheating yourself—

and drink plenty of water, even if you don't feel particularly thirsty. (By the time you do, you're on the way to dehydration.) Intense heat inspires heavy perspiration, which, in practical terms, means people need to drink at least one gallon of water per day. Wear a hat, sunglasses, and loose long pants and long-sleeved shirts to minimize sun exposure. Slather on the sunscreen. Wear (or at least carry) good sturdy shoes to protect your feet in case you'll need to walk any distance. When the ambient air temperature is 120°F or so, the temperature of the desert's surface is up to 40 percent higher.

Should you become stranded in the desert heat, even if within a few miles of a highway, remember the first rule of survival: Take care of yourself first. In other words, tend to basic survival needs before worrying about repairing your vehicle or otherwise seeking rescue. Stay with your vehicle and stay out of the sun (underneath your car if there's no other available shade). Wait until the day cools to work on the car or walk for help—if you must, and if you know where you're going. Even if you're hopelessly stuck, in most cases it's wiser to wait for help to come to *you.* Don't wander away from your car and get lost.

If stranded in cold weather, the same "personal survival first" rule applies. Dress warmly and stay dry to avoid hypothermia (a dangerous drop in body temperature). Build a fire if possible, wrap yourself in blankets or a sleeping bag, eat well, drink warm liquids, and move around—walk briskly, do jumping jacks—to maintain body temperature and circulation. Do *not* drink alcohol, which may make you feel warmer but actually lowers body temperature—starting with the heart, lungs, and other vital organs.

---

holly, for example, fades to nearly white during summer heat, helping to reduce transpiration.

The ultimate drought-tolerance strategy is dormancy, often in conjunction with one or more other adaptations.

The third primary desert-survival strategy is gluttony followed by long-term water storage—the way of desert succulents, the cacti and their close relatives. These plants take in as much water as possible when it rains, through far-reaching and very shallow root systems, then store it in stems, leaves, or roots until needed for survival.

An oddity of most succulents—and, in a sense, another survival strategy—is their unique method of photosynthesis: crassulation acid metabolism or CAM. In typical photosynthetic gas exchange, plants take in carbon dioxide and release oxygen during the daytime—in the process losing water, or transpiring, through plant "pores" or stomates. In succulents, stomates open at night to take in carbon dioxide; plants use it for photosynthesis during the day, then, when the stomates open again at night, release oxygen. Since temperatures are cooler and the air more humid at night, much less water is lost during the process. Plants that use CAM photosynthesis also have the remarkable ability to "idle," without lapsing into dormancy, during periods of extreme heat or drought—sealing off stomates day and night and recycling both carbon dioxide and oxygen within a tightly closed and self-contained photosynthetic system. Unlike dormant plants, which can take weeks to revive once external conditions improve, CAM succulents can function normally within 12 to 24 hours—allowing them to take full advantage of light or unseasonal rainfall.

But even if succulents and other plants succeed in stashing away or otherwise acquiring an adequate water supply, that success comes to nothing if thirsty critters decide to share the wealth. So it's not surprising that cacti, other succulents, and many nonsucculent species have devised defenses against predators—sharp "hairs," thorns, and porcupine-like spines as well as bitter-tasting flesh and effective toxins.

Animal Survival Strategies

Like plants, desert animals have evolved various strategies to survive the extreme climate. For mammals, chief among these is nocturnal habit—coming out only at night to eat, drink, and procreate—thereby avoiding the hottest, driest daylight hours. Some mammals hibernate. The round-tailed ground squirrel, for example, takes time off both in summer and winter, emerging in spring to eat, drink, and mate, then again in fall to feast again. Others have special adaptations to survive the heat and limited water supply. Because of a unique evolutionary adaptation in body-temperature tolerance, the chipmunklike antelope ground squirrel is one of few mammals seen out and about during the heat of the day. When the ground squirrel's internal temperature exceeds 110 °F, it retreats to a cool burrow; when the excess heat has dissipated, it scurries out again to continue foraging. And the kangaroo rat requires no water

beyond what it absorbs from seeds and can "recycle" from basic metabolism because of its advanced water-conservation adaptations, these including low water loss in urine and feces and a special nasal passage that condenses water from the air.

Birds of the desert, with internal body temperatures naturally higher than those of other animals and the ability to fly to available water sources, have less need of desert-specific adaptations. Desert reptiles, including lizards, snakes, and the threatened desert tortoise, are unable to regulate their body temperatures internally; to avoid the predator- and prey-related dangers of sluggishness, they hibernate during the winter. During active periods, however, they respond to climatic conditions almost constantly. Most snakes are nocturnal. Many lizards scurry around during the day, lowering their body temperatures by slipping under rocks or otherwise retreating to the shade as needed. Nocturnal lizards, like snakes, avoid the heat of day and maintain body heat at night by absorbing solar heat from rocks. And the desert's famous fish—the pupfish, prehistoric species remaining in and around Death Valley—have adapted to changing times and more limited circumstances, surviving both in highly saline water and hot springs.

Insects and other desert invertebrates are also well-adapted desert survivors. In summer, species including many moths and butterflies escape through "estivation," a form of suspended animation that can extend for years when conditions are particularly extreme. Some insects require no water, obtaining what they need from food alone; others excrete no water, instead eliminating uric acid in solid form. And when times are so bad that adults can barely survive, before their ultimate recycling many species produce substantial numbers of eggs—the next generation. Like desert-adapted plant seeds, most insect eggs can survive inhospitable conditions for indefinite periods.

GREATER PALM SPRINGS

THE DESERT RIVIERA

In the beginning was the desert—the wide and sandy Coachella Valley of the Colorado Desert, where Mount San Jacinto, the San Jacinto Mountains, and the scenic and steep Santa Rosa Mountains served as the scenic backdrop for scattered fan-palm oases. The city of Palm Springs, still considered a "village" by locals, took its name from the Cahuilla people's sacred palm-shaded hot springs, atop which the Spa Hotel and Casino stands today.

Then came the movie stars. Palm Springs was renowned as a winter playground of the famous and the rich almost since its discovery by Hollywood in the 1920s. Aside from more sensible Cahuilla cultural traditions, the most fundamental history of Palm Springs is largely secret. This is the town, after all, where former President John F. Kennedy's illicit liaison with Marilyn Monroe purportedly took place, in March of 1962. The local attitude has always been that if movie stars, starlets, singers, dancers, rock stars, politicians, and just plain rich people want to get doped up, crazy drunk, or just plain crazy in reasonable privacy, then so what?

So what, indeed.

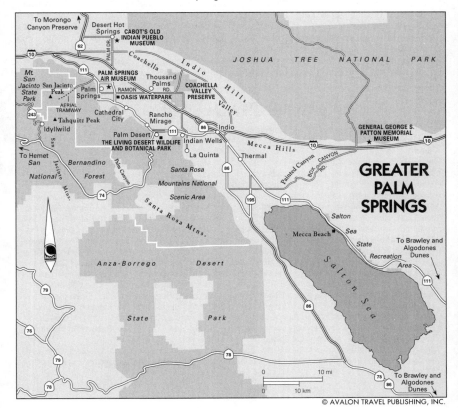

Then came everyone else. Since its early days the very idea of Palm Springs has influenced middle-class America's more innocent, more romantic ideals—many of these inspired by the thoughtful yet clearly promotional 1920 book *Our Araby: Palm Springs and the Garden of the Sun* by J. Smeaton Chase. Who wouldn't love a balmy valley surrounded by snow-covered peaks in winter, exotic desert, date gardens, and citrus and avocado groves? A place where the air is clean and the sun shines year-round? A place where, on Christmas Day, people sun themselves and frolic in swimming pools?

Who, indeed.

Of Greens and Green

One wag has described Palm Springs as "a theme park masquerading as a city, with the themes being money, sunshine, and a wistful proximity to fame." Particularly among the wealthy, money is the magic. According to abbreviated local social history, *new* new money chased the new money that chased the movie money to Palm Springs. Nowadays, though, the tourist dollar is chasing it all—a middle-brow economic reality best symbolized by the new convention center in downtown Palm Springs.

But people still covet fame, or some connection to it. These days more celebrities appear on area street signs than anywhere else. Even an incomplete list is impressive: Arthur Ashe Lane; Gene Autrey Trail; Bob Hope, Frank Sinatra, Dinah Shore, and Gerald Ford Drives; and Danny Kaye, Greer Garson, and Burns & Allen Roads. As in Hollywood and Los Angeles movie-industry neighborhoods, it seems everyone here knows someone who bathed Liberace's poodles, changed the sheets in Michael Jackson's suite at a local resort, or bartended a recent celebrity gala. (Palm Springs may have attracted its reclusive wealth by looking the other way, officially, but just plain folks who live here do look.) Charity balls, benefits, and celebrity sporting events keep society circles spinning; the winter season produces about one major event per week—astonishing amounts of "society" for what is, still, a very small community. The total Coachella Valley population is somewhere around 200,000.

GOLFING PALM SPRINGS

Newcomers sometimes gasp at Palm Springs' general greenness, its greens, and its green. It does seem a bit garish. To justify the general atmosphere of excess, everyone eagerly explains that the Coachella Valley sits atop a massive underground lake. Even if the Colorado River Aqueduct were snipped tomorrow, they say, the valley's cities, agriculture, and golf courses would stay green for at least 200 years.

So—water is abundant in and around Palm Springs, and so is world-class golf. The region passed its golf course century mark in November 2000, with the opening of its 100th course—the Rancho La Quinta Country Club in La Quinta, designed by Jerry Pate. All Palm Springs golf courses are way above par, designed by the likes of Robert Trent Jones, Jack Nicklaus, Gary Player, and Billy Casper. Most courses play through even in summer, though hot-season visitors should try for very early or very late (evening) tee times. And most are private and/or limited to resort guests, though at least limited public access is sometimes offered. Area standouts include the **Indian Wells Country Club** in Indian Wells, site of the Bob Hope Chrysler Classic; **PGA West** and the **La Quinta Resort Golf Club** in La Quinta; and the **Mission Hills North Golf Course** in Rancho Mirage.

Unlike other top-rated area golf courses, at which play is typically restricted to private club members and/or a resort's paying guests, the 18-hole **Tahquitz Creek Resort Golf Course** in Palm Springs is owned by the city of Palm Springs and available for the general public—including visitors. The 140-acre Tahquitz Creek course was designed by Ted Robinson and is managed by Arnold Palmer Golf Management in conjunction with the city's older public course. High-season green fees run $85 on weekends, less during the week. Call for current rates (seasonal) and reservations. For more information, contact Tahquitz Creek Resort, 1885 Golf Club Dr. in Palm Springs, 760/328-1005; www.palmsprings.com/golf/tahquitz.html.

For information on other golf course options and availability, contact local visitor bureaus.

Then there's the sunshine. In and around Palm Springs, major attractions include tennis, world-class golf, and swimming. Palm Springs boasts some 600 tennis courts. Golf courses are also legion—90-some at last count, many of them world-class and class-consciously exclusive. There's even a putting green at the local airport. Statistically speaking, what with the number of local hotels and resorts, there's about one swimming pool for every six residents—an amazing fact in any season but especially comforting to anyone who happens to be here during the searing summer months.

Golf courses and swimming pools require abundant water, of course, typically not available in the middle of the desert. Unlike much of Southern California, Palm Springs has plenty of water—and comes by it almost honestly, since the entire Coachella Valley sits atop a giant underground lake replenished by mountain runoff and (via aqueduct) the Colorado River.

The Palm Springs Appeal

Palm Springs has its peculiarities, including an excessive number of plastic surgeons, psychiatrists, and T-shirt shops. Palm Springs also has its charms—and an undeniable appeal. This sprawling rich people's retreat is also friendly to middle-income retirees, frugal sun-loving families, and a growing gay clientele. Though Easter week cruising and other once-riotous spring break celebrations were all but banned in the early 1990s, even college students are once again welcome. These days everyone but gang members from L.A. and Las Vegas are welcome in Palm Springs. And everything's cool—even under the influence of an incredible two million visitors per year.

There's plenty to do in and around Palm Springs, what with countless world-class golf and tennis resorts, swimming pools, cultural diversions, and shopping venues. Hot-spring spas, hikable canyons and mountains, botanical gardens and parks, museums, and almost endless outdoor activities connect the community to the region's unique natural history. The Coachella Valley is also still agricultural, or at least semiagricultural, especially farther east in the less affluent communities of Coachella, Indio, and Thermal, where agricultural workers and many of the hotel industry's maids, gardeners, and restaurant employees live. At least in cooler months, stopping at roadside produce stands and date groves is a pleasurable reprieve from garrulous glitz.

Best of all is the social acceptability of doing nothing, or next to nothing—a major attraction. Unlike Los Angeles, with its hectic hipness, here no one will think less of you for just sitting around the pool reading a good book.

When to Come

Winter is high season for Palm Springs tourism, also the peak season for spotting celebrities. Fall is the winter lead-in season, when the community's sociability comes out of heat-related hibernation. Spring is also party time. But you *can* enjoy summer here, despite the searing heat, thanks to moderating evening breezes, swimming pools, near-universal air-conditioning, and those nifty outdoor micro-misting systems. In fact, summer is the hot new season to do the town, with some businesses and attractions—even the Palm Springs Desert Museum—now open year-round. Better yet, summer prices are low and crowds are light. (The other "best bargain" times are early in fall and late in spring.) But people do tend to skip town during the blast-furnace days of August, and some businesses still close up shop. If it matters, check it out before setting out.

SEEING AND DOING PALM SPRINGS

Since Palm Springs is an attitude more than an easily definable place, it's not surprising that the entire Coachella Valley shares the city's mythic identity to some degree. Directly north of Palm Springs proper, for example, is Desert Hot Springs, atop the San Andreas fault—a geologic fact that explains why most of the valley's natural hot springs and historic health spas are here. But the Palm Springs cachet isn't confined to the valley's northwest side. Both new money and "new new" money have migrated down valley into neighboring Coachella Valley communities retaining their fair share of celebrity.

Palm Springs the Village

Palm Springs proper, where the celebrity-watching and scandalous wild parties began, is like an aging movie star who's finally found the fountain of youth. Just years after being declared all but dead, not only is downtown still alive and kickin', it's *lively,* an inimitable mix of settled "old Palm Springs" and increasingly hip "new Palm Springs" in its neighborhoods, restaurants, shops, and entertainment venues.

A symbol of 21st-century Palm Springs is the famous 1963 **Tramway Oasis Gas Station** near the town's northern entrance, designed by noted Palm Springs architect Albert Frey. This modern architectural landmark has been completely restored, and is now the **Montana St. Martin Art, Design, and Sculpture Gallery,** complete with sculpture garden. Retro is big in Palm Springs.

Though prices in stylish-again Palm Springs are increasing, this area is still the most central location for affordable accommodations and eateries. Get oriented by strol-

ling **Palm Canyon Drive,** also the **Palm Springs Walk of Stars,** and by following downtown's new pedestrian- and bike-friendly one-mile **Heritage Trail.**

For the dramatic "big picture" view of Palm Springs and vicinity, just outside town is the world-famous Palm Springs Aerial Tramway, which carts people straight up the face of Mount San Jacinto.

Major downtown attractions include the Palm Springs Desert Museum, a combination art, history, and natural history museum that also serves as a major area performance venue. For more historical perspective, head for the Village Green Heritage Center and adjacent Agua Caliente Cultural Museum Information Center. Fairly new is the Spa Hotel Casino, owned and operated by the Agua Caliente Band of Cahuilla Indians on

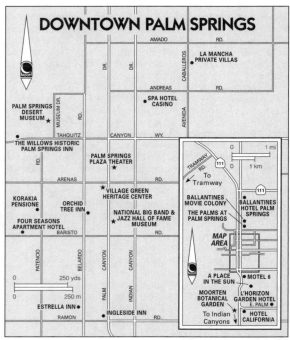

DOWNTOWN PALM SPRINGS

CAHUILLA COOL: THE AGUA CALIENTE PEOPLE

The Agua Caliente Band of the Cahuilla Indians (ka WEE ya) is quite prominent in Palm Springs political, social, and business affairs. The Cahuilla people's influence is partially due to their status as landed gentry. It wasn't always thus, of course; as typical elsewhere in California, the Cahuillas were effectively shoved off their own lands with the arrival of early settlers. But when the railroad blew into town, in exchange for their territorial losses the Cahuilla people were granted alternating tracts of land—then prevented by the federal government from selling it.

All in all, it was a fortunate turn of events. Collectively, the band now owns 32,000 acres of land in and around Palm Springs—roughly 42 percent of the entire Coachella Valley—including 6,700 acres within Palm Springs city limits. Many of the area's noted resorts are renters, essentially, with luxury hotels, golf courses, and tennis courts built on land owned, and leased out, by the local Cahuilla tribal council until the year 2025. Because of its wise stewardship of this very valuable real estate, the net worth of the Agua Caliente Band—"hot water" in Spanish, a reference to area hot springs—is substantial.

Stop by the free **Agua Caliente Cultural Museum Information Center,** part of the Village Green Heritage Center on South Palm Canyon Drive in downtown Palm Springs, to learn more about Cahuilla culture—including plans to build an impressive cultural museum complex in Tahquitz Canyon. The information center, 219 S. Palm Canyon Drive, 760/323-0151, fax 760/322-7724, is open weekends only in summer.

the site of their original sacred palm spring. Newer still is the Palm Springs Air Museum, one of the world's largest collections of rare World War II–era aircraft. New in 2001: the National Big Band & Jazz Hall of Fame Museum.

South of downtown on Palm Canyon Drive is long-running Moorten Botanical Garden, an impressive cactus and desert plant collection started more than 50 years ago by "Cactus Slim" Moorten and his wife. Beyond are the Cahuillas's Indian Canyons, tribal lands featuring some of the most striking natural palm oases and best hiking around.

Big doings in Palm Springs proper include the January **Nortel Palm Springs International Film Festival,** an event first launched in 1990 by then-mayor and late U.S. Congressman Sonny Bono, and the fairly new **Palm Springs International Shorts Film Festival** usually held in early August. During the traditional Palm Springs "season" the historic **Plaza Theatre,** restored to its original 1930s flash, hosts the fabulous **Fabulous Palm Springs Follies** vaudeville revue. **Palm Springs Village Fest**—with crafts, clothing, produce, food stands, and a certified Farmers Market—convenes along Palm Canyon Drive on Thursday evening year-round, 7–10 P.M., and look for free evening **Concerts in the Park,** blues and bluegrass to swing bands, in Sunrise Park on Ramon Road. Special events include the **Senior Softball World Series** in fall, the **Palm Springs Celebrity Golf Tournament** in December, and, substituting for spring break chaos, the annual **Palm Springs SunFest** during the weeks before and after Easter.

Greater Palm Springs

Just north of Palm Springs, almost astride the San Andreas fault, is Desert Hot Springs. Set apart from other Palm Springs-area resort cities both physically and socially, Desert Hot Springs is famous for its rejuvenating "waters"—hot mineral springs bubbling up from the ground, the main local draw since the 1930s. Hot Springs Park commemorates this "hot" local asset. The area's ritziest resorts are down valley, east of Palm Springs on the way to La Quinta, but most hot springs spas—laid-back, sometimes historic shrines of healthy self-indulgence—are in Desert Hot Springs. Also here: the eccentric Cabot's Old Indian Pueblo, a gift shop cum museum that's more "old Palm Springs" than just about anything around.

Just east of Palm Springs is Cathedral City, with most of the area's gay bars and craziest clubs. "Cat City," as locals call it, has a respectably renegade social history. During the 1920s and '30s, for example, Cat City was famous for its illicit gambling clubs and infamous for the very illegal—and very exclusive—Dunes Club casino.

TOURING PALM SPRINGS

Palm Springs is a great "tour town," as is true of the entire Coachella Valley. Here, unusual and unique tours are the norm. Quite timely, in these California days of deregulated power woes, is the ultimate power trip—the **Palm Springs Windmill Tour,** in which guests tour the terrain of the local "wind farm" caravan-style, in electric cars. This particular "ecoadventure" travels through sunny, metallic forests of wind-powered turbines, demonstrating the basics of wind energy, a nonpolluting, renewable resource. Wind power is not without its drawbacks; for one thing, turbines tend to be rather deadly for hapless birds. Still, this is no doubt one aspect of a sustainable future for California, so check it out. In peak season (fall through spring), tours are offered four times daily, at 9 and 11 A.M. and 1 and 3 P.M. Tours are also offered in summer, but in air-conditioned coaches (schedule varies). Reservations are required for all tours. At last report prices were $23 adults, $20 seniors, $15 high school and college students, $10 children (infants free), with a 20 percent discount for AAA members. For more information and reservations, contact: Windmill Tours, 62-950 20th Ave., North Palm Springs, CA 92258, 760/251-1997 or toll-free 877/449-WIND (group tours only), fax 760/323-0688; www.windmill-tours.com. The tour site is located at the intersection of I-10 and Indian Avenue, on 20th Avenue (North Frontage Road).

There are other unusual tours—backcountry jeep trips, covered wagon rides, mountain bike excursions, and nude moonlight hikes. Contact local visitor bureaus for complete current listings. **Desert Adventures Wilderness Jeep Tours,** 760/324-6530 (324-JEEP) or toll-free 888/440-6539 (440-JEEP), www.red-jeep.com, is immensely popular for its informative and entertaining backcountry jeep tours. Specific adventures include Indian Culture, Lost Legends of the Wild West, Mystery Canyon, and Sunset-Nightwatch. Among other awards, Desert Adventures has been honored with the Phoenix Award from the Society of American Travel Writers (SATW), for its active conservation, preservation, and promotion of natural resources, and with the Public Spirit Award from U.S. Bureau of Land Management. A good bet for guided area hikes is **Trail Discovery/Desert Safari Hiking Guide Service,** 760/325-4453 (325-HIKE) or toll-

free 888/324-4453 (324-HIKE), www.desertsafari.com, which also offers treks into Joshua Tree National Park. For toll-free information, call 888/867-2327 (TO-SAFARI).

Covered Wagon Tours, 760/347-2161 or toll-free 800/367-2161, www.coveredwagontours.com, offers authentic, educational, and very enjoyable tours of the Nature Conservancy's Coachella Valley Preserve by, yup, covered wagon. Fun, too, is **Adventure Bike Tours** in Rancho Mirage, and fax 760/328-2082, offering guided mountain bike tours into the outback (kids and groups welcome), bikes and helmets included. **Bighorn Bicycles** in Palm Springs, 760/325-3367, fax 760/325-5585, email: bighornbikes@webtv.net, offers guided hikes to spectacular outback destinations. And this one's free: Even if you don't stay at **Marriott's Desert Springs Resort and Spa** in Palm Desert, known for its immense indoor pools and interconnecting outdoor lakes, you can come for a free afternoon boat tour—that's right, *boat* tour—of the grounds. For information, call 760/341-2211.

It's not everyone's idea of a good time—and the kids might squirm—but since present-day Palm Springs was created by and for celebrities, you could go celebrity touring. (In a sense these tours are actually historical home tours, since most places along the route are where famous people *once* lived.) A best bet in this category is **Palm Springs Celebrity Tours,** headquartered in Palm Springs at 4751 E. Palm Canyon Dr., Ste. C, 760/770-2700, fax 760/770-2707; www.welcome.to/celebritytours.com. In addition to amusing star stories, this fun tour shares some entertaining lesser-known local lore. Find out where Hedy Lamarr, Marilyn Monroe, Elvis Presley, and Frank Sinatra lived; who golfs where; and what it all costs—quite enlightening, even for those who typically don't do this type of thing. Take either the one-hour or the two and a half-hour tour. For the short tour, rates are $17 adults, $15 seniors (60 and older), and $8 children (16 and under). The two-hour tour is $23 adults, $20 seniors, and $10 children. The regular schedule operates October–May, but summer tours are also offered; call for current details and reservations. Closed Thanksgiving, Christmas, and New Year's Day.

A MAP TO THE STARS' GRAVES

Sometimes people make the trip to great Palm Springs determined to visit people who aren't there anymore—thus the popularity of the free "Cemetery to the Stars" map provided by the Desert Memorial Cemetery in Cathedral City.

A major recent draw is the grave of entertainer Frank Sinatra, who died in May of 1998 and is buried in a family gravesite near the graves of his parents. Also buried here is former U.S. Congressman and former Palm Springs mayor Sonny Bono—known in a previous life as the shorter half of Sonny and Cher—who died in a skiing accident in January 1998.

Other celebrities at Desert Memorial include actor William Powell of *The Thin Man* fame; actor Cameron Mitchell; song and dance man Busby Berkeley; and songwriters Frederick Lowe and Jimmy Van Heusen.

For more information and directions, contact: **Desert Memorial Cemetery,** 69-920 E. Ramon Rd. (near I-10) in Cathedral City, 619/328-3316. Or just stop by and request a map; directly across the road from the cemetery is the Palm Springs Mortuary.

Down valley and in the big money, Rancho Mirage is a major golf mecca, home to the annual **Nabisco Dinah Shore LPGA golf tournament.** It has been called the "playground of the presidents," and can claim one as a resident—Gerald Ford. Other famous residents include billionaire philanthropist Walter Annenberg, U.S. ambassador to Great Britain during Richard Nixon's presidency, and Nixon's ex-vice president, the late Spiro Agnew. Rancho Mirage is also noted for first-class medical facilities, including The Eisenhower Medical Center, the Barbara Sinatra Children's Center, and the now-famous Betty Ford Clinic.

Boasting the most golf courses in the Coachella Valley is Palm Desert farther down valley, also famous for its country clubs, upscale shopping, November **Golf Cart Parade,** and summer **Haute Nites, Cool Sounds,** concerts. Palm Desert's major natural attraction is its naturalistic zoo—The Living Desert Wildlife and Botanical Park. Among the major annual events in Indian Wells, which boasts the area's highest

per-capita income, are the **Bob Hope Chrysler Classic Golf Tournament** (played concurrently at other area courses as well), the **Newsweek Champions Cup** and **State Farm Evert Cup** tennis tourneys, and the annual **New Year's Jazz at Indian Wells** festivities. Fast-growing La Quinta was named for its namesake forebear—the elegant Spanish-style La Quinta Hotel, the only place for miles around when it was built in 1926, still going strong as the ritzy La Quinta Resort and Club.

The oldest city around is Indio at the southern end of the valley. Indio's attractions include date gardens and polo fields, the Coachella Valley Museum and Cultural Center, and two Indian gaming centers—Fantasy Springs Casino and Spotlight 29 Casino. Among fun annual events: the **National Date Festival,** part of the Riverside County Fair, and the **International Tamale Festival.**

SEEING AND DOING GREATER PALM SPRINGS

Palm Springs Desert Museum

This superb regional museum, downtown at 101 Museum Drive, between Amado and Tahquitz Canyon, has benefited from Palms Springs–area wealth in general and its world-class private art collections in particular. Excellent dioramas and displays explore local natural history (kids love the live tarantula exhibit) and also showcase Palm Springs history and culture. The permanent art collection emphasizes both contemporary American and western Native American art; changing exhibits keep things lively. The museum's **Annenberg Theater** (separate admission required) schedules dance, music, theater, and other performances and hosts an excellent film series. The Palm Springs Desert Museum also boasts a great museum store and an on-site cafée (the café open weekdays only).

The museum is open Tues.–Sun. 10 A.M.–5 P.M. (Friday until 8 P.M.), closed Thanksgiving, Christmas, and New Year's Day. Hours are subject to change for selected special exhibits. Admission is $7.50 adults, $6.50 seniors (62 and over), and $3.50 children (6 to 17; age 5 and under free with adult). Free admission on the first Friday of every month. For current exhibit information, call 760/325-0189 (recorded). For other information, contact: Palm Springs Desert Museum, 101 Museum Dr., Palm Springs, CA 92263, 760/325-7186, fax 760/327-5069; www .psmuseum.org.

Spa Hotel Casino

The recently renovated **Spa Hotel,** 100 N. Indian Canyon Drive, now owned and operated by the Agua Caliente Band of Cahuilla Indians, stands on the site of the hot-springs palm oases for which Palm Springs was named. These springs are the source of the hotel's famed hot mineral water "swhirlpool" soaks. The hottest news these

---

DESERT ADVENTURING~BY JEEP

Even four-wheeling wannabes can do the desert's most adventurous backroads—by hitching a ride with Desert Adventures.

The flaming red Jeeps of this award-winning ecotour company take intrepid travelers into otherwise inaccessible areas of the Santa Rosa Mountains, scenic backdrop for Palm Springs and vicinity. Tour guides are knowledgeable and entertaining, providing a substantial introduction to local cultural and natural history, useful medicinal plants, and desert survival while tossing off tall tales and amusing trivia tidbits at every turn. Backroad trips into Joshua Tree National Park—thrilling for desert adventurers of all ages—and other tour options are offered, all including pickup and dropoff at area hotels. Also available through Desert Adventures: guided hiking tours, ecohiking, and hosted barbecues.

Tours typically last from two to four hours (lunch included on longer trips), so bring your wide-brimmed hat, sunscreen, and jacket if you'll be out during early morning or evening. Also bring your camera. The price depends on the tour and the number of people on board, but most trips run $79–$129 per person. Reservations are required.

For more information contact: **Desert Adventures Wilderness Jeep Tours,** 67-555 E. Palm Canyon Dr., Ste. A104, Cathedral City, CA 92234, 760/324-6530 (324-JEEP) or toll-free 888/440-6539 (440-JEEP); www.red-jeep .com.

---

days, though, is the adjacent Spa Hotel Casino, where pleasures run to video gaming, poker, and Spa 21 (similar to blackjack). The casino, which accommodates nonsmokers, is downtown between Andreas Road and Tahquitz Canyon Way (enter the casino from Indian Canyon). It's open 365 days per year, 24 hours per day. For casino information, call 760/323-5865 or toll-free 800/258-2946. For hotel information and reservations, call toll-free 800/258-2846. For spa information, call toll-free 888/293-0180.

Fabulous Palm Springs Follies

Vaudeville may be dead elsewhere, but in Palm Springs it's alive and kickin'—sky high, too, thanks to the Ziegfield Follies–style chorus line of the Fabulous Palm Springs Follies. All performers, including the dancers, are at least "50 to 80 years young, " and famed burlesque queen Tempest Storm is among more recent arrivals. The follies are staged at the historic 1930s' **Palm Springs Plaza Theatre,** 128 S. Palm Canyon (100 Jack Benny Plaza), also home to the **Palm Springs Hollywood Museum.** (Museum admission is free with show admission.) Follies tickets range from $35 to $65 or so, and the performance season runs from November through May. Both matinee and evening performances are scheduled. For more information and tickets, call 760/327-0225 or point your browser to www.palmspringsfollies.com.

Village Green Heritage Center

What nonmovie star history Palm Springs does have can be summed up in a very small amount of space. That space is right downtown at Village Green Heritage Center, 221 S. Palm Canyon Drive, where two historic homes and a facsimile 1930s' general store are on display. The 1884 **McCallum Adobe** and **Cornelia White House,** built from old railroad ties in 1893, give present-day desert pilgrims a cleaned-up look at life in Palm Springs during its cowboy days. Though the Depression-era **Ruddy's General Store** has nothing to do with Palm Springs in particular, this small museum does offer an amazingly authentic look at the wares and the wherefores of the good ol' days of American shopping—Prince Albert tobacco in a can (really), Rinso detergent, Uneeda biscuits packaged in a cracker barrel, ancient sewing notions, and snake-oil patent

SOME FAMILY FUN

In addition to appropriate attractions and diversions mentioned elsewhere, Palm Springs and vicinity offers plenty of family-style fun. **Camelot Park Family Entertainment Center,** 67-700 E. Palm Canyon Dr. (at Golf Club) in Cathedral City, 760/321-9893, fax 760/770-7525, features three separate miniature golf courses (each with its own theme), bumper boats, go-carts, batting cages, and a video games and arcade games pavilion. It all adds up to good, clean, family-style fun. Parents can play, too—but bring money. Park admission is free, but each attraction has a separate price tag.

Also in Cathedral City is the **Big League Dreams Sports Park,** 33-700 Date Palm Dr., 760/324-5600 or toll-free 888/390-7275, www.bigleaguedreams.com, which boasts scaled-down replicas of famous ballparks—Yankee Stadium, Fenway Park, and Wrigley Field—for baseball and softball, largely local league play. Big League Dreams also features batting cages, soccer fields, flag football fields, covered basketball courts, roller hockey rinks, and sand volleyball courts.

Some people think the **Oasis Waterpark,** 1500 Gene Autry Trail in Palm Springs (but quite close to Cathedral City), 760/327-0499 or toll-free 800/247-4664, is a water-conservation obscenity—21 acres of incessant evaporation with a whitewater river, giant waterslides and inner tube rides, a wave pool, body- and board-surfing, even beachlike amenities including sand volleyball. Other people, especially kids, just love this place. The **Centipede** water slide is now open-air and sans inner tubes, but the tandem **Black Widow** is still a tuber's darkest dream, with a 50-foot drop. Once tubed-out, visit Monte Carlo Beach with micro-mist-cooled private cabanas, gift shop, and food concessions. Oasis is open daily open at 11 A.M. from early March through Labor Day; after Labor Day, weekends only through October. Cost can be daunting, so be sure to make a full day of it: adults $18.95 (five-feet tall and up); $11.95 children three- to five-feet tall; free for those under three-feet tall. Parking $4. Also here is the **Uprising Rock Climbing Center,** 760/320-6630, offering beginner lessons and open-air, shaded, micro-misted climbing all year.

medicines. Though hours can change, all three museums are usually open at least Thurs.–Sun. 10 A.M.–4 P.M. from October through June. Small admission donation.

In many ways more fascinating than the Village Green's official history are the tidbits of local Native American culture on display at the adjacent **Agua Caliente Cultural Center Information Center**—Cahuilla basketry, cultural beliefs, ceremonial tradition, and plans for the cultural center and museum planned for Tahquitz Canyon near downtown. Since Tahquitz was the Cahuilla guardian spirit of the shamans, the location should prove propitious. Most of the year the information center, 219 S. Palm Canyon Dr., 760/323-0151, is open Thurs.–Sat. 10 A.M.–4 P.M. and Wednesday and Sunday noon–3 P.M. It's open weekends only in summer, Fri.–Sun. noon–3 P.M.

National Big Band & Jazz
Hall of Fame Museum

Scheduled to open in April 2001, Palm Springs' jazzy new museum is a 16,000-aquare-foot venue at 296 S. Palm Canyon Dr. (the former Home Savings of America building), 760/320-3128 or toll-free 877/425-5633. An event as much as a destination, the museum includes a dance floor, a bandstand with room for a 12- to 17-piece orchestra, the Java Jazz coffee lounge, and One Bourbon Street—an outdoor patio area with live entertainment—along with the exhibits, education center, and theater. The museum is open Sun.–Wed. 10 A.M.–6 P.M., Thurs.–Sat. 10 A.M.–10 P.M. Admission is $12. You can't miss the place, especially after dark. Just look for the 17-foot "water and fire" saxophone out front.

Moorten Botanical Garden

Calling itself the "world's first cactarium," the Moorten Botanical Garden features more than 3,000 species of cacti and other desert plants in its circa-1938 arboretum and garden complex. Wander along the nature trail, where something is always in bloom. Exhibits are added regularly. Nursery-grown plants are available for sale. Small admission. It's open Mon.–Sat. 9 A.M.–4:30 P.M., Sunday 10 A.M.–4 P.M. Admission is $2

The Historic Cornelia White house offers a glimpse of life in Palm Springs during its cowboy days.

KIM WEIR

adults, $.75 for children ages 5–15. The garden is south of downtown on the way to Indian Canyons, on the west side of Highway 111 at the South/East Palm Canyon Drive "split." For more information, contact: Moorten Botanical Garden, 1701 S. Palm Canyon Dr., 760/327-6555.

Palm Springs Air Museum

A fairly new museum in town, the $5 million Palm Springs Air Museum at the Palm Springs Regional Airport has a venerable starring cast. One of the world's largest collections of World War II–vintage fighters and bombers still in flight form, the exhibits here include the rotating Robert J. Pond collection—everything from the Boeing B-17 Flying Fortress and Stearman PT-17 Kaydet to the Chance Vought F4U Corsair and the Russian Yakovlev YAK-11 Moose. Regular flight demonstrations are offered, of both the museum's planes and visiting aircraft. Other exhibits include rare, original combat photography, original artwork and murals, and video documentaries as well as artifacts, memorabilia, and uniforms. Admission is $7.50 adults, $6 seniors and military, $3.50 children ages 6–11 (under 6 free). The museum is open daily 10 A.M.-5 P.M., closed on Thanksgiving and Christmas Day. For more information, contact: Palm Springs Air Museum, 745 N. Gene Autry Trail, 760/778-6262; www.air-museum.org.

For still more World War II memorabilia, hit the freeway and head for Chiriaco Summit near the southern entrance to Joshua Tree National Park, where the star attraction is the **General George S. Patton Memorial Museum.**

Cabot's Old Indian Pueblo Museum

Aided by his faithful burro, Merry Christmas, and a pick and shovel, Cabot Yerxa took 20 years to build this eccentric, intentionally asymmetrical Hopi-style adobe in what is now Desert Hot Springs. The adobe, four stories tall, features 35 rooms, 150 windows, and walls two feet thick. These days the pueblo serves as an eclectic private museum, "trading post," and the town's pride and joy. Admission is $2.50 adults, $2 seniors, $1 children (16 and under). Cabot's, 67-616 E. Desert View Ave., 760/329-7610, is usually open Wed.–Sun. 10 A.M.–4 P.M. To get to Desert Hot Springs from the Palm Springs airport, head north on Gene Autry Trail.

Palm Springs Aerial Tramway

You might as well begin your area tour with the big picture. To get it, simply climb aboard the Palm Springs Aerial Tramway—and climb a vertical mile in under 15 minutes. Now a historic civil engineering landmark, "Crocker's Folly" took electrical engineer Francis Crocker 28 years to design and build. For families, this white-knuckle aerial adventure is effortless, once the kids are convinced they really *do* want to ride a cable-driven gondola on a swinging trip up into the pines. The views are spectacular, especially from the new 80-passenger Rotair tramcars from Switzerland, which slowly rotate to offer pas-

SANTA ROSA AND SAN JACINTO MOUNTAINS NATIONAL MONUMENT

New in October 2000 was the Palm Springs area's newest federal preserve, the Santa Rosa and San Jacinto Mountains National Monument. This 227,000 -acre monument, which protects land previously designated as a national scenic area, is jointly administered by the U.S. Bureau of Land Management (BLM), the U.S. Forest Service (USFS), the California Department of Fish and Game, the California Department of Parks and Recreation, the Agua Caliente Band of Cahuilla Indians, and the Coachella Valley Conservancy, in cooperation with the county, adjacent cities, and private landowners.

Despite their stark first imnpression, these desert mountains support an immensely diverse ecosytem —including five distinct "life zones," from Sonoran Desert to Arctic Alpine—and great biodiversity, providing habitat for a number of federally listed threatened and endangered species, magnificent fan palm oases, and more than 500 plant species.

Notable among mountain residents are Peninsular Ranges bighorn sheep, *(Ovis canadensis cremnobates),* listed as endangered by the federal government in 1998. Other species found—and protected—here include the southern yellow bat; the desert tortoise *(Gopherus* or *Xerobates agassizii),* California´s official reptile; the desert slender salamander, found only in the Santa Rosa Mountains; and the least Bell's vireo, a small songbird dependent on riparian habitat—once abundant, now listed as endangered by both the state and federal governments.

The area also has great cultural and historical significance, particularly the Santa Rosa Mountains, homeland of many generations of the Cahuilla people. The three Indian Canyons and Tahquitz Canyon are listed on the National Register of Historic Places. Significant prehistoric and historic sites in the Santa Rosa Mountains include Agua Alta Canyon; the Clark Lake Dune Village archaeological site; Ataki, or Hidden Spring Village; Big Falls in Palm Canyon; the Cactus Spring area; the Clark Lake petroglyphs; the ruins of Cottonwood Springs Village; the Lake Cahuilla fishtraps (listed on the National Register of Historic Places); Deep Canyon; the Martinez Canyon Rockhouse (also on the National Register); and the Santa Rosa Mountains rock tanks.

In related news, in early 2001 President George W. Bush endorsed President Clinton's previous decision to designate a larger area—some 845,000 acres of land, both public and private—in Riverside, Imperial, and San Diego Counties as "critical habitat" for the peninsular bighorn sheep.

For detailed information about the Santa Rosa and San Jacinto Mountains National Monument, call the BLM's California Desert District Office at 909/697-5200, or see www.ca.blm.gov/palm-springs /santa_rosa_national_monument.html. In addition to highlighting the new national monument's main features, the website also includes a map. Even better, stop by the **Santa Rosa Mountains Visitor Center** in Palm Desert, on the south side of Highway 74.

sengers "360 degress of wow!" Once on top of the world—having traveled through five different climate zones, like driving between Mexico and Alaska—sit down for a meal at the station restaurant, picnic outdoors, or set off on a hike into **Mount San Jacinto State Park** or surrounding **San Bernardino National Forest** wilderness.

Tram cars leave at least every half hour. First car goes up at 10 A.M. weekdays, 8 A.M. weekends and holidays; last car goes up at 8 P.M. (9 P.M. during daylight saving time). The Tramway closes for two weeks in August. Admission is $19.65 adults, $17.65 seniors, and $12.50 children (5 to 12). "Ride 'n' Dine" tickets are extra.

Group rates are available. To get here from downtown Palm Springs: head northwest via Highway 111, turn west onto Tramway Road, and continue to the end (steep climb). For more information, call 760/325-1391 (recorded) or 760/325-1149; www.pstramway.com.

The Living Desert Wildlife and Botanical Park

This 1,200-acre spread, both innovative zoo and educational park, includes both desert plant and animal life on display in naturalistic settings. The **Indian Garden** explains how the Cahuilla people used native plants for medicine, food, clothing, and shelter. The 26,000-square-foot **Eagle Canyon** exhibits native wildlife, including mountain lions, bobcats, and golden eagles, and is also a breeding center for endangered species, including the cheetah, the fastest land animal on earth. Also new: the **Animal Wonders** live animal show. Wander the park's six miles of trails or take a guided tram tour. Lucky visitors may spot bighorn sheep (an endangered species) scrambling around on the surrounding craggy hillsides. The native plant nursery here offers some intriguing desert plants for sale. Come in late October for the Living Desert's **Howl-O-Ween,** four days of carnival-style booths and costume contests. Other special events are scheduled year-round.

The Living Desert is in Palm Desert, about 1.5 miles south of Highway 111 at 47-900 Portola

---

HIKING PALM SPRINGS

Palm Springs, near sea level, is fringed by high mountains—one of the few areas in California where the distance between low desert and snow-dusted mountain peaks can be managed in a matter of minutes.

Desert hiking possibilities abound. Directly west of Palm Springs are the **San Jacinto Mountains** and newly-opened Tahquitz Canyon and the three Indian Canyons—superb for hiking, details below—unlike the steep Santa Rosa Mountains directly south of the Coachella Valley. East past Indio is the U.S. Bureau of Land Management's impressive **Mecca Hills,** where Painted Canyon is a hiking standout. Almost directly north of Desert Hot Springs by Hwy. 62 is the Nature Conservancy's very hikable **Big Morongo Canyon Preserve.** For long-distance desert hiking and backpacking, though, the best bet is **Joshua Tree National Park** For information on both Joshua Tree and Big Morongo, see the Joshua Tree National Park section, below.

Hikers heading into the high country can either drive up via Highway 74, the inimitably snakelike **Palms to Pines Highway,** or hitch a ride on the **Palm Springs Aerial Tramway.** However you get there, wilderness awaits—miles and miles of trails winding through **Mount San Jacinto State Park** and surrounding sections of **San Bernardino National Forest.** (Wilderness permits, available at area ranger stations, are required for serious treks.) Campgrounds abound in the area too. For more information about the area, see Beyond Palm Springs, below.

Indian Canyons and Tahquitz Canyon

The premier, practically in-town destination for hiking, picnicking, and up-close exploration of desert palm oases—most enjoyable in spring and fall—are the accessible Indian Canyons in the San Jacinto Mountains, just beyond downtown Palm Springs.

Sacred lands of the Agua Caliente Band of Cahuilla Indians, "Indian Canyons" consist of the abundant plant life, palm oases, and remote high-country scenery of **Andreas, Murray,** and **Palm Canyons.** Best bet for oasis lovers and distance hikers is Palm Canyon, with 3,000 native fan palms. The entrance to Indian Canyons is at the end of S. Palm Canyon Drive. At last report admission was $6 adults; $3.50 active military, students, and seniors; and $1 children (6 to 12), age 5 and under free. Group rates and season passes are available. The canyons are usually open fall through spring 8 A.M.–5 P.M.; the summer schedule varies. Prices and hours are subject to change.

Tahquitz Canyon—site of the Cahuilla people's new Tahquitz Canyon Visitor Center—was Shangri-La in the classic 1937 film *Lost Horizon.* Most sacred place of all to the Cahuilla, Tahquitz is the mythic home of Tah-kwish, the spirit of a powerful medicine man. In recent years the Cahuilla have ousted the homeless, cleaned up accumulated garbage, erased graffiti, erected fences, and otherwise prepared to protect the canyon—and to offer limited public access. Tahquitz Canyon is open daily 8 A.M.–5 P.M. Two-hour guided hikes, on which visitors see ancient rock art, native irrigation systems, and a 60-foot waterfall, leave from the visitor center on the hour, 8 A.M.–3 P.M. Canyon admission is $10 adults, $5 children. For reservations, stop by the visitor center at 500 W. Mesquite or call 760/416-7044.

For more information, contact: **Agua Caliente Band of Cahuilla Indians,** 760/325-3400 or toll-free 800/790-3398; www.aguacaliente.org. Better yet, contact the Tahquitz Canton Visitor Center, located just west of downtown at 500 W. Mesquite, 760/416-7044. For current information on the canyons themselves, see www.indian-canyons.com and www.tahquitzcanyon.com.

Ave. (near its intersection with Haystack Rd.), 760/346-5694; www.livingdesert.org. It's open 9 A.M.–5 P.M. from September 1 through mid-June, and just 8 A.M.–1 P.M. in summer. Closed on Christmas. Admission is $7.50 adults, $6.50 seniors (62 and over), and $3.50 children (ages 3–12). Guided 50-minute tram tours are available, as well as group tours and special programs (by reservation).

ARTFUL, ENTERTAINING PALM SPRINGS

In Palm Springs proper, the Palm Springs Desert Museum (listed above) is the center of the local art world. In addition to its changing exhibits, films, theater events, and other performances, educational and guest lectures are staged at the museum's **Annenberg Theater.** The historic 500-seat **Plaza Theatre** downtown on S. Palm Canyon Drive, primary venue for the **Fabulous Palm Springs Follies** vaudeville revue (also listed above), stages other events too. But the Coachella Valley's primary performance venue is the **McCallum Theatre for the Performing Arts** at the Bob Hope Cultural Center, 73-000 Fred Waring Dr. in Palm Desert, 760/340-2787 (340-ARTS). If what's up at the McCallum seems too high brow—not always the case—then head back to Palm Springs and the new **National Big Band & Jazz Hall of Fame Museum** (listed above) to see what's shakin' downtown.

Since almost everything else in Palm Springs is staged outdoors, why not art? The regions's newest sculpture garden and gallery is the **Montana St. Martins Art, Design, and Sculpture Gallery,** 2901 N. Palm Canyon Dr., 760/323-7183 or toll-free 877/767-6337, at home at the retro landmark Tramway Oasis Gas Station designed by noted Palm Springs architect Albert Frey. Also a fascination, for outdoor sculpture, is the **Aerie Art Garden** near Palm Desert at 71-255 Aerie Dr., open only Sept.–May by appointment; for information call 760/568-6366. At both places, what you see is also for sale.

The city of Palm Springs and the surrounding Coachella Valley communities boast a year-round calendar of arts and performing arts events. To find out what's up when you'll be in town, contact local visitor bureaus (see below).

As for entertainment, look around to see what's happening. Lolling around downtown joints such as **Peabody's Coffee Bar & Jazz Studio,** 134 S. Palm Canyon Dr., 760/322-1877, or swingin' at **Muriel's Supper Club,** 210 S. Palm Canyon (at Arenas) 760/325-8839, is action enough for many, but Palm Springs also has its discos, piano and sports bars, country-western dance venues, and gay clubs. And movie theaters. And gambling casinos. And billiard halls. Even bowling alleys, including **Palm Springs Lanes,** 68-051 Ramon Rd. in Cathedral City, 760/324-8204, where you can bask in the fluorescent glow of LazerBowling.

SHOPPING PALM SPRINGS

If shopping isn't a recreational pastime in and around Palm Springs, then nothing is. And if you can't find it for sale here, it probably doesn't exist.

For a free peek at local arts and crafts—not to mention a certified farmers' market—head for the entertaining **Palm Springs VillageFest** held downtown along Palm Canyon Drive every Thursday evening 7–10 P.M., 760/320-3781 or 323-8272. On weekend mornings bargain hunters head to the **College of the Desert Street Fair,** 43-500 Monterey Avenue, 760/568-9921 (weekdays only), operated by the college alumni association and featuring some 300 vendors and a certified farmers' market. Something of a change-up but also fun during its fall-through-spring season is the themed monthly **La Quinta Main Street Marketplace** on Calle Estabo, with arts, crafts, food, beer, a "wine garden," and music.

Major shopping venues in Palm Springs proper include shops along **Palm Canyon Drive** as well as **Loehmann's Plaza,** the **Palm Springs Promenade** (formerly the Desert Fashion Plaza), and the **Palm Springs Mall.** In Palm Desert, serious shoppers have seemingly endless choices, including the **Palm Desert Town Center,** the Moorish **Desert Crossing Shopping Center** (marked by three faux camels in a faux oasis), where you'll find Old Navy and Target, and chi-chi two-level, open-air **The Gardens on El Paseo** in Palm Desert (often referred to as the "Rodeo Drive of the desert"), featuring Brooks Brothers, Saks Fifth Avenue, and bunches of boutiques and art galleries. An immense presence is Palm Desert's **Westfield Shoppingtown,** 72-840 Hwy. 111 (at Mon-

terey), 760/568-0248 (concierge: 568-0248), the desert's largest shopping extravaganza, with 120 specialty stores and restaurants, department stores, a 10-theater multiplex, and the Coachella Valley's only ice-skating rink. In Indio,

INTO THE OASIS: TOURING THOUSAND PALMS

This is the last natural, virtually untouched watershed in the Coachella Valley—a 20,000-acre preserve system protected from off-road vehicles and golf-course developments alike, part of the Nature Conservancy's Coachella Valley Preserve in the Indio Hills. The preserve offers wonderful outdoor opportunities: hiking, horseback riding, bird-watching, and general nature appreciation. Come in spring for wildflowers, in spring and fall for migratory-bird watching. Get oriented, any time of year, at the small on-site visitor center at Thousand Palms Oasis.

The preserve's 500 acres of blow-sand fields and dunes are the last protected habitat of the endangered Coachella Valley fringe-toed lizard—its scaly toes a sand-related adaptation (for better traction), like its shovel-like snout (for quicker escapes into the sand). The lizards are so fast, and so successful at avoiding detection, that few preserve visitors ever see one. Visitors have many other animal species to look for throughout the preserve, though, including the rare flat-tailed horned lizard, the Coachella round-tailed ground squirrel, rattlesnakes, the endangered desert pupfish, and 183 species of birds.

Beyond the sand and arid plains are the palm oases. At 2,383 acres, **Thousand Palms Oasis** is one of the state's largest groves of California fan palms *(Washingtonia filifera),* also known as Washingtonia palms. Cecil B. DeMille filmed his *King of Kings* here, and the terrain also served as backdrop for the 1969 movie *Tell Them Willie Boy Is Here.* Like Thousand Palms, other palm oases at the preserve exist because of slippage of the San Andreas earthquake fault, which traverses the entire Colorado Desert but is quite visible here. Five of these—**Macomber, Biskra, Pushawalla, Hidden** and **Horseshoe**—lie within the state's 2,200-acre **Indian Hills Palms** wilderness park, steep canyonlands strung together by trails straddling the fault line (accessible only on foot and, with some exceptions, horseback).

Another way to tour the territory is onboard a mule-drawn **Covered Wagon Tour.** These days the wagon wheels are well-inflated rubber, instead of wood, but otherwise tours are quite authentic—much like those taken by early desert tourists more than a century ago. They're also quite enlightening, thanks to the knowledgeable naturalist on board. If you sign on for the special Chuck Wagon Cookout Tour, wagoneers return at sunset for genuine cowpoke fare—steaks and such—plus marshmallow roasting and a campfire sing-along.

Covered wagon trips into the preserve are offered daily from October through May, by reservation only, with a 20-person minimum except on Saturday (no minimum). At last report the two-hour tour was $40 adults, $20 children ages 7 to 16 (kids 6 and under free, on the tour only), and the chuck wagon cookout (including tour) was $55 adults, $35 seniors (Saturday only; adult rate at other times), and $27.50 children. Reservations are required for all tours; group tour rates and theme parties are also available. For more information, contact: Covered Wagon Tours, P.O. Box 1106, La Quinta, CA 92253, 760/347-2161 or toll-free 800/367-2161.

To get to Thousand Palms Oasis: From I-10, exit east at Ramon Road; after four miles turn north onto Thousand Palm Canyon Drive. From Ramon Road, it is about two miles to the oasis and visitor center (street address: 2900 Thousand Palms Canyon Road). The preserve is open daily, sunrise to sunset, for hiking, horseback riding, and bird-watching; groups are welcome by arrangement. Pick up a trail guide, which also shows horseback routes, at the visitor center. No collecting, hunting, camping, or pets allowed at the preserve. No smoking, either. For more information, call the local **Nature Conservancy** office, 760/343-1234—donations to the Nature Conservancy are always welcome—or the U.S. Bureau of Land Management's **Palm Springs Field Office,** 760/251-4800.

the **Indio Fashion Mall** is a bit more down-to-earth, with Harris-Gottschalks, Miller's Outpost, and Sears among its many offerings. For outlet shopping, head west on I-10 to dinosaur-studded Cabazon and the 120-plus-store **Desert Hills Premium Outlets.**

Shopping for "Previously Loved" and "Gently Used" Items

Quite productive in and around Palm Springs is the opportunity to pick through a chi-chi selection of "previously loved," "gently used," and used clothing, furniture, and miscellaneous household items. Even rich people redecorate, and celebrities need periodic makeovers.

For top-drawer secondhand furnishings, the place to start is **The Estate Sale Company,** 4185 E. Palm Canyon Dr. in Palm Springs, 760/321-7628, fax 760/327-6187. The Estate Sale is the largest of the lot—22,000 square feet of consignment space—and you'll occasionally find the former furniture of the rich and famous, fine jewelry, and interesting odds and ends. Most stock here is local—and it moves fast. For clas-

sic collectors' clubs and affordable golf equipment, try **Golf Alley,** 74-040 El Paseo in Palm Desert, 760/776-4646.

And when upscale Palm Springs closets overflow, glamorous glad rags end up in local consignment shops. **Re-Deux Designer Resale Boutique,** 71-598 Hwy. 111 in Rancho Mirage, 760/776-9662, features "gently used" designer-label gowns and top-of-the-line sportswear. Other resale clothing stores—the pickin's are great in these parts—include **Suzy's Repeat Boutique,** also in Rancho Mirage, at 71-610 Hwy. 111, 760/776-8733; **Dora's Boutique Second Time Around** on El Paseo in Palm Desert, 760/340-4673; and **Collectors Corner** at 71-280 Hwy. 111 in Rancho Mirage, 760/346-1012, where proceeds benefit the Eisenhower Medical Center. Best bets in Palm Springs proper include **Patsy's Clothes Closet,** 4121 E. Palm Canyon Dr. (next to The Estate Sale), 760/324-8825, and **Celebrity Seconds,** 333 N. Palm Canyon Dr. (in the Amado Center), 760/416-2072, boasting Ginger Rogers' private collection.

STAYING IN AND NEAR PALM SPRINGS

Whatever you have in mind, it's here. Palm Springs offers an impressive array of historic lodgings—including a hotel built on the site of the city's namesake palm springs, and the desert resort that inspired Frank Capra's *It Happened One Night*—but budget travelers can also find some good choices. Motel 6 and other budget motels are hard to beat for frugal families, but special packages, off-season deals, and great children's programs sometimes make major area resorts quite competitive. For longer stays, apartment, condo, and home rentals are also options.

There's also the Palm Springs "resort spa" experience—a phenomenon once derogatorily called going to the fat farm—for fighting the battle of the bulge in style and with dignity. For other "special interest" clientele, Palm Springs offers both clothing-optional (nudist or naturist) and gay- and lesbian-oriented hotels and resorts.

For help in sorting out available options—and in getting the best available deals for your particular needs—contact either (or both) local vis-

itor bureaus. In addition to fairly complete local listings, each also offers free toll-free reservations assistance.

BUDGET STAYS AND GOOD DEALS

A large, attractive, and well-located **Motel 6** sits right downtown in Palm Springs at 660 S. Palm Canyon Drive, 760/327-4200 or toll-free 800/466-8356 (central reservations), fax 760/320-9827, www.motel6.com, with weekend rates from $45 for two (lower when business dries up in summer, higher on special-event weekends). There's another on Highway 111 (E. Palm Canyon Drive), 760/325-6129, another in **Rancho Mirage,** 760/324-8475, and still another in **Desert Hot Springs,** 760/251-1425.

The 17-room **Hotel California** motel, 425 E. Palm Canyon Dr., 760/322-8855, fax 760/323-0694, is a best bet for a budget stay and the basics, with rates as low as $49 in the off-season. High season rates are $69 and up. Some kitchen units are available.

Place in the Sun, 754 San Lorenzo Rd., 760/325-0254 or toll-free 800/779-2254, fax 760/325-0254, is a very pleasant and unpretentious place to park oneself, old Palm Springs style. Offering a mix of studio and one-bedroom apartments (most with full kitchens), Place in the Sun is smack dab in the middle of a private garden paradise (fruit trees included). Several blocks east of Palm Canyon via Mesquite Avenue and Random Road, it's quiet here yet close (but not too close) to the hustle and bustle of downtown. And it features all the basic diversions: pool, whirlpool, putting green, and TV. Small pets are accepted ($10 fee), and a family plan is available year-round. High-season rates begin at $79.

Another great choice for an apartment-style stay is the 11-unit **Four Seasons Apartment Hotel,** 290 San Jacinto Dr. (at Baristo), 760/325-6427, fax 760/325-0658. High-season rates are expensive but drop as low as $70 at other times.

And at least in the summer, some rooms are quite reasonable at the very nice 1930s **Orchid Tree Inn,** 261 S. Belardo Rd., 760/325-2791 or toll-free 800/733-343, fax 760/325-3855. High-season rates start at $125, but drop to $80 in the off-season.

Fairly inexpensive for a hot springs-spa vacation is the **Desert Hot Springs Spa Hotel,** 10-805 Palm Dr. in Desert Hot Springs, 760/329-6495 or toll-free 800/843-6053, fax 760/329-6915; http://dhsspa.com. This two-story motel complex offers the requisite palm-tree landscape and more than its share of Desert Hot Springs healing waters: four natural hot mineral pools, four hot mineral whirlpools, a sauna, even a wading pool for the kids. The rest of the spa treatment—body wraps, facials, and massage—is extra. High-season rates start at $69–79.

Palm Desert has its good values, too, particularly in the off-season—these including the **International Lodge** "studio condos" at 74-380 El Camino, 760/346-6161 or toll-free 800/874-9338 (reservations only), fax 760/568-0563, from $80 in winter, $55 in summer.

HISTORIC STAYS

Stuck so long in the 1950s and 1960s, Palm Springs is discovering that styles recently considered passè are hip again. Notable is the **Ballantines Hotel Palm Springs,** 1420 N. Indian Canyon Dr., 760/320-1178. Plenty retro here in the 14 individual rooms and suites are the furnishings—Eames, Miller, Knoll, Loewy—the art, the B and 1950s classic movies, even the poolside scene. Dig that blue Astroturf on the sundeck. New again in late 2000 was the old San Jacinto Hotel, now the Bauhaus-style **Ballantines Movie Colony,** 726 N. Indian Canyon Dr., 760/320-6340, a split-level 1937 Albert Frey-designed hotel with a total of 16 rooms (kitchens available). Danish House and Tiki House are among the three villas. For a preview of both hotels, see www.ballantineshotels.com. To make reservations at both, call toll-free 800/780-3454.

Another retro option, open since early 2001, is the **Orbit In,** five blocks from downtown in the city's Tennis Club District at 562 W. Arenas, 760/323-7575 or toll-free 877/99-ORBIT; www.orbitin.com. In addition to the mid-century modernism—furnishings by Eames, Saarinen, Bertoia, Nelson, Noguchi, and Schultz—as well as contemporary designs by Pepe Cortez and Russell Baker, suites here feature in-room data ports, CD players, VCRs, and both private patios and kitchens. Full breakfast. Extras include a fab pool with a view, complete with boomerang-shaped bar, and Schwinn cruisers. Rates start at $189.

Korakia Pensione, 257 S. Patencia Rd., 760/864-6411, fax 760/864-6423, was built in the 1920s by a Scottish artist whose visitors included both bohemians and dignitaries. Winston Churchill stayed here. Restored in 1989, this spectacular bed-and-breakfast villa is arty and colorful and still attracts a spirited crowd. Rooms at Korakia ("crows" in Greek) are distinctive and furnished with antiques and North African airs; each features a kitchen and refrigerator, but no TV or phone (both are available upon request). Children are welcome on the family plan—sharing your room—but for this romantic trip into the past, it's usually best to leave the kids at home. Rates start at $119 (two-night minimum). At last report Korakia, on Patencio (off Palm Canyon Dr.) between Arenas and Baristro, was closed in August and September.

Winston Churchhill may have stayed at Korakia, but Albert Einsten was once a guest at **The Willows Historic Palm Springs Inn,** 412 W. Tahquitz Canyon Way, an elegant Mediterranean villa built in 1927 as the winter estate of Samuel Untermeyer, former U.S. Secretary of the Treasury. Now an exquisite eight-room bed-and-breakfast, the Willows has its lore—including the rumor that Carole Lombard and Clark Gable honeymooned here. Luxury. For more information or reservations, call 760/320-0771 or toll-free 800/966-9597; www.thewillowspalm-springs.com.

In its heyday the **Estrella Inn,** 415 S. Belardo Rd., 760/320-4117 or toll-free 800/237-3687, www .estrella.com, one block west of Palm Canyon downtown, was renowned for the wild parties thrown by Clark Gable and Carole Lombard. And Bing Crosby was often a guest in this recently renovated 1930s motel-style holn addition to regular guest rooms, the Estrella features 10 two-bedroom suites and four bungalows with private outdoor whirlpools. Three pools, whirlpools, volleyball court, shuffleboard, and lovely grounds complete the setting. Continental breakfast is included in the rates, (two-night minimum stay on weekends, three- or four-night minimum for holidays). Look for off-season deals. Weekly and monthly rates are also available.

The **Ingleside Inn,** 200 W. Ramon Rd. (at Bellardo), 760/325-0046 or toll-free 800/772-6655, www.inglesideinn.com, originally a private estate, was declared "one of the world's ten best hotels" by the TV show *Lifestyles of the Rich & Famous.* This place is swell despite that fact. The Ingleside's hotel history began in 1935, its star clientele including Greta Garbo, Greer Garson, Elizabeth Taylor, and Salvador Dalí. This small full-service hotel is less restrictive these days. Rooms are individually decorated with antiques; all include a private whirlpool and sauna. Suites and villas feature fireplaces and private terraces. High-season rates begin at $95 (two-night minimum on weekends) and are typically much higher—though summer rates drop.

The **Spa Hotel and Mineral Springs,** 100 N. Indian Canyon Dr. (at Tahquitz Canyon Dr.), Palm Springs 92262, 760/325-1461 or toll-free 800/854-1279, www.spahotelandcasino.com, sits atop the hot springs for which Palm Springs was named. Owned and operated by the Agua Caliente Band of Cahuilla Indians, this 1960s-vintage spa hotel was completely renovated and redecorated in 1993, spiffed up even outside with lush landscaping and a striking salmon-and-teal paint job. Also improved: the sunken marble "swhirlpool" tubs and other full-service spa facilities, including the classic rooftop solarium for private sunbathing (clothing optional). For spa information, call toll-free 888/293-0180.

La Quinta Resort and Club

For Old California romance and present-day celebrity appeal, the quintessential Palm Springs–area resort is the very elegant, very expensive La Quinta Resort and Club, 49-499 Eisenhower Dr. in La Quinta, 760/564-4111 or toll-free 800/854-1271; www.laquintaresort.com.

The La Quinta of today is a virtual city of simple yet simply stunning adobe-style "casitas." Legend has it that Irving Berlin was inspired to write "White Christmas," and Frank Capra the classic films *It Happened One Night* and *Lost Horizon,* while staying here. (Capra liked La Quinta so much, in fact, he moved in permanently. He and his wife lived at La Quinta until the end of their days.) In addition to the usual litany of illustrious Hollywood stars who sought desert refuge, La Quinta also hosted American business barons—the DuPonts, the Vanderbilts, and the Gianninis (of Bank of America fame).

But in those days La Quinta boasted a mere 56 casitas. Today it has 640. The grounds alone, a 90-acre riot of annual color, bougainvillea vines, and evergreen lawns, require the attention of 40 full-time gardeners. Despite its immense size—with 25 swimming pools, 35 spas, 30 tennis courts, on-site shopping, children's center, new 23,000-square-foot **Spa at La Quinta,** and several affiliated world-class golf courses—La Quinta is still surprisingly intimate. And popular with celebrities, who typically stay incognito. High-season rates start at $250. If you don't mind the heat, summer rates can be a comparative bargain.

The 90 acres of grounds at the La Quinta Hotel Resort and Club require the attention of 40 full-time gardeners.

LA QUINTA HOTEL GOLF AND TENNIS RESORT

Adding appeal are the resort's five great restaurants, including the four-star French-Mediterranean **Azur,** casual 1920s-style American **Morgans,** and, for authentic regional Mexican, the **Adobe Grill.**

Two Bunch Palms

Equally beloved yet earthier is Two Bunch Palms, 67-425 Two Bunch Palms Trail in Desert Hot Springs, 760/329-8791 or toll-free 800/472-4334; www.twobunchpalms.com. This spot on the map was named (for its two bunches of palms) in 1907 by a U.S. Army Camel Corps survey team. One of those "secret" celebrity getaways everybody knows about, secluded Two Bunch Palms was voted one of America's top-10 spas in *Condé Nast Traveler* magazine's 1995 readership survey. According to local lore, even famed mobster Al Capone once hid out here in the 1930s, at a swank villa supposedly built for him—though some locals, including a former Palm Springs mayor, point out that Capone was in prison at the time.

Be that as it may, this *is* a great hideout. Simple bungalows and suite-style villas cluster around the lovely stone mineral pools, a main attraction. The full spa—massage, steam bath, and more—is among the best anywhere. Luxury, continental breakfast included (other meals available), spa services extra.

OTHER STYLISH STAYS

If money isn't an issue—and if you tire of the scenery elsewhere—there is no shortage of stylish stays throughout the Coachella Valley. Not particularly expensive though, by Palm Springs standards, is wonderful little **L'Horizon Garden Hotel,** 1050 E. Palm Canyon Dr. in Palm Springs, 760/323-1858 or toll-free 800/377-7855, www.lhorizonhotel.com, a walled garden enclosing seven buildings, each with two or three guest rooms (one with a kitchen/studio). Groups or extended families sometimes rent an entire building or two. The decor here is airy and contemporary. Each room has a private patio; some bathrooms feature a small, private atrium. Other attractions: a library, bocce ball, croquet, horseshoes, and loaner bicycles. Continental breakfast is delivered to your door along with the morning paper. Lunch can also be delivered, though plenty of restaurants are a stroll away. Expensive (two-night minimum on holiday weekends).

Need to evade celebrity hunters and the paparazzi, or just want to pretend you do? Try **La Mancha Private Villas,** 444 Avenida Caballeros in Palm Springs, 760/323-1773 or toll-free 800/255-1773; www.la-mancha.com. La Mancha is a state-of-the-art hideout, secluded (security gates and all) as well as lovely and luxurious. Rooms here are actually private villas—from one-bedroom "casitas" to four-bedroom tennis villas with private tennis court, swimming pool, courtyard patio, and endless indoor comforts (the latter very expensive). Absolutely private restaurant and other top-drawer facilities. La Mancha is about three-fourths of a mile east of Palm Canyon Drive, via Alejo Road.

Always elegant, in its trademark conservative style, is the **Ritz-Carlton, Rancho Mirage** up the hill at 68-900 Frank Sinatra Dr. in Rancho Mirage, 760/321-8282 or toll-free 800/241-3333; www.ritzcarlton.com. The view from the top of the hill here, which takes in almost the entire Coachella Valley, is stunning, particularly at sunset, but nothing is more surprising than the brazen (protected) bighorn sheep that come down out of the hills to graze the high-priced landscaping. Here, the Ritz-Carlton is a full-out resort, with a nine-hole on-site pitch and putt, preferred tee times at the Rancho Mirage Country Club, tennis courts—and a tennis program directed by U.S. Olympic Coach Tom Gorman —croquet, fitness center, pool, whirlpool spa, aerobics classes, and full-service health spa and salon. For folks who can't leave work at home, there's also a business center. And for folks who can't leave the kids at home, the **Ritz Kids** program provides endless activities and outings along with day care and baby-sitters. Also here: great restaurants, lounge, and gift shops. Summer rates can be a real deal.

RESORTING TO RESORTS

Golf Resorts

If families that play together really do stay together, then even the desert's most glorious golf sanctuaries now promote family values. The main point of a resort vacation, of course, is that once you arrive you never need to leave—not a travel style that suits everyone.

A standout in this golf-and-kids getaway category is sprawling, 512-room **The Westin Mission Hills Resort** at Dinah Shore and Bob Hope Dr. in Rancho Mirage, 760/328-5955 or toll-free 800/335-3545, www.westin.com, quite contemporary, with an art deco Moroccan sensibility. The three golf courses here include a Gary Player signature course (Mission Hills North) and a Pete Dye–designed course. The three

swimming pool/spa complexes include a 60-foot waterslide. A 20-acre resort park and the children's program cover just about everything else. And everywhere is that grand Southern California commitment to greening the desert, whether it wants to be green or not, the fountains and waterfalls here inspired by the region's natural oases and desert canyons. Expensive with bargain summer rates. Inquire about specials and packages.

Another grand golf star is the **Hyatt Grand Champions Resort,** 44-600 Indian Wells Ln. in Indian Wells, 760/341-1000 or toll-free 800/233-1234 (reservations only), www.hyatt.com, with luxury accommodations, good restaurants, two "champion" Ted Robinson golf courses, 12 tennis courts (grass, clay, or hard surface)—the country's third largest tennis stadium—four swimming pools, health and fitness club. You name it. And for the kiddos, for a price: **Camp Hyatt** diversions from dawn to dusk. Peak golf-season rates are expensive (golf extra).

Practically next door and similarly well endowed is the **Renaissance Esmeralda Resort,** 44-400 Indian Wells Ln. in Indian Wells, 760/773-4444 or toll-free 800/468-3571; www.renaissancehotels.com. **Sirocco** here may be the best restaurant in the desert. Room rates: $250–300 in the fall and winter, dropping to $150 or so in summer.

Newest in the Indian Wells neighborhood and absolutely deluxe is the **Miramonte Resort,** 45000 Indian Wells Ln. in Indian Wells, 760/341-2200 or toll-free 800/237-2926, www.miramonteresort.com, a 226-room Tuscan Village with two swimming pools and every imaginable amenity, including on-site spa services. Though the Miramonte doesn't boast its own golf courses or tennis courts, it does provide access to neighboring facilities. Call for details.

For sheer unreality out in the desert, nothing beats huge **Marriott's Desert Springs Resort and Spa,** 74-855 Country Club Dr. in Palm Desert, 760/341-2211 or toll-free 800/228-9290, marriotthotels.com, with its indoor lagoon and eight-story atrium, pools, waterfalls, hanging gardens, indoor and outdoor lakes (boat tours available), golf courses, putting green, five swimming pools, 21 tennis courts, and endless other recreation facilities. High-season rates run $250 but drop substantially in summer.

Resort Spas

The big-bucks buzz in Palm Springs lately has a French accent, what with the 1996 arrival of the region's newest ultraswank health spa, this one for both men and women. That accent has been Americanized by new owner Merv Griffin. **Merv Griffin's Resort Hotel and Givenchy Spa,** the first Givenchy outpost in the U.S., is modeled after the spa at Trianon Palace in Versailles, France. At home at the revamped old Gene Autry Resort, 4200 E. Palm Canyon Dr. in Palm Springs, 760/770-5000 or toll-free 800/276-5000, www.merv.com/hotel/givenchy_spa, the spa's emphasis is on active and enjoyable exercise as well as refined and gentle body care. The key words here: *beauty, luxury,* and *voluptuousness.* Also served: very good, very healthful French food. Ask about weekend packages and specials.

The long-running classic local health and fitness spa is **The Palms at Palm Springs,** 572 N. Indian Canyon Dr. (at Alejo) in Palm Springs, 760/325-1111 or toll-free 800/753-7256, www.palmsspa.com, which rates as one of the country's best by no lesser authority than *Condé Nast Traveler.* People typically stay a week or more, eating low-calorie meals and exercising, exercising, exercising; massages, manicures, and other spa services are available. Rooms are spacious and comfortable—and cheaper ($145 per person per day) if you're willing to share. Otherwise, rates begin at $210 per day (higher on weekends), all extras extra.

Another time-honored alternative is **Two Bunch Palms** in Desert Hot Springs. For more information, see listing above.

Clothing-Optional Options

Sun worship being the unofficial religion of Palm Springs, some people prefer to enjoy the sun without undue restrictions. The balmy possibilities include the Naturist Society's **Desert Shadows Inn Resort & Villas,** the clothing-optional couples' retreat **Villa Escondida,** the 10-room **Morningside Inn,** and the **Terra Cotta Inn** (formerly the Monkey Tree Hotel, rumored onetime rendezvous of Marilyn Monroe and John F. Kennedy). For more details and to make reservations, contact the Palm Springs visitor center (listed below) or see the website: www.palm-springs.org.

Gay Resorts

Palm Springs offers an array of resorts and other accommodations for a gay and/or lesbian clientele, many of these included in the city's annual visitors guide. Some have wink-wink suggestive names, including **Bachannal, Chestnutz,** the **Triangle Inn,** and **Bee Charmer Inn,** not to mention **Inndulge, Inntimate, Inntrigue,** and **Inn Exile.** Other possibilities include **Abbey Las Palmas, Casitas Laquita, El Mirasol Villas,** and **Queen of Hearts.** For more details and current information, and to make toll-free reservations, contact the Palm Springs visitor center (listed below) or see the city's website: www.palm-springs.org.

EATING IN AND NEAR PALM SPRINGS

CHEAP EATS

Inexpensive Downtown

Unlike Palm Desert and Rancho Mirage, where community is defined by walled high-security compounds and empty streets, in Palm Springs people actually amble around and do things. And one of the things they do is eat.

A snazzy yet simple choice downtown is **Capra's It's A Wonderful Life Deli,** 204 N. Palm Canyon Dr., 760/325-7073, opened by film director Frank Capra's son—Tom Capra, formerly a producer of NBC's *Today Show*— and his wife, Kris. If what you're looking for is something wholesome and tasty, the predominantly housemade fare here—everything from pastas and salads to soups and sandwiches—is just what the director might have ordered. (In the latter department, meatball lovers should try the Mr. Smith—a reference, of course, to Frank Capra's *Mr. Smith Goes to Washington.)* And yes, there in the glass case, that's the real Oscar from *It's a Wonderful Life.* Frank Capra memorabilia covers the walls. Other highlights of a visit to Capra's include the wondrous breads and the tiramisu. Beer and wine available.

Ever popular is landmark **Louise's Pantry,** 124 S. Palm Canyon Dr. (between Tahquitz Canyon and Arenas), 760/325-5124. Breakfast is the real deal here, but people wait in line for burgers and milkshakes at lunch, and homestyle meat loaf, pork chops, and fresh roasted turkey at dinner. Grab a booth, then let the kids sidle up to the Formica counter to peruse the pies. Since 1946, Louise's has been famous for its homemade cream pies—especially the banana split pie.

Palm Springs—the people's Palm Springs— is a coffee-shop kind of town, favoring places with sunny attitudes and patios. It's just assumed that such places will serve generous helpings of good food at reasonable prices, as does **Bit of Country,** 418 S. Indian Canyon Dr., 760/325-5154, starting with hearty breakfasts. Open for breakfast and lunch.

A true local hot spot is **Elmer's Pancake and Steak House,** 1030 E. Palm Canyon, 760/327-8419, open daily for breakfast, lunch, and dinner. The Coachella Valley produces 95 percent of the dates consumed each year in the United States—so come to breakfast at Elmer's to polish off your share. The date-nut pancakes are great, as are the cheese blintzes. Elmer's specialty, though, is German pancakes. The only drawback to this place is its popularity; on weekends, the wait can be considerable.

Then there's **Las Casuelas—The Original,** 368 N. Palm Canyon (between Amado and Alejo), 760/325-3213, open for lunch, dinner, and Sunday brunch. Kids like this place because it's cheerful and colorful. Parents like it for the same reasons, but also because the food at this Casuelas—at last count, there were three others in the area—is predictably good. Standards include tacos, tostadas, enchiladas, and burritos, but try a homemade tamale. Beloved for its "wild coyote" margaritas and immensely popular for imaginative Southwestern is the **Blue Coyote Grill,** 445 N. Palm Canyon Dr., 760/327-1196, where you'll dive right into the tortilla soup and savor the enchiladas. Eat indoors or, weather permitting, outdoors.

And if you're hungry for all-American burgers and such, on the way into or out of Palm Springs you can't miss **The Wheel Inn** off I-10 in Cabazon, 909/849-7012, a gussied-up 24-hour truck stop famous for its humongous dinosaurs—the real reason the kids will want to stop here.

Inexpensive and Other Options Elsewhere

For south-of-the-border fare near Palm Springs, most authentic are some of the *taquerías* and tiny storefronts in and around Indio. Getting there from Palm Springs is some drive, however—so try **El Gallito Cafe,** 68-820 Grove St. in Cathedral City (two blocks south of Hwy. 111, via Cathedral Canyon Rd.), 760/328-7794, a popular local hangout with down-home decor— piñatas, funky paintings, and lit-up beer signs— and very good, inexpensive food. A real deal here is the "burrito especial."

The **Trader Joe's** chain, with an outpost here at 44-250 Town Center Way in Palm Desert, 760/340-2291, was once described by its founder, "Trader" Joe Coulombe, as catering to "the overeducated and underpaid." If that sounds relevant, stop by to stock up on baked goods, coffee, cheese, nuts, all-natural snacks, and assorted beers and wines. A little flashier in the neighborhood: L.A.'s popular **Daily Grill,** 73-061 El Paseo, 760/779-9911. Pricier still, beloved for dinner by meat-eaters everywhere, is **Ruth's Chris Steak House,** 74-040 Hwy. 111, 760/779-1998. There's also a **Morton's of Chicago** in town, 74-880 Country Club Dr., 760/340-6865.

Quite affordable in La Quinta is the **Beachside Cafe** in the Von's Shopping Center at 78-477 Hwy. 111, 760/564-4577. With the Salton Sea so far away, the most obvious question is: *What* beach? (It's on the wall, near the big beach umbrellas outside.) The fare is sunny and California-style, with fresh-baked pastries and breads—killer banana-nut bread, delectable pies and cakes—homemade soups and imaginative salads. Fresh fish too. Open daily 7 A.M.–9 P.M. Also a best bet, in Palm Desert, is **Mario's on El Paseo** 73-399 El Paseo, 760/346-0584, where the wait staff sings for your supper.

Devane's, 80-755 Hwy. 111 in Indio, 760/342-5009, is named after its owner, actor William Devane. This casual California-style joint serves some unusual salads and generous portions of pasta, great chicken, seafood. But Devane's real claim to fame is its pizza. People drive here from all over the Coachella Valley just to get some, whether traditional pepperoni or vegetarian combinations. Full-service bar, too.

THE CUISINE SCENE

A dazzling fine-dining star downtown is **St. James at the Vineyard,** 265 S. Palm Canyon Dr., 760/320-8041, where the eclectic decor just about covers the map—the entire map of the world—as does the creative fare. From bouillabaisse Burmese and grilled Australian rack of lamb to the shrimp curry, come on in and prepare to be surprised.

Swingin' **Muriel's Supper Club,** 210 S. Palm Canyon Dr., 760/325-8839, is both dining destination and dance club. The daily changing dinner menu, emphasizing seasonal ingredients, might include George Banks sea scallops, pan-seared blue prawns, or grilled elk medallions. Delectable desserts. The entertainment menu also changes constantly—both Eartha Kitt and the Cherry Poppin' Daddies have taken their bows here—but generally includes jazz, Latin jazz, salsa, and swing.

As hot with seniors as it is with its gay clientele, immensely popular **Shame on the Moon,** 69-950 Frank Sinatra Dr. in Rancho Mirage, 760/324-5515, is all but impossible to get into unless you book well in advance. Also a big hit is **The Left Bank** in Palm Springs proper, 150 E. Vista Chico Rd., 760/320-6116, a dinner-only French bistro.

Otani—A Garden Restaurant in downtown Palm Springs at 266 Avenida Caballeros, 760/327-6700, a relative of A Thousand Cranes in L.A., is the most beautiful shogun's palace in Palm Springs. Savvy diners don't even try to choose between the teppen-yaki and yakitori menus. Sushi lovers have a field day here (the California rolls are quite good). Tempura selections include calamari and clams. Early-bird dinner specials are the real deal. Across from the convention center, three blocks east of Indian Canyon, Otani is open for dinner daily, lunch weekdays only, Sunday brunch. Also fine for fancy dining in Palm Springs proper is romantic French **Le Vallauris,** 385 W. Tahquitz Canyon Way, 760/325-5059, open daily for both lunch and dinner.

Another favorite, for French-Mediterranean, is **The Dining Room** up the hill from the highway at the Ritz-Carlton, Rancho Mirage, 68-900 Frank Sinatra Dr., 760/321-8282. The Ritz-Carlton is a superb desert resort destination and—if you're in the mood for semiformal attire, formal atmosphere, and great food—a superb dinner destination. The menu includes three prix-fixe options and menu selections such as fresh black mussel soup with saffron and the house bouillabaisse. Full bar, excellent wine list. Reservations are highly recommended. For something more easygoing, consider one of the Ritz-Carlton's more casual dining options. Call for the current dinner schedule. Coming or going, perhaps you'll meet the Ritz-Carlton's regulars—bighorn sheep from the surrounding preserve grazing the flower beds.

DATE SHAKES AND OTHER DELICACIES

Few people in and around Palm Springs argue about how delectable a date milkshake tastes. They do quibble, however, over just which local enterprise makes the best date shakes—a blender brew of vanilla ice cream, milk, crystallized date sugar and, sometimes, chunks of fresh dates. You can get gussied-up dates in shops all around Palm Springs. Many specialize in the retail sale of dates—Medjools, Deglet Noors, Barhis, Black Abbadas, and honey dates—and date-related delicacies, such as marzipan-stuffed Medjools, date nut rolls, and chocolate date truffles.

The best place to go date hunting, though, is at the other end of the Coachella Valley, near Indio and Thermal—where most of the area's date palms are, and have been, since the first were imported from the Middle East in the late 1800s.

At **Oasis Date Gardens** just south of Thermal on Highway 111, the Laflin family has been growing dates—the oldest known domesticated fruit—since 1912. However, it wasn't until 1939 that the clan began growing the superb Medjool dates for which Oasis has become known. Attractions here include a retail shop and a small café serving thick, creamy, and truly delectable date shakes. It's a fun drive to Thermal—and, with a picnic under the palms, a relaxing half-day outing. Open daily 8:30 A.M.–5 P.M.,

closed on Easter and Christmas, Oasis Date Gardens is one-and-a-half miles south of Thermal at 59-111 Highway 111. For more information call 760/399-5665 or toll-free 800/827-8017; www .oasisdate.com.

Always popular in Indio is **Shields Date Gardens,** famous for its "Black Date" ice cream—rich vanilla swirled with date puree. This 1950s-vintage shop, starring Abdullah the mechanical camel, actually harks back to 1924. That's when the late E. Floyd Shields joined the local legion of date-growing pioneers. Shields narrates the aging but ever-popular *Romance and Sex Life of a Date* slide show, which is shown regularly. Shields Date Gardens is on the south side of Highway 111, just east of Jefferson Street, at 80-225 Highway 111, Indio 92201, 760/347-0996 or toll-free 800/414-2555; www .shieldsdates .com. The shop is open daily 8 A.M.–6 P.M. (closed on Christmas).

To do dates socioculturally, in mid-February come to the **National Date Festival** in Indio, part of the Riverside County Fair, where the theme since 1947 has been "1,001 Arabian Nights." The family-friendly fun here includes ostrich and camel racing—a species of California craziness hard to find elsewhere.

For a stylistic change-up, there's **Palomino Euro Bistro,** 73-101 Hwy. 111 in Palm Desert, 760/773-9091. Stepping into a cutting-edge eatery with California style and European attitude usually costs plenty. Not so at uptown Palomino, one of the hippest places around. Beloved for its imaginative pizzas and pastas (wonderful coffee and desserts too), this bistro is reasonably relaxed. For a horse of a different color, step up to the full-service bar for some house wine. From Iron Horse Vineyards, it carries the Palomino label. Palomino, on Highway 111 near Highway 74 (also known as Monterey Ave.), is usually open for dinner 6 P.M. to 10 P.M.; call for current schedule.

For French, consider **Cuistot** in Palm Desert's Galleria Centre at 73-111 El Paseo, one block south of Highway 111 between Ocotillo and Sage, 760/340-1000. Palm Springs has its venerated French restaurants, most of them quite

classical and fairly formal. But Cuistot's "continental drift" combines Old World flavor with eclectic Californian attitude, with choices such as salmon with ginger-chervil sauce and duck in black currant and apricot sauce. Good wine list, full bar. Closed Monday and in summer, at last report. Otherwise, it's open for lunch and dinner Tues.–Sat., dinner only on Sunday. Reservations are required, especially during the winter.

An Indian Wells attraction is **Le St. Germain,** 74-985 Hwy. 111, 760/773-6511, contemporary bistro-style sibling of the long-running local Le Vallauris. It's open nightly for dinner.

Then there's Mediterranean **Sirocco** just off Highway 111 at the Renaissance Esmeralda Resort, 44-400 Indian Wells Ln., 760/773-4444. Named for the hot Saharan wind, this premier dining establishment is something of an international oasis for food lovers. Sirocco's specialties include unique interpretations of standards, such as gazpacho and paella, and an exceptional wine list. Casual dining, reservations strongly advised. Sirocco regularly attracts celebrity chefs, so inquire about special events. At last report lunch was served on weekdays only, dinner every night, but call for current information on schedule and seasonal closings.

For other fine dining choices, consider other area luxury resorts.

TRANSPORTATION AND INFORMATION

Getting Here, Getting Around

San Gorgonio Pass, just northwest of Palm Springs, is such an effective wind funnel that local windshields are literally pitted and scarred by sandblasting storms, particularly when Santa Anas blow hot off the desert. No wonder, then, that the region is such a productive power-generating windmill field—quite the striking scene. And you'll see it, too, especially driving. (If the setting looks familiar, this is the site of the opening scenes in *Rain Man,* with Tom Cruise and Dustin Hoffman.) By road, the primary route into the Coachella Valley from Los Angeles is I-10; heading into Palm Springs from the freeway, most folks take the Highway 111 cutoff through the windmills. That route becomes one-way **Palm Canyon Drive** heading south, which (1) loops around onto downtown's other central artery, one-way **Indian Canyon,** heading north and (2) continues, from the right-hand lanes, as E. Palm Canyon—still Highway 111, the main thoroughfare connecting the various valley towns. Most intersecting streets, shown on local maps, are usually well marked and visible. To avoid the often crushing traffic along Highway 111, use your map to plot alternative routes via the bigger cross-valley roads.

Most car rental agencies are at the airport (see below). Sans car, you can come via bus. There's a **Greyhound** terminal in downtown Palm Springs, 311 N. Indian Canyon Dr. (at Amado), 760/325-2053, and another in Indio, 760/347-5888; www.greyhound.com. **Amtrak** offers direct train service to Palm Springs—it's an undeveloped, unstaffed station, with all arrivals and departures between midnight and 5 A.M., at last report—so you can also come by train. The only trains stopping at this station are those of the *Sunset Limited,* which operates three days a week between Los Angeles and Florida. The station is located on the Union Pacific (former Southern Pacific) Railroad tracks just south of I-10 west of Indian Avenue, about four miles north of downtown Palm Springs. For current information on Amtrak trains, call toll-free 800/872-7245 or try www.amtrak.com or www.amtrak-west.com.

Palm Springs lacked airplane service until 1945, and what was available wasn't convenient even from Los Angeles until the 1950s. Flights here from any distance typically required so many transfers and "short hops" that it was all too tedious for most people's tastes. That fact of Palm Springs life is fast changing, even though some service is still "high-season" (winter) only. (Check with your travel agent or with the airlines.) At last report **Palm Springs Regional Airport,** at the out-there east end of Tahquitz

KIM WEIR

Hitch a ride on a covered wagon to tour Thousand Palms Oasis.

Canyon Way, was well served by **American Airlines/American Eagle** and **Alaska Airlines.** American offers a Los Angeles hop and nonstop Chicago and Dallas/Ft. Worth service. Alaska offers nonstop San Francisco and Seattle service. Other carriers include **America West,** which offers jet service connecting to its hub in Phoenix, **Delta/Skywest** (Salt Lake City), **U.S. Airways/United Express** (Los Angeles), and **United Airlines** (Denver). New in late 1999 was **Continental Airlines** seasonal service from its Houston hub, with daily flights in winter. Contact relevant airlines for current details.

Palm Springs Area Information

For information about the city of Palm Springs, contact the **Palm Springs Visitor Information Center,** 2781 N. Palm Canyon Dr., Palm Springs, CA 92262, 760/778-8415 or toll-free 800/347-7746,, fax 760/325-4335. In addition to providing all essential local information, the center also assists with motel, hotel, and resort reservations. New in 1999 was the city tourism department's *Gay Guide to Palm Springs,* available here. For visitor info via the Web, try www.palm-springs.org.

For information on the greater Palm Springs area—including, but not limited to, Palm Springs—contact **Palm Springs Desert Resorts Convention and Visitors Authority,** The Atrium, 69-930 Hwy. 111, Ste. 201, Rancho Mirage, CA 92270, 760/770-9000 or toll-free 800/417-3529, www.desert-resorts.com and (new website) www.palmspringsusa.com, which offers a 24-hour reservations service for hotels, golf, and other activities and services. The bureau also offers a visitor information desk downtown at the Palm Springs Regional Airport. For 24-hour recorded information (message updated monthly), call 760/770-1992.

Local newspapers, and freebie tabloids, deliver the small-town goods. And such a glossy place deserves at least one glossy mag—in this case, **Palm Springs Life.** Many more intriguing celebrity-story details are available in the gossipy but hard-edged *Palm Springs Babylon: Sizzling Stories from the Desert Playground of the Stars* by Ray Mungo (St. Martin's Press), a local boy who happily sweeps the dirt on local legends right out into the open. Talk about a wild town.

BEYOND PALM SPRINGS

Immediately south of the Coachella Valley is one of the nation's newest national monuments, a craggy collection of spires that seem to leap straight up out of the desert. The rugged 227,000-acre Santa Rosa and San Jacinto Mountains National Monument, which includes the earlier Santa Rosa Mountains National Scenic Area, was established in October 2000. According to the U.S. Fish and Wildlife Service, this general area—part of a 1,370-square-mile region extending from the Coachella Valley to the Mexican border—is "critical habitat" for endangered Peninsular bighorn sheep, a population that had declined by mid-2000 to about 335.

Taking the spectacularly winding and scenic Palms to Pines Highway (Hwy. 74) south from Palm Desert and up into the Santa Rosa Mountains leads to Idyllwild, a tiny resort town in the woods popular for its sweet mountain air and just general coziness. The route eventually leads to Hemet, site of the annual Ramona Pageant

each spring. Roads soon spin off in all directions, like the spokes of a wagon wheel; Highway 79, for example, takes you to the wine country near Temecula and then on an extensive backcountry tour of San Diego County, including Julian and both Anza-Borrego and Cuyamaca State Parks.

Heading east from the Coachella Valley via Highway 111 leads past the date groves of Indio and Thermal to the Salton Sea, yet another backroad route into Anza-Borrego (Hwy. 78), and the vast Imperial Valley and its farm towns, a sandy breadbasket responsible for much of the delicate produce and fruit Americans enjoy in winter. East of the Imperial Valley, via Highway 78, is an almost endless sea of sand—and the Algodones Dunes.

North and east from greater Palm Springs is the rest of California's desert, including its most famous natural attractions: Joshua Tree National Park, the new Mojave National Preserve, and Death Valley National Park.

Idyllwild

The main attraction is the alpine scenery and the cool, fresh air—and a little vacation-related shopping in downtown Idyllwild, which features some stunning crafts shops, including the **Feats of Clay Gallery**, 54225 N. Circle Dr., 909/659-2692. Not only that, you can get here via the **Palm Springs Aerial Tramway** and then along hiking trails through **Mount San Jacinto State Park** and surrounding **San Bernardino National Forest** wilderness—altogether a radical transition between desert and thick conifer forest. (Wilderness permits, available at area ranger stations, are required. For information, call the state park office, listed below.) From near Idyllwild, a favorite trek is up **Mount Tahquitz,** about 10 miles round-trip. **Tahquitz Rock** near the summit is a rock-climbing hot spot. There's also a great summer "environmental exploration" program for kids, through both of Riverside County's regional parks here, **Idyllwild** and **Lawler.**

Once hiked out, comfort lovers can head for a bed-and-breakfast overnight at the welcoming **Strawberry Creek Inn**, 26370 Hwy. 243, 909/659-3202 or toll-free 800/262-8969, www.strawberrycreekinn.com, featuring nine rooms and one cottage. Rates are $85 and up (some rooms slightly higher in winter). The **Creekstone Inn Bed and Breakfast** at Fern Valley corners (N. Circle and Pine Crest), 909/659-3342 or toll-free 800/409-2127, features nine large guest rooms all with private baths, most with fireplaces, and several with a large Jacuzzi tub. Rates are $105 and up. Contact the chamber for other choices.

Cabin-style stays are a time-honored local tradition. The charming and woodsy **Fireside Inn,** 54540 N. Circle Dr., 909/659-2966 or toll-free 877/797-3473, www.thefireside-inn.com, is often booked up to a year ahead for holiday weekends. Fireside features seven duplex-style cottages and one separate cottage, most with fireplaces and furnished kitchens. Rates are $60–110. Another possibility is the **Quiet Creek Inn**, 26345 Delano Dr., 909/659-6110 or toll-

THE RAMONA PAGEANT: RACIAL INJUSTICE AS ROMANCE

Helen Hunt Jackson was an early activist on behalf of California's downtrodden native peoples. In despair that so few cared about the Indians' plight, Jackson decided to tell the story as a romance—an interracial romance. As she put it: "I am going to try to write a novel, in which will be set forth some Indian experiences in a way to move people's hearts. People will read a novel when they will not read serious books." The resulting *Ramona* was a national sensation when it was first published in 1884.

Jackson's story, about the beautiful young maiden Ramona and Alessandro, her Indian love, has been staged as an outdoor play since 1923. The remote Hemet-area locale is fitting, since the San Jacinto Valley was the setting for some of the novel's original scenes. Alessandro's murder, for example, was modeled after an all-too-true killing here in 1883. Though the story is the stuff of Hollywood movies—in 1959, showcasing the charms of Raquel Welch, the 1969 version starring Anne Archer—*Ramona* the novel became *Ramona* the play in 1923. It was dramatized by Garnet Holme, who also scripted the "Bracebridge Dinner" for Yosemite National Park's Awahnee Hotel Christmas celebration and Marin County's Mount Tamalpais *Mountain Play.*

Now the official California State Play, the Ramona Pageant is presented on select weekends each spring at the open-air **Ramona Bowl and Museum** in the rocky hills just south of Hemet. (Dress casually, wear a hat, and bring sunscreen.) Nothing much has changed over the years, except that the "cast of hundreds" often includes young girls in young-boy roles because of increasing lack of interest in the Y-chromosome crowd. The Ramona Pageant is staged each year over several consecutive weekends, typically mid-April to May, matinee performances only. At last report ticket prices were $14–$23. The Ramona Bowl is about three miles south of Florida Avenue via Girard. The museum is open weekends only, January through May, 10 A.M.–4 P.M.

For more information, contact: **Ramona Pageant,** Ramona Bowl, 27400 Ramona Bowl Rd., Hemet 92544, 909/658-3111 or toll-free 800/645-4465 for tickets and current information, or go to www.ramonapageant.com.

free 800/450-6110, www.quietcreekinn.com, with five duplex-style cabins sitting alongside reasonably quiet Strawberry Creek. Each cabin includes a studio unit and a one-bedroom suite, all with a wood-burning fireplace and kitchenette. Rates are $80–90. **Woodland Park Manor,** 55350 S. Circle Dr., 909/659-2657 or toll-free 877/659-2657, www.woodlandparkmanor.com, offers open-beamed redwood cottages with floor-to-ceiling windows—to let all that outdoors in— and rental homes as well. Heated pool too. Cottages are duplex-style; the larger side features a wood-burning fireplace and a fully equipped kitchen, the smaller a fireplace, refrigerator, and coffeemaker. For families or groups, the two units can be connected. The separate and secluded Cottage in the Woods and rental homes and cabins are also available. Rates are $75–165.

For a good sit-down meal, look around the village and see what's new. Always a best bet is casual **Restaurant Gastrognome,** in the Village Center at 54381 Ridgeview Dr., 909/659-5055, where the fare includes rack of lamb, beef tournedos, fresh fish, and chicken Kiev, though you certainly won't go wrong with pastas and salads. And don't forget the pecan pie. Children's menu, full bar, great Sunday brunch. Just south of the Village center at 26345 Hwy. 243 is **Antonelli's Seafood,** 909/659-5500, where you can dine out on the patio in summer.

For more information about the area, contact the **Idyllwild Chamber of Commerce,** 54295 Village Center Dr. (downstairs in the same building as the local *Idyllwild Town Crier* newspaper), P.O. Box 304, Idyllwild, CA 92549, 909/659-3259; www.idyllwildchamber.com. For more information about Mount San Jacinto State Park, call 909/659-2607 or try www.sanjac.statepark .org. For state park camping reservations, contact ReserveAmerica at toll-free (800) 444-7275; www.reserveamerica.com.

For San Bernardino National Forest information, contact the **San Jacinto Ranger District** office, at Hwy. 243 and Pine Crest Ave., 909/659-2117; www.r5.fs.fed.us/sanbernardino (website under construction, at last report). Area campgrounds offer some campsites on a first-come, first-served basis, along with campsites by reservation. To reserve campsites, call toll-free 800/ 280-2267. Fees are $8–24. "Dispersed camping" is also available.

Salton Sea

From a distance one might assume it to be a massive desert mirage, a shimmering imaginary lake. But the Salton Sea is quite real—California's largest body of water, 35 miles long and twice the size of Lake Tahoe. This very salty inland lake, on the site of long-extinct Lake Cahuilla, exists because of a greed-inspired engineering accident. In 1905 engineers working to divert Colorado River water decided to also siphon off some of Mexico's share. The disastrous diversion attempt caused river water to pour north—in a rampaging torrent that lasted 18 months—into this sink, which is more than 200 feet below sea level.

At one time, the Salton Sea was an immensely popular recreation area, attracting a half-million visitors each year for water sports and sportfishing. The shorter half of Sonny and Cher, the late U.S. Congressman Sonny Bono, water-skied here as a teenager. Even in the 1970s the water in this desert lake was fresh enough to support rainbow trout. These days, though, the Salton Sea is 30 percent saltier than the Pacific Ocean and becoming saltier all the time, due to accumulating salts from irrigation runoff. And such salty, nutrient-rich water has become a turnoff for visitors—not to mention a potential danger to the fish and wildlife of Salton Sea State Recreation Area. Though waterfowl and other migrating birds have turned the Salton Sea into a bird-watching mecca, sometimes there are disastrous bird die-offs—caused by selenium-related water toxicity in the late 1980s and, more recently, suspected botulism in the lake's fish. Almost 20,000 birds died in late 1996 from eating sick fish; scientists later announced that the bacteria that caused the die-off could be harmful to humans.

Yet the Salton Sea may again become a recreational hot spot. A federally supported effort is now underway to save the Salton Sea, a project expected to cost hundreds of millions of dollars. This future Salton Sea may be vastly reduced in size; Colorado River water that once replenished the lake is now being conserved and diverted to other uses. Options for reducing salinity including pumping water out of the lake for salt extraction, then returning the desalted water, and building dikes to turn one-third of the lake into a solar salt-concentration sump.

WAY OUT THERE: PICACHO STATE RECREATION AREA

Looking for an out-there California desert destination? Consider Picacho State Recreation Area, some 24 miles north of Winterhaven, California, just across the border from Yuma, Arizona.

Over a century ago, Picacho was a gold-mining town with some 100 citizens. Gold may have been discovered along the Colorado River as early as 1862, but it wasn't until 1890 that a large stamp mill was built near the river at Picacho. Soon the Picacho Mine opened in the Picacho Basin; a narrow gauge railroad hauled ore from the mine to the mill. By 1904, Picacho had grown to some 2,500 people, the river itself and paddle-wheel ferries the town's main transportation links to the outside world.

Not much of early Picacho remains today, though just east of park headquarters and the developed campground a one-mile self-guided trail leads to the ruins of the old Picacho Mill. Today Picacho, with its beavertail cacti and wild burros, is primarily popular with hikers, campers, boaters, and fisherfolk;

the area's eastern border is formed by a eight-mile length of the Colorado River. In winter, bird-watchers take advantage of its location along this section of the Pacific Flyway.

The 54-site campground at Picacho features drinking water, chemical toilets, a solar-heated shower, picnic tables, and fire rings. Also here: two boat-in campsites and a group campground. Five smaller campgrounds, located upriver, have no drinking water.

Picacho is definitely "out there." Only the first six miles of the road from Winterhaven are paved; the dirt road to Picacho is usually fine for cars, trucks with trailers, and motorhomes, but summer thunderstorms and flash flooding can make sections of the road temporarily impassable. Since climate can be extreme in any season, layered clothing is wise. Always carry extra water and essential supplies.

For more information about Picacho State Recreation Area, call the Salton Sea State Recreation Area at 760/393-3052.

Do stop by in the meantime. Most visitors come during the mild winter months, when it can be a bird-watcher's paradise. More than four million birds, some 400 species, have been tallied here. For organized birding, come for the **Salton Sea International Bird Festival** in February, 760/344-5359, www.imperialcounty.com/birdfest, which features both guided and self-guided tours of more than 100 bird species and five habitats reaching from the Salton Sea and Imperial Valley into northern Baja California.

Other recreational attractions at the Salton Sea include boating, fishing, swimming, and water-skiing. Picnicking, shore walks, nature trails, and camping (be prepared for high winds) round out the action. The Salton Sea features five developed and primitive campgrounds near the lake's shoreline; the Varner Harbor campground, near the visitor center, includes complete hook-ups.

For more information about the Salton Sea, contact **Salton Sea State Recreation Area,** 100-225 State Park Rd., North Shore, CA 92254, 760/393-3052 or 760/393-3059; www.saltonse

.statepark.org. Day use is $2 per vehicle. To reserve available campsites—many are first-come, first-camped—contact **ReserveAmerica** at toll-free 800/444-7275; www.reserveamerica .com. The recreation area is open year-round, but the visitor center closes in summer.

And while you're in the area, visit the Nature Conservancy's **Dos Palmas Oasis** preserve, a freshwater oasis frequented at various times by the Cahuilla Indians, the legendary Wyatt Earp, and General George S. Patton. Now managed by the U.S. Bureau of Land Management, the 1,372-acre preserve, at the base of the Orocopia Mountains near the town of North Shore, is open daily from sunrise to sunset. Call 760/343-1234 for more information.

Algodones Dunes

California's most extensive sand dune system, also known over the years as the Imperial Dunes and Glamis Dunes, Algodones Dunes Natural National Landmark is an impressive sight—the kind of desert that allows one to imagine being Lawrence of Arabia or General Patton, say, or

Cleopatra. But most of these dunes are open to the mind-numbing racket of off-road and all-terrain vehicles, especially near Glamis. Some off-road areas—including a large interior section of the southern dunes—were closed to dune buggy enthusiasts in 2000, as part of a lawsuit settlement aimed at protected an endangered species of vetch. A small percentage—including the 32,000-some acres north of Highway 78, now the U.S. Bureau of Land Management's **North Algodones Dunes Wilderness**—is open only for on-foot exploration. To get here: From the junction of Highways 86 and 78 in Brawley, head east via Highway 78 to the ranger station and visitor center (closed in summer); from I-8,

head west on Highway 78. And head south for Gray's Well Road, on the south side of I-8 (Gray's Well exit, then west), to see remnants of the desert's historic **Old Plank Road.** One car wide (with turnouts every quarter mile) and constructed of heavy wooden planks, this was the only route across the dunes from 1916 to 1926.

For more information about the area, contact the BLM's El Centro office, 1661 S. Fourth St., El Centro, CA 92243, 760/337-4400 or 760/337-4490. For detailed information on all of the BLM's new desert wildernesses, contact the California Desert District Office, 6221 Box Springs Rd., Riverside, CA 92507, 909/697-5200.

JOSHUA TREE NATIONAL PARK

Joshua trees, the kinky agaves for which this fairly new national park is named, spooked early desert immigrants. Perhaps to express that anxiety they attached derogatory names and descriptions. But Mormon pioneers envisioned inspiration, perhaps even divine intervention, where others saw only grizzly grotesques. Thus the trees' given name, prompted by the Bible's Book of Joshua: "Thou shalt follow the way pointed for thee by the trees." Equally inspiring are Joshua Tree National Park's giant granite formations—eccentric arrangements of fat, khaki-colored stone as smooth and aesthetically well rounded as Henry Moore sculptures.

The strange landscape here is solid and timeless yet in perpetual transition, a scenic backdrop for an endless juggling act. With airs both prehistoric and futuristic, the park embraces the Mojave and Colorado Deserts as it defines the weird no-man's-land connecting them.

"Weird" is a common descriptive term for Joshua Tree. Even its human dimension can be somewhat strange, since the oddball and outlandish visit fairly frequently—and always have, judging from the murders and miscellaneous treacheries that dogged early settlers. To keep track of current inexplicable events, park rangers keep an ongoing "weird file." Some blame the lunacy of the landscape and its proximity to Los Angeles. Spiritualists believe the area is veined with earth-energy "power centers," explanation enough in some quarters.

Perhaps all of the above—or none of the above—explain the 1973 outdoor cremation of mythic musician Gram Parsons, former Byrd, Flying Burrito Brother, and significant other of Emmylou Harris. Parsons had died in Twenty-nine Palms of a drug and alcohol overdose; both coffin and body were shipped off to Los Angeles pending return to his next of kin. But before Gram Parsons could board his final flight from L.A., his remains were stolen and spirited back to Joshua Tree. The following day, a park employee discovered his blazing corpse near Cap Rock. Parsons's after-death immolation left a long-lived stain that served, for years, as ground zero for his fans' de facto shrine.

For most of us, the Joshua Tree experience is much less dramatic. Yet this surreal and spacious landscape, with its oddly expressive trees and serene stone, is a holy place, its central shrine dedicated not to human idols but to the enduring wonders of everyday creation.

Protecting "Desert Beauty Spots" from Progress

Before Joshua Tree became a national park in 1994, it was a national monument—established by President Franklin D. Roosevelt in 1936 to protect these beleaguered giants and the legions of other desert life suddenly threatened by progress.

In the 1920s California's new love affair with the automobile had reinvented the desert as

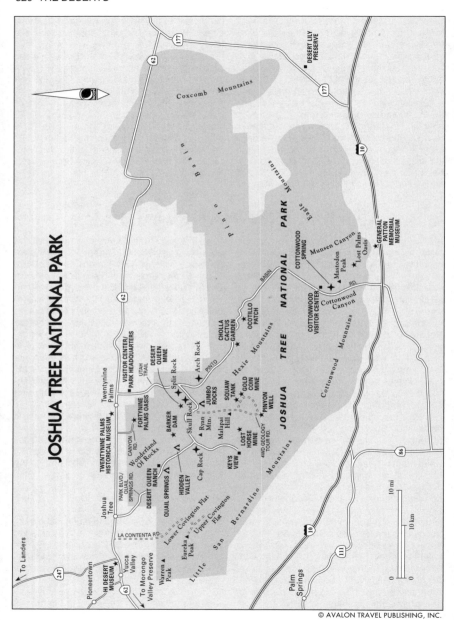

JOSHUA TREE NATIONAL PARK

urban playground—and as no-cost neighbor-hood nursery. Cactus collections that soon bloomed in and around Southern California bungalows, even full-grown palm trees, were dug out of their desert habitats and dragged back to the city at alarming rates. Almost overnight, the massive Devil's Garden along Highway 62 near Morongo Pass—a concentration of thousands of cactus and yucca varieties described by George Wharton James in his 1906 *Wonders of the Colorado Desert*—was decimated by domestic plant predators.

Joshua trees, too, were threatened, both by active vandalism and by garden-variety exploratory enthusiasm; at night, otherwise well-meaning travelers torched them to light the way for fellow motorists. Crass commerce also had a hand. In the 1880s 5,200 acres of Joshua trees surrounding Palmdale were harvested by a London-based paper company, though the "cactus paper" enterprise failed because of the product's inferior quality. Fortunately for the Joshua tree, furniture makers met with similar fates.

Beginning in the late 1920s, Minerva Hamilton Hoyt, a proper Pasadena matron, launched the public education campaign to preserve what is now Joshua Tree National Park and surrounding "desert beauty spots." She was assisted by noted biologists Philip Munz and Edmund Jaeger and their documentation, in word and photograph, of the desert's rich diversity. Endless "desert exhibitions," both in the United States and England, desert tours for VIPs, and lobbying by Hoyt's International Deserts Conservation League achieved their aim on August 10, 1936, when President Roosevelt set aside 825,000 acres as Joshua Tree National Monument.

Bearing early witness to the political power that desert mining interests would wield throughout the 20th century—and on into the 21st—in 1950 the original monument was whittled by 289,000 acres in exchange for federal funds to acquire private lands still within monument boundaries, a compromise engineered by conservationists to prevent the loss of Joshua Tree entirely. Yet the campaign by miners and other "multiple use" advocates to "open up" the national monument and other sensitive desert areas began again in 1951—a struggle side-lined only in 1994 with the passage of the Desert Protection Act, which established Joshua Tree as a national park.

With national park status came more stringent desert protections and new wilderness designations—and 234,000 additional acres, for a new park total of 793,955. Now included within the national park are the Coxcomb, Cottonwood, and Eagle mountains, minus a few active mining areas.

LAND IN TRANSITION

Perched upon a high-desert escarpment surrounded by sand and mountains, Joshua Tree National Park represents the "high" or Mojave Desert as it shape-shifts into the "low" Colorado Desert.

The Joshua tree, primary indicator plant of the Mojave Desert, is a highlight of ecological transition in the park's central and northwestern regions. But there are others, including two groves of native fan palms thriving well north of their typical Colorado Desert context: the **Oasis of Mara** adjacent to the park's main visitor center outside Twentynine Palms, and the **Fortynine Palms Oasis** tucked into a canyon some four miles west of town. Other citizens of the botanically rich Colorado dot the landscape to the south and east—ironwood, green-barked palo verde (an oversized legume), and smoke trees, along with the indicators ocotillo and teddy-bear cholla. At higher mountain elevations within both deserts, where rainfall is greater, junipers and piñon pines flourish.

Yet at Joshua Tree the range and distribution of plant and animal species is somewhat unpredictable, depending on microclimatic and other local factors—which makes birding and botanizing that much more inviting.

Geological Movements

As an open-air natural history exhibit, Joshua Tree offers more than its oddly anthropomorphic yuccas. One can also study geology—some of California's most intriguing desert formations, in fact. Most noticeable are the mountains and mounds of exposed monzogranite, also known as quartz monzonite.

In his 1906 *Wonders of the Colorado Desert,* George Wharton James described such formations as "one wild chaotic upheaval and tumblement of disintegrating coarse granite. Great masses, of irregular size and shape, thrust their heads above the general mass, and stand, split, seamed, creviced, shattered, jagged, and rough, and in some cases rounded by water and weather, in dumb protest against the fierceness of the desert sun."

The scientific creation story is substantially less poetic. About a hundred million years ago this molten, light-colored granite rose up to push aside its ancient predecessor, the darker metamorphic "pinto gneiss" still atop the area's higher mountains. As the young granite cooled and crystalized beneath the earth's surface, it also cracked—in endless vertical and horizontal patterns. The blocks of monzogranite rose to the surface; groundwater seepage transformed much of the new rock into softer clays, particularly at fracture points. Once exposed to the elements, the clay quickly eroded—leaving the characteristic rounded stone shapes so visible today, with columns and stony spires where the granite fractured vertically and stacked pancakelike formations where it cracked horizontally. Ongoing erosion—the wheeling cycles of sunlight and scorching heat, ice, rain, and relentless wind—continues to create variations on these themes.

Joshua Trees Point the Way

Joshua trees are an endless fascination—which is why visitors spend day after day just wandering among them, studying their eccentric shapes, shadows, and unintended impersonations. Yet early California travelers had few kind or poetic words for these desert giants. Early Spanish and Mexican explorers called them "cabbage palms." According to the intrepid John C. Frémont in 1844, "their stiff and ungraceful form makes them. . . the most repulsive tree in the vegetable kingdom." The scurrilous slurs continued into the next century, when J. Smeaton Chase observed:

> *It is a weird, menacing object, more like some conception of Poe's or Dore's than any work of wholesome Mother Nature.*

> *One can scarcely find a term of ugliness that is not apt for this plant. A misshapen pirate with belt, boots, hands, and teeth stuck full of daggers is as near as I can come to a human analogy. . . . A landscape filled with Joshua trees has a nightmare effect even in broad daylight; at the witching hour it can be almost infernal.*

Mormon immigrants redeemed Joshua trees. As the story goes, a party of parched pioneers led by Elisha Hunt crossed the region in late spring of 1851, en route to San Bernardino. As they came upon a forest of the trees, a cloud suddenly blocked the sun—halting its course across the sky—as if commanded by Joshua, the settlers thought. With their many "arms" raised in supplication, "Joshua trees" seemed an apt name for the odd plants that bore witness to this event and seemed to be pointing the way.

Joshua trees can live to be 700 to 800 years old or more, and may stand 30 to 60 feet tall at maturity—though you'll see few true elders or giants here, since early settlers chopped the largest for fence posts and firewood. While they are trees, they are also wildflowers. These *Yucca brevifolia* specimens, or short-leafed agaves, are slow-growing members of the lily family that bloom in sync with the rest of the desert.

Peculiar perennials, these particular yuccas are also noteworthy for their odd growth and reproductive habits. Joshua trees don't begin to take on their characteristic shape until age 30 or so. With the onset of flower formation, or when there is damage to the terminal bud, vertical growth ends and the Joshua tree's characteristic freeform branching begins. Two or more growth buds—future branches—form just below the terminal bud, these branches eventually sprouting branches in the same way. Plant growth is slow, however, averaging only a half-inch per year.

Flowering is not an annual event. Joshua trees bloom only in years of sufficient rainfall, typically in March. The immense blossoms are most inspiring to the nectar-collecting yucca moth, whose symbiotic relationship with the plant is solely responsible for pollination; to humans, the clustered cream-colored blooms give off a slightly foul, musty scent. Plants reproduce from seed and vegetatively. By May the huge green pecan-shaped pods, used pharmaceutically for steroid manufacture, hang from branch ends like fat fingers. Young Joshua trees established by underground runners grow up, slowly, in the slim shadows of their elders.

Despite unwholesome associations imagined by early explorers and settlers, the Joshua tree is central to Mojave Desert life. At least 25 bird species are known to nest in it—thanks in large part to woodpeckers, which bore holes and hollow out nesting cavities in its limbs. Birds of prey use it as a hunting perch; the loggerhead shrike uses it also as a hunting tool, impaling and then storing its prey on the daggerlike leaves. Woodrats use Joshua tree leaves to build their own nests. Snakes, lizards, and an endless march of insects also use the Joshua tree—living and dead—for shelter.

SEEING JOSHUA TREE

Seeing and doing Joshua Tree National Park requires some strategic planning, since the park's key features and diversions are fairly far-flung. If coming from the north, get oriented at the park's main **Oasis Visitor Center** on National Park Drive (Utah Trail) in Twentynine Palms, just off Highway 62. Stroll the short nature trail through the native fan palms and mesquite of the adjacent **Oasis of Mara.** To the Serrano and Chemehuevi peoples who called it home when explorers and settlers first passed through, this once well-watered oasis was known simply as *mara,* or "place of small springs and much grass." (The natural water source still exists, though diminished by the area's pumping of groundwater, which pools here as the direct result of earthquake faulting.) Early explorers and settlers called the oasis, and the town that soon sprang to life in its shadows, Twentynine Palms. Birdwatching is almost always fruitful here, but more so during annual migrations. For several days in spring and fall, for example, the turkey vultures convene; hundreds make the several-day migratory stop at Mara before moving on.

Other northern attractions include the remote **Fortynine Palms Oasis** near Twentynine Palms, and the **Wonderland of Rocks** near

Joshua trees are among the world's weirdest wildflowers.

Indian Cove Campground, geological magnet for hands-on mountaineers. Farther west, in the Little San Bernardino Mountains near Yucca Valley, is the pleasant high-country **Black Rock Canyon Campground** area and, nearby, dirt-road access from the highway to **Covington Flat**—featuring the park's largest Joshua trees and wonderful picnicking—and **Eureka Peak.** The view from the peak, most spectacular in spring, takes in 10,000-foot **Mount San Jacinto,** beyond Palm Springs to the southwest, and, directly west, Southern California's tallest, **San Gorgonio Mountain,** looming above its siblings at an elevation of 11,499 feet.

The central park includes a multitude of just-the-basics campgrounds—**Hidden Valley, Jumbo Rocks, Ryan, Belle,** and **White Tank**—and most of the park's major natural and historic attractions.

The short hike/scramble through surrealistic, stone-circled **Hidden Valley** also wanders into the dark side of local lore, since this was said to be the historic hideout and hidden grazing headquarters of the horse-rustling McHaney Gang during the late 1800s.

North of Hidden Valley is the southern jumble of the vast **Wonderland of Rocks,** scenic setting for the storied **Desert Queen Ranch** which can be seen only on guided tours. The serene Desert Queen is most infamous for the murder conviction of its owner Bill Keys, prospector, family man, and friend of Death Valley Scotty. For the best general on-foot introduction to the stony surroundings, hike the trail to **Barker Dam**— once associated with the Desert Queen, and one of the park's remaining "tanks" or artificial reservoirs. Equally pleasant for picnicking, if you're heading northwest, is **Quail Springs.**

South of Hidden Valley is the Joshua Tree wonderland of **Lost Horse Valley,** named for the **Lost Horse Mine**—the area's most successful gold mine, a claim purportedly "discovered" by prospector Johnny Lang (through Frank Diebold) while Lang was tracking his runaway horse. Farther south, and best for getting the indescribable big picture of the park, is mile-high **Keys View,** a vista sweeping the landscape from high to low—from San Gorgonio Mountain in the north to lonely Salton Sea in the south. The route south to Keys View begins at **Cap Rock,** a huge granite dome topped by a stone-brimmed baseball cap.

East from Cap Rock is Ryan Campground, near remnants of the old Ryan Ranch; farther east, just before the turnoff to Sheep Camp Group Campground, is the rousing three-mile round-trip trek to the top of **Ryan Mountain,** where the views are most dramatic at dawn and dusk.

Still farther east is broad **Queen Valley,** crowned on the north by the Queen Mountains and ending far to the south at intersecting Pleasant Valley. The ideal soils and elevations between Sheep Pass and Jumbo Rocks Campground support one of the park's most impressive forests of Joshua trees—thousands and thousands of them, pointing off in all directions. A short dirt road leads north to the ruins of the **Desert Queen Mine,** another historic Joshua Tree enterprise accompanied by murder, mysteries, and miscellaneous intrigues. The 18-mile **Geology Tour Road** loop shoots straight south

through the valley to demonstrate key geological processes, intersecting the **California Riding and Hiking Trail** en route. Black **Malapai Hill** (a wannabe volcano), an impressive **balanced rock,** and the stunning stones surrounding **Squaw Tank** are tour highlights. To continue the loop, follow the road east toward the Hexie Mountains and the ruins of the **Gold Coin Mine** then south onto the clay Pleasant Valley playa (unwise after rain) and the trail to the onetime **Pinyon Well** gold camp.

Once back on paved road, next east is aptly named **Jumbo Rocks,** where the stone impersonations rival the best efforts of Joshua trees. Even nonhikers enjoy the quarter-mile interpretive stroll from the Jumbo Rocks Campground to the specter of **Skull Rock.** From here, the more adventuresome scramble north on Skull Rock Trail across the park road and through the silent stone canyons before returning to the campground entrance. Just east and north, across the highway from the **Live Oak Picnic Area,** is huge, neatly fractured **Split Rock** and its namesake picnic sites.

Pinto Basin Road ambles south past Belle Campground and nearby **Bread Loaf Rock** then White Tank Campground and its associated **Arch Rock** on the way to the **Cholla Cactus Garden** and **Ocotillo Patch**—clear indicators of the Colorado Desert. The road continues south through the stark basin, past its small sand dunes and on to **Cottonwood Spring,** where, beyond the small **visitor center,** camping, picnicking, and hiking are the main attractions. (Fresh water is available here too.) Continuing south over Cottonwood Pass leads to the onetime site of World War II–era **Camp Young** and, just east along I-10, the **General Patton Memorial Museum** at **Chiriaco Summit.**

Bill Keys's Wonderland: The Desert Queen Ranch

Open to the public only for guided tours, the Desert Queen Ranch is like a well-preserved ghost town—this one preserving the memories of prospector and homesteader Bill Keys, his wife, Frances, and their family and friends.

One of Teddy Roosevelt's fabled Rough Riders, William F. Keys worked as a bodyguard, sheriff, and cowboy before abandoning civilization altogether and picking his way across the California desert as a gold miner. If Keys imagined that desert life would be uncomplicated, his thinking was soon corrected. He was first arrested, along with Death Valley Scotty, for his involvement in the "Battle of Wingate Pass" ambush—a staged shootout aimed at preventing Scotty's actual gold-mine financier Albert Johnson of Chicago, from discovering he'd invested in a nonexistent mine. For lack of evidence, neither Keys nor Scotty was prosecuted. That luck didn't hold, however. In 1943 he was arrested and convicted of manslaughter after gunplay with neighbor Worth Bagley. At the age of 64, Keys was sentenced to 12 years in San Quentin. His cause championed by mystery writer Erle Stanley Gardner, father of the Perry Mason mysteries, and his claims of self-defense ultimately bolstered by Bagley's ninth wife, Keys was freed in 1948 at age 69; he received a full pardon in 1956. Among other achievements before his death at age 90, Bill Keys starred as a grizzled old prospector in the Walt Disney movie *The Wild Burro of the West.*

Keys's ultimate achievement, of course, was the simple but gracious life he and his wife created for their family in the high desert. The ranch house and outbuildings are preserved by the park service much as the Keys family left them in the 1960s, from the original adobe barn built by the McHaney brothers to the schoolhouses, windmill, junked cars, and antique mining equipment scrounged from abandoned claims. The practical value of Joshua trees—crafted into sturdy corrals, fences, and gateposts—is also on display at the Desert Queen Ranch.

Guided tours of the Desert Queen Ranch, offered by the Joshua Tree Natural History Association, are offered daily from October through May, on weekdays at 10 A.M. and 1 P.M. and on weekends at 10 a.m, 1 P.M., and 3 P.M. (Should times change, the tour schedule is posted at park visitor centers, ranger stations, and campgrounds.) In summer, tours are offered by reservation only. The cost is $5 per person. Buy tour tickets up to five months in advance by calling 760/367-5555, Mon.–Fri. 9 A.M.–5 P.M., or buy tickets at the Oasis Visitor Center.

Near the Desert Queen:
Barker Dam and Vicinity
Then there's Bill Keys's dam—Barker Dam to the east, actually constructed by cattleman C. O.

Barker, which Keys renamed **Bighorn Dam** when he raised its height during the 1950s. Water is essential to all life in all places, but in the desert it somehow takes on divine stature. Assuming adequate recent rainfall, here you can soak up some of its life-giving significance. Get here via the short one-mile interpretive trail that begins northeast of Hidden Valley Campground, reached by dirt road. (For a longer hike, strike out from the campground.)

Below the dam and beyond Piano Rock are the park's **movie petroglyphs,** so called after a Hollywood film crew in the 1950s intentionally "enhanced" (painted) the ancient rock art here for the sake of cinematography. Petroglyphs, or symbols carved into rocks, and pictographs, or rock paintings, are fairly common in the Wonderland of Rocks and elsewhere throughout the park. The desecration of these park petroglyphs, which occurred when this area was still privately owned, illustrates why these and other cultural artifacts need absolute protection.

The dam's loop trail also offers the chance for up-close appreciation of the **Wonderland of Rocks**—a stone jumble so chaotic and confusing that no trail cuts through it. Relying on keen wits and known landmarks, even experienced mountaineers get turned around in the wonderland's disorienting interior.

Fortynine Palms Oasis
A few miles west of Twentynine Palms proper, Fortynine Palms is *the* springtime destination for wildflower aficionados in years of high rainfall—though fans of native fan palms make the trip any time. Next to carpets of ephemeral desert annuals, the barrel cacti along the trail produce stunning blooms. At the end of the trail and gracing a canyon pool are the palm trees, the hike's main attractions—noticeably blackened from fires that long since torched their skirtlike lower fronds. These palms survive, even thrive, despite severe burns, suggesting that fire is generally an aspect of local ecology. But do not build a fire (even light a match) anywhere near this area. Fires have been prevented at park palm oases for many decades, in most cases, allowing mesquite and dense scrub growth to replace long grasses and herbs. Area ecologists now fear that oasis wildfires would burn too hot and devastate the palm groves.

From the parking area at the end of short Canyon Road, which shoots south from Highway 62, the fairly strenuous 1.5-mile trail heads up and over the ridge—dotted with barrel cacti—before dropping down into the oasis. Even with limited access the area is quite popular, so pack out all litter—other people's too—and leave behind only your thoughts. There is little shade along the way, so wear a hat and bring sunscreen and water. The trail may be closed during periods of high fire danger.

Cholla Cactus Garden and Ocotillo Patch

Cactus, cactus, cactus. The creosote bush may be the chief indicator plant for the Colorado Desert, but here the cacti star. The seemingly fuzzy "teddy bear" or "jumping" cholla, more formally known as *Opuntia bigelovii,* is most infamous of the collection. Keep your distance. These teddy bears hitch rides on hapless passersby with uncanny skill. Miniscule barbs at the end of its spines hook into the skin or clothing of any creature that so much as brushes against it—and a prickly chunk of cactus goes along for the ride, an ingenious if painful plant dispersal method. Other cactus species here: the buckhorn cholla, the pencil cholla, and the calico cactus.

Fans of agriculture and alternative energy, also note the evergreen jojoba (ho-HO-ba) or goatnut plants here—a Colorado Desert native plant now being grown commercially in the nearby Coachella Valley for the high-quality oil of its seeds, already used commercially in cosmetics, high-test engines, and precision instruments.

An intriguing feature of local ecology are the packrat nests built from cholla cactus segments, these typically built two to three feet high around the bases of creosote bushes. Each well-armored, complicated dwelling includes a living room, hallways, bathroom, food storage areas, and (for females only) a nursery. One nest may survive for many, many generations, requiring constant maintenance and repair. Astonishingly, researchers have found some still in use after 25,000 years. The generous supply of cholla cactus here, which provides food for packrats in addition to shelter and a rather cunning security system, supports about 16 rats per acre. The rats are also good to the cholla. While transporting cholla segments, sometimes they lose them—inadvertently increasing the cactus population, since each segment takes root and grows into a new plant.

Just down the road is the park's Ocotillo Patch, a noticeable population of the dramatic spiny-stemmed desert shrub most noted for its stunning spring flowers in clusters of flaming red—these favored by hummingbirds. Known also as Jacob's staff, candlewood, coachwhip, and vine cactus, the ocotillo loses its leaves under the severe stress of drought.

Cottonwood Canyon

The highlight of southern Joshua Tree is Cottonwood Canyon and its aptly named Cottonwood Spring Oasis. The liquid heart of the oasis here is quite natural—the water seeps up through area earthquake faults. The palms are not, however, which is not to say they aren't appreciated, particularly by the many birds and other wildlife frequenting the area. Campers at **Cottonwood Campground** also have the luxury—in Joshua Tree, at least—of on-site water. The small visitor center and interpretive nature trail introduce the area. Two worthwhile hikes—the three-mile round-trip hike to **Mastodon Peak** and the more challenging all-day trip to **Lost Palms Oasis** (advisable only in cool weather)—begin at Cottonwood Spring.

DOING JOSHUA TREE

For all its sacred detachment, Joshua Tree is quite sporting. Popular outdoor activities vary from campground loafing and leisurely hiking to biking and rock-climbing. Winter climbing in Joshua Tree, in fact, has achieved international stature, this being one of the few appropriate off-season spots in North America for "bouldering" and big wall climbing outdoors. The truly intrepid climb in other seasons too. Also popular: bird-watching, botanizing, general nature study, and just staring up into the starry, starry night.

Joshua Tree Hiking

Most Joshua Tree trails, particularly interpretive loops, are family friendly and fairly easy, but the park also serves up athletic challenge.

Short interpretive trails start near park campgrounds—including **Arch Rock, Skull Rock,**

Cap Rock, Hidden Valley, Black Rock Canyon, Indian Cove, and **Cottonwood Spring**— or other attractions, such as **Oasis of Mara, Barker Dam,** and **Keys View.**

In addition to self-guided trails detailed under Seeing Joshua Tree, above, don't miss **Hidden Valley.** The surreal landscape, a giant stone fortification and gallery of human, animal, and abstract images autographed by ancient peoples with pictographs and petroglyphs, is circled by a fairly easy mile-long loop trail (though in some spots you'll have to scramble over and around boulders). Hidden Valley is also sublime at night—a prime location for watching stars, planets, and meteor showers, which is why the park's "star programs" often meet here in spring. The vigorous three-mile trudge up **Ryan Mountain** and back is a good workout with great eagle-eye views of surrounding valleys, most picturesque at sunrise and sunset. Also challenging among the park's shorter hikes, and a spring tradition for desert wildflower fans, is the three-mile round-trip trek to **Fortynine Palms Oasis,** described in some detail above.

The half-day hike to **Lost Horse Mine** showcases remnants of the park's mining history—in this case, a ten-stamp mill and lonely foundations—though the walk to the **Desert Queen Mine** site, with its rusting machinery, is much easier. For mining relics with a grand desert view—not to mention a shady cottonwood oasis —take the fairly challenging three-mile loop from the southern park's Cottonwood Spring to **Mastodon Peak,** an elephantine presence named for its animistic profile. Or use the Mastodon Peak walk as a warm-up for Lost Palms; the trails interconnect. Athletic aficionados of native fan palm oases set their lug soles on the rugged trail to **Lost Palms Oasis** and nearby **Munsen Canyon** (the latter requires a boulder scramble), an eight-mile round-trip well worth the effort.

Also great for lung expansion is the six-mile round-trip to Warren Peak via **Black Rock Canyon Trail** in the park's northwestern section, a trek that takes in cacti, Joshua trees, and piñon pines on the way to some inspiring views of the San Bernardino Mountains, the Little San Bernardinos, and Coachella Valley. Good for a one- to two-day walking workout is the 13-mile **Scout Trail** (still shown on some maps, stubbornly, as the Boy Scout Trail) along the western edge of the Wonderland of Rocks; this route also starts in the north, just south of the Indian Cove Ranger Station, and continues to Quail Springs.

And 35 miles of the **California Riding and Hiking Trail** traverse the park, from Covington Flat in the west to its eastern terminus near the junction of the main park road with Pinto Basin Road. It takes two to three days to hike the entire route, but you can turn it into multiple day trips by hopping on or off at Ryan Campground, the Geology Tour Road, White Tank Campground, and other intersections along the way.

This and other vigorous treks, particularly in the Colorado Desert, are recommended only in winter and early spring, when temperatures are mild. Longer, more remote trails, including the California Riding and Hiking Trail, require backcountry registration as a safety precaution. For current trail information, contact park visitor centers or ranger stations.

Joshua Tree Mountain Biking

With its wide-open horizons and woolly, Wild West vegetation, Joshua Tree is a beacon for present-day rough riders. Most of the park is designated as wilderness, however, so the opportunity for outback biking adventures is limited to established (however tenuously) roads

---

HELPING EVERYONE "SEE" AT JOSHUA TREE

The **Bajada All-Access Nature Trail** at Joshua Tree National Park, near the Cotton Spring entrance (coming from Indio and I-10), offers physically and visually challenged visitors the chance to "see" Joshua Tree's wonders, via scent and sound.

The quarter-mile loop trail offers wheelchair access without pavement; the trail is "paved" instead with biodegradeable road oil. Information about audiocassettes for this self-guided tour of the Colorado Desert, with some 15 exhibits, is available by calling the Oasis Visitor Visitor Center at 760/367-5500. Or stop by the Cottonwood Visitor Center, open daily year-round, 8 A.M.– 4:30 P.M.

and four-wheel-drive routes. Precautions for hikers and four-wheelers—such as packing plenty of water, sun protection, and emergency supplies and provisions, as well as avoiding solo travel and flash floods—also apply to backcountry cyclists. Before setting out, check with visitor centers or ranger stations for current road and weather conditions.

Joshua Tree Rock-Climbing
Though wandering through airy forests of Joshua trees is fascination enough for most folks, a special attraction at Joshua Tree National Park is winter rock-climbing—a pastime pursued religiously here by climbers from around the world, especially those temporarily frozen out of their regular rocky turf. Climbing routes at Joshua Tree aren't particularly high, but they are almost endless; more than 4,500 (an estimated 4,000 bolting routes) have been established, with more pioneered every year. Since 1993, there has been a moratorium on new bolting routes, due to concerns about complying with provisions of the Wilderness Act of 1964. The park's climbing management plan now allows the replacement of unsafe climbing bolts on existing routes and the installation of new ones in nonwilderness areas only (by permit). Respect for the sanctity of unmolested stone means that "free" climbing— without the aid of pitons and hacked-in hand holds—is otherwise the standard here. For permit applications, current regulations, restrictions, and equipment requirements, contact park headquarters—or see the official park website.

Seasoned climbers favor locales including **Saddle Rocks** at **Ryan Mountain,** the **Astro Dome** in the **Wonderland of Rocks,** and various spots near **Hidden Valley Campground.** Even beginners can scramble up easier formations scattered along main park roads and near campsites—even *in* campsites, so long as affected campers give their consent—and sign on for private lessons.

When just watching climbers at play is no longer exciting enough, lessons are available. **Vertical Adventures,** 949/854-6250 or toll-free 800/514-8785, www.vertical-adventures.com, offers beginning and intermediate classes at Joshua Tree from September to May along with four-day "rockcraft" seminars and guided climbs. **Joshua Tree Rock Climbing School** in Joshua Tree, 760/366-4745 or toll-free 800/890-4745, offers courses in basic rock-climbing as well as advanced seminars and privately guided climbs.

PRACTICAL JOSHUA TREE

A Park Primer
Joshua Tree National Park, open year-round, is about 50 miles northeast of Palm Springs and 140 miles east of Los Angeles via I-10. Most visitors enter from the north, via Twentynine Palms Highway (Hwy. 62) and the desert highway towns of Joshua Tree or Twentynine Palms. Joshua Tree aficionados prefer entering from Highway 62 at the town of Joshua Tree, reaching the park's **West Entrance**—the most dramatic first impression—via Park Boulevard/Quail Springs Road. But for newcomers a proper introduction is required, sooner or later. Just outside the park's **North Entrance** is the **Oasis Visitor Center** at the Oasis of Mara in Twentynine Palms (at the eastern edge of town; from Hwy. 62 follow the signs), the place for general park orientation. Visitors also enter the park from the Coachella Valley (Palm Springs and vicinity) and I-10 in the south, heading north through Cottonwood Canyon to **Cottonwood Spring,** where there is another but smaller visitor center.

Time spent at the Oasis Visitor Center is time well spent. Displays and exhibits—and the Oasis of Mara, adjacent—introduce area geology and ecology. In addition to a good selection of desert books, useful and inexpensive pamphlets include *The Oasis Story, The World of the Joshua Tree,* and keys to cacti, wildflowers, snakes, other reptiles, and amphibians. Free fact sheets on hiking trails, biking routes, and climbing regulations, as well as climbers' bolting permits, are also available. Inquire here about upcoming guided tours, walks, and campfire and stargazing programs, scheduled primarily in the fall and spring "interpretive season."

All park visitor centers are open daily 8 A.M.–5 P.M. Park admission is $10 per vehicle per week ($5 for walk-ins and bike-ins). A 12-month admission pass is $25. Park admission includes a map/brochure and the current edition of the tabloid *Joshua Tree Journal,* which highlights local natural and cultural history and current park programs and regulations.

For current information, and to receive maps and other park information by mail, contact: **Joshua Tree National Park,** 74485 National Park Drive, Twentynine Palms, CA 92277, 760/367-5500; www.nps.gov/jotr. For a current publications list, and to support park interpretative and preservation activities, contact the **Joshua Tree National History Association** at the same address; www.joshuatree.org. For additional California desert information, see www.california desert.gov.

When to Come, What to Bring, How to Behave

Fall and spring constitute prime time at Joshua Tree, the only seasons that invite all-day explorations. Officially, the park's interpretive seasons are mid-October through mid-December and mid-February through May. The peak time to see the blooming desert, a phenomenon dependent on rainfall and temperature, is usually mid-March through April—a justifiably popular time to visit the park. Even the air sparkles.

Since summer is like a bake oven—reaching 115°F in the Colorado Desert—Joshua Tree's brisk winter temperatures sometimes surprise visitors. From December through February in the low desert, average daytime high temperatures range from 55 to 65°F and nighttime lows can drop below freezing. In the high desert, which includes most of the park's northern and central areas, temperatures typically run about 10 degrees cooler. April and May are balmy, with days in the 70s and 80s and nights averaging 40–50°F. (Though everything's much less green, temperatures are similar in October and November.) Summer holds sway from June through September, 95–105°F during the day, 60–70 at night. Elevations within the park range from 1,000 to 6,000 feet, a fact that also affects area temperatures.

Though it can cook in summer, the season least attractive to visitors, sudden thunderstorms are not unusual. So come prepared for—and dress in layers for protection from—the cold in winter, and unobstructed sun and savage high winds in any season. Basic personal gear even in balmy seasons: broad-brimmed hat, broken-in hiking shoes or boots, T-shirts, shorts, long-sleeved shirts, long pants, long johns, and a sweater or jacket.

It's tempting to toss sleeping bags right onto the ground for snoozing and late-night stargazing, but tents (and campers) offer better wind protection. If you plan to camp, bring everything—food, water, all essential supplies, even firewood. No collecting is allowed in the park, a prohibition that includes any and all downed plant matter.

Water is largely unavailable in Joshua Tree—in most campgrounds, along the road, and on the trail—so pack plenty. For drinking purposes alone, the recommendation is at least one gallon per person per day (two gallons during hotter months). Water is available only in the park's "edge" areas: at Black Rock Canyon and Cottonwood campgrounds, Indian Cove Ranger Station, and Oasis Visitor Center.

Absolutely no services or supplies are available within Joshua Tree National Park. Gasoline, groceries, and other supplies are available in the greater Palm Springs area, Yucca Valley, and the towns of Joshua Tree and Twentynine Palms.

Now that Joshua Tree is protected as a national park, attendance is up substantially—more than 1.3 million visitors in 1999, and counting—which means increasing strain on the park's campgrounds, limited visitor facilities, and personnel. Be respectful to other people and to the park—and remember that the rules and regulations exist to protect the park and its wonders for future generations.

While exploring, always bring more water than you think you'll need, never travel alone, and stay on established trails and roads. Given the park's vastness and extreme temperatures, getting lost can be deadly. Scofflaw four-wheelers and motorcyclists typically discover that off-limits old roads end in sand pits or steep-sided washes and discover themselves suddenly mired in immediate danger at worst, eventual embarrassment at best. The nearest hospital in the north is in the town of Joshua Tree, 26 miles from Jumbo Rocks; in the south, in Indio, 25 miles from Cottonwood Spring.

Camping at Joshua Tree

At Joshua Tree you feel the "bigness" of this big-sky country even in the campgrounds. Most campsites are tucked into and around towering granite boulders that offer protection from desert winds and provide some degree of soundproof-ing. Campfires—bring your own firewood—cast enchanting and eerie shadows onto boulder backdrops.

Camping is free (first-come, first-camped) yet spartan at the park's central campgrounds, which feature pit toilets, fire rings, and tables but no running water, no showers, and no electricty. These central campgrounds—**Jumbo Rocks, Hidden Valley,** and **Ryan**—tend to overflow with rock-climbers. Nearby **Belle** and **White Tank** campgrounds, on Pinto Basin Road, were originally developed as "overflow" sites; White Tank is usually closed in summer.

Individual campsites at **Indian Cove Campground** and **Black Rock Canyon Campground,** $10 per night, and group sites at **Sheep Pass Group Camp,** $20–35 per night, are reservable through the National Park Reservation Service, toll-free 800/365-2267 or http://reservations.nps.gov.

Only Black Rock Canyon, Indian Cove, and Cottonwood campgrounds have potable running water. Once a private campground, 4,000-foot Black Rock Canyon just outside Yucca Valley is perfect for campers who prefer to make mealtime a side trip to a local restaurant. In addition to drinking water, the 101-site campground here has flush toilets (but no showers) and an RV dump station—all the comforts of home, comparatively speaking. Ditto for 62-campsite **Cottonwood Campground** at Cottonwood Spring, $10 per night, which is first-come, first-camped (no reservations). At isolated Indian Cove Campground at the northern edge of the Wonderland of Rocks—near Highway 62 between the communities of Joshua Tree and Twentynine Palms—drinking water is available at the nearby ranger station.

There is a 14-day camping limit from fall through spring (October through May), 30 days in summer. For more information about Joshua Tree campgrounds, contact park visitor centers.

PRACTICAL OPTIONS NEAR JOSHUA TREE

Accommodations, food, and services are available in the nearby Morongo Basin towns of Twenty Nine Palms, Joshua Tree, and Yucca Valley. For information about what's available in towns bordering Joshua Tree, contact local chambers of commerce—**Twentynine Palms,** 6455-A Mesquite Ave. in Twentynine Palms, 760/367-3445, www.29chamber.com; **Joshua Tree Village,** 61325 Twentynine Palms Hwy. in Joshua Tree, 760/366-3723, www.desertgold.com/jtcc/jtcc.html; and **Yucca Valley,** 55569 Twentynine Palms Hwy. in Yucca Valley, 760/365-6323, www.yuccavalley.org.

Traditional desert tourist kitsch such as "jackalope" memorabilia is still widely available, of course, but these days it's not that difficult to hunt down urban essentials such as café latte and pasta. And if it's not quite what you might find in L.A. or San Francisco, zip those critical lips, you spoiled city sophisticates. Even electricity didn't exist in these parts until the 1940s. That said, for a good meal the relaxed restaurant at the circa-1928 **Twentynine Palms Inn,** 73950 Inn Ave., 760/367-3505, is a long-running local favorite for lunch and dinner. Neighboring towns have their high points, too, including small, kid-friendly **Stephano's** Italian restaurant on the highway in Yucca Valley (two miles west of the Hwy. 247 junction), 760/228-3118. A hip Yucca Valley find is the **Water Canyon Café** and cybercoffeehouse, located at the corner of Pioneertown Road and Highway 62, 760/365-7771, famous for its coffee drinks and open for breakfast, lunch, snacks. Live entertainment on weekends.

Staying in Twentynine Palms

If staying cheap is the main consideration, Twentynine Palms boasts a **Motel 6,** 72562 Twentynine Palms Hwy. (near 49 Palms Rd.), 760/367-2833 or toll-free 800/466-8356, fax 760/367-4965, www.motel6.com, featuring just the basics, air conditioning, swimming pool, and spa. Rates: $45 for two. Always a safe bet in Twentynine Palms is the very nice **Best Western Gardens Inn and Suites,** 71487 Twentynine Palms Hwy., 760/367-9141, fax 760/367-2584, with spring high-season rates $79 and up and extras including a heated swimming pool. Quite comfortable for a noncamping overnight is the **Circle C Lodge,** a motel at 6340 El Rey Ave., 760/367-7615, fax 760/361-0247; for reservations, call toll-free 800/545-9696. This attractive, intimate motel features just 11 rooms—all large, with kitchens—featuring cable TV, video players, and free movies. Best of all, after a day spent scrambling over rocks and around Joshua trees: the landscaped pool and whirlpool area plus outdoor barbecue and dining setup. Rates are $70–85. The Circle C is 1.5 miles west of town via Highway 62, then one block north.

The in-town classic for artsy desert lovers is the 1928 **Twentynine Palms Inn** near the park visitor center at 73950 Inn Ave., 760/367-3505, fax 760/367-4425, www.29palmsinn.com, a serene 30-acre spread within the Oasis of Mara featuring both simple, flat-topped adobe cabins that once attracted Hollywood escapees—the likes of James Cagney, Bette Davis, and Jimmy Durante—and wood-frame cabins. Both now appeal to the tastefully spartan tastes of desert adventurers hot on the trail of solitude. Most cabins feature a wood-burning fireplace and a private, walled-in sun patio. And the inn's pool is the perfect antidote to a dry, wind-whipped day in Joshua Tree, not to mention the hot tub and hammocks. High-season rates for the cabins are $85–115 from mid-Sept. to mid-June, with higher rates on weekends (rates are for two, though some cabins sleep four). Summer rates are $75–100. Also available are **The Guest House** and **Irene's Historic Adobe,** the latter a landmark 1930s' adobe home. The inn also boasts a good home-style restaurant (featuring homegrown vegetables and fresh-baked breads) and poolside bar.

For something more out there, quite fascinating are the four isolated and eccentric cabins offered at **Mojave Rock Ranch** ("Established Way Back") near Joshua Tree National Park, P.O. Box 552, Joshua Tree, CA 92252, 760/366-8455, fax 760/366-1996; www.mojaverockranch.com. How many cabins, after all, are "elegantly rustic" and "cozy, funky, whimsical" at the same time? Yet hanging one's hat in the Mojave Desert does *not* mean abandoning creature comfort. All cabins at Mojave Rock Ranch feature a wood-burning stove or fireplace (firewood provided), fully equipped kitchen, private bathroom, unique decor (some combination of antique and eclectic), at least two bedrooms and two king-size beds (one also has a sleeping porch and a queen bed), and down comforters and pillows, linens, towels, and toiletries. Not to mention, for warm days, ceiling fans and evaporative coolers.

Little extras include telephones with private numbers, stereo systems and CD players, satellite TV, outdoor barbecues or fire pits, and enclosed areas for dogs. Rates are $275–325 for up to four people.

Other area stays include bed-and-breakfast inns, such as the romantic 1928 **Roughley Manor** on the onetime Campbell Ranch, 74744 Joe Davis Rd., 760/367-3238, fax 760/367-4483; www.roughleymanor.com. The main house includes two elegant suites with private baths; there are four cottage rooms, all with private baths and kitchenettes. Rates are $125–150. The seven-room **Homestead Inn Bed & Breakfast,** 74153 Two Mile Rd., 760/367-0030, fax 760/367-1108, features four B&B rooms and suites, all with private baths, and three "executive rooms" featuring TV, telephones, microwave, refrigerator, private entrance, and a private courtyard patio suitable for sunbathing. Rates: $125–150, midweek specials sometimes available. Full breakfast included.

Staying in Joshua Tree and Yucca Valley

The desert's traditional minding-your-own-business-is-good-business philosophy reigned supreme in the 1960s and '70s when *Saturday Night Live* cast and crew members, rock 'n' rollers, including the Rolling Stones and the Flying Burrito Brothers, and slumming Palm Springs celebrities used to high-tail it to Joshua Tree and their favorite desert moThough you can still stay in the room where former Byrd and Flying Burrito Brother Gram Parsons died of a drug and alcohol overdose—it's Number 8—the hacienda-style motel has been reincarnated as a relaxed but quite proper bed-and-breakfast. Rooms and suites are tastefully decorated in antiques and high-backed chairs (private bathrooms with showers). Breakfast is delectable; dinners available upon request. Rates for rooms and suites are $65–220, with private cottages and cabins also available. Pet rooms, too. For more information, contact the **Joshua Tree Inn,** 61259 Twentynine Palms Highway, P.O. Box 340, Joshua Tree, CA 92252, 760/366-1188, fax 760/366-3805; www.joshuatreeinn.com. For reservations, call toll-free 800/366-1444. While the days of rock 'n' roll are gone here, they're not necessarily forgotten. Right next door is the Hi-Desert Playhouse, 760/366-3723, where the inn cosponsored the first annual "Gramfest" on October 26, 1996—what would have been Gram Parsons's 50th birthday. That event was still going in Joshua Tree, as of 2000, though known as the annual Cosmic American Music Festival.

And if there's no room at *that* inn, try the **Oasis of Eden Inn,** 56377 Twentynine Palms Highway, 760/365-6321 or toll-free 800/606-6686, fax 760/365-9592, www.oasisofeden.com, an attractive and modern motel most notable for its special "theme rooms," decorated to help guests get in the mood for just about anything—from Greece and Tahiti to the local landscape. Basic guest facilities include swimming pool, whirlpool, cable TV, free movies. Rates are $60–200, with theme and spa rooms on the high end.

An entirely different kind of escape, popular with writers, artists, and creative types, is available just beyond Pioneertown, north of Yucca Valley—the inviting 1940s-vintage **Rimrock Ranch Cabins,** P.O. Box 313, Pioneertown, CA 92268, 760/228-1297, fax 818/956-0268, www.rimrockranchcabins.com, where the hiking and bouldering is sublime. The area's first homestead, located just at the snowline (much cooler in summer), Rimrock Ranch offers four knotty pine-paneled cabins cozied up with antiques, quilts, and "desert eclectica," each featuring a fully-equipped modern kitchen, shower bathroom, private patio, and lots of little extras. Outside are other essentials for a successful urban escape, from the rope hammock, BBQ, and picnic tables to the hot tub—filled with the ranch's own natural mineral water and a perfect setup for stargazing. Rates are $75–145 for one or two people, with higher rates on weekends. Well-socialized, neutered dogs are welcome ($10 fee plus deposit).

SIGHTS NEAR JOSHUA TREE

National park visitors inevitably make gas and supply stops in the Morongo Basin towns along Highway 62 north of Palm Springs and Desert Hot Springs—Morongo Valley, Yucca Valley, Joshua Tree, and Twentynine Palms, each tucked into its own desert valley. The military flavor of Twentynine Palms and, to a lesser extent, the town of Joshua Tree, is best explained by the proximity of the **Twentynine Palms Marine Corps Air-Ground Combat Center,** just north of Twentynine Palms. Twentynine Palms is also appreciated for its impressive gallery of outdoor murals. To get a feel for the longer reach of local history, stop by the Twentynine Palms Historical Society's **Old School House Museum** at the Oasis of Mara in Twentynine Palms and the nature-oriented **Hi Desert Museum** on the highway in Yucca Valley. Both are free, as is the **Joshua Tree and Southern Railroad Museum,** a memorabilia-rich stop in Joshua Tree featuring several restored railroad cars and a collection of steam train models.

Yucca Valley is most famous for the towering white biblical statuary of the **Desert Christ Park,** which includes a 16-ton Jesus, among other biblical characters. Old Town has its own charms, including antique and collectible shops.

North of Yucca Valley is **Pioneertown,** a residential community intended as a permanent Wild West movie set when it was built in the late 1940s. Aside from the still-surviving OK Corral featured in many Westerns and some unique street signs—including Mane Street and Roy Rogers Road—the Pioneertown dream failed to fully materialize, and by the 1960s Hollywood abandoned it to the high desert winds. These days Hollywood is interested again, but Pioneertown is ambivalent about going back to the good ol' days of being taken over by semis, floodlights, and film crews—an issue that's become less pressing since the nonprofit Wildland Conservancy purchased some 35 square miles surrounding the town as protected wildlife habitat. Highlights of Pioneertown these days include Pappy and Harriet's **Pioneertown Palace,** the "best honky-tonk west of the Colorado River," serving up wholesome home-style food and live music and dancing on the weekends.

A desert dream that almost succeeded, in nearby **Landers,** was the brainchild of George Van Tassel, a former test pilot for eccentric billionaire Howard Hughes. Following instructions Van Tassel said he received from UFO contacts—and using no nails, just wooden dowels—he took 18 years to piece together his creation, the 38-foot-tall **Integratron.** The impressive wood dome was intended as a rejuvenation machine, a cosmic fountain of youth, but Van Tassel died before completing his work. One local vision brought to successful completion is the Nature Conservancy's **Big Morongo Canyon Preserve,** a bird-watcher's paradise south of the highway in Morongo Valley.

South of Joshua Tree National Park, just off I-10 at Chiriaco Summit, is the **General Patton Memorial Museum,** which honors the desert's large-scale contributions to World War II combat training. Farther east and then northeast along Highway 177 is the **Desert Lily Preserve,** a fenced protectorate for this striking spring Colorado Desert beauty.

Desert adventurers heading all the way east to Arizona via I-10 should track down the **Giant Figures National Historic Landmark** situated on two mesas about 15 miles north of Blythe—astonishingly huge human, horse, and abstract intaglios mysteriously made by ancient artisans some 450 to 2,000 years ago and now fenced to protect them from being overrun by off-road vehicles.

Big Morongo Canyon Preserve

This 4,500-acre canyon preserve, managed cooperatively by the Nature Conservancy, San Bernardino County, and the U.S. Bureau of Land Management, once served as an ancient freeway—the most convenient migration route between low and high deserts for nomadic native peoples and one with abundant food and beverage stops. Attracted by the canyon's water, birds and other game animals thrived here. Even the stone was endlessly enduring; some of the rock formations here are the oldest in California, dated at nearly two billion years old.

Visitors can still appreciate Big Morongo's natural cornucopia, noteworthy for its fine Mojave riparian forest—cottonwoods and willows—and desert springs ecosystems. Beyond the short looping nature trails—all trails begin near the kiosk—the Canyon Trail extends the entire length of the canyon, an 11-mile round-trip. (If you plan to go the distance, beat the heat by getting an early start.) Bird-watching is the preserve's biggest attraction, particularly during spring and fall migrations. In summer the canyon's steady water supply attracts rare desert bighorn sheep

and other thirsty mammals, among them raccoons, bobcats, and California's omnipresent coyotes. Amphibians and reptiles also thrive here. Watch for rattlesnakes in warmer months; do not disturb snakes or other residents.

To get here from Twentynine Palms Highway (Hwy. 62): At the northern edge of Morongo Valley's business strip, turn east on East Drive then, after about 200 yards, left into the preserve parking lot. The preserve is open year-round, daily from 7:30 A.M. to sunset, though fall through spring are the best seasons to visit. For more information, contact: Big Morongo Canyon Preserve, P.O. Box 780, Morongo Valley, CA 92256, 760/363-7190; www.bigmorongo.org.

General Patton Memorial Museum

Just off I-10 at Chiriaco Summit, about 30 miles east of Indio, this fascinating and quirky collection of World War II–era memorabilia honors Gen. George S. Patton. Patton established the 18,000-square-mile Desert Training Center here at the former Camp Young in 1942; his objective was to get both men and machines ready for the harsh combat conditions of the North African deserts. On display outside is a crusty veteran from Patton's Sicily campaign, an M-47 tank donated by the U.S. Army. Admission is $4 adults and $3.50 seniors; children under age 12 get in free if accompanied by an adult. For more information, contact: General Patton Memorial Museum, 760/227-3483. The museum is open daily 9 A.M.–5 P.M. (closed Thanksgiving and Christmas).

Desert Lily Preserve

Among the most regal of the desert's wildflowers, this pale and fragrant desert perennial blooms profusely only in warm spring weather after abundant winter rains. Prime bloom time, which can vary from year to year, generally comes from February to April—and in a good year you'll see desert lilies throughout the sandy Colorado Desert. To get to the preserve from Joshua Tree: From the junction of Cottonwood Spring Road and I-10 head east 23 miles to Desert Center and head northeast via Highway 177. After about 8.5 miles you'll see the fenced preserve and pull-off parking to the right (east).

MOJAVE NATIONAL PRESERVE

Easily accessible from I-40 in the south and I-15 in the north, 1.4 million-acre Mojave National Preserve stretches east from Baker to Highway 95 and the Nevada border near Nipton. In deference to its freeway delimitation, this sublime slice of desert life is affectionately known as "The Lonesome Triangle," though it was lonesome out here long before there were freeways.

In a sense, the entire area is a historic thoroughfare. Petroglyphs and other signs of early human habitation in the East Mojave date from at least 11,000 years ago. In more recent times native peoples, Mojave and Paiute traders alike, trekked back and forth across the desert to participate in California's earliest coastal commerce. The most credible predecessor of present-day freeways was created from this original Native American trading route—the Mojave Road, first dubbed the Old Government Road, which ran from Prescott, Arizona, to somewhere south of Los Angeles. But first came Spanish explorers, traveling to San Francisco from Mexico in 1776, and Kit Carson, Jedediah Smith, and other early 19th-century American explorers and traders. This vast desert, more mountain than sand, also watered and sheltered stagecoaches and wagon trains and the lonely military outposts quickly built to protect them. The Mojave Road was also a freeway for camels. In one of the oddest chapters in the history of the West, from 1857 to 1860 Jefferson Davis attempted to introduce camels as desert-hardy American pack animals—a business venture that might have succeeded had it not been for impatient teamsters and the onrushing Civil War. Camels were already California history when Davis became president of the Confederacy.

Present-day signs of human habitation include shotgun shell casings, graffiti, mining mementos, rutted old roads, railroad tracks, and range cattle. Yet here the desert abides, an endless landscape of ancient mountains and youthful lava dotted with sand dunes and grasslands. As the western Mojave Desert is tamed by suburbs and military and space-age technology, the eastern Mojave is as lonely as ever—happy news for the city-weary. While it's possible to see, if not experience, most of the Mojave's main attractions in two to three days, it takes at least several days to shake off the side effects of urban worry and overscheduling—whatever it is that blinds people to the desert's graces. Stay a while.

Preserving the Status Quo

Previously managed by the U.S. Bureau of Land Management (BLM) as the multiple-use East Mojave National Scenic Area, the new Mojave National Preserve is still a political minefield. In the spirit of the Sagebrush Rebellion the region's residents—or at least many landowners, hunters, miners, ranchers, and off-road vehicle enthusiasts among them—generally take the view that this is *their* land, by virtue of tradition. They resent the fact that the federal government regulates both land use and access with an eye toward preserving the Mojave's resources. That the area was granted national preserve, rather than national park, status when the Desert Protection Act was approved by Congress in 1994 is one measure of local political heat. Unlike national park protection, preserve status allows continued cattle grazing, hunting, and mining,

Even looser levels of preservation failed to cool preserve opponents. After the Republican takeover of Congress in late 1994—just days after the Desert Protection Act was passed—and during federal budget battles of 1995 and early 1996, U.S. Representative Jerry Lewis of Redlands continued to champion the cause of unhappy desert constituents. Lewis, who owns land within the preserve, first managed to transfer preserve administrative funds from the park service to the BLM. Then he successfully inserted budget language that directed the park service to loosen commercial and recreational regulations—in effect, to return to BLM-style multiple-use management. But in the end Lewis lost his war to U.S. Senator Dianne Feinstein, final political midwife for the Desert Protection Act, and to President Clinton, who waived implementation of Lewis's maneuvers.

Despite overwhelming public support in California for the state's newest national parks, count on this war continuing—at least rhetorically. It's a touchy topic hereabouts.

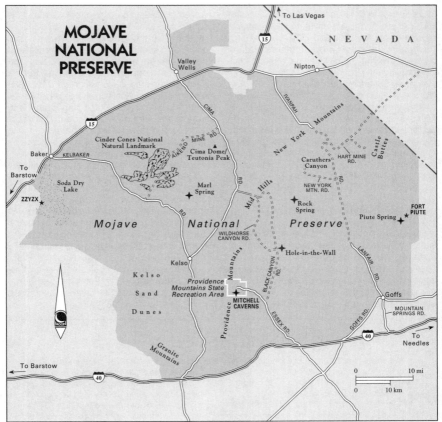

MOJAVE
NATIONAL
PRESERVE

To Las Vegas

NEVADA

Valley Wells

Nipton

CIMA

Cinder Cones National
Natural Landmark

MINE RD.

AIKENO

Cima Dome/
Teutonia Peak

IVANPAH

New York Mountains

Castle Buttes

Baker   KELBAKER

Caruthers
Canyon

HART MINE
RD.

To
Barstow

Soda Dry
Lake

Marl
Spring

NEW YORK
MTN. RD.

NEW YORK
MTN. RD.

ZZYZX

Rock
Spring

Piute Spring

FORT
PIUTE

Mojave   National   Preserve

WILDHORSE
CANYON RD.

Mid Hills

LANFAIR RD.

Kelso

Hole-in-the-Wall

Providence
Mountains State
Recreation Area

MITCHELL
CAVERNS

Providence Mountains

BLACK CANYON RD.

Goffs

MOUNTAIN
SPRINGS RD.

Kelso
Sand
Dunes

ESSEX RD.

GOFFS RD.

To
Needles

Granite
Mountains

To Barstow

0   10 mi

0   10 km

© AVALON TRAVEL PUBLISHING, INC.

Practical Mojave National Preserve

The preserve ranges in elevation from 1,000 to 8,000 feet. Summer temperatures can exceed 100°F, which is why October through May is the most popular time to come. Even in spring and fall be prepared for subfreezing temperatures and, in winter, snow. Popular activities include backpacking, hiking, camping, back-roads ambling, and stargazing. Legal game hunting is permitted, but no other gunplay (including target shooting).

Come prepared for anything, and bring everything. No services or gasoline and minimal water supplies are available within the preserve. Some

roads are unpaved, or partially paved; high-clearance vehicles are recommended. You'll be on your own in very remote country, so be sure your vehicle is in good repair.

For more information about the area's attractions, recreation, hiking, and camping, contact: **Mojave Desert Information Center,** Mojave National Preserve, 72157 Baker Blvd., P.O. Box 241, Baker, CA 92309, 760/733-4040, www.nps .gov/moja—or stop by the center, conveniently located beneath the **World's Tallest Thermometer** adjacent to the Bun Boy restaurant in Baker. (Look up. You can't miss it.) There's also the walk-in **Needles Information Center,** 707

W. Broadway in Needles (closed Mon.), 760/326-6322. Another park service information center is at Hole-in-the-Wall, 760/928-2572, open at least on weekends and at other times as staffing allows, particularly from November through April. To contact park headquarters: Mojave National Preserve, Superintendent's Office, 222 E. Main St., Ste. 202, Barstow, CA 92311, 760/255-8800.

For basic campground information, see Mid Hills, Hole-in-the-Wall, and Vicinity, below. In addition to campgrounds, "no trace" backcountry camping—at least a half-mile from a road and 1,000 feet back from any water source—is permitted throughout the preserve. For other practical information, see Baker and Vicinity, below.

ALONG KELBAKER ROAD

Kelbaker Road introduces a few of the Mojave National Preserve's natural wonders. The route starts at I-15 near Baker and then meanders east and south for some 50 miles, eventually intersecting I-40, the preserve's southern boundary. Some sections of Kelbaker Road are unpaved to allow bighorn sheep to cross the road—they disdain pavement—but the route is typically passable even for passenger cars.

Kelbaker's first major sight: the Mojave Cinder Cones, also known as **Cinder Cones Natural National Landmark,** a very young volcanic formation atop older lava flows. (A side trip via Aiken's Mine Road takes you there.) About 35 miles from Baker is **Kelso,** where cottonwoods, palms, and the graceful **Kelso Depot** have long been the main attractions. Though the depot was still delapidated, at last report, and funding seemed somewhat dubious, plans to restore it as a visitor center were in the works.

Even before reaching Kelso, to the southwest you'll see the **Kelso Dunes,** wonderful for dune walks. To the southeast are the Providence Mountains, where the focal point of the **Providence Mountain State Recreation Area** is **Mitchell Caverns State Reserve.** Last stop before I-40: the stunning stone sculpture of the **Granite Mountains,** a desert research area reminiscent of Joshua Tree National Park. Among the protected species here is a cave-dwelling Venus hair fern—typically at home above 7,000 feet in the Sierra Nevada—trapped here since the end of the Ice Age.

WITHER THE DESERT?

A quiet drama surrounding a radical new proposal to supply water to Southern California's ever-thirsty Metropolitan Water District (MWD) is playing out near the Mojave National Preserve.

In a proposed $1 billion deal with the MWD, Cadiz, Inc., a publicly traded agriculture and water firm, proposes to tap the aquifers of the Mojave Desert and to store water for MWD agencies for use in years of lower water availability from the Colorado River—a prospect it says will cause no ecological problems, given what it says will be adequate aquifer recharge rates. Environmentalists disagree mightily, arguing that the MWD would be launching an ecological disaster on the scale of the historic Owens Valley water grab on the eastern slopes of the Sierra Nevada—here as there, essentially killing off the underground rivers that support all life.

The MWD's main scientific experts—the same consulting firm working for Cadiz, Inc.—contend that the desert's water recharge rate will approach 50,000 acre-feet, while it proposes to pump some 60,000 acre-feet. Other scientists say the reality is even more unbalanced, suggesting that the MWD would be pumping water out at a rate 15 to 30 times greater than the land's ability to replenish itself; the U.S. Geological Survey suggests the extraction rate is 6 to 35 times greater than recharge. And some scientists question the practical application of desert water replenishment entirely, pointing out that natural water recharge has not occurred in some desert basins for thousands of years.

In January 2001, member agencies of the MWD postponed a vote on the project, pending further review of the Cadiz, Inc. proposal.

Should the MWD ultimately approve the project, there will surely be a lawsuit—one in which the environmental and scientific precepts underlying the desert water pumping proposal will go on trial.

Stay tuned.

Cinder Cones Natural National Landmark

Southeast from Baker and visible from the interstate, the Mojave Cinder Cones consist of more than 30 colorful cinder cones "clustered" within a 25,000-acre area. The age range of these cones is dramatic, geologically speaking, with some formations created in the very recent volcanic past. The slightly smaller cones—reachable by car from Kelbaker Road and then Aiken's Mine Road—are a mere 800 to 1,000 years old, while the old-timers close to the freeway near Halloran Summit are approximately 10 million years old.

Kelso Dunes

Second tallest dune system in the California desert, rising some 600 feet to 700 feet above the desert floor and fanning out over 45 square miles, the isolated Kelso Dunes were created from fine wind-driven sand—golden rose quartz—blown down from the Mojave Sink in the northwest. Winds come from all directions, though, which accounts for the massive sand accumulation and for the circular patterns "drawn" in it by tall grasses. The hike up and back takes about two hours, not counting time spent making the dunes "sing." When sand slides down from the steep slopes at a dune's peak the entire dune vibrates and then sounds off—a reverberation something like that of a Tibetan gong, not typical of all sand dunes.

To get here: About seven miles south of Kelso turn west (signed road) and continue three miles to the parking pullout. After more than a mile of struggling through the sand, ascend the tallest dunes indirectly, via a lower saddle, then hike up along the crest. The most effective way to walk in deep sand is flat-footed (don't dig in) and fast, without breaking the sand's crust. To fully appreciate shapes and shadows, do the dunes in the indirect light of early morning or late afternoon. Sunrise or sunset is best.

MID HILLS, HOLE-IN-THE-WALL, AND VICINITY

Cima Dome, the first thing visitors notice when approaching the preserve's central stone fortresses of Mid Hills and Hole-in-the-Wall, is actually much easier to see from a distance. Because of its perfect and gradual slope, under foot it's all but invisible. Despite its proximity to the Mojave Cinder Cones, Cima does not share their volcanic history. This nearly symmetrical, 1,500-foot-tall mound of granitelike quartz monzonite, once a mass of molten rock, is a batholith 75 square miles in size (10 miles in diameter). Outcroppings of the original bedrock include **Teutonia Peak,** 5,755 feet tall; for up-close appreciation, scramble up the two-mile trail (marked) that starts just north of Sunrise Rock. Cima Dome also features one of the world's finest—and largest—forests of Joshua trees, a species distinct from those in Joshua Tree National Park.

To get here: From I-15, exit south at Cima road in Valley Wells and continue heading southeast about seven miles; follow the signed turnoffs.

Mid Hills and Hole-in-the-Wall

Named rather unimaginatively for their location midway between the New York and Providence Mountains, the mile-high Mid Hills serve cool, pine-scented mountain air with some grand desert views—the shimmering Kelso Dunes to the west, Cima Dome and the Pinto Mountains to the north. According to local lore, the rock outpost to the south known as Hole-in-the-Wall was named by a member of Butch Cassidy's outlaw gang, since it resembled his favorite Wyoming hideout. Another Hole-in-the-Wall attraction is the iron-ring-in-the-wall handholds for the short, steep trail into odd **Banshee Canyon,** a natural amphitheater.

For one of the best hikes around, take the eight-mile (one way) **Mid Hills to Hole-in-the-Wall Trail,** which you can shorten to a three-mile loop at the cutoff (marked) and which is also convenient for car shuttles. Along the fairly rugged route: petroglyphs and a ceremonial Native American "birthing hole" (for spiritual, not actual, births). If you'd rather drive the distance, horseshoe-shaped **Wild Horse Canyon Road** meanders for 11 miles through the volcanic mesas and low-desert cactus land connecting Hole-in-the-Wall and Mid Hills—the nation's first official Back Country Byway, most scenic during spring wildflower season.

Marvelous **Mid Hills Campground,** tucked into the juniper and piñon pine at an elevation of 5,600 feet, can be downright cold—if not buried in sudden snow—during winter, sometimes also during the peak spring and fall camping season. Be prepared. The 26 campsites feature tables, fire rings, and pit toilets; as the road is a bit treacherous, RVs are not recommended. **Hole-in-the-Wall Campground,** with 37 campsites at 4,200 feet, is more RV friendly, with some pull-through campsites as well as dump station. Both campgrounds are $12 per night, first-come, first-camped, with a 14-day limit; both now feature potable water. But bring extra water if you can (supplies are limited) along with firewood, and anything else you think you'll need in the middle of nowhere. If preserve campgrounds are full, head for the BLM's **Afton Canyon Campground** west of Baker (see Near the Preserve, below.) By reservation only, group camping is available within the preserve at **Black Rock Canyon Group Campground,** $25 per night.

Mitchell Caverns State Reserve

Eons of calcium carbonate deposits created the graceful stone curtains, stalactites, and stalagmites at El Pakiva and Tecopa caves; these days, stairs and railings offer easy access. The limestone caves at Mitchell Caverns State Reserve, high on the craggy slopes of the Providence Mountains about 16 miles north of I-40 via Essex Road, are the only Southern California caves developed for visitors. That fact makes them attractive to the occasional film crew. In 1990, for example, Oliver Stone filmed part of the Jim Morrison art-rock bio *The Doors* here.

Either before or after the guided tour, walk the short **Mary Beal Nature Trail** and—for the views—the more challenging **Crystal Spring Trail** up the canyon. Rock-climbing is also popular year-round. The park day-use fee is $2 per vehicle. Access to the caves is possible only on guided tours, which are offered from mid-September through mid-June at 1:30 P.M. on weekdays, and at 10 A.M., 1:30 P.M., and 3 P.M. on weekends and state holidays. Tours are $3 adults, $1 children ages 6 to 17 (under 6 free). And no matter what the temperature may be outside, always bring a sweater or light jacket on cave tours; the temperature is a constant and cool 65°F.

The on-site visitor center here is staffed only part-time. So for more information and to arrange group tours, contact: **California Department of Parks and Recreation,** Mojave Desert Sector, 1051 W. Ave. M, Ste. 201, Lancaster, CA 93535, 805/942-0662; www.calparksmojave.com.

THE MOJAVE ROAD AND OTHER HIGHLIGHTS

The Mojave Road

The Mojave and Paiute people originally blazed this trail from the Colorado River to near what is now Los Angeles—the most logical business route from desert to ocean, weaving together watering holes and shelter from sun and storms. Then came Francisco Garces, a Spanish missionary, and Kit Carson and Jedediah Smith—and the U.S. military, which carved out the east-west Old Government Road that survives today as rugged Mojave Road. Since the route is quite challenging (almost nonexistent) in places, four-wheel-drive travel is recommended—and that only after checking with rangers for current road and weather conditions. (Sudden flash floods or mountain snowstorms can be as life-threatening as too much sun and too little water.) If you're serious about making this trip, try to get a copy of Dennis Casebier's *Mojave Road Guide* (Tales of the Mojave Road Publishing Company). Thanks to Friends of the Mojave Road, the route has been marked with cairns at all key points.

The route through the Mojave National Preserve officially begins in Arizona, on the west bank of the Colorado River directly across from **Fort Mojave.** The route bisects the preserve as it winds west via natural springs—Piute Spring, Rock Spring, Marl Spring—past Mid Hills, south of the Mojave Cinder Cones and Soda Lake, then on toward the Barstow area. Notable within the preserve: **Fort Piute,** a Mojave Road outpost staffed by the U.S. Army in 1866 and 1867. Near ancient petroglyphs and ruins of the stone fort is **Piute Creek,** a half-mile-long ribbon of water with willows and cottonwoods—the Mojave Desert's largest perennial riparian habitat, a natural haven for birds and wildlife. A most memorable hike—and almost unimaginable as a wagon route, despite the wagon-wheel grooves worn into the stone—is the hellish scramble over the Piute Range and down Piute Hill into **Piute Gorge.**

New York Mountains
With their own gold-mining history and, at higher elevations, an isolated white fir population, the New York Mountains are most famous as a sure bet to beat the heat in summer. If you get this far, don't miss the red volcanic **Castle Buttes**—one of the most remote areas remaining in this most remote reach of desert. "Residents" here include some of California's most beleaguered natives—desert tortoise, bighorn sheep, the golden eagle, and prairie falcon. Mojave Indian creation stories center on the buttes and the surrounding New York Mountains; parts of the region still serve as traditional hunting grounds. Ancient cultural remnants include well-trodden trails, rock art, rock shelters, and a village site. Another popular destination is **Caruthers Canyon** near the base of New York Mountain, popular for camping, easy hikes, and bouldering.

To get to Castle Buttes: Exit I-15 at Nipton Road and continue 3.5 miles to Ivanpah Road; head south on Ivanpah for about 17 miles, then turn east onto Hart Mine Road. To get to Caruthers Canyon: From Goffs or I-40, head north via Lanfair Road, which becomes Ivanpah; at the historic Ox Ranch (private) turn left onto rough New York Mountain Road. The road ambles through Joshua trees for just over five miles before angling north; keeping to the right, look for parking turnouts in another two miles. Follow the road on foot for a hike into the canyon.

Near the Preserve
Grand **Afton Canyon** just off I-15 33 miles northeast of Barstow (southwest of Baker) is one of very few places the shy Mojave River flows—above ground, any way. If it's not a hectic weekend full of off-roaders gathered for a desert assault, nice for an overnight is the BLM's **Afton Canyon Campground**, $6 per night (no reservations). To get here: Take the Afton exit from I-15 and continue south three miles (dirt road). Equestrian trails too.

On the south side of the Mojave National Preserve, easily reached from I-40 east of Barstow, are various attractions accessible from old **Route 66** (now known as the National Trails Highway. Notable among them: black **Amboy Crater,** a very young volcano, and the nearby **Cadiz Valley Dunes.**

BAKER AND VICINITY

Baker is primarily a gas and supply stop for I-15 travelers, certainly the last chance for fast food or lottery tickets before heading north into Death Valley via Highway 127. Baker is also the proud hometown of the **World's Tallest Thermometer,** which cost $750,000 to construct and which looms 134 feet above the adjacent Bun Boy restaurant parking lot. The thermometer's height honors the highest temperature ever recorded in the United States—134°F, at Death Valley in 1913. (To "talk" to the thermometer, call 800-204-TEMP.) At the thermometer's base is the visitor information center for the **Mojave National Preserve,** open daily, 760/733-4040.

Aside from the spectacular desert scenery in nearby Death Valley National Park, attractions near Baker include the vast Mojave National Preserve; the remains of **Zzyzx,** an infamous onetime hot springs health resort now home to the Desert Studies Center; and **Tecopa Hot Springs,** an odd enclave of desert "Snow Bird" culture on the way to Death Valley.

Weekend traffic note: As Angelenos head home from Las Vegas on Sunday afternoons and evenings, westbound traffic on I-15 is often bumper-to-bumper, like one endless parking lot. Ditto, some Fridays and on holiday weekends, for the eastbound flow. At such times Baker can resemble a three-ring consumer circus; to avoid it, get gas and snacks elsewhere en route. But if you're feeling lucky—or unlucky, should Las Vegas refuse to share the wealth—stop at Baker's **Will's Fargo Country Store** for a lottery ticket. Will's Fargo is the state's busiest Lotto outlet and, at least in some years, proportionately the luckiest.

For more information about the community and available services, contact: **Baker Chamber of Commerce,** P.O. Box 131, Baker, CA 92309, 760/733-4469.

Baker Eats, Baker Stays
The **Bun Boy** on Baker Blvd., 760/733-4660, is the burg's most familiar feature, a 24-hour burger and basic eats family-style restaurant that also serves as social center for this vast section of desert. Next to the World's Tallest Thermometer and the Mojave National Preserve's visitor infor-

mation center, this is the place to find out what's going on. For a refreshing change, try the **Mad Greek,** 760/733-4354.

For an overnight, of course there's the **Bun Boy Motel** on Baker Boulevard (more or less marking the intersection of I-15 and Hwy. 127), 760/733-4363, fax 760/733-4595—just the basics, but clean and air-conditioned with color TV and free movies. Rates are $55–65 (plus tax), with the higher rates on weekends.

Something different, farther out there in the desert, is the Southwestern-style **Hotel Nipton Bed and Breakfast Inn,** 72 Nipton Rd., Nipton, CA 92364, 760/856-2335; www.nipton.com/hotel .html.The 1904 Hotel Nipton is the most civilized sight for miles around, a modest rectangle with foot-thick Spanish Territorial-style adobe walls to keep the desert heat and winds at bay. Four guest rooms share two baths down the hall. Each room is named for a local celebrity—

including silent film star Clara Bow, the "It Girl," who once owned a nearby ranch. Rates: $55. For reservations, call between 8 A.M. and 6 P.M., or email the hotel at hotel@nipton.com. To get here: exit I-5 at Wheaton Springs and head toward Nevada; it's about 10 miles to Nipton. The Hotel Nipton also offers campsites with picnic and BBQ area, hot showers, flush toilets, laundromat, even a hot tub, for $15 per night for one or two people. Platform tent cabins and a few RV hookups are also available.

Otherwise, public camping is the best local choice—in the **Mojave Desert Preserve** (see Mid Hills, Hole-in-the-Wall, and Vicinity, above) or at any number of BLM desert sites, including **Afton Canyon** just 33 miles east of Barstow. Or continue to **Death Valley National Park,** which offers luxury hotel, standard motel, and camping options.

THE ROAD TO ZZYZX

In 1944 Curtis Howe Springer, a colorful character in Mojave Desert history and the self-described "last of the old-time medicine men," established Zzyzx Mineral Springs. Here, 11 miles south of Baker at the end of 4.5-mile Zzyzx Road, on 12,000 acres of land that belonged to the U.S. government, Springer built his 60-room hotel, health spa, church, castle, and radio station. Ever the promoter, he chose the name "Zzyzx"—pronounced ZYE-Zix, to rhyme with "size six"—because he wanted his resort to be the last listing in the telephone book.

Neither a doctor nor Methodist minister, Springer claimed to be both. He solicited cash donations, over the radio, to cure ailments. And he sold his elixirs and potions internationally—until 1974, when he was arrested for unauthorized use of federal land and various violations of food and drug laws.

Since 1976, Zzyzx has served as the Desert Studies Center of the California State University system. Stop by the visitor center (unstaffed), and then wander the grounds and study exhibits to learn about the endangered Mojave chub (a fish) and other aspects of area natural history. For a picturesque view of dry Soda Lake and the mountains beyond, look east through the old bathhouse windows.

At Zzyzx Mineral Springs you can dip into the past of an old charlatan's desert resort, now part of the California State University system.

DEATH VALLEY NATIONAL PARK

To stargazers, Death Valley is the closest thing to heaven in light-blinded Southern California. To rockhounds, it's a timeless monument to very grounded geologic grandeur. To botanists and bird-watchers, it's a study in successful adaptation. Its vast spaces sprinkled with petroglyphs, ghost towns, mine ruins, and other enduring marks of human aspiration, to hikers and history buffs it's one endless discovery trail.

The essence of Death Valley, however, is its remoteness—and its aloof indifference to all things civilized.

Though this otherworldly landscape has been protected as a national monument since 1933, after decades of political wrangling California's astonishing Death Valley was re-created, as a national park, in 1994. With national park status came a near-doubling in size—that much more room to roam.

THE LAY OF THE LAND

Squeezed on all sides by bold, bare mountains, as the crow flies Death Valley extends about 90 miles from north to south; by road, following the valley's curves and canyons, the distance is 130 miles or more. Though the park boundaries are far more expansive, the valley itself measures less than a mile across at its narrowest point, about 10 miles at its widest. The nation's hottest, driest, and most dramatically desolate summer landscape, about 500 square miles of the valley floor lie below sea level. Not surprisingly, the lowest elevations in the United States are in Death Valley. Until the 1950s, Badwater was considered the lowest point in the United States, measured at 279 feet below sea level. More careful measurement revealed two lower spots in the park—one west-northwest of Badwater and the other north-northwest of Badwater, both

> *please refer to the Death Valley National Park map on page vii*

measured at 282 feet below sea level. Death Valley's depths are all the more impressive when one considers that the highest point in the continental United States, Mount Whitney, is about 100 miles away, in the southern Sierra Nevada near Lone Pine.

In the south, Death Valley's floor is one vast and sandy salt flat, whitewashed over the eons by mineral deposits. This inhospitable landscape, this naturally toxic environment, is home to an astonishing array of alkali-adapted plants and animals. The Amargosa River (bitter one in Spanish) is the valley's one and only, an alkaline stream that flows south from Nevada, winds around the Black Mountains, and then heads north to percolate into oblivion. In the north, salt flats give way to sand dunes, white clay, and ghostly flatlands.

Surrounding the valley are more than 100 steep and narrow canyons, gorges, gulches, and washes leading up into colorful, craggy landscapes. At the mouths of many canyons are vast and sometimes stunning alluvial fans. Water-borne boulders blend with sand and gravel sediments—testimony to the power of water crashing down from the mountains.

The Panamint Range, from 6,000 to more than 11,000 feet in elevation, borders Death Valley on the west; the range's northern section is also known as the Cottonwood Mountains. On the east is the Amargosa Range, a stone-faced dirge composed of the Grapevine, Funeral, and Black Mountains. The equally optimistic Last Change Range closes in on the valley from the northwest, the Owlshead Mountains from the southwest.

With the area's low rainfall—and keeping in mind that the potential evaporation rate here is about 150 inches per year—there's a surprising amount of water in Death Valley, provided by surrounding mountain springs. Furnace Creek visitor facilities sit astride a generous and historic freshwater spring, as does Scotty's Castle, though most of the valley's water is "bad" (as in "Badwater"), tainted by toxic concentrations of mineral salts.

Death Valley's Story: The Landscape

In many ways a Death Valley visit is also a trip through time, an exploration of an impressive open-air natural history museum narrated by the land itself. The landscape in Death Valley tells the story of the slow but dramatic passage of geologic time—a tale writ large here and flamboyantly illustrated by startling shapes and odd angles, everything brushed with vivid color and then etched by water and wind.

Death Valley's landscape began to emerge some 60 million years ago. Angry earthquakes re-created the Sierra Nevada—forcing the new granite blocks of that range up through the earth's crust where wild magma flows cemented them into place. This creative violence blew south too; tiny fissures spread throughout the earth like the spindly threads of a spider's web. Rocked and rolled by the Sierra Nevada commotion, the molten rock of the inner earth broke through the earthquake faults here, too, rising and falling and tilting and twisting until the underground firestorm finally died out.

The stone-faced new landscape, later named the Mojave Block, covered 15,000 square miles. Time chipped away at it for the next 25 million years, eroding strong features into near oblivion and then feverishly creating them anew. During the next two million years, with the arrival of the Ice Age and the Pleistocene epoch, Death Valley and the rest of the region rested.

As the ice receded, the land awakened. Rivers of ice-melt sliced through the stony landscape before racing to the sea or pooling into vast inland lakes. In a small corner of the Mojave Block, unrelenting erosion scoured out a deep but narrow trough almost 100 miles long from north to south, its low profile dramatized by resurging rocky ranges on both the east and west—the terrain we know today as Death Valley.

But Death Valley wasn't always dry, wasn't always a valley. Some 10,000 years ago it was a lake—actually, a series of lakes, separated by giant steps in time. (In recent history, the large northern lake was posthumously named Lake Rogers, its large southern cousin, Lake Manly—after two heroes in early Death Valley settlement.) By 6,000 years ago the region's great lakes, including Death Valley's, had become mere puddles, the landscape watered only by streams and sweetwater springs. About 3,000

WILDFLOWERS: THE MOST EPHEMERAL DESERT BEAUTY

When first introduced to the California desert, neophytes typically see only sand, scrub brush, and an otherwise empty horizon of desolate mountain ranges. Yet California's Mojave and Colorado Deserts both boast an abundance of drought-adapted plant and animal life.

Most accessible for a natural history introduction is California's desert flora—more than 2,000 native species, including grasses, annuals, perennial herbs, shrubs, and trees. To appreciate desert plant life at its most dazzling, visit during spring's ephemeral wildflower season. Dramatic desertwide displays require early and fairly constant rain, through March—a rare phenomenon occurring only about once per decade. Because of local microclimates, some areas may put on a snazzy show in other years, however.

Popular areas to observe the desert flower frenzy—largely, but not exclusively, a Mojave Desert phenomenon—include the **Antelope Valley California Poppy Reserve** west of Lancaster; **Anza-Borrego Desert State Park** east of San Diego; **Death Valley National Park** southeast of the Sierra Nevada; the **Mojave National Preserve** in the high desert; and **Joshua Tree National Park** and other natural areas near **Palm Springs.** Call local parks for more information, including peak-bloom projections for a particular year. To avoid the wildflower-crazed crowds, arrive on a weekday.

---

years ago the lakes, streams, and springs had all disappeared, the scenery taking on its contemporary salt-crusted characteristics. Then it rained again, the new deluge creating a 30-foot-deep lake. But by 2,000 years ago Death Valley's vast interior was once again bone-dry. Done with molten fire and water, for its further work time experimented with wind and intense dry heat.

The Land as Interpreter

Though the language of time is challenging to master, at Death Valley the land itself is a useful interpreter. The ancient lake shoreline is marked by terraces along the valley's walls, for example, and the work of big and boisterous rivers memorialized by monstrous alluvial fans. The vast salty bottomlands represent eons' worth of minerals washed down into the ancient lake from the mountains and then concentrated in one place, through evaporation. And the endlessly creative work of erosion and the adaptive evolution of plants and animals appears everywhere—on every mountain, in every canyon, atop every sand dune, even in streams flowing with toxic levels of minerals.

Death Valley Climate: Warm, Hot, and Hotter

One glance at the desolate terrain convinces most people that Death Valley is a desert. Scientifically speaking, such classifications can be complicated, since "desert" does not apply to all hot, bleak landscapes nor to all areas of low precipitation. Death Valley is indeed a desert, however, for several official reasons. Its distance from the moderating effects of the California current virtually guarantees that cool Pacific Ocean air is well heated by the time it reaches the valley. Death Valley is also tucked away behind multiple rain shadows. Storms blowing in off the ocean must get up and over several major mountain ranges to reach the valley; few have any moisture left if and when they do arrive. Death Valley is also defined by stable subtropical high pressure, with the air descending and warming.

"Warming" is a euphemism. Winter is the traditional travel season here for good reason—extremely inhospitable summer temperatures. Though winter is the "rainy season," not much rain falls; Death Valley's average annual rainfall is just 1.84 inches. What moisture does arrive often comes all at once. (Watch for flash flooding at all times after desert rainstorms.) In January of 1995, 2.59 inches of rain fell—the wettest month ever recorded in Death Valley—though record high rainfall came in 1913 and again in 1983, with annual totals of 4.54 inches.

The year 1913 was a record-breaker in terms of temperature, too, graced both with Death Valley's lowest recorded temperature—15°F, recorded in January—and highest temperature—134°F, recorded on July 10, a temperature extreme expected only once every 650 years, according to weather experts. Average daytime winter temperatures are 60–70°F, summer temperatures 90–100°F. But white-hot misery is

common enough in summer. In 1974 the park recorded 134 days when temperatures exceeded 100°F, and in 1994, 31 days over 120°F and 97 days over 110°F.

After scaring visitors silly with such statistics, people here typically soften the blow by saying: "But at least it's *dry* heat," meaning that the heat-related discomfort is much less severe than it would be in more humid climates. True enough, though summer perspiration rates can be astounding. (Drink water, drink water, drink water.) Dry heat or no, don't walk barefoot in and around Death Valley, particularly in summer. Ground temperatures generally exceed the ambient air temperature by about 40 percent; the highest ground temperature ever recorded here was 201°F, at Furnace Creek on July 15, 1972, on a day when the overall temperature was 128°F.

But Death Valley's extremist temperament shows in the winter, too. Though it rarely freezes here, it can get quite chilly during the November-to-March peak travel season; if you'll be camping out, come prepared for nighttime temperatures dipping into the 30s—not counting wind chill, which can make it feel much colder.

LIFE IN DEATH VALLEY: FLORA AND FAUNA

"Death Valley" might seem apt to describe the natural neighborhood. Yet "Life Valley" is more like it. The variety of plants and animals in Death Valley is astonishing. A total of 900 plant species, many quite ephemeral, have been recorded here, and the most recent count of endemic plants was 15. (The number of endemic species—those which occur nowhere else on earth—may increase with national park status, which brings with it much new territory and new levels of national and international research interest.) The impressive number of unique plant species may seem peculiar in a place so often perceived as barren, but, botanically speaking, isn't at all odd. These plants—the successful ones, the survivors—have adapted to the extremes of a unique and isolated environment.

Animal life, too, is fairly specialized—and amazingly abundant. Hundreds of animal species, including 300 different birds, have adjusted to life in this land. Many are found only here, including several species of tiny, very aggressive fish known as "pupfish."

For more detailed study of Death Valley plant and animal life, sign on for ranger-guided hikes and/or attend campfire programs—and stop by the park visitor center at Furnace Creek for additional information, field guides, and other good books.

Death Valley Plant Communities

Death Valley's plants congregate in distinct communities, each of these with characteristic features. Below sea level, Death Valley's salt flats prove toxic to most plant species; there is no community here per se, unless one prefers fantastic possibilities—always popular in California—such as extraterrestrial salt-spire colonization. Nonetheless, even at notoriously inhospitable spots such as Badwater and Salt Creek you'll find salt-adapted algae, ditch grass (salt grass) in the water, and pickleweed at water's edge.

The valley's lower elevations are otherwise included within either the desert dry wash woodland or the creosote bush scrub communities.

Predominant plant species in and around the valley's dry washes include the omnipresent creosote bush, desert holly, turtleback, and the historically noteworthy mesquite. Though they also grow in canyonlands and at higher elevations, deep-rooted mesquite groves crop up on alluvial fans, in canyon washes, and other valley areas in the path of at least occasional water. Stoic and scraggly mesquite trees, a source of firewood, building materials, and beans for native peoples and of shade and shelter for valley wildlife, made their mark on modern history by fueling the fires of valley borax works. But here and elsewhere, the dominant lower-elevation plants in Death Valley are the ephemeral spring wildflowers that germinate, grow, and then burst into glorious bloom in years of relatively heavy, well-spaced winter rain. Dramatic in a good wildflower year are the huge desert sunflowers known as "desert gold," typically found atop alluvial fans. More subtle but also easy to spot: the prostrate, purple-flowering sand verbena and the equally colorful, upright phacelia. A wide variety of rusty-colored *Eriogonum* species grow along washes and in canyonlands, the most striking being the canopied Rixford.

The creosote bush scrub community stars the humble creosote bush, whose ranks include some of the earth's oldest living individual plants. This low-desert survivor is found everywhere below 2000 feet except on salt flats and sulphur-poisoned soils. Rounded in form and regularly spaced to take fair advantage of limited water, the creosote bush often sports small, leafy, walnut-sized galls, protected larval home of the creosote gall midge. Growing in close association is burroweed (white bursage) and a variety of sages. Succulents show up in less arid areas. The most common in Death Valley are beavertail and cholla cacti, succulents that store water in viscous stem tissue and typically found above 1,000 feet. Gourd lovers will appreciate the desert's coyote melons; when the fruit sets, these prostrate vines and tiny melons could easily pass for miniature watermelon patches.

the towering stalk of a century plant

KIM WEIR

This plant is radically deviant, however; unlike the domesticated melons and gourds it resembles, the coyote melon is considered a "root succulent," since it stores its annual supply of water underground within a huge turniplike root.

At higher elevations creosote bush scrub can segue into shadescale scrub and sagebrush scrub. A notable member of the latter community, typically found on alluvial fans, is the long-jointed, seemingly leafless *Ephedra,* also known as Mormon tea, Mexican tea, and desert tea; *Ephedra* leaves are tiny "scales" growing at the stem nodes.

At still higher elevations, particularly in the hills of the Panamint Valley, is Joshua tree woodland—featuring the Mojave Desert's most striking indicator plant. Found in areas with reasonably good drainage at elevations of 2500 to 4000 feet, in community with cactus, creosote bush, and sage, the dramatic and strangely evocative Joshua tree is actually an agave. Joshuas are named after the biblical Joshua for their characteristic near-human pose, "limbs" raised skyward as if beseeching God.

A less obvious trait of the Joshua tree is its intriguing symbiotic relationship with the female yucca moth; the two depend upon each other for reproductive success. When the Joshua tree is in bloom, the small white moth—disinterested in all other plant species—sets out at dusk to collect Joshua tree pollen from at least several agaves. She selects one plant for her own purposes; laying her eggs inside a flower's ovary, the moth then deposits enough collected pollen to both cross-pollinate the plant (ensuring seed production) and feed her own young (upon hatching, the moth larvae eat some of the seeds). Though established Joshua trees can resprout from their roots, they can reproduce—produce seeds for dispersal—only in this way.

Not technically a desert plant community, piñon-juniper woodland is nonetheless fairly common at higher elevations—above 6000 feet—throughout the California desert region. Typical plants include the single-needle piñon (or pinyon) pine, scrub oaks, and junipers. Rare bristlecone pines also grow at high elevations.

Low-elevation desert oases with impressive stands of native California fan palms and other lush water-loving vegetation are fairly common in and around Palm Springs and Joshua Tree National Park—but not in Death Valley or most parts of the Mojave Desert. "Oases" here are man-made, for the most part, such as Furnace Creek, with its dramatic date palms and tamarisk groves (both introduced species). Natural springs, waterfalls, and spring-fed pools are surprisingly abundant, however, typically tucked away in protected canyons. One notable example is Darwin Falls on the eastern edge of the Panamint Valley, a refreshing riparian oasis of cottonwoods, willows, and waterfalls.

Death Valley Animals

Insects are the predominant animal presence in Death Valley—which is not to suggest that you'll see many, busy as they are with the serious business of survival. A notable exception is the black *Eleodes* beetle, sometimes known as the "circus bug" because of its tendency to stand on its head and otherwise clown around during its very active daylight hours. Also not always seen are Death Valley's successful armies of harvester ants, though their colonies are easy to spot; look for piles of seed husks and hulls that circle their nests. Unfortunately for wildlife and human visitors alike, one of the valley's nastiest insects is a biting black fly found wherever there is surface water—creeks, natural springs, some mesquite groves—during warm weather.

Among the invertebrates most perturbing to human beings is the hairy, scary-looking tarantula—here, a perfectly harmless member of the arachnid or spider clan—and the less friendly scorpion, whose sting is not poisonous but nonetheless painful. Reptiles here include the chuckwalla lizard, a traditional delicacy for the Shoshone. Capturing one is some challenge, however, because of the chuckwalla's clever strategy for foiling predators: crawling into tight crevices and then inflating itself to substantial size. (Don't try to catch one. No collecting is permitted in the park; even the attempt is not allowed.) Other unusual reptiles spotted here include the harmless desert iguana—which bears an uncanny resemblance to its poisonous cousin from Panama—the hard-to-find gecko, and the "horned toad," actually the desert horned lizard, one among many other lizard species.

Snakes snack on lizards, mice, rats, and other small mammals, so it's no surprise that Death Valley has its fair share of slitherers. Since desert snakes are typically nocturnal, humans usually must make an effort to encounter any. To avoid an unfortunate confrontation with Death Valley's two troublesome, toxic snakes—the Panamint rattlesnake, usually found at higher elevations in the Panamint Range, and the fascinating yet smaller "sidewinder" of American cowboy mythology—don't wander at night without benefit of shoes and a good flashlight, and be cautious during early-morning or evening hikes during cooler months. The sidewinder is named for its undulating sideward motion—an advantage for quick traction across unsteady sand and stone, moves made possible by unique segmented muscles—and its distinctive S-shaped track, easily recognizable. Like all reptiles, both rattlesnake species are cold-blooded. To cool off during the heat of day rattlers retreat into deep shade and rocky crevices; to warm themselves at night or on cool mornings and evenings, they curl up on exposed rocks to absorb radiant heat. In canyons and mountain country, they tend to coil up on similarly colored gravel or stone—right out in the open, perfectly camouflaged. In sandy areas they bury themselves under the sand, only their eyes and a part of their heads visible. Rattlers avoid human contact when possible, so the best way to avoid a confrontation is to avoid them. The watchwords of rattlesnake safety: heads up, eyes open, watch for snake tracks, and be careful where you put your feet and hands.

Among mammals, the smaller species predominate—rodents, primarily. Because of its collecting habits, among the most entertaining is the pack rat, usually found by finding its home: in the mountains, a rocky crevice stuffed with sticks and perhaps protected by cactus spines; on alluvial plains, an entire mound of cholla cactus parts piled high against other cacti or shrubs.

Larger wild things include the never-popular spotted skunk, the kit fox, and the coyote. Should you spot a foxlike apparition in the night, keep in mind that the adaptable and wily coyote—essentially a wild dog, a survivor equally at home in the suburbs of Los Angeles—typically tucks its tail between its hind legs when on the run. The now-

rare kit fox, almost trapped into oblivion because of its beautiful fur, can sometimes be spotted in the valley and near sand dunes; kangaroo rats are a favorite meal.

Among the most ruggedly dramatic of Death Valley mammals is the desert bighorn sheep, rarely seen by the casual sight-seer. Most of the northern Mojave Desert's sheep are protected here, where mountain ranges create the craggy corridors necessary for migratory herd movement. Burros, beasts of burden long freed from their tasks as mining assistants, successfully competed with native sheep for scarce water and food—a competition that further threatened the already diminished herds. In recent decades feral burros have been herded up and "adopted out," with only the wiliest of the wily remaining in the remote backcountry here and elsewhere throughout the desert.

In general, the most observable animals in Death Valley are the birds, from hawks and owls to hummingbirds. Some species are migratory, some are seasonal visitors, but many are year-round residents. Unlike other categories of desert wildlife, most birds are most visible during the day. Early morning and late afternoon are usually best for bird-watching; let your field guide be your guide.

DEATH VALLEY HISTORY: BADLANDS, BAD WATER, AND BORAX

Prehistoric Human Presence

The dazed and disoriented settlers who first descended into this bone-dry desert found the land in the mid-19th century much less hospitable than did the people living here during previous eons. Anthropologists are still unsure when and how the first people arrived in the region; early archaeological evidence unearthed throughout the desert—pottery shards, fragments of bone, stone tools—suggested widespread human habitation, near ancient streams and lakes, 9,000 to 10,000 years ago. But Dr. Louis S. B. Leakey's excavations at the Calico "early man" site near Barstow, an ongoing dig begun in the 1960s, unearthed Pleistocene chipped-stone tools encrusted in calcium carbonate dated to at least 200,000 years ago. The discoveryforced some radical theoretical revisions about just when humanity, and what species of humanity, first arrived on the North American continent.

It is generally agreed that the earliest *Homo sapiens*—known to early anthropologists as the Lake Mojave People, primarily hunters less poetically known now as the Death Valley I culture—came about 10,000 years ago to what is now Death Valley, when the deep lakes and lush landscape supported an abundance of prehistoric plants and animals. About 5,000 years ago, when the valley's original lakes had disappeared, the Mesquite Flat People—or the Death Valley II culture, also primitive hunters who brought down game without benefit of bow and arrow—had emerged in the northern part of the valley. Some 2,500 years ago, before the valley's most recent large lake appeared, the Saratoga Spa People, or the Death Valley III culture, appeared throughout the region. Adapted to much harsher conditions, and assisted by the advent of the bow and arrow, these farmer-gatherers/sometimes hunters nonetheless declined because of the valley's increasingly hot, dry climate and its increasingly sparse nature. By the beginning of the 11th century the Death Valley IV culture, a similar desert-adapted people skilled at pottery making, had arrived.

Badlands Nomads: The Shoshone

During California's onrushing gold rush of the 1850s, the Tumbisha Shoshone were quite well established in and around Death Valley. Like most California Indians, the Tumbisha, known as the Koso or Panamints by earlier anthropologists, lived as extended families within a loosely affiliated clan culture rather than as a unified "tribe." The Paiute people maintained a seasonal hunting camp south of Saratoga Springs yet did not share the territory. But according to old Shoshone stories, Paiute hunters occasionally breached the cultural barrier created by the Grapevine Mountains to hunt game and launch unprovoked attacks.

The Shoshone lived in Death Valley proper only in winter, migrating to cooler mountain elevations in summer. In every season they made good use of the land's limited abundance. Dietary mainstays from the plant kingdom included beavertail cactus, mesquite, and the piñon pine—plants that provided sweet-fleshed boiled or dried vegetable "steaks," beans, and pine nuts, respectively. (Sweathouses were constructed of arrowweed and then covered with soil.) Almost anything that moved—insects, lizards, rats, birds—was considered edible, if not necessarily a delicacy. Favored game animals included bighorn sheep, coyotes, and rabbits. Hunters relied on deadfall traps as well as the bow and arrow, with bows crafted from juniper and strung with wild hemp, arrows fashioned from willow with greasewood points. Other Shoshone arts—basketry, weaving nets, and tanning animal hides—were also the arts of survival. Baskets woven from willow and sumac, sometimes waterproofed with piñon pitch, were essential for gathering plants and seeds and for holding water; plant-fiber carrying nets were also useful in the endless task of food collection; and animal hides provided clothing and blankets.

After settlers arrived, the Shoshone continued their nomadic traditions as best they could—a tendency that, in the late 1800s, earned particular notoriety for "Panamint Tom." Known to forage for horses as far away as Los Angeles, Panamint Tom divided his catch fairly between families—for what was, for a time, the Shoshone's special annual horsemeat feast.

Badlands and Bad Water: Stumbling into "Death Valley"

Earlier signs had suggested that the Shoshone's hunting and gathering traditions would continue—starting with attempts to bring down, with bow and arrow, the oxen of the first white settlers to traverse the valley.

Early California explorers and trappers had avoided Death Valley; even at the time of California statehood the region was vaguely, and inaccurately, mapped. John C. Frémont, Kit Carson, and company shimmied around the valley's southern reaches in April of 1844, but not until the gold rush of 1849 was the treacherous terrain tested by impatient fortune-hunters heading west by wagon train.

The misadventure that gave Death Valley its name began in Salt Lake City in September of 1849. Captain Jefferson Hunt of the honored

Mormon Battalion had signed on to lead the 110 wagons of the Sand Walking Company west, following a new southern route to San Bernardino that avoided the Salt Desert. Intent on arriving in California's gold fields as soon as possible—and hoping to pursue a more direct but rumored route—almost immediately Hunt's sand walkers began agitating for a change in course. Unable to sway their leader, group after group of settlers broke away from the main party and headed west sans guide, returning within days when their chosen paths proved impossible. But the conflict only escalated. At one point the wagon train itself went renegade, with only seven wagons opting to follow Hunt. After dead-ending in a canyon, however, most of the dissatisfied settlers resigned themselves to Hunt's slow but sure leadership and rejoined his group.

Three groups stubbornly struggled and straggled on, over uncharted territory. With little water and limited food, the route rebels encountered endless mountains and high-desert plains before reaching absolute desolation—a vast and barren saline valley fringed by frightening, unfriendly mountains. The tremendously difficult terrain, boxed in by steep canyons, was bad news enough. But the bad water was almost worse; the laxative effects of Epsom-salt overdose almost undid the exhausted travelers before they found the valley's freshwater springs.

Some of these ill-fated adventurers, their wagons and worldly goods abandoned or burned to barbecue their oxen, died in the struggle to escape Death Valley. But, after trudging hundreds of desperate miles to Los Angeles, most lived to tell the tale—including many of the Jayhawkers, a group of young men from Illinois, and the women, children, and men of the Arcane, Bennett, Biers families.

Members of these three families were saved from starvation by William Lewis Manly and John Rogers, who had gone ahead to find help. Manly and Rogers returned 25 days later with supplies provided by a California rancho near Tehachapi—the beans, rice, and other staples supplemented by fresh oranges, the first the children had ever seen. As the survivors crested the Panamints and looked back over their landscape of manifest misery, someone murmured: "Good-bye, Death Valley."

So Death Valley got its name.

Mining, Mule Teams, and Borax

The first travelers' tales easily deterred other settlers, even the U.S. government; no official expeditions explored Death Valley until the 1870s. Dread of the desert didn't diminish the lust for overnight wealth, however. That fever was fanned by one Death Valley survivor's story of a mountain of silver-veined ore—a mythic lodestar that came to be known as the Gunsight Mine—and the equally elusive Breyfogle Mine, a forgotten place that befuddled blacksmith Jacob Breyfogle reported to be rich in gold ore. But the Death Valley area had its share of boomtime mining towns, mines, and miners, particularly from the 1870s into the early 1900s. The most famous miner of them all was Walter Scott, better known as "Death Valley Scotty," a 20th-century prospector mighty mysterious about his gold mines but otherwise fairly flamboyant. A turn-of-the-20th-century trick rider in Buffalo Bill's western revue who gained national celebrity for his 45-hour cross-country train race, Scotty and partner Albert Johnson left a more lasting legacy—Scotty's Castle, Death Valley's eccentric 1920s Moorish mansion, still open to the public.

Borax mining was less romantic than the lure of gold and silver but, at least for a time, proved more profitable. The Harmony Borax Works, Death Valley's most successful operation, produced the trademark 20-Mule Team Borax, a laundry product long associated with the *Death Valley Days* western radio and television programs.

The Desert as Tourist Attraction, Research Lab, and Preserve

By the early 1900s wild Death Valley attracted its first tourists, who arrived by train. Motorized vehicles also gained a tirehold. Touring Death Valley by automobile was an adventure even in terms of simple mechanics, since the rugged roads repeatedly sacrificed tires, axles, and oil pans on the rocky altar of nature appreciation. Early visitor facilities, including the Furnace Creek Inn, were owned and operated by the Pacific Borax Company—even for a time after 1933, when the valley gained national and international acknowledgment for its uniqueness, and a new level of protection, as Death Valley National Monument.

In late 1994 Death Valley's status was elevated again—to national park—with passage of the California Desert Protection Act. Along with Death Valley's new moniker came new land—an additional 1.3 million acres, for a total of almost 3.4 million acres (1,347,000 hectares), making this the largest national park outside Alaska.

Onetime Bureau of Land Management (BLM) lands in Eureka Valley, Saline Valley, the Panamint Mountains, the northern Panamint Valley, Hunter Mountain, the Nelson Range, Greenwater Valley, and the Owlshead Mountains are now included in Death Valley National Park.

SEEING AND DOING DEATH VALLEY

You can do Death Valley in a day—if a tour of Scotty's Castle and an exhausting all-day road trip will assure you that you've "done it." Better by far is a longer stay—a week to 10 days, if possible, or at least a long weekend—for in-depth exploration and more experiential memories of this and other highlights of the northern Mojave Desert. Another, quite personal benefit of a longer visit—rarely acknowledged even in park literature—is its salutary effect on mental health. Especially if you stay away from the fray, the tortoiselike pace of life here can help unwind even a packrat's nest of fret.

Before setting out to discover Death Valley and vicinity, stop by the visitor center at Furnace Creek—then set priorities. Even with fairly few stops it can easily take an entire day just to get from one end of the valley to the other. Much more pleasant is charting, over a period of several days, various looping, long-distance road trips. With even minimal planning one can manage an early-morning hike, a pleasant picnic, and some leisurely sight-seeing before heading back for a relaxed evening in the thrall of a Death Valley sunset.

"Big Picture" Viewpoints

Taking in Death Valley's stunning vistas from vantage points well above the valley itself—experiencing the "big picture"—is particularly spectacular at sunrise or sunset, when light and landscape are at their most dramatic. But getting the big picture involves mileage and, in some cases, shoe leather. Save at least some miles and time by stopping at the following panoramic (and semipanoramic) "big picture" viewpoints on your way to or from elsewhere.

Just a few miles southeast of Furnace Creek via Highway 190, and therefore quite popular, is **Zabriskie Point.** The view here is toward the west—the Amargosa Range's yellow-clay hills, onetime lake-bottom sediments, and the towering Panamint Mountains beyond. It's a fairly easy downhill hike, about 2.5 miles, from here to Golden Canyon and then on to Badwater Road.

For another perspective on the grandeur of Death Valley, try mile-high **Dante's View,** a name inspired by purgatory's poetic description in *The Divine Comedy,* Dante Alighieri's classic 14th-century spiritual allegory. Just getting here, a 25-mile drive from the visitor center, is an awesome allegory on the true nature of time—starting with minute-by-minute self-absorption: "Did I pack the snacks? Enough water? Sunscreen? A jacket for the cool mountain air?" Climbing via Highway 190, the route passes both old and new reminders of human enterprise—in this case, historic Twenty-Mule Team Canyon and, later, the fresh open-pit mine tailings of the Boraxo mine—and then weaves through the odd beauty of Black Mountains' canyonland. Earlier worries seem less pressing, suddenly, though the human clock keeps ticking. Below the road's last steep, hairpin climb is a place to park one's excess baggage (in this case, hindrances such as motor homes and trailers) and slow down yet again. At the overlook—at the edge of the visible world—comes the surprising sensation that time, human time, has stopped altogether.

Directly below is **Badwater,** an impressive puddle of same famous for its locale—near the lowest elevations in the continental United States—and connected to the green of Furnace Creek by a thin asphalt string. Directly across the valley, about a mile above one's head, is notched Telescope Peak, the most prominent presence in the Panamints; beyond to the northwest are the Sierra Nevada and triangular Mount Whitney (visible on a clear day), the highest point in the Lower 48. Between these highs and

Death Valley views can offer some perspective.

KIM WEIR

lows is almost everything else in Death Valley's careful crazy-quilt of color—nature at its most elemental. Most identifiable: the vast salt sink, at its blinding, borax-bright whitest in summer, and the valley's immense and impressive alluvial fans, boulders bounced down out of the canyons by water and gravity and then neatly piled high by inertia.

Aguerreberry Point, just north of Emigrant Pass on the road to Wildrose, is named after Pete Aguerreberry, Basque shepherd turned prospector, who along with his friend Shorty Harris found gold—and inadvertently founded the short-lived mining camp of Harrisburg. (The original intended name was Harrisberry.) Long after fair-weather fortune seekers had moved on to Skidoo and other strikes, Aguerreberry returned, alone, to work the Harrisburg mine. During his many years of solitary labor, Aguerreberry's most constant companion was this unobstructed panoramic view looking east over Death Valley; the miner himself scraped out a forebear of the current road.

For the best roadside view of the rugged Panamint Mountains, pull off at **Father Crowley Point** adjacent to Highway 190, on the edge of Rainbow Canyon. (To get here from the west and Highway 136, continue east for 21 miles on Highway 190. If coming from Death Valley, this viewpoint is about eight miles west of Panamint Springs.) Below in the Panamint Valley are the serene and sandy Panamint Dunes, supremely hikable. Look to the southeast for another view of

Telescope Peak. Some say the best Death Valley view of all is from **Telescope Peak,** looking east from the summit—an experience you'll miss if uninspired by the idea of making the long-day's hike up from Wildrose Canyon (best in spring and fall). The peak was named for the clarity and "up-closeness" of the view looking east, as if through a telescope. An easier climb, with great views of both east and west, is **Wildrose Peak** nearby.

IN AND AROUND FURNACE CREEK

Especially for first-time visitors, the best place to start a Death Valley adventure is at the **Death Valley National Park Visitor Center** at Furnace Creek, 760/2331, open daily 8 A.M.–6 P.M. The museum introduces both the lay of the land—with a huge three-dimensional relief map, to scale—and the area's cultural and natural history. Current exhibits include the infamous "false 49er trunk" that recently made the news. Park orientation programs are scheduled daily (12-minute slide program shown every half-hour, with special daytime talks, evening programs, and ranger-guided hikes throughout Death Valley offered from October into April. The visitor center is also *the* place to stop for maps, books, and current road and trail information—the latter absolutely mandatory if you'll be leaving the blacktop behind, since conditions can change radically overnight. (Call for daily updates, posted each morning.) Other essential visitor facilities and services are nearby, so fill up on gas, emergency water, and trail snacks while in the neighborhood.

The Borax Story: Memorabilia and Memorable Sights

The story of borax and related borates—essential ingredients in soaps and detergents, boric acid, photographic chemicals, porcelain enamel, solder, optical lenses, insulation, even antifreeze—is one of the world's less exciting tales. But Death Valley's contribution to borax mining mythology is legendary—the stuff of Hollywood legend, at any rate. Get the complete and unabridged borax story at the park's free **Borax Museum**, just north of the Furnace Creek Ranch entrance and southwest of the post office. The building itself, built in 1883 as a combination kitchen, office, and boarding house, was relocated here from its original site at the borax operations in Twenty-Mule Team Canyon. With historical photos and miscellaneous memorabilia—elegant Shoshone basketry, railroad schedules, prospecting tools, and peculiar mining contraptions—the impacts of the local borax business, and mining in general, are well documented. But borax, too, is on display, an astonishing collection of mineral samples. Out back is still more historical amazement—a virtual barnyard of wagons, buckboards, stagecoaches, and an oxen-shoeing rig keeping company with the original Greenwater **Chuckwalla** printing press, a Baldwin locomotive from the Death Valley Railroad, and the original 1880s 20-mule team barn from Mojave.

Two miles north of the visitor center are the remains of the **Harmony Borax Works,** where the interpretive quarter-mile path winds past an 1880s-vintage 20-mule team borax wagon, crumbling adobes, and antique equipment. Harmony was the "cottonball" borax processing center of the W. T. Coleman Company, Death Valley's first successful borax operation, established here in 1882. Harmony was too hot for summer work, so in 1884 Coleman moved its borax works to the high-desert Amargosa area; but by 1888 Coleman was bankrupt, its assets controlled by the Pacific Coast Borax Company (now the U.S. Borax and Chemical Corpora-

tion) by 1890. Harmony's most lasting contribution to borax mining history was the 20-mule team wagon rig—an innovation that allowed the mules, hitched in pairs, to pull two loaded borax wagons plus a 1200-gallon water tank, a total load of 36.5 tons, from here across the desert to Mojave, some 180 rough and rugged miles distant.

It's a fairly easy, level five-mile hike from Harmony through the **Borax Haystacks** to the north, stacked by Chinese laborers to establish Harmony's mining claim—a sight most striking at sunrise.

East on Highway 190

The jaunt east from Furnace Creek via Highway 190 is perfect for a late afternoon tour. First stop is **Zabriskie Point,** with its panoramic view of the badlands below. (Bring camera and film.) Next stop, about two miles along, is the one-way side loop through **Twenty Mule Team Canyon,** a onetime mecca for borax mining and miners. The colorful undulating hills here were sculpted from mud—ancient lakebed sediments—that were folded, faulted, and uplifted before being smothered by lava flows. About five miles farther on is the turnoff to **Dante's View,** one of the park's most popular panoramic vistas and prime end-of-day destination for sunset seekers.

Before paved Dante's View Road jogs westward toward purgatory, unpaved **Furnace Creek Wash Road** shoots off to the southeast to **Greenwater Canyon** and its ridge-top petroglyphs (some damaged by present-day cretins), other petroglyph sights, and the cholla-dotted landscape near what remains of the **Greenwater** copper mining camp. Beyond the four-wheeling route into **Gold Valley,** the road eventually intersects Highway 178 east of Salsberry Pass near Shoshone.

Back on Highway 190 from Dante's View Road, 19 miles to the east and outside the park is spot-in-the-road **Death Valley Junction,** known as Amargosa before becoming a de facto company town for the Tonopah and Tidewater Railroad. In the cooler months the hottest entertainment act around is staged at the **Amargosa Opera House,** a small theater included in the original **Amargosa Hotel** complex built by the Pacific Coast Borax Company in 1923–25.

HEADING SOUTH: BAD WATER, BETTER VIEWS

Just south of Furnace Creek is the 60-acre fenced enclave of Depression-era adobes and modern mobile homes now home to the valley's remaining Timbisha Shoshone—members of a federally recognized tribe since 1983.

Heading due south from Furnace Creek via scenic Badwater Road (Hwy. 178) leads to Badwater—a desert pond of variable size not nearly as "bad" or as devoid of life as it might appear—and its surreal salt-flat surroundings. On the way to Badwater but off the main road are other intriguing features, including hikable Golden Canyon, the one-way Artists Palette driving tour, the Devil's Golf Course salt formations, and the Natural Bridge stone arch shaped by ancient waterfalls.

Below Badwater the paved road continues south along the big toes of the Black Mountains—some notable alluvial fans—to the ruins of World War I–era Ashford Mill, then veers east to climb up and over Salsberry Pass and roll on to the tiny town of Shoshone just beyond the boundaries of Death Valley National Park—a total distance of over 70 miles from Furnace Creek. Some five miles south of Shoshone, via Highway 127, is Tecopa Hot Springs, a somewhat surreal snowbird hotspot; about 28 miles north of Shoshone is the one-actress town of Death Valley Junction famous these days for its Amargosa Opera House. For more information about both the hot springs and opera house performances, see Near Death Valley, below.

Gravel-road adventure is also available in Death Valley's southern reaches. From Badwater Road near Artists Palette, West Side Road ambles southwest and then skirts the western edge of the valley before rejoining the paved road just north of Ashford Mill. Attractions along the way include the ruins of the failed Eagle Borax Works and the Cinder Hill cinder cone, in addition to four-wheel-drive roads into Warm Springs and other canyons. Another worthwhile four-wheel-drive route, starting just southeast of Ashford Mill, ambles south from Highway 178 along the Amargosa River to Saratoga Spring—a day-use destination that one can also reach, by better (unpaved) road, from Highway 127.

Golden Canyon and Artists Drive

If the ambient air temperature is tolerable, hike Golden Canyon in the late afternoon, when the sun's rays spin the sandy brown stone into gold —more accurately, warm-hued iron oxides. A 1.5-mile spur road leads to the parking lot; from there, hike right on in. At the end of the steep, narrow canyon, up the wash to the right, is aptly named **Red Cathedral** (also known as Cathedral Wall), a natural amphitheater created from an ancient, iron-capped Funeral Mountains alluvial fan—most dramatic in the late-day sun. Explore Golden Canyon's various side canyons for more colorful surprises and odd rock formations. The fairly gradual trail up through **Gower Gulch** leads to the scenic vistas of **Zabriskie Point,** though the hiking views are better—and the walking even easier—heading downhill. Happy hoofers can also hike to the base of **Manly Beacon,** a self-guided geology lesson.

Back on the main road heading south, ancient lake shorelines are visible in the basalt foothills of the Black Mountains. The flat point at the northern end is **Manly Terrace,** believed by archaeologists to be one of the first inhabited areas of Death Valley. Around the point to the east is **Mushroom Rock,** an apt name for an unusual lava formation once resembling a massive mushroom. The forces of erosion and vandalism have chipped away at that form; some say 'Shroom Rock now more closely resembles a well-known extraterrestrial film star.

Late afternoon is also the best time to dabble in **Artists Palette,** the next major attraction, where primary colors shade into badlands pastels. One-way, nine-mile Artists Drive (enter at the south end) winds through mud hills splashed with mineral oxides and chlorides, lasting testament to nature's creativity.

Devil's Golf Course, Natural Bridge

About 10 miles south of the Artists Drive exit is the short dirt spur leading to Devil's Golf Course. But even the devil might get mighty teed off if trying to whack a few across this ungodly salt-pocked landscape. These crusty salt spikes, from several inches to several feet tall, were created by evaporation and erosion. As the most recent lake receded more than 2,000 years ago, thick layers of salt crystals—here, almost pure table salt, or sodium chloride—sealed the lake-bottom sediments. Centuries of wind, rain, and heat have continued this creation. Wind and rain whittle the salt pinnacles, yet they continue to "grow"; in the presence of underground moisture, dissolved salts are drawn through capillary action back to the surface, where they recrystalize. When it's hot, the salt-crystal crust breaks up anew—crackling, popping, and pinging.

Just two miles south on the main road and several steep dirt-road miles east, much quieter Natural Bridge is a short stroll up the canyon from the parking lot. This 50-foot-high formation—sculpted by a rushing waterfall—is a true Death Valley ancient, composed of sedimentary stone more than two million years old.

Badwater

Make way for the tour buses, because this is one place they all stop. Badwater is actually more famous for its long-time, if slightly inaccurate, billing as the lowest elevation in the Lower 48—the valley's two lowest points are actually a few miles away—and its earnest candidacy for hottest place on earth than for its "bad" water. How bad is bad? The water in the pool is not toxic, though it's none too tasty—the chemical equivalent of a very strong dose of Epsom salts. (Since Epsom salts are an effective laxative, sampling the water could prove quite distressing. Not recommended.) And it is capable of supporting life—soldier fly larvae, water beetles, water snails, algae, ditch grass, and (beyond the water's edge) pickleweed.

For some instant on-site perspective, look directly west across the valley to the Panamints's Telescope Peak—standing tall at an elevation of 11,049 feet but rising more than 11,300 feet above where you're standing.

HEADING NORTH: STOVEPIPES AND SCOTTY'S CASTLE

As you head north from Furnace Creek, three possible tour routes present themselves. Following **Highway 190** as it snakes north and then southwest/west leads first to **Salt Creek,** one of the park's few remaining pupfish habitats, on the way to Stovepipe Wells Village, Death Valley's other primary visitor services center. Well before the village is the dirt-road turnoff to the lovely **Death Valley Sand Dunes** (picnic area), near the sand-proofed original **Stovepipe Well** for which this area is named. Farther west along the highway is **Devil's Cornfield,** the vaguely agricultural ambience created by 10-foot-tall arrowweed "stacks." Facilities at historic **Stovepipe Wells Village** include a pleasant Western-style motel, a fall-to-spring campground, restaurant and saloon, general store, and gas station. Worth exploring near Stovepipe Wells Village: hikable **Mosaic Can-**

Old Scratch himself would find himself in the rough at this badlands golf course.

KIM WEIR

yon and, for four-wheelers, **Cottonwood** and **Marble Canyons.**

Alternatively, head northeast toward Daylight Pass Road (Hwy. 374) via **Beatty Cutoff** to reach the remains of **Keane Wonder Mill** and **Keane Wonder Mine** (dirt road and then foot trail) and the striking **Chloride Cliff** viewpoint at the end of the four-wheeling route to ghost-town **Chloride City.** (A longer but much better road to Chloride City begins at the south side of the highway at the park's Highway 374 entrance.) East from the cutoff's junction with the highway and the **Hell's Gate** rest area/information stop, Highway 374 twists up and over Daylight Pass and down into the Amargosa Desert and **Beatty** in Nevada (gas, food, ranger station). More interesting attractions are en route, however, including the one-way (westward) dirt-road tour of Death Valley's **Titus Canyon** and the Nevada ghost towns of **Rhyolite,** where the beer-bottle adobe **Bottle House** still stands, and **Bullfrog.**

Heading north from Highway 190 past another information stop (just north of its junction with Highway 374) is **Death Valley North Highway,** which continues about 36 miles to grand **Scotty's Castle** and surrounding oasis, the park's most popular destination and tour (fee; gas available during the day).

From Scotty's Castle, take the road less traveled up narrow Grapevine Canyon via Highway 267 to reach spot-in-the-road Scotty's Junction (no services) in Nevada. Or continue west to nearby **Ubehebe Crater** for a quick geology lesson. A gravel road angles south from Ubehebe for some 20 miles through Racetrack Valley to **The Racetrack**—an odd and intriguing sun-blistered playa where stones "race" each other, though no one has actually seen the competition.

From near Ubehebe Crater, unpaved (and very rough) Death Valley Road snakes north into recently acquired park territory, eventually making its way up and over the Last Chance mountains. Make sure you've filled up on gas, water, and current weather and road information before setting out. The two most popular features north of Scotty's Castle are the **Eureka Dunes** in Eureka Valley and the clothing-very-optional hot springs in **Saline Valley** (actually more accessible from the west, via a very rough access road).

Salt Creek Pupfish Tour

Pity the poor Salt Creek pupfish, seasonal survivors doomed in summer to inhabit only pools, as if these creek puddles were the entire universe—because, for this species, seasonal Salt Creek *is* the entire universe. When mastodons and saber-toothed tigers roamed the neighborhood, vast freshwater Lake Manly dominated a lush landscape. But as the lake evaporated, only salty desert, isolated springs, and a few spring-fed waterways remained; with rare exceptions, established plant and animal species either moved on or died out.

Among Death Valley's salt-adapted exceptions is the Salt Creek pupfish, *Cyprinodron salinus,* most numerous, active, and observable in March or early April. The half-mile boardwalk and interpretive trail leads you into their limited world. (These tiny silvery slivers shy away from lurking shadows, so stand still.) Spawning season begins in February, with flashy blue males fighting for females and territory. With several new generations in the swim, summer heat and evaporation grimly reap; only those fish in deeper pools survive. When Salt Creek is again recognizable as a creek, in winter, dormant pupfish wait out the cold nestled into the muddy bottom.

Near Stovepipe Wells: The Dunes, the Well

Until the Eureka Dunes and Panamint Dunes were added to the park's holdings in 1994 (see listings below), the Death Valley Sand Dunes were known as "the sand dunes," with little confusion. Covering roughly 25 square miles, these dunes are created—and constantly re-created—by crosswinds and eddies. Though most sand dunes migrate over time, this whirling wind-riffed sand is more or less stationary; major movement is "corrected" by seasonal changes in wind direction. Especially after heavy winter rains, spring wildflowers are a major draw. But a sandy stroll is a pleasure—and a challenge—any time temperatures are reasonably moderate. You'll find no trail, since shifting sands would soon obliterate any trace; here, you can blaze your own. You can even blaze a barefoot trail, if possible encounters with superheated sand, sidewinders, and thorns are no deterrent. (Carry shoes, just in case.) Distances are deceiving, so slather on the sunscreen and carry water.

The historic **Stovepipe Well** farther north along this road was named for the length of stovepipe once poked into the well here to prevent dune sand from choking off the water supply.

Mosaic and Other Area Canyons

Just west of Stovepipe Wells Village and then several miles south via unpaved road is dramatic **Mosaic Canyon,** popular for guided park service tours of the stunning polished stone "mosaics" for which it was named. As recently as the 1970s Mosaic Canyon featured unusual "whirlpools" and greater depth—even iron hand-railings for precipitous passages—but heavy rains and accelerated erosion have silted things up considerably. Intrepid trekkers can make a challenging four- to five-mile hike out of excursions into side canyons.

Cottonwood Canyon beyond the Stovepipe Wells airstrip is immensely popular with four-wheelers—cottonwoods grow near a creek at the end of the road—but hikers use this road (and topo maps) to create longer looping routes through adjacent **LeMoigne** and **Marble** canyons.

The Titus Canyon Tour

This one-way dirt-road adventure through Titus Canyon begins at Highway 374 in the Nevada desert, the turnoff several miles south of Rhyolite and east of the park proper. Highlights of the dramatic 28-mile, two- to three-hour tour include the scant remains of **Leadfield,** a few tattered tin buildings built as props for Charles Courtney Julian's 1920s mining investment scam, the **When Rocks Bend** sign, petroglyphs at **Klare Spring,** and the canyon's narrow and steep stone-mosaic walls. The entire route is walkable, of course, but an immensely long trek requiring water caches and other forms of prudence. More popular with hikers is a round-trip walk starting from the canyon's Death Valley side; the road from the highway is two-way until the parking lot.

Because the road through Titus Canyon is very narrow, with very few turnouts, be sure your vehicle is up to the trip—gas, water, good tires—to avoid stranding yourself and others in the canyon; a stall during Easter Week, or on almost any busy spring weekend, could conceivably create a single-file parking lot.

Scotty's Castle and Gas House Museum

Toward the end of his days, Death Valley Scotty was perturbed that the expansive desert mansion named in his honor garnered more public attention than he did. "I'm the one-man circus," he reportedly said. "The castle is just the tail of my kite."

Some tail.

According to popular assumption in the 1920s and '30s, this vaguely Spanish tile-roofed mansion at Grapevine Springs was built with profits from Death Valley Scotty's fabled gold mine. But the gold mine never existed. And Death Valley Scotty had no money, aside from the sums he conned from various backers. The two-million-dollar castle complex, started in 1922 but never finished, was the brainchild and desert health retreat of Albert Mussey Johnson of Chicago, a millionaire insurance executive who became Scotty's most enthusiastic supporter. When the

---

DEATH VALLEY FISH STORY: PREHISTORIC PUPFISH

One of Death Valley's most astonishing creatures is the desert pupfish, a relict species—actually a collection of relict species and subspecies, of the genus *Cyprinodon*—first hatched here when the valley was still a vast lake country in well-watered wilderness. Some biologists speculate that the endangered pupfish of the Death Valley region were originally all one widespread species, its survivors suddenly isolated in separate small streams and springs when the valley's great lakes disappeared some 20,000 years ago. The passage of time and evolutionary adaptation to distinct environments are responsible for current species variation. Some pupfish are adapted to highly saline conditions, for example—up to six times saltier than seawater—and others can tolerate water temperatures up to 111°F, making survival possible even in hot springs.

Endemic here and in adjacent Nevada territory, Death Valley pupfish are easy to see at Salt Creek—a lively feature along the self-guided nature trail. These finger-long omnivorous fish, aggressive and fierce, also live at Saratoga Springs, Cottonball Marsh, and Devil's Hole.

Johnsons wintered at the castle—entertaining guests including Will Rogers and Norman Rockwell while also offering tours of "Scotty's" castle to the public—Death Valley Scotty held court as if he owned the place, regaling his audiences with tall tales and dubious deeds. Though he sometimes stayed as a guest, Death Valley Scotty actually lived elsewhere—in his own cabin, several miles to the west.

These days, guides dressed in 1930s garb lead living history tours of the main house, also sharing anecdotes about and insights into the peculiar long-lived partnership between Death Valley Scotty and the Johnsons.

Centerpiece of the castle complex, officially known as Death Valley Ranch, is the 25-room main house with its immense Great Hall (de facto living room) and indoor waterfall, 18 fireplaces, music rooms, and guest suites. Elaborate tile work, wrought-iron accents, carved wooden doors, and beamed ceilings set the stage for exquisite Old World antiques, elaborate fakes

Elaborate as it is, Scotty's castle stands unfinished.

KIM WEIR

(no original paintings here), and eccentric collectibles—the latter including the Welte-Mignon theater organ in the Upper Music Room. Either before or after the castle tour, wander the grounds (free) to appreciate other quirks and charms of the complex. Death Valley Scotty's grave site is up the hill, at the end of Windy Point Trail. The Gas House Museum exhibits new materials from the Castle collection, emphasizing history and personalities.

The Scotty's Castle grounds are open 7 A.M.–6 P.M. year-round. The 50-minute guided castle tours are offered daily, on the hour from 9 A.M. to 5 P.M.; each is limited to a maximum of 19 people. Tickets are sold here on a first-come basis, on the date of the tour only, and are $8 adults, $6 seniors, and $4 children (age 5 and under free); expect to wait. To improve the odds of landing tour tickets during busy times, arrive early—and be flexible about plans for the rest of the day. Late morning and early afternoon tours, for example, are easily sandwiched around a picnic (tables available) and a leisurely exterior tour of the grounds. Securing tickets for a late afternoon tour leaves the earlier part of the day open for excursions farther afield. A self-guided tour (of the grounds) is also an option; pick up a tour brochure at the Castle Ticket Office. In summer months—from April through October—the Gas House Museum, which also offers a great Death Valley and desert book selection, serves as the ticket office for guided tours. For more information about Scotty's Castle, tours, and special events, visit the park service website (see below) or call 760/786-2392.

Ubehebe Crater

This notable upside-down cone eight miles from Scotty's Castle—800 feet deep, 450 feet across at bottom, and a half-mile wide at ground level—is still the subject of scientific quibbling. Formed by a massive volcanic steam explosion, Ubehebe Crater is assumed to be about 1,000 years old, though some say 4,000 to 10,000 years old and others contend that the crater is a mere 300 years old, like Little Hebe and similar smaller craters just south. Whenever Ubehebe blasted its way into existence, the force of creation was so intense that the colorful earth was sliced clean, like a megalayered cake. Examine those layers by taking the trail to the bottom. Another route

"DEATH VALLEY SCOTTY": A MAN AND HIS MYTH

A true celebrity among Death Valley's ever-quirky cast of characters, Walter "Death Valley Scotty" Scott has been memorialized as more colorful than even the desert's most garish sunset. And Death Valley Scotty ensured the world knew of his exploits, his self-promotional flair making him the darling of the Los Angeles press corps during the early 1900s.

After a youthful stint with Buffalo Bill Cody's Wild West Show, according to the myth, the Kentucky-born Scott headed west to Death Valley. In no time at all he laid claim to what he boasted was a fabulously rich gold mine, vaguely located in the south, somewhere near the modern ruins of Ashford Mill. All he lacked, subsequent backers were convinced, was sufficient capital to unearth this vast wealth. The myth itself proved to be a gold mine for Scott, despite his lasting inability to produce either the mine or its gold. As practiced prospector Pete Aguerreberry once put it, other people's pockets were all Death Valley Scotty ever mined.

And so it was, starting with Julian M. Gerard, conned into backing Scott's mining venture with the help of Ella Josephine McCarthy Milius Scott (Scotty's wife, known as "Jack") and two nuggets she'd brought west from Colorado. Death Valley Scotty's next benefactor was E. Burdon Gaylord, an L.A. mining engineer who in 1905 paid the freight for Scott's record-breaking cross-country train trip aboard the Coyote Special—a spectacularly successful publicity stunt for Gaylord, who was desperately seeking a buyer for his Death Valley mine, and for Walter Scott. The nation celebrated Death Valley Scotty's accomplishment, though he was merely a passenger aboard the Chicago-bound Coyote.

Scott's celebrity attracted the attention of Chica-go financier Albert M. Johnson, who was soon convinced to back Scotty's nonexistent gold-mining venture. Johnson headed west to examine the mine. Though the trip erupted in scandal and ended in arrests—an armed "ambush" near Wingate Pass had been arranged by Scott, to scare off the mine investigation—Johnson was not deterred. He and his wife became Death Valley Scotty's life-long benefactors, also putting up the money for elegant "Scotty's Castle" and other 1920s construction at Death Valley Ranch. Even Johnson's financial losses in the stock market crash of 1929, which introduced the Great Depression to Death Valley, failed to diminish their relationship. As to why he served as Death Valley Scotty's "gold mine" for so many years, in 1941 Johnson said it was because Scott was such a "swell companion," something money couldn't buy. "He repays me in laughs."

Aside from his enduring friendship with the Johnsons, Death Valley Scotty's most lasting accomplishment was the creation of a romantic 20th-century Western desert mythology—and his success in permanently placing that myth on the map of the nation's imagination.

By the time Death Valley Scotty died at the age of 81—in 1954, just six years after his good friend Albert Johnson passed on—his mythic persona had taken on a life of its own. Scotty had specified a fairly pedestrian message for his epitaph: *Here he is.* But those in charge of marking his memory instead inscribed: *I got four things to live by: Don't say nothing that will hurt anybody. Don't give advice—nobody will take it anyway. Don't complain. Don't explain.*

The fact that Death Valley Scotty consistently failed to live by such posthumous posturing is, in the realm of mythology, inconsequential.

circumnavigates the black perimeter before jogging on to Little Hebe.

The Racetrack

After a long, leisurely gravel-road sojourn up to a few Joshua tree stragglers and down again—the trip in can easily take a half-day—Racetrack Valley Road finally arrives at its surreal destination. One of the park's most mysterious features, the Racetrack hosts a "race" so slow that it's never been observed. What you do see here, though, are the racers—rocks seemingly tossed at random atop the fine-clay playa, their tracks indicating how far each contender has come. Some the size of baseballs, others boulders, the hardened competitors rest motionless and silent. Yet the sense that everything just moved—just *then,* when one's back was turned—is eerie, almost overwhelming. Scientists theorize that the race resumes with the arrival of strong winds on those rare days when the clay surface is just moist enough to become slick.

Eureka Sand Dunes

Eureka Sand Dunes National Natural Landmark, boasting California's tallest sand dune, is among the park's newly acquired attractions. Standing about 700 feet tall, Sand Mountain at the north end is notable, its ghostly pale sands a dramatic contrast to the Last Chance Range in the background. Like the Kelso Dunes in Mojave National Preserve, the dunes here "sing" when sand particles cascade from the summit—a rare sand dune feature and a real kick for the kids. Unusual also are the area's endemic plant species. (Do not molest plants or animals.) Because of the hellacious summer heat, the dunes are best visited in late fall, winter, and early spring.

To reach the Eureka Dunes from Scotty's Castle, head north on rough-and-tumble Death Valley Road—up and over the Last Chance mountains—then turn south onto South Eureka Road (gravel, high-clearance vehicles preferable). Continue for ten miles; there are no services at the dunes or en route. To reach the dunes from Big Pine and Highway 395, head east on Highway 168 and turn southeast onto Death Valley Road. After about 39 miles, turn south onto South Eureka. (If making a side trip from the north end of Saline Valley, also follow these general directions). Roads may be impassable after storms, so check with rangers before setting out.

HEADING WEST:
INTO THE PANAMINTS

Present-day park visitors can find their way west from Stovepipe Wells by virtually the same route early immigrants did—into the Panamint Mountains via the steep and deeply twisted **Wildrose Road** (Hwy. 178) along the alluvial fan and then into and out of Emigrant Canyon. Too treacherous for campers, trailers, and large RVs, the road continues from Emigrant for about 21 miles to the Wildrose ranger station and campground. Worthy side trips along the way include the mining ghost town of **Skidoo,** the site of short-lived **Harrisburg,** and **Aguerreberry Point,** with its spectacular sunset views of Death Valley below. At Wildrose, take **Mahogany Flat Road** (pavement, then dirt) for a still higher climb into Wildrose Canyon, a gain of 4,000 feet in a mere eight

miles. On the left, after seven miles, are the imposing stone **Wildrose Canyon Charcoal Kilns,** beehivelike furnaces built by Chinese laborers for the task of transforming wood into charcoal. (Wildrose charcoal fueled the silver smelters at the Modoc Mine—owned by George Hearst, father of William Randolph Hearst, and an early contributor to the Hearst family fortune—on Lookout Mountain across the Panamint Valley.) Popular for its stunning vistas is the vigorous 14-mile round-trip hike or backpack into the piñon pines atop **Telescope Peak,** best for wildflowers from May through July (snow and ice gear usually required for winter climbs). Easier and equally scenic is the eight-mile round-trip **Wildrose Peak** hike.

For some extra excitement on the way west, take winding **Wildrose-Trona Rd.** (gravel in places) down into the southern Panamint Valley.

The route west from Stovepipe Wells via Highway 190 quickly leads up and over the Panamint Mountains and then down into the Panamint Valley before rolling on toward Lone Pine and the eastern slope of the Sierra Nevada. Reasonably accessible national park attractions include the **Panamint Dunes** (visible from Father Crowley Point) in the northern Panamint Valley, **Darwin Falls,** and **Lee Flat Joshua Tree Forest.** Intrepid travelers in search of solitude might seek the road less traveled past Lee Flat and on into **Saline Valley,** a wild wonderland equally accessible from near Lone Pine in the north.

Panamint Dunes

About five miles east of Panamint Springs, on the north side of the highway, is Panamint Dunes Road. To reach these lovely sand dunes, take the road skirting the dry lake as far as feasible, then walk the rest of the way—a four-mile drive followed by a vigorous four- or five-mile hike (as always in these parts, bring water) and an all-day journey, almost enjoyable in cooler months. Though not California's tallest dunes, these are among the most beautiful—a sea of undulating sand stars, some reaching to 250 feet tall. Come for the peak wildflower bloom in spring, for sunrise and sunset photo ops anytime but summer.

Darwin Falls

A genuine surprise in the midst of bone-dry desert, 60-foot-high Darwin Falls serves as focal point for the park's Darwin Canyon oasis. Fresh, cool water cascades onto moss-covered rocks, pooling here as a rare year-round water source critical for both area and migratory wildlife. Named for Dr. Darwin French, who led a party of prospectors through the area in the 1860s, the waterfalls' source is several miles away at Miller Springs.

To get here, via good dirt road, turn south from Highway 190 onto Darwin Canyon Road; the turnoff is one mile west of Panamint Springs. Continue 2.5 miles and turn southwest onto a rougher dirt spur. The parking area is about a half-mile farther. From the trailhead, Darwin Falls is a quarter-mile walk/scramble. Equipped and experienced rock climbers can heft their way up the falls. It's also possible to drive to Upper Darwin Falls and China Gardens; follow the main road up the wash.

Saline Valley
Though a recent addition to Death Valley National Park, Saline Valley is one of the area's most spectacular "secrets"—and at least regionally famous for its long-running and very popular people's hot springs spa—a laid-back, clothing-optional collection of concrete pools that comes complete with pit toilets and primitive campgrounds.

Bordered on the west by the Inyo Mountains and on the east by the Saline and Last Chance Ranges, north-south Saline Valley roughly parallels the distance between Big Pine and Lone Pine, just to the west. Aside from the hot springs, attractions include hikes up **Saline Peak** and into **McElvoy, Beveridge,** and **Hunter canyons** (all three feature waterfalls) as well as the historically curious 1913 **salt tram** designed for Daisy Canyon.

Elevations along the way range from the valley floor's 1100 feet to 7200 feet; temperatures can range from a low of 20°F in winter to 120°F in summer. Though much of the road is graveled or graded, four-wheel-drive or high-clearance vehicles are highly recommended. Aside from bad patches in the road itself, flash floods, snow, devilish dust storms, and the hot sun are the primary potential hazards. Be sure to gas up, bring water, food, and other essentials—no services available—and check road conditions and weather reports before heading out. Also check at the park visitor center or area ranger stations for current maps and use guidelines. Spring and fall are most pleasant.

To start the trip from the north, from Highway 168 turn south onto Eureka Valley Road then south again about 16 miles later, at the pass atop the Inyo Mountains (gravel road, not necessarily marked). To start the trip from the south, take the Saline Valley Road turnoff (between Panamint Springs and Owens Lake) east from Highway 190, bear left at the first Y (about four miles in), then take the Grapevine Canyon branch (west) about ten miles farther along.

Lee Flat Joshua Tree Forest
If you're entering Saline Valley from the south, Lee Flat Joshua Tree Forest is a major attraction en route. Noted for its exceptionally tall Joshua trees—these oddly shaped yucca plants grow to more than 30 feet tall—this vast forest thrives in the northern Mojave Desert because of the high elevation and cooler temperatures. From Highway 190 about 14 miles west of Panamint Springs, turn north onto Saline Valley Road. At the end of the pavement on Saline Valley Road, take either gravel road; the one to the left goes deeper into the forest, all the way up to Lee Flat. Best visited any time but summer.

PRACTICAL DEATH VALLEY

STAYING AND EATING IN DEATH VALLEY

More than 1.2 million visitors make the desert trek to Death Valley each year, most of these arriving during the mild-weather winter season. Since the park takes in 3.3 million acres, you'd think there would be plenty of room for everyone. But 90 percent of the park is wilderness, after all, and visitor facilities are appropriately limited. Though Death Valley offers deluxe and family-style digs, due to an abundance of area campgrounds it's possible to do Death Valley on the cheap. Without some strategy, though, don't be too surprised if there's no room at the inn—or at area campgrounds.

Staying at Furnace Creek

As the human-centered hub of Death Valley, Furnace Creek is the park's most popular accommodations and restaurant option. Star of the show is the elegant and appropriately eccentric **Furnace Creek Inn,** snuggled into a hillside palm-tree oasis a mile south of the park visitor center. Originally part of Greenland Ranch, the 68-room hotel at Furnace Creek was built by the Pacific Coast Borax Company in 1927 as part of its package-tour railroad travel promotion. An adobe-and-stone villa with red-tiled roofs and lush landscaping, this onetime tourist lure is still some attraction. Stylishly refurbished and decorated in pastel desert hues, most rooms feature fireplaces, ceiling fans, cable TV, refrigerators, and tiled bathrooms with whirlpool tubs. The Furnace Creek Inn also offers full fitness facilities, an 18-hole golf course (fee), horseback riding (fee), archery, tennis, spring-fed pool (heated naturally to 84°F), saunas, the superb Inn Dining Room—*the* Death Valley dining destination, elegant casual; no jeans, shorts, or T-shirts—and the new Lobby Lounge. This adult-oriented resort is now open year-round, for the first time in its history. Rates can drop some during off seasons, but are still $230–350 per night in the high season for two (higher with meals),

with minimum stay requirements on weekends, holidays, and other peak times. Make reservations at least two months in advance.

A decent family-friendly choice year-round is the **Furnace Creek Ranch** motel, up the road near the visitor center. With comfortable, attractive motel rooms conveniently located near the visitor center in the middle of the park, Furnace Creek Ranch is quite popular with retirees, foreign tourists, and families—thus the playground, spring-fed pool, tennis courts, hayrides, and relatively inexpensive restaurants. Rates are $97–174, $5 higher on holidays and some weekends. There's also a small first-come, first-served campground with hookups.

For ranch-style fare, mosey on over to the **Wrangler Buffet,** which serves cafeteria-style breakfast and lunch by day—nothing fancy, just inexpensive and filling. Come nightfall it's a more ambitious **Wrangler Steak House,** specializing in steaks, chicken, and desert-style seafood. Another option is the **49er Café,** serving breakfast, lunch, and dinner. As might be expected, on prime-time weekends hungry hordes descend on available food service facilities; at times it can be a long wait.

For information about both the Furnace Creek Inn and the Furnace Creek Ranch, contact: **Furnace Creek Inn & Ranch Resort,** P.O. Box 1, Death Valley, CA 92328; call 760/786-2345 or toll-free 800/236-7916 (central reservations); www.furnacecreekresort.com. To dial the Inn directly, call 760/786-2361.

Campers have several national park campgrounds to choose from, with some campsites—in little more than an elaborate parking lot—designed for wintering "snowbirds" and their RVs. For camping information, see Camping in Death Valley, below.

Staying at Stovepipe Wells

Twenty-four miles from the maddening crowds, **Stovepipe Wells Village** in many ways offers the quintessential Death Valley stay. Launched in the lonesome desert as "Bungalow City" in 1926, this venerable 83-room motel features the basic modern comforts—sans TVs and telephones—along with steer-head light fixtures, oxen-yoke headboards, and other eccentric decorative touches that honor Death Valley's history. And it's still quiet and unhurried here.

Amenities and associated facilities include a swimming pool, general store, restaurant (in summer, breakfast and dinner only) and the colorful Badwater Saloon—built with timbers from an old area mine. (Ranger station, gas station, campground, and airstrip nearby.) Rates:$88 per couple. For information and reservations call 760/786-2387 (fax 760-786-2389) or write to Furnace Creek Inn & Ranch Resort (see above).

Staying at Panamint Springs

The newest resort destination *in* Death Valley National Park is the private **Panamint Springs Resort,** (775) 482-7680, www.deathvalley.com, just inside the park's new western boundary, 48 miles east of Lone Pine and 31 miles west of Stovepipe Wells. The Western-style facilities include 14 motel rooms (Moderate), campground with RV sites (full hookups $20) and tent sites ($10), store, and restaurant and bar. Pets welcome (deposit).

Camping in Death Valley

Some people would happily pitch tents or park their RVs in Death Valley and stay the entire winter—which is why there's a 30-day total limit for the October 1 through September 30 "camping year" (14-day limit at popular Furnace Creek Campground). Year-round **Furnace Creek Campground** just north of the visitor center offers 136 campsites, some shaded, open all year. Sites are $16 per night in winter, $10 in summer, and the facilities are limited to water, flush toilets, dump station, tables, and fireplaces. These are the only individual Death Valley campsites that are reservable, essential from Oct. 15–April 15; call toll-free 800/365-2267 or reserve online at http://reservations.nps.gov. Almost overwhelming: the 1,000 RV and tent sites across the highway at **Sunset Campground** (access road across from Furnace Creek Ranch), $10 per night, strictly first-come, first-camped (no fires allowed), open October through April. Take the same turnoff to reach **Texas Springs Campground,** nestled into the hills above the Furnace Creek Inn. For the 92 sites

here—tent camping with limited RV sites (and dump station)—it's $12 per night on a first-come basis, open only Oct. 15–April 15. Facilities include potable water, flush toilets, tables, and fireplaces. Tent campers, get as close to the hills as possible for some protection from the wind. The two group camping sites here are reservable ($40 per night), even in summer, by calling 760/786-3247.

In the far north, near Scotty's Castle, is year-round **Mesquite Spring Campground,** small (30 sites), unshaded, but scenically situated, with all the basics—picnic tables, fireplaces, water, flush toilets—for $10 per night.

In the west, large, open **Stovepipe Wells Campground** north of the highway near the village has water and flush toilets but most sites comes sans picnic tables and fireplaces, $10 per night. Dump station available. In March, April, and other times the winds—and sand from the dunes just a few miles to the east—can create unsettling sandstorms. For tent campers, hunkering down near perimeter trees is the best defense. Open Oct. 15–April 15. Campers also will find 10 free tents-only campsites at **Emigrant Junction Campground** with picnic tables, potable water and flush toilets, open April through October. No fires are allowed at either.

Death Valley's other three campgrounds are sky-high, comparatively, at Wildrose and beyond—not an area suitable for campers, trailers, or RVs. Even some passenger cars have a rough time with the S-turns on this twisted road. But a special reward waits for those who can make the grade; all three are free. **Wildrose Campground,** with 30 campsites, is open all-year (weather permitting) but has no drinking water. The other two—**Thorndike** at an elevation of 7500 feet, and **Mahogany Flat** at 8200 feet—are quite small, with no water available. Other facilities at all three are quite basic—just tables, fireplaces, and pit toilets. No campfires were allowed at either of the latter, at last report.

At all Death Valley campgrounds, campfires are allowed only in designated fireplaces (no wood collecting allowed) though portable stoves are fine even in the backcountry. "Quiet time" is 10 P.M.–7 A.M.; generators are allowed in all campgrounds except Texas Springs, 7 A.M.–7 P.M. Pets must be leashed.

Other Area Accommodations

New in 1997, the 10-bed **HI-AYH Desertaire Hostel** is in Tecopa, just an hour drive from Death Valley. Rates are $13–15 per person per night. For more information, contact: HI-AYH Desertaire Hostel, 2000 Old Spanish Trail Hwy., P.O. Box 306, Tecopa, CA 92389, 760/852-4580 or toll-free 877/907-1265; www.hostelweb.com. Another hosteling option, for those who don't mind some driving, is the charming HI-AYH-affiliated **Winnedumah Hotel** in Independence (northwest from Death Valley, in the eastern shadow of the Sierra Nevada), 760/878-2040, fax 760/878-2833, www.hostelweb.com, where hostel beds are $18, linen and breakfast included. Quite reasonable and homey hotel rooms are also available

If you'll be attending a performance at Marta Becket's Amargosa Opera House—see Death Valley Area Diversions, below—why not stay in her hotel? The sometimes-open-sometimes-not **Amargosa Hotel** in Death Valley Junction, east of Death Valley at the junction of Highways 190 and 127, won't be mistaken for Death Valley's upmarket Furnace Creek Inn. But here you pay for a different kind of atmosphere, something simpler and probably more comfortable for artsy desert adventurers. The 12 rooms here do have private bathrooms. The hotel is open for business only from October through mid-May (closed after Mother's Day). Rates: $50–70. For more information: Amargosa Hotel, P.O. Box 8, Death Valley Junction, CA 92328, 760/852-4441, fax 760/852-4138.

Motel accommodations are also available in a variety of towns within 50 to 150 miles of Death Valley, from Shoshone and Beatty to Ridgecrest, Lone Pine, and Independence. The visitor center can provide a complete listing. Or contact the **Death Valley Chamber of Commerce**, in Shoshone, at 760/852-4524; www.deathvalley-chamber.org.

DEATH VALLEY AREA DIVERSIONS

Most people come to Death Valley to unplug themselves from urban concerns. Reading a good book, hiking, sight-seeing, and attending interpretive ranger talks are entertainment enough, though anyone undergoing electronic withdrawal can easily find TV sets and electrical outlets. Close to Death Valley are two social compromises—the **Amargosa Opera House** in Death Valley Junction and **Tecopa Hot Springs.**

The social event of the year, though, is the annual **Death Valley Encampment,** usually scheduled during the second week in November—a five-day Western fest celebrating the valley's first pioneers and sponsored by the Death Valley '49ers. Events include competitions such as the Old Prospectors Race, Gold Panning Championships, Artists' Quick-Draw, several rounds of the Fiddlers Contest, even a Horseshoe Tournament. Midfestival, survivors of the Encampment's 125-mile Desert Trail Ride from Ridgecrest straggle in—too late for the Pioneer Dress-up Parade and the Hootenanny Hoedown Breakfast but just in time for cowboy poetry, country-western music, dancing, and the Tale Tales Contention & Sing-along at Stovepipe Wells. Proceeds from this event and other '49er projects provide college scholarships for students at Death Valley High School in Shoshone. For current details, see www.deathvalley49ers .org.

Tecopa Hot Springs

Hot mineral springs once popular with the Paiute Indians are the main attraction here. Free public baths—featuring separate men's and women's bathhouses and a "no swimsuits" policy—are surrounded by a surreal landscape of travel trailers (typically painted white to reflect the sun's heat) parked atop the white borax-crusted ground. Baths are free, open daily, 24 hours (except when closed for cleaning). Campsites with hookups are $8 per night; $6.50 without. The park also has weekly and monthly rates. The activity center is open 9 A.M. to 9 P.M. To get here: From Highway 127 beyond the southeastern entrance to Death Valley National Park, exit at Old Spanish Trail Highway and turn north onto Tecopa Hot Springs Road. For more information, contact: **Tecopa Hot Springs County Park,** P.O. Box 158, Tecopa, CA 92389, 760/852-4264.

Amargosa Opera House

Certainly the most unusual entertainment attraction in the California desert is the cleverly cornball one-woman show performed by Marta Becket at the Amargosa Opera House, a stand-up presence at the junction of Highway 127 and Highway 190. Becket, whose original "On with the Show" dance-pantomimes tell the story of life in Death Valley Junction, was a ballet dancer in New York City before arriving here in 1968. She owns the opera house and hotel—and painted the astonishing surrealistic murals that decorate both.

Doors open at 7:45 P.M., and performances start at 8:15 P.M. Admission is $10 adults, $8 children (ages 1–12). But get your tickets early since the show is often sold out. At last report— the schedule here can change from year to year—shows were offered on Saturday night only in October, December and January, and on both Saturday and Monday nights in November, February, March, and April. For more information, contact: Amargosa Opera House, P.O. Box 8, Death Valley Junction, CA 92328, 760/ 852-4441, fax 760/852-4138.

DEATH VALLEY INFORMATION AND ESSENTIALS

Death Valley Information
Among basic practical facts affecting Death Valley visitors: General park admission is $10 per vehicle ($20 for an annual pass) and $5 for walk-ins, bike-ins, motorcyclists, and people on horseback. All vehicles—including bicycles—must stay on established roads at all times. No target practice or other weapons use is allowed in the park. Collecting, damaging, or disturbing any park feature, be it plant, animal, or mineral, is strictly forbidden. Abandoned mine areas are designated for day use only. Pets must be leashed at all times. Backcountry hiking, backpacking, and camping are allowed in many areas, with no permits required; check with park rangers for current regulations. Considering the unforgiving nature of the terrain, it's prudent to complete a backcountry registration form (voluntary) before setting out on any independent trek.

The **Death Valley National Park Visitor Center** and museum at Furnace Creek, 760/2331, open daily 8 A.M.–6 P.M., is the essential all-purpose information stop. After an introduction to local history and natural history, inquire here about road, trail, and weather conditions—and about any special safety or other precautions deemed prudent for more obscure trips and backcountry travel. Maps, books, hiking guides, and various other useful publications are available here. There's another official Death Valley visitor center at the ranger station in Beatty, Nevada, at the junction of Highways 95 and 374, (775) 553-2200, with abundant information but more limited exhibits. Other park ranger stations are at **Grapevine** (near Scotty's Castle), **Stovepipe Wells**, and **Wildrose**.

For current park information, write **Death Valley National Park**, P.O. Box 579, Death Valley, CA 92328, or call 760/786-2331, fax 760/ 786-3283; www.nps.gov/deva.

Death Valley Essentials
Get gasoline, water, and at least basic supplies at either Stovepipe Wells or Furnace Creek. Within the park, gas is also available at Scotty's Castle (during regular business hours only). Beyond the park, fuel stops include Shoshone (and Baker) to the southeast; Amargosa Valley (formerly known as Lathrop Wells) and Beatty in Nevada to the east; Trona (and Ridgecrest) to the southwest; and Lone Pine to the northwest.

Furnace Creek is also the place for just general gabbing, getting your hair done, getting towed (by AAA-affiliated service stations), going to church, grabbing a hot shower, gift and grocery shopping, and golfing 200 feet below sea level. Other Furnace Creek amenities and services include a 24-hour Laundromat, full-service post office, swimming pools, horseback and carriage rides (seasonal), and guided Death Valley bus tours. For current information, refer to the tabloid *Death Valley Visitor Guide* distributed at park entrances.

OTHER HIGH DESERT HIGHLIGHTS

BARSTOW

A big city by Mojave Desert standards, present-day Barstow is the de facto desert crossroads—the place I-15, I-40, Highway 58, Highway 257, and the Union Pacific and Santa Fe Railroads converge. It's no real surprise that the town was named for the 10th president of the Santa Fe Railroad, William Barstow Strong, though it first made the map as a stop for cross-country wagon train expeditions. It was later a supply station for Death Valley adventurers. Barstow's historical heyday came during the gold and silver mining boom of the 1880s and '90s, when nearby Calico—now a gussied-up ghost town—was in its prime.

Conveniently situated halfway between Los Angeles and Las Vegas, these days Barstow is still the desert's central information, service, and supply stop. Barstow even has two factory outlet shopping malls. Aside from air-conditioned motels and restaurants—including the highly unusual McDonald's franchise here, housed in railroad cars—until recently Barstow's primary attraction was the **Mojave River Valley Museum,** 270 E. Virginia Way, 760/256-5452, open daily 11 A.M.–4 P.M. Definitely worth a look is the "Headless Horseman," a hapless human skeleton found, butcher knives stuck between his ribs, still astride the bones of his mount. (Horseman's skull was eventually found by the contractor who dug him up, some distance away.) Newly rebuilt downtown, from the original bricks, is Barstow's classy Santa Fe Railroad depot, **Casa del Desierto** ("House of the Desert"), which housed a Harvey House restaurant from 1911 through the 1950s. For some idea of Harvey House's other-era significance, watch the 1946 Judy Garland film *Harvey Girls.* Barstow's Harvey House now houses the new two-room **Mother Road Museum,** 681 N. First Ave., 760/255-1890, commemorating the city's Route 66 highway history.

For more information about the area, contact the **Barstow Chamber of Commerce** at the Mercado Mall, 222 E. Main St., Ste. 216, P.O. Box 698, Barstow, CA 92312, 760/256-8617; www.barstowchamber.com. For area recreation and camping suggestions, contact the **Barstow Field Office,** U.S. Bureau of Land Management, 2601 Barstow Rd., Barstow, CA 92311, 760/252-6000; www.ca.blm.gov /barstow.

Practical Barstow

Beyond bare desert camping, the cheapest available stay is **Calico Ghost Town** on Ghost Town Road about 10 miles northeast of Barstow off I-15 near Yermo. This San Bernardino County park offers full RV hookups and off-highway camper and tent sites with the luxuries of restrooms, running water, and hot showers. Also available: small cabins and a bunkhouse that sleeps up to 20 people. (For details, see Calico Ghost Town, below.) If you're heading west to Rainbow Basin, pitch the tent at the BLM's first-come, first-camped **Owl Canyon Campground,** at the beginning of the loop near Fossil Bed Road. If heading east toward Joshua Tree, consider **Afton Canyon Campground.** Both are $6 per night. Water is trucked in weekly, but it's advisable to bring your own. For more information, contact the BLM's Barstow Field Office (see above).

In Barstow, "motel row" is Main Street—Route 66 in the Mother Road's glory days. Most motels are scattered along E. Main, easily accessible to I-15 and I-40; decent, quite inexpensive choices abound. For an economical overnight, best bets include the **Best Motel,** 1281 E. Main, 760/256-6836, and the **Stardust Inn** farther from the freeway at 901 E. Main, 760/256-7116. Both are $34–45 and feature clean rooms, cable TV, and swimming pools. A bit more upmarket are the **Holiday Inn Express,** 1861 W. Main, 760/256-1300, fax 760/256-6807, www.basshotels.com/holiday-inn, rates: $75–101, and the **Best Western Desert Villa Inn,** 1984 E. Main (adjacent to I-40, east of I-5), 760/256-1781, fax 760/256-9265, www.bestwestern.com, rates: $58–149. Both have swankier rooms with cable TV and free movies, swimming pools and hot tubs, and plenty of restaurants in the neighborhood if not on-site.

Barstow has its share of restaurants and fast fooderies, most of these near freeway exits in town. *The* place, though, is the **Idle Spurs Restaurant** outside town at 29557 W. Hwy. 58, 760/256-8888. Like the desert itself, from a distance the restaurant seems nondescript. Inside, though, the eclectic decorative memorabilia collection revives the Wild West—just the right ambience for generous steaks, chicken, and other meat-and-potatoes selections. Meat is the main attraction—dig that Spur Burger—but try to leave room for homemade apple pie. Special menu for the Little Spurs too. Idle Spurs is open weekdays for lunch, daily for dinner; closed Thanksgiving, Christmas, and New Year's Day.

NEAR BARSTOW

A number of attractions near Barstow are worth exploring. These include, to the north, Rainbow Basin National Natural Landmark, nearby Inscription Canyon (Black Canyon), the largest Native American petroglyph (rock art) "gallery" still open to the general public, and NASA's **Goldstone Deep Space Communications Complex** at

---

GETTING SOME KICKS ON ROUTE 66

America's most famous roadway in the days before the interstate system, Route 66 once stretched west from Chicago, Illinois, to Santa Monica, California, sauntering through dozens of other cities and towns en route. Known also as the nation's "Mother Road" (thanks to John Steinbeck) and the "Main Street of America," the highway was immortalized in the popular imagination—a fact captured in music by Bob Troupe's *Route 66!*, performed by Nat King Cole and the King Cole Trio.

But even immortals have a short shelf-life in America. Route 66's days were numbered by 1956, when the U.S. Congress approved the Interstate Highway Program. Its official epitaph came in 1985, when the federal government "decertified" the 2,400-mile route as a national highway. Swaths of old Route 66 were paved over by faster freeways; some remnants were unofficially reassigned to scenic ghost town status.

In recent years America seems ready, again, to roll down its favorite highway, with new historical markers making it much easier to retrace the Mother Road. In California, the desert highway well beyond present population centers is most interesting; the route is all but lost from coastal Santa Monica through the streaming chaos of Los Angeles. But if coming from that direction, pick up old Route 66 in Pasadena. On Fair Oaks Avenue in South Pasadena, the **Fair Oaks Pharmacy** boasts an authentic soda-fountain interior transplanted here from Joplin, Missouri—a Route 66 shrine from the other end of the line. The main Pasadena route, though, passes through **Old Pasadena,** the city's vibrant historic district along Colorado Boulevard—the Rose Bowl parade route—before heading east and becoming Foothill Boulevard.

Surviving highlights along Foothill include the aging Mayan-Toltec **Aztec Hotel** in Monrovia, the down-home downtown surrounding **Claremont Colleges** in Claremont, the sadly seedy **Wigwam Motel** in Rialto (a sign here says: "Do It in a Tee Pee"), and the stunning **California Theater** in downtown San Bernardino.

In San Bernardino, Cajon Boulevard technically defines the route. The alternative way up and over Cajon Pass is I-15, which overlays much of the original road. Beyond the pass ribbons of old Route 66 are now called the **National Trails Highway.** In Barstow the route becomes Main Street. Beyond Barstow (off I-40) the National Trails Highway rolls almost all the way into Arizona.

To make a commemorative stop along Route 66, there are at least two choices. Victorville pays homage to America's Main Street at the **California Route 66 Museum** on D Street in the town's spruced-up downtown, 760/951-0436; http://califrt66museum.org. To get there, exit I-15 at D Street (Hwy. 118); the museum is on D between Fifth and Sixth. Barstow, too, has a Route 66 museum—the two-room **Mother Road Museum,** 681 N. First Ave., 760/255-1890, honoring the city's Route 66 highway history. The museum is housed in the newly rebuilt (from the original bricks) Santa Fe Railroad depot, **Casa del Desierto** ("House of the Desert"), which housed a Harvey House restaurant from 1911 through the 1950s.

Fort Irwin, where the **Fort Irwin 11th Armored Cavalry Regiment Museum** memorializes local U.S. Army history and Vietnam's Blackhorse Regiment. To the east via I-15 is Calico Ghost Town, a gift from Walter Knott (of Knott's Berry Farm) to San Bernardino County, and the Calico Early Man Archaeological Site. To the east via I-40, amid other Daggett-area solar developments, is the site of the innovative **Solar Two Power Plant,** an experimental research project successfully undertaken by the U.S. Department of Energy in conjunction with Southern California Edison and other companies. Considered the world's most advanced solar power plant, while it was in operation Solar Two used a molten salt technology to collect and store the sun's energy—at an effiiiency of 97 percent—and, unlike other solar piwer plants, even at night delivered electricity "on demand." Farther along

is the odd old desert town of **Newberry Springs,** a spot in the road along old Route 66 (National Trails Hwy.) where the movie *Bagdad Café* was filmed. In real life, the café's name is the Sidewinder.

Rainbow Basin National Natural Landmark

The rainbows here are solid stone—sedimentary coats of many colors within canyon walls that have been folded and faulted under great geologic stress. Exceptional insect fossils and the encrusted remains of camels, dog-bears, mastodons, three-toed horses, and other 15-million-year-old creatures also grace the area. (Look but don't touch.) The geological record is so visible, and the fossil supply so rich, that geologists and paleontologists are never too rare in these parts. Scientists from around the world date both fossil and stone samples from the framework established at Rainbow Basin. To stay long enough to understand why, park yourself at **Owl Canyon Campground,** at the beginning of the loop near Fossil Bed Road, $6 per night. If you have the time—and a four-wheel-drive vehicle—also plan an all-day excursion via Black Canyon to the BLM's **Inscription Canyon** petroglyph site.

Rainbow Basin is about eight miles northwest of Barstow. To get here from there, head west on Highway 58 to Fort Irwin Road; turn north and continue 5.5 miles to Fossil Bed Road. Turn left (west) and continue for several more miles. From Fossil Bed Road, take the scenic six-mile loop, or explore various washes on foot—though not after a rainstorm, since the area is vulnerable to flash flooding. For more information about Rainbow Basin, contact the BLM's Barstow Field Office, 760/252-6000; www.ca.blm.gov /barstow.

Calico Ghost Town

Not many genuine ghost towns still offer sit-down meals, hot fudge sundaes, live theater, or craft and gift shops. But not many California mining camps survive as long as Calico. Most don't live long enough to worry how—or even if—history will remember them.

According to Calico's official biography, this wild (and wildly successful) silver mining town was born in 1881, wounded in 1893 when silver prices fell—and again in 1896 when borax fal-

ROY ROGERS–DALE EVANS MUSEUM

Movie-cowboy kitsch displayed here includes Roy Rogers lunch boxes, comic books, and jigsaw puzzles. Most memorable, though, is Roy's famous palomino horse Trigger, co-star of countless TV shows and westerns. After Trigger died in 1963 he was stuffed—the museum prefers the term "mounted"—and then saddled up as if ready to hit the trail. Fresh from a million-dollar renovation, the museum now includes new exhibits, interactive video displays, and two theaters.

The Roy Rogers–Dale Evans Museum, 15650 Seneca Rd. in Victorville, 760/243-4547 (recorded) or 760/243-4548, www.royrogers .com ("the first cowboy in cyberspace"), is open daily 9 A.M.–5 P.M. (closed Easter, Thanksgiving, and Christmas). Admission is $8 adults, $7 seniors and students, $5 children 6–12 (age 5 and under free). You can't miss it—"It's a big ol' fort sittin' out in the field." Even from I-15 you'll see the giant Trigger rearing up outside the fort.

Keep your ears peeled for news about **ROGERSDALE, U.S.A.,** a huge entertainment and retail complex to be located somewhere in Southern California—near Temecula, at last report.

ghost town

TOM MYERS PHOTOGRAPHY

tered—and then finally declared dead and buried in 1907. In its heyday Calico was populated by 4,000 people, some 400 houses, 22 saloons, and six railroads, the entire metropolis tucked into Wall Street Canyon in the many-colored Calico Mountains. The legendary Wyatt Earp used to show up from time to time just to play poker.

Though the Calico mining district at one time registered 500 mines and mining claims, the town's own noteworthies included the Bismarck, Maggie, Odessa, Oriental, and Silver King. The Silver King *was* king—the town's first and richest mine. Of the $130 million in mineral wealth harvested here—$86 million in silver, $44 million in borax—$10 million came from the Silver King alone. So rich was the King's ore that much of it was carted out in almost pure half-ton hunks.

In a sense, the Silver King saved Calico.

Only old mine shafts, rusted railroad tracks, and a few faltering structures would stand here today but for the intervention of Walter Knott (of Knott's Berry Farm fame) and his passion for ghost towns and Wild West lore. Knott, whose uncle made his fortune as a partner in the Silver King, bought and began resurrecting the 60-acre Calico site in 1951. After restoring the few surviving original structures and reconstructing some of the rest, Knott gave Calico to the county in 1966.

Though Calico has been spit-shined and prettied up for visitors—sometimes entire tour buses full—beyond its cornball kitsch is an underlying authenticity. Wander the entire town and imagine its past. Explore the excavated ruins of Calico's **Chinatown.** The narrow gauge **Calico-Odessa Railroad** tours the town's history, passing even the cavelike mountain dwelling where miners once lived. A walk through the **Maggie Mine,** with its low ceilings and thin air, is a realistic reminder of the good ol' days. Miners worked as employees of company-owned mines; some did get rich—or very well off—by working 12-hour days, hammering away at hard rock with a pick and shovel for $25 per week.

During special seasonal events—extra admission charged—Calico becomes so popular that the campground here and the entire town of Barstow are overrun with Wild Westerners. These family-friendly celebrations include the **Civil War Reenactment** held on Presidents Day Weekend in February; the **Calico Spring Festival,** a bluegrass festival and hootenanny held on Mother's Day weekend in May; the **Calico Days** Wild West parade, National Gunfight Stunt Championships, burro run, and 1880s-vintage games on Columbus Day weekend in October; the **Ghost Haunt** in late October; the **Heritage Fest** on Thanksgiving Weekend; and **Christmas in Calico** in early December.

Calico is about 10 miles northeast of Barstow, just off I-15. Exit at Ghost Town Road and follow the signs. Calico is closed on Christmas but otherwise "open" daily 8 A.M. to dusk, its shops, services, and tours in business from 9 to 5. Regular admission is $6 adults, $3 children. The campground comes complete with restrooms and hot showers ($22 per night with full hookups, $18 otherwise). Small camping cabins are also available ($28 per night plus deposit refundable at checkout), and, for groups of up to 20, a bunkhouse ($60 for 12 people, $5 each extra person). Camping fees include park admission.

For more information—and to make group tour arrangements or overnight reservations—contact: Calico Ghost Town, P.O. Box 638, Yermo, CA 92398, 760/254-2122 or toll-free 800/862-2542, fax 760/254-2047; www.calico-town.com.

Calico Early Man Archaeological Site

Since the "Calico Dig" began in November 1964, unearthing a variety of Pleistocene chipped-stone tools, archaeologists have radically revised theories about when humanity arrived on the continent. One of the most important archaeological finds in North America, this is the only continental dig directed by Dr. Louis S. B. Leakey—best known for his discoveries in East Africa's Olduvai Gorge—who worked here until his death in 1972. Scientists subsequently dated the calcium carbonate surrounding the encrusted artifacts as about 200,000 years old. The current speculation is that Calico Early Man may have been a now-extinct species, perhaps *Homo erectus* or *Homo sapiens neandertalensis*. Tour the excavation pits and stone-tool exhibits on either guided or self-guided tours—a chance for the kids to really "dig" the science of archaeology.

The Calico Early Man Site is open Wednesday 12:30 P.M.–4:30 P.M., Thurs.–Sun. 9 A.M.–4:30 P.M., closed Monday and Tuesday (also closed on July 4th, Thanksgiving, Christmas Eve, Christmas Day, and New Year's Day). Admission is $5 adults (one or two persons; $2.50 each additional adult in group), $2 seniors, and $1 children (age 12 and under). Additional donations are always appreciated. Guided site tours are offered on Wednesday at 1:30 and 3:30 P.M. and Thurs.–Sun. at 9:30 and 11:30 A.M. as well as 1:30 and 3:30 P.M. To get here: Head east from Barstow via I-15 for 12 miles and exit at Minneola Road; continue north about three miles (dirt road, by the dump).

For more information, contact: Calico Early Man Archaeological Site, P.O. Box 535, Yermo, CA 92398, 760/256-5102, or the San Bernardino County Museum, Friends of Calico Early Man Site, Attn. Maggie Foss, 2024 Orange Tree Ln., Redlands, CA 92374, 909/798-8570; www.co.san-bernardino.ca.us/museum.

RIDGECREST AND VICINITY

A shimmering mirage of concrete and condominiums, modern-day Ridgecrest sprang up out of the desert to keep company with the adjacent China Lake Naval Air Warfare Center, Weapons Division (NAWCW PNS). A major attraction here, in fact, is the new China Lake Weapons Museum, where all species of naval warfare innovation are on display. Another draw is the small Maturango Desert Museum, also the Northern Mojave Visitor Center, with its excellent introductory natural history and history exhibits and programs. Also nearby, just off Highway 178 on Randsburg-Wash Road about four miles east of Ridgecrest, are the Bureau of Land Management's **Wild Horse and Burro Corrals,** where nonnative wild things captured throughout the Southwest are penned pending adoption (open weekdays 7:30 A.M.–4 P.M., closed on federal holidays, tours by arrangement). The pens hold up to 1,300 animals. Peak seasons for the horse and burro roundup are fall through early spring.

For Ridgecrest area visitor information, stop by the Maturango Desert Museum (open daily; see below for details) or contact the **Ridgecrest Area Convention and Visitors Bureau,** 100 W. California Ave., Ridgecrest, CA 93555, 760/375-8202 or toll-free 800/847-4830; www.ridgenet.net. For information about nearby U.S. Bureau of Land Management attractions, and to find out about the Wild Horse Adoption program, contact the BLM's **Ridgecrest Field Office,** 300 S. Richmond Rd., 760/384-5400; www.ca.blm.gov/ridgecrest.

China Lake Weapons Museum

Officially known as the **U.S. Naval Museum of Armament and Technology,** the impressive new China Lake Weapons Museum officially opened in 2000—the result of a decadelong effort to establish a permanent Command center exhibit. Housed in the onetime Commissioned Officers' Mess building, the new museum includes refurbished exhibits once displayed at the China Lake Exhibit Center—a virtual menagerie of military might including the Bat, the first homing missile, used in World War II; the Sidewinder, a dogfight missile; the Shrike anti-radiation missile; and the Vietnam-era Walleye. But it also offers much more, in its efforts to chronicle six decades of naval weapons and technological history—including the Lunar Soft Landing Vehicle, first test-driven at China Lake. Outdoor exhibits include a submarine-launched Polaris missile and a BOAR atomic rocket, projects with which China Lake was also heavily involved. The museum is in Building 500 on Pearl Harbor Way. For more information call 760/939-3105.

Maturango Desert Museum

This excellent regional museum was established in 1961 to help preserve the natural heritage of the Indian Wells Valley—historic and prehistoric. Exhibits illustrate the upper Mojave Desert's past and present—fossils, petroglyphs, gemstones, mining memorabilia, and the first space shuttle landing. Public education is one of museum's main missions. Real prizes here are the unusual museum-sponsored outings, including very popular tours of Little Petroglyph Canyon (a destination otherwise off-limits to the general public); reservations are required (fee). Also here: an art gallery, gift shop, Children's Discovery Area, and the Northern Mojave Visitor Center/Death Valley Tourist Center. Small museum admission.

The Maturango Desert Museum is right off China Lake Boulevard (Hwy. 178, the main drag) at 100 E. Las Flores Ave. in Ridgecrest, and is open daily 10 A.M.–5 P.M. (closed major holidays). For further information call 760/375-6900, fax 760/375-0479, or point your browser to www.maturango.org.

Trona Pinnacles

Fans of *Star Trek V: The Final Frontier* and other sci-fi flicks will recognize this otherworldly landscape—500 tufa towers, some more than 140 feet tall, rising from the bone-dry Searles Lake basin. Scientists speculate that these calcium carbonate spires formed 10,000 to 100,000 years ago, when this dry lake was a substantial inland body of water. These are the finest examples

of tufa towers in the United States. The area has been extensively mined since the 1870s, when borax was discovered. The predominant mineral, though, is trona—a double salt used in baking powder, soaps, and solvents.

Wear sturdy shoes when exploring Trona Pinnacles—an easy walk from the parking area—since tufa neatly slices human flesh. Avoid coming in summer, when the sun will broil whatever else is exposed, and after rains, since this low-lying area is vulnerable to sudden flash floods. To get here from Ridgecrest, continue east of Ridgecrest via Highway 178 for about 20 miles and turn right onto Pinnacles Road; you'll reach the pinnacles in 5.5 miles, but it's another mile or so to the parking area. The dirt road—slow going, washboardy sand, then gravel—is suited for passenger cars with good ground clearance, but can be treacherous after a heavy rain. For more information, call the Ridgecrest BLM office at 760/384-5400.

Fossil Falls

Northwest from Ridgecrest and north of Little Lake, just off Highway 395 about 20 miles north of the Highway 14 junction, is another intriguing natural attraction—Fossil Falls, a section of the Owens River Gorge lava field where the lava "falls"—actually, the fossil of a waterfall—were sculpted and smoothed by the once-rushing waters of the ancient river. To get here: Exit at Cinder Cone Road, head east a half-mile; turn right and head south for about a quarter-mile on dirt road; then turn left (east again) and continue a half-mile to the parking lot. Paint blots mark the trailhead and the short trail.

Rand Mining District

Due south of Ridgecrest, **Randsburg,** a "living ghost town" with tired tin buildings and eccentric antique shops, is typically the focal point of the Mojave Desert's historic Rand Mining District—late-1800s gold mining territory named after the Witwatersrand of South Africa. Nearby **Red Mountain** also grew up from mining camps, and **Johannesburg**—the only place around with right-angle intersections and straight streets—was built to serve both camps. The excellent **Randsburg Desert Museum** on Butte Avenue, affiliated with the Kern County Museum in Bakersfield and open only on weekends and long-weekend holidays, 10 A.M.–5 P.M., tells the whole story. (The town is "open" daily.) A small shaded picnic area is adjacent to the museum.

Stop by the **Randsburg General Store** for supplies and to find out what's going on. Another best bet for area information and supplies is the **Frontier Market** on Highway 395 in Johannesburg.

Red Rock Canyon State Park

The opening archaeological scenes of *Jurassic Park* and countless Westerns were filmed here in 4,000-acre Red Rock Canyon, something of a miniature Grand Canyon featuring some of the California desert's most unusual scenery. Fossil remains (no collecting) and ancient petroglyphs represent earlier historical periods. Though most people sightsee from the freeway—four-lane Highway 14 runs through Red Rock Canyon—stop at the visitor center for a proper introduction. On-foot exploration of these colorful "badlands"—a geologic transition zone between the Sierra Nevada and the Mojave Desert—is the main attraction. Day-use fee $2. **Ricardo Campground** is a fairly primitive, 50-unit camping facility at the base of Whitehouse Cliffs. Each campsite features a table and fire ring; drinking water is available (first-come, first-camped, $8 per night). To avoid the intense heat, visit any time but summer. Ranger-guided nature hikes are offered Feb.–May and Oct.–Nov. on Sunday at 9 A.M. Campfire programs are offered on Saturday nights, Feb.–May and Oct.–November.

Red Rock Canyon State Park is 25 miles northeast of Mojave on Highway 14. You can also get here from Randsburg, via two-lane desert Redrock-Randsburg Road straight across the desert (not advisable after rains, because of the danger of flash floods). For more information, contact: **California State Parks/Mojave Desert Information Center,** 43779 15th St. W. (at Ave. K) in Lancaster, 661/942-0662, www.calparksmojave.com. The center is open daily 10 A.M.–4 P.M. (closed on major holidays). Also inquire about **Tomo-Kahni** ("Winter Home"), the historical site of a Kawaiisu (Nuooah) village atop a ridge in the Tehachapi Mountains, open to the public only on guided tours.

Desert Tortoise Preserve

In 1994 the federal government designated more than six million acres of public lands, a dozen distinct areas, most of them in California—as critical habitat for the threatened desert tortoise. Twenty years earlier, the 21,000-acre Desert Tortoise Natural Area north of California City was established by the Nature Conservancy and other concerned citizen groups to protect *Gopherus agassizi,* the official state reptile. That preserve, now some 39.5 square miles, still protects the desert tortoise, listed as threatened on the federal Endangered Species list. Yet the population has plummeted. According to researchers, the preserve tortoise population dropped 91 percent between 1988 and 1995. The number of tortoises per square mile had dropped from 195 to 18. Researchers have since established that an upper respiratory infection is the likely culprit, the result of poor tortoise nutrition (due to habitat degradation), drought, and the release of captive desert tortoises—already ill with the disease—into the wild.

All the more reason for increased public awareness—and serious tortoise protection measures. If you're lucky enough to see a tortoise here, you're most likely to see one in spring, the season for mating, laying eggs, and grazing on the tender shoots of ephemeral wildflowers and grasses. Preserve visitors must slow to a tortoise's pace—watching, walking, and watching some more. Prime tortoise-watching time in the western Mojave Desert is March through May, when the desert tortoises are out from mid-morning to mid-afternoon—during the warm part of the day. Get more information at the preserve's Interpretive Center, with parking lot, information kiosk, restroom, and access to the preserve's self-guiding trails. Bring water (none is available here), camera, binoculars, sunscreen, and a hat with a brim.

The preserve's Interpretive Center is located about four miles northeast of California City, just off unpaved Randsburg-Mojave Road. To get here: From Highway 14 north of Mojave, exit onto California City Boulevard and head east 10 miles. Turn left (northeast) onto 20 Mule Team Parkway; after 1.5 miles, turn left onto Randsburg-Mojave Road. It's another 4.5 miles (dirt road) to the parking lot.

For more information, contact the nonprofit **Desert Tortoise Preserve Committee, Inc.** 4067 Mission Inn Ave., Riverside, CA 92501, 909/683-3872, fax 909/683-6949; www.tortoise-tracks.org.

MORE DESERT HIGHLIGHTS

Air Force Flight Test Center Museum

Edwards Air Force Base boasts many test-flight firsts—breaking the sound barrier for the first time, firing rocket engines for the first time, and bringing the U.S. space shuttle back to earth for the first time. These and other accomplishments are chronicled here. Outside and adjacent is three-acre **Blackbird Park,** the only place in the world displaying the Lockheed SR-71A, the A-12, and the once top-secret D-21 Drone.

The museum, 1100 Kincheloe at Edwards Air Force Base, is open Tues.–Sat. 9 A.M.–5 P.M., admission free. For more information, contact: **Air Force Flight Test Center Museum,** 661/277-8050, fax 661/277-8051. Access to Edwards is controlled; request a pass to visit the museum at any of the three base entrances. Free tours of air base operations and of NASA's **Dryden Flight Research Center** are also available. The 90-minute Dryden tours are offered Mon.–Fri., at 10:15 A.M. and 1:15 P.M., on a "reservation-only" basis. U.S. citizens must make reservations at least 72 hours in advance; foreign nationals, at least two weeks in advance. For information and reservations, call 661/276-3446 or 661/276-3460; www.dfrc.nasa.gov.

Antelope Valley California Poppy Reserve

This 1,745-acre Antelope Valley open-space preserve is famous for its fabulous spring display of the California poppy—the state flower—and other native wildflowers. Best visited during peak bloom from March to May, the poppy preserve features a picnic area and seven miles of trails, including a paved section for wheelchair access. In spring visitors can appreciate the state-of-the-art visitor center—dug into the hillside to conserve energy. During the ephemeral wild-flower season the preserve is open 24 hours a day, though the visitor center is open mid-March through mid-May only, 9 A.M.–5 P.M. on weekends, 9–4 on weekdays. In season, guided walks are scheduled on Saturday and Sunday at 11 A.M. and 1 P.M.; other nature walks are also scheduled. Call the visitor center at 661/742-1180 for wildflower bloom updates (spring only).

The preserve is 15 miles west of Highway 14. on Lancaster Road—an extension of Lancaster's Avenue I. Day-use is $2 per vehicle, $1 for seniors (mini buses $10, tour buses $20). A few miles west of the poppy reserve, on Lancaster Road at 210th Street W., is the state parks' 566-acre **Ripley Desert Woodland,** an unusually impressive stand of native Joshua trees and junipers open for hiking. For more information on both parks, contact: **California State Parks/ Mojave Desert Information Center,** 43779 15th St. W. (at Ave. K) in Lancaster, 661/942-0662; www.calparksmojave.com. The center is open daily 10 A.M.–4 P.M. (closed on major holidays).

Saddleback Butte State Park

This 2,955-acre Joshua tree woodland preserve suggests sights once common throughout Antelope Valley—even after the antelope disappeared. Stroll the short nature trail for an introduction to high-desert botany. Longer trails loop to the top of Saddleback Butte. Come in spring for wildflowers and the chance to spot a desert tortoise. A new 4.5-mile horse trail offers an equestrian option. Picnic areas feature ramadas for sun and wind protection, and include tables and char-wood grills. The 50-site family campground (no hot showers) features tables, cooking grills, flush toilets, and water, as well as protective ramadas. Saddleback Butte also features a reservable group camp.

Saddleback Butte is 17 miles east of Lancaster; the park entrance is on E. Avenue J at 170th Street. Day-use fee is $2, camping $8 per night (call for reservation information). For more information, contact: **California State Parks/ Mojave Desert Information Center,** 43779 15th St. W. (at Ave. K) in Lancaster, 661/942-0662; www.calparksmojave.com.

Antelope Valley Indian Museum

Near Saddleback Butte State Park and housed in a handcrafted chalet literally carved into the bedrock of Paiute Butte, the Antelope Valley Indian Museum was originally the home of its builder. The artist Howard Arden Edwards started this homesteading project in 1928 and filled his new home with artifacts representing the native cultures of California and the Southwest. Anthropologist Grace Oliver bought the Edwards homestead in 1938 and—adding her own substantial collection to his—established this museum.

Open weekends only, 11 A.M.–4 P.M., from late September to mid-June for self-guided tours (small fee), the museum is on E. Ave. M between 170th and 150th Sts., 2.5 miles southwest of Saddleback Butte State Park. For more information, call 661/946-3055; www.avim.av.org. Or contact **California State Parks/Mojave Desert Information Center,** 43779 15th St. W. (at Ave. K) in Lancaster, 661/942-0662; www.cal-parksmojave.com.

COURTESY AISLINN RACE

INLAND EMPIRE: SAN BERNARDINO AND RIVERSIDE

A TALE OF TWO CITIES AND COUNTIES

Boosterism, that brand of civic self-promotion aimed at boosting local business, built contemporary Southern California. All but passé in L.A., that philosophy is still embraced, unabashedly, in California's "Inland Empire" counties of San Bernardino and Riverside. It's no accident that their namesake cities are also serious rivals.

The city of Riverside boasts a University of California campus, while greater San Bernardino is home to California State University, San Bernardino and the private University of Redlands and Loma Linda University and Medical Center campuses.

The renowned and recently restored Mission Inn hotel is centerpiece of historic Riverside, yet downtown San Bernardino showcases the exquisite California Theatre for the Performing Arts.

San Bernardino hosts the annual National Orange Show Citrus Fair, as it has since 1911, but Riverside is the actual historic center of the area's navel orange industry—a status confirmed by the new California Citrus State Historic Park.

In at least one sense, both San Bernardino and Riverside are absolutely in step. As society marches on, so do the suburbs—shimmering, miragelike waves of vaguely Spanish-style red tile roofs stretching toward all horizons, threatening to landscape the desert with smog and other decidedly urban concerns.

Both San Bernardino and Riverside face radical population growth and demographic change. The region has long served as an affordable housing option for anyone willing to sacrifice family for "freeway flying" time to and from Los Angeles. In recent years the exodus from L.A. has become more multicultural, with over 40 percent of the counties' newest arrivals black, Asian, and Latino. Here as elsewhere, the heritage of the West is complex. These days it's often easier to find a traditional Mexican *charreada* than American-style rodeo.

Beyond the Two Cities
While the region twists into knots of freeway traffic, transforming itself into yet another new California, both Riverside and San Bernardino Counties offer surprising entrée into the great outdoors. From San Bernardino, possible getaways include the Big Bear and Lake Arrowhead mountain resort areas, plus San Gorgonio Mountain, centerpiece of the San Gorgonio Wilderness and the highest peak in Southern California.

Also in San Bernardino County: the southernmost part of Death Valley National Park, the vast Mojave National Preserve, and the California side of Lake Havasu along with other remnants of the Colorado River. In Riverside County, great escapes include Joshua Tree National Park and the vast desert, oases, and high-mountain majesty accompanying the golf and glitz of Palm Springs and idyllic Idyllwild and vicinity.

For more information on nearby mountain attractions, see Into The Mountains: Big Bear And Vicinity, below. For other nearby attractions, see The Deserts chapter.

SAN BERNARDINO: BIRTHPLACE OF McDONALD'S

Now a sprawling desert city of some 65 square miles, stretched out between old Route 66 and the Santa Ana River and invisibly sliced by the San Andreas Fault, San Bernardino was first an outpost of Mission San Gabriel and then settled, in the 1850s, by Mormons. This 4000-acre spread, the state's first significant "irrigation colony," was also once home to legendary lawman Wyatt Earp. In modern times San Bernardino is noteworthy as birthplace of both the Hell's Angels motorcycle clubs and the McDonald's fast-food restaurant chain.

More fascinating, though, is natural history—particularly San Bernardino's prehistoric **Arrowhead,** emblazoned into a hillside six miles northeast of town near the original Arrowhead Hot Springs Hotel (now a Christian conference center). The Arrowhead measures 1,115 feet long and 396 feet wide, totaling about seven acres in size. Made of light gray granite and decomposed white quartz with a vegetative veneer of white sage and weeds, the Arrowhead is quite distinct from both surrounding geology and adjacent greasewood chaparral. Though the Cahuilla and other native peoples tell various stories to explain

You can hook up with Historic Route 66 in Barstow.

GET YOUR KICKS ON

MAIN ST. USA — HISTORIC ROUTE 66 — BARSTOW CA.

CENTER

TOM MYERS PHOTOGRAPHY

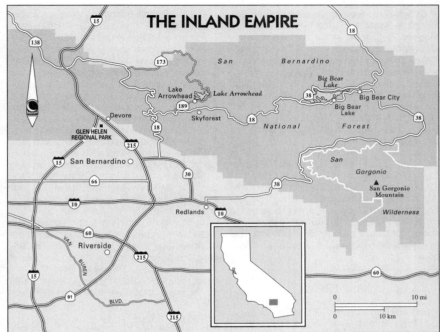

THE INLAND EMPIRE

© AVALON TRAVEL PUBLISHING, INC.

its creation, scientists speculate that the Arrowhead was created by water. Given the unusually thin soil layer, an unusually powerful cloudburst was all it took.

DOING SAN BERNARDINO AND VICINITY

Downtown San Bernardino, near the Radisson Hotel San Bernardino Convention Center on E Street, is trying to renovate and revitalize itself. If you have extra time, take a look around. An early vaudeville stage and venue for Hollywood "sneak previews," drawing stars such as Joan Crawford, Jean Harlow, and Clark Gable, the **California Theatre of the Performing Arts** still stands downtown at 562 W. Fourth St., 909/885-5152. This 1928 Spanish colonial is performance venue for the **San Bernardino Symphony Orchestra,** 909/381-5388.

Golden arches and other fast fooderies now span the globe, but it all started here at the original McDonald Brothers restaurant downtown (at 14th and E Streets. In the 1940s Maurice and Richard McDonald decided to phase out their carhops and offer "fast food." (A burger cost 15 cents, fries 10 cents, both promised within 20 seconds.) Ray Kroc, then based in the Midwest, worked as a milkshake machine salesman. To find out why the McDonald brothers bought so many machines, Kroc went west—and was so smitten with the concept that he bought the business in 1961, paying the McDonald brothers the then-princely sum of just over $1 million each. The rest is fast-food history. And though the original McDonald Brothers restaurant is long-gone, since December 1998 a new facsimile McDonald's—a veritable museum, with Route 66 and other memorabilia dating from the 1830s—has stood in its place, an inductee into the San Bernardino Route 66 Cruisin' Hall of Fame.

Generally more evocative of regional history, though, is **Redlands** just to the east, where the biggest thing going is the **San Bernardino County Museum,** 2024 Orange Tree Ln., 909/798-8570, www.co.san-bernardino.ca.us /museum, a three-story parade of natural history, history, and art, including a hands-on "discovery hall" for children. Among more noteworthy wonders: the renowned Wilson C. Hanna ornithology collection, with 40,000 bird eggs. Affiliated satellite museums and exhibit halls are scattered throughout the county.

Home to the only Lincoln memorial west of the Mississippi, the **Lincoln Memorial Shrine** in Smiley Park behind the A. K. Smiley Library at 125 W. Vine St., Redlands is also known for its architecture, which includes everything from Arts and Crafts bungalows and fantasy cottages to exquisite Victorians. Countless commercial shows, TV shows, and movies—including *How to Make an American Quilt*—have been filmed here.

One of the most celebrated Victorian personalities is the 1897 **Kimberly Crest House and Gardens,** 1325 Prospect Drive, 909/792-2111, www.kimberlycrest.com, onetime family home of the Kimberly half of the Kimberly-Clark Corporation. It's closed during the suffocating month of August, but otherwise open for tours Thurs.– Sun. 1–4 P.M., $5 admission. Quite special, too, is the elegant, onion-domed **Morey Mansion Inn,** 190 Terracina Blvd. in Redlands, an 1890 Victorian built by retired shipbuilder David Morey. The home's hand-carved orange blossom motif is best explained by the fact that Sarah Morey started Southern California's first orange seedling nursery. Tours are offered; for more information, call the Morey Mansion Inn at 909/793-7970. And if you'd like to stay, that can also be arranged.

To tour local Victoriana and other architecture—the city boasts more than 300 citrus-era mansions—pick up the **Historic Redlands Driving Tour** (fee) at the Redlands Chamber of Commerce office, 1 E. Redlands Blvd., 909/793-2546; www.redlandschamber.org. Or buy tickets for the annual **Holiday Home Tour,** 909/793-2957.

The Renaissance Pleasure Faire

In many ways the San Bernardino area is more event than destination—a truism even at local parks. North of the Indio Freeway (I-10) at the conjunction of the Devore Freeway (I-15) and the Barstow Freeway (I-215), **Glen Helen Regional Park** features grassy rolling foothills, scattered oak forests, a lake, even campgrounds and picnic areas. Every spring it also features Southern California's **Renaissance Pleasure Faire,** considered the most "historically correct" Renaissance-period U.S. event of its kind, like its Northern California sister celebration held every fall.

First held in the woods near Agoura Hills more than 30 years ago, Southern California's Elizabethan rite of spring now unfolds in Glen Helen. What's on tap, besides authentic ale? A cast of thousands—many in Elizabethan costume, acting strictly in character—plenty of merriment in the marketplace, traditional food and drink, plus 16th-century song, dance, theater, children's games, and other diversions, including elephant rides and jousting tournaments. The Renais-

---

LAKE PERRIS

An attractive Southern California storage facility for Northern California water, thanks to California's State Water Project, **Lake Perris State Recreation Area** near Riverside also offers recreational respite. More than a million people each year come to Lake Perris for water recreation—swimming (two sandy beaches and a waterslide), fishing (shore, pier, and boat), boating, sailing, water-skiing, even limited scuba diving.

To avoid the crowds, though, come some other time. A nine-mile bike meanders around the lake, all the better for wildlife viewing (migratory bird-watching in winter, guided wildlife hikes in spring). Or hike into the boulder-rugged Bernasconi Hills; it's two miles to the top of Terri Peak. Just south of the dam, Lake Perris also boasts some impressive rock-climbing. If you happen to be here midweek or a weekend, stop by *Ya'i Heki'* **Regional Indian Museum,** with exhibits on Luiseño and other area Native American peoples. The museum is open Wednesday 10 A.M.–2 P.M., until 4 P.M. on weekends.

Day use at Lake Perris is $3. For more information, call the park at 909/657-0676.

sance Pleasure Faire, a program of the publicly traded Renaissance Entertainment Corporation, typically runs for eight consecutive weekends, May through June. At last report admission at the gates was $17.50 adults, $15 seniors and juniors (ages 12–16), $7.50 children (ages 5–11), and free for ages 4 and under. Parking $10. For current information and advance discount ticket sales (slightly cheaper), call 909/880-0122 or try www.renfair.com. Whether or not you and yours come in costume, be sure to bring plenty of cash. If you fully indulge, this blast from the past gets expensive.

Another main "event" here, year-round, is the ever-changing parade of major-league musical groups and other entertainers onstage at the park's 40-acre **Glen Helen Blockbuster Pavilion,** a 1993 $15-million open-air amphitheater on its way to becoming the nation's largest. For current events information, call 909/886-8742.

Other San Bernardino Events

San Bernardino events kick off in May, spring renewal all but guaranteed by the annual **Renaissance Pleasure Faire** at Glen Helen Regional Park near Devore, held on consecutive weekends through June. (See above.) But *the* major San Bernardino event, since 1911, is the annual **National Orange Show Citrus Fair,** held in May at the 170-acre National Orange Show grounds at 689 S. E St., 909/888-6788; www .nationalorangeshow.com. What began as the city's citrus-scented answer to Pasadena's Tournament of Roses has become a rollicking regional festival with exhibits, games, rides, and big-time entertainment. Look for other events here throughout the year, too, from NASCAR stock car racing to cat shows and gun shows.

When the withering summer heat starts to subside in September, the city hosts the family-friendly **Route 66 Rendezvous.** Vintage street 'rods—American-made only, excluding low riders and mini trucks—are the central focus, even during the World's Best Mystery Poker Run, Best Sounding Exhaust Contest, and the "legal" Open Header Cruise down E Street (patrolled by police in vintage squad cars who pull people over for the crime of not having enough fun). Also on the revelry roster for the Route 66 Rendezvous: a golf tournament, classic car show, and downtown street dance with tunes including Bobby Troupe's classic "Route 66." Be there or be square.

The main event in October is the **Festival de Mariachis.** Come in November for the **Wildlife West Festival** at the San Bernardino County Museum and the local **Harvest Fair.**

PRACTICAL SAN BERNARDINO

Staying in San Bernardino

Camping is a good bet in and around San Bernardino, with public campgrounds in various regional parks (some sites with hookups) and in nearby San Bernardino National Forest. For contact information, see San Bernardino Information and Into the Mountains: Big Bear and Vicinity, below.

Redlands is a good bet for inexpensive, quite decent motels, especially along and near W. Colton Avenue (exit I-10 south at Tennessee Street). One good choice is the **Best Western Sandman Motel,** 1120 W. Colton (at Tennessee), 909/793-2001 or toll-free 800/528-1234, fax 909/792-7612. Rates: $50 and up, discounts possible during slower times. Heated pool and whirlpool, continental breakfast. Another possibility is the **Redlands/San Bernardino Super 8,** 1160 Arizona St. (north of I-10 between Tennessee and Alabama Sts.), 909/335-1612 or toll-free 800/800-8000 (central reservations), fax 909/792-8779; www.super8.com. Rates: $36–45.

Most motel-type accommodations in San Bernardino are clustered, with numerous restaurants, along Hospitality Lane, just north of and parallel to I-10 (exit at Waterman). Among these are the **La Quinta Inn,** 205 E. Hospitality, 909/888-7571 or toll-free 800/531-5900 (central reservations), fax 909/884-3864, where the basics include in-room coffee and data ports, and the nearby **Comfort Inn,** just north of Hospitality at 1909 S. Business Center Dr., 909/889-0090 or toll-free 800/228-5150, fax 909/889-9894. Rooms at both are $69 and up (sometimes discounted).

The biggest thing going downtown, just two blocks from the California State Theatre, is the **Radisson Hotel Convention Center,** 295 N. E St., 909/381-6181 or toll-free 800/333-3333 (central reservations, United States and Canada), fax 909/381-5288; www.radisson.com. Primarily a business-oriented enterprise, the Radisson does offer some weekend deals—such as the spring weekend Renaissance Fair rate and the family-with-breakfast package—summer rates: $89 and up.

Eating in and near San Bernardino

A long-running locals' favorite at lunch and dinner is **Nena's Mexican Restaurant,** 642 N. D St., 909/885-4161. A long-running local favorite for Italian is **Isabella's,** 201 N. E St., 909/884-2534, open for both lunch and dinner. (There's another Isabella's in Redlands, on N. Sixth St. in Mission Plaza, 909-792-2767.) Also a best bet is charming **Michaels Bon Appetito Restaurant,** 246 E. Base Line, 909/884-5054. For French, try **Le Rendezvous Restaurant,** 4775 N. Sierra Way, 909/883-1231. Immensely popular for California-style American and quite good is casual **La Potiniere** at the San Bernardino Hilton Hotel, 285 E. Hospitality Ln., 909/889-0133. Great for Sunday brunch.

Hospitality Lane hosts a multitude of restaurants, however, everything from San Bernardino–style Chinese at the **Lotus Garden,** 111 E. Hospitality Ln., 909/381-6171, to **El Torito** across the way at 118 E. Hospitality, 909/381-2316. For the best beer and jukebox, definitely worth a stop is **The Pig's Ear** British-style pub at 1987 S. Diners Court (just off Hospitality, around the corner from Tony Roma's), 909/889-1442, where billiards and darts are also on tap.

Worth looking for in Redlands is dinner-only **Joe Greensleeves** downtown at 222 N. Orange St., 909/792-6969, a fairly casual, very California place with the wine list to prove it. Or try the stylish American **Wild Rabbit** in Brookside Plaza, 1502 Barton Rd. (at Alabama), 909/793-2038. Beer and wine. For stylish bistro fare, consider **Citrone,** 347 Orange St., 909/793-6635. For European-style Middle Eastern and a real deal in Redlands, the place is **Cafe Caprice,** 104 E. State St., 909/793-8787, open for both lunch and dinner. Marvelous for Thai: **Rama Garden,** 309 W. State, 909/798-7747, open for lunch on weekdays, for dinner every night.

San Bernardino Information

For current information on San Bernardino and vicinity, contact the **San Bernardino Conven-** **tion and Visitors Bureau,** downtown at 201 N. E St., Ste. 103, San Bernardino, CA 92401, 909/889-5998 or or toll-free 800/867-8366; www.sanbernardino.org. At last report, the visitors bureau also handled scheduling for guided **Redlands Historical Tours.** For a copy of the self-guided **Historic Redlands Driving Tour** (audio cassette also available), stop by the **Redlands Chamber of Commerce** office (weekdays only) at 1 E. Redlands Blvd., 909/793-2546; www.redlandschamber.org.

For area parks information—and the city's public **Shandin Hills Golf Course** is one of Southern California's top 20—contact **San Bernardino County Regional Parks,** 777 E. Rialto Ave., 909/387-2757 (38 PARKS); www.co.sanbernardino.ca.us/parks. For other local recreation information, contact **San Bernardino Parks and Recreation,** 547 N. Sierra Way, 909/384-5233. For information about **San Bernardino Stampede** California League baseball games, Class A affiliate of the Los Angeles Dodgers, played downtown at "The Ranch," 280

RILEY'S: STAYING IN COLONIAL NEW ENGLAND

Riley's Farm & Orchard in Southern California's San Bernardino Mountains offers a unique living history experience. Celebrating the colonial culture of New England—a scene from the movie *Amistad* was filmed here—Riley's Farm offers historically authentic hand-hewn log and post-and-beam cabins furnished with rope beds, corn husk mattresses, feather ticking, wool blankets, and fireplaces or Franklin stoves. Read yourself to sleep by candlelight. A stay includes three colonial-style meals per day, served in the local tavern, and encouragement to participate in the farm's ongoing living history theater. Scripts, costumes, and muskets are provided, so there's no excuse to shirk your part. Don't shirk the work, either. Farm work—including hitching up the horses, working in the garden, and stoking the blacksmith forge—is also offered. For details, contact: Riley's Farm & Orchard, 12261 S. Oak Glen Road, Oak Glen, CA 92399, 909/797-7534; www.rileysfarm.com.

S. E St., call 909/888-9922 or try www.stampedebaseball.com. For information on the Anaheim Angels' California League **Rancho Cucamonga Quakes,** call 909/481-5000 or try www.rcquakes.com.

For transportation information, see Riverside and Regional Transport under Riverside: Navel of the Inland Empire, below.

INTO THE MOUNTAINS: BIG BEAR AND VICINITY

With more than 810,000 acres, all within easy reach of greater Los Angeles, San Bernardino National Forest attracts more than six million visitors every year—earning it greater popularity, by the numbers, than any other national forest. The terrain and the life it supports are quite diverse, ranging from high desert Joshua tree landscapes and scrub-covered chaparral to pine, fir, and cedar forests and lush mountain bogs and lakes. Popular southern California mountain resort areas, including Big Bear Lake and Lake Arrowhead, are included in the forest's northern section.

Popular Southern California downhill ski resorts (some offer night skiing) include **Big Bear Mountain Ski & Summer Resort,** 909/585-2519, www.bearmtn.com, where high-altitude golf is a popular summer pursuit; **Snow Summit,** 909/866-5766 or toll-free 888/786-6481 (SUMMIT-1), www.snowsummit.com; and **Snow Valley,** 909/867-2751; www.snow-valley.com. Other winter sports are a big recreational draw, along with summertime mountain biking (at ski resorts and elsewhere), camping, picnicking, hiking, backpacking, fishing, and boating. National forest day use is free; fees for campgrounds and picnic areas vary.

The separate southern section of San Bernardino National Forest is adjacent to **Palm Springs,** and includes forests surrounding the mountain retreat of **Idyllwild.**

For more detailed information and necessary wilderness permits, contact: **San Bernardino National Forest Headquarters,** 1824 S. Commercenter Circle, San Bernardino, CA 92408, 909/383-5588; www.r5.fs.fed.us /sanbernardino.

Rent a sailboat and take lessons at the marinas of Big Bear Lake.

BIG BEAR RECLAIMS ITS BEARS

Big news in Big Bear recently has been big bears—grizzly bears. California hasn't had any grizzly bears, except on the state flag, since early settlers and hunters hounded the state's native species into extinction nearly a century ago. But grizzlies have returned to Big Bear, the result of this mountain resort community's all-out campaign to save a few Montana misfits from the death penalty. Big Bear's new bears—a mama grizzly with a lengthy federal rap sheet, plus two now-grown cubs she had led astray early in their lives—had been on death row in Seattle pending the availability of a permanent bear-proof prison. In early 1996, Big Bear fundraising raised the $55,000 needed to build an appropriate den here.

But there's more to Big Bear than bears. Built around man-made Big Bear Lake high in the San Bernardino Mountains, this is a popular filming location and year-round L.A. getaway—a pine-scented village surrounded by vacation cabins and tall trees. Active diversions include downhill and cross-country skiing in winter and, in summer, swimming, fishing, wildflower and bird walks, canoe tours, horseback rides, hayrides, even carriage rides. **Big Bear Jeep Tours,** 909/878-5337, offers its own brand of backcountry adventure. For inveterate shoppers, Big Bear also has its antique and gift shops.

Events and performances are scheduled year-round. Come in May for the annual **Trout Classic,** in June for the **Open Sky Music Festival.** One of the year's biggest big deals is the two-week-long **Old Miners Days** celebration in late July/early August, with everything from burro races and barbecues to log-rolling contests. Cool August events include the **Festival of Jazz** and the **Peddler's Market Antique & Collectibles Show.** The **Big Bear International Film Festival** is screened in September.

For more information about Big Bear and vicinity, contact: **Big Bear Resort Association,** 630 Bartlett Rd., Big Bear Lake, CA 92315, toll-free 800/424-4232, www.bigbearinfo.com, also a visitor reservation service.

Staying in Big Bear

Weekend rates at all local lodgings tend to be highest, especially in the peak summer and winter seasons. To beat the crowds and get the best prices, plan a midweek visit either before or after the summer-vacation and ski seasons. Most Big Bear accommodations require a two-night minimum stay on weekends (three-night on holiday weekends). Cancellation policies vary greatly, so be sure to ask when you make reservations.

A variety of pleasant cabin-style accommodations are available in and around Big Bear, good setups for families and groups, including the very nice **Grey Squirrel Resort** west of town on Highway 18, 39372 Big Bear Blvd., 909/866-4335 or toll-free 800/381-5569, fax 909/866-6271, www.greysquirrel.com, with year-round rates $75–425, slightly higher in winter. Cabins are all named after forest critters; the smallest sleep only 2, the largest up to 14. Pets are OK—contact Grey Squirrel for details—and midweek, senior, and off-season discounts are available. Private rental homes are also available.

Sleepy Forest Cottages, 426 Eureka Dr., 909/866-74444 or toll-free 800/544-7454, www.sleepyforest.com, feature a unique Jacuzzi-in-front-of-the-fireplace setup, perfect for romance or soothing those screaming muscles after a day on the slopes. Rates: $119 and up, but ask about packages and specials. The small **Hillcrest Lodge** in Big Bear City at 40241 Big Bear Blvd. (Hwy. 18), 909/866-6040 (front desk) or 909/866-7330 and toll-free 800/843-4449 for reservations, fax 909/866-1171, www.hillcrestlodge.com, offers rooms from $39–$64 and up in summer, $44–$79 and up in winter, with higher prices on weekends. Cabins higher.

In addition to many motels, lakeside condos, and other vacation rentals, Big Bear also has a good selection of bed-and-breakfast inns. Perhaps most famous is the historic **Knickerbocker Mansion Country Inn,** 869 S. Knickerbocker Rd., 909/878-9190 or toll-free 877/423-1180, fax 909/878-4248; www.knickerbockermansion.com. This imposing log cabin, built by Big Bear's first dam keeper, sits on two-plus acres just blocks from town and the lake. It features halved logs, installed vertically, for outdoor siding; more logs and original cedar panelling inside; and huge stone fireplaces. Four rooms are in the main house and four more plus a suite in the Carriage House. Rates are $110 and up.

Newest in Big Bear is the elegant and sophisticated yet relaxed **Alpenhorn Bed and Breakfast,** 601 Knight Ave. (midway between the village and Ski Summit), 909/866-5700 or toll-free 888/829-6600, fax 909/878-3209, www.alpenhorn.com. The seven inviting, individually decorated rooms all feature fireplaces, stall showers and separate spa tubs "for two," king or queen feather beds, private balconies, phones, quality linens, and abundant little luxuries. A video library boasting all Academy Award-winning "Best Pictures" since 1939 increases the interest of in-room TVs and VCRs. Handicapped-accessible rooms. Complimentary hors d'oeuvres and wine are served in the early evening, and after-dinner liqueurs and chocolates later. And don't pass on the four-course breakfast. Rates from $149.

Other B&B possibilities include the 1928 **Gold Mountain Manor,** 1117 Anita, 909/585-6997 or toll-free 800/509-2604, fax 909/585-0327, www.goldmountainmanor.com, another vintage log mansion, this one with boisterous Old West style. Rates: $120 and up. The charming Ponderosa pine-log **Eagle's Nest** next to Snow Summit at 41675 Big Bear Blvd., 909/866-6465, fax 909/866-6025, features five lodge rooms right out of your favorite Westerns—named after them, too, from Cat Ballou to Rio Bravo—and five cottage suites (one available for people with pets). Rates: $85 and up.

For more information about accommodations options in and around Big Bear, contact the local resort association (listed above).

Eating in Big Bear

You definitely won't starve here. Exceptional in Big Bear is **Mozart's Bistro,** 40701 Village Dr., 909/866-9497, where the contemporary American comes with German and other accents at both lunch and dinner. For lunch, how 'bout a Heidelburger, with Black Angus burger, Swiss cheese, grilled red and yellow onions, and mushrooms, served on sourdough bread? Or the German knockwurst or portobello mushroom sandwiches, the Santa Fe wrap, the Asian chicken salad, the veggie pizza? At dinner, consider the smoked salmon linguine, the wild mushroom fettuccini, the roasted half-chicken marinated in

orange honey mustard sauce, or—a house specialty—pork crown roast rack. Housemade desserts include caramelized pecan upside-down spiced apple pie. Full bar. Children's menu too. Another stylish yet casual possibility, with early American decor, is the continental **Iron Squirrel,** 646 Pine Knot Blvd., 909/866-9121, where the early-bird specials are the real deal. Full bar.

Popular for steaks and seafood at dinner, and for Sunday brunch, is the **Blue Whale Lakeside,** 350 Alden Rd., 909/866-5771. Casual cafés, often serving breakfast, lunch, and dinner, abound in and around Big Bear. For Italian, try **Paoli's Italian Country Kitchen,** 40821 Pennsylvania Ave., 909/866-2020. Best bet for Mexican (lunch and dinner only) is **La Montaña Mexican Restaurant,** 42164 Moonridge Rd., 909/866-2606, for pizza, **Maggio's Pizza** in the Interlaken Shopping Center on Big Bear Blvd., 909/866-8815. Casual hot spots in Big Bear City include rustic **Thelma's Family Restaurant and Bakery,** 337 W. Big Bear Blvd., 909/585-7005, and **Madlon's,** 829 W. Big Bear Blvd., 909/585-3762.

RIVERSIDE: NAVEL OF THE INLAND EMPIRE

San Bernardino may have remnants of the nation's "Mother Road," old Route 66, but Riverside has the surviving Mother Tree—actually, Parent Tree—for much of the world's supply of seedless oranges now known as Washington navels, named for the characteristic "belly button."

Father of Riverside's astonishing agricultural prosperity was Judge John Wesley North, an abolitionist who in 1870 established the Southern California Colony Association here. Mother of California's orange industry—and, in a sense, mother of the Southern California myth—was Eliza Tibbetts, who in 1873 planted the first two U.S. "bud sports" (mutant bud stock) of the Selecta orange that originated in Bahia, Brazil. The trees flourished, and the fruit was clearly superior to any other commercial orange variety of the day—in size, appearance, texture, and flavor. The fact that navel oranges were also

seedless further enhanced their prospects as popular table fruit. Mother Tibbets's orange was originally christened the Riverside navel by the U.S. Department of Agriculture, but other Southern California citrus growers objected, vehemently, and campaigned for a name of more "national" scope. Thus navel oranges—and all their descendants—were named after the nation's father, George Washington.

One of the original two trees was acquired by Frank A. Miller, founder of the famed Mission Inn. With the hands-on assistance of President Teddy Roosevelt, Miller transplanted it to the inn's courtyard on May 8, 1903. That tree died in 1921, however, and was replaced by an 11-year-old descendant.

Ownership of Eliza Tibbets's surviving sport reverted to the city of Riverside in 1902, and the tree was transplanted to its current home on the corner of Arlington and Magnolia (across from

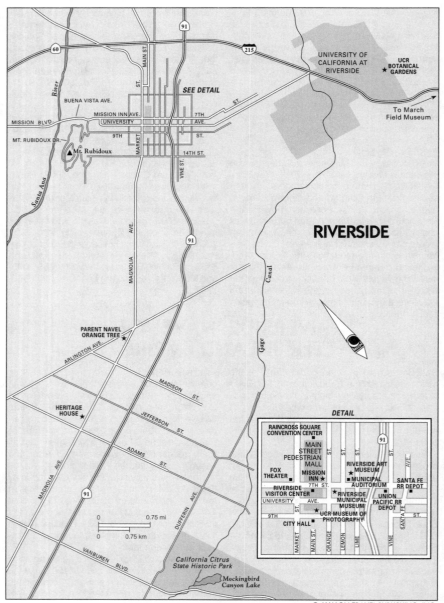

© AVALON TRAVEL PUBLISHING, INC.

the southeast corner of the Tibbets homestead). With help from a horticultural technique called "inarching," Riverside's **Parent Navel Orange Tree** has been revivified with new roots at least three times since.

THE MISSION INN

Exploring the courtyards and labyrinthine byways of Riverside's Mission Inn, with its baroque arches, bell towers, and buttresses, endless odd angles, and occasional stairways to nowhere, is something like strolling through a three-dimensional M. C. Escher sketch. Fine-tune the mental picture by imagining the hotel's illustrious guests—presidents, kings, queens, and 20th-century celebrities, including Sarah Bernhardt, Booker T. Washington, Amelia Earhart, Humphrey Bogart, and Rin Tin Tin. The Carnegies, Rockefellers, Fords, Huntingtons, and other turn-of-the-20th-century industrialists considered the Mission Inn their personal West Coast retreat. Richard and Pat Nixon got married here (in the Presidential Suite, no less), as did Ronald and Nancy Reagan, who honeymooned here. John Steinbeck finished at least one of his novels here. And Will Rogers called the Mission Inn "the most unique hotel in America."

So Southern Californians cheered the news that this grand old hotel, a national historic landmark, would reopen, finally, in the 1990s, after a $50 million facelift and complications including multiple bankruptcies and abrupt changes in ownership.

Making Southern California's Mission Days Myth

The official founding date for Riverside's famed Mission Inn is November 22, 1876, the date the first boarder moved into the Miller family's "Glenwood Cottage" downtown. The home's humble adobe origin was hidden by clapboard siding— but not for long. After young Frank A. Miller bought the Glenwood from his father in 1880, he began his lifelong task of transforming the family home into one of the world's most theatrical luxury hotels.

The myth Frank Miller pursued was California's romanticized Hispanic past, the style, variations on the new mission revival architectural

---

SUNRISE NEAR THE ON-RAMP

Dig and I sat on lead-sprayed
 cinderblocks
watching semis and Subarus, Chryslers
and Porsches slide beneath the dawn

along the eight oil-streaked lanes
that bordered our world,
chewing slow dogs and children
like so much Big Red,

four lanes leading to Riverside,
four others to Newport Beach.

Which way, one of us asked,
would you go
if you could fly
with vanity plates

from the smog alerts,
gray lawns, and Quonset hut schools
of our drive-by subdivision?
In answer, we pointed,
my first true friend and I,

one to the desert, the Rockies,
the plains, the swamps, and beyond
a rumored second sea,

the other to Newport Beach.

—MICHAEL SIGALAS

---

theme. With financial backing from Henry E. Huntington (of Huntington Hotel fame), in 1902 Miller began building the "New Glenwood," an adobe-colored four-story stucco hotel surrounding a mission-style quadrangle. At the center of the courtyard stood the original Glenwood, stripped of its wooden siding and remodeled with red tile roof and a campanile copied from the bell tower at Mission San Gabriel. In no time at all the New Glenwood was known, descriptively, as the Glenwood Mission Inn, then simply the Mission Inn.

The hotel was wildly successful from the start, satisfying California's need for some sense of history, real or imagined. Frank Miller's Mission Inn, which he continued to build and rebuild through 1931, offered both—a synthesis of historical sincerity and sentimental showmanship that somehow managed to capture California's emerging myth about itself. Miller's family traipsed all over Europe collecting antique furniture, tapestries, and art to illustrate this newly created California sensibility. Early additions—such as the Cloister Wing and the Cloister Walk or "Catacombs"—reflected guests' preference for the illusion of sleeping in a mission that had been converted into a hoLater additions were increasingly sophisticated, such as the Spanish Wing (designed by architect Myron Hunt), the Spanish Art Gallery, and the five-story Rotunda with its spiral staircase. Building nooks and crannies was a constant necessity, just to keep up with the family's compulsive collecting of antiques, armor, bells, fountains, sculpture, stained glass, wrought ironwork, even sections of entire buildings.

The Modern-Day Mission Inn

Though much of the original collection was auctioned off in the 1950s, after Miller's heirs lost interest and sold the Mission Inn, there's still plenty to see, since the recent restoration preserved the hotel's charm. For a proper introduction, take a docent-led tour, or stop by the **Mission Inn Museum** on the corner of Mission Inn Avenue and Main. Guided 75-minute tours are offered Mon.–Fri. at 10:30 A.M., 1:30 P.M., and 2 P.M. On Saturday and Sunday, tours are offered every half-hour, 10 A.M.–3 P.M. For more information on hotel tours—at last report, $8 per person, beginning in the hotel lobby—and to make reservations, call 909/788-9556 or see www.missioninnmuseum.com. The museum is open daily 9:30 A.M.–4 P.M., $2 donation.

If at all possible, plan to stay a day or two. Accommodations range from spacious motel-style rooms to stunning rooftop suites. Rates start at $139, junior suites at $225, and presidential suites at $500, but ask about discounts, weekend packages, and seasonal specials. Rooms feature all modern comforts plus conveniences including hair dryers, irons and ironing boards, phones with two lines and data-privacy modem capabilities, and color TV with HBO and pay-per-view movies. Hotel amenities include

heated pool, whirlpool, fitness facilities, the exceptional, dress-up **Duane's Prime Steaks and Seafood Restaurant**—winner of the Wine Spectator Award for Excellence in 1999—as well as the more casual, California-style **Mission Inn Restaurant** and the **Mission Inn Coffee Company.**

For more information about the hotel and its attractions, contact: The Mission Inn, 3649 Mission Inn Ave., Riverside, CA 92501, 909/784-0300 or toll-free 800/843-7755 for reservations, fax 909/683-1342; www.missioninn.com.

SEEING AND DOING DOWNTOWN

Downtown Riverside

Though Riverside was famous for its Mission Inn hotel and Riverside Raceway, both closed in the 1980s. These days the raceway is a shopping mall. But now that the Mission Inn is back in

KIM WEIR

The Mission Inn started out as a clapboard-covered adobe.

business, downtown is also back. Strolling the pedestrian-friendly streets near the Mission Inn is like an over-the-shoulder glance into the city's very civil, very civilized citricultural past.

Regional cultural center of long standing, the city of Riverside was the wealthiest per capita in the nation in 1895. That wealth spread itself out, domestically, along palm-lined boulevards perfumed by 20,000 acres of orange blossoms and, in town, created multiple monuments to civility —and to the success of the landed gentry.

Most of Riverside's historic sites and structures lie within the original one-square-mile downtown district along the Santa Ana River designated as "Riverside" by the Southern California Colony Association.

Notable throughout downtown are Riverside's "raincross" street lamps, incorporating the city's symbol—another gift from Frank Miller. Working with L.A. architect Arthur B. Benton, Miller created the symbol for the Mission Inn's logo— framed Spanish mission bells crowned by the double-armed Navajo raincross—as a romantic marriage of mission and Indian history.

From the Mission Inn, get a basic downtown orientation by wandering aimlessly along the **Main Street Pedestrian Mall** between City Hall and the Riverside Convention Center. In eclectic college-town style, an intriguing array of unusual shops, coffeehouses, and restaurants dot Main and intersecting streets. The main attraction, though, is the old art-deco Kress Co. store, now home to the impressive **UC Riverside/California Museum of Photography,** 3824 Main (between University Ave. and Ninth St.), 909/784-3686 (784-FOTO) for recorded information or 909/787-4787 for administrative offices, www.cmp.ucr .edu, open Tues.–Sun. 11 A.M.–5 P.M. The comprehensive website details current exhibits and photography programs, including "Senior Eye." The museum's permanent collections include the world's largest, most complete holding of vintage stereographs; a 10,000-item collection of cameras and viewing devices, including classics from the 19th and 20th centuries; and images by over 1000 photographers, both contemporary and historical. Admission is free.

More Downtown Riverside

Many noteworthy buildings are concentrated within several blocks of Mission Inn Ave. (Seventh Street). On Mission Inn at Market, for example, is Riverside's venerable **Fox Theater,** a 1929 grande dame dressed in Spanish colonial revival style, once a popular venue for Hollywood previews and film debuts. *Gone with the Wind* had its first public screening here, in 1939. In recent years the Fox featured artsy and other eclectic films in conjunction with the Riverside Film Festival, but at last report the theater was closed and looking for a buyer. For historical details and updates, see the website www.fox-riverside-theater.com.

Across from the Mission Inn is the **Riverside Municipal Museum,** 3580 Mission Inn Ave. (at Orange), 909/782-5273, www.ci.riverside.ca .us/museum, an imposing Italian renaissance –style U.S. post office when constructed in 1912. It became the city's combined police department/museum starting in 1945, but has strictly been a museum since 1966. The emphasis here is anthropology, history, and natural history, drawing primarily upon local Native American culture, settlement history since the De Anza expeditions of 1774–76, and the local culture of agriculture, in addition to special rotating exhibits. It's open Tues.–Fri. 9 A.M.–5 P.M., Saturday 10 A.M.–5 P.M., Sunday 11 A.M.–5 P.M., Monday 9 A.M.–1 P.M., closed on major holidays. Free.

Another cultural and architectural find is the **Riverside Art Museum,** 3425 Mission Inn Ave. (at Lime), 909/684-7111, www.riversideartmuseum.com, housed in the 1929 Young Women's Christian Association (YWCA) building designed by noted California architect Julia Morgan, most famous for her work on William Randolph Hearst's San Simeon "castle." The building is included on the National Register of Historic Places. The museum itself is a genuine community resource—supporting public arts education, offering visual arts classes and lectures, and displaying local artists' work (some of it also for sale, in the Museum Shop and Gallery). For a pleasurable meal, try the **City Cuisine** restaurant in the museum's atrium, open during museum hours. The Riverside Art Museum hosts an average of 10 curated shows every year, typically well worth a stop. At last report the museum was open Mon.–Sat. 10

A.M.–4 P.M., at other times for special events. Small admission (by donation). Next door (at Lemon) is the **Municipal Auditorium,** designed by Arthur Benton and G. Stanley Wilson, built in the late 1920s, and principal venue for the Riverside County Philharmonic.

On the university side of the Riverside Freeway (the 91), at Mission Inn Ave. and Vine, is the onetime **Sutherland Fruit Company Packinghouse,** now home to the family-friendly Old Spaghetti Factory restaurant. Across the street, at 3751 Vine, is a 1904 mission revival building once home to the **Union Pacific Railroad Depot.** A block away, at Mission Inn and Santa Fe, is the 1927 Spanish revival **Santa Fe Railroad Depot.** Riverside's **Metrolink** mass transit train station is in the same general vicinity, at 10th and Vine.

Semiurban Hikes

Aside from its calendar of cultural events, most appealing for most visitors to the **University of California at Riverside** campus, across the Riverside Freeway (Hwy. 91) from downtown, is a stroll through the 39-acre **UCR Botanic Gardens.** The main path, meandering through roses, irises, subtropical fruit trees, and succulents, is wheelchair accessible; hiking trails wind up into the alder-shaded canyon. It's open daily 8 A.M.–5 P.M. (closed major holidays), free admission and parking. For information, call 909/787-4650.

For a more ambitious urban hike, particularly worthwhile on a crisp, clear winter day, head to the top of "downtown's mountain," **Mount Rubidoux,** where the nation's first interdenominational Easter sunrise service was held in 1909. The cross erected here in honor of Father Junípero Serra—and other spiritual shrines, including Frank Miller's World Peace Tower, a symbol of his post–World War I international peace activism—were preceded by centuries of other holy use, particularly sun worship by Cahuilla and Serrano native peoples. Mount Rubidoux, closed to cars but open to hikers and mountain bikers, is west of downtown. It can be reached via the Pomona Freeway (Hwy. 60) or, from downtown, via Mission Inn Avenue (which becomes Mission). The walking trail to the summit begins at Ninth Street and Mount Rubidoux Drive.

OTHER RIVERSIDE ATTRACTIONS

Heritage House

Southwest of downtown, just blocks beyond the Parent Navel Orange Tree, is another outpost of Riverside's Victorian past—the astonishing Heritage House, a very special project of the Riverside Municipal Museum sponsored by the Riverside Museum Associates. This eclectic 1892 Queen Anne–style Victorian was designed by John Walls, of the prominent L.A. firm of Morgan and Walls, and is one of the most authentic "museum houses" in California. Heritage House offers a rare glimpse into the self-consciously comfortable lives of affluent early orange growers—from the hand-carved oak and redwood, gold leaf, and tambour lace to the indoor bathroom with period plumbing and marble countertop.

Heritage House, 8193 Magnolia Ave., 909/7 82-5273, www.ci.riverside.ca.us/museum/rmm/ hh.html, is open for 45-minute, docent-guided tours from Labor Day until July 4th, Thurs.–Fri. 12–3 P.M. and Sunday 12–3:30 P.M. From July 4th until Fourth of July until Labor Day, tours are offered only on Sunday, 12–3:30 P.M. With notice, tours can be arranged at other times. Donations are greatly appreciated. Parking is available behind the house; turn into the narrow driveway.

To get here from downtown, follow Market Street south; Market becomes Magnolia—the first "parkway"-style boulevard, precursor to the freeway. Heritage House sits on the right (north) side of Magnolia Avenue, between Jefferson and Adams Streets. Alternatively, from the Riverside Freeway (Hwy. 91) exit at either Adams or Madison and head north to Magnolia.

California Citrus State Historic Park

Though the citrus industry in and around Riverside has been all but eliminated by the dual scourges of smog and suburban sprawl, its memory lives on. The most recent historical repository is a new state park, this one carved into the remaining navel orchards and palm-lined old promenades of Riverside's Arlington Heights area.

A work in progress, the park opened to the public in 1993 and at present is best suited for picnics and as a peaceful respite from freeway travel. The general landscape of 377-acre California Citrus State Historical Park includes 150 acres of oranges, lemons, and grapefruit, Mockingbird Canyon Reservoir, and a section of the historic Gage Canal that first provided—and still provides—irrigation water for local orchards. A perfect introduction to both the park's concept and content is the ersatz early 1900s' "Giant Orange" fruit drink stand marking the park's entrance.

One of the first buildings constructed at the park was the craftsman-style Sunkist Activity Center. The center, and the adjacent Orange Court and Gazebo, host various special events.

The park amphitheater and attached interpretive center sometimes offer open-air presentations. The picnic areas were among the first park development projects. Still to come, pending the availability of funds are a restaurant and visitor center disguised as a grower's house; a worker's camp and company store (not everyone got rich on the citrus crop); and an orange packing house emphasizing the industry's early cooperative marketing ventures. A living history program, with park facilities and exhibits staffed by historically correct volunteers, is also planned.

The park, 909/780-6222, is open daily 8 A.M.–5 P.M., until 7 P.M. from April through September. Admission is free. To schedule weddings or events at the Sunkist Center, call 909/352-4099 or 909/784-0456.

To get here from the Riverside (91) Freeway, exit at Van Buren Boulevard and head south, just over a mile, to Dufferin Avenue, then turn left. A giant orange marks the spot.

March Field Museum

Worth a visit in the same general neighborhood, a few miles east of the state park at the conjunction of Van Buren Boulevard and the I-215 freeway—look for the red-and-white checkered roof—is the March Field Museum. First established as March Air Force Base, this was the oldest operational Air Force base on the West Coast until its recent transformation into the March Air Reserve Base. The life-sized dioramas here feature airmen's dramas and footlockers full of aeronautical memorabilia, now housed in a new hangar-type building. But most of the stars are still outside—dozens of warbirds and other heritage aircraft, from the SR-71 "Blackbird" reconnaissance plane and Bell P-59, the first U.S. jet fighter, to the World War II–era Boeing B-17 "Flying Fortress" and the replica Vultee BT-13 rebuilt as a Japanese carrier plane for the movie *Tora, Tora, Tora*. Go for the "G-Force" thrill at the museum's new **Flight Simulator** ride. The museum is open daily 10 A.M.–4 P.M., until 5 P.M. in summer (closed major holidays). Admission is $5 adults, $2 children. Other contributions are always appreciated. For more information, call the March Field Museum at 909/697-6600 or try www.pe.net/~marfldmu.

PRACTICAL RIVERSIDE

Staying in Riverside

The **Mission Inn,** of course, is *the* place to stay in Riverside. (See above.) But if for some reason there's no room at that inn, there's always the **Holiday Inn Select** at the convention center, 3400 Market St., 909/784-8000 or toll-free 877/291-7519, fax 909/369-7127, www.holidayinn .com, most popular with conventioneers and business folks. The regular $99 room rate is discounted as low as $69, subject to availability.

Less expensive accommodations are near the university, including **Motel 6,** 1260 University Ave. (just west of I-215/Hwy. 60), 909/784-2131 or toll-free 800/466-8356, fax 909/784-1801, www.motel6.com, which offers just-the-basics rooms at $43 for two. Inexpensive. The very comfortable **Dynasty Suites** is a block from the university at 3735 Iowa Ave., 909/369-8200 or toll-free 800/842-7899 (central reservations), fax 909/341-6486, www.dynastysuites.com, with rooms $60 or so for two, but ask about discount programs. Some choices in the same general vicinity include **Courtyard by Marriott,** 1510 University, 909/276-1200 or toll-free 800/321-2211 in the United States and Canada (central reservations), fax 909/787-6783; http://marriotthotels.com.

Eating in Riverside

You won't go wrong with a meal at the **Mission Inn.** (See above.) The downtown area offers other good choices, however, including the tasty pastries, homemade soups, fresh salads, and succulent sandwiches—honey-baked ham, roasted turkey, or vegetarian selections on slabs of house-baked bread—from nearby **Simple Simon's,** on the pedestrian mall at 3639 Main St., 909/369-6030, open Mon.–Sat. 9 A.M.–5 P.M. (lunch served 11–4). Such a deal. Weather permitting, eat outside on the tables and benches provided along the mall. Brewpub fans, taste the local wares at the **Riverside Brewing Company,** 3397 Mission Inn Ave. (at Lime), 909/784-2739, which at last count served six homemade brews plus a "handcrafted rootbeer," not to mention some fairly decent pub fare.

Beyond downtown, the possibilities include **Ciao Bella,** at 1630 Spruce St., 951/781-8840, known for its Northern Italian. Not far away is also-Italian **Mario's Place** bistro, 1735 Spruce St., 909/684-7755. For dress-up French, the place is **Gerard's,** 9814 Magnolia Ave., 909/687-4882. Great for mesquite-broiled seafood is the **Market Broiler,** 3525 Merrill Ave., 909/276-9007.

Riverside Events and Information

Something's always going on in Riverside, especially during the University of California's regular session, from September through May. Riverside's cultural calendar also includes performances by the **Riverside Community Players,** the **Riverside Ballet,** and the **Riverside County Philharmonic,** not to mention endless galas and benefits. For more information about regional attractions, special events, and practicalities, contact the **Riverside Visitor Center,,** 3660 Mission Inn Ave. (Mission Inn Ave. and Main), 909/684-4636, www.riverside-chamber.com, or the **Riverside Convention Bureau** inside the convention center at 3443 Orange St., 909/222-4700 or toll-free 888/748-7733; www.riversidecb .com.

Riverside and Regional Transport

Most everyone gets here by freeway. The north-trending Riverside Freeway (Hwy. 91) bisects downtown before converging, north of town, with the Escondido–San Bernardino Freeway (I-215). Making area freeway transitions even more confusing is the fact that the eastward-trending Pomona Freeway (Hwy. 60) does the same thing —bisecting downtown from another angle before joining with the southeasterly leg of I-215. Both I-10 and I-15 also swing through the general vicinity.

To avoid the crushing freeway traffic heading this direction from L.A. on a Friday, consider taking the train. Riverside was the first desert community linked into L.A.'s **Metrolink** commuter train system, with two local terminals— one downtown in the Marketplace, at 10th and Vine, the other north of town in Pedley (Van Buren Blvd. at Limonite Avenue). For information on the current Metrolink schedule and fares, call toll-free 800/371-5465 or try www.metrolinktrains .com. Metrolink also serves **San Bernardino.** For information on how to hook into Amtrak train service from Riverside, call toll-free 800/872-7245 or see www.amtrak.com. To otherwise leave the headache of driving to someone else, the **Riverside Regional Transit Agency,** with its terminal downtown at 3425 Mission Inn Ave., toll-free 800/800-7821, www.rrta.com, also provides **Greyhound** bus connections and **Inland Empire Connection** bus service to San Bernardino, Los Angeles and Orange Counties.

Flying is the other nonfreeway option. The incredibly busy **Ontario International Airport** just west of San Bernardino, 909/988-2700 (909-988-2737 for parking information), is served by low-budget **Southwest Airlines** and many other major carriers.

UP THE COAST FROM L.A.

Here's a thought to ponder while fueling that gas hog for a cruise up the coast from Los Angeles to Ventura, Santa Barbara, and beyond. Scientists from USC now predict that rising sea levels caused by global warming will create havoc along much of the Ventura County coastline in the coming 50 years, with coastal military bases, power plants, harbors, hotels, businesses, and residential areas increasingly battered and left to bail out after major storms and associated floods. Because the coastal Oxnard Plain is so level, and so near sea level, the effects of global warming will be felt here sooner than elsewhere along the California coastline. By the year 2040, they say, sea level here will be permanently two feet higher than it is today. A 10-foot increase in sea level is "highly unlikely"—except during serious storms.

Road trippers not yet running on empty because of fossil-fuel guilt will find much to enjoy here along the coast north of Los Angeles.

The scenic route into Ventura County from

please refer to the South-Central Coast map on page vi

the south is via the Pacific Coast Highway (PCH) from Malibu, though most people come via the Ventura Freeway through the San Fernando Valley—one of L.A.'s most congested freeways. A more serene if roundabout inland alternative is Highway 126 through Piru, Fillmore, and Santa Paula; or take the Ronald Reagan Freeway (Hwy. 118) through Simi Valley. Ventura County highlights include Ventura, with its San Buenaventura Mission and a welcoming old-fashioned downtown, state beach, and pleasant boat harbor—headquarters for Channel Islands National Park and point of departure for most park visitors. Fun for harbor hounds, too, is nearby Oxnard, with its downtown Heritage Square and historical museums. Highlights of inland explorations include very Victorian Santa Paula, home to the Santa Paula Union Oil Museum, and artsy Ojai, home to the annual Ojai Music Festival.

Rolling north along the coast on Highway 101 leads to Santa Barbara County, one of California's newest "wine countries," and the balmy city of Santa Barbara, always near the top of the Californians' Favorite Places To Get Away From It All list. Attractions beyond Santa Barbara include sunny Solvang, still an authentic transplanted slice of Denmark; Lompoc, site of California's most meticulously restored mission complex, now a state historic park; and Santa Maria, the one and only authentic home of Santa Maria–style barbecue. Wandering farther north

leads to San Luis Obispo, birthplace of the motel, and its surrounding attractions, and to Hearst San Simeon State Historic Monument, the famous "Hearst Castle" just south of Big Sur.

VENTURA COUNTY

OXNARD AND VICINITY: SEABEE CENTRAL

One notices in Ventura County the immense impact of recent and continuing growth—subdivisions and commercial developments all but consuming the county's once sleepy, agricultural past. Oxnard, still known for its annual May **California Strawberry Festival,** was once known for its sugar beet, bean, and strawberry fields, along with mile after mile of citrus orchards and packing sheds. The vanishing fruit industry is memorialized at the stylized Oxnard Factory Outlet mall at Rice Avenue off Gonzales Road.

The center of civic pride downtown is impressive **Heritage Square,** a collection of immaculately restored, landmark historic local buildings and replicas now home to shops, law offices, and such. A stroll away is the neoclassical **Carnegie Art Museum,** 424 S. C St., 805/385-8179, which showcases local arts and artists Thurs.–Sun. (call for current hours, small admission), and the **Ventura County Gull Wings Children's Museum,** 414 W. Fourth St., 805/483-3005, www.gullwingsmuseum4kids.org, open Wed.–Sun. 1–5 P.M. (small admission). Or head for the waterfront and Oxnard's surprisingly tony **Channel Islands Harbor,** where the **Ventura County Maritime Museum** at Fisherman's Wharf, 2731 S. Victoria Ave., 805/984-6260, open daily 11 A.M.–5 P.M., offers an overview of maritime history, ship models, and ocean-themed artwork. Among the treasures collected here: a copy of the map of Anacapa Island drawn by James Whistler. Most appealing of all is **Oxnard State Beach,** broad and sandy, backed by dunes and comfortably weathered beach bungalows.

For more information about the area, contact: **Oxnard Convention & Visitors Bureau,** Heritage Square, 711 S. A St., Oxnard, CA 93030,

805/385-7545 or toll-free 800/269-6273; www.oxnardtourism.com. For harbor information, contact: **Channel Islands Harbor Visitor Center,** 3810 W. Channel Islands Blvd., Ste. G, Oxnard, CA 93035, 805/985-4852; www.channelislandsharbor.com.

NEAR OXNARD: PORT HUENEME

The area's military-industrial development is most notable just south of Oxnard in and around Port Hueneme (wy-NEE-mee), about 60 miles north of L.A. and 40 miles south of Santa Barbara. A Chumash word meaning "halfway" or "resting place" and previously spelled Y-neema, Wyneema, and, officially, Wynema until 1940, when the U.S. Post Office altered it, Hueneme is still sometimes pronounced "way-NAY-ma" by old-timers here. A major military and civilian port—the only deepwater port between San Francisco and Los Angeles—Hueneme is most noted for its **Point Mugu Naval Air Weapons Station,** at last report still a survivor of U.S. defense budget cuts. The **Naval Construction Battalion Center,** "Home of the Pacific Seabees," has been at home here since 1942. If naval history fans first stop at the Ventura Road gate for a visitor pass, the free **U.S. Navy Civil Engineer Corps/Seabee Museum** on the base at Ventura Road and Sunkist Avenue, 805/982-5165, is well worth a visit—one of the finest military museums around. Open Mon.–Sat. 9 A.M.–4 P.M., Sunday 12:30–4:30 P.M. Free. Port Hueneme also boasts a small city history museum downtown next to the chamber of commerce, but adjacent **Grandpa,** the city's most aged downtown resident, a 375-year-old Monterey cypress, was finally recycled into walking sticks and such in 1997.

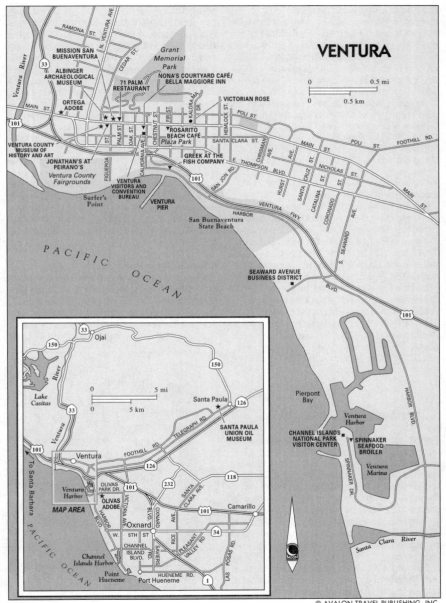

VENTURA

0   0.5 mi

0   0.5 km

MISSION SAN BUENAVENTURA

ALBINGER ARCHAEOLOGICAL MUSEUM

71 PALM RESTAURANT

ORTEGA ADOBE

NONA'S COURTYARD CAFÉ/ BELLA MAGGIORE INN

Grant Memorial Park

VICTORIAN ROSE

VENTURA COUNTY MUSEUM OF HISTORY AND ART

ROSARITO BEACH CAFÉ
Plaza Park

JONATHAN'S AT PEIRANO'S
Ventura County Fairgrounds

GREEK AT THE FISH COMPANY

VENTURA VISITORS AND CONVENTION BUREAU

Surfer's Point

VENTURA PIER

San Buenaventura State Beach

HARBOR

SEAWARD AVENUE BUSINESS DISTRICT

PACIFIC OCEAN

Ventura River

RAMONA ST.
N. VENTURA AVE.
CEDAR ST.
MAIN ST.
PALM ST.
OAK ST.
CALIFORNIA AVE.
CHESTNUT ST.
FIR ST.
KALORAMA DR.
HEMLOCK ST.
POLI ST.
SANTA CLARA ST.
CHRISMAN AVE.
MAIN ST.
POLI ST.
FOOTHILL RD.
FIGUEROA
E. THOMPSON BLVD.
HURST AVE.
SANTA CRUZ ST.
NICHOLAS ST.
CATALINA ST.
CORONADO ST.
MAIN ST.
SAN JON RD.
VENTURA FWY.
S. SEAWARD AVE.
BLVD.

Inset Map

Ojai

33
150
150
126

Lake Casitas

River

Santa Paula

SANTA PAULA UNION OIL MUSEUM

Pierpont Bay

CHANNEL ISLANDS NATIONAL PARK VISITOR CENTER

Ventura Harbor

SPINNAKER SEAFOOD BROILER

Ventura Marina

0   5 mi

0   5 km

TELEGRAPH RD.

FOOTHILL RD.

Ventura

33
101

Ventura Harbor

MAP AREA

OLIVAS PARK DR.

OLIVAS ADOBE

VICTORIA AVE.
OXNARD BLVD.
SANTA CLARA AVE.

232
101
118

Camarillo

34

Oxnard

W. 5TH ST
CHANNEL ISLAND BLVD.
SAVIERS
RICE AVE.
PLEASANT VALLEY RD.
LAS POSAS RD.

Channel Islands Harbor

Point Hueneme

Port Hueneme

HUENEME RD.

1

Santa Clara River

To Santa Barbara

PACIFIC OCEAN

101

HARBOR BLVD.

SPINNAKER DR.

MooN

Staying in and around Oxnard

Oxnard is fairly affordable, compared to other coastal locales. For a fairly complete accommodations list, contact the visitors bureau. Very nice is the **Best Western Oxnard Inn,** 1156 S. Oxnard Blvd., 805/483-9581 or toll-free 800/469-6273, fax 805/483-4072, www.bestwestern.com, with in-room refrigerators, microwaves, coffeemakers, and all the usual motel amenities plus swimming pool and whirlpool spa. Rates: $89–99. A best bet for a harbor stay is the **Casa Sirena Marina Resort,** 3605 Peninsula Rd., 805/985-6311 or toll-free 800/447-3529, fax 805/985-4329. Rates: $79–99, but look for off-season specials.

Eating in and around Oxnard

If you don't have time to drive area back roads in search of fresh produce, the **Oxnard Certified Farmers' Market,** 805/483-7960, is held in Downtown Plaza Park at Fifth and B Streets on Thursday, 10 A.M.–1 P.M. The **Oxnard–Channel Islands Harbor Certified Farmers' Market,** 805/652-2089 is held on Sunday 10 A.M.–2 P.M. at the foot of Harbor Boulevard in the harbor. Otherwise, almost anyone will tell you that **The Whale's Tail** in the harbor at 3950 Blue Fin Circle, 805/985-2511, is the best place around. Also decent for seafood is **Tugs** upstairs in the Marine Emporium at 3600 S. Harbor Blvd., 805/985-8847, open for breakfast, lunch, and dinner.

VENTURA: HOMETOWN ADVENTURES

Travelers on Highway 101 are typically in such a hurry to get either to or from Santa Barbara that they miss Ventura, still one of the most pleasant surprises along the coast north of Los Angeles. Its surrounding farmlands are fast being lost to the usual California housing developments and shopping centers, but historic downtown Ventura retains both its dignity and serenity. Stopping here is like visiting an old friend's oft-described hometown, since you'll feel like you've been here before.

Fun local events include the annual **Fourth of July Street Faire** downtown, the weekend **Summer by the Sea** music, entertainment, and arts

and crafts offerings every Saturday and Sunday from mid-July through August at the Ventura Pier and Promenade; and the August **California Beach Festival** at San Buenaventura Beach and the **Ventura County Fair** at Seaside Park. If you're here in early October, don't miss Southern California's own two-day **Kinetic Sculpture Race at Ventura,** www.ventura-kinetic-race.com, a people-powered artistic event to benefit the local homeless. Come in December for the **Parade of Lights** at Ventura Harbor.

For more information, contact: **Ventura Visitors and Convention Bureau,** 89 S. California St., Ste. C, Ventura, CA 93001, 805/648-2075 or toll-free 800/333-2989, fax 805/648-2150; www.ventura-usa.com. Among available information: local guides to antique shops and art galleries, and listings of sportfishing and whale-watching tour companies, shopping centers, local golf courses, and parks and other area recreational facilities.

Adventuring in Downtown Ventura

The centerpiece of Ventura's homey downtown Main Street business district is **Mission San Buenaventura,** 211 E. Main St., 805/643-4318, the ninth mission established in California and the last founded by Father Junípero Serra. Nearby is the very enjoyable **Ventura County**

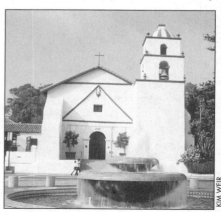

Mission San Buenaventura, the ninth mission established in California, was Father Junipero Serra's last.

Museum of History and Art, 100 E. Main, 805/653-0323, www.vcmha.org, open Tues.–Sun. 10 A.M.–5 P.M. (closed major holidays). Beyond the excellent exhibits—the Chumash, mission-era, and California statehood exhibits of the Huntsinger Gallery, the "three-dimension portraits" of the Smith Gallery, the contemporary local art on display in the Hoffman Gallery—the museum's gift shop is unusually fine. Admission is $4 adults, $3 seniors and AAA members, $1 children (under age 6 free). Nearby, at 113 E. Main, is the small but fascinating **Albinger Archaeological Museum,** 805/648-5823 or 805/658-4726, where an ongoing dig into one city block has unearthed artifacts from more than 3,500 years of coastal civilization; in 1974 and 1975 alone, more than 30,000 prehistoric, Chumash, Spanish, Mexican, American, and Chinese artifacts were unearthed. Admission is free. The Albinger museum is open Wed.–Sun. 10 A.M.–4 P.M. in summer; call for current off-season hours.

A few blocks away is the simple **Ortega Adobe,** 215 W. Main St., 805/658-4726, the 19th-century birthplace of the Ortega chile and salsa company, the first commercial food concern of its kind in California and originator of both the chile fire-roasting and canning processes. More evocative of the days of the Mexican ranchos, however, is the two-story Monterey-style **Olivas Adobe** hacienda east of the harbor at 4200 Olivas Park Dr., 805/644-4346, once the main house of vast Rancho San Miguel. Grounds are open daily 10 A.M.–4 P.M.; the house is open weekends only 10 A.M.–4 P.M.

The visitors bureau can suggest more local attractions. But since Erle Stanley Gardner, prolific author of the Perry Mason mysteries, was once a notable local presence, consider taking the **Erle Stanley Gardner Tour** of Ventura. Suggested stops are included on the website: www.erlestanleygardner.com.

The Beach, the Pier, the Harbor

Not all of Ventura's pleasures are downtown, however—at least not right downtown. A popular surfing locale, Ventura also boasts fine two-mile-long **San Buenaventura State Beach,** within strolling distance of downtown, extended by miles and miles of beach access up and down the coast. The recently restored 1,958-foot-long

Ventura Pier, just south of downtown and east of California Street off Harbor Boulevard, reopened in 1993 after a seven-year renovation and unveiled anew in 2000 following the addition of a new octagonal extension, is the state's oldest and longest wooden pier. Still popular for fishing, the pier boasts a large restaurant, snack bar, the blowholelike copper kinetic sculpture *Wavespout,* and lights that illuminate the beach after dark. West of the pier, at the end of Figueroa Street, is **Surfer's Point,** one of the state's premiere point breaks—a good place to watch longboard surfing.

South along the coast, past the beach-scene **Seaward Avenue Business District,** is relaxed **Ventura Harbor,** just off Harbor Boulevard. For information on the Channel Islands and permitted recreational activities, see Islands in Time: Channel Islands National Park, below.

Staying in Ventura

Stylish downtown is the historic **Bella Maggiore Inn,** 67 S. California St. (on the west side of California between Main and Santa Clara), 805/652-0277 or toll-free 800/523-8479, fax 805/648-5670. This three-story bed-and-breakfast hotel, built in 1924, has a breezy Mediterranean style—with fireplace, potted palms, and Italian chandeliers in the lobby, and shuttered windows, Capuan beds, ceiling fans, and fresh flowers in the graceful guest rooms. Rates: $75–150. Weather permitting—and it usually is—breakfast is served outside, in the lovely interior courtyard. In fact **Nona's Courtyard Cafe** here, a snazzy little Californian with a Northern Italian accent, is reason enough to stay. Breakfast can be a simple matter of coffee, pastries, and fresh fruit, or, for hearty appetites, omelettes and egg dishes. Expect good salads, sandwiches, and pastas at lunch, and chicken, fresh fish, and seafood at dinner (menu changes weekly). Nona's is open daily for breakfast, Mon.–Sat. for lunch, and Friday, Saturday, and Sunday for dinner.

Ventura's newest B&B is the **Victorian Rose,** 896 E. Main St., 805/641-1888, fax 805/643-1335, www.victorian-rose.com, a very Gothic onetime church where the five gorgeous guest rooms all feature private baths. Full breakfast included. Rates: $99–145.

Ventura offers a number of surprising reasonable hotels and motels; for a complete listing, ask at the visitors bureau. One good choice is the local outpost of **Country Inn & Suites,** 298 Chestnut St., 805/653-1434 or toll-free 800/456-4000, fax 805/648-7126, www.countryinns.com, along with all the usual amenities plus refrigerators, microwaves, wet bars, in-room coffee, remote-control color TVs with videocassette players, even hairdryers. Full country breakfast included. Rates: $89–119 (but ask about specials).

Eating in Ventura

Johnny's, 176 N. Ventura Ave., 805/648-2021, is famous for its burritos. People come from miles around just to sink their teeth into *chile verde* burritos, *chile relleno* burritos, and other intriguing possibilities. Another local draw is the **Rosarito Beach Café,** 692 E. Main St., 805/653-7343, where fresh fish is a main attraction. For more seafood at lunch or dinner, head to the harbor and the **Spinnaker Seafood Broiler,** Ventura Harbor Village, 1583 Spinnaker Dr., 805/339-0717, or the nearby **Greek at the Harbor,** 805/650-5350. Better yet is California-style **Eric Ericsson's Fish Company,** 668 Harbor Blvd., 805/643-4783.

Back downtown, consider very attractive **Nona's Courtyard Café** at the historic Bella Maggiore Inn, 67 S. California St. (see above), just the California-style Italian antidote for too much freeway-flying. Quite fine is **Jonathan's at Peirano's,** 204 E. Main St., 805/648-4853, where the style is also Mediterranean. The **71 Palm Restaurant,** 71 N. Palm St., 805/653-7222, specializes in French classics.

ISLANDS IN TIME: CHANNEL ISLANDS NATIONAL PARK

Privately owned **Santa Catalina Island** is the only truly populated island among Southern California's eight Channel Islands. Populated by humans, that is. Many of the rest are inhabited by, or surrounded by, such rare, endangered, and endemic animals and plants—various whale and seal species, the island fox, the giant coreopsis "tree" (tree sunflowers), and the Santa Cruz Island ironweed among them—that biologists describe the Channel Islands, collectively, as North America's Galápagos.

San Miguel, Anacapa, Santa Cruz, and Santa Rosa Islands are seaward extensions of the east-west-trending Transverse Ranges (Santa Monica Mountains), and Santa Barbara, San Clemente, and San Nicolas are the visible ocean outposts of the Peninsular Range. Out-there **San Nicolas** and **San Clemente Islands,** property of the U.S. Navy, have rarely been visited. San Clemente has the unfortunate history of being used for bombing runs and military target practice. In the 1950s San Nicolas, inspiration for the book *Island of the Blue Dolphins,* was a top-secret post for monitoring submarines from the USSR Since San Nicolas still contains ancient petroglyphs of dolphins, sharks, and whales, it's entirely appropriate that this same Cold War technology is now used to track the movements of migrating whales.

Channel Islands preservation efforts first succeeded in 1938, when President Franklin D. Roosevelt protected Anacapa and Santa Barbara Islands as a national monument. The five northernmost Channel Islands are now included in Channel Islands National Park, 250,000 acres of isolated Southern California real estate set aside in 1980 by President Jimmy Carter for federal preservation. (Odd, by national park standards, is the fact that half these acres are below the ocean's surface.) With some planning, visitors can set out for **San Miguel, Santa Rosa, Santa Cruz, Anacapa,** and **Santa Barbara Islands.** Primitive camping is allowed on all five islands.

Islands in Time

The Channel Islands discovery of a complete fossilized skeleton of a pygmy or "dwarf" mammoth generated major excitement in the summer of 1994. Scientists speculate that this unusual miniature species, standing only four to six feet tall, was descended from woolly mammoths who swam here from the Southern California mainland during the Pleistocene, when the islands were "one" and just a few miles off the coast.

These islands in time reveal more surprises. For one thing, they are still on the move. Satellite measurements in the early 1990s showed that Santa Catalina, San Clemente, and San

CHANNEL ISLANDS TOURS AND TRIPS

Unless you have your own boat, if you're shoving off from Ventura you'll be going via **Island Packer Cruises,** which offers the rare opportunity to get up close and personal with Channel Islands National Park, an area otherwise all but inaccessible for the average traveler. Since island access is limited, extra benefits of an Island Packer trip—some trips, anyway—include the chance to hike, snorkel, or kayak. Camping drop-offs can also be arranged. Whale-watching (January through March) is particularly popular, especially since whales, dolphins, seals, and sea lions favor the protected waters and abundant food supplies near the Channel Islands. But every season has its unique pleasures. Spring, for example, offers the chance to see wildflowers and rare endemic plants in bloom.

For current information, contact: Island Packer Tours, 1867 Spinnaker Dr., Ventura, CA 93001, 805/642-7688 (recorded) or 805/642-1393, fax 805/642-6573; www.islandpackers.com. The compa-

ny's office is adjacent to the park's visitor center in Ventura Harbor (closed Thanksgiving and Christmas). Reservations are required for all trips, but are subject to last-minute cancellation in case of big waves or bad weather. For popular weekend outings, reserve well in advance. In spring and summer, Island Packer operates tours to—or around—all five islands. Call for specific information about "transport" services for backpackers and long-term campers.

If you're departing from Santa Barbara, the official Channel Islands trip concessionaire there is **Truth Aquatics,** 301 W. Cabrillo Blvd., Santa Barbara, CA 93101, 805/962-1127, fax 805/564-6754; www .truthaquatics.com.

Channel Islands Aviation offers day-trip transportation, tours, and "drop-offs" to and from Santa Rosa Island (and Santa Catalina Island). For current information, contact: Channel Islands Aviation, 305 Durley Ave., Camarillo, CA 93010, 805/987-1301.

Nicolas Islands are moving northwest about one-half inch per year, and that a section of California's coastline is slowly converging with Santa Cruz and Santa Rosa islands—narrowing the Santa Barbara Channel by the same one-half inch each year.

For another, the Channel Islands provide some of the earliest North American evidence of human habitation. Prehistoric cooking pits found in conjunction with mammoth bones on Santa Rosa Island point to a neighborhood barbecue bash about 30,000–40,000 years ago.

Humans, other animals, and plant species have been introduced to the islands over the vast expanse of time; some failed, and some evolved into unique species as geographical isolation led to genetic isolation; 145 species of Channel Islands plants and animals are found nowhere else on earth.

Unusual animals found on the islands today include the island fox—a distant relative of the mainland's gray fox and about the size of a cat—various rodents, bats, and feral goats and pigs. (Of the islands' endemic mammals, the deer mouse is known to carry hantavirus.) More than 260 bird species have been spotted on and around Santa Cruz Island alone. Brown pelican

rookeries and the largest U.S. colony of Xantus's murrelet and black petrels are Channel Islands highlights.

Channel Islands National Park is also a national marine sanctuary and international biosphere preserve, an ecosystem protectorate including all five islands and a six-mile area surrounding each one. During its annual migration south to Baja, Mexico, between January and March, the California gray whale appears in large numbers throughout the Channel Islands. In recent years a fairly large population of the rare and endangered blue whale, the world's largest creature, has tarried here as well. More than two dozen species of marine mammals—whales, sharks, dolphins and porpoises, various seal and sea lion species, sea otters—inhabit these waters during at least part of the year. Because of "upwelling" along California's coast and the Pacific Ocean's rich nutrient levels, vast kelp and other marine "forests" provide food and shelter for vast numbers of animals. Island tide pools also teem with sea life.

San Miguel Island

The most westerly of the Channel Islands, 9,325-acre San Miguel in the north is most famous for the thousands and thousands of seals and sea lions—up to 30,000 in summer, the population including the once-rare northern elephant seal—that bask in the sun at Bennett Point. Also notable for hikers are its giant coreopsis "trees" and ghostly caliche forests, the latter an odd moonscape of calcified plant fossils—a natural variation on sand casting—of up to 14,000 years old. Local landmarks include a modest memorial to Cabrillo, believed to have died here in 1583, and the ruins of the Lester Ranch of caretaker Herbert Lester, "King of San Miguel," who committed suicide here in 1942 rather than be forcibly evicted by the military. The weather here can be wicked—always windy, foggy, often rainy—so come prepared. Primitive camping, hiking, beach exploration, and ranger-led hikes are the main attractions, but be sure to stick to established trails. San Miguel was once used for bombing practice, and live ordnance is constantly being discovered beneath the island's shifting sands.

Santa Rosa Island
The national park system has owned 52,794-acre Santa Rosa since 1986. The island's main attractions aren't the usual tourist trappings, particularly some 2,000 archaeology sites (strictly off-limits) related to Chumash Indian and Chinese abalone fishing settlements. Ruthlessly wind-whipped, Santa Rosa nonetheless protects rare and endangered plants, including one of only two surviving natural stands of Torrey pines (the other is near La Jolla). Despite federal ownership, overgrazing has recently a problem on Santa Rosa. In addition to primitive camping and kayak beach camping, hiking, ranger-guided hikes, and vehicle tours are Santa Rosa's main attractions.

Santa Cruz Island
In 1997, preservationists finally took complete possession of 24-mile-long, 60,645-acre Santa Cruz Island, the largest of the eight Channel Islands. Island Adventures, a private firm that had offered private bow-hunting trips and bed-and-breakfast overnights on the east end of Santa Cruz, was evicted and the National Park Service bought its part of the island, to the east. The Nature Conservancy owns the other 90 percent and manages it as the **Santa Cruz Island Preserve,** to date a noticeably healthier ecosys-

tem. But park officials are restoring damaged east-end habitats, long overgrazed by sheep, goats, and feral pigs, and the historic Gherini Ranch. The ranch will eventually become the human-oriented hub of the park's five islands.

Already the park's primary draw, Santa Cruz is the most luxuriant of the Channel Islands. Two mountain ranges traverse Santa Cruz, one red, one white, and the island's picturesque Central Valley is an active earthquake zone. (According to local lore, terror created by the great California earthquake of 1812 finally convinced the native Chumash to leave Santa Cruz for life in the mainland's Franciscan missions.) This slice of the French Mediterranean right off the coast of California is the onetime ranching empire of Justinian Caire. Caire's winery here, finally closed during Prohibition, was at that time one of Southern California's largest. The Caire family's chapel and other buildings of the subsequent Santa Cruz Island Company ranch were preserved by subsequent owners, members of the Stanton family, and by The Nature Conservancy.

The island's curvaceous coastline boasts many natural harbors, bays, and popular dive spots, along with some spectacular sea caves. The landscape features 10 distinct plant communities, about 650 plant species scattered from pine forests, oak woodlands, and riparian streams and springs to meadows, sandy beaches, and dunes. The seascape features many more plant and animal communities, which makes Santa Cruz paradise for divers, kayakers, snorkelers, and tidepoolers. (Look, but don't touch.) More than 260 bird species have been spotted on and around the island, including the endemic Santa Cruz Island scrub jay, bigger and bluer than its mainland cousins. Hike, camp, and explore on the park's property. Private boaters, call The Nature Conservancy, 805/964-7839, to request permission to land on the west side of Santa Cruz.

Anacapa Island
Wind-whipped Anacapa Island is most accessible from the mainland, just 11 miles from Oxnard. Quite popular for day-trippers, 699-acre Anacapa is actually three distinct islands divided by narrow channels. **East Anacapa** is the usual human destination. On the way to Landing Cove is 80-foot-tall **Arch Rock,** an immense eroded

volcanic "bridge" with a 50-foot arch, unofficial emblem of the Channel Islands since James Whistler sketched it during his stint in the U.S. Coast Guard. Once ashore it's a quick 154 steps straight up to the bluff-tops, where the meandering nature trail begins. Beyond the visitor center, standing vigil at the entrance to the Santa Barbara Channel, is the U.S. Coast Guard's restored, solar-powered **East End Lighthouse** and associated museum, open for public tours. (Inquire at the park's mainland visitor center for details.) If time, weather, and water conditions permit, **Landing Cove** and **Frenchy's Cove** are popular for snorkeling and swimming. Guided **kayak tours** are also popular here.

On **Middle Anacapa** the stands of giant coreopsis ("tree sunflowers") are stunning when in bloom—on a clear day, their vibrant color is visible from the mainland. Craggy **West Anacapa**, the largest of the three, is off-limits to the public, protected as a brown pelican rookery and reserve.

Santa Barbara Island

Ever fantasized about being stranded on a desert island? Want to play *Survivor*? Here's a possible destination. Unlike the lushly landscaped, socially sophisticated mainland city of the same name, 639-acre Santa Barbara Island is a piece of California in the raw. Smallest of the park's five islands, Santa Barbara has no trees, no natural beaches, and no fresh water. Its sheer cliffs rise abruptly from the sea. It's often windy and foggy in quick succession; in winter Santa Barbara's thin thatch of grass and scrub is green. Most popular with birders, divers, and kayakers, in warm weather Santa Barbara also attracts pinniped peerers (including sea lions), hikers, and campers. (Bring *everything,* including water.) A lonely 25 miles west of Catalina, a long, often choppy three hours from Ventura Harbor, Santa Barbara is most appreciated by avid island and/or wildlife aficionados.

Practical Channel Islands

For more information on the islands and permitted recreational activities, contact: **Channel Islands National Park Visitors Center,** 1901 Spinnaker Dr., Ventura, CA 93001, 805/658-5730; www.nps.gov/chis. Or sign on for an island tour (see below). The visitor center in Ventura

Harbor is *the* stop for relevant books, maps, and a good general introduction to the history and natural history of the islands. For hiking permits for San Miguel Island, call 805/658-5711.

At last report primitive park campgrounds were available on all five islands. If you're planning to camp or hike (permits required), come prepared for anything—wind, in particular—because the weather can change abruptly. For current information, inquire at the park's visitor center; for camping permits—free, though there is a $2.50 reservation fee per campsite per day—are available by calling Biospherics, Inc., at toll-free 800/365-2267.

SANTA PAULA: BLAST FROM THE PAST

Like nearby Fillmore, Santa Paula is most famous for its delightful 19th-century downtown, both in its architecture and ambience. The Victorian-era buildings along well-manicured Main Street, in other respects representing an antiquers' holiday, are constructed, uniquely, of weathered red brick and Sespe sandstone. Queen Anne and Victorian homes line nearby streets, blending here and there with Mediterranean and craftsman styles. Yet Santa Paula offers its historic eccentricities; on the four-sided clock tower downtown, notice the bullet holes on the clock's north face, a distinguishing feature. Even the privately owned airport here is a surprise, a relic from the heyday of open-cockpit aviation; planes in the air on any weekend here comprise an ever-changing antique plane museum.

Still surrounded by orange and lemon groves and occasional oil derricks—and so far spared the indignities of suburban sprawl—Santa Paula was built from the wealth generated by the California oil boom of the late 1800s and the subsequent success of area agriculture. The free **Santa Paula Union Oil Museum,** 1001 E. Main St. (10th and Main), 805/933-0076, open Wed.–Sun. 10 A.M.–4 P.M., tells part of the story. The museum store sells copies of the Santa Paula Historical Society's "Neighborhoods and Neighbors of the Past," which tells some of the rest by guiding visitors through historic residential neighborhoods. A drive through Santa Paula's surrounding citrus groves completes the tale. Ventura County is still California's largest lemon producer (California is the largest producer in the United States), and Santa Paula is the industry star. Santa Paula's Limoneira Co. is the county's largest lemon grower, with 40 percent of its crop—the most perfect oval fruit—exported to Hong Kong and elsewhere in Asia, where the lemons can fetch a price of $2 each.

For more information about the area, stop by the **Santa Paula Chamber of Commerce** at the historic train depot, 200 N. 10th St. (10th and Santa Barbara Sts.), 805/525-5561.

Practical Santa Paula
Notable among Santa Paula's notable bed-and-breakfasts is the Spanish revival **Fern Oaks**

NEAR SANTA PAULA

Another of Southern California's "last best small towns" is historic **Fillmore,** east of Santa Paula via Highway 126, also noted for its intriguing brick-and-masonry downtown. But Fillmore sits astride the Oak Ridge earthquake fault. Right after a costly downtown spruce-up campaign, in early 1994 came the devastating Northridge earthquake. About $200 million in structural damage later—much of it to downtown buildings—Fillmore is still putting itself back together again. Family-style fun here includes rides on the **Fillmore and Western Railway,** 250 Central Ave. (red caboose on the north side of city hall), 805/524-2546 or toll-free 800/773-8724, www.fwry.com, where special-event trains include the Summer Sunset BBQ and the Spaghetti Western Dinner Train.

Directly south of Fillmore via Highway 23 is the affluent suburb of **Moorpark,** most famous as the first town in the United States to be completely powered by nuclear energy—a 1957 event that actually lasted only about an hour but which 20 million people watched on TV two weeks later, thanks to newsman Edward R. Murrow. Moorpark's nuclear adventure was an early Southern California Edison experiment that lasted just a couple of years. A small nuclear plant in the Simi Hills supplied only a part of the city's energy during most of the experiment.

Inn, 1025 Ojai Rd., 805/525-7747, fax 805/933-5001; www.fernoaksinn.com. Rates: $95–130, breakfast included. For a decent meal, try **Familia Diaz,** 245 S. 10th St., 805/525-2813, a local tradition for decades. In 1996 this cheerful restaurant, known for its homemade red *chile colorado* tamales, celebrated its 60th anniversary with a special tamale (such as shrimp) each month. But you can't go wrong with anything here, from the *carnitas, chile verde,* and *chiles rellenos* to fish dishes. Kids' menu, too. It's open daily for lunch and dinner. For fine dining, head to Ojai, a mere 20 minutes away. Or continue to Santa Barbara.

OJAI: SVELTE SHANGRI-LA

To the native Chumash peoples, Ojai (OH-hi) was the spiritual center of the world. Plenty of later arrivals shared similar beliefs, which is why the Krishnamurti Foundation and Library, the Krotona Institute of Theosophy and Library, Aldous Huxley's Happy Valley School, and so many other philosophical and religious icons have centered themselves in this lovely valley. Southern California's newest religion, the quest for svelte health, is also reasonably well represented here—particularly at The Oaks at Ojai health spa downtown, sister to The Palms at Palm Springs.

The mountain-ringed Ojai Valley nests in the shadows of the Topatopa Mountains. According to local lore, Ojai means "the nest" in Chumash, though linguists say "moon" is the word's actual meaning; some residents now interpret the name of their spiritual nesting place as "valley of the nesting moon." Also according to local lore, Frank Capra set up his cameras at Dennison Grade east of town to shoot Ronald Coleman's first impressions of lush Shangri-La, the valley of eternal youth, for his 1937 film *Lost Horizons*—a film fact still in some dispute, since most of Capra's filming actually took place near Palm Springs.

But no one disputes the truth of Ojai's fabled "pink moment," that magical time close to sunset when the entire valley glows pink in the light of the waning sun—the community's most unifying spiritual event. Visitors can pay homage at least indirectly by signing on for a trip with **Pink**

Moment Jeep Tours, 805/646-3227, which offers around-town tours as well as rugged back-country jaunts.

For more information about the area, contact: **Ojai Valley Chamber of Commerce and Visitors Bureau,** 150 W. Ojai Ave., Ojai, CA 93023, 805/646-8126; www.the-ojai.org. For area hiking, camping, and other national forest information, stop by the **Ojai Ranger District Office** of Los Padres National Forest, 1190 E. Ojai Ave., 805/646-4348; www.r5.fs.fed.us /lospadres.

Seeing and Doing Ojai

Artsy and laid-back downtown Ojai is neat but nondescript, architecturally distinguished by its mission revival architecture, particularly the clock tower atop the downtown post office and the pergola fronting Libbey Park. For a brief community introduction, stop by the **Ojai Valley Museum,** 130 E. Ojai Ave., 805/646-1390. Or explore the various antique shops, art and pottery galleries, boutiques, and bookstores. A local institution is **Bart's Corner,** 302 W. Matilija, 805/646-3755, an open-air used bookstore not known for bargains but for its inimitable ambience.

Ojai's inhabitants seem to share a striking love of the land. Join in with a visit to Ojai's 275-acre **International Center for Earth Concerns** at the headwaters to Lake Casitas, 805/649-3535, www.earthconcerns.org, "a place to know and work for nature." Included here are 30 acres of botanical gardens, a parrot sanctuary, and a small retreat center. Open to the public by reservation only for bird walks and garden and herb tours. (Pack a lunch and bring water.) For a current walk schedule and reservations, call or consult the website. Also intriguing for a stroll in nature is the **Studio in the Hills,** 805/646-2000, where "The Walk" means an arty, spirit-expanding experience walking through the chaparral.

People here also love the arts. Find out what's going on, artistically speaking, at the **Ojai Center for the Arts,** 113 S. Montgomery St., 805/646-0117, which sponsors monthly art shows and community theater. Except in July, August, and December, the **Ojai Film Society,** 805/646-8946, www.ojai,net/film, presents fine films every Sunday at 4:30 P.M. at the Ojai Playhouse. The society also debuted its first **Ojai International Film Festival** in November 2000.

OJAI MUSIC FESTIVAL, OTHER EVENTS

As famous as The Pink Moment is Ojai's three-day Ojai Music Festival, "the class act of all California music festivals" since the 1940s, held either on the last weekend in May or in early June under the oaks at the Libbey Park Bowl. Along with the classics, the Ojai festival distinguishes itself by showcasing post–World War II works, including progressive and avant-garde compositions. Single-performance ticket prices are $15–65, depending on where you sit, and series tickets are $70–290. Hard wooden benches are the "good seats" (bring a cushion, or buy one); cheap-seaters get to sprawl out on the lawn behind the bowl. For current schedule information or to buy tickets, contact: **Ojai Festivals, Ltd.,** 805/646-2053, fax 805/646-6037; www.ojaifestival.org.

But you can hear music free in summer at the **summer band concerts** held in Libbey Park every Wednesday in July and August, starting at 8 P.M. Other worthwhile local events include the big-deal **Ojai Valley Tennis Tournament** in late April, the **Ojai Garden Tour** in May, the **Ojai Valley Mexican Fiesta** in September, and the **Bowlful of Blues** festival in October.

Lake Casitas

Central to outdoor Ojai life is lovely Lake Casitas to the west off Highway 150, a 6,200-acre regional recreation area and reservoir most famous for its trout and bass fishing. The 1984 Olympics rowing and canoeing events were held here. Prime for camping and fun for picnicking and letting the kids let off a little steam—there are many playgrounds here—Lake Casitas has never been open for public swimming, but officials are at least considering changing that policy, much to the dismay of fisherfolk. Campgrounds and group camps here are quite nice, featuring both basic tent camping sites and full hookups for RVs. Two- or three-night minimum stays are required on weekends. Camping fees begin at $12 per campsite per day (up to six people) and climb to $22 for full hookups on a holiday weekend. Hiker/biker campsites are $2 per person. Other facilities include boat launch and docking facilities, a full-service marina, snack bar, store, and coin-operated showers. Boat rentals are available.

The lake's day-use fee is $5 per vehicle ($6 on holiday weekends), $1 extra for pets (on leashes). For general park information, contact: Lake Casitas Recreation Area, 11311 Santa Ana Rd., Ventura, CA 93001, 805/649-2233. You can reserve campsites up to several days, but no more than 90 days, in advance of your arrival.

Staying in and near Ojai

If you're not camping at Lake Casitas, consider the national forest's **Wheeler Gorge Campground** on Matilija Creek, about eight miles north of Ojai on Highway 33, near Wheeler Springs; for information call the Ojai ranger station, 805/646-4348; for reservations, from 7–120 days in advance, call toll-free 800/280-2267. Another possibility is woodsy **Camp Comfort** on San Antonio Creek two miles south of town at 11969 N. Creek Rd., 805/646-2314 or 805/654-3951 for reservations. With tent sites and some RV hookups, extras here include hot showers, laundry, and a small store.

Good choices among midrange area motels include the **Hummingbird Inn,** 1208 E. Ojai Ave., 805/646-4365 or toll-free 800/228-3744, fax 805/646-0625, www.hummingbirdinnofojai .com, with clean rooms, a pool, and on-site spa; pets are allowed on approval. High-season rates: $76–145. The comfortable **Best Western Casa Ojai** nearby at 1302 E. Ojai Ave., 805/646-8175 or toll-free 800/255-8175, fax 805/640-8247, www.bestwestern.com, also includes a pool and spa. Rates: $80–120. A real deal in the neighborhood, though, is the **Oakridge Inn** east of Lake Casitas at 780 N. Ventura Ave., 805/649-4018, fax 805/649-4436, www.oakridgeinn.com, rates: $55–95.

Just about the hippest place around, though, is a onetime motor court south of town, restyled into the artsy **Blue Iguana Inn,** 11794 N. Ventura Ave., 805/646-5277, fax 805/646-8078, www .blueigianainn.com, where you can meet Iggy the iguana yourself at the tiled mosaic fountain in the courtyard. The inn, carefully crafted in old mission style—arched designs, terra cotta tile roofs, handmade Ojai tile work—showcases the work of local artists. Rates for rooms and kitchen suites $99–160.

For peeling away the pounds and inches, one place is **The Oaks at Ojai,** "the affordable spa" at 122 E. Ojai Ave., 805/646-5573 or toll-free 800/753-6257, www.oaksspa.com, where the total fitness and stress management program comes with all meals—about 750 calories per day—and a fairly hefty tab. Rates from $145 per person.

For the most luxurious local stay, just west of town is the historic 220-acre **Ojai Valley Inn,** appropriately situated on Country Club Road, 805/646-5511 or toll-free 800/422-6524 (hotel), toll-free 888/772-6524 (spa), fax 805/646-7969; www.ojairesort.com. In 1923 the wealthy glass manufacturer Edward Drummond Libbey, whose name crops up frequently in these parts, commissioned architect Walter Neff to design the stylish Spanish colonial golf course clubhouse here. The rest of the Ojai Valley Inn, with its 18-hole golf course (now featured on the Senior PGA Tour), putting green, tennis center, riding stables and "ranch," Camp Ojai for kids, and complete health spa, exercise, business, and conference facilities, has grown up around Neff's original contribution. Completely renovated and restyled in the 1980s and updated since, this Spanish-style grande dame features 207 rooms and suites, two swimming pools, two restaurants, 24-hour room service, bike rentals, and hiking and jogging trails. Rooms start at $245, suites at $390, though discounts and off-season specials can drop the tab considerably.

Eating in Ojai

The weekly **Ojai Certified Farmers' Market,** with local baked goods and pastries in addition to the usual cornucopia of fresh produce and flowers, convenes every Sunday morning in summer 9 A.M.–1 P.M. downtown behind the Arcade, 300 E. Matilija, 805/646-4444. Put together an impromptu picnic with help from **Bill Baker's Bakery,** 457 E. Ojai Ave., 805/646-1558, which features the famed and flavorful wheat-free breads and other baked goods originally invented by Bill Baker in the 1930s. Poke around town for pizza places and café-style possibilities. French-influenced California-style **Suzanne's Cuisine,** 502 W. Ojai Ave., 805/640-1961, is a best bet at lunch and dinner (closed on Tuesday). Another long-standing local favorite is **Boccali's,** 3277 Ojai–Santa Paula Rd., 805/646-

6116, where the vegetables accompanying the pizza and traditional Italian come from the restaurant garden.

For natural food elevated to fine dining *experience,* the place is the **Ranch House** restaurant on S. Lomita Avenue, 805/646-2360. Founder Alan Hooker first came to Ojai in 1946 to hear Krishnamurti speak, and within a few years he was catering the event—and thus the original Ranch House was born. Since it moved to a spot closer to the highway, the restaurant still serves the finest, freshest natural foods anywhere, here often accompanied by rich sauces and—gasp!—real creamery butter. (Herbs still come from the restaurant's herb garden.) The Ranch House is open for dinner only Wed.–Sat., for lunch and dinner on Sunday, closed Monday and Tuesday. Expensive. To take this place home with you, pick up a copy of *California Herb Cookery: From the Ranch House Restaurant.*

Other possibilities for fine dining include the Belgian **L'Auberge,** 314 El Paseo, 805/646-

2288, open for dinner Wed.–Mon. and for lunch and dinner on weekends (closed Tuesday). Or head to the Ojai Valley Inn and the **Oak Grill and Terrace,** 805/646-5511, ext. 700, open for lunch and dinner.

From Ojai

It's a quick trip from Ojai back to Santa Barbara via Highway 50 and then either Highway 192 or Highway 101 along the coast—the usual route, for day-trippers. For a much longer alternative road trip to Santa Barbara, head north past Wheeler Springs on Highway 33, up the switchbacks to Pine Mountain Summit, then drop down into Cuyama Valley; follow Highway 166 past the badlands burg of New Cuyama into Santa Maria. From there, dabble in Santa Barbara County's boutique wine country around Los Alamos and Los Olivos before cruising past Cachuma Lake and into Santa Barbara via Highway 154.

SANTA BARBARA AND VICINITY

Santa Barbara is beautiful, rich, and proud of it. Though her past is somewhat mysterious (she goes by the name "Santa Teresa" in the works of mystery writers Ross MacDonald and Sue Grafton), her presence hints at natural luck almost as incredible as her beauty, cosmic beneficence only briefly perturbed by unavoidable misfortune. If she were a flesh-and-blood woman, she would sway down the brick sidewalks, her aristocratic nose pointed upward, a satisfied smile on her face.

But such easy grace is no accident, of course; Santa Barbara's beauty regimen is strict. She insists that the façades of all buildings (including McDonald's) reflect the Spanish style she favors. Death, decay, or other disarray in her environment displeases her; the only time she curses is when she spits out the words "developer," "development," and "oil companies," these latter responsible for the 1969 oil spill that fouled 20 miles of her pristine beaches. Her most peculiar personality quirk is that she secretly believes she lives in Northern California, despite social intercourse with everything Southern Californian.

Santa Barbara is generous with her gifts, and she has everything: beautiful beaches and understated, stark chaparral slopes, colleges and universities, a celebrated arts and entertainment scene, fine restaurants (more restaurants per capita than any other U.S. city, in fact) and luxury resorts, trendy boutiques, antique shops. Though her sun shines brightest on celebrity residents—among them, in recent history, Cher, Julia Child, Michael Douglas, Jane Fonda, Kenny Loggins, Steve Martin, Priscilla Presley, and John Travolta—she magnanimously allows the middle class to bask in her glow.

But the shadow side to Santa Barbara's radiance is the basically ugly belief that she must shun any and all things unsightly. Poverty is unsightly and Santa Barbara doesn't want to see it. So her people passed laws prohibiting the homeless from sleeping in public on the sidewalks.

Santa Barbara Natural History: Dignified But Dry

The city itself faces south, spreading back toward the dry but dignified Santa Ynez Mountains like

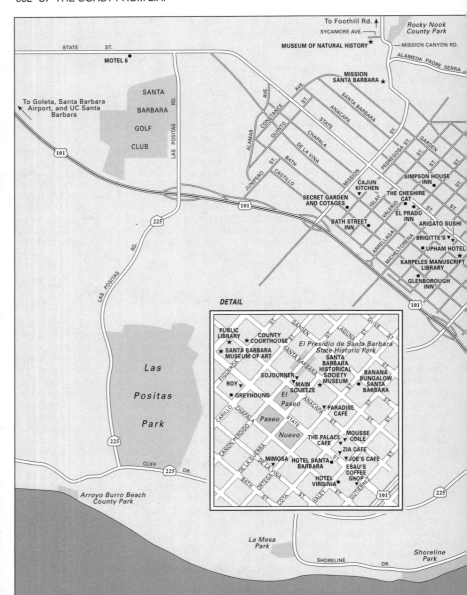

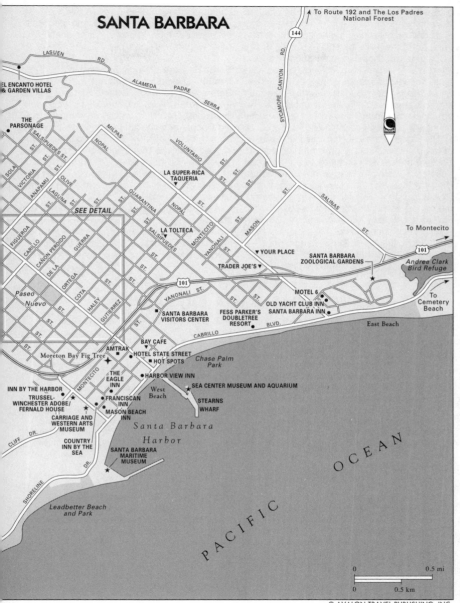

SANTA BARBARA

To Route 192 and The Los Padres
National Forest

144

LASUEN RD

ALAMEDA PADRE SERRA

SYCAMORE CANYON RD

EL ENCANTO HOTEL
& GARDEN VILLAS

THE
PARSONAGE

MILPAS

NOPAL

VOLUNTARIO ST

SALSIPUEDES ST

SOLA ST
VICTORIA ST
ANAPAMU ST
OLIVE ST
LAGUNA ST

LA SUPER-RICA
TAQUERIA

SALINAS

ST

QUARANTINA

NOPAL ST

SEE DETAIL

FIGUEROA
CARILLO
CANON PERDIDO
DE LA GUERRA
GUERRA ST

ST

LA TOLTECA

SALSIPUEDES ST

MONTECITO ST

YANONALI ST

MASON ST

To Montecito

YOUR PLACE

SANTA BARBARA
ZOOLOGICAL GARDENS

101

Andree Clark
Bird Refuge

Paseo
Nuevo

ORTEGA
COTA
HALEY ST
GUTIERREZ ST

ST

101

TRADER JOE'S

YANONALI ST

MOTEL 6

OLD YACHT CLUB INN
SANTA BARBARA INN

To
Cemetery
Beach

SANTA BARBARA
VISITORS CENTER

FESS PARKER'S
DOUBLETREE
RESORT

CABRILLO BLVD

East Beach

BAY CAFE

Moreton Bay Fig Tree

AMTRAK

HOTEL STATE STREET

HOT SPOTS

Chase Palm
Park

INN BY THE HARBOR

TRUSSEL-
WINCHESTER ADOBE/
FERNALD HOUSE

CARRIAGE AND
WESTERN ARTS
MUSEUM

MONTECITO

THE
EAGLE
INN

HARBOR VIEW INN

FRANCISCAN
INN

MASON BEACH
INN

West
Beach

SEA CENTER MUSEUM AND AQUARIUM

STEARNS
WHARF

CLIFF DR

COUNTRY
INN BY THE
SEA

SHORELINE DR

SANTA BARBARA
MARITIME
MUSEUM

Santa Barbara
Harbor

OCEAN

Leadbetter Beach
and Park

PACIFIC

0   0.5 mi

0   0.5 km

a Spanish fan. The Channel Islands offshore protect Santa Barbara's sublime coastal bay and unruffled beaches. Despite the genuine devastation of the 1969 oil spill here, the gooey blobs of tar on shoreline rocks and white sand are primarily natural, from Monterey shale petroleum deposits hundreds of feet thick in some areas. Near Santa Barbara, earthquake fault lines run east-west, like the mountains whose deformed rock formations hint at the intensity of underground earth movement.

The palms and eucalyptus trees, in fact *most* of the plants commonly growing along Santa Barbara streets and beaches, are introduced species. Native plants in and around Santa Barbara today include live oaks, pines, and California bay trees, also toyon, greasewood, manzanita, and other chaparral shrubs. Shadier valleys and grassy hillsides are dazzling with wildflowers in spring. About 400 species of birds are found in the Santa Barbara region.

The most common "city birds" include the western mockingbird, California jays, house finches, sparrows, and hummingbirds. At the beach, sandpipers, terns, gulls, and other seabirds are common. Migrating ducks, geese, and other waterfowl visit the city's lake refuge.

Santa Barbara History: Basking in Gentility, Beset by Troubles

Before there even was a Santa Barbara, before the Bronze Age, an ancient Oak Grove people lived here. Then later, equally mysterious Hunting People arrived with improved technology: arrows, clubs, spearheads, and tools used for digging shellfish. These hunters and gatherers slowly merged their society with still later arrivals to become the industrious Chumash, whose few descendants today live inland and along nearby coasts.

As with many native California peoples the central focus of the Chumash was spiritual, though they nonetheless found time for their industries: boat making, fishing, and trading with island residents across the channel. Only remnants of the rich ancient Chumash culture

NATURAL SANTA BARBARA

The best of natural Santa Barbara and vicinity is on display at the exceptional **Santa Barbara Museum of Natural History** two blocks north of the mission at 2559 Puesta Del Sol Rd., 805/682-4711; www.sbnature.org. This Spanish-style cluster of buildings and courtyards includes excellent exhibits on the Chumash and other indigenous peoples, collections of fossils, geology displays, nature exhibits (including a busy beehive), even some original Audubon lithographs. In addition to the museum's classes on every natural history topic under the sun, there's a planetarium and observatory here, 805/682-3224, offering a popular Sunday afternoon program. The museum also sponsors a year-round schedule of films and special events—including **monarch butterfly tours** in January (by reservation) and the **Wine Festival** in August. On the way in or out, stop outside near the parking lot to appreciate the 72-foot-long skeleton of a blue whale, recently restored. The natural history museum is open 9 A.M.–5 P.M. daily (from 10 A.M. on Sunday and holidays), closed Thanksgiving, Christmas, and New Year's Day. Admission is $6 adults, $5 seniors and students (ages 13–17), and $4 children age 12 and under, free on the first Sunday of every month. Nearby and perfect for an almost-country picnic is **Rocky Nook County Park.**

The 65-acre **Santa Barbara Botanic Garden**, 1212 Mission Canyon Rd., 805/682-4726, www.sbbg.org, is "dedicated to the study of California's native plants." Too many people miss this natural Santa Barbara treasure. Plants native to Santa Barbara and vicinity are the main event (don't miss the spectacular spring wildflowers) but cacti, other succulents, even redwoods are at home in the gardens here. Good gift shop—particularly popular with gardeners and plant lovers. Lectures, classes, trips, and special events are often scheduled, and docent-guided tours are offered daily at 2 P.M., also on Thursday, Saturday, and Sunday at 10:30 A.M. Best, though, is showing up when nothing's going on and just wandering the grounds—a stroll that can easily become a brisk five-mile hike. The botanic garden is open daily 9 A.M.–sunset (gift shop open until 4 P.M. in winter, 5 P.M. in summer). Small admission (under age 5 free), and once you're in docent-guided tours are free, but donations and membership support are always appreciated.

*Santa Barbara's
"Queen of the Missions"*

KIM WEIR

remain—baskets, beads, charms, and money—many of these items now in museums. Forced into Christianity by zealous Spanish missionaries, the Chumash near Santa Barbara were all but wiped out by foreign diseases, their own social and spiritual decline, and alcoholism.

Despite its aura of established comfort, Santa Barbara has suffered two major earthquakes (the first flattened the original mission), a tidal wave, direct enemy attack during World War II, an ecologically devastating offshore oil spill, and fires—many, many fires. Vizcaíno was the first to Europeanize the place. He named the channel after Saint Barbara in 1602, though the name "Santa Barbara Virgin and Martyr" didn't have much to stick to until it was later applied to the presidio in 1782 and the mission four years later.

For many years, aristocratic Spanish families basked in their own gentility here, making Santa Barbara the social capital of Alta California even if Monterey was designated the political capital. With mission secularization, Santa Barbara high society became landed gentry—but only briefly. The grand ranchos all but dried up, littered with cattle bones picked clean by condors and vultures during the devastating drought of the 1860s. Upstart Americans then snatched up the land and with it, local political power. In the late 1880s the industrialists arrived along with old money, banks, brokerage houses, and the Southern Pacific Railroad. When oil was discovered offshore in the 1890s and the first offshore oil well started pumping near Summerland in 1896, they kept coming.

No sooner had the Montecito mansions and Santa Barbara power palaces settled onto their new foundations than they were removed from those foundations—suddenly, shockingly. From the present-day perspective the earthquake of June 1925, which left the city in ruins, was the best thing that ever happened to Santa Barbara. During the city's reconstruction, a quickly formed architectural review board declared that new buildings in Santa Barbara would henceforth be Mediterranean in design and style, appropriate to the area's balmy climate and sympathetic to its Hispanic cultural heritage. The town's trademark old Spanish California adobe look—cream-colored stucco, sloping red-tile roofs, and wrought-iron grillwork—is a unified effect of fairly modern origin.

Santa Barbara had barely rebuilt itself when a Japanese submarine surfaced offshore in 1942 to attack an oil refinery nearby. Oil was the issue again in 1969, when a massive spill from an offshore oil rig blackened 20 miles of beaches in and around Santa Barbara, killing thousands of birds and destroying the local marine ecology. That event fired up ocean lovers all over California and helped launch the successful 1972 California Coastal Protection Initiative, which created the California Coastal Commission to protect the coast as well as the public's access. Starting in the 1980s, a seven-year drought forced Santa Barbara residents to drain their swimming pools and paint their dried-up lawns green. (Water conservation is a serious concern in these parts.) Then, in 1990, the devastating

Painted Cave arson fire killed one person and torched 4,900 acres, racing through the chaparral near San Marcos Pass and then seaward, down into the residential canyons of Goleta and northern Santa Barbara. Sometimes change is a challenge to survival.

Yet even change-wary Santa Barbara welcomes innovation, as it did in the early 1990s when CalTrans coughed up $58 million to widen U.S. Highway 101 through the city to six lanes, remove all four freeway stoplights, and route crosstown traffic either over or under the freeway instead of across it—thus eliminating one of California's most complicated and nightmarish traffic bottlenecks. Innovation is also a byword in the local business community—increasingly high tech, increasingly cutting edge.

SEEING SANTA BARBARA: DOWNTOWN

Since the founding of **Mission Santa Barbara** in 1786 at the upper end of what is now Laguna Street, the altar light has never been extinguished—and that's saying something. Originally a collection of simple adobes, Santa Barbara's "Queen of the Missions" and California's 10th was named for a Roman virgin beheaded by her pagan father. The mission was subsequently all but flattened by the 1812 earthquake, the same year the town on the coastal plain below was all but swept away by a huge tidal wave. Another earthquake, in 1925, did its best to bring the mission down.

The Queen of the Missions still stands—indeed queenly, presiding over the city and sea below with two massive squared towers, arcades, and domed belfries. The dignified Ionian columns, arched entrance, and double-paneled doors add to the mission's grace. The genesis of the city's original water system is also here, an impressive network of aqueducts, filter house, and Spanish gristmill. The larger of the mission's two reservoirs, circa 1806, is still in use by the city, and the 1807 mission dam is now part of the Santa Barbara Botanic Garden just up the canyon. The **museum** tells the mission's story with history displays, photographs, and a reconstructed kitchen. Self-guided tours

SANTA BARBARA MUSEUM OF ART

Along with history, downtown offers it own perspectives on the history of art at the **Santa Barbara Museum of Art,** 1130 State St. (between Anapamu and Figueroa), 805/963-4364, www.sbmuseart.org, an outstanding regional museum that attracts impressive traveling exhibits. The permanent collection here boasts 19th-century Impressionists including Chagall, Matisse, and Monet; O'Keeffe, Eakins, Hooper, and other major American artists; and an eclectic assortment of classical antiquities, Asian art, photography, prints, and drawings. Good bookstore and on-site café. The museum is open Tues.–Sat. 11 A.M.–5 P.M. (until 9 P.M. on Thursday) and Sunday noon–5 P.M. Docents guide free gallery tours at 1 P.M. Tours of special exhibitions are offered Wednesday and Saturday only, at noon. Admissions is $5 adults, $3 seniors, $2 students with ID and children ages 6–17. The museum is free to everyone, though, every Thursday and on the first Sunday of every month (under age 6 always free).

are offered daily 9 A.M.–5 P.M., small admission fee (children under age 12 free). For details or more information, stop by the mission at 2201 Laguna St., call 805/682-4149, or try www.sbmission.org.

There's more historical Santa Barbara downtown, just down the hill. Get oriented at the **Santa Barbara Historical Society Museum,** 136 E. De La Guerra, 805/966-1601, an impressive regional history museum featuring everything from antique toys to vaquero-style saddles within its collection of period costumes, documents, and Santa Barbara memorabilia. The museum is open Tues.–Sat. 10 A.M.–5 P.M., Sunday noon–5 P.M. Guided tours are offered; call for details. Admission is free, though nonmembers must pay for use of the historical society's associated **Gledhill Library** (call for current hours). The museum's adjacent 19th-century **Casa Covarrubias** and **Historic Adobe** also offer a peek into the past. (Museum docents can also tell you about the society's restored **Trussell-Winchester Adobe** and the 1862 Queen Anne **Fer-**

nald House, located together at 412-414 W. Montecito St. and usually open for guided tours on Sunday only, 2–4 P.M. Nearby is the **Carriage and Western Arts Museum,** 129 Castillo St., 805/962-2353, at the north end of Pershing Park, open by donation Mon.–Sat. 9 A.M.–3 P.M. and 2–4 P.M. on Sunday.) Most of Santa Barbara's other surviving adobes, now private residences or office buildings, are included on downtown's self-guided **Red Tile Walking Tour,** outlined in the visitor guide and also available on the website.

The walking tour's traditional starting point is the **Santa Barbara County Courthouse,** a must-see destination one block from State Street at Anapamu and Anacapa, 805/962-6464, an L-shaped Spanish-Moorish castle with spacious interiors decorated with murals, mosaics, ceramic Tunisian tile, and hand-carved wood, quite possibly the most beautiful public building anywhere in California. County supervisors meet in the Assembly Room, with its romantic four-wall historic mural created by a Cecil B. DeMille set designer, and sit in comfortable leather-covered, brass-studded benches and chairs under handmade iron chandeliers. The spectacular views of the city from the clock tower or the *mirador* balcony alone are worth the trip. The courthouse is open 8 A.M.–5 P.M. on weekdays, 9–5 on weekends and holidays, with free guided tours offered at 2 P.M. Mon.–Sat., also at 10:30 A.M. on Friday.

Across the street at 40 E. Anapamu St. sits the stunning Spanish-style **Santa Barbara Public Library,** 805/962-7653, with its grand Peake-Warshaw murals and both the Faulkner Gallery and Townley Room art displays. It's open Mon.–Thurs. 10 A.M.–9 P.M., Friday and Saturday 10 A.M.–5:30 P.M., and Sunday 1–5 P.M. Well worth a stop in the other direction is the unusual **Karpeles Manuscript Library,** 21 W. Anapamu, 805/962-5322, a free museum featuring an extensive collection of both original and facsimile manuscripts—music, letters, maps, illustrations, books, treaties, and such. It's open daily 10 A.M.–4 P.M., closed Thanksgiving and Christmas.

El Presidio de Santa Barbara State Historic Park, 123 E. Cañon Perdido St. (between Anacapa and Santa Barbara Sts.), 805/966-9719, an ambitious reconstruction, is now under way. The project was undertaken by the private Santa Barbara Trust for Historic Preservation to re-create the original 1782 Presidio Real, imperial Spain's last military outpost in California. Before restoration began, all that remained of the original presidio were two crumbling adobe buildings; one, El Cuartel, is Santa Barbara's oldest building and the second oldest in the state. The renovation started in 1961, and the project was expected to be completed by the year 2000. To date two buildings have been restored and five reconstructed.

Confusing the line between real and faux history are downtown's many stylish shops—art galleries galore and **Brinkerhoff Avenue,** famous for its antiques—and, now, two shopping centers. **El Paseo,** California's first shopping center and the originator of the city's distinctive architectural "look," is a clustered two-story collection of Spanish colonial revival shops built in the early 1920s around courtyards, fountains, and gardens (enter from State St., near De La Guerra). The stylish new **Paseo Nuevo** mission-style mall, anchored by Nordstrom and The Broadway between State and Chapala Streets and Ortega and Cañon Perdido, offers upscale shops and shopping. Particularly worthwhile here is the 4,500-square-foot **Contemporary Arts Forum,** 805/966-5373, an adventurous contemporary arts gallery and exhibition space often sponsoring traveling shows, other special exhibits, and lectures.

To the benefit of visitors and residents alike, Santa Barbara is generous with public parking downtown. Park in any of 10 various lots, and the first 90 minutes is free; the incorrigibly cheap could, conceivably, move their cars from lot to lot at precise intervals and stay downtown all day for free.

SEEING SANTA BARBARA: AROUND TOWN AND BEYOND

The **Moreton Bay Fig Tree** at Chapala and Montecito Streets (where Hwy. 101 rolls by) is considered the nation's largest. Affectionately called "the old rubber tree" by some, though it produces neither rubber nor figs, this Australian native is large enough (they say) to shelter 10,000 people from the noonday sun. Street people and transient philosophers are attracted to its welcoming attitude, much to the rest of the community's chagrin.

Nearby is the Santa Barbara harbor area; the city's "bay" is little more than a curvaceous beach front. **Stearns Wharf,** 805/564-5518, at the foot of State Street and the oldest operating wharf on the West Coast, offers pier fishing, shops, restaurants. Worthwhile here is the **Sea Center Museum and Aquarium,** 805/962-0885, a branch of the Santa Barbara Museum of Natural History open daily 10 A.M.–5 P.M. The emphasis here is on the marine life of the Santa Barbara Channel, just offshore, with seawater tank exhibits, a computer learning center, and an outdoor "touch tank" for an up-close-and-personal introduction to underwater wonders (touch-tank exhibit open noon–4 P.M. every day except Wednesday). Small admission. Also worth a stop on the wharf, if you care to learn more about California's endlessly threatened natural environments, is **The Nature Conservancy Visitor Center,** 213 Stearns Wharf, 805/962-9111, open on weekdays noon–4 P.M., on Saturday and Sunday 11 A.M.–5 P.M.

To the east of the pier is pleasant **East Beach,** buffered from busy Cabrillo Boulevard by the manicured lawns, footpaths, and bike trails of expanded **Chase Palm Park,** which stretches along the north side of Cabrillo Boulevard from Garden Street to Calle César Chávez. At the east end of East Beach is **Cemetery Beach,** a popular nude beach (one of four in the area). Also reasonably secluded is Montecito's **Butterfly Beach,** below the Four Seasons Biltmore HoWest of Stearns Wharf is the municipal harbor, protected by a long stone breakwater, and **West Beach.** The promising new **Santa Barbara Maritime Museum,** 805/962-8404, www .sbmm.org, is situated at the harbor entrance, in the Waterfront Center. Pending the museum's grand opening in 2002, the "preview center" and other exhibits (in progress) are open in summer Wed.-Sun. 11 A.M.-5 P.M. (closed Monday and Tuesday); call for hours at other times. Admission is $5 adults; $3 seniors, students, and youth (age 7-17); $1 children (ages 1–5); or $15 families (5 or more people). Farther west are **Leadbetter Beach** and **Shoreline Park,** also tiny **La Mesa Park** and **Arroyo Burro Beach,** popular for swimming and surfing.

Overlooking West Beach is the **Santa Barbara Zoological Gardens,** a onetime estate at 500 Niños Dr. (off E. Cabrillo Blvd.), 805/ 962-6310 (recorded) or 805/962-5339, www .santabarbarazoo.org, with more than 600 exotic animals in almost natural habitats—one of the best smaller zoos anywhere. Santa Barbara's zoo has an outstanding walk-through "aquatic aviary," a portholed Sealarium, and islands for squirrel monkeys and gibbons. Nocturnal Hall, a walk-in tropical aviary on the outside, houses nocturnal animals within. Also here: a peaceful picnic area, small botanic garden, farmyard, Wild

You'll know you've found the Santa Barbara Museum of Natural History when you spot the whale skeleton.

KIM WEIR

West playground, and zany minitrains. The zoo is open daily 10 A.M.–5 P.M., adults $7, children and seniors $5 (under age 2 free). The **Andree Clark Bird Refuge** is a landscaped 50-acre preserve of reclaimed marshland at the east end of E. Cabrillo Boulevard adjoining the zoo, with freshwater fowl, also bike trails and footpaths; if you really like to bike it, the paved **Cabrillo Bikeway** runs to the refuge from the harbor. Guided refuge tours are sometimes offered by the local Audubon Society chapter.

North and West of Santa Barbara

Just up the coast from Santa Barbara proper on a beautiful stretch of beachfront property in Goleta is the **University of California at Santa Barbara** campus. Bordered on two sides by the Pacific Ocean, miles of white-sand beaches, and a natural lagoon, the campus itself is a beauty. Noted for its comprehensive environmental studies program—one of the first of its kind in the nation—and its engineering, education, and scientific instrumentation programs, the university gained national attention in the late 1960s and early '70s for anti–Vietnam War activities in the adjacent "student ghetto" of **Isla Vista,** still jam-packed with stucco apartment buildings and bustling with student-oriented businesses and activities.

Diversions in nearby **Goleta** include the **South Coast Railroad Museum,** 300 N. Los Carneros Rd., 805/964-3540, featuring a restored 1901 Southern Pacific depot, antiques and artifacts, a 300-square-foot model railroad, miniature train rides for the kiddies, and handcar rides for older kids. Open Wed.–Sun. 1–4 P.M. Next door is the historic Victorian **Stow House,** 805/964-4407, open weekends only 2–4 P.M. from February through December (museum closed on rainy days), though the grounds are open year-round. Popular local events staged at Stow House include the annual **Goleta Valley Lemon Festival** and the **Old-Time Fiddlers' Convention.** Another area attraction is the two-acre **Santa Barbara Orchid Estate,** 1250 Orchid Dr., 805/967-1284, www.sborchid.com, with more than 100 varieties on display (plants and cut flowers available for sale), an entire acre of them under glass.

Attractions along the coast north of Santa Barbara and Goleta include three spectacular state "beach" parks. Farthest north is **Gaviota State Park,** about 22 miles north of Goleta, a small beach area that also includes 3,000 associated acres of chaparral, campsites, picnic areas, hiking trails, and hike-in hot springs. Next down-coast and perhaps loveliest of all, just 12 miles north of Goleta, is breathtaking **Refugio State Beach,** a white-sand cove fringed by palm trees and protected from the pounding surf by a rocky point. Here are more campsites—just five facing the beach—plus a glorious group camp. Two miles south, connected by paved bike path to Refugio, is **El Capitan State Beach,** most popular for year-round camping. All three beaches are open daily dusk until dark for day use ($5 per vehicle fee). For current information on all three beaches, call 805/968-1033. For campground reservations—essential in summer and on weekends, prudent any time—call ReserveAmerica at toll-free 800/444-7275.

About 18 miles northwest of Santa Barbara, on the way to Solvang and Santa Ynez via Highway 154, is **Lake Cachuma,** the largest manmade lake in Southern California, a 3,200-acre, trout-stocked, oak woodland reservoir open for day use 6 A.M.–10 P.M. daily. Stop by the **Cachuma Nature Center** to get oriented. Also a county park, Cachuma is ripe for year-round recreation: boating, sailing, hiking, and swimming in pools (Memorial Day through Labor Day only). No "body contact" with the lake is allowed, since this is the city of Santa Barbara's primary water supply. Fishing is a year-round draw, as is bird-watching; more than 275 bird species have been spotted here. A major new attraction here is the two-hour **Eagle Cruise** led by the park's naturalist, offered only November to March when the bald eagles arrive for their own winter respite (fee, by reservation only). The lake has pleasant picnic areas and developed campsites for both tents and RVs, also group camps. Day use is $3.50 per vehicle, camping $12 and up. And a quarter will get you a three-minute hot shower. For more information, contact: Cachuma Lake Recreation Area, HC 58—Hwy. 154, Santa Barbara, CA 93105, 805/686-5054 (recorded) or 805/686-5050 for information, weekend events, and Fish Watch, 805/686-5055 (voice/TDD); www.sbparks.com.

Remote **Gibraltar Reservoir** off Paradise and Camuesa Roads farther south is open for long-weekend trout fishing January through March, but reservations and permits from the city of Santa Barbara are necessary. Also worth seeing, for dedicated backroaders, is **Chumash Painted Cave State Historic Park** off Painted Cave Road, with its characteristic black, red, and yellow pictographs. Gaze in through the iron grating now in place to discourage vandals, or call 805/968-3294 for tour information. Parking on the road's narrow shoulder accommodates only one or two cars (definitely no trailers or RVs).

South and East of Santa Barbara

The balmy beaches, yacht harbor, and wooded estates of **Montecito,** just south of Santa Barbara, seem tailor-made for the people behind commercial trademarks such as DuPont, Fleischmann, Pillsbury, and Stetson—and they were. Especially worth seeing in Montecito is surreal **Lotusland,** created by the flamboyant and independent Madame Ganna Walska, thwarted opera singer and compulsive marrier of millionaires. Here you'll find the world's finest private collection of cycads (relatives of pine trees that look like palms), also cacti and succulents, a luxuriant fern garden lacking only prehistoric dinosaurs, an eccentric "Japanese" garden, a fantastic aloe-and-abalone-shell "forest," weeping euphorbias, 20-foot-tall elephant's feet, lily and lotus ponds, bromeliads, orchids, and roses. Casual or drop-in garden tours are not possible, but the gardens are open by reservation to those interested in horticulture or botany. Make reservations for the two-hour tours ($10 per person, no children under age 12) by contacting the Ganna Walska Lotusland Foundation, 695 Ashley Rd., Santa Barbara 93108, 805/969-3767. Because the house and gardens are in a residential area, there is an annual limit of 9,000 visitors (no drive-by lookie-loos, please; such voyeurism upsets the neighbors, and you can't see anything anyway). Beginning on or about November 15, reservations are taken for the following year—and the entire year's tours are typically booked by January 15.

The burg of **Summerland** just south along the coast is the site of California's first offshore oil drilling in the 1890s. The Spiritualists, a sect known for its séances and merriment, settled here first on former mission lands (thus the locals' derogatory nickname, "Spookville"). Most archi-

tectural evidence of Summerland's past was bulldozed during the 1925 construction of Highway 101 and 15 years later, when the highway became a freeway. Summerland offers a county park, a nice beach, and a boom in antique shops, restaurants, and bed-and-breakfast inns, but the town's most entertaining feature somehow disappeared in the last decade—the sign reading: Population 3,001, Feet Above Sea Level 280, Established 1870, Total: 5,151. Following Lillie Avenue east (it becomes Villa Real) leads to the **Santa Barbara Polo and Racquet Club,** where exhibitions and tournaments are scheduled on Sunday, sometimes on Saturday, spring through fall.

Carpinteria farther south on the way to Ventura was once a Chumash village. Cabrillo stumbled upon it in August of 1542, and Portolá later called it Carpinteria or "carpenter shop" because of the natives' industrious canoe making. People say **Carpinteria State Beach,** a onetime bean field now complete with large campground and hiker/biker campsites, sports the "safest beach in the world" because the surf breaks 2,000 feet out from shore, beyond the reef, and there's no undertow. Other local attractions include the free **Carpinteria Valley Museum of History,** 956 Maple Ave., 805/684-3112 (free, but donations appreciated). Carpinteria's main streets also boast an abundance of antique shops.

For more information about Summerland and Carpinteria, call the **Carpinteria Valley Chamber of Commerce** at 805/684-5479 or toll-free 800/563-6900; www.carpcofc.com.

From south of Carpinteria, Highway 150 leads to Lake Casitas and to Ojai, made famous as a setting for Shangri-La in the movie *Lost Horizon.* For more information on these areas and the coast south of Carpinteria, see Venturing Ventura, above.

DOING SANTA BARBARA

Eventful Santa Barbara

Come in January for the annual **Hang Gliding Festival** in Mesa Flight Park. Held in late February or early March (usually March), the four-day **Santa Barbara International Film Festival** is quite the bash, with premieres and screenings of both international and U.S. films, followed by the city's three-month theater festival. Also in

March comes the **Whale Festival & Week of the Whale.** In April, Santa Barbara hosts the annual **International Orchid Show,** a major flower fest. (The Santa Barbara Orchid Fair comes in July.) Also in April: the **Santa Barbara County Vintners' Festival,** a spring wine aficionado and foodie fest, and the three-day multiethnic **Presidio Days,** Santa Barbara's annual birthday party.

A main event in May—there are many, including **Cinco de Mayo,** the **Santa Barbara Harbor Festival** (formerly the Fishermen's Festival), and the **Santa Barbara Arts and Crafts Show**—is the *I Madonnari* **Italian Street Painting Festival,** a chalk art festival, the first in the nation, named for the 16th-century Italian street painters and held at the Santa Barbara Mission courtyard. June brings the **Summer Solstice Parade,** a sometimes sunny longest-day-of-the-year lunacy including wacky floats, giant puppets, fantasy costumes and masks, dance, mime, and a festive street fair, and the **Big Dog Parade and Block Party** on State Street. Also in late June: **Semana Nautica,** a two-week summer sports festival featuring air, sea, land, pool, and adaptive sports. (The winter Semana Nautica, reduced to just a few days, comes in early February.)

Santa Barbara's **Fourth of July** includes a parade downtown, fireworks along the waterfront, and festivities all over town—including the Santa Barbara Symphony's free pops concert at the Santa Barbara Courthouse. The Santa Barbara **National Horse Show** in July is one of the top five horse events in the United States, followed by the black-tie **Charity Hunt Ball.** Also in July: the **Chinese Festival** in Oak Park, the annual **California Outrigger Championships,** the **Old Mission Art Festival,** and the annual **Santa Barbara County Fair** in Santa Maria. August's **Old Spanish Days Fiesta** is a classy five-day celebration of the city's heritage with parades, carnival, rodeo, herds of horses, performances, other special events, and two colorful marketplaces—festive but dignified, a festival featuring plentiful freebies. Come in August also for the annual **Mariachi Festival,** the **Santa Barbara International Wine Auction,** and the annual **Kite Festival** at Shoreline Park.

The prestigious **Pacific Coast Open Polo Tournament** is held on three consecutive weekends in August. The elegant **Santa Barbara Concours d'Elegance** in September features spit-polished antique and classic cars, a winner's parade, and picnic. In late September or early October comes the **Santa Barbara International Jazz Festival and World Music Beach Party** at Stearns Wharf. In October comes the Santa Barbara Vintners' Association **Celebration of Harvest,** another foodie and wine festival, this one also featuring dancing, exhibits, and storytelling, and the **Santa Barbara Art Walk** fine arts show and sale. But don't miss the **California Avocado Festival** and the annual Goleta Lemon Festival. Santa Barbara's **National Amateur Horse Show** in November has a few days of Western events and a week of English-style riding competition in the largest amateur show in the nation. *Una Pastorella,* a re-creation of the traditional shepherd's nativity play, is staged in December inside the Presidio Chapel, and the **Yuletide Boat Parade** lights up Stearns Wharf. Also show up for **Winterfest** at the Santa Barbara Botanic Garden.

Artful, Entertaining Santa Barbara

The main arts event every March is the annual **Santa Barbara International Film Festival,** 805/963-0023, www.sbfilmfestival.org, with movie screenings at various local theaters. Local bookstores, cafés, and college campuses boast their fair share of poetry readings and other literary events; come in May for the **Santa Barbara Poetry Festival,** a regional and national poetry forum. The **Santa Barbara Writers' Conference,** which in the past has attracted popular scribes including Ray Bradbury and Amy Tan, convenes in June.

Public concerts have a long history in Santa Barbara. Native peoples greeted Portolá and company not with arrows, after all, but with "weird noises" on bowl flutes and whistles. Such tradition is perhaps why the small city of Santa Barbara offers an astounding array of arts events—including more concerts per capita than anyplace else in the country, from the classics and jazz to rock and pop.

Performances by the **Santa Barbara Symphony,** 805/898-9626, www.thesymphony.org, and Montecito's **Music Academy of the West,** 805/969-4726, www.musicacademy.org, are held throughout the year, throughout the community. The symphony holds its summer concerts at the Santa Barbara County Bowl, its regular series performances at the spectacular Arlington Center for the Performing Arts (for more on these venues, see below). The academy's eight-week summer music festival, held at various venues in Santa Barbara and at a private estate in Montecito, is one of the world's most acclaimed. The **Los Angeles Philharmonic** also performs fairly regularly in Santa Barbara, along with an ever-changing roster of world-class and regional performers. The **UC Santa Barbara Arts and Lectures** program, 805/893-2080, www.ucsb.edu, sponsors a lengthy calendar of special events, including readings and lectures, ballet, modern dance, and chamber music. If you're in the Goleta area, stop by to appreciate changing exhibits at the fine **University Art Museum,** 805/961-2951. **Santa Barbara City College** in Santa Barbara proper has a modern performing arts complex, the **Garvin Theatre,** 805/965-5935, www.sbcc.net, which stages dozens of performances each year. **La Casa de la Raza** on the city's lower east side at 601 Montecito, 805/965-8581, is the local Latino cultural center, sponsoring films, plays, lectures, and special concerts.

Santa Barbara's **Lobero Theatre,** 33 E. Cañon Perdido St., 805/963-0761, www.lobero .com, the city's first fashionable theatrical venue, was first established in 1873 in an old adobe schoolhouse. Headquartered here are the **Contemporary Music Theatre,** the **Santa Barbara Grand Opera Association,** the **Santa Barbara Dance Theater,** the **Santa Barbara Chamber Orchestra,** and the **Gilbert and Sullivan Company of Santa Barbara,** though various other groups and series—including **Sings Like Hell**— also call the Lobero home. The **Santa Barbara Civic Light Opera,** 805/962-1922, performs at the **Granada Theatre,** 805/966-2324. Another popular local venue is the sylvan **Santa Barbara County Bowl** outdoor amphitheater—cutstone seating, revolving stage, great visibility and acoustics—which hosts a wide variety of contemporary and classical acts, usually from May through September.

But Santa Barbara's cultural gem is the Alhambra-like Arlington Theatre, also known as the **Arlington Center for the Performing Arts,** built on the site of the old Arlington Hotel at 1317 State St., 805/963-4408, a onetime 1930s movie palace where the domed ceiling still sparkles with electric stars; in its heyday there was even a cloud-making machine here. An arched passageway leads into the lobby, and the stage is flanked by two Spanish "villages," part of its architectural allure. In addition to regular Santa Barbara Symphony performances, the Arlington also hosts touring symphonies sponsored by the **Community Arts Music Association,** 805/966-4324.

For advance tickets for most local arts performances, call **State of the Arts,** toll-free 800/398-0722 or **Ticketmaster,** 805/583-8700 or toll-free 800/765-6255.

After touring the **Santa Barbara Museum of Art,** 1130 State St., 805/963-4364, and poking into nearby galleries—the **Contemporary Arts Forum** at the Paseo Nuevo mall downtown, 805/966-5373, exhibits both established and up-and-coming artists—head to Montecito and the **Western States Museum of Photography** at the renowned **Brooks Institute of Photography,** 1321 Alameda Padre Serra, 805/966-3888, www.brooks.edu, with its outstanding rotating exhibits plus a collection of historic shutterbug stuff. The museum is open weekdays 8 A.M.–5 P.M. daily, closed weekends and holidays. Also, on select Fridays the institute sponsors a public open house; guided campus tours can usually be arranged as well. To dabble in more artsy-craftsy fare, every sunny Sunday there's a **Beach Arts and Crafts Show** in Santa Barbara at Palm Park along Cabrillo Boulevard, just east of Stearns Wharf, from 10 A.M. to dusk.

Santa Barbara hosts an amazing number of arts and crafts fairs, benefits, cat, dog, and horse shows, community festivals, and other events throughout the year. To find out what's going on while you're in town—and what might be hip or happening in local nightlife—pick up a current issue of the free *Santa Barbara Independent,* www.independent.com, published on Thursday each week and offering local news coverage and excellent arts and entertainment features, reviews, and calendar listings. The daily *Santa Barbara News-Press,* www.newspress.com, also features calendar listings and a special Friday *Scene* magazine insert.

SANTA BARBARA WINE COUNTRY

Santa Barbara County is premium wine country. The county's wine-making history reaches back more than 200 years, though small vineyards and wineries established since the 1970s and 1980s are responsible for the area's regional viticultural revival. The unusual east-west orientation of the Santa Ynez Mountains and associated valleys allows fog-laden ocean air to flow inland—creating dry summers with cool nights and warm days. Cabernet sauvignon, sauvignon blanc, pinot noir, chardonnay, and riesling are among the wine grapes that thrive here, though Rhône varietals are a new trend.

Yet when does a good thing become too much of a good thing?

This is a question asked more frequently here and elsewhere along the central coast, especially following a nearly successful local ballot initiative in fall 1998 that would have severely restricted local wine grape growers' ability to clear-cut native oaks and other vegetation to plant vineyards. Environmentalists, grape growers, and county planning officials are trying to come up with a collaborative solution to this particular problem, to avoid the possibility of another public—and vitriolic—political battle.

Most of Santa Barbara County's wineries—well over 50 and counting—are scattered throughout the Santa Ynez Valley, beyond San Marcos Pass northwest of Santa Barbara and southeast of Santa Maria.

Award-winning **The Gainey Vineyard,** 3950 E. Hwy. 246, P.O. Box 910, Santa Ynez 93460, 805/688-0558, fax 805/688-5864, is noted for its cabernets, chardonnays, and pinot noirs. The contemporary 12,000-foot winery and tasting room and adjacent picnic area is open daily 10 A.M.–5 P.M. for tours and tasting (very informative tours). The vineyard also sponsors a variety of evening concerts—popular regional jazz bands and the likes of Randy Newman—which sell out fast.

Almost everyone stops at the **Fess Parker Winery,** 6200 Foxen Canyon Rd. in Los Olivos, 805/688-1545 or toll-free 800/841-1104, fax 805/686-1130, www.fessparker.com, open for tasting and sales daily 10 A.M.–5 P.M. (closed Thanksgiving, Christmas, and New Year's Day) and for group tours only (by arrangement). Most popular here is syrah, which tends to sell out almost instantaneously every year, and a very good chardonnay. And anyone with a yen for the good ol' days of 1950s television will have fun in the gift shop, featuring Davy Crockett "coonskin" caps and other Fess Parker TV-star memorabilia. On most weekends Parker is available in person to autograph wine bottles. Tours and admission to the gift shop are free, but there is a fee for tastings.

Also popular in Los Olivos is **Firestone Vineyard,** 5000 Zaca Station Rd., 805/688-3940, fax 805/686-1256, open daily 10 A.M.–5 P.M. for tasting (closed major holidays), tours also offered. Firestone was the first in the country to produce estate-grown wines. People go out of their way to pick up Firestone's award-winning cabernet sauvignon, though the winery is actually best known for Johannesburg riesling. Picnicking here is a pleasure, with picnic tables surrounding a fountain in the courtyard. Tastings and tours are free, but a fee is charged for groups of 15 or more.

Not far southeast of Santa Maria is the **Byron Vineyard and Winery,** located at 5230 Tepusquet Rd., 805/937-7288, named 1992 "Winery of the Year" by *Wine and Spirits* magazine and now owned by Robert Mondavi.

But with 50 or so member wineries in the local vintners' association—and major events such as the spring **Santa Barbara County Vintners' Festival,** the fall **Celebration of Harvest,** and other galas to help introduce them—it takes more than a few stops to fully appreciate the region. For a current winery map and guide, and for current events information, contact: **Santa Barbara County Vintners' Association,** P.O. Box 1558, Santa Ynez 93460, 805/688-0881 or toll-free 800/218-0881, fax 805/686-5881; www.sbcountywines.com.

And the region's wineries don't begin or end in Santa Barbara County, thanks to the mild central coast climate. Small wineries also cluster farther north near San Luis Obispo—in the **Edna** and **Arroyo Grande Valleys**—and, more famously, north of San Luis Obispo near **Paso Robles** and **Templeton.** For more information, see San Luis Obispo and Vicinity, below.

Recreation, Tours, and Other Adventures

If it's remotely related to sky, sea, sand, or sand trap, Santa Barbara has it. Popular local recreational pursuits vary from in-line skating, strolling, and cycling to sailing and scuba diving, from kayaking to lawn bowling, hiking and horseback riding to polo. Winter whale-watching tours, windsurfing, golf—a major regional pastime, judging from the number of world-class courses scattered throughout Santa Barbara County—and tennis also keep people out and about.

For a complete listing of boat and charter rentals, also organized tours in and around Santa Barbara, stop by local visitor centers—or consult the current phone book. An official concessionaire for trips to offshore Channel Islands National Park is Santa Barbara's own **Truth Aquatics,** 301 W. Cabrillo Blvd., 805/962-1127 or toll-free 800/927-4688, fax 805/564-6754, www.truth-aquatics.com, an award-winning scuba diving fleet that also offers island hiking, camping, and natural history tours. If you'd rather shove off from Ventura, **Island Packer Cruises,** headquartered at 1867 Spinnaker Dr., Ventura 93001, 805/642-7688 (recorded), fax 805/642-6573, www.islandpacker.com, offers fair-weather trips and winter whale-watching tours to the Channel Islands. Reservations are required for all trips which, unfortunately, can be cancelled at the last minute because of inclement weather. (For more on what to see and do offshore, see Islands in Time: Channel Islands National Park, above.) The **Santa Barbara Museum of Natural History,** 805/682-4711, also offers whale-watching tours, along with **Captain Don's Harbor Tours,** 805/969-5217.

PRACTICAL SANTA BARBARA

STAYING IN SANTA BARBARA

Santa Barbara is a popular destination year-round—a wonderful winter getaway when the rest of the nation is snowbound—but the "high season" is July and August, extending into balmy fall weekends, when warm weather coastal fog all but disappears. Most accommodation rates, fairly high any time, are highest in the summer, on weekends, and during major special events. If you plan to arrive in summer and are particular about where you'll be staying—an issue for budget travelers and families as well as the affluent—book your reservations many months, even a year, in advance. Though the practice has long been business as usual at area bed-and-breakfasts, increasingly even motels and hotels require a two-night minimum stay on weekends (three-night minimum on holiday weekends).

For help in sorting out the possibilities, try local no-fee booking agencies, including **Coastal Getaways,** 805/969-1258, **Central Coast Reservations,** toll-free 800/557-7898, and **Santa Barbara Hot Spots,** 805/564-1637 or toll-free 800/793-7666.

Campgrounds, Yurts, a Hostel, and a Monastery

Nearby **Los Padres National Forest** offers plenty of campgrounds. A complete campground listing and forest map, $2, is available at the National Forest headquarters in Goleta, 6755 Hollister Ave., Ste. 150, 805/968-6640, www.r5.fs .fed.us/lospadres; all are first-come, first-camped (no reservations taken) with a two-week maximum stay. Closer to the ocean are the three developed state beach campgrounds northwest of Santa Barbara—**Gaviota, Refugio,** and **El Capitan.** All are popular and quite nice, even for sunny winter camping (popular with snowbirds). For general information on all three, call 805/968-1033. Reserve campsites at all three—well-worn El Capitan is especially popular year-round—through ReserveAmerica, toll-free 800/444-7275; it's first-come, first-camped from December through February. Gaviota has the smallest campground, and El Capitan and Refugio are like Siamese twins, sharing the palm-lined shoreline and a bike trail but featuring distinct identities otherwise (some campsites at Refugio are sublime, but Gaviota is most pleasant and reclusive). All offer sites with hot showers and flush toilets, some have RV hookups. Also within reasonable range of Santa Barbara is huge—262 total campsites, 126 with RV hook-ups—**Carpinteria State Beach** 12 miles southeast of Santa Barbara and just off Highway 101, local 805/684-2811 or 805/968-3294, toll-free 800/444-7275 for reservations. Dogs (six-foot leash) are permitted at all of these state campgrounds for an extra $1 per day, but are not allowed on beaches or trails.

The biggest campground around is a bit farther away and inland via Highway 154: the county's very pleasant **Cachuma Lake Recreation Area,** with a total of almost 1,000 family and group campsites available on either a first-come or reservation basis, $12 and up (hookups extra). Cachuma offers tent, yurt, and RV camping. The fabric-covered yurts feature platform beds, electric lights and heating, lockable doors, and wood-framed screened windows. General camping amenities include hot showers, restrooms, fireplaces with grills, picnic tables, swimming pools (summer only), and nonswimming lake recreation opportunities. Primitive and hiker/biker campsites are less expensive. Dogs—on leashes—are welcomed, for a $1-per-day fee and current proof of rabies vaccination; pets are not allowed on trails. For current reservation information and other specifics, call 805/686-5054 or 686-5055; www.sbparks.org.

Santa Barbara also boasts a 60-bed **Banana Bungalow Santa Barbara,** 210 E. Ortega St., 805/963-0154 or toll-free 800/346-7835, fax 805/963-0184, www.bananabungalow.com, within an easy stroll of both the bus and train stations. Guests can stay in private, four-bed dorms with shared restrooms, or in large dorms. Rates: $16–22.

For a peaceful retreat, consider the **Mount Calvary Guest House** at 2500 Gilbraltar Rd., 805/962-9855, www.mount-calvary.org, a palatial 1940s mountaintop Spanish-style villa with incredible vistas, great hiking access, plenty of comfortable spare bedrooms, and Benedictine monks happy to serve you. Rates are $70 per person suggested donation (all meals included, on the American plan), with both single and double rooms (singles share an adjoining bath). Individuals—no partiers, please—are welcome for personal retreats.

In addition to the yurts available at Lake Cachuma, there's also the **White Lotus Foun-** **dation,** 2500 San Marcos Pass, 805/964-1944, www.whitelotus.org, a yoga-teaching institute that makes theirs available on a space available basis, $70 couple per night.

Inexpensive–Moderate Motels and Hotels

Beyond hostels and such, finding inexpensive accommodations in Santa Barbara is a challenge. There's always Motel 6, which here isn't all that inexpensive. The **Motel 6 Santa Barbara,** 443 Corona Del Mar, 805/564-1392 or toll-free 800/466-8356 (nationwide), fax 805/963-4687, www.motel6.com, is close to the beach and downtown, newly renovated, and small, featuring the usual basic accommodations plus color TV and HBO, phones, free local calls. Very popular; for the summer-fall season, book at least six months in advance. Rates: $63–84, depending on the season (weekends in summer and fall are highest). If there's no room here, there's another Motel 6 downtown, 3505 State St., 805/687-5400, still another north of town near Goleta, and two more south of town near Carpinteria.

The once stately old hotels at the beach end of State Street are other low-end possibilities, though these are rapidly becoming boutique hotels. Of the rest, some places look better than they are, passing trains offer unwanted wake-up calls in the middle of the night, and it's a little sleazy here after dark (pack your street smarts). A best bet for an inexpensive stay, still, is the **Hotel State Street,** 121 State St., 805/966-6586, where high-season rates for clean rooms with shared baths are $50, with private baths $90 and up, continental breakfast included.

Midrange Motels and Hotels

Most medium-priced motels here are pricey compared to similar accommodations elsewhere. But since this is Santa Barbara, who can complain? The following offer exceptional value, including good location, for the money.

Appealing and fairly affordable among Santa Barbara's burgeoning downtown boutique hotel roster is the 1926-vintage **Hotel Santa Barbara,** 533 State St. (at Cota), 805/957-9300 or toll-free 888/259-7700, fax 805/962-2412; www.hotelsantabarbara.com. Rooms are light, airy, and attractively decorated. An abundance of great restaurants are just a stroll away from the welcoming lobby. Rates: $99–209, but look for good seasonal specials.

Santa Barbara's newest downtown boutique, open since late 1999, is the very stylish Holiday Inn Express **Hotel Virginia,** just a hop and skip from the beach at 17 W. Haley St. (east of State St.), 805/963-9757 or toll-free 800/549-1700, fax 805/963-1747, www.hotelvirginia.com, listed on the National Register of Historic Places. Decor in this 1916-vintage, 61-room hotel emphasizes the spectacular Malibu and Catalina tile work now preserved and restored here—including the striking mosaic fountain in the lobby—and also showcases local art and artists. Rooms, decked out in a contemporary take on classic art deco style, feature all the modern comforts, from state-of-the-art phones and data ports to hair dryers and in-room irons and ironing boards; some have balconies with wrought-iron railings and French windows. A stay includes expanded continental breakfast, with good coffee, fresh juices and fruit, locally baked goods, cereals, and yogurt. Rates: $159–199, though specials can drop the tab to as low as $99.

A classic in the Santa Barbara area is the historic blue-roofed **Miramar Hotel,** in Montecito at 1555 S. Jameson Ln., 805/969-2203 or toll-free 800/322-6983 for reservations (in California), fax 805/969-3163; www.sbmiramar.com. The Miramar was more tranquil in prefreeway days, but it's nonetheless still charming, perfect for unfussy families. Semitropical gardens and beachfront location add to the appeal. Regular rooms are $89 and up in summer, with cheaper, fairly spartan rooms closer to the thundering traffic, quieter ones clustered around the pool or along the 500-foot beachfront. Cottage and parlor suites with one, two, or three bedrooms (some have kitchens) start at $159. But even with a simple room you can enjoy the tennis and shuffleboard courts, the two swimming pools, the health spa, the on-site restaurants—and the beach. For burgers and such, the kids will love the **Miramar Diner,** open 11 A.M.–6 P.M. This venerable diner cum ice cream fountain, snuggled into a 1950s' Pullman car with a view, adds an element of olden-days excitement to the simple menu of burgers, sandwiches, soups, salads, and ice cream creations—especially realistic when real trains rumble by.

The attractive 53-room **Franciscan Inn,** 109 Bath St. (just south of Hwy. 101), 805/963-8845, fax 805/564-3295, www.franciscaninn.com, offers high-season rates of $105–200, with tasteful decor and all the country-style comforts plus swimming pool and whirlpool, just a block from the beach. Almost half the rooms here have kitchenettes (extra).

Another find is **The Eagle Inn,** 232 Natoma Ave. (three blocks south of Hwy. 101, at Bath), 805/965-3586 or toll-free 800/767-0030, fax 805/966-1218; www.theeagleinn.com. Most rooms at this very attractive Spanish-style motel, a onetime apartment complex, are more like apartments, with full-stocked kitchens and the homey, well-kept kind of comfort that makes you want to stay longer than you'd planned. Even better is the fact that the Eagle Inn is only a block and a half from the beach. On-site laundry, cable TV, and free movies (no air-conditioning). Rates: $89–160, with off-season and weekday rates the real deal. For summer, book rooms by mid-May.

Also quite appealing and close to the beach is the **Inn by the Harbor,** 433 W. Montecito St., 805/963-7851 or toll-free 800/626-1986, fax 805/962-9428, www.sbhotels.com, a classic Mediterranean-style moMany units have kitchens. Rates: $102–168. See the website for the rundown on sister motels nearby.

Another good value, a gussied-up motel done up in appealing country-French décor, well situated for a beach-oriented vacation, is the smoke-free 45-room **Country Inn by the Sea** two blocks south of Highway 101 at 128 Castillo St., 805/963-4471 or toll-free 800/455-4647, fax 805/962-2633; www.countryinnbythesea.com. Most rooms come with a balcony or patio plus color TV, VCRs, free movies, and tasty continental breakfast. Extras include a small swimming pool, saunas, spa, and a nearby city park with tennis courts. Rates: $149–209, though off-season and discounted rates drop down as low as $99.

Other good midrange possibilities include the **Coast Village Inn** in the center of Montecito at 1188 Coast Village Rd., 805/969-3266 or toll-free 800/257-5131, fax 805/969-7117, www.coastvillageinn.com, rates: $125–165, though specials drop to $89; the **El Prado Inn** downtown at 1601 State St., 805/966-0807 or toll-free 800/669-8979, fax 805/966-6502, www

.elprado.com, rates: $85–170; and the **Mason Beach Inn** just south of Highway 101 at 324 W. Mason St., 805/962-3203 or toll-free 800/446-0444, fax 805/962-1056, rates: $85–195.

High-End Motels and Hotels
Lacking the history of other upscale area hotels but little else, 360-room **Fess Parker's Doubletree Resort**, previously the Red Lion Inn, is a luxurious Spanish-style resort motel across from the beach at 633 E. Cabrillo Blvd., 805/564-4333 or toll-free 800/879-2929, fax 805/564-4964; www.fpdtr.com. The huge resort motel, situated on 24 acres, features basketball and shuffleboard courts, a putting green, lighted tennis courts, exercise facilities, rental bikes, heated pool, sauna, and whirlpool. **Maxi's** restaurant is another mainstay. Rooms include all the usual comforts plus in-room coffeemakers, honor bars, color TV with cable and movies, and radios. Room rates start at $195, but inquire about specials and seasonal discounts.

Also fronting the beach, adjacent to Stearns Wharf, is the 80-room **Harbor View Inn** just west of State Street at 28 W. Cabrillo Blvd., 805/963-0780 or toll-free 800/755-0222, fax 805/963-7967. Very attractive rooms feature the usual deluxe amenities plus in-room coffeemakers, refrigerators, safes, and color TV with cable. In addition to the swimming pool and whirlpool, there's a heated wading pool for the kiddos and skate rentals. On-site restaurant. High-season rates $180 and up (ocean-view rooms most expensive).

Though it's really just a spiffed-up Santa Barbara beach motel, dedicated foodies are drawn to the 71-room **Santa Barbara Inn**, 901 E. Cabrillo Blvd., 805/966-2285 or toll-free 800/231-0431, fax 805/966-6584; www.santabarbarainn .com. That's because after filling up on the fine California-French fare at **Citronelle,** chef Michel Richard's on-site restaurant, guests can just waddle right over to their rooms—or across the street to the beach—and rest until mealtime comes around again. Rooms here are spacious and attractive, with refrigerators, coffeemakers, and color TV with cable TV. Some have kitchens, some have air-conditioning. In addition to the heated pool and whirlpool, there's a sundeck on the third floor. Rates: $219–309; discounts and off-season specials can drop the tab con-

siderably. Weekly and monthly rates are available.

In 1928 the little tramp himself, Charlie Chaplin, and his later scandal-plagued partner Fatty Arbuckle established the **Montecito Inn,** 1295 Coast Village Rd., 805/969-7854 or toll-free 800/843-2017, fax 805/969-0623, www.montecitoinn .com, as a Hollywood hideout. These days an attractive and trendy small hotel with Mediterranean-provincial style, the Montecito Inn features somewhat small rooms with all the usual amenities—no air-conditioning, but there are ceiling fans—plus an attractive pool and spa area out back. Seven spacious new Mediterranean-style luxury suites feature bathrooms of Italian marble plus whirlpools; some suites have fireplaces. The inn sits close to the freeway, right in town—an easy stroll to most of Montecito's action. Rates starting at $185.

Especially Fun for Families
The **Circle Bar B Guest Ranch** at 1800 Refugio Rd. beyond Goleta, 805/968-1113, www.circle-barb.com, is a place the kids will get excited about—a genuine ranch dedicated to horseback rides (extra) and all kids of family-appropriate fun, hiking, picnicking, and diving into the neighborhood swimming hole. And the dinner theater does drama down at the barn, spring through fall. Accommodations, some cabin-style, are Western themed and quite comfortable. High-season rates starting at $186 double. (two-night minimum on weekends, three nights on holiday weekends). In summer, plan to book at least six weeks in advance on weekends, four weeks otherwise. The ranch is about three and a half miles inland from Refugio State Beach, via Refugio Road, 20 miles north of Santa Barbara via Highway 101.

Just the basics for a camping-style stay but considerably less pricey is a stay at **Rancho Osos Stables & Guest Ranch**, 3750 Paradise Rd. in Santa Barbara, 805/683-5686 or toll-free 800/859-3640, adjacent to the Santa Ynez River and Los Padres National Forest. Overnight options at "Western Town" include colorful tongue-and-groove pine cabins complete with beds, coffeemaker, and small refrigerator or any of 10 Conestoga covered wagons circled around the campfire. Each wagon features electricity, hardwood floors, and four Army-style cots. Cabins $46 a night, wagons $27. Hot showers, bathrooms, charcoal barbecue pits, and abundant picnic tables are nearby. Hearty meals are available on weekends at the on-site Chuck Wagon and nearby Stone Lodge Kitchen.

If money is no object and you and the lil' dogies will be moseyin' north, within easy reach is the luxurious **Alisal Guest Ranch and Resort** just outside Solvang, 805/688-6411 (for details, see Solvang and Vicinity, below). Also, the 4200-square-foot ranch house at the family-owned **Cottontail Creek Ranch,** 805/995-1787, www.cottontrailcreek.com, is available 12 weeks of the year as a vacation rental.

Santa Barbara–Area Bed-and-Breakfasts

Santa Barbara is a B&B bonanza—that phenomenon quite rare in and around Southern California. Many local bed-and-breakfasts and B&B–style inns are as reasonably priced as local motels, if not more so, and most offer reduced rates, specials, or packages for off-season and/or weekday stays. Many require a two-night minimum stay on weekends and/or a three-night stay over longer holiday weekends. Here as elsewhere, most bed-and-breakfasts are smoke-free—though you may be allowed to smoke on a terrace or patio, or on a nearby street corner.

Quite appealing and a great value by Santa Barbara standards is the **Secret Garden and Cottages,** 1908 Bath St., 805/687-2300, fax 805/687-4576, www.secretgarden.com, a collection of craftsman-style cottages with most of the 11 rooms are named after particular birds. Weather permitting, breakfast is served out in the shady private garden. Rates: $115–225.

Near the beach is the award-winning **Old Yacht Club Inn,** 431 Corona Del Mar Dr., 805/962-1277 or toll-free 800/549-1676 (California) or 800/676-1676 (U.S.), fax 805/962-3989, www.oldyachtclubinn.com, actually once a yacht club, though this homey 1912 stucco craftsman was built as a private home. Santa Barbara's first bed-and-breakfast, open since 1980, the Yacht Club's main house features yachting memorabilia and five rooms decorated in period furnishings of various moods. Four more rooms, all with private entrances, are available in the adjacent tile-roofed Hitchcock House. Just two blocks from the beach, the Yacht Club also provides bikes to tour the neighborhood. Fabulous breakfasts and

famous Saturday night dinners (extra, by reservation). Rates: $110–190.

The gracious three-story Queen Anne **Bath Street Inn** is just south of Mission Street at 1720 Bath St., 805/682-9680 or toll-free 800/341-2284, fax 805/569-1281; www.travel-seek.com. Some of the 12 rooms, in the main house and summer house out back, feature fireplaces and whirlpool tubs; some also have in-room refrigerators and coffeemakers; one features a kitchen, whirlpool tub, and separate entrance. In addition to full breakfast, tea is served in the afternoon, wine in the evening. Rates: $100–190 (20 percent discount Sun.–Thurs., summers and holiday weeks excepted).

Other bed-and-breakfast possibilities include the **Glenborough Inn,** 1327 Bath St., 805/966-0589 or toll-free 888/966-0589, fax 805/564-8610, www.silcom.com/~glenboro, actually a combination of five turn-of-the-20th-century homes and cottages with 14 rooms (rates: $100–380); **The Parsonage,** 1600 Olive St., 805/962-9336, fax 805/962-9336, with six rooms in an 1892 Victorian (rates: $125–325); and **The Cheshire Cat,** 36 W. Valerio St. (at Chapala), 805/569-1610, fax 805/682-1876, www.cheshire-cat.com, a collection of houses and cottages with rooms named after characters in Alice's adventures (rates: $140–350).

For those uncomfortable with the forced social intimacy of most bed-and-breakfast inns, the historic **Upham Hotel,** 1404 De La Vina St., 805/962-0058 or toll-free 800/727-0876, fax 805/963-2825, www.uphamhotel.com, offers a friendly alternative. Built in 1871 by Amasa Lincoln, a Boston banker who set sail for California to build himself a New England–style inn, these days the Upham is still more hotel than bed-and-breakfast. This Victorian hotel features 50 rooms and garden cottages on an acre of land in the heart of town, just a stroll from State Street. The Upham's primary eccentricity is in its guest register—an incongruous celebrity collection including Richard Nixon, Aldous Huxley, and Agatha Christie. Rooms in the main building are smallish but comfortable, with nice antique touches; more contemporary, more expensive rooms and suites are situated in various outbuildings and garden cottages. The fireplace-cozy lobby resembles an English parlor. The buffet breakfast can be taken indoors, out on the wraparound veranda, or out in the garden in an Adirondack chair. Wine and cheese are served in the evening. The on-site **Louie's** restaurant is quite good. Rates: $140 and up.

Truly exceptional among Santa Barbara's bed-and-breakfast celebrities is the landmark **Simpson House Inn,** 121 E. Arrellaga St., 805/963-7067 or toll-free 800/676-1280 (U.S.), fax 805/564-4811; www.simpsonhouseinn.com. Centerpiece is the uncluttered 1874 Eastlake Italianate Victorian, exquisitely restored with period furnishings, oriental rugs, and English lace. Other rooms are in a onetime barn—the 19th-century "barn suites," complete with authentic interior walls—and three separate garden cottages with stone fireplaces and English charm. The gardens here, an entire acre of horticultural adventure sculpted into various semi-private "outdoor rooms," are most charming of all. Full gourmet breakfast is served on the veranda or in the formal dining room, along with afternoon or evening hors d'oeuvres (including Santa Barbara County wines). Rates: $195–500.

Quite nice is the 16-room English country-style **Inn on Summerhill** south of Montecito at 2520 Lillie Ave. south of town in Summerland, 805/969-9998 or toll-free 800/845-5566, fax 805/565-9948, another award-winning bed-and-breakfast. This one boasts suite-style rooms with canopied beds and all the contemporary comforts—in-room refrigerators, hot tubs, color TV with cable and VCRs—plus full homemade breakfast and, come evening, hors d'oeuvres and dessert. Rates: $215 and up.

And if you're pushing farther on down the coast, a bed-and-breakfast gem along the way—particularly for fans of T. S. Eliot—is **Prufrock's Garden Inn,** 600 Linden Ave. in Carpinteria, 805/566-9696 or toll-free 877/837-6257, fax 805/566-9404; www.prufrocks.com. Rates: $120–250, but in the off-season weekday rates can drop quite a bit.

Luxury Hotels and Resorts

If money is no object—if this is a once-in-a-lifetime visit and you want something close to guaranteed bliss—*the* place is the **Four Seasons Biltmore Hotel** in the Montecito area at 1260 Channel Dr., 805/969-2261 or toll-free 800/332-3442 (United States) and 800/268-6282 (Canada), fax 805/969-4212; www.fourseasons.com. Even *Condé Nast Traveler* says this is one of the finest resorts in the nation. The vast but intimate tile-roofed 1927 resort, designed in "Spanish ecclesiastical" style with endless other Mediterranean details by architect Reginald Johnson, just oozes luxurious old-money charm. Visitors could spend an entire stay just appreciating the craftsmanship, from the hand-made decorative Mexican tiles and the irregular mission-style *ladrillos* (tile floors) to the massive oak doors at the hotel's entrance. Endless archways, stairways, low towers, fountains, loggias, and bougainvillea-draped walkways threaded through the lush 21-acre grounds make just finding your room an architectural adventure. Yet for all its understated elegance and luxury—and its Olympic-sized swimming pool, lighted tennis courts, kids program, excellent restaurants, multilingual staff, full conference and business facilities—a stay can be almost reasonable. And for sheer extravagance, nobody beats the Biltmore's Sunday brunch. High-season rates are $290–600, with larger ocean-view rooms and cottages most expensive; inquire about special packages and off-season specials.

Or head to the **San Ysidro Ranch,** in Montecito at 900 San Ysidro Ln. (at Mountain Dr.), 805/969-5046 or toll-free 800/368-6788, fax 805/565-1995; www.sanysidroranch.com. The ranch is an honorable member of the Relais at Châteaux international hotel association, one of the few in the United States, which explains its current exclusive cachet. But actor Ronald Colman owned the ranch in the 1930s and, in those rowdier years it was a popular Hollywood trysting place. One can still see why. These romantic cottages—the ultimate rooms with a view, scattered throughout some of Santa Barbara's most stunning gardens—are prized for their seclusion as well as their understated luxury. John and Jackie Kennedy honeymooned here, Laurence Olivier and Vivien Leigh were married here, and ink-stained scribes including Somerset Maugham and Sinclair Lewis hid out here to write. Winston Churchill wrote his memoirs here. Individually decorated rooms feature wood-burning fireplaces and endless little luxuries—such as in-room massage and other spa and beauty services (extra)—and the grounds include a swimming pool, wading pool, tennis courts, and stables. Horseback riding is immensely popular here. You can also golf, with privileges at the nearby Montecito Country Club. If you can't afford to stay here, a special breakfast, lunch, dinner, or spectacular Sunday brunch at the excellent California-style American **Stonehouse** restaurant at least gets you a look around (reservations highly recommended). Cottage rooms start at $375 and luxury cottages top out at $3,750, with a two-night minimum stay on weekends, a three- or four-night minimum on holiday weekends.

Just as enchanting in its own way, and a tad less expensive, is the 10-acre hilltop **El Encanto Hotel & Garden Villas,** 1900 Lasuen Rd. (at Alameda Padre Serra), 805/687-5000 or toll-free 800/678-8946, fax 805/687-3903; www.nthp.org. This sprawling country inn, just a half-mile from the Santa Barbara Mission, once served as student and faculty housing for the original University of California at Santa Barbara campus; when the university headed north to Goleta in 1915, El Encanto was born. A charter member of the National Trust for Historic Preservation's Historic Hotels of America, El Encanto is a maze of tile-roofed Spanish colonial revival-style *casitas* and craftsman-style cottages tucked in among the oaks and luxuriant hillside gardens. (Don't lose the map the staff gives you when you check in; you'll definitely need it to find your way around.) Over the years El Encanto has welcomed endless celebrities and dignitaries, including Franklin Delano Roosevelt. But just about anyone will feel at home in these under-stated yet pleasant lodgings, decorated in French country style. Many rooms feature wood-burning fireplaces, quite cheering on rain- or fog-chilled evenings; hotel staff regularly replenishes the wood supply on the porch. Some have refrigerators and kitchens. "View" rooms are higher on the hillside, some distance from the main building. A private, reclusive resort, El Encanto's amenities include a year-round solar- and gas-heated swimming pool, tennis courts and full-time tennis pro, library, and lounge. Views from the excellent on-site restaurant—open daily for breakfast, lunch, and dinner—and the hotel lobby overlook the city and the vast Pacific Ocean, a dazzling sight at sunset. Rooms $239–419, cottage suites $379–1,200. Ask about off-season and midweek packages and specials.

EATING IN SANTA BARBARA

Farmers' Markets, Trader Joe's

The **Santa Barbara Downtown Certified Farmers' Market,** 805/962-5354, is the place to load up on premium fresh flowers, herbs, vegetables, fruits, nuts, honey, eggs, and other farm-fresh local produce. The market is held on the corner of Santa Barbara and Cota Streets every Saturday 8:30 A.M.–12:30 P.M. The **Santa Barbara Old Town Certified Farmers' Market** (same phone) convenes along the 500-600 blocks of State St. on Tuesday, 4–7:30 P.M. in summer and 3–6:30 P.M. in winter. Other area farmers' markets are held in Goleta and Carpinteria on Thursday afternoon, and in Montecito on Friday morning; call for locations and current hours.

Though Santa Barbara has its share of gourmet delis—see food listings below—it also has a **Trader Joe's,** 29 S. Milpas St., 805/564-7878, which means just about anybody can afford to put together a stylish picnic dinner for the beach.

Inexpensive and Good

Even people who can't afford to sleep in Santa Barbara can usually find a good meal here. For "gourmet tacos," Santa Barbara's most famous dining destination is **La Super-Rica Taqueria,** 622 N. Milpas, 805/963-4940, an unassuming hole-in-the-wall and long-running favorite of chef Julia Child and appreciative fellow foodies. This mom-and-pop place serves the best soft tacos around—fresh house-made corn tortillas topped with chorizo, chicken, beef, or pork—and unforgettable seafood tamales. For Santa Barbara at its best, grab a taco and a cold beer and head for the patio—or head for the beach and a sunset picnic. Also worth a takeout stop: **La Tolteca** restaurant and deli, 614-616 E. Haley, 805/963-0847, not real close to downtown but cheap—a tortilla-factory restaurant serving great home-made tamales, tostadas, tacos, and burritos (call for current hours).

Santa Barbara is a health-conscious city, and people from all walks of life tend to appreciate foods that'll do their bodies good. Been-there-forever **Sojourner,** 134 E. Cañon Perdido St., 805/965-7922, serves inexpensive vegetarian and vegan fare, from vegetable-rich homemade soups and black-bean stew to veggie lasagna. Also good for healthy and veggie basics, including juices and smoothies, is the **Main Squeeze** two doors down at 138 E. Cañon Perdido, 805/966-5365.

Super for inexpensive all-American breakfast is the people's favorite **Esau's Coffee Shop,** 403 State St., 805/965-4416, where everything is homemade, right down to the biscuits and home fries. It's open until 1 P.M. for breakfast and lunch (most people do breakfast).

The oldest place in town is reportedly **Joe's Cafe** and bar, 536 State St. (near Cota), 805/966-4638, a reasonably inexpensive local institution—marked by the eagle—that keeps shuffling around downtown. (Since Joe's is often mobbed, come at an off hour.) Check out the history on the walls while you enjoy excellent ravioli, steaks, fried chicken, sometimes-fresh swordfish, rainbow trout, and Santa Maria–style barbecue. Good pasta salads. *Big* meals, no desserts, and notoriously potent drinks. It's open for lunch and dinner daily.

Stylish Yet Affordable

Santa Barbara loves its restaurants served up with some style. The city's better restaurants also tend to cluster downtown, making many city blocks irresistible for foodies. For the best quiche in town, for example, head to **Mousse Odile,** 18 E. Cota St., 805/962-5393, actually a French deli serving breakfast, lunch, and dinner. The chocolate dessert mousse drives people wild. For California-style French bistro fare, the place is **Mimosa,** 700 De La Vina St., 805/682-2272, open for lunch weekdays only, for dinner nightly. For Thai, **Your Place,** 22 N. Milpas St., Ste. A, 805/966-5151, is a best bet. Fabulous and locally famous for sushi is **Arigato Sushi,** 11 W. Victoria St. #16, 805/965-6074.

For Southwestern, seek out the blue-corn tortillas and marvelous cheese *chiles rellenos* is the **Zia Cafe,** 532 State St., 805/962-5391, open daily for both lunch and dinner. **Roy,** 7 W. Carillo, 805/966-5636, is famous for serving stylish and fresh California-style American at astonishingly low prices.

Fish, fish, fish—the ocean around here is still full of them, even after the Bay Cafe has had

its way. The **Bay Cafe,** 131 Anacapa St., 805/963-2215, serves all kinds of charbroiled fish at dinner, from salmon to swordfish, plus the Bay's rendition of surf 'n' turf, paellas, and shrimp and other seafood pastas. At lunch, expect some of the same but also fish and chips, tostadas, crab melts, and seafood salad. Just about everything tastes better if you're sitting out on the patio. The Bay Cafe is open for lunch and dinner daily.

Fun at breakfast, lunch, and dinner is the other-era **Paradise Café,** 702 Anacapa St., 805/962-4416, specializing in new renditions of predominantly all-American fare—eggs and omelettes, beefy burgers, and woodfire-grilled chicken, chops, fish, and steaks. But the Paradise Café is most famous for its steamed mussels—fresh from the Santa Barbara Channel, scraped off the legs of offshore oil rigs—and for the fact that it serves an exceptional selection of Santa Barbara County wines. Lively bar scene. Half the town shows up on Sunday (starting at 9 A.M.) for the Paradise Café's killer breakfast/brunch. Breakfast is served only on Sunday.

Locally beloved for Cajun is the original **Cajun Kitchen,** 1924 De la Vina, Ste. A (near Mission St.), 805/965-1004. Those in the know say to show up early on Saturday morning—before everyone else gets there—for the unforgettable chile verde. There are Cajun Kitchens all over, elsewhere in town at 901 Chapala St., 805/965-1004, and also in Goleta and Carpinteria. **The Palace Cafe,** 8 E. Cota St. (at State), 805/966-3133, is Santa Barbara's other New Orleans niche, serving imaginative and exceptionally well-prepared fish, crawfish, "Cajun popcorn," and other Cajun-Creole and Caribbean fare. The menu changes nightly. It's open daily for lunch and dinner.

Busy **Brigitte's** California-style bistro at 1325 State St., 805/966-9676, serves everything one would expect—pizzas with pizzazz, refined pastas, grill specialties, grand salads—along with an impressive California wine list. For something simpler, stop by the associated bakery and deli adjacent for sandwiches, takeout salads, fresh-baked breads, and other bakery items.

Then there's always **The Patio** at the Four Seasons Biltmore, 1260 Channel Dr., 805/969-2261, open daily for breakfast, lunch, and dinner. Even if a stay at Santa Barbara's venerable Biltmore is impossible, almost anyone can swing a meal here—at least at The Patio, reasonably relaxed and quite good. A wonderful French, Mediterranean, or Italian buffet is served every evening. If money's no object, of course, the ultimate is dress-up dinner in the Biltmore's ocean-view **La Marina** restaurant. Either choice offers an excuse to appreciate the lobby and explore the grounds of this stunning 1927 Spanish-Mediterranean hotel, exquisitely restored in 1987.

Stylish Yet Affordable Nearby

For something different on the San Marcos Pass route between Santa Barbara and the Solvang area, stop at **Cold Spring Tavern,** an old stagecoach stop at 5995 Stagecoach Rd. off Highway 154, 805/967-0066. The evocative Old West ambience here comes with some fairly sophisticated fare—such things as charbroiled quail—along with more traditional meat, potatoes, and biscuits with gravy. It's open daily for lunch and dinner, on weekends only for breakfast.

Otherwise, beyond Santa Barbara proper and the Santa Ynez Valley (see Solvang and Vicinity, below), the place to go is Montecito. This uptown Santa Barbara suburb has its share of snazzy restaurants, many of them strung out along Coast Village Road, the main drag—also home to the Friday morning farmers' market—and many of them reasonably priced. Always a best bet is the California-style **Montecito Cafe** at the stylish Montecito Inn, 1295 Coast Village Rd., 805/969-3392, open daily for lunch and dinner.

For fashionable deli and café fare, the place is **Tutti's,** 1209 Coast Village Rd., 805/969-5809, open daily for breakfast, lunch, and dinner. Poke around the neighborhood for other possibilities, since restaurants sometimes come and go quite quickly. Such is the nature of style.

Or try **Piatti** in Montecito at 516 San Ysidro Rd. (at E. Valley Rd.), 805/969-7520, open for lunch and dinner daily. This cheerful Italian was cooked up by the owners of Auberge du Soleil and the local San Ysidro Ranch, two of California's most prestigious resorts. But anybody can feel comfortable here, what with colorful vegetables on the walls and a sunny-patio sense of place. Sit down and celebrate the Santa Barbara good life with homemade pastas, good salads, and chicken, fish, and other entrees. Piatti is open daily for both lunch and dinner.

Pane e Vino, 1482 E. Valley Rd. in Montecito, 805/969-9274, is another popular local Italian, this one serving good Northern Italian—perfect pasta and fine chicken and fish dishes. Bread and wine too. For something still simpler—pizzas, pasta, sandwiches, and such—head next door to Pane e Vino's kissing cousin **Via Vai,** 805/565-9393.

For fine deli and cafe fare or to pack a gourmet picnic basket, don't miss the **Pierre LaFond** food market at 516 San Ysidro Rd. #1, 805/565-1503, where you'll find it all—and then some. There's another Pierre on State Street in downtown Santa Barbara, 805/962-1455.

Ye Cold Spring Tavern, outside Santa Barbara, was once a stagecoach stop.

KIM WEIR

Super-Fine Dining

In Santa Barbara, perennially laid-back, even fine dining is often a reasonably casual affair. Jackets are required in some dining rooms; if you're concerned about being too dressed up or down, call ahead.

Santa Barbara's all abuzz about Michel Richard's French **Citronelle** restaurant at the Santa Barbara Inn, 901 Cabrillo Blvd., 805/963-0111, coastal sibling to the famous Citrus in Los Angeles. This attractive, upbeat, and airy oceanside bistro, associated with the Santa Barbara Inn, the gussied-up motel adjacent, serves quiche Lorraine, eggs Benedict, and variations on more traditional American fare for brunch. Lunch and dinner selections include such choices as salmon fettuccine with saffron sauce, chicken ravioli, and Caesar salad with scallops. Wonderful appetizers and soups, exceptional California wine list, and unforgettable desserts—such as the famed chocolate hazelnut bar. It's open daily for lunch and dinner, for brunch on weekends, and sometimes for weekday breakfast; call for current details.

Also at the top of the local food chain is dinner-only **La Marina** at the Four Seasons Biltmore Hotel, 1260 Channel Dr., 805/969-2261. Seafood typically stars on the menu but roasted pheasant, chicken, steaks, even delectable vegetarian selections are also available. And the stylish Sunday brunch here is something to write home about.

Also exceptional is the **Stonehouse** restaurant at the San Ysidro Ranch in Montecito, 900 San Ysidro Ln., 805/969-5046, open daily for breakfast, lunch, and dinner, also serving wonderful Sunday brunch. Another, more casual possibility at the ranch is the **Plow & Angel Bistro.**

Charming and quite romantic for California-style is the **El Encanto Dining Room** at the El Encanto Hotel and Garden Villas, 1900 Lasuen Rd., 805/687-5000, though **Downey's** downtown at 1305 State St., 805/966-5006, is more innovative and consistent.

TRANSPORTATION AND INFORMATION

Santa Barbara Transportation

Many of the region's finest pleasures, including the Santa Barbara wine country and the lovely state beaches 20-plus miles north of town, can't be reached by public transit. Look in the telephone yellow pages or contact the local chamber of commerce or visitor bureau for car rental agencies.

To get around town without a car, **Santa Barbara Metropolitan Transit District** buses offer mainly commuter services but connect with most nearby destinations, including Goleta and Carpinteria. The transit center, 1020 Chapala St. at Cabrillo, is behind Greyhound. Call 805/683-3702 for current route and fare information, or try www.sbmtd.gov. But for many people the transit district's electric **Downtown-Waterfront Shuttles,** which run along State Street between Cabrillo Boulevard (at Stearns Wharf) and Sola Street, 10:15 A.M.–6 P.M., and along the Waterfront (Cabrillo Blvd.) 10 A.M.–5:45 P.M.; at last report the all-day fare was still just 25 cents. The less frequent morning and early evening service (times vary depending on the day) runs between the zoo on the east and the Arlington Theatre on the west. Also convenient in many cases is the **Santa Barbara Trolley,** 805/965-0353, which connects most of downtown's sights with destinations as far-flung as the Santa Barbara Mission and nearby botanic gardens with the waterfront, the zoo, and downtown Montecito. All routes start and end at Stearns Wharf. Pick up a current trolley schedule and route map; at last report all-day trolley fare was $3 adults, $2 children.

Greyhound, 34 W. Carrillo, 805/965-7551, offers good bus connections to and from L.A. and San Francisco. Even better than buses, though, is the opportunity Santa Barbara provides for traveling by train. The **Amtrak** station is downtown at 209 State St., 805/687-6848, with trains rolling south to Los Angeles and north to San Francisco; for current schedule and fare information, call toll-free 800/872-7245 or try the websites: www.amtrak.com or www.amtrakwest.com.

Limited air transport is available at the **Santa Barbara Municipal Airport** just north in Goleta at 601 Firestone Rd., 805/967-7111. But you can also arrange a ride to or from LAX with **Santa Barbara Airbus,** 805/964-7759. For prepaid reservations—usually the cheapest way to go—call toll-free 800/733-6354.

Santa Barbara Information

To request information before your trip, contact the **Santa Barbara Conference and Visitors Bureau,** 510 State St., Santa Barbara 93101, 805/966-9222, fax 805/966-1728; www.santabarbaraca.com. For a copy of its comprehensive current visitor guide, call toll-free 800/927-4688—or download a PDF version from the website. (There's also a downtown parking map on the web.) Or stop in for visitor information when you arrive. The visitors bureau sponsors two walk-in visitor centers: the **Santa Barbara Visitor Information Center,** 1 Garden St. (at Cabrillo Blvd., across from Chase Palm Park), 805/965-3021, open Mon.–Sat. 9 A.M.–5 P.M. and Sunday 10 A.M.–5 P.M., and **Hot Spots,** 36 State St., 805/564-1637 or toll-free 800/793-7666; the lobby is open 24 hours, and there's an ATM here and a coffee machine. Among the informational offerings typically available: the current edition of the *Santa Barbara County Wineries* brochure and touring map and the *Antiques Map and Guide* for Santa Barbara, Montecito, and Summerland. Also pick up the *Red Tile Walking Tour* brochure (information and route also available on the website) and ask about bike rentals and such. People here are passionate about renting those "pedalinas," for example, for wheeling slowly along the beachfront bike path.

The **main post office** is at 836 Anacapa, 805/564-2266 or toll-free 800/275-8777, and the attractive **Santa Barbara Central Library** is at 40 E. Anapamu, 805/962-7653. For current entertainment and events information, pick up current copies of the weekly *Santa Barbara Independent* and the daily *Santa Barbara News-Press.* You'll find other publications around town too.

NORTH OF SANTA BARBARA

SOLVANG AND VICINITY

Solvang, "sunny meadow" or "sunny valley" in Danish, was founded in 1911 by immigrants from Denmark seeking a pastoral spot to establish a folk school. This attractive representation of Denmark is now a well-trod tourist destination in the otherwise sleepy Santa Ynez Valley, complete with Scandinavian-style motels, restaurants, shops, even windmills. Recent history has also had its impact here. Though national media always put former President Ronald Reagan's Western White House in Santa Barbara, it was actually closer to Solvang, off Refugio Road. The Reagans don't live at the ranch anymore. But when they did, they made quite an impression. When Ron and Nancy arrived at the Solvang polls to vote, for example, SWAT teams took over the town.

In summer and on many weekends, tourists take over the town. To appreciate the authentic taste of Denmark here—and, surprisingly, the experience is largely authentic—come some other time, in winter, spring, or fall. Come in February for the **Flying Leap Storytellers Festival,** in March for **Taste of Solvang,** in April for the **Vintners Festival.** And in September Solvang hosts **Danish Days,** a colorful community celebration honoring the old country since 1936, with authentic dress, outdoor dancing and feasts, roving entertainers, and theater. Yet there is a special compensation for those who do come in summer: **Summer Theaterfest** performances by the **Pacific Conservatory of the Performing Arts** in Solvang's 700-seat outdoor Solvang Festival Theatre. For current information, call the theatre at 805/922-8313 or try the website, www.pcpa.org. And about four miles from the Reagan ranch, the **Circle Bar B Guest Ranch,** 805/968-1113, www.circlebarb.com, stages dinner theater productions in an old barn (now a 100-seat theater) from May into November; call for current information.

For more information on attractions and events in and around Solvang, contact: **Solvang Conference and Visitors Bureau,** P.O. Box 70, Solvang, CA 93464, toll-free 800/468-6765, www.solvangusa.com, or the **Solvang Chamber of Commerce,** P.O. Box 465, Solvang, CA 93464, 805/688-0701; www.solvangcc.com.

Seeing and Doing Solvang and Vicinity

A wander through Solvang offers thatched-roofed buildings with wooden roof storks, almost endless bakeries and gift shops, and surprises such as the **wind harp** near the **Bethania Lutheran Church,** where services are still conducted in Danish once each month. The **Wulff Windmill** on Fredensborg Canyon Road northwest of town is a historic landmark, once used to grind grain and pump water. For an appreciation of Danish culture, stop by the **Elverhøj Danish Heritage and Fine Arts Museum** on Elverjoy Way, 805/686-1211, an accurate representation of an 18th-century Danish farmhouse open Wed.–Sun. 1–4 P.M. Perfect for picnics: **Hans Christian Andersen Park** off Atterdag Road, three blocks north of Mission Drive, complete with children's playground.

New in Solvang, open for tours by reservation only, is the free **Western Wear Museum,** 435 First St., 805/693-5000 or 805/688-3388, 10 rooms of silver-screen cowboy regalia and other Western wear themes; most fun for the kiddos is the "cowkids" room.

Mission Santa Inés just east of Solvang off Highway 246 (on Mission Dr.), 805/688-4815, www.missionsantaines.com, was established in 1804, the 19th of the state's 21 missions and the last in the region. Get a more complete story on the tour of this rosy-tan mission with its copper roof tiles, attractive bell tower, original murals, and decent museum. It's open daily; small donation requested. Bingo and such are the main attractions at the otherwise almost invisible **Santa Ynez Indian Reservation,** on the highway in Santa Ynez. More interesting for most folks is the **Santa Ynez Valley Historical Society Museum** on Sagunto Street in Santa Ynez, 805/688-7889, open Fri.–Sun. 1–4 P.M., a respectful look at local tradition. Also here is the **Parks-Janeway Carriage House,** with a restored collection of horse-drawn buggies, car-

ROBERT HOLMES/CALIFORNIA DIVISION OF TOURISM

Solvang's Danish history is evident in the architecture around town.

riages, carts, and stagecoaches; at last report the carriage house was open during museum hours, and also open Tues.–Thurs. 10 A.M.–4 P.M.

Seeing and Doing the Santa Ynez Valley

Rancho San Fernando Rey near Santa Ynez is noteworthy as the birthplace of Palomino horses, one of the few "color" breeds, golden creatures descended from Arabian stock with flaxen manes and tails. Horse ranches, in fact, whether specializing in Arabians, American paints, quarterhorses, thoroughbreds, Peruvian *paso finos* or other breeds, are big business in these parts. Monty Roberts of *The Man Who Listens to Horses* fame, is headquartered in the valley at 110-acre **Flag Is Up Farms,** a thoroughbred racing and training ranch and event center.

Most Santa Ynez Valley back roads offer wonderful cycling, increasing numbers of small wineries, and sublime pastoral scenery. **Santa Barbara County wineries**—a cornucopia—are becoming big business, and a major regional attraction. For more on area wineries, see Santa Barbara Wine Country later in this chapter.

Nojoqui Falls County Park, www.sbparks .com, is about six miles south of Solvang on Alisal Road, a beautiful bike ride from town but more easily accessible from Nojoqui Pass on Highway 101. Some say the Chumash word *nojoqui* (nah-HO-wee) means "honeymoon," a possible reference to a tragic love story staged here in Chumash mythology. The park itself includes 84 acres of oaks, limestone cliffs, and a sparkling 168-foot vernal (spring only) waterfall, in addition to hiking trails and picnic and playground facilities.

Los Olivos, once a stage stop at the end of a narrow-gauge railroad rolling down from the north, is now a tiny Western revival town seemingly transplanted from the Mother Lode. If the town looks familiar, it may be because its main street served as a set for TV series *Mayberry RFD.* Nowadays, the county's booming boutique wine trade is quite visible from here. Well worth a stop for wine aficionados is the **Los Olivos Wine & Spirits Emporium** on Grand Avenue south of town, 805/688-4409 or toll-free 888/729-4637 (SB-WINES), www.sbwines.com, which definitely purveys some of the area's finest. Also check out the **Wilding Museum—America's Wilderness in Art,** in town across from St. Mark's, 805/688-1082. The main attraction in nearby **Ballard** is the Ballard School, a classic little red schoolhouse still used for kindergarten classes. **Los Alamos** off Highway 101 northwest of Buellton is another spot in the road experiencing a Western-style wine country renaissance. From Los Alamos, take a spin through the Solomon Hills, hideout for the notorious antigringo *bandito* Salomon Pico, Pio Pico's cousin, a native Northern Californian and inspiration for the mythical Zorro of comic book and movie fame. Head south on Highway 101, and then turn left on little-traveled Alisos Canyon Road to Foxen Canyon Road, which leads past the granite **Frémont-Foxen Monument** commemorating John C. Frémont's bloodless December 1846 capture of Santa Barbara (with the help of local guide Benjamin Foxen). To take in more of the area's charms, try an alternate route to Highway 101 between Santa Barbara and the Solvang area, the locally favorite but bustling backroads route (via Hwy. 154 just beyond Santa Ynez) over San Marcos Pass to Lake Cachuma.

PRACTICAL SOLVANG

Staying in and near Solvang

In the Solvang-Buellton area, camp off Foxen Canyon Road at **Zaca** ("peace and quiet" in Chumash) **Lake,** actually two natural lakes, both privately owned and surrounded by abundant plant and wildlife, great hiking trails, and good swimming. The facilities include a rustic resort, picnic areas, horseback riding, good swimming. No motor boats allowed, but visitors can rent canoes, sailboats, fishing skiffs. For more information, contact: **The Lodge,** Zaca Lake, P.O. Box 187, Los Olivos, CA 93441, 805/688-4891. To get here, take Foxen Canyon Road from near Los Olivos (or Zaca Station Rd. from just north of Solvang on Hwy. 101), and then turn down the marked dirt road beyond the gate.

You'll find a **Motel 6** in Buellton just off Highway 246 as it slides into Solvang at 333 McMurray Rd., P.O. Box 1670, Buellton 93427, 805/688-7797 or toll-free 800/466-8356 fax 805/686-0297, www.motel6.com, with pool, color TV, and movies. Reserve well in advance. Rates: $58–68 from mid-June through September—lower in the off-season, higher on special-event weekends. Look around in the same general vicinity for other less expensive possibilities and along Highway 101, also just outside Solvang on Alisal Road. Also quite basic but right in the middle of town is the 12-room **Viking Motel,** 1506 Mission Dr., 805/688-1337, fax 805/693-9499. Rates: $42–125. The 14-room **Hamlet Motel,** 1532 Mission Dr., 805/688-4413 or toll-free 800/253-5033, fax 805/686-1301, is also a good deal. Rates: $50–175.

Most lodgings in Solvang proper tend to be pricier, especially in summer. Weekend rates are often higher too. The **Best Western Kronborg Inn,** 1440 Mission Dr., 805/688-2383 or toll-free 800/528-1234, fax 805/688-1821, features pleasant, redecorated rooms, refrigerators and coffeemakers in all rooms, color TV with cable, heated pool, and spa. Some "pet rooms" available too. Rates: $60–95. **Inns of California,** 1450 Mission Dr., 805/688-3210, fax 805/688-0026, has comfortable rooms and a heated pool. Rates: $60–$195.

Quite appealing in that Solvang style is the **Chimney Sweep Inn,** 1564 Copenhagen Dr.,

805/688-2111 or toll-free 800/824-6444, fax 805/688-8824, which features individually decorated rooms, loft rooms, suites, and garden cottages. Complimentary Danish bakery breakfast. And there's a spa in the gazebo. Rates: $90 and up. Still a great value is **Country Inn & Suites,** 1455 Mission Dr., 805/688-2018 or toll-free 800/446-4000, fax 805/688-1156, with attractive, spacious rooms, abundant amenities, and free country breakfast and "hospitality reception" refreshments and snacks daily. Rates: $128–148, but ask about specials. Solvang's full-service hotel is the **Solvang Royal Scandinavian Inn,** 400 Alisal Rd., 805/688-8000 or toll-free 800/624-5572, fax 805/688-0761, featuring large rooms and heated pool. Summer rates of $99 and up ($79 and up in winter). An impressive newcomer is the 40-room **Petersen Village Inn,** 1576 Mission Dr., 805/688-3121 or toll-free 800/321-8985, fax 805/688-5732, featuring all the amenities, including European buffet breakfast and evening dessert buffet.

For more complete listings of accommodations, contact the local chamber of commerce or visitor bureau.

Special Solvang-Area Stays

Since 1946 Solvang's 10,000-acre cattle ranch, **The Alisal Guest Ranch and Resort,** has become one of California's premier resorts—offering absolute peace and rustic luxury, with no phones, no television sets, and no radios. Though the "cottages" here are quite comfortable, the real appeal is out of doors: long hikes, wrangler-led horseback rides, tennis, horseshoes, shuffleboard, croquet, badminton, volleyball, pool, table tennis, swimming, and just lounging around the pool. The Alisal even has its own lake. But some come just for the exceptional 18-hole golf course here. And some come just to loaf in the mild climate—bestirring themselves only to head for the excellent ranch-house restaurant (breakfast and dinner are included; lunch is also available). The Alisal provides a children's program in summer. For summer, book six months in advance. Rates (two-night minimum) aren't affordable for most real cowpokes, though, at $375 and up. For more information, contact The Alisal Ranch, 1054 Alisal Rd., 805/688-6411 or toll-free 800/425-4725 for reservations, fax 805/688-2510; www.alisal.com.

Among other Solvang-area entries in the "very special stay" category is the historic Western-French **Fess Parker's Wine Country Inn** in Los Olivos, formerly the Los Olivos Grand Hotel country inn, a luxurious 21-suite turn-of-the-20th-century hostelry with rooms named after the Western artists or French Impressionists whose works decorate the walls. The hotel's elegant but casual **Vintage Room** restaurant is open for lunch and dinner daily, breakfast on weekends. Rooms, with gas fireplaces, are $175–400 and up, but inquire about discounts and off-season specials. For more information and reservations, contact Fess Parker's Wine Country Inn, 2860 Grand Ave., P.O. Box 849, Los Olivos, CA 93441, 805/688-7788 or toll-free 800/446-2455, fax 805/688-1942; www.fessparker.com.

Quite nice, too, and also smack dab in the middle of Santa Barbara County wine country, is **The Ballard Inn**, 2436 Baseline Ave., Ballard, CA 93463, 805/688-7770 or toll-free 800/638-2466 for reservations, fax 805/688-9560, www .ballardinn.com, a contemporary two-story country inn with 15 rooms and all the amenities. Rates: $170–250. The inn offers breakfast cooked to order, afternoon hors d'oeuvres, and wine tasting. The inn's dinner-only **Cafe Chardonnay** serves well-prepared fish, chicken, chops and other wine-enhancing possibilities.

Eating in and near Solvang

Solvang's Danish bakeries are legendary, and many visitors manage to eat reasonably well without going much farther. The **Solvang Bakery**, 460 Alisal Rd., 805/688-4939, is one good choice. Farm-style breakfast places and pancake houses are also big around town. A solid café-style choice is **The Mustard Seed** ("Good Home Cookin' Naturally"), 1655 Mission Dr., 805/688-1318, a warm and casual family- and country-style place with outdoor patio, open for breakfast and lunch seven days a week, and for dinner every night but Sunday. Expect good egg "scrambles" or Danish omelettes at breakfast, sandwiches and salads at lunch, and homestyle cooking at dinner (beef stew, beef liver, chicken fried steak, even a vegetarian platter) though the best deal of all is the Seed's full-meal homemade chicken pot pie, served with either soup or salad. Inexpensive choices, too, for "seedlings" (children ages 10 and under). For

sophisticated Solvang fare, the place is the **Brothers Restaurant** inside the Storybook Inn, 409 First St., 805/688-9934. Always special for a fine dine is the **River Grill** at the Alisal Ranch, outside town at 1054 Alisal Rd., 805/688-7784.

Though the general consensus is that it's not as good as it used to be, now that it's become a restaurant chain, the original **Andersen's Pea Soup** is in nearby Buellton (you can't miss it on Hwy. 246, with its own Best Western motel). But Buellton won't disappoint. Best bet for breakfast, for miles around, is **Ellen's Danish Pancake House,** 272 Avenue the Flags, 805/688-5312. For Mexican, the place is **Javy's Café**, 406 E. Hwy. 246, 805/688-7758. Buellton also boasts the sequel to the original Hitching Post barbecue palace and steakhouse in Casmalia (see below), the dinner-only **Hitching Post II**, 406 E. Hwy. 246, 805/688-0676.

Other great eating possibilities are scattered throughout surrounding vineyard country. The casual French country-style **Ballard Store** restaurant in block-long Ballard closed in late 1999, alas. But there are other possibilities, including the small **Cafe Chardonnay** in the Ballard Inn, 2436 Baseline Rd., 805/688-7770, open for dinner Wed.–Sun. nights. Reservations are advisable. Or head to Los Olivos.

About five miles north of Solvang on Highway 154 in Los Olivos is historic **Mattei's Tavern,** 805/688-4820, once a train depot and stage stop, now a white-frame dinner house specializing in steak, seafood, and other hearty fare. It's open noon–3 P.M. for lunch too, Fri.–Sun. only. Reservations advisable. Or try the **Los Olivos Café,** 2798 Grand Ave., 805/688-7265, open daily for lunch and dinner. For something simple, stop by **Panino,** 2900 Grand Ave., 805/688-9304, for smoothies, any one of the 30-something sandwiches, and picnic supplies. Exceptional in these parts for fine dining is the elegant yet casual **Vintage Room** at Fess Parker's Wine Country Inn, 2860 Grand Ave., 805/ 688-7788, open for breakfast, lunch, and dinner.

As elsewhere in the Santa Ynez Valley, in Santa Ynez the tried-and-true bumps up against the new—though wine country sensibility is fast outpacing cowboy-style steak and eggs. Still going strong, though, for basic 1950s-style breakfast along with great burgers and fries is the **Longhorn Coffee Shop & Bakery,** 3687

Sagunto St., 805/688-5912. Also here is **Maverick Saloon,** 805/688-5841, kind of a country-western juke joint popular for line dancing and karaoke. At home in the same complex yet cultural and culinary worlds away is world-class **Trattoria Grappolo,** 805/688-6899, famous for its homemade pastas and wood-fired pizza. Other foodie destinations include the **Santa Ynez Feed & Grill,** 3544 Sagunto St., 805/693-5100, and **Vineyard House,** 3631 Sagunto, 805/688-2886.

Los Alamos also has its attractions, but still down-home and kicked-back, including **Charlie's,** 97 Den, 805/344-4404, and the fairly mellow biker tavern **Ghostriders,** 550 Bell, 805/344-2111.

LOMPOC AND VICINITY

Probably Chumash for "shell mound," Lompoc these days is a bustling military town amid blooming flower fields, a commercial crazy-quilt patchwork of fragrant sweet peas, larkspurs, asters, poppies, marigolds, zinnias, and petunias adding vivid bloom to the city's cheeks from June through September. The local flower seed business is under pressure from foreign agricultural production, but the bloom boom is still healthy enough to make the tourists smile. At **Vandenberg Air Force Base** just west of town —home of the 30th Space Wing, and the only U.S. military installation that launches unmanned government and commercial satellites in addition to intercontinental ballistic missiles (ICBMs)— evening launches create colorful sky trails at sunset. Free tours of Vandenberg, which might include a former space shuttle launch site, an underground missile silo, and a shipwrecked 1923 naval destroyer, are offered Wednesday at 10 A.M. (pending missions permitting). For details and reservations, call 805/606-3595.

Another significant but subtler local presence is the area's medium security prison—until recently also a comfortable minimum security prison camp known fondly as Club Fed, historic home away from home for white-collar criminals, including Nixon-era Watergate scandal alumni Dwight Chapin, John Dean, H. R. Haldeman, and Donald Segretti. Inside trader Ivan Boesky, former San Diego Chargers running

POINT CONCEPTION

Just below Vandenberg Air Force Base is the place California turns on itself. Point Conception, an almost inaccessible elbow of land stabbing the sea about 40 miles north of Santa Barbara, is the spot where California's coastal "direction" swings from north-south to east-west, the geographical pivotal point separating temperature and climate zones, northstate from southstate. A lone wind-whipped lighthouse teeters at the edge of every mariner's nightmare, California's Cape Horn.

Inaccessible by car, Point Conception can be reached by hikers from **Jalama Beach County Park** just south of Vandenberg (from south of Lompoc, take Jalama Rd. west from Hwy. 1). Some hike along the railroad right-of-way on the plateau—illegal, of course, so you've been warned—but with equal caution one can take the more adventurous route along the beach and cliffs to commune with startled deer, seals, sea lions, and whales offshore.

back Chuck Muncie, and convicted Soviet spy Christopher Boyce (of *The Falcon and the Snowman* fame) did some time here, too.

Mission La Purísima Concepción (see below) is the area's main attraction, but stop by the **Lompoc Museum,** 200 S. H St., 805/736-3888, open afternoons Tues.–Sun., to review the city's pioneering Prohibitionist history. And poke around town to appreciate the **Lompoc Valley Mural Project** (more than 60 and counting) and the city's unique Italian stone pines. Beach hikers can head south for miles from **Ocean Beach County Park** at Vandenberg Air Force Base, reached from Lompoc via Highway 246 (heading west) and then Ocean Beach Road; often windy, so come prepared. Also locally famous for beach walks, good picnics, fishing, and fabulous sunsets is isolated, windswept, and wicked-waved **Jalama Beach County Park** about five miles south of Lompoc via Highway 1 and Jalama Road, site of the annual **Heavy Wind Surfing Championships** in May. Come to town in June for the annual **Lompoc Flower Festival** and associated **Valley of the Flowers Half-Marathon.**

For more information about the area, contact the **Lompoc Valley Chamber of Commerce,** 111 S. I St., Lompoc, CA 93436, 805/736-4567, www.lompoc.com, which offers a "flower drive" brochure/map (routes also available on the website), events, and practical information.

Practical Lompoc

For absolutely budget travelers, the best bet is camping. Near Lompoc, camp south of Vandenberg at **Jalama Beach County Park,** once the site of a Chumash village, where campsites are first-come, first-camped; for more information call 805/736-3504. Other possibilities include **Lopez Lake** to the north and state park campsites near **Morro Bay** (for area information, see below).

Motels in Lompoc are fairly inexpensive, most of them along H Street. One choice in Lompoc is the **Best Western Vandenberg Inn,** 940 E. Ocean Ave., 805/735-7731, fax 805/737-0012, www.bestwestern.com, with color TV with cable and in-room refrigerators, heated pool, spa, and sauna. Free breakfast. Rates: $70–100. Also a good value is the attractive **Inn of Lompoc,** 1122 N. H St., 805/735-7744, fax 805/736-0421. Rates: $79–89.

The **Lompoc Certified Farmers' Market** is held Friday 2 P.M.–dusk on the corner of I Street and Ocean Avenue. For more information, call 805/343-2135. **Tom's** in Lompoc at 115 E. Cottage Ave., 805/736-9996, is everybody's favorite burger joint. For burgers fresh off the oak-fired barbecue pit, the place is the **Outpost,** 118 S. H St., 805/735-1130. But, for café society, head for the **South Side Coffee Company,** 105 S. H St., 805/737-3730. As unlikely as it may seem to find a good Japanese restaurant in these parts, don't pass up **Oki Sushi,** 1206 W. Ocean Ave., 805/735-7170.

For other dining options in the area, just ask around.

La Purísima Mission State Historic Park

The largest mission complex in the state, now situated on 1,000 unspoiled acres about four miles east of Lompoc on Highway 246, Misión de la Concepción Purísima de María Santísima ("Mission of the Immaculate Conception of Most Holy Mary") was the 11th in California's chain of coastal missions when it was built in what is now downtown Lompoc in 1787. Almost all of the original Mission La Purísima was destroyed just before Christmas Day in 1812 by a devastating earthquake and deluge. Another traumatic year was 1824, when rebellious Chumash, angry at their exploitation by soldiers, captured the mission and held it for a month. Ten years later, the mission was essentially abandoned.

Now an impressive state historic park and California's only complete mission complex, the new La Purísima (built between 1813 and 1818) is unusual in its layout. All buildings line up like ducks in a row along El Camino Real, rather than occupying more traditional positions surrounding an interior courtyard. Also unique here is the fine Depression-era restoration work accomplished primarily by the Civilian Conservation Corps under state and national parks supervision. Completely rebuilt from the ground up with handmade adobe bricks, tiles, and dyes essentially identical to the originals, the mission's hand-hewn redwood timbers, doors, and furniture, even the artwork and decorative designs, also come as close to authenticity as well-disciplined architectural imagination allows.

At La Purísima, secular existence has been emphasized over the religious life. Workshops and living quarters, the soldiers' quarters, and simple cells of the padres offer a sense of the unromantic and less-than-luxurious life in mission times. More interesting, though, are the shops where the mission's work went on: the bakery, the soap and tallow factory, weaving rooms, olive press, and grain mill. The mission's museum includes an excellent collection of artifacts and historical displays. Wander along remnants of El Camino Real, past the livestock corrals, the cemetery, and the long, narrow church. (Inside, notice the abalone shells for holding holy water and the absence of benches; worshipers knelt on the adobe brick floor.)

Mission gardens, at one time irrigated by an ingenious water system, include scarecrow-guarded vegetables mixed with flowers and herbs, native plant gardens, even Castilian roses. The old pear orchards and vineyards have been replanted though a few ancient specimens remain.

Main mission events include the **Fiesta** in mid-May, spring and summer demonstrations of mission arts, crafts, and daily life—Purísima's **Peo-**

KIMWEIR

Mission La Purísima is the state's largest and only complete mission complex.

ple's Days—and the luminaria-lit **Founding Day** celebration in December (very popular, so plan; advance tickets required). The mission is open daily, from May through September 9 A.M.–6 P.M., otherwise 9 A.M.–5 P.M.; $5 per vehicle day-use fee. During the off-season, come later in the afternoon to avoid school tours and take the 90-minute recorded tour. Guided tours are available by appointment. For more information, contact: **La Purísima Mission State Historic Park,** 2295 Purisima Rd., 805/733-3713.

SANTA MARIA AND VICINITY

This onetime ranch-country hitching post on the northern fringe of Santa Barbara County is quickly growing out into its flower fields, thanks in part to the proximity of Vandenberg Air Force Base. Built on sand flats, Santa Maria has an abundance of trees, unusually wide streets—originally to more easily reverse eight-mule wagon rigs—and one of the West's best repertory theater programs.

Come in April for the annual **Santa Maria Valley Strawberry Festival** at the county fairgrounds, and the **Santa Maria Bluegrass Festival.** The "West's Best Rodeo," Santa Maria's **Elks Rodeo and Parade,** is the big event in late May or early June. The **Santa Barbara County Fair** in late July is old-fashioned family fun complete with carnival, exhibits, entertainment, and horse show. Biplanes, hot-air balloons, and sky divers all converge in September for Santa Maria's **Air Fair.** But good times anytime are almost guaranteed by the fine **Pacific Conservatory of the Performing Arts,** which offers Shakespeare, musicals such as *Narnia* and *I Do, I Do,* and dramas such as *Amadeus* and Eugene O'Neill's *Long Day's Journey into Night.* Performances are also held in Solvang, but the troupe's headquarters are at the local Allan Hancock College, 800 S. College Dr. in Santa Maria, www .pcpa.org, 805/922-8313 or, for tickets, toll-free 800/727-2123.

Fairly new in the neighborhood is the two-hangar **Santa Maria Museum of Flight,** 3015 Airpark Rd., 805/922-8758, open Fri.–Sun. 9 A.M.–5 P.M. (until 4 P.M. in winter), which documents general flight history with both antique and model planes, with an emphasis on local contributions to aviation history. (Santa Maria was a basing station during World War II.) The once-secret Norden bombsight, the Fleet Model 2, and the Stinson V77-Reliant are among the treasures on display. The Early Aviation Hangar houses aircraft, memorabilia, models, and photos chronicling the years stretching between the Wright Brothers' first flights to World War II. A veritable flock of antique planes perches here in July for the **Primary Trainer Fly-In.** For broader local historical perspective, the **Santa Maria Valley Historical Museum** is downtown adjacent to the visitor bureau/chamber of commerce office at 616 S. Broadway, 805/922-3130, and is open Tues.–Sat. noon–5 P.M. A fascination here: the Barbecue Hall of Fame.

For more information about Santa Maria and vicinity, contact: **Santa Maria Visitor and Convention Bureau,** 614 S. Broadway, Santa Maria, CA 93454, 805/925-2403 or toll-free 800/331-3779, fax 805/928-7559, www.santamaria.com, which offers accommodations, food, and regional wine-tour information. Also pick up a copy of the *Walk Through History* local walking tour guide. For area camping and regional recreation information, contact the **Santa Lucia Ranger District** office of the Los Padres National Forest at 1616 N. Carlotti Dr. in Santa Maria, 805/925-9538; www.r5.fs.fed.us/lospadres.

Staying in Santa Maria

If you need to spoil yourself but don't have big enough bucks to do that in places like Carmel or Santa Barbara, consider the **Santa Maria Inn,** a half-mile south of Main Street at 801 S. Broadway, 805/928-7777 or toll-free 800/447-3529 for reservations, fax 805/928-5690; www.santamariainn.com. This historic English Tudor–style hostelry, built in 1917, is Santa Maria's pride and joy—a grande dame that once hosted California luminaries such as William Randolph Hearst and actress Marion Davies on their way to and from San Simeon and Hollywood stars

IN SEARCH OF *THE TEN COMMANDMENTS*

The coastal dunes due west of Santa Maria provide habitat for California brown pelicans and the endangered least terns, though Cecil B. DeMille probably didn't think much about such things in 1923 when he built, and then buried, a dozen four-ton plaster sphinxes, four statues of Ramses the Magnificent, and an entire pharaonic city here—the original movie set for *The Ten Commandments.* Referred to as the dune that never moves, Ten Commandment Hill is now part of the **Guadalupe –Nipomo Dunes Preserve** and the first thing visitors see at the Guadalupe entrance.

This large coastal dunes preserve is part of the seemingly simple yet quite complicated and fragile Nipomo Dunes ecosystem, which stretches from Pismo Beach south to Vandenberg. Created by howling wind and enormous offshore swells, the seaward dunes are sizable parabola-shaped mounds of sharp-grained sand in almost perpetual motion. The more stable back dunes stand 200 feet tall and offer more hospitable habitat for the 18 endangered and rare endemic coastal scrub species counted to date by members of the California Native Plant Society. Among the most instantly impressive is the yellow-flowered giant coreopsis, which grows only on the Channel Islands and on the coast from Los Angeles north to the Nipomo Dunes.

Oso Flaco Lake to the north of Guadalupe is a surprising sparkling blue coastal oasis, actually a group of small lakes fringed by shrubs and surrounded by sand dunes (and the din from dune buggyists penned up just northwest at the Oceano Dunes State Vehicular Recreation Area).

To the south is **Mussel Rock,** at 500 feet the tallest sand dune in California. Sit and watch the

sunset while the surf spits and sputters across the sand. Or hike to Point Sal and **Point Sal State Beach,** a wonderfully remote stretch of headlands, rocky outcroppings, and sand (the treacherous surf is unsafe for swimming) just north of Vandenberg. (To get there, head west on the Brown Road turnoff three miles south of Guadalupe, and then take Point Sal Road.) Good whale-watching.

Though the preserve holdings started with 3,400 acres, including the critical central section relinquished by Mobil Oil Corporation, the preserve now embraces a total of 20,000 acres owned by the Nature Conservancy and various public agencies. The San Luis Obispo–based People for Nipomo Dunes led the dunes preservation effort with the idea of creating a Nipomo Dunes National Seashore, protected federally like Point Reyes to the north. The dunes are now recognized as a National Natural Landmark.

The preserve is accessible from Highway 101 in Santa Maria (via Hwy. 166) or from Highway 1 farther west near Guadalupe. There are two preserve entrances. To reach the Guadalupe entrance, from Guadalupe continue to the west end of W. Main Street. To reach the Oso Flaco Lake entrance, from Highway 1 about three miles north of Guadalupe turn left onto Oso Flaco Lake Road. The Oso Flaco Lake area is handicapped accessible, with a mile-long boardwalk. The preserve is open dawn to dusk 365 days each year. No overnight camping, dogs, or four-wheel drive vehicles are allowed.

For more information, stop by the **Dunes Center,** in downtown Guadalupe at 951 Guadalupe St. (Hwy. 1), 805/343-2455; www.dunescenter.org. The center is open Friday 2–4 P.M. and on weekends noon–4 P.M.

including Charlie Chaplin, Mary Pickford, Douglas Fairbanks, Rudolph Valentino, Marlene Dietrich, Marilyn Monroe, John Wayne, and Jimmy Stewart. More recently, even Demi Moore. The Santa Maria Inn, renovated and redecorated in Old English style, now includes full fitness facilities in addition to the swimming pool. Rooms in the older hotel section are smaller yet more "historic"; more spacious accommodations are situated in the hotel's newer Tower. All accommodations feature abundant amenities, from color TVs with video players and hair dryers to in-room coffeemakers and refrigerators. Rooms are $89–119 and suites are $149–259, with discounts, specials, and golf, theater, and wine packages also available. The inn's restaurant and lounge are also local stars. Come on Sunday for the hotel's famous brunch, usually including Santa Maria–style barbecue.

Among less expensive motel options is the **Santa Maria Motel 6,** 2040 N. Preisker Ln. (Broadway at Hwy. 101), 805/928-8111 or toll-free 800/466-8356, fax 805/349-1219; www.motel6 .com. Rates: $44–48.

Eating in and near Santa Maria
Since the area boasts agricultural abundance, you can usually count on good pickin's at local farmers' markets. The **Santa Maria Certified Farmers' Market** is held Wednesday 1–5 P.M. in the Mervyn's parking lot, Broadway and Main. For more information, call 805/343-2135.

Otherwise, Santa Maria is a difficult place for vegetarians to avoid feeling deprived. But there are compensations—like the great Cajun fare at **Chef Rick's Ultimately Fine Foods,** in the Lucky Shopping Center at 4869 S. Bradley Rd.,

805/937-9512. Meat eaters might want to track down some world-famous **Santa Maria-style barbecue.** A tradition passed down from the days of the vaqueros, real local 'cue includes delectable slabs of prime sirloin beef barbecued over a slow red-oak fire, then sliced as thin as paper—and served with the chunky *salsa cruda* people drown it in—pinquito beans (grown only in Santa Maria Valley), salad, toasted garlic bread, and dessert, unquestionably the ultimate in California cowboy fare. Especially on Saturday, barbecue is the easiest meal to find in and around Santa Maria. The most authentic local version is served on weekends at local charity affairs of one sort or another, but several steakhouses serve it anytime.

The best of the Santa Maria barbecue bunch is the **Hitching Post,** open 5–9:30 P.M. at 3325 Point Sal Rd., 805/937-6151, in Casmalia, a tiny town southeast of Santa Maria more recently famous as the state's Class I toxic waste landfill. (The big sign at the landfill reads: Casmalia Toxic Dump—It's A Resource.) Back at the Hitching Post, you can watch the meat being barbecued over the oak fire from the other side of the glass wall. Though the wine selection is good—full bar, too—they say it's okay to drink the water here because it's pumped in from the Santa Maria Valley. Another best bet, just north of Santa Maria, is **Jocko's,** 125 N. Thompson St. in Nipomo, 805/929-3686, a Santa Maria–style steakhouse also known for its spicy beans, open daily.

West of Santa Maria is tiny Guadalupe, a Latino-Italian-Swiss-Filipino-Chinese colony also famous for its small and authentic ethnic eateries.

SAN LUIS OBISPO AND VICINITY

Before freeway arteries pulsed with California car traffic, when trips between San Francisco and Los Angeles took at least two days, north-south travelers naturally appreciated San Luis Obispo (known locally as "SLO") as the most reasonable midpoint stopover. So it's not surprising that San Luis Obispo gave birth to both the concept and the word "motel," a contraction of "motor hotel."

In 1925 when the Spanish colonial **Milestone Mo-tel** (now the Motel Inn) opened, it was the first roadside hostelry to call itself a motel. A sign at the entrance told travelers how to pronounce the new word, and Pasadena architect Arthur Heineman, who designed the place, even copyrighted it.

Playwright Sam Shepard uses motels as symbols of all that is déclassé, desolate, and depressing in the United States. Vladimir Nabokov vilified motels from a continental perspective in *Lolita:* "We held in contempt the plain white-washed clapboard Kabins, with their faint sewerish smell or some other gloomy self-conscious stench and nothing to boast of. . . ." J. Edgar Hoover, former FBI director and self-styled arbiter of the nation's personal and political morality, attacked motels in 1940 as "assignation camps" and "crime camps" contributing to the downfall of America. From that perspective, then, seemingly innocent San Luis Obispo is where the downfall of America began.

SLO Then and Now

Hoover's opinions aside, San Luis Obispo is a peaceful and pretty college town that has so far escaped the head-on collision with urban and suburban traffic under way in places such as Monterey and Ventura. **California State Polytechnic University** (Cal Poly) here is a major jewel in the community's crown, though the college is still snidely referred to as "Cow Poly" or "Cow Tech" in some circles. The Beef Pavilion, crops, swine, and poultry units do collectively clamor for center-stage attention on the campus just northeast of town, but the college is not just an agricultural school anymore. Cal Poly's architectural school is excellent, the largest in the country, as are the engineering and computer science departments. And since students here "learn by doing," there's almost always something fascinating doing on campus—particularly now that the impressive new $30 million **Performing Arts Center** has opened its opera house-style doors.

San Luis Obispo as a mission fortress was established in 1772 and named for the 13th-century Saint Louis, bishop of Toulouse, who also inadvertently lent his name to this California city and county in 1850. But San Luis Obispo's saintly antecedents have been overshadowed, politically speaking, by Pacific Gas & Electric's (PG&E) Diablo Canyon Nuclear Power Plant. Diablo, in Spanish, means "the devil." Though some claim Diablo Canyon has tarnished the town's halo of rural serenity, most of the forward-looking folks of San Luis Obispo don't seem bothered. They assume, like the rest of us, that the devil's due won't come due anytime soon.

San Luis Obispo's rip-snortin' intercollegiate rodeo and livestock competitions in April, the notorious **Poly Royale,** is no more, since locals got a bit tired of the out-of-control crowds and partying. But there's always **La Fiesta** at the Mission Plaza Park in May, with Spanish-era music, costumes, feasting, and dancing. In July, come

HIKING THE DIABLO COAST

The 10 miles of coast north of Port San Luis is pristine and rugged, home to sea lions, pelicans, and cormorants. The presence of the **Diablo Canyon Nuclear Plant** means this entire area has long been off-limits to coast walkers for security reasons. But now the **Pecho Coast Trail** traverses several miles of this once-lost coast, from just north of Avila Beach to Point San Luis Lighthouse and the marine terrace just beyond. Before you strap on those hiking boots, though, pick up the phone and call 805/541-8735; the area is accessible on guided hikes only, and only by reservation.

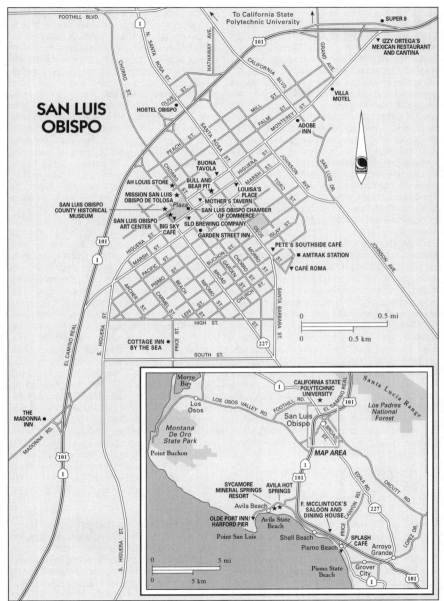

SAN LUIS OBISPO

To California State
Polytechnic University

SUPER 8

IZZY ORTEGA'S
MEXICAN RESTAURANT
AND CANTINA

VILLA
MOTEL

ADOBE
INN

FOOTHILL BLVD.

HATHAWAY AVE.

CALIFORNIA BLVD.

GRAND AVE.

N. SANTA ROSA ST.

CHORRO ST.

OLIVE ST.

HOSTEL OBISPO

PEACH ST.

SANTA ROSA ST.

HIGUERA ST.

MILL ST.

PALM ST.

MONTEREY ST.

JOHNSON AVE.

SAN LUIS DR.

JOHNSON AVE.

BUONA
TAVOLA

AH LOUIS STORE

BULL AND
BEAR PIT

MISSION SAN LUIS
OBISPO DE TOLOSA

SAN LUIS OBISPO
COUNTY HISTORICAL
MUSEUM

Plaza

SAN LUIS OBISPO
ART CENTER

BIG SKY
CAFÉ

LOUISA'S
PLACE

MOTHER'S TAVERN

SAN LUIS OBISPO CHAMBER
OF COMMERCE

SLO BREWING COMPANY

GARDEN STREET INN

MARSH ST.

TORO ST.

OSOS ST.

ISLAY ST.

PETE'S SOUTHSIDE CAFÉ

AMTRAK STATION

CAFÉ ROMA

HIGUERA ST.

MARSH ST.

PACIFIC ST.

PISMO ST.

ARCHER ST.

CHORRO ST.

BUCHON ST.

GARDEN ST.

BROAD ST.

MORRO ST.

CHORRO ST.

CHURCH ST.

BEACH ST.

NIPOMO ST.

LEFF ST.

CARMEL ST.

HIGH ST.

SANTA BARBARA ST.

S. HIGUERA ST.

EL CAMINO REAL

PRICE ST.

COTTAGE INN
BY THE SEA

SOUTH ST.

THE
MADONNA
INN

MADONNA RD.

0   0.5 mi

0   0.5 km

(inset map)

Morro
Bay

Los
Osos

Montana
De Oro
State Park

Point Buchon

CALIFORNIA STATE
POLYTECHNIC
UNIVERSITY

Santa Lucia
Range

Los Padres
National
Forest

LOS OSOS VALLEY RD.

FOOTHILL RD.

EL CAMINO REAL

San Luis
Obispo

BROAD ST.

MAP AREA

ORCUTT RD.

EDNA RD.

PRICE CANYON RD.

LOPEZ DR.

SYCAMORE
MINERAL SPRINGS
RESORT

AVILA HOT
SPRINGS

Avila Beach

OLDE PORT INN/
HARFORD PIER

Avila State
Beach

F. McCLINTOCK'S
SALOON AND
DINING HOUSE

Point San Luis

Shell Beach

SPLASH
CAFÉ

Pismo Beach

Arroyo
Grande

Grover
City

Pismo State
Beach

0   5 mi

0   5 km

for the **Central Coast Renaissance Faire.** One of the West Coast's finest cycling events is the **SLO Criterium,** also in July. The biggest arts event of the year is the annual **Mozart Festival** (www.mozartfestival.com) in late July and early August. The 20 or more intimate concerts are held at the on-campus Performing Arts Center, at the mission, and in cafés, parks, and wineries throughout the area, from Arroyo Grande to San Miguel. Composers, conductors, and musicians from around the world come to town to evoke the spirit of Amadeus. Free public Mozart Akademie lectures by various distinguished visitors are part of the week's program; the **Festival Fringe** activities include free art exhibits, concerts, and poetry readings. Come in August for the **Central Coast Wine Festival,** in November for the annual **Harvest Celebration.**

For more information about attractions and events throughout the county, contact: **San Luis Obispo County Visitors and Conference Bureau,** 1041 Chorro St., Ste. E, San Luis Obispo 93401, 805/541-8000 or toll-free 800/634-1414, fax 805/543-1255; www.sanluisobispo-county.com. Alternatively, stop by or contact the adjacent **San Luis Obispo Chamber of Commerce and Visitor Center,** 1039 Chorro St., 805/781-2777; www.visitslo.com. The visitor center is open Tues.–Fri. 8 A.M.–5 P.M. and Sat.–Mon. 10 A.M.–5 P.M. The chamber also sells tickets for Hearst Castle tours at San Simeon up the coast, if you're thinking of heading that way and don't have reservations. For information about area arts events, contact the **San Luis Obispo County Arts Council,** 805/544-9251; www.sloartscouncil.org. For whatever else is happening here and in northern Santa Barbara County, pick up a copy of *New Times* magazine; www.newtimes-slo.com.

SEEING AND DOING SAN LUIS OBISPO

Downtown San Luis Obispo

The creekside **Mission San Luis Obispo de Tolosa** downtown, founded by Father Junípero Serra in 1772 and still central to community life, was the fifth in the chain. Originally built of tules and logs, then of five-foot-thick adobe walls with tiled roofs to prevent native peoples from torch-ing the place, this isn't one of California's most intriguing missions. The stars on the parish church ceiling *are* different, though, and the mission's combination belfry and vestibule is another unique feature. The museum, once the priest's quarters, is worth a short stop for the arrowheads, baskets, Father Serra's vestments, and tangential trivia: books, portraits of mission workers, a winepress, handmade knives, and 1880s office furniture carved by the Cherokee. The mission itself, at 751 Palm St. on the edge of the downtown Mission Plaza area between Chorro and Garden and Monterey and Higuera Streets, is open 9 A.M.–5 P.M. in summer, 10 A.M.–4 P.M. otherwise (closed Easter, Thanksgiving, Christmas, and New Year's Day). Small donation requested. Call 805/543-6850 for more information.

From the mission, San Luis Obispo's historic walking tour leads through parts of hip and homey downtown, past Victorians, adobes, and the old-time train depot. Court Street is the site of the old **Bull and Bear Pit,** an early California "sporting" arena. The **San Luis Obispo County Historical Museum** at the far end of Mission Plaza in the old Carnegie library, 696 Monterey St., 805/543-0638, open Wed.–Sun. 10 A.M.–4 P.M., houses a collection of local memorabilia, including Chumash artifacts and settlers' glassware, antique clothes, even hair wreaths, also an extensive historical photo archive and research library. Just across the street is the **San Luis Obispo Art Center.** On the other side of the public bathrooms is the historic **Murray Adobe.** The **Ah Louis Store,** 800 Palm St., is all that remains of San Luis Obispo's once-thriving Chinatown. Established in 1874, Ah Louis's store was the county's first Chinese general store and the bank, counting house, and post office for the many Chinese employed by the Southern Pacific Railroad between 1884 and 1894 to dig eight train tunnels through the Cuesta Mountains.

Touring the County's Bounty

The "Ag's My Bag" bumper stickers on cars and pickup trucks you'll see throughout San Luis Obispo don't lie; agriculture seems to be everybody's bag here. In San Luis Obispo County, local produce *is* local and remarkably diverse because of the mild and varied climate. Bring

JAMES DEAN DIED HERE

Rebels otherwise without a cause might spend a few minutes in Cholame (sho-LAMB), 27 miles east of Paso Robles on the way to Lost Hills via hustle-bustle Highway 46. At the onetime intersection of Highways 41 and 46 (the exact routing of the roads has since changed), actor James Dean met death at the age of 24. The star of only three movies—*East of Eden*, his trademark *Rebel without a Cause*, and *Giant*—Dean, heading west into the blinding sun, died instantly when his speeding silver Porsche slammed head-on into a Ford at 5:59 P.M. on September 30, 1955.

And every September 30th since 1979, members of a Southern California car club trace the route of Dean's last road trip, starting in Van Nuys, during the annual en masse migration to Cholame on the James Dean Memorial Run—just about the ultimate experience for 1950s car enthusiasts.

But in front of Cholame's postage stamp-sized post office and outside the restaurant a half mile from the actual place Dean died, there's an oddly evocative stainless-steel obelisk in his memory, paid for by a businessman from Japan. The memorial is wrapped around a lone tree and landscaped with 9,000 pounds of imported Japanese gravel, a concrete bench, and engraved bronze tablets—a pilgrimage site for fans from around the world. (Inside, Dean fans can buy memorial T-shirts, sun visors, posters, and postcards. The proceeds go toward maintaining the monument.)

Seita Ohnishi's explanation etched on the tablets reads:

> *This monument stands as a small token of my appreciation for the people of America. It also stands for James Dean and other American Rebels. . . . In Japan, we say his death came as suddenly as it does to cherry blossoms. The petals of early spring always fall at the height of their ephemeral brilliance. Death in youth is life that glows eternal.*

But in keeping with James Dean's own favorite words—from Antoine de Saint-Exupéry, "What is essential is invisible to the eye"—what was important about Dean's life is not necessarily here.

---

bags and boxes along and take home seasonal produce, everything from almonds to zucchini. To find the best of the county's bounty, pick up pamphlets at the visitor bureau or chamber offices—or attend any of the eight weekly area farmers markets.

The biggest and some say the best of these, a cross between a no-bargains-barred shopping spree and a street party, is San Luis Obispo's main event. The **San Luis Obispo Higuera Street Certified Farmers' Market,** 805/544-9570, is held in downtown San Luis Obispo every Thursday 6:30–9:30 P.M., weather permitting, along the 600–900 blocks of Higuera (between Osos and Broad Streets). Show up early to find a parking place, since the whole county comes to the city on Thursday evenings—the main reason area shops and restaurants are open late on this particular weeknight. On tap Thursday evenings: live entertainment, arts, crafts, and good food in addition to fine fresh fruits, vegetables, and flowers.

Particularly worth it, too, from late summer into early November, is the 13-mile **See Canyon apple tour** of the half-dozen 1900s-vintage orchards in the narrow canyon southwest of town. Apples grown here are not the kind usually found in supermarkets: old-time Arkansas Blacks, Splendors from Tasmania, and Gravensteins plus more modern "Jonalicious," New Zealand Galas, and the very tart Tohuku variety so popular in France. Among the most popular apple stops in See Canyon: Gopher Glen Apples, Daisy Dell Apple Ranch, and Ruda's Apples. To take the See Canyon tour: head south from San Luis Obispo on Highway 101 and then west on San Luis Bay Drive; after a mile or so turn right onto See Canyon Rd., which eventually becomes Prefumo Canyon Road—with great views of Morro Bay—and connects farther north with Los Osos Valley Road. A left turn here leads to Morro Bay, a right back to Highway 101 just south of San Luis.

SEEING AND DOING THE BAY

Bayside Diversions
Gentler than Big Sur's, the coastline near San Luis Obispo offers rocky terraces, sandy dunes, and a big-picture view of the Seven Sisters, volcanic peaks that saunter seaward from San Luis Obispo to "the rock" at Morro Bay. By car, the coastal communities of Morro Bay, Avila Beach, and Pismo Beach are all less than 15 minutes away from San Luis Obispo.

The pier at **Port San Luis,** old Port Hartford and once a regular steamship stop on San Luis Obispo Bay, is now a favorite fishing spot. **Avila Beach** just east along the bay is a favorite surfers' beach town on the way to becoming trendy, its protected beaches tucked into the cove. (Try to ignore the oil tanks looming overhead.) These days Avila Beach is still recovering from Unocal Corp.'s massive "oil change" on the beach, a multi-million-dollar project that involved excavating then replacing tons of soil and sand soaked with some 420,000 gallons of petroleum, and relocating (or demolishing then replacing) many of those famously funky beach-shack Front Street businesses and other buildings. Stop by and see how clean a cleaned-up beach town can get. Less appealing but definitely private is clothing-optional **Pirate's Cove** beaches a mile south of Avila Beach (weirdos possible, so bring a friend). But before leaving Avila Beach, do the hot springs. Relaxed, funky, and family-friendly **Avila Hot Springs,** also an RV and tent-camping resort at 250 Avila Beach Dr., 805/595-2359 or toll-free 800/332-2359 or

TOURING THE COUNTY'S WINERIES

When you're done with the local apple tour, try some fruit of the vine. Together the **Edna Valley** and **Arroyo Grande Valley** comprise yet another upstart wine region just inland from the California coast; the small wineries here were first successful with chardonnay and pinot noir grapes. **Edna Valley Vineyard,** for example, specializes in both, while **Meridian** features an exceptional Edna Valley chardonnay. Most of these regional wineries lie between San Luis Obispo and Arroyo Grande, on small agricultural holdings and hillsides east of Highway 227. Come the first weekend in May for the annual **Roll Out the Barrels** winery barrel tasting and "passport" event. For a current tour map or other information, contact: **Edna Valley Arroyo Grande Valley Vintners,** 5825 Orcutt Rd., San Luis Obispo, CA 93401, 805/541-5868, fax 805/541-3934; www.thegrid.net/vintners. Some area wineries are not vintner association members, however. For a reasonably comprehensive listing of wineries within the larger Central Coast appellation—which ranges from the southern San Francisco Bay Area to Santa Barbara—see www.villacreek.com/region_winerys.html.

North-county wineries are also well worth looking for. Another of California's newer small winery regions lies near **Paso Robles, Templeton,** and **Atascadero,** throughout the hills and valleys both east and west of Highway 101, a region where cabernet, chardonnay, merlot, syrah, and zinfandel grapes do well. As in Edna Valley and Arroyo Grande, most wineries here are small, family-run operations producing 5,000 or fewer bottles per year—casual and "country," as different from the now-big-business Napa and Sonoma county wine industries as well-broke cowboy boots are from Bruno Maglis. Many offer tours only with reservations, especially during the hectic autumn harvest season. Among the many possible stops: **Justin Vineyards and Winery** on Chimney Rock Road, specializing in barrel-fermented chardonnays and known for its Isosceles, a blend of cabernet franc, cabernet sauvignon, and merlot, and the **Martin Brothers Winery** on Buena Vista Road, known for its award-winning Italian-style cabernet sauvignon, chardonnay, and zinfandel as well as summer Opera under the Stars and occasional jazz concerts. Come in mid-May for the **Paso Robles Wine Festival Weekend.** For current regional wineries information, contact the **Paso Robles Visitors & Conference Bureau,** 1225 Park St., Paso Robles, CA 93446, 805/238-0506 or toll-free 800/406-4040, fax 805/238-0527, http://pasorobleschamber.com, open weekdays and on Saturday 10 A.M.–4 P.M., and the **Paso Robles Vintners and Growers Association,** 622 12th St., 805/239-8463, fax 805/237-6439; www.pasowine.com.

800/543-2359 for reservations, www.camp-grounds.com, features a large freshwater swimming pool in addition to private step-down tiled hot mineral tubs in the original 1930s bathhouse and the hot outdoor pools. (Rent inner tubes and float in the warm pool.) Spa services are also available. The more uptown and historic **Sycamore Mineral Springs Resort,** 1215 Avila Beach Dr., 805/595-7302 or toll-free 800/234-5831 for reservations, www.smsr.com and www.sycamoresprings.com, offers pleasant motel-style rooms, suites, and bed-and-breakfast stays—not to mention a swimming pool, volleyball courts, and The Gardens of Avila restaurant—in addition to hot mineral soaks, massage, facials, and other spa services. The very private lattice-screened redwood hot tubs, which rent by the hour 24 hours a day, are strategically scattered around the landscaped wooded hillside (hot tub reservations advised).

Shell Beach south of Pirate's Cove and north of Pismo Beach is a marine-terrace town with lots of antique shops and two wooden staircases leading to the rocky coast below. Primo is shoving off from Shell Beach for ocean kayaking, an adventure easily undertaken with help from **Central Coast Kayaks** on Shell Beach Road, 805/773-3500.

Pismo Beach and Other Bayside Communities

Shell Beach segues into **Pismo Beach** proper, once a haute destination for 1930s celebrities, now a cleaned-up, family-friendly, and fairly affordable beach community. Pismo Beach was first famous for its pismo clams, a population now nearly decimated. The Spanish *pismo* means "a place to fish," but the Chumash *pismu* means "a place where blobs of tar wash up on the beach." Since good fishing is a historical fact and, in the absence of major coastal oil spills, beach tar from here to Santa Barbara is a natural phenomenon, pick your own derivation. For more information about the area and its attractions, contact: **Pismo Beach Chamber of Commerce & Visitors Center,** 581 Dolliver, 805/773-4382, fax 805/773-6772, www.pismochamber.com, open Mon.–Sat. 9 A.M.–5 P.M. and Sunday 10 A.M.–4 P.M.

The six miles of shoreline from Pismo Beach to Oceano is primarily **Pismo State Beach,** with

a small dunes preserve tacked on to the southern end. Dominated by the **Oceano Dunes State Vehicular Recreation Area** dune-buggy heaven, Pismo offers little for solitude-seeking beach and dune lovers beyond pier fishing. Such souls will feel considerably more comfortable at the Nature Conservancy's now extensive **Guadalupe-Nipomo Dunes Preserve** farther south (see Santa Maria and Vicinity, below) or at isolated **Point Sal State Beach,** reached from Highway 101 south of Santa Maria via Betteravia and Brown Roads.

Oceano and vicinity, just south of Pismo Beach, have seen wilder days. Sneaky sand dunes advanced on the town's famous dance pavilion, cottages, and wharf years ago, destroying them all. The dunes here are the highest and whitest in the state, blocked from straying farther south by the Point Sal cliffs. Inland are marshes and shallow lagoons, resting areas for mallards and teal and home during the Depression to the "Dunites," an eclectic group of artists, astrologers, loners, nudists, and writers. These days Oceano's most notable attraction is **The Great American Melodrama,** 805/489-2499, where old-fashioned entertainment comes with dinner.

Inland from Oceano and the Pismo Beach area is **Arroyo Grande,** nothing but a stage stop in 1877, now an attractive village with Old West–style antique and other shops, some bed-and-breakfasts, and surrounding flower seed farms. At the Village Green near city hall, you'll see a small park and a 71-foot-long swinging bridge built in 1875. For more information, contact: **Arroyo Grande Chamber of Commerce & Visitors Center,** 800 W. Branch, 805/489-1488, fax 805/489-2239, open weekdays 10 A.M.–5 P.M.

PRACTICAL SAN LUIS OBISPO

Camping near San Luis Obispo

Camp at Lopez Lake about 11 miles northeast of Arroyo Grande, a pretty little reservoir also good for fishing, swimming (waterslide, too), sailing, and windsurfing. Primitive tent campsites, shaded by oaks, are $13, sites with full hookups $21. For more information, call **Lopez Lake Recreation Area** at 805/489-8019 or 805/489-

TOURING DIABLO CANYON

Since guards at the two-unit Diablo Canyon Nuclear Power Plant control the traffic flow here near Port San Luis, don't plan on walking in for a casual look-see. Years of antinuclear protest have made security serious business. Trouble was Diablo's middle name for 20 years, thanks to relentless antinuclear energy protesters. Critics of the plant, built just a few miles from the Hosgri offshore earthquake fault, have consistently attempted to shut down construction—then, later, the online plants—with lawsuits and civil disobedience.

In 1997, Pacific Gas & Electric (PG&E) agreed to pay $14 million to settle charges it had deliberately underreported damage to sea life at Diablo Canyon, the indirect result of the 2.5 billion gallons of seawater sucked into the plant each day.

Despite environmentalists and antinuke naysayers, PG&E promotes the plant as "solid as the Rock of Gibraltar," a good neighbor until the end of time; PG&E also hopes its rock is a rock-solid investment, with its total $5.8 billion construction price tag financed through Northern California customers' utility bills. Though both are now online, Diablo's first nuclear reactor set a nationwide performance record during its first year of operation, producing more than eight billion kilowatt-hours of electricity while operating at capacity 93 percent of the time.

How do local people feel about Diablo Canyon? You'll find both gung-ho support and absolute opposition but primarily, in the typically apolitical American tradition, a "let's-wait-and-see" attitude prevails.

The utility's pretty, Spanish-looking **PG&E Community Center** about 12 miles south of San Luis Obispo via Highway 101 at 6588 Ontario Rd. (exit at San Luis Bay Dr.) in Avila Beach, 805/546-5280, open 9 A.M.–5 P.M. daily, offers simple but flashy presentations on fission nuclear energy, also three-to four-hour **overlook tours** of the plant site by bus, including stops at the marine biology lab and a simulated control room. But if you want to hear what a nuclear-meltdown siren sounds like, you'll have to make reservations.

2095, www.centralcoast.com/lakelopez. For hikers and fisherpeople, the day-use fee at Lopez Lake is $5; pets (on leashes) are $2 extra, boat launch fees are $2–4.

Beach camping is also a good bet. State park campsites are available at Morro Bay, with the best developed ones at **Morro Bay State Park** and primitive ones at **Montaña de Oro.** For details, see Morro Bay and Vicinity, below. The hot mineral tubs and pools are the main attraction at **Avila Hot Springs** on Avila Beach Drive in Avila Beach, but you can also pitch a tent here for $18 (up to six people) or park your RV, $19 with electricity, $23 for full hookups.

Contact the visitors center in San Luis Obispo for more camping suggestions.

A Hostel and Affordable "Motor Hotels"

San Luis Obispo has a new HI/AYH hostel location—**Hostel Obispo,** 1617 Santa Rosa St. (Hwy. 1), San Luis Obispo, CA 93401, 805/544-4678, fax 805/544-3142, www.hostelweb.com, with a per-bed rate of $15–17 for dorm beds, $37.50–40 for private rooms. Reservations accepted by mail or fax, with deposit (no credit cards). Extras here include laundry, bike rentals, on-site parking, and a garden and patio with barbecue. Hostel Obispo also offers group trips and hiking and biking "adventure tours."

The quite decent **Motel 6** here, 1433 Calle Joaquin (take the Los Osos Valley Rd. exit from Hwy. 101), San Luis Obispo 93401, 805/549-9595, fax 805/544-2826, or toll-free 800/466-8356 for reservations (nationwide), www.motel6 .com, is convenient for hikers planning to head out early for the Los Osos Preserve and other Morro Bay area parks. Beyond the basics, facilities include a pool and laundry. Regular high-season weekend rates are $50, higher during major local events, lower most of the year. Another, larger Motel 6 is just a stroll away, on the other side of Los Osos Valley Rd., 805/541-6992, with similar rates.

Most San Luis Obispo motels are on or near Monterey Street, including the local **Super 8,** 1951 Monterey St., 805/544-7895 or toll-free 800/800-8000 for reservations (nationwide), fax 805/546-7895, with summer double rates $55 and up. Also quite reasonable in the neighborhood: the small **Villa Motel,** 1670 Monterey (at

Grand), local 805/543-8071 or toll-free 800/554-0059, fax 805/549-4389, which also offers a heated pool and free breakfast. Summer rates of $49 double and up, winter rates as low as $40 double. Weekly rates available. Quite inviting is the friendly Southwestern B&B-style **Adobe Inn**, 1473 Monterey, 805/549-0321 or toll-free 800/676-1588, fax 805/549-0383, www.adobeinns .com, with summer weekday rates $75 double, weekend rates $95, homemade breakfast included. (But off-season rates can be as low as $55—a real deal.)

More luxurious accommodations are available, too, particularly on Monterey Street and also on Madonna Road; contact the visitors bureau for a current listing. For other affordable options, head for Pismo Beach, where bargains abound—especially in the off-season.

Memorable Local "Motor Hotels" and Inns

The **Motel Inn**, San Luis Obispo's first and original "mo-tel," closed some years back for historic renovation and eventual expansion. In the meantime, the next best thing is right next door—the **Apple Farm Inn**, 2015 Monterey St., San Luis Obispo 93401, 805/544-2040 or toll-free 800/374-3705 for reservations, fax 805/546-9495; www.applefarm.com. Behind the locally famous **Apple Farm Restaurant** is the rest of the ranch—in this case, a quaint three-story motel with contemporary country-inn airs. Rooms feature fireplaces, four-poster beds, and other period furnishings, even armoires. Equally pleasant but less expensive are the more motel-like rooms in the **Apple Farm Trellis Court**, adjacent. Inn rooms start at $169 in the high season, dropping to $149 in winter. Motel rooms start at $119 in summer, $99 at other times.

The Cliffs at Shell Beach, 2757 Shell Beach Rd. in Pismo Beach 93449, 805/773-5000 or toll-free 800/826-7827, fax 805/773-0764, once offered the only seaside-resort accommodations in the San Luis Obispo area. The Cliffs, a hotel-style motel, sits right on the beach (actually, the cliffs above the beach). Rooms are spacious and attractive, done in day-at-the-beach colors, and feature the usual modern amenities plus in-

room coffeemakers. Most have private patios and ocean views. The suites are something special, complete with in-room hot tubs. Regular room rates start at $130, but ask about discounts, off-season specials, and packages. To get here from Highway 101: If coming from the north, exit at Shell Beach Rd.; from the south, exit at Spyglass Road. Other area options include the **Spyglass Inn**, 2705 Spyglass Dr., 805/773-4855 or toll-free 800/824-2612, fax 805/773-5298, www.spyglassinn.com; and **Cottage Inn by the Sea**, 2351 Price St., 805/773-4617 or toll-free 888/440-8400; www.cottage-inn.com.

Fun for bed-and-breakfast fans: the 13-room **Garden Street Inn**, 1212 Garden St. in San Luis Obispo, 805/545-9802 or toll-free 800/488-2045, fax 805/545-9403, www.gardenstreetinn.com, an 1887 Italianate Queen Anne Victorian, was originally centerpiece of the local mission vineyard. Rooms and suites are individually decorated; Valley of the Moon commemorates the life and times of Jack London, Walden is a Thoreau tribute, and Amadeus remembers Mozart. No phone, no TVs, so prepare to truly relax. Suites include extras such as Jacuzzi bath/showers, private decks, separate bedrooms. Full breakfast is served every morning, wine and cheese every evening. Rooms start at $100, suites at $150, with a two-night minimum stay on weekends.

For something to write home about, consider **The Madonna Inn**, 100 Madonna Rd., San Luis Obispo 93405, 805/543-3000 or toll-free 800/543-9666, fax 805/543-1800; www.madonnainn .com. One of the most unusual motels anywhere, the Madonna is noted for quirky "theme" rooms and suites, some with waterfalls and other dramatic elements, each one of the 109 rooms here unique. Some sample themes: the Daisy Mae Room, the Caveman Room, the Cloud Nine Suite, the Love Nest. You get the idea—immensely popular with newlyweds and couples tired of the same old anniversary celebration. This Madonna is getting a bit tired these days, too, but still, a stay here is *different*. Rates: $127–310. Those who don't stay should satisfy their curiosity by wandering the halls and peeking into any open rooms. Men—and undaunted

WORTHWHILE NORTH OF SAN LUIS OBISPO

North of San Luis Obispo proper, Santa Margarita was once a small outpost of the mission, with a chapel, grain storage, and lodging rooms. The biggest thing around today, though, is tiny **Santa Margarita Lake,** which offers camping, picnicking, and fishing. For info, call 805/438-5485 or check www.centralcoast.com/santamargaritalake/. East via Highway 58 is the fascinating **Carrizo Plain Natural Area,** sometimes referred to as "California's Serengeti," much of the land now protected within a vast Nature Conservancy preserve. Though almost everything else in California has been endlessly exploited, the Carrizo Plain somehow missed out on the march of progress. The San Andreas Fault is on the plain's eastern edge, and the region is hot in summer and cold in winter. Yet the plain, once a prehistoric lake, was sacred to the Chumash, whose Great Spirits lived here—and shook the earth, when angered. Eight miles wide and 50 miles long, the Carrizo Plain preserves the last large remnant of the San Joaquin Valley's natural terrain, where sandhill cranes winter and some 600 pronghorn antelope roam native grasslands. The best time to come for a look is in late winter and early spring.

North via Highway 101 are **Atascadero** and **Paso Robles,** center of another notable California wine country. Still farther north on the main highway is sleepy little **San Miguel** with its fine old mission and, to the west, **Lake Nacimiento.** As the highway hums northward through the Salinas Valley, to the west lies **Lake San Antonio,** popular for bald eagle watching in winter.

Beyond Jolon, smack in the midst of Fort Hunter-Liggett, is **Mission San Antonio de Padua,** 831/385-4478, not the biggest nor most ravishingly restored mission, certainly not the most popular, but somehow the most evocative of Spanish California—well worth the detour. For a simple yet special stay less than a half-mile away, consider the **Hacienda Guest Lodge,** 831/386-2900, the original ranch house designed for William Randolph Hearst by Julia Morgan, built in 1922. Later an officers club, the Hacienda is now a combination hotel, restaurant, bar, bowling alley with snack bar, and campground. Nothing fancy, but a tremendous value. A steak dinner is $10 or so. Rooms or suites with private baths start at $46; those with shared baths are $33. Weather and road conditions permitting, from Fort Hunter-Liggett it's possible to take the back-roads route, Nacimiento -Fergusson Road, over the mountains to Big Sur.

---

women—should also check out the men's bathroom off the lobby, most notable for its free-flowing waterfall urinal and seashell washbasins. Other attractions include a very good restaurant, bar, and on-site bakery.

More relaxing, in its unpretentious way, is **Sycamore Mineral Springs Resort** in Avila Beach at 1215 Avila Beach Rd. in San Luis Obispo, 805/595-7302 or toll-free 800/234-5831, fax 805/781-2598, www.sycamoresprings.com, or with very private rent-a-hot tubs (clothing optional) tucked into the oak-covered hillsides and available 24 hours per day. Spa services including acupressure, reflexology, polarity therapy, shiatsu, facials, and Swedish massage are also available. Motel-style rooms here, each with a private hot tub outside on the patio or deck, are $119 and up. The resort's new two-room suites, with four-poster beds, fine wood furnishings, and wet bars, marble fireplaces, and sofas, start at $209. A stay also includes a $12 credit toward breakfast at very good, reasonably priced California-style **The Gardens of Avila** restaurant here, which also serves lunch and dinner daily and Sunday brunch. Bed-and-breakfast rooms are also available, $169–300.

Dining Downtown and Around

San Luis Obispo boasts more than 60 eateries, so look around—especially downtown, where delis, small cafés, and restaurants surround the plaza area. Good for breakfast is **Louisa's Place,** 964 Higuera St., 805/541-0227, a countertop-style café locally popular for its buckwheat pancakes and lunch specials. **Pete's Southside Cafe,** 1815 Osos St., 805/549-8133, is an outpost of the original Avila Beach Pete's all gussied up for more stylish times. But the fresh seafood is still fresh, the Mexican selections still good, and the atmosphere still bright and bustling. It's open for lunch and dinner, on Sunday for dinner only.

The **Big Sky Café,** 1121 Broad St., 805/545-5401, serves great Southwestern selections and other eclectic New American fare. Justifiably popular, too, is **Mother's Tavern,** 725 Higuera St., 805/541-3853, where the specialty is "California tavern food"—everything from burgers and steaks to pastas, salads, and sandwiches. Another hit at Mother's is the tavern's house band, the jump blues and swing band Sugar Daddy Swing Kings. So cool. The cool destination for the weekday "Happy Hour and a Half" is the old-brick **SLO Brewing Co.** downtown at 1119 Garden St. (between Higuera and Marsh Streets), 805/543-1843, open for lunch and dinner daily (just noon–5 P.M. on Sunday). Brewpub fans believe the main attractions here are the Amber Ale, Pale Ale, and Porter—and at least one seasonal brew, on tap. Live entertainment later too, most nights.

Stylin' it in San Luis Obispo might include lunch or dinner at **Cafe Roma,** in a new location at Railroad Square near the train station, 1020 Railroad Ave., 805/541-6800, open Tues.–Fri. for lunch and Tues.–Sun. for dinner. Noted for its authentic northern Italian fare, Cafe Roma is one of San Luis Obispo's most popular fine food destinations. The pastas are always good, though you won't go wrong with the Tuscan chicken or osso bucco. The wine list is also a treat, a mix of classy regional Californians and classic Italians. Also quite good, downtown next to the Fremont Theater, is **Buona Tavola,** 1037 Monterey St., 805/545-8000, also open for lunch and dinner.

A fun family-style place convenient to motel row is **Izzy Ortega's Mexican Restaurant and Cantina** next to the Holiday Inn at 1850 Monterey St., 805/543-3333, open daily 11:30 A.M. until at least 9 P.M. (bar open later). Colorful and cheerful with a party-hearty American attitude, Izzy's is one of San Luis Obispo's most popular restaurants. The food's quite good, and considerably more authentic than most Americanized Mexican. Try the shrimp or fish tacos, for example, the pork tamales, or the tasty bean soup. Entrées get more ambitious, including steak ranchero and broiled garlic shrimp. Children's menu available.

Another place to take the kids, especially if you can get them to pay: the original **F. McClintocks Saloon and Dining House,** 750 Mattie Rd. in Pismo Beach, 805/773-1892, open daily (after 3 or 4 P.M.) for dinner, and on Sunday at 9:30–9 P.M., for "ranch breakfast," early supper, and dinner (closed some major holidays). Beef—aged, "hand-cut," and then barbecued over oak wood—is the secret to the success of this kicky outpost of commercialized mom-and-pop cowboy kitsch. (The gift shop overfloweth.) Everything here is pretty good, however. The machismo challenge, typically issued by men to men, is eating the oddest menu item—fried turkey nuts—without squawking. And if you like that sort of thing, come in mid-July for the Annual Mountain Oyster Feed, held out back. But kids are more impressed by the wait staff, who pour water by holding the pitcher at least two feet above the table—and never spill a drop. And don't miss the Birthday Picture Gallery. Or mosey on over to the other area F. McClintocks locations; there's one here in SLO at 686 Higuera St., 805/541-0686, and others in Paso Robles and Arroyo Grande.

The classic surfers' fuel center in Pismo Beach is the **Splash Café,** just a block from the pier at 197 Pomeroy Ave., 805/773-4653, where you can get a bread bowl full of wonderful New England–style clam chowder for under $5. A bit more stylish for seafood is the **Olde Port Inn,** in Avila Beach at Port San Luis's Pier #3, 805/595-2515. Well worth looking for in nearby Arroyo Grande is **Massimo's,** 640 Oak Park Blvd., 805/474-9211, where northern Italian is the specialty.

And if you're heading north from the area, **Villa Creek** in Paso Robles, 1144 Pine St., 805/ 238-3000, specializes in early Californian, and **McPhee's Grill** at 416 Main St. in Templeton, 805/434-3204, is known for its regional American.

MORRO BAY AND VICINITY

The first thing visitors notice is the Rock, spotted by Cabrillo in 1542. Morro Reef has been a significant navigational landfall for mariners for more than three centuries and was noted in the diaries of Portolá, Crespi, and Costanso. (That wouldn't impress the native peoples, though; Chumash artifacts found here date to 4700 B.C.) Morro Rock is the last visible volcanic peak in the 21-million-year-old series of nine cones that stretch to San Luis Obispo; the chain is known as the **Seven Sisters** (one is submerged and one is out of line). Before extensive quarrying, this "Gibraltar of the Pacific" stood much higher than its current 576 feet and, until the 1930s, was an island at high tide. The height of the Rock seems reduced even more by the proximity of the three 450-foot-tall power plant smokestacks jutting from the edge of the bay like giant gun barrels, part of the scenery since 1953.

Until the rise of tourism, commercial fishing, especially for abalone and albacore, was Morro Bay's major industry. But intrepid amateurs can try clam digging for geoducks (Washington clams) or some barehanded grunion snatching during full-moon high tides from March through August. Pier fishing is also good here on the city's three T-piers, north of the Embarcadero and opposite the Rock. Morro Bay also boasts a thriving nature-oriented tourism industry—and a kitsch- and gift-shop-oriented tourism industry, perfect for shopaholics. Or watch the boats in the bay from **Tidelands Park,** at the south end of the Embarcadero, or take a ride on the *Tiger's Folly II* replica river boat. Laid-back **Baywood Park** on the bay just a few miles south of Morro Bay is a better choice for those determined to avoid the crowds.

Thanks to a few local bars and the Morro Bay Chess Club, Morro Bay also has *culture.* The star in that department is the chess club's **giant outdoor chessboard,** especially eye-catching when demonstration tournaments are under way after noon on Saturday along the Embarcadero. With each of the game's carved redwood pieces weighing between 18 and 30 pounds, playing chess here offers more than a mere mental workout. Anyone can play, by reservation, either on the giant board or on punier standard-sized chess tables along the perimeter. During the town's **Harbor Days Celebration** in October, local drama buffs in full costume *become* chess pieces. Another major event is the **Morro Bay Winter Bird Festival.** And come to Morro Bay in December for the **Christmas Parade** of lighted boats on the bay's waters.

For more information about local attractions, events, and practicalities, contact the **Morro Bay Chamber of Commerce,** 880 Main St., 805/772-4467 or toll-free 800/231-0592, and the **Los Osos/Baywood Park Chamber of Commerce,** 781 Los Osos Valley Rd., 805/528-4884.

SEEING AND DOING MORRO BAY

The entire town of Morro Bay, including Morro Rock, is a bird sanctuary and nature preserve in deference to the endangered peregrine falcons, great blue herons, and other bird species that have selected the Rock and vicinity as a rookery. The bay and adjacent mudflats create a fertile wetland, one of the most significant along the California coast for sheer number of resident bird species and one of the top 10 national bird-watching spots. Guns are banned throughout Morro Bay—the rock, the town, and the state park.

Morro Bay State Park

A multifaceted park dominating the entire bay area, Morro Bay State Park includes the sand dunes on the spit, dual Morro Strand State Beach farther north, a natural history museum, adjacent golf course, and the Los Osos Oaks State Reserve just inland from the bay on Los Osos Valley Road. The park's campgrounds and picnic areas seem like value-added bonuses.

Eucalyptus trees shade the bay near park headquarters and attract monarch butterflies after the October bloom. A more interesting first stop for most people, though, is the park's excellent **Museum of Natural History** on Country Club Dr., 805/772-2694, www.mbspmuseum.org, which emphasizes the wildlife of the headlands

KIM WEIR

Besides the rock, the coastal town of Morro Bay is noted for its giant chess board.

and adjacent aquatic environments, offers guided natural history hikes, and features fun hands-on touch pools and other nature exhibits, a good bookshop, and great views of Morro Bay below. It's open daily 10 A.M.–5 P.M., closed Thanksgiving, Christmas, and New Year's Day; free for campers, otherwise small admission.

Next, explore the mouth of **Los Osos Creek,** one of the largest natural coastal marshlands remaining in California. Wildflowers on adjacent grassy hills are most striking in spring, but their blooms, seeds, and vegetation attract birds year-round. Rent a canoe or kayak for some unforgettable eyeball-to-eyeball encounters. (Get an area bird checklist and other local bird-watching information at the museum.) Take a boat to reach the **Sand Spit Wild Area,** the pristine peninsula separating Morro Bay from the ocean (protected shell mounds, good birding), or come the long way from Montaña de Oro State Park to the south. For the adventurous: Hike the entire Morro Bay sand spit, an eight-mile round-trip from the Sunset Terrace golf course around the inlet and over the sand dunes toward Morro Rock.

Once known separately as Morro Strand and Atascadero state beaches, the two sections of **Morro Strand State Beach** north of Morro Bay, 805/772-2560, feature several broad miles of sandy strand with small naked dunes along Estero Bay and adjacent to residential areas; the beach is popular for surfing, skin diving, surf fishing, swimming, and sunning (clam digging prohibited). Another spot of state beach, with picnic tables, pier, and playground, is in family-friendly **Cayucos** just north.

Los Osos Oaks State Reserve, southeast of the bay at the end of Los Osos Valley Road, is a 90-acre grove acquired in 1972 to preserve one of the few old stands of coast oaks remaining in the area. These gnarled oldsters, coast live oaks, scrub oaks, and various hybrids, create an eerie impression on early morning hikes. Stay on the trail: the understory here is mostly poison oak.

The park is open for day use sunrise to sunset daily. The park's day-use fee is $6 per vehicle (camping and museum admission extra). For camping information, see below. For other park information, stop by the natural history museum (above) or call 805/772-2560 or 805/772-2694.

Montaña de Oro State Park

Just south of the sand spit is Montaña de Oro State Park ("Mountain of Gold"), its name particularly apt in spring when the hills are ablaze with yellow and orange wildflowers, from California poppies and yellow mustard to goldfields and fiddleneck. Any time of year, 8,000-acre Montaña de Oro is a hiker's park. The seclusion here also means abundant wildlife: sea lions, harbor seals, and sea otters at sea; gray foxes, mule deer, bobcats, and sometimes even mountain lions on land. From near **Point Buchon** (private property), the whale-watching is superb, but you can find other good vantage points along the Bluff Trail.

The area's wild beauty stretches from the seven-mile shoreline of 50-foot bluffs and tide pools, surging surf, and sandy beaches inland to Valencia Peak (great ocean views looking north to Piedras Blancas, south to Point Sal) and up Islay Creek to the waterfalls. The best tide-pools are at **Corallina Cove,** though **Quarry Cove** comes in a close second. There's good tide-pooling after the five-minute creekside scramble down from Hazard Canyon, also access to the entire sand spit and silent beaches. South of the **Spooner's Cove** visitor center, part of the old ranch, is an old Chumash campsite.

HEARST'S CASTLE: PLEASURE HE COULD AFFORD

The **Hearst San Simeon State Historic Monument** northwest from San Luis Obispo along the coast, ranks right up there with Disneyland as one of California's premier tourist attractions. Somehow that fact alone puts the place into proper perspective. Media magnate William Randolph Hearst's castle is a rich man's playground filled to overflowing with artistic diversions and other expensive toys, a monument to one man's monumental ego and equally impressive poor taste.

In real life, of course, Hearst was quite a wealthy and powerful man, the man many people still believe was the subject of the greatest American movie ever made, Orson Welles's 1941 *Citizen Kane.* (These days even Welles's biographers say the movie was about the filmmaker himself.) Yet there's something to be said for popular opinion. "Pleasure," Hearst once wrote, "is worth what you can afford to pay for it." And that attitude showed itself quite early; for his 10th birthday little William asked for the Louvre as a present. One scene in the movie, in which Charles Foster Kane shouts across the cavernous living room at Xanadu to attract the attention of his bored young mistress, endlessly working jigsaw puzzles while she sits before a fireplace as big as the mouth of Jonah's whale, won't seem so surreal once you see San Simeon.

Designed by Berkeley architect Julia Morgan, the buildings themselves are odd yet handsome hallmarks of Spanish renaissance architecture. The centerpiece La Casa Grande alone has 100 rooms (including a movie theater, a billiards room, two libraries, and 31 bathrooms) adorned with silk banners, fine Belgian and French tapestries, Norman fireplaces, European choir stalls, and ornately carved ceilings virtually stolen from continental monasteries. The furnishings and art Hearst collected from around the world complete the picture, one that includes everything but humor, grace, warmth, and understanding.

The notably self-negating nature of this rich but richly disappointed man's life is somehow fully expressed here in the country's most ostentatious and theatrical temple to obscene wealth. In contrast to Orson Welles's authentic artistic interpretation of either his own or Hearst's life, William Randolph's idea of hearth, home, and humanity was full-flown fantasy sadly separated from heart and vision.

Touring Hearst's Castle

In spring when the hills are emerald green, from the faraway highway Hearst's castle appears as if by magic up on the hill. (Before the place opened for public tours in the 1950s, the closest view commoners could get was from the road, with the assistance of coin-operated telescopes.) One thing visitors *don't* see on the tour shuttle up to the enchanted hill is William Randolph Hearst's 2,000-acre zoo—"the largest private zoo since Noah," as Charles Foster Kane would put it—once the country's largest. The inmates have long since been dispersed, though survivors of Hearst's exotic elk, zebra, Barbary sheep, and Himalayan goat herds still roam the grounds.

The four separate tours of the Hearst San Simeon State Historic Monument take approximately two hours each. Theoretically you could take all the San Simeon tours in a day, but don't try it. So much Hearst in the short span of a day could be detrimental to one's well-being. A dosage of two tours per day makes the trip here worthwhile yet not overwhelming. Visitors obsessed with seeing it all should plan a two-day stay in the area or come back again some other time. Whichever tour, or combination of tours, you select, be sure to wear comfortable walking shoes. Lots of stairs.

Tour One is a good first-time visit, taking in the castle's main floor, one guest house, and some of the gardens—a total of 150 steps and a half mile of walking. Included on the tour is a short showing in the theater of some of Hearst's "home movies." Particularly impressive in a gloomy Gothic way is the

To get to Montaña de Oro, head west on Los Osos Valley Road from San Luis Obispo back roads or Highway 101, and then follow Pecho Valley Road south to the end. For basic information and to get oriented, stop by the natural history museum at Morro Bay State Park (see above) or call 805/528-0513 or 805/772-7434.

Montaña de Oro's facilities are appropriately limited but picnic tables overlook the cove. Nearby is the valley **Islay Creek Campground,** 50 primitive, environmental, and hiker/biker sites, with pit toilets. Call for information.

---

dining room, where silk Siennese banners hang over the lord's table. The poolroom and mammoth great hall, with Canova's *Venus,* are also unforgettable. All the tours include both the Greco-Roman Neptune Pool and statuary and the indoor Roman Pool with its mosaics of lapis lazuli and gold leaf. It's hard to imagine Churchill, cigar in mouth, cavorting here in an inner tube.

Tour Two requires more walking, covering the mansion's upper floors, the kitchen, and Hearst's Gothic Suite, with its frescoes and rose-tinted Venetian glass windows (he ran his 94 separate business enterprises from here). The delightfully lit Celestial Suite was the nonetheless depressing extramarital playground of Hearst and Marion Davies. **Tour Three** covers one of the guest houses plus the "new wing," with 36 luxurious bedrooms, sitting rooms, and marble bathrooms furnished with fine art.

Gardeners will be moved to tears by **Tour Four** (offered April–Aug. only), which includes a long stroll through the San Simeon grounds but does not go inside the castle itself. Realizing that all the rich topsoil here had to be manually carried up the hill makes the array of exotic plant life, including unusual camellias and about 6,000 rosebushes, all the more impressive—not to mention the fact that gardeners at San Simeon worked only at night because Hearst couldn't stand watching them. Also included on the fourth tour is the lower level of the elegant, 17-room Casa del Mar guest house (where Hearst spent much of his time), the recently redone underground Neptune Pool dressing rooms, the never-finished bowling alley, and Hearst's wine cellar. David Niven once remarked that, with Hearst as host, the wine flowed "like glue." Subsequently, Niven was the only guest allowed free access to the castle's wine cellar.

Fairly new at San Simeon are the **Hearst Castle Evening Tours,** two-hour adventures featuring the highlights of other tours—with the added benefit of allowing you to pretend to be some Hollywood celebrity, just arrived and in need of orientation. (Hearst himself handed out tour maps, since new-

comers often got lost.) Guides dress in period costume and show you around. It's worth it just to see the castle in lights. At last report, evening tours were offered on Friday and Saturday nights March–May and Sept.–Dec., but call for current details. December **Christmas at the Castle** tours are particularly festive.

Practical Hearst's Castle

San Simeon is open daily except Thanksgiving, Christmas, and New Year's Day, with the regular two-hour tours leaving the visitor center area on the hour from early morning until around dusk. Tour schedules change by season and day of the week. Reservations aren't required, but the chance of getting tickets on a drop-in, last-minute basis is small. For current schedule information and reservations, call ReserveAmerica toll-free at 800/444-4445 and have that credit card handy. (For international ticket reservations, dial the U.S. telephone code then 1-880-444-4445.) Wheelchair-access tours of San Simeon are offered on a different schedule; call 805/927-2070 for reservations and information.

Admission to each of the four San Simeon day tours is $10 adults, $5 children (ages 6–17). Evening tour rates are $20 adults, $10 children. A special brochure for international travelers (printed in Japanese, Korean, French, German, Hebrew, Italian, and Spanish) is available. With a little forethought (see Near San Simeon below), visitors can avoid eating the concession-style food here.

Adjacent to the visitor center is the Hearst Castle's giant-screened **National Geographic Theatre,** 805/927-6811, where at last report the larger-than-life *Hearst Castle—Building the Dream* and *Everest* were showing on the 70-foot by 52-foot screen. Call for current times and details (no reservations required).

For other information, contact: Hearst San Simeon State Historic Monument, 750 Hearst Castle Rd., San Simeon, CA 93452, 805/927-2020 or 805/927-2000; www.hearstcastle.org.

PRACTICAL MORRO BAY

Morro Bay Camping

Basic beach camping is the setup at **Morro Strand State Beach** north of the bay, 104 barren beachfront RV parking lot sites (no hookups) featuring some tent camping sites; campsites include tables, stoves, restrooms, and cold outdoor showers. Considerably more comfortable is camping at **Morro Bay State Park** near park headquarters, 135 tree-shaded campsites with tables, stoves, hot showers, restrooms, and laundry tubs, also RV hookups (20 sites) and sanitation station. **Montaña de Oro State Park** also offers camping at its Islay Creek Campground—50 wooded primitive (tents and RVs) and environmental sites, pit toilets only. Call each park for further details. For reservable campsites, ReserveAmerica reservations, toll-free 800/444-7275, are advisable year-round; at Morro Strand reservations are taken only for summer.

Staying in Morro Bay

In addition to camping, Morro Bay offers comfy real-bed alternatives—most of these fairly reasonable. The ever-affordable **Motel 6,** about a mile from the beach at 298 Atascadero Rd. (Hwy. 1 at Hwy. 41), 805/772-5641 or toll-free 800/466-8356 for reservations (nationwide), fax 805/772-3233, www.motel6.com, is $56 double on summer weekends, lower at other times. Much closer to the bay scene and a best bet is the tiny, two-story **Best Western Tradewinds Motel,** 225 Beach St. (at Market Ave.), 805/772-7376 or toll-free 800/628-3500, fax 805/772-2090, rates are $79 and up in summer, though smaller rooms go for as low as $49 double in the off-season. All rooms have in-room refrigerators and coffeemakers and color TV with cable (free movies). Other midrange motel favorites include the **Breakers Motel,** 780 Market Ave. (at Morro Bay Blvd.), 805/772-7317 or toll-free 800/932-8899, fax 805/772-4771, with rates from $78; and **La Serena Inn,** 990 Morro Ave., 805/772-5665 or toll-free 800/248-1511, fax 805/772-1044; www.laserenainn.com.

Uptown for these parts is **The Inn at Morro Bay** a mile south of town just outside the entrance to Morro Bay State Park, 805/772-5651 or toll-free 800/321-9566 for reservations, fax 805/772-4779, www.innatmorrobay.com, where attractive rooms are $99 and up—bay views come at a premium, especially on summer weekends—though discounts and specials are possible. A less stylish but quite pleasant alternative is the small **Beachwalker Inn** motel just a block from the beach at 501 S. Ocean Ave. in Cayucos, 805/995-2133 or toll-free 800/750-2133 for reservations, fax 805/995-3139, www.beachwalkerinn.com, where double rooms are $85 and up in summer, as low as $65 in winter.

Pleasant choices in Baywood Park include the 13-room **Back Bay Inn,** 1391 Second St., 805/528-1233 or toll-free 877/330-2225; www.backbayinn.com, (continental breakfast included); and the 15-room **Baywood Bed & Breakfast Inn,** 1370 Second, 805/528-8888, www.baywoodinn.com.

For more complete lodging listings, contact local chambers of commerce (see above).

Eating in Morro Bay

A local tradition is **Dorn's Original Breakers Cafe,** 801 Market St., 805/772-4415, with wonderful pecan waffles, buttermilk pancakes, and veggie omelettes for breakfast, an impressive Boston clam chowder and marinated seafood salads and various sandwiches at lunch. Generous seafood dinners are served with good views of the bay.

People could drown in the aquatic ambience around Morro Bay. For more fresh fish, stop off at **Giovanni's Fish Market** right in front of the boat docks at 1001 Front St., open 9 A.M.–6 P.M. Seafood places leap out all along the Embarcadero, many of them open for lunch and dinner and many featuring early-bird dinner specials. Very good and very popular is **Rose's Landing Restaurant,** 725 Embarcadero, 805/772-4441, on the waterfront overlooking the bay. Good specials, but come early or make reservations because people pack in here like sardines, probably because the bar is shaped like a boat. Also on the waterfront: the **Great American Fish Company,** 1185 Embarcadero, 805/772-4407, which specializes in mesquite-grilled seafood. The place for sushi and such is **Harada,** 630 Embarcadero, 805/772-1410. For pasta and vegetarian selections as well as seafood, jockey for a patio table at **Hoppe's Hip Pocket Bistro,** 901 Embarcadero, 805/772-5371.

For something a bit fancier at dinner—yet still casual—consider **Hoppe's Marina Square,** overlooking the bay at 699 Embarcadero, 805/772-5371, where the steak and seafood are served with continental flair. Or head for the popular **Paradise Restaurant** at The Inn at Morro Bay near Morro Bay State Park, 805/772-2743, for fine dining American style and an inviting Sunday brunch.

BOOKLIST

The virtual "publisher of record" for all things Californian is the **University of California Press,** 2120 Berkeley Way, Berkeley, CA 94720, 510/642-4247 or toll-free 800/777-4726 and fax 800/999-1958 for orders, www.ucpress.edu, which publishes hundreds of titles on the subject—all excellent. Stanford University's **Stanford University Press,** 521 Lomita Mall, Stanford, CA 94305, 650/723-9434, fax 650/725-3457, www.sup.org, also offers some books of particular interest to Californiacs—especially under the subject categories of American Literature, California History, and Natural History—though in general these are books of academic interest.

Other publishers offering California titles, particularly general interest, history, hiking, and regional travel titles, include **Chronicle Books,** Division of Chronicle Publishing Co., 85 Second St., Sixth Floor, San Francisco, CA 94105, 415/537-3730 or toll-free 800/722-6657, www.chronbooks.com, and **Heyday Books,** 2054 University Ave., Ste. 400, P.O. Box 9145, Berkeley, CA 94709, 510/549-3564, fax 510/549-1889. **Avalon Travel Publishing,** 5855 Beaudry St., Emeryville, CA 94608, 510/595-3664, fax 510/595-4228, www.foghorn.com, publishes Foghorn Outdoors, which includes a generous list of unusual, and unusually thorough, California outdoor guides, including Tom Stienstra's camping, fishing, and "getaways" guides. **Sierra Club Books,** 85 Second St., Second Fl., San Francisco, CA 94105, 415/977-5500 or toll-free 888/722-6657 for orders, www.sierraclub.org/books, and **Wilderness Press,** 1200 Fifth St., Berkeley, CA 94704, 510/558-1666 or toll-free 800/443-7227 for orders, fax 510/538-1696, www.wildernesspress .com, are the two top publishers of wilderness guides and maps for California. Among their titles are some particularly handy for exploration of Southern California. Definitely useful from the Sierra Club, for example, is Lynne Foster's *Adventuring in the California Desert.* Wilderness Press publishes some good regional hiking guides, including Jerry Schad's county-by-county hiking guides **(Afoot**

and Afield in San Diego County, etc.) and Nancy Salcedo's unique **A Hiker's Guide to California Native Places.**

Contact these and other publishers, mentioned below, for a complete list of current titles relating to California.

The following book listings represent a fairly basic introduction to books about California history, natural history, literature, recreation, and travel. The interested reader can find many other titles by visiting good local bookstores and/or state and national park visitor centers. As always, the author would appreciate suggestions about other books that should be included. Send the names of new candidates—or actual books, if you're either a publisher or an unusually generous person—for *Moon Handbooks: Southern California*'s booklist, not to mention possible text additions, corrections, and suggestions, to: Kim Weir, c/o Moon Handbooks, Avalon Travel Publishing, 5855 Beaudry St., Emeryville, CA 94608, USA.

COMPANION READING, GENERAL TRAVEL

Abbey, Edward. *Desert Solitaire.* Ballantine Books, 1991. One of the classic books, a prose poem for seekers of solitude, inspired by Abbey's half year as a park ranger in Utah's Arches National Monument.

Austin, Mary. *Land of Little Rain.* Albuquerque: University of New Mexico Press, 1974. Originally published in 1903. Before it was likely that one would be such a person, Mary Austin was an ecologist, feminist, and mystic. The essays in *Land of Little Rain,* a classic of Southwestern literature, still reveal Austin to be something of a philosopher: "It is a question whether it is not better to be bitten by the little horned snake of the desert that goes sidewise and strikes without coiling than by the tradition of a lost mine." More than anything else Mary Austin was a superb writer, a writer utterly in love with the Owens Valley and the nearby deserts she called home for many years.

Austin, Mary, with a foreword by John Walton. *The Ford.* Berkeley: University of California Press, 1997. Appreciating Mary Austin's "bold and original mind" in reviewing this novel for the *New York Times,* Carey McWilliams also said: "Of her novels, *The Ford,* which deals with the battle for the water of the Owens Valley, [is] perhaps the best."

Baldy, Marian. *The University Wine Course.* San Francisco: The Wine Appreciation Guild, 1993. A classic, designed for both instructional and personal use, this friendly book offers a comprehensive education about wine. *The University Wine Course* explains it all, from viticulture to varietals. And the lips-on lab exercises and chapter-by-chapter examinations help even the hopelessly clueless develop the subtle sensory awareness necessary for deeper appreciation of the winemaker's art. Special sections and appendixes on reading (and understanding) wine labels, combining wine and food, and understanding wine terminology make it a lifelong personal library reference. Definitely "do" this book before doing any of California's winery regions. For college wine appreciation instructors and winery personnel, the companion *Teacher's Manual for The University Wine Course* may also come in handy.

Bright, William O. *1,500 California Place Names: Their Origin and Meaning.* A revised version of the classic *1,000 California Place Names* by Erwin G. Gudde, first published in 1949. University of California Press, 1998. Though you also get the revised edition of Gudde's original masterpiece (see below), this convenient, alphabetically arranged pocketbook—now in an expanded and updated edition—is perfect for travelers, explaining the names of mountains, rivers, and towns throughout California.

Buckley, Christopher, and Gary Young, eds. *The Geography of Home: California's Poetry of Place.* Berkeley: Heyday Books, 1999. This contemporary anthology showcases the work of 76 California poets. In addition to multiple selections of each poet's work, the poets also talk about their history in California, and the state's influence on their poetry.

Cain, James. *Three Novels.* New York: Alfred A. Knopf, 1941. Los Angeles classics, all: *Double Indemnity, Mildred Pierce,* and *The Postman Always Rings Twice.*

Chandler, Raymond. *The Big Sleep.* New York: Vintage Books, 1992. The first mystery writer to be initiated into the Library of America—the U.S.A.'s literary hall of fame—Raymond Chandler and his legacy have been all but put to sleep by successors in the genre, including parodies such as the film *Dead Men Don't Wear Plaid.* But if one hasn't succumbed to today's trendy nihilism—if one understands that pain hurts and life matters—then *The Big Sleep,* first published in 1939, is still spellbinding and fresh. And Philip Marlowe, Chandler's alter ego and private-eye protagonist, is still the L.A. insider's outsider. (As James Wolcott puts it, to Marlowe the rich are risen scum.) Lesser works by Chandler include *Farewell, My Lovely, The Long Goodbye,* and *The Little Sister.*

Dana, Richard Henry, Jr. *Two Years Before the Mast.* New York: New American Library, 1990. A classic of early California literature. After recovering from a bout with the measles, young Harvard man Richard Henry Dana sailed off to complete his convalescence—not as a privileged ship passenger but as a sailor. On August 14, 1834, he boarded the *Pilgrim* in Boston Harbor and was underway on what was to be the greatest adventure of his life. This realistic depiction of life on the high seas offers an accurate firsthand account of what it was like to see the California coastline for the first time—and to tie up in San Francisco *before* the gold rush. Some of the earliest written descriptions of California—and still an exceptional read.

Darlington, David. *The Mojave.* New York: Henry Holt & Co., 1996. Part history, part oral history, and part natural history, the sum total of this book is marvelous—the tale of the Mojave

Desert writ almost as large as the otherworldly landscape itself.

Drinkard, Michael. *Disobedience*. Berkeley: University of California Press, 1996. According to no lesser authority than the *New York Times Book Review*: "Orange groves are a metaphor for nothing less than creation and apocalypse in this sharply funny and affecting novel set in Redlands, California." An intriguing take on the myth of oranges.

Ellroy, James. *My Dark Places: An L.A. Crime Memoir*. New York: Alfred A. Knopf, 1996. Best known for his crime fiction, Ellroy this time is telling a real-life story. A lifetime after childhood, the author returns to the scene of his mother's murder in what he calls the "White Trash Heaven" of El Monte in the San Gabriel Valley—to unravel the mystery of that event, to understand the strange legacy of her life and death. This dark and disturbing memoir is the result, a writer's excavation of his own painful past.

Fitzgerald, F. Scott. *The Last Tycoon*. New York: Charles Scribner's Sons, 1940. The golden boy of American letters had a heck of a time as a screenwriter in Hollywood—people still say Tinseltown did him in—but, after this (unfinished) novel, there was never any question that he knew the place as well as his own skin. In this, the barely disguised story of MGM genius Irving Thalberg, Fitzgerald demonstrates his genius and supreme talent as a writer.

Gebhard, David, and Scott Zimmerman. *Romanza: The California Architecture of Frank Lloyd Wright*. San Francisco: Chronicle Books, 1988. Accompanied by color photographs, architectural renderings, and floor plans, this book provides an analysis of 24 California buildings—public and private—designed by the noted American architect.

Gilbar, Steven. *Natural State: A Literary Anthology of California Nature Writing*. Berkeley: University of California Press, 1998. This hefty and dazzling collection includes many of the writers you'd expect—Gretel Ehrlich, M.F.K.

Fisher, John McPhee, John Muir, Gary Snyder, and Robert Louis Stevenson—but also a few surprises, including Joan Didion, Jack Kerouac, and Henry Miller.

Gioia, Ted. *West Coast Jazz: Modern Jazz in California, 1945-1960*. Berkeley: University of California Press, 1998. Reprint edition.

Gudde, Erwin G. Edited by William O. Bright. *California Place Names: The Origin and Etymology of Current Geographical Names*. Berkeley: University of California Press, 1998. Did you know that *Siskiyou* was the Chinook word for "bobtailed horse," as borrowed from the Cree language? More such complex truths await every time you dip into this fascinating volume—the ultimate guide to California place names (and how to pronounce them). A revised and expanded fourth edition, building upon the masterwork of Gudde, who died in 1969.

Hamilton, Ian. *As Good as Their Words: Writers in Hollywood*. New York: Harper & Row, 1990. A primer on the literary world of Hollywood, including vignettes about the reluctant screenwriting lives of Chandler, Faulkner, and Fitzgerald. Aldous Huxley, on the other hand, loved writing for the silver screen—and was actually good at it.

Hart, James D. *A Companion to California*. Berkeley: University of California Press. Revised and expanded, 1987 (OP). Another very worthy book for Californiacs to collect, if you can find it, with thousands of brief entries on all aspects of California as well as more in-depth pieces on subjects such as literature.

Hicks, James, James D. Houston, Maxine Hong Kingston, and Al Young, eds. *The Literature of California: Writings from the Golden State, Volume I—Native American Beginnings to 1945*. Berkeley: University of California Press, 2000. This long-awaited anthology is a California landmark, as the publisher says, "unmatched by any existing collection and distinguished by its breadth, variety of sources, and historical sweep. The editors have been refreshingly inclusive and imaginative in their selection: some of the writers are internationally known, others are anthologized here for the first time." The book is subdivided in four sections—starting with stories, legends, and songs of the indigenous tribes; continuing with letters, diaries, reports, and early travel narratives; sharing early signs of California as an identifiable place in U.S. society, from the Mother Lode tales of Mark Twain and Bret Harte to California women's narratives, from the the nature writings of John Muir and Mary Austin to the earliest prose from writers of Asian background and the fiction of Jack London and Frank Norris; and tracing the period between the World Wars, when California literature came into its own. Expect Volume II in 2002.

Houston, James D. *Californians: Searching for the Golden State.* Santa Cruz, CA: Otter B Books, 1992. 10th reprint ed. Good prose, good points in this collection of personal essays about Californians in their endless search for the meaning of their own dream.

Huxley, Aldous. *After Many a Summer Dies the Swan.* London: Chatto and Windus, 1939. As an expatriate in Southern California, Huxley never did entirely warm up to the place. But he understood it, as he so deftly demonstrated in this literary masterpiece, inspired by the larger-than-life life of William Randolph Hearst.

Jackson, Helen Hunt. *Ramona.* New York: New American Library, 1988. The author was an early activist on behalf of California's native peoples. Despairing that so few cared about the Indians' plight, Jackson decided to tell the story as a romance—an interracial romance. As she herself put it: "I am going to try to write a novel, in which will be set forth some Indian experiences in a way to move people's hearts. People will read a novel when they will not read serious books." The resulting *Ramona* was a national sensation when it was first published in 1884. It is now the official California State Play, staged since 1923 at the annual outdoor Ramona Pageant near Hemet.

Kadohata, Cynthia. *In the Heart of the Valley of Love.* New York: Penguin Books, 1993. A new edition is published by the University of California Press. This gritty, stunning novel envisions a future Los Angeles in which almost nothing—food, water, clean air, education—is available to the multiethnic multitudes. Yet humanity abides. A beautifully written and inspiring, if disturbing, book.

Kael, Pauline, Herman J. Mankiewicz, and Orson Welles. *The Citizen Kane Book: Raising Kane.* New York: Limelight Editions, 1984. Includes an excellent essay on the classic American film, plus script and stills.

Kahrl, William. *Water and Power: The Conflict over Los Angeles' Water Supply in the Owens Valley.* Berkeley: University of California Press, 1982. Perhaps the best book available for anyone who wants to understand the politics of water and power in California, and how water and political power have transformed the state's economy and land.

Kirker, Harold. *California's Architectural Frontier.* San Marino, CA: The Huntington Library, 1970 (OP). Perhaps more useful and easier to find is Kirker's 1991 *Old Forms on a New Land: California Architecture in Perspective.*

Krutch, Joseph Wood. *The Desert Year.* Tucson: University of Arizona Press, 1985. Originally published in 1951, this classic by the noted naturalist describes his year in the desert. A good general companion for desert travel.

Kutler, Stanley I., and Richard M. Nixon, eds. *Abuse of Power: The New Nixon Tapes.* Carmichael, CA: Touchstone Books, 1998. Whether one cherishes or despises the memory of Richard Nixon, Stanley Kutler's *Abuse of Power: The New Nixon Tapes,* offers some revelation. These transcripts cover more than 200 hours of Nixon's secret tapes of conversations held in the White House—including crude and devasting details about the extent of Nixon's hands-on involvement, from the beginning, in the Watergate cover-up.

Le Guin, Ursula K. *Dancing at the Edge of the World: Thoughts on Words, Women, Places.* New York: Grove Press, 1989. This delightful collection of essays includes some rare sidelong glances into the soul of the state—and why not? The daughter of UC Berkeley anthropologist Alfred L. Kroeber and Ishi's biographer Theodora Kroeber, Le Guin offers a unique perspective on California as a place, then, now, and in the times to come. Particularly enjoyable in this context: "A Non-Euclidian View of California as a Cold Place to Be"; "The Fisherwoman's Daughter" (about, among other things, her mother); and "Woman/Wilderness."

MacDonald, Ross. *The Moving Target.* New York: Alfred A. Knopf, 1967. In this, one of MacDonald's many Southern California intrigues, private dick Lew Archer encounters Los Angeles criminals at their most entertaining.

McNamee, Gregory, ed. *Sierra Club Desert Reader: A Literary Companion.* San Francisco: Sierra Club Books, 1995.

Michaels, Leonard, David Reid, and Raquel Scherr, eds. *West of the West: Imagining California.* New York: HarperCollins, 1991. Though any anthology about California is destined to be incomplete, this one is exceptional—offering selections by Maya Angelou, Simone de Beauvoir, Joan Didion, Umberto Eco, Gretel Ehrlich, M.F.K. Fisher, Aldous Huxley, Jack Kerouac, Maxine Hong Kingston, Rudyard Kipling, Henry Miller, Ishmael Reed, Kenneth Rexroth, Richard Rodriguez, Randy Shilts, Gertrude Stein, John Steinbeck, Octavio Paz, Amy Tan, Gore Vidal, Walt Whitman, and Tom Wolfe.

Mitchell, Greg. *Tricky Dick and the Pink Lady—Richard Nixon vs. Helen Gahagan Douglas: Sexual Politics and the Red Scare, 1950.* New York: Random House, 1998 (OP). This fascinating account of Richard Nixon's rise to power revisits the 1950 political battle for the U.S. Senate between California contenders Richard Nixon and progressive, onetime actress Helen Gahagan Douglas, who was the first to use the phrase "Tricky Dick"—a well-worn label by the 1970s and the Watergate scandal. Other books by Mitchell include *The Campaign of the Century,* about Upton Sinclair's failed 1934 California gubernatorial campaign; *The Birth of Media Politics*; *Hiroshima in America*; and *Truth and Consequences.*

Mosley, Walter. *Devil in a Blue Dress.* New York: W.W. Norton & Co., 1990. Easy Rawlins, the reluctant private-eye hero of Walter Mosley's noir Los Angeles, reveals post-World War II truths from the perspective of Watts and South-Central L.A. But beyond the plot—black detective takes job from white man to find a mysterious woman—the story of African American migration into Los Angeles is also told here, a depth of experience, and mistrust, grounded in the Deep South. Even after you've seen the movie (starring Denzel Washington as Easy Rawlins) and vicariously relived L.A.'s jazz club cultural heyday, you can follow Easy on more Los Angeles adventures in Mosley's *Black Betty, White Butterfly, A Red Death,* and *A Little Yellow Dog.*

Parker, T. Jefferson. *Laguna Heat.* New York: St. Martin's Press, 1985. So, who says only L.A. does down and dirty whodunits? Orange County's own T. Jefferson Parker, in his bestselling national debut, certainly did Laguna Beach proud. And when you're done untangling this tale, there's always *Little Saigon, Pacific Beat,* and *Summer of Fear.*

Sale, Kirkpatrick. *Dwellers in the Land: The Bioregional Vision.* San Francisco: Sierra Club Books, 1985 (OP). One of the first books putting forth the bioregional philosophy, envisioning a world based not on political borders but on natural geographic regions.

See, Carolyn. *Dreaming: Hard Luck and Good Times in America.* Berkeley: University of California Press, 1996. A bittersweet reevaluation of the American dream, presented as memoir. Also by See, and well worth a read: *Golden Days,* a provocative fictional look at life in 1970s and '80s L.A., as linked to an "iffy" future, and *Mother, Daughter.*

Sinclair, Upton. *Oil!* Berkeley: University of California Press, 1997. Reprise of the original 1927 edition, in which journalist and socialist gadfly Sinclair fictionally recreates the Signal Hill oil fields of Long Beach and the Teapot Dome oil reserve scandals.

Southern, Terry. *Flash and Filigree.* New York: Grove Press, 1958. Just so you know what you're in for, Terry Southern was also the screenwriter for that hilarious cinematic celebration of apocalypse, *Dr. Strangelove: Or How I Learned to Love the Bomb.* No one else quite captures the banality of Los Angeles with such affectionate horror.

Stegner, Wallace. *Where the Bluebird Sings to the Lemonade Springs.* New York: Random House, 1992. It's certainly understandable that, at the end of his days, Wallace Stegner wasn't entirely optimistic about the future of the West, bedeviled as it is, still, by development pressures and insane political decisions. In these five thoughtful essays, he spells out his concerns—and again pays poetic homage to the West's big sky and bigger landscapes. In the end he remains hopeful that a new spirit of place is emerging in the West—and that within a generation or two we will "work out some sort of compromise between what must be done to earn a living and what must be done to restore health to the earth, air, and water."

Theroux, Peter. *Translating L.A.: A Tour of the Rainbow City.* New York: W.W. Norton & Co., 1994. Here, Paul Theroux's cousin takes the reader on an affectionate and quirky personal tour of Los Angeles as adopted hometown. Wearing the various hats of journalist, translator, and literacy tutor, Theroux visits earthquakes, mass transit, Beverly Hills, Hollywood, and Watts.

Van Dyke, John C. *The Desert.* Layton, UT: Gibbs Smith Publishing, 1991. First published in 1901, this is Van Dyke's tale of his three-year solo trek through the desert landscapes of Arizona, California, and Mexico.

Wambaugh, Joseph. *The New Centurions.* Boston: Little, Brown, 1970. Los Angeles cops on patrol in East L.A.—a fictional look from a veteran of the Los Angeles Police Department.

Ward, Elizabeth, and Alain Silver. *Raymond Chandler's Los Angeles.* New York: The Overlook Press. Reissue ed., 1997. This literary tour of a Los Angeles that doesn't exist—and never actually did, outside the writer's imagination—is pretty fun, if you've got some extra time. A tour of Silver Lake becomes a return visit to Raymond Chandler's (and Philip Marlowe's) Gray Lake, and the fabled Bradbury Building (as seen in the 1969 film *Marlowe)* is transformed into the Belfont. Reissued to commemorate the 50th anniversary of film version of *The Big Sleep,* this evocative collection of 100 black-and-white photographs is interwoven with Chandler's own text about Los Angeles, the city he described as "no worse than others, a city rich and vigorous and full of pride, a city lost and beaten and full of emptiness."

Waugh, Evelyn. *The Loved One.* Boston: Little, Brown, 1948. Pet cemeteries and people cemeteries with that eternal touch—nobody denies death better than L.A. And nobody writes about it better than Waugh.

West, Nathanael. *The Day of the Locust.* New York: New Directions, 1962. Before West and his wife were killed in a car accident, he published this surreal novel of L.A. apocalypse. This 1939 tale of terror premieres in Hollywood, naturally, but the story is about the troublesome troupes no longer needed by the silver screen.

WPA Guide to California: The Federal Writers Project Guide to 1930s California. New York: Pantheon Press (an imprint of Random House), 1984. The classic travel guide to California, first published during the Depression, is definitely dated as far as contemporary sights but excellent as a companion volume and background information source.

HISTORY AND PEOPLE

Anger, Kenneth. *Hollywood Babylon*. San Francisco: Straight Arrow Books, 1975. Along with Anger's sequel, this is the classic catalog of juicy gossip about Hollywood's glitterati.

Balio, Tino. *Grand Design: Hollywood as a Modern Business Enterprise, 1930-1939*. Berkeley: University of California Press, 1995. Part of UC Press's History of the American Cinema series, *Grand Design* explores the development of the Hollywood system during the Great Depression.

Barlett, Donald L., and James B. Steele. *Empire: The Life, Legend and Madness of Howard Hughes*. New York: W.W. Norton & Co., 1979. He of obsessive habits and unclipped fingernails wasn't always a madman. Earlier, Hughes was a noted Hollywood gadfly cum empire builder. This is the definitive work on the man and his mission.

Bean, Lowell John, and Lisa J. Bourgeault. *The Cahuilla*. New York: Chelsea House Publishers, 1989. Part of Chelsea's Indians of North America Series, this book explores the culture and history of the native peoples near Palm Springs. From rock art, pottery, and other details of daily life to contemporary history, *The Cahuilla* is a good, very readable introduction.

Brady, Frank. *Citizen Welles*. New York: Scribner, 1989. One of the noted few in Hollywood's genius genre, even Orson Welles had a tough time of it in Tinseltown.

Brownlow, Kevin. *Hollywood: The Pioneers*. New York: Alfred A. Knopf, 1979. The textbook of early Hollywood history, chronicling the era of silent films. Brownlow's trilogy also tells the story, in still more depth: *The Parade's Gone By, The War, the West, and the Wilderness,* and *Behind the Mask.*

Carnes, Mark C., ed. *Past Imperfect: History According to the Movies*. New York: Henry Holt & Co., 1995. Published under the aegis of the Society of American Historians, this historical peek into Hollywood's version of reality is offered via eclectic essays from about 60 writers, including Frances Fitzgerald, Stephen J. Gould, Antonia Fraser, Anthony Lewis, and Gore Vidal. *Past Imperfect* is as entertaining as it is educational.

Cleland, Robert Glass. *A History of California: The American Period*. Westport, CT: Greenwood Press, 1975. Originally published in 1922.

Cleland, Robert Glass. *From Wilderness to Empire: A History of California*. New York: Alfred A. Knopf, 1944 (OP).

Dalton, David. *James Dean: The Mutant King*. San Francisco: Straight Arrow Books, 1974. Dean's cult has grown larger and more disaffected since the actor's violent death on the highway after completing only three films for Hollywood. This pulpy bio digs into the Dean legend.

Davis, Margaret Leslie. *Rivers in the Desert: William Mulholland and the Inventing of Los Angeles*. New York: HarperCollins, 1993 (published in paperback by HarperPerennial). The astonishing and meticulously researched story of how self-taught water engineer William Mulholland masterminded massive water supplies for present-day Los Angeles, told with admiration and respect. Davis sidesteps the temptation to demonize Mulholland with 20/20 hindsight, though she does acknowledge more pointed current criticisms. In her epilogue she also takes care to exonerate Mulholland for the grievous sins history had tarred him with—the St. Francis Dam Disaster and the multitude of lives lost.

Davis, Mike. *City of Quartz: Excavating the Future in Los Angeles*. With photos by Robert Morrow. New York: Vintage Books, 1992. Something of a surprise bestseller in Southern California, as historical dust-up *City of Quartz* takes issue with the idea of California as an innocent and sunny paradise lost. From the book's prologue: "The pattern or urbanization here is what design critic Peter Plagens once called 'the ecology of evil.' Developers don't grow homes in the desert—this isn't Marrakesh or even Tucson—they just clear, grade and pave, hook up some pipes to the artificial river (the federally subsidized California Aqueduct), build a security wall, and plug in the 'product.' With generations of experience in uprooting the citrus gardens of Orange County and the San Fernando Valley, the developers . . . regard the desert as simply another abstraction of dirt and dollar signs." And with that, he's just warming up. Though Davis has been taking some heat lately from his detractors, this is a must-read for anyone who loves Los Angeles—or even the idea of Los Angeles.

Ellison, William Henry. *A Self-Governing Dominion, California 1849-1860.* Berkeley: University of California Press, 1978.

Farquhar, Francis P., ed. *Up and Down California in 1860-1864: The Journal of William H. Brewer.* Berkeley: University of California Press, 1974. Reprint of 1966 edition.

Fogelson, Robert M. *The Fragmented Metropolis: Los Angeles, 1850-1930.* With a new foreword by Robert Fishman. Berkeley: University of California Press, 1993. This new UC Press edition of an urban history classic includes a new preface and updated bibliography.

Fradkin, Philip L. *A River No More: The Colorado River and the West.* Berkeley: University of California Press, 1996. Revised ed. It's not as if California is the only state that helps itself to the waters of the once mighty Colorado River. This, the definitive history, traces the tale from the river's headwaters in Wyoming's Rockies to the Arizona and California borders. Would there be any cities in the desert without the Colorado?

Frederick, David C. *Rugged Justice: The Ninth Circuit Court of Appeals and the American West.* With a foreword by U.S. Supreme Court Justice Sandra Day O'Connor. Berkeley: University of California Press, 1994. Now that the Republican U.S. Congress is trying to muzzle the independent and oft-overturned judicial voice of the West's Ninth Circuit Court—still half Democrat, half Republican, the only federal appeals court not yet dominated by party-line Republicans—what better time to read this colorful history?

Frémont, John Charles. *Memoirs of My Life.* New York: Penguin Books, 1984. Originally published in Chicago, 1887. The old Bearflagger himself tells the story of early California—at least some of it.

Friedrich, Otto. *City of Nets: A Portrait of Hollywood in the 1940s.* New York: Harper & Row, 1986. In 1939 provincial Hollywood almost went international, as expatriates from war-strafed Europe—the likes of Bertolt Brecht and Arthur Schoenberg—came to town. In one of the best books ever written about Tinseltown, Friedrich chronicles the following decade—a significant, substantive period for filmmaking.

Griswold del Castillo, Richard. *The Los Angeles Barrio, 1850-1890: A Social History.* Berkeley: University of California Press, 1980.

Guiles, Fred Lawrence. *Norma Jean: The Life of Marilyn Monroe.* New York: McGraw-Hill, 1969. The tragic life of Marilyn Monroe, studio creation, could have been scripted by Hollywood. Equally enlightening: *Legend: The Life and Death of Marilyn Monroe,* also by Guiles.

Gutiérrez, David G. *Walls and Mirrors: Mexican Americans, Mexican Immigrants, and the Politics of Ethnicity.* Berkeley: University of California Press, 1995. Reaching back more than 100 years, this probing history examines the cultural transformation of the U.S. Southwest in relationship to Mexico from multiple angles.

Gutiérrez, Ramon A., and Richard J. Orsi, eds. *Contested Eden: California Before the Gold Rush.* Berkeley: University of California Press, 1998. In this first volume of a projected four-part series, essays explore California before the gold rush.

Harlow, Neal. *California Conquered: The Annexation of a Mexican Province, 1846-1850.* Berkeley: University of California Press, 1982.

Hart, John. *Storm Over Mono: The Mono Lake Basin and the California Water Future.* Berkeley: University of California Press, 1996. While a fairly happy ending to the story is now being written on the pages of California newspapers, *Storm Over Mono* covers the fight to save Mono Lake as comprehensively as anyone. Illustrated with dozens of striking color photographs plus black-and-white photos, maps, and illustrations.

Heizer, Robert F. *The Destruction of the California Indians.* Layton, UT: Gibbs Smith Publishing, 1974.

Heizer, Robert F., and Martin A. Baumhoff. *Prehistoric Rock Art of Nevada and Eastern California.* Berkeley: University of California Press, 1976.

Heizer, Robert F., and Albert B. Elsasser. *The Natural World of the California Indians.* Berkeley: University of California Press, 1980. As an adjunct to the rest of Heizer's work, this fact-packed volume provides the setting—the natural environment, the village environment—for California's native peoples.

Heizer, Robert F., and M.A. Whipple. *The California Indians.* Berkeley: University of California Press, 1971. A worthwhile collection of essays about California's native peoples, covering general, regional, and specific topics— a good supplement to the work of A.L. Kroeber (who also contributed to this volume).

Hine, Robert V. *California's Utopian Colonies.* Berkeley: University of California Press, 1983.

Holiday, James. *The World Rushed In: The California Gold Rush Experience: An Eyewitness Account of a Nation Heading West.* New York: Simon and Schuster, 1981. Reprint of a classic history, made while new Californians were busy making up the myth. While it's true that the gold rush had little direct impact on Southern California, it certainly set the stage for the nation's radical tilt westward.

Houston, James, and Jeanne Houston. *Farewell to Manzanar.* New York: Bantam Books, 1983. A good goodbye to California's World War II internment of Japanese immigrants and American citizens of Japanese descent, a nightmarish experience that lives on in the cultural memory of Southern California's large population of Japanese Americans.

Hutchinson, W.H. *California: The Golden Shore by the Sundown Sea.* Belmont, CA: Star Publishing Company, 1988. The late author, a professor emeritus of history at CSU, Chico known as Old Hutch to former students, presents a dizzying amount of historical, economic, and political detail from his unique perspective in this analysis of California's past and present. Hutchinson saw the state from many sides during a lifetime spent as "a horse wrangler, cowboy, miner, boiler fireman, merchant seaman, corporate bureaucrat, rodeo and horse show announcer, and freelance writer."

Irons, Peter. *Justice at War: The Story of the Japanese-American Internment Cases.* Berkeley: University of California Press, 1993. Irons examines the internment of Japanese Americans and noncitizen immigrants in World War II "relocation" camps as historical travesty in a brilliantly researched, beautifully written book.

Jackson, Helen Hunt. *Century of Dishonor: A Sketch of the United States' Government's Dealings (with some of the Indian tribes).* Irvine, CA: Reprint Services, 1988. Originally published in Boston, 1881.

Jackson, Joseph Henry. *Anybody's Gold: The Story of California's Mining Towns.* San Francisco: Chronicle Books, 1970. A lively history back in print after a 30-year hiatus.

Kling, Robert, Spencer Olin, and Mark Poster, eds. *Postsuburban California: The Transformation of Orange County Since World War II.* Berkeley: University of California Press, 1991. Most appropriate for the academically inclined, this is a multidisciplinary look at Southern California's foremost example of "postsuburbia."

Kroeber, Alfred L. *Handbook of the Indians of California.* New York: Dover Publications, 1976 (unabridged facsimile version of the original work, *Bulletin 78* of the Bureau of American Ethnology of the Smithsonian Institution, published by the U.S. Government Printing Office). The classic compendium of observed facts about California's native peoples by the noted UC Berkeley anthropologist who befriended Ishi—but also betrayed him, posthumously, by allowing his body to be autopsied (in violation of Ishi's beliefs) then shipping his brain to the Smithsonian Institution.

Lewis, Oscar. *The Big Four.* Sausalito, CA: Comstock Editions, 1982. Originally published in New York, 1938.

Lingenfelter, Richard E. *Death Valley and the Amargosa: A Land of Illusion.* Berkeley: University of California Press, 1986.

McDonald, Linda, and Carol Cullen. *California Historical Landmarks.* Sacramento, CA: California Department of Parks and Recreation, 1997. Revised ed. Originally compiled in response to the National Historic Preservation Act of 1966, directing all states to identify all properties "possessing historical, architectural, archaeological, and cultural value," this updated edition covers more than 1,000 California Registered Historical Landmarks, organized by category—sites of aboriginal, economic, or government interest, for example—and indexed by county. A wide variety of other publications is available from the Department of Parks and Recreation. To order, call toll-free (800) 777-0369.

McWilliams, Carey, with a foreword by Lewis H. Lapham. *California, the Great Exception.* Berkeley: University of California Press, 1999. Historian, journalist, and lawyer Carey McWilliams, editor of *The Nation* from 1955 to 1975, stepped back from his other tasks in 1949 to assess the state of the Golden State at the end of its first 100 years. And while he acknowledged the state's prodigious productivity even then, he also noted the brutality with which the great nation-state of California dealt with "the Indian problem," the water problem, and the agricultural labor problem—all issues of continuing relevance to California today. McWilliams' classic work on the essence of California, reprinted with a new foreword by the editor of *Harper's* magazine, is a must-read for all Californians.

McWilliams, Carey. *Southern California Country: An Island Upon the Land.* New York: Duell, Sloan & Pierce, 1946. The classic of pre-World War II L.A. history, still the best in terms of placing the city's seeming peculiarities in their proper contexts.

Monroy, Douglas. *Thrown Among Strangers: The Making of Mexican Culture in Frontier California.* Berkeley: University of California Press, 1990.

Mungo, Ray. *Palm Springs Babylon: Sizzling Stories from the Desert Playground of the Stars.* New York: St. Martin's Press, 1993. It's tacky to pry into the private lives of Hollywood celebrities, politicians, and rich people, even when they're at play in Palm Springs. But Mungo does it so well—managing to spew out chapter after chapter of substantive local social history along with the snide asides (such as the caption for a photo of Sonny Bono: "Former Cher Bimbo Goes His Own Way"). All in all this book is a hoot—and you'll find out more about the sleazier side of Palm Springs than you ever wanted to know.

Nadeau, Remi. *City-Makers.* Garden City, NY: Doubleday, 1948. Hey, *Chinatown* fans. Here's the dark side of L.A. history in book form—the tale of the boosters, promoters, and sleazy business deals that together created present-day L.A., much to the detriment of the place and its people.

Pitt, Leonard. *Decline of the Californios: A Social History of the Spanish-Speaking Californians, 1846-1890.* Berkeley: University of California Press, 1966.

Powers, Stephen. *Tribes of California.* Berkeley: University of California Press, 1977.

Reisner, Marc. *Cadillac Desert: The American West and its Disappearing Water.* New York: Penguin Books, 1993. Revised ed. Inspiration for the four-part PBS documentary of the same name, first broadcast in 1997, this is the contemporary yet classic tale of water and the unromantic West—a drama of unquenchable thirst and reluctant conservation, political intrigue and corruption, and economic and ecological disasters. How Los Angeles got its water figures prominently—the histories of William Mulholland and the Owens Valley as well as the Colorado River. A must-read book.

Ridge, John. *The Life and Adventures of Joaquin Murrieta.* Norman, OK: University of Oklahoma Press, 1986.

Riva, Maria. *Marlene Dietrich: By Her Daughter.* New York: Alfred A. Knopf, 1993. Marlene Dietrich was an alcoholic, bedridden ghost of a woman when she died. But that was no call for her daughter to betray her or the fond memories of their complex mother-daughter relationship. Though, as Riva puts it: "At the age of three, I knew quite definitely that I did not have a mother, that I belonged to a queen. Once that was settled in my head, I was quite content with my lot." Serious Dietrich fans must also read the definitive biography, *Marlene Dietrich: Life and Legend,* by Steven Bach (William Morrow, 1992).

Robinson, W.W. *Land in California: The Story of Mission Lands, Ranchos, Squatters, Mining Claims, Railroad Grants, Land Scrip, Homesteads.* Berkeley: University of California Press, 1979.

Royce, Josiah. *California from the Conquest in 1846 to the Second Vigilance Committee in San Francisco 1856.* New York: AMS Press. Originally published in Boston, 1886.

Santa Barbara Museum of Natural History. *California's Chumash Indians.* San Luis Obispo, CA: EZ Nature Books, 1988. A fascinating overview of Chumash culture, innovation, trade, and tradition.

Sinclair, Upton. *American Outpost: A Book of Reminiscences.* New York: 1932. A reprint edition of the original is now available through Reprint Services.

Sinclair, Upton. *I, Candidate for Governor: And How I Got Licked.* Berkeley: University of California Press, 1994. Reprint of the original edition. This is a genuine treasure of California history—a first-person account of California's liveliest and most notorious gubernatorial race, in which California business employed Hollywood's tools to defeat muckraking journalist and socialist Democratic candidate Sinclair in the too-close-to-call 1934 campaign. Sinclair's platform was EPIC—End Poverty in California—and he almost got the chance to try. Though it's hard to imagine in these days, at other times in its history—certainly during the Great Depression—California as place got seriously agitated over issues of social justice, giving the good ol' boys quite a scare.

Starr, Kevin. *Americans and the California Dream: 1850-1915.* New York: Oxford University Press, 1973. A cultural history, written by a native San Franciscan, former newspaper columnist, and current professor, historian, and California State Librarian. The focus here is on Northern California. Yet this book taps an impressively varied body of experiences and sources as it seeks to "suggest the poetry and the moral drama of social experience" from California's first days of statehood through the Panama-Pacific Exposition of 1915 when, in the author's opinion, "California came of age." Annotations suggest rich possibilities for further reading.

Starr, Kevin. *Endangered Dreams: The Great Depression in California.* New York: Oxford University Press, 1996. "California, Wallace Stegner has noted, is like the rest of the United States, only more so." And so begins the fourth volume of Starr's imaginative and immense California history, in which the author delves into the Golden State's dark past—a period in which strikes and unions were forcibly suppressed, soup kitchens became social institutions, and both socialism and fascism had their day. The "therapy" that finally cured California involved massive transfusions of public capital in the form of public works projects. Yet some things don't change: San Francisco is still a strong union town, and Los Angeles barely tolerates unionism.

Starr, Kevin. *The Dream Endures: California Enters the 1940s.* New York: Oxford University Press, 1997. This, the fifth volume in Kevin Starr's impressive California history series, traces the history of the California good life— in architecture, fiction, film, and leisure pursuits—and how it came to define American culture and society. Chosen Outstanding Academic Book of 1997 by *Choice,* and one of the best 100 books of 1997 by the *Los Angeles Times Book Review.*

Starr, Kevin. *Inventing the Dream: California Through the Progressive Era.* New York: Oxford University Press, 1985. Second in Starr's projected five-part series on California history, *Inventing the Dream* addresses Southern California's ascendancy in the late 19th and early 20th centuries.

Starr, Kevin. *Material Dreams: Southern California Through the 1920s.* New York: Oxford University Press, 1990. The third book in Starr's lively symbolic celebration of California history chronicles the most compelling period of explosive growth in Los Angeles—which the author affectionately calls "the Great Gatsby of American cities"—made possible by the arrival of water.

Stein, Ben. *Hollywood Days, Hollywood Nights.* New York: Bantam Books, 1988. Forget the fact that Stein was once a speechwriter for Richard Nixon. He also knows the mentality ("soul" too high-flown a phrase) of Hollywood, from paranoia to script punctuation, and is happy to share his secrets.

Stone, Irving. *Men to Match My Mountains.* New York: Berkeley Publishers, 1987. A classic California history, originally published in 1956.

Walton, John. *Western Times and Water Wars: State, Culture, and Rebellion in California.* Berkeley: University of California Press, 1992.

Winner of both the Robert Park and J.S. Holliday Awards, Walton's compelling chronicle of the water wars between Los Angeles and the farmers and ranchers of the Owens Valley is a masterpiece of California history.

NATURE AND NATURAL HISTORY

Alden, Peter. *National Audubon Society Field Guide to California.* New York: Alfred A. Knopf, 1998. A wonderful field guide to some 1,000 of the state's native inhabitants, from the world's smallest butterfly—the Western Pygmy Blue— to its oldest, largest, and tallest trees. Well illustrated with striking color photography.

Bailey, Harry P. *The Weather of Southern California.* Berkeley: University of California Press, 1966.

Bakker, Elna. *An Island Called California: An Ecological Introduction to Its Natural Communities.* Berkeley: University of California Press, 1985. Expanded revised ed. An excellent, time-honored introduction to the characteristics of, and relationships between, California's natural communities. New chapters on Southern California, added in this edition, make *An Island* more helpful statewide.

Balls, Edward K. *Early Uses of California Plants.* Berkeley: University of California Press, 1962.

Barbour, Michael, Bruce Pavlik, Susan Lindstrom, and Frank Drysdale, with a foreword by Pulitzer Prize-winning California poet Gary Snyder. *California's Changing Landscapes: Diversity and Conservation of California Vegetation.* Sacramento: California Native Plant Society Press, 1993. Finalist for the Publishers Marketing Association's 1994 Benjamin Franklin Award in the Nature category, this well-illustrated, well-indexed lay guide to California's astonishing botanical variety is an excellent introduction. For more in-depth personal study, the society also publishes some excellent regional floras and plant keys.

Belzer, Thomas J. *Roadside Plants of Southern California.* Missoula, MT: Mountain Press,

1984. If as a nature lover you rarely venture far from the family car, this is the plant guide for you. From trees to cacti and wildflowers, the most likely roadside specimens are described in reasonable detail and illustrated with full-color photos.

Blake, Tupper Ansel, and Peter Steinhart. *Two Eagles/Dos Aguilas: The Natural World of the United States-Mexico Borderlands.* Berkeley: University of California Press, 1994. One of those rare books well worth reading *and* displaying on the coffee table for everyone's appreciation. This award-winning book is a revelation, sharing its secrets through fine writing and stunning photography (color and black and white).

California Coastal Commission, State of California. *California Coastal Resource Guide.* Berkeley: University of California Press, 1997. This is the revised and expanded fifth edition of the California coast lover's bible, the indispensable guide to the Pacific coast and its wonders—the land, marine geology, biology—as well as parks, landmarks, and amusements. But for practical travel purposes, get the commission's *The California Coastal Access Guide,* listed under Enjoying the Outdoors below.

Clarke, Charlotte Bringle. *Edible and Useful Plants of California.* Berkeley: University of California Press, 1977. With this book in hand, almost anyone can manage to make a meal in the wilderness—or whip up a spring salad from the vacant lot next door.

Cogswell, Howard L. *Water Birds of California.* Berkeley: University of California Press, 1977.

Collier, Michael. *A Land in Motion: California's San Andreas Fault.* Berkeley: University of California Press, 1999. An intriguing geologic tour of the world's most famous fault, which cuts through the Southern California desert then parallels the entire edge of western California. Wonderful photographs.

Crampton, Beecher. *Grasses in California.* Berkeley: University of California Press, 1974.

Dale, Nancy. *Flowering Plants of the Santa Monica Mountains: Coastal and Chaparral Regions of Southern California.* Santa Barbara: Capra Press, 1986. With 214 color photos, dozens of illustrations and maps, and suggested wildflower walks, this is an invaluable book to tuck into the daypack for anyone spending serious time in the Santa Monicas.

Dawson, Yale E. *Cacti of California.* Berkeley: University of California Press, 1966.

Dawson, Yale E., and Michael Foster. *Seashore Plants of California.* Berkeley: University of California Press, 1982.

DeSante, David, and Peter Pyle. *Distributional Checklist to North American Birds.* The most accurate and up-to-date information ever assembled on the abundance and status of birds north of Mexico—indispensable to serious birders—but hard to find. It is sometimes available through the Mono Lake Committee, P.O. Box 29, Lee Vining 93541, 760/647-6595, fax 760/647-6377.

Duremberger, Robert. *Elements of California Geography.* Out of print but worth searching for. This is the classic work on California geography.

Farrand, John Jr. *Western Birds.* New York: McGraw-Hill Book Co., 1988. This birding guide includes color photographs instead of artwork for illustrations, conveniently included with descriptive listings. Though the book contains no range maps, the "Similar Species" listing helps eliminate birds with similar features.

Fitch, John E. *Tidepool and Nearshore Fishes of California.* Berkeley: University of California Press, 1975.

Fitch, John E., and Robert J. Lavenberg. *California Marine Food and Game Fishes.* Berkeley: University of California Press, 1971.

Fradkin, Philip L. *The Seven States of California: A Natural and Human History.* New York: Henry Holt & Co., 1995; subsequently published in paperback by the University of California Press. Both personal and historical exploration of California.

Fuller, Thomas C., and Elizabeth McClintock. *Poisonous Plants of California.* Berkeley: University of California Press, 1987.

Garth, John S., and J.W. Tilden. *California Butterflies.* Berkeley: University of California Press, 1986. At long last, the definitive field guide and key to California butterflies (in both the larval and adult stages) is available, and in paperback; compact and fairly convenient to tote around.

Grillos, Steve. *Fern and Fern Allies of California.* Berkeley: University of California Press, 1966.

Grinnell, Joseph, and Alden Miller. *The Distribution of the Birds of California.* For those interested in serious study, this is the definitive California birder's guide. Out of print but it may be available through the Mono Lake Committee; see contact information under the DeSante listing, above.

Hale, Mason, and Mariette Cole. *Lichens of California.* Berkeley: University of California Press, 1988.

Hall, Clarence A., Jr., ed. *Natural History of the White-Inyo Range, Eastern California.* Berkeley: University of California Press, 1991. This impressive 560-page tome covers all the natural wonders of the extraordinary landscape that rises up from the eastern edge of the Owens Valley—from native culture and the oldest living species on earth, the bristlecone pine, to hundreds of flowering plants and area fish, reptile, and bird species. Also well covered here: archaeology, geology, geomorphology, and meteorology.

Hickman, Jim, ed. *The Jepson Manual: Higher Plants of California.* Berkeley: University of California Press (with cooperation and support from the California Native Plant Society and the Jepson Herbarium), 1993. New in the early 1990s but at least 10 years in the making, *The Jepson Manual* is already considered the bible of California botany. The brainchild of both Jim Hickman and Larry Heckard, curator of the Jepson Herbarium, this book is a cumulative picture of the extraordinary flora of California, and the first comprehensive attempt to fit it all into one volume since the Munz *A California Flora* was published in 1959. The best work of almost 200 botanist-authors has been collected here, along with exceptional line drawings and illustrations (absent from the Munz flora) that make it easier to identify and compare plant species. This book is the botanical reference book for a California lifetime—a hefty investment for a hefty tome, especially essential for serious ecologists and botanists, amateur and otherwise.

Hill, Mary. *California Landscape: Origin and Evolution.* Berkeley: University of California Press, 1984. An emphasis on the most recent history of California landforms. Also by Hill, if you plan to poke around farther north: *Geology of the Sierra Nevada.*

Hinton, Sam. *Seashore Life of Southern California.* Berkeley: University of California Press, 1988. Revised and expanded.

Houk, Walter, Sue Irwin, and Richard A. Lovett. *A Visitor's Guide to California's State Parks,* Sacramento, CA: California Department of Parks and Recreation, 1990. This large-format, very pretty book includes abundant full-color photography and brief, accessible basic information about the features and facilities of the state's parks and recreation areas. *A Visitor's Guide* is available at retail and online bookstores and at the state parks themselves.

Hunt, Charles B. *Death Valley: Geology, Ecology, Archaeology.* Berkeley: University of California Press, 1975.

Jaeger, Edmund C. *The California Deserts.* Palo Alto: Stanford University Press, 1965. Fourth ed. A true classic in natural history, first published in 1933, and a surprisingly poetic read. Example: "Let me have the delicious odors of the creosote bush and the saltbush when they are wetted with desert rains, look upon the endless variety and beauty of the clouds' far-flung forms, have the silence of the uninhabited mesas, and I am in a land enchanted."

Jaeger, Edmund C., and Arthur C. Smith. *Introduction to the Natural History of Southern California.* Berkeley: University of California Press, 1966. A must-have for the southstate naturalist's bookshelf.

Johnston, Verna R. *California Forests and Woodlands: A Natural History.* Berkeley: University of California Press, 1994. For beginning botany students, a very helpful general introduction to the plants, animals, and ecological relationships within California's varied types of forests.

Kaufman, Kenn. *Lives of North American Birds.* New York: Houghton Mifflin Co., 1997. Sponsored by the Roger Tory Peterson Institute. A bit bulky for a field guide but already considered a classic, this 674-page hardbound tome focuses less on identifying features and names and more on observing and understanding birds within the contexts of their own lives. Now, there's a concept.

Klauber, Laurence. *Rattlesnakes.* Berkeley: University of California Press, 1982.

Knute, Adrienne. *Plants of the East Mojave.* Cima, CA: Wide Horizons Press, 1991. A good botanical introduction to the plants of the Mojave National Preserve, well-organized and easy to follow.

Latting, June, and Peter G. Rowlands, eds. *The California Desert: An Introduction to Natural Resources and Man's Impact. Volumes I and II.* June Latting Books, 1995 (distributed by the California Native Plant Society). This compendium includes just about everything known about California desert resources, a project unofficially started by June Latting in 1978 when the first Desert Conservation Area Advisory Committee meetings convened in Riverside. Published posthumously with the assistance of Peter Rowlands and June Latting's family, this is a must for any desert aficionado.

Leatherwood, Stephen, and Randall Reeves. *The Sierra Club Handbook of Whales and Dolphins.* San Francisco: Sierra Club Books, 1983.

Lederer, Roger. *Pacific Coast Bird Finder.* Berkeley: Nature Study Guild, 1977. A handy, hip-pocket-sized guide to birding for beginners. Also available: *Pacific Coast Tree Finder* by Tom Watts, among similar titles. All "Finder" titles now available through Wilderness Press.

McCauley, Jane, and the National Geographic Society staff. *National Geographic Society Field Guide to the Birds of North America.* Washington, D.C.: National Geographic Society, 1993. One of the best guides to bird identification available.

McConnaughey, Bayard H., and Evelyn McConnaughey. *Pacific Coast.* New York: Alfred A. Knopf, 1986. One of the Audubon Society Nature Guides. More than 600 color plates, keyed to region and habitat type, make it easy to identify marine mammals, shorebirds, seashells, and other inhabitants and features of the West Coast, from Alaska to California.

McGinnis, Samuel M. *Freshwater Fishes of California.* Berkeley: University of California Press, 1985. Including a simple but effective method of identifying fish, this guide also offers fisherfolk help in developing better angling strategies, since it indicates when and where a species feeds and what its food preferences are.

McMinn, Howard. *An Illustrated Manual of California Shrubs.* Berkeley: University of California Press, 1939. Reprint ed. An aid in getting to know about 800 California shrubs, this classic manual includes keys, descriptions of flowering, elevations, and geographic distributions. For the serious amateur botanist, another title for the permanent library.

Miller, Crane S., and Richard S. Hyslop. *California: The Geography of Diversity.* Palo Alto, CA: Mayfield Publishing Company, 1999. Second ed.

Munz, Philip A. *A Flora of Southern California.* Berkeley: University of California Press, 1974. This hefty hardcover tome, 1,086 pages, should be more than enough to help any plant lover explore every square inch of unpaved Southern California.

Munz, Philip A. *California Desert Wildflowers.* Berkeley: University of California Press, 1962. A very useful and informative desert travel companion for wildflower aficionados, amateur and beginning botanists in particular. Entries are organized by flower color, so you don't have to do any "keying," and plants are listed first by common name. Line drawings illustrate each entry, and the book also includes 96 color photos.

Munz, Philip A., and David D. Keck. *A California Flora and Supplement.* Berkeley: University of California Press, 1968. Until quite recently this was it, the California botanist's bible—a complete descriptive "key" to every plant known to grow in California—but quite hefty to tote around on pleasure trips. Generally more useful for amateur botanists are Munz's *California Desert Wildflowers* (see above), *California Mountain Wildflowers,* and *Shore Wildflowers,* as well as other illustrated plant guides. Serious amateur and professional botanists and ecologists are ecstatic these days about the recent publication of the *new* California plant bible: *The Jepson Manual,* edited by Jim Hickman. (For more information, see above.)

Nilsson, Karen B. *A Wildflower by Any Other Name.* Yosemite National Park: Yosemite Association, 1994. This engaging book tells the story of pioneering Western naturalists whose names—Eschscholtz and Chamisso, for example—often define either genus or species in the Latin names of many native plants. In an age of mass-marketed information, this is a gold mine for serious botany students and trivia buffs alike.

Ornduff, Robert. *Introduction to California Plant Life.* Berkeley: University of California Press, 1974. An essential for native plant libraries, this classic offers a marvelous introduction to California's botanical abundance.

Orr, Robert T., and Roger Helm. *Marine Mammals of California.* Berkeley: University of California Press, 1989. Revised ed. A handy guide for identifying marine mammals along the California coast—with practical tips on the best places to observe them.

Pavlik, Bruce, Pamela Muick, Sharon Johnson, and Marjorie Popper. *Oaks of California.* Santa Barbara: Cachuma Press, 1991. In ancient European times oaks were considered spiritual beings, the sacred inspiration of artists, healers, and writers since these particular trees were thought to court the lightning flash. Time spent with this stunning book will soon convince anyone that this truth lives on. Packed with photos and lovely watercolor illustrations, maps, even an oak lover's travel guide, this book celebrates the many species of California oaks.

Peterson, Roger Tory. *A Field Guide to Western Birds.* Boston: Houghton Mifflin Co., 1990. The third edition of this birding classic has striking new features, including full-color illustrations (including juveniles, females, and in-flight birds) facing the written descriptions. The only thing you'll have to flip around for are the range maps, tucked away in the back. Among other intriguing titles in the Peterson Field Guide series: *A Field Guide to Western Birds' Nests* by Hal Harrison.

Peterson, Victor P. *Native Trees of Southern California.* Berkeley: University of California Press, 1966.

Powell, Jerry A., and Charles Hogue. *California Insects.* Berkeley: University of California Press, 1980.

Raven, Peter H. *Native Shrubs of California.* Berkeley: University of California Press, 1966.

Raven, Peter H., and Daniel Axelrod. *Origin and Relationships of the California Flora.* Sacramento: California Native Plant Society Press, 1995. Reprint of the 1978 original, another title most appropriate for serious students of botany.

Robbins, Chandler, Bertel Brown, Herbert Zim, and Arthur Singer. *Birds of North America.* New York: Western Publishing, 1983. A good field guide for California birdwatching.

Schmitz, Marjorie. *Growing California Native Plants.* Berkeley: University of California Press, 1980. A handy guide for those interested in planting, growing, and otherwise supporting the success of California's beleaguered native plants.

Schoenherr, Allan A. *A Natural History of California.* Berkeley: University of California Press, 1992. With introductory chapters on ecology and geology, *A Natural History* covers California's climate, geology, soil, plant life, and animals based on distinct bioregions, with almost 300 photographs and numerous illustrations and tables. An exceptionally readable and well-illustrated introduction to California's astounding natural diversity and drama written by an ecology professor from CSU Fullerton, this 700-some page reference belongs on any Californiac's library shelf.

Schoenherr, Allan A. and C. Robert Feldmeth. *A Natural History of the Islands of California.* Berkeley: University of California Press, 1999. A comprehensive introduction to California's Año Nuevo Island, Channel Islands, Farallon Islands, and the islands of San Francisco Bay—living evolutionary laboratories with unique species and ecological niches.

Starker, Leopold A. *The California Quail.* Berkeley: University of California Press, 1985. This is the definitive book on the California quail, its history and biology.

Stebbins, Robert. *California Amphibians and Reptiles.* Berkeley: University of California Press, 1972.

ENJOYING THE OUTDOORS: RECREATION, TOURS, TRAVEL

Bakalinsky, Ada, and Larry Gordon. *Stairway Walks in Los Angeles.* Berkeley: Wilderness Press, 1995. Update edition. This guide to 18 walks and some 200 public stairways leads to diverse, older neighborhoods and parts of L.A. the car-bound can't go—all in all a delightful education in history, architecture, and nature, as well as invigorating exercise.

Brown, Ann Marie. *Foghorn Outdoors: California Waterfalls—Your Key to Accessing the State's Most Spectacular Falls.* Emeryville, CA: Avalon Travel Publishing, 2000. Second ed. This trail guide points the way for thorough enjoyment of some 225 California waterfalls, whether you prefer to get there via hike, bike, backpack, or drive.

Bryan, T. Scott, and Betty Tucker-Bryan. *The Explorer's Guide to Death Valley National Park.* Boulder, Colorado: University Press of Colorado, 1995. First edition. A handy companion for up-close exploration in Death Valley, including mileage markers for hunting down obscure features, even in the desert outback. No maps, alas, so hustle those up elsewhere.

California Coastal Commission, State of California. *The California Coastal Access Guide.* Berkeley: University of California Press, 1997. Fifth revised ed. According to the *Oakland Tribune*, this is "no doubt the most comprehensive look at California's coastline published to date." A must-have for serious Californiacs.

Clark, Jeanne L. *California Wildlife Viewing Guide.* Helena, MT: Falcon Press, 1996. Second ed. This revised and expanded guide tells you where to go for a good look at native wildlife, and what to do once you're there. Color photos, overview maps.

Collins, Andrew. *Fodor's Gay Guide to Los Angeles and Southern California.* New York: Fodor's, 1997.

Culliney, John, and Edward Crockett. *Exploring Underwater.* San Francisco: Sierra Club Books, 1980.

Darvil, Fred, Jr., M.D. *Mountaineering Medicine and Backcountry Medical Guide.* Berkeley:

Wilderness Press, 1998. 14th revised ed. Written specifically for mountaineers, this small manual is indispensable for all outdoorsfolk and wilderness travelers.

Dirksen, D.J. *Recreation Lakes of California.* Port Angeles, WA: Recreation Sales Publishing, 1999. 12th ed. A very useful guide to the multitude of recreation lakes in California, complete with general maps (not to scale) and local contact addresses and phones. A worthwhile investment for boaters and fisherfolk.

Fein, Art. *L.A. Musical History Tour: A Guide to the Rock and Roll Landmarks of Los Angeles.* London: Faber and Faber, 1990.

Foster, Lynne. *Adventuring in the California Desert: The Sierra Club Travel Guide to the Great Basin, Mojave, and Colorado Desert Regions of California.* San Francisco: Sierra Club Books, 1997. Revised and updated edition. So, you wanna do the desert? This book is the best overall guide for figuring out where to go, when, and how. Out-there desert hikes are the book's obvious strength. But along with such sage advice you'll also find out plenty about desert history and natural history.

Gayot, André, ed. *The Best of Los Angeles and Southern California.* Los Angeles: Gault Millau, 2001. Updated every three to four years. The bible for what to see and do, where to shop, and where to eat in L.A. and Southern California. Even Angelenos always have a copy on hand.

Gebhard, David, and Robert Winter. *Los Angeles: An Architectural Guide.* Layton, UT: Gibbs Smith, 1994. This is the Baedeker for devotees of Los Angeles architecture, encyclopedic in scope, though you may find the error quotient a bit high, even by everything-always-changes L.A. standards. Also worth it, from the same authors, with a broader reach: *A Guide to Architecture in Los Angeles and Southern California.*

Gehman, Pleasant, ed. *The Underground Guide to Los Angeles.* San Francisco: Manic D Press, 1999. So, you really want to get down and dirty in L.A.? This will get you started—a great guide for the too-cool-for-themeparks, too-cool-for-guidebooks crowd. Still, even helped along by guides such as this—pointing out where to eat cheap, to buy clothes and music, to party hearty—it'll be something of a challenge to discover all the dives and delights of "real" L.A. since, by definition, what's hip is ever-changing. Good luck.

Gersg-Young, Marjorie. *Hot Springs and Hot Pools of the Southwest.* Berkeley: Aqua Thermal Access (distributed by Wilderness Press), 1998. Revised and updated ed. A useful guide to California's commercial as well as unimproved (natural) yet accessible hot springs, including those in Arizona, Nevada, New Mexico, Texas, and Baja Mexico.

Gold, Jonathan. *Where to Eat in the Real Los Angeles.* New York: St. Martin's Press, 2000. New York never tires of mocking all things Los Angeles—when they aren't somehow appropriating them. And so it is that L.A.'s beloved people's eats connoisseur has finally been dragged away to New York, where he surveys the city's cuisine scene for *Gourmet* magazine. Before that culinary kidnapping, though, Gold ate it all, and all over L.A. *Counter Intelligence,* also the title of Gold's long-running restaurant review column in the *L.A. Weekly,* collects more than 200 of Gold's best restaurant discoveries—from inexpensive lunch counters, best burgers, best 'dogs, and the most exotic, international cuisines to undiscovered dishes at more mainstream establishments. If you eat your way around L.A. with Gold as your inspired companion, you'll finally understand the place.

Jardine, Ray. *The Pacific Crest Trail Handbook: Innovative Techniques and Trail Tested Instruction for the Long Distance Hiker.* Berkeley: Adventure Lore Press, 1992 (OP). The author and his wife have hiked the entire 2,500-mile route between Mexico and Canada *twice,* so the information included here—on everything from equipment and clothing to mosquitos, ticks, and bears—is all a serious hiker needs to know. Also by Jardine—and still available, at last report—is *Beyond Backpacking: Ray Jardine's Guide to Lightweight Hiking.*

Jeffrey, Nan, and Kevin Jeffrey. *Adventuring with Children: The Family Pack-Along Guide to the Outdoors and the World.* San Francisco: Foghorn Press, 1992. This enthusiastic guide to getting out and about with children—and without fear and loathing—is invaluable for parents determined to see the world as sanely as possible.

Keator, Glenn. *Complete Garden Guide to the Native Shrubs of California.* San Francisco: Chronicle Books, 1994. California's native plants are under siege just about everywhere in the Golden State—so help nature out by stashing some natural biological diversity in your own backyard. More than 500 native shrub species are listed here, some beautifully represented by turn-of-the-century line drawings.

Kegan, Stephanie, and Elizabeth Pomada. *Fun Places to go with Children in Southern California.* San Francisco: Chronicle Books, 1997. Sixth ed. As important as finding a place to eat with kids is finding appropriate places to take them before and after meals.

Kelton, Simon St. Goar. *The Rich Bastard's Guide to Los Angeles.* London: RBG Publications Ltd., 1998. In these heady days of all-American greed, this book would seem to be a natural. (The term "rich bastard" is far from being pejorative, the author assures us: "Rich Bastards tend to be loved, loathed and admired in equal amounts not just because of the size of their bank accounts or their recently purchased smiles, but because they've come from the Outside: outside family, outside community, and perhaps even from outside the very fabric of society. Yet despite the odds stacked against them at birth, RBs join the game of life, struggle and win. They are, therefore, a combination of the adorable mutt and the lone wolf, a beast to be both cherished and feared.") As loveable and frightening as they may be—and it's attitude, more than money, that defines a rich bastard—there *still* aren't as many of them as there are the

rest of us, which may be why, at last report, no one was home at the Rich Bastard's website. Still, if you can find this book, give this overeducated, rich bastard wannabe a break and buy it. The text is wonderful, well worth adding to your travel collection—as much for its incisive, hilarious takes on the habits and hangouts of the rich in L.A. as for its promo blurbs, from the likes of Princess Birgitta von Liechtenstein; Dr. Carole Lieberman (psychiatrist to the Stars, author of *Bad Boys)*; Micky Dolenz of The Monkees; Tom Bailey, president of Janus Mutual Funds; and writer and producer Rob Long.

Kirkendall, Tom, and Vicky Springs. *Bicycling the Pacific Coast.* Seattle: The Mountaineers, 1998. Third ed. A very good, very practical mile-by-mile guide to the tricky business of cycling along the California coast (and north).

Koenig, David. *Mouse Tales: A Behind-the-Ears Look at Disneyland.* Irvine, CA: Bonaventure Press, 1994. Disneyland is still one of Koenig's happiest places on earth, but that doesn't mean there aren't unofficial tales to tell—unsavory stories such as labor and discrimination disputes, gang fights, stabbings, shootings, a full-tilt riot, accidents, and of course lawsuits. And then there was the time the Yippies—Youth International Party anti-war activists—flew the Viet Cong flag over Tom Sawyer Island and turned Monsanto's Adventure through Inner Space into a pot-smoking den of druggy iniquity. Too much like real life, sure, and more than the average reader would care to know about Disneyland, but a good read nonetheless.

Larson, Lane, and Peggy Larson. *Caving.* San Francisco: Sierra Club Books, 1982.

Lindsay, Lowell, and Diana Lindsay. *The Anza-Borrego Desert Region: A Guide to the State Park and Adjacent Areas.* Berkeley: Wilderness Press, 1998. Fourth ed. This guide will take you wherever you want to go— responsibly, whether on foot or in four-wheel drive— and bring you back amazingly well-informed about the life and lore of this immense and lovely desert.

Lovett, Anthony R., and Matt Maranian. *L.A. Bizarro: The Insider's Guide to the Obscure, the Absurd and the Perverse in Los Angeles,* New York: St Martin's Press, 1997. As *Los Angeles Times* book reviewer D. J. Waldie put it, this book "continues the tradition of seeing Los Angeles as a toxic playground, best observed slightly unconscious. The book is largely about body parts, cracks (wise and otherwise) and drinks. L.A. Bizzaro! approves of consuming them all. Just below the cheerful pornography, however, is a satire of post-middle-class consumption in a city waiting to explode again. Anthony R. Lovett and Matt Maranian have found interesting things to buy in L.A. while they wait for something terrible to happen." So, like, if you plan to take this tour, better make it quick.

McKinney, John. *Coast Walks: 150 Adventures Along the California Coast.* Santa Barbara: Olympus Press, 1999. The new edition of McKinney's coast hiking classic contains plenty of new adventures, from Border Field State Park at the Mexican Border north to Damnation Creek and Pelican Bay. Along the way, you'll also learn about local lore, history, and natural history—a bargain no matter how you hike it. Maps and illustrations.

McKinney, John. *Day Hiker's Guide to California State Parks.* Santa Barbara: Olympus Press, 2000. All you need to know to stretch your legs *and* see the sights in the Golden State's hikable parks and recreation areas.

McKinney, John. *Day Hiker's Guide to Southern California,* Santa Barbara: Olympus Press, 1998. Second revised ed. Out in new, updated form, McKinney's Southern California hiking guide covers it all, from beach to desert badlands. Helpful maps (to scale) and black-and-white photos.

McKinney, John, and Cheri Rae. *Walking the East Mojave.* New York: HarperCollins, 1994 (OP). A good introduction to the hiking trails of the Mojave National Preserve.

Mitchell, Linda, and Allen Mitchell. *California Parks Access.* Berkeley: Cougar Pass Publications, 1992 (distributed by Wilderness Press). A very useful guide to national and state parks in California for visitors with limited mobility. Both challenges and wheelchair-accessible features are listed. Informationally accessible appendixes are helpful, too.

National Register of Historic Places, *Early History of the California Coast.* Washington, D.C.: National Conference of State Historic Preservation Officers, 1997. Map. This fold-out introduction to the California coast serves as a travel itinerary with 45 stops illustrating the coast's earliest settlement and culture.

Ostertag, Rhonda, and George Ostertag. *California State Parks: A Complete Recreation Guide.* Seattle: The Mountaineers, 1995. Moving from north to south, this readable companion serves as a good general introduction to the state parks—and guide to what to do while you're there, with an emphasis on hikes. Here California is divided into six regions. Helpful maps, some entertaining photos.

Perry, John, and Jane Greverus Perry. *The Sierra Club Guide to the Natural Areas of California.* San Francisco: Sierra Club Books, 1997. Second ed. A just-the-facts yet very useful guide to California's public lands and parks—a book to tuck into the glovebox. Organized by regions, also indexed for easy access.

Rae, Cheri, ed. *Death Valley: A Guide. The 1938 WPA Guide Updated for Today's Traveler.* Santa Barbara: Olympus Press, 1991. Originally written and compiled by the Federal Writers' Project of the Works Progress Administration of Northern California, and published as part of the WPA's American Guide Series by Houghton Mifflin Co., Boston, 1939. For enlightenment, entertainment, and the surprising historical perspective of a mere half-century or so, this book is hard to beat as a general interest guide to Death Valley.

Rizzo, David "Dr. Roadmap." *Freeway Alternates.* Baldwin Park, CA: Gem Guides Book Co., 1990. So, you plan to get around Southern California without venturing onto the fearsome freeways? It can be done—and this book shows you how.

Roberts, Brian, and Richard Schwadel. *L.A. Short-cuts: The Guidebook For Drivers Who Hate To Wait.* Los Angeles: Red Car Press, 1989. Hey, road warriors. Here's another book that'll help you master the mysteries of L.A. driving. This one does indeed offer some great L.A. short-cuts—making it possible to get from Burbank to Los Feliz without freeways, for example, avoid crazed surface streets on the way to Hollywood, and take the "back door" route into Dodger Stadium. And with this book you get just the basics—brief descriptions of what you're doing plus maps—so you won't get slowed down by history, social issues, and shopping, etc.

Robinson, John W. *San Bernardino Mountain Trails.* Berkeley: Wilderness Press, 1999. Fourth ed. An essential companion for on-foot exploration of the San Bernardino, the San Jacinto, and the Santa Rosa Mountains and their incotporated wilderness areas—including easy day hikes as well as more ambitious backpack trips.

Robinson, John W. *Trails of the Angeles.* Berkeley: Wilderness Press, 1998. Seventh ed. The definitive guide to hiking in the San Gabriel Mountains, only an hour or two from Los Angeles. Covering nearly every major trail in these. Included here are some 100 hikes, from short, popular hikes to longer, back-country treks.

Salcedo, Nancy. *A Hiker's Guide to California Native Places.* Berkeley: Wilderness Press, 1999. First ed. Visit those places throughout California that resonate with the truth of native cultures in their natural state, assited by 103 author-guided walks, both long and short.

Schad, Jerry. *Afoot and Afield in San Diego County.* Berkeley: Wilderness Press, 1998. Third ed. Well-written, informative hiking guide offering a wide variety of hikes (rated for difficulty) along the coast and inland both in mountainous areas and desert. Also by Jerry Schad: *Afoot and Afield in Los Angeles County* (2000) and *Afoot and Afield in Orange County* (1996).

Schad, Jerry. *California Deserts.* Helena, MT: Falcon Press, 1997. Second ed. A good out-and-about guide to the desert, from the Mojave to Death Valley. Lots of lore, lots of hikes.

Schaffer, Jeffrey. *Hiking the Big Sur Country: The Ventana Wilderness.* Berkeley: Wilderness Press, 1988. Other good hiking and backpacking guides by this prolific pathfinder are primarily in Northern California.

Silverman, Goldie. *Backpacking with Babies and Small Children.* Berkeley: Wilderness Press, 1998. Third ed. Everything adventurous parents need to know, or consider, before heading to the woods with youngsters in tow.

Stevens, Barbara, and Nancy Conner. *Where on Earth: A Guide to Specialty Nurseries and Other Resources for California Gardeners.* Berkeley: Heyday Books, 1999. Fourth ed. Ever wondered where to get that unusual color of iris or that exotic azalea, or where to find the state's best native plant nurseries? Wonder no more. California gardeners won't be able to live for long without *this* essential resource.

Stienstra, Tom. *Foghorn Outdoors: California Camping—The Complete Guide to More Than 1,500 Campgrounds in The Golden State.* Emeryville, CA: Avalon Travel Publishing, 2001. Twelfth ed. This is undoubtedly the ultimate reference to California camping and campgrounds, public and private. Every single one is in here. Also included here are Stienstra's "Secret Campgrounds," an invaluable list when the aim is to truly get away from it all. In addition to a thorough practical introduction to the basics of California camping—and reviews of the latest high-tech gear, for hiking and camping comfort and safety—this guidebook is meticulously organized by area, starting with the general subdivisions of Northern, Central, and Southern California. Even accidental outdoorspeople should carry this one along at all times.

Stienstra, Tom. *Foghorn Outdoors: California Fishing.* Emeryville, CA: Avalon Travel Publishing, 1999. This is it, *the* guide for people who think finding God has something to do with strapping on rubber waders or climbing into a tiny boat;

making educated fish-eyed guesses about lures, ripples, or lake depths; and generally observing a strict code of silence in the outdoors. As besieged as California's fisheries have been by the state's 30 million-plus population and the attendant devastations and distractions of modern times, fisherfolk can still enjoy some world-class sport in California. This tome contains just about everything novices and masters need to know to figure out what to do as well as where and when to do it.

Story, David, and Laurie and Chris Leman. *Mountain Bike! Southern California: A Guide to the Classic Trails,* Birmingham, AL: Menasha Ridge Press, 1999. Second ed. A worthy investment for fat-tired bikers heading south.

Varney, Philip. *Southern California's Best Ghost Towns: A Practical Guide.* Norman, OK: University of Oklahoma Press, 1990. For anyone intrigued by the vastness of California's deserts, particularly those empty areas once home to human enterprise, this book is a treasure. Lively, informative histories combine with photographs and maps to take you there. The large-format presentation of this book is its only drawback—an awkward, impractical size to pack along.

Wallis, Michael. *Route 66: The Mother Road.* New York: St. Martin's Press, 1990. Worthwhile purchase for those obsessed with the almost vanished two-lane visage of the Mother Road, ol' Route 66 from Illinois to California. Though *Route 66* is a bit heavy on diners and waitresses and anti-interstatism, what is also here is the species memory of what it was like to take that lonely road west—accompanied by hang-on-the-door canvas water bags to make sure you and yours didn't die before you'd arrived.

Winnett, Thomas, and Melanie Findling. *Backpacking Basics.* Berkeley: Wilderness Press, 1994. Fourth ed. Everything you need to know about going the distance on foot—with an emphasis on getting (and staying) in shape, the principles of low-impact camping, and how to save money on just about everything you'll need.

Zagat Survey, ed. *Los Angeles/Southern California Restaurants.* New York: Zagat Survey. An eater's survey of the best and most beloved southstate dining destinations in Los Angeles and beyond (Orange County, Palm Springs, San Diego, Santa Barbara), annually updated.

ACCOMMODATIONS INDEX

CAMPING/CAMPGROUNDS

FOOD INDEX

INDEX

ARCHITECTURAL HIGHLIGHTS

BEACHES

COLLEGES/UNIVERSITIES

MISSIONS

MUSEUMS

STATE PARKS

THEATER/PERFORMING ARTS VENUES

UNUSUAL ATTRACTIONS/CLAIMS TO FAME

WHALE-WATCHING

ABOUT THE AUTHOR

Kim Weir is a California native, born in Southern California though a longtime resident of the far north. She is also a journalist and writer, a curious generalist by nature. Weir is most happy when turning over rocks—literally and figuratively—and poking into this and that to discover what usually goes unnoticed. Her formal study of environmental issues began at the University of California at Santa Barbara and continued at California State University, Chico, where she studied biology and obtained a degree in environmental studies and analysis. Since all things are interconnected, as a journalist Weir covered the political environment and the natural and unnatural antics of politicians. Before signing on with Moon Handbooks she also worked as an editor at Scholars Press, now on the Emory University campus in Atlanta, Georgia. More recently she served as communications director for the Faculty Association of California Community Colleges (FACCC) in Sacramento.

Weir is a member of the Society of American Travel Writers (SATW). Her award-winning essay on ecotourism was published in the 1993 international *American Express Review of Travel*. Weir is also the author of *Moon Handbooks: Northern California* and *Moon Handbooks: California*. She threatens to write fiction.

U.S.~METRIC CONVERSION

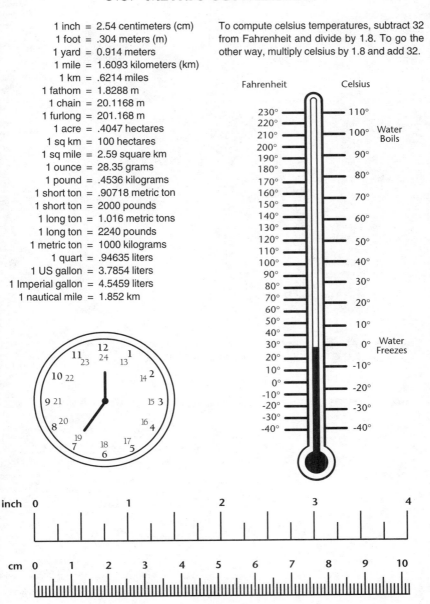

1 inch = 2.54 centimeters (cm)
1 foot = .304 meters (m)
1 yard = 0.914 meters
1 mile = 1.6093 kilometers (km)
1 km = .6214 miles
1 fathom = 1.8288 m
1 chain = 20.1168 m
1 furlong = 201.168 m
1 acre = .4047 hectares
1 sq km = 100 hectares
1 sq mile = 2.59 square km
1 ounce = 28.35 grams
1 pound = .4536 kilograms
1 short ton = .90718 metric ton
1 short ton = 2000 pounds
1 long ton = 1.016 metric tons
1 long ton = 2240 pounds
1 metric ton = 1000 kilograms
1 quart = .94635 liters
1 US gallon = 3.7854 liters
1 Imperial gallon = 4.5459 liters
1 nautical mile = 1.852 km

To compute celsius temperatures, subtract 32 from Fahrenheit and divide by 1.8. To go the other way, multiply celsius by 1.8 and add 32.

Will you have enough stories to tell your grandchildren?

Yahoo! Travel

Do You YAHOO!?